HANDBOOK OF CHURCH HISTORY

IV

HANDBOOK OF CHURCH HISTORY

Edited by
HUBERT JEDIN
and
JOHN DOLAN

Volume IV

FROM THE HIGH MIDDLE AGES TO THE EVE OF THE REFORMATION

by

HANS-GEORG BECK

KARL AUGUST FINK

JOSEF GLAZIK

ERWIN ISERLOH

HANS WOLTER

Translated by
Anselm Biggs

HERDER AND HERDER

1970

HERDER AND HERDER

232 Madison Avenue, New York, N. Y. 10016

BURNS & OATES LIMITED

25 Ashley Place, London S. W. 1

Translated from the *Handbuch der Kirchengeschichte*, edited by Hubert Jedin,
Vol. III, "Die mittelalterliche Kirche",
Part 2, "Vom kirchlichen Hochmittelalter bis zum Vorabend der Reformation".
Herder, Freiburg

Library of Congress Catalog Card Number: 64–15929
First published in West Germany © 1970 Herder KG
Printed in West Germany by Herder

CONTENTS

CONTENTS

CONTENTS

CONTENTS

CONTENTS

The treatment of the Church History of the High and Late Middle Ages, offered in this volume, starts from the close of the Investiture Controversy and the slowing down of the Gregorian reform and concludes with the Renaissance papacy. As explained in the prefaces to Volumes III and V, by Professors Kempf and Iserloh respectively, the original plan of the entire work, outlined by the collaborators in conferences at Trier and Freiburg in 1958–1960, envisaged a different arrangement: the Early and High Middle Ages (700–1300) were to be in one volume (III), while the Late Middle Ages, the Reformation, and the Catholic Reform were to provide the content of Volume IV. External circumstances, not least of all the compass of mediaeval Church History, brought about the present arrangement of volumes, which, as Kempf and Iserloh have noted, has an equally valid basis: the Western Church in her making, her development, her crises and in her relations with the Eastern Churches is treated in Volumes III and IV, while the shattering of Western Christendom in the Reformation and in the Age of Confessionalism, together with the opening up of new lands through the voyages of discovery and the missions, constitutes the matter of Volume V.

Nevertheless, it seems appropriate to state the connecting links extending from the present volume to those preceding and following it and thereby to bring together what was externally sundered by the existing arrangement of the volumes. For the mediaeval system which was constructed in the Ottonian Age and in the Gregorian reform was brought to full maturity in the twelfth and thirteenth centuries both as regards the position of the papacy and in its intellectual and devotional life. Nevertheless, the hierarchical Church encountered a growing opposition: the poverty movement, only partially caught up and "baptized" in the mendicant orders, and the radical hostility of the Cathari. The grand theme of Western history, the confrontation of the two powers, did not come to rest with the defeat of the Hohenstaufen. The Avignon papacy fell into an oppressive dependence on France, while the papacy of the Great Western Schism, divided against itself, had to come to terms with the secular powers in order to retain the "obediences".

The causal relationship to the Reformation, it seems to me, will be even more clear in this volume. The unrealized reform of the Church, conciliarism, the decisive role of the states in liquidating the Council of Basle, the papacy's entanglement in Italian territorial politics — these were as much immediate predispositions for the Reformation as were the appearance of the new humanist education and the Renaissance and the social and economic restratifications in the course of the fourteenth and fifteenth centuries. The whole complex of "causes" or, more correctly, of "presuppositions" for the Reformation becomes transparent. However, the roots of the Catholic renewal in the sixteenth century also extend back to this period. From the *devotio moderna,* to which, probably for the first time, justice is amply done here, a line reaches to Ignatius Loyola; the reforms of the religious orders in the sixteenth century were frequently related to those of the Late Middle Ages; the Tridentine reform was to a great extent the carrying out of reform programs proposed in the Late Middle Ages. Without Christian humanism the development of positive theology in the sixteenth and seventeenth centuries is unthinkable. The beginnings of missionary work in Asia, Africa and America, which belong chronologically to the present volume, are only treated in Volume V.

The Church History of the Middle Ages, which is here completed, is obliged to treat ecclesiastical events and situations in the context and the reciprocal action of the general, and especially the political, history of the Middle Ages. One cannot write the history of the papacy in the twelfth and thirteenth centuries without investigating its position at the head of the Western family of nations; one cannot understand the history of the Renaissance papacy if one disregards its involvement in Italian territorial politics. However one may feel in regard to these phenomena, they are, and they remain, historical facts which must be respected. As certain as it is that Church History must never be only a factual report of the Church's past and that it must always be also a confrontation with that past, we still believe that this confrontation must not, in a handbook, lead to a constricting and contracting of the field of vision, such as would be permissible in accounts for a wider circle of readers. The readers and users of this *Handbook* must be fully informed of the facts and contexts as they are known in the present state of research; then they can form their own judgment and draw pragmatic conclusions for the present. On this point the collaborators and the editors are in basic agreement.

In accord with the principles relating to the writing of the *Handbook,* each author is at liberty to present his own scholarly opinions; he alone assumes responsibility for the part composed by him. Hence there are certain differences in the judgments on events and persons, which the reader and user of this volume will quickly notice. The editors' task is limited to the maintaining of the total plan which was sketched by the collaborators in common.

Hubert Jedin

PREFACE TO THE ENGLISH EDITION

The present volume of the *Handbook of Church History* embraces a period that for many appears to have been the high-water mark of Christian civilization. The dream of a papally dominated Europe that followed Rome's triumph over the Hohenstaufen *imperium* was reflected in the Crusades, the works of the schoolmen, and the charters of the universities. Yet the very triumphs, spiritual and temporal, of the reinvigorated papacy contained the seeds of its own decline. Neither the highly legalized and centralized governing apparatus of the Church nor the proliferation of clerical corporations as agents of its authority were successful. The recovery of Hellenic philosophy, the great mediaeval synthesis, while providing a rational basis for the superstructure of revelation, fostered a mentality that diminished interest in the very font of that revelation, the Scriptures.

At the same time that the ambitions of the Vicar of Christ to direct secular affairs were blunted by nascent nationalism and the economic and social revolutions that weakened feudalism, the failure of the Crusades facilitated the resurgence of the Ottoman Turk and the eventual engulfment of Byzantium. Yet the great debates on the nature of authority, the empirical shift in philosophy and the brief contacts with the Far East created the impetus for many of the achievements of the modern world—democracy, scientific inquiry, and a sense of world mission. There can be little doubt that during this period of transition the Church in spite of its limitations was still the focal point of the historical process in Europe.

As in previous volumes of the *Handbook* the authors have avoided the pitfalls of merely chronicling the activities of the hierarchy. The Church's successes and its failures are seen in the *plebs sancta* as well as in the *sacerdotium*.

Although limited by its very nature in scope and subject matter, the work nevertheless opens up avenues of study for historians of all hues. Its treatment of such varied subjects as Northern Humanism, Hesychasm and Palamism, the mediaeval hospital and the Jew in mediaeval Christendom are indicative of this wide spectrum. Certainly the *Handbook* will do much to support the claim that Western history is unintelligible apart from the history of the Church. This is especially true during the period of the late Middle Ages and Renaissance when the Church, though often in open opposition to the changes taking place, nonetheless remained the most powerful spiritual and intellectual force of the age.

John P. Dolan
University of South Carolina

LIST OF ABBREVIATIONS

The references within brackets indicate the General Bibliography of this volume.

AAB	*Abhandlungen der Deutschen* (till 1944: *Preussischen*) *Akademie der Wissenschaften zu Berlin.* Phil.-hist. Klasse, Berlin 1815 ff.
AAL	*Abhandlungen der Sächsischen Akademie der Wissenschaften in Leipzig* (till 30, 1920: *AGL*), Leipzig 1850 ff.
AAM	*Abhandlungen der Bayerischen Akademie der Wissenschaften.* Phil.-hist. Klasse, Munich 1835 ff.
AAMz	*Abhandlungen (der geistes- und sozialwissenschaftlichen Klasse) der Akademie der Wissenschaften und der Literatur,* Mainz 1950 ff.
AAug	*Analecta Augustiniana,* Rome 1905 ff.
ActaSS	*Acta Sanctorum,* ed. Bollandus *et al.,* (Antwerp, Brussels, Tongerloo) Paris 1643 ff., Venice 1734 ff., Paris 1863 ff.
ADipl	*Archiv für Diplomatik, Schriftgeschichte, Siegel- und Wappenkunde,* Münster and Cologne 1955 ff.
ADRomana	*Archivio della Deputazione Romana di Storia Patria,* Rome 1935 ff. (1878–1934: *ASRomana*).
AElsKG	*Archiv für elsässische Kirchengeschichte,* published by the Gesellschaft für elsässische Kirchengeschichte, edited by J. Brauner, Rixheim im Oberelsass 1926 ff.; from 1946 edited by A. M. Burg, Strasbourg.
AER	*The American Ecclesiastical Review,* Washington 1889 ff.
AFP	*Archivum Fratrum Praedicatorum,* Rome 1931 ff.
AFranc	*Analecta Franciscana sive Chronica aliaque varia Documenta ad historiam Fratrum Minorum spectantia,* edita a Patribus Collegii S. Bonaventurae, Quaracchi 1885 ff.
AFrH	*Archivum Franciscanum Historicum,* Florence and Quaracchi 1908 ff.
AGAU	*Archief voor de Geschiedenis van het Aartsbisdom Utrecht.*
AGL	*Abhandlungen der Sächsischen Gesellschaft der Wissenschaften Leipzig* (from 31, 1921: *AAL*), Leipzig 1850 ff.
AH	*Analecta Hymnica,* edited by G. Dreves and C. Blume, 55 volumes, Leipzig 1886–1922.
AHD	*Archives d'histoire doctrinale et littéraire du moyen-âge,* Paris 1926 ff.
AHPont	*Archivum Historiae Pontificiae,* Rome 1963 ff.
AHR	*The American Historical Review,* New York 1895 ff.
AHVNrh	*Annalen des Historischen Vereins für den Niederrhein, insbesondere das alte Erzbistum Köln,* Cologne 1855 ff.
AkathKR	*Archiv für Katholisches Kirchenrecht,* (Innsbruck) Mainz 1857 ff.

AKG	*Archiv für Kulturgeschichte,* (Leipzig) Münster and Cologne 1903 ff.
ALKGMA	*Archiv für Literatur- und Kirchengeschichte des Mittelalters,* edited by H. Denifle and F. Ehrle, 7 volumes, (Berlin) Freiburg im Breisgau 1885–1900.
ALMA	*Archivum Latinitatis Medii Aevi,* Brussels 1924 ff.
AMrhKG	*Archiv für mittelrheinische Kirchengeschichte,* Speyer 1949 ff.
AnBoll	*Analecta Bollandiana,* Brussels 1882 ff.
Angelicum	*Angelicum,* Rome 1924 ff.
AnGr	*Analecta Gregoriana* cura Pontificiae Universitatis Gregorianae edita, Rome 1930 ff.
AnOCist	*Analecta Sacri Ordinis Cisterciensis,* Rome 1945 ff.
Antonianum	*Antonianum,* Rome 1926 ff.
AnzAW	*Anzeiger der österreichischen Akademie der Wissenschaften,* Vienna 1864 ff.
AÖG	*Archiv für österreichische Geschichte,* Vienna 1865 ff.
APhilHistOS	*Annuaire de l'Institut de Philologie et d'Histoire Orientales et Slaves,* Brussels 1932 ff.
APraem	*Analecta Praemonstratensia,* Tongerloo 1925 ff., from 1953 Averbode.
ARG	*Archiv für Reformationsgeschichte,* (Leipzig) Gütersloh 1903 ff.
ASRomana	*Archivio della Reale Società Romana di Storia Patria,* Rome 1878–1934 (from 1935: *ADRomana*).
AST	*Analecta Sacra Tarraconensia,* Barcelona 1925 ff.
AstIt	*Archivio storico Italiano,* Florence 1842 ff.
AttiPontAc	*Atti della Pontificia Accademia Romana di Archeologia,* Rome 1923 ff.
AUF	*Archiv für Urkundenforschung,* Berlin 1908 ff.
AZ	*Archivalische Zeitschrift,* Munich 1876 ff.
BAC	*Biblioteca de Autores Cristianos,* Madrid 1945 ff. (thus far 138 volumes).
Baluze-Mollat	S. Baluze, *Vitae Paparum Avenionensium,* edited by G. Mollat, 4 volumes, Paris 1916–28.
Baudot-Chaussin	Baudot et Chaussin, *Vies des Saints et des Bienheureux selon l'ordre du calendrier avec l'historique des fêtes* (par les RR. PP. Bénédictins de Paris), 12 volumes, Paris 1935–56.
BÉCh	*Bibliothèque de l'École des Chartes,* Paris 1839 ff.
Beck	H. G. Beck, *Kirche und theologische Literatur im Byzantinischen Reich,* Munich 1959.
BÉH	*Bibliothèque de l'École des Hautes Études,* Sciences philologiques et historiques, Paris 1869 ff.
Benedictina	*Benedictina,* Rome 1947 ff.
BGPhMA	*Beiträge zur Geschichte der Philosophie* (after 1930: *und Theologie*) *des Mittelalters.* Texte und Untersuchungen, 39 volumes, first edited by C. Baeumker, now by M. Schmaus, Münster 1891 ff.
BHL	*Bibliotheca hagiographica latina antiquae et mediae aetatis,* ed. socii Bollandiani, 2 volumes, Brussels 1898–1901; Suppl. editio altera, *ibid.* 1911.
BiblThom	*Bibliothèque Thomiste,* Le Saulchoir 1921 ff.
BISI	*Bollettino dell'Istituto storico Italiano,* Rome.
BIStIAM	*Bollettino dell'Istituto storico Italiano per il Medio Evo e Archivio Muratoriano,* Rome 1886 ff.
BJRL	*The Bulletin of the John Rylands Library,* Manchester 1903 ff.
BLE	*Bulletin de littérature ecclésiastique,* Toulouse 1899 ff.
BRN	*Bibliotheca Reformatoria Neerlandica,* edited by S. Cramer and F. Pijper, 10 volumes, The Hague 1903–14.
BThAM	*Bulletin de Théologie ancienne et médiévale,* Louvain 1929 ff.

Bullarium Taur.   *Bullarium Romanum,* edited by A. Tomassetti, 24 volumes, Turin 1857–72.

BullFr   *Bullarium Franciscanum,* Vols. I–IV edited by H. Sbaralea and B. de Rossi, Rome 1759–68; V–VII, by K. Eubel, Rome 1898–1904; VIII (new series, I), by U. Hüntemann, Quaracchi 1929; IX–X (new series, II–III), by J. Pou y Marti, Quaracchi 1939–49; Suppl. I, edited by F. Annibali de Latera, Rome 1780; Suppl. II, by K. Eubel, Quaracchi 1908.

BullSocAHLiège   *Bulletin de la Société d'Art et d'Histoire du Diocèse de Liège,* Liège.

BullThomiste   *Bulletin Thomiste,* Paris and Le Saulchoir.

ByZ   *Byzantinische Zeitschrift,* Leipzig 1892 ff.

Byz(B)   *Byzantion,* Brussels 1924 ff.

Byzslav   *Byzantinoslavica,* Prague 1929 ff.

BZ   *Biblische Zeitschrift,* Freiburg im Breisgau 1903–29; Paderborn 1931–39; 1957 ff.

CahiersCivMéd   *Cahiers de Civilisation Médiévale,* Poitiers.

CambrHJ   *The Cambridge Historical Journal,* Cambridge 1923 ff.; from 1958: *The Historical Journal.*

CCivMéd   *Cahiers de la Civilisation Médiévale,* Poitiers 1958 ff.

CH   *Church History,* New York and Chicago 1932 ff.

CHR   *The Catholic Historical Review,* Washington 1915 ff.

CICfontes   P. Gasparri and I. Serédi, *Codicis Iuris Canonici Fontes,* 9 volumes, Rome 1923–39.

Cist   *Cistercienser-Chronik,* edited by the Cistercians of Mehrerau, Mehrerau 1889 ff.

COD   *Conciliorum oecumenicorum decreta,* published by the Centro di Documentazione Bologna, Freiburg im Breisgau, 2d ed. 1962.

CollFr   *Collectanea Franciscana,* Rome 1931 ff.

CollOCR   *Collectanea Ordinis Cisterciensium Reformatorum,* Rome and Westmalle 1934 ff.

CSEL   *Corpus Scriptorum ecclesiasticorum latinorum,* Vienna 1866 ff.

CSHB   *Corpus Scriptorum Historiae Byzantinae,* Bonn 1828 ff.

CTom   *Ciencia Tomista,* Madrid 1910 ff.

D   H. Denzinger and A. Schönmetzer, *Enchiridion Symbolorum, Definitionum et Declarationum de rebus fidei et morum,* Barcelona and Freiburg im Breisgau, 34th ed. 1967.

DA   *Deutsches Archiv für Erforschung des Mittelalters* (1937–43: *für Geschichte des Mittelalters,* Weimar), Cologne and Graz 1950 ff. *(cf. NA).*

Dahlmann-Waitz   F. C. Dahlmann and G. Waitz, *Quellenkunde der Deutschen Geschichte,* 9th edition by H. Haering, Leipzig 1931–32; new edition in preparation.

DDC   *Dictionnaire de droit canonique,* edited by R. Naz, Paris 1935 ff.

Denzinger-Schönmetzer   *D.*

DHGE   *Dictionnaire d'histoire et de géographie ecclésiastiques,* edited by A. Baudrillart *et al.,* Paris 1912 ff.

DölgerReg   *Corpus der griechischen Urkunden des Mittelalters und der neueren Zeit.* Reihe A: *Regesten.* Abteilung 1: *Regesten der Kaiserurkunden des oströmischen Reiches,* edited by F. Dölger. 1. Teil: from 565 to 1025, Munich 1924; 2. Teil: from 1025 to 1204, Munich 1925; 3. Teil: from 1204 to 1282, Munich 1932.

DOP   *Dumbarton Oaks Papers,* published by Harvard University, Cambridge, Mass. 1941 ff.

DSAM	*Dictionnaire de spiritualité ascétique et mystique. Doctrine et Histoire*, edited by M. Viller, Paris 1932 ff.
DTh	*Divus Thomas* (before 1914: *Jahrbuch für Philosophie und spekulative Theologie;* from 1954: *Freiburger Zeitschrift für Theologie und Philosophie*), Fribourg.
DThC	*Dictionnaire de théologie catholique*, edited by A. Vacant and E. Mangenot, continued by É. Amann, Paris 1930 ff.
DTh(P)	*Divus Thomas*, Piacenza 1880 ff.
Duchesne LP	*Liber pontificalis*, edited by L. Duchesne, 2 volumes, Paris 1886–92; supplementary Volume III, edited by C. Vogel, Paris 1957.
DVfLG	*Deutsche Vierteljahresschrift für Literaturwissenschaft und Geistesgeschichte*, Halle 1923 ff.
DZGw	*Deutsche Zeitschrift für Geschichtswissenschaft*, Freiburg im Breisgau 1889–98 (from 1898: *HV*).
ECarm	*Ephemerides Carmeliticae*, Florence 1947 ff.
ECatt	*Enciclopedia Cattolica*, Rome 1949 ff.
Éfranc	*Études franciscaines*, Paris 1909–40; new series, Paris 1950 ff.
EHR	*English Historical Review*, London 1886 ff.
EIC	*Ephemerides Iuris Canonici*, Rome 1945 ff.
ELit	*Ephemerides Liturgicae*, Rome 1887 ff.
ÉO	*Échos d'Orient*, Paris 1897 ff.
EThL	*Ephemerides Theologicae Lovanienses*, Bruges 1924 ff.
FDG	*Forschungen zur Deutschen Geschichte*, 26 volumes, Göttingen 1860–86.
Feine RG	H. E. Feine, *Kirchliche Rechtsgeschichte*, I: *Die katholische Kirche*, Cologne and Graz, 4th ed. 1964.
FF	*Forschungen und Fortschritte*, Berlin 1925 ff.
Fliche-Martin	*Histoire de l'église depuis les origines jusqu'à nos jours*, publiée sous la direction de A. Fliche et V. Martin, Paris 1935 ff. [General Bibliography, II, 3].
FlorPatr	*Florilegium Patristicum*, edited by J. Zellinger and B. Geyer, Bonn 1904 ff. (thus far 44 Hefte).
FontiStIt	*Fonti per la storia d'Italia*, published by the Istituto storico Italiano per il medio evo, 94 volumes, Rome 1887 ff.
FreibDiözArch	*Freiburger Diözesan-Archiv*, Freiburg im Breisgau 1865 ff.
FreibGeschBl	*Freiburger Geschichtsblätter*, Fribourg.
FStud	*Franziskanische Studien*, (Münster) Werl 1914 ff.
FStudies	*Franciscan Studies*, St. Bonaventure, New York 1940 ff.
FZThPh	*Freiburger Zeitschrift für Theologie und Philosophie* (before 1914: *Jahrbuch für Philosophie und spekulative Theologie;* 1914–54: *DTh*), Fribourg.
Gebhardt-Grundmann	B. Gebhardt, *Handbuch der Deutschen Geschichte*, 8th edition by H. Grundmann, Stuttgart, I (1954), II (1955).
Giesebrecht	F. W. Giesebrecht, *Geschichte der deutschen Kaiserzeit*, I–V, Munich 1855–88; VI, 1895, by B. von Simson; partly in 5th edition.
Gilson-Böhner	É. Gilson and P. Böhner, *Die Geschichte der christlichen Philosophie von ihren Anfängen bis Nikolaus von Cues*, 3 volumes, Paderborn, 2d ed. 1952 f.
GlorieuxR	P. Glorieux, *Répertoire des maîtres en théologie de Paris au XIIIe siècle*, I–II, Paris 1933.

Glotz	Histoire générale, edited by G. Glotz (and his successors) [General Bibliography, II, 1].
Grabmann G	M. Grabmann, Die Geschichte der katholischen Theologie seit dem Ausgang der Väterzeit, Freiburg im Breisgau 1933.
Grabmann MGL	M. Grabmann, Mittelalterliches Geistesleben, I–III, Munich 1926–56.
Grousset	R. Grousset, Histoire des Croisades et du royaume de Jérusalem, 3 volumes, Paris 1934–36.
Grumel Reg	V. Grumel, Les Regestes des actes du patriarcat de Constantinople, Kadiköi and Bucharest, I, 1 (1932), I, 2 (1936), I, 3 (1947).
GuL	Geist und Leben. Zeitschrift für Aszese und Mystik (until 1947: ZAM), Würzburg 1947 ff.
Haller	J. Haller, Das Papsttum, 5 volumes, corrected and expanded edition, Stuttgart 1950–53.
Hauck	A. Hauck, Kirchengeschichte Deutschlands, Leipzig, I–IV, 3d and 4th ed. 1906–14, V, 2d and 4th ed. 1929; Berlin and Leipzig, I–V, 8th ed. 1954.
Hefele-Leclercq	Histoire des conciles d'après les documents originaux, by C. J. Hefele. Translated by H. Leclercq. I–IX, Paris 1907 ff.
Heimbucher	M. Heimbucher, Die Orden und Kongregationen der katholischen Kirche, 3 volumes, Paderborn, 2d ed. 1907–08; 3d ed. 1932–34, ibid., in 2 volumes.
Hinschius	P. Hinschius, Das Kirchenrecht der Katholiken und Protestanten in Deutschland, 6 volumes, Berlin 1869–97, reprint 1959.
HJ	Historisches Jahrbuch der Görres-Gesellschaft, (Cologne 1880 ff.) Munich 1950 ff.
Hochland	Hochland, Munich 1903 ff.
Holzapfel	H. Holzapfel, Handbuch der Geschichte des Franziskanerordens, Freiburg im Breisgau 1909.
HPBl	Historisch-politische Blätter für das katholische Deutschland, edited by F. Binder and G. Jochner, 171 volumes, Munich 1838–1923.
HS	Hispania Sacra, Madrid 1948 ff.
HStud	Historische Studien, edited by E. Ebering, Berlin 1896 ff.
HV	Historische Vierteljahresschrift, Leipzig 1898–1937 (till 1898: DZGw).
HZ	Historische Zeitschrift, Munich 1859 ff.
IER	The Irish Ecclesiastical Record, Dublin 1864 ff.
Istina	Istina, Boulogne-sur-Seine 1954 ff.
IThQ	The Irish Theological Quarterly, Dublin 1906–22, 1951 ff.
JA	Journal Asiatique, Paris 1822 ff.
Jaffé	P. Jaffé, Regesta Pontificum Romanorum ad annum post Christum natum MCXCVIII, Leipzig 1851; 2d ed. 1881–88 in two volumes prepared by S. Löwenfeld, F. Kaltenbrunner, and P. Ewald; photographic reproduction, Graz 1956.
JbbDG	Jahrbücher der deutschen Geschichte, published by the Historische Kommission der Bayerischen Akademie der Wissenschaften, 1862 ff.
Jedin	H. Jedin, Geschichte des Konzils von Trient, Freiburg im Breisgau, I, 2d ed. 1951, II, 1957. English translation: H. Jedin, A History of the Council of Trent, translated by E. Graf, St. Louis, Mo., I, 1957; II, 1961.
JEH	The Journal of Ecclesiastical History, London 1950 ff.
JJS	Journal of Jewish Studies, London 1948 ff.
JL	JLW

JLW	*Jahrbuch für Liturgiewissenschaft*, Münster 1921–41 (now: *ALW*).
JÖByzG	*Jahrbuch der österreichischen byzantinischen Gesellschaft*, Vienna 1951 ff.
JRAS	*Journal of the Royal Asiatic Society of Great Britain and Ireland*, London 1833 ff.
JRelH	*The Journal of Religious History*, Sydney.
JThS	*The Journal of Theological Studies*, London 1899 ff.
JungmannK	J. A. Jungmann, *Katechetik*, Vienna, 2d ed. 1955.
JungmannMS	J. A. Jungmann, *Missarum Sollemnia. Eine genetische Erklärung der römischen Messe*, I–II, Vienna, 3d ed. 1952. English translation: *The Mass of the Roman Rite: Its Origins and Development*, translated by F. A. Brunner, 2 vols., New York 1951–55.
Katholik	*Der Katholik*, Mainz 1821 ff. (general index for 1821–89).
Lavisse	*Histoire de France depuis les origines jusqu'à la Révolution*, Paris 1900 ff. [General Bibliography, II, 2].
Le Bras D	*Histoire du droit et des institutions de l'Église en Occident*, edited by G. Le Bras, I: *Prolégomènes*, Paris 1955.
LM	*Lexikon der Marienkunde*, edited by K. Algermissen, L. Böer, C. Feckes, and J. Tyciak, Regensburg 1957 ff.
LPM	J. P. March, *Liber Pontificalis completur ex codice Dertusensi*, Barcelona 1925.
LThK	*Lexikon für Theologie und Kirche*, edited by J. Höfer and K. Rahner, Freiburg im Breisgau, 2d ed. 1957 ff.
LuJ	*Lutherjahrbuch. Jahrbuch der Luthergesellschaft*, 1919 ff.
MA	*Le moyen-âge. Revue d'histoire et de philologie*, Paris 1888 ff.
MAH	*Mélanges d'archéologie et d'histoire*, Paris 1880 ff.
Manitius	M. Manitius, *Geschichte der lateinischen Literatur des Mittelalters*, Munich, I (1911), II (1923), III (1931).
Mansi	J. D. Mansi, *Sacrorum Conciliorum nova et amplissima Collectio*, 31 volumes, Florence and Venice, 1757–98; reprinted and continued by L. Petit and J. B. Martin, in 60 volumes, Paris 1899–1927.
Maria	*Maria. Études sur la Sainte Vierge*, sous la direction d'H. Du Manoir, I–IV, Paris 1949–56.
MartèneC	E. Martène, *Veterum Scriptorum et monumentorum ecclesiasticorum et dogmaticorum amplissima Collectio*, 9 volumes, Paris 1724–33.
Med et Hum	*Mediaevalia et Humanistica*, Boulder, Colorado.
MF	*Miscellanea francescana*, Rome 1886 ff.
MG	*Monumenta Germaniae Historica inde ab a. C. 500 usque ad a. 1500;* Indices by O. Holder-Egger and K. Zeumer, Hanover and Berlin 1826 ff. Sections:
MGConst	*Constitutiones.*
MGDD	*Diplomata.*
MGEp	*Epistolae.*
MGEp. sel.	*Epistolae selectae.*
MGFont. iur.	*Fontes iuris germanici.*
MGLiblit	*Libelli de lite.*
MGLL	*Leges.*
MGSS	*Scriptores.*
MGSS rer. Germ.	*Scriptores rerum Germanicarum in usum scholarum ex Monumentis Germaniae historicis recusi* or *separatim editi* (octavo).

MGSS rer. Germ. NS   MG, *Scriptores rerum Germanicarum* Nova series.

MIÖG   *Mitteilungen des Instituts für österreichische Geschichtsforschung,* (Innsbruck) Graz and Cologne 1880 ff.

MiscFranc   MF

Misc. Hist. Pont.   *Miscellanea Historiae Pontificiae.*

MiscMercati   *Miscellanea Giovanni Mercati,* 6 volumes, Rome 1946.

Mitteis   H. Mitteis, *Der Staat des hohen Mittelalters,* Weimar, 4th ed. 1953.

MOP   *Monumenta ordinis Fratrum Praedicatorum historica,* edited by B. M. Reichert, 14 volumes, Rome 1896–1904; continuation, Paris 1931 ff.

MRS   *Mediaeval and Renaissance Studies,* London 1949 ff.

MS   *Mediaeval Studies,* published by the Pontifical Institute of Mediaeval Studies, Toronto 1939 ff.

MthSt   *Münchener Theologische Studien,* edited by F. X. Seppelt, J. Pascher, and K. Mörsdorf, Munich 1950 ff.

MThZ   *Münchener Theologische Zeitschrift,* Munich 1950 ff.

Muratori   L. A. Muratori, *Rerum italicarum Scriptores ab anno aerae christianae 500 ad 1500,* 28 volumes, Milan 1723–51; continued by Tartini, 1748–70, and N. G. Mittarelli, 1771; new edition by G. Carducci and V. Fiorini, Città di Castello 1900 ff.

NA   *Neues Archiv der Gesellschaft für ältere deutsche Geschichtskunde zur Beförderung einer Gesamtausgabe der Quellenschriften deutscher Geschichte des Mittelalters,* Hanover 1876 ff. (from 1937: *DA*).

NAG   *Nachrichten von der Akademie der Wissenschaften in Göttingen* (till 1940: *NGG*), Göttingen 1941 ff.

NAKG   *Nederlands Archief voor Kerkgeschiedenis.*

NDB   *Neue Deutsche Biographie,* Berlin 1953 ff.

NGG   *Nachrichten von der Gesellschaft der Wissenschaften zu Göttingen* (from 1941: *NAG*), Berlin 1845–1940.

NRTh   *Nouvelle Revue Théologique,* Tournai, Louvain, and Paris 1879 ff.

NZM   *Neue Zeitschrift für Missionswissenschaft,* Beckenried 1945 ff.

OGE   *Ons Geestelijk Erf,* Antwerp and Thielt, 1927 ff.

OrChr   *Oriens Christianus,* (Leipzig) Wiesbaden 1901 ff.

OrChrP   *Orientalia Christiana periodica,* Rome 1935 ff.

OstKSt   *Ostkirchliche Studien,* Würzburg 1951 ff.

Pastor   L. von Pastor, *Geschichte der Päpste seit dem Ausgang des Mittelalters,* 16 volumes, Freiburg im Breisgau, 1885 ff. and at other times. English translation: L. Pastor, *The History of the Popes from the Close of the Middle Ages,* 40 volumes, St. Louis, Mo., I–VI, edited by F. I. Antrobus, 1891–98; VII–XXIV, by R. F. Kerr, 1908–33; XXV–XXXIV, by E. Graf, 1937–41; XXXV–XL, by E. F. Peeler, 1950–53.

PhJ   *Philosophisches Jahrbuch der Görres-Gesellschaft,* Fulda 1888 ff.

PL   *Patrologia Latina,* edited by J. P. Migne, 217 volumes and 4 index volumes, Paris 1878–90.

PotthastR   A. Potthast, *Regesta Pontificum Romanorum inde ab anno 1198 ad annum 1304,* 2 volumes, Berlin 1873–75; from 1911 in Paris.

Pourrat   P. Pourrat, *La spiritualité chrétienne,* 4 volumes, Paris 1947.

Preger   J. W. Preger, *Geschichte der deutschen Mystik im Mittelalter,* 3 volumes, Leipzig 1874–93.

QFIAB   *Quellen und Forschungen aus italienischen Archiven und Bibliotheken*, Rome 1897 ff.

RAC   *Reallexikon für Antike und Christentum*, edited by T. Klauser, Stuttgart 1941 (1950) ff.

RAM   *Revue d'ascétique et de mystique*, Toulouse 1920 ff.

RBén   *Revue bénédictine*, Maredsous 1884 ff.

RDC   *Revue de droit canonique*, Strasbourg 1951 ff.

RDL   *Reallexikon der deutschen Literaturgeschichte*, edited by P. Merker and W. Stammler, 4 volumes, Berlin 1925–31; 2d ed., revised by W. Kohlschmidt and W. Mohr, 3 volumes, Berlin 1955 ff.

RE   *Realencyklopädie für protestantische Theologie und Kirche*, founded by J. J. Herzog, edited by A. Hauck, 24 volumes, Leipzig, 3d ed. 1896–1913.

RÉB   *Revue des études byzantines*, Paris 1946 ff.

RecHistCrois   *Recueil des historiens des croisades*, 16 volumes, Paris 1841–1906.

RepFont   *Repertorium fontium historicorum medii aevi*, Rome 1962 ff.

RepGerm   *Repertorium Germanicum*, published by the Königliches Preussisches Historisches Institut in Rom, 4 volumes, Berlin 1916–43, Volumes VI and VII in preparation.

RevSR   *Revue des Sciences Religieuses*, Strasbourg 1921 ff.

RFN   *Rivista di filosofia neoscolastica*, Milan 1909 ff.

RH   *Revue historique*, Paris 1876 ff.

RHÉF   *Revue d'histoire de l'Église de France*, Paris 1910 ff.

RHD   *Revue d'histoire diplomatique*, Paris.

RHE   *Revue d'histoire ecclésiastique*, Louvain 1900 ff.

RHM   *Revue d'histoire des missions*, Paris 1924 ff.

RHPhR   *Revue d'histoire et de philosophie religieuses*, Strasbourg 1921 ff.

RHR   *Revue de l'histoire des religions*, Paris 1880 ff.

RI   J. F. Böhmer, *Regesta Imperii* (1831 ff.), revised by E. Mühlbacher, J. Fischer, *et al.*, I, Innsbruck 1889, 2d ed. *ibid.*, 1901–08; II/1, Innsbruck 1893; II/2, Graz 1950; II/3 in preparation; III/1, Graz 1951; V–VI, VIII, IX, Innsbruck 1877–1948.

RivAC   *Rivista di archeologia cristiana*, Rome 1924 ff.

RMA   *Revue du moyen-âge latin*, Strasbourg 1945 ff.

RMab   *Revue Mabillon*, Ligugé 1921 ff.

RNPh   *Revue néoscolastique de philosophie*, Louvain 1894 ff.

ROC   *Revue de l'Orient chrétien*, Paris 1896 ff.

Rolls Series   *Rerum Britannicarum medii aevi Scriptores*, published by the Master of the Rolls, 99 volumes, London 1858–96.

RömHM   *Römische Historische Mitteilungen*, Graz and Cologne 1958 ff.

RQ   *Römische Quartalschrift für christliche Altertumskunde und für Kirchengeschichte*, Freiburg im Breisgau 1887 ff.

RQH   *Revue des questions historiques*, Paris 1866 ff.

RSF   *Rivista critica di Storia della Filosofia*.

RSIt   *Rivista storica Italiana*, Naples 1884 ff.

RSPhTh   *Revue des sciences philosophiques et théologiques*, Paris 1907 ff.

RSR   *Recherches de science religieuse*, Paris 1910 ff.

RSTI   *Rivista di storia della chiesa in Italia*, Rome 1947 ff.

RThAM   *Recherches de théologie ancienne et médiévale*, Louvain 1929 ff.

RThom   *Revue Thomiste*, Paris 1893 ff.

Runciman   S. Runciman, *A History of the Crusades*, 3 volumes, Cambridge 1951–54.

SA   *Studia Anselmiana*, Rome 1933 ff.

SAB   *Sitzungsberichte der Deutschen* (till 1944: *Preussischen) Akademie der Wissenschaften zu Berlin*. Phil.-hist. Klasse, Berlin 1882 ff.

Saeculum   *Saeculum. Jahrbuch für Universalgeschichte*, Freiburg im Breisgau 1950 ff.

SAH   *Sitzungsberichte der Heidelberger Akademie der Wissenschaften*. Phil.-hist. Klasse, Heidelberg 1910 ff.

SAM   *Sitzungsberichte der Bayerischen Akademie der Wissenschaften*. Phil.-hist. Abt., Munich 1871 ff.

SAW   *Sitzungsberichte der* (from 225, 1, 1947: *Österreichischen) Akademie der Wissenschaften in Wien*, Vienna 1831 ff.

SC   *Scuola Cattolica*, Milan 1873 ff.

SchmausThGG   *Theologie in Geschichte und Gegenwart* (M. Schmaus zum 60. Geburtstag), edited by J. Auer and H. Volk, Munich 1957.

Scholastik   *Scholastik*, Freiburg im Breisgau 1926 ff.

Schottenloher   K. Schottenloher, *Bibliographie zur deutschen Geschichte im Zeitalter der Glaubensspaltung 1517–85*, 6 volumes, Leipzig 1933–40, Stuttgart, 2d ed. 1956 ff.

Seppelt   F. X. Seppelt, *Geschichte der Päpste von den Anfängen bis zur Mitte des 20. Jahrhunderts*, I, II, IV, V, Leipzig 1931–41; I, Munich, 2d ed. 1954, II, *ibid.*, 2d ed. 1955, III, *ibid.*, 2d ed. 1956, IV, ibid., 2d ed. 1957 (revised by G. Schwaiger).

SM   *Studien und Mitteilungen aus dem Benediktiner- und Zisterzienserorden bzw. zur Geschichte des Benediktinerordens und seiner Zweige*, Munich 1880 ff. (from 1911, new series).

SourcesChr   *Sources chrétiennes*, edited by H. de Lubac and J. Daniélou, Paris 1941 ff.

Speculum   *Speculum. A Journal of Mediaeval Studies*, Cambridge, Mass. 1926 ff.

Stammler-Langosch   *Deutsche Literatur des Mittelalters. Verfasserlexikon*, 5 volumes, Volumes I–II edited by W. Stammler, Volumes III–V edited by K. Langosch, Berlin and Leipzig 1933–55.

StC   *Studia Catholica*, Roermond 1924 ff.

StdZ   *Stimmen der Zeit* (before 1914: *Stimmen aus Maria-Laach)*, Freiburg im Breisgau 1871 ff.

Stegmüller RS   F. Stegmüller, *Repertorium commentariorum in sententias Petri Lombardi*, I–II, Würzburg 1947.

SteT   *Studi e Testi*, Rome 1900 ff.

StG   *Studia Gratiana*, edited by J. Forchielli and A. M. Stickler, I–III, Bologna 1953 ff.

StMis   *Studia Missionalia*, Rome 1943 ff.

Streit   *Bibliotheca Missionum*, begun by R. Streit, continued by J. Dindinger, (Münster, Aachen) Freiburg im Breisgau 1916 ff. (up to 1968: 26 volumes).

StRom   *Studi Romani.*

StudFr   *Studi francescani*, Arezzo and Florence 1903 ff.

StudGreg   *Studi Gregoriani*, edited by G. B. Borino, I ff., Rome 1947 ff.

StudMed   *Studi Medievali*, Turin 1904 ff., new series 1928 ff. (*Nuovi Studi Medievali*, Bologna 1923–27); 3d series, Spoleto 1961 ff.

StudMon   *Studia Monastica*, Montserrat (Barcelona).

TG   *Tijdschrift voor Geschiedenis*, Groningen.

ThGl   *Theologie und Glaube*, Paderborn 1909 ff.

ThL   *Theologische Literaturzeitung*, Berlin.

ThLZ   *Theologische Literaturzeitung*, Leipzig 1878 ff.

ThPQ	*Theologisch-praktische Quartalschrift*, Linz an der Donau 1848 ff.
ThQ	*Theologische Quartalschrift*, Tübingen 1819 ff.; Stuttgart 1946 ff.
ThRv	*Theologische Revue*, Münster 1902 ff.
ThZ	*Theologische Zeitschrift*, Basel 1945 ff.
Tr	*Traditio*, New York 1943 ff.
TThZ	*Trierer Theologische Zeitschrift* (till 1944: *Pastor Bonus*), Trier 1888 ff.

Ueberweg   F. *Ueberwegs Grundriss der Geschichte der Philosophie*, Berlin I, 12th ed. 1926 by K. Praechter; II, 11th ed. 1928 by B. Geyer; III, 12th ed. 1924 by M. Frischeisen-Köhler and W. Moog; IV, 12th ed. 1923 by K. Österreich; V, 12th ed. 1928 by K. Österreich.

VigChr	*Vigiliae christianae*, Amsterdam 1947 ff.
ViVr	Vizantijskij Vremennik, Leningrad 1894 ff.
VS	*La vie spirituelle*, (Ligugé, Juvisy), Paris 1869 ff.

WA	M. Luther, *Werke. Kritische Gesamtausgabe* ("Weimar Edition"), 1883 ff.
WaTr	*D. Martin Luthers Werke, Tischreden*, 6 volumes, Weimar 1912–21.
Waas	A. Waas, *Geschichte der Kreuzzüge*, 2 volumes, Freiburg im Breisgau 1956.
Watterich	J. B. Watterich, *Pontificum Romanorum qui fuerunt inde ab exeunte saeculo IX° usque ad finem saeculi XIII* vitae ab aequalibus conscriptae ...*, I (972–1099) and II (1099–1198), Leipzig 1862.
Wulf	M. de Wulf, *Histoire de la philosophie médiévale*, Louvain and Paris, I, 6th ed. 1934, II, 6th ed. 1936, III, 6th ed. 1947.
WZKM	*Wiener Zeitschrift für die Kunde des Morgenlandes*, Vienna 1887 ff.

ZAM	*Zeitschrift für Aszese und Mystik* (from 1947: *GuL*), Innsbruck, Munich) Würzburg 1926 ff.
ZBKG	*Zeitschrift für bayerische Kirchengeschichte*, Gunzenhausen 1926 ff.
ZBLG	*Zeitschrift für Bayerische Landesgeschichte*, Munich 1928 ff.
ZdAdL	*Zeitschrift für deutsches Altertum und deutsche Literatur*, (Berlin) Wiesbaden 1841 ff. (till 1874: *Zeitschrift für deutsches Altertum*).
ZGObrh	*Zeitschrift für die Geschichte des Oberrheins*, Karlsruhe 1851 ff.
ZKG	*Zeitschrift für Kirchengeschichte*, (Gotha) Stuttgart 1876 ff.
ZKTh	*Zeitschrift für Katholische Theologie*, (Innsbruck) Vienna 1877 ff.
ZMR	*Zeitschrift für Missionswissenschaft und Religionswissenschaft*, 34 ff., Münster 1950 ff. (*Zeitschrift für Missionswissenschaft*, 1–17, ibid. 1911–27; *Zeitschrift für Missionswissenschaft und Religionswissenschaft*, 18–25, ibid. 1928–35; *Zeitschrift für Missionswissenschaft*, 26–27, ibid. 1935–37; *Missionswissenschaft und Religionswissenschaft*, 28–33, ibid. 1938–41, 1947–49).
ZRGG	*Zeitschrift für Religions- und Geistesgeschichte*, Marburg 1948 ff.
ZSavRGgerm	*Zeitschrift der Savigny-Stiftung für Rechtsgeschichte*, Germanistische Abteilung, Weimar 1863 ff.
ZSavRGkan	*Zeitschrift der Savigny-Stiftung für Rechtsgeschichte*, Kanonistische Abteilung, Weimar 1911 ff.
ZSKG	*Zeitschrift für Schweizer Kirchengeschichte*, Fribourg 1907 ff.
ZSTh	*Zeitschrift für systematische Theologie*, (Gütersloh) Berlin 1923 ff.
ZThK	*Zeitschrift für Theologie und Kirche*, Tübingen 1891 ff.

PART ONE

The High Middle Ages

The Post-Gregorian Epoch (1124—53)

CHAPTER 1

Honorius II, the Schism of 1130, and the Second Lateran Council

The Concordat of Worms (1122) and its ratification by the Church at the First Lateran Council (1123), which put an end to the Investiture Controversy in Germany and Italy also, meant for Christendom the beginning of an age of peaceful growth. Now the forces of reform, as represented by the new orders, were able to develop everywhere. The relationship of the Roman Church to the Empire and to the Western Kings was under the aegis of a trusting cooperation. However, an exception was constituted by the growing area of Norman rule in South Italy that was subject to the vigorous policies of Count Roger II. Its northward expansion could not but be a source of constant anxiety for the Curia. And yet the Normans had also been, since their enfeoffment by the Pope in 1059, a support for the Roman Church when the imperial pressure from the north jeopardized the autonomy of the *Patrimonium*.

The external peace which, as has just been mentioned, the Church had won was, to be sure, affected by a severe crisis within the Roman Church's leadership, which occurred in the Schism of 1130–38 and for the settlement of which the decision of the whole of Christendom had to be invoked. Research in recent decades[1] has made it clear that there was here involved not so much any strictly Roman rivalries, such as had often decided the fate of the papacy in the holders of that office during the tenth and eleventh centuries, but rather a partisan struggle within the College of Cardinals, which in its new form had gained an important influence on the government of the Church. The new representatives of the reform movement — Cîteaux, Prémontré, and the canons regular — had already, under Calixtus II, found a friend in the college in the person

---

[1] *Cf.* the report on research (till 1961) in F. J. Schmale, *Studien zum Schisma des Jahres 1130* (Cologne 1961), 2–12. Also, G. Tellenbach, "Der Sturz des Abtes Pontius von Cluny und seine geschichtliche Bedeutung," *QFIAB*, 42 f. (1963), 13–55, and P. F. Palumbo, "Nuovi studi (1942–62) sullo scisma di Anacleto II," *BIStIAM*, 75 (1963), 71–103.

of the Cardinal Chancellor Aimeric.[2] It was due to his resolute policy that within the Curia the circle of Old Gregorians, as they were called, who were inclined to continue in the ideas of the militant period of the Investiture Controversy, was faced by a growing front composed of cardinals who were linked to the concerns of the age of peace that had just been gained and to the religious reform now more strongly circulating in the new orders.

The tumultuous election following the death on 13 December 1124 of Calixtus II served as a sign of the changing situation at the Curia. Candidates for the succession were Lambert, Cardinal Bishop of Ostia, and the Cardinal Deacon Saxo of Santo Stefano. Both had taken part in the discussions which had led to the concluding of the Concordat of Worms. However, the electors decided on the Cardinal Priest Theobald of Sant'Anastasia, who was invested with the red mantle under the name of Celestine II. The *Te Deum* had already been intoned when the gathering was thrown into an uproar by Leo Frangipani, and the newly elected Pope was subjected to grave indignity. The Cardinal Chancellor Aimeric, whose connection with the Frangipani was well known, was able to induce Celestine to abdicate and succeeded in uniting the votes of the electors on Lambert of Ostia on 21 December 1124, especially after Cardinal Peter Pierleoni officially renounced the candidacy which seems to have been urged upon him. The new Pope, Honorius II (1124–30), confirmed Aimeric in his office and thus facilitated his further rise. Of the ten cardinals created[3] in this pontificate, seven strengthened the chancellor's group, as would appear in 1130. For the most part men were also selected for the legations to Germany, England, Lombardy, Venice, Benevento, and Castile up to 1130 who, as the decision of that year showed, were on Aimeric's side. To the very end of the pontificate Aimeric was able to win for the "new course" a strong minority of the college, almost one-half. As a Burgundian, Aimeric came from the heartland of the monastic reforms of Cluny and Cîteaux and was himself a canon regular, as was Lambert of Ostia, whose election he had decisively brought about.

A few months after the accession of Honorius II to the papal throne the Emperor Henry V died in Germany (23 May 1125). The election of his successor in the presence of the papal legate, Cardinal Gerard of Santa Croce, and under the authoritative guidance of the electoral assembly by Archbishop Adalbert of Mainz ended in favour of the Duke of Saxony, Lothar of Supplinburg. The princes passed over Frederick of Hohen-

---

[2] F. J. Schmale, *op. cit.*, 93–191, provides the first detailed sketch of his life.

[3] Following the method of H. W. Klewitz, *Ende des Reformpapsttums*, F. J. Schmale (*op. cit.*, 29–90) achieved searching analyses of all members of the College of Cardinals before 1130; he gives here a concise characterization of the rivals of 1130, in which the stress is definitely favourable to Innocent II.

staufen, Duke of Swabia, who as nephew of the dead Emperor would have had the expectation of the crown by hereditary right. But it was feared that he would continue the Salian ecclesiastical policy, and Lothar, who had no son and at the age of fifty was, for those days, an old man, seemed to offer a better assurance of the princes' right of free election. The new King Lothar (1125–37) announced his election to the Pope and even asked its confirmation. But the opposition of the disregarded Hohenstaufen soon made itself known. While Duke Frederick had done homage to King Lothar, his brother Conrad had not, and at Nürnberg in December 1127 the Swabian and Franconian princes elected Conrad as anti-King. On an expedition to Italy Conrad received the iron crown of the Lombard Kingdom from Archbishop Anselm of Milan at Monza on 29 June 1128. Pope Honorius II now came out for Lothar. He sent Cardinal John of Crema to Pisa, where at a synod Archbishop Anselm was excommunicated. Thereby the Pope's repudiation of Conrad was made clear, and in 1130 the anti-King returned to Germany without having achieved his Italian aims.

In South Italy Honorius had to deal with Count Roger II. For when Duke William of Apulia died in 1127 the Count of Sicily aspired to enter upon the inheritance. The Curia planned an expedition against Roger, but nothing came of it. Negotiations, conducted on behalf of the Curia by Cardinal Aimeric and Cencio Frangipani and necessitated by Roger's forcible occupation of Apulia in 1128, ended with the Treaty of Benevento, a compromise which confirmed the growth of Roger's power. The Sicilian bound himself to respect the County of Capua and the papal property in Benevento. The Peace of Benevento (22 August 1128) revealed, however, where the definitive frontiers of Norman Italy would lie. It was really only an armistice, like so many peace treaties of the epoch.

More instructive for the inner Church policies of the pontificate were the proceedings in regard to Cluny and Montecassino. Abbot Pons de Melgueil, [4] who had succeeded Abbot Hugh at Cluny in 1109 and up to the time of the Concordat of Worms had been one of the prelates most favoured by the Curia, had gone to Jerusalem *via* Rome in 1122. Whether Calixtus II had succeeded in inducing him to renounce the abbacy cannot be proved. In any event the Pope allowed a new election at Cluny. The monks chose Hugh of Marcigny and, after his early death, Peter the Venerable. The return of Pons from Jerusalem was followed at Cluny by a violent struggle over the abbacy. Honorius II cited the rivals before his tribunal at Rome. Abbot Pons was condemned and died the same year, 1126, in papal custody. The most recent research sees in these events proof that the trend at the Curia "from monachism to episcopate," already

---

[4] On this see especially Tellenbach, *loc. cit.*

5

discernible under Calixtus II, was growing stronger,[5] and points to the strong tensions between Cluny and the bishops, which had come to light under Pons. A similar interpretation is probably to be given to the Curia's proceedings at Montecassino, where Honorius II forced the Cardinal Abbot Oderisius to resign the abbatial office. Here too the *gravamina* of the bishops against the powerful abbey seem to have been taken seriously. A further change in the Curia's ecclesiastical policy became clear in the growing number of privileges for the canons regular.[6] But because of their recognition of episcopal jurisdiction the Cistercians and the Premonstratensians were in their first years spared from having to oppose this new direction at the Curia. The papacy had to make it its business to gain everywhere the energetic collaboration of the episcopate for the religious reform of the West.

At Rome this change, simultaneously involving the disappearing of a generation in the College of Cardinals, led to strains, which became worse toward the close of Honorius's pontificate because of the interference of the competing noble factions, the Frangipani, who favoured the trend represented by the Cardinal Chancellor Aimeric, and the Pierleoni, supporters of the Old Gregorians. The fateful year 1130 released these tensions, not for peace but for a schism of the type that the Church had been spared since the dark days of the feudalized papacy up to 1046. The Schism of 1130 was not imposed on the Church from without but originated within the Church's own bosom. Nevertheless, the history of this schism was to show how very much times had changed since the *saeculum obscurum*. What at first seemed to be a purely Roman confrontation between two claimants to the papacy was quickly cited before the forum of the Universal Church and there decided.

When Pope Honorius II fell gravely ill at the beginning of 1130, Cardinal Aimeric, probably recalling the tumultuous election of 1124, proceeded to make preparations[7] which should facilitate a free and canonical election. The dying pontiff was conveyed to the monastery of San Gregorio all'Aventino, which was protected by the strongholds of the Frangipani. The College of Cardinals selected from its three orders representatives who would constitute an electoral commission of eight. On this group,

---

[5] *Ibid.*, 55.

[6] Under Calixtus II the ratio of privileges for Benedictines to privileges for canons regular had been 4:1; under Honorius II it became 1.6:1 and under Innocent II 1.1:1. Cf. Schmale, *op. cit.*, 139 f.

[7] In *Die streitige Papstwahl des Jahres 1130* (Innsbruck 1876), E. Mühlbacher compiled an exhaustive collection of the sources for the double election. Her criticism was retained in all later works on the schism. Most recent in importance has been the investigation by F. J. Schmale of the writings transmitted in the *Codex Udalrici*, which he was able with a high degree of probability to demonstrate as forgeries in "Die Bemühungen Innozenz' II. um seine Anerkennung in Deutschland," ZKG, 65 (1953 f.), 240–65.

following the death and burial of the Pope, would devolve the election of a successor. Five members of this commission belonged to Aimeric's faction; only three came from the ranks of the Old Gregorians.[8] The church of Sant'Andrea was to be the place of the election, and the fortresses of the Frangipani were to be turned over to the College of Cardinals for the time of the election.

Actually, these arrangements were not adhered to. Honorius died during the night of 13–14 February and was buried with the utmost haste in a temporary grave. The commission was unable to meet in full strength, for two of its members, Cardinals Peter Pierleoni and Jonathan, were absent. But at daybreak, with the assent of his friends and despite the protest of Cardinal Peter of Pisa, Aimeric acclaimed as Pope the Cardinal Deacon Gregory of Sant'Angelo. Invested with the red mantle of his predecessor, Innocent II (1130–43) was enthroned at the Lateran.

When during the morning of 14 February people in Rome learned what had happened during the night, Cardinal Peter Pierleoni convoked the other cardinals, the majority of the college, at San Marco, protested against the uncanonical method of the election, and invited the gathering for its part to provide Honorius II with a successor. He himself designated as a candidate the Cardinal Bishop Peter of Porto, who, however, refused to be considered and in turn nominated Peter Pierleoni. The latter was unanimously elected by the cardinals present and acclaimed by the clergy and people who were at hand. Anacletus II (1130–38) was conducted to Saint Peter's for his enthronement. And so Rome had elected two Popes on one day. Both were likewise consecrated on the same day, 23 February: Innocent II by the Cardinal Bishop of Ostia in Aimeric's titular church, Santa Maria Nuova; Anacletus II by the Cardinal Bishop Peter of Porto in the Lateran.

Both rivals were Romans. Innocent II belonged to the Papareschi of Trastevere, Anacletus II to the powerful Pierleoni.[9] The Pierleoni were of Jewish origin — hence Anacletus is known as "the Pope from the ghetto" — but they had been Christians since the days of Leo IX. They

---

[8] The two Cardinal Bishops, William of Preneste and Conrad of Sabina, the Cardinal Priest Peter Rufus, and the Cardinal Deacons, Aimeric and Gregory of Saint'Angelo, belonged to the first group. The other three were the Cardinal Priests, Peter Pierleoni and Peter of Pisa, and the Cardinal Deacon Jonathan.

[9] The most thorough studies on the Pierleoni are those of P. F. Palumbo (see the bibliography for this chapter). The picture of the Cardinal's character was so distorted by the harsh polemics of the period of the schism that its real lines can be determined only with difficulty. His intellectual preeminence seems to have gained him only slight sympathy among his opponents, the majority of whom were French; they condemned him in a rare unanimity. (Here should be recalled the Cluniac Cardinal Matthew of Albano in the presentation by U. Berlière in RBén, 18 [1901], 113–40.) The then stirring national feeling may have played a role.

had rendered great services to the Popes up to Calixtus II inclusively and were closely bound to the Old Gregorians. Cardinal Peter, who had studied at Paris and had become a monk at Cluny, had been created a cardinal by Paschal II and had risen steadily in influence. Without any doubt he was intellectually outstanding, energetic and quick at making decisions, and, thanks to his experience at the Curia and on important legatine missions in England and France, he was also conversant with the government of the Church, and the adversary and match of the Cardinal Chancellor Aimeric. Beside Anacletus, Innocent was pale and middling. People praised his pleasing devotion and his blameless conduct. He too was experienced as a legate: he had taken part in the negotiations preceding the Concordat of Worms and together with Cardinal Pierleoni he had carried out a legatine mission in France. Neither election had taken place canonically, even if one can speak at all of an election law in force at that time. The papal electoral law of 1059 had not been in effect for a long time, if it ever had been; in any event, the guidelines and conditions previously agreed upon and sworn to had not been observed. There was no court of arbitration to which appeal could be made. And so there remained only one way, if neither rival could impose himself in Rome by excluding the other or getting him to resign: an appeal to the Universal Church, on gaining whose recognition both claimants now concentrated all their energies. Innocent II had to leave Rome, for the Frangipani abandoned him and did homage to Anacletus II. Innocent was a canon regular and hence, together with Aimeric, he was friendly toward the influential circles of the new orders. Anacletus expected to have on his side Cluny, the most powerful monastic order of the West, to which he himself belonged. But the majority decision of the Church favoured Innocent, especially since Cluny under Peter the Venerable let itself be ranged against Anacletus.

Innocent first wooed France, where Bernard of Clairvaux came out for him. Not all of France followed, it is true, for Aquitaine, Archbishop Hildebert of Tours, and Bishop Gerard of Angoulême were at first on the side of Anacletus. England too, which initially hesitated, could eventually be brought over to Innocent by Bernard's influence on King Henry I, but Scotland, both King and clergy, held to Anacletus. Spain and Portugal acknowledged Innocent. Information is lacking in regard to Scandinavia and the churches of Eastern Europe. While the crusader states and their Latin Patriarchs finally adhered to Innocent, the Greek Patriarch of Constantinople appears to have recognized Anacletus.[10]

Especially important became the stand of the German Church and of

---

[10] Both rivals boasted of the assent of the Eastern Churches; their contradictory statements were investigated by Schmale, op. cit., 248, footnote 2. Complete clarification is impossible in the present state of the sources.

King Lothar. Both claimants announced their election to the King and invited him to Rome. But it was only at the Diet of Würzburg in October 1130 that Lothar acceded to the majority decision of the bishops and prelates and recognized Innocent, whom he met in person in March 1131 at the Diet of Liège; here he promised the requested journey to Rome. In Germany Innocent's cause had been especially seconded by Norbert of Magdeburg and Conrad of Salzburg, who were kept informed by Archbishop Walter of Ravenna, Bishop Hubert of Lucca, Aimeric, and Bernard of Clairvaux.

Anacletus could rely on Rome, Milan, and South Italy, in particular on Roger II, for whom he confirmed the royal title that the Count of Sicily had just assumed.[11] The connection with the Normans allowed Anacletus to continue to act as Pope from Rome until his death on 25 January 1138. On his first expedition, in 1133, King Lothar did, it is true, gain at least the Lateran basilica, where on 4 June Innocent crowned him Emperor, but, once the Germans had again left Rome, Innocent could not maintain himself and in September he went to Pisa. There in 1135 he held a synod, which was well attended from beyond the Alps; Anacletus and Roger of Sicily were excommunicated.

When, finally, thanks to the efforts of Bernard of Clairvaux, Milan was gained for Innocent, the route was open for a second journey to Italy by the Emperor (1136–37). This time also Rome could not be taken, and the campaign against Roger II ended indecisively. Lothar died on 4 December 1137, *en route* back to Germany, without having seen the end of the schism. Meanwhile, the Innocentians had undertaken negotiations with Roger. The outcome was that both rivals sent embassies to present the claims and rights of their respective principals before the King as arbiter at Salerno in November 1137, but they were unable to bring him to a definitive stand.

Success in these debates was achieved only by Bernard of Clairvaux, who contrived to get Cardinal Peter of Pisa, hitherto one of the most loyal adherents of Anacletus, to submit to Innocent.

Only the death of Anacletus II ended the schism; his successor, Cardinal Gregory Conti of Santi Apostoli, chosen in March 1138 and styling himself Victor IV, renounced the pontificate as early as 29 May of the same year. His electors and the Pierleoni now recognized Innocent II, who had thus finally won the long and arduous fight for the assent of all of Christendom. The virtually unanimous consent of the old and the new orders, the confidence of the great congregations of canons regular, the

---

[11] On this *cf.* what is so far the best exposition: L. R. Ménager, "L'institution monarchique dans les États Normands d'Italie," *Cahiers de Civilisation médiévale*, 2 (1959), 445–48 (La promotion royale).

recognition accorded by the leading princes of the West and their episcopates, had especially contributed to this success. The dynamic propaganda, fully displayed in these years, of the great Abbot of Clairvaux, who effectively supported the exertions of Innocent II in all aspects, above all in regard to Italy, must not be passed over in silence.[12]

Innocent II summoned a general synod to meet at Rome in the Lateran in April 1139. Now following the model of Lateran I (1123), which had liquidated the confusion resulting from the Investiture Controversy, all problems growing out of the Schism of 1130 were to be settled. Like Lateran I, Lateran II obtained recognition as an ecumenical council only much later.[13] In attendance were more than one hundred bishops, some of them from the crusader states; the number of abbots and of superiors of chapters of canons must have been far larger but it has not come down to us. At the opening of the Council Innocent spoke on the unity of the Church, the mutilation of which he branded as a sin against the Holy Spirit. He refused to recognize any legitimacy in the pontificate of Anacletus II, since it had not obtained the assent of the Church, and so the synod declared that all acts, decisions, ordinations, and consecrations performed by Anacletus and his adherents were null and void. These adherents, including even Peter of Pisa, for whom Bernard had interceded, lost all offices and dignities. Bishop Godfrey of Chartres was made legate in France and Aquitaine to enforce these decisions. At the Council Innocent canonized Sturmi of Fulda at the request of the German episcopate. The synod's thirty decrees again comprised the reform program of the last decades and repeated the canons of Lateran I and of the Synods of Clermont (1130), Reims (1131), and Pisa (1135), but the sanctions were made more severe.

With its renewed rejection of lay investiture and of every sort of simony, with its tightening of religious and clerical discipline, with its concern for family and social morality, including its stress on the Peace of God, with its measures against simony and heresy, this Council has been called the "Epilogue of the Gregorian Age."[14]

---

[12] B. Jacqueline, "Bernard et le schisme d'Anaclet II," *Bernard de Clairvaux* (Commission d'Histoire de l'Ordre de Cîteaux, 3) (Paris 1953), 349–54, 375–77. However, this author apparently does not know the German research, and there are numerous inexact statements. Reference should be made to the account of Saint Bernard in Chapter 2.

[13] Cf. *Conciliorum Oecumenicorum Decreta*, ed. J. Alberigo *et al.* (Freiburg, 2nd ed. 1962), 163 (Lateran I) and 171 (Lateran II); R. Foreville, *Latran I, II, III, et Latran IV* (Paris 1965), 10–12.

[14] Thus A. Fliche in *Fliche-Martin*, IX, 1 (Paris 1944), 178.

CHAPTER 2

The Reform Orders of the Twelfth Century and
Bernard of Clairvaux

The origins of the new orders, during the period of the Gregorian reform, were discussed in the preceding volume. Though in some respects the papacy contributed to their founding, fundamentally involved was a religious movement coming from below, the heroic striving of monks, canons, and laymen to realize the spirit of the Gospel and of the primitive Church in the most austere poverty, in solitude, or as wandering preachers. The fact that not a few new foundations were again satisfied with the mitigated manner of life of the older Benedictinism did not necessarily imply decadence, for the Benedictines were still at a respectable level. Some of their monasteries even displayed an openness to the new ideas, as did even Cluny, whose congregation achieved its widest extent under the important Abbot Peter the Venerable (1122–56).[1] Just the same, the future belonged to those new communities of monks and canons, who preserved more purely the ideal of the *vita evangelica* and slowly established it institutionally. Their amazingly rapid diffusion throughout the entire West, the deeply appealing seriousness of their lives, and to an extent their pastoral and missionary efforts enabled these orders to rank with the most important historical factors of this period.[2] They profoundly reshaped Christian piety, including that of the people, and in their copious literature are to be heard many *motifs* that remained vital long after this age. They were the bridges leading from the Gregorian reform to the epoch of the mendicant orders.

[1] G. Constable and J. Kritzek, "Petrus Venerabilis (1156–1956). Studies and Texts Commemorating the Eighth Centenary of his Death," *Studia Anselmiana*, 40 (Rome 1956). On the conflict between Cluny and Cîteaux in regard to the authentic understanding of monastic perfection, *cf.* A. Wilmart, "Une riposte de l'ancien monachisme au manifeste de S. Bernard," *RBén*, 46 (1934), 296–344, where the best known texts are analyzed; however, still other witnesses are known. See M. A. Dimier, "Un témoin tardif peu connu du conflit entre cisterciens et clunisiens," Constable and Kritzek, *op. cit.*, 81–94; "Dialogus inter Cluniacensem monachum et Cisterciensem de diversis utriusque ordinis observantiis," ed. Martène, *Thesaurus novorum anecdotorum*, V, 1569–1654, and W. Williams, "A Dialogue between a Cluniac and a Cistercian," *JThS*, 31 (1930), 164–75, and A. Wilmart, *op. cit.*, 302 f.

[2] On the development of both the Benedictine and the reform orders in the twelfth century, *cf.* B. Bligny, *L'Église et les Ordres Religieux dans le royaume de Bourgogne aux XIᵉ et XIIᵉ siècles* (Paris 1960); the investigation is restricted to Burgundy, but it basically concerns the whole Church, especially since Burgundy was the heart of the West in regard to monasticism.

Hence, the development to be related here was reflected a great part of the course taken by the reform in the post-Gregorian period.

The Cistercians

No other community can give so clear an idea of the reform energies operating within the sphere of monasticism as the Cistercian Order. The beginnings and the first and decisive decades are, unfortunately, far more obscure than scholarship was aware until recently.[3] To be regarded as established are: the founding of Cîteaux by Robert of Molesme in 1098; Robert's return to his former monastery; the government of Cîteaux by Abbot Alberic and, after his death, probably in 1109, by Stephen Harding (1109–34). Born at Sherborne in England, Stephen had studied at Paris, was acquainted with Rome, and had become a monk at Molesme under Robert. The ideas of the founding generation are adequately known to us: concerned with strict poverty and a life in an isolated and poor locality. The monks of Cîteaux sought nothing different from what many other communities originating at that time were looking for. They were able to found La Ferté, the first daughter house, in 1113, not far from Cluny. Then, in quick succession, came Pontigny in 1114 and Clairvaux and Morimond in 1115. With La Ferté they constituted the group of so-called "primary abbeys," from which, in extensive ramifications, all Cistercian monasteries derived their origin. In 1119 the order counted ten houses, in 1123 there were twenty, and at the death of Stephen Harding in 1134 — he had resigned his abbacy in 1130 — the number was eighty.

This rapid growth presented Stephen Harding and the other Cistercian abbots with the question of how unity was to be preserved in so many foundations. From the bull of confirmation issued in 1119 by Calixtus II it appears that a first outline of an organization had been laid before the Pope, but we do not know its details. Undoubtedly it involved the matrix of the so-called *Carta Caritatis* and not, as was previously held, that document itself. Its original form must now be regarded as lost, and the most recent efforts to construct it from available texts have not succeeded. So long as a more certain pinpointing in time of the three extant texts, the *Carta Caritatis Prior*, its *summa*, and a *Carta Caritatis Posterior*, is not forthcoming, one must be satisfied with the following results: Until the bull of Alexander III of 5 August 1165, the *Carta Caritatis* had

---

[3] On the beginnings of the Cistercian Order now see P. Zakar in *AnOCist*, 10 (1964), 103–38; the development of the constitution, the *Carta Caritatis*, is best presented by J. B. Van Damme, "Formation de la constitution cistercienne. Esquisse historique," *Stud Mon*, 4 (1962), 111–37, and *AnOCist*, 21 (1965), 128–37.

undergone changes, the stages of which can be pretty well established from the bulls of Eugene III in 1152 and 1153 but not, at least for the present, for the preceding period. Even after Alexander III the constitutional development did not cease. There were no further changes in the text of the *Carta* but they were expressed in the decrees of the general chapters, which, compiled at rather long intervals, were published in the *Libellus definitionum* (1202–12) and the *Institutiones capituli generalis* (*ca.* 1256, supplemented in 1298).

The Cistercians sought to observe the Rule of Saint Benedict in its original purity. To avoid the charge of novelty they emphasized this return to the old, to the sources. But in fact the new observance was not in all respects an adhering to the letter of the Rule. *Oblati* were no longer accepted, the institute of *conversi*, or lay brothers, was elaborated, and the limiting of the abbatial authority by the constitution was new.

New also was the annual general chapter, attendance at which was obligatory on all abbots. Presided over by the Abbot of Cîteaux, it possessed and exercised full power over the order — legislative, executive, and judicial — but left to the abbeys complete financial and administrative autonomy. Annual visitation provided supervision, even in regard to the instructions of the general chapter. Within each filiation group it was taken care of by the mother abbey. The visitation of Cîteaux pertained to the four "primary abbeys."

In contradistinction to the predominantly personal organization of the Order of Cluny, with its dependence of priors and, to a degree, of abbots on the Abbot of Cluny, the Cistercians succeeded in establishing their order on an objectively co-operative basis. Individual abbeys, autonomous in themselves, associated according to filiation groups, and corporately united in the general chapter attended by all abbots — these constitutional principles gave rise to an order in which both the rights of the individual monastery and the interests of the entire order were assured. Hence it should cause no surprise that other reform orders of the period, such as the Premonstratensians and the Carthusians, took the *Carta Caritatis* as model.

While, also contrary to the Cluniac and older Benedictine ideal, there was desired until the mid-century a subordination to local episcopal jurisdiction, there then appeared papal exemption, so that, under the Pope, the general chapter became the highest court of appeal in the order.[4] The abbeys promised one another mutual economic help, the preservation of a

---

[4] Already foreshadowed in the *Privilegium Romanum* of Paschal II (1100), clearer in the confirmation of the *Carta Caritatis* by Calixtus II (1119), the exemption was made absolute by the bull of Lucius III of 21 November 1184; *cf.* K. Spahr, *Die Anfänge von Cîteaux* (Mainz 1953).

uniform discipline, and the cultivation of a simplified liturgy, whose externals — church buildings, vestments, vessels, chant — were to be kept as unpretentious as possible.

Since the order wanted to keep itself free from the feudal ties prevailing in the Cluniac system, it declined benefices and reintroduced manual labour. The white habit, the strict seclusion from the world by means of settlement in deserted areas, the austerity of the life in food, dwelling, and clothing, and the simplicity of the liturgy gave the order a great reputation as something new in the monastic world. The observance of the Benedictine rule enabled it to remain interiorly a part of this world.

The dynamism of Cistercian expansion was determined up to the mid-century by the personality of Saint Bernard of Clairvaux. When he died in 1153, there were already 350 abbeys, and he alone had founded sixty-six of them. In quick succession the order was established in Italy from 1120, in Germany from 1123, in England from 1128, and in Spain from 1132. Then followed Belgium (1132), Switzerland (1133), Savoy (1134), Scotland (1136), Portugal (1138), Hungary (1142), Ireland (1142), and Poland (1143.) The order appeared in Sweden in 1143, in Denmark in 1144, in Norway in 1146. In some abbeys the number of members reached an astounding figure: at Clairvaux 700, at Rievaulx 650, at Les Dunes in Flanders 530, at Walkenried 260. But in these and other monasteries the majority of members were lay brothers.

The origin of the institute of lay brothers was treated in the preceding volume. Cîteaux made particular use of this new institution, which had long before been introduced into other communities. As elsewhere, the Cistercian lay brothers made the monastic renunciations, without thereby becoming monks in the strict sense; they had neither an active nor a passive vote in their community. They shared in the choral liturgy only on Sundays and holy days. With few exceptions they came from the ordinary folk. Their dedication to work gave the order a high economic prosperity in the twelfth century and was especially irreplaceable in the foundations penetrating the eastern frontier area with the clearings that had to be created there. The *conversi* lived in the abbey and on the granges more or less remotely surrounding it.[5] Tensions with the real monastic community were not lacking and from the middle of the century there were revolts, boycotts, and even murderous attacks on abbots and superiors. The disciplinary problem could scarcely be controlled because of the partly widely scattered groups and the large numbers — Pontigny, for example, had 100 monks and more than 300 *conversi*.

---

[5] Exemplary for the elaboration of the granges is now the work by R. A. Donkin, "The Cistercian Grange in England in the 12th and 13th Centuries, with Special Reference to Yorkshire," *StudMon*, 6 (1964), 95–144.

The new order contributed powerfully to the development of the spiritual life in the Church.[6] Important French Cistercians, in addition to Saint Bernard, were William of Saint-Thierry (d. 1148), Guerric of Igny (d. 1157), and Isaac of Stella (d. 1169), and in the thirteenth century Adam of Perseigne (d. 1221) and Hélinand of Froidmont (d. 1235). In England the outstanding name is that of Aelred of Rievaulx (d. 1167); in Germany, that of the historian, Otto of Freising (d. 1158). The literary history of the twelfth century extols not only the order's historiographers but also its poets, Hélinand of Froidmont and Theobald of Marly. Troubadours made their appearance: Bernard of Ventadour, Bertrand of Born, Fulco of Marseilles; here belong also Alain de Lille and Serlo of Wilton.

The Popes utilized the services of the order in the most varied ways, Bernard's career becoming the model here too. The wide and very thickly woven network of houses, with their regular intercommunications, especially in their general chapters, constituted an excellent medium of active and passive communication. The order was very soon represented in the College of Cardinals, and Pope Eugene III was a Cistercian. The order furnished many bishops, and outstanding members were entrusted with legatine functions, the most important of which was the combat with heresy in the Midi in the second half of the century. The preaching of the crusade was often committed to the order; here too Bernard's famed preaching of the Second Crusade supplied the inspiration. In the course of the Curia's centralization of the ecclesiastical juridical system, many Cistercian abbots were assigned tasks as judges delegate. An eventual result of this recourse to the order by the Curia was a wealth of privileges, despite Bernard's warning against this very thing. The growth of the order's exemption in the course of the later twelfth century can be read in the history of the bestowal of these privileges.

And so criticism was not absent; it came not only from the Cistercians' own ranks but also from without.[7] Well known is the polemic between Cluny and Cîteaux, represented respectively by Peter the Venerable and Bernard of Clairvaux. Toward the close of the twelfth century Walter Map, archdeacon of Oxford, and Giraldus Cambrensis spoke out in biting satire against the order that was by then, of course, no longer supported by the enthusiasm of its beginnings.

---

[6] Cîteaux's alleged aversion to study and literary activity was investigated by A. Dimier, "Les premiers Cisterciens étaient-ils ennemis des études?" *StudMon*, 4 (1962), 69–91. There was no such aversion. Corresponding instructions of the general chapters have also been misunderstood.

[7] *Cf.* C. H. Talbot, "The English Cistercians and the Universities," *StudMon*, 4 (1962), 197–220, who stresses the less fortunate consequences for religious life in the monastery in the case of monks who studied at the universities.

The Canons Regular

Only after the conclusion of the Investiture Controversy could the institute of canons regular, whose beginnings were described in the preceding volume, develop freely. From the pontificate of Urban II it was already clear that it would have a great future. For the greater the number of reform-minded bishops became in the course of the Gregorian reform, the more urgent became the task of introducing the reform among clergy and people. The bishops themselves had to try to solve the problem in their dioceses, but of course they needed numerous helpers. Because of their cloister-centred lives, the Benedictines and other monastic communities were not too frequently considered for this work, and, besides, the relations between the episcopate and at least the older type of Benedictines were compromised by the monks' efforts to obtain exemption. The tensions were exposed both in the conflicts over exemption and the attempt to exclude monks from all pastoral activity. And so it was understandable that the bishops should turn to the canons regular. Here at first there were no difficulties about exemption. The reform of the higher clergy was assured for the future by the canons regular, and these could directly take part in the care of souls.

The importance of the canons regular movement was early grasped by the papacy and effectively fostered, above all from the time of Urban II. The climax of this favour came while Aimeric, who was one of them, was chancellor. Privileges were bestowed in an increasing amount. The number of votes of canons regular in the College of Cardinals grew, and, except for Celestine II and Eugene III, all the Popes from Honorius II to Hadrian IV were canons regular. They were thereby clearly distinguished from the five Benedictine Popes of the Gregorian reform, from Gregory VII to Gelasius II, because, significantly, Anacletus II, whose elevation in 1130 produced a schism, had been a monk of Cluny and accordingly could be regarded as the exponent of the old and now outdated tradition.

Together with the Popes, many bishops now also favoured the canons regular. In the new institute special prominence was achieved by the foundation made by Saint Norbert of Xanten, which was able to develop into a real order.

The Premonstratensians

Its origin, sketched in the preceding volume, was at first greatly influenced by the founder, especially after Norbert had become Archbishop of Magdeburg in 1126. In the same year he obtained from Honorius II the solemn confirmation of his order. He turned over the government of Prémontré to his disciple, Hugh of Fosses, in 1128. Norbert's friendship with Bernard of Clairvaux may explain the extensive dependence on the Cistercian *Carta Caritatis* that is to be noted in the oldest known statutes of the order, dating from about 1140. The result was that under Hugh of Fosses the desire to engage in the care of souls, otherwise a special characteristic of canons regular, was restricted and the *vita contemplativa* was more strongly emphasized. The organization knew the general chapter and a uniform direction, as in the case of Cîteaux, but the system of filiation was not adopted. Instead the order was divided into "circaries," or provinces, each headed by a *circator,* later called vicar general. Since Norbert demanded a subordination to the local ordinary in the case of Magdeburg — the circaries corresponded to the ecclesiastical provinces —, a similar relation was also imposed on many new foundations, and the Premonstratensians obtained exemption rather late, in 1409. The Abbot of Prémontré ranked as the Abbot General, and the three Abbots of Saint-Martin de Laon, Floreffe, and Cuissy were assigned to him as advisers. The original title of provost for the superior of a monastery was retained only in Saxony and Hungary. The cathedral chapters of Brandenburg, Riga, Havelberg, Ratzeburg, Börglum, and Leitomischl were made up of Premonstratensians. In addition to the general chapters at Prémontré there gradually appeared provincial chapters also. The right of visitation pertained to the Abbot General and also to the vicars general of the provinces.

In accord with Norbert's wish, all Premonstratensian foundations were originally double monasteries, in which the nuns were to occupy the position of *conversae;* and lay brothers were also envisaged. But the system of double monasteries was abolished as early as 1140. However, the now autonomous Premonstratensian nuns settled close to a community of canons, who retained their spiritual direction. In Germany the number of houses of nuns soon surpassed that of the abbeys.

The order experienced its strongest expansion in Germany, Bohemia, Belgium, and France; it was almost as widespread in England and Spain, but in other countries it was much less. Among the most important German monasteries were Steinfeld, Wadgassen, Knechtsteden, Arnstein, Roggenburg, Schussenried, Obermarchtal, Ursberg, Rot, and Weissenau; the last six of these later became royal abbeys.

Like the Cistercians, the canons regular also displayed a vigorous and special spirituality. Leadership here belonged to the school of Saint-Victor de Paris in France and to the Brothers of Reichersberg in Germany. Augustine, John the Evangelist, Paul, and Gregory the Great were held in particular veneration. Devotion to the Passion and to the Sacred Heart and a mysticism of the Cross were congenial to them; these were to some extent related to the attitude of Saint Bernard, but they are also to be viewed in the light of the crusade piety proper to the time. Especially noteworthy representatives of ascetical and mystical literature from the ranks of the canons, in addition to Norbert of Xanten and the theologians of Saint-Victor, were Luke of Mont-Cornillon at Liège and Philip of Harvengt, Abbot of Bonne-Espérance in Hainaut.

Emphasis upon the parochial care of souls especially by the Premonstratensians, who were themselves often nobles, meant a rise in the social level of the ministry in the lesser churches and at the same time the opening up of an important reservoir of recruits. Since the Premonstratensians, like the Cistercians, participated in the work of colonization and evangelization of the eastern territories, the parochial care of souls could only have contributed to the permanent effects of their exertions.

Bernard of Clairvaux

The most powerful ecclesiastical personality during the decades between 1120 and 1150 came from the Cistercian reform. With Norbert of Xanten and the Chancellor Aimeric he was one of the leaders of the late Gregorian reform and so stamped his features on his age that it has often been called the Age of Saint Bernard.

Bernard came from Dijon, almost on the frontier between the Imperial County of Burgundy and the French Duchy of Burgundy. Through his father, Tescelin Sorrel, and his mother, Aleth de Montbard, he belonged to widely ramified Burgundian knightly families.

He grew up with five brothers and one sister. He went to school with the canons of Notre-Dame de Saint-Vorles and devoted himself to literary and theological studies. His definite choice of a vocation was only made, after much hesitation, in 1111–12. It was probably determined by the strict asceticism of newly founded Cîteaux. He entered there, not by himself, but with thirty relatives and friends, whom he contrived to gain for the same ideal. For Cîteaux and its now rapidly starting expansion their entry was a turning point.

In April 1112 Bernard began his novitiate under Stephen Harding. He completed it in 1113 when Cîteaux founded its first daughter abbey, La Ferté. Its founder was a cousin of Bernard's, Josbert the Red de Châtillon. Bernard's friend, Hugh of Mâcon, became Abbot of the second daughter abbey, Pontigny, founded in 1114. Finally, in 1115 Bernard himself was entrusted with the founding of Clairvaux. Four of his brothers, his uncle Gaudri de Montbard, and his cousin Godfrey de la Roche-Vanneau followed him there.

Clairvaux was founded on the property of Bernard's uncle, the Viscount of Dijon, and lay in the diocese of Langres, 116 kilometres northwest of Cîteaux. Since Joceran, Bishop of Langres, was absent, Bernard received the abbatial blessing from William of Champeaux, Bishop of Châlons-sur-Marne, who became the most effectual patron of the young monastery.

Although Bernard was often ill and bedridden, we know of much travelling. Up to 1125 he went twice to Langres and visited Dijon, Auxerre, Foigny, Châlons, Reims, Igny, and Châteaulandon. Clairvaux was able to think of making foundations as early as 1118. In place of the Abbot, who was so often away, the community was governed by the prior, Bernard's cousin, Godfrey de La Roche-Vanneau. In 1138 he was elected Bishop of Langres.[8] Bernard was able to end the opposition to this. Hence for Clairvaux was assured the favour of the local Ordinary, while the good will of the territorial lord, Theobald of Champagne, was secured through Bernard's mediation between Theobald, the Bishops of Langres, and the Dukes of Burgundy. Clairvaux grew rapidly because of permanent foundations made by Bernard's kin and the great nobles friendly to him.

The spiritual authority of its Abbot likewise grew amazingly fast and spread far, first of all in the order itself, where he was one of the signers of Cîteaux's first organizational charter, the *Carta Caritatis*. His influence was unchallenged in the group of filiations of Clairvaux and also in the related groups proceeding from La Ferté and Morimond.

He was closely bound with the founder of Prémontré until the latter's death as Archbishop of Magdeburg and likewise with Peter the Venerable of Cluny. But the second of these friendships had to weather serious problems, for Bernard criticized the manner of life of the great Burgundian abbey and its congregation. It was to the credit of the Abbot of Cluny that he not only did not break off relations with Bernard but even allowed Bernard to influence him in reforming his congregation. Something similar occurred in the circles of canonical reform, where Bernard advocated transformation from chapters of secular canons to those of canons regular. This often came about through favouring elections which resulted in the choice of reform prelates, as at Toussaint-en-l'Isle at Châlons.

How powerful the authority of the Abbot of Clairvaux had become by 1130 appeared when he decided for Innocent II at the Synod of Étampes. Through his active role in liquidating the Schism of 1130-38 in France and Italy, through his constantly growing correspondence with the leading personalities of Western Christendom, through his ever more frequently requested and obtained intervention in ecclesiastical crises, Bernard gradually became "le personnage le plus en vue de l'Europe," as he has been termed,[9] the adviser of the great in Church and state. His friends and

---

[8] On the contested episcopal election at Langres, see now G. Constable, "The Disputed Election at Langres in 1138," *Tr*, 13 (1957), 119-52.

[9] *Fliche-Martin*, IX, 1 (1944), 13-41 (Saint Bernard).

relatives soon occupied the most influential positions in the Church. Hugh of Mâcon, Abbot of Pontigny, became Bishop of Auxerre. For his cousin, Godfrey of La Roche-Vanneau, prior of Clairvaux, Bernard obtained the see of Langres in a successful struggle against Peter of Cluny. Hugh, Abbot of Tre Fontane, Clairvaux's first daughter house, became Cardinal Bishop of Ostia in 1150. Bernard of Pisa, Abbot of Sant'Anastasio at Rome, was eventually elected Pope as Eugene III. The brother of the French King, a monk of Clairvaux, became Bishop of Beauvais in 1149.

Bernard was closely connected with the Roman Curia because of his friendship with the Chancellor Aimeric. [10] His letters to Honorius II, Innocent II, and Eugene III show the Abbot's intimate relations with the reform movement of canons regular that was favoured under these Popes, especially by Aimeric. Bernard was always the friend and adviser of the congregations of Saint-Ruf d'Avignon, Saint-Victor de Paris, and Arrouaise in Artois. This was true also of the founder of Saint-Victor, William of Champeaux, and of the great theologians at Paris, Hugh and Richard. The order established by Saint Gilbert of Sempringham in England was permanently influenced in its organization by Cîteaux. To the Curia such a man, who had gained so powerful a prestige, not only in his own order, but in the Cluniac, the Premonstratensian, and the Carthusian orders, among the canons regular, and even in the world of hermits, [11] must have seemed almost irreplaceable. It is true that friction could not always be avoided between him and Roman prelates, and, in view of Bernard's temperament, this is not to be wondered at, but identity of spiritual interests constantly brought about peace again.

The preparations for the Second Crusade furnished further proof of this. Bernard had long been familiar with the world of the crusade. In 1128, at the Council of Troyes, he had collaborated on the constitution of the Knights Templars, whose first grand master was related to him, and in De laude novae militiae he had sketched a spiritual program for the order. It had been suggested to him that Cistercian abbeys should be established in the Holy Land but he had declined, suggesting instead Prémontré, which he regarded as better suited for this. He corresponded with Queen Mélisende of Jerusalem. When, after the fall of Edessa in 1144, King Louis VII of France decided to provide the requested armed assistance and asked Pope Eugene III to send crusade preachers, Bernard

[10] F. J. Schmale, *Studien zum Schisma des Jahres 1130* (Cologne and Graz 1961), gives a cautious estimate of Bernard's relationship with the Chancellor Aimeric and even plays down his influence on the recognition of Innocent II in comparison with that of the canons regular.

[11] Bernard's relations with the various religious institutes is presented in special detail in *Saint Bernard* (Paris 1953), 193–338.

received the commission to preach the cross in France. He did so for the first time at Vézelay on 31 March 1146. But his enthusiasm led him beyond the French frontiers to Flanders and to the Rhine as far as Switzerland. At Speyer during the Christmas festivities he managed, but only after rather lengthy discussions, to gain the German King Conrad III for the crusade, though this was probably contrary to the intentions of the Pope. It was not until 6 February 1147 that Bernard returned to Clairvaux, travelling *via* Cologne, the Netherlands, and Flanders, preaching and working miracles. But as early as 13 March he took part in a Diet at Frankfurt am Main, where he was induced to approve the Wend Crusade, to declare that it deserved to be preached, privileged, and carried out, as the equal of the crusade to the East. It was only with hesitation that Eugene III confirmed the Frankfurt decisions. The extraordinary preaching journey of the saint of Clairvaux provided both contemporaries and later observers with a sharply outlined picture of the great Abbot. But the decisive depths of his spiritual being were revealed even more unambiguously in his literary work.

"The last of the Fathers," as Bernard has been called, left a bulky *corpus* of letters, sermons, and treatises, masterpieces of spiritual literature. Most of the treatises deal with questions of monastic spirituality, such as the *Degrees of Humility and Pride* (1124), the defense of the Cistercian ideal of life in comparison with that of Cluny (1125), several works on the love of God (1128–36), the explanation of *Precept and Dispensation* (before 1144), the *Praise of the New Knighthood* (before 1130), and the treatise on *Grace and Free Will* (before 1128). In 1135 Bernard began his chief work, the *Sermones super Canticum Canticorum*, of which he managed to finish eighty-six by the time of his death. The work of his old age, *De consideratione* in five books, was written for Pope Eugene III. Finally, he also composed the biography of his friend Malachy, Archbishop of Armagh in Ireland.

Despite the variety of literary form Bernard was basically concerned with only one thing: like the Fathers, he sought to present to his environment the teachings of Scripture, in whose world of ideas he himself lived and whose language he managed to appropriate because of an identification of spirit.[12] Students such as A. Dimier and J. Leclercq have extolled him as the clearest mirror of the spiritual life of his age. So long as he was alive and, even more, after his death there proceeded from him a far-reaching and enduring influence on the life of the entire Church.

John of Salisbury referred to Bernard without irony as the "sanctissi-

---

[12] On Bernard's language and style, see C. Mohrmann, "Observations sur la langue et le style de Saint Bernard," *Sancti Bernardi Opera*, ed. J. Leclercq *et al.*, II (Rome 1958), ix-xxxiii.

mus abbas." [13] As a saint, Bernard of Clairvaux was a moving force of his age. From his love of God he obtained the ceaseless impulses that determined his activity as well as his contemplation. He always regarded his business as God's business. The Cistercian way of life and the faithfully observed Benedictine rule were the framework for the *schola caritatis* of strict asceticism, where the spiritual father and Abbot knew how to operate better by example than by word. He became the "holy Abbot," though he was not lacking in human frailties, which he confessed and sought to eradicate. Experiences with himself and with his monks and friends throughout the Church taught him to understand and use ever better the Benedictine *discretio*. This experience was, demonstrably, a mystical experience of the nearness of God, from which there poured out upon him the wisdom of the final knowledge of God. Its most important presupposition, he taught, was humility, which had to inform all spiritual exertions. From it begins the ascent to God and it conditions all further stages, because it is basically the attitude of Christ: "habes commendatam a Deo humilitatem in Christo." This ascent is a constant growing in love, an incessant search for union with the triune God, which Bernard has described, as though in his last will, in the final sermons on the Canticle, as a union of the spirit with the Word who is God.

CHAPTER 3

*The Papacy and the Western Kings in
the Age of Saint Bernard*

The peace brought to the Empire by the Concordat of Worms in 1122 had been preceded in the other countries of Christendom by similar agreements between the Church and the secular authority — in England in 1106–07 and in France at the same time but without any formal treaty. [1] Following the intensive disputation of the Investiture Controversy views were to some extent theoretically clarified and even in agreement as to the function of kings and other secular powers within the Church, regarded as the Church of clerics and monks, of bishops and abbots, and of the Ro-

---

[13] *Historia ecclesiastica*, ed. M. Chibnall (London 1956), 25; *ibid.*, further judgments on Bernard: "abbatem, cuius tunc summa erat auctoritas, cuius consilio tam sacerdotium quam regnum pre ceteris agebatur" (16) and "erat religiosissimus et dissertissimus" (17).

[1] Volume III, Chapter 45. For England, see N. F. Cantor, *Church, Kingship and Lay Investiture in England* (Princeton 1958); for France, A. Becker, *Studium zum Investiturproblem in Frankreich* (Saarbrücken 1955); T. Schieffer, "Investiturstreit," *LThK*, V (2nd ed. 1960), 742–46. *Cf.* Volume III, Chapter 50, and the bibliography given there.

man Pontiff. Protection and in particular cases even extensive defense with means suited to the secular power were meant: preservation of the order which was a legal order embracing the whole of Christendom in all its members and classes by means of a readily offered, or at least not refused, support of the ecclesiastical judgment through sanctions extending beyond purely spiritual measures and intervening in the civil sphere. Saint Bernard himself, in his letters to the Emperor Lothar and King Conrad III, discovered a formula for this, to be understood entirely in a Gregorian sense. [2]

But in reality, even if one were to follow a stricter interpretation of Bernard's concept as Walter Ullmann sketches it, [3] bishops and Popes in their relations with Emperors, kings, and princes had to submit to the law of the politically possible. In the age of the unambiguous power of the reform spirit, which, represented by the orders of Cîteaux and Prémontré and the other congregations of canons regular, carried the day in the entire Church, and hence in the entire political field, in the crisis of the Schism of 1130—38, this law lay often in the hands of the clergy. It can be best discovered in the interventions, not always successful, it is true, but in many cases very important, of Bernard of Clairvaux [4] in conflicts, such as disputed episcopal elections, negotiations for settlements between princes and kings, the implementation of papal judgments which impinged upon the political sphere, and so forth. It is from this viewpoint that the relations now to be discussed must be examined.

The Empire

The age of Saint Bernard corresponds in German history to the reigns of the Emperor Lothar (1125–37) and King Conrad III (1138–52). Both reigns were under the influence of the prevailing reform spirit and the aegis of peace with the papacy. By his decision for Innocent II Lothar had made it clear that he was in agreement with this new tendency in the Church. In his two journeys to Italy, in 1133 and 1136–37, he complied with the desires of the Holy See, even if, especially in 1137, friction was not absent. [5] Episcopal elections in Germany were free, for example, those at Eichstätt in 1125 and Magdeburg in 1126. Lothar renounced any

[2] Ep. 139 and 140 (to Lothar), 183 and 244 (to Conrad), PL, 182.
[3] The Growth of Papal Government (London, 2nd ed. 1955), 426–37.
[4] Bernard de Clairvaux (Commission d'Histoire de l'Ordre de Cîteaux, 3) (Paris 1953), Table analytique II: Bernard et l'épiscopat, 627–47; Table analytique III: Bernard, les princes et la société féodale, 649–57; B. Jacqueline, Papauté et Épiscopat selon Saint Bernard de Clairvaux (Paris 1963).
[5] Gebhardt-Grundmann, I, 292; Seppelt, IV, 182.

royal interference in ecclesiastical disputes, even though, because of the constitution of the Empire, they touched upon the crown's interests, such as those at Trier, Verdun, and Halberstadt.[6] At Würzburg he left the initiative to Archbishop Adalbert of Mainz. Gebhard of Henneberg, supported by the Emperor Henry V, and Rugger, supported by Adalbert, contended for the see, but Rugger died in 1125. After lengthy negotiations the provost Embrich of Leiningen was consecrated Bishop on Christmas 1127. An appeal by Gebhard to Lothar was ineffectual. Only in the dispute over the see of Strasbourg did Lothar impose his will, when at the end of 1129 he recognized Bruno, whom Henry V had earlier had consecrated to replace the deposed Bishop Conrad and whose position had become precarious with the death of that Emperor.[7]

At this period the activity of the papal legates[8] was devoted no longer preferably to political but rather to expressly ecclesiastical questions and revealed an intimate co-operation of the German episcopate with the Curia. They convoked and directed provincial synods, adjusted disputes among bishops, confirmed elections and consecrated bishops, visited dioceses and regulated questions of Church discipline, and transmitted papal privileges. Year after year there came at least one legate, and sometimes three or more acted at the same time. The powerful Rhenish archbishops were reprimanded, many disputes pertaining to the jurisdiction of the metropolitan were immediately sent to the Holy See, the number of exemptions increased, many bishops went to Rome to be consecrated. The election of Conrad III at Koblenz on 7 March 1138 was determined by Archbishop Adalbero of Trier. The new King also adhered to the prescriptions of the Concordat of Worms, but, unlike Lothar, he proved to be no help to the Holy See in Rome nor against the Normans of the Sicilian Kingdom.[9]

France

A map of twelfth-century France shows the royal *demesne*, where alone the King really ruled, as a strikingly small enclave in comparison with the entire Kingdom, hemmed in by the lands of the powerful Counts of Blois-Champagne. Flanders, Normandy, Brittany, Anjou, Poitou, Aquitaine (or

---

[6] *Hauck*, IV (5th ed.), 126–29.

[7] *Ibid.*, 133 f.

[8] W. Janssen, *Die päpstlichen Legaten in Frankreich vom Schisma Anaklets II. bis zum Tode Cölestins III. (1130–98)* (Cologne and Graz 1961), 1–54; J. Bachmann, *Die päpstlichen Legaten in Deutschland und Skandinavien* (Berlin 1913), 21–116.

[9] H. Gleber, *Papst Eugen III. (1145–53) unter besonderer Berücksichtigung seiner politischen Tätigkeit* (Jena 1936); see the critical remarks by E. Jordan in *RHE*, 33 (1937), 367–72.

Guienne), Gascony, Toulouse, Auvergne, and Ducal Burgundy — the great vassals of the crown — evaded the royal influence. Upper and Lower Lorraine, the County of Burgundy, and the Kingdom of Arles (Provence) pertained to the Empire. Hence, ecclesiastical life depended for its development upon a co-operation with many princes, among whom the King of France appeared as little more than one among many, and certainly not the most powerful one. This becomes clear in the correspondence of Bernard of Clairvaux with the princes of his day.

In 1137 Louis VI was succeeded by his son, Louis VII (1137–80). No Western prince was so much under the influence of the Church and the papacy as was this King, who, however, as husband of Eleanor of Aquitaine until 1152, sought at least for a time to extend the royal authority. Goaded by the Queen, he began to pursue a personal policy in various episcopal elections that was in opposition to the Roman views.[10] But the alliance of Count Theobald IV of Champagne, arranged by Bernard of Clairvaux, with the episcopate and the Curia forced him to yield. This appears in the matrimonial case of Raoul of Vermandois, who, having married a niece of Theobald's, had repudiated her for a sister of Queen Eleanor. A papal legate[11] declared the second marriage invalid, excommunicated Raoul and Petronilla, and laid an interdict on Vermandois. Urged by Eleanor, Louis declared war on Theobald, who took his niece's part. Thirteen hundred persons perished in the flames of Vitry in 1144. Bernard arranged peace between the King and Theobald; Louis abandoned Raoul and decided to submit to Rome. The Queen's influence thereafter yielded to that of the clergy, Bernard's authority was enhanced, and Suger, Abbot of Saint-Denis, acquired ascendancy. During Louis's absence on the Second Crusade Suger looked after the royal interests. (It would probably be an anachronism to speak of a real royal government.) Not the crown but the French Church, especially the new orders and the canons regular, must be regarded as the leading influences in public life.

Anarchy in England

Following the peaceful settlement of the Investiture Controversy in 1107, King Henry I contrived until his death in 1135 to control the English Church with the firm hand characteristic of his father, William the Conqueror. While one cannot speak of an English territorial Church, still both in England and in Normandy it was customary that the participation of the bishops in councils beyond the King's territory depended upon his

[10] *Lavisse*, III, 1, 1–11.
[11] The Cardinal Priest Ivo of San Lorenzo in Damaso; *cf.* W. Janssen, *Legaten*, 35–37.

express permission. Without the same express permission no legate of the Pope might enter his lands. By a benevolent attitude to the monasteries Henry had assured himself a favourable judgment in ecclesiastical historiography, but the Church was certainly not free as this was understood by the Gregorians. Still, it was to her advantage that the peace in a Kingdom which was vigorously governed and, in contrast to the other West European countries, was united could only be of service in the development of ecclesiastical life.

The situation changed in the long period of the struggle over the throne between Henry's daughter Matilda, widow of the Emperor Henry V and wife of Count Geoffrey of Anjou, to whom her father had forced the barons to do homage by reason of heredity before his death, and Stephen of Blois, grandson of the Conqueror through his daughter Adele. A new era of political calm did not begin again until the accession of Henry II in 1154.

During the confusion of King Stephen's reign (1135–54) the Holy See guarded its authority by the conferring *permanenter* of legatine powers on the Archbishops of Canterbury, William of Corbeil (1123–36) and Theobald (1139–61), and for a time (1139–43) on Henry of Blois, Bishop of Winchester and brother of King Stephen. In 1138 Cardinal Alberic acted as legate with unlimited authority, even in regard to political questions. His assistant in the south was the Augustinian canon, Robert of Hereford; in the north, the Cistercian Abbot Richard of Fountains. Thanks to the struggle over the succession to the throne, the episcopate was at last able to secure its freedom and to make extensive use against the crown of that right which Henry I had conceded to it: to appeal to Rome in doubtful cases.

At the same time there occurred an influx of recruits for the Cistercians and the canons regular, which had been prepared under Henry I but only now became a mighty stream. William of Corbeil was a canon regular, as was Henry I's confessor, Aldulf, who in 1133 became Bishop of Carlisle. The first Cistercians had settled at Waverley in 1128–29 and at Rievaulx in 1131–32. Fifty-seven abbeys were founded by 1153, if the monasteries of the Congregation of Savigny are counted. In the contest for the archiepiscopal see of York [12] the Cistercians were able, following the Langres model of 1138, to impose their candidate, Henry Murdach,

---

[12] *Cf.* D. Knowles, "The Case of Saint William of York," *CambrHJ*, 5 (1936), 162–77, and also *The Historian and Character* (Cambridge 1963), 76–97; A. L. Poole, *From Domesday Book to Magna Carta* (Oxford, 2d ed. 1964), 191; D. Nicholl, *Thurstan, Archbishop of York (1114–40)* (York 1964). For the analogous case of the election at Langres, in which, against the will of the King, the election, already confirmed, was quashed by Innocent II, and the prior of Clairvaux, Godfrey de la Roche-Vanneau, obtained the see in 1138, *cf.* E. Vacandard's study on Bernard of Clairvaux.

against William Fitzherbert, nephew of Henry of Blois, by means of the support provided by letters of Bernard of Clairvaux in both Rome and England. The Cistercian Pope Eugene III spoke the final word in 1146–47.[13]

The Iberian Peninsula

In the Iberian peninsula the difficult course of the *Reconquista* was scarcely the most favourable climate for a calm development of ecclesiastical life. Aided by French knights and accompanied by the benevolent interest of the Holy See — at the First Lateran Council Calixus II empowered Archbishop Olegar of Tarragona as Papal Legate to proceed against the Muslims — Alfonso I of Aragón pushed farther to the south. After his death in 1134, Raymond Berengar IV of Catalonia managed to secure the succession in Aragón and continued the struggle against Islam, acquiring Tortosa in 1148. The papal legates of these decades seem not to have been particularly concerned with the struggles of the *Reconquista,* although Cardinal Guido of Santi Cosma e Damiano took part in the Council of Gerona in 1143. Through their ecclesiastical activity they enhanced the total European influence of the Curia in the course of the centralization of the Roman administration and jurisdiction. During the Schism of 1130 Archbishop Diego Gelmírez of Compostela was decisive in supporting Innocent II.[14] Of great importance was the withdrawal by Afonso Henriques, Count of Portugal, from his vassalage to Castile. Having assumed the royal title in 1139,[15] he in 1143 declared his land to be a fief of the papacy and took the oath of fealty in the presence of the Cardinal Legate Guido. With the aid of the crusaders of 1147 he almost managed to free the country from Muslim domination. The final confirmation of his royal title, which Lucius II did not use in his correspondence with Portugal, probably out of regard for King Alfonso VII of Castile, came only under Alexander III.

[13] After Eugene III, Bernard of Clairvaux, and Archbishop Henry Murdach were dead, William Fitzherbert was able again to occupy the see with the consent of Anastasius IV. He died on 8 June 1154, and in 1226 was canonized by Honorius III. Without regard for the agreement of 1107 between her father and Anselm of Canterbury, the Empress Matilda in 1141 invested William Cummin with the see of Durham by ring and staff; *cf.* A. L. Poole, *op. cit.,* 191.

[14] See Anselm G. Biggs, *Diego Gelmirez, First Archbishop of Compostela* (Washington 1949), 299–302.

[15] Afonso Henriques (1128–85), called The Conqueror. The acceptance of Portugal as a fief of the Holy See took place on 12 December 1143, through the agency of the legate, Guido de Vico. Lucius II ratified it in 1144 and at the same time recognized the royal title which Alexander III confirmed by the bull "Manifestis probatum" of 23 May 1179. *Cf.* Rui de Azevedo, *Documentos Medievais Portugueses,* I (Lisbon 1958), 114 ff.

The connection between Portugal and the papacy became ever more intimate, thanks to the work of the Cardinal Legate. Even the conclusion of peace between Castile and Portugal was due to papal initiative. Under Innocent II there was an understanding in regard to the organization of the Portuguese episcopate and the introduction of papal protection of monasteries. The canons regular constituted an important element for the development of Church life, and the most recent research proves that it was they who saw to the care of the pilgrimage route to Compostela.[16] The Congregation of Saint-Ruf d'Avignon also played a leading role.

The important and successful legatine journey of the Cardinal Bishop of Albano, Nicholas Breakspear, in 1152, to Scandinavia presupposed the co-operation of the crown and the Curia.[17]

Christian Expansion Eastward

Otto, Bishop of Bamberg, set out upon his so-called first missionary journey (1124–25) to Pomerania on behalf of Poland, under the protection of the Emperor Henry V and with papal assent, but a pagan reaction largely destroyed his success. In 1128 he was able to carry out a second missionary journey on behalf of and under the protection of King Lothar, who regarded Pomerania as belonging to the Empire. Norbert of Magdeburg had had him promise to respect the metropolitan rights of his see and insisted that the Bishop of Bamberg not undertake a mission among the pagan Liutizians, who belonged to Magdeburg's territory. The Bishop of Bamberg retained the direction of the missionary district, and Christianity was definitely assured in Pomerania, but the diocesan organization was only begun after Otto's death (1139) by Innocent II, who in 1140 established the see of Wollin. Poznań, which he had subordinated to Magdeburg, and Gniezno, which was to lose its metropolitan status, again became independent after Norbert's death in 1134. In 1136 Innocent confirmed Archbishop James as Metropolitan of Gniezno.

Association with German eastward colonization decisively favoured the missionary work. At the same time as Otto of Bamberg, Archbishop Adalbero of Hamburg-Bremen began a mission whose chief representative was Vizelin, canon and *scholasticus* of Bremen; his activity is reported in Helmold's *Chronicon Slavorum*. Beginning his work together with the canons Rudolf of Hildesheim and Ludolf of Verden and, out of the

---

[16] F. J. Schmale, *Studien zum Schisma des Jahres 1130*, 217 f. (hitherto it was thought that the Cluniacs had provided this protection).

[17] W. Holtzmann, "Krone und Kirche in Norwegen im 12. Jahrhundert," *DA*, 2 (1938), 341–400; likewise the literature relevant to Cardinal Breakspear's legatine journey in the bibliography for this chapter.

country parish which Adalbero had conveyed to him in 1125, he created the foundation at Neumünster as the base for further missionary work. The Emperor Lothar sent him help. But the Wend Crusade of 1147 halted the effort. In 1148–49 Cardinal Guido undertook a legatine journey to Poland and Moravia,[18] and in 1149 the sees of Oldenburg and Mecklenburg were once more occupied, by Vizelin and Emmenhard respectively. Vizelin received investiture from the hands of Duke Henry the Lion in 1150.[19] In 1154 this measure was approved by Frederick I, but restricted in the sense that the Duke was to give investiture, not as the territorial prince, but in the exercise of the royal power granted to him. In this question the Roman Curia seems not to have taken the part of Archbishop Hartwig of Bremen–Hamburg, who felt that as metropolitan of the Wend bishoprics he was authorized to act independently of any consent by Henry the Lion.

The service of the *Imperium* and the *Regna* to the Church in these decades of the age of Saint Bernard are seen in the rapid and unequivocal decision for Innocent II, in the freedom conceded to the Church after the Investiture Controversy, especially in the matter of episcopal elections, abbatial elections, and the relations of the higher clergy to the Roman Curia, and in the legal protection which kings and princes accorded to cathedrals, abbeys, and collegiate churches.

In France the close relationship of the crown with the bishops in the great principalities was the only way by which the crown could exercise its influence beyond the limits of the *demesne*. Accordingly, it was cultivated there as a relationship of mutual service. It is well known how intimately Louis VI was bound to the Church, which assisted him and his son in the direction of the Kingdom, especially in the person of Stephen of Garlande and Suger of Saint-Denis. Bishoprics, chapters, and abbeys were richly endowed, and both Kings made a point of promoting the new orders of Cîteaux, Prémontré, Tiron, and Fontevrault. Saint-Victor de Paris received its substantial endowment from Louis VI. Both Kings afforded the Curia hospitality in the crises of the pontificates of Innocent II and Eugene III. Tensions, even with Bernard of Clairvaux, were not wanting, but the overall view showed the kingship in France in a productive cooperation with the Church of the Kingdom and with the Roman Church as the representative of Christendom. The same can be said of Germany and, with certain restrictions, of England and the Iberian peninsula. Italy, on the other hand, remained an agitated land of variety,

---

[18] R. Wenskus, "Zu einigen päpstlichen Legationen nach Böhmen und Mähren im 12. Jahrhundert," *ZKG*, 70 (1959), 141–46 (corrective of J. Bachmann, *op. cit.*); L. Spätling, "Kardinal Guido und seine Legation in Böhmen und Mähren (1142–46)," *MIÖG*, 66 (1958), 306–30.

[19] K. Jordan, *Die Bistumsgründungen Heinrichs des Löwen* (Schriften des Reichsinstituts für ältere deutsche Geschichtskunde, 3) (Stuttgart 1939, reprinted 1952), 81–91.

with the constantly changing relations of the Curia to the Normans and its unstable connections with the North Italian communes and revolutionary Rome, which at the close of this period became a difficult problem in curial policy.

CHAPTER 4

Elaboration of the Curia and
Criticism of Church and Papacy

The Gregorian reform had involved changes in the structure of the Roman ecclesiastical administration that were not completed before the middle of the twelfth century. But now the main lines of what people began to call the Curia were clearly discernible: court, household, and meeting all in one, as in the Germanic royal model, the pattern for the Roman development. Proper, that is, Roman traditional elements were added in the course of the renewal of the idea of Rome, reminiscences of the reorganization of Senate and courts by Diocletian. At the same time this Curia had a rapid expansion in size. [1]

On the occasion of the double election of 1130, there being no tribunal above the two claimants which could have decided between them authoritatively or by arbitration, it was left to the Church as a whole, to Christendom itself, to give the final judgment. The Church did so in recognizing Innocent II by a great majority. For the first time Christendom had acted as a unity, as the *corpus mysticum Christi*,[2] to use the term that persons began to apply to it in the early twelfth century. Christendom had, of course, been assisted in arriving at this knowledge of its unity by the crusade experience, which made Christians of many countries acquainted with one another; the sufferings endured in common for it and the common use of spiritual and physical energies attested one goal to be striven for by all in the same way. At the same time the crusade had impressively brought into prominence the head of the *corpus mysticum*, Pope Urban II, organizer and, in his legates, leader of the expedition. The Second Crusade confirmed the idea that Christendom still retained this experience as a lasting awareness, for people then turned to Eugene III, who, following the model of Urban II, summoned the crusade, appoint-

[1] See Volume III, Chapters 34, 35, and 49.
[2] For the Church as *corpus mysticum*, see E. H. Kantorowicz, *The King's Two Bodies. A Study in Mediaeval Political Theology* (Princeton 1957), 194–206 ("Corpus Ecclesiae mysticum").

ed crusade preachers, named legates, and, a new element in the development, in the absence of the Kings intervened in political matters in France and Germany.[3] He there elevated, as it were, to the highest plane that protection — and thereby, according to the mediaeval view, that dominion — which the Church guaranteed at home to the absent crusader for his rights, property, and family. A logical effect of this was, of course, that the failure of this crusade was at first imputed to the Pope himself.

The new Curia served these constantly increasing functions of the papacy in the social, political, and ecclesiastical spheres; from them the Curia received the impulse to further development.[4] The change from the Roman urban clergy and administration to an instrument of government that could be used for all of Christendom was, it is true, already essentially complete at the beginning of this period. The College of Cardinals had taken shape, and the total numbers grew.

The charters now make known, in the signatures of the cardinals,[5] how the college as an advisory body assisted the Pope in the government of the Church. The chiefs of the earlier offices of *arcarius* (treasurer), *saccellarius* (paymaster), *nomenculator* (care of the poor), *protoscriniarius* (archives), *bibliothecarius* (chancery), and the two *primicerii* of the *schola notariorum* (correspondence) and the *schola defensorum* (legal matters) — the so-called *iudices de clero* or *iudices palatini* — retained only judicial functions as the College of Seven. In their places appeared the Pope's *camerlengo* (for finances) and chancellor (for correspondence). Just as at royal courts, so there were also at the Curia the *dapifer* or seneschal, the *pincerna* (cupbearer), the marshal.[6] And, like the northern courts, the Curia too was often itinerant. The broad outlines of a papal *capella* were also discernible,[7] apparently in imitation of the Frankish court chapel. While at first its members were still called *subdiaconi sanctae Romanae ecclesiae* and *subdiaconi domini nostri papae,* soon they were *subdiaconi et capellani* and in the thirteenth century merely *capellani*. A nucleus of this new structure was the *schola notariorum,* or *notarii palatini.* Under the chancellor, who united in himself the functions of the earlier *scriniarius* and of the *primicerius notariorum,* this college took charge of the Pope's correspondence. Other groups carried on the tradition of the earlier seven

---

[3] H. Gleber, *Eugen III.* (Jena 1936), who, however, exaggerates in interpreting these facts as "erstmalige Durchsetzung des päpstlichen Weltherrschaftsgedankens" (83).

[4] *Fliche-Martin*, 12, 2 (Paris 1964), 349–62).

[5] B. Katterbach and W. M. Peitz, "Die Unterschriften der Päpste und Kardinäle in den 'Bullae majores' vom 11. bis 14. Jahrhundert," *Miscellanea Francesco Ehrle*, IV (Rome 1924), 177–274.

[6] *Fliche-Martin*, 12, 2, 359–61; E. Eichmann, *Die Kaiserkrönung im Abendland*, II, 247–49.

[7] R. Elze, "Die päpstliche Kapelle im 12. und 13. Jahrhundert," *ZSavRGkan*, 36 (1950), 145–204.

palatine subdeacons (liturgy), of the regionary subdeacons (social service), of the subdeacons of the *schola cantorum*. Now, as each occasion demanded, missions were also probably required of all of them in addition to their liturgical and administrative duties. They accompanied legates on their journeys. They constituted a college at the Lateran, where they lived and worked in common and were provided for by the papal kitchen. Each obtained a benefice to provide for his proper support, but, unlike the cardinals, they were not attached to titular churches. In so far as they received judicial functions as *advocati* or *auditores,* they could participate in the consistory, which in these decades replaced the earlier Roman Lenten synods and, as a regular meeting of the cardinals under the presidency of the Pope, considered and settled *causae maiores*. The overall direction of the college of subdeacons or chaplains was in the hands of the *camerlengo*. Hence the chancellor, who headed only one group of them, was subordinate to him. Probably for this reason in the thirteenth century a vice-chancellor conducted the real business in place of the chancellor, who was a cardinal. In the late twelfth century the College of Cardinals obtained its own *camerlengo* for its own financial administration, which was separating itself from that of the papacy.

This imposing structure grew steadily.[8] Especially from the pontificate of Innocent II the number of processes at the Roman Curia increased rapidly, over and above *causae maiores* in the strict sense. The enhanced prestige of the Pope in the whole of Christendom, the canon law that was gaining ground everywhere, the intensified drive for exemption on the part of monasteries and particular churches — all contributed to this. To the papal Curia belonged not only ecclesiastics but also, as earlier, lay persons, most of them from the great Roman families. The College of Cardinals and the *capella*, both of them together with the Pope constituting the Curia, displayed in the twelfth century, even in the lower echelons, a personnel that was remarkably international and no longer merely Roman.

Like the first reform Pope, Leo IX, the Popes of the twelfth century were often on the move, but not always voluntarily; frequently enough they were forced to this by Roman disturbances or by the general ecclesiastical situation. In this way the important contact between the Pope and Christendom was maintained and deepened, but likewise the operations of the Curia and its very personnel were exposed to the Church's critical faculty, which had been sharpened by the reform.

If for some time fault had been found with the situation at Rome[9] — during the Investiture Controversy this had, of course, been intensified

---

[8] K. Jordan, *Die Entstehung der römischen Kurie,* 148.
[9] On the beginnings, see P. Lehmann, *Parodie,* pp. 25–30.

by polemics — but the blame was quite often levelled rather at the Romans as such, now the reform papacy itself had to learn, from the representatives of the most important factors in this reform, how hard it was for a demand to improve the life and promote the sanctification of the people to maintain itself in this Church "of sinners and saints" if it was raised by sinners rather than by saints. The Curia, both cardinals and chaplains, and the Pope too now found themselves in the crossfire of criticism without being really able to mount a defense, because this criticism was based on quite simple and undisputed facts. The force of criticism is, of course, characteristic of reform movements, just as it is essential to the Church to reform herself so long as she is on pilgrimage. But if now the reform itself or at least some of its results encounter harsh judgments from irreproachable spokesmen, persons pay attention.

This criticism was represented not by Arnold of Brescia, the canon regular inclining to spiritual radicalism,[10] but by Saint Bernard, by John of Salisbury and his "common sense" with its orientation to humanistic moderation, and by Gerhoh of Reichersberg with his testimonials and treatises dedicated to Eugene III and Hadrian IV. Whereas Arnold demanded that the Pope and the bishops renounce property and dominion in order to keep themselves free for the care of souls exclusively, for the others the solution lay in the human. They required the right use of institutions which were not found to be blameworthy in themselves and seem not to have taken any offense at the feudalism[11] which had established itself since 1059 in increasing measure in the life of the Roman Church. They apparently saw in them those *elementa mundi* which the Church makes use of, which indeed she must assimilate in order to remain true to her inner law as a representation of the mystery of the Incarnation. As *corpus mysticum Christi* the Church of necessity assimilates in space and time the forms of existence characteristic of this precise time and space. Arnold's radicalism, on the other hand, moved, with its spiritualism, entirely on that line whose beginnings were to be found in the poverty movement of the turn of the century — the *pauperes Christi*, the *vita apostolica* — and from which heretical extremes often enough developed and not first with Arnold.

Bernard of Clairvaux possessed a high regard for the authority of the Pope and the bishops in the Church of Christ. For that very reason he urgently warned against any misuse of this authority and combatted tendencies at the Curia,[12] for example that of becoming too liberal with

---

[10] For Arnold of Brescia, see Chapter 8.

[11] K. Jordan, "Das Eindringen der Lehnsidee in das Rechtsleben der römischen Kurie," *AUF*, 12 (1932), 13–110.

[12] *De consideratione*, I, 4 (secular business), *PL*, 182, 732 f.; III, 2 (abuse of appeals), *ibid.*, 761–64; III, 4 (suppression of stages in appeals), *ibid.*, 766–69.

privileges of exemption, which would restrict episcopal freedom and authority, as a perversion of the traditional order established by God himself. Even the system of appeals was an abomination to him, not in itself but its excess, its practical operation. He made himself the spokesman of the grievances of all the churches: abbots were withdrawn from the bishops, bishops from the archbishops, archbishops from the patriarchs. To his way of thinking appeals mainly served to circumvent the local courts, which, however, possessed a more exact knowledge of the place and the case and had often already given a judgment in accord with equity and law. In the highest court of all was sought a pardon or an advantage, and in this way episcopal authority was gravely injured. And Rome was finally overburdened with business which, for the most part or to a degree, fell entirely within the temporal and secular spheres: with questions of the payment of tithes, of building regulations in regard to the minimum distance between houses, barns, stables, with the authorization of fishing in this or that pond. The Curia, so Bernard wrote, was on the point of becoming a great secular business centre. Dealers penetrated into the temple, an army of officious lawyers and solicitors with every quarrel and controversy in Christendom. Hildebert of Lavardin, Archbishop of Tours, had already written in a similar vein.[13] To the same complaints Gerhoh of Reichersberg added the bitter remark that "apparently these appeals were not unwelcome to the Romans":[14] "Gravatur iam ecce universa terra, fastum et avariciam Romanorum non sustinens."[15] One detects the real concern, and at the same time the tactful tendency, to attribute the guilt, not to the Pope, not even to the Curia, but only to those of its personnel who were Romans. John of Salisbury demanded especially an incorrupt conduct of processes in Rome so as to avoid any exerting of influence by money or gifts. Especially in regard to the official conduct of legates, who by virtue of judicial and extensive administrative powers were able to make the government of the Curia omnipresent in Christendom, the future Bishop of Chartres sketched in the *Policraticus,* from his own experience or from excellently attested material, a picture of the contemporary Church government whose deep shadows filled even the loyal friends of the Roman Church, of the Pope, and of the Curia with great anxiety.

---

[13] *Epistolae Hildeberti,* II, 41, PL, 171, 265–67.

[14] *De investigatione Antichristi,* I, 52 (abuse of appeals), *MGLiblit,* III, 358 f.

[15] Here Gerhoh had in mind chiefly the insatiable Romans, whom the Pope had to accommodate for the sake of peace in the city: "Romanus Pontifex compellitur undecumque colligere, quod expendat in Romanos, plus Crasso tyranno avaros" (*Opusculum ad Cardinales,* ed. D. and O. Van den Eynde, 312); *De investigatione Antichristi,* I, 49, *MGLiblit,* III, 356 f.

CHAPTER 5

The Second Crusade and
the Wars in Spain and the Slavic East

The papacy, the Curia, and the West saw themselves faced around the middle of the century with a new task, which called upon all their resources: the peril of the crusader states.[1] When word of the fall of Edessa reached Jerusalem, Queen Mélisende contacted Antioch for the dispatch of an envoy to Rome to apprise the Pope and ask for a new crusade. Bishop Hugh of Gabala (Djeble) met Eugene III at Viterbo in the fall of 1145. At the same time there arrived a delegation of Armenian bishops from Cilicia, come to gain support against Byzantium. Otto of Freising, who was present at this audience, has left a report of it.[2] The Pope decided to summon a crusade, while Hugh proceeded to France and Germany. On 1 December 1145 a bull was sent to King Louis VII of France,[3] inviting him and all the princes and faithful of the Kingdom to aid the East. Because of disturbances in Rome[4] Eugene was unable at the moment to emulate Urban II in activating the organizing process beyond the Alps, supervising it, and preaching the crusade. He did not appeal to King Conrad III of Germany, because he needed his help in Rome and against King Roger II of Sicily, and of course not to Roger, whose untrustworthiness and self-willed policy were sources of fear.[5] Also, Roger aspired to continue his undertakings in North Africa against Tripoli.

A first appeal by Louis VII from Bourges at Christmas of 1145 had little effect. The King thereupon asked the support of Bernard of Clair-

[1] Cf. Volume III, Chapter 51.
[2] Chronica, VII, 32, ed. Hofmeister, 360 f. The meeting took place at Vetralla near Viterbo; cf. also Chronica, VII, 3, ed. Hofmeister, 363–67.
[3] E. Caspar, "Die Kreuzzugsbullen Eugens III.," NA, 45 (1924), 285–300; cf. also U. Schwerin, "Die Aufrufe der Päpste zur Befreiung des Heiligen Landes," HStud (Berlin 1937).
[4] Originating in the north, the communal movement reached Rome in 1143 (cf. C. W. Previté-Orton in The Cambridge Medieval History, V [Cambridge 1926], 208–41). In the summer the citizens proclaimed the "Holy Senate of the City" on the Capitol. After the death of Innocent II (23 September 1143) his successors, Celestine II and Lucius II, were likewise unable to suppress the movement, which was consolidated under Eugene III; he had to take up residence outside the city, at Viterbo. F. Bartolini, "Codice diplomatico del Senato Romano," FontiStIt (Rome 1948); idem, "Per la storia del Senato Romano nel secolo XII," BIStIAM, 60 (1946); A. Frugoni, "Sulla 'Renovatio Senatus' del 1143 e l'ordo equestris," BIStIAM, 62 (1950), 159–74; A. Rota, "La costituzione originaria del commune di Roma. L'epoca del commune liber (Luglio 1143–Dicembre 1145)," BIStIAM, 64 (1953), 19–131.
[5] E. Caspar, Roger II., 370–98.

vaux, who was willing to comply if ordered to by Eugene III. The papal command was, of course, quickly forthcoming, and at Vézelay on 31 March 1146 Bernard began his amazingly effective crusade preaching, of which mention has already been made.[6] The Pope went to France in 1147 and at first Bernard had to reassure him in regard to the extension of the recruiting for the crusade to Germany. Eugene met twice with Louis VII — at Dijon in April, at Saint-Denis in June — but a meeting with Conrad III,[7] suggested for Strasbourg by the King, did not materialize.

Under the leadership of the two Kings, the German army at the end of May and the French army at the end of June took the land route to the East. An offer by Roger II to transport them to the Holy Land by sea was turned down. Conrad III was in Byzantium in September, Louis VII on 4 October. Since Louis had come by the same route that the Germans had already traveled, and for this reason had not been suitably provisioned and dealt with, because of excesses by the Germans, which apparently could not have been avoided, relations between the two crusading armies were permeated with bitterness and suspicion even in Constantinople. Both were likewise not kindly disposed to Byzantium. The beginning gave little to hope for.

Louis VII was accompanied by his wife, Eleanor of Aquitaine, and Bishops Arnulf of Lisieux and Godfrey of Langres, of whom John of Salisbury sketches a discreditable picture in his *Historia Pontificalis.*[8] In the army of Conrad III Duke Frederick of Swabia led the nobility, Bishops Stephen of Metz and Henry of Toul the Lotharingians. Otto of Freising was later able to write a participant's account. Conrad III joined the Byzantine Emperor Manuel in a common policy against Roger II of Sicily, and Conrad's sister-in-law, Bertha of Sulzbach, married Manuel. Manuel urged haste, for the crusaders were a heavy burden on the city. Louis VII was also amicably received and had no scruples about delivering possible conquests to the Byzantines as their own property. He had all his barons swear the same sort of oath.

When at the beginning of November the French army reached Nicaea, Conrad had lost almost all of his army and all his camp provisions in the battle of Dorylaeum on 25 October. The remnant joined the French army. They went on together as far as Ephesus, where Conrad fell sick and was invited to Constantinople by Manuel. He there recovered and in March

[6] *Supra*, Chapter 2.
[7] Influenced by Bernard of Clairvaux, King Conrad III had taken the cross at Speyer on 27 December 1146, and with him Welf VI and many other princes and bishops. At Frankfurt in March 1147 Henry the Lion had promised that he would put aside his claims to Bavaria until the ending of the crusade. A detailed presentation of the German role is given by. W. Bernhardi, *Konrad III.* (Leipzig 1883), 503–684.
[8] *Historia Pontificalis*, ed. M. Chibnall, 54–56.

1148 was able to continue on to Palestine with his entourage on Byzantine ships. Acre was reached in mid-April. The French army, which had melted away to less than half its original strength through severe losses, made Antioch in the late spring of 1148. Here occurred the well known serious matrimonial crisis between Louis and Eleanor, provoked by the Queen's intimacy with Prince Raymond of Antioch.[9] The King compelled her to proceed with him and the army to Jerusalem; they entered the city in May and were cordially received by Queen Mélisende. Never had Jerusalem seen so brilliant a gathering of knights and ladies.

A great council was arranged for 24 June at Acre, with King Baldwin III, the Patriarch Fulcher, the Archbishops of Caesarea and Nazareth, and the grand masters of the Templars and the Hospitallers acting as hosts. It was decided to unite all the forces for an attack on Damascus. Correct as the project was from the point of view of strategy — for with Damascus a wedge would have been driven between Egyptian-African and North Syrian-Eastern Islam — it was nevertheless a political blunder, for at that moment it was of great importance to the Burid Kingdom of Damascus to maintain friendship with the Franks against the common enemy, Nur-ed-Din. But now Damascus too was driven into the Caliph's camp. The city was besieged in vain, the Western lords departed in deep humiliation, and the legend of the invincibility of the Western knights was destroyed. A new confidence awoke in the world of Islam.

On 8 September 1148 Conrad III left Acre by sea for the journey home and, at the invitation of the Emperor Manuel, spent Christmas at Constantinople, where the marriage of Duke Henry of Austria with Manuel's niece, the Princess Theodora, was celebrated. A firm alliance was concluded between the two Empires against Roger II, the partition of whose lands on the Italian peninsula was planned.

Louis VII put off his homeward journey. He wanted to keep Easter in Jerusalem and feared the inevitable confrontation with Eleanor, who was pressing for the dissolution of their marriage. Conrad's friendship with Manuel induced Louis to seek an alliance with Roger II, especially since he could thereby give vent to his dislike of Byzantium. He left the Holy Land on Sicilian vessels at the beginning of summer 1149 and met Roger at Potenza early in August. At once they decided on a new common crusade, but this time first against Byzantium — a preview of what was to happen in 1204. Pope Eugene III was not greatly impressed by the plan, but the Curia eagerly promoted it. At Paris Louis was able to convince even Abbot Suger of the reasonableness of the idea, and Bernard of

---

[9] *Ibid.*, 52 f. *Cf.* F. McNimm Chambers, "Some Legends concerning Eleanor of Aquitaine," *Speculum,* 16 (1941), 459–68. Despite many attempts, there is still no biography of Eleanor that is satisfactory to scholars.

Clairvaux, deeply disillusioned by the wretched outcome of "his" crusade, seemed ready to take up once again the burden of crusade preaching. But King Conrad, whose cooperation would have been essential, this time refused his consent. He feared the hand of Roger II, which he rightly believed he saw in the outline of the project. And so it had to be dropped.

No enterprise of the Middle Ages[10] began with more brilliant expectations. Planned by the Pope, proclaimed and fired by the golden eloquence of Saint Bernard, and led by the two chief powers of the West, the crusade had promised so much for the glory and safety of Christendom. But when it came to a shameful end with the difficult retreat from Damascus, it had done nothing but push relations between the West and Byzantium almost to the breaking point, sow distrust and suspicion between the newly arrived crusaders and the Franks who were living in the East, divide the Western princes, bring the Muslims closer together, and irreparably damage the military reputation of the Franks. A new epoch began in Syria, for now the Christians had been forced to the defensive. In the West itself the reports of the returned soldiers spread a deep distrust of the Franks of the Holy Land, resident in the crusader states, by whom they felt they had been left in the lurch. The failure of the Second Crusade had an effect on the intellectual and religious life of Latin Christendom in that the crusade idea lost its lustre. Persons no longer wanted to aid the Franks in Palestine. The indignation was even directed against the Pope and Saint Bernard, who had summoned to the expedition. The esteem of the Abbot of Clairvaux declined, at least in Germany. He wrote his *apologia*[11] in the introductory chapter to Book II of *De Consideratione,* taking himself seriously to task. In it a deep psychological need becomes apparent, betraying something that the saint was able to establish even in his own entourage: that this misfortune caused men to entertain doubts of faith.

The Wend crusade, to which Bernard had given his assent at the Diet of Frankfurt in March 1147 and to which he had issued a summons, was also a failure.[12] An inner contradiction became visible here, together with an ambiguity as to goals and planning. For some of the Slavs whom it was desired to subjugate proved to be good Christians, and hence a war against them could not be termed a crusade. Or if the Slavs who were subdued were and intended to remain pagans, it appeared senseless to destroy them and devastate their land, from which persons aspired to derive profit under their own rule. This contradicted Bernard's express instructions for

---

[10] Thus Steven Runciman, *History of the Crusades,* II, 277.

[11] *De consideratione,* II, 1, PL, 182, 741–45. Otto of Freising also reflected on the failure in his *Gesta,* I, 65, ed. Waitz-Simson, 91–93.

[12] The Wend Obodrite Prince Niklot anticipated the attack in 1143. The projected crusade took the field against his invasion but achieved merely a feigned baptism of the Wends. *Cf.* H. Beumann, *Heidenmission und Kreuzzugsgedanke,* 275–316.

the crusade. He had called for "extermination or conversion of the heathens"[13] and had forbidden a concluding of peace or of a treaty so long as the people were still pagans. The princes did not adhere to Bernard's directions.

An enduring success was granted only to the taking of Lisbon[14] and to the completion, thereby made possible, of the new Kingdom of Portugal. In this way the right wing of the campaign against Islam, comprising the entire Mediterranean, was consolidated. Roger II was able to establish himself in the centre sector at Tripoli, first in 1143 and then definitively in 1146.[15] Meanwhile, the left wing, the crusader states, was in increasing difficulty.

CHAPTER 6

Monastic Humanism

The twelfth century was an age of social restratification, of urban development, and of the communal movement. The horizon of the West was extended by the drive eastward in colonization and crusade, and contacts with the intellectual world of Islam became more frequent. Young clerics began to move restlessly from school to school, that is, from one celebrated teacher to another, apparently oblivious of any diocesan or territorial boundaries. Until the mid-century monastic humanism,[1] predominant from time immemorial, still maintained its primacy in the field of intellectual disputation and of literary creativity, despite the versatility of the new clerical personnel. This fact must be connected with the preeminence which the new orders of Cîteaux and Prémontré, that is, the reformed Benedictine and the reformed canonical life,[2] occupied in the second phase of ecclesiastical reform.

In this period, when the enthusiasm of the beginnings was still operative in both orders, a sociological law procured for them not only the pious but also the intellectually most active forces. While the growth of the

---

[13] *Epp. Bernardi*, no. 457, *PL*, 182, 651 *D:* "ad delendas penitus aut certe convertendas nationes illas."

[14] Here a group of English, Flemish, and Frisian crusaders, who were *en route* to the Holy Land by sea and had sailed up the Tagus, had assisted in the siege of Lisbon, lasting several months, and had made possible the taking of the city.

[15] E. Caspar, *Roger II.*, 415–23.

[1] The term was coined by Jean Leclercq, who describes it in many individual essays and above all in *L'amour des lettres et le désir de Dieu* (Paris 1957); English translation, *The Love of Learning and the Desire for God* (New York 1961).

[2] Although the canons regular and the Premonstratensians do not belong to the monastic world in the proper sense, they can be included in the same intellectual trend because of their literary works.

cathedral schools and of the schools of the unreformed chapters continued,[3] the intellectual and literary achievement of Cluny, Cîteaux, and the congregations of canons regular maintained its lead, and especially among the last named group a public teaching activity was often to be found, as at Saint-Victor de Paris.[4]

The cultivation of the *artes liberales* still dominated the entire educational process of the West but it was gradually restricted at the cathedral schools. In these began a sort of withering in the direction of pure utility aiming at rapid preparation for a real specialization in theology, law, and medicine. Also now apparent was the isolation of one of their elements, dialectics, as it was transformed into a special discipline with its own laws. After the mid-century John of Salisbury vigorously fought this tendency.[5]

But in the abbeys and in the chapters of canons regular, as earlier, the *artes liberales* were seen as the best way to a deeper understanding of Scripture and to a full mastery of the patristic and ecclesiastical tradition. In addition, this "humanistic" pursuit of grammar, rhetoric, and dialectic suggested a fostering of those literary forms which were used with predilection by the representatives of monastic humanism: the *sermo,* the dialogue, the letter, the *florilegia,* the biography, and in fact all forms of historical writing in general. At the same time mediaeval Latin acquired that flexibility, liveliness, and poetic precision, so praised by J. de Ghellinck and P. Lehmann.[6] At the moment when vernacular languages took their first important steps toward literary expression, Latin, as the language of Western Christendom, was still enjoying a wealth of experience, whose brilliance recalls the colours of autumn.

Since this linguistically elegant dress served for the most part to express concepts of a deepened religious feeling, of mystical theology, of reform austerity, of enhanced claims in the area of the challenged freedom of the Church, the works of the monastic humanism of this epoch acquired greater importance as literary, journalistic, and theological achievements. The wealth of names can be divided among the already mentioned party-slogans: Cluny, Cîteaux, Prémontré, Saint-Victor, and so forth.

Cluny was represented especially by Abbot Peter the Venerable

---

[3] *Cf.* the next chapter.

[4] Here monastic theology continued the study of the Fathers and moved parallel to early scholasticism. *Cf.* Leclercq, *op cit.,* 1 ff., where he refers to the agreement of A. M. Landgraf.

[5] Especially in his great works: *Metalogicon* and *Policraticus. Cf.* H. Liebeschütz, *Mediaeval Humanism in the Life and Writings of John of Salisbury* (London 1950). The *Metalogicon* has now been translated and commented on by D. D. MacGarry (Berkeley-Los Angeles 1955).

[6] J. de Ghellinck, *L'essor de la littérature latine au XIIᵉ siècle,* II, 300–21; P. Lehmann, "Die Vielgestalt des zwölften Jahrhunderts," *Erforschung des Mittelalters,* III, 225–46, especially 228–31.

(d. 1156), in whom the reform of the famed monastic congregation found a protagonist in the spirit of the new orders. His literary work was chiefly concerned with this reform, and its greatest part, the collection of letters, clearly betrays the pen of the humanist. His apologetic treatises — *Adversus Iudaeos* and *Adversus sectam Saracenorum* — and the projected translation of the Koran and of other Arabic writings display the candour of the supreme superior responsible for a monastic union that was spread over many lands. This union involved, especially in the southern monasteries, numerous contacts with the non-Christian world which had to be intellectually assimilated.

The writing of history, alongside the letter an especially characteristic literary form of humanism, was, as earlier, cultivated within the Benedictine world, even outside the Cluniac union. Deserving of mention are: Ordericus Vitalis (d. 1142) of Saint-Évroul in Normandy, Guibert de Nogent (d. 1124), William of Malmesbury (d. 1142), Hariulf of Saint-Riquier (d. 1143), Leo (d. 1115) and Peter (d. 1140) of Montecassino, Hugh of Reading, later Archbishop of Rouen (d. 1164), Heimo of Michelsberg (d. 1139), Bernard of Morlay (d. *ca.* 1150), Suger of Saint-Denis (d. 1151), and Wibald of Stavelot (d. 1158). Only the most important have been named. All of them are at the same time representative of many others, and in the wide range of their native lands they give an idea of the intensity of the Western culture of this epoch. Both poetry and prose were cultivated.

Benedictine theology at this period found its most important name in Rupert of Deutz (d. 1129). The humanistic element in his point of departure lay in his view that an appreciation of salvation history rather than dogmatic abstraction was the proper concern of research. A visual concept determined his exegesis: a viewing of divine mysteries in the scenes of salvation history. Rupert ranks as the founder of biblical theology. As a monk at Liège and then in Siegburg and as Abbot of Deutz, he acted as a connecting link for the two most important districts along the Rhine. His influence traveled east and south and through Gerhoh of Reichersberg it moved also in the world of the canons regular.[7] With Bernard of Clairvaux and the Cistercians, Rupert had a high esteem of Holy Scripture, alongside which the Church Fathers, while important representatives of ecclesiastical tradition, possessed only a lesser probative force in theology. Bernard's relationship to Scripture was, however, much more intimate than Rupert's; his meditative study penetrated more deeply and acted more dynamically.

Mediation between Cîteaux and Cluny was undertaken not only by the irenic Peter the Venerable, but also by William of Saint-Thierry, who,

---

[7] *Cf.* P. Classen, *Gerhoh von Reichersberg*, 36–40.

like Rupert, came from Liège. He became a Benedictine at Saint-Nicaise de Reims and in 1119 Abbot of Saint-Thierry. In 1135 he entered the Cistercian Order and was active at Signy until his death in 1148. For La Grande Chartreuse he wrote the famous "Golden Letter." Thus he stood, as it were, at the centre of all the spiritual concerns of the new orders in his capacity of theologian of the mystical life.[8]

What was more important for monastic humanism was life, not knowledge and doctrine, as was the case with the teachers in the urban schools. And so Bernard of Clairvaux took his place among historians with his *Vita Malachiae*, and William of Saint-Thierry became the biographer of his still living friend, Bernard of Clairvaux. Among Cistercians mention must be made of Aelred of Rievaulx (d. 1167), whose literary work has come again into esteem through modern research. The same may be said of Isaac of Stella (d. 1169), Guerric of Igny (d. 1157), Amadeus of Lausanne (d. 1159), and Gilbert of Hoyland (d. 1172), the first continuer and imitator of Bernard's *Commentary on the Canticle of Canticles*.[9]

First place among the canons regular was occupied in France by Hugh of Saint-Victor (d. 1141) and in Germany by Gerhoh of Reichersberg (d. 1169). Hugh's surpassing theological preeminence was undisputed. The encyclopedic breadth of his creativity justifies his being included in the humanism here under consideration, even though his teaching activity and the systematization of his theological works assign him also to early scholasticism. But with him too the exegetical-theological proposition revolves around a scene from salvation history. His creativity served the spiritual life, the reform of souls. Hugh and his entire Victorine school — Richard (d. 1173), Achard (d. 1171), Godfrey (d. *ca.* 1195) — combined their emphatically biblical theology with a rich spiritual experience.[10]

Gerhoh of Reichersberg came from the school of Rupert of Deutz, from whom he took the salvation-history orientation of his theology. His typological interpretation of time, his exegesis related to the present, his historical-critical method, to the extent that it can be so called, set him apart from the nascent scholastic method. He may be regarded not only as a conservative theologian but as a representative of humanism, even though he was not a monk; for the canons regular, because of their strict poverty

---

[8] This was especially pinpointed by M. M. Davy; see the bibliography for this chapter.

[9] On Isaac of Stella, see L. Ott, *LThK*, V (2nd ed. 1960), 777 f., with bibliography of the works by W. Meuser, J. Beumer, J. Debray-Mulatier, and M. R. Milcamps. The works of Guerric of Igny are in *PL*, 185, 11–214. *Cf.* D. De Wilde, *De Beato Guerrico* (Westmalle 1935); "Guerric et l'école monastique," *Collectanea O. Cist. Ref.*, 19 (1957), 238–47. On Amadeus of Lausanne, see A. Dimier, *Amédée de Lausanne* (Saint-Wandrille 1949). The works of Gilbert of Hoyland are in *PL*, 184, 11–298. On the whole Cistercian school see J. Leclercq, *Histoire de la spiritualité chrétienne*, II, 233–72.

[10] On the Victorine school see F. Vandenbroucke, *Histoire de la spiritualité chrétienne*, II, 282–98.

and their claustral mode of life, were very close to the monastic style — "pene eiusdem propositi," as Urban II put it. And both types of reform orders were equally aloof from rising scholasticism.

Norbert of Xanten, the founder of Prémontré, left no writings of his own, but he communicated his attitude to pupils who attested it, among them Anselm of Havelberg (d. 1158).[11] The latter's three books on his religious discussions in Constantinople became famous. Again, as in the case of Rupert, Gerhoh, and Hugh, with Anselm there is involved a salvation-history concept of the world-mowing events of the past and the present. Also Premonstratensians were Philip of Harvengt (d. 1183), Abbot of Bonne-Espérance, and Adam the Scot of Dryburgh (d. 1212); the last named later became a Carthusian at Witham. In the *Magna Vita* of Hugh of Lincoln it is said of Adam that he possessed an "incomparanda eruditio et doctrina."[12]

Even the silent Grande Chartreuse could at least write. Its founder, Bruno of Cologne, was regarded at Reims as a *doctor doctorum,* and something of his delight in elegant diction maintained itself in his foundations. Guigues de Châtel (d. 1137), fifth prior of La Grande Chartreuse, wrote letters, a life of Saint Hugh of Grenoble, meditations, and the constitution of the order. Jean Leclercq ranks him among the most noteworthy spiritual writers of his century.[13]

Chapter 7

The New Theology:
Abelard, Peter Lombard, Gratian

Parallel with monastic humanism there developed in the twelfth century a new theology in the world of the cathedral and chapter schools. In contradistinction to the abbeys, where theological knowledge appeared as oriented to the religious life itself, to prayer, meditation, and mystical union with God, the new theology sought to throw light on the mysteries of the faith, transmitted in Scripture and the patristic tradition, to acquire a systematic total view of the truths of faith by means of intensive rational reflection. It thereby corresponded to an urgent need of the time, in which economic, social, and political changes were forming a type of man

[11] On Anselm of Havelberg, see F. Petit, *La spiritualité des Prémontrés,* 56–64.
[12] On Adam the Scot see J. Bulloch, *Adam of Dryburgh* (London 1958); F. Petit, *Ad viros religiosos, 14 sermons d'Adam Scot* (Tongerloo 1934); most of his works are in *PL,* 198, 20–872.
[13] J. Leclercq, *Histoire de la spiritualité chrétienne,* II, 193.

different from that known to previous centuries. The great pilgrimages of the eleventh century and the crusades of the twelfth, the colonization getting under way on the Germanic-Slavonic frontier areas, the numerically not very important but still considerable interchange of men and institutions such as was connected with the founding of Norman states in England, South Italy, and the Levant — all this meant that in the ever expanding awareness of Western Christendom, above all through the upsetting contact with non-Christians, the vital questions of the traditional *milieu* of faith were put more critically and more anxiously.

The new theology cannot be understood only from the mentality of its first proponents, as though here men less inclined to contemplation or scholars especially equipped for reasoning accounted for a new method of gaining insights into the faith. Far more importantly, it was entirely in accord with a more comprehensive new intellectual need, which made itself known in the questions of students and in the problems of journalism, as, for example, in the Investiture Controversy. The continuity of intellectual development precludes any surprise that the initial steps of the new theology were associated with the names of monks, that Anselm of Bec and Canterbury ranks as the father of scholasticism, that Anselm of Laon came from his school, that Abelard in turn was a student of the younger Anselm. Nor is it without symbolic significance that Abelard lived as a monk of Saint-Denis and as Abbot of Saint-Gildas and died under the protection of Cluny, in Cluny's priory of Saint-Marcel near Chalon-sur-Saône.

Later this new theology was given the name "scholasticism" and attributed as "early scholasticism" to the twelfth and as "high scholasticism" to the thirteenth century. It was called the "theology of the schools," because it was at home in the urban schools from which the universities were to develop at the turn of the twelfth to the thirteenth century and because its leading teachers founded schools which were concerned to cultivate the theological specialization of their founders. Thus one speaks of the school of Anselm of Laon, of the school of Abelard, of the school of Gilbert de la Porrée, of the school of Saint-Victor, of the schools of Orléans, Chartres, Paris, Bologna. These numerous schools emerged almost simultaneously. The earliest appeared in the eleventh century — that of Bec with its two great teachers, Lanfranc and Anselm of Canterbury. Since the school of Bec does not fall within the scope of this presentation, the closely related school of Laon may be considered first.[1]

Anselm of Laon (*ca.* 1050–1117) and his brother Raoul, both of them pupils of Anselm of Canterbury, taught at the cathedral school of Laon.

---

[1] See S. Otto, *Die Funktion des Bildbegriffs in der Theologie des 12. Jahrhunderts* (Münster i. W. 1963), 24–69, and the bibliography for this chapter.

Research has rediscovered many works of the "sentence" *genre* from their sphere of influence; John of Tours is identified, but most of the other works have come down anonymously. Among the famous students of Laon were Adam du Petit Pont, Gilbert *universalis*, Abelard, and Gilbert de la Porrée. Since students came to Laon, just as they did to Bec, from great distances, including even the Slavic lands, the manuscripts of the school of Laon, scattered over the entire West, testify to a radiation over all of *christianitas latina*. Anselm's name was denigrated for contemporaries by Abelard's cuttingly critical withdrawal from Laon; in fact, the succeeding centuries forgot him. But John of Salisbury[2] rendered a very favourable judgment on the "clarissimi doctores fratres" of Laon.[3] New in the collections of sentences of the school of Laon was the manner in which the lecture notes of the *magistri* themselves were now set beside the patristic texts; in the further course of the development these notes acquired such great authority that the patristic texts were treated rather in the framework of the *theologoumena* of the teachers. Likewise discernible were the beginnings of the famous form of the *quaestio*, the classical method of teaching and of dealing with problems in scholastic theology.

Together with Anselm of Laon there is always simultaneously mentioned William of Champeaux (1068–1122), like Abelard a pupil of Roscelin of Compiègne. William taught at the cathedral school of Paris until a dispute with Abelard in 1108 induced him to withdraw to the left bank of the Seine. He settled down at the chapel of Saint-Victor, where soon arose the canonical institute of which he was the founder. Like many another celebrated teacher of these decades, he was made a Bishop, receiving the see of Châlons-sur-Marne in 1113, and as the friend and patron of the young Abbot of Clairvaux he could later enjoy a better publicity than that which overtook Anselm of Laon. His *Sententiae vel Quaestiones*, which are not merely concerned with topics such as the problem of universals, but, bearing an Augustinian stamp, treat in an original manner especially questions of moral theology, were able to produce long-range effects through his pupils, above all in Germany.[4] Even Bernard of Clairvaux found William's outlook congenial.

Important as a connecting link between France and Germany was the school of Liège.[5] Its great age occurred, it is true, in the eleventh century,

---

[2] *Metalogicon*, I, 5, ed. C. C. Webb (Oxford 1929), 18.

[3] *Historia Pontificalis*, c. 8, ed. M. Chibnall (London 1956), 19.

[4] H. Weisweiler, "Das Schrifttum der Schule Anselms von Laon und Wilhelms von Champeaux in deutschen Bibliotheken," *BGPhMA*, 33 (Münster i. W. 1936).

[5] "Les écoles liégeoises," in E. Lesne, *Histoire de la propriété ecclésiastique en France*, V (Lille 1940), 349–61.

but its best known teacher was Alger,[6] who became a monk at Cluny in 1126, was ordained a priest, and died there in 1131–32. His still unpublished, but in his own day much used, *florilegium*, the *Liber sententiarum magistri Algeri*, belongs to the prehistory of the *Liber sententiarum* of Peter Lombard.

Of greater significance than the founder of Saint-Victor for the new theology was the young community's greatest teacher, Hugh (d. 1141).[7] He probably came from Germany, for he received his first formation at Sankt Pankraz in Hamersleben, together with his introduction to the ideals of the canons regular; by his entry into the chapter of Saint-Victor de Paris between 1115 and 1120 he definitely adopted these ideals as his own. An encyclopedic mind,[8] an esteemed teacher, an author on a broad range of subjects, Hugh, especially with his systematically organized theological works, in particular *De sacramentis christianae fidei*, his scriptural commentaries, and the *Summa sententiarum*, which originated in his school, exerted a decisive influence on the century's history of theology, even on Peter Lombard, who often followed him. In addition to the surpassing influence of the Latin patristic theology, above all that of Saint Augustine, the thought of pseudo-Dionysius also carried weight with Hugh, as his commentary on the *Hierarchia coelestis* shows. Through Richard of Saint-Victor Hugh acted as a stimulus on mediaeval mysticism down to Gerson and Dionysius the Carthusian.

Together with Hugh, Abelard was celebrated by contemporary historians as one of the two *luminaria* who lectured on theology in France before audiences from the entire West. Abelard stands beside Anselm of Canterbury as the real founder of scholastic theology — not of its doctrines but of its scientific method. The very name "theology" probably came from him; previously the expressions *divina pagina* and *sacra doctrina* had been used. Through Abelard the *ratio*, schooled in dialectics, moved up beside the *auctoritas patrum*, and with him especially began the speculative penetration of the individual truths of the traditional faith, hitherto arranged in a superficial classification according to points of view.

Just as the investigations of individuals in the past thirty years have led to new evaluation of the theological achievement of Anselm of Laon and his school, in which not only the cosmopolitan radiation and the variety of the works but also the theological certainty of the evidence and the originality of the continuing theological reflection could find their

---

[6] Peter the Venerable terms Alger, Hezelo, and Tezelin "magnos suis temporibus magistros" (*Epp.*, III, 2, *PL*, 189, 278 f.).

[7] On Hugh, see R. Baron, *Études sur Hugues de Saint-Victor* (Paris 1963).

[8] For Hugh's scientific teaching see R. Baron, *Science et sagesse chez Hugues de Saint-Victor* (Paris 1957), 35–96.

scientific recognition, so too Abelard and his theological school now increasingly find a more positive stress than previously in the history of theology.

Born at Pallet near Nantes in 1079, Abelard emerged into the light of the history of theology with his criticism of Anselm of Laon and William of Champeaux. Under the cloud of his twofold condemnation at Soissons in 1121 and at Sens in 1141, his reputation was long tarnished, despite his writings and despite praise from contemporaries, by the overpowering fame of his opponent, Saint Bernard, especially since his relationship to Héloise was of more interest to a later age than was his significance within the new theological movement of the twelfth century. His name in theology owes its restored brilliance to the exertions of Denifle, Geitl, Vacandard, Geyer, and others. Modern research especially devotes its attention to his school, its personalities, and their works. J. de Ghellinck remarks that the history of theology in the twelfth century, and above all the history of Peter Lombard and his *Sentences,* could not be written without giving Abelard and his theological work an essential place within them.[9]

With Abelard and his school the climax is reached between patristic and scholastic theology. Especially in method, but also in content, as, for example, by stressing the essential position of the theology of the Sacraments in the total structure of the scientific study of the faith, they caused an advance which was capable of assuring the future of theology as a science, even though it was William of Auxerre (d. 1231) who first expressly posed and discussed the problem of "theology as a science." Research has contributed to the theological reassessment of Abelard especially by providing an exact chronology of his works and their various editions and by more clearly pinpointing the philosophical presuppositions of Abelard's thought processes, in particular his dialectic. Abelard's theological errors and daring conclusions, such as he drew in applying his method, are not eliminated by this new knowledge. Above all, the far too optimistic recourse to what must be called an almost exclusive intellectualism concealed their dangers; Bernard of Clairvaux felt obliged to meet them. Arno Borst was able to show[10] that in this matter, culminating in the Sens condemnation of 1141, there was involved an objective and not a personal confrontation and that one must not speak of bad blood between the two great theologians.

The theology of Gilbert de la Porrée was subjected to ecclesiastical judgment at almost the same time as Abelard's was. And like him,

---

[9] *Le mouvement,* 151. *Cf.* The bibliography for this chapter.
[10] A. Bornst, "Abälard und Bernhard," *HZ,* 186 (1958), 497–526. R. Klibanski, "Peter Abailard and Bernard de Clairvaux," *MRS,* 5 (1961), 1–27, independently arrived at a similar conclusion.

Gilbert,[11] who died as Bishop of Poitiers in 1154, was one of those power-ful figures who founded the schools. In him speculative theology was first discernible and active in a sense proper to scholasticism. If Abelard became the dialectician of theology, Gilbert became its metaphysician. Gilbert, who came from the circle of disciples surrounding Anselm of Laon, was equally under obligation to the school of Chartres.[12] His dialectical method, already successfully resorted to by Abelard, his *Liber sex principiorum*, which established itself as a textbook, and his theo-logical concepts made an impact through his school into the thirteenth century.

The school of Chartres,[13] where Gilbert taught, fostered by virtue of its Platonism a Christian humanism of encyclopedic scope, but also sought, with the aid of all secular sciences, to arrive at a deeper understanding of revelation. It belonged to the new theology, which was represented and enriched by all the great schools of the time. The fame of the schools of Chartres, connected with the names of the brothers Bernard and Thierry of Chartres, Bernard Silvestris, Clarenbald of Arras, and John of Salis-bury, was only diminished in the second half of the twelfth century by the growing repute of the schools of Paris.

In Paris, where Hugh of Saint-Victor had taught until 1141, originated the most famous theological work of the century: the *Four Books of Sentences* of Peter Lombard. First appeared the *Summa Sententiarum*, in which the theological movements of Abelard and Hugh of Saint-Victor met and united. As a brief, precise, and systematically composed treatise on all of theology, it found an extraordinarily intensive use.

With Peter Lombard (d. 1160) and his chief work, the course of development of the new theology reached its culmination, in so far as it called for classification, for a codification, so to speak, and for an orderly synthesis of the traditional doctrine, now theologically assimilated. Theol-ogy emerged from the spell of the biblical and patristic tradition and the unique *auctoritas* into the pungent atmosphere of the critical reason and was now opening the gate to the great *summae* of high scholasticism.

Peter Lombard, who came to Paris between 1135 and 1139, was hospitably received at Saint-Victor. In Paris he may have listened to

[11] On Gilbert de la Porrée and his school, see S. Otto, *Die Funktion des Bildbegriffs*, 176–94, 224–50; S. Gammersbach, *Gilbert von Poitiers und seine Prozesse im Urteil der Zeitgenossen* (Cologne and Graz 1959); N. M. Häring, "Zur Geschichte der Schulen von Poitiers," *AKG*, 47 (1965), 23–47.
[12] The Council of Reims (1148) refrained from a condemnation of Gilbert's doctrine of the Trinity, which Bernard of Clairvaux had rejected.
[13] The classic work by A. Clerval, *Les écoles de Chartres au moyen âge* (du Ve au XVIe siècle) (Paris 1895) was reprinted at Frankfurt am Main in 1965; E. Lesne, *op. cit.*, V, 152–72.

Abelard, and he certainly knew his works. During a stay at the Curia (1148–50) he became acquainted with the theological work of John Damascene in the translation of Burgundio of Pisa. At the Council of Reims in 1148 he belonged to the group of theologians hostile to Gilbert de la Porrée. His *Four Books of Sentences* were probably completed in 1157.[14]

It is surprising that the author of this celebrated work, differing from his more famous contemporaries whom we have already mentioned, was hardly named by contemporary chroniclers and historians. It may be assumed that his teaching activity did not arouse an equally lively echo.[15] The first book of the *Sentences* treats of God and the Trinity; the second, of creation, the angels, the six days, original sin, and grace; the third, of the Incarnation, virtues, sins, the commandments; the fourth, of the sacraments and the last things. The work displays none of the genius of Anselm, the originality of Hugh of Saint-Victor, the keenly speculative clear-sightedness of Abelard. It adopted Abelard's method but not his *theologoumena*. Because of the lucid arrangement, the rich and well ordered fulness of its texts, and the *via media* of its theological propositions, it managed, not without first having been exposed to some criticism, to establish itself universally as a textbook for theological instruction in the West and maintained itself unchallenged until the sixteenth century. It was then replaced by the *Summa theologica* of Saint Thomas Aquinas.[16]

Before the Lombard had composed his *Sentences,* the Camaldolese Gratian compiled at Bologna his *Decretum:* the *Concordia discordantium canonum.* Finished immediately after the Second Lateran Council (1139), it appeared in the context of the new theology, for it too was characterized by a process of systematization and synthesis. With it was born the new science of canon law, which met on equal terms the new science of theology of the French schools. Like the latter, Gratian sought to master the alleged contradictions of the assembled *auctoritates* by the light of reason. He discussed, critically but with an eye to harmonization, the value of passages in the texts and drew compelling conclusions. The *Decretum* did not know a real system in the sense of the classical canon law, but rather a line of thought that was logically planned and developed. Only Gratian's pupils and commentators understood the *Decre-*

---

[14] This is now held by D. Van den Eynde, "Essai chronologique sur l'œuvre de Pierre Lombard," *Miscellanea Lombardiana* (Novara 1957), 45–64.

[15] Peter's scriptural commentaries are frequently called the *Glossa magna,* and in particular the commentary on Saint Paul was later called simply the *Glossa.*

[16] A. M. Landgraf did not regard Peter Lombard "exactly as an independent thinker" (*Einführung,* 94), while he thought that Gilbert's school "gave its own stamp to the theology of the twelfth and thirteenth centuries in many points" (*ibid.,* 91).

tum as having a threefold division into persons *(ministri)*, procedure *(negotia)*, and Sacraments.

As the successor of Ivo of Chartres, Bernold of Constance, Alger of Liège, and Abelard, Gratian sought to resolve disagreement among the canons. This had become a burning problem the moment that the reform papacy had established itself, Christendom had become more keenly aware of its unity than earlier, and a universally accepted juridical order appropriate to it and taking precedence over particular customs and privileges seemed to be required. Since the authority of the papacy itself seemed not yet sufficiently effective everywhere, reason, or the dialectical method, came to its aid and with the new science of the decretists created a serviceable instrument.

The *Decretum* meant a substantial beginning, but for the moment only a beginning, for Gratian's wise rules of distinctions were by no means handled consistently, even by him. But, alongside the *lacunae,* defects, and inconsistencies of the *Decretum,* contemporaries saw especially its excellences: it contained everything essential in the numerous previous collections and took the place of a library. Reason reached useful conclusions and pointed out important groups of problems. The *Decretum,* assembling all texts of the Church's first millennium in an intelligible and ordered whole, fulfilled a double function: certainty was imparted and questions still open were indicated.

The new sciences, closely related through their sources, continued in this intimacy in the next stages of their development, especially since some of their topics, such as the sacraments, overlapped.[17] What was new in both was the dialectical method, by virtue of which a structured order could be introduced into the apparently formless mass of traditional texts and an impetus was to be expected for the further elucidation of the context of the teachings of faith, morals, and law. Thus Peter Lombard drew from Ivo of Chartres and from Gratian's *Decretum,* and he may have observed Gratian's work coming into being at Bologna. He accepted some of Gratian's teachings in his own work, but at the same time he energetically rectified certain conclusions of the *Decretum.*

If Gratian was less successful than the Lombard in mastering the mass of texts, it may be recalled that he had no model, whereas Peter Lombard could go back to Hugh of Saint-Victor, Abelard, the *Summa Sententiarum,* and finally to the *Decretum* itself.

---

[17] J. de Ghellinck, *Le mouvement,* 203–13; A. M. Landgraf, "Diritto canonico e teologia nel secolo XII," *StG,* I (1953), 371–413.

The Threats to the Freedom of the Church
(1153—98)

CHAPTER 8

The Popes, the Emperor Frederick I, and the Third Lateran Council

Eugene III died at Tivoli on 8 July 1153, and a whole epoch drew to a close. In this Pope from the Cistercian Order in its spectacular development, the reform papacy produced its last representative. A long succession of monks and canons regular had for a whole century guided the destinies of the Roman Church, which more and more represented the Universal Church. The heirs to the successes of this century were very clearly distinguished from their predecessors. They were a new generation, stamped by the new theology and the new science of canon law, by the mentality of a cooler rationalism and a more soberly realistic political planning. The Church and the *Patrimonium Petri,* in which, as before, they saw the decisive guarantor of the freedom of the Universal Church, they intended to govern with as much centralization as possible.

Bernard of Clairvaux died on 20 August 1153, almost at the same time as Eugene III. Seldom has a new generation made its appearance in world history so unmistakably as at this moment. Henry II began his reign in England officially on 19 December 1154, though he had been designated as King after the death of Stephen's son Eustace on 17 August 1153. Roger II of Sicily died at Palermo on 26 February 1154. In these first years of the second half of the century there also died Abbot Suger of Saint-Denis (1151), Wibald of Stavelot (1158), Anselm of Havelberg (1158), Archbishop Adalbero of Trier (1152), and Gilbert de la Porrée, Bishop of Poitiers (1154).

A change occurred also on the German royal throne. Eugene III lived to see the death of Conrad III on 15 February 1152; the King had not been able to undertake the journey to Rome, urgently requested by the Pope because of the unruly state of the Eternal City and planned for the fall of 1152. Eugene had given his approval of the election of Frederick I Barbarossa on 4 March 1152; it had actually not been sought, and Frederick had merely sent an announcement. The negotiations then ensuing between Frederick and the Curia occurred toward the close of Eugene's pontificate and terminated in the novel bilateral Treaty of Constance[1] of 23 March 1153, which stipulated a strictly mutual cooperation between King and Pope. Both parties obliged themselves to political solidarity *vis-à-vis* the City of Rome and the Normans. Neither was to declare himself prepared for territorial concessions to Byzantium. Each promised to protect and guarantee the other's *honor*, that is, his sovereign rights. The Concordat of Worms was not mentioned. Frederick was, nonetheless, disposed to exercise authority over the Church of the Empire to the extent that the Worms guide-lines allowed. The Curia displayed a willingness to be accommodating when Eugene III also gave his two legates full authority to annul, on the ground of too close relationship, the childless marriage of Frederick with Adele of Vohburg, whom the King wanted to divorce for infidelity. While a suspension of Archbishop Henry of Mainz was agreeable to the King, he opposed the intervention of the legates in the question of the disputed election to Magdeburg, which he intended to settle by promoting Wichmann, Bishop of Zeitz-Naumburg. Anastasius IV finally confirmed Wichmann, who had come to Rome and there obtained the pallium.

Anastasius, a Roman, had been Cardinal Conrad of Suburra. In his brief pontificate, from 12 July 1153 to 3 December 1154, he disappointed others as well as Gerhoh of Reichersberg, who said of him: "After Eugene there was not found his like on the papal throne to keep the law of the Most High, as is proved by the letters and deeds of his successor, Pope Anastasius, a feeble old man."[2] His was a pontificate of transition and, as such, significant that a new epoch was beginning.

Hadrian IV

Hadrian IV (1154–59), who inaugurated the new age, also came from the ranks of the canons regular — he had been provost of the famed chapter of Saint-Ruf d'Avignon —, but he guided it into paths different from those hitherto trodden. His activity was determined, not by the *consideratio* called for by Bernard, the commitment of the Supreme Shepherd, derived from the depth of spiritual meditation, but rather by the awareness of the fulness of power bestowed by God, the dispassionately cool eye for the politically attainable and for the juridical claim. Ever more to the fore moved the chancellor, Roland Bandinelli, pupil of Abelard and jurist, who, by reason of his intellectual background, could not

---

[1] Reprint of the text of the Treaty of Constance in P. Rassow, *Honor imperii* (Darmstadt 1961).

[2] *Commentarius in Ps. 65*, MGLiblit, III, 493 (footnotes 25–27).

52

but arouse mistrust in such men of the old school as Gerhoh of Reichersberg.[3]

Nicholas Breakspear, thus far the only Pope of English origin, had been a fellow-student and friend of John of Salisbury and, presumably, a pupil of Abelard and of Gilbert de la Porrée at Paris, as were John and Roland Bandinelli. After entering the chapter of the canons regular of Saint-Ruf d'Avignon, he rose to the position of provost. He left there, not entirely peacefully, when Eugene III made him Cardinal Bishop of Albano in 1149. His community had complained to Rome of his excessive strictness. In 1152 he was in Norway as papal legate.[4] He there convoked and directed a large council, established the archiepiscopal see of Nidaros (Trondheim), and sought to regulate the ecclesiastical situation in the spirit of the reform movement. In the spring of 1153 he presumably went to Sweden and convoked a council to Linköping. The King, bishops, and magnates took part but unfortunately the decrees are not extant. He managed to introduce Peter's Pence in both Norway and Sweden, but in the latter kingdom he did not succeed in erecting an ecclesiastical province as he had probably planned.

Immediately after his election[5] Hadrian IV displayed great firmness in Rome. By laying an interdict on the city shortly before Easter of 1155 he induced the Senate to expel Arnold of Brescia and his adherents. In January 1155 he had renewed with Frederick I the Treaty of Constance on behalf of himself and his successors. This step was of great importance for the Pope, since William I of Sicily, Roger II's successor, had meanwhile occupied Benevento and was beginning incursions into the Roman *campagna*. Hadrian excommunicated him.

At Sutri on 8 June 1155 occurred the first meeting of the Pope with Frederick, who was *en route* to Rome for his imperial coronation. The interview, which acquired notoriety because of the affair of the service of bridle and stirrup, owed by the German King but at first refused and then performed by Frederick, has been eagerly discussed by scholars.[6] Only after rather long discussions, in which older princes as well as the Curia itself referred to the purely ceremonial nature of the marshal's service "out of deference for the blessed Apostles Peter and Paul," could the incident be closed. An offer by the Romans to confer the imperial crown at the Capitol, against a payment of 5,000 pounds of gold, was rejected

---

[3] *Cf.* P. Classen, *Gerhoh von Reichersberg* (Wiesbaden 1960), 156.

[4] G. Inger, *Das kirchliche Visitationsinstitut im mittelalterlichen Schweden* (Lund 1961), 222–28.

[5] 4 December 1154.

[6] *Cf.* R. Holtzmann, *Der Kaiser als Marschall des Papstes* (Berlin and Leipzig 1928); also E. Eichmann, "Officium stratoris et strepae," *HZ*, 142 (1930), 16–40, and R. Holtzmann's reply, "Zum Strator- und Marschalldienst," *HZ*, 145 (1932), 301–50.

by Frederick, who pointed out that the *Imperium* had long since passed to the Germans. On the day of the imperial coronation, 18 June 1155, Frederick had to put down in blood a rising of the Romans. Arnold of Brescia,[7] whose extradition Frederick had achieved, was executed on the orders of the prefect of the city. Without having aided the Pope in his quarrel with the Normans, as provided by the Treaty of Constance, the Emperor, at the request of the German princes, returned home in the late summer. He had not brought Rome back under the Pope's control, though he had turned over Tivoli, which had placed itself under the Emperor's authority, to the Pope, reserving the rights of the Empire. There was no agreement on the key ideas of the Treaty of Constance, *honor imperii* and *honor Sancti Petri* (or *papatus*), nor in regard to the Normans and their Kingdom.

In his disappointment over Frederick's premature return to Germany, Hadrian IV gave to his policy that turn which Frederick had aimed to prevent by the Treaty of Constance. In 1156 he concluded the Peace of Benevento with King William I of Sicily.[8] In it William's royal title, which had at first been denied him, was recognized, as was his legitimate authority over Capua, Apulia, Calabria, and Sicily. Extensive rights over the Church in his territories were conceded to him, substantially as a renewal of the privilege granted to Count Roger I for Sicily by Urban II. For his part, William acknowledged the feudal suzerainty of Saint Peter and obliged himself to a considerable annual *census* of 1,000 gold pieces to the Pope for South Italy. Naples, Salerno, Amalfi, and Marsia were awarded to William as a hereditary possession. Thanks to the peace with the Normans the Pope was able, with the assistance of the prudent and energetic Cardinal *Camerlengo* Boso,[9] to consolidate papal authority in the various *terrae Sancti Petri*, and even his return to Rome became possible in November 1156.

In order to apprise the Emperor of the Peace of Benevento the Pope then dispatched two legates, the Cardinal Chancellor Roland Bandinelli,

---

[7] Arnold of Brescia (*ca.* 1100–55) became provost of a chapter of Augustinian canons in Brescia following his studies at Paris. He defended the radical poverty of the reform clergy and demanded that clergy and bishops renounce possessions, ecclesiastical property, and *regalia*. Banished in 1139, perhaps by the Second Lateran Council, he left Italy and taught at Paris but was expelled through the efforts of Bernard of Clairvaux. He went *via* Zurich to Bohemia, where the Cardinal Legate Guido of Castello received him and in 1145 arranged a reconciliation with Eugene III. He then took part in the commune's rising against the Pope and in 1147 preached in Rome against the simony and worldliness of the clergy. He remained in Rome, despite his excommunication by the Pope in 1148, and in his preaching seconded the citizens' demand for autonomy. See R. Foreville, *Latran I, II, III, et Latran IV* (Paris 1965), 86 f., 105 f., 111.

[8] Text of the Treaty of Benevento in *Constitutiones*, I, nos. 413 f.

[9] *Cf.* F. Geisthardt, "Der Kämmerer Boso." *HStud*, 293 (Berlin 1936), 41–59.

and Bernard, Cardinal Priest of San Clemente. They were also to concern themselves with the case of the imprisoned Archbishop Eskil of Lund. While *en route* from Rome to the north, this prelate had been arrested in Imperial Burgundy and imprisoned in the expectation that he would be ransomed at a high price. Eskil, to whom Hadrian, when legate in the north, had brought the pallium and whom, when Pope, he had constituted Primate of Sweden and Legate of the North, was regarded as an enemy of the Empire, because, in his new dignities, he was in opposition to the Nordic ambitions of Hamburg–Bremen, which were supported by Frederick. These were based on old papal privileges and through them Frederick intended to assure his influence in Scandinavia. At the Diet of Besançon in October 1157 occurred the well known incident, brought on by an expression in Hadrian's letter to the Emperor, which was translated, perhaps deliberately, by Rainald of Dassel, Frederick's chancellor since 1156, as "fief". In the letter, with reference to the *beneficium* of the imperial coronation, already conferred, still further *maiora beneficia* were held out to the Emperor by the Pope, if the former should be accommodating in regard to Rome's concerns, for example, the liberation of the Archbishop of Lund and the projected visitation of the German Church by the legates. Alleging the excitement of his magnates, the Emperor sent the legates back empty-handed, but not without having thereby seriously compromised his relations with the Curia by misunderstandings and tensions.

In the manifestoes sent out by the imperial chancery concerning the events at Besançon, the "Empire consciousness" in the circle around Frederick I for the first time found expression as a program. The independence of the imperial office from the Roman Church was proclaimed: the Emperor, it was maintained, owes his crown only to the grace of God and the free choice of the princes. An appeal by the Pope to the German episcopate obtained an unexpected reply: a corroboration of the imperial view and the request that Hadrian IV would appease the Emperor by another, milder letter, for the good of the Church and of the Empire. In June 1158 the Pope had such a letter delivered to the Emperor at Augsburg by two legates, the Cistercian Henry of Santi Nereo et Achilleo and Hyacinth of Santa Maria in Cosmedin. In this he stated that the term *beneficium* in the letter read at Besançon should have been translated not as "fief" but as "benefit," while the use of *conferre* in regard to the imperial crown did not mean "to confer" but "to impose". The Emperor accepted this explanation, especially since the legates were able to assure him that the Pope would continue to be concerned for the *honor imperii* and to maintain the rights of the Empire.

Just as Hadrian IV renewed his feudal relationship to the Normans and appealed to the *Constitutum Constantini* in regard to Sicily, so, according to John of Salisbury, whom he used as middleman, did he also dispose of Ireland by virtue of his authority over the western islands, investing Henry II of England with the rule of Ireland by sending him an emerald ring.[10]

Meanwhile the Emperor, having entrusted the defense of the Empire's interests on its eastern frontiers to new princely families in order to be free to devote himself entirely to the Italian problem, proceeded southward again. At the Diet of Roncaglia near Piacenza in November 1158 he again enforced the old imperial rights in the Kingdom of Lombardy, as he had had them verified by the Four Doctors of Bologna and the representatives of twenty-eight cities — that is, the crown *regalia,* which had not been claimed for decades. Milan, which had submitted on 7 September 1158, had already surrendered them. If implemented, the Roncaglia decrees would have meant, not only the restoration of the old royal authority and a loss by the cities of their freedom and autonomy, but also an excessive increase in the economic and political power of the crown. Hence Milan, Brescia, and Piacenza undertook negotiations with Hadrian IV for an alliance against the Emperor, who was now beginning to apply the Roncaglia decrees also in Tuscany and even in the north of the *Patrimonium Petri.* Hadrian allowed him a respite of forty days within which to annul these measures; otherwise he would be compelled to excommunicate the Emperor. But before the interval had expired, the Pope died at Anagni on 1 September 1159.

Shortly before his death Hadrian had had his interpretation of *honor Sancti Petri* expounded to the Emperor by the Cardinal Legates Octavian and William: the Pope's authority was unrestricted over Rome and the entire *Patrimonium Petri,* where Frederick intended to occupy a position like that of Charles the Great or Otto the Great; the Roncaglia decrees were not to be applied to the Italian bishops; and the Treaty of Constance was to be renewed, especially since the Treaty of Benevento had in no way offended against the letter and the spirit of Constance. Hadrian had naturally rejected an arbitration court, suggested by the Emperor, which would discuss and clarify the opposing views of the two powers.

Hadrian's corpse was transported to Rome and interred in Saint Peter's. He had contrived to consolidate his rule in the *Patrimonium* by means of a consistent continuation of the exemption policy of his predecessors, but in the case of abbeys and chapters reserving the rights of the bishops. He had further developed the actual government of the Universal Church by the Roman Curia. In Ireland, Scotland, and Spain he had renewed the ecclesiastical bonds and brought them more firmly into connection with

---

[10] *Metalogicon,* IV, 42: *cf.* A. L. Poole, *From Domesday Book to Magna Carta,* 303, footnote 1; P. Sheehy, "The Bull Laudabiliter," *Galway Archaeological and Historical Society Journal,* 29 (1961), 45–70.

Rome, just as he had done earlier as cardinal legate in the North. By means of Peter's Pence he had caused the unity of Christendom and the relationship of individual Christians, and not merely of princes and prelates, with the See of Peter to become more vivid in the awareness of the faithful. He had quite intentionally defended the jurisdictional primacy of the Roman Church, especially against Byzantium, and had been able to exercise it, despite manifold difficulties. Finally, toward the close of his pontificate he had sought, by means of an understanding between the Emperor Manuel and William I of Sicily in 1158, to erect a dam against Frederick I's Italian policy, which was preparing systematically to advance from Lombardy *via* Tuscany to the south. And just before the Pope's death the Emperor's moderate advisors had all died in 1158: Wibald of Stavelot in July on his last embassy to Byzantium, Anselm of Havelberg and Ravenna on 12 August, and Otto of Freising. A new phase of the Roman Church's struggle for her freedom was ushered in.

Alexander III

The double papal election of 7 September 1159[11] took place under the influence of the methodically pursued Italian policy of the Emperor Frederick I. The frontiers of the *Patrimonium* had already been violated, contact had been made with circles in Rome, and Otto of Wittelsbach lingered in the city during the election. The majority of the Sacred College, at least two-thirds, decided on the chancellor, Cardinal Roland Bandinelli; a minority, favourably disposed to the Emperor, preferred Cardinal Octavian of Monticello (Tivoli). The stormy course of the election allowed doubts to rise, as in the double election of 1130, as to the legitimacy of both claimants. Bandinelli styled himself Alexander III (1159–81), while his rival took the name Victor IV (1159–64).

Once again a judgment by the Universal Church had to decide, since there was no institutional organ qualified to clarify such cases by arbitration.[12] If the double election of 1130 had been determined by inner ecclesiastical motives, the existence in the College of Cardinals of opposing views of the tasks and methods of Church reform, this time clearly political considerations predominated. Alexander's electors wanted to continue what Hadrian IV had begun, whereas Victor's partisans displayed their agreement with the Emperor's imperial and Italian policy. Nevertheless,

[11] Since the now outdated dissertation of M. Meyer, *Die Wahl Alexanders III. und Viktors IV.* (Göttingen 1871), this topic has not been the subject of a monograph; see J. Haller, *Das Papsttum,* III (2nd ed. 1962), 503 f.

[12] See Chapter I, pp. 8 f.

the developments of the next years made clear that more deeply grounded basic concepts were dialectically encountered in this double election and its consequences and pressed for a settlement in severe struggles that shook the Church. As Frederick's idea of the function of the imperial office in the Christian world was largely shaped by the revived Roman law as modified by Justinian and Christianity, so did the pontificate of Alexander III seem to be determined by a canon law, developing consistently and establishing itself in practice, which was entirely able to make methodical use of Roman juristic categories. At issue was the settlement of the question: which principle of order should have the primacy in the Christian world, *auctoritas sacrata pontificum* or *regalis potestas*? The inclusion of the celebrated statement of Gelasius in Frederick's first message to the Pope was not unpremeditated. [13]

The obediences were quickly distinguished. In the Council of Pavia, meeting from 5 to 11 February 1160, summoned by the Emperor and attended for the most part by the imperial episcopate of Germany, Burgundy, and Lombardy, Frederick had Victor IV recognized, while Alexander was excommunicated. In the autumn of the same year the episcopates and monastic orders of the Western countries, including Spain, met at Toulouse in the presence of Henry II of England and Louis VII of France and, after a detailed inquiry into the elections, declared for Alexander III, and, as was to be expected, excommunicated Victor. Contrary to the procedure in the Empire, the Western kings had yielded to the pressure of their clergy, who for the most part saw a kindred spirit in Alexander, pupil of Abelard and representative of the new theology; [14] certain national hesitations were also expressed in regard to a Pope acting under imperial protection, not to mention imperial pressure. [15]

In the religious orders the reaction was less uniform. Cîteaux and La Grande Chartreuse adhered to Alexander; Cluny, to Victor. Prémontré was divided. The canons regular went along with the rest of the clergy of their countries or, like Gerhoh of Reichersberg, remained neutral. And there was an Alexandrian enclave in Germany: the province of Salzburg under Archbishop Eberhard I of Biburg and Hipoltstein, a Benedictine.

[13] *MGConst*, I, no. 137, 192 (footnotes 7–14).

[14] J. de Ghellinck, *Le mouvement théologique du XIIe siècle* (Bruges and Paris 1948), 250–58.

[15] John of Salisbury, Letter 124 to Magister Ralph of Sarre (June-July 1160) in *The Letters of John of Salisbury (1153–61)*, ed. W. J. Millor, H. E. Butler, C. N. L. Brooke (London 1955), 204–15. This letter, a commentary on the imperial Council of Pavia (February 1160) and referring to an analysis of the double election of September 1159, passionately took the part of Alexander III and the freedom of ecclesiastical elections: "... electio pastoris est in ecclesia a clero libere et sine mundanae potestatis praenominatione celebranda, sic eadem in ecclesia a iudicibus ecclesiastics, amotis saecularibus terribilibusque personis, libere et secundum regulas ecclesiasticas examinanda est" (208).

Since the Emperor Frederick's power continued to grow in Italy, especially with the fall of Milan on 1 March 1162, and the Norman Kingdom, in which rebel vassals declared for Victor while the King upheld Alexander, offered no effective protection, Alexander left Italy. At Milan Archbishop Eberhard of Salzburg had previously sought to bring about an understanding between Frederick and Alexander. When the effort failed, Alexander proceeded to Genoa and in April 1162 sailed for southern France. In this country, where Innocent II had sought and found help, he remained for three years. But Bernard of Clairvaux had been dead for almost ten years and Frederick was reigning in the Empire instead of Lothar. Furthermore, the loyalty of Henry II of England and Louis VII of France appeared to be quite different from that of their predecessors of 1130. For them the new schism was almost a welcome opportunity, which promised them freedom of action and various possibilities in domestic and foreign politics. Henry II could, among other things, restore the crown's diminished authority over the Church, while Louis VII could correspondingly require a price for his support.

At first Alexander stayed at Montpellier, for Louis was negotiating with the Emperor. Agreement was reached on a meeting of the monarchs on the Saône bridge at Saint-Jean-de-Losne,[16] with the rival claimants to the papacy participating. But Alexander declined to submit to the projected arbitration court. A new date had to be selected: 19 September 1162. This too came to nothing, for shortly before, on 7 September, Frederick had had Alexander again excommunicated at a synod at Dôle, presided over by Victor. Thus Louis VII alone turned up; on the bridge he met the chancellor, Rainald of Dassel. A violent exchange between them wrecked any agreement for the moment. In fact, Alexander was now able to reconcile Louis with Henry II of England. The two Kings met at Coucy-sur-Loire, south of Blois. They planned a council, which met at Tours in May 1163 and turned into an impressive demonstration in favour of Alexander. The excommunication of Victor IV, Rainald of Dassel, and others was repeated, but the Emperor was spared. Alexander resumed his efforts for an understanding. In the summer of 1163 he sent representatives to Nürnberg and in April 1164 two cardinals, Hyacinth and William, to Susa, where Frederick was residing. Both attempts failed because Frederick insisted on the idea of an arbitration court, which Alexander had repeatedly rejected as unacceptable.

When Victor IV died at Lucca on 20 April 1164, Rainald of Dassel, without awaiting a word from the Emperor, hastened to procure the election of Cardinal Guido of Crema, who became Paschal III (1164–68).

[16] W. Heinemeyer, "Die Verhandlungen an der Saône im Jahre 1162," *DA*, 20 (1964), 155–89.

Whether he entirely enjoyed the Emperor's approval is controverted, but Frederick subsequently ratified what his chancellor had done.

For in Upper Italy there was being formed, at the instigation of Venice, a league of Lombard cities, led by Verona, in opposition to the strict implementation of the Roncaglia decrees, especially the harsh taxation by imperial *podestàs*. Alexander got into contact with this League of Verona that together they might meet the pressure of the imperial policy — successfully, as it turned out. In addition, after Victor's death there began in Germany a crumbling of the ecclesiastical front. In Burgundy the bishops refused Rainald of Dassel's demand that they recognize Paschal III. In the summer of 1164 the new Archbishop of Salzburg, Conrad, who as Bishop of Passau had adhered to Victor, now recognized Alexander. Gerhoh of Reichersberg followed suit. Conrad of Wittelsbach, Archbishop of Mainz, on the occasion of a pilgrimage to Santiago de Compostela, had sought out Alexander in France. And Archbishops Hillin of Trier and Wichmann of Magdeburg gradually became alienated from the imperial policy because of the serious harm done to the churches by the schism. At the Diet of Würzburg, at Pentecost 1165, the Emperor endeavoured to compel the loyalty of the bishops by having them swear under oath never to acknowledge Alexander. He was himself the first to take the oath, and the secular princes, headed by Henry the Lion, followed. Conrad of Wittelsbach fled to Alexander in France during the night preceding the swearing, and his see was given to Christian of Buch. Conrad of Salzburg was outlawed when he refused to take the oath within the delay granted to the absent princes. The year 1165 ended with the solemn raising at Aachen of the remains of Charles the Great, whom Rainald of Dassel, as the competent metropolitan, canonized in the presence of the Emperor.

The manifestoes of 1165 showed clearly in what sense Frederick intended to have his imperial office respected in the Church: perhaps not in the crude sense of binding the episcopate and the papacy to a mere function of service to the Empire, but certainly in the sense that he intended to fulfill his service to the Church as *defensor* only if the *honor imperii* could be brought into harmony with the *honor papatus*. In practice this appeared in Frederick's eyes to imply that only the *honor imperii* was sovereign, while the *honor papatus* was at most autonomous within the unity of the universal Empire, which was regarded, at least in theory, as identical with Christendom. Here ideas were so radically different that Alexander with reason had to continue the struggle without compromise in principle, if he was concerned for the liberty of the Church. In this connection the ending of the schism itself was to be understood only as a precondition; the restored unity would require a right ordering.

Meanwhile, in April 1165 Alexander III had left Sens, where he had resided for two years, in order to return to Italy. This time he found in the Normans a strong support. Negotiations had been begun with the Emperor Manuel, who held out the offer of a union of the Greek and Latin Churches in the event that Alexander would crown him Emperor. France and the Normans were to be included in the great coalition between Rome and Constantinople. But Louis VII and William I declined for obvious reasons. And Alexander himself was not prepared to abandon the Western imperial tradition.

In view of this lively diplomatic activity by his opponents, Frederick determined to force a decision in Italy. With a large army, which included mercenaries from Brabant, he set out on his fourth expedition to Italy in the fall of 1166. In the spring of 1167 he proceeded south. He took Ancona, which was allied with the Byzantines, and on 29 May defeated the Romans near Tusculum. He occupied the Leonine City at the end of July, thereby acquiring possession of Saint Peter's. Paschal III was solemnly enthroned there and on 1 August he gave the imperial crown to Frederick's wife, Beatrice of Burgundy. Alexander had fled to the protection of the Normans in Benevento.

A few days after the celebrations at Saint Peter's malaria broke out in the imperial army. More than 2,000 knights, princes, and bishops died, including Rainald of Dassel, and the Emperor himself fell ill and returned to Germany with the rest of the army. In Lombardy there began a rapid defection from the Emperor, which spread far. Milan was rebuilt and in 1168 there was founded near Tortona a league stronghold, which was named Alessandria in the Pope's honour. Italy was lost to the Emperor; the attempt to reestablish the imperial power in Italy, against the Curia and the cities, was wrecked. It is true that Paschal III acquired a successor in Calixtus III (1168–78), but from the death of Rainald of Dassel Frederick seemed more inclined to negotiate anew with Alexander. Bishop Eberhard of Bamberg, who was accompanied by the Abbots of Cîteaux and Clairvaux, was delegated for this purpose. It was only the two Abbots who succeeded in contacting the Pope in 1169, for Bishop Eberhard did not obtain permission from the Lombard League to pass through its territory. It was not until the end of March 1170 that he was able to meet the Pope at Veroli. Since the Lombard League was not to be included in the projected peace, Eberhard's mission foundered against the Pope's loyalty to his commitment.

And so at the Diet of Fulda in June 1170 the Emperor renewed his declaration, made at Würzburg, that he would never recognize Alexander and again made diplomatic overtures to the Western powers, England and France. He met Louis VII at Vaucouleurs in February 1171 and also opened negotiations with Byzantium. However, it was only too natural that the real decision had to be sought again in Italy. Hence Frederick moved south for the fifth time in September 1174. After several military engagements with the Lombard cities had taken place, a truce was agreed to at Montebello on 10 April 1176.[17] But a definitive peace could not be achieved, for this time the Lombards insisted on including the Pope. The war continued. Since Duke Henry the Lion, whom Frederick had gone to Chiavenna to see at the end of January 1176, refused to provide armed aid, Frederick went into the final phase of the long quarrel weaker than he had expected to be, and on 29 May 1176 he lost the battle of Legnano, northwest of Milan.

Frederick exploited the long drawn out peace negotiations to acquire by diplomacy what his arms had denied him. In the preliminary treaty of Anagni, in the negotiations for which representatives of the Lombard League had not been consulted, he was able to conclude a separate agreement with the Pope, which was to serve as the basis for the definitive discussions by all qualified parties. This preliminary treaty stipulated that Frederick should recognize Alexander as the lawful Pope, hand over to him the *regalia* of the *Patrimonium*, restore the confiscated properties, and renounce the Mathildine lands in Tuscany. It was agreed that the Lombards, the Normans, and the Byzantines should be included in the general peace. The Pope would release Frederick from excommunication and recognize him as Emperor and his son Henry as King of the Romans. All ecclesiastical decisions made by Frederick and his bishops during the schism were to retain their validity.

The final negotiations took place at Venice after Alexander had exerted himself, not without difficulty, to dispel the misgivings of his Lombard allies. The very secretly conducted preliminary negotiations at Anagni caused this mistrust to appear as only too justified. The agenda were determined by the Pope. There was first to be a discussion of peace between the Emperor and the Lombard League, and simultaneously a discussion of peace between the Emperor on the one hand and the King of Sicily and the Roman Church on the other hand. Hence, when the negotiations between the representatives of the Lombards and the Emperor's envoys came to a standstill, the Pope was able to propose the compromise that was later accepted: that instead of a peace an armistice of ten years might be agreed to, and similarly a fifteen-years' armistice between the Emperor and Sicily. The preliminary peace of Anagni was ratified, except that the arrangements in regard to the Mathildine lands were suppressed; Frederick contrived to have these territories remain in his hands for a further fifteen years. The negotiations lasted from 10 May to 21 July, during which time the Emperor resided at Pomposa and then at Chioggia. From here he seemed inclined, almost at the final hour, to proceed against Alexander by force, with the aid of the Venetian *popolani*.

---

[17] W. Heinemeyer, "Der Friede von Montebello (1175)," *DA*, 11 (1954), 101–39.

But the hesitations and opposition of his own war-weary entourage induced him to drop the project.

The Emperor, having been absolved from excommunication, entered Venice on 24 July. The Pope awaited him before San Marco. Frederick prostrated himself, but Alexander lifted him up, gave him the kiss of peace, and blessed him, while the Germans present sang the „Te Deum". The next day the Pope celebrated Mass in San Marco and preached in the Emperor's presence. Before and afterwards Frederick performed the honorary service he had once objected to at Sutri. On 1 August in the episcopal palace the Emperor took an oath to abide by the peace and the armistice. Then a cardinal proceeded to Rovigo to obtain corresponding assurances from the Empress and King Henry, both of whom had been included in the Peace of Venice.

Thus was the schism ended. All of Christendom breathed a sigh of relief. While the peace did not bring a decision in principle in regard to the relations between *Imperium* and papacy, and the Emperor came out of it practically unimpeded, still Alexander may be regarded as the winner, even though he too, in order definitely to end the schism, renounced any clarification of the disputed ideologies. He had to be less concerned with that than with the peace, which at the moment contributed more for the welfare of the Universal Church than did a formal but revocable word from the Emperor.

The Third Lateran Council

A general council had been agreed upon both in the preliminary treaty of Anagni of October-November 1176 and in the Peace of Venice of 21 July 1177. Both treaties say in identical terms:

The Lord Pope, together with the cardinals, bishops, and other devout men [abbots], who take part, will excommunicate at the council soon to be summoned, all who seek to break this peace. The same thing will then be done at the general council.

The council first mentioned took place in San Marco at Venice on 14 August. The Emperor occupied a throne beside the Pope, who pronounced excommunication on all who should violate the peace or armistice and did not present themselves for penance within forty days. At the same time Alexander renewed the excommunication of all who still adhered to the schism. When the torches were cast on the ground and extinguished, the Emperor, with the rest, cried aloud: "Fiat, fiat."

Archbishop Christian of Mainz conducted the Pope back to the *Patrimonium*. The Antipope Calixtus III was outlawed by imperial authority when he refused to submit. Alexander received a delegation of Romans at

Anagni and was able to entrust to Christian's care the conditions for the return to Rome. The city's autonomy, a result of the revolution of 1143, was maintained, but the senators had to take an oath of fealty to the Pope, restore the *regalia,* and guarantee the safety of the Pope and of the pilgrims. *Via* Tusculum Alexander at length reentered his city on 12 March 1178. He had not hurried. The Romans were apparently enthusiastic, but Alexander had no confidence in them. He soon returned to Tusculum, where on 29 August 1178 Calixtus III finally submitted.

The Emperor had already made his way back to Germany in September 1177 and held aloof from the stipulated general council. The Curia's preparations for it began with the return to the *Patrimonium.* In the autumn of 1178 several legates visited the European states in order to invite bishops and abbots to the council, which was to meet in the Lateran. The overall political situation was not unfavourable. Louis VII and Henry II had concluded peace at Nonancourt on 25 September 1177, shortly after the peace between Emperor and Pope. Baldwin IV was still reigning in Jerusalem, and seven bishops and a delegation of Templars and Hospitallers were *en route* to Rome. Sicily authorized its prelates to attend the council, while Henry II granted permission to the Irish and to six English bishops.

The Pope opened the council on 5 March 1179. The inaugural address was delivered by the Bishop of Assisi, Magister Rufinus, one of the leading canonists of the age. Present were some 300 bishops from Italy, Germany, and Burgundy, from France, Spain, England and Ireland, from Sicily and the crusader states, even from Denmark and Hungary. Among them was John of Salisbury, now Bishop of Chartres. From Germany had come the Bishops of Mainz, Bamberg, Augsburg, Constance, Worms, Speyer, Chur, Salzburg, Regensburg, Passau, Trier, Metz, Liège, Zeitz, Meissen, Brandenburg, Hamburg-Bremen, and Schwerin — an impressive witness to the peace.[18] Cologne, Magdeburg, and the Westphalian sees were not represented because the troubles between the Emperor and Henry the Lion kept them at home. Nectarius of Casula arrived as envoy of the Byzantine Church. Also present was a group of Waldensians from Lyons. If note is taken also of the uncounted abbots, priors, scholars, and attendants of bishops, it was an impressive gathering, a real representation of the Universal Church, before which, in his opening discourse, Rufinus of Assisi developed the principles underlying the primacy of the Roman Church and extolled the personality and work of Alexander III.

Unfortunately, no real conciliar acts have been preserved[19], and the

[18] List of participants in *Mansi,* 22, 213–17, 239 f., 458–68 summarized in R. Foreville, *op. cit.,* 387–90.

[19] What is relatively the best account is given by Roger of Howden, *Chronicle,* ed. W. Stubbs, I (London 1868), 171–89 (also given in Rolls Series, 51, 1).

notes of Archbishop William of Tyre are lost. Only the jejune remarks of historians and some allusions by participants, such as Peter of Blois, Peter Comestor, and Walter Map, inform us about this or that point.[20] Twenty-seven canons were the fruit of discussions at three sessions on 5, 14, and 19 March.[21]

The formulation, the lucid and carefully chosen language of these decrees, is thought, probably correctly, to betray the hand of the jurist Pope. The diversity of their contents reflects the aim of evaluating the great events and decisions of the pontificate and having them ratified by the Universal Church. The measures agreed to in Anagni and Venice for the liquidation of the schism were confirmed. It was recalled that every cathedral was to have a school of its own, no cleric was to be without a benefice, the bishop was to look out for the welfare of his clergy. Canon 1, which regulated the papal election, was important and of permanent validity. Clearly inspired by the experience of 1159, it demanded a two-thirds majority for validity. At the same time the distinction insisted on in 1059 between bishops and non-bishops in the College of Cardinals was tacitly set aside and the election was restricted to the College exclusively, for neither the rest of the clergy nor the people was mentioned. "[It] is still in force and will probably remain so as long as Popes are elected."[22] Canons 3 and 8 became the bases on which was developed the right of devolution: if a benefice was not filled within six months, the right to fill it passed to the concurrent or next highest tribunal.

Decrees still had to be issued against simony and on celibacy (canons 7, 10, 15). Thus a century had not been long enough for correcting abuses, nor, as is well known, would the succeeding centuries suffice. Canon 18 promised exemption from fees for instruction, and Canon 25 forbade usury and traffic in war materials with infidels. Canons 24 and 25 regulated social relations of Christians with Jews or Muslims. The last canon dealt with heresy — the prelude to the trying episode now beginning, which was to find its climax in the Albigensian wars of later pontificates. Canon 27 was in effect the charter of the crusade against heretics: the privileges hitherto intended for crusaders, the indulgences, the papal privi-

[20] Albert of Stade, *Annales MGSS*, 16, 348 (the assertions of loyalty by Christian of Mainz and Philip of Cologne); Walter Map, *De nugis curialium*, D. 1, c. 31, ed. M. R. James (Oxford 1944), 60 f. (Peter Waldo of Lyons and his disciples); Peter Cantor, *Verbum abbreviatum*, PL, 205, 158, 235 f. (attitude of the Bishop of Chartres, John of Salisbury, at the Council).

[21] The complicated and still not fully clarified history of the transmission of the conciliar decrees is briefly sketched in *Conciliorum Oecumenicorum Decreta* (Basel, Barcelona, Freiburg, Rome, Vienna, 2nd ed. 1962), 182–86. The decrees themselves, *ibid.*, 187–201.

[22] J. Haller, *Das Papsttum*, III (2nd ed. 1962), 242.

leges accorded to them and their possessions were from now on granted to those who made themselves available for the armed struggle against heresy.

Alexander received the Waldensians who were present sympathetically and graciously, and praised their voluntary poverty, but he did not grant them permission to preach. The competent bishops were to decide this question. But the very first attempt at Lyons failed, since the Archbishop rejected the request and thus drove the Waldensians into opposition.

Like the case of the Waldensians, still other problems occupied the Council without being mentioned in the canons: for example, the reconciliation of schismatic bishops. The Council's measures in regard to the papal election, the right of devolution, the prosecution of heretics, and the care of lepers were of permanent validity.

CHAPTER 9

Thomas Becket and Henry II of England

In the Angevin Kingdom of England a confrontation between King Henry II and the Primate Thomas Becket, Archbishop of Canterbury, ran its course between 1162 and 1170. In many ways intertwined with the eighteen-year struggle between Alexander III and Frederick I, in certain of its moments of crisis it cannot be fully understood apart from that contest. The English struggle concerned the threat to that liberty of the Church that had been firmly established since the confusion of 1135–52 over the succession to Henry I. Especially at issue were episcopal elections, communication with Rome, and ecclesiastical courts. Because of its dramatic *dénouement* and the powerfully drawn personalities who figured in it, this struggle occupied the field of vision of contemporary observers even more than did the turning-points of the schism.

On the one side was a saint, who was likewise a man of brilliant intellect, a skillful diplomat, a reliable administrator, and a socially sensitive prelate, rising from the new social strata of an urban and mercantile self-consciousness, formed in the schools of the new theology and of the just then developing science of canon law, representative of all that was striving to establish itself in the world and in the Church.

On the other side was a still young King, the husband of the most important and best known lady of the epoch, Eleanor, former wife of the French King. Of a none too praiseworthy repute because of the Second Crusade, she had brought Aquitaine along when she married the future English monarch. Henry II (1154–89) was a son of the Empress Matilda, widow of Henry V, by her second marriage with Count Geoffrey of

Anjou. Immediately after his accession to the throne in 1154 he had begun to restore the rights and claims of the crown which had been usurped during the anarchy. Among these was control of the English bishoprics and abbeys because of their importance in the feudal social and political constitution of the Kingdom. His guiding idea was to recover the position occupied by Henry I in Church and state, if not to win back the authority once exercised by William the Conqueror.

From 1155 Henry II had at his side as chancellor the archdeacon of Canterbury, Thomas Becket. Born in London in 1108,[1] Thomas had been educated by Robert of Merton, then in France by Robert of Melun, a pupil of Abelard, and at Bologna. Archbishop Theobald had made him archdeacon when that position became vacant by the election of Roger de Pont-l'Évêque as Archbishop of York. Theobald died on 18 April 1161, whereupon Henry saw to it that his chancellor Thomas was chosen Metropolitan and Primate of the English Church in a canonically proper election on 27 May 1162.[2]

The Archbishop

As chancellor Thomas Becket had been a friend of the King. But he had carefully represented the interests of the Church and had exerted himself with Henry in favour of Alexander III. While his conduct was blameless, he appeared at court and while hunting and traveling with the display appropriate to his position. But from his consecration Thomas seemed to be another man. Prayer, study, and spiritual discussions with his cultured and reform-minded clerics filled his days. He resigned the chancellorship and sent the seals back to the King at the end of 1162. People praised his grand-scale hospitality and his solicitude for the poor; the latter was enhanced by his personal participation. He also practised strict mortifications, the forms of which were in some cases discovered only after his death, such as the wearing of a hairshirt and self-flagellation. The Archbishop took his new position seriously and wanted to be only priest, bishop, pastor, theologian. Neither contemporaries nor later research has been unanimous in judging his career; to some it seemed to be a mere change of role, to others a genuine *conversio*.[3]

The King, appealing to the customary law and to precedents in the common law, intended to restore the crown's authority in the English

---

[1] R. Foreville tried to establish 21 December 1120 as the date of his birth ("Tradition et comput dans la chronologie de Thomas Becket," *Bulletin historique et philologique* [1957], 7–20).

[2] On Gilbert Foliot's opposition, which became apparent at the time of the election, see A. Morey and C. N. L. Brooke, *Gilbert Foliot and His Letters* (Cambridge 1965), 147–87.

[3] *Cf.* R. Foreville, *L'église et la royauté en Angleterre*, 111–13.

Church, to limit ecclesiastical jurisdiction and keep it in check and probably to subordinate it eventually to the royal justice, and to keep royal control over appeals to the Curia.

The Archbishop, on the contrary, did not hesitate to stand up for rights and liberties of the Church hitherto acquired or won under King Stephen and to afford greater scope for the canon law that had been entering England since the appearance of Gratian's *Decretum* around 1140. But just as the reviving canon law was of great significance for the Archbishop, so too did the reviving Roman law play a great role for the King, following the example of the Emperor Frederick I, even though outwardly there was mention only of the restoration of the customs of the Kingdom. A confrontation was inevitable and it had to be all the sharper and more dramatic since both men, King and Archbishop, regarded themselves as representatives of the good and valid law, and both, for the sake of the highest goals, were prepared to make use of high intelligence, diplomatic skill, a will that expressed itself vigorously and even tempestuously, and at the same time all the intellectual, material, and personal helps which state or Church put at their disposal.

The Constitutions of Clarendon

Immediately after entering upon his office, Thomas asked for and obtained the pallium from Alexander III, who was staying at Montpellier. Along with his suffragans he was able to take part, with the King's permission, in the Council of Tours in 1163, which again strengthened Alexander's case and deepened in Thomas the awareness that the interests of the Roman Church and of the Church of Canterbury were identical. To be sure, the Council of Tours made clear the irreconcilable opposition between Canterbury and York in the question of the primacy in England. Archbishop Roger was to remain on the King's side to the last, an opponent of Thomas Becket. [4]

The conflict with the crown began with measures of the King which limited ecclesiastical jurisdiction over clerics. At a council at Westminster on 1 October 1163 Henry complained of the increase in the number of crimes committed by clerics and the leniency of the spiritual courts. In February 1162 he had had the old customary law, which had been promulgated at Lillebonne in 1080 and renewed by Henry I, again enforced for Normandy. Something analogous was to have happened at Westminster but the attempt was shattered on the united opposition of the episcopate under the leadership of the Archbishop of Canterbury.

---

[4] *Cf.* D. Knowles, *The Episcopal Colleagues,* 12–14. On the incident at Tours, see R. Foreville, *L'église et la royauté,* 277 f.

Henry II summoned the royal council to meet at the end of January 1164 at Clarendon, and here the bishops were to express themselves on the renewal of the English customary law from the time of Henry I. After long discussions Thomas was able finally to induce the episcopate to agree, and he himself gave his consent orally. But when the King intended to have the written codification of the customs signed and sealed by the bishops, Thomas was alone in his refusal. For he was able tacitly to allow or dissimulate much in practice, just as the Curia was accustomed to do, but not to approve by signature and seal measures which clearly violated the prevailing canon law.

The sixteen articles of the Constitutions of Clarendon,[5] different as were the particular points treated, aimed as a whole at nullifying the growing independence of the English Church from the crown. The feudal dependence of the episcopate was emphasized, episcopal elections were to take place under royal control, bishops-elect were to take the oath of fealty before being consecrated, bishops' rights of disposal of Church property were restricted, they were bound by the same services to the crown as were the secular vassals. Ecclesiastical courts had to accommodate themselves to the judicial procedures of the secular courts and their competence was considerably restricted, while that of the secular courts was extended to matters of debt, perjury, disputes over benefices, questions of patronage, and the criminal and civil cases of clerics. Bishops' powers of excommunication were curtailed in regard to the crown's tenants-in-chief and members of the royal household and of the courts. Every appeal from English courts to the Curia was subject to the King's examination and consent, as were also journeys by bishops to the Curia or to councils. None of this was new in regard to details, but here it was juridically formulated for the first time and made a law with the written assent of the episcopate.

Appealing to the canonical principles expressed in Gratian's *Decretum*, Thomas Becket protested this diminution of ecclesiastical jurisdiction and of episcopal liberties. In the Constitutions of Clarendon he feared a complete feudalization of the English Church, which was exposed to the danger of gradually losing both of its essential privileges, — *privilegium fori* and *privilegium canonis*, — of being excluded from the jurisdictional sphere of the Universal Church, and of experiencing a lessening of its ties with its faith and its head.

Disenchanted with his chancellor, who as Archbishop first gave up the chancellorship and then rejected the King's policy of a restoration of the royal authority, Henry in October 1164 cited him before the council at Northampton on the basis of Article 9 of the Constitutions of Clarendon.

---

[5] For the Constitutions of Clarendon see W. Stubbs (ed.), *Select Charters* (London, 9th ed. 1913; *reprint* 1921), 163–67.

The Archbishop did not accept the judgment but appealed to the Pope and thereby placed himself and his church under the protection of the Holy See. The episcopate held itself aloof. Protected by the people, who had long been grateful for the social welfare provided by the chancellor and Archbishop, Thomas left the royal castle of Northampton. The devotion of the canons regular of Sempringham enabled him to flee to the coast during the night following the judgment and then to France, where he was to spend six years.

Exile and Reconciliation

The fleeing Primate of England obtained a place of refuge from King Louis VII. Then at Sens he explained his case to Pope Alexander III and the cardinals and read to them the Constitutions of Clarendon; the Pope condemned nearly two-thirds of the articles: numbers 1, 3, 4, 5, 8, 9, 10, 12, 15. The Pope also absolved him from the oral promise he had earlier made to observe them. He refused the Archbishop's offer to resign his office, confirmed him in it, and at the same time recognized the primatial status of Canterbury.

Thomas took up residence in the Cistercian abbey of Pontigny near Auxerre, not far from Sens. He stayed there from the end of November 1164 to November 1166. Wearing the Cistercian habit, he devoted himself to prayer and to the study of theology and canon law. Meanwhile Henry II confiscated the ecclesiastical property of Canterbury and expelled from the Kingdom the Archbishop's family and the clerics who remained loyal to him, together with their relatives. Efforts at mediation came to nothing, even when undertaken by the Empress Matilda, the Pope, and King Louis VII (at Easter 1166). Before returning to Italy Alexander III solemnly annulled the judgment of Northampton.

Since in 1165–66 there occurred a *rapprochement* on Henry's part to the imperial policy of Frederick I and at Würzburg in 1165 English envoys signed the proclamation of intransigence in regard to Alexander, it was not to be expected that the Angevin would give in. The English episcopate, it is true, declined for its part to honour these signatures, but the King was satisfied with the pressure on Alexander that was made possible by his friendship with Frederick. He demanded that the Pope either depose Thomas or assign him another see. In spite of several compromises with the English King that depended on trivial circumstances, Alexander in the end upheld the Archbishop, confirmed him as Primate on 5–8 April 1166, and on 24 April 1166 even named him legate in England, a post he had refused to Roger of York, despite the King's intervention. But in order to accommodate Henry, he made Roger legate in Scotland and removed the province of York from the territory subject to the legate in England.

At Vézelay on Pentecost 1166, Thomas as legate solemnly excommunicated the King's councillors and officials, but not Henry himself. He thereby laid claim to a right which was denied him by the Constitutions of Clarendon. Henry's answer was to bring pressure to bear on the general chapter of the Cistercians, threatening to expel all members of the order from England if Thomas continued to obtain hospitality at Pontigny. The Archbishop left Pontigny and spent the remaining years of exile with the Benedictines of Sainte-Colombe de Sens. There followed the most varied negotiations, conducted by papal legates[6] especially designated for this purpose, with Henry II; in these were at times reflected the complexities of Alexander's political situation *vis-à-vis* the threatening enterprises of Frederick I. In this connection the Pope displayed a strangely hesitant technique that was ready for compromise and to an extent even underhanded, an attitude which was even blamed by contemporaries.

From 1169 on several encounters between Henry and Thomas became possible — on 6 January at Montmirail, on 18 November at Montmartre — but there was no actual reconciliation nor adjustment of viewpoints.

On the contrary, from the beginning of 1170 Henry completely isolated England from the continent and especially from the Curia. The Constitutions of Clarendon were strictly enforced. The coronation of Henry the Younger was prepared. In defiance of the prohibition obtained from the Pope by Thomas, the Archbishop of York crowned the Prince on 14 June at Saint Peter's, Westminster, with the assistance of Bishops Gilbert Foliot of London, Jocelin de Bohun of Salisbury, Walter of Rochester, and Hugh du Puiset of Durham. It was an intentional affront by the King in the face of repeated prohibitions by the Pope, just recently renewed, and of the rights of the ancient metropolitan see of Canterbury. Henry, who now had to fear that Thomas would make use of his right to lay an interdict on England or other parts of the Angevin realm, proceeded to the continent for a personal discussion with the Archbishop, at Fréteval-en-Dunois in the Orléanais on 22 July 1170. He assured the Primate peace, safety, the return of the church and the property of Canterbury, as these last were at the time of the rupture; he promised the restoration of all the rights of the primatial see and a repetition of the coronation by Thomas. They parted, seemingly reconciled. But the King had not given sureties, and the fulfilling of the various promises seemed almost

---

[6] On the legateships in connection with the strife over Thomas Becket, see H. Tillmann, *Die päpstlichen Legaten in England*, 56–72, and W. Janssen, *Die päpstlichen Legaten in Frankreich*, 84–88.

hopeless, especially since the bishops from the time of the coronation were risking everything to prevent a reinstatement of the Archbishop. Before his return to England Thomas had himself provided by the Pope with the widest powers, but he excommunicated the bishops even before setting out on his journey, for he had to reckon with the possible confiscation of his papers by the officials when he landed.

His return to Canterbury in December 1170 was a profound satisfaction for the Archbishop, especially as it was celebrated by the people as a triumph. Only complications proceeded from the King and the bishops. The bishops appealed to the Pope against their excommunication and declined to make an oath of obedience to their Metropolitan and Primate. The Archbishop was forbidden to visit the young King at Winchester and was commanded to stay within the limits of his own bishopric and to keep silent about personal insults offered by royal officials and attendants. Furthermore, the excommunicated prelates proceeded at once to Henry II in Normandy. Irritated by the excommunication of these bishops, which he had not anticipated, Henry impetuously expressed his mind: "Isn't there anyone to deliver me from this hateful priest?"[7]

Murder in the Cathedral

Four knights of the King's entourage, at whose disposal Ranulf de Broc, administrator of the sequestered Canterbury property, placed a few armed men, forced their way into the episcopal residence, always open to guests and the poor, on the afternoon of 29 December 1170. They found the Archbishop in conversation with his clerics and began a long dispute with him, blaming him for having excommunicated members of the royal court without previous consultation with the King. At the hour of Vespers the Archbishop's attendants urged him to go to the cathedral, where the monks were just assembling. The Archbishop refused to have the gates barricaded behind him. The knights had departed to get their weapons. After the Archbishop and his retinue had reached the north transept, where a huge pillar upheld a gallery and there stood an altar dedicated to Saint Benedict, the knights sought to drive the prelate and his entourage out of the church. His back to the pillar, Thomas replied to the demand that he absolve the bishops from censure: "I can absolve them only when they have made satisfaction." "Then," said the four, "receive the death you deserve." "I am ready to die for my God, if thereby liberty and peace are restored to the Church."[8] They then killed him amid the glow

[7] *Materials*, VII, 440, 476, 443, and *Gesta regis*, I, 32 *(PL*, 190, 42 A, 97 C, 177 B).
[8] *Materials*, II, 430–40 *(PL*, 190, 46 A–47 C). See also the report by John of Salisbury to Bishop John of Poitiers, *Materials*, VII, 462–65.

of torches. The assassins plundered his residence and departed late that night. Only then did the monks and clerics venture forth to bury the remains of the martyr in a marble coffin in the crypt before the altar of Saint John the Baptist and Saint Augustine, Apostle of the English. The blood was carefully collected.

The Sequel to the Martyrdom

Christendom very quickly learned of what had happened at Canterbury, and everywhere people were shocked. Responsibility for the murder was assigned to the English King, the Archbishop of York, and Gilbert Foliot, Bishop of London. On 25 January 1171 the Archbishop of Sens, as papal legate, laid an interdict on the continental lands of Henry II. The King, personally shaken by the consequences of his angry words, sent to Rome a delegation which was able to prevent the laying of an interdict on England but could not stop the Pope from excommunicating on Holy Thursday all who had contributed directly or indirectly to the murder. Alexander confirmed the sentence issued by the Archbishop of Sens and punished Henry with a personal interdict; only legates who should be expressly named would be able to release him from it. The King set out on his expedition to Ireland; he was able to conquer part of the island and was hailed as King by its subkings.

Meanwhile, negotiations were taking place with the Curia in regard to the reparation to be made by the King because of Thomas's murder. He had had the expedition to Ireland declared to be a crusade, an undertaking which would subject the Irish Church to the Holy See. After his return in the spring of 1172 he met the papal legates in Normandy.[9] On 21 May Henry and the accused bishops purged themselves with an oath that they had neither commanded nor desired the death of the Archbishop of Canterbury. Henry further swore that he would hold 200 knights in readiness for a year for the defense of the Holy Land, that at Christmas of 1172 he would take the cross for three years and personally set out on the crusade the following summer, and that in any event he would keep himself at the disposal of the Pope. If a journey to Jerusalem should be impossible, he would carry out his vow in Spain against the Muslims. He would permit appeals to Rome in cases before ecclesiastical courts. He would disavow customs hurtful to the Church as these had been enforced under his authority. He would restore to the Church of Canterbury all its prop-

---

[9] Cardinals Albert of San Lorenzo in Lucina and Theodin of San Vitale; cf. H. Tillmann, op. cit., 68–74, and W. Janssen, op. cit., 85–88.

erty. And finally he would receive in peace all clerics and lay persons who had remained loyal to Thomas and give back their possessions.

After Henry and his son had sworn to these promises he was absolved and reconciled with the Church.[10] The promises of Avranches were confirmed by Alexander III in a bull of 2 September and ratified on 27 September by Henry at Saint-André. The Constitutions of Clarendon were not disavowed in their entirety, but appeals to Rome were allowed, and this was of the greatest importance. For the papal decretals that were issued for England from now on in great numbers laid the basis of an English canon law within the framework of the development in the Universal Church.

The grave of the murdered Archbishop very soon became the goal of the greatest pilgrimage movement of the High and the Late Middle Ages. Alexander III solemnly canonized Thomas Becket on 21 February 1173. King Henry himself made a pilgrimage to Canterbury in July 1174 and again did penance for his share in the saint's death. At his wish the Pope sent Hugh Pierleoni[11] to England as Cardinal-Legate. He was not only able to arrange the filling of the many vacant sees but also reached a compromise with the King in regard to the disputed ecclesiastical jurisdiction. Only questions concerning clerics' fiefs and violations of the forest laws by clerics were for the future to be handled by a secular judge. The total result of the long conflict should not be estimated as meagre. The Archbishop did not die in vain.

CHAPTER 10

The Heritage of Alexander III

The Peace of Venice was only a truce, made possible by a compromise. The German Church remained in the hands of the Emperor, who continued to exploit the *ius spolii* and placed the *regalia* at the service of the Empire. Alexander's legates let matters take their course. The Pope himself mediated between Frederick and the Lombard League.[1] The League disintegrated, and such recent enemies as Milan and Alessandria allied with the Emperor. Alexander loyally observed the stipulations of the peace until his death, but he left behind as open questions the unclari-

---

[10] On the Concordat of Avranches, see R. Foreville, *L'église et la royauté*, 356–61.

[11] On the legatine activity of the Cardinal Deacon Hugh Pierleoni of Sant'Angelo, see Tillmann, *op. cit.*, 73–76.

[1] The Peace of Constance (25 June 1183) was Frederick's renunciation of the Roncaglia decrees. The alliance with Milan was concluded at the beginning of 1185.

fied juridical and political situation of the Mathildine lands, the validity of the schismatic ordinations in Germany and Italy, and the relations of the Holy See with the Roman commune. In flight from rebellious Viterbo, he died at Città Castellana.[2] Nevertheless, his heritage did not consist merely of unsolved difficulties. Thanks to the tenacious struggle at the time of the schism and his consistently pursued government of the Universal Church, despite his always disputed legitimacy, it also meant the establishment of the prestige of Roman legal decisions in Christendom and the recognition of the Roman See as the supreme judge and legislator. At the same time the competence of this highest jurisdiction had been enlarged, and appeals from all countries to the Holy See had increased. Like Eugene III and Hadrian IV earlier, Alexander III at the Lateran Council sought to take measures against excess in appeals, but without any noticeable effect.

The Cardinal Bishop Ubaldo Allucingoli of Ostia was elected Alexander's successor on 1 September 1181 and styled himself Lucius III (1181–85). An old and prudent Cistercian, as a friend of Bernard of Clairvaux he was so identified with the reform ideas of that saint's age that he declined to make the money gifts to the Romans that were expected at every change of pontificate, for he regarded this as an abuse. In November 1181 he arrived in Rome, where a college of twenty-five senators had control of the government. He was received cooly and remained only five months. A conflict erupted in regard to Tusculum, which the Romans wanted either to subjugate to their own rule or to destroy. Lucius appealed for aid to Archbishop Christian of Mainz, who was always close at hand. But in September 1183 he lost this helper, who ever since the Peace of Venice had loyally looked after the interests of the papacy in the *Patrimonium* and against the Roman commune. The warrior prelate succumbed to a fever before Tusculum. The Curia moved northward, for a meeting with the Emperor Frederick I had been arranged in Verona.

The Emperor had made peace with the Lombards at Constance in 1183 and, since it was important to him to settle with Alexander's successor the questions left open at Venice, he showed himself to be accommodating. Lucius III waited at Verona from 22 July 1184. The Emperor did not arrive until the end of September, after having spent some time at Milan, his new ally. The Pope profited by the presence of Heraclius, Patriarch of Jerusalem, and of the grand masters of the military orders, who, as envoys of King Baldwin IV, candidly expounded the situation of the Holy Land, to urge a crusade on the Emperor. Frederick assured him that the preparations would get under way by Christmas of that year. A uniform procedure by *regnum* and *sacerdotium* was also planned at Verona for the

[2] 30 August 1181.

struggle against heretical movements, which were spreading ever more powerfully and becoming more threatening, especially in the Midi and North Italy. In the decretal "Ad abolendam" of 4 November 1184 was found the classical formula, according to which the Church was to institute proceedings against heretics and, if the occasion arose, to condemn them, leaving or recommending the carrying out of the judgment and of the penalty to the secular arm. An imperial edict, whose text is not extant, corresponded to the papal decree. This papal-imperial decision has been called the charter of the Inquisition.[3]

But Lucius did not obtain a definite promise of imperial assistance in his struggle for Rome, and the questions relevant to the Mathildine lands remained unclarified. On the other hand, the Pope, referring to a new council to be held at Lyons, did not give in to the imperial pressure to settle the existing ambiguity in regard to schismatic orders. Nor did Lucius decide the conflict over the see of Trier between Folmar, who had been elected in May 1183, and Rudolf zu Wied, whom Frederick had invested; instead, he summoned both claimants to the Curia. He likewise refused the Emperor's demand that his son Henry be given the imperial crown at once.[4] If it is remembered that the discussions of Verona had been suggested by the Pope himself, this emphatic reserve may cause surprise. The blame has been assigned to both the Curia and those German bishops who opposed the Emperor. The leader of this group was Philip of Heinsberg, Archbishop of Cologne, to whom Frederick had granted the Duchy of Westphalia in 1180. But the real reason must be ascribed to Frederick's making known at Verona a fundamental change in his Italian policy: his intention of reaching an understanding with the Norman Kingdom in South Italy. This was promoted by the engagement of his son Henry to Constance of Sicily, daughter of King Roger II and hence aunt of the reigning King William II. The engagement took place at Augsburg on 29 October 1184. Its consequences were not at all apparent when it was officially made known toward the end of the discussions and shortly before

---

[3] "Ipse [Lucius] et Imperator Veronae convenientes, ut inter spiritualem patrem et filium miscentur colloquia, et tamquam ex duabus principalibus curiis et duobus orbis capitibus una Republica effecta, ecclesiastica simul et saecularia inter eos tractantur negotia; ubi etiam vicissim alterutrius delectati praesentia et vigore suffulti communi consilio omnium qui convenerant... contra diversas haereses et eorum auctores... insurgunt et suo eos fine condemnant." (From the decretal "Ad abolendam" of 4 November 1184; cf. H Maisonneuve, Études sur les origines de l'Inquisition [Paris, 2nd ed. 1960], 151.)

[4] As early as 1169 the Emperor Frederick had negotiated in vain with Alexander III relevant to Henry's becoming coemperor. Like Lucius III, Urban III would likewise refuse. "The Curia rejected the office of coemperor for the Western Imperium"; cf. W. Ohnsorge, "Das Mitkaisertum in der abendländischen Geschichte des frühen Mittelalters," ZSavRG germ, 67 (1950), 309–39; also, now, idem, Abendland und Byzanz (Darmstadt 1958), 261–99 (especially 281).

the Emperor's departure from Verona. The wedding was to take place at Milan, which had allied with the Empire. It was solemnized on 27 January 1186.

It may with great probability be assumed that Pope Lucius himself was not unwilling to regard this connection as being in the interests of peace and of the plans for a crusade, and even that he personally fostered it. Nevertheless, the Curia may have feared, even if at the moment there was really no cause to expect Constance to succeed to the throne, that such an alliance of the Empire with Sicily concealed additional threats to the existence of the *Patrimonium*.

Following the Emperor's departure from Verona the discussions between the two courts continued. But Lucius III died on 25 November 1185, without having reached any final decisions. On the very same day the cardinals elected Archbishop Uberto Crivelli of Milan, an avowed opponent of the Emperor, thereby making clear how little they agreed with Frederick's new course. He called himself Urban III (1185–87), and as Pope did not resign his archbishopric in order not to allow the *regalia* to accrue to the Empire during a vacancy. The Pope kept aloof from the Hohenstaufen-Hauteville marriage at Milan, and Henry was crowned King of Italy by the Patriarch of Aquileia. There is no doubt that this was intended as an affront to the Pope, who reacted by consecrating the anti-imperial Folmar for the see of Trier on 1 June 1186. A break between Pope and Emperor seemed inevitable. Frederick ordered his son to occupy the *Patrimonium* and so to isolate the Pope and Curia at Verona as to prevent any contact with the Church. At the Diet of Gelnhausen in November 1186 the Emperor also succeeded in paralyzing the opposition around Philip of Cologne and of isolating the Archbishop. The German episcopate was again united behind the throne.

In 1187 Frederick decided to send an embassy to Verona to submit new proposals to the Pope. But Urban avoided it. He had consecrated the city's new cathedral and had been prevented by the wary people of Verona from proclaiming Frederick's excommunication. He now left Verona for Venice but *en route* he died at Ferrara during the night of 19–20 October. The Church was thereby spared a new and disagreeable crisis.

The brief pontificate of his successor, Gregory VIII (21 October– 17 December 1187) was entirely preoccupied with preparations for the crusade. As Cardinal Chancellor, Albert de Morra had founded a congregation of canons regular of an austere observance in his native city of Benevento, and, like his predecessor Lucius III, he belonged to the group representing the Bernardine reform. In accord with its leading idea, he intended to work for a renewal of the Curia, but his early death saved him from failure and disappointment. Just the same, he had been able at least to put an end to Urban III's intransigent policy toward the Empire.

In view of the organizing of the crusade, then getting under way, the election of the new Pope could fall only on a conciliatory personality, in view of the fact that the Emperor Frederick himself was to be the most important leader. The Cardinal Bishop Paul Scolari, who became Clement III (1187–91), was a Roman by birth and related to several influential families of the Eternal City. He contrived to find a compromise between the Curia and the city, while a definitive peace with the Empire was also achieved. The Trier dispute was ended when the two rivals, Folmar and Rudolf, were discarded to make way for the Imperial Chancellor John.[5]

Clement had to negotiate for quite some time with the Romans before the treaty of 31 May 1188 could be signed. With a considerable financial output and the loss of rights the Curia purchased a peace which still remained precarious and could be assured only by unending new payments.

In the Treaty of Strasbourg of April 1189 the Empire restored the *Patrimonium* to the Pope, reserving the *honor imperii,* and in return Clement held out the prospect of the imperial crown for King Henry. Again the Mathildine lands remained in the hands of the Emperor, who, however, dispensed with an express recognition of his proprietorship. In order to prepare for and carry out the crusade Clement put up with all the disadvantages of these treaties.

William II of Sicily died childless on 18 November 1189. His legitimate heir was Queen Constance, wife of Frederick's son Henry, who had just assumed the regency of the Empire for the absent Emperor.

Shortly before his death William had taken the vassal's oath to the Pope for Sicily. Would Henry, soon to succeed his father as ruler of the *Sacrum Imperium,* be prepared to do the same? While Apulia decided for Constance and Henry, the Sicilian magnates proclaimed as King a bastard cousin of William, Count Tancred of Lecce. The Archbishop of Palermo crowned him with Clement's consent.

Henry was determined to take possession of his wife's entire inheritance. Through the mediation of the Archbishop of Mainz he was reconciled with Henry the Lion at Fulda in July 1190 and, accompanied by the Duke of Saxony, set out for Italy. But the news of his father's death in Asia Minor produced a delay and it was only in January 1191 that he entered Lombardy. Meanwhile, the presence in Messina of the Kings of France and England, who had set up winter quarters there *en route* to Palestine, so strengthened Tancred's position that in April he crossed to

---

[5] M. Corsten (*née* Lönartz), "Erzbischof Johann I. von Trier (1189–1212), "*Zeitschrift für die Geschichte der Saargegend,* 13 (1963), 127–200. *Cf.* J. Heinrich, *Kaiser Heinrich VI.,* 193–99, 215 f., 221–23.

Apulia and began to conquer this part of the Norman Kingdom also in order to be armed for his confrontation with Henry.

Clement III died at the end of March 1191, and his successor could not avoid the fateful decisions following from the proximity of Henry, who was on his way to Rome for the imperial crown and was already at Anguillara. The aged Cardinal Hyacinth Bobone, an eighty-five-year-old curial prelate, who had belonged to the College of Cardinals for forty-seven years, was elected; he assumed the name of Celestine III (1191–98). A pupil of Abelard's, he had been critical of Bernard of Clairvaux. He had been the Curia's successful diplomat in embassies of reconciliation, notably that to Frederick I for settling the misunderstandings of Besançon and that to Henry II after the murder of Thomas Becket, and he had remained loyal to Alexander III during the schism. And so, despite his advanced age, he seemed to be the right man for a conciliatory policy toward the harsh new ruler of the Empire, who was consistently pursuing his father's Italian projects.[6]

After some initial hesitations Celestine III gave Henry VI the imperial crown on Easter Sunday, 14 April 1191. He advised him not to continue southward, where the attempt to overthrow Tancred foundered before Naples, while Salerno even delivered the Empress Constance as a prisoner to Tancred. At the end of 1191 Henry had to return to Germany empty-handed. Celestine decided to recognize Tancred. He invested him with the Kingdom of Sicily and in June 1192 concluded with him the Concordat of Gravina, that was favourable to the Curia.

Back in Germany, the Emperor Henry was asked for a decision in the disputed election to the see of Liège.[7] He rejected both claimants and in January 1192 gave the bishopric to Lothar of Hochstaden. Albert of Brabant, the choice of the majority of the chapter, proceeded to the Curia, and Celestine III confirmed his election. Since Albert was prevented from setting foot in the diocese of Liège, he had himself consecrated by the Archbishop of Reims and placed himself under his protection. At Reims he was assassinated by *ministeriales* of Liège. The blame was universally attributed to the Emperor, who took an oath of purgation but let off the assassins with a reprimand. Hence, suspicion was not allayed and the Rhenish episcopate united with some of the secular princes in opposition to the Emperor. Contact was also established with England, Sicily, and the Curia. Henry had himself been allied with King Philip II of France since the fall of 1191; they had met at Milan, when the French King was returning from the crusade. The Emperor's critical situation was corrected

[6] *Cf.* the studies by V. Pfaff (see the bibliography for this chapter).

[7] On the double election at Liège and its outcome, see E. Moreau, *Albert de Louvain, prince-évêque de Liège* (Brussels 1946).

when Duke Leopold V of Austria delivered to him the English King, whom he had taken prisoner near Vienna.[8] Richard, who thus had to pay dearly for his tactlessness in Syria, could purchase his freedom only by promising a huge ransom and agreeing to accept England as a fief of the Empire. And the episcopal and princely opposition in the Rhineland lost its decisive support.

The vast amount of money by which Richard obtained his liberty now enabled the Emperor to resume the conquest of Sicily. Tancred had died on 20 February 1194, and his wife Sibyl had assumed the regency for her minor-aged son, William III; hence no serious opposition was to be expected. Henry set out from Trifels for Italy in May 1194 and as early as Christmas of the same year he could be crowned King at Palermo. The next day Constance gave birth to a son, who as Frederick II was destined to succeed to his father's kingdoms. The assembly of Bari in March 1195 published the new arrangement: the Empress Constance became regent of Sicily, with Conrad of Urslingen, named Duke of Spoleto by Frederick I, at her side as governor. Henry's brother, Duke Philip of Tuscany, was to administer the Mathildine lands; he had renounced in 1193 the see of Würzburg that had been given to him earlier. The High Steward of the Empire, Markward of Anweiler, became Margrave of Ancona and Duke of Romagna.

Contact with the Curia had been interrupted since the recognition of Tancred and the confirmation of Albert of Brabant as Bishop of Liège by Celestine III. In an effort to renew it, Henry VI offered to launch a well organized crusade. At the Curia it was clearly perceived that this crusade would at the same time further the Emperor's far-reaching Mediterranean projects of empire. Leo of Armenia and Amauri of Cyprus had already received their crowns as vassals of the Emperor. Hence Celestine was hesitant to enter into Henry's plan, though to reject it entirely was, of course, outside the realm of the possible. He had the crusade preached in England, Bohemia, Denmark, Poland, and Spain, thereby in a sense involving all of Christendom and eliminating the political thorn from the Emperor's crusade.

Henry's negotiations with the Curia also included his plan to have the Empire now recognized as an hereditary monarchy. He had offered the German princes extensive privileges, especially the heritability of the great fiefs, and he may have proposed to the Curia that the Empire as a whole be held as a fief of the Holy See. Protracted negotiations enabled Celestine to evade any decision on so tricky a question. Meanwhile there broke out

[8] K. A. Kneller, "Des Richard Löwenherz deutsche Gefangenschaft," *Stimmen aus Maria Laach,* ErgH, 59 (Freiburg 1893), and the literature listed in Dahlmann-Waitz under no. 6671; also G. Bullinger, *König Richard Löwenherz und Kaiser Heinrich VI.* (typed dissertation, Tübingen 1947).

in Sicily serious disturbances, which the Emperor succeeded in harshly suppressing in the summer of 1197. But on 6 August, before he was able to join his crusade, he fell mortally ill. During his sickness he is said to have drawn up his last will, which is not uniformly evaluated by scholars. According to this document, Sicily was to be acknowledged as a fief of the Roman Church,[9] and Constance and Frederick were to take the oath of vassalage to the Pope. If the dynasty should become extinct, the Kingdom should escheat to the Pope. Duke Philip was to evacuate the *Patrimonium* and recognize the Pope's feudal suzerainty of Ancona and Ravenna, held by Markward of Anweiler.

The Emperor died at Messina on 26 September 1197 and was buried in the cathedral of Palermo. A few months later, on 8 January 1198, Celestine III followed him to the grave. At Christmas he had expressed his intention of resigning the papacy if the College of Cardinals would declare its agreement to accept as Pope his designated successor, Cardinal John of San Paolo. The cardinals rejected both the abdication and the designation. The heritage of Alexander III seemed assured. If Celestine III and his predecessors, when compared with the forceful personalities of the two Hohenstaufen, had always sat on the shorter arm of the lever so far as power politics were concerned, especially since Rome was always a burden to them and never a help, they still had managed to assure the continuity of what Alexander had begun in regard to the Church Universal.

In particular Celestine's "inner pontificate" merits notice.[10] The Pope, all along an administrator rather than a politician or one endowed with charisms, possessed an outstanding coworker in Cardinal Cencio Savelli, who, thanks to the influence of the future Celestine III, had been made *camerlengo* of the Roman Church under Clement III. Under Celestine the *camerlengo's* office increased in importance, since no chancellor was appointed. To introduce order into the Church's finances, which had suffered greatly ever since the schism and the uneasy pontificates that followed, Cencio drew up a comprehensive property register of the Roman Church, such as had been long before introduced in cities, monasteries, and principalities. This *Liber censuum* became an official survey and record of all spiritual institutions — sees, abbeys, chapters — and secular lordships that were dependent on the Roman Church and owed *census* to her. It was finished in 1192 and was of amazing, though not of complete, accuracy — out of 682 actually existing dependents Cencio was able to include all but 154. Moreover, the Cardinal *Camerlengo* succeeded not only in ordering the Curia's finances but also in actually increasing them.

[9] The testament was transmitted in fragments in the *Gesta Innocentii III*, printed in *Constitutiones*, I, no. 379. It was not a last will valid in law, but an instruction for Markward of Anweiler in his negotiations with the Curia.

[10] Thus V. Pfaff, "Papst Cölestin III.," *ZSavRGkan*, 47 (1961), 109–28.

As in previous pontificates, legal cases streamed from all of Christendom to Rome under Celestine III, especially since he solemnly declared that anyone who felt that he was threatened by others could and should seek justice at Rome. Thus Celestine made the Curia the central office for all final legal decisions in the Church, placed the written law ahead of customary law, made his judgments up-to-date, as has been remarked, and especially exercised control over their execution. More than previously, the papal jurisdiction was exercised by judges delegate, so that the Curia's routine became less burdensome and the way was made ready for central legislation. Chancery and *Camera* obtained their stable organization, and the importance of the College of Cardinals and its share in the government of the Universal Church grew.

It was as though all the preliminaries could be said to have been created for Celestine's successor, who as Innocent III would inaugurate a new epoch in the historical process of Christianity's development.

CHAPTER 11

The Third Crusade

The Third Lateran Council, in contrast to the other general synods of the twelfth and thirteenth centuries, referred only indirectly to Christendom's responsibility for the crusade. Six bishops and two abbots from the crusader states had taken part in it, but not even Archbishop William of Tyre, the most distinguished among them, intimates that the Council concerned itself in any detail with the situation of the Kingdom of Jerusalem. William, chancellor of the leprous King Baldwin IV (1174–85), knew only too well the crisis produced by the energetic advance of Saladin (1171 to 1193).[1] Propagandizing in Sicily, France, and England was not neglected, and many French knights under Peter of Courtenay sailed to the East along with the prelates returning home from the Council. One might entertain the opinion that the peace between Pope and Emperor, the ending and liquidating of the schism, would have again aroused in the West the readiness for common assistance to Jerusalem. Even Alexander III, during his agitated pontificate, had attentively followed the

[1] Imad ad-Din, *Conquête de la Syrie et de la Palestine*, ed. C. von Landberg (Leiden 1888); H. A. R. Gibb, "The Achievement of Saladin," *Bulletin of the John Rylands Library*, 35 (1952 f.), 44–60; J. Kraemer, *Der Sturz des Königreichs Jerusalem in der Darstellung des Imad al-Din* (Wiesbaden 1952); H. A. R. Gibb, "The Rise of Saladin (1169–89)," *History of the Crusades*, I (1958), 563–89; M. W. Baldwin, "The Decline and Fall of Jerusalem," *ibid.*, 590–621.

developments in Syria and Palestine and on 16 January 1181, shortly before his death, which occurred the following 30 August, he had been able to direct an appeal to Christendom. His successors, likewise with an eye on the crusade, sought a comprehensive policy of peace in the West: between Curia and Empire, between Curia and Rome, and between kings and princes, above all between England and France. Louis VII of France had died in 1180, and his successor, Philip II, had begun his energetic reign.

But only the catastrophe of the battle of Hattin in Galilee and Saladin's[2] capture of and entry into Jerusalem in 1187 were of a nature to shock the West so violently that the emotional presuppositions for a general European crusade were again present. The papacy once more undertook the duty of preaching the crusade but declined the actual leadership of the expedition, which was to lie in the hands of three monarchs: the Emperor and the Kings of England and France. The ephemeral pontificate of Gregory VIII (21 October — 17 December 1187) was entirely marked by this preoccupation, and the first legates proceeded at once to Germany, France, Denmark, and even Poland to preach the crusade. Clement III (1187–91) consistently continued these initial moves with his summonses of 10 February and 27 May 1188.

The Cistercian Cardinal Henry of Albano, who was accompanied by Archbishop Josias of Tyre, set to work with special zeal.[3] He contrived to bring about the English-French armistice of Gisors of 21 January 1188, on which occasion both Kings took the cross under pressure from public opinion. At Cologne he succeeded in reconciling Archbishop Philip with the Emperor Frederick I. At the "Diet of Jesus Christ" at Mainz on Laetare Sunday, where the legate and Godfrey I of Helfenstein, Bishop of Würzburg, preached, the Emperor, his oldest son and namesake, who was Duke of Swabia, and numerous princes took the cross. The expedition was to set out in the spring of 1189, and the liberation of the Holy Sepulchre was to crown the Emperor's life work. Counts Philip of Flanders and Baldwin of Hainaut agreed to take part. A crusade tax, the Saladin Tithe, was raised for the first time in France and England.[4] Scotland contributed nothing, for King William the Lion was unable to persuade his thrifty barons. The German expedition was financed by the participants. Clement III demanded a money contribution from members of the higher clergy, but the amount was not specified. This measure foreshadowed a

---

[2] *PL*, 200, 1294–96.

[3] Y. M. J. Congar, *Henri de Marcy*, 43–54, 77–90.

[4] For the controversial crusade tax in England and France, see F. A. Cazel, "The Tax of 1185 in Aid of the Holy Land," *Speculum*, 30 (1955), 385–92, and J. H. Round, "The Saladin Tithe," *EHR*, 31 (1916), 447–50.

development which in the next century led to the financing of crusades almost entirely by means of taxation of ecclesiastical incomes.

Crusade preaching was supplemented by literary propaganda, notably the crusade song in both courtly and popular form.[5] The parish clergy even recruited with the aid of vivid pictures representing scenes from the Holy Land and the struggle with the Muslims in order to stimulate participation by the illiterate.

The German expedition got under way at Regensburg on 11 May 1189. It unquestionably supplied the mightiest fighting force and was praised by contemporaries for its good discipline and its careful preparation. Meanwhile, King William II of Sicily had dispatched the first assistance, thereby helping to save the cities of Tyre and Tripolis, but he died on 18 November 1189. English crusaders, in advance of the royal expedition, and Flemings and Danes went by sea. While the Emperor Frederick was moving through Hungary and the Balkans, the English and the French enterprises had bogged down because of the recent renewal of the struggle between the two Kings; it ended only two days before Henry II's death with a peace that was deeply humiliating to the English King, since his sons Richard and John were aligned with his French opponent.[6] The Emperor Frederick wintered in the vicinity of Constantinople, where the new Byzantine Emperor, Isaac II Angelus, unexpectedly created difficulties, but in the spring of 1190 he could cross over to Asia Minor. The march across the interior made slow progress. After the Cilician foothills had finally been crossed and Cilician Armenia had been reached, the Emperor met his death in the river Saleph on 10 June 1190. Saladin could rightly see in this tragedy his own salvation. The dead Emperor's son, Duke Frederick of Swabia, was unable to hold the army together. A part of it returned home, others went on by ship; he led the remnant to Antioch, where on 21 June 1190 he fell sick and died. The Emperor's remains were interred at Antioch.

King Richard I Lionheart of England assumed his father's obligation to the crusade.[7] The English and French hosts met at Vézelay on 4 July 1190 and decided to go to Syria by sea. The armies wintered on Sicily at Messina, where an English crusade fleet had turned up. *En route* to the Holy Land, King Richard managed to conquer the island of Cyprus, to which the political centre of gravity of the crusader states was later to be transferred.

---

[5] See F. W. Wentzlaff-Eggebert, *Kreuzzugsdichtung des Mittelalters* (Berlin 1960).

[6] A. L. Poole, *From Domesday Book to Magna Carta*, 347 f., where the date of the agreement is given as 4 July 1189 and the place as Colombières between Tours and Azay-le-Rideau.

[7] F. J. West, *The Justiciarship in England, 1066–1232*, Cambridge Studies in Medieval Life and Thought, 12 (Cambridge 1966), 64–74.

First of all, the English-French expedition on 13 July 1191 relieved Acre, which had been besieged for two years. Dissension then broke out among the crusaders, for the Kings, who had become enemies during the winter on Sicily, took sides in the quarrel over the succession to the throne of Jerusalem: Richard supported Guy of Lusignan; Philip, Conrad of Montferrat. But when the King of France chose to regard his crusade vow as having been fulfilled with the fall of Acre and returned home *via* Rome, where he had himself expressly absolved *ad cautelam* by Celestine III, Richard was able to assume the direction of the expedition against Saladin. Jerusalem could not be recovered, but Richard's brilliant victories near Jaffa and in the battle of Arsuf obtained for the Franks at least a military breathing-space, especially since Saladin died in 1193 and left a disintegrating state. The armistice of 2 September 1192 marked the end of the Third Crusade. Saladin assured pilgrims free access to Jerusalem and a corresponding protection, but the Holy Sepulchre remained for the time being in Muslim hands.

Only a narrow coastal strip from Beirut to Ascalon could be saved and even its political existence depended on the good pleasure of the mighty Islamic realm. Furthermore it could be maintained only in the most intimate contact with the Latin West. Hence from now on the leading monarchs of Christendom at the moment wore also the crown of Jerusalem, first the Hohenstaufen, then Saint Louis IX, and finally Charles of Anjou. The crusader states themselves, now only a collection of individual cities and castles, often administered from Cyprus, constituted from the Third Crusade the Kingdom of Acre, whose history came to a definitive end with the fall of that city in 1291.

The severe losses of the Third Crusade and the meagre results disillusioned Christendom, even if to a lesser degree than had the Second Crusade. Before the end of the century the diminished Kingdom of Jerusalem obtained further help from the West in the crusade of the Emperor Henry VI, which must be viewed in the context of his Mediterranean policy. The Kings of Cyprus and Armenia were accepted as vassals of the Empire. The Emperor could not lead the crusade in person, for he died in September 1197. His chancellor, Bishop Conrad of Hildesheim, and Archbishop Conrad of Mainz, who had been named papal legate, came with a large army from the Rhineland and the Hohenstaufen lands. Individual groups arrived in Syria from August 1197 on. It was possible to take Sidon and Beirut and to preserve the coast, but the death of the Emperor and the anarchy ensuing in Germany with the double election prematurely ended the undertaking. Before the crusaders departed, what had been a German hospital brotherhood was organized in Acre on 5 March 1198 as a military religious order, which, as the Order of the Teutonic Knights, was to face an important future, but not in the Holy Land.

A glance at a century of military operations under the sign of the cross presents the question of whether and how these events formed and developed the devotional outlook of Christians. The history of piety in the twelfth century not only encounters that enrichment which was occasioned by an intensification and further development of monastic spirituality in the new orders. There also opened up to it entirely new fields of devout deportment, of generous self-sacrifice, even of mystical experience. Alongside the monk and the canon appeared the layman,[8] not too often, to be sure, as a new spokesman in the sense of being writer or theologian, but usually as the actor, whose motives, attitudes, and prayers are disclosed only indirectly by the sources. Only when he was a poet did the layman directly give expression to the new piety.

It participated in the tendencies common to all proponents of the ecclesiastical reform movement and arose out of a longing for a *vita apostolica* and a desire to belong to the *pauperes Christi*. But its forms were determined by the fact of crusading, the great epoch of which belonged preeminently, though not entirely, to the age of Saint Bernard. The fact that the appeals to the crusades were so overwhelmingly successful among all classes of the Christian population and, in the well-nigh universal opinion of scholars, the religious motive predominated in the determination to take the cross[9] can hardly be otherwise explained than by the awakening and strengthening of a pious frame of mind, in which the elements of religious insights and decisions, to be set forth below, became effective.

There had long been pilgrimages to Compostela, Rome, and Jerusalem, motivated by penance, devotion, and vow. What was new was the armed pilgrimage, conditioned by the notion in the Latin West of the now more deeply Christianized class of knighthood. The unique origin of religious orders whose members by vocation bore arms testifies to this. Their beginnings lay also in the hospital idea,[10] which knew its richest and most spontaneous development parallel to the crusades, in the whole of Christendom, first of all in the twelfth century. Characteristic features of this preparedness for hospital work recur among the hermits, who also belong to the many-sided picture of the piety of this epoch. The binding force that united such individual tendencies, at first glance incompatible

[8] *Cf.* J. R. Strayer, "The Laicization of French and English Society in the Thirteenth Century," *Speculum,* 15 (1940), 76–86, who traces it to the twelfth century.
[9] Even S. Runciman, *History of the Crusades,* III, 478, holds that the "chief motive that impelled the Christian armies eastward was faith."
[10] G. Schreiber, *Gemeinschaften des Mittelalters, Recht und Verfassung, Kult und Frömmigkeit* (Münster 1948), 3–80.

even if not entirely contradictory, was a lively devotion to Christ, of an orientation different from what it had been earlier. The preaching and the pastoral contact of monks, canons, bishops, and diocesan clerics, stamped by a greater familiarity with Holy Scripture, especially the New Testament, began to complete the change from the Lord King Christ to Jesus of Nazareth, wandering, suffering, humanly close, redeeming, and not holding sway, in the characteristic attitude to piety. This had awakened in the laity the demand for the *vita apostolica*, that is, for personal nearness to Christ, who showed them the way to salvation, made it possible, and had already lived it directly as exemplar. All catechetical instruction, as recent research shows,[11] was based from the twelfth century on the fundamental theological schema of the *via salutis*. It is no longer surprising that the concrete aspect of this *via salutis* now became the crusade. Accordingly, crusade piety appears as a characteristic form of the Christian's seeking after salvation, which he found in a threefold union: a union with God in obedient service — "God wills it" — with Christ in a suffering, dying, and triumphing imitation — for Christ and with him — with the Holy Spirit in the enthusiasm of the reorientation, esteemed as a newly experienced Pentecost.

It was above all the way of penance and prayer that led to this three-fold union with God. Penance belonged to the central themes of crusade preaching and crusade piety, just as it was also predominant in the basically soteriological schema of popular catechesis. Ennobled by the idea of the imitation of Christ, the penitential desire freed itself from the sphere of a striving directed solely to one's own salvation, all the more as the crusader was filled with an awareness of doing penance as the representative of those who remained at home. For crusading as such was a duty imposed, of itself, on all of Christendom. Corresponding to this was the attitude of the homeland, which supported the *expeditio sacra* by means of alms, money and other real contributions, intercessory prayer, fasting, and freely undertaken penitential works, and thereby participated in it. This self-sanctification, viewed as participation in the *via salutis* of crusading, united all of Christendom in a common pious undertaking and made crusade piety stand out as the first uniform type of Christian lay spirituality in Church History. The *Gesta Francorum*, composed by a layman, begin with the informative sentence:

When that time had come to which the Lord Jesus daily referred his faithful, especially when it is said in the Gospel, "If anyone wishes to come after me, let him deny himself, take up his cross, and follow me", a powerful movement spread throughout the lands of the Franks,

---

[11] B. I. Kilström, *Den kateketiska undervisingen i Sverige under medeltiden* (Uppsala 1958), 147–62, 318 f.

so that anyone who eagerly wished to follow God with a pure heart and mind and faithfully to carry the cross after him did not delay to enter as quickly as possible upon the route to the Holy Sepulchre. [12]

A fruit of this crusade piety was the military religious orders, which at the same time realized a predominant motive of the piety of the age in hospital service. People saw in the sick the *pauperes Christi,* saw the Lord in them, served him by serving them. The grand master of the Hospitallers described himself as *servus pauperum Christi.* William of Malavalle (d. 1157), returning from the crusade, settled as a hermit in the Silva Livallia on Monte Pisano and began the construction of a "hospitale ad dei venerationem et pauperum Christi refectionem"; by „pauperum Christi" he meant especially pilgrims going to Rome. [13] The Hospitallers of Saint Lazarus were founded at Jerusalem around 1120 and lived according to the Augustinian rule. The late twelfth century saw a whole group of lay associations for the service of the sick, such as the Brothers of Saint John the Baptist at Beauvais (before 1185), the Hospitallers of Our Dear Lady, or della Scala, at Siena (1194), the Brothers of the Order of the Holy Spirit at Montpellier (*ca.* 1180). Paul Alphandéry also places in this context the building movement, *la croisade monumentale,* which arose from the spirit of the new piety. Proceeding from Chartres, it spread through Normany and a great part of France. [14] In it too the idea of penance was the central motive. The pilgrims assembled their vehicles at the building site, as though it were a spiritual camp, and regarded themselves as an "army of the Lord". This piety, in relation to the experience of the whole Church in the crusades, also encountered stimulation in the very monasteries of the new orders, though here it was intensified and more powerfully spiritualized.

Out of a movement in many ways turbulent, determined by eschatological fear but at the same time driven by an honouring of Christ and a love of God that were deepened by the Gospel and elevated to enthusiastic surrender, a movement which especially affected the masses of Latin Christendom, there proceeded a form of popular piety which extended throughout the period of the crusades themselves and far beyond it and became the root of many forms of devotion of the following epoch.

[12] *Gesta Francorum et aliorum Hierosolimitorum,* ed. R. Hill, Nelson's Medieval Texts (London 1962), 1.
[13] K. Elm, *Beiträge zur Geschichte des Wilhelmitenordens* (Cologne and Graz 1962), 11–33.
[14] *La chrétienté et l'idée de croisade,* 163–65.

CHAPTER 12

Scholasticism, Canon Law, and the Universities

Early Scholasticism

Of the various works of the "sentence" type, which in the first half of the twelfth century constituted the special character of theological endeavour, especially outside the realm of monastic education, the work of Peter Lombard at Paris [1] was outstanding. With its recourse to the dialectical method that had reached its important maturity in Abelard, it was almost as though it was the last word, the ultimate norm of these expositions of theological scholarship. In it Augustine was regarded as the principal witness of theological tradition. Basically conservative, it was a systematic and clearly and precisely organized summary of all the chief truths of the Christian faith that had been hitherto discussed by theologians. To every question it brought the relevant patristic citations and reliable solutions. In a relatively long period of reception, which ended with the celebrated text of the Fourth Lateran Council in 1215, [2] Peter's work became the first and for centuries the leading theological textbook. His opponents, John of Cornwall [3] and Gerhoh of Reichersberg, [4] especially rejected his Christological theses or, like Joachim of Fiore, [5] his formulation of the theology of the Trinity. More effective as journalism was the powerful indictment by the prior of Saint-Victor, Walter, [6] who in *Contra quatuor labyrinthos Franciae* came out against dialectical theology at the Third Lateran Council of 1179, but the reputation of the theologians whom he attacked, Peter Lom-

[1] See Chapter 7.

[2] COD, 208 (footnotes 4–6), Constitutio 2: De errore abbatis Ioachim. "Nos autem, sacro et universali concilio approbante, credimus et confitemur cum Petro [Lombardo] ..."

[3] John of Cornwall (1125/30–1199/1200) especially in his *Eulogium ad Alexandrum Papam III* (1177/79) against Christological nihilism; cf. N. M. Häring, *MS*, 13 (1951), 253–300 (edition); biographical material in E. Rathbone, *RThAM*, 17 (1950), 46–60.

[4] See P. Classen, *Gerhoh von Reichersberg* (Wiesbaden 1960), 261, where it is stressed that, despite all criticism, Gerhoh referred to the Lombard as an outstanding teacher and collector, whom he was not attacking as the head of a heretical school, as he did in the case of Abelard and Gilbert de la Porrée. On the whole question, see *ibid.*, pp. 248–72.

[5] He was condemned at the Fourth Lateran Council as an opponent of the Trinitarian doctrine of Peter Lombard; see *supra*, footnote 2, and E. Bertola, "La dottrina trinitaria di Pietro Lombardo," *Miscellanea Lombardiana* (Novara 1957), 129–35 (investigated from the viewpoint of Joachimite criticism); J. de Ghellinck, Le mouvement, 263–67.

[6] Walter of Saint-Victor (d. after 1180), prior of the community from 1173. His polemic in *PL*, 199, 1129–72, ed. by P. Glorieux, *AHD*, 27 (1952), 187–335; also, *idem*, "Mauvaise action et mauvais travail. Le 'Contra IV labyrinthos Franciae'," *RThAM*, 19 (1954), 179—93; J. de Ghellinck, *op. cit.*, 258–63.

bard, Gilbert de la Porrée, Peter of Poitiers, and Peter Abelard, could not be impaired with contemporaries.

Dependent on Peter Lombard, there appeared up to 1200 still other collections of sentences and questions, theological *summae*, based on early excerpts from his work, and *abbreviationes*, as they were produced in this form also at Bologna by the *Decretum* of Gratian. A work by the *magister* Bandinus[7] and the *abbreviatio* "Filia magistri," which at the same time displayed dependence on the *Summa aurea* of William of Auxerre, quickly became known. In many copies of *The Sentences* of Peter Lombard, as produced by enterprising groups of copyists for school use, are marginal glosses, which were later compiled, as occasion offered, into complete and separately published commentaries. Widely scattered, and for the most part still unpublished, in many manuscript collections, at Bamberg, Munich, Rome, Paris, and elsewhere, they are witnesses of the early school of Peter Lombard.

Beside the Lombard stood another noteworthy theological scholar, Robert of Melun, who died in 1167 as Bishop of Hereford. He was one of Abelard's creative pupils and his successor in the directing of the *schola artium* at Sainte-Geneviève.[8] His *Quaestiones de divina pagina* on the text of Saint Matthew's Gospel and his *Sentences*, which appeared at the same time as those of Peter Lombard (1152–60), were praised. And the *Sentences* of *magister* Udo (1160–65) must also be mentioned. Their plan corresponded to Hugh of Saint-Victor's outline in *De sacramentis fidei*. They were excerpted, found their *abbreviatores*, and indicate to what a great extent the school of Paris developed into the leading centre of European theological learning.

Leader among the glossators of Peter Lombard, his successors in the teaching office, was *magister* Peter Comestor,[9] with his *Historia scholastica*, gloss on the Gospels, and treatise on the Sacraments. In the last mentioned work he first introduced the concept of *transubstantiatio*, later adopted by the Fourth Lateran Council. The Lombard's influence extended as far as Bologna, where it can be detected in Gandulf (after 1160).[10]

Following Peter Comestor another pupil of Peter Lombard assumed the post of master of *The Sentences* as theological *magister* at Paris. This

---

[7] *PL*, 192, 965–1112; J. de Ghellinck, *op. cit.*, 270.

[8] H. Horst, *Die Trinitäts- und Gotteslehre des Robert de Melun* (Mainz 1963; bibliography).

[9] Peter Comestor (or Manducator) (*ca.* 1100–after 1179), called "Magister historiarum": *Historia scholastica* (*PL*, 198, 1053–1644, supplemented by Peter of Poitiers, *ibid.*, 1645 to 1722); S. R. Daly, "Petrus Comestor, Master of Histories," *Speculum* (1957), 62–73; bibliography in L. Hödl, *LThK*, VIII (2nd ed. 1963), 357 f.

[10] On Gandulf, see especially J. de Ghellinck, *op. cit.*, 297–373.

was Peter of Poitiers (1130–1205). [11] As chancellor he was to exercise a deciding influence on the genesis of the university. His *Five Books of Sentences* appeared around 1170; more than a mere commentary on the Lombard, they became a theological compendium of a special character. To the school of Peter Lombard [12] belonged also *magister* Martin, Simon of Tournai, Prévotin of Cremona, and Peter of Capua. In a sense the century ended with the *Summa* of Prévotin (1190–94), a collection of previously separately treated particular questions. [13] So far forty manuscripts of it are known. All still unpublished and widely scattered, they also point to the unity of Western theological endeavour.

Outside the circle of pupils of Peter Lombard there worked at Paris around 1170 Peter Cantor (d. 1197), [14] who left abundant writings on many aspects of theology; based on an intensive study of Scripture, they were above all oriented to moral theology. Educated in theology at the cathedral school of Reims, probably under *magister* Alberic, and familiarized by him with the thought of Anselm of Laon, Peter became a canon of Notre-Dame de Paris and in 1178 obtained the capitular post of chanter, from which he got his nickname. His works, still for the most part unpublished, pertain to dogmatic and moral theology, to the theological encyclopedia, and especially to exegesis. His chief work is his *Summa de sacramentis et animae consiliis*. From canon law he received important suggestions as to form and content. Most widely circulated seems to have been his *Verbum abbreviatum*, with important remarks on the method of theological research. A mine of information in regard to cultural history, it became the important source for the condition of the clergy at Paris and at the same time, thanks to his familiarity with the authors of antiquity, a late witness of the Renaissance of the twelfth century.

Martin Grabmann mentions as pupils of Peter Cantor the Benedictine Liebhard of Prüfening, Guy of Orchelles, and especially the Englishmen,

---

[11] Peter of Poitiers *(ca.* 1130–1205); his *Sentences* in *PL*, 211, 789–1280; new ed. of Book I by P. S. Moore and M. Dulong (Notre Dame 1943), of Book II by P. S. Moore, M. Dulong, and J. N. Garvin (Notre Dame 1950); P. S. Moore, *The Works of Peter of Poitiers* (Notre Dame 1936).

[12] On the Lombard's school, now see S. Otto, "Die Funktion des Bildbegriffs in der Theologie des 12. Jahrhunderts," *BGPhMA*, 40, 1 (Münster 1963), 200–23.

[13] G. Lacombe, *Praepositini Cancellarii Parisiensis opera omnia*, I: *La vie et les œuvres de Prévostin, Bibl Thom*, 11, 1927. Praepositinus (born between 1130 and 1135 at Cremona; died at Paris in 1210), was chancellor of the University of Paris from 1206 to 1209; S. Otto, *loc. cit.*, 251–54; J. N. Garvin, *LThK*, VIII (2nd ed. 1963), 696 (bibliography).

[14] Peter Cantor *(ca.* 1130–97) was elected Bishop of Tournai but was not confirmed; the most recent treatment is that by P. Delhaye in LThK, VIII (2nd ed. 1963), 353 f. (bibliography); J. A. Dugauquier, *Pierre le Chantre. Summa de Sacramentis et animae consiliis*, so far 4 vols. (*Analecta Mediaevalia Namurcensia*, 4, 7, 11, 16 [Louvain and Lille 1954 to 1963]).

Robert de Courçon, William de Montibus, and Richard of Leicester, who take us into the thirteenth century, and Stephen Langton (d. 1228), Cardinal and from 1206 Archbishop of Canterbury, who was one of the most celebrated theologians of his age.[15]

Besides the theologians of the Lombard circle, scholars of the entourage of Gilbert de la Porrée[16] also taught and wrote, such as Jordan de Fantasma, the Archdeacon Ivo of Chartres, and John Beleth. Outstanding among them was Alain de Lille (1120–1202),[17] Cistercian, teacher at Paris, and later active in the Albigensian mission. With his *Regulae de sacra theologia* he wrote a much used theological compendium, a series of theses, which, established by argumentation as occasion called for, were an innovation in form alongside the previously preferred *quaestiones*. The *Distinctiones dictionum theologicalium* were a sort of theological lexicon, which collected and explained biblical expressions and especially the current theological terminology. Alain's voluminous literary work also includes poetry, treatises on penance, sermons, the much commented *Summa de arte praedicatoria*, and the *Liber poenitentialis*.

To the school of Gilbert de la Porrée also belonged Eudes (d. 1171),[18] Abbot of the Cistercian monastery of Ourscamp from 1167 to 1170 and before that a teacher of theology at Paris. A shrewd dialectician, he opposed Peter Lombard in fundamental questions of theology, Christology, and the doctrine of the Sacraments. He died in 1171 as Cardinal Bishop of Tusculum. Through his influence on Simon of Tournai (d. 1201)[19] his theology found a far-reaching response. Various collections of *quaestiones* from the group of his hearers prove that he founded a school. Simon of Tournai's chief work, the *Institutiones in Sacram Paginam* (1170/75), so far unpublished, displays Abelard's stock of ideas; new in Simon were the *disputationes*, which took their place beside the hitherto customary *lectiones*, *quaestiones*, and theses. Through him Aristotle obtained entry into theological speculation.

The *Ars catholicae fidei*, formerly attributed to Alain de Lille, was the

---

[15] *Die Geschichte der katholischen Theologie seit dem Ausgang der Väterzeit* (Freiburg 1933), 46.

[16] On the school of La Porrée, see now S. Otto, *loc. cit.*, 224–50, with reference to E. Bertola, *La scuola di Gilberto de la Porrée* (Padua 1951); N. M. Häring, "Zur Geschichte der Schulen von Poitiers," *AKG*, 47 (1965), 23–47.

[17] Alain de Lille, works in *PL*, 210; J. Longère, *Alain de Lille: Liber poenitentialis, I: Introduction doctrinale et littéraire* (*Analecta Mediaevalia Namurcensia*, 17 [Louvain and Lille 1965].

[18] On Eudes of Ourscamp, see L. Hödl, *Geschichte der scholastischen Literatur und der Theologie der Schlüsselgewalt*, I (Münster 1960), 116–41, 210–14.

[19] On Simon of Tournai, see S. Otto, *loc. cit.*, 238–50; L. Hödl, *Schlüsselgewalt*, I, 240.

work of Nicholas of Amiens, who thereby enlarged the la Porrée circle. Peter Cantor, already mentioned, seems also to have belonged to it because of his intellectual proximity to Alain de Lille. Dependent on Nicholas is one of the most exhaustive presentations of ethics in the twelfth century, the *Speculum universale* of Raoul Ardent,[20] a grand-scale theological encyclopedia, which remained unfinished. Abundant use was made of Gilbert de la Porrée. Thus far only a survey of the chapters of this work, famed for its originality, is in print. Raoul died before the end of the century.

Early Canon Law

Whereas *The Sentences* of Peter Lombard were able only gradually and not without opposition to establish themselves in the world of higher education, the *Decretum Gratiani*[21] succeeded very quickly and almost without effort in becoming at Bologna the basic text of the new science of canon law. Alongside the legists, who concentrated from the time of Irnerius and his four great pupils on the Roman law of late antiquity, stood the decretists, who dealt in detail, according to the scholastic method, with the *Decretum* and its content in lectures and treatises. As was true of *The Sentences* at Paris, so too here the *Decretum* obtained interlinear glosses, the textual exegesis was condensed in *summae,* legal *quaestiones* were treated, legal rules were drawn up, and in this way the practical application of the sources was taught. Complete, detailed expositions of the entire text, the so-called *apparatus,*[22] later appeared, based on the glosses and *summae.* In addition to the decretists of Bologna, there were canonists in France also, above all in Normandy.[23]

Gratian's best known pupil, Paucapalea, to whom is attributed the subdividing of Part I and Part III of the *Decretum* into *distinctiones,*

---

[20] Raoul Ardent, homilies in *PL*, 155, 1301–1626, 1667–2118; the *Speculum Universale* (1193–1200) is still unprinted; see J. Gründel, *Das Speculum Universale des Radulf Ardens* (Munich 1961); *idem, Die Lehre von den Umständen* (Münster 1963), 204–15.

[21] See Chapter 7.

[22] S. Kuttner, *Repertorium der Kanonistik* (SteT, 71) (Rome 1937); J. Rambaud-Buhot, "Les divers types d'abrégés du Décret de Gratien," *Recueil de travaux offert à M. Clovis Brunel* (Paris 1955), 397–411. On the literary forms of the academic proposition *(glossa, apparatus, notabilia, generalia, brocarda, distinctiones, quaestiones, casus),* cf. G. Le Bras, C. Lefebvre, and J. Rambaud, *L'âge classique,* 270–73.

[23] S. Kuttner, "Les débuts de l'école canoniste française," *Studia et documenta historiae et iuris,* 4 (1938), 1–14; S. Kuttner and E. Rathbone, "Anglo-Norman Canonists of the Twelfth Century," *Tr,* 7 (1949 f.), 279–358.

began with a *summa* (1145–48).[24] The *summa,* known as *Stroma,* of *magister* Roland Bandinelli was ready in 1148, the *abbreviatio* of Ognibene of Verona around 1156. John of Faenza (d. 1190) relied on the formerly much used work of *magister* Rufinus (shortly before 1159), which was generally regarded as the first great gloss of the *Decretum.* Even before John of Faenza Stephen of Tournai (d. 1203) around 1160 had utilized both Bandinelli and especially Rufinus. Also a pupil of Gratian was Simon of Bisignano, whose *summa* was written in 1177–79. But without any doubt the "greatest of the decretists" was Huguccio of Pisa, termination and climax of the school of Bologna. His *summa* was finished in 1188–90 and he died in 1210 as Bishop of Ferrara. As a matter of fact, most of the teachers of law at Bologna became bishops, while some, such as Bandinelli, Albert de Morra, and, above all, Lothar di Segni became Popes. Rufinus obtained the see of Assisi, Ognibene Verona, John Faenza, Sicard Cremona, Stephen Tournai. Others rose to be cardinals, such as Laborans and Gratian (d. 1197), namesake of the author of the *Decretum.* The age of the jurist Popes and jurist bishops had begun.

The French *summae* of the *Decretum* have all come down anonymously. They are often distinguished from their Italian counterparts by their arbitrary division of the content and their method. Their titles — *Summa Coloniensis, Monacensis, Parisiensis, Lipsiensis,* and so forth — denote the location of the manuscripts, but they were not necessarily written where they were later found; thus the *Summa Coloniensis* was written at Paris around 1170, the *Summa Monacensis* in Carinthia in 1175–78. The *summa* of Sicard of Cremona (1179–81) is also reckoned as belonging to the French school. The French school (Paris and Normandy) and the wide diffusion of its manuscripts prove the rapid and general reception of the *Decretum* and its adaptations in all of Christendom. Under Alexander III the *Decretum* even came into use at the Curia.

The *Decretum* itself did not acquire any strictly legal force, but the copious literature on it, the intensive work of comparing and clarifying the law that it achieved, and its diffusion by the leading schools to all centres of ecclesiastical life laid the groundwork for the legislative accomplishment of the papal leadership, which from the time of Alexander III and especially of Innocent III showed itself as ever more universal in activity and as determining the whole ecclesiastical order.

---

[24] The older literature in A. van Hove, *Prolegomena* (Malines and Rome, 2nd ed. 1945) (Commentarium Lovaniense in Codicem Iuris Canonici, I, 1), 423–35. On the *summae* on the *Decretum* by the Bologna and French schools, see S. Kuttner, *Repertorium,* 123–207; on the *summae* of the Anglo-Norman and Cologne schools, see S. Kuttner and E. Rathbone, "Anglo-Norman Canonists" (note 23): Magister Honorius, the circle around John of Tynmouth with John of Cornwall and Simon of Southwell, Thomas of Marlborough, and others belonged to it. Richard Anglicus taught at Bologna.

The Rise of the Universities

The two new sciences here described, that of theoretical and practical theology and that of canon law, by the force of their attraction on students from all parts of Western Christendom and by the constantly more intensively developing cooperation of teachers and their students, especially though not exclusively at Bologna and Paris, laid the foundation for an institution whose proper history belongs to the thirteenth century, but whose beginnings occurred in the twelfth: the universities, or *studia generalia*, of the West.

In the wake of the general changes in the social, economic, and political structure, the educational system of the West also experienced a significant transformation in the twelfth century. Whereas previously clerics, monks, and lay persons had received a humanist and theological training at abbey, cathedral, or chapter schools, but, apart from a few exceptions, only the requirements of the current personnel of the monastery, chapter, or bishopric were envisaged, the picture quickly changed in the course of the twelfth century. The importance of the monastic schools yielded to the growing influence of the urban schools, because the primacy of the agrarian organization was supplanted by the development of the urban culture.

If for the moment the cathedral and chapter schools were predominant in the cities, there were already in places like Salerno, Montpellier, and Bologna schools that were not really ecclesiastical institutions. At Paris from the beginning of the century there was an increase in the number of teachers who still instructed their students on ecclesiastical premises — the cloisters of the cathedral or of Sainte-Geneviève — but neither they nor their students were included in the personnel of the cathedral or the collegiate chapter. Such groups grew especially at Paris, but also elsewhere. The number of teachers rose in proportion as a rapidly growing movement of wandering scholars set in, a movement that can hardly be reckoned in numbers but was in accord with the general intellectual restlessness. It started in all parts of Christendom but moved especially westward to Paris and southward to Bologna. What is to be said of Bec, Chartres, and Orléans in the eleventh century, though on a more modest scale, now became visible in a broad movement. Persons wandered from the Empire to Liège first, then to Reims, to Laon and Orléans, and finally to Paris especially.

It was as yet not the schools themselves as institutions which exerted the power of attraction but the names of teachers who had become renowned, such as Anselm at Laon and William of Champeaux and especially Abelard at Paris. The cities themselves expanded and offered greater possibilities as residences of teachers and students. In the second half of the century there emerged centres which were no longer dependent on the renown of an outstanding teacher but where the schools themselves became permanent institutions; the teachers changed and whole groups of teachers gathered. Extant are long lists of names for Paris, where teachers of the *artes liberales* and of theology taught in specified sections, such as the masters of arts on the Petit-Pont and on Mont-Sainte-Geneviève, and the theologians at Saint-Victor, at the cathedral, at Sainte-Geneviève, at Saint-Germain-des-Prés. The *scholasticus canonicus* or chancellor of the cathedral chapter of Notre-Dame — and this was also true of other cathedral and collegiate chapters — could give the teachers the authorization to teach; it had to be asked from him. Every qualified aspirant, so Alexander III had had the Third Lateran Council declare,[25] was to obtain it.

Accordingly, the institutional nucleus of the University of Paris was present here. The chancellor retained supervision of the teachers, who even in the twelfth century, in accord with the tendency of the age, began to unite as a gild — *societas* or, later, *universitas*. The admission of new members usually took place in such a way that the *magister* introduced through the ceremony of *inceptio,* or commencement, his pupil who had completed his study. The twofold element of an official licensing by the chancellor and an academic cooptation thus remains to be noted.

The situation developed similarly at Bologna.[26] But it is controverted whether the teachers of Roman law, Irnerius and his pupils, were allowed to teach with or without official attestation by the authorities of city and Church. In any event, the well known *constitutio* "Habita" of Frederick I, which he published at the Diet of Roncaglia in 1158, not expressly for Bologna but for all *scholares* of the Kingdom of Italy, seems to have presupposed a sort of union of the teachers of law, from which, in cases of dispute, justice could be sought in competition with the episcopal jurisdiction. It had no written statutes but lived according to rules of customary law and, as at Paris, replenished itself through cooptation by the *magistri.* Most likely the teachers of Roman law constituted a single *universitas* together with those of canon law. Only later were there also formed the unions of the students, upon which in the course of time was to devolve the control of the university as a whole. These called themselves *universitates,* while the teachers became a *collegium.* The *magistri* retained the important right of judging the scholarly qualification of those who

---

[25] Canon 18, *COD*, 196.

[26] The contributions to the *Studi e memorie per la storia dell'Università di Bologna* (NS, 1) (Bologna 1954) elucidate the beginnings of the University of Bologna; besides the work by G. de Vergottini, mentioned in the bibliography to this chapter, U. Gualazzini reports on the origin ("L'origine dello Studium bolognese nelle più antiche vicende della licentia docendi," 97–115), G. Rossi on the relations of the students to the city (" 'Universitas scholarium' e commune," 173–266), and G. Le Bras on Bologna as one of the chief intellectual cities of the West ("Bologne, monarchie médiévale des droits savants," 1–18).

wished to be coopted to their *collegium* in the *conventus,* which corresponded to the Paris *inceptio,* but in all else the gilds of students retained the primacy.

Apart from a few generally observed imperial and papal decrees which were issued in the twelfth century with regard to studies, the royal and ecclesiastical, the communal and imperial privileges for particular universities began only from 1200. Until then there were found, especially at Paris, Bologna, Montpellier, Salerno, and Oxford, those communities of teachers and students out of which in the thirteenth century developed the universities, endowed especially by the papacy with specific rights. Hence they appeared as a spontaneous growth, not as an institution planned and set up by the highest authorities. Their beginnings belong to the twelfth century and its intellectual outburst, in which there became manifest not so much an interest directed to vocational training but rather the desire for a knowledge of the truth, for a knowledge transcending the needs of daily life.[27] Of course, the general rapid development of urban culture and the increased connections among nations in the wake of the crusades contributed something to this. There is no question of a continuity in Italy or in the Midi of the late classical Roman or Near Eastern educational institutions; even Byzantine or Muslim influences have not been demonstrated by research. It is true that there arose relatively early a legend of the *translatio studii,*[28] similar to the *translatio imperii,* from Athens to Rome, from there to Byzantium, and finally to Paris, traces of which are found in Alcuin and Notker in Carolingian times and which was familiar in Germany and France in the twelfth and thirteenth centuries, but it is without any historical foundation. The early history of the universities as properly defined institutions belongs to the thirteenth century.

---

[27] Especially stressed by H. Grundmann, *Vom Ursprung der Universitäten im Mittelalter* (Darmstadt, 2nd ed. 1960).

[28] Allusion was made to this *translatio* by É. Gilson, *Les idées et les lettres* (Paris 1932), 183–85, then by E. R. Curtius, *Europäische Literatur und lateinisches Mittelalter* (Bern, 2nd ed. 1954), 388–90; by H. Grundmann, "Sacerdotium — Regnum — Studium. Zur Wertung der Wissenschaft im 13. Jahrhundert," *AKG,* 34 (1952), 5–21; then, in detail, by F. J. Worstbrock, "Translatio artium," *AKG,* 47 (1965), 1–22: "The migration of the *studium* from Greece *via* Rome to France — this view may have come to flower in the soil of the Paris schools. It was understood, as Hugh of Saint-Victor indicates, as a continuation of the ancient theories and *schemata* of translation" (18).

CHAPTER 13

Heresy and the Beginnings of the Inquisition

The epoch of the Gregorian reform had known radical preachers under the auspices of the *vita apostolica*. Their anti-ecclesiastical and anti-sacramental tendencies had found some response among the lower classes. Such demagogues had followed the reform preachers. Among them was Peter of Bruys in the Midi from around 1105; before 1126 he was burned by an enraged mob.[1] Anti-sacerdotal sentiments also characterized the preaching of Tanchelin[2] in Flanders and Brabant and were found among the peasants of Bucy-le-Long near Soissons. Similar ideas appeared at Florence in 1117 and at Orvieto in 1125 and in the bishopric of Trier in 1122. The traces were first lost at the time of the Schism of 1130, but it was curious that, while radical elements made themselves known everywhere, they were apparently independent of one another.

After 1135 a powerfully emerging new wave of heresy moved through the southern and western areas of Christendom. Henry of Lausanne[3] preached penance at Le Mans, Lausanne, Pisa, Poitiers, Bordeaux, and finally Albi till 1145. Like Peter of Bruys, he spoke against the Church and had his adherents desecrate church buildings, destroy altars, burn crosses, and beat priests. He called for an apostolic life, but the multitude of his hearers could not be permanently organized. In Brittany from 1145 Eudes de l'Étoile[4] was more effective among the ordinary folk in denouncing the Church and the monasteries and in uniting groups of believers into communities living a penitential life. His fantastic doctrine impressed theologians as the product of a sick mind. He died soon after 1148 in the prison of the Archbishop of Reims.

The most important of the radicals of this period was Arnold of Brescia (d. 1155),[5] pupil of Abelard and canon regular, who carried the reform

---

[1] *Cf.* R. Manselli, *Studi sulle eresie del secolo XII* (Rome 1953), 25–43. Manselli prefers 1132–33 as the year of his death.

[2] W. Mohr, "Tanchelm von Antwerpen, eine nochmalige Überprüfung der Quellenlage," *Annales Universitatis Saraviensis* [Saarbrücken], 3 (1954), 234–47; most important is the letter from the Utrecht cathedral clergy to Archbishop Frederick of Cologne (1112–14) in *Codex Udalrici*, no. 168, ed. P. Jaffé, *Bibl. rer. Germ.* V, 296–300.

[3] R. Manselli on Henry of Lausanne in *BIStIAM*, 65 (1953), 1–63; *idem, Studi sulle eresie del secolo XII*, 45–67.

[4] On Eudes de l'Étoile (Eudo de la Stella), see L. Spätling, *De Apostolicis, Pseudo-Apostolicis, Apostolinis* (Munich 1947), 67–69; H. Maisonneuve, *Études*, 106–08; N. Cohn, *The Pursuit of the Millennium* (London 1957), 38–40.

[5] C. W. Greenaway, *Arnold of Brescia* (Cambridge 1931); A. Ragazzoni, *Arnoldo da Brescia nella tradizione storica* (Brescia 1937); P. Fedele, *Fonti per la storia di Arnoldo da Brescia* (Rome 1938); F. Bartolini, *Codice diplomatico del senato romano (1144–1347)*, I (Rome

ideas of his age to the ultimate consequences, called for an itinerant Church of apostolic poverty, and demanded contempt of the world and humility in priests and bishops. Arnold met defeat not only because his requirements were so extreme but also because of his imprudent attempt to lay the ground for them by political means. Frederick I had him arrested and turned him over to the Roman authorities, who made short work of him. His followers, like those of Henry of Lausanne and Eudes de l'Étoile, scattered. Common to them all was the fact that their preaching was not really a reaction against the Church reform but rather an exaggeration of the reform into the heretical and the radical.

Heresy first became a mass movement, no longer dependent on the presence of one or the other demagogic preacher, with the appearance of the Cathari[6] from 1140. As a mass movement they belonged to this century of the crusades, of penitential journeys for the building of churches in northern France, of the communal movement everywhere, in the Midi and North Italy, on the Rhine and in Flanders, and in all regions with a rapidly developing urban organization.

It was probably merchants and crusaders who first brought back Bogomile[7] ideas from the East. From Bulgaria Bogomiles had migrated to Byzantium; then, persecuted and expelled by the government of the Emperor Manuel Comnenus (1143–80), they had moved to the West. The Cathari, a name known from 1163, held as doctrine a dualism of Manichaean allure in the twofold direction of an absolute and a moderate form. The good God as creator of spirits and the evil God[8] as creator of the visible world represented orders which were intermingled by the activity of Satan. The activity of Saint Michael and of Christ, who defeated the demon and thereby redeemed souls from Satan's dominion, dualistic, existing in division, would restore the old order. This was absolute Catharism. The moderate form knew only a creator God, whose

1948); A. Frugoni, *Arnoldo da Brescia nelle fonti del secolo XII* (Rome 1954); A. Suraci in *AnOCist* (1957), 83–91.

[6] The authoritative monograph is by A. Borst (Stuttgart 1953), but research and exposition continue: S. Savini, *Il catarismo italiano ed i suoi vescovi* (Florence 1958); R. Nelli, *Écritures cathares. Textes originaux traduits et commentés* (Paris 1959); J. Russell, "Les cathares de 1048–54 à Liège," *BullSocAHLiège*, 42 (1961), 1–8; D. Walther, *Survey* (see the bibliography for this chapter); E. Werner, "Die Entstehung der Kabbala und die südfranzösischen Katharer," *FF*, 37 (1963), 86–89; C. Thuzellier, *Un traité cathare inédit du début du XIII*e *siècle d'après le Liber contra Manicheos de Durand de Huesca*, Bibliothèque de la *RHE*, 37 (Louvain 1961).

[7] A. Solovjev, "Autour des Bogomiles," *Byz(B)*, 22 (1952); *idem*, "Le symbolisme des monuments funéraires Bogomiles et Cathares," *Actes du X*e *Congrès Internat. d'Études byzantines* (Istanbul 1957), 162–65; B. Primov, "Medieval Bulgaria and the Dualistic Heresies in Western Europe," *Études historiques* (Sofia 1960), 79–106. See vol. III of this *Handbook*, p. 340.

[8] H. Rousseau, *Le Dieu du Mal*, Mythes et Religions, 47 (Paris 1963).

order was disturbed by the revolt of Satan, who seduced the angels and inserted them as souls into the bodies of men. They were released from this prison of the flesh by Christ, who is not the Son of God but an angel who seemed to become man in Mary. This Christ lived, suffered, and died in an apparent body. At his baptism in the Jordan the Spirit dwelt in him and remained there until Christ's glorification. He then descended upon the Apostles. He communicated himself to believers through baptism; with the Cathari this was not a baptism of water, but an exorcism, a contact with the text of the Gospels, and an imposition of hands — the *consolamentum*. It imparted righteousness to the *perfecti*, the *élite* of leaders, while the simple *credentes* could be freed of their sins from time to time by the *apparellamentum*, a sort of penance. Death freed the angels for paradise, but it seems that a type of transmigration of souls was not excluded. The demons and the damned were to be annihilated at the end of the world, and there was no bodily resurrection. Thus God's victory was seen as all-embracing. The Trinity was denied, the Incarnation was rejected, and many early heresies, such as Gnosticism, Monarchianism, Docetism, and Manichaeism, were revived.

Perhaps even the heretics who were brought to trial at Liège in 1144 and then left for final judgment by Pope Lucius II were the first representatives of this new but soon increasingly threatening movement, for in the trial a regular hierarchy of hearers, believers, priests, and prelates was discovered among them. Similarly, Cathari bishops were active in Champagne and at Albi; they were able quietly to organize a growing membership. They cropped up in the neighbourhood of the monastery of Steinfeld in the archbishopric of Cologne; the Premonstratensian provost Eberwin corresponded on their behalf with Bernard of Clairvaux, who replied in Sermons 65 and 66 on the Canticle of Canticles. After a three-day religious discussion with the Catholics, the Cathari were burned by the people,[9] despite the resistance of the clergy. They had already gained many clerics and monks of Cologne and had their elect, believers, apostles, *continentes*, and missionaries; it was asserted that they all lived under a supreme authority, a sort of Pope of Heretics. Bernard's advice was to instruct, to warn, and finally to excommunicate heretics. If the canonical penalties did not suffice, the secular power should be asked to proceed against heretics, following advice given long before by Augustine.

From 1165 Catharism spread in North Italy, in the cities of Lombardy and Tuscany. Around 1162 it had even appeared in England. It was able to open schools at Cologne, and a great religious discussion took place at Lombez in 1165. In its radical, absolute form Catharism penetrated the

---

[9] "...tormentum ignis non solum patientia, sed et cum laetitia introierunt et sustinuerunt," wrote Eberwin: *PL*, 182, 676—80 (especially 677c).

Midi by the agency of the Bulgarian Bishop Nicetas and his Italian disciple, Mark; it was possible to hold a council at Saint-Félix de Caraman in 1167.

Independently of the Cathari, there appeared in southern France a lay movement which had been founded as a community of penance and poverty by the Lyons merchant, Peter Waldo, around 1175.[10] He had had the New Testament and several books of the Old Testament translated into Provençal and, after having provided for his wife and daughters, gave away his property. Then he turned to itinerant preaching and soon attracted numerous followers from all classes of society. In groups of two they preached apostolic poverty and the imitation of Christ on the streets and squares, in houses and churches. At the Third Lateran Council Alexander III praised Peter Waldo's call for poverty but forbade doctrinal preaching and allowed preaching on moral subjects only under the supervision of the clergy. When this consent of hierarchy and parish clergy was not obtained, Waldo and his followers declared their independence and then began to preach against the sins of ecclesiastics. They incurred excommunication at the Synod of Verona in 1184. At first they had repudiated and attacked the Cathari, but from 1184 they came under their influence. They now began to reject the Church's teaching authority and to denounce hierarchy, tradition, Sacraments, and the veneration of saints, images, and relics. They rejected indulgences, oaths, tithes, military service, and the death penalty. Their strict moral conduct, oriented to the Gospel, gained them an increasing number of adherents. They too were divided into two classes: the perfect, who were preachers, supervisors, and pastors, and the believers, who were friends, promoters, sympathizers, and ordinary followers. On his own authority Waldo ordained bishops, priests, and deacons. The spread of the Waldensians in the twelfth century was connected especially with the Poor Lombards in North Italy, where they became more radical in their anticlerical outlook than they had been in the Midi. They are mentioned early at Metz and Strasbourg, but their farthest expansion occurred in the thirteenth century.

Densely populated Flanders, flourishing commercially and industrially, became a centre of settlement for heresy. Its missionaries were active in the Rhine valley and along the Danube. The waves of this sinister movement smashed into Gascony, Burgundy, Champagne, and everywhere else in Christendom, becoming a flood that threatened the Universal Church. How was the Church to react?

---

[10] A. Dondaine, "Aux origines du Valdéisme," *AFP*, 16 (1946), 191–235; after the Third Lateran Council (1179), Waldo in 1180 made a profession of faith, probably in the presence of the Cardinal Legate Henry of Albano and Archbishop Guichard of Lyons, as reported by an eyewitness, the Cistercian Gaufrid of Auxerre, Abbot of Hautcombe; *cf.* J. Leclercq in *Analecta Monastica, 2, SA*, 31 (Rome 1953), 194–97.

The people in northern France and the Rhineland killed heretics,[11] whereas the hierarchical Church for the most part correctly instituted proceedings against them. Nevertheless, among both people and Church officials a keen instinct indicated that the movement was foreign to the faith and to the Church.

The situation was different in the Midi. Here the people remained indifferent and uninterested when they did not join in considerable numbers a movement that knew no sins, denied hell, and promised easy redemption by means of a *consolamentum* on the deathbed. If Henry of Lausanne and, before him, Peter of Bruys had been able quickly to gather a following there, this was even easier for organized Catharism. Alexander III repeatedly took a stand against it, at the Synod of Montpellier in 1162, at Tours in 1163. In his correspondence with Archbishop Henry of Reims and King Louis VII[12] he had already outlined the main features of a systematic intervention against heresy, and these were put into fixed form at the Council of Tours.[13] A definite change of methods was thereby announced. Instead of waiting for accusations to be made before officials by the people or the clergy, now the officials were themselves to proceed *ex officio* against heretics. The Inquisition was thereby sketched in principle.

In this way Alexander III, a former professor of canon law, made the teaching of Bologna the teaching of the whole Church. It called for active intervention in view of the danger to the purity of the Church's faith and the unity of her organization. It held that bishops and priests had the duty to inquire into the life and activities of heretics, to obtain information on the existence and type of their gatherings, and to proceed against them with canonical penalties. It seems certain that this last point refers to a search for heretics and the institution of a process.

Later, postponing a crusade to the Holy Land, Alexander III, under pressure from a report by Abbot Henry of Clairvaux, sought through his legate, Cardinal Peter of San Crisogono, to bring about an ecclesiastical and military action in the Midi against the Cathari.[14] Clergy, magistrates, and all orthodox citizens were invited to point out heretics. Those pointed out were excommunicated and imprisoned, their property was confiscated, their castles were destroyed; the penalties inflicted had already been envisaged by the Council of Tours. Count Raymond V of Toulouse was to carry out these measures. When the Cardinal returned to Italy, an actual Inquisition tribunal had met for three months in the County of Toulouse. The activity of the embassy of 1178 was reflected in the legislation of the

[11] See W. Maurer, *Bekenntnis und Sakrament* (Berlin 1939), 60–124 (especially 67–70).
[12] *Bouquet*, Vol. 15, *Epistolae Alexandri papae*, December 1162–January 1163, nos. 66, 67, 69.
[13] *Mansi*, XXI, 1177 f. (canon 4).
[14] *Cf.* H. Maisonneuve, *Études*, 129–33.

Third Lateran Council of 1179. Canon 27[15] described the religious situation in Gascony and Languedoc, admonished the princes to carry out the Church's instructions, and finally called for a crusade in the areas infected by heresy. The same indulgences were announced as for the crusade to the Holy Land. The leadership of the army was to pertain to the bishops. During the Council Alexander made Abbot Henry Cardinal Bishop of Albano and dispatched him as legate to the Midi to inaugurate the crusade. In Canon 27 there was no mention of what was the specific characteristic of the Inquisition procedure: the seeking out of heretics, the *ex officio* denunciation by the ecclesiastical authorities, and the instituting of the process. On the other hand, the cooperation of the secular and ecclesiastical powers in the effort to suppress heresy by means proper to them respectively was clearly and emphatically demanded. The legate's crusade brought only meagre and no enduring results.

In his decisions Alexander III was taking as his point of departure principles already found in Gratian and the decretists.[16] Gratian saw in heresy a serious assault on the dogmatic and social structure of the Church and an attack on the public welfare — the *bonum commune* of both Church and state. In the common defense against such an attack the secular power seems to have been subordinated to the spiritual power of direction and to have been the executor of its judgments. Gratian likewise mentioned the war against heresy as a crusade. The heretic was equated with the infidel, and war against him was meritorious, a holy war. A Christian who fell while participating in it died a martyr. Paucapalea, Gratian's pupil, defended the view that "malos ad bonum cogendos," as did also Roland Bandinelli and the *Summa* of Stephen of Tournai. Through the war on heresy the death penalty was clearly suggested for the convicted heretic.

Similarly, Rufinus in his *Summa Decretorum* defended the opinion: "Armis etiam haeretici compellendi sunt." While Huguccio, like his predecessors, commented on the *Decretum* with reference to Roman law, he nevertheless added one remark that his great pupil, Pope Innocent III, was to take up: that heresy was to be regarded as *maiestas laesa*. Sicard of Cremona regarded the death penalty as justified in the case of obstinate and hopeless heretics, but it should be carried out by the secular power. All the decretists stressed that persons should proceed against heretics not "zelo ultionis, sed amore correctionis." The holy war against them, and hence the death penalty, continued to be considered as the *ultima ratio*, but they were systematically pondered and classified into an emerging penal law for heresy.

---

[15] *COD*, 200 f.; *cf.* R. Foreville, Latran I, II, III (Paris 1965), 146–51.

[16] On what follows *cf.* Maisonneuve, *op. cit.*, 65–91.

After the Peace of Venice in 1177 and its confirmation at Verona in 1184, these beginnings received a first legislative formulation in the decretal "Ad abolendam" of Lucius III, issued 4 November 1184.[17] In it, first of all, a number of heretical groups were condemned *nominatim* by Pope and Emperor: Cathari, Patari, Humiliati, Poor Men of Lyons (Waldensians), Arnoldists, and others. Then the bishops were instructed to take penal action; but apparently it was as yet an accusing procedure rather than one of inquiring. In this respect the decretal comprised only elements of law hitherto in existence. The decretal "Vergentis in senium,"[18] issued for Viterbo by Innocent III on 25 March 1199, first carried the development further by describing heresy as "crimen laesae maiestatis." Thereby the Roman and the Germanic lines of legal transmission converged and set up the presuppositions for the creation of the Inquisition, which was completed in the thirteenth century.

It is plain that the Church clearly saw the threatening danger of an invasion by disintegrating forces into her organism and armed herself so as to meet it vigorously. This she did by inner reforms, by a crusade under her leadership, by an increasing juridical clarification of the possibilities of the penal process against heretics, by stepping up her legislation. The pontificate of Innocent III would bring into prominence the grand-scale counterattack.

CHAPTER 14

Lay Movements of the Twelfth Century,
Christian Knighthood,
Pastoral Care, Popular Piety, and Mystical Theology

From the beginning of the twelfth century the layman[1] became much more prominent than before, alongside the cleric, in the life of the Church. This was a product of the crusades and especially of the vigorously developing urban culture. In Western society the city community, organized in patriciate and crafts, appeared as a new element which clearly acted not entirely in opposition to the structure — made up of nobility and peasantry —

---

[17] See *supra* p. 76. *Mansi*, XXIII, 476–78; Jaffé, II (2nd ed.), 469 (nos. 15, 101); Maisonneuve, *op. cit.*, 151.
[18] *Potthast R*, no. 643, p. 61; *PL*, 214, 537.

[1] The decrees of Vatican II have given rise to a wealth of literature on the laity in the Church, both preparatory and interpretative. *Cf.* Y. Congar, "Laie," *Handbuch theologischer Grundbegriffe*, II, ed. H. Fries (Munich 1963), 7–25, and the bibliography for this chapter.

of the feudal and agrarian organization, but was integrated with it above all in Italy and even in Germany, by means of the families of ministerial rank.[2] To the constantly growing international relations among armies, merchants, and scholars was added the migration of peasants to the cities.[3]

The great response which the preaching of itinerant clerics[4] had found around the turn of the eleventh century showed itself not only in the crowds of listeners who gathered but also in the not inconsiderable groups that attached themselves to the preachers when they moved on and, as occasion offered, settled down as colonies of ascetics. It is, therefore, not surprising that among the laity there was a desire to undertake the proclaiming of the teaching of Christ as a fulfilling of the *vita apostolica* that had been preached to them and was being practised by them in poverty and common life. It was not enough for them to proclaim by example; they now wanted "to preach to the whole world" by word also. Out of the private profession of the faith emerged the public profession in the form of preaching. If Hildebert of Lavardin[5] had pointed to the obvious realization of this aim in the family circle, where parents in a sense officially carried out an ecclesiastical proclamation of doctrine in regard to their children, soon many persons, especially those who had not founded a family or no longer had one, were demanding other fields of action. Heretical movements felt this impulse, and it is not to be wondered that, in addition to clerics, lay persons especially had a chance to speak in them.[6]

Lay activity in the ecclesiastical sphere was seen in this century especially in the cities where, within the unity constituted by an association, the various professions of merchants and artisans joined in fraternities, gilds, corporations, and lodges;[7] these, both in their purpose and even in

---

[2] K. Bosl, *Die Reichsministerialität der Salier und Staufer. Ein Beitrag zur Geschichte des hochmittelalterlichen deutschen Volkes, Staates und Reiches* (Schriften der *MG*, 10), 2 vols. (Stuttgart 1950 f.).

[3] E. Ennen, *Frühgeschichte der europäischen Stadt* (Bonn 1953); H. Planitz, "Die deutsche Stadtgemeinde," *ZSavRGgerm*, 64 (1944), 1–85.

[4] On itinerant preaching, see Volume III, Chapter 52; M. D. Chenu, "Moines, clercs, laïcs au carrefour de la vie évangélique (XIIe siècle)" *RHE*, 49 (1954), 59–89; L. Spätling, *De Apostolis, pseudoapostolis, apostolinis* (typed dissertation, Munich 1947); E. Werner, *Pauperes Christi. Studien zu sozial-religiösen Bewegungen in der Zeit des Reformpapsttums* (Leipzig 1956).

[5] Hildebert of Lavardin, *Sermo 130 ad populum*, PL, 171, 923 A; on Hildebert, see P. von Moos, *Hildebert von Lavardin (1067–1133). Humanitas an der Schwelle des höfischen Zeitalters* (Pariser Hist. Studien, 3) (Stuttgart 1965); on teaching the catechism at home, cf. L. Bopp, "Katechese," *LThK*, VI (2nd ed. 1961), 27–31 (especially 28).

[6] Cf. Chapter 13.

[7] H. Planitz, "Kaufmannsgilde und städtische Eidgenossenschaft ... im 11. und 12. Jahrhundet," *ZSavRGgerm*, 60 (1940), 1–116. K. Bosl in *Gebhardt-Grundmann*, I, 669,

their statutes, made clear the tendency toward a religious and ecclesiastical expression of aim. This was probably most evident among the hospital associations, in which brothers and sisters united for the exercise of charity to the sick and the aged. They were lay persons who did not thereby intend to found a new order and did not assume any such monastic obligations as vows.[8] Gerhoh of Reichersberg thus expressed what was common to all of them: "Iudices, milites, praefecti vectigalium, mercatores, rustici regulam apostolicam sequuntur."[9] The Gospel itself became for them, as later for Saint Francis, the rule of life.

In the new schools also, whose clerical character was long predominant, lay persons appeared among the teachers of medicine, law, and the liberal arts as well as among the students. In this way the laity gained something they had hitherto lacked for the most part: the possibility of expressing their concerns orally and especially in writing. The school and the city naturally aroused in lay persons especially the taste for freedom, and so one can understand why the new canon law sought, among other things, to determine more clearly the frontiers between laity and clergy.[10]

At first the distinction was stressed, and then also the subordination of the laity to the clergy. The rights of the laity in the Church appeared, in their crudest expression, as concessions made by the clergy. The layman could have possessions, but only as much as he needed for his support. He could marry, go to court, make offerings, and tithe. Lay persons had a right to ask from the clergy the spiritual aid envisaged in the order of salvation as organized by the Church. In case of necessity they could baptize and confess one another. It had now been made clearer that the contracting parties administered the Sacrament of matrimony to each other. But the laity had no share in the *ministerium verbi*, which remained reserved to the clergy. Innocent III would merely allow them to criticize the clergy to the bishop in the event of a neglect of this *ministerium*. With a clarity that had been achieved at great cost, the canon law now insisted that lay persons had no right whatsoever over ecclesiastical property and ecclesiastical persons. But at the same time there was also now developing the institute of the guardianship of churches, whereby the laity acquired a very important share of the responsibility for the administration of Church property and the care of ecclesiastical buildings and real estate.

In the eliminating of the law of the proprietary church there appeared in Gratian the initial steps in the development of the right of patronage,

discusses the association-building force of the gild idea as supported by the Church; P. Wilpert - W. P. Eckert, *Beiträge zum Berufsbewusstsein des mittelalterlichen Menschen (Miscellanea Mediaevalia*, 3) (Berlin 1964).

[8] *Cf.* Chapter 24, pp. 183 ff.

[9] *De aedificio Dei*, c. 43 (*PL*, 194, 1302).

[10] For what follows see G. Le Bras, *Institutions*, I, 171–77, 404–23 (*Fliche-Martin*, 12).

whereby an important right of lay persons in the Church was defined. But on the other hand they were ousted from ecclesiastical electoral bodies, from chapters, and from the sphere of ecclesiastical notaries, and above all they were now forbidden in principle to take the clergy to court — they were not permitted to denounce them nor to testify against them, to say nothing of judging them. On the whole, of course, the laity retained an important secular function in the service of the Church: the protecting of religion, especially by the Emperor and the kings as *defensores ecclesiae*, and the protecting of the moral order by the secular administration of justice to the extent that the clergy were not exempt from it by the *privilegium fori*. The position of the King or of the Emperor continued to be ambivalent for in the twelfth century the quasi-sacred status of rulers, despite the Investiture Controversy and the enduring tension between the powers, was still asserted, and hence kings should still not be reckoned merely as laymen. [11]

In general, the juridical prescriptions of the *Decretum* and the ideas of the decretists seem to imply an attitude of mistrust in regard to the laity and cause this delimitation to appear as a sort of defense against encroachments. But one probably cannot say that in the social realities of the century, despite all the canonical depreciation of the lay state and all the high esteem lavished in theological theory on the clerical state and especially on the monastic and canonical ideals, the laity were repressed, despised, or scorned. Particular study of the attitude of a Rupert of Deutz, a Bernard of Clairvaux, and others yields instead an entirely positive evaluation of the ecclesiastical mission of the laity within the limits of their profession and their vocation. [12]

This becomes clear if one looks into the Christian values of knighthood, [13] which appeared in sharp outline in this century, and its estimation by the clergy.

Western knighthood, the chief representative of the crusade movement,

---

[11] W. Ullmann, *A History of Political Thought: Middle Ages* (Harmondsworth 1965), 130–58; *idem, Papst und König, Grundlagen des Papsttums und der englischen Verfassung im Mittelalter* (Salzburg and Munich 1966), 34 (the king as *persona ecclesiastica* or as *rex canonicus;* refer to J. Fleckenstein, "Rex canonicus," *Festschrift P. E. Schramm,* I [Wiesbaden 1964], 57).

[12] M. Bernards, "Die Welt der Laien in der kölnischen Theologie des 12. Jahrhunderts. Beobachtungen zur Ekklesiologie Ruperts von Deutz," *Die Kirche und ihre Ämter und Stände. Festschrift Kardinal Frings* (Cologne 1960), 391–416 (copious bibliography); H. Wolter, "Bernard von Clairvaux und die Laien. Aussagen monastischer Theologie über Ort und Berufung des Laien in der erlösten Welt," *Scholastik,* 34 (1959), 161–89.

[13] C. Erdmann, *Die Entstehung des Kreuzzugsgedankens* (reprint, Darmstadt 1955); F. L. Ganshof, *Qu'est-ce que la féodalité?* (Brussels, 3rd ed. 1957); *idem,* "Qu'est-ce que la chevalerie?" *Revue générale Belge,* 25 (Nov. 1947), 77–86; also, the bibliography to this chapter. A. Borst, "Das Rittertum im Hochmittelalter. Idee und Wirklichkeit," *Saeculum,*

opened itself in a special degree to the tendency toward a sacralization of the states of life and of calling.[14]

It is true that the tension between idea and reality is unmistakable. And at no period of the Middle Ages was there a universally obligatory ideal of knighthood — beside the early fighting man there stood later the courtly knight and then the crusader, — but one can speak, at least for the age of the flowering of mediaeval knighthood (1150–1300), of uniformly constituted values, which were binding on the knights of all the lands of Christendom. In every country knighthood had its special characteristics and hence it was many-sided in its social appearance. But the values produced by the common experience of the crusade saw in the knight the fighter for God, *miles christianus*, in whom piety and the urge to do great deeds merged.

In his treatise *De laude novae militiae* Bernard of Clairvaux describes the religious outlook, even if one bears in mind the restriction that his expressions apply first of all and especially to the Templars. The Christian knight is subject to Christ as the Lord of hosts, the cross is his banner, death is his witness to the faith *(martyrium)* and his prize (certain beatitude). In this way the earlier, and not strictly ecclesiastical and Christian, demands of knightly morality — loyalty and service — were sanctified, just as weapons and standards were blessed and the ceremony of knighting became the consecration of the knight. Adolf Waas even thinks that the knight found his strictly proper character in the crusader and that, without the experience and the stake in the crusade, the Christian ideal of knighthood in the West would not have achieved its full development.[15] God's fighter protected the Church and her goods, fought against the heathen, shielded the weak, widows, and orphans, and unselfishly established God's order on earth. That the reality did not fully correspond to this ideal and not all knights felt themselves obliged by it cannot detract from the fact that in the majority, and especially in the military orders, it acted as a determining motive. Since it found an echo in all of Christendom in its theological refinement at the hands of Bernard of Clairvaux and John of Salisbury,[16] it may be regarded as a type of lay religious culture characteristic of the twelfth century, its probably most impressive form with the most enduring historical impact.

A powerful sympathy on the part of the world of women has been

---

10 (1959), 213–31, refers, like Ganshof, to the many-faceted figure of the mediaeval knight; *cf.* also S. Painter, *French Chivalry* (reprint, Ithaca, N. Y. 1957). Borst is preparing a comprehensive history of mediaeval knighthood.

[14] M. D. Chenu, *Moines, clercs, laïcs,* 77–80.

[15] *Geschichte der Kreuzzüge,* I, 1–52, II, 57–70.

[16] *Policraticus,* Book VI, ed. C. C. I. Webb. II, 1–89. The entire Book VI develops a detailed moral code of the knight in the royal service.

identified in the lay movement in regard to the itinerant preachers at the beginning of the century.[17] Accordingly, one must ask what role woman played in the lay participation thus far intimated in the religious and ecclesiastical life of the twelfth century. Naturally, we are not referring to women religious as such, since they belonged to the strictly monastic sphere, which must be reckoned as a third estate alongside clergy and laity, even if a certain overlapping is to be observed here, as for example in the institute of lay brothers and lay sisters.

Woman began to play a more active role in the social life of this century,[18] above all in the Midi, where the troubadours recognized her central position. A person such as Eleanor of Aquitaine, whose career was able to exert a powerful influence over almost the whole century, can be proposed as a model. The praise of woman dominated lyric poetry among both the French and Catalan troubadours and the German minnesingers. In regard also to woman's delight in education one speaks for many in the career of Héloise, pupil, wife, and intimate of Peter Abelard. Within the family and the kindred a great share of responsibility devolved upon the woman if she was of a correspondingly strong character. One thinks especially of Adele, Countess of Blois, William the Conqueror's daughter, whose picture can be drawn convincingly and impressively from the few extant letters that she received from her crusader husband. And the letters of Bernard of Clairvaux to women acquaint us with noteworthy sketches that point to woman's autonomous position in the family.

The lively tendency to forms of cultivated piety led numberless women of this century to the monasteries of the Premonstratensians and later to the Cistercian nuns. When these were no longer in a position to take care of them, groups of virgins and widows united for a common life near hospitals and leprosaria; from them arose the movement of the Beguines, which experienced its first and strongest growth in the thirteenth century. And the recluse type, in which women followed an eremitical life in cells, according to monastic tradition, often in several cells adjoining under a superioress, experienced a flowering in the twelfth century and also contributed to the beginnings of the Beguine movement.[19]

---

[17] H. Grundmann, *Religiöse Bewegungen im Mittelalter* (Darmstadt 1961), is fundamental; G. Schreiber, *Gemeinschaften des Mittelalters* (Munster 1948, Reg.).

[18] R. Gout, *Le miroir des dames chrétiennes* (Paris 1935); M. R. Bezzola, *Les origines et la formation de littérature courtoise en occident*, I (500–1200) (Paris 1944); M. de Montoliu, "San Bernardo, la poesía de los trobadores y la 'Divina Comedia'," *Spanische Forschungen*, first series, 12 (Münster 1956); E. Russel, "Bernard et les dames de son temps," *Bernard de Clairvaux* (Paris 1952), pp. 411–28.

[19] L. Oliger, *Speculum inclusorum* (Rome 1938); the well known English *Ancren Riwle* was frequently edited in recent times (English edition by A. C. Baugh, London 1956; Latin edition by R. M. Wilson, London 1954); C. H. Talbot, "The 'De institutis inclusarum' of Ailred of Rievaulx," *AnOCist*, 7 (1951), 167–217.

The laity's more intensive participation in ecclesiastical life did not have its origin only in changes in the social structure in the twelfth century. Rather it can be surmised that the care of souls was attended to in these changes in a more responsible manner than persons have commonly been inclined to admit for that century because of the impression created by the pastoral successes of the mendicant orders in the thirteenth century. The Christian people received religious instruction, were made receptive to the sacramental life, and through the cult of the saints and the pilgrimage had a manifold connection with the totality of the Church's piety.

Religious instruction began in the family. Hildebert of Lavardin impressively explained the duty of parents carefully to provide this initial proclamation as a participation in the teaching office of the Church. This instruction was taken up and carried further in the church building by means of worship and preaching. An abundant sermon literature also from this century attests the uninterrupted tradition, even if in the case of bishops this aspect of their official mission often yielded to other duties. Even learned theologians naturally preached to the laity in the vernacular — for example, Peter Comestor, Peter Lombard, Maurice de Sully, Peter Cantor, Stephen of Tournai and Peter of Blois. In twelfth-century England Anglo-Saxon was still used in preaching.[20] Alain de Lille, through allusions in his *Ars praedicatoria,* lets us surmise that sermons intended for particular classes were known. He supplies model sermons for *milites, advocati (oratores), principes (iudices), coniugati, viduae, virgines, sacerdotes.*[21] For the most part they were homilies or catechetical sermons. Only to persons at the universities were questions of any real theological depth addressed. A special type of popular preaching, which was very widespread and effective, must be mentioned: crusade preaching, the organizing of which got under way and developed its basic forms in this century. Organized according to dioceses, entrusted there to the most celebrated preachers, and carried out not merely in churches but also in public squares, on bridges, and at cross-roads, it aimed at as widespread and all-embracing a proclamation as possible. Because it had as its point of departure a uniform theme, through it the piety of the people in all parts of Christendom came to know a definite form, which, together with Saint Bernard's turning to the suffering Lord, can be characterized as a movement from a Christ-piety to a Jesus-piety.

The sacramental life of the people grew to the extent that private auric-

---

[20] Abbot Samson of Bury St. Edmunds (1182–1210) preached in the Norfolk dialect: "... anglice sermocinare solebat populo, sed secundum linguam Norfolchiae" (*Cronica* of Jocelin of Brakelond, ed. H. E. Butler, Nelson's Medieval Texts [London 1962], 40).
[21] *Summa de arte praedicatoria,* cc. 40–42, *PL,* 210, 185–89.

ular confession even included the recommendation of confession to lay persons. Theology was as yet unable to arrive at any completely clear rejection of the sacramental character of such confession. Especially in battles and combats, if no priest was available, was this form of confession of sins suggested, in conformity with James 5:16: "Confess, therefore, your sins to one another . . ." Communion, on the other hand, became more rare. It was restricted to the great feasts and to a part of the rite of reconciliation, in which the parties received the broken Host. It was likewise received on solemn occasions, such as a knighting and a wedding. Baptism, formerly specified for Easter and Pentecost, now had to be conferred soon after birth, if possible on the same day. Now, as earlier, reception into a religious community, the *professio ad succurrendum*, continued to be for the nobles the method of preparation for death that was in keeping with their social position, and the question of burial in the family vault in a monastery seems to have been solved at the same time.

The cult of the saints developed remarkably in the twelfth century, and the royal saints became especially prominent.[22] Of particular interest are the political canonizations of Charles the Great in 1164, Edward the Confessor in 1161, Olav II Haraldson of Norway, and Knut of Denmark in 1100–01. The amazingly rapid spread throughout Christendom of the veneration of the Archbishop of Canterbury, Thomas Becket, assassinated in 1170 and canonized in 1173, marks the climax.[23] Together with Jerusalem, Rome, and Compostela, Canterbury became one of the most important European places of pilgrimage, followed by Vézelay with the alleged grave of Saint Mary Magdalen.[24] Since in the change from the very liberally granted commutations to the indulgence, the practice of which spread powerfully in the twelfth century and even before the end of the century knew of the "plenary indulgence," the pilgrimage, especially the crusade, was recommended as an appropriate penitential work, this form of piety became very widely known, even as a sort of by-product of the growing international commerce. Above all, pilgrimages to shrines of the Blessed Virgin sprang up everywhere,[25] probably as a consequence of the outspoken Marian devotion of the new orders. Even more strongly than in regard to Marian devotion, Saint Bernard's influence is seen in the turning of popular piety to the mysteries of the Redeemer's life and death.

[22] J. Schlafke, "Das Recht der Bischöfe in Causis Sanctorum bis zum Jahre 1234," *Die Kirche und ihre Ämter und Stände. Festschrift Kardinal Frings,* 417–40 (the older literature is given also).

[23] R. Foreville, *La jubilée de Saint Thomas de Cantobéry (1220–1470)* (Paris 1958).

[24] V. Saxer, *Le culte de Marie-Madeleine en occident,* 2 vols. (Paris 1959); G. Schreiber "Die heilige Maria Magdalena als Volksheilige und Bergwerksbesitzerin," *Festschrift Karl Eder* (Innsbruck 1959), 259–75.

[25] E. Baumann, *Histoire des pèlerinages de la Sainte Vierge* (Paris 1941); B. Kötting, "Wallfahrt," *LThK,* X (2nd ed. 1965), 941–46 (bibliography).

Mystical Theology [26]

At the beginning of the century Anselm of Canterbury inaugurated the series of theologians of mysticism, which reached its climax in Bernard of Clairvaux, William of Saint-Thierry, and Aelred of Rievaulx, and was cultivated in the school of Saint-Victor, especially by Richard. Philip of Harvengt (d. 1183) and Guerric of Igny (d. 1157) show that mystical theology was especially at home in the new orders, but monks and canons regular were definitely not the only ones to unite theological speculation with a certain degree of experienced love. [27]

The Church is still living on this spiritual wealth of the twelfth century. In Germany the representatives of mystical theology included especially Rupert of Deutz (d. 1130) and, in his footsteps, Gerhoh of Reichersberg (d. 1169), even though in the latter the bellicose tone often drowns out the prayer. More vigorous in expression were the women, such as Herrad of Landsberg (d. 1195) with her *Hortus deliciarum* (1159–75), and Hildegard of Bingen (d. 1179) with her mystical works that resemble revelations: *Liber Scivias, Liber vitae meritorum,* and *Liber divinorum operum.* [28] Elizabeth of Schönau (d. 1164), with her three books of visions and the *Liber viarum Dei* that was edited by her brother Ekbert, was enabled to exert a great influence through the wide circulation of these writings. [29] But without any doubt the most important contribution to the mystical theology of the twelfth century was made by the great Cistercians in France and England who were mentioned at the beginning of the preceding paragraph, especially since their works soon became the most significant elements in the theological libraries of the West. The systematic theology of the next decades was also promoted by them in essential questions.

[26] Monastic theology is a theology of devotion in its essence and a mystical theology in its more important propositions. The best expositions are in J. Leclercq, F. Vandenbroucke, and L. Bouyer, *La spiritualité du moyen-âge* (*Histoire de la spiritualité chrétienne,* 2) (Paris 1961), and in the articles that have thus far appeared in the *Dictionnaire de spiritualité* (41 fascicles, Paris 1966). The literature is immense and is listed in the bibliographies of the *RHE* and elsewhere.

[27] J. Leclercq, *The Love of Learning and the Desire for God* (New York 1961).

[28] On Hildegard of Bingen, see *Scivias. Übersetzung und Bearbeitung* by M. Böckler (Salzburg 1954). *Gott ist am Werk. Aus dem Buch De operatione Dei,* translation and commentary by H. Schipperges (Olten-Freiburg 1958).

[29] On Elizabeth of Schönau, see *Schönauer Elisabeth-Jubiläum 1965,* ed by the Premonstratensian Canons of Tepl in the monastery of Schönau (Limburg 1965), in particular "Elisabeth von Schönau, Leben und Persönlichkeit," "Das visionäre Werk, seine Überlieferung, Verbreitung und Wirkung in der mittelalterlichen Welt," 17–46 (with bibliography), by K. Köster.

The Byzantine Church in the Epoch of the Crusades

CHAPTER 15

The Byzantine Church from 1054 to 1203

While the date 1054 has quite firmly established itself in historiography as that of the definitive separation of the Byzantine Church from Rome, it was, however, only slowly fixed as such in the awareness of contemporaries and of the next generation. In any event, little was at first changed in the relations of the two Churches, for such relations had lost all cordiality long before 1054. The faithful on both sides and even a large part of the clergy did not at first take note of this date. Impressive evidence for this statement can be adduced, [1] such as pilgrimages from West to East and East to West and translations of relics. The best proof of the confessional impartiality of these latter is afforded by the dossier of the conveying of the relics of St. Nicholas of Myra to Bari or the canonization by Pope Urban II of St. Nicholas of Trani, an itinerant "fool in Christ" from central Greece. Other testimonies are the unhesitating *communicatio in sacris* of pilgrims *en route* from the West *via* Constantinople to the Holy Land and back, the monastic interchange, Montecassino's position of mediator between the papacy, the Normans, and Byzantium, and the not infrequent marriages between partners of the Western and the Orthodox communions. Even the theologians experienced little desire to play up dogmatic differences. They were content to blame the disciplinary peculiarities of the Western Church and were inclined to charge the differences in belief to the Latins' defective knowledge of languages. [2]

---

[1] A good collection of material on this theme is provided by B. Leib, *Rome, Kiev et Byzance à la fin du XIe siècle* (Paris 1924). *Cf.* also the report on the literature in F. Dölger, "Byzanz und das Abendland vor den Kreuzzügen," Παρασπορά (Ettal 1961), 73–106.

[2] The chief role in the controversies of the period was played by the dispute over unleavened bread. Especially interesting for the positions on the dogmatic questions is Archbishop Theophylact Hephaestus of Ochrida in Bulgaria (d. after 1126). He was a champion of the Photian teaching of the procession of the Holy Spirit, but he condemned any disputatious dogmatic hair-splitting by his Orthodox coreligionists and all arrogance, and conceded to the Latins that in their tongue it was not possible to express all the refinements of the doctrine of the Trinity (*PG*, 126, 245–49).

113

Of course, the dissatisfaction existing between the heads of the two Churches could hardly be concealed, and even on the political plane there long prevailed an attitude of more than annoyance. The fault here lay with the Normans. Persons at Constantinople may have been able to understand that the Popes had to make an arrangement with these intruders, but they could only regard it as an act of hostility when, following the Synod of Melfi in 1059, Pope Nicholas II invested Robert Guiscard with territories which were former Byzantine lands and in fact were still partly under Byzantine rule. Thereby the sworn enemy of the Byzantine holdings in South Italy received the Pope's blessing on his further attacks. Furthermore, the Norman conquests in Italy meant, at least in the beginning, a systematic retreat of the Greek hierarchy and the Byzantine rite, and Constantinople had no reason not to suspect that the papacy was also behind this process.

Nevertheless, after the severe defeat administered by the Seljuk Turks to the imperial forces at Manzikert in 1071, the same year in which Bari, the last Byzantine bulwark in Italy, fell to the Normans, the Byzantine Emperor had to swallow his pride and seek peace with the Normans and the Popes in order to assure his rear in the West for the sake of the struggle in the East. Pope Gregory VII was all the more ready for such an understanding, since his own relations with the Normans were none too good. At the same time he was preoccupied with ambitious plans for a crusade, for which he could not dispense with Byzantine cooperation. Not the least significant element in these plans was the hope that in the course of such an expedition the papal claim to the primacy would be accepted at Constantinople and the separation of the Churches would be ended.[3]

In view of the Norman threat to cross over to Greece, there was nothing left for the Emperor Michael VII (1071–78) except to go along with the papal plans. He seems to have made Gregory an offer of ecclesiastical and political negotiations,[4] which induced the Pope to support the Emperor's offer of a marriage alliance to Robert Guiscard: Robert's daughter Helena was to marry the Byzantine Crown Prince Constantine, and Robert himself was to be brought into the imperial family and bind himself to fealty. Such at least is the content of a document of the Byzantine chancery, which, it is true, is not free from all suspicion.[5] From December 1074

---

[3] *Cf.* G. Hofmann, "Papst Gregor VII. und der christliche Osten," *StudGreg*, 1 (1947), 169–81; *cf.* also W. Holtzmann, "Studien zur Orientpolitik des Reformpapsttums und zur Entstehung des ersten Kreuzzuges," *HV*, 22 (1924 f.).

[4] *Dölger Reg.*, 988.

[5] *Ibid.*, 1003; text in *ViVr*, 6 (1899), 140–43. On its authenticity see *Dölger Reg., loc. cit.* The suspicions refer only to the document; the fact of the treaty is confirmed by Anna Comnena (I, 10).

people even had to reckon with the likelihood that Gregory VII would go to Constantinople in person.

The Pope's plans quickly came to nothing, but Byzantium had gained a reprieve. It is true that Michael VII was toppled in 1078 because of his incompetence, and his successor, Nicephorus III Botaneiates (1078–81), annulled the marriage treaty. Robert now prepared for war, and the Pope excommunicated the Emperor in what was the first formal break between the Curia and the Emperor in centuries. This was a serious mistake, not least of all because Rome thereby lost the possibility of carrying on the diplomatic game with two Byzantine partners — Patriarch and Emperor — who at the proper time could be played off against each other. But not even from these events were any conclusions drawn which would merit the label of a formal schism. The next years provide noteworthy proofs of this.

The successor of Nicephorus III, Alexius I Comnenus (1081–1118), was also excommunicated by Gregory VII and from 1081 to 1085 the Normans sought to make their way to Constantinople *via* the Balkan peninsula. But Gregory died and Alexius was victorious over the Normans. The prudent Urban II lifted the censure and extended peace-feelers to Byzantium. Apparently he would have been satisfied with a mention in the Byzantine liturgy, that is, if his name were included in the diptychs. His inquiry, therefore, had to do with why this had thus far been neglected and why the churches of the Latin rite in Constantinople had been closed. The Emperor caused an investigation into these complaints to be made in the *patriarchium* with the aim of determining whether a document on the separation of the two Churches could be found in the archives. The search was a failure, according to the report of the ecclesiastical authorities. In other words, it seems that the Patriarch and his synod regarded the exchange of anathemas between the Patriarch Michael Caerularius and Cardinal Humbert as a personal matter between the two prelates, without consequences for the two Churches. The difficulty, it was said, lay in disciplinary differences between the two Churches, but these could be adjusted. The failure to mention Urban in the diptychs was connected with his not having sent notice of his elevation by means of the traditional synodical. Not all of the Latin churches had been closed, but only those of the Normans, because of the acts of war. The Patriarch suggested that the Pope should send on his synodical, to which a profession of faith was customarily attached; then the inscription in the diptychs would follow and a discussion of the disciplinary differences could get under way.[6] The

---

[6] The official documents were rediscovered by W. Holtzmann, "Die Unionsverhandlungen zwischen Kaiser Alexios I. und Papst Urban II. im Jahre 1089," *ByZ*, 28 (1928), 38–67 (with edition and critique). *Cf. Grumel Reg.*, 953 f.

plan was not carried out. The Patriarch's envoy, Bishop Basil of Reggio, combined this official business with his own fight to restore the Byzantine rite in his see, and it was no longer at that time in accord with the papal idea to submit a profession of faith in such a context.

These events occurred in 1089. It is significant that, despite this failure, relations between Urban and Alexius in no way cooled, but instead the Emperor apparently obtained from the Pope at that time the prospect of military aid. There was agreement, not on the basis of strict law or of dogma, but on the more useful basis of *oikonomia,* of mutual *laissez-faire*. And this was the basis for the common preparation of the First Crusade. And precisely this crusade had the duty and would have possessed the ability to bring the two parts of Christendom together in common distress and hope. That the Pope and the Emperor planned and prepared together can no longer be doubted — Alexius was by no means struck by the arrival of the crusaders as by a bolt from the blue.[7] And the aims and ideas of the Pope and the Emperor must have been basically the same.

But the enterprise slipped not only out of Urban's hands but also out of those of Alexius, and what would have been able to lead to peace actually produced a deepening of the schism. What was decisive in this respect was not, as has been claimed, the discrepancy of the fundamental idea — that the Byzantines were expecting auxiliary troops for their struggle against the Seljuks, while the crusaders had set as their immediate goal the capture of Jerusalem, which even for Urban II had been only a long-range goal and for Alexius was of little importance in view of the state of his diplomatic relations with the Fatimids. The trouble lay rather with the formalities. It is true that Alexius continued to assure, by means of a flexible system of feudal forms,[8] his claims to sovereignty over the territories to be conquered as far as a bit south of Antioch, but the fact that the vanguard of the crusade possessed more enthusiasm than a sense of order or a talent for organization, and indeed that whole crusade armies took the land route going north to south through the Balkan peninsula, which was not prepared for them, led to ever more irksome tests of nerves. And if Alexius finally had to send home the vanguard, which had been routed by the Turks precisely because of its lack of discipline, the *perfidia Graecorum* was there alleged as the excuse for this misfortune.

More dangerous was the fact that the old enemy of the Byzantines, Bohemond of Tarentum, began to play before Antioch a role with which neither Godfrey of Bouillon nor even Raymond of Toulouse would have

---

[7] Cf. C. Erdmann, *Die Entstehung des Kreuzzugsgedankens* (Stuttgart 1935, reprinted 1955), 299 ff.; P. Charanis, "Byzantium, the West and the Origin of the First Crusade," *Byz(B),* 19 (1949), 17–36.

[8] See F. Ganshof, "Recherches sur le lien juridique qui unissait les chefs de la première croisade à l'empereur byzantin," *Mélanges M. P. E. Martin* (Geneva 1961), 49–63.

had anything to do.[9] The papal legate, Adhémar of Le Puy, had been able time and again to adjust the tensions that arose between the Byzantine escort and the crusade army, acting from the notion of a Universal Church that was not torn by schism. Thus it was at first taken for granted by the crusaders that the liberated Orthodox Patriarch of Antioch should be recognized as the only Bishop of that city.[10] But when the legate died, Bohemond was able openly to promote his own policy, which amounted to a withholding of Antioch from the Byzantine Emperor. He started a deliberate propaganda against Byzantium, in which now the theme of the schism and the differences of belief played a great role. The Orthodox Patriarch of Antioch was forced to withdraw to Constantinople.[11] Daimbert of Pisa, who was determined to succeed Adhémar and was sailing to the Holy Land with a Pisan squadron which *en route* had already treated the Ionian islands as enemy territory, joined Bohemond. He supported the formation of a Latin hierarchy and the expulsion of the Greek, and he even partly excluded the Greeks from worshipping at the church of the Holy Sepulchre in Jerusalem. Finally, Bohemond even succeeded in gaining the new Pope, Paschal II, for his idea of the *perfidia Graecorum*, and the papal legate Bruno, who accompanied Bohemond to France in 1104, received the commission to preach the holy war against Byzantium. This was both a turning point and a catastrophe. The reply of the Byzantine hierarchy was not slow in coming, the theological opposition hardened, and Latin bishops, who, passing through Constantinople, entered into theological dispute, ran into a resistance that became less and less possible to overcome.[12]

If, despite everything, the age of the Comneni was an uninterrupted series of attempts to reach an adjustment on the religious plane with the Holy See and hence with the West, these efforts almost always proceeded from the Emperors. They liked to surround themselves even with Western theological advisors, the best known being Hugh Eteriano and his brother Leo, two Pisans at the court of Manuel I.[13] The Emperors sought contacts everywhere, and when they could no longer break the resistance of their

[9] Cf. A. C. Krey, "A Neglected Passage in the Gesta," *The Crusades and other historical essays, presented to D. C. Munro* (New York 1928), 57–78.
[10] Albert of Aachen: "... nostrae vero latinitatis patriarcham eo vivente qui pridem ibi ordinatus fuerat, eligere vel consecrare non praesumpserunt" (*Hist.*, VI, 23).
[11] The new Latin Patriarch of Antioch was named, not after, but before the Greek Patriarch had abdicated. The latter only abdicated in Constantinople. Cf. *Runciman*, I, 307, and now P. Gautier, "Jean V l'Oxite, patriarche d'Antioche," *RÉB*, 22 (1964), 128–35.
[12] Thus, for example, Peter Grossolano of Milan in 1112; cf. V. Grumel, "Autour du voyage de Pierre Grossolanus à Constantinople," *ÉO*, 32 (1933), 22–33. Also, Anselm of Havelberg in 1154; see G. Schreiber, "Anselm von Havelberg und die Ostkirche," *ZKG*, 60 (1942) 354–411.   [13] Cf. O. Volk, *LThK*, V (2nd ed., 1960), 512 f. (with bibliography).

own hierarchy, they still reduced it for the time being to silence. To put it simply, the Emperors had to handle the successive waves of the crusade. Under all circumstances they had to prevent their own capital from becoming the goal of an attack. And they had to avoid aggravating the danger which Paschal II had opened up; hence they could not afford to have the reproach of being schismatics hurled at them by the crusaders in addition to that of being untrustworthy.

And so from the time of the Comneni the policy of union became an element in a policy of self-preservation and eventually a diplomatic weapon which persons used without paying any too much attention to its essentially religious concept. Thereby began also the game over the time-relationship between Western political and military aid and the Church union that depended on it. The help which the Emperor received in this connection from the hierarchy of his Empire was meagre. Sometimes it reluctantly obeyed, but on the whole it did whatever was possible to obstruct the concluding of a union.

Without a doubt the closest affinity to the Western mentality was displayed by the Emperor Manuel I Comnenus (1143–80). His intensive and far-reaching political plans led finally to a special type of union endeavour. His ambition aimed at the reconquest of Byzantine Italy. His first military successes were soon followed by a serious setback: the defeat of the Byzantine troops at Brindisi by the Normans in 1156. But the Emperor did not abandon his plans and he even tried to turn the struggle between Pope Alexander III and the Emperor Frederick Barbarossa to his own advantage. In 1166 or 1167 he laid before the Pope a plan that was as grandiose as it was unrealistic: the Pope should crown him Universal Roman Emperor, since the opportunity was now favourable and he rather than Frederick had a right to this. In return Manuel promised the Pope protection and aid against Barbarossa and also an offer of union, reported by the Roman informant in the following terms: "ut sub una divinae legis observantia et uno ecclesiae capite uterque clerus et populus latinus videlicet et graecus, perpetua firmitate subsisteret."[14] The Pope could not but be greatly embarrassed by this offer, and his acceptance would have meant a complete change of papal policy. However, he did not reject the plans a limine but sent an embassy to Constantinople, probably to drag out the negotiations. Why the plans then failed completely cannot be determined.[15]

[14] On the entire matter see P. Lamma, *Comneni e Staufer*, II (Rome 1957), 123–43; W. Ohnsorge, *Das Zweikaiserproblem im früheren Mittelalter* (Hildesheim 1947), 104 ff.; A. van der Baar, *Die kirchliche Lehre der Translatio imperii romani bis zur Mitte des 13. Jahrhunderts* (Rome 1956), especially 78 ff.

[15] *Grumel Reg.*, 1121 f.; *cf.* also G. Hofmann, "Papst und Patriarch unter Kaiser Manuel I. Komnenos," Ἐπετ. Ἑτ. Βυζ. Σπουδ. 23 (1953), 74–82.

With the death of Manuel I the opposition solidified in regard to Latin and especially Venetian influence in the Empire; economic and national viewpoints probably played a stronger role than religious. The point of departure for a union became ever worse, and a crusade against Byzantium itself became more and more likely. The Emperors of the House of the Angeli wavered indecisively between the various political possibilities. Whatever the reasons why the Fourth Crusade finally moved directly against Constantinople, it was certainly not Pope Innocent III who gave it this direction. The sources in any event make it clear that, for the ordinary participants in the crusade, this turn of the expedition could be sufficiently justified by the schism of the Greeks. And so the catastrophe of 1204.

CHAPTER 16

The Byzantine Church from 1203 to 1282

The Fourth Crusade brought the most important parts of the Byzantine Empire, including Constantinople, its capital, into the hands of "the Latins." This victory, destined to reveal itself as, in the words of Steven Runciman, "an act of gigantic political folly," produced no enduring advantages either for the crusade idea as such or for the security of the Frankish East, while for the notion of the reunion of the separated halves of Christendom it proved to be one of the worst hindrances. Pope Innocent III[1] at first vacillated between indignation over the "abomination of desolation" which the crusaders had perpetrated on a Christian territory and a scarcely restrained satisfaction that this Empire, which had sought to pass itself off as Christian without being actually willing to acknowledge the papal primacy, had finally been brought low. Satisfaction clearly gained the upper hand and gave birth in the Pope to a legal concept, which in this trained lawyer can be explained only in the light of that gratification and which can appropriately be reduced to the dangerous phrase, cuius regio, eius religio. In any event, the papal instructions for the legate, Benedict of Santa Susanna, contained the unmistakable sentence: "... translato ergo imperio necessarium, ut ritus sacerdotii transferatur, quatenus Ephraim reversus ad Iudam in azymis sinceritatis et veritatis expurgato fermento veteri epuletur ..."[2]

National and cultural differences have always been charged with

[1] Cf. W. de Vries, "Innozenz III. (1198–1216) und der christliche Osten," AHPont, 3 (1965), 87–126.
[2] Innocentii III epp., VIII, 55 (PL, 215, 623 f.).

119

responsibility for the divergent disciplines of the two Churches. But these differences only now became decisive, when the self-esteem of the Byzantines was pierced to the heart. The Greek resistance was consolidated on the frontiers of the new Latin Empire, and there arose political structures, all of which aspired to the succession to the old Byzantine Empire: Trebizond, Nicaea, and Epirus. Their rivalries prevented a unified action against the Latin Empire and delayed the recovery of Constantinople and restoration in the former geographical extension. But they were all agreed on a new, specifically Greek Orthodox national sentiment, in which "Greek" and "Orthodox" more and more became convertible terms and which, for all the recognition of the political rights of the conquerors, was directed precisely against the convertibility of the terms "Frankish" and "papal," which can be ascertained with equal ease. All efforts for union were fundamentally shattered on this fatal combination of ideas.

Little as most of the conquerors and papal agents were aware of this dangerous situation, they were equally unmindful of the ancient religious unity of the Balkan peninsula. It is true that the Bulgarian Tsar Kalojan had obtained from the Pope recognition of the ecclesiastical primacy of Tirnovo in 1203 and of himself as ruler of the "Bulgars and Vlachs" in 1204 and that he had even received the crown from the hand of a papal legate. But when he then made contact with the Latin conquerors of Constantinople, he could not fail to note that the Emperor Baldwin, the haughty successor of the Byzantine *autokrator*, made completely unrealistic territorial claims on Bulgarian Thrace and Macedonia. Under the circumstances it was not difficult for the Bulgars' old coreligionists in Orthodoxy, the Greeks, to gain the Tsar to their side. In Easter week of 1205, hardly a year after the fall of Constantinople, Kalojan inflicted on the crusaders a severe defeat at Adrianople, which cost the Emperor Baldwin his liberty and plunged the young Empire into the greatest difficulties. Baldwin's brother, Henry of Flanders, who now mounted the throne (1206 to 1216), drew from this occurrence the not unimportant conclusion that he should deal more indulgently with the sensitivities of the Greeks of his Empire than his predecessor did,[3] and so he conducted even religious discussions not so much in the spirit of the far-away Pope as with that discretion which political expediency forced on him.

And finally it must be emphasized that the papal legates who came to Constantinople with projects of union found there no fully legitimate partners for a dialogue.[4] The last Patriarch of the Byzantine Empire, John

---

[3] *Cf.* especially J. Lognon, *L'empire latin de Constantinople* (Paris 1949), 89 ff.

[4] On the following discussions of union and embassies see especially A. Heisenberg, *Neue Quellen zur Geschichte des lateinischen Kaisertums und der Kirchenunion*, I–III, *SAM*, 1922, 5; 1923, 2; 1923, 3 (Munich 1922 f.), and the most recent presentation in J. M. Hoeck, *Nikolaos-Nekatarios von Otranto, Abt von Casole* (Ettal 1965), 30 ff.

Kamateros, had fled at the arrival of the crusaders and could not be induced to return to Constantinople.[5] He died in 1206 in voluntary exile. This was the opportunity of Byzantine monachism, which could now pose as the spokesman of Orthodoxy without being further obstructed by the Patriarch and his attitude, always powerfully determined by political considerations. This hour of monachism remained decisive: for the future the ultimately determining word in all these questions very frequently was not that of the hierarchy. As early as 1204 the effort to organize a discussion of union, arranged by Cardinal Peter of Capua, foundered on the resistance of the monk John Mesarites. Cardinal Benedict of Santa Susanna arrived in Constantinople at the end of 1205 or early in 1206 as papal emissary. At first he organized gatherings of the Byzantine clergy, in which it seems that John's brother, the deacon Nicholas Mesarites,[6] was the Greeks' spokesman. But then, apparently in the understanding that the monks counted for more than did the diocesan clergy of the capital, he arranged a meeting of the monks, and here again John Mesarites played the decisive role.[7] The monks seem to have been prepared to a certain degree to acknowledge the Emperor Henry as their sovereign but not to recognize the Pope's primacy of jurisdiction or to yield in dogmatic questions.

A weak prospect of success showed itself when the Patriarch John Kamateros had died. The Greeks applied, not to the legate, but to the Emperor Henry for permission to elect a Patriarch. Henry seems not to have been unwilling but he still had to require a certain recognition of the Pope. Two drafts of letters to Pope Innocent III were drawn up by the Orthodox, in the second of which at least an acclamation after the liturgy was conceded to the Pope. It is doubtful that either of these letters was really dispatched,[8] but, if they were, Innocent certainly did not take them into account. A favourable opportunity was lost, for now the clergy of Constantinople contacted Theodore Lascaris, Emperor of Nicaea, and in Nicaea there took place the election of an Orthodox Patriarch, who was recognized also in Orthodox Constantinople. A further and portentous step in the consolidation of Orthodoxy had thereby been taken.

The sequel was that the next papal legate, Cardinal Pelagius of Albano, had to get into touch with Nicaea. After his arrival at Constantinople in 1214 he seems first to have tried to bring the monks to reason, if necessary

---

[5] John Kamateros never abdicated, but neither did he accept the invitation to Nicaea; cf. *Grumel Reg.*, 1202.

[6] On Nicholas Mesarites see *Beck*, 666. A report on a disputation with Cardinal Benedict in Heisenberg, *op. cit.*, II, 15–25.

[7] Report of the conference in Heisenberg, *op. cit.*, I, 52 ff.

[8] The first draft of the letter, from the pen of John Mesarites, in Heisenberg, *op. cit.*, I, 63 ff. The second draft in *PG*, 140, 291 ff. On the date see Hoeck, *op. cit.*, 51.

by force. Now they no longer lodged their complaints with the Emperor Henry but with Theodore Lascaris. And so there was an exchange of intermediaries with Nicaea.[9] Theodore Lascaris was not averse to the negotiations, for the mere *de facto* recognition of his sovereign dignity by the papal legate was a gain at the expense of the Latin Empire. And that is all it was; there can be no question of a success. After the dead pledge, Constantinople showed itself in every discussion with Nicaea as the greatest obstacle, for the recovery of the ancient capital was for the Greek Emperor, admittedly or not, a *conditio sine qua non,* while for the Pope this Latin Empire, that was unable both to survive and to die, constituted an irritating burden. And when at length Innocent IV (1243–54) seemed ready to give up Constantinople he died before he could carry out his plans. In any event people at Nicaea could now believe with reason that the city would soon fall to the Greek Emperor like a ripe fruit.[10] Hence, in the confrontations in the eastern Mediterranean, union soon played merely the role of a political attendant circumstance, to be manipulated according to the situation of the respective opponents.

It was only logical, then, for an Emperor such as John III Vatatzes (1222–54) to undertake to exploit for his own ends the conflict between the Hohenstaufen Frederick II and the Pope. Authentically ecclesiastical disputes played only a slight role; enthusiasm for the crusade had long ago cooled off and a cavalier system of coalitions and countercoalitions with the single aim of one's own advantage became more widespread. The Emperor of Nicaea not infrequently gained his victories by means of Latin mercenaries, and the Latin Empire just as often was allied with the Seljuks. Religious policy in the principalities of the Latin Empire was determined less by papal directives than by the advantage of the dukes and counts who had acquired sovereignty and property. A special position was, in any event, occupied by Mount Athos, over which Innocent III himself had assumed the protectorate, even though scarcely a single monastery apart from the Iberon probably acknowledged his primacy.

In general there prevailed in the entire territory of the Empire the rule that every Greek bishop who had made the oath of obedience to the Pope could continue in office — and a group of bishops had made it. The others for the most part resigned voluntarily or sought to govern their flocks from some safer place. For the monasteries it was probably enough if they paid taxes to the new bishops, and the lower clergy on the whole very likely got off with this tangible gesture. Of course, there were so many Latin clerics in the train of the conquerors who coveted the ecclesiastical property of Orthodoxy that we must allow for a large-scale bestowal of

[9] Report of Nicholas Mesarites in Heisenberg, *op. cit.,* III, 19 ff.
[10] Evidence in W. Norden, *Papsttum und Byzanz,* 359 ff.

Greek benefices and a general impoverishment of the remaining Greek higher and lower clergy. On Crete, which had fallen to the Venetians, only two of ten bishops were still functioning in 1224, and they soon disappeared. And if Venice also made no serious efforts to force union upon the Cretans, neither did she let them have a hierarchy but only *protopapades* in the larger cities, while the monasteries enjoyed autocephaly. Eight Latin sees, including the archbishoprics of Patras and Corinth, were established in the Frankish Peloponnesus, and so not much room was left for the Greek hierarchy. The Greek Metropolitan of Patras sought from time to time to rule his people from the monastery of Megaspelaion. Michael Choniates directed his Athenian flock from the island of Ceos, while a Latin archbishop resided in Athens itself. These examples are typical of the entire ecclesiastical organization in the conquered territory: here and there arrangements with the conquerors, exterior submission, perhaps even opportunism, but just as often stiff resistance and involuntary exile, underground activity, missionary work from a distance. Neither Church turned out to be the victor.[11]

On 25 July 1261 Constantinople fell to the Greek Emperor. A nightmare was over, a dream fulfilled. But it soon became clear that the situation was something less than rosy, for Michael VIII (1259–82) was a usurper, and the opposition, especially that of the average and lower clergy,[12] made serious difficulties for him in the name of the dethroned Lascarids. Trebizond remained outside the restored Empire, and the "Great Comneni" there could bring themselves to show no more than marks of respect to the Emperor at Constantinople. Epirus likewise escaped more and more from Byzantine sovereignty. At most the reconquest was successful in the Peloponnesus. Worst of all for Michael was the fact that the Latin West, which had at first looked on calmly as Constantinople and the shrinking Latin Empire became ever weaker until they fell an easy prey for the Greeks, now suddenly remembered the deserted Empire again and exerted itself, from the most varied reasons, to retrieve the booty from the Greeks.[13] Above all, the Hohenstaufen Manfred pursued this aim, unmindful of the alliance between Frederick II and John III Vatatzes. A power basis which included South Italy and the Greek lands across the Adriatic seemed to him to be important for his own ambitious plans, which were intended to lead to the imperial throne. And if Genoa was prepared to side with Michael VIII, this automatically meant the

[11] For a general view of the situation of the Orthodox Church under direct Latin rule, see Lognon, *op. cit.*, 135 ff.

[12] On this opposition see V. Laurent, "Les grandes crises religieuses à Byzance: La fin du schisme arsénite," *Bulletin Soc. Hist. Acad. Roum.*, 26 (1945), 225–313.

[13] *Cf.* E. Dade, *Versuche zur Wiedererrichtung der lateinischen Herrschaft in Konstantinopel im Rahmen der abendländischen Politik 1261 bis etwa 1310* (Jena 1937).

dangerous hostility of Venice. And Charles of Anjou, successor of the Hohenstaufen in South Italy, assumed all the hereditary claims of Manfred and, through a skillful policy, added new ones.

For Michael VIII there was only one possible, but difficult, ally: the Pope, who, in the ceaseless conflict with the Hohenstaufen, would, in the circumstances, be pleased with a Greek confederate. While in Charles of Anjou the papacy had found the right man to free it from the Hohenstaufen, at the same time it had to dread that there might be no limit to the aggrandizement of this new lord of South Italy. Naturally, an alliance with the papacy meant union, and so Michael VIII was quickly aware of the necessity of concluding one.[14] The point of departure may have been political, but the Emperor took his duty seriously and pursued it honestly and persistently. The difficulties never lay in his good will but always in the circumstances. The monastic world, hostile to union, was, as always, conscious of its own importance, while the hierarchy, in order not to lose the people, had to yield time and again to the monks and at most could go along with the Emperor's plans only from afar and in a diplomatically zigzag course. Despite what the Pope believed to the contrary, the Byzantine Emperor was no longer in a position to impose on his people union in matters of faith by his mere authority. And so Michael VIII went his way, more or less alone. He sought by severity and even by ruthlessness[15] to enforce the Pope's desire in his Empire; so long as he was alive, many a resistance could be eliminated, but with his death his work at once collapsed.

The greatest difficulty in regard to Rome came from the question of priorities. The Byzantine Emperor was at first mostly interested in the papacy's diplomatic and military help and argued that this would best prepare the way for union. But Pope Urban IV flatly rejected this arrangement and demanded ecclesiastical submission as the first step.[16] With Clement IV, Michael tried the promise of having all controverted points discussed at a general council, but again without success.[17] Even his offer to take part in the crusade of Louis IX of France did not dissuade the Pope from his primary requirement of ecclesiastical submission.

The situation changed only with the pontificate of Gregory X (1271–76).

---

[14] Summary of the whole problem in B. Roberg, *Die Union zwischen der griechischen und der lateinischen Kirche auf dem II. Konzil von Lyon* (Bonn 1964).

[15] Occasionally the severity of the persecution of anti-unionists by the Emperor Michael has been exaggerated; for example, it can be proved that there was no real persecution of the Athos monks. On this point see J. Anastasiu, Ὁ θρυλούμενος διωγμὸς τῶν Ἁγιωρειτῶν ὑπὸ Μιχαὴλ Η′ τοῦ Παλαιαλόγου (Salonika 1963), reprinted in Ἡ Ἀθωνικὴ πολιτεία (Salonika 1963), 207–57.

[16] Cf., for example, Urban's letter in Tautu, no. 6, 21.

[17] Tautu, no. 69.

Whatever judgment may be rendered on this Pope, in his Eastern policy he possessed something of the greatness, the restraint, and the clarity of the Pope of the First Crusade, Urban II. Above all, he had an unfailing sympathy for the difficult situation of his Byzantine partner in dialogue, and, even if he found himself unable to yield in matters of principle, still the style of his policy was entirely in the spirit of *oikonomia*. Even Byzantine anti-unionists such as George Pachymeres frankly admitted this. It was Gregory himself who acted *motu proprio* to renew the contact with Michael VIII. It was important that the Pope offered discussions at a general council but was at the same time prepared to enter at once upon political negotiations. Furthermore, he declared that he would be satisfied if at first only a part of the Byzantine episcopate would recognize the union; a universal personal taking of the oath to the union need take place only after the full realization of a *rapprochement* at a time to be determined by the Pope. What he first regarded as necessary was not an oath but a mere promise to acknowledge the Roman faith and the papal primacy after the conclusion of peace in the secular sphere. "Agnoscere desideramus" was the formula which he proposed as his minimal demand.[18] Thereby was created a model case of a *modus procedendi* which is virtually unique in Church history.

Michael now had to work to gain at least a minority of the hierarchy for the union but he actually tried to obtain a majority. A first inventory among the higher clergy did not yield half a dozen partisans of the Emperor. The Patriarch Joseph (1267–75) demanded too much in dogmatic questions and in the disputations availed himself of the aid of a monk, Job Jasites, who was an outspoken opponent of the Latins. The Patriarch even let himself be induced to swear not to assent to union. He seems later to have regretted this oath but regarded himself as bound by it.[19] Just the same, he made it clear that he did not wish to stand in the way of union.

More serious was the fact the *chartophylax* John Beccus,[20] the most learned theologian of the day, was unwilling to support the Emperor's efforts. Since he expressed himself only too frankly, he was imprisoned; but he was allowed a small theological library that he made use of to examine his theological views. This measure produced its effect. To me it

---

[18] Tautu, nos. 101 f. The Pope would have preferred the formula "catholicae fidei veritatem agnoscimus"; as second choice he proposed the possibility of "convenimus in suprascriptam catholicae fidei veritatem," but he was finally satisfied with "desideramus eandem fidem agnoscere, suscipere, et profiteri."

[19] V. Laurent, "Le serment antilatin du patriarche Joseph Ier (juin 1273)," *ÉO*, 26 (1927), 396–407.

[20] On Beccus and his importance see *Beck*, 681–83. V. Laurent is preparing a monograph.

hardly seems probable that his conversion was political in nature, for we know that in prison Beccus read the works of a Byzantine theologian who died just around this time (1272), Nicephorus Blemmydes by name.[21] While vacillating in regard to ecclesiastical politics, Nicephorus in his theological writings occasionally achieved an approach to the Latin position in the question of the procession of the Holy Spirit, in which *a filio* and *per filium* were equivalent, an approach of the greatest importance. And it was this very Blemmydes to whom Beccus would later appeal. Be that as it may, he left his prison to become the skillful and theologically unbeatable champion of union, to whose writings it is due that for the future a small but important party of *Latinophrones* could no longer be disregarded in Byzantine intellectual history. The archdeacon Constantine Meliteniotes, already a staunch advocate of union, now became the closest collaborator of Beccus. The archdeacon George Metochites must also be mentioned as the third member of the group. In the higher civil hierarchy Michael VIII found a champion of his ideas in the esteemed historian George Acropolites, who, while he lacked theological depth, made his own the Christian idea of union as such. In addition there was doubtless a whole group of clerics and lay persons who intended to follow the Emperor's lead, some out of conviction, others out of indifference or opportunism. Finally, in February 1274, the imposing number of forty-four bishops, together with the higher clergy of Hagia Sophia, dispatched to the Pope a letter which recognized his primacy — "primum et summum pontificem esse et nominari" — and expressed their preparedness for union.[22] At the same time the Emperor signed with purple ink the profession of faith that had been sent to him from Rome.[23]

The Byzantine delegation, consisting of the former Patriarch Germanus III, the Metropolitan Theophanes of Nicaea, and the grand logothete George Acropolites, set sail on 11 March 1274 and entered Lyons on 24 June. The Emperor's profession of faith, which they brought, contained the dogmatic formulas of the Latin Church, including the *Filioque*. However, the Emperor asked the Pope to avoid any altering of the Creed in regard to the Greeks and to guarantee their rites. The solemn act of union was proclaimed on 29 June.[24] The question of the addition to the Creed and of rites was presumably arranged, orally but successfully, between the Pope and the Greek delegates.

---

[21] *Beck*, 671–73.

[22] Roberg, *op. cit.*, 235–39, provides a new edition of this letter. *Cf.* also the editions in *Mansi*, XXIV, 74–77, and Tautu, nos. 124–27.

[23] *Dölger Reg.*, 2006, ed. in *Mansi*, XXIV, 67–74.

[24] *Cf.* A. Fliche, "Le problème oriental au second concile œcuménique de Lyon," *OrChrP*, 13 (1947), 475–85; A. Franchi, *Il concilio II di Lione* (Rome 1965).

Shortly afterwards the Patriarch Joseph resigned at Constantinople and on 16 January 1275 a union liturgy was solemnly celebrated in the imperial palace church. In May 1275 the Byzantine Church received, in the person of the *chartophylax* John Beccus, a new Patriarch in the spirit of the reunion of the Churches. But on 10 January 1276 death overtook Pope Gregory X, whose personality was so very necessary for the continuance of the reconciliation of the Greek Church.

Hostility to the Greeks once more gained the upper hand at the Curia.[25] If Michael VIII had approached Gregory X in a manner which pushed the complex of political questions virtually to second place behind the ecclesiastical question, Gregory's successors were disinclined to honour the situation; on the contrary, they were prepared rather to recognize the old hereditary claims of Latin princes to Constantinople. And so the agreement was preparing to collapse. It has been suspected, and not incorrectly, that behind the Curia lurked Charles of Anjou, for whom the union of Lyons could only be a hindrance. Despite all the increased demands of the next Popes, despite all the multiplied formalities and demands for oaths, Michael VIII long continued to be the classical politician of unconditional fulfillment, even though Rome gave him none of the promised aid in the sphere of foreign policy. The resistance of the ecclesiastical opposition at Constantinople became ever harder. A rather vague recognition of the primacy, of the right to appeal to Rome, and of the commemoration of the Pope in the liturgy was all that could be obtained from a majority. But now the Popes were concerned not merely for these points but also for the express addition of the *Filioque* in the Creed, which thus afforded the opponents of union the satisfaction of arguing about a papal or imperial breach of faith.

The fateful development reached its climax with Pope Martin IV, who not only made no objection to an alliance of Charles of Anjou, Philip de Courtenay, and Venice for the reconquest of Constantinople, but removed any last religious scruples when, without any plausible reason, he excommunicated the Emperor Michael VIII on 18 November 1281, and on 26 March 1282, under pain of excommunication and interdict, forbade Catholics to have any contact with Michael or to send him any war material. There can be no doubt as to who it was that so unscrupulously trampled down the weak plant of the new union, for the papal bull of excommunication affected no guilty person, but only the one Greek who, despite his political interests, had done and sacrificed the most for the union.

---

[25] V. Grumel, "Les ambassades pontificales à Byzance après le II⁰ concile de Lyon," *ÉO*, 23 (1924), 437–47; *idem*, "En orient après le II⁰ concile de Lyon," *ÉO*, 24 (1925), 321–25.

CHAPTER 17

The Inner Life of the Byzantine Church in the Age of the Crusades

Whereas in the preceding periods the Byzantine Imperial Church made its importance felt, collectively in synods or in assemblies with the Emperor, only occasionally and for the rest remained curiously amorphous as a population group and particular estate becoming distinctive only in individual personalities, from the middle of the eleventh century a profound change revealed itself. A new *esprit de corps* pervaded the clergy and even made itself noticeable in the constitutional life of the Empire.[1] The causes were varied. The manner in which, for example, the Patriarch Michael Caerularius prevailed *vis-à-vis* the imperial power was certainly due to his own high-handed personality and not to the traditions of his office. Even though he finally failed, dying in 1058 after the Emperor had had him deported, the very action taken against him betrayed his importance. The hierarchy first appeared on the political stage as a compact group under this Patriarch on the occasion of the usurpation of the throne by the Emperor Isaac I Comnenus in 1057.[2] The decisive electoral gathering which enabled Isaac to seize the capital now included not merely the earlier electoral elements — Senate, people, and representatives of the army, — but also the clergy, and it was the Patriarch who presided. And the initiative in the constitutional acclamation of Isaac was taken by a cleric, the Patriarch of Antioch. What had taken place somewhat tumultuously in 1057 was still so impressed on the memory in 1078 that it could be repeated almost as though required by protocol: Senate, people, and synod cooperated harmoniously on a footing of equality to pave the way for the candidate, Nicephorus III Botaneiates.[3] And throughout the twelfth century, whenever the succession to the throne was not assured, and of course only then, the Emperors always sought to induce not only the Senate, army, and people, but also the synod of the clergy, with or without the Patriarch, to join in the formal acclamation.[4]

When the "synod" is mentioned, it is the so-called "permanent synod," *synodos endemousa,* that is usually meant. It consisted of the highest dignitaries of the patriarchal see in deacon's orders and of all archbishops and bishops of the Empire who happened to be staying in the capital. Under the presidency of the Patriarch they regularly discussed and de-

---

[1] *Cf.* H. G. Beck, "Kirche und Klerus im staatlichen Leben von Byzanz," *RÉB,* 24 (1966), 1–24.
[2] Skylitzes, II, 636 (Bonn); Attaleiates, 57 (Bonn).
[3] Skylitzes, II, 733; Attaleiates, 270.
[4] For example, Manuel I, *cf.* Nicetas Choniates, 66 f.; Alexius III, *cf.* Choniates, 601; Michael VIII, *cf.* Pachymeres, I, 74.

cided the business of the Church. The constantly increasing exemptions of bishoprics from metropolitan authority, which led to the creation of ever more "autocephalous" archbishoprics, the pernicious bent of Byzantine provincial prelates for going to the capital as often as possible and staying there as long as possible, and finally the ever growing number of prelates fleeing before the Seljuk occupation of Asia Minor to Constantinople, where they lived on some sort of income, must have caused the number of persons entitled to take part in this synod to grow remarkably at the close of the eleventh century and the beginning of the twelfth. It was only natural that many of these unoccupied fugitive bishops should zealously throw themselves into the political bustle of the capital, which offered them a new and hitherto unknown field of activity, and that, as permanent guests of an institution which was only as such regarded as permanent, they should foster the constructing of a self-conscious *esprit de corps* — even if it was only because of the dissensions that soon appeared within the group. These last were promoted not least of all by the so-called *exokatakoiloi*, that is, the five (later six) highest deacons of Hagia Sophia, who not infrequently combined with the newly elected archbishops against the Patriarch and the representatives of the old, classical metropolitan sees in the synod.[5]

The weapon of these higher clerics of Hagia Sophia was not least of all the canon law, the renaissance of which is perhaps to be seen in connection with the reorganization of the higher school system of Constantinople by the Emperor Constantine IX Monomachus in 1045. The first director of the law faculty,[6] which of course served especially the constitutional law and the formation of the secular officials, was John Xiphilinus, who soon became Patriarch (1064–75) and as such gave new stimulation to the canon law. The special cultivation of this branch of law then found its home above all with the Patriarch's *chartophylax*, who had meanwhile developed from librarian and archivist to being a sort of vicar general of the Patriarch, precisely because of his knowledge of law. Of the three great canonists of the twelfth century, Zonaras,[7] Aristenus,[8] and Balsamon,[9] who commented on the entire *corpus* of canonical sources, the last

---

[5] Under the Emperor Alexius I the *chartophylaces* preferred to resort to this policy in order to consolidate their own position in the synod against the old metropolitans. *Cf.* *Dölger Reg.*, n. 1175, and J. Nicole, "Une ordonnance inédite de l'empereur Alexis I Comnène sur les privilèges du chartophylax," *ByZ*, 3 (1894), 17–20.

[6] Statute for the head of the jurists (*Dölger Reg.*, n. 863). On John Xiphilinus *cf.* K. Bonis, Ἰωάννης ὁ Ξιφιλῖνος (Athens 1938).

[7] On Zonaras see F. Dölger, *LThK*, X (2nd ed., 1965), 1402 f. (with the literature); his commentaries and those of Aristenus and Balsamon constitute Vols. II–IV of Rhallis as well as *PG*, 137 and 138.

[8] P. P. Joannou, *LThK*, I (2nd ed. 1957), 852.

[9] *Beck*, 657 f.

two belonged to the higher clergy of Hagia Sophia, and the greatest among them, Balsamon, was *chartophylax* before he was promoted to the see of Antioch. There began a scholastic and casuistic reflection on the canonical sources which, while it never led, because of the different ecclesiological development, to that sovereignty of the canonical method of thought such as the *Decretum* of Gratian introduced in the West, constituted a counterpoint to the civil law and laid the foundation for a confrontation of state and Church which the early Byzantine epoch had not known in this form. Even the greatest of these canonists, Theodore Balsamon, did not develop in this regard any harsh antithesis to imperial law, and he followed no consistent line in the distribution of powers. But he introduced a manner of investigation which, despite all assurances of the Emperor's privileges in the Church, tended to see in these privileges a concession by the Church rather than a divine right.

The number of clerics at Hagia Sophia and the other great churches in Constantinople in all probability exceeded that at any cathedral in the West. Whether they sought to kill time or to increase their incomes, in any event they provided a great part of the higher instruction in the capital.[10] It is not correct to speak of a reform of the study of theology by the Emperor Alexius I — there was no real study of theology as a discipline of higher education in Constantinople —, since the imperial decree of 1107, which called for the installing of various *didaskaloi*, referred not to the teaching profession but to preaching and catechesis.[11] Nevertheless, it can be established for the twelfth century that classical studies flourished under the care of the clergy of Constantinople, but it cannot be determined whether or not this was in any way connected with the decree. Typical in this regard was the great figure of Eustathius, commentator of Homer, Pindar, and other classical authors, and, before his promotion to the see of Thessalonica, a deacon of the great church.[12] The dogmatic controversies that filled this whole period show also that the pursuit of theology was not unfamiliar to these clerics.

Here too must be sought the starting point in the reorganization of the so-called university at the middle of the eleventh century. Alongside the teaching of law under John Xiphilinus stood the teaching of philosophy under Michael Psellus, the "consul of the philosophers," whose effort to continue the traditional instruction in the direction of a platonizing, "liberal" philosophy is unmistakable.[13] With the successor of Psellus, John

---

[10] Cf. F. Fuchs, *Die höheren Schulen von Konstantinopel* (Leipzig 1926); R. Browning, "The Patriarchal School at Constantinople in the Twelfth Century," *Byz(B)*, 32 (1962), 167–202, 33 (1963), 11–40.   [11] *Dölger Reg.*, n. 1236.

[12] *Beck*, 634–36, and the Introduction of S. Kyriakides, *Eustazio di Tessalonica, La espugnazione di Tessalonica* (Palermo 1961).

[13] On Psellus see C. Zervos, *Un philosophe néoplatonicien du XIe siècle: Michel Psellos*

Italus,[14] this trend, which must not be condemned as a movement toward mere verbiage, was halted by a keen logician with a marked interest in the question of universals, which probably went back to his early education in the spirit of the new scholasticism in his Italian homeland. Something of Abelard's *Sic et Non* can be detected in his method of philosophizing. Conflict with the Orthodox Church, which perceived a danger to the truths of revelation in his free philosophical investigation, did not fail to materialize. Proceedings, not unmixed with politics, were instituted against him. To some extent his pupils remained loyal to him, and they were probably not molested for some time. Without any doubt the best among them was Eustratius,[15] who later became Metropolitan of Nicaea and enjoyed the favour of the Emperor Alexius I. Going beyond his teacher, he measured his dialectical skill on questions of Christology, but without neglecting the fundamental study of the new age, the writings of Aristotle. But this led to the reappearance of the problem of nominalism, and even the Emperor's protection was unable to save him from ecclesiastical condemnation in 1117. From the purely Christological viewpoint the exertions of Eustratius can be explained thus: he aspired to lead back to a tolerable degree the theses propounded with an ever decreasing prudence by a conventional and not carefully pondered "neo-Chalcedonianism."

Despite his condemnation the Christological quarrels were not settled, and it was always basically the same problem, even though with variations, that occupied minds. Furthermore, the result of theological encounter with persons from the Latin West, who were stopping in Constantinople or settled there permanently and did not dispute only the *Filioque*, became evident. Especially worthy of mention in this connection were Peter Grossolano of Milan, Anselm of Havelberg, Moses of Bergamo, James of Venice, and the Pisans, Burgundio, Leo Tuscus, and Hugh Eteriano.[16]

A first controversy was concerned with this question: From what point of view can Christ be at the same time the one who offered and the one who accepted the Sacrifice of the Cross. Soterichus Panteugenes, a candidate for the patriarchal see of Antioch, became entangled in distinctions which gained for him the reproach that he was confusing the unity of

---

(Paris 1919); *Beck*, 538–42; P. P. Joannou, *Die Illuminationslehre des Michael Psellos und Joannes Italos* (Ettal 1956).

[14] P. Stephanou, *Jean Italos, philosophe et humaniste* (Rome 1949); P. P. Joannou, *Ioannes Italos: Quaestiones quodlibetales* (Ettal 1956).

[15] *Cf.* S. Salaville, "Philosophie et théologie ou épisodes scolastiques à Byzance," *ÉO*, 29 (1930), 142 ff.; F. Dölger, *LThK*, III (2nd ed., 1959), 1206 (with literature and sources).

[16] V. Grumel, "Autour du voyage de Pierre Grossolanus à Constantinople en 1112," *ÉO*, 32 (1933), 22–33; K. Fina, "Anselm von Havelberg," *APraem*, 32 and 33 (1956 and 1957) in several continuations; W. Berges, *Jb. für die Geschichte Mittel- und Ostdeutschlands*, 1956, 39–57; A. Dondaine, "Contra Graecos," *AFP*, 21 (1951), 320–446; *idem*, "Hugues Étherien et Léon Tuscus," *AHD*, 19 (1952), 67–134.

person with the duality of natures in Christ, and in 1157 he was disqualified for any ecclesiastical dignity.[17] Implicated in his case were even a couple of bishops, in particular the one who brought on the confrontation, Nicephorus Basilakes, one of the *didaskaloi* of the patriarchal see, but of course they got off scot-free. Soon afterwards the controversy blazed forth under new auspices: Christ's saying that "the Father is greater than I." It can be proved that this dispute reflected the attacks by Gerhoh of Reichersberg on the French and Austrian Gilbertines.[18] A certain Demetrius of Lampe had returned from a diplomatic tour of the West with the relevant information and introduced the dispute into the Byzantine theological world, but we have no exact knowledge of his own position. The question was treated in a whole series of synods, and in 1166 the theological caprices of the Emperor Manuel I Comnenus finally forced a decision. It lacked precision and Hugh Eteriano termed it a sheer scandal, but at Reichersberg people were of the opinion that in it Gerhoh's theses would find support. A final echo of these controversies, called by J. Gouillard "les déviations des didascales," was heard in the theses of a monk, Michael (Myron) Sikidites, who is said to be identical with Michael Glykas. In these was broached the question of the corruptibility of Christ's body and blood in the Eucharist. Synods in 1199 and 1200 basically avoided these theses and reverted to positions which no one questioned.[19]

What is noteworthy in these controversies is that, in spite of certain "early scholastic" tendencies, they avoided the trend toward systematization, proving that persons did not care to have recourse to the newly discovered instrument of logic with ultimate consistency. So far as systematization was concerned, the twelfth century confined itself to the systematizing of heresies and their refutation, as proved by the great *Panoplia* of the monk Euthymius Zigabenos[20] and its revision and continuation by Nicetas choniates.[21] Of tle classical heresies, Monophysitism at most was still a living issue because the political *rapprochement* with Armenia made ecclesiastical pacification desirable. Bogomilism, on the other hand, raised its head.[22] At the very time when the higher Byzantine hierarchy in the capital was attaining to a new self-awareness, it saw itself attacked more severely than ever by the Bogomiles — and, characteristically, the oppo-

[17] *Grumel Reg.*, nn. 1039–44.
[18] P. Classen, "Das Konzil von Konstantinopel 1166 und die Lateiner," *ByZ*, 48 (1956), 339–68; *Grumel Reg.*, nn. 1059–67.
[19] *Grumel Reg.*, n. 1195.
[20] *Beck*, 614 f.; J. Wickert, "Die Panoplia dogmatica des Euthymios Zigabenos," *OrChr*, 8 (no year), 278–388.
[21] *Beck*, 663 f.
[22] Cf. D. Angelov, *Der Bogomilismus auf dem Gebiet des byzantinischen Reiches*, 1, 2 (Sofia 1948–50); D. Obolensky, *The Bogomils* (Cambridge 1948).

nents were found even in the ranks of the provincial bishops of Asia Minor. Alexius I himself was personally involved in the process against a certain Basil, in whom it was thought that a leader of the Bogomiles had been discovered. Its outcome was the synod's assent to death by burning (*ca.* 1110). There remain traces of the writings of a monk, Constantine Chryso-mallus,[23] which point to a disdain for the Sacraments administered by the clergy. In the sees of Sasima and Balbissa in 1143 Bogomilism was even detected among the bishops themselves.[24]

The monastic life of the time still suffered from the evil consequences of the charistikariate.[25] In the reign of Alexius I there proceeded from the pen of the resigned Patriarch of Antioch, John Oxeites, one of the most important reform writings against this institution.[26] Among the best known monastic founders of the age was Christodulus, who, after a number of attempts, finally in 1088 obtained from Anna Dalassena, mother of Alexius I, the island of Patmos,[27] where he established the celebrated monastery of Saint John, bestowing on it complete exemption from any supervision by state or Church. He also gave it a rule, in which he laid down his own strict principles. In the capital in 1136 the Emperor John II Comnenus founded the monastery of the Pantokrator, whose charitable institutions — an infirmary and a home for the aged — were among the most ambitious of any in the Middle Ages, at least according to the tenor of the foundation charter, but they were not directly administered by the monastery.[28] The other monastic foundations of the period also betray the trend to an association between themselves and charitable institutions. At the same time they appear to force the principle of "autodispotism" and to guarantee independence on all sides. The first Serbian foundation on Mount Athos belongs to the close of the twelfth century. This was Chilandarion, which Saint Savas, together with his father, the retired Kral Stephen Nemanja, made the centre of "Serbianism" in the monastic republic.

In spite of many new foundations, which cannot be enumerated here in detail, and of a steady increase of monastery property, which was accompanied by a constant granting of privileges, the moral situation of monasticism left much to be desired. Conditions on Athos again and again called for intervention by Emperors and Patriarchs. The generosity with which the Athos monks granted pasture rights to the Vlach shepherds, together with their families and herds, had as consequences a situation that was totally incompatible with the ideals of the holy mountain. The Patriarch's intervention was impeded by the way in which the monks appealed to

---

[23] *Grumel Reg.*, no. 1007.   [24] *Ibid.*, nn. 1011, 1012, 1014.

[25] *Cf.* Volume III, 423 f.   [26] *PG*, 132, 1117–49.

[27] *Beck*, 646 f.

[28] G. Schreiber, *Gemeinschaften des Mittelalters* (Münster 1948), 1–80.

their canonical independence; in doing so they were supported by metropolitans and bishops, who apparently intended to oppose any extension of patriarchal authority, even at the price of discipline. The Emperor too could be called upon to frustrate intervention by the Patriarch.[29] The complaints of the Metropolitan Eustathius of Thessalonica[30] cast special shame on the status of monastic culture. Above all he deplored that the recruits in the monasteries came for the most part from persons who were interested only in a guaranteed livelihood. He was especially irritated by the turning from the contemplative ideal to a strong economic activity and to the complete neglect of all intellectual interests, which even led to the squandering of the treasures of the monastic libraries. It is worthy of note that to a certain degree Eustathius excluded the monasteries of the capital. Since these monasteries were supported chiefly by pensions for the individual monks, they were probably not obliged to take up the economic reconstruction of their means of subsistence as were those houses which had been jeopardized by the charistikariate.

Some mention has already been made of the ecclesiastical and theological literature of the age. Among dogmatic theologians whose writings were not confined to polemics special mention must be made of Bishop Nicholas of Methone with his work, which, whatever may be thought of its originality, supplies us with a valuable testimony for the renaissance of Neoplatonism at this time through his polemic against Proclus.[31] Also to be noted is the probably never entirely completed attempt at a total exposition of the work of Christian salvation by one Doxopatres, probably Nilus, of whose great undertaking in five books the manuscripts, so far as they are available, have preserved only two with 466 chapters.[32]

While the preceding period was the great age of hagiography, characterized by the work of Simeon Metaphrastes, there now began in the great contemporary homiliaries the "codification" of the homiletic tradition. In the first place stood John Xiphilinus, nephew of the Patriarch Xiphilinus; making copious use of Chrysostom he compiled the standard homiliary.[33] The Patriarch John IX Agapetus (1111–34), following the work of Xiphilinus, compiled what is today called the "Patriarchate homiliary."[34] Italo-Greek homiletics was represented by Philagathus of Cerami,[35] whose col-

[29] P. Meyer, *Die Haupturkunden für die Geschichte der Athosklöster* (Leipzig 1894), especially 166–69.
[30] L. F. Tafel, *Eustathii opuscula* (Frankfurt 1832), 214–67; *PG*, 135, 729–909.
[31] *Cf.* T. Niggl, *LThK*, VII (2nd ed. 1962), 993; *Beck*, 624 ff.
[32] *Beck*, 620 f.
[33] A. Ehrhard, *Überlieferung und Bestand der hagiographischen und homiletischen Literatur der griechischen Kirche*, I, 3 (Berlin 1943), 525–59.
[34] *Ibid.*, 559–631.
[35] *Ibid.*, 631–81; G. Rossi Taibbi, *Sulla tradizione manoscritta dell'omiliario di Filagato da Cerami* (Palermo 1965).

lection of sermons was also accepted in the eastern half of the Empire. The south was represented by Neophytus Enkleistus, who founded a monastery on Cyprus and left a three-volume *Panegyrikon*.[36] The period under consideration was the climax of an extensive Byzantine scriptural exegesis; an example is the work of Theophylact, Archbishop of Bulgaria, an epitome of Saint John Chrysostom, in the form of a commentary on the books of the Bible but with a strongly pronounced *catena* characteristic.[37] The Metropolitan Nicetas of Heraclea, a contemporary of Theophylact, was the last great Byzantine catenist, whose influence not even Thomas Aquinas could escape.[38]

In short, the time seemed full of most promising beginnings. How they would have developed if the Fourth Crusade had not been diverted can, of course, not be determined. The twelfth century was a period when the West was drawing closer than ever before to the Byzantine East, here and there provoking dangerously, elsewhere ready for symbiosis. The incipient economic "sell out" to the Italian maritime cities, forced by the needs of foreign policy, could not but nourish the animosity felt in many circles for all that was Western, and it is here that the reason is to be sought why Byzantine resistance was especially stiff in the spheres of theology and Church unity. This was no longer, it is true, a resistance which drew its strength from an absolute feeling of superiority. Men like Hugh Eteriano gave Byzantium an idea of the theological potentiality of the West, and hence in Byzantine theological circles of the century a not insignificant nervousness was apparent. To be regarded not as a cause but as concomitants, the to some extent painful confrontations on the already mentioned "déviations des didascales" were a reason why the distrust of whatever was regarded as "scholasticism" became stronger rather than weaker. But in this way official Byzantium permanently excluded itself from the great Western progress in scientific theology. Elsewhere, however, for example in the world of mysticism and of monastic spirituality, this Byzantine century did not dispose of those leading minds who in concentration on this field would have been able to build a counterweight equal to scholasticism, such as Hesychasm and Palamism formed — whether legitimately or not is undecided — in the late Byzantine period. And if the twelfth century made available to Byzantium for the first time a real encounter with the freer Western ecclesiastical organization, the political presuppositions were lacking for deducing sound consequences for its own ecclesiastical system. The presuppositions were not present until a generation later. Then persons would take up the experiences of the twelfth century but without having enough time left.

[36] Ehrhard, *op. cit.*, 681–86.   [37] *Beck*, 649–51.
[38] *Ibid.*, 651–53.

The Papacy at the Height of its Power
(1198—1216)

The period known as the High Middle Ages was without any doubt dominated by the personality of the Pope whose pontificate joined the twelfth and thirteenth centuries together. In it there matured those energies in theology and canon law which had begun to unfold in the twelfth century. At the same time the main features of the thirteenth-century development appeared in the ecclesiastical decisions of this reign. Rarely has a Pope found in his contemporaries so unanimously favourable a judgment as did Innocent III,[1] and later historiography has wondered why the distinction of "the Great" has not been accorded him.[2] Most of the problems pertaining to the basic stock of the intellectual life of Church History in the High Middle Ages found under Innocent a settlement which seemed to approach a real solution. He sought to bring the relationship of *regnum* and *sacerdotium*, even in its special form of tension between the papacy and the imperial office, to a practical and a theoretical solution. The Church's commission to foster the sanctification of the world through the proclaiming of the Gospel and the administration of the Sacraments obtained in Innocent an extraordinarily talented pontiff, who made this commission the program of his reign. The demand for poverty, made energetically and angrily on the Church of the poor Saviour by the saints, the laity, the heretics of the twelfth century, did not die away unheard by this Pope. If the irresistible march of canon law presented the Church with a danger, with the institutionalizing of what must properly be filled by the charism of love, namely the religious life of Christendom, then Innocent sought not unsuccessfully to find the balance between law and love. Between theology as a science and the mystical knowledge of God in the

---

[1] Critical voices, such as that of Walther von der Vogelweide, come from the sphere of polemics. *Cf.* K. Burdach, "Der Kampf Walthers von der Vogelweide gegen Innocenz III. und gegen das vierte Lateranische Konzil," *ZKG*, 55 (1936), 445–522.

[2] *Haller,* III, 471, and *Seppelt,* III, 389.

imitation of Christ there was developing a tension which threatened to lead to a diastase, perhaps even to an alienation of the two. Here too Innocent could intervene as mediator. It was his great merit to see the reform needs of the Church in their full compass and in his constant exertions for them to be in accord with the justified concern of criticism, including that of heretics; at the same time he thereby made the most positive contribution to overcoming this dangerous threat to the unity and the truth of Christendom.

The presupposition for these exertions was not merely a claim, but a really exercised authority over Christendom, the possession of a real *dominium orbis christiani*, with which was joined the possibility of enforcing a planning, adjusting, and clarifying will as far as the frontiers of Christendom. Hence, the motto of this unique pontificate of the High Middle Ages can be concisely stated by saying that it sought to realize a "spiritual *dominium mundi*."

CHAPTER 18

Personality and Program of Innocent III

The Cardinal Deacon Lothar dei Conti di Segni was not yet thirty-eight years old when, on the day of the death of his predecessor, Celestine III, 8 January 1198, in the Septizonium of Septimius Severus, whose ruins had been turned into a stronghold by the Frangipani, he received a majority of votes in the first balloting and all of them in the second. Accepting the election he styled himself Innocent III, probably in memory of Innocent II, whom he highly esteemed, together with Saint Bernard of Clairvaux, as a Pope of reform and the one who had convoked the Second Lateran Council.

The son of Trasimondo di Segni, he was born at the castle of Gavignano at the end of 1160 or the beginning of 1161. Through his mother, who was of the Scotti family, he was closely linked with the Roman patriciate. His family's early move to Rome enabled him to obtain his first education there. It was later entrusted to Peter Ismael, probably in the monastery of Sant'Andrea, and was then completed with his philosophical and theological studies at Paris, which lasted till 1187.

Among his teachers at Paris was Peter de Corbeil, whom he was later to appoint as Bishop of Cambrai and eventually as Archbishop of Sens. His fellow-students included Stephen Langton and Robert de Courçon, both of whom he later promoted to the cardinalate, and Eudes de Sully, who, as Bishop of Paris, was eventually his man of confidence in France.

At the Fourth Lateran Council he set up a monument to the school of Paris under the auspices of the Master of the Sentences through the mention of the Lombard in a context that gave him the highest praise. Occasional remarks in sermons and letters indicate how much Paris meant to him, even though later he did not show the same confidence in the dialectical method which he had clearly entertained during his studies. In 1187 he left Paris in order to pursue law at Bologna, especially under the most celebrated of the decretists, Huguccio of Pisa. Innocent later made him Bishop of Ferrara.

In November of the year when he transferred to Bologna Lothar received the subdiaconate from Pope Gregory VIII. In 1189 his maternal uncle, Clement III, brought him into the College of Cardinals, bestowing on him the deaconry of Santi Sergio e Bacco,[3] which Clement had himself formerly administered. Lothar's activity at the Curia, more in matters of ecclesiastical jurisdiction than in political questions of any great moment, allowed him time for literary works on ascetical and moral, dogmatic, and canonical topics. Best known and much read until the sixteenth century was his *De miseria humane conditionis*,[4] which sketches a picture of man under the shadow of sin. A corresponding treatise on the dignity of man in the light of grace, which was to round out the work by supplementing and completing it, was not finished. As Pope, he revised his *De missarum mysteriis*[5] and the *De quadripartita specie nuptiarum*.[6]

---

[3] This deaconry, also called *diaconia Fori Romani*, was suppressed by the Constitution "Religiosa" of Sixtus V of 13 April 1587; cf. *CICfontes*, I (1923), no. 160, p. 295.

[4] *PL*, 217, 701–46, now critically edited by M. Maccarone, *Lotharii Cardinalis (Innocentii III) De Miseria humane conditionis* (Lugano 1955). Maccarone was able to enumerate 435 manuscripts but still others are being discovered; cf. D. R. Howard, "Thirty New Manuscripts of Pope Innocent III's De Miseria humanae conditionis," *Manuscripta*, 7 (1963), 31–35. Monographs on this work by: A. Nagy, *De tractatu de miseria humanae conditionis Innocentii III* (Budapest 1943); W. Will, "Innocenz III. und sein Werk 'Über das Elend des menschlichen Daseins,'" *Humanismus, Mystik und Kunst in der Welt des Mittelalters*, ed. J. Koch (Leiden and Cologne 1953), 125–36; M. Di Pinto, "Il 'De miseria conditionis humanae' di Innocenzo III,'" *Studi medievali A. De Stefano* (Palermo 1956), 177–201; R. Bultot, "Mépris du monde, misère et dignité de l'homme dans la pensée d'Innocent III," *CCivMéd*, 4 (1961), 441–56.

[5] *PL*, 217, 763–916, under the title: *Mysteriorum Evangelicae Legis et Sacramenti Eucharistiae Libri Sex*, also called *De Sacro Altaris Mysterio*. In "Innocenzo III prima del pontificato," *ADRomana*, 66 (1943), 59–134, Maccarone established the identity of the work under these different titles.

[6] *PL*, 217, 921–68. H. Tillmann calls the work "a less personal occasional writing" (*Papst Innocenz III.*, 14). It was made use of by M. Wilks, "Chaucer and the Mystical Marriage in Medieval Political Thought," *BJRL*, 44 (1961 f.), 489–530. His works show the young Cardinal in accord with the theological tradition of the twelfth century: les with the Parisian dialectical systematization than with the Bernardine-Victorine mysticism and the conservative moral and hortatory sermon literature. The six books *De missarum mysteriis*, an allegorical and mystical interpretation of the Roman liturgy, represent a literary and

Toward the close of the pontificate of Celestine III the Cardinal Deacon Lothar must have been more active than before in the strictly political discussions and decisions of the Curia, for otherwise the attention of the electors of 8 January 1198, which was so quickly concentrated on him, is inexplicable.

Innocent III postponed his episcopal consecration and coronation till the feast of Saint Peter's Chair, 22 February, a date that naturally suggested itself because of its symbolic importance. In this he recalls Gregory VII, who after his election on 22 April 1073 waited till the feasts of Saints Peter and Paul, 29 and 30 June, for his consecration and coronation.

The electors must have observed extraordinary qualities of intellect and character in Lothar di Segni in order to give all their votes to the youngest of their number. If they had expected that he would be capable of leading the Church out of the prevailing stagnation into which a series of weak pontificates of superannuated Popes after Alexander III had led her, their hopes were confirmed by history. Innocent III took up his office in the consciousness of a divine summons, and from it apparently derived that much admired sureness of decision and the essentially invariable consistency of his administration — qualities that endured to the end. His superb theological formation enabled him in almost every one of his innumerable letters and decretals to stamp with fundamentally theological explanations a word of instruction which revealed him as the supreme herald of conservative ecclesiastical doctrine. To this was added his equally outstanding command of canon law whose methods he so perfecthy dominated both in his proceedings and his decisions and was able to carry out so masterfully that in his hand the papal judicial practice was regarded by many experts as a higher school of their discipline. Furthermore, he possessed, perhaps from his mother's Roman family, a sophistication in politics and its ways, especially the instinct for the possible, the famed "snap judgment," which "in every situation caused [him] to desire only the possible, but all of it." Innocent

> was born to rule. Fate had bestowed on him all the gifts for this
> purpose: an inexhaustible wealth of invention, the most skilful
> handling of men, an unrivalled combining of tenacity of will with
> flexibility in execution, the boldest energy in endeavour and the most
> sober calculation of the means, the vision of a genius for what was
> great, and painstaking diligence in details. [7]

theological *genre* going back to the Early Middle Ages. Innocent's manner of preaching was determined by the Paris tradition; *cf.* J. Chatillon, "Sermons et prédicateurs victorins de la seconde moité du XIIᵉ siècle," *AHD*, 32 (1965), 7–60.

[7] *Haller*, III, 301 f.

From his years at Paris and Bologna — and at Bologna because of Huguccio[8] especially — he possessed a clearly reasoned notion, which would be a decisive factor in his pontificate, of the fulness of the authority pertaining to him as Pope, of its relationship to the power of secular rulers, above all to that of the Emperor, in whom authority as King in Germany, Burgundy, and Italy differed from the function and power which were his as ruler of the *Sacrum Imperium Romanum*.[9]

To speak of a program of government in the strict sense would be as much a mistake in regard to the accession of Innocent III as at any other change of pontificate. But from the decrees and letters of the first months one can form a sketch of the most important problems which, even in a survey of the entire pontificate, must be regarded as the Pope's chief concerns: order in the Papal State, its protection *vis-à-vis* the threats of expansion from south and north, intensification of the crusade idea and promotion of the project of a crusade, overcoming of the progressively stronger and more dangerous heretical movements, and, finally, what lay at the basis of all the rest and took precedence over them, the reform of the Church in head and members. No one of these four concerns nor all of them together were new. They somehow made their presence known as a program, and as an effort to do justice to the program, in all the pontificates of the twelfth century and determined the legislation of the three Lateran Councils. Innocent III again took up the themes of the Gregorian reform and sought to realize them on a lasting basis.

Celibacy was always, or perhaps even again, a remote and only defectively realized ideal in the Latin West. Simony had by no means been eradicated but again and again emerged in various forms on the lowest and the highest plane. The freedom of the lesser churches, of the bishoprics, and even of the papacy itself remained, as before, either a postulate or at most a precarious achievement. In the monastic world the Cistercian *élan*, which more than anything else had distinguished the twelfth century, was in danger of dying out; had not Alexander III already sent letters of admonition to the general chapter? The canons regular and the Premonstratensians also stood in urgent need of new impulses. The Pope may have

---

[8] *Cf.* M. Ríos Fernández, "El primado del Romano Pontífice en el pensamiento de Huguccio de Pisa decretista," *Compostellanum*, 6 (1961), 47–97, 7 (1962), 97–149, 8 (1963) 65–90. G. Catalano, *Impero, regni e sacerdozio nel pensiero di Uguccio da Pisa* (Milan 1959).

[9] F. Kempf, *Papsttum und Kaisertum bei Innocenz III., Miscellanea Historiae Pontificiae*, 19 (Rome 1954), is fundamental. It has been further elaborated by its author in other articles, the latest being "Kanonistik und kuriale Politik im 12. Jahrhundert," *AHPont*, 1 (1963), 11–52. But Kempf's theses must be looked at together with the results of the researches of Walter Ullmann and his school and now with B. Tierney, "The Continuity of Papal Political Theory in the Thirteenth Century. Some Methodological Considerations," *MS*, 27 (1965), 227–45, and W. Ullmann, *Papst und König. Grundlagen des Papsttums und der englischen Verfassung im Mittelalter* (Salzburg and Munich 1966).

entertained little hope that the comfortable peace of the Benedictines could be aroused to life again. Nevertheless, his letters betray a lively awareness of his expecting substantial help from the cooperation of the orders precisely for his work of renewal in the Church. In many respects Innocent III suffered especially from the political and human strife within Latin Christendom, the ceaseless quarrelling of kings and princes, and the interminable feuds of barons and knights, of cities and communes. Internal peace, not only for its own sake, but also for the sake of the external tasks on the frontiers of Christendom became one of his central concerns.

From the outset and, without interruption, to the end of his pontificate, Innocent III carried out his *officium pastorale* in the consciousness of possessing the full authority necessary for it. This corresponded to the comprehensive extent of the office, which was to bear responsibility first for the Roman Church and its property, the *Patrimonium Petri,* and then for all of Christendom. The most recent research[10] has rendered obsolete the previous idea prevailing in historiography, namely that Innocent intended to develop this office into a sort of world rule or that he felt he could exercise it only in an actual world dominion. Neither the extant texts of his official letters, his sermons, and the acts of his councils nor his legal, pastoral, and political decisions permit such an interpretation of his administration. Quite the contrary: the more profoundly they are all investigated in the context of the development of the pontificate and the individual records in their context of situation and document, there definitely emerges an essentially spiritual profile of this Pope. The *plenitudo potestatis* was understood by Innocent, just as it had been taught by his mentor Huguccio, as a *plenitudo potestatis ecclesiasticae,* not as a fulness embracing all spiritual and secular power whatever. It must be regarded as a defining of what is today termed the primacy of jurisdiction of the Bishop of Rome. An overlapping of this power on to the sphere of secular law was not excluded in Innocent's mind, but it happened only in a subsidiary way, when, in accord with the current theory of emergency, cases were referred to the Pope's decision in which the secular stages of appeal had broken down; for example, in a case of strife between kings, when no superior judge, deciding with authority, could be called upon. Emperor

---

[10] See the works of S. Mochy Onory, *Fonti canonistiche dell'idea moderna dello stato* (Milan 1951); A. Hof, "'Plenitudo potestatis' und 'Imitatio imperii' zur Zeit Innocenz' III.," *ZKG,* 66 (1954 f.), 39–71, and the contributions of H. Tillmann, F. Kempf, A. M. Stickler, *et al. Cf.* also the summary by A. Walz, "'Papstkaiser' Innocenz III. Stimmen zur Deutung," *Sacerdozio e Regno da Gregorio VII a Bonifacio VIII, Misc. Hist. Pont.,* 18 (Rome 1954), 127–38. B. Tierney, *loc. cit.,* best summarizes the state of the discussion: "Innocent III and Innocent IV expressed substantially the same opinion on problems of church and state ... their position cannot be adequately characterized by the two currently fashionable terms, 'dualistic' and 'hierocratic'" (p. 234).

and kings received their power, as Innocent recognized, directly from God, just as the papacy did. The kingship claimed by Innocent himself as a secular dominion referred to the royal possessions of the Roman Church in Central Italy, the *Patrimonium Petri*, where he considered himself as a King among kings, and not, following the Carolingian model, as the autonomous ruler of a territory. Perhaps the claim to possess not only spiritual but also secular power referred to the coercive power of the Church intervening even in secular legal relationships, to papal intervention, by means of instructions, *ratione peccati*.

Innocent had his idea concisely formulated at the Fourth Lateran Council:

> Just as we do not want the laity to usurp the rights of clerics, similarly we must see to it that clerics do not claim the rights of the laity. And so we forbid all clerics to extend their privileges to the prejudice of secular authority, under the pretext of the liberty of the Church. On the contrary, they should be content with the written law and the previously approved customs, so that what is Caesar's will be rendered to Caesar and what is God's to God, in accord with the objectively right order which is proper to each.[11]

In addition to the separation of powers, Innocent stressed the higher unity of Christendom and the consequent rights of the Holy See, and he likewise intended to maintain his own rights relevant to the Empire,[12] which in his view did not affect the principle that the imperial authority was derived directly from God. Kings, princes and magistrates within the frontiers of Christendom were to the Pope not merely bearers of an independent power of jurisdiction but at the same time outstanding members of the mystical body of the Church. As such, not only as private persons but precisely as officials, they were subject to the pastoral care of the Roman Bishop. Only thus can one interpret the official statements of emperors and kings when in their correspondence with the Pope they spoke of obedience, devotion, and readiness to carry out the mandates of the Holy See. Innocent himself defined the limits of his full authority, which lay fixed on the one hand in the *ius divinum*, on the other hand in the conscience of the individual. By its very nature as *potestas ecclesiastica* it was clearly distinct from the *potestas saecularis*. Canon law still indicates that any clearer delimitation of boundaries is not always possible

---

[11] COD, 229 (footnotes 25–31) (Constitutio 42). "Sicut volumus ut iura clericorum non usurpent laici, ita velle debemus, ne clerici iura sibi vindicent laicorum. Quocirca universis clericis interdicimus, ne quis praetextu ecclesiasticae libertatis suam de caetero iurisdictionem extendat in praeiudicium iustitiae saecularis, sed contentus exsistat constitutionibus scriptis et consuetudinibus hactenus approbatis, ut quae sunt Caesaris reddantur Caesari, et quae sunt Dei Deo recta distributione reddantur."
[12] F. Kempf, *Papsttum und Kaisertum*, 314–25.

in practice.[13] The decision as to whether a matter pertained to the sphere of divine or of human law, in which the Pope possessed the power of dispensing, was left by Innocent to tradition and in practice to deliberation by a council.

Under Innocent III the Pope's position in the Church did not become something basically different. But he gave to the doctrine of the primacy a strict formulation and systematic justification and deeply impressed on the consciousness of the Western Church the Roman Bishop's position as the ordinary holder of all ecclesiastical power...[14]

CHAPTER 19

The Spiritual Monarch as Arbiter Mundi

The order of Christendom — *pax et iustitia* — was entrusted to two powers, the spiritual power, which belonged in its fulness to the Pope, and the secular power, which was shared by a number of bearers: kings, princes, magistrates. Among these secular authorities, the imperial dignity was, in accord with tradition, confided to the German King. To the imperial office, because of its function as *advocatus* of the Roman Church, pertained a certain universality that had never been precisely defined.[1] The intimate interrelationship of the spiritual and the secular in the whole of Christendom in the High Middle Ages thus caused the Pope, whose plenitude of spiritual power was undisputed, to appear as its real monarch. The real power of the Emperor, on the other hand, never went beyond the bounds of those areas over which he reigned as King: Germany, Burgundy, Lombardy. Since, moreover, the spiritual power, because of the interrelationship just mentioned, maintained also in the secular areas claims which were partly of public law or of a political nature, there belonged to the monarchy of its holder an enhanced importance, which was asserted in many ways, if not always successfully, during the pontificate of Innocent III, thanks both to his statesmanlike personality and also to the total political situation at the turn of the century, which

---

[13] *CIC*, c. 1553, par. 2: "... in causis in quibus tum Ecclesia tum civilis potestas aeque competentes sunt, quaeque dicuntur mixti fori, est locus praeventioni."

[14] H. Tillmann, *Innocenz III.*, 38. O. Hageneder, "Über das Sonne-Mond-Gleichnis bei Innocenz III.," *MIÖG*, 65 (1951), 340–68; *idem*, "Exkommunikation und Thronfolgeverlust bei Innocenz III.," *RömHM*, 2 (1957 f.), 9–50.

[1] *Cf.* F. J. Schmale, "Römisch-deutsches Kaisertum," *LThK*, V (2nd ed. 1960), 1247–50 (bibliography), and especially F. Kempf, "Das mittelalterliche Kaisertum," *Mainau-Vorträge*, ed. T. Mayer (Constance 1956), 225–42; T. Mayer, "Papsttum und Kaisertum," *HZ*, 157 (1959), 1–53; H. Grundmann, "Kirchenfreiheit und Kaisermacht um 1190 in der Sicht Joachims von Fiore," *DA*, 19 (1963), 353–96.

was favourable to him. Innocent did not have his gaze fixed on world domination in the strict sense of the phrase; he always acted ultimately from motives deriving from his all-embracing and universal responsibility for the welfare of all of Christendom: for *pax et iustitia*. He aspired to promote this *mundus christianus* and its peace as arbiter, able, it is true, to dispose of only a limited and by no means always effective coercive power, but also in possession of the moral power of his universally acknowledged primacy as the Vicar of Christ. Whoever confessed Christ — and this included kings, princes, and magistrates — was for that very reason subject, in respect to his thinking and acting as a Christian, to that directing authority of the Vicar of Christ[2] which Innocent made use of with amazing assurance and in countless cases everywhere throughout Christendom.

The Papal State

The freedom of the Roman Church, her Curia, and her Bishop was a presupposition for an effective exercise of this directing authority. In accord with current notions, the guarantee of this freedom was the possession and revenues of the *Patrimonium Petri,* that territorial complex whose real frontiers were always in dispute and whose constitutional structure, also involved in constant change, was at that time tending toward complete feudalization. And so Innocent began his pontificate by establishing peace and order in the *Patrimonium* and in those states that had long been vassals of the Holy See.

The *Patrimonium,* which Innocent aimed to rule with the forms of a strictly secular royal authority, had to be again subjugated because of the confusion produced under Henry VI. The Pope placed at the head of Rome's commune a senator who took an oath of loyalty to him. The barons in the Roman Duchy were prepared to follow suit. The Romans were victorious, thanks to the Pope's support, in their quarrel with Viterbo, but Innocent also contrived to bind Viterbo to himself. Basing himself on the titles of donation and privileges compiled by Cencio in the *Liber censuum,* Innocent then began his so-called policy of recovery,[3] which, not without resistance, brought again under the papacy's control the Duchy of Spoleto and the Marches of Ancona. The objections of the Archbishop of Ravenna kept Romagna from also submitting. Nor was he able to establish his authority in the Mathildine lands and the rest of Tuscany,

[2] On the use of this title, especially stressed by Innocent III, *cf.* M. Maccarone, "Il Papa 'Vicarius Christi,'" *Miscellanea Pio Paschini*, I (Rome 1948), 427–500.

[3] The recovery was started by Celestine III immediately after the death of Henry VI; *cf.* V. Pfaff, "Coelestin III.," *ZSavRGkan*, 47 (1961), 109–28.

except to recover the frontier strip around Radicofani and Montefiascone. But what was recovered lay like a bar, from sea to sea, between the Kingdom of Sicily to the south and North Italy, disputed between the cities and the imperial power. In this territory Innocent regarded himself as the sovereign lord, not even subject to the feudal suzerainty of the Emperor.

The Vassal States

In accord with the arrangements made by the Emperor Henry VI[4] in his last will, the Empress Constance, as regent, received the Kingdom of Sicily in fief from the Pope in her own name and that of the young King Frederick. For her part she disposed by her own last will that, following her death, which occurred on 28 November 1198, the Pope should assume the regency and the wardship of Frederick, who had been crowned on 17 May 1198. Innocent carried out this office for ten years. He first of all obtained from the crown, in a concordat at the end of 1198, the renunciation of the state's ecclesiastical supremacy. The personal union of the Empire and Sicily had been dissolved when Constance, in May 1198, renounced for herself and her son the title of King of the Romans. Innocent obtained the ratification of this separation by the imperial authority. First, the envoys of Otto of Brunswick in 1198 made the appropriate promises. Negotiations with Philip of Swabia procured Philip's readiness, shortly before his assassination in 1208, to renounce the imperial claims to Sicily. The moment that the Emperor Otto IV moved to conquer the Kingdom of Sicily he was excommunicated by Innocent on 18 November 1210, and the sentence was solemnly published on 21 March 1211. Finally, Frederick II, whom Innocent declared the champion of the Church against the excommunicated Emperor, repeated in the Golden Bull of Eger on 12 July 1213 a promise given earlier to leave Sicily independent. Moreover, he swore before a cardinal legate at Strasbourg on 1 July 1216 that after his imperial coronation he would relinquish the Kingdom of Sicily to his son Henry, who had already been crowned, and renounce both the title and the royal authority there, for "the supreme power over the Kingdom belongs to the Roman Church alone."[5] To the end of his life, accordingly, Innocent was able to maintain the order that he sought in

---

[4] Now see V. Pfaff, "Die Gesta Innozenz' III. und das Testament Heinrichs VI.," *ZSav RGkan*, 50 (1964), 78–126. There is no original text of the testament and the fragment transmitted in the *Gesta Innocentii* (c. 27, *PL*, 214, III) gives reason for serious hesitations in criticism. A testament, or the draft of one, is not excluded, but what has come down to us is drawn up in an anti-imperial tone and is certainly a falsification to some extent.

[5] "... ad quam [ecclesiam Romanam] solummodo ipsius regni dominium noscitur pertinere." (*Promissio Argentinensis* of 1 July 1216, *MGLL, Const II*, no. 58, p. 72, footnotes 29, 30).

Sicily. And even after King Frederick had been declared of age on 26 December 1208, the Pope contrived in every single case to prevent him from restoring the ecclesiastical regime of his forebears.

Nevertheless, the ten-years' regency meant for Innocent a heavy financial and political burden, implicated as he was in unending struggles with the great vassals of the crown, above all with Markward of Anweiler until 1202. Genoa and Pisa exploited the chaos and gained a footing on the island of Sicily. With the support of the Pope, Walter of Brienne conquered the mainland part of the Kingdom for Frederick; he had had to bind himself under oath to do so for the young King. Despite everything, at the end of the regency Innocent could hand over to Frederick only a seriously disorganized Kingdom. This attempt at real rule, even though it was made for and in the name of another, was basically such a failure that if Innocent had really entertained the notion of a "world dominion," he would in due time have given it up.

The Holy See regarded all the Spanish kingdoms as its vassal states. Of them, Aragón under King Peter II showed itself to be especially loyal and from 1207 it forever gave up control of ecclesiastical elections. As early as 1199 Innocent had felt called upon to intervene there, when, by a treaty of peace between Sancho VII of Navarre and Peter, a marriage between Sancho's sister and the King of Aragón had been envisaged. To live up to the agreement, Peter would have had to separate from his wife, Mary of Montpellier. The consequence was a long marriage process, which was still being dragged out at the time of Peter's death in 1213.

The other Spanish kingdoms showed themselves less inclined to comply with the Pope's wishes. Thus it was only after five years that Innocent prevailed upon Alfonso IX, King of León, to separate from his wife Berengaria, daughter of his cousin, Alfonso VIII of Castile, whom he had invalidly married. It was also contrary to the Pope's wish that Sancho VII of Navarre allied with the Muslims, and, when Alfonso VIII of Castile occupied Navarre, Innocent made no protest. The Pope also proceeded unsuccessfully against the political supremacy crudely exercised by Sancho I of Portugal over the Church, but he did not refuse pardon to the penitent dying King in 1210. In other respects he worked constantly, for the sake of the *Reconquista,* to preserve peace among the kingdoms, even if occasionally he felt that he had to endanger this peace himself in order to maintain the Church's matrimonial laws. In 1214 he solemnly confirmed a treaty of peace between Alfonso VIII of Castile and Alfonso IX of León. In 1209 he obtained for young King Frederick of Sicily his first wife in the person of Constance, widow of King Emeric of Hungary and sister of King Peter II of Aragón.

Hungary was not a vassal of the Holy See in the strict sense, although Gregory VII, referring to the crowning of Stephen I with a diadem sent to him by Pope Silvester II, seems to have assumed a feudal dependence. Hence the Curia regarded itself as especially closely bound to Hungary since this Kingdom was an important route for the crusades, for which, so to speak, the papacy had a special responsibility. In the pontificate of Innocent III the country was suffering from the disorders arising on the one hand from the rival claims to the throne of Emeric and his brother Andrew and on the other hand from the tension between the Kings and the opposing nobles. After Emeric's death Innocent approved the regency of Duke Andrew for his short-lived nephew Ladislas and, after the death of Ladislas, Andrew's accession to the throne. But first he had obliged Andrew, for the pacification of the country, personally to fulfill his father's crusade vow which had not been carried out because of his death. Innocent appealed more than once to the Hungarian episcopate, which he reminded of the loyalty due to Andrew, to work for the internal peace of the Kingdom. In the other Christian lands also Innocent often and not without success called for a like cooperation of the territorial episcopate in his effort to assure the peace and order of Christendom.

A sort of vassalage relationship seemed about to be established between Bulgaria and the Holy See. Innocent had become interested in the Balkan peninsula for the sake of the reunion of the Western and Eastern Churches. The pressure of political circumstances brought about a *rapprochement* of the Serbs, Albanians, Armenians, and Ruthenians with the papacy. When the Tsar Johannitsa of Bulgaria turned to Innocent as a result of this movement, the Pope was able to write on 25 February 1204: "We appoint you King of the peoples of Bulgaria and of Wallachia." [6] In doing so he was aware that Johannitsa was already in possession of sovereign power over his people and as Tsar already bore the royal title. When the situation changed and a Latin Emperor at Constantinople adopted as his own the policy of his Byzantine predecessor in regard to these peoples, they again turned away from the West during Innocent's pontificate.

The Empire

Central in more than one sense in the Pope's thoughts, plans, and decisions throughout his pontificate was his concern for the *Imperium* and for the theoretical and practical relations between the papacy and the imperial

---

[6] "... regem te statuimus eos [Bulgaros et Blacos]" (*Reg.*, VII, 1, *PL*, 215, 279 C); cf. R. L. Wolff, "The 'Second Bulgarian Empire.' Its Origin and History to 1204," *Speculum*, 24 (1949), 167–206 (especially pp. 190 and 198); L. Tautu, "Le conflit entre Johanitsa Asen et Éméric roi de Hongrie (1202–04)," *Mélanges Eugène Tisserant*, III (*SteT*, 233) (Vatican City 1964), 367–93. Innocent III's correspondence with Johanitsa Asen was edited by I. Duicev, *Innocentii III epistolae ad Bulgariae historiam spectantes* (Sofia 1942).

office. The Empire became vacant on the death of Henry VI in 1197. The sequel was the double election of 1198: of Philip of Swabia on 8 March and of Otto of Brunswick on 9 July. A decision could, as always, be reached only by a clear preponderance of power on the part of one of the rivals, that is, by an appeal to arms. While Innocent was apprised of the elections he was not asked to give a decision as arbiter. In regard to the imperial crown the Pope reserved the freedom to bestow it on the one whom he would regard as the "more suited." With this crown was involved the duty of aiding the Roman Church, and so the Pope felt it was up to him to determine which claimant could best fulfill this task. When both men applied to Rome for the imperial crown, Innocent at first postponed a decision. When Archbishop Conrad Wittelsbach of Mainz returned from the crusade, Innocent had him try to induce both claimants to renounce the throne in favour of a third party, probably Frederick of Sicily, but without success.

Meanwhile, Otto of Brunswick had made important promises, among others the recognition of the papal recovery of territory in Italy and the renunciation of the controverted *ius spolii* in Germany. Philip of Swabia, on the other hand, did not commit himself during his negotiations with the Curia. Despite the fact that in Germany the decision was already beginning to favour Philip, Innocent decided for Otto toward the end of 1200 or early in 1201. In a rather long, shrewdly thought out, and ingeniously dialectical consistorial address,[7] he made known this decision and so informed Otto on 1 March 1201.

Through Otto's relations with England, where his uncle, King Richard Lionheart, though not the latter's brother King John, supported him, and Philip's alliance with France, the quarrel assumed European proportions. Philip's prospects of establishing his claims in Germany by force constantly improved, despite the papal decision for Otto. Meanwhile, the negotiations of the Curia with the still excommunicated Hohenstaufen continued. In 1207 cardinal legates sought to get Otto to renounce his claims and absolved Philip from censure. Plenipotentiaries of both Kings went to Rome, where an understanding was reached: Otto's retirement was agreed upon and Philip's recognition as King and Emperor-elect was decided. But Philip's assassination at Bamberg on 21 June 1208 by the Count Palatine Otto of Wittelsbach eventually led to the general recognition of Otto of Brunswick in Germany, and this was ratified by his unanimous election at Frankfurt on 11 November.

---

[7] "... te in regem recipere" is supposed to mean, not that the Pope was here making an inner German decision but that, among the three kings, he regarded Otto as the "rex in imperatorem coronandus." The "Deliberatio super facto imperii de tribus electis" is in F. Kempf, *Regestum Innocentii III papae super negotio Romani imperii*, Misc. Hist. Pont., 12 (Rome 1947), no. 29.

Otto IV received the imperial crown from Innocent III on 4 October 1209. But then, contrary to the Pope's expectations and his own earlier assurances, Otto launched an attack on the Kingdom of Sicily. The moment that the Emperor violated the Sicilian frontier, on 18 November 1210, Innocent excommunicated him; the sentence was renewed in stronger terms on the following Holy Thursday and all persons were released from oaths they had taken to the Emperor. In September of the same year, 1211, Innocent obtained the election at Nürnberg of Frederick of Sicily as King of Germany. When the latter arrived in Germany in the autumn of 1212, there ensued an unending defection of the German princes from the Emperor Otto. In November 1212 Frederick, in accord with good Hohenstaufen tradition, allied with Philip II of France against Otto, who had, for his part, allied with King John Lackland of England, under papal excommunication since 1209. The decision taken at Nürnberg was confirmed by a new election at Frankfurt in December 1212, and then Frederick was crowned at Mainz. The decision between him and the Emperor Otto was made at the battle of Bouvines on 27 July 1214, in which Otto, who had taken the field on behalf of the English, was defeated by the French. This was, at the same time, the end of the contest over the German throne, for now even the princes of the lower Rhineland accepted King Frederick II.

In the Golden Bull of Eger, on 12 July 1213, Frederick promised the Pope all that Otto IV had promised at Speyer in 1209: recognition of the recovery of papal territory in Central Italy, abandonment of the *ius spolii* and the *regalia* in regard to the spiritual princes, renunciation of intervention and participation in elections of abbots and bishops, allowing of appeals to the Curia, and, finally, aid in the struggle against heresy. The Golden Bull created imperial law, legalized the Pope's territorial policy in regard to the Papal State, and replaced the Concordat of Worms by a new regulation that was far more favourable for the Church. Frederick's position as King of Germany was confirmed by the Lateran Council of 1215.

Isolated and abandoned, but reconciled with the Church, the Emperor Otto IV died in the Harzburg on 19 May 1218. Without the Pope's knowledge Frederick had taken the cross at his second coronation at Aachen on 23 July 1215. Shortly before his death Innocent obtained from Frederick the promise that, after receiving the imperial crown, he would turn over the Kingdom of Sicily to his son Henry, who had already been crowned. In this connection Frederick again acknowledged the feudal suzerainty of the Roman Church over Sicily. Innocent probably died in the awareness of having acted, not unsuccessfully, as arbite in regard to the imperial office.

England

England had played an important role in the contest over the German throne, both because of King Richard I's active involvement in the candidacy of his nephew, Otto of Brunswick, and because of the later association of King John with Otto in his struggle against Frederick II, who was supported by Philip II of France. In an effort to strengthen Innocent's inclination toward Otto, Richard had, at the Pope's demand, concluded a five-year armistice with the French King in 1199 since peace in Christendom for the sake of the crusade was one of the Pope's basic concerns.

After Richard's death on 6 April 1199, war broke out again, since Philip II was promoting the succession of John's nephew, Prince Arthur, to the Angevin fiefs in France. In the Peace of Le Goulet (May 1200) John had to bind himself not to support Otto of Brunswick. Innocent annulled this article of the treaty and admonished the English King to give effective aid to his nephew. War between John and Philip was resumed in 1202, despite the Pope's threats, and ended with the conquest of Normandy and most of John's other French fiefs by Philip Augustus. So long as the contest over the German throne remained undecided, Innocent was indulgent toward John despite the King's brutal ecclesiastical policy, especially since John occasionally showed himself submissive in the face of papal threats. But when the Curia undertook to effect an understanding with Philip of Swabia, the Pope's forbearance in regard to John changed.

Conflict erupted over the succession to Archbishop Hubert Walter of Canterbury, who died in July 1205. The monastic chapter elected its subprior, Reginald, and asked the Pope to confirm him. The suffragan bishops who had thus been disregarded claimed that by prescription they were entitled to take part in the election. They got the King to compel the monks to drop Reginald and in his place to elect John, Bishop of Norwich, the King's candidate, who thereupon took possession and was invested with the see by the crown. In December 1206 Innocent annulled both elections and had some of the monks who were then in Rome elect a candidate of his own, the English curial Cardinal Stephen Langton. Though King John angrily rejected Langton, the Pope consecrated him in June 1207 and invested him with the pallium despite the absence of the royal approval. He intended to force his admission to Canterbury by threat of interdict. In March 1208 the Pope actually laid on England an interdict that was in general carefully observed. The King expelled the Canterbury monks, confiscated the property and revenues of clerics and bishops who obeyed the interdict, and left sees and abbeys which became vacant unfilled. Negotiations for a settlement broke down and King John was excommunicated in January 1209.

The King ruthlessly continued his oppressive policy in regard to the

Church, and the resumed negotiations collapsed in the summer of 1211. Complaints by the banished bishops induced the Pope at the end of February 1213 to absolve the King's subjects from their oaths. No actual deposition of the King, however, was pronounced, even though Innocent had threatened it, but the Pope declared the war of Philip II of France against John a crusade. Since Philip strenuously pushed forward his preparations, while John was not sure of the support of his barons, the English King accepted the papal conditions of peace on 13 May 1213: to recognize Archbishop Langton, to permit the return of the fugitive bishops, to restore all the confiscated Church property. Two days later, on his own initiative, he placed the Kingdom under the protection of the Holy See as a papal fief, promising 700 pounds sterling for England and 300 for Ireland as an annual *census*. This payment, in addition to which the customary Peter's Pence continued to be paid, was not definitely abolished until 1366.

Innocent thereupon deprived the French undertaking against England of its character as a crusade and forbade any attack on England, which was now under his protection. The ordering of the ecclesiastical situation lay in the hands of the papal agent Pandulf and Cardinal Nicholas of Tusculum. In the war with France, recently begun by John himself, which resulted in the previously mentioned battle of Bouvines, the Cardinal Legate Robert de Courçon was able, despite the French victory, to arrange a five-years' armistice on the basis of the *status quo* (18 September 1214). In the war against the rebel barons, who on 15 June 1215 compelled John to issue the *Magna carta libertatum,* which restricted the crown's feudal and sovereign rights, Innocent stood by the King, who had, moreover, taken the cross on 4 March 1215 in order to assure himself even more of the Church's protection. On 24 August 1215 Innocent declared *Magna carta* null and void. But this judgment was disregarded in England, even by Archbishop Langton, who was thereupon suspended.

In Rome Langton strove in vain for the lifting of his suspension, and the Pope forbade his return to England. At the Fourth Lateran Council Innocent renewed the excommunication of the rebel barons, laid an interdict on London, and rebuked the French King for supporting the rebels. These had offered the English throne to the French Crown Prince Louis, whose wife was a niece of John's.[8] Even though the Cardinal Legate Gualo again forbade an attack on England at the assembly of Melun, Louis landed in England on 21 May 1216. He was excommunicated by Gualo and the areas already occupied fell under interdict. While the letters in which Innocent asked the French bishops for their part to publish these sentences were *en route,* the Pope died on 16 July. John Lackland

[8] Blanche of Castile, daughter of John's sister Eleanor; she became the mother of Saint Louis IX.

followed him to the grave on 19 October. The Cardinal Legate was able to have John's under-age son, Henry III, crowned and to induce the barons to take the oath of loyalty to him on 11 November. Louis was obliged to abandon the English enterprise, and the Cardinal Legate arranged the Peace of Kingston on 12 September 1217. Louis left England, and Henry III obtained general recognition. The unusual course of events in England, culminating in what was at least an external success on the part of Innocent III, shows the Pope in almost every phase of the dramatic succession of events not merely as the tenacious "master of politics" but also at the same time as guided by the religious concerns and motives of his pontificate: freedom of the Church, the crusade, and peace among nations.

France

The Curia and the papacy had long been bound to France by especially active and cordial relations. Alexander III had found asylum there; for a short time during the Second Crusade Eugene III had governed the West from Paris; and Innocent II had achieved his definite recognition in France. But the Church's "eldest daughter" was also her most demanding. After a long resistance King John had conceded the freedom of the Church in England; the Empress Constance had promulgated the renunciation of interference by the crown in the Sicilian Kingdom; and the contest over the throne had produced the same result in Germany. But in France the Church continued to be strictly dependent on the crown.

King Philip II Augustus (1180–1223) of France was one of the most self-willed princes who ever resisted the measures of Innocent III. He abandoned his second wife, Ingeborg of Denmark, the day following their marriage in 1193 and sought to obtain an annulment, thereby beginning a matrimonial case which clouded his relations with Innocent throughout that Pope's pontificate. Occasionally the King found himself compelled to make a seeming submission, as, for example, on the occasion of the interdict which was laid on the royal *demesne* on 13 January 1200, even though the Pope could not count on the loyalty of all the bishops there. The Pope tried several times to mediate in the ceaseless strife with England. But when Philip undertook measures against John on the basis of feudal law — the war ended with the conquest of Normandy in May-June 1204 — he resisted an intervention by the Pope and at the assembly of Mantes on 22 August 1203 made the celebrated declaration that, according to feudal law, he was not bound in what pertained to his relations with his vassals to heed the admonitions of the Holy See.[9] The Pope then expressly con-

[9] "Nihil ad pontificem pertinere de negotio, quod vertitur inter reges" (*Reg.* VI, 163, *PL*, 215, 177 B C).

firmed this. But within the royal *demesne* itself Philip was not at all willing to let the Church be governed by the Pope; he regarded himself as her master first of all and only then the Pope. Innocent's consistently affable language in his correspondence with this King, his great gentleness *vis-à-vis* the French crown, is amazing in view of the fact that in his scandalous marriage case Philip did not retreat, he did not submit to the Pope's will, and the final settlement proceeded from his free decision, based on political motives, in April 1213. The King defended his clergy against the claims of the princes and the demands of the communes, but he insisted on their subordination to the crown and the services corresponding to this. He seldom interfered in elections, but the clergy remained subject to the royal tribunal. Philip Augustus intended to be, and was, master of the Church in France, and Innocent tolerated the situation.

Scandinavia, Poland, and the Balkan Peninsula

While in Sweden Innocent III supported the legitimate King, or at least the one he regarded as legitimate, against a real, or alleged, usurper,[10] in Norway he decided against the claims of King Sverre and aided the opposition to him in the country. Whether he acted rightly can no longer be decided.[11] He commanded King Knut VI of Denmark and King Sverker II Carlsson of Sweden — "per apostolica scripta mandamus" — to support the Baglar party, which was friendly to the Church, in order to assure the protection of the churches, the freedom of the clergy, and the care of the poor.[12] The generally opposed Birkebein Sverre, however, did not yield, despite excommunication and interdict, and it was only under his successor, Haakon IV, that an agreement, based on the arrangement of 1152, was reached.

In Denmark Innocent found a sympathetic collaborator in the clever, energetic, and powerful Archbishop Absalom of Lund,[13] the founder of Copenhagen, until the latter's death in 1201. Primate of Denmark and Sweden from 1177, Absalom was one of the strongest personalities in Scandinavian ecclesiastical history.

Like Absalom in the north, in Poland the Primate, Archbishop Henry Kietlicz of Gniezno (1199–1219), a friend of the Pope from his school days in Paris, worked in close union with the Holy See. Through him

---

[10] H. Tillmann, *Innocenz III.*, 57, with reference to *Reg.*, XI, 174, *PL*, 215, 1485 f.

[11] *Ibid.*, 76.

[12] *Register*, ed. Hageneder, *Briefe*, I, 383, p. 579.

[13] Absalom, Archbishop of Lund (1177–1201), received his first letter from the Pope as early as 22 September 1198 (*Register*, ed. Hageneder, *Briefe*, I, 372, pp. 564 f.).

Innocent deprived the refractory Vladislas III of authority by excommunicating him in 1206. In 1210 the Pope even achieved the recognition of Poland's feudal dependence on the Roman Church, already prepared for earlier.

Besides the Bulgarians, already mentioned, Innocent was approached in 1198 by King Vulk of Dalmatia and Vulk's brother, the Great Zupan Stephen of Serbia. He declared that he was prepared to regulate ecclesiastical conditions in Dalmatia by erecting a separate province. The tension existing between Hungary and Serbia-Dalmatia and between Hungary and the Ruthenians of Volhynia, in addition to the political changes in Greece from the time of the Fourth Crusade, rendered impossible a continuation of the Pope's policy.

CHAPTER 20

The Fourth Crusade and The Latin Empire

Concern fort the East dominated the entire pontificate of Innocent III.[1] In the Pope were united a number of goals, the legacy of the Gregorian ideas: reunion of the Greek and Latin Churches, safety of the holy places, recovery of lost areas of the crusader states, peace among Western princes and within their respective dominions, both as a prerequisite for participation in the crusade and as a value in its own right, the *bonum pacis*, that is, as the optimum essential condition of an orderly ecclesiastical life.[2] Furthermore, the Kingdom of Jerusalem[3] was a vassal state of the Holy See, which was therefore obliged to aid it actively. In the Empire there was no Emperor and the contest for the throne monopolized all the resources of the princes. The Kings of France and England were in conflict over the succession to Richard Lionheart. The Kingdom of Sicily had been turned over by the Empress Constance to the Pope as regent and guardian of her son, Frederick. So the year 1200 appeared favourable for the arranging of a crusade as a repetition of that of Urban II a century before.

The preparations began with a letter from the Pope to the Emperor

---

[1] For the relations of Innocent III with the Eastern Church see Chapter 16.

[2] For the papacy's exertions for peace, *cf.* J. Gaudemet, "Le rôle de la papauté dans le règlement des conflits entre états aux XIII⁰ et XIV⁰ siècles," *La Paix*, II (*Recueils de la Société Jean Bodin*, 15) (Brussels 1961), 79–106.

[3] On the fate of the crusader states after 1192, see M. N. Hardwicke in K. M. Setton, *A History of the Crusades*, II (Philadelphia 1962), 522–56. The Kingdom of Jerusalem had had to transfer its capital to Acre. See also S. Runciman, *History of the Crusades*, III, 78–108.

Alexius III Angelus on behalf of reunion.[4] Fulk of Neuilly preached the crusade in France, Abbot Martin of Pairis in Germany. Not the Kings but the barons and manorial lords were gained for the cause. These included great princes of France, such as the Counts of Champagne, Flanders, Blois, and Montfort, and Geoffrey de Villehardouin, historian of the expedition; in Germany Bishop Conrad of Halberstadt and Count Berthold of Katzenelnbogen with their neighbours. Great lords from North Italy also joined, the chief one being the Margrave Boniface II of Montferrat. Since the land-route through Asia Minor was not practicable, a fleet had to be provided. The Flemish vessels did not suffice and sailed off by themselves. Following the death of Theobald III of Champagne in 1201, Boniface of Montferrat was chosen leader. He was a friend of Philip of Swabia and father of the heiress of the Kingdom of Jerusalem.

Egypt, as the most vulnerable part of the Ayubite Empire, had been selected as the immediate goal of the crusade. But at a meeting between Montferrat and Philip of Swabia, which was attended also by the latter's brother-in-law, Alexius,[5] it was discussed whether the expedition could not intervene *en route* to place Alexius on the Byzantine imperial throne. Meanwhile, Geoffrey de Villehardouin had concluded a treaty with Venice in regard to the means of transportation. In return for 85,000 silver marks of Cologne the Republic of Venice agreed to supply ships and provisions for one year from 28 June 1202 for 4,500 knights and their horses, 9,000 squires, and 20,000 infantry;[6] in addition, fifty galleys were promised as convoy on condition that one-half of all conquests was awarded to Venice. When the arm gathered at Venice in June 1202, the money agreed upon was not forthcoming, and so the expedition was at Venice's mercy.

The crusading army, which did not put to sea until 8 November, had first of all to recover Zara from Hungary for the Republic — an enterprise that Innocent had formally forbidden. Then it also had to winter there. Venice or, rather, the Doge Henry Dandolo, was excommunicated. Philip of Swabia now made known that responsibility for the crusaders' debt to

---

[4] *Register,* ed. Hageneder, *Briefe,* I, 353, pp. 525–28. *Cf.* the commentary on it by Haluscynsky, *Acta Innocentii III,* 105 f. Innocent put his own words, complaints, and requests into the mouth of the Christian people themselves. "Murmurat populus Christianus," he said, that the Emperor does not submit to Rome and does not aid the Kingdom of Jerusalem, that the Greek Church has separated from Rome and made herself independent. The Christian people invite the Emperor to give energetic aid for the *terra Christi* and ask him to reconcile the Greek Church with the Holy See again.

[5] Alexius IV, son of the Emperor Isaac II Angelus, who had been dethroned by his brother Alexius III Angelus on 8 April 1195, and brother of Irene, wife of Philip of Swabia.

[6] The estimated figures, on which the treaty was based, were grossly exaggerated and were never reached by the number of crusaders who actually assembled at Venice. Just the same, Venice held to the price agreed upon.

Venice would be accepted if the expedition were to make for Constantinople and enthrone Alexius; furthermore, the crusade to the Holy Land would then be provisioned and supplied with a military force of 10,000 men. Despite some hesitations and a papal warning the majority of the crusaders allowed themselves to be gained for this project.

Accompanied by the young Prince Alexius, the fleet appeared before Constantinople on 24 June 1203. While the usurper, Alexius III, fled, the officials he had deserted brought his blinded predecessor and brother, Isaac II, out of prison and reinstated him on the throne, thinking that they had thus deprived the Venetians and the leaders of the crusade, who had come to restore the deposed Emperor, of the essential motive for conquering the city. And in fact it sufficed to have Alexius crowned as co-Emperor in Hagia Sophia on 1 August 1203. His government had first bound itself to pay the Venetians the promised money, but this was impossible. Then it obliged itself to work for the recognition of Rome by the Greek Church, but the clergy and people protested. The presence of the crusaders in the city and its environs aggravated the situation.

In February 1204 a palace revolution gave the imperial throne to a new usurper, Alexius V Mourtzouphlos. Then in April the crusaders took the city, which was given over to a three-days' sack. The plundering and bloodshed reduced the vast and beautiful city to a heap of rubble. "Even the Muslims," wrote Nicetas Choniates,[7] "would have been more merciful." The Latin leaders, together with the Venetians, chose as Emperor, not Montferrat, but the weaker Count Baldwin IX of Flanders; he was supposed to become suzerain of all the conquered territory except for the areas assigned to the Doge of Venice, such as the three-eighths of Constantinople, administered by a Venetian *podestà*. Since a Frank had become Emperor, then, according to the arrangement, a Venetian had to become Patriarch; Thomas Morosini thus obtained that office. A constitution, the *Assises of Romania*, made the Emperor the chairman of an hereditary House of Lords. Almost all the European provinces of the Byzantine Empire were conquered and divided among several hundred crusade barons; the most powerful among them was Boniface of Montferrat, who became King of Thessalonica. In the remnant of the Byzantine dominions beyond the straits Greek successor states were set up[8] at Trebizond and Nicaea, and some of Epirus was preserved. The recovery was planned and carried out from Nicaea, where Theodore Lascaris, son-in-law of the Emperor Alexius III, reigned as Emperor, and from Epirus.

---

[7] *Cf.* the account of the city's fate after its conquest in F. Grabler, *Die Kreuzfahrer erobern Konstantinopel* (based on the history by Nicetas Choniates), 161–230.

[8] A. A. Vasiliev, "The Foundation of the Empire of Trebizond," *Speculum*, 11 (1936), 3–37; G. Ostrogorsky, *Geschichte des byzantinischen Staates* (Munich 1940), 298–322.

Following a first report from the new Emperor Baldwin, Innocent III gave his assent to what was happening at Constantinople, but more exact information evoked energetic protests and threats from the Pope, who was deeply shocked by the sack of Constantinople and who, as a statesman, had a presentiment of unhappy results.[9] But meanwhile his legate had dispensed all the crusaders from continuing to the Holy Land if they would oblige themselves to support for two years the new Latin Empire, which was called Romania. If, nevertheless, the Pope had hoped that the happenings at Constantinople would result in reunion with the Greek Church, the negotiations were unsuccessful, especially as the tactlessness of the Cardinal Legate Pelagius was not an appropriate means of effecting reconciliation. The city's fate and the misguided policy of the Latin hierarchy deepened the breach instead of helping to close it. The policy of imposing Latinization on Greece was a fatal mistake.

And so the ill-advised enterprise that was the Fourth Crusade turned out to be an immense folly and brought the Holy Land itself no aid but instead a further burden in so far as, from now on, many crusaders preferred to assist Romania in Greece instead of keeping alive the collapsing rule of the Franks in Palestine. With the Byzantine Empire a powerful bulwark against the advancing Turks had been almost ruined. Something that could not be erased from memory had been allowed to take place and a great hatred had been born, which was to envenom the relations of the Christian East and the Christian West for generations to come.

However, indirect help had been provided the Holy Land by the fall of Byzantium. The frightened Sultan concluded a ten-years' armistice with the Kingdom of Jerusalem. In 1210 John de Brienne married Mary, the heiress of King Amauri, and on this occasion received from both the French King and Pope Innocent the sum of 40,000 silver pounds. In 1212 he was able to have the armistice extended for five more years. Mary died giving birth to Yolande in 1212, and John, who acted as regent, married Stephanie of Armenia in 1214.

The Pope sought to mediate at Antioch between Bohemond IV and his nephew, Raymond Ruben. Bohemond remembered that Antioch was formally a fief of Byzantium, but his nephew's part was vigorously taken by King Leo of Armenia, who then entered into personal negotiations with the Pope. The long drawn out contest was left for settlement by the Patriarch of Jerusalem, since Innocent became weary of it, above all when Bohemond rejected his intervention as unjustified on the ground that a

---

[9] The contradictory approach of Innocent III to the developments in this crusade are well worked out by H. E. Mayer, *Geschichte der Kreuzzüge* (Stuttgart 1965), 170–87.

157

question of pure feudal law was at stake. Despite these and many other difficulties in the Christian remnant in Syria-Palestine, Innocent continued to exert himself to realize a new crusade, without being discouraged by the catastrophe of that of 1203–04.

That the mood of the West could still be directed to one was probably made evident to him by the singular story of the French and German Children's Crusade of 1212.[10] Many youngsters from Lower Lotharingia and the Rhineland, from ten to eighteen years of age, made their way south. They aspired to recover the Holy Land, unarmed and penniless. The undertaking has been called the "triumph and defeat of the poverty idea."[11] Nicholas of Cologne had gone as far as Rome with what was left of his band, but Innocent sent them home. The French groups under Stephen of Cloeys reached Marseilles and were then taken on board ships by merchants; some of them perished in a storm, the others were sold into slavery in Egypt and North Africa.

Pope Innocent finally utilized the Fourth Lateran Council as a new means of arousing interest in the crusade. It may characterize the intensity of his effort if one realizes that he died at Perugia as he was preparing to reconcile the maritime cities of Genoa and Pisa with each other in order to provide the crusade with a base more solid than that supplied by Venice fourteen years previously.

[10] On the Children's Crusade, see R. Röhricht, "Der Kinderkreuzzug 1212," *HZ*, 36 (1876), 1–9; P. Alphandéry, "Les croisades d'enfants" *RHR*, 73 (1916), 259–82; D. C. Munro, "The Children's Crusade," *AHR*, 19 (1913 f.), 516–24 (critical evaluation of the sources); J. E. Hansbery, "The Children's Crusade," *CHR*, 24 (1938), 30–38; P. Alphandéry, *La chrétienté et l'idée de croisade (L'évolution de l'humanité,* 38) (Paris 1959), 115–48; G. Miccoli, "La 'crociata dei fanciulli' del 1212," *StudMed*, 3, series 2 (1961), 407–43; the best is now N. P. Zacour, "The Children's Crusade" in K. M. Setton, *A History of the Crusades*, II (Philadelphia 1962), 325–42, where the children's expeditions are appraised as manifestations of popular piety. There was no lack of critical reserve on the part of the clergy. H. E. Mayer, *Geschichte der Kreuzzüge*, 188–91, stresses that the children's expeditions did not have the official blessing of the Church and hence theoretically could not be termed a crusade. But they show that there was among the people a strong readiness to fight for the faith.

[11] H. E. Mayer, *op. cit.*, 189.

CHAPTER 21

Reform and the Struggle against Heresy

Like the crusade, the will for reform also dominated the thought and activity of Innocent III. The opening words of his letters contain many references to his unremitting concern to cure what is sick in the ranks of the diocesan and the regular clergy and in all classes in the Church, to assure order, to straighten up again the bent reed, and to rekindle the glowing spark.[1] This care embraced the whole Christian world. Thus, in the first year of his pontificate, Innocent wrote to Iceland[2] to admonish the episcopate and the clergy that "certain things are to be extirpated with particular effectiveness so that thorns and thistles may not suffocate the seed of the Gospel."

Canonical obedience was enjoined; prelates were urged to an exemplary life in order to facilitate such obedience on the part of their subjects; murder, arson, incontinence were mentioned as common crimes; contact with the excommunicated Norwegian usurper Sverre was denounced; the bishops were advised to display courage in rebuking, "for a shepherd who is unwilling to rebuke those who do wrong leads them to death by his silence."

Concern for the maintaining of the purity of ecclesiastical morals and discipline recurs like a leitmotif in many letters, admonishing the episcopate and religious superiors, individuals and groups, princes and magistrates. The crusades had evoked new needs and introduced an oriental and Byzantine luxury into the West. The courtly love of the troubadours had begun to exercise a destructive influence on family and marriage morality. The amendment of prostitutes and the arranging of marriages for them

---

[1] *Register,* ed. O. Hageneder, *Briefe,* I, 6 (Innocent subjects the monastery of Telki to Archbishop Job of Esztergom and commissions him to reform it): "Circa reformationem monasteriorum et augmentum eorum tanto potius tenemur esse solliciti et ipsorum gravaminibus precavere, quanto ad nos specialius pertinet et plantare religionem in Dei ecclesiis et fovere plantatam" (p. 13); *Briefe,* I, 22: "Pastoralis officii debitum nos invitat et ipse rationis ordo deposcit, ut ea sollicitudine utilitatibus ecclesiarum intendere debeamus, quod ipsis ecclesiis ordo debitus conservetur et clerici earum ministerio deputati, sicut ab eis stipendia militie clericalis accipiunt, ita eis obsequia militie clericalis impendant" (p. 33); *Briefe,* I, 31: "... de grege nobis commisso sollicitam curam debemus gerere et tamquam pastores seduli faciente Domino providere, ne ovis morbo infecta incurabili oves ceteras suo cogat contagio morbo simili laborare" (pp. 44 f.).

[2] *Register,* ed. Hageneder, *Briefe,* I, 320, of 30 July 1198, to the Bishops Paul of Skalholt and Brando of Holar and all the clergy of Iceland (pp. 464–66). *Cf.* G. Gathorne-Hardy, *The Royal Impostor. King Sverre of Norway* (Oslo 1956).

was clearly a problem.[3] Usury was eating into the economic and social structure like a cancer and had to be resisted. The clergy were greatly exposed to the general moral decay. Their avarice, especially among the lower clergy, who saw the worst example in the higher ranks, compromised the care of souls. Celibacy was scarcely observed any more among both the higher and the lower clergy,[4] and the hankering after luxury and a comfortable life persisted in showing itself in their ranks. Hunting, drunkenness, luxurious dress, gambling, and even dancing were among the abuses denounced. Divine worship was carelessly celebrated, the care of souls was neglected. The secularization of the higher clergy increased, and monasteries, such as those belonging to the orders of Cluny, Cîteaux, Grandmont, and Prémontré, were in need of reform.

Innocent III inaugurated reform with himself and with the Curia. The centralization of ecclesiastical administration and legislation had in the course of the twelfth century reached a degree which began to involve an intolerable burden for the Curia. The episcopate had become accustomed to apply to the Curia for decisions even in regard to questions of detail. Innocent sought to restore the balance between episcopal administration and final recourse to the Holy See, and so he insisted on limiting or abolishing improper appeals to Rome: an appeal should be a legal remedy for the injured, not an expedient for the guilty, in view of the fact that, with an appeal, judgment was suspended. In cases that were clear any appeal to Rome was forbidden — "omni appellatione remota" — and all appeals were curtailed. Legates were sent only for limited times so that metropolitans could again intervene more vigorously. Ordinarily, legates *a latere* received exactly defined mandates. Metropolitans, on the other hand, were admonished of their duty of visitation. If there appears here a certain tendency toward decentralization of the administrative power, Innocent, very keenly mindful of his *plenitudo potestatis*, still reserved *causae maiores* to himself: the rearrangement of diocesan boundaries and jurisdiction in Spain (Compostela and Braga), in France (Dol and Tours), in Hungary (Esztergom and Kalocsa), and in Germany, where he detached Prague from the province of Mainz and created the autonomous province of Prague; the rendering of decisions in disputed episcopal elections; and the confirmation of elections. Only the Pope was qualified to approve a transfer from one see to another, only he could remove a bishop from

---

[3] *Register*, ed. Hageneder, *Briefe*, I, 112, of 29 April 1198, in which Innocent grants an indulgence to all the faithful who marry prostitutes and thereby rescue them from their former mode of life.

[4] H. Winterer ascertained that in Spain there was a strong reaction against the immoral conduct of clerics from the time of the Fourth Lateran Council in 1215; on the marriage of priests in Spain, see *ZSavRGkan*, 52 (1966), 374 f.

office. Hence the episcopate was closely bound to the Holy See, but in their dioceses the bishops' freedom of action was guaranteed.

Together with administrative reform the moral renewal of the Church was Innocent's weightiest concern: he simplified the living standard of the Curia, sought to revive propriety and honesty at the Curia, established an exact tariff of fees, and forbade the ecceptance of bribes. In the episcopate he was interested in the choosing of candidates of such quality that a morally sound generation could arise, and hence candidates who were too young, too little educated, or of an evil reputation were rejected. Related to this was his persistent struggle against princes and lords for the chapters' freedom of election, since their interference was the source of abuses. But admonition was not enough; it was necessary to see to it that admonitions were put into practice. Hence Innocent stressed bishops' duty of making the *visitatio ad limina* every four years in order to report on the state of their dioceses. In the event that the frequently inculcated duty of visitation was fulfilled, a report was not difficult to obtain. In admonishing negligent bishops, Innocent often resorted to fraternal reproof, given by a neighbouring bishop. In regard to erring prelates or those who had been accused in Rome, Innocent took action prudently. He first sought to clarify the actual state of affairs, either directly interrogating the person concerned or having an inquiry made. He then proceeded sternly against those really found guilty. His basic principle was expressed thus: the bishop is for the Church, not the Church for the bishop. Especially in regard to the lower clergy he demanded of the bishops a firm hand and a stubborn enforcing of law and precept. Violation of celibacy, a secularized mode of life in dress and appearance, avarice, forgery, pluralism, simoniacal practices — such were some of the offenses that had to be reprimanded and eliminated in the lower clergy. The bishop was to remember to convoke diocesan synods again; the metropolitan was to hold provincial synods.

In the lay world, Innocent made himself the defender of the indissolubility of marriage and stressed that the *consensus de praesenti* established the matrimonial bond. His procedure in regard to royal marriage cases in France, Aragón, Bohemia, and Castile proved that he made no distinction between high and low and for the sake of the sanctity of marriage put up with political difficulties and losses. He took a stand against usury and supported the bishops' measures against this widespread evil.

He wanted to lead monasteries, monks, and canons back to fidelity to their rule and their particular constitutions in order here also to pave the way for reform. The road to this reform of monasteries was indicated by means of excellent canons at the Council of Paris in 1212 under the presidency of the papal legate, Cardinal Robert de Courçon.[5] Poverty, en-

---

[5] The family name of the English-born Cardinal is written in various ways: Curzon, Courson, Courçon; *cf.* M. and C. Dickson, "Le Cardinal Robert de Courson. Sa vie," *AHD*, 9

closure, stability, hospitality, a fair paternal administration on the part of the superiors, and obedience were again demanded and enjoined. Innocent encouraged the founding of new orders, as, for example, the Hospitallers of the Holy Spirit,[6] which owed its origin to Guy of Montpellier (1180) and whose rule was confirmed by Innocent in 1213. For it he founded the Hospital of the Holy Spirit at Rome. He likewise encouraged John of Matha, who established the Order of the Most Holy Trinity for the ransom and exchange of captives. This society was completely in accord with the age of the crusades. Innocent had Bishop Eudes of Paris and Abbot Absalom of Saint-Victor draft its rule, which he then confirmed on 17 December 1198.[7] The growing danger from heresy, above all in France, even induced the Pope to call upon the Cistercian Order to undertake preaching even outside the monastery. However, the general chapter of 1213 found it difficult to harmonize the Pope's desire with its ideal of pure contemplation. But at this moment other assistants were already flocking to the Pope[8] and so he could drop the idea.

The reform of the Church was the more necessary since the critical forces, which were competing in the breakdown of ecclesiastical morality and were driven even to doubt the Church herself, managed to appeal to ever wider circles in the Church and win them for themselves. Various groups had already been specified and condemned by one of Innocent's predecessors.[9] The Cathari especially became the real danger to the unity of the Church's faith around the turn of the century. Apart from the Balkan Bogomiles,[10] they were found mainly in Lombardy, Tuscany, the Marches of Ancona, Romagna, and even in the *Patrimonium*. A particularly close and well organized social class caused alarm in the Midi, especially in the County of Toulouse and the neighbouring areas. In the cities, above all Albi, which thus contributed to them the name "Albigensians," and even in the country they often enjoyed the protection of magistrates and lords. Count Raymond VI of Toulouse, however, seems never to have joined them formally. The aristocratic bishops of Narbonne, Carcassonne, Béziers, and other sees showed themselves indifferent and uninterested in fighting against error, which, spread by many preachers and

---

(1934), 61–142. On the reform of the orders at the councils held by Robert during the period of his legatine activity in France, see *ibid.*, 124–27.

[6] On the Hospital Order of the Holy Spirit, *cf.* G. Brune, *Histoire de l'ordre hospitalier du S. Esprit* (Paris 1892); P. De Angelis, *L'ospedale di S. Spirito in Saxia*, I (Rome 1960); on the Trinitarian Order, see P. Deslandres, *L'ordre des Trinitaires*, 2 vols. (Paris 1903); Antonin de l'Assomption, *Les origines de l'ordre de la Très S. Trinité* (Rome 1925).

[7] *Register*, ed. Hageneder, *Briefe*, I, 481, of 17 December 1198, pp. 703–08.

[8] See *infra*, Chapter 23.

[9] Lucius III in his decretal "Ad abolendam" of 4 November 1184; *cf. supra*, Chapter 13.

[10] On the question of the Bogomiles, see now E. Werner, "Bogumil," *Balkan Studies*, 7 (1966), 49–60. "There is no reason to doubt the historicity of the founder" (*ibid.*, 60).

effectively supported by the charitable works of the „perfect," increased powerfully in number and influence. Even monasteries of nuns were influenced. The parochial clergy were often sympathetic with the ideas of the Cathari because of daily contact with them, and hence all the decisive forces — hierarchy, religious, parish clergy, and secular powers — appeared to have broken down. Thus Innocent III, appealed to by an apprehensive minority in the district, was moved to intervene.

Innocent exerted himself in an all-embracing manner everywhere in Christendom for an energetic attack on heresy, with recourse to all the spiritual and secular means that were at his disposal. In the countries beyond the Alps, such as Bosnia, in Aragón, and in Italy, and above all in the Midi his efforts were clearly to be seen. He began with admonitions to the bishops to make themselves conversant with the increasing danger from heretical movements and to take action against them. He gave the proper example in person in the districts and cities of the *Patrimonium*, as at Viterbo in 1199. This is the background of the later celebrated decretal "Vergentis in senium," of 25 March 1199, in which for the first time heresy was equated with the *crimen laesae maiestatis* of Roman Law.[11] But he modified the strictness of the law, which judged, condemned, and punished, by expanding the Roman Law's *misericordia*, which allowed the descendants of the condemned their lives but not the confiscated family property, by restoring their possessions to these in the event of a sincere conversion. In the fight against heresy [12] the Church saw herself dependent on a close collaboration of the spiritual and secular powers, as had been envisaged at Verona by Lucius III and Frederick I in 1184.[13] But in the event that princes and cities, especially in Italy and the Midi, were either too indolent for such collaboration or were opposed to it, there was still a final, radical means: the crusade against heretics.

At first Innocent commissioned members of the Cistercian Order to proceed against heretics, as his legates to the bishops and princes, as his theologians to the heretics themselves. At Carcassonne in 1204 there occurred a public religious disputation with Bernard Simorre, one of the Cathari bishops, in the presence of King Peter II of Aragón, who acted as arbiter.

The behaviour of the Cistercians — from 1204 they were Abbot Arnaud-Amaury of Cîteaux [14] and two monks of Fontfroide, Rudolph and Peter of

---

[11] *Register*, II, 1, *PL*, 214, 537–39: "... cum longe sit gravius aeternam quam temporalem laedere maiestatem" (*PL*, 214, 539 B).

[12] On the combatting of heresy through the measures taken by Innocent III, *cf.* H. Maisonneuve, *Études sur les origines de l'Inquisition* (Paris, 2nd ed., 1960); for the areas between the Loire and the Rhine, 158–65; Bosnia, 169 f.; Aragón, 170; Italy, 171–75; the Midi, 179–97.

[13] *Cf.* the observations of H. Maisonneuve, *op. cit.*, 151–55.

[14] Arnaud-Amaury became Archbishop of Narbonne in 1212.

Castelnau — evoked criticism from Diego de Acebes, Bishop of Osma, and Saint Dominic Guzmán, who in 1206 sought out the Pope at Rome with practical proposals and, furnished by him with corresponding instructions and mandates, returned to the Midi.[15] They represented the view, long shared by the Pope too, that it was necessary to make use of those means which the heretics themselves successfully employed in their cause: preaching and, especially on the part of the preachers, a simple mode of life.

Meanwhile, the Pope himself was proceeding with disciplinary measures against the careless episcopate, which he succeeded in almost entirely renewing in the course of the years up to the Fourth Lateran Council. He then took action also against Raymond VI, Count of Toulouse, the most important prince in the French Midi. Raymond was excommunicated in 1207 because of his neutral attitude toward the heretics. When Peter of Castelnau was assassinated on 14 January 1208, the whole situation became aggravated to such an intolerable degree that the Pope felt constrained to have recourse to the ultimate means at his disposal, the crusade. Innocent had made it clear to the princes from the start of his pontificate that their fight against heresy was a crusade. He now turned to King Philip II Augustus of France, feudal suzerain of the Count of Toulouse, and requested military intervention. Innocent promised him support and for this purpose declared that the war was a crusade. He arranged crusade preaching in order to encourage enlistment and promised a plenary indulgence to the participants and the protection of the law for their possessions and their families. The King was permitted to collect a tenth and a twentieth of the annual income of ecclesiastical benefices. Nevertheless, Philip, whom the Pope had already approached for help several times since 1204, declined to participate in person because of his strained relations with England.

Nevertheless, the preaching of the crusade was so successful that Raymond VI in 1209 sought to immobilize the impending campaign by a spectacular reconciliation with the Church, agreeing to put himself, as a crusader, at the head of the approaching contingents. He intended to use the expedition especially to suppress a vassal who opposed him, Raymond-Roger, Viscount of Béziers and Carcassonne. Leadership of the expedition was formally vested, it is true, in the legates, but they needed the services of an expert for military strategy and tactics, and so they accepted Raymond VI's offer. Béziers was taken on 21 July 1209. The massacre of 7,000 women, children, and old persons in the church of La Madeleine[16] and the burning of the cathedral became ineffaceable memories of the

---

[15] Cf. now the biography by M. H. Vicaire, Geschichte des heiligen Dominikus, I (Freiburg 1962), 86–130.

[16] The figures were probably grossly exaggerated, for the total population of Béziers at that

harshness of these struggles. Carcassonne fell on 8 August 1209, and the Viscount Raymond-Roger was captured and imprisoned. His fiefs were acquired by Simon de Montfort, Earl of Leicester, who, following the renewal of the excommunication of the Count of Toulouse at the Synod of Avignon on 6 September 1209, also received the leadership of the crusade.

Raymond went to Rome to justify himself. The Pope dealt kindly with him and had his case reexamined by a legatine court in the Midi, which ratified the sentence of Avignon. Once again Innocent tried to save the Count. But at a synod held at Montpellier on 22 January 1211, in which the Count's brother-in-law, King Peter II of Aragón, took part, Raymond's excommunication was renewed, and finally, on 15 April 1211, the sentence was ratified by the Pope. On Raymond had been imposed conditions, the acceptance of which would have meant nothing less than political suicide.[17] Apparently the legates had collaborated with Simon de Montfort, who now turned the crusade against Toulouse itself. Simon was eventually able to conquer the entire county, except for the city of Toulouse itself and Montauban. In the statutes of Pamiers, of 1 December 1212, the freedom of the Church was guaranteed and a reorganization of the entire district was regulated. Nothing was said of the heretics.

Peter II of Aragón sought to obtain from the Pope an alteration of the verdict of Montpellier and of Simon's policy. Innocent admonished Simon to war in earnest against heretics rather than Catholics and to evacuate the territories of Foix, Comminges, and Béarn, which were fiefs of the King of Aragón and in which, besides, there were no heretics. At the Synod of Lavaur in January 1213, the legates succeeded in thwarting Peter's mediation and in convincing the Pope of the correctness of their procedure. Innocent thereupon definitely abandoned Raymond's cause. The King of Aragón perished at Muret on 12 September 1213, while aiding his brother-in-law to defend Toulouse. Finally the cities of Toulouse and Montauban also fell into Simon's hands. Innocent, frequently misled by his legates and probably too accommodating toward Simon de Montfort, sent the Cardinal Legate Peter of Benevento to neutralize Simon's victory and again make the war a real struggle against heretics. Though Simon was able to gain the legate Robert de Courçon to his views, the sensible attitude of Peter of Benevento prevailed and the first steps were taken toward a settlement of the enterprise. The Fourth Lateran Council was to wind up the affair.

time must have been no more than 9000; cf. A. P. Evans, The *Albigensian Crusade*, 289, footnote 14.

[17] Raymond was supposed to dismiss all mercenaries, expel or surrender heretics, raze his fortresses, assure the crusaders unrestricted permission to stay in his lands, and go to the Holy Land as a Templar; cf. *Register*, XII, 106, 107, 152, 153 (*PL*, 216, 124–28, 171, 173).

One of the religious colloquies with which it was hoped to gain converts at the beginning of the efforts to win the Cathari achieved a notable success. It took place at Pamiers in September 1207, in the castle of Count Raymond-Roger of Foix, and ended with a judgment in favour of the Catholics, rendered by the arbiter, Arnold of Camprahan.

As a consequence of this colloquy, a group of Waldensians, or Poor Men of Lyons, returned to the Church under the leadership of Durandus of Huesca. Innocent III received them sympathetically and had them swear to the same profession of faith which he had already required of the converted Poor Men of Milan. As Catholics, the Poor Men [18] spread in Languedoc, Lombardy, and Aragón under the protection of the Pope, who often had to defend them against the distrust of the bishops. Around Milan they encountered groups of similarly converted heretics, the Poor Catholics, who, likewise supported by the Pope's sensible and tactful instructions, could live undisturbed according to their prudent ideal of perfection.

Innocent wanted to win back the heretics, not to exterminate them. In his decretals he did not call for their death. Far from being made stricter, this legislation was toned down by the stress on the principle of mercy in regard to the posterity of those condemned. If Innocent's pontificate appears to be compromised by the Albigensian Crusade, the high-handed proceedings of his legates and the uncontrollable truculence of the North French crusaders under Simon de Montfort were equally responsible. Despite rather small gains and the seemingly definitive conquest of the Midi, his pontificate did not really achieve a clear success in regard to the heresy, which continued to make progress. The problem long continued as an unending task, difficult to master, for his successors.

Chapter 22

The Fourth Lateran Council

At the very beginning of the pontificate of Innocent III, a general council was envisaged, in the correspondence between Rome and Byzantium, as a possible and desirable framework for reunion discussions.[1] These, however, were considered, not in themselves, but rather as the presupposition for the requested participation of Byzantine resources in the crusade that

---

[18] On the Poor Catholics, see H. Tillmann, *Papst Innocenz III.*, 182 f. and the editions by C. Thouzellier (see the bibliography for this chapter).

[1] *Register*, ed. Hageneder, *Briefe*, I, 353 (Innocent III to the Emperor Alexius III, August-September 1198: admonition to free the Holy Land from the Muslims and to unite the Greek Orthodox Church with the Roman), 525–28; *Briefe*, I, 354 (Innocent to the Patriarch George of Constantinople in the same sense), 528–30.

the Pope was planning. While he was expecting from the Eastern Church reunion as a return to the *Mater et Magistra,* to a Christendom united in and guided by the papacy, the Patriarch and, at his suggestion, the Byzantine Emperor[2] were pointing to the differences in the concept of the Church and in dogma that were to be clarified by the synod. The dialogue that had just begun stopped quickly, and the general council only met toward the end of the pontificate and in entirely changed circumstances.

To be sure, the crusade was still, or even more, one of the determining motives for the summoning of the Synod. The occurrence of 1204 could not be regarded by anyone as a fulfilling of the program of the pontificate: the Holy Sepulchre had not yet been liberated. Together with the call for the West to make ready for a new crusade,[3] there now went out an invitation to take part in a general council,[4] which was to provide the publicizing, organizational, and legal basis for the expedition.

Over and above this, Innocent planned the Council as a summarizing of his previous reform activity, which, expressed in carefully prepared and systematically pondered legislation and ratified by the Council, could prove that it was capable of supplying constructive impulses for the future. Both the experiences of his own administrative, legislative, and disciplinary action over the years and those of all the bishops and prelates who had been invited were to contribute to the establishing of a model of renewal which should be suited for and obligatory on the Universal Church. And that is why the invitation went out so early — 19 April 1213 — and so urgently.

The whole Church was asked to meet in Rome on 1 November 1215: clergy and laity, bishops and princes, monasteries and chapters, the orders and cities of Christendom. All were to be there, either in person or, in the case of the corporate bodies — chapters, orders, cities, — by proxy.

For the bishops in particular, participation in the Council was a canonical duty, from which they were dispensed only in the event of demonstrable necessity. In each province one or the other suffragan could remain at home because of necessary pastoral work. The time before the date of convocation was to be utilized not only for zealous promoting of the crusade but also for amassing all the *gravamina,* for the settling of which the Council was summoned.

The bull of convocation, *Vineam Domini Sabaoth,* clearly outlined the Council's program. It would deal with the welfare of all of Christendom; vices were to be uprooted, virtues planted, abuses eliminated, morals renewed; heresies were to be suppressed, the faith to be strengthened; and

---

[2] *Register,* II, 208–11 (*PL,* 214, 756–71).
[3] *Register,* XVI, 28 (*PL,* 216, 817–32).
[4] *Register,* XVI, 30 (*PL,* 216, 823–25).

peace was to be assured so that Christian princes and peoples could hasten to the assistance of the Holy Land. The Pope sent personal invitations to the abbots and general chapters of Cîteaux and Prémontré, to the grand masters of the Templars and Hospitallers. A new development was his emphatic request that cathedral and collegiate chapters should send proxies, for the Council was to deal with questions that especially concerned these bodies. Kings, princes, and city magistrates were invited especially because of the crusade, in regard to which the Pope stressed that he retained the responsibility for the organization and goals of the expedition.

We have no information as to details of the preparations on the diocesan level, apart from the crusade preaching. But the unusually large number of those who accepted the invitation and the wealth of problems settled at the Council, together with the extant legislative work, allow us to surmise that the ample time allowed before the opening was fully utilized.

More than 400 bishops from eighty provinces and over 800 abbots and superiors of chapters took part in this greatest medieval Council.[5] The Eastern Church, to be sure, was represented, apart from the Primate of the Maronites, only by the Latin episcopate of Greece and the crusader states. Frederick II, the Latin Emperor Henry, the Kings of France, Hungary, Jerusalem, Cyprus, and England, and Simon de Montfort sent envoys, while the Counts of Toulouse, Foix, Béarn, and Comminges and their vassals came in person.

Innocent III could rightly assume that this unique representation of the West was a ratification of his efforts over many years to bring the papal primacy to effective recognition as far as the outermost frontiers of Christendom. The seventeen Irish, four Scottish, five Polish, and eleven Hungarian bishops were an especially impressive testimony to this.

The Council completed its work in the three solemn sessions of 11, 20, and 30 November, and hence it lasted one month. Merely from the viewpoint of organization, considering the large number of participants and the relatively meagre possibilities of lodging and provisions, it must be regarded as a masterful achievement by the Curia and the Pope; the chroniclers hardly mention complaints. Some mishaps had to be put up with. Before and between the solemn sessions proceeded discussions and deliberations and even decisions on many pending disputes. Thus for England the excommunication of the rebel barons and the suspension of Archbishop Stephen Langton of Canterbury — a measure taken by the papal

---

[5] List of participants in R. Foreville, *Latran*, 391–95, with reference to J. Werner, "Die Teilnehmerliste des Laterankonzils vom Jahre 1215," *NA*, 31 (1906), 577, 584–92; cf. also J. F. Rivera, "Personajes hispanos asistentes en 1215 al IV concilio de Letrán," *Hispania Sacra*, 4 (1951), 335–55; H. Krabbo, "Die deutschen Bischöfe auf dem vierten Laterankonzil von 1215," *QFIAB*, 10 (1907), 275–300.

legates in the Kingdom — were ratified, even though Langton had gone to Rome in person. Waldemar, Archbishop-elect of Bremen, and Dietrich, excommunicated Archbishop of Cologne, who had remained loyal to the Emperor Otto IV, were not admitted to the Council, while the election of Ulric of Passau was confirmed. The see of Chiemsee, recently established by Salzburg, now obtained its recognition. The double election at Constantinople, following the death of the Patriarch Thomas Morosini in 1211, was decided in favour of Gervase, Archbishop of Heraclea, and a successor at Heraclea was immediately named. Similarly clarified was the contested succession to York, where, instead of Simon Langton, who had been elected first, the Bishop of Worcester, Walter Gray, was appointed as Archbishop.

At the opening of the Council Innocent III delivered a sermon, transmitted by Richard of San Germano,[6] on the text: "I have greatly desired to eat this passover with you before I suffer" (Luke 22:15). Reform of the Church and the crusade were stressed as the Council's chief topics. Immediately afterwards the Patriarch of Jerusalem commented on the help requested for the Holy Land, while Bishop Thedisius of Agde reported on the proceedings against the Albigensians. The majority of the Council approved Simon de Montfort and his conquests, and so Raymond VI — but not his son, Raymond VII — lost all his claims. Following tumultuous discussions in the second solemn session the decision on the imperial schism went to Frederick II, but it was not proclaimed by the Pope until the last solemn session, when he confirmed Frederick's election at Frankfurt and definitively abandoned Otto IV.

This session was begun with a solemn profession of faith (canon 1), the rejection of heresy (canon 2), and the unanimous acceptance of the decrees.[7] A general peace was proclaimed, the crusade was summoned, and the decisions already given in the affairs of England, the Empire, and the Midi were published. The *Te Deum* and the papal blessing with a relic of the true cross closed the Council.

The union with the Eastern Church, which Innocent believed had been achieved by the establishing of the Latin Empire, was indirectly ratified by canons 4 and 5.[8] The constitution *Ad liberandam* (canon 71) con-

---

[6] In addition to the report of Richard of San Germano, *Chronica priora*, ed. A. Gaudenzi (Naples 1888), 90–94, see now especially the Giessen fragment, edd. S. Kuttner and A. García y García, "A New Eyewitness Account of the Fourth Lateran Council," *Tr*, 20 (1964), 115–78 (text, 123–29).

[7] The latest edition of the conciliar decrees is in *COD* (Freiburg, 2nd ed. 1962) 203–47, with critical introduction and the most important bibliography.

[8] Canon 9 ("De diversis ritibus in eadem fide") and canon 14 must also be considered. In canon 14 it must have been tacitly assumed that the less severe rule of celibacy operating in the Eastern Church was recognized: "qui autem secundum regionis suae morem non ab-

tained the planning of the crusade. First came the assessment of a general three-years' crusade tax, then the commission to the bishops to preach the expedition and induce the princes to agree to a four-years' armistice. There followed the laying of an embargo on commerce in war materials and the prohibition of any commerce at all with Islamic states for the next four years. No particular military enterprise, not even the continuation of the *Reconquista* in Portugal, was to interfere with the collective effort. The departure was set for 1 June 1217, and for this purpose everyone was to assemble at Brindisi in South Italy or at Messina in Sicily; hence Venice was excluded. No previous crusade had been planned in so practical a manner or sketched on so broad a basis.[9] What the Council made obligatory on all bishops Innocent III intended to realize in his fervent zeal, and in this preoccupation he died at Perugia.

The other conciliar constitutions had to do with the purity of the faith and the renewal of ecclesiastical discipline. The introductory profession of faith (canon 1) repeated, almost *verbatim*, the formula which in 1210 Bernard Primus had had to swear to on behalf of himself and his adherents, the Poor Men of Lombardy; but added to it were some elements from the profession taken by Durandus of Huesca. Much space was occupied by the doctrine of the Eucharist and of the official priesthood, and into this was inserted the term *transsubstantiatio*, coined by the early scholastics. Also contained in this profession was the orthodox doctrine of baptism, penance, and matrimony. In the complementary second canon the Council rejected the ideas of Joachim of Fiore on the Trinity and the heresy of Amaury of Bène. And finally canon 3 condemned all heresies and formulated measures against them, especially stressing the collaboration of the spiritual and temporal powers for their suppression. Canon 3 included nothing new; it was merely a statement of the procedure that had developed in the Midi. The episcopal Inquisition, already introduced and in operation, was now declared obligatory for the whole Church.

In anlyzing the Council's legislation reference has been made to the preparatory work, and especially to the third of the celebrated five collections of decretals which preceded Gregory IX's *Liber Extra*. Commissioned by the Pope, *Magister* Peter of Benevento had assembled them in 1209, and Innocent sent them to Bologna for use in academic instruction. The entire experience of his long pontificate was incorporated into the conciliar decrees, which in many respects took up and further developed the synodal decisions of the twelfth century.

dicarunt copulam coniugalem, si lapsi fuerint, gravius puniantur, cum legitimo matrimonio possint uti" (*COD*, 218, footnotes 24–26).
[9] On the preparations for the Fifth Crusade *cf.* T. C. Van Cleve, "The Fifth Crusade," K. M. Setton, *A History of the Crusades*, II (1962), 377–428 (especially 377–84).

The guide-lines of the conciliar legislation affected clergy, religious, and laity, and the Church's administration and law. The responsibility of the episcopate was often stressed, especially in regard to synods, visitations, preaching, the education of priests, and the conferring of benefices. The law on ecclesiastical elections obtained its definitive regulation, whereby the role of the chapters was strengthened. Some decrees gave detailed demands in the matter of the moral discipline of the clergy. These conciliar desires for improvement applied also to monks. The institution of general chapters, which had proved their worth in the Cistercian Order, was recommended to them. The duty of reform and visitation of non-exempt monasteries was made incumbent on the bishops and specifically insisted upon. New orders and rules were rejected, but the practice of succeeding Popes was to prove that this was not regarded as an absolute prohibition.

The imposition on all Christians of the obligation of annual confession, which included a stricter inculcation of the seal, and of Easter communion are among the best known regulations of the Council.[10] The spiritual care of the sick was impressed on physicians as a duty taking precedence over their medical treatment; it was enjoined under strict sanctions, apparently against possible scruples in the physicians.

Opposing the swelling flood of appeals to Rome, the Council referred energetically to the normal juridical procedure and added clarifications on ecclesiastical processes. The important forty-second canon supplied a clear distinction of ecclesiastical and secular courts. And ecclesiastical courts were warned against extending their competence at the cost of the proper secular authorities.

In its nineteenth canon the Third Lateran Council had already demanded the immunity of the clergy in the cities from taxation, but it had urged them to make voluntary contributions in time of need to the burdens of their city. This was now confirmed in canon 46, but a previous consultation of the ecclesiastical authorities was made a necessary condition. Measures taken by excommunicated urban officials were declared null and void in this context.

In regard to matrimony, the Council limited the impediments of consanguinity and affinity, renewed the prohibition of clandestine marriages, and introduced the obligation of the banns.

The legislation on tithes was completed by references to the existing privileges of religious orders, and in this the relationship of the regular clergy and the hierarchy was more precisely defined in the sense of a strengthening of episcopal authority.

Canon 62 attacked abuses in the cult of relics and decreed that new relics could be exposed for veneration only with the express consent of

---

[10] P. Browe, *Die Pflichtkommunion im Mittelalter* (Münster 1940).

171

the Holy See. Other decrees sought to put a stop to simony, which was still practised, and attacked the clerical vice of avarice. The concluding decrees, which took cognizance of the practice of usury[11] by Jews and prescribed for them a special dress, must be viewed in a certain connection with the previous mention of avarice. This regulation and the declaration of the Jews' second-class citizenship were not innovations of the Council.[12] They are understandable in the climate of preparation for the crusade. Racial grounds were not the determining causes of them; rather they were probably intended to prevent Christians from having social contacts with Jews because of a lack of knowledge of the difference of religion. Muslims in Christian lands were subject to similar prescriptions. Hence, there was question of a pastoral measure.[13]

While the Council's political decisions were not of lasting importance and soon appeared out of date because of events, its legislation persisted because it was taken into the general law of the Church. A vigorous synodal activity, instituted everywhere right after the Council, contributed to this. More important still was the adoption of fifty-nine of the seventy decrees into the law book of Gregory IX. Lateran IV holds the first place after Trent in the conciliar sources of the modern *Codex Iuris Canonici*.

Chapter 23

The Mendicant Orders

Throughout his pontificate Innocent III had exerted himself for a renewal of the monastic life in the Church. Not only had the Benedictine abbeys fallen, economically and religiously, into a threatening crisis, but even the reform orders of the twelfth century, Cistercians and canons regular, seemed to have succumbed to a similar loss of spiritual substance. The Pope appealed to the orders themselves, commissioned the episcopate to undertake visitations, and had his legates investigate and try to deal with emergencies. At the same time Innocent encouraged new foundations, such as the Hospitallers of Guy of Montpellier and the order established by John of Matha for the exchange of captives between Islam and the Christian nations. Furthermore, the Teutonic Knights obtained papal confirmation on 19 February 1199.

[11] On the problem of usury cf. T. P. McLaughlin, "The Teaching of the Canonists on Usury (XII, XIII and XIV Centuries)," *MS*, 1 (1939), 81–147, 2 (1940).

[12] Cf. the important work by S. Grayzel, *The Church and the Jews in the XIIIth Century* (Philadelphia 1933).

[13] Cf. H. Tillmann, *Innocenz III.*, 163.

Above all, however, Innocent sought prudently to devote to the service of the Church the gift for founding communities that was manifesting itself in many areas of France and Italy in the poverty movement of his age, notably among heretical groups. He succeeded to a degree in winning back the Humiliati of Lombardy; likewise, parts of the Waldensian movement were reincorporated into the unity of the Church under Durandus of Huesca in Spain.

To this total context belong the beginnings of the two great mendicant orders, foundations which in the course of the thirteenth century were the models for other religious foundations. It should cause no surprise that both had their origin where the most dangerous centres of the crisis were found, in the Midi and Central Italy. However, contact with heresy was far more decisive for Saint Dominic than was a grasp of the corresponding phenomena in the environment of his Umbrian homeland for Saint Francis.[1]

On the one hand they attested the uninterrupted *élan* of the movement for apostolic poverty. On the other, they demonstrated the interdependence of ecclesiastical and heretical forms within this impulse toward the realization of the *vita apostolica*.

The Dominicans

The very title "Order of Preachers" indicates the origin and aim of the Dominican friars. Dominic Guzmán, born around 1170 at Caleruega in Old Castile, had, as subprior of the cathedral chapter of canons regular of Osma, accompanied his Bishop, Diego, on journeys to Denmark and Rome. Both men, apostolic in spirit and theologically well grounded, had become acquainted in the Midi with the Cathari movement, so full of peril for the Church. At first, it is true, at Rome in 1206 they asked Pope Innocent III for permission to undertake missionary work among the Cumans in Hungary, but he directed their attention to the more urgent tasks in the Midi. Diego of Osma returned home in 1207 and died there the same year. Dominic, joined by a few companions, at first took charge of the house established at Prouille by Diego for converted women, who not only continued there the common life of pious poverty which they had already followed among the Cathari, but also interested themselves thereafter in the education of girls. This tactic of taking over from the enemy his own instrument, so to speak, of grasping his own spiritual concerns and making them one's own, and, like him, of proclaiming *verbo et exemplo* the Lord's

---

[1] *Cf.* K. Esser, "Franziskus von Assisi und die Katharer seiner Zeit," *AFrH*, 51 (1958), 225–64; J. Toussaert, *Antonius von Padua* (Cologne 1967), 360–63.

glad tidings, became the unique characteristic of the Dominican institute. Prouille[2] had to serve also as the temporary lodging of the itinerant preachers, Dominic and his companions, until they could establish a house of their own near Saint-Romain at Toulouse under Bishop Foulque. The Bishop appointed them as diocesan preachers but this did not measure up to the original *élan* of Saint Dominic, and so the Bishop and the preachers sought to obtain at Rome confirmation and encouragement of the incipient religious community from the Pope. Out of regard for canon 13 of the Fourth Lateran Council, just concluded, Innocent got them to accept the Augustinian rule and then gave the brotherhood the requested confirmation. However, official confirmation came only from Honorius III in bulls of 22 December 1216 and 21 January 1217. The first general chapter of the new order, held in Bologna at Pentecost 1220, drew up a constitution which could be supplemented and made definitive during the generalships of Raymond of Peñaforte (1241) and Humbert of Romans (1259).

Dominic died at Bologna on 6 August 1221. Following the first papal confirmation he had sent friars from Toulouse to Paris and Spain, thereby demonstrating his intention of now having his diocesan missionaries become preachers for the Universal Church. In the last years of his life he was tireless in his journeys from country to country in order everywhere to provide for the rapidly spreading order, which was soon in a position to found houses in Italy, Germany, and England, to acquire experience, to represent the needs of the home as well as of the foreign mission, to acclimatize the order at the universities, especially at Paris and Bologna. This last was of particular importance for Dominic. From his very first encounter with the Cathari of the Midi it had been clear to him that a solid theological formation was essential for preaching, not only for apologetics but for catechesis within the Catholic fold. The lay preacher movement, which so often ended up in heretical side-roads, had, of course, made known the need of the word of God among the faithful, but, as unsupervised proclamation, it had at the same time shown only too vividly the necessity of a clear grasp of dogmatic and moral theology in the preacher. The declared intention of pursuing a theological approach in the renewal of the preaching of Christian doctrine gained for Saint Dominic from the very start many companions from the university circles, as, for example, his successor in the government of the order, Blessed Jordan of Saxony (1222–37),[3] who had studied at Paris. Under Jordan the order spread to Syria and to Scotland.

---

[2] *Cf.* now especially *Saint Dominique en Languedoc (Cahiers de Franjeaux,* 1) (Toulouse 1966).

[3] The letters of Jordan of Saxony were edited by E. Bayonne, *MOP,* VII, German translation by J. Mubauer (Vechta 1927); biography by H. C. Scheeben (Vechta 1937).

The constitution stressed the poverty of both the individual and the community. It adopted traditional elements from the congregations of canons regular, above all the Premonstratensians, and was oriented also to the monastic life, especially the Cistercian. New, however, was the requirement of living on alms; fixed revenues and landed property were rejected. The church building was to be as unpretentious as among the early Cistercians. The first houses were founded in university cities and in episcopal and commercial cities. Here were found the hoped for fields for attracting recruits, for the care of souls, for study, and also for livelihood. Here were held the annual general chapters, by turns in all countries where the friars settled. The general chapter, apparently derived from the Cistercian model, which Innocent III had made of obligation for the other orders also at the Fourth Lateran Council in canon 12, was the supreme legislative authority in the order and elected the master general, whom it could also depose. The provincial superiors were likewise elected by the provincial chapters; in regard to them the master general had only the right of confirmation. From 1228 there were provinces in Spain, Provence, France, Lombardy, Rome, Germany, England, Hungary, the Holy Land, Greece, Poland, and Scandinavia. To the general chapter and the provincial chapters pertained the function of supervising the superiors elected by them. Hence there existed a unique and, as was to appear, a very effective combination of monarchical and democratic elements in the overall construction of the organization.

The central role of preaching in the order's program caused the legislative authority to demand for every house a lecturer in theology and a director of studies, to establish in every province a *studium generale,* and finally to have the best recruits formed at Saint-Jacques in Paris. The strict subordination to the Pope — the master general resided in Rome — and to the national episcopates was to serve the work of preaching and assured to the founding generations a far-reaching support by the local bishops and to preaching a secure place within the Church. Their strict mode of life, their poverty, fasting, abstinence, and personal penance gained for the Friars Preachers the notice of the faithful and a steadily growing number of vocations, above all in the university circles and the upper middle class.

Dominic clearly stamped his order with the traits of his own character. He lived according to "the rule of the Apostles" and was a "man of the Gospel in the footsteps of his Redeemer," as Gregory IX said in 1234 in the bull of canonization. He wanted not only to realize this evangelical outlook in his own life but also, as a "man of the Church," to establish institutionally in her the forms of the apostolic life. He knew the canon law and accepted the Pope's universal directing authority. For Dominic the Gospel and the hierarchical Church belonged together. He joined a charming humanity with a keen intellectuality, a strict asceticism of prayer and fidelity to his chosen rule with a capacity for objective, individual decision corresponding to the many-faceted apostolate. The "born preacher" forever remained the model for his brothers as well as the theologically trained disputant with heretics and the apostle faithful till the end of his life to the desire to win pagans, the Cumans, for Christ.

Under the energetic leadership of his first successors, Jordan of Saxony (1222–37), Raymond of Peñaforte (1238–40), John the German (1241–52), Humbert of Romans (1254–63),[4] the order experienced a rapid and astounding rise. At the end of the thirteenth century there were 557 convents in eighteen provinces and the number of members amounted to about 15,000. Under Humbert of Romans the constitution acquired its definitive form, a framework for the further legislative development of the order, which did not need to be changed until 1924. By 1259 a proper liturgy, within the framework of the Roman liturgical tradition, was drafted.

While at first the friars carried on a missionary apostolate among the people in a close collaboration with the bishops and the parochial clergy, from 1240 on the convents themselves appeared as pastoral centres, with preaching, administration of the Sacraments, the confraternity system, and so forth. The Popes, notably Gregory IX and Innocent IV, lavished rich privileges on the order, drew many of their advisers from it — one thinks of Raymond of Peñaforte and Gregory IX, — and made use especially of Dominicans in constructing the Inquisition.

Service on the tribunal of the Inquisition did not exclude discussions in controversial theology or preaching; on the contrary, it fostered theological scholarship. The new order's special achievement lay in this field of education, university, and theological literature. The convents at Paris, Orléans, Bologna, Cologne, and Oxford especially lodged the leading theologians of the century. Dominican missionary ardour found fields in Prussia, the Holy Land, Spain, and North Africa. In Greece it was directed, in accord with the mind of the Popes, to the problem of reunion with the Orthodox Church. Missions to the Cumans and Mongols are to be noted.

The Second Order of Saint Dominic,[5] originating at Prouille and at San Sisto in Rome, became the model for other establishments of communities of women. The constitutions of San Sisto were, alongside the rule of the Cistercian nuns, decisive for the Order of the "Penitents of

---

[4] K. Michel, *Das opus tripartitum des Humbert von Romans* (Graz, 2nd ed., 1926); *Opera de vita regulari*, ed. J. J. Berthier, 2 vols. (Rome 1888 f.); biography by F. Heintke (Berlin 1933).

[5] J. Vesely, *Il secondo Ordine di S. Domenico* (Bologna 1943); H. Wilms, *Geschichte der deutschen Dominikanerinnen* (Dülmen 1920).

Saint Mary Magdalene,"[6] which spread quickly, especially in Germany. Its founder, at the urging of the Cistercian Cardinal Conrad of Urach, was the canon Rudolf of Hildesheim (1226–27).

The Third Order of Brothers and Sisters of Penance of Saint Dominic grew out of a lay brotherhood of the *Militia Christi*.[7]

The Franciscans

Fed by similar sources and running its course before the same historical background, but obtaining its inspiration from an even more powerfully charismatic personality, the poverty and preaching movement of the Friars Minor of Saint Francis made its appearance at the same time as did that of the Friars Preachers.

Francis of Assisi, born around 1181–82, was the son of a well-to-do cloth merchant, Peter Bernardone, and of Pica, daughter of a respected French family. Baptized John, he was called "Francesco" by his father. He was of a sensitive nature, of more than average intelligence, endowed with intuition, gifted musically, open, and generous. He obtained the ordinary education of the day in the city school of Assisi. A rather long captivity due to the war between Assisi and Perugia in 1202 and a subsequent illness brought about a profound change in his religious development, the stages of which cannot easily be pinpointed. It was marked by an experience of the majesty of God the Father, by an awakening concern for the deterioration of the Church, concretely realized by the rebuilding of decayed chapels, and by the distress of the poor and the sick, especially the lepers, in the environs of wealthy Assisi. Conflict with his father in 1206–07 ended with his being disinherited. Francis placed himself as a poor man under the protection of the Bishop. To his devotion to poverty was added the desire for the apostolate, aroused by reading Matthew 10:5–16, the account of the mission of the twelve Apostles. The imitating of the Lord — poor, preaching, aiding — became the life program of Saint Francis.

Companions joined him from Assisi; they went in twos through the cities and countryside, preaching the good news. The bishops' reserve in regard to a movement so similar to the heretical lay preaching could be

---

[6] *Heimbucher*, 3rd ed., 646–48; H. Grotofend, "Die büssenden Schwestern der heiligen Maria Magdalena in Deutschland," *Mitt. des Vereins für Geschichte und Altertumskunde Frankfurt am Main*, 6 (1881), 301–16; A. Simón, *L'ordre des Pénitentes de Ste-Marie-Madeleine en Allemagne* (Fribourg 1918); J. Schuck, *Die Reuerinnen* (Paderborn 1927); O. Decker, *Die Stellung des Predigerordens zu den Dominikanerinnen* (Vechta and Leipzig 1935).

[7] *Cf.* especially the studies by G. Meersseman, "Études sur les anciennes confréries dominicaines," *AFP*, 20–23 (1950–53) (bibliography for this chapter); P. Mandonnet, *Les Règles et le gouvernement de l'Ordre de Paenitentia au XIIIᵉ siècle* (Paris 1902).

overcome only by papal approval. Francis, who had already visited Rome as a pilgrim in 1206, was able to obtain a verbal confirmation of his first rule from Innocent III through the good offices of the Bishop of Assisi, who was in residence there, and of Cardinal John Colonna. It is not extant and was probably only a brief collection of scriptural passages. The Pope took the friars under the jurisdiction of the Church by giving them the tonsure, and Francis himself was ordained a deacon. The brothers called themselves Friars Minor and lived part of the time at the Portiuncula, where Clare of Assisi, foundress of the Second Order, or Poor Clares,[8] also turned up with her sister Agnes in 1212. The movement was everywhere well received and the number of friars grew rapidly. Francis, who also envisaged the preaching of the word to non-Christians, left for the East in 1212 but got only as far as Dalmatia. He wanted to go to North Africa but fell sick in Spain around 1213–15, and finally joined the Fifth Crusade in 1219. He contrived to preach in person before the Sultan al-Kamil, who was not converted, it is true, but allowed Francis to preach in his lands. The latter went to Palestine before returning to Italy, probably in the fall of 1220.

There awaited him the need to give an organization to his now very large brotherhood, but, quite unlike Saint Dominic, he lacked all planning and organizational ability. The Curia interested itself in the matter. The so-called Chapter of Mats in 1221, with more than 3,000 participants, promulgated the new second rule, likewise a collection of scriptural passages in twenty-four chapters. It is extant and is known as the *regula non bullata*. It was only the *Regula bullata* of 1223, more strictly juristic in character, that became the real fundamental law of the new order. Cardinal Ugolino of Ostia had played a decisive role in drawing it up. It was incorporated in its entirety into Honorius III's bull of confirmation of 29 November 1223. The home and foreign mission was mentioned as the order's chief goal, and the poverty of the individual and of the communities, including a strict prohibition of accepting money, was sternly demanded. The Chapter of Mats sent out friars to all countries of Europe.

Francis himself had already turned over the direction of the friars to one of his first companions, Peter Catanii, had asked the Pope to give the order a Cardinal Protector, and had obtained one in Ugolino of Ostia. While the *regula non bullata* knew nothing of a Cardinal Protector, the *regula bullata* required one. Hence the institution must have been projected between 1221 and 1223. Peter Catanii died on 10 March 1221 and was succeeded by Elias of Cortona. In the same year Francis founded the Third

---

[8] E. Wauer, *Entstehung und Ausbreitung des Klarissenordens* (Leipzig 1906); J. Ancelet-Hustache, *Les Clarisses* (Paris 1924); *Santa Chiara d'Assisi, Studi e Cronaca del VII Centenario* (Perugia 1954); biographies of Saint Clare by F. Casolini (Assisi 1953) and E. Schneider (Paris 1959).

Order,[9] a community of lay persons, even married, who sought to realize the Franciscan ideal of life outside a religious order.

After his return from the East, Francis had dissolved the house of studies which had been founded at Bologna. The Cardinal Protector intervened for its restoration and Francis yielded, even naming its first lecturer, Anthony of Padua.[10] The necessity of theological studies for a fruitful preaching apostolate could not have remained unknown to him, above all as more and more priests were joining the order. The beginnings proper to a trend of the apostolic lay movement seemed to have been left behind.

Francis stayed at Greccio until April 1224 and at Pentecost took part in the general chapter at which the *regula bullata* was promulgated. Then, with a few companions he withdrew to Monte Alverno for a life of prayer, penance, and contemplation, and there on 14 September 1224 he received the stigmata. Much sickness plagued his poor body. In particular he had contracted a serious malady of the eyes in the East. He had it treated, but in vain, at Rieti on the suggestion of Cardinal Ugolino and at Siena at the command of Brother Elias. From February 1226 he stayed at Assisi, where he was the Bishop's guest. He was unable to take part in the Pentecost Chapter of 1226; instead, in August of that year he wrote his "testament," which again inculcated the strictest poverty and, above all, obedience to the Roman Church. Before his death on 3 October 1226 he was able to make peace between the Bishop and the municipal council of Assisi and to complete his celebrated "Canticle of the Sun." He died in a hut near the Portiuncula and was buried in the church of San Giorgio. Pope Gregory IX, the former Cardinal Ugolino, canonized him less than two years later, on 29 July 1228. He found his last resting place in the lower church of the Assisi basilica. After previously fruitless efforts, it could be identified under Pius VII in 1818.

The figure of the *Poverello* interested his own and later ages much more than did that of Dominic, who withdrew far more decidedly behind his work. Whereas the Dominican Order was already an institution when Dominic died, the Franciscan remained even after 1226 still a sort of movement. Francis was just not an organizer, but, according to Dante, "he rose on the world like a sun." He was a mystic, poet, singer, man of prayer, but no canonist, theologian, or controversialist. Nor was he a fool,

[9] The Third Order originated in brotherhoods which united under the influence of St. Francis. Probably at Florence or Bologna Cardinal Ugolino of Ostia, perhaps after consultation with Francis or at least with recourse to an already existing version, published the official rule under the title *Memoriale propositi fratrum et sororum de paenitentia in domibus propriis existentium*. In a revised form it was confirmed by Nicholas IV in 1289. Cf. F. van den Borne, *Die Anfänge des franziskanischen Dritten Ordens* (Münster 1925); idem, *LThK*, IX (2nd ed., 1964), 1375 f.

[10] See now the critical monograph by J. Toussaert, *Antonius von Padua* (Cologne 1967), 348–54.

as has been supposed, but an intelligent, shrewd, and deeply religious man, who knew his limitations and hence so early desired the cooperation of the Curia. The Cardinal Protector was not forced on him; he himself asked for this "gubernator, protector et corrector." In his testament Francis declared expressly that it was the Cardinal Protector's duty, among other things, to keep from the order any shadow of heresy. At the same time he fulfilled the function of representing the order at the Curia and to the hierarchy and of smoothing its path in the Church. Such a notion hardly reveals in Francis any ignorance of the world. And the sources display much evidence of a good knowledge of men in the seraphic saint, even if this did not amount to genius. When in 1219 he travelled to the East he appointed as vicars Matthew of Narni and Gregory of Naples, who in his absence introduced new rules and instituted the house of studies at Bologna. Had Francis not perceived their attitude earlier? When he abandoned the actual direction of the order, Peter Catanii and then Elias of Cortona became his vicars general. Even if the image of Elias has been deformed by later polemics, there is still a puzzle with regard to the choice of this particular man, who likewise received the final blessing of the dying saint. Today, it is true, research transfers the activity of Elias that was injurious to the order to the period after his being voted out of office at the Chapter of 1227, which made, not him, but John Parenti the minister general, or successor of Saint Francis.[11]

It was only then that those trends[12] which determined the destiny of the order after 1226 began to show themselves more clearly. The zealots for poverty defended the literal observance of the rule, appealing especially to the testament of the saint. In response to inquiries Gregory IX in 1230 declared that the testament possessed no legal standing. From this trend were later to spring the Spirituals.

Especially during his time as minister general (1232–39), Elias of Cortona advocated assimilation to other orders, as the model of the Dominican Order permanently gained influence in the course of the years, for example, in the assurance of the organization through the position of the minister general and in the order's turning to the cultivation of scholarship.

The middle party was represented by Anthony of Padua, Bonaventure, John Pecham, and others, who, while maintaining the original ideals so far as possible, demanded and carried through an accommodation to changing conditions of the time. The tensions among these tendencies were

[11] The problem of Elias was most recently presented by R. B. Brooke, *Early Franciscan Government* (Elias to Bonaventure) (Cambridge 1959).
[12] M. D. Lambert has now made a careful study dealing with the development of the various notions of poverty held by the early Franciscans: *Franciscan Poverty, The Doctrine of the Absolute Poverty of Christ and the Apostles in the Franciscan Order (1210–1323)* (London 1961).

at first not very severe and did not become aggravated until after 1250, to develop into a serious crisis for the entire order at the beginning of the fourteenth century.

Until then the Friars Minor had been able to spread everywhere in the Church — to Ireland, Scotland, Scandinavia, Syria, the Holy Land — so that by 1300 they must be reckoned as having from 30,000 to 40,000 members. Due to the close ties which Francis, like Dominic, maintained from the start with the Roman Curia, the order's influence was from the beginning geared to the Universal Church. Freedom of movement, contrary to the *stabilitas loci* hitherto cultivated by the old orders, enabled all the chief convents to have an international composition. A lively exchange from country to country, in all offices of the order and for all sorts of missions, remained characteristic. The Franciscan school, especially at Oxford and Paris, was soon able to serve theological scholarship on an equal footing with the Dominican.

Naturally, the Friars Minor displayed their chief influence in the ministry of the word (popular and crusade preaching) and of the Sacraments (confession) and in fostering popular devotions centring on the Lord's Incarnation and Passion. They preached in cities, soon in their own churches, and, like Francis, in the country as itinerant preachers. The thirteenth century especially has transmitted great names: in Italy Anthony of Padua and Bonaventure of Jesi, in France Hugh of Digne and Odo Rigaldus, in Germany Conrad of Saxony and Berthold of Regensburg.

Following both the example and the desire of Saint Francis, the Friars Minor could especially take part as pioneers in the work of evangelizing pagans. As Francis, preaching before the Sultan, aspired to prepare a change from the crusade as military offensive and defense of Christian positions to a Way of the Cross as a peaceful concern for the faith of non-Christian peoples, so too the Friars Minor went as preachers to North Africa, Syria, and Palestine to the Muslims, and, under a papal mandate, to the Mongols — John of Piano di Carpine (1245–47), William of Ruysbroeck (1253–55), and John of Montecorvino (1294).[13]

For the Holy See they, like the Dominicans, meant an important assistance in Church reform, in the struggle against heresy, and in politics, such as the undertaking of embassies and interventions on behalf of peace.

Other Mendicant Orders

The two orders just discussed set the pattern for other foundations in the course of the century. In 1247 Innocent IV included the Carmelites among the mendicant orders. Simon Stock became their first general (1247–65). But their origins go back to the twelfth century, to a hermit colony, which

[13] *Cf.* Chapter 29.

the crusader, Berthold of Calabria (d. 1195), had instituted on Mount Carmel in 1185. From the Patriarch Albert of Jerusalem they had received in 1207–09 a strictly contemplative rule, which Honorius III confirmed in 1226. When, hard pressed by Islam, they emigrated to Cyprus, Sicily, France, and England and from 1238 reorganized themselves as cenobites, it was natural to give them a constitution corresponding to that of the mendicant orders.

The Order of Hermits of Saint Augustine likewise developed out of eremitical groups. First, Innocent IV in 1243 united the hermits living in Tuscany, then in 1256 Alexander IV brought all the others into one community, the Order of Hermits of Saint Augustine. But the Williamite Order, originating in the twelfth century, withdrew from the union in 1266. Peter Nolasco (d. 1256) and the Dominican general, Raymond of Peñaforte (d. 1275), were the founders of the Order of Mercedarians, which, beginning at Barcelona in 1222 as a union of pious laymen, concerned itself, like the Trinitarians, to arrange exchanges of captives. Under King James I of Aragón it became a military religious order, which Gregory IX confirmed as such in 1235. It could not be regarded as a mendicant order until 1318, when John XXII decided that only a priest might be its superior general; the knights withdrew and the order assumed an exclusively religious character.

In 1233 there appeared at Florence the Order of Servants of the Blessed Virgin Mary, or Servites. It too originated in a lay brotherhood of merchants and urban patricians. It adopted the Augustinian rule in 1240 and in 1255 was confirmed by Alexander IV, but it did not rank as a mendicant order until Martin V declared it one in 1424. The fifth superior general, Philip Benizi (d. 1285), founded a Second Order. In addition, there were tertiaries, Mantellates, living a religious life, who went back to Saint Juliana Falconieri (d. 1341). They devoted themselves especially to the care of the sick.

Summary

The mendicant orders decisively stamped the ecclesiastical and religious life of the thirteenth century, certainly more powerfully than did the reform orders of the twelfth century in their day. On the one hand, by virtue of the centralization of their organization, which was tempered by the relative autonomy of the several provinces, and, on the other hand, by the freedom of movement of their personnel on the international plane, and, especially in the case of the Friars Minor, their broad pastoral contacts with all strata of society, above all in the cities, they presented the papacy with incomparable resources for the government of the Church — many bishops and cardinals and even Popes came from their ranks as early as the thirteenth century — for the renewal of popular piety, especially through the influence of the three types of orders which they had created, and for the growth of theological scholarship, whose most important representatives at all universities were soon Dominicans and Franciscans, from Alexander of Hales to Bonaventure and Duns Scotus, from Hugh of Saint-Cher to Albert the Great and Thomas Aquinas. They accomplished very much, especially the Friars Preachers, in the struggle against heresy through the Inquisition and in the repeated efforts to reunite the Eastern and Western Churches. The first phase of the history of the world mission was determined by them. Ecclesiastical literature was enriched by them, with, to some extent, immortal works in all fields: homiletics, catechesis, apologetics, philosophy, theology, historiography, exegesis, liturgy, poetry.

While it is true that their integration into university life and the pastoral ministry was not achieved without friction, especially at Paris between 1250 and 1260, still the main difficulties could be surmounted, at least in principle, by papal intervention. The human shadows could in this first century of their history be steadily eclipsed by the uncontested brilliance of their accomplishments.

CHAPTER 24

The Medieval Western Hospital

In the early Middle Ages it was the canons and monks who had received the poor and the sick, the pilgrim and the traveller into their houses and cared for them. In these *hospites* was to be seen and served Christ himself, according to the prescriptions of rule and constitution. Alongside the *opus Dei* in worship, work, and self-sanctification — the *vita contemplativa* — the service of guests and the infirm had, it is true, only a secondary significance and was scarcely anywhere regarded as a central preoccupation of religious communities.

A change occurred in the age of the Gregorian reform, when there began a more active participation by the laity in the public life of the Church. Prominent among the motives of the *vita apostolica* was the example of Christ as healer and helper: the *pauperes Christi* wanted to become poor in order to succour others in their necessities. At the same time the crusades produced homelessness, sickness, physical disability, and poverty wherever they played a role, at home and abroad. *Caritas* in the hitherto familiar form was in no position to provide ample assistance in such massive need, and so new forms had to be found for dealing effectively with it.

One such form was the renewed hospital service in West and East under the auspices of chapters and monasteries, above all in cities and along pilgrimage routes. The source of this renewal in the West was, among other factors, the Augustinian rule followed by the canons regular, including the cathedral chapters. Especially among the Premonstratensians it produced a vigorous impact on hospital work. [1]

In the cities were formed hospital confraternities of men and women, at first in already available hospitals and usually connected with a chapter or monastery. However, there soon appeared a tendency to become autonomous, and this was facilitated by the expansion or transfer of the hospital. The confraternities were frequently inclined to adopt a monastic organization, and from such confraternity hospitals there developed foundations of Augustinian canons or independent monasteries of nuns.

Alongside this process in the thirteenth century, whereby confraternities became religious orders, in the cities there occurred also the so-called "communalization" of the confraternity hospital,[2] in the case of both civic foundations and already existing religious houses. Hospital service thereby became all the more urgent, when transformation into a religious order caused it to be neglected.

From the twelfth century hospitals directed by confraternities were encountered in all countries of the West in a relatively ample distribution that was favoured by the urban development then getting under way. They were even established wherever cities appeared in the colonial and missionary area beyond the Elbe by Cistercians, Premonstratensians, and the Teutonic Knights. The climax of the new foundations was achieved by the middle of the thirteenth century.

Founders of hospitals came from all classes of Christian society. The bishops for the most part revived and enlarged the old hospitals of their territory. Secular lords of the most varied strata, from kings to *ministeriales*, took part chiefly in new foundations. A founder often joined his institution as a hospital brother. Clerical or lay confraternities were formed for the administration of existing hospitals, and from them new orders sometimes developed: the military and the non-military orders of this epoch.

The Military Hospital Orders

The Hospitallers and the Templars were treated in the previous volume. Far clearer is the hospital origin of the Teutonic Knights, who proceeded from the hospital erected by citizens of Bremen and Lübeck during the siege of Acre in 1189–90. Even more impressive are the beginnings of the

---

[1] N. Backmund, "Prämonstratenser," *LThK*, VIII (2nd ed. 1963), 638–94: "... die caritative Tätigkeit des Ordens im MA war bedeutend, fast alle Stifte unterhielten Spitäler ... auch eine wahre Kette von Pilgerhospitälern in Südfrankreich und Spanien" (691).

[2] *Cf.* also S. Reicke, *Das deutsche Spital*, I, 196–277.

Order of Lazarus from a leprosary at Jerusalem in 1120. This hospital association likewise followed the Augustinian rule, but it did not become a military order, on the model of the others, until the thirteenth century. Since in the course of time these institutes devoted themselves especially to military service, their original hospital apostolate yielded often enough to military and economic preoccupations without, however, being entirely given up.

In their very title the Hospitallers maintained a constant connection with their original aim, and after their transformation into a military order their principal house at Jerusalem remained for a while dedicated to the care of the infirm and the poor. Their rapidly appearing houses in the West served rather for the military and economic maintenance of their warfare in the East than for the direction and growth of hospitals. Thus, for example, only a few hospitals can be discovered among their numerous German houses, but these were busy as hospices. While the competition of the Teutonic Order in the thirteenth century may be attributed in Germany to the lack of hospitals among the Hospitallers, the fact remains that the claims of the East on the homeland demanded a pooling of all available financial means with the result that there were far-reaching restrictions on the strictly charitable apostolate.

The Teutonic Order, even after its removal to the West, always maintained the care of the infirm. In fact, its first decades, up to 1230 when it assumed its fateful task in Prussia, stood expressly under the auspices of hospital work in regard to gifts, undertakings, and foundations. Care of the sick was an essential element in its constitution. This ordered that a permanent hospital should be established at the principal house, but elsewhere only if the grand master and the chapter should so decide. It knew those *hospitalia oblata*, which marked the path of its advance into Germany, and subjected them to the local commandant. Houses without hospitals might be erected as such only with the special permission of the grand master. As a matter of fact, in Germany and later in its own principality the Teutonic Order accomplished far more in the sphere of public assistance than did the other military hospital orders.[3]

Of these others, the Order of Lazarus was able to establish itself in Europe only later, after its expulsion from Syria in 1253, especially in France, where the grand master settled at Boigny near Orléans, in England, Scotland, Italy, Switzerland, Hungary, and Germany. It continued faithful

---

[3] Rule of the order, 4–6 (*Die Statuten des Deutschen Ordens nach den ältesten Handschriften*, ed. by M. Perlbach [Halle 1890], 31–34): "Von den spitâlen zu haldene," "Wie man die siechen in die spitâl entphâhe," "Wie man der sîchen phlegen sule in den spîtâlen." Cf. also P. G. Thielen, *Die Verwaltung des Ordensstaates Preussen* (Cologne and Graz 1965), 74 f. (Der Oberstspittler: obirster spittaler, summus hospitalarius). "The order's example was decisive also for the urban hospital system" (Thielen, *op. cit.*, 75, footnote 20).

to its origin in so far as it devoted itself above all to the care of lepers. In 1266 Clement IV granted it a monopoly of this apostolate, which, however, could not really be maintained in view of the wide spread of this disease.[4]

The Non-Military Hospital Orders

At the close of the eleventh century there appeared in the Midi the Hospital Order of Saint Anthony at the church of La Motte-des-Bois at Saint-Didier. Until 1297 its hospital confraternity had to work in dependence on the Benedictine monastery of Saint-Pierre-de-Montmajeur. As early as 1247 the members had bound themselves to the Augustinian rule and adopted the organization of the Augustinian canons regular. From the beginning of the thirteenth century they spread everywhere, especially in lands of Romance speech but also in Germany: Upper Swabia, Hesse, Alsace, Mecklenburg. Their contribution, however, to strictly hospital work was relatively meagre — they had hospitals at Strasbourg, Basel, and Memmingen. Elsewhere the infirm were attended to in the houses of the order itself or by visits. On the other hand, their almsgiving was famous and made the Antonians very popular.

The Hospital Order of the Holy Spirit, which also originated in the Midi, at Montpellier, made a more significant contribution to the care of the sick. In 1198 Innocent III confirmed the order, which then had ten daughter houses and had its centre in Rome at the Hospital of Santo Spirito *in Sassia*. Its rule made the service of the poor and the infirm its first duty. Most of its houses were in Italy and France, though it had ten houses in Germany, especially South Germany, in the thirteenth century. The numerous Hospitals of the Holy Spirit found elsewhere in Germany had no connection with the order; for example, many hospitals of the Teutonic Order in Prussia were dedicated to the Holy Spirit.

The Order of Bearers of the Cross with the red star, which had grown out of a hospital association at Prague, spread in Bohemia and the adjacent countries around the middle of the thirteenth century. Like many other hospital orders, it followed the Augustinian rule. Its members made foundations also in Silesia and Poland. In the fourteenth century the apostolate to the infirm often flagged among them, as among the other hospital orders.

Finally, mention should be made here of the Order of the Brothers of

---

[4] *Cf.* A. Englisch, *Über Leproserien in Württemberg* (typed dissertation, Frankfurt a. M. 1951); J. H. Mundy, "Hospitals and Leprosaries in the Twelfth and Early Thirteenth Centuries," *Essays in Medieval Life* (New York 1955), 181–205; also, the older work by L. LeGrand, *Statuts d'hôtels-Dieu et de léproseries* (Paris 1901); also A. Viaene, *Leprozen en leprozerijen in het oude Graafschap Vlaanderen* (Bruges 1962), supplemented critically

the Holy Sepulchre at Jerusalem, to be distinguished from the Military Order of the Holy Sepulchre. But since the brothers did not move to the West until after the fall of Acre in 1291 — earlier they had had only isolated houses there — their activity as a hospital order belongs to the late Middle Ages.

The Municipal Hospital

The Western urban middle class, powerfully growing and aspiring to autonomy especially in the thirteenth century, made important contributions to the development of the hospital system.

The old ecclesiastical institutes proved to be inadequate *vis-à-vis* the constantly increasing city population. Consequently, the bourgeoisie itself assumed the duty of public assistance, for which it possessed amply growing means. The allotment of such means naturally implied the claim to share in or entirely to assume the direction or control of the hospital system. Thereby the bourgeoisie came into competition with the Church. However, the communalization, now beginning, of the hospital system did not involve anything such as secularization. Alongside the ever stronger pervading, in the first half of the thirteenth century, of the ecclesiastical hospitals conducted by confraternities or by religious institutes by municipal organs in the form of supervisors, there often appeared new municipal foundations. In these the connection with the Church and her apostolate to the sick was always maintained. To quote Reicke: "A hospital without accommodations for worship was unknown to the Middle Ages." The municipality assumed the secular administration and direction, the Church retained the spiritual care under the bishop's supervision.

This development got under way first of all in Italy, the Low Countries, and to a degree in France. It took place in Germany especially in the thirteenth century, though it was not completed before the fourteenth century. It can even be said that in Germany in the first half of the thirteenth century the ecclesiastical type of hospital organization was still entirely preponderant. The hospitals of confraternities and the hospital orders were to so great a degree in the public interest that even purely municipal foundations were entrusted to them for their administration.

In general, after the mid-century lay bourgeois emerged as supervisors *(procuratores)* and administrators of hospital property, especially where such institutions originated from purely municipal means. Such superintendencies possessed the future, not only in regard to hospitals but in the case of all other ecclesiastical institutes and even churches.

by H. Huyghebaert, "L'origine ecclésiastique des léproseries en Flandre et dans le Nord de la France," *RHE*, 58 (1963), 848–57. Privileges granted in favour of leproseries in the twelfth century are indicated by B. Bligny, *L'Église et les ordres religieux dans le royaume de Bourgogne aux XIᵉ et XIIᵉ siècles* (Paris 1960), 433, footnote 199.

The Contest for the Leadership of the West
(1216—74)

CHAPTER 25

The Papacy's Victory over Frederick II

For a brief moment in world history the papacy in Innocent III had acted as the leading power responsible for order in Western Christendom; the Fourth Lateran Council could be regarded as the visible sign of this domination. With Innocent's death on 16 July 1216, the grand-scale experiment did not at once collapse, but in Frederick II the Holy See found an ever more demanding competitor, in Italy if not in the Latin West. Frederick, whose tenure of the German throne had been ratified by the Council, had not yet been crowned Emperor. Besides, at the eleventh hour, on 1 July 1216, he had promised the Pope to turn over to his son Henry, who had already been crowned King in 1212 at Innocent's bidding, the Kingdom of Sicily, whose political separation from the Empire he had guaranteed. It was now incumbent on the successors of the great Innocent to continue and bring to completion what he had achieved in this question as well as in the other policies he had formulated: crusade, reform, and fight against heresy.

Cencio Savelli, *camerlengo* of the Roman Church and compiler of the *Liber censuum,* succeeded to the papacy as Honorius III (1216–27). Aged and sickly, he was the first one to be called upon to continue and complete Innocent's work. The crusade planned and called for at the Fourth Lateran Council was an overriding task of his pontificate. To assure it he let the election of Frederick's son Henry as King of the Romans at Frankfurt in April 1220 go unchallenged and crowned Frederick Emperor in Saint Peter's on 23 November 1220. The Emperor again took the cross from the hand of Ugolino of Ostia and promised to set out on the expedition in 1221. But the settlement of the affairs of the Kingdom of Sicily, which the Emperor now turned to, probably with a view to creating an assured point of departure for the crusade, claimed more time than the brief period that had been set. Hence Honorius consented to numerous postponements, as at Veroli in April 1222 and at Ferentino in March 1223, until the Treaty of San Germano in July 1225 definitely set the term for the summer of 1227. The Emperor agreed under oath that he would regard himself as excommunicated if this date was further postponed.[1]

Meanwhile, the crusade planned by the Fourth Lateran Council had frittered away its strength in isolated operations and ended with failure in the defeat at Mansurah, for peace could be bought from Malik al-Kamil only with the evacuation of Egypt and the surrender of Damietta, the single gain in these operations. It is true that the Emperor had sent aid under Duke Louis of Bavaria and Hermann of Salza, but his intervention was fruitless. And so responsibility for the outcome was charged to him and not to the ill-starred Cardinal Legate Pelagius.[2]

Concern for the crusade also induced Honorius III to mediate between France and England. King John, dying on 19 October 1216, had left England to his minor son, Henry III, under the guidance of the Cardinal Legate Gualo, and the country was afflicted by the invading army of the heir to the French throne, Louis. Louis's defeat led to the Peace of Kingston on 12 September 1217.

Honorius had especially to continue the struggle against heresy, which had in no sense been ended by the measures of the Fourth Lateran Council but rather was spreading further, energetically and in the most varied forms. The Albigensian War flared up again. Simon de Montfort perished in the siege of Toulouse on 25 June 1218, and the Pope vainly asked King Philip II Augustus for a military intervention. Only Louis VIII, who had already intervened as heir to the throne, promised effective aid. In 1226 he conquered the Midi, except for Toulouse. The episcopate threw in its lot with the King, as did also the nobility. The Cathari among the common folk fled to the mountains, to Lombardy, and even to Aragón. However, Louis VIII died that same year on 8 November. The ending of the Albigensian War with the Peace of Paris of 12 April 1229 meant for France an extension of the power of the crown, but for the Church it in no way implied the definite overcoming of heresy in the Midi.

When Honorius III died on 18 March 1227, the preparations for the Emperor's crusade were in full swing. Gregory IX (1227–41), cousin of Innocent III and friend of Saint Francis, was, in contrast to his gentle predecessor, a high-spirited, obstinate, and energetically active personality. He took up in their true sense the program of the Innocentian ideas. His pontificate was to present the first phase of the Curia's fight against Frederick II's aspirations for hegemony, especially in Italy. The raising of the curtain came with the first excommunication of the Emperor. When in August 1227, on the date set by the Treaty of San Germano, a large

---

[1] MGConst, II, no. 102: "Promissio de expeditione in Terram Sanctam," p. 130, 38–45.
[2] The best presentation of the crusade is now that of T. C. van Cleve, "The Fifth Crusade," in K. M. Setton, A History of the Crusades, II (Philadelphia 1962), 377–428.

crusade army, which had however been weakened by epidemics, set to sea, the Emperor became ill and returned to Pozzuoli for treatment; he had the fleet sail on without him. His excuses were not accepted by Gregory; in fact, the Pope declared on 29 September 1227 that the penalty of excommunication, as stipulated by the Treaty of San Germano, had been incurred.

Nevertheless, Frederick held to his crusade.[3] He replied to the Pope's accusing manifesto in a circular of 6 December 1227, which calmly and objectively denied Gregory's charges and declared that the Emperor would start on the crusade in May 1228. And even when on Holy Thursday, 23 March 1228, Gregory renewed the censure, this did not stop Frederick from carrying out his declaration. He left Brindisi for the voyage to the East on 28 June 1228, with forty galleys. On Cyprus he renewed the feudal sovereignty of the Empire over the island as established by the Emperor Henry VI, and on 7 September he reached Acre. After long negotiations he was able on 18 February 1229 to conclude a treaty with the Sultan al-Kamil, who had meanwhile conquered Jerusalem. By the terms of the agreement the Holy City, except for the mosque of Omar, was relinquished to the Christians, as were also Bethlehem, Nazareth, and a strip of coast from Jaffa to Acre with the pilgrim routes to Jerusalem and Nazareth. The treaty was to be in force for ten years and en visaged a mutual assistance by the contracting parties.

In Jerusalem Frederick, without any ecclesiastical solemnity, placed on his own head the crown of the Kingdom of Jerusalem, which, strictly speaking, belonged to his son Conrad through the latter's mother Yolande, the real heiress of the Kingdom. He had dispensed with any sacred rite because he was still under excommunication and was in need of an understanding with Gregory IX.

For the Pope, by no means satisfied with a renewal of the Emperor's excommunication, had had recourse to further measures. He sought to have an antiking set up in Germany, released Frederick's subjects in the Kingdom of Sicily from their oaths of loyalty, and, when Frederick's vicar in Tuscany and the Marches of Ancona, Rainald of Urslingen, Duke of Spoleto, attacked the *Patrimonium Petri*, excommunicated the latter and hastened to take military countermeasures. Papal mercenaries under John of Brienne drove out Rainald; others under Cardinal Pelagius occupied large parts of the Kingdom of Sicily.

Having returned on 10 June 1229, the Emperor was able without too much difficulty to save the situation, but without violating the frontiers of the *Patrimonium Petri*. He succeeded in entering into negotiations with

---

[3] For Frederick's crusade see T. C. van Cleve, "The Crusade of Frederick II," Setton, *op. cit.*, 429-62, and H. E. Mayer, *Geschichte der Kreuzzüge* (Stuttgart 1965), 204-14.

Gregory IX; they were conducted by Hermann of Salza in Frederick's name, while Cardinal Thomas of Capua acted for the Pope. In July 1230 they ended in the Treaty of San Germano, which was ratified at Ceprano.[4] Frederick was absolved from censure on 28 August, and a meeting with Gregory IX at Anagni on 1 September sealed the reconciliation of the two universal powers. The Lombard question continued to be excluded. Frederick's extensive concessions in the Sicilian Kingdom, in addition to the Pope's military defeat and fruitless exertions in Germany, provided Gregory with the presuppositions for the Emperor's absolution. For the Emperor himself his release from the ban was an important preliminary to the realizing of his total political aspirations, which amounted basically to a unification of Italy under his rule. In this regard at least the neutrality of the Church was necessary; in any event her opposition could only mean an extremely serious hindrance.

The Peace of San Germano-Ceprano endured for almost nine years. During this period the two powers aided each other in various ways and simultaneously both found time to carry out the constructive aspect of their own administrative programs in their respective spheres. Nevertheless, they always regarded each other with suspicion, for the tension continued, despite all protestations of peace.

Frederick was successful in consolidating the basis of his power: the Sicilian Kingdom. In September 1231 he published the *Liber Augustalis,*[5] containing his Constitutions of Melfi. This grand-scale legislative work amalgamated the older constitutional and administrative law and the financial legislation of Norman origin with his own decrees. Then he consistently completed the construction of the Kingdom into a tightly organized bureaucratic state, in which only his will counted and all law proceeded from him.

In the Peace of San Germano he had exempted the Sicilian clergy from the jurisdiction of the state, freed them from general taxes, and even renounced the royal right of assent to episcopal elections — all of this obviously in opposition to the building up of a centralized state. Here, always ready, lay the centres of conflict between Emperor and Pope, for the actual exercise of Frederick's absolutist notion of the state could hardly allow so far-reaching an exemption of most important elements — there were 140 sees in the Kingdom — from his authority.

Together with the reorganization of the Sicilian Kingdom Frederick again took up the question of North Italy, the restoration of the imperial

---

[4] *Acta pacis ad S. Germanum anno 1230,* ed. K. Hampe (*MG Epistolae selectae,* 4) (Berlin 1926; reprint 1964).

[5] For the *Liber Augustalis* cf. the important account by E. H. Kantorowicz, *The King's Two Bodies. A Study in Medieval Political Theology* (Princeton 1957), 97-107.

authority in Lombardy. Just as he had summoned an imperial diet to Cremona in 1226, so now he ordered one to meet at Ravenna in November 1231, and as in 1226 once again the cities resisted, whereupon Frederick laid them under the ban of the Empire. Gregory IX tried repeatedly to mediate as arbiter, but with no real success, because the demands of the two sides were mutually exclusive. With the aid of the Pope, who excommunicated the rebel King Henry in Germany for having even joined the Lombards against his father, Frederick managed to put down the revolt in the north in 1235; until his death in 1252, Henry was his father's prisoner in Apulia. From Germany the Emperor announced his campaign against the Lombards, though he knew that Gregory was seeking by diplomatic means to prevent such a war of the Empire against the cities.

In September 1236 Frederick was able to extend the area of his rule in the eastern part of North Italy. In the summer of 1237, he proceeded with new recruits from Augsburg through the Brenner Pass, after having had his nine-year-old son Conrad elected King of Germany and King of the Romans at the Diet of Vienna in the previous February. The final negotiations between representatives of the Pope, the Emperor, and the cities had failed. At Cortenuova on 27 November Frederick defeated a Lombard army as it was returning home from Brescia. The victory appeared to secure for him domination in North Italy, but his success was ruined by his demand, made especially on Milan, for unconditional surrender. Milan, in alliance with Alessandria, Brescia, Piacenza, Bologna, and Faenza, continued the struggle. The Emperor besieged Brescia in vain for three months, until 9 October 1238. On this occasion he had managed to reinforce his German, Sicilian, and Muslim contingents with mercenaries from England, France, Castile, Burgundy, Hungary, Greece, and Egypt. The Emperor's increasing power, the fact that in October 1238 he arranged the marriage of his son Enzio to the heiress of a great part of Sardinia without consulting the Pope, who regarded himself as suzerain of the island, and that he thus seemed to be striving to assume control even in Rome in order to make it, as far as possible, the real or at least the theoretical centre of a renewed Empire — all this contributed to strengthen the opposition to Frederick in the Curia, above all by the Pope. He dispatched as legate to Lombardy Gregory of Montelongo, who brought together the anti-imperialist cities. The Pope was successful in allying Venice and Genoa and in again establishing his own authority in Rome.

When Frederick, in a decree of February 1239 against the Empire's rebels, as he termed them, issued a summons to a total war against the Lombards and to a social and economic boycott, binding all subjects of the Empire, Gregory IX decided on 20 and 24 March to renew the Emperor's excommunication. Without mentioning the Lombards he justified this step especially by referring to Frederick's ecclesiastical policy in the Sicilian Kingdom, which was contrary to the promises of the treaty of 1230, and to his efforts to establish his rule in Rome.

With this decision began the final struggle of the Curia against the Emperor and his dynasty. Frederick answered Gregory's measures with the occupation of the *Patrimonium* and the encirclement of Rome. For his part, Gregory decided to appeal to Christendom and summoned a council to meet in Rome at Easter of 1241. But Frederick countered by arresting most of the non-Italian participants, who were traveling in a Gedoese fleet, after a sea-battle near Montecristo, not far from Elba, on 4 May 1241.[6]

At the beginning of August the Emperor drew near to Rome, but his intended attack on the city did not take place, for the Pope died on 21 August 1241. Frederick returned to the Sicilian Kingdom to await the outcome of the new election.

By virtue of the official journalism of the immediately preceding years, which had striven to bring the struggle before the forum of Christendom by solemn manifestoes issued by both Pope and Emperor, the conflict between the papacy and the imperial office seemed to have been elevated to the plane of a confrontation in fundamentals. Nevertheless, Frederick had constantly stressed that there was question, not of a conflict with the Church, but with the personality of the Pope, whereas Gregory, for his part, did not attack the role of the *Imperium* in its function as universal *defensor* and *protector* of the Roman Church, but rather rejected the present holder of the office, who, instead of being a defender, attacked the Church, instead of being an orthodox Emperor, lived under the suspicion of heresy without clearing himself.

But the language of the manifestoes, with its apocalyptic hues, did nothing to alleviate the conflict. On the contrary, in its predominant motives it indicated that on both sides persons were prepared to take up the decisive principles that lay behind questions of personality, principles affecting the relationship between the secular and the spiritual powers in their claim to the leadership of the West.

The Milanese Cardinal Goffredo Castiglioni was not elected Pope until 25 October 1241; he styled himself Celestine IV, but on 10 November he died. The cardinals refused to proceed to a new election until the Emperor had released the two of their number whom he was holding prisoner since

---

[6] *Cf.* H. M. Schaller, "Das letzte Rundschreiben Gregors IX. gegen Friedrich II.," *Festschrift Percy Ernst Schramm*, I (Wiesbaden 1964), 309–21. The Pope reports to an archbishop on Frederick's violent procedure, especially the imprisonment of the prelates journeying to Rome for the council, and asks the recipient to summon the bishops and other clergy of his province in order to discuss the inclosed *capitula*. These last, probably a series of complaints against the Emperor, are not extant.

the battle of Montecristo. Otto of Tusculum was freed in August 1242, James of Praeneste in May 1243. On 25 June 1243 the Genoese Cardinal Sinibaldo Fieschi was unanimously elected Pope Innocent IV (1243–54).

Frederick hailed the election, believing that in Innocent IV a representative of the peace party in the Sacred College had been elevated. But he soon had to realize that "no Pope [could] be a Ghibelline."[7] Innocent IV, an outstanding jurist and, as a diplomat, entirely in sympathy with his native city, shrewd, objective, tenacious, and far-sighted, took up the legacy of Gregory IX, which included not only the conflict with the Emperor but also the threat to the West from the expansion of the Mongols, concern for the disintegrating Latin Empire, and the repressing of heresy. He was determined to harmonize them with one another, including the crusade. The settlement of the conflict with Frederick presented itself as the most urgent problem. The Emperor himself initiated the negotiations,[8] which, with interruptions, were protracted for years. They almost brought about peace in Holy Week of 1244 (31 March), when Frederick's envoys solemnly swore to the stipulations of a provisional treaty. The Emperor was to be released from excommunication and in return evacuate the Papal State, perform ecclesiastical penance, give the imprisoned prelates their freedom and compensation, and assure immunity to the Church's adherents. Once again the Lombard question was left unsolved, and the mistrust between Emperor and Pope was not eliminated. In fact, both sides attempted to improve their positions. The Treaty of Rome was not ratified. Instead, Innocent decided on the decisive step of leaving Italy and convoking outside Frederick's sphere of power, even though on imperial territory, the council intended by Gregory IX but obstructed by the Emperor, in order to lay the conflict before the forum of Christendom and bring it to a binding solution.

On 28 June 1244 the Pope sailed to Genoa in a Genoese fleet that was already at hand. He fell ill and stayed there several months; then in the late autumn he crossed the Alps and at the beginning of December took up residence at Lyons with the canons regular of Saint-Just. Without his being able to anticipate it, he was to rule the Church from Lyons until the Emperor's death six years later.

How very much this step implied liberation can be inferred from the accelerated activity of the papal chancery, the lively visits to the Curia, the abundance of far-reaching decisions which occurred almost immediately after the arrival at Lyons and led in the most varied sectors

[7] E. Kantorowicz, *Kaiser Friedrich der Zweite*, supplement, 225: the Emperor's words, "Nullus papa potest esse Gibellinus," reported by Galvanus Flamma, are in *Muratori, Scriptores*, XI, 680.

[8] The best presentation of these negotiations is by A. Folz, *Kaiser Friedrich II. und Papst Innocenz IV. Ihr Kampf in den Jahren 1244 und 1245* (Strasbourg 1905).

of Church life to new starts and new ways of life. This showed, as would also be the case later at Avignon, that Rome could not for a long time be regarded basically as the centrally located residence of the Popes, not to speak of the continuing difficulties which the city's local politics caused — hardly the climate suited for a peaceful government.

The First Council of Lyons (1245)

Innocent IV announced on 27 December 1244 that he would convoke a general council, which was to meet at Lyons on 24 June 1245.[9] The invitations were sent out from 3 January 1245 to the episcopate, to cathedral chapters and abbots, to princes and cities. The matters to be treated were reform ("status debitus ecclesiae romanae"), the crusade, aid to Constantinople, measures against the Mongols, and finally the conflict with the Emperor ("de negotio, quod inter ecclesiam et principem vertitur"). Since, besides the Mongols, also "other despisers of the faith and persecutors of the Christian people" were mentioned, it may be surmised that the reference was to heretics, against whom, despite a half-century of persistent struggle, the Church still had to fight. In addition to the conflict with the Emperor, these were the classical conciliar themes of the Middle Ages.

The Emperor, the Pope wrote, had been called upon by him in his sermon of 27 December to come to the Council, not as a participant, as were the other kings and princes, but as a defendant („citavimus"), who was to justify himself ("responsurus") there to the Pope and the others.

When the reports of the severe setbacks in the Holy Land — the taking of Jerusalem by the Khwarazmian Turks and the defeat of the knights at Gaza and Ascalon — reached Italy around the end of the year through the Patriarch of Antioch, and the Emperor in a circular appealed to the Christian princes for help, there simultaneously began the final peace negotiations between Emperor and Pope, in which the Patriarch was involved. It is true that on Holy Thursday Innocent renewed Frederick's excommunication, probably because of pressure from the Archbishops of Mainz and Cologne, who kept aloof from the Emperor in Germany. Still, we possess a letter of 6 May 1245, in which the Pope declared his readiness to lift the censure if Frederick would really take his promises seriously. But simultaneous encroachments of the imperial troops in the *Patrimonium* and the Emperor's clumsy diplomatic maneuvers in England, where the Pope's request for financial help was to be thwarted, brought to nothing these attempts of the eleventh hour.

[9] On the preparation for the Council, its course, and its outcome *cf.* H. Wolter and H. Holstein, *Lyon I et Lyon II (Histoire des Conciles Oecuméniques, 7)* (Paris 1966).

And so the Council assembled with its program unchanged. Attendance by the bishops of lands ruled by Frederick was naturally meagre. Some exiled prelates did come, but from the Empire only the Bishops of Prague and Liège and those of the Kingdom of Burgundy. Spain, France, and England, on the other hand, were well represented. Altogether there were present 150 bishops and, in addition, abbots, the generals of the new orders, deputies of invited chapters, of cities, and of princes. Baldwin II, Emperor of Constantinople, Raymond VII, Count of Toulouse, and Raymond Berengar, Count of Provence, attended in person.

Between 26 June and 17 July 1245, there were four sessions of the Council, which of course continued its work between sessions in discussions, consistories, and committee meetings. On 28 June, in the first of the three principal sessions, which took place in the cathedral of Lyons, Innocent IV delivered the introductory address, outlining the program, after the Solemn Mass in the brief liturgical ceremony of inauguration: the decay of ecclesiastical discipline among clergy and laity ("status debitus ecclesiae"), the distress of the Holy Land because of the arrogance of the Muslims, the Greek Schism as reflected in the problem of the Latin Empire, the Mongol problem, and finally the persecution of the Church by the Emperor Frederick II.

At all the sessions the Emperor's case was pleaded especially by the Grand Justiciar, Thaddeus of Suessa, who exerted some influence on the assembly in his discourses. In addition, Frederick was championed by the Patriarch of Aquileia and the English envoys. The closing session, intended for 12 July, was postponed by the Pope till 17 July at the request of Frederick's agents in order to await the arrival of the Emperor, who was thought to be *en route* to Lyons. But he came no nearer than Turin, for he clearly had no intention of appearing in person at the Council.

And so there was handed down in the final session the decision which the Pope had previously discussed thoroughly with the prelates individually and which was approved by most of them without any objection. First of all, Innocent announced that the feast of Our Lady's Birthday, 8 September, should henceforth be celebrated with an octave by the entire Church. He then had the decisions of the Council read; issued in the form of juridical decrees and constitutions, they addressed themselves to the various problems considered, as laws, instructions, admonitions, and proclamations. The Council promoted reform by its clarification of juridical, especially procedural, problems, its tightening of administrative controls, chiefly in regard to an improvement of monastic economic management, and its more precise definition of the powers of papal legates. It tried to meet the Mongol peril by its call for intensive measures of defense. Ecclesiastical taxes were prescribed for the safety of the Latin Empire, while in regard to the crusade the decrees of Lateran IV were renewed, but, significantly, no concrete planning was attempted. Then, before Innocent could have the bull of deposition read, Thaddeus of Suessa lodged a formal appeal against it to the next Pope and to an authentic general council. Innocent calmly defended the universality of the Council of Lyons, to which, he said, all in Christendom who were qualified had been invited; he also noted that Frederick himself was the reason why certain regional episcopates had been unable to attend.

The Council's final act was the reading of the bull of deposition and its confirmation by the assembly. Because of the four crimes of perjury, breach of peace, sacrilege in imprisoning prelates, and suspicion of heresy, Frederick II was deposed as Roman Emperor, King of Germany, and King of Sicily; he was stripped of all honours and dignities, his subjects were released from their oaths of loyalty, and the German princes were invited to proceed to a new election. The Pope, with the advice of the cardinals, intended himself to decide the future of the Sicilian Kingdom.

The session ended with the *Te Deum*. Incidentally, Frederick's excommunication had purposely not been renewed, and so there was here involved what was until now the single case of an implementation of statement 13 of Gregory VII's *Dictatus Papae*.[10]

The First Council of Lyons was a turning point. Despite harsh words the Emperor did not cease, even after the Council, his efforts for peace with the Curia. But the sentence of Lyons intensified the breach between him and the Pope. The struggle for hegemony in Italy and the reaction of the Curia, which feared for its ecclesiastical independence, had now become a struggle over the continuance or non-continuance of the imperial office in the House of Hohenstaufen and at the same time over the validity of the Hohenstaufen concept of the Empire. The Pope mobilized all of his strength in Germany, Italy, and the Sicilian Kingdom in order to enforce the sentence of Lyons. Henry III of England, who was Frederick's brother-in-law, and Louis IX of France maintained a strict neutrality. The Pope contrived to win back Hungary, which had expected help from the Emperor against the Mongols. As had already been clear at the Council, Spain was entirely on the Pope's side, even though Ferdinand III of Castile remained neutral.

But the Emperor made his presence felt everywhere by means of envoys, letters, threats, demands. The journalism of 1239–42 was resumed but its tenor had changed. The question now was whether the Pope had a right

---

[10] "Quod illi liceat imperatores deponere," *Reg.* II, 55a, ed. E. Caspar, 204, 5; see Volume III of this *Handbook,* p. 369 and footnote 4.

to depose the Emperor. Innocent IV maintained that he did, pointing to the authority whereby he constituted the Emperor. The Pope "makes" the Emperor, he said, and hence in a given case he can again deprive him of office and dignity.[11]

The Emperor likewise argued from principle, while coming forward with a reform plan, which relegated the Church, and in her the Pope, to properly spiritual functions, to the apostolic ideal of the Primitive Church, with its subordination to the divinely established authority of kings. Frederick's letter of February 1246[12] was, of course, not intended as a plan for a reform actually to be carried out but as an element in a journalistic confrontation. It found an echo in a manifesto of French barons of November 1246, which even led to a league of the barons against the Clergy.[13]

In Germany[14] Innocent managed powerfully to arrange the fronts in his own favour, thanks to a consistent personal policy on a high level. In the Kingdom of Sicily he had a crusade preached against Frederick. But the struggle could not be decided until Frederick's death on 13 December 1250. Innocent returned to Italy in order to oppose first Conrad IV, who died on 21 May 1254, before the Pope's death, and then Manfred.[15] But Manfred continued to cause anxiety for the papacy until his death at Benevento in 1266. When on 29 October 1268 Conradin was executed at Naples, the male line of the Hohenstaufen Dynasty was extinguished. Italy did not lay eyes on another Emperor in the thirteenth century.

---

[11] Innocent IV gave a detailed explanation of the Council's decree of deposition in his *Apparatus (Commentaria super libros quinque Decretalium)* (ed. Frankfurt 1570), lib. II, tit. XXVII, cap. XXVII, 316^v–317^v: "papa iure deponit imperatorem." Innocent developed the bold notion that Christ is the "dominus naturalis" of emperors and kings and hence can institute and depose them. Christ has fully transmitted this power to his Vicar on earth.

[12] Huillard-Bréholles, *Historia diplomatica*, VI, 391 f.

[13] C. Petit-Dutaillis, *La Monarchie Féodale en France et en Angleterre, X^e–XIIIe siècle* (Paris 1950), 295 f.

[14] *Cf.* P. Aldinger, *Die Neubesetzung der deutschen Bistümer unter Papst Innocenz IV. (1243–54)* (Leipzig 1900), and H. Kroppmann, *Ehedispensübung und Stauferkampf unter Innocenz IV.* (Berlin 1937).

[15] M. Finano, "La città di Napoli nelle lotte tra Innocenzo IV e Manfredo," *Studi in onore di Ricardo Filangeri*, 3 vols. (Naples 1961), I, 259–82.

CHAPTER 26

The Veering of the Papacy to France and the Angevin Domination in Italy

After the deposition of Frederick II at the Council of Lyons, Innocent IV had left the succession to the Hohenstaufen in the Empire to the qualified electors, but he had reserved the new order in the Kingdom of Sicily to himself and the cardinals.[1] The "Sicilian question" was greatly to embarrass the Curia's policy until the end of the century. There were two possibilities for solving it: The Roman Church could either undertake the administration of the Kingdom or enfeoff a new dynasty with it. At first Innocent seemed to be inclined to assume the direct rule, even though the scarcely happy experiences of his predecessor, Innocent III, as guardian of the young Frederick, with a direct administration of his sort must have been known to him. As a matter of fact, the Curia's financial, military, and personnel resources quickly proved to be too weak, and so the second possibility had to be seriously considered.

First, the Pope offered the Kingdom to Earl Richard of Cornwall,[2] and then, almost simultaneously, to the brother of Louis IX of France, Charles of Anjou, Count of Provence. Both declined, whereupon Innocent began negotiations with King Henry III of England.[3] Through *Magister* Albert of Parma he suggested that Henry should accept the Kingdom for his eight-year-old son Edmund.

After the death on 21 May 1254 of Conrad IV, the Pope felt he was in a position to incorporate Sicily into the Papal State, and hence he broke off the negotiations with England. The envisaged conquest of Sicily under the leadership of the papal nephew, Fieschi, failed. Its collapse was the last message given to Innocent IV, who died at Naples on 7 December 1254. The Hohenstaufen policy was quickly taken up and continued by Manfred, independently and successfully. Without having any support in Germany, Manfred sought to realize in their fulness the Italian plans of his imperial father.

---

[1] Bulla depositionis Friderici II imperatoris: "Illi autem, ad quos in eodem imperio imperatoris spectat electio, eligant libere successorem. De praefato vero Siciliae regno providere curabimus cum eorundem fratrum consilio, sicut viderimus expedire" (*COD*, 259, 30–35).

[2] H. Marc-Bonnet, "Richard de Cornouailles et la Couronne de Sicile, " *Mélanges L. Halphen* (Paris 1951), 483–89, points out that Innocent IV's first contacts with Richard, if they were not made as early as 1247, probably occurred at Lyons in April 1250.

[3] The best account of the English candidacy for Sicily is A. Wachtel, "Die sizilische Thronkandidatur des Prinzen Edmund von England," *DA*, 4 (1941), 98–178; *cf.* M. Powicke, *The Thirteenth Century (1216–1307)* (Oxford, 2nd ed. 1962), 110–23, 136, 167, who labels the enterprise "the Sicilian business."

Because of this turn of events, Alexander IV, who had succeeded Inno-cent IV on 12 December 1254, resumed the negotiations with England. He excommunicated Manfred on 25 March 1255, and on 9 April enfeoffed Edmund with Sicily. When Henry III was unable to meet the high finan-cial and military commitment he had contracted, Alexander cancelled the agreement in 1258, but he had no alternative solution ready. In the same year Manfred had himself crowned King at Palermo on 10 August. His influence grew steadily in Spoleto, the Marches of Ancona, and Romagna. Even at Rome the Ghibellines contrived in the spring of 1261, at the very time when Richard of Cornwall was elected Senator,[4] to secure this dignity for Manfred also.

Alexander IV died on 25 May 1261. For three months the conclave sweated over the succession, which was finally bestowed on an outsider, the Patriarch of Jerusalem, James Pantaléon, a Frenchman from Troyes in Champagne. He had taken part in the Council of Lyons as Archdeacon of Liège; then, in the service of the Curia he had got to know North and East Germany and Poland on extensive legatine journeys. An energetic, shrewd, and diplomatically patient ruler, Urban IV (1261–64), being a Frenchman, was not compromised by the problems of Italy and hence he was freer. He was determined to solve the Sicilian question in order to free his hands for the problems of the whole Church. Under him was completed the papacy's veering to France.

He first succeeded in again strengthening papal influence in North and Central Italy to the detriment of Manfred. He abandoned the English candidacy and asked Louis IX to permit one of his sons to accept enfeoff-ment with Sicily. The French King refused, referring to Edmund's rights and to the claims of Conradin of Hohenstaufen. Hence Urban turned to Charles of Anjou. The treaty with England was formally annulled, the consent of Louis IX was won, and on 17 June 1263 a treaty was drawn up which sketched in broad outline the Curia's ideas about the envisaged solution of the Sicilian question. South Italy and the island of Sicily were to remain united, and Charles of Anjou would be enfeoffed with the Kingdom in return for a single payment of 50,000 marks sterling. A yearly *census* of 10,000 ounces of gold was anticipated. The freedom of the Church in the Kingdom was to be assured, and Charles promised the Curia military aid. He had to oblige himself to reject any offer of the German or the imperial crown, and there was to be no question of

---

[4] From the time of his election as King of the Romans in 1257 Richard had sought corona-tion as Emperor. His designation as one of the two Senators of Rome, urged by Cardinals Ottobuono Fieschi and John of Toledo, was intended to induce the hesitant Pope to make a decision. *Cf.* A. Wachtel, *loc. cit.*, 165, N. Schöpp, *Papst Hadrian V. (Kardinal Otto-buono Fieschi)* (Heidelberg 1916), 72–75, and F. R. Lewis, "The Election of Richard of Cornwall as Senator of Rome in 1261," *EHR*, 52 (1937), 657–62.

his ruling the imperial provinces in Italy or the Papal State. Other stipulations explained the aid which the Curia expected from Charles, who was to take possession of his fief within one year. When Manfred, in view of the now clear candidacy of the Angevin, seriously harassed the Pope, Charles was easily able to have the draft of the treaty modified in his favour. Even before it was signed Charles had violated its stipulations by accepting election as Senator of Rome. Nevertheless, Urban confirmed the election, which made it obvious that there would be other complications. Before the Pope died on 2 October 1264, the Curia's treaty with Charles of Anjou had been signed. The Angevin domination had been established, not only in the Sicilian Kingdom, but, as events were to prove, also in Italy.

The long vacancy of the Holy See, which lasted until 5 February 1265, facilitated the assuming of power by the new lord of Sicily. He prepared for this by underpinning it with a long series of alliances which he concluded with North Italian rulers and cities. Such a procedure hardly corresponded to the spirit of the treaty he had just signed with the Roman Church. But the new Pope, Clement IV (1265–68), less vigorous than his predecessor, had also, as a Frenchman, close personal ties with the House of Anjou. On 28 June 1265 he solemnly invested the new King of Sicily at Rome. Thanks to his good offices, Charles was able to make contacts with Tuscan bankers, who granted him extensive credit against a thirty-years' tithe on the French Church. In this way Tuscany became involved in the new Sicilian policy: Charles opened up his new Kingdom to economic exploitation. The confrontation with Manfred led to the decisive battle of Benevento, where on 26 February 1266, the last Hohenstaufen ruler of Sicily lost both Kingdom and life. The route into the Kingdom was now open for its new master.

But Conradin of Hohenstaufen, Duke of Swabia and King of Jerusalem, was still alive and he claimed the succession in Sicily. After Manfred's death a diet at Augsburg in October 1266 decided on an Italian expedition by the youthful Conradin. All who were unhappy with the papacy's award to Anjou had turned to him: the Hohenstaufen faction in Sicily, the opposition in the Papal State, and the Ghibellines of Tuscany under Pisa's leadership. Condottieri of every sort joined him, including two Infantes of Spain, Henry and Frederick, brothers of King Alfonso X of Castile, who had himself been elected King of the Romans in 1257.

Papal objections had thus far prevented Conradin's election as King. Clement IV now tried to stop Conradin's expedition. He threatened excommunication and interdict, in April 1267 appointed Charles paciarius generalis to safeguard disinterestedly the rights of all during the vacancy of the Empire, permitted the Angevin to hold power for six years as podestà in Florence and other cities of Tuscany, and in the cathedral of

Verona on 18 November 1267 declared that Conradin had incurred excommunication for having disregarded the prohibition of coming to Italy;
if he advanced farther, he would be deprived of the Kingdom of Jerusalem.
On Holy Thursday, 5 April 1268, Clement formally deposed him from the
throne of Jerusalem, had a crusade preached against him, and, finally, on
17 April, named Charles imperial vicar in Tuscany. But meanwhile Conradin moved from Verona *via* Pavia, Pisa, and Siena to Rome, where on
24 July 1268 he was elected Senator. When he set out to conquer the
Sicilian Kingdom he lost the decisive battle of Tagliacozzo on 23 August.
He was overtaken in flight. Charles put him on trial and had him
beheaded at Naples on 29 October 1268.[5] Exactly one month later
Clement IV died at Viterbo.

Charles of Anjou, now unchallenged master of the Kingdom of Sicily,
in possession of Tuscany, and influential in Lombardy, prepared to gain
all of Italy as heir of the Hohenstaufen. Persons had already heard of his
intention of supporting the powerless Emperor Baldwin II in reconquering
Byzantium, whereupon Jerusalem was to be liberated. A comprehensive
imperialist scheme unfolded itself.[6]

For almost three years — from 29 November 1268 to 1 September
1271 — the Holy See remained vacant. Charles of Anjou utilized this
time to suppress opposition in his Kingdom, to arrange the affairs of Tuscany as its master, to hold in check his Ghibelline opponents in North Italy.
At Rome he was elected Senator for life. Hence in 1270 he seemed to rule
all of Italy. The papacy saw him as its assistant, but now he had risen to
become master. Innocent IV's mighty exertions had been apparently in
vain.

For twenty years after its victory over the Hohenstaufen the Curia had
been so seriously hampered by its concern for the succession to Sicily and
by the unrest in the other parts of Italy that important tasks in the East
and in the government of the Universal Church had been neglected. In
1261 Constantinople was lost, as far as the West was concerned. In the
Empire the double election of 1257 had inaugurated the dark age of the
Interregnum. Alfonso X of Castile never entered the Empire, while
Richard of Cornwall in his brief visits could gain recognition only in the
West. Christendom, which had seemed united and strong on the morrow
of the papal victory over Frederick II, began to display symptoms of

---

[5] A. Nitschke did painstaking research into Conradin's fate, the "trial," and the Pope's
position in regard to it in *ZSavRGkan,* 42 (1956), 25–54. H. M. Schaller, "Zur Verurtei-
lung Konradins," *QFIAB,* 37 (1957), 311–27, challenged him in particular points, but in
QFIAB, 38 (1958), 268–77, Nitschke was able to maintain his theses.

[6] *Cf.* E. Dade, *Versuche zur Wiedererrichtung der lateinischen Herrschaft in Konstantinopel im Rahmen der abendländischen Politik 1261 bis etwa 1310* (Jena 1937), and S. Runciman, *The Sicilian Vespers* (Cambridge 1958), 135–47.

inner uncertainty because of a lack of firm leadership. A religious and moral deterioration in many strata of Christian society made itself felt. The territorial prince's authority over the Church was everywhere consolidated. Reform was needed and persons looked for a man who could master the confusion of the age and restore order.

CHAPTER 27

Pope Gregory X and the Second Council of Lyons

The election of Tedaldo Visconti on 1 September 1271 ended the longest vacancy of the Holy See in the thirteenth century. Archdeacon of Liège, he was then in the Holy Land; he arrived in Viterbo in February 1272 and was crowned at Rome on 26 March. As early as 13 April invitations went out for a general council, which once again was to meet in Lyons.[1] Reform of the Church, union with the Greeks, and aid for the Holy Land were to be the principal themes of the gathering. They were also the essential concerns of the program laid down for his pontificate by Gregory X (1271–76).

The leitmotif was the liberation of the Holy Places, and peace with Byzantium was regarded as its prerequisite. The renewal of ecclesiastical life in Western Christendom was likewise to serve this end. The schemes of Charles of Anjou with regard to Byzantium had to be stopped. While still in Syria Gregory X had initiated negotiations[2] with the Emperor Michael VIII Palaeologus.[3] To protect himself against the threat from Charles of Anjou, the Emperor was ready for far-reaching concessions, even for the recognition of the Roman Primacy. However, his clergy and people made it clear to the Emperor that he would find no support among them for his policy, and the Patriarch Joseph abdicated.

In Italy, Gregory, while allowing Charles of Anjou to continue as Roman Senator and as imperial vicar in Tuscany, avoided giving any appearance that the papacy was dependent on Charles. He aimed at an energetic effort to settle the strife between Guelfs and Ghibellines, which

[1] Lyons was selected in order to exclude the influence of Charles of Anjou. The Pope's journey is described by A. Callebaut, "Le voyage du B. Grégoire X et du S. Bonaventure au Concile de Lyon," *AFrH*, 18 (1925), 169–80.

[2] George Pachymeres, *De Michaele Paleologo*, V, 11 (*PG*, 143, 823A).

[3] C. Chapman, *Michel Paléologue, restaurateur de l'Empire byzantin (1261–82)* (Paris 1926); also D. J. Geanakoplos, *Emperor Michael Paleologue and the West (1258–82). A Study in Byzantine-Latin Relations* (Cambridge, Mass. 1959), and H. D. Nicol, "The Greeks and the Union of the Churches. The Preliminaries to the Second Council of Lyons (1261–1274)," *MS*, presented to A. Gwynn (Dublin 1961), 454–80.

was tearing all of Italy to pieces. The principal factor in settling this difficult complex of problems was to be the election of a new Emperor. By means of a friendly cooperation with him, the Pope intended to try to restore peace to Italy. Furthermore, the growing anarchy in Germany during the reigns of the rival Kings, Richard of Cornwall and Alfonso of Castile, had done the greatest harm to the Church as well as to the nation. Richard died on April 1272. When Alfonso now sought to obtain recognition by the Pope as King of Germany, Gregory referred him to the German electoral princes, whose business it was, he said, to decide who should be King.

Since Richard's death the Electors had been concerned about the succession. As candidates there came forward King Ottakar II of Bohemia, King Philip III of France, Duke Henry of Bavaria, Conradin's uncle and heir, and the Duke's brother, the Count Palatine Louis, himself one of the Electors. However, agreement was eventually reached on the Landgrave of Alsace, Rudolf of Habsburg, who was elected at Frankfurt on 1 October 1273 and crowned at Aachen on 24 October. Ottakar had been too powerful, Philip had been rejected by the Pope, Henry had withdrawn, and no one had wanted Louis. Ottakar had not appeared for the election, and for this one occasion his vote had been awarded to the Duke of Bavaria.

The Electors informed the Pope of Rudolf's election and coronation and asked that he be given the imperial crown. Rudolf sent an embassy to Rome to convey his respects and assured the Pope of his readiness to take the cross. Ottakar protested and lodged an appeal against the outcome of the election. Gregory cordially accepted the messages from Germany but postponed a decision until the Council.[4]

The preparations for the Council were aided by testimonials on the state of the Church, which the Pope requested from everywhere. Of the extant replies the most useful were those of Bishop Bruno of Olomouc and of the former general of the Dominicans, Humbert of Romans.[5] They sketched

---

[4] A. Zisterer, *Gregor X. und Rudolf von Habsburg in ihren beiderseitigen Beziehungen* (Freiburg 1891); H. Otto, *Die Beziehungen Rudolfs von Habsburg zu Papst Gregor X.* (Innsbruck 1895); O. Redlich, *Rudolf von Habsburg* (Innsbruck 1903); K. and M. Uhlirz, *Handbuch der Geschichte Österreich-Ungarns*, I (Graz and Cologne, 2nd ed., 1963), 263–66, 274–78 (bibliography).

[5] The *Opus tripartitum* deals systematically with the three points of the Council's program: crusade, union with the Greeks, and reform of the Church. A fourth testimonial came from the Franciscan Fidentius of Padua; composed at the request of Gregory X, it did not become known until 1291, but it was probably written at the time of the Council. It is entitled *De recuperatione Terrae Sanctae*, ed. G. Golubovich, *Biblioteca bio-bibliografica della Terra Santa*, II (Quaracchi 1913), 1–60. Among the works preparatory to the Council must also be included Thomas Aquinas's *Contra errores Graecorum* (1260). Thomas, invited to take part, died, as is well known, *en route* to Lyons on 7 March 1274 in the Cistercian Abbey of Fossanuova. The last edition of his work is by P. Glorieux (Tournai and Paris 1957).

a gloomy picture of the religious condition of both clergy and people. Bruno's reform proposal amounted to a strengthening of episcopal authority, notably *vis-à-vis* the richly privileged mendicant orders. Humbert demanded especially a reform of the Curia.

The Council met in Lyons on 7 May 1274. Almost 300 bishops, sixty abbots, generals of orders, and prelates, and leading theologians attended,[6] but Thomas Aquinas had died *en route*. King James I of Aragón was the only prince to accept the invitation in person; the others were represented by envoys. The Greek embassy made its belated appearance on 24 June, and eventually a group of Mongols also arrived.

Gregory X had not desired a mass-meeting, and the monasteries and collegiate churches were originally supposed to be represented only by an abbot or provost respectively, but he probably did want a gathering that properly represented all of Christendom in all its social classes. Of the three principal topics, the most important, Church reform, for which the best preliminary work had been done, seems to have been the least discussed. The union with the Greeks was realized because the Emperor had already previously declared for it in principle. For the crusade there was at hand Michael VIII's promise to participate in it if the West would first make a lasting peace with him, a condition aimed at frustrating the projects of Charles of Anjou and Baldwin II. With the envoys of the Khan of Persia was made a treaty which provided for a common front against Islam. The Kings of France, England, Aragón, and Sicily agreed in principle to take part in the crusade. At the conciliar consistory of 6 June 1274, the Chancellor Otto swore, on behalf of King Rudolf, to maintain the privileges and promises made to the Roman Church by Otto IV and Frederick II; included was the renunciation of the Sicilian Kingdom.[7] Rudolf's recognition by the Pope was given on 26 September; it had been delayed because Gregory had hoped that Ottakar of Bohemia and Alfonso of Castile would in the meantime have dropped their claims.

In agreement with the cardinals at Lyons the Pope appointed 23 May of the following year for the imperial coronation, but the date was soon put off until 1 November 1275. By means of stubborn negotiations, Gregory X succeeded in inducing King Alfonso to renounce the imperial crown. In October 1275 the Pope and King Rudolf met at Lausanne, where Rudolf in person made the promises already sworn to by his chan-

---

[6] J. Guiraud, *Les Registres de Grégoire X*, no. 220, contains the list of prelates; among them, in addition to the bishops, were the Patriarchs of Jerusalem and Constantinople, the Abbots of Cluny, Prémontré, Cîteaux, and Clairvaux, the generals of the Dominicans, Franciscans, and Augustinian Hermits, and the grand masters of the three military orders.

[7] "Cum prorsus intentionis sit Romane ecclesie, ut regnum ... nullo umquam tempore imperio uniatur, ut scilicet unus Romanus Imperator et Sicilie rex existat"; thus the oath taken by Charles of Anjou on 7 October 1276 (J. Guiraud, *Registres*, no. 163).

cellor; he also intended, if necessary, to preserve and defend the Kingdom of Sicily for the Church, but not to assume the government himself, as this is usually understood. Now 2 February 1276 was agreed upon as the date of the imperial coronation and then Rudolf, together with the princes present and 500 knights, took the cross. But this date also could not be kept, for Gregory X died at Arezzo on 10 January 1276.

The Council met from 7 May to 17 July, longer than any of its predecessors. The proxies of the chapters were dismissed after the second session, 18 May. The Byzantine embassy arrived a month late. The discussions between the Pope and the cardinals relative to the rules of the conclave were protracted, and the meetings with the representatives of Alfonso of Castile and of Rudolf of Habsburg claimed much time. On 4 July the Pope received the sixteen envoys of the Mongol Khan Abaga. The publication of the conciliar decrees was distributed among several sessions, and so the impression is created that the Council worked intensively. The Pope himself and his two trusted collaborators, the Franciscan Cardinal Bonaventure and the Dominican Cardinal, Peter of Tarentaise[8], which is reflected in the *professio fidei*,[9] were the preparations for the Among the results of the Council, in addition to the union with the Greeks, which is reflected in the *professio fidei*[9], were the preparations for the crusade. Provision was made for a tithe on all ecclesiastical incomes over a period of six years. No fundamentally new considerations were brought forward, but the texts of 1215 and 1245 were used. Princes and kings had promised to take part, and Michael Palaeologus also seemed ready to cooperate under certain conditions. More detailed plans were not outlined, nor was a date appointed. The Pope's early death was a severe blow to the enterprise.

The Council's decrees continued the legislative work of 1215 and 1245. First place among them belongs to the constitution *Ubi periculum*,[10] which made new rules for the papal election. Frequently revised, it is still in force today. The cardinals were not to wait more than ten days from the Pope's death for the arrival of the absent. The election was to occur in the place where the Pope died. The cardinals were to stay together, cut

---

[8] For Peter of Tarentaise see M. H. Laurent, "Le bienheureux Innocent V (Pierre de Tarentaise) et son temps," *SteT*, 129 (Rome 1947); for Bonaventure see R. Ménindès, "Saint Bonaventure, les Frères mineurs et l'unité de l'Église au concile de Lyon," *La France franciscaine*, ser. II, 18 (1935), 363–92.

[9] Constitutio "Fideli ac devota," *COD*, 290; see also the comments of H. Holstein in H. Wolter and H. Holstein, *Lyon I et Lyon II*, 192–96.

[10] Constitutio "Ubi periculum," *COD*, 290-94; *cf.* E. Ruffini-Avondo, "Le origini del conclave papale," *Atti della R. Accademia delle scienze di Torino*, 62 (Turin 1927), 409–30; O. Jölson, *Die Papstwahlen des 13. Jahrhunderts bis zur Einführung der Conclaveordnung Gregors X.* (Berlin 1928).

off from all contact with the outside world, until they had completed the election. The longer the election took, the more scanty should their provisions become. In addition, the constitution deprived the cardinals of all revenues during the vacancy. Such stern conditions explain the resistance of those affected. For the constitution was annulled by Gregory's successors and only put back into effect by Celestine V. It was included in the *Liber Sextus* by Boniface VIII and from then on was an element of the canon law that is still valid.

The other decrees attacked abuses, as these were specified in the various testimonials. Excessively long vacancies, especially of benefices connected with the care of souls, were to be stopped, and only worthy and educated candidates were to be named, above all for parishes. The duty of residence was inculcated, and pluralism was made more difficult. An effort was made to eliminate abuses in elections. The Council exerted itself for the renewal of the capitular liturgy, which was deteriorating, and turned its attention to the piety of the faithful. The constitution *Religionum diversitatem* [11] repeated the prohibition made in 1215 of founding new orders and congregations and suppressed all establishments made since that time without the consent of the Holy See; the others were subjected to severe restrictions. Only the two oldest mendicant orders were excepted from this strict legislation; the Carmelites and the Augustinian Hermits had to await further instructions. The Pope reserved for a later regulation the relations of the new orders to the episcopate, especially in regard to the much disputed pastoral privileges. All the military orders were supposed to be combined into one single order, but this effort collapsed on the opposition that was to be expected from Spain. This constitution was to have a great impact on the further development of relations between the regular and the diocesan clergy.

Finally, usury was again reprobated, the penal law was made more precise, and decrees were issued for the course of trials; these last were directed especially against excessive prolonging. The Pope was unable to see to the implementation of these decrees, but they were almost all adopted into the *Corpus Iuris* and hence acquired permanent validity. In his closing address Gregory X charged the bishops especially to tackle the reform of the parochial care of souls; they should so reform themselves and, by a careful personal policy, their estate, that the anticipated overcoming of the decay of Church life, complained of and described on all sides, might now begin and its permanence might be assured. It is the tragedy of Gregory X that the union with the Greeks was not lasting, the crusade did not take place, and the sought for reform was not realized.

---

[11] Constitutio "Religionum diversitatem," *COD*, 302 f.

207

CHAPTER 28

Heresy and the Inquisition in the Thirteenth Century

Waldensians, Humiliati, Cathari — a legacy of the late twelfth century — were not regained to the unity of the Church, despite Innocent III's policy of conciliation and the measures of the Fourth Lateran Council. On the contrary, they again spread throughout Europe, apart from England. The Cathari continued to be in congenial surroundings especially in Languedoc and to a lesser degree in Lombardy.[1] Related to them were the Albanenses on Lake Garda under John di Luglio.[2] The Garatenses and Bagnolenses were regarded as moderate dualists. Groups of Cathari were formed around Vicenza and in Tuscany. Mutually hostile, they nevertheless occasionally closed ranks on the outbreak of persecution. Cathari were encountered also in Catalonia, Aragón, and Castile. They were often organized into churches: three in Languedoc, six in Italy, others in the Balkan peninsula and the Near East and in France, Germany, and Spain. In 1250 the Dominican Rainer Sacconi[3] mentioned sixteen. The Cathari often formulated their doctrine during the crusades against them and in the conflict with the Inquisition. They published Latin writings. Little of this is extant; for the most part it is known from quotations in Catholic literature.[4] The ex-Waldensian Durandus of Huesca cited a statement of doctrine composed in Languedoc in 1220.[5] The former Cathar Rainer Sacconi made use of the work of John di Luglio (1230). The *Liber de duobus principiis*, written after 1240, contains a Cathar ritual in Latin; corresponding to it is a ritual drawn up in Provençal around 1280. These works could not have contributed any new impulse to the Cathar movement itself. Following the wars in the Midi they could maintain themselves only as harmless sectaries. The last proceedings against them took place around 1300 in the Midi and North Italy.

The Waldensians, who have maintained themselves until the present, were more tenacious. As the "Poor Lombards" they began to play a role of their own in North Italy and distinguished themselves from the French "Poor Men of Lyons." They were connected with the Humiliati, flatly rejected

[1] *Cf.* A. Dondaine, "La Hiérarchie cathare en Italie," *AFP*, 19 (1949), 280–312, 20 (1950), 234–305.

[2] Before 1190 they had combined into a bishopric — Desenzano on Lake Garda — and belonged to the radical dualistic faction of the Cathari.

[3] Rainer Sacconi (d. 1262) grew up as a Cathar, was converted by Peter Martyr, and from 1254 was director of the Inquisition in Lombardy. His *Summa de catharis et de pauperibus de Lugduno,* composed *ca.* 1250, was edited by A. Dondaine, *Un traité néo-manichéen du XIIIᵉ siècle. Le Liber de duobus principiis* (Rome 1939), 64–78.

[4] By these are meant the works by Peter of Verona, James de Capellis, Moneta of Cremona, Salvo Burci, and others, which are given in the bibliography for this chapter.

[5] A. Dondaine, "Durand de Huesca et la polémique anti-cathare," *AFP*, 29 (1959), 228–76.

Men of Lyons." They were connected with the Humiliati, flatly rejected the notion of Sacraments, and aspired to live, not by begging, but in communities of workers. They also refused any control of their beliefs by the French Waldensians. In Germany they made their appearance as *Runcarii*, apparently so called from John of Ronco, the first leader of the "Poor Lombards." The German Waldensians maintained a rather slight contact with the Lombard brethren and bishops and sent them money. In Lombardy, France, and Spain they were liquidated by the Inquisition. But Waldensian communities survived in Calabria and Apulia and in the Alpine valleys of Piedmont and Savoy.

The German Waldensians reached Bohemia, Poland, and Hungary in the wake of the eastern colonial movement. Berthold of Regensburg preached[6] and David of Augsburg wrote against them, but without enduring success. Around 1315 they were encountered in more than forty Austrian communities in the bishopric of Passau.

Alongside Cathari and Waldensians there everywhere emerged in the thirteenth century, at first in isolation, then in variously increasing numbers, heresies of another sort, which did not, however, organize themselves as sects. Their basic sources included theological and philosophical speculations of learned circles, while spiritualistic tendencies, above all among the women, became apparent. It should be recalled that the Fourth Lateran Council had rejected the Trinitarian doctrine of Joachim of Fiore and the teachings of the Parisian master, Amaury of Bène. Innocent III is said also to have condemned David of Dinant and Ortlieb of Strasbourg. Joachim's doctrine[7] was first popularized around the mid-century by Franciscans, by, among others, Gerard of Borgo San Donnino in 1254.[8] William of Saint-Amour, on the other hand, attacked it at Paris. Gerard's introduction to the *Evangelium aeternum* of Joachim of Fiore[9] was condemned and burned, but so also was the attack on it by William of Saint-Amour. The long dead Joachim himself was investigated by a commission of cardinals under Alexander IV, but he was not branded a heretic. His writings continued

---

[6] L. Casutt, *Die Handschriften mit lateinischen Predigten Bertholds von Regensburg (1210–72)* (Freiburg 1961).

[7] But *cf.* M. W. Bloomfield and M. E. Reeves, "The Penetration of Joachimism into Northern Europe," *Speculum*, 29 (1954), 772–93, where it is established that Joachim and his ideas were known and discussed beyond the Alps long before 1256.

[8] For Franciscan Joachimism see Chapter 32.

[9] For the bibliography of the strife over the *Eternal Gospel* see M. W. Bloomfield and M. E. Reeves, *op. cit.*, 772, footnote 2; especially H. Denifle, "Das Evangelium Aeternum und die Commission zu Anagni," *ALKGMA*, 1 (1885), 49–142; M. Perrod, "Étude sur la vie et sur les œuvres de Guillaume de Saint-Amour...," *Mémoires de la Société d'Émulation du Jura*, 7ᵉ sér., 2 (Lons-le-Saunier 1902), 61–252; A. van den Wyngaert, "Querelles du clergé séculier et des ordres mendiants à l'université de Paris au XIIIᵉ siècle," *La France Franciscaine*, 5 (1922), 257–81.

to be influential among the "Spiritual" Franciscans. The "Joachimites" were especially numerous under the general John of Parma, but Bonaventure was able to get rid of them.

Joachim's doctrine of the Three Ages — the Old Testament as the Age of the Father, the New Testament as the Age of the Son, and an epoch of a monastically coloured spirituality as the Age of the Holy Spirit — influenced also a Parisian heretical circle of disciples of Amaury of Bène, who was first condemned in 1210. They regarded the Holy Spirit as incarnate in themselves, and a pantheistic ontology, as propounded by Amaury, became among them a fanaticism which found a response among both lay men and women. At the University of Paris a line of so-called Averroists led from David of Dinant to Siger of Brabant and others. They understood their Aristotle as a concept of being which was independent of the faith and theology, as a truth apart from theological truth — the "double truth."[10] Averroism continued to be influential among lay scholars, jurists and physicians, though it was repeatedly forbidden and the Inquisition proceeded energetically against its proponents, among others Siger of Brabant.

Analogous notions, similar to those represented by the disciples of Amaury and by David of Dinant, appeared also in Ortlieb of Strasbourg, who intended to obey only the Holy Spirit revealing himself to him most intimately. Ortlieb's followers[11] in Germany did not believe in creation, taught the eternity of the world with the Averroists, and denied the resurrection and the last judgment. They held that whoever did not join them in Noah's Ark was lost. They understood the sacraments and the articles of faith in a mystical sense and the Gospels in a moral sense, but not literally or sacramentally in the sense of tradition. Like the Waldensians and the Cathari, they rejected oaths and every form of lying and killing, but they permitted marriage and called for asceticism, in particular fasting and penance. They did not organize a sect. They were everywhere and nowhere. Wandering scholars, friars and preachers who were weary of the religious life, itinerant Beghards and Beguines may have transmitted such notions. As the opportunity arose, they were arrested, interrogated, and punished. Soon after 1270 Albert the Great wrote at Cologne an opinion on about one hundred statements of heretics in Swabian Ries near Nördlingen, which, as the *Compilatio de novo spiritu*, was included in the collection of the so-called Passau Anonymous and was there supplemented by a list of errors of this "heresy of the new Spirit."

The Beghard-Beguine movement of the thirteenth century[12] was also early infected by heretical elements, which, however, were not seen to be

[10] A. Hödl, "Siger de Brabant," *LThK*, IX (2nd ed. 1964), 746 f., denies that Siger of Brabant ever defended the doctrine of the double truth.

[11] On Ortlieb's followers see now H. Grundmann, *LThK*, VII (2nd ed. 1962), 1256 f.

[12] On the Beguines and the Beghards see Chapter 32.

dangerous until the fourteenth century. Because of the wide distribution and varied organization of the Beguines, these elements could not be localized and at first seemed to be merely enthusiastic admixtures in the fabric of what was in itself a pious and orthodox organization. Still, so far as the Church was concerned, these groups had to be kept under surveillance, because they quickly settled especially in the great cities, but these centres were located in those regions where heresy was at home by predilection: Byzantium, the Danube districts, the valleys of the Rhine, Meuse, Rhone and Saône, and Loire, Champagne, Flanders, North Italy, Provence, Languedoc, and Aragón.

The papal reaction against these heretical movements that were spreading everywhere proved to be ineffective. The secular arm was called upon for help in France, Spain, Italy, and the Empire, and warlike methods were employed under the guise of a crusade.[13] But then the papacy developed an institution whose origins go back to the twelfth century but which first obtained its organization in the second quarter of the thirteenth century: the Inquisition. At Verona in 1184 Lucius III, in the presence of the Emperor Frederick I, took up a decision rendered by Alexander III at the Council of Tours in 1163 and made it universally binding in his bull "Ad abolendam," which was later included in the decretals of Gregory IX. According to this, the bishop, as the ordinary judge in questions of heresy, was to search out heretics in biennial visitations of his diocese in order to prosecute them on his own authority, without waiting for a formal accusation. Thus, inquisition proceedings were to replace accusation proceedings. Here were the beginnings of the Inquisition. In his bull "Vergentis in senium" of 1199 Innocent III had confirmed these directives of 1184 and their strict sanctions, declared the offense of heresy to be *crimen maiestatis*, a concept of Roman law, and regulated the penalties there provided, stressing, it is true, that the Church may not disregard her obligation to exercise mercy. The Fourth Lateran Council made these rules law for the Universal Church,[14] emphasized the lawfulness of investigations from parish to parish, demanded that processes be initiated *ex officio*, without awaiting charges, and required the confiscation of the goods and the relinquishing, not the surrendering, of the condemned to the secular power for punishment, but with the *animadversio debita*. In this way the procedure of the Inquisition was essentially determined.

Honorius III proceeded further. He first intensified the Albigensian Crusade, for which the heir to the French throne made himself available. As King

---

[13] Cf. A. P. Evans, "The Albigensian Crusade," and J. R. Strayer, "The Political Crusades of the Thirteenth Century," *A History of the Crusades*, ed. K. M. Setton, II (Philadelphia 1962), 277–324, 343–76.
[14] COD, 213–15.

Louis VIII, the latter brought it to a close to the great advantage of the crown. In April 1226 Louis issued an ordinance[15] of significance for the development of the Inquisition: that every heretic condemned by the episcopal court was to be forthwith punished through the *animadversio debita,* while the penalty of infamy was to be the lot of followers and abettors. The bishop was thus the judge of heretics, and the canonical formula, *animadversione debita,* of Verona in 1184 became an element of French royal law. This ordinance of 1226 can be regarded as the model of all later legislation.

As in France, so also in Aragón Honorius III gained the help asked from the crown. At the request of the Cardinal Legate Romanus King James I forbade his vassals to receive heretics and commanded them to refuse any aid to them and their friends. But the essential support of the papal action against heresy was to be the Emperor. At his coronation Frederick II issued some laws, concerning which it has been possible to establish that they were formulated by the Curia. Among them was an edict against heretics.[16]

Heretics condemned by the Church were exiled and they and their heirs suffered confiscation of property. Persons suspected of heresy incurred, as provided by the Fourth Lateran Council, infamy, excommunication, and, in the case of the obstinate, the same penalties as heretics. City authorities were obliged under oath to expel them. If lords were involved, their land and possessions were liable to seizure, reserving the rights of the respective overlord. With this edict the canons of the Fourth Lateran Council became the law of the Empire. Frederick II sent the edict to Bologna to be inscribed in the University's register and proclaimed as the norm of instruction. A year later Honorius III did the same. In 1224 Frederick II introduced the penalty of burning. In a reply of March 1224 to an inquiry from Archbishop Albert of Magdeburg, who was acting as imperial legate in Romagna, occurs the following:[17]

> Anyone who has been convicted of heresy by the bishop of his diocese must immediately, on the bishop's demand, be arrested by the secular judicial authority and delivered up to the pyre. Should the judges mercifully spare his life, he must at least suffer the loss of his tongue, by which the Catholic faith has been assailed.

[15] Text of the ordinance in *Fliche-Martin,* X, 300, footnote 1: "Statuimus quod haeretici qui a catholica fide deviant, quocumque nomine censentur, postquam fuerint de haeresi per episcopum loci vel per aliam personam ecclesiasticam quae potestatem habeat condemnati, indilate animadversione debita puniantur, ordinantes et firmiter decernentes ne quis haereticos receptare vel defensare quomodolibet aut ipsos fovere praesumat, et, si quis contra praedicta praesumpserit facere, nec ad testimonium nec ad honorem aliquem de caetero admittatur, nec possit facere testamentum, nec successionem alicuius hereditate habere; bona ipsius mobilia et immobilia ipso facto [sint confiscata] ad ipsum vel ad ipsius posteritatem nullatenus reversura."
[16] *MGConst,* II, 106–09.
[17] *Ibid.,* 126 f.

This order was to rank, not as a simple rescript, but as an imperial constitution for all of Lombardy. While it is true that in 1197 Peter II of Aragón had decreed the penalty of fire, James I had not admitted it into his legislation of 1226. Likewise, in Languedoc the penalty of burning had been decreed at the beginning of the century, but the royal ordinance of 1226 did not mention it.

In Italy, however, Frederick II called for recourse to the pyre, whereas the Curia hesitated to do so. The imperial municipal councils of Rimini and Macerata in 1226 surrendered a few heretics to Frederick, who had them burned. Still, the imperial constitution of 1224 appeared neither in the *Compilatio quinta* nor in Gregory IX's collection of decretals. Hence the papacy did not adopt it officially, though it tacitly tolerated its implementation. The cities remained more than cool, especially when from 1226 they again began to unite against the Emperor.

Honorius III, acting as arbiter between Lombard League and Emperor, commanded the envoys of the cities to adopt both the papal conciliar decrees and the imperial constitutions against heresy into their municipal legislation. [18]

The Lombard cities complied in their peace proclamation of 26 March 1227. Included in the recommended imperial constitutions was certainly that of 1224, which provided death by fire for condemned heretics.

Gregory IX energetically pursued the policy of his predecessor, who had made the canons of the Fourth Lateran Council respected in France, Spain, and the Empire but had abandoned the restrictions favouring mercy as laid down by Innocent III.

Since he made the Lombards' peace formula a guiding principle and imposed it upon all cities, through him the Church officially recognized death at the stake as a penalty. Hesitant and negligent bishops in Lombardy were ordered by Gregory to procure the aid of preachers who could edify the people by word and example. Whether the new Order of Preachers was meant cannot be determined from the texts, which seem rather to refer to preachers among the diocesan clergy. However, Gregory now expressly gave the task of inquisitor to religious, for example, to the Dominican prior of Santa Maria Novella at Florence against the heretic Paterno and in Germany to Conrad of Marburg, a Premonstratensian. [19]

On 12 April 1229 there was concluded at Paris between King Louis IX

---

[18] *MGEp, sec. XIII*, I, no. 327 (5 January 1227): "Constitutiones vero, leges et statuta ab Ecclesia Romana et Romanis imperatoribus et specialiter ab ipso imperatore contra haereticos, receptatores, defensores, credentes et fautores eorum, hactenus promulgata vel in posterum promulganda, recipiant et observent inviolabiliter et efficaciter exequantur."

[19] Conrad's membership in the Premonstratensian Order (Abbey of Arnstein) has been made probable by the studies of K. H. May in *Hess. Jb. für Landesgeschichte*, 1 (1951), 87–109.

and Count Raymond VII of Toulouse a peace which is to be regarded as the definitive end of the Albigensian wars. The royal ordinance of 1229, which dealt with the procedure against heretics in connection with the peace treaty, repeated the order of 1226. The collaboration of ecclesiastical and secular authorities in discovering and punishing heretics, established at Verona in 1184, sanctioned in the Empire in 1220 and 1224 and in France in 1226, was now officially recognized and confirmed by Louis IX in 1229.

Since the Emperor was thereafter often obstructed by his quarrel with the Curia, the policy with regard to heretics in France became of special importance for the further development of legislation on heresy and hence of the Inquisition. The Council of Toulouse in the year of the Peace of 1229 — in the autumn under the presidency of the Cardinal Legate Romanus — played a great role in this, since there for the first time the assembling of a permanent law court was decreed, a permanent college of judges with delegated episcopal authority, whose task consisted solely in seeking out heretics and bringing them before the court. About twenty of the Council's forty-five articles were concerned with the question of heretics.

These dealt with the episcopal Inquisition, the duties of the commission of pastors, which traced the accused and took them to the court, and the duty of all believers to put themselves at the court's disposal as witnesses.

Following the Peace of Paris and the Council of Toulouse the Cathari and other heretics went underground and open resistance ceased.

Gregory IX carried further the Curia's legislation on heretics. In January 1231 he accepted Frederick II's constitution of 1224, including the punishment by fire, into his register[20] and in February 1231 incorporated it into his own constitution "Excommunicamus,"[21] so that from then on *animadversio debita* became synonymous with the penalty of death at the stake. Elements from Verona (1184), Narbonne, and Toulouse were adopted in this constitution. Public and private discussions of faith among the laity were forbidden, and ecclesiastical burial was denied to those put to death. Immurement, or life-imprisonment for penitent heretics, prohibition of any appeal to other tribunals, denial of any legal assistance for the accused, and finally social ostracism of the descendants of the condemned — to the second generation they lost the ability to hold any ecclesiastical offices — were among the fundamental components of this legislation. Gregory also had the Roman Senate's decision in cases of the condemnation of relapsed heretics included in his register immediately after his constitution of February 1231, so that, together with his own and the imperial enactment of 1224, it constituted in a sense one *corpus*. It gave the secular arm a delay of eight days for the carrying out of the *animadversio debita,* ordered the

[20] L. Auvray, *Registres de Grégoire IX*, no. 535.
[21] *Ibid.*, no. 539.

destruction of the immovable property, assigned one-third of the goods to those making the denunciation, and expelled from the city all followers of the condemned, confiscating one-third of their possessions also.

With the 1231 edicts of Gregory IX the basic legislation for the procedure of the Inquisition was complete. All the essential elements can be identified in it: infamy, loss of civil and political rights, banishment, deprivation of feudal holdings, and *animadversio debita* as death at the stake, so far as the series of penalties was concerned. The Pope also made universally binding the wearing of the cross by the condemned, the secrecy of trials and the withholding of the names of witnesses, the prohibition of lodging an appeal and of asking legal assistance from lawyers. The duty of maintaining prisoners was defined, and the exhuming of the remains of heretics who had gone undetected in their lifetime was ordered. The episcopal judges and those from the diocesan clergy thereby obtained their manual of penal procedure and penal law for the future. From now on there was question of its use and of the activation of Inquisition tribunals everywhere in the Church.

In addition to the episcopal Inquisition, such as it had been decided upon, though, of course, to a great extent ineffectively, at Verona in 1184, Gregory IX now appointed papal inquisitors with the permanent duty of seeking out heretics systematically, of bringing them to trial, of condemning them if they were unable to free themselves of suspicion, and of relinquishing them to the secular power for burning.

From 1232 on Gregory IX, and later his successors, turned over the Inquisition to the new orders, especially to the Dominicans, who, to quote Grundmann, "with a downright scientific zeal for the faith built up an inescapable legal procedure in their special tribunal." Textbooks and manuals for inquisitors appeared, in which were to be found fundamental, even if often one-sided and polemical explanations of heresy and the harsh methods for combatting it. But this systematically organized Inquisition, becoming everywhere effective, was unable completely to eradicate heresy. Still, because of it a keener defensive struggle was possible in the event of any deviation from the faith of the Church.

In South Germany the episcopal Inquisition and that entrusted to specified religious or to individual commissioners worked side by side under Gregory IX. The Dominicans, soon to be commissioned by preference, always had to act under the control of the bishops. It was the same in Flanders, Prussia, Bohemia, and Bavaria.

In France also, for the time being, the episcopal Inquisition continued to operate; it was effectively administered by most bishops. In the Midi, it is true, Gregory IX in 1233 named papal inquisitors such as Peter Cella and William Arnaud of Montpellier for the dioceses of Toulouse and Cahors. They were immediately subject to the Pope, control of their activity lying in the hands of papal legates.

The episcopal and the legatine Inquisition and that administered by religious were intended by the Pope to co-operate in principle, even though there were shifts of emphasis according to the various territories. Under Innocent IV occurred the completion of the Inquisition as an institution of canon law. In this connection he frequently modified the procedure, whose original severity had evoked opposition, not only in Germany and the Midi, but among princes and cities generally. A more respectable conduct of processes had been set forth in the decrees of the Synods of Narbonne (1243) and Béziers (1246), and Innocent IV confirmed these. In the struggle against Frederick II he had to be concerned about a rapid and thorough settlement of the many disturbances in the Midi, about a reconciliation with Count Raymond VII of Toulouse, and about the co-operation of the German bishops. He was able to arrange a harmonious collaboration of crown and papacy in France, and in Spain and Germany the episcopates were prepared to support the Inquisition. After the Emperor's death in 1250, Innocent IV was able to establish the Inquisition as a permanent institution in Italy. All earlier papal and imperial enactments were combined in the bull "Ad exstirpanda" of 15 May 1252.[22] The introduction of torture in the process was new. But the Pope's actual policy brought many modifications and amnesty for all who were reconciled to the Church within a year. The arrest of relatives, introduced by Gregory IX in 1231, was abolished. All this was, one might say, a return to the merciful firmness of Innocent III.

The establishing of the Inquisition and its activity, the collaboration of ecclesiastical and secular power in the fight against heresy, the harshness of the procedure, and the cruelty of the penalties — none of this can be understood apart from the assumptions of the social order in the High Middle Ages. The bond unifying them was the faith, which heresy threatened to destroy. With all the means provided by its ecclesiastical and secular powers Christendom waged a war to maintain itself against this threat. Perhaps a real Christian self-understanding was obscure in some circles. These shadows remain and should have served as a warning to coming generations. A better understanding demands a more refined but at the same time more generous judgment of the past.

CHAPTER 29

The Missionary Work of the Church in the Twelfth and Thirteenth Centuries

The epoch of the elaboration of legal structures and of religious renewal, of theological scholarship and of mystical emotion, could not neglect a task so central to the very being of the Church as was that of announcing salvation

[22] *Potthast*, 14592; text in *Bullarium Taur.*, III, 552–58.

to all peoples. This was all the more urgent as the crusade movement constantly brought new peoples into view on the frontiers of Christendom, from the Muslims to the Mongols. In addition, there took place from Scandinavia to Central Germany a constant encounter with the still pagan world of the Elbe Slavs, the Baltic Sea area, and Finland.[1] While efforts had begun there as early as the ninth and tenth centuries to press eastward,[2] and Adalbert of Prague in 997 and Bruno of Querfurt in 1009 had died as martyrs,[3] still, with the exception of Poland in 966, no North Slavic people could be won. Wends, Pomeranians, Prussians, Livs, Esthonians, and Finns were not to be incorporated into Christendom until the twelfth and thirteenth centuries.

Missionary work among these peoples was influenced by the idea then current of a *dilatatio imperii christiani* and continued necessarily to be characterized by the intimate interrelationship of political and religious motives that marked the contemporary self-awareness of the Church. The mission of the sword and the mission of the word were inextricably combined; conquest, constructing of an ecclesiastical organization, and a comprehensive pastoral activity on the part of monastery and parish succeeded one another. Protection by the state remained essential both for beginning and for continuing any Christianization The results were not due chiefly to the papacy, as one would have expected, but to the reform orders of the twelfth century — Cistercians, Premonstratensians, and canons regular — and to the mendicant orders of the thirteenth century, even though the overall responsibility remained that of the Holy See through the grant of privileges and the dispatch of legates. As regards secular powers, the initiative passed from the Emperor to the princes of the marches and the northern kings and, especially in the Baltic area, to the military orders, in particular to the Teutonic Knights in Prussia. During this entire period the crusade played a role only once and then negatively: in the Wend Crusade of 1147. Of course, the military exertions of Albert of Riga in Livonia were also authentic crusade enterprises.

The resumption of Christian evangelization in the twelfth century began in Pomerania, which King Boleslas III of Poland conquered in 1122. He asked assistance from Bishop Otto of Bamberg, who in two sojourns, 1123–24 and 1128–29, baptized and preached in Pyritz, Wollin, Stettin, Kammin, and elsewhere. The see of Wollin, founded in 1140 after Otto's death,

---

[1] G. Stökl, *Geschichte der Slavenmission (Die Kirche in ihrer Geschichte,* ed. K. D. Schmidt - E. Wolf, II/E) (Göttingen 1961), 90 f.

[2] See Volume III, Chapters 30 and 31.

[3] H. D. Kahl, "Compellere intrare. Die Wendenpolitik Bruns von Querfurt im Licht hochmittelalterlichen Missions- und Völkerrechts," *Zeitschrift für Ostforschung,* 4 (1955), 161–93, 260–401, now also in H. Beumann, *Heidenmission und Kreuzzugsgedanke in der deutschen Ostpolitik des Mittelalters* (Darmstadt 1963), 177–274.

was made subject neither to Gniezno nor to Magdeburg but directly to the Curia at Rome.

Not much later than in Pomerania an effort was made from Hamburg-Bremen to convert the Slavs beyond the Elbe. Archbishop Adalbero sent the Bremen canon Vizelin, who began to preach in Wagria in 1126. Northwest of Lübeck he founded the chapter of Neumünster. From the 1140's Henry the Lion of Saxony and Albert the Bear of Brandenburg especially became the decisive protectors in the marches.

The Wend Crusade of 1147[4] involved not only an interruption of the missionary endeavours but also a hardening of fronts and an impeding of later pastoral work among the Slavs. The expression, "death or baptism", as ascribed to Bernard of Clairvaux, who preached the crusade, sounded harsh but was also to be understood as a criticism of the policy thus far pursued by the princes, who seemed disposed, *vis-à-vis* an unconverted but subjugated population, to maintain a freer hand in regard to taxes and tribute. Actually, the expression was really applied in very few cases.

In questions relating to the organizing of bishoprics, which was carried on from Hamburg-Bremen and Magdeburg, there occurred a confrontation between the Archbishop of Bremen, Hartwig of Stade, and Duke Henry the Lion, who claimed the right to institute the bishops.[5] Vizelin, whom Hartwig had consecrated as Bishop of Oldenburg, accepted investiture from the Duke in 1151 after long hesitation. The Duke, in investing him, exercised a mandate from the Emperor. Besides Oldenburg, which was transferred to Lübeck in 1160, the sees of Ratzeburg and Mecklenburg, widowed since 1066, were restored; in 1161 Mecklenburg was transferred to Schwerin. Premonstratensians settled at Leitzkau and Jerichow, Cistercians at Doberan and Lehnin — to mention only the most important abbeys.

Albert the Bear's expansion policy, which, as everywhere else, was likewise one of colonization, — Hollanders and Flemings were invited to the country beyond the Elbe, — allowed the occupation of Brandenburg in 1150.[6] The old sees of Brandenburg and Havelberg had been restored since the 1130's and were administered by Premonstratensians. Particular attention was devoted to completing the parish organization; in its main lines this was achieved by 1200. But an actual consolidation of the situation was delayed until the middle of the thirteenth century.

[4] *Cf.* H. D. Kahl, "Zum Ergebnis des Wendenkreuzzugs von 1147. Zugleich ein Beitrag zur Geschichte des sächsischen Frühchristentums," *Wichmann-Jahrbuch*, 11/12 (1957 f.), 99–120, now in Beumann, *op. cit.*, 275–316. Kahl thinks he can establish "that the crusade itself ... achieved on the whole the goal set for it" (314).

[5] *Cf.* K. Jordan, *Die Bistumsgründungen Heinrichs des Löwen (Schriften der MGH*, 3) (Leipzig 1939).

[6] M. Treiter, "Quellen und Darstellungen zur Geschichte der Mark Brandenburg im Mittelalter," *Wichmann-Jahrbuch*, 1 (1930), 5–73; G. Wentz, *Das Bistum Brandenburg*, I *(Germania Sacra*, I/1) (Berlin 1929).

The Augustinian canon, Meinhard of Segeberg, was active in Livonia [7] from 1180. He resided at Üxküll on the Dvina as a suffragan of Bremen. A pagan reaction put an end to this start until Albert of Buxhövden, consecrated Bishop of the Livs in 1199, organized a crusade, which was successful under his leadership. In 1201 Albert founded Riga, which became his episcopal city. He founded the Military Order of the Knights of the Sword, *Fratres militiae Christi,* with whose help he subjugated parts of Esthonia, Semigallia, Courland, and the island of Ösel. The see of Dorpat, like that of Riga, was made an imperial prince-bishopric in 1225 by King Henry, son of the Emperor Frederick II. In 1255 Alexander IV made Riga an archbishopric, the first metropolitan being Albert Suerbeer, former Archbishop of Armagh. [8] For the protection of the whole territory that was evangelized from Riga crusaders were recruited throughout the thirteenth century for the struggle against pagan attacks. Bishop Albert's dominion — it has been said that he intended to found an ecclesiastical state — was divided through the intervention of the Curia. The Bishop, the Knights of the Sword, and the city of Riga each obtained one-third. Albert had declared Livonia to be the "property of the Mother of God" and had thereby in principle subjected it to the Church. Even after the division of power this idea remained the unifying bond among Bishop, city, and knights.

Farther north the intervention of the Danes had continued the Church's missionary work among the Esths since 1170. The regions conquered were at first added to the province of Lund; the Franciscan friar Fulco became the first Bishop. Questions controverted between Danes and Germans were settled by the Papal Legate William of Modena in the Treaty of Stenby in 1237. The see of Reval remained subject to Lund, but Dorpat and Ösel-Wiek became suffragans of Riga.

Christian influence had made itself felt in Finland in the eleventh century but it required Swedish crusades, in 1157 under King Eric IX Jedvardson and in 1239 and 1295, to subjugate the country. Bishop Henry of Uppsala, [9] English by birth, accompanied Eric as missionary. He was murdered in 1160 and became Finland's patron saint. The see of Abo, founded in 1276, remained a suffragan of Uppsala. The Dominicans played a substantial role in the Christianization of Finland, and the see even adopted their liturgy.

---

[7] For Livonia see now the biography by G. Gnegel-Waitschies, *Bischof Albert von Riga* (Hamburg 1958) and the large-scale monograph by F. Benninghoven, *Der Orden der Schwertbrüder* (Cologne and Graz 1965); also the sketch by T. Grentrup, "Der Zisterzienser Dietrich in der altlivländischen Mission (1219)," *ZMR*, 40 (1956), 265–81. While Gnegel-Waitschies regards Albert as the founder of the order (66), Grentrup (268) and Benninghoven stress the decisive role of Dietrich.

[8] For Albert Suerbeer see M. Hellmann, *Das Lettenland im Mittelalter* (Münster and Cologne 1954), 176–85.

[9] For Saint Henry of Uppsala see A. Maliniemi, *De Sancto Henrico,* II (Helsinki 1942).

The first attempts at the evangelization of the pagan Prussians between the Vistula and the Memel were ordered by Boleslas I of Poland toward the end of the tenth century. But it was due to the initiative of Innocent III that the work was seriously continued. Christian of Lekno, a Cistercian, went there before 1210 and in 1215 was consecrated Bishop of the Prussians by the Pope. When the Chelmno district, which belonged to Mazovia, was conquered by the Prussians, Duke Conrad, with the consent of Bishop Christian, called upon the Teutonic Knights for assistance. Hermann of Salza, grand master from 1209 to 1239, accepted the offer; the Emperor Frederick II granted him the imperial protection, and Pope Gregory IX approved. The struggle to subjugate the Prussians lasted from 1230 to 1283. The Livonian Knights of the Sword provided military assistance, as, to a lesser degree, did also the Knights of Christ of Dobrin, founded by Bishop Christian in 1228. German peasants, especially Westphalians, were invited into the country, and the mendicant orders, again the Dominicans in particular, took charge of the pastoral work. The Papal Legate William of Modena erected sees in 1243 at Chelmno, Pomesania, Ermeland, and Samland. At first they were combined into one Archbishopric of Prussia, but when Riga was made a metropolitan see in 1255 they were incorporated into that province. Except for Ermeland, these sees became part of the territory of the Teutonic Order. The still young Order of the Hospital of Our Lady of the German House in Jerusalem — it had been founded at Acre in 1198 — had for some time been on the lookout for work outside Syria-Palestine, even though the castle of Montfort near Acre remained the residence of the grand master until 1271. At first, in 1211, it obtained from King Andrew II of Hungary the protectorate of the Burzenland in Transylvania against the pagan Cumans. Since it began to create there an autonomous territory, it had to give way in 1225. Almost at once, in 1226, arrived the call to the north. Probably at the instigation of Hermann of Salza, the Emperor Frederick II had already in 1224 placed the peoples of Livonia, Esthonia, Samland, Prussia, and Semigallia under the protection of the Empire, very likely in order to counteract Danish influence. In 1225 Pope Honorius III also placed them under his personal protection, in particular the new converts in Prussia and Livonia. In the Golden Bull of Rimini in 1226 Frederick II bestowed on the Order dominion over the territory to be conquered, and the grand master became a prince of the Empire. The territory gained by the Order was entrusted to it in perpetuity as the "property of Saint Peter" by Gregory IX in 1234. It was due to the grand master that in this matter the competing interests of Pope and Emperor did not conflict but rather proceeded in peaceful co-operation. In 1236 the remnant of the Knights of the Sword of Livonia was united with the Teutonic Order, which thus became responsible also for Livonia. Esthonia remained in the hands of the Danes. A revolt of the Prussians in 1242 could not be suppressed until 1247. In the Peace of

Christburg in 1249[10] the Prussians, thanks to the intervention of the Curia, obtained personal freedom and equality with the Germans. The legate on that occasion was James of Troyes, the later Pope Urban IV. From Livonia the Order also subjugated Courland and in 1252 founded Memel. The Lithuanians remained unconquered and for the time being unconverted, even though Prince Mindaugas received baptism in 1250 and obtained the royal title from Innocent IV. In 1260 he apostatized. Not until toward the end of the thirteenth century was the strength of the Teutonic Order's state so secure that the grand master could in 1309 transfer his residence from Venice to the Marienburg.

If the missions among the Slavs and in the Baltic area remained closely tied to conquest and domination, if here the crusade developed from a means of defense into an instrument of forcible expansion, the situation was different in the eastern Mediterranean and on the African coast. Only in the Spanish *Reconquista* can analogous developments be surmised, even if a quite different social and historical context must be considered: that of Christian communities on Islamic territory.[11]

The crusader states in Syria and Palestine, it is true, had non-Christian populations under their rule, but apart from a few indications in the twelfth century, there was very little eagerness to preach the Gospel to them. Pastoral activity, to the extent that it was taken seriously, was directed to the Christian population, which, extraordinarily mixed, — Latins and Greeks, French and Italians, long resident families and pilgrims, — resisted any systematic care. The experiences in 1216–18 of James of Vitry, Bishop of Acre, showed this only too clearly.[12]

Serious reflection to the effect that the warlike contacts with Islam, though they might have been pursued with the noblest defensive aims, could not free the West from the responsibility of seeking to preach Christianity even in Islamic territory first occurred in the thirteenth century. Well known are the attitude of Saint Francis of Assisi and his discussion from Damietta in 1219 with the Sultan al-Kamil, which at least obtained for him personally the freedom to preach.[13] He also sent friars to Morocco, where five of

---

[10] H. Patze, "Der Frieden von Christburg vom Jahre 1249," *Jahrbuch für die Geschichte Mittel- und Ostdeutschlands,* 7 (1958), 39–91, now in Beumann, *op. cit.,* 417–83.

[11] For the *Reconquista* see R. Menéndez Pidal, *La España del Cid,* 2 vols. (Madrid, 4th ed. 1947); J. Goñi Gaztambide, *Historia de la bula de la cruzada en España* (Vitoria 1958; literature).

[12] *Cf.* James of Vitry, *Lettres,* ed. R. B. C. Huygens (Leiden 1960).

[13] On this *cf.* M. Roncaglia, *Biblioteca bio-bibliografica della Terra Santa e dell'Oriente Francescano,* I: *Storia della provincia della Terra Santa,* Part I: *I Francescani in Oriente durante la crociata* (Cairo 1954); for the meeting of Saint Francis and the Sultan *cf.* G. Golubovich, "San Francesco e i Francescani in Damiata (5. 11. 1219–2. 2. 1220)," *Studi Francescani,* 23 (1926), 307–30, supplemented by L. Lemmens, "De Sancto Francisco

them were killed in 1220.[14] From now on, especially in the new orders, it was seen ever more clearly that, wherever the crusade made it possible, there was a duty to activate an evangelization. As is well known, this effort nowhere led to real successes when it had to face Islam, whose attitude was one of fundamental rejection and obstruction. Toward the end of the century the bases of the problem of the mission to Islam were grappled with by the Franciscan tertiary, Raymond Lull (d. 1316).[15] With him the holy war clearly retired in favour of an intellectual campaign to win unbelievers. On Mallorca he established a missionary college for Franciscans. Himself fluent in Arabic, he worked for the setting up of chairs of Greek, Arabic, Hebrew, and Syriac at the universities. After the fall in 1291 of Acre, which settled the fate of the Crusader Kingdom, Lull sent to Pope Nicholas IV his treatise on the converting of infidels. His plan was sufficiently comprehensive: the erecting of houses for the study of languages by missionaries, a uniform direction of missionary activity by a cardinal, amalgamation of the military orders, religious renewal of clergy and laity. Naturally, the crusade itself also played a role in all this. Lull himself made extensive missionary journeys: in North Africa in 1281—82, 1292, 1307, and in 1314 until he was stoned to death in 1316; among the Jews and Arabs at Naples in 1293–94; on Mallorca in 1300–01; and on Sicily in 1313–14. He offered suggestions to Pope Celestine V in 1294 and to Pope Boniface VIII in 1296 and dedicated his *Liber de acquisitione Terrae Sanctae* to Pope Clement V. To his satisfaction, the Council of Vienne in 1311 adopted his suggestions and decreed the establishing of chairs of languages. To a great extent he too viewed conquest and conversion as one, and hence he quite approximated the practice of northern Europe.

Like the Franciscans, the Dominicans also sought to promote the mission to Islam. Raymond Lull took part in their general chapters of 1283, 1285, and 1294, and he was invited by the Franciscans in 1287, 1289, and 1295.

The actual results of such missionary activity were, it is true, meagre. The scanty reports are frequently limited to individual conversions and to work among Arabs and Muslims in lands under Christian rule. In North Africa there were only occasional contacts, for there, with the assent of the princes, the strictly pastoral activity served the Christians. If the Popes, notably Gregory IX and Innocent IV, had messages delivered by mendicant friars

Christum praedicante coram sultano Aegypti," *AFrH*, 19 (1926), 559–78; also M. Roncaglia, "San Francesco d'Assisi in Oriente," *Studi Francescani*, 50 (1953), 97–106.

[14] On the preaching by the Franciscans in Morocco and their martyrdom see now J. Toussaert, *Antonius von Padua* (Cologne 1967), 191–201.

[15] For Raymond Lull *cf.* the excellent article by E. W. Platzeck in *LThK*, VIII (2nd ed. 1963), 974–76, with copious bibliography. Raymond's anonymous *Vita coetana* was ed. by B. de Gaiffier in *AnBoll*, 48 (1930), 130–78; E. W. Platzeck, *Raimund Lull*, 2 vols. (Düsseldorf 1962 f.), is the most comprehensive biography.

to the Sultans of Damascus, Iconium, Aleppo, and Baghdad between 1233 and 1250, in all probability no missionary preaching could be included on these diplomatic occasions.

As early as the pontificate of Gregory IX the Curia was aware of the danger from the Mongols, who had already invaded Eastern Europe.[16] Hungarian Dominicans had gone to the Volga region to investigate the missionary possibilities. They came back with extremely upsetting news. Berthold of Andechs, Patriarch of Aquileia, had appropriate warnings read from all pulpits. The Mongol storm fell upon Poland and Hungary in 1240 to 1241. The German defeat at Liegnitz in Silesia in 1241 appeared to present the worst threat, but actually it was the turning point, for the death of the Great Khan Ogdai in 1242 caused the Mongols to evacuate Central Europe, though they remained in Russia.

It was known in the West that in Asia there had long been living Persian Nestorians, who had penetrated as far as India and China. In the eleventh century they had contrived to convert the Turcoman prince of Kerait on Lake Baikal, who then led his people to Christianity. This vassal of the Chinese Empire is to be regarded as the historical nucleus of the legend of Prester John, which arose at that time and was widely believed.[17] The view that beyond the frontiers of Europe there were Christian kingdoms in the Far East may have contributed to the Curia's determination to send messengers of its own to the East at the very moment of the farthest advance of the Mongols to the West. It could learn from previous reports that the Mongols, belonging to none of the known world religions, practised an extensive toleration toward them, including that of the Christian Nestorians. The wife of the Khan Hulagu (1259–65) was a Nestorian.

And so on several occasions Innocent IV and King Louis IX of France sent Franciscans and Dominicans to the Mongols. John of Piano di Carpine in the Abruzzi went in 1245–47 *via* Russia to Karakorum, chief residence of the Great Khan; William of Ruysbroeck in Flanders also went there, *via* Anatolia, in 1253–55. Probably there was no question of missionary activity; inquiries and contacts were envisaged. The mission in the sense of a preaching of the faith was first taken up by the Franciscan John of Montecorvino, who from 1294 to 1328 worked at Cambalu (Peking) among Nestorians and Buddhists with a group of confrères, notably Arnold of Cologne and Odoric of Pordenone. He was named Archbishop by Clement V in 1307. Of the many auxiliary bishops sent to him from the Franciscan Order only four reached Peking. The end of the Mongol domination in China and the

---

[16] H. Dörrie edited the relevant texts: *Drei Texte zur Geschichte der Ungarn und Mongolen. Die Missionsreisen des Fr. Julianus O.P. ins Uralgebiet (1234/35) und nach Russland (1237)* (Göttingen 1956).

[17] For Prester John cf. F. Zarncke, *AGL*, phil. Kl., 7 (1879), 827–1030, 8 (1883), 1–186; R. Hennig, *Terrae incognitae*, II (Leiden, 2nd ed. 1950), 438–60.

assumption of power by the Ming Dynasty in 1368 destroyed the Peking mission.[18]

Missionary zeal was kept aglow among the Dominicans, especially by the master general Humbert of Romans (1254–63). Toward the close of the thirteenth century the Order established the *Societas fratrum peregrinantium propter Christum*, which was active particularly in the lands around the Black Sea and in Asia Minor.[19]

In general it can be established in regard to the Church's missionary endeavour in this period that, in connection with the political opening up of the Baltic countries for the West, Christianity was also able to take root there. The encounter with Islam continued, because it was for the most part of a military and political nature, to be without particular impact because of its exclusion of any religious propaganda, if one disregards the catechetical efforts in the reconquered parts of Spain. The advance in the countries under Mongol rule was merely casual, except for the Franciscan mission in Peking.

CHAPTER 30

Canon Law and the Constitution of the Church in the Thirteenth Century

Since the appearance of Gratian's *Decretum* around 1140 the scientific study of canon law had developed at Bologna and Paris and later also at Montpellier, Oxford, and Salamanca. Applying the scholastic method, the decretists had prepared the material in glosses, *quaestiones*, treatises, and *summae* for use in academic instruction and the courts. The collaboration of theory and practice gave rise to what Gabriel Le Bras calls the "new law." The legislative activity of the papacy in the decretals and of councils in constitutions contributed the most to this development. These new decisions became especially numerous from the pontificate of Alexander III. Collections were made, at first privately,[1] then with papal authorization. More than eighty such collections have been discovered; the best known are the five great compilations made between 1191 and 1226. Two of them were officially approved: the *Compilatio tertia* of Peter of Benevento by Innocent III in 1209 and the *Compilatio quinta*, perhaps of Tancred, by Honorius III in 1220; they were sent to the courts and schools for their use. Gregory IX

[18] On the Chinese mission in the Middle Ages see now C. W. Troll, *FStud*, 48 (1966), 109–50, 49 (1967), 22–79.
[19] R. Loenertz, *La Société des Frères Pérégrinants. Étude sur l'Orient dominicain* (Rome 1937).
[1] *Cf.* C. Duggan, *Twelfth-Century Decretal Collections and their Importance in English History* (London 1963).

decided to unify the decretal legislation of the last century. He entrusted Raymond of Peñaforte with the codification in 1230 and it was published by the Pope on 5 September 1234. Thus Gregory IX's *Liber Extra (Liber decretalium extra decretum vagantium)* became the first "official, authentic, uniform, universal, and exclusive" law book of the Church. Innocent IV, Gregory X, and Nicholas III then published collections of decretals *(novellae)*, and other private and inadequate compilations also appeared. Once again the legal situation became so complicated that at the end of the century Boniface VIII decided to publish a law book that would include all collections made since the *Liber Extra*. A commission of three, under William of Mandagout, Archbishop of Embrun, produced this work, which contained not only 108 decretals of his predecessors but 251 decretals of Boniface himself and the canons of the two Councils of Lyons. The Pope published this *Liber Sextus* on 3 March 1298; Gregory IX's *Liber Extra* retained its legal force. These two codifications of the thirteenth century stimulated and provided the models for the legislation of kings and princes that was now everywhere in process.[2]

The methods employed in systematic instruction in canon law were similar to those developed at the theological faculties, above all that of Paris. In addition to the lecture *(lectio, praelectio, lectura), disputatio* was also practised. In it the *quaestiones* already treated in the lecture were discussed again between teachers and students, mostly in an analytical and exegetical manner. Both found expression in the literature as *lecturae* composed by the teacher himself or as *reportatio* (student's notes) or *quaestiones (disputatae)* respectively. As in theology, the works of the glossators — collections of glosses, later apparatus — became important. Eventually there appeared the great *summae*, real commentaries, intended as texts and manuals for practice. Among them the *summae* of apparatus had special prestige. Innocent IV had composed one, which gained him the title of *princeps iuristarum*. The commentaries dealt to some extent only with restricted fields, such as matrimonial law, judicial procedure, penal law, electoral law. Also noteworthy were the *summae* of confession, or penitential *summae*, whose importance was more and more in the field of moral and pastoral theology, so that their strictly canonical character was obscured.

The decretalists of the thirteenth century were concerned first of all with the five great compilations: those of Bernard of Pavia (d. 1213), Tancred (d. 1234–36), John Teutonicus (d. 1245–46), and James of Albenga (d. *ca.* 1273). England produced a group of scholars, such as Richard Anglicus (d. 1237), Gilbert Anglicus, Alan Anglicus, and others, as did Spain with Law-

[2] *Cf.* S. Gagnér, *Studien zur Ideengeschichte der Gesetzgebung* (Uppsala 1960), 288–340; criticism in W. E. Brynteson, "Roman Law and Legislation in the Middle Ages," *Speculum*, 41 (1966), 420–37.

rence Hispanus (d. *ca.* 1248), Vincent, and Peter Hispanus. Even Hungary was represented by Damasus, who was a professor at Bologna between 1210 and 1220. The Golden Age of the decretalists began with the promulgation of the *Liber Extra* in 1234 and included the career of the celebrated John Andreae (1270–1348). Hence it lasted a century and was at the same time the expression of the most vigourous period of the constructing and consolidating of the ecclesiastical organization of the High Middle Ages and of the acceptance by the West of the canon law as the universally valid and effective legal order of Christendom.

To the decretalists of this period — they are also called the "later" decretalists — belonged, to name only a few, Raymond of Peñaforte (d. 1275), Godfrey of Trani (d. 1245), Bernard de Botone of Parma (d. 1266), Sinibaldo Fieschi (Pope Innocent IV, d. 1254), and, the most celebrated among them, Henry of Susa (Hostiensis, d. 1270). Many decretalists worked and wrote also in France, Spain, and Germany. The canonists did not develop a comprehensive theory of the Church as legislator; rather, they presupposed this, so to speak, and in their lectures, disputations, and commentaries were more concerned with the thousand particular problems that resulted from the ceaseless alteration of structures. Theology also knew no real treatise on the Church but understood quite well that the legislative Church of the jurists was to be identified with the Church experienced in faith, which, as the *corpus Christi mysticum*, to use an expression of Aquinas, constituted the proper ontological basis for all ways of life in Christendom that became visible in the law. The historical development led to this, that the hierarchical order of divine institution gained preeminence in the thought and action of the High Middle Ages, while the concept of the Church as the "people of God on earth," which was engaged in its journey to God, retired to the background. And so there was sketched a picture of the constitution of the Church in this period which was determined by one of the stable institutional elements in her. In this connection it must, of course, be remembered that all of them and every particular aspect of them, by virtue of the dynamics of historical transformation, changed, withdrew, were renewed, and occasionally, by the exaggerating of their functions, improperly displaced others or at least crippled them.

The great epoch of classical canon law was at the same time the epoch of the papacy as the authoritative guide of the destinies of Christendom, from Innocent III to Boniface VIII.[3] Neither before nor after was the papacy able to raise its claim so effectively, thanks precisely to the successful activity of canon lawyers and their students in the various offices — the

---

[3] See now J. A. Watt, *Papal Monarchy in the Thirteenth Century* (London 1965). M. Wilks, *The Problem of Sovereignty in the Later Middle Ages* (Cambridge 1963), looks back to the thirteenth century development.

papacy itself, the Curia, bishoprics, abbeys, and chapters — which converted theory into practice, to act and to lead as the universally acknowledged teacher, judge, and guide of *christianitas*.

The fundamental lines of the ecclesiastical organization did not change in the thirteenth century. The distinction between the power of orders and the power of jurisdiction in the one *potestas ecclesiastica* was worked out more clearly, again chiefly by Aquinas. The legislative power was exercised more firmly and more consciously, especially by the Pope. In the case of the Pope it found its limits in the divine law, both positively revealed and naturally known, but it could be developed beyond the conciliar law of earlier centuries. The Pope's sovereignty *vis-à-vis* the Council remained undisputed so long as he did not fall into heresy, which meant that he ceased to be Pope. He summoned general synods, directed them and promulgated their decisions as his decrees. There was no longer any question of an essential co-operation of the laity, such as the Emperor.

The papal right to legislate included the right to bestow privileges and grant dispensations from papal and universal as well as from particular law. Celestine II (1143–44) had introduced the legal reservation *salva Sedis Apostolicae auctoritate*.[4] To be sure, in the case of unrestrained exercise of the right to dispense there lay grave dangers for the security of the legal structures, but for the time being these did not seem to be threatening.

All clerical and non-clerical members of Christendom were subject to the supreme judicial authority. There had developed, in particular since the time of Alexander III (1159–81), the institution of delegated jurisdiction. Judges delegate undertook especially the investigation of disputed cases but occasionally also received authority to render decisions. Certain legal and penal cases were reserved exclusively to the Pope.

The Pope's supreme administrative rights were completed. To them belonged the right of supervision for the Universal Church. The canonization of saints was reserved to the Holy See from Alexander III and definitively by a regulation of Gregory IX. The system of ecclesiastical indulgences was concentrated in the Curia and restricted in regard to bishops. The Pope also had a leading role in the educational system of the age through the founding of universities and the conferring of privileges on them. The most important division of administration was that dealing with the filling of offices, in which there began a development leading to the Pope's universal right to fill all ecclesiastical benefices. At first specific classes were reserved. A vigorous opposition, which flared up because of the practice of Innocent IV during his struggle with the Hohenstaufen, was overcome. The Curia more and more made its own appointments, bestowed expectatives to benefices that were yet to be vacated, developed a right of devolution, and received postu-

---

[4] *Cf.* G. Le Bras, *L'âge classique* (Paris 1965), 487–506.

lation from everywhere. This universal competence of the Pope in the disposing of all offices and benefices in the Church was, however, not fixed in law until later.

The papal election law, first regulated under Nicholas II in 1059, was modified by Alexander III at the Third Lateran Council in 1179 in the sense that now the election was declared to be the exclusive prerogative of all the cardinals. If unanimity could not be achieved, a two-thirds majority was to suffice. There was no mention of any assent or participation by Emperor or by clergy and people of Rome. And the election did not have to take place in Rome. The one elected could exercise the papal rights as soon as he had accepted the election. While all clerics had a passive vote, still, with few exceptions, only cardinals were elected. At the Second Council of Lyons in 1274 the law was extended to include the rules for the conclave, which probably had its model in the Italian communes or the electoral constitution of the Dominicans. The arrangement was suspended by John XXI (1276 to 1277) but it was reintroduced, this time for good, by Celestine V (1294). The two-thirds majority and the conclave were maintained with a few modifications and proved their worth in the succeeding centuries.

To the general councils, convoked and held under papal control, were invited, in addition to the cardinals, the metropolitans, bishops, abbots, and the deans of cathedral and collegiate chapters. Only cardinals and bishops had a deliberative vote; all others were competent in an advisory function only, which pertained also to princes and representatives of cities who were present. There was no strict regulation for councils but it became the practice that statements of principle were heard and decrees were promulgated in a few solemn sessions; they were prepared in consistories and in committee consultations that took place between sessions. The final decision in regard to conciliar decrees lay with the Pope, who was under no obligation to accept them. Councils which were summoned by legates in connection with their function could also be regarded as papal synods. In its canon 6 the Fourth Lateran Council had ordered the annual meeting of provincial councils, which especially saw to the promulgating and implementing of the decrees of ecumenical synods and at the same time served, as earlier, for the further growth of particular law proper to their area.

The papal registers of the thirteenth century reveal the constant contacts between the Holy See and the Western episcopate. These were due, not only to the increasing prestige of the papacy, the completing of a universally valid canon law, and the regular meeting of general synods, but also to the emancipation of the bishops from control by the princes. It is true that the legal and spiritual concentration of ecclesiastical power in the Pope's hands restricted the position of the bishops, but it could not but be important to the Pope that he should strengthen the position of the bishop within each diocese. As successor of the Apostles, the bishop retained unchallenged, even in the epoch of the canon law, the autonomous right to act within his bishopric as chief priest, judge, and ruler of his people.[5] The erecting, dividing, or suppressing of a see had become a papal prerogative, which extended also to an ecclesiastical province, but within the boundaries of this diocese the bishop governed according to his own decrees, but, of course, in conformity with the requirements of the general canon law. The circumstances of jurisdiction were naturally more complex in those bishoprics where the temporal endowment was involved with state functions, as in the bishoprics in the Empire and some of those in France (Sens, Langres), England (Durham), and Spain. Often the boundaries of the barony pertaining to the bishopric did not coincide with those of the diocese.

The institution of *Chorepiscopus* was suppressed; on request, neighbouring bishops rendered assistance as auxiliaries. Often they were even bishops expelled from the crusader states or from the Eastern colonial areas. From this situation later developed the so-called auxiliary bishops, whose territory lay *in partibus infidelium*. They had only spiritual functions to perform. If he were impeded by sickness, absence, or activity outside his diocese, a bishop could be given a coadjutor. Boniface VIII laid down the basic rules for this. The right of succession did not necessarily belong to the coadjutor but, if requested, it could be granted by the Pope.

During the crusade centuries patriarchs of the Latin rite were appointed at Jerusalem, Antioch, and from 1204 at Constantinople. They functioned either alone or parallel with the corresponding Greek patriarch. After the collapse of the crusader states these functions continued as merely titular offices.

In the West many a metropolitan sought the rank of primate, but the instituting of such primates did not achieve any uniform and weighty significance in the history of canon law.[6] The dignity of primate became a mere title, often connected with that of *legatus natus*. It existed at Mainz, Cologne, Trier, Magdeburg, and Salzburg, at Saint Andrew's in Scotland, Armagh in Ireland, Lund in Scandinavia, Gniezno in Poland, Toledo and Tarragona in Spain, and Esztergom in Hungary.

As metropolitans these archbishops had the right to confirm the election of their suffragans and to consecrate them. They had to summon and direct

---

[5] On the relationship of the episcopate to the secular power and its efforts, necessary even in the thirteenth century, to preserve the freedom of the Church *cf.* W. R. Jones, "Bishops, Politics, and the Two Laws: the Gravamina of the English Clergy (1237–1399)," *Speculum*, 41 (1966), 209–45.

[6] *Cf.* G. Le Bras, *Institutions*, 536 f. (literature); A. Felbinger, "Die Primatialprivilegien für Italien von Gregor VII. bis Innocenz III.," *ZSavRGkan* (1951), 95–163; A. Matamic, *De origine tituli "Dalmatiae et totius Croatiae primas"* (Rome and Subiaco 1952); J. F. Rivera Recio, "La primacía eclesiástica de Toledo en el siglo XII," *Anthologia annua 1962*, 11–88.

them at provincial synods, to be held annually. Their right of visitation was undisputed, but Innocent IV decreed in 1246 that they were not allowed to exercise it until they had visited their own dioceses. Furthermore, a visitation of the whole province required the consent of the *comprovinciales*. In cases of failure of duty, jurisdiction devolved on the metropolitan, whose court was also that of second instance in orderly judicial procedure. The metropolitan possessed no direct power of jurisdiction over the subjects of his suffragans. He was supposed to request the pallium in person from the Pope, who occasionally granted it to simple bishops.

Many bishops were bound to the Pope in law by their oath of obedience. The growing papal legislative activity, especially the right to dispense, could not but limit the bishop's rights within his diocese. The custom, originating earlier in a visit of devotion to the tombs of the Apostles, of regularly calling on the Pope and reporting to him became of obligation from Gregory IX as the *visitatio liminum*. If impeded, bishops could perform it by means of accredited proxies.

In the course of the consolidation and completion of the judicial and administrative system larger dioceses were divided into districts which were directed by archdeacons. Originally the archdeacon had been the closest collaborator and even the other self of the bishop, but as director of a district he became in the thirteenth century a prelate with quasi-episcopal power, to whom were subject the clergy of his territory. Possessing ordinary jurisdiction, though the development varied by countries, the archdeacon conducted the annual visitations and supervised the discipline of the clergy, their manner of life, financial administration, and performance of duty. Several times a year the clergy met for the archidiaconal chapters. Even parts of the episcopal judicial authority were handed over to the archdeacon. There gradually occurred among the bishops a reaction against this institution that threatened their autonomy. The episcopal rights of reservation were more firmly stressed, such as nomination of rural deans, visitation of monasteries, jurisdiction in the external forum and in the forum of conscience in serious offenses of clerics and laity, jurisdiction over religious, in disputes over property, and in marriage cases. Bishops appointed an *officialis* for the judicial system and a vicar general for administration as their personal official representatives, thereby reducing the competence of the archdeacon. The period of the decline of the archdeacon's office began with the end of the thirteenth century.

Rural deaneries, which comprised several parishes, were in part subdivisions of archdeaconries, in part subject immediately to the bishop. The dean, also called archpriest, had to intervene in various ways between bishop and parishes, make known episcopal regulations, visit his deanery, and supervise the discipline of the clergy. Like the archdeacon, he convoked meetings of the clergy of the deanery several times a year. In the gild-conscious thirteenth century the parochial clergy also organized into rural chapters. The number of parishes grew because of the dividing up of cities.[7] Even parochial associations of persons — gilds, confraternities, national groups, especially in Eastern Europe and the crusader states — were temporarily established, but only the territorial organization of parishes endured. Their erection lay with the bishop. The care of souls — administration of the Sacraments, preaching, ministry to the sick, burial — was incumbent on the pastor, who, as the prelate over his church, possessed also a power of jurisdiction to a certain extent.

The pastor obtained his post through appointment by the bishop or the one enjoying the *ius patronatus*, and not infrequently also by election by the congregation. All three elements might co-operate. If a pastor was not resident, he had to name and pay a vicar. This duty was incumbent upon the chapter or monastery in the case of parishes incorporated with such bodies. To be distinguished from these vicars were the assistants necessary in larger parishes and known as *capellani, viceplebani, socii in divinis*. In the thirteenth century they were appointed by the pastor, who could even call them from another diocese. Apart from the parish, other chaplains served in a particular pastoral capacity as court chaplains, chaplains in the castles of nobles, in hospitals, and in subsidiary churches.

In this organization of the Church the clergy occupied a position superior to that of the laity, constituted a special *ordo*, and regarded themselves as an *élite*. Besides special duties they also had special rights[8] and, thanks to the subdivision of Church property into an enormous number of benefices, were quite secure economically.

Associations of clerics, grouped around the various functionaries already mentioned, did not fit in the strict sense into the hierarchical order of pastors, bishops, metropolitans, and Pope. They extended from the College of Cardinals downward, through cathedral chapters and deanery chapters, to the gilds of vicars that would later be organized in the large urban churches. Since the College of Cardinals will be discussed later, reference must now be made to the significantly growing power of the cathedral chapters at this period. An outgrowth of the *presbyterium*, the cathedral chapter already had a long history. In the High Middle Ages it perfected its legal structure and influence and became an integral element in the diocesan organization. Naturally, in the 800 dioceses of Christendom its concrete forms displayed much variety, but the decretal law sketched a common plan for all of them. The cathedral chapter consisted of canons, who were responsible for the

---

[7] K. Fröhlich, "Kirche und städtisches Verfassungsleben im Mittelalter," *ZSavRGkan*, 22 (1933), 188–287; *cf.* also the chapter on the urban parish in *Feine*, 414–27 (bibliography).

[8] The survey in G. Le Bras, *Institutions*, 150–71, must be supplemented by what he says on the autonomy of the clergy within Christian society (271–82). The *privilegium fori* and the *privilegium canonis* are the bases of the special rights of the clergy.

liturgy, canonical hours and Mass, in the cathedral and service in the episcopal administration. They elected the bishop. Thanks to the Roman law,
received since the twelfth century, they became a corporation, a legal person.
As such they had rights of ownership and of property, could enter into
contracts, could be represented in court. Their common property increased
considerably. Their chapters were presided over by their elected dean. They
had a seal of their own and regarded themselves as constituting, alongside
the bishop, an autonomous legal structure, with their own statutes and proper
jurisdiction over the capitulars. Direction belonged to a provost or, more
commonly, to the dean. Elected by the chapter, he had to belong to it and
be a priest. To him pertained pastoral authority over all the cathedral clergy.
He had his own seal, and occasionally his income exceeded that of the bishop.
There were also a chanter, a *camerarius*, a treasurer, and in the large chapters
the subdean and subchanter substituted for the dean and chanter. When
absent, capitulars had to appoint vicars for the choir service. In Germany
the cathedral chapters were often reserved to nobles. They also possessed the
special right of co-optation but usually had to share it with the bishop as the
ius simultaneae collationis. Candidates were selected early, sent to famous
universities, and well prepared.

From the time of Alexander III the consent of the cathedral chapter was
required for the alienation of the goods of the bishopric and from that of
Clement III for exchange of goods. Innocent III decreed that the cathedral
chapter was to be heard in cases of the conbining of benefices. This development finally reached the point where Boniface VIII decreed that an aging
or sick bishop could ask for a coadjutor only with the consent of the chapter.
Thus the rights of the cathedral chapter grew, especially since the administration of the bishopric, *sede vacante*, fell to it. An indication of its enhanced
importance was its right to be represented at the provincial synod and,
through its dean, to be invited to general councils. The amazingly extensive
correspondence between the Holy See and the cathedral chapters in the
twelfth and thirteenth centuries shows the consistently increasing importance of these corporations, which was even occasionally displayed in
their exemption from the bishop and direct subordination to the Holy See.
At this period the cathedral chapter became a real power in the Church and
in civil society.

The laity, the mass of the Christian people, were apparently taken less
into consideration in ecclesiastical legislation than the privileged class that
was the clergy,[9] and finally canon law came to look like a clerical law.

_____

[9] Y. M. Congar, *Jalons pour une théologie du laïcat* (Paris 1953), provides historical material for the laity's position in the mediaeval Church; L. Leitmaier, "Der Laie in der Kirche
im Mittelalter und im 20. Jahrhundert," *ZSavRGkan*, 39 (1953), 28–45; R. J. Cox, *A
Study of the Juridic Status of Laymen in the Writings of the Medieval Canonists* (Washington 1959).

However, this law often regulated the relations of the layman to the clergy; many of its decrees referred to all Christians, not exclusively to the clergy. One of the five books of the decretals had to do with matrimonial law. And, in addition to the written law, the customary law, valid in very many areas, also served the laity. In the thirteenth century, which in many aspects of social life experienced a rapid upsurge of new, educated, wealthy, and politically active strata among the urban bourgeoisie, the ecclesiastical self-awareness of the laity also increased. It not infrequently revealed itself in opposition to the clergy.

Still, despite the great separation from the clergy, who reserved to themselves the *magisterium* in the Church and extended their jurisdiction over the laity to purely secular spheres, the rights of the laity were real and could grow. Lay persons administered the Sacraments of baptism and matrimony; lay confession continued to be controverted. In regard to the clergy the laity had a positive right to pastoral care in all its forms: Sacraments, preaching, burial. They were especially active in the administration of Church property, above all in the cities. In the replacing of the proprietary church right by the *ius patronatus*, from the time of Gratian, the laity retained a determining influence on personnel policy in the Church. The contemporary tendency to form associations led to many such groups of lay persons, the confraternities, with a well developed religious orientation — direction of hospitals, defence of the faith, piety — and a gradually growing autonomy.

Despite many a dispute and much tension between clergy and laity the basic feature of the age was the peaceful co-operation and common exertions for the spiritual, economic, and social welfare of *christianitas*, into which all were equally incorporated by baptism and which intended for all the same goal of sanctification and perfection.

The Crisis of the Papacy and of the Church
(1274 — 1303)

CHAPTER 31

The Papacy Subject to Angevin Influence

Gregory X died on 10 January 1276, too soon to be able to continue with the energy proper to him the things the Second Council of Lyons had initiated and the program of his pontificate. His immediate successors, Innocent V (1276), Adrian V (1276), and John XXI (1276–77), were in no position to do anything decisive because of the brief time allowed them on Saint Peter's throne. The aims of Gregory X were not taken up again and an effort made to shield the independence of the Curia against the expanding imperialism of the House of Anjou until the pontificate of Nicholas III (1277–80). But since, immediately after him, the French Martin IV (1281 to 1285) turned the helm completely around and placed himself unreservedly at the service of the interests of Anjou, even to the extent of terminating the reunion of the Churches that had been agreed upon at Lyons, this final phase of the Church's development in the thirteenth century was under the sign of dependence on Anjou and France.

Innocent V, formerly Peter of Tarentaise, was French, even though born within the frontiers of the Empire, a scholar, and, as the first Dominican to ascend the papal throne, a proof of the importance which the Order of Preachers had achieved in the Church. He confirmed Charles of Anjou in his functions as Senator of Rome and Imperial Vicar in Tuscany and thereby seemed to indicate a return of curial policy to the line abandoned by Gregory X. The election of his successor, Adrian V, Ottobono Fieschi, was a result of the pressure of Charles of Anjou on the conclave, which took place in Rome. His sole administrative act was the annulment of Gregory X's rules on the conclave. John XXI, Peter of Spain, did the same, even though he cannot be regarded as a creature of Charles of Anjou. [1] But because of the brevity of their pontificates neither was able to issue a new electoral constitution. As

---

[1] The cancelling of Gregory X's conclave regulations was due to the severity of the conclave that elected Adrian V. Adrian's charter is not extant but it seems to have been used in the corresponding constitution of John XXI: *Reg.* no. 159, ed. E. Cadier, 51 (30 September 1276); *cf.* N. Schöpp, *Papst Hadrian V.* (Heidelberg 1916), 300 f.

a consequence, the next conclaves were again to be of intolerable duration. The election of John Gaetano Orsini as Nicholas III meant a return to the policy of Gregory X. As a Cardinal, it is true, he had supported the invitation of the Angevin into the Hohenstaufen Kingdom of Sicily, but when he perceived in King Charles's struggle for power a threat to the freedom of the Papal State he conformed himself to Gregory X's resistance and was inclined as Pope to act as Gregory had. Like the latter he intended to find in a collaboration with Rudolf of Habsburg, King of Germany, a counterweight to Anjou and to weaken Charles's position in Italy itself. Negotiations with the German King secured Romagna as a part of the Papal State, while Rudolf on 14 February 1279 renounced the imperial interests in that province. A series of charters of the German princes, requested and granted, supported this important decision. King Rudolf was again promised the imperial crown. With Romagna the Papal State definitively rounded out its frontiers, as thy were to be maintained until 1860.

In Rome Nicholas III was able to induce Charles of Anjou, when the King's office as Senator of Rome expired on 16 September 1278, not to seek it again. Shortly before, an electoral regulation had provided that for the future no outside king or prince might be elected as Senator; instead, the dignity was to be held by Romans for a year at a time, and on assuming office they had to take an oath of loyalty to the Pope. Actually, Nicholas had the dignity of Senator conferred upon himself for his lifetime, and appointed his relative, Matthew Orsini, to act as his deputy. Thus began the papal *signoria* over Rome; the one or two Senators were only the deputies of the Pope, who at his election also assumed the dignity of Senator of Rome.

In Lombardy and Tuscany, where Charles of Anjou had been able to consolidate his position, Nicholas likewise sought to check his influence. In this aim he was assisted by the renewal of the Ghibelline opposition at Genoa and in Piedmont, in co-operation with King Alfonso X of Castile, and the assumption of power at Milan by the Visconti, which was likewise of a Ghibelline hue. In Tuscany Charles made himself leader of the Guelf faction. Nicholas first induced the King of Sicily to resign the imperial vicariate. He then devoted himself to relaxing the various tensions among factions and cities in the province in order not to provide the King with any reason for further interference. At Florence, for example, where the Guelfs had come to power in 1267, the diplomacy of the Pope's nephew, Cardinal Latino Malabranca, contrived a reconciliation at the end of 1279 and the beginning of 1280. The exiled Ghibellines were allowed to return.

In the interests of an agreement between Charles of Anjou, leader of the Italian Guelfs, and Rudolf of Habsburg, presumptive leader of the Italian Ghibellines, Nicholas worked for the realization of a project already discussed under Gregory X. Rudolf's daughter Clementia was to marry Charles Martel, grandson of Charles of Anjou, and to receive the Kingdom of Arles as her dowry. In 1280 Rudolf actually enfeoffed Charles of Anjou with the Counties of Provence and Forcalquier, and in March 1281 Clementia was handed over to Charles's envoys at Orvieto. But on 27 August 1280 the Pope died during the negotiations.

Simon de Brie was elected Pope as Martin IV on 22 February 1281, after a six-months' vacancy and a conclave that was powerfully influenced by pressure from Charles of Anjou. He not only abandoned the policy of his predecessor but was prepared to make the most far-reaching concessions to the Angevin. This most French of all the thirteenth-century Popes had risen in the service of the French crown, as a Cardinal had played a substantial role in the transfer of power in Italy to Charles of Anjou, and as Pope was to be a willing tool in the hand of the King of Sicily. He placed himself wholly at the service of the Guelfs and their leader, believing that he was thereby serving the interests of the French Kings. Far from concealing his antipathy toward Germany and the Ghibellines, he availed himself of every opportunity to show it.[2]

He first named Charles Senator of Rome and delivered the Papal State to him by appointing officials of Charles as rectors of the provinces. In the faction struggles in Romagna he supported the Guelfs, removed his predecessor's nephew from the rectorate, and appointed a Frenchman from Charles's retinue. This man, John d'Eppe, obtained at the same time investiture as *generalissimo* of the papal troops. The Pope named as vicar general the French canonist, William Durandus,[3] who became the political adviser of the new rector before he went to France to recruit troops for Charles. The army, made up of mercenaries from all Western countries, suffered a defeat at the hands of the Ghibelline leader, Guy of Montefeltro, on 1 May 1282. If the latter had not, oddly, withdrawn from the conflict in 1283, the Ghibellines would have acquired control of Romagna.

Charles of Anjou took no part in these confrontations, for he was again preoccupied with his far-reaching plans in regard to the East. When Martin IV in 1281 excommunicated the Byzantine Emperor Michael VIII Palaeologus and thus undid the reunion accomplished by the Second Council of Lyons, he was serving the Eastern policy of the King of Sicily. It is true, of course, that since 1274 it had been ever clearer that the Union of Lyons was not accepted by the people. Gregory X had urged it for the sake of the crusade; Michael VIII, to hamstring Charles of Anjou.[4] While the union had

[2] The Pope's pro-French attitude was criticized in the writings of the Cologne canon, Alexander of Roes (cf. bibliography for this chapter).

[3] William Durandus the Elder, Bishop of Mende (ca. 1230–96), was one of the most important canonists of the thirteenth century. His *Speculum iudiciale*, an exposition of the entire canon law in the framework of court procedure (A. M. Stickler), had an enduring influence. Cf. L. Falletti, "Guillaume Durand," *DDC*, 5 (1953), 1014–75.

[4] On 15 October Charles had given his daughter Beatrice in marriage to Philip de Cour-

been proclaimed at Constantinople in April 1277, the Greek bishops had been unwilling to take the personal oath of loyalty required by Gregory X and had refused to insert the *Filioque* in the Creed, as had been agreed.

When Nicholas III in October 1278 demanded the taking of the oath by the bishops and also by the whole of the Greek clergy and at the same time hinted that he intended to tolerate the Byzantine rite only to the extent that it could be brought into harmony with the current canon law of the Latin Church, the tensions became worse. Meanwhile, Charles of Anjou was treating with the heir of the Emperor Baldwin and with the *Signoria* of Venice. A papal notary drew up a treaty at Orvieto on 3 July 1281; this act implied the consent of Pope Martin IV. Hence the excommunication of the Byzantine Emperor in the autumn of the same year came as no surprise. It had at the same time the aim of deterring King Peter III of Aragón from an alliance with the Emperor Michael, which the latter sought to conclude as a counterweight to the alliance between Charles and Venice. Instead of being a crusade for the liberation of the Holy Land, Charles's expedition against Byzantium now assumed, with the Pope's co-operation, the character of a holy war.

In 1277 Charles had purchased from the heiress of Jerusalem, Mary of Antioch, her claim to the Kingdom. He assumed the title of King of Jerusalem and sent to the East the Count of Marseilles, Roger of San Severino, as his *bailli*. Hugh III of Cyprus had in practice given up his claim to Jerusalem and returned to his island. With Conradin the last legitimate King of Jerusalem died in 1268. Charles maintained friendly commercial relations with the Sultan of Egypt. In the Balkan peninsula he was Lord of Albania, he had taken over the administration of the County of Achaia in the name of his daughter-in-law, and he had imposed himself as suzerain on the Duke of Athens and other Latin princes. And so, in 1281, after the signing of the treaty which bound Venice to him, Charles appeared to be on the point of reestablishing the Latin Empire of Constantinople.

The Sicilian Vespers of Easter Monday, 30 March 1282, wrecked all these plans. This revolt of Sicily brought the island under the rule of the King of Aragón, restricting Charles of Anjou to the mainland, thereafter usually known as the Kingdom of Naples. But Pope Martin upheld Charles. He and his immediate successors did all they could, though in vain, to procure for the Angevins their rights. In reality the revolt delivered the papacy from the peril presented by Angevin imperialism, which was thereafter able to gain influence only during the brief pontificate of Celestine V. Boniface VIII would get rid of it entirely.

tenay, who, following the death soon after of his father Baldwin, the last Latin Emperor of Constantinople, assumed the imperial title himself. In the marriage agreement it was provided that Charles should invade the Empire before the summer of 1274; cf. Runciman, *The Sicilian Vespers*, 137.

Steven Runciman has now definitively presented the history of the Sicilian Vespers. The absolute rule, exercised by Frenchmen for the absent King, had pushed the Sicilians into a revolt in which Aragón, aiming to establish an extensive domination in the western Mediterranean, came to their aid. The Kingdoms of Mallorca and Valencia had served as a bridge to Sicily since 1250. King Peter III had married Constance, daughter of King Manfred of Sicily, and had thereby announced his claim to the succession of the Hohenstaufen. In 1281 Peter made an alliance with the Emperor Michael VIII, whom Charles of Anjou was threatening by his treaty with Venice. Peter kept in constant touch with Sicily through refugees, representatives of the national pro-Hohenstaufen party.

The Sicilian revolt was directed against Charles, not against the papacy, to which the rebel government, representing a communal union of the most important cities of the island, offered itself in vassalage. Martin IV rejected the offer, called upon the island to submit to Charles, and promised the King his assistance in recovering it. Cardinal Gerard of Parma, the papal legate, intended to act with this aim at Messina, but neither the proposal of a modified constitution nor the intercession of the Pope was successful, and so Charles had no alternative to winning back the island by force. Meanwhile, the Sicilians had proffered the crown to King Peter of Aragón. He sailed with his fleet and on 1 September 1282 had himself crowned at Palermo. Charles of Anjou raised the blockade of Messina because he was afraid of being cut off from Naples by the Aragonese fleet. He thereby abandoned this part of his Kingdom forever. In prolonged guerilla fighting Peter of Aragón tried to conquer Calabria, but he was excommunicated by Martin IV, who threatened, in the event of disobedience, to deprive him of his Kingdom of Aragón. His deposition[5] was proclaimed by the Pope on 21 March 1283, and the Kingdom was offered by Martin to the King of France, Philip III, for his younger son, Charles of Valois.

When Charles of Anjou died in January 1285, his son and heir, the Prince of Salerno, Charles the Lame, was being held prisoner by the Sicilian Aragonese, who had twice thwarted his attempts to reconquer the island. Calabria was in their hands and revolt was threatening in the rest of the Kingdom around Naples. Charles died a thoroughly beaten man. He had designated as heir his twelve-year-old grandson, Charles Martel, for whom Robert of Artois was to act as regent. He governed the Kingdom of Naples, by papal mandate, together with the Papal Legate Gerard of Parma, until 1289, when Charles II returned from captivity. Pope Martin died on 28 March 1285, three months after his friend, leaving to his successor the irksome legacy of the Sicilian question. The Roman James Savelli, who styled himself Honorius IV (1285

---

[5] O. Hageneder, "Das päpstliche Recht der Fürstenabsetzung: seine kanonistische Grundlegung (1150–1250)," *AHPont*, 1 (1963), 53–95.

to 1287), was elected on 2 April in order to free the Curia from the Angevin connection. The position of Senator of Rome was given to him for life and he had his brother, Pandulf Savelli, act as his deputy. He abandoned the warlike policy of his predecessor in Romagna, pacified the Ghibellines, and received the submission of their leader, Guy of Montefeltro, to whom he granted Asti as his residence.

King Philip III of France had accepted Martin IV's proposal that he take possession of Aragón, of which the Pope had solemnly deprived Peter III, for his son, Charles of Valois. A real crusade was made ready in France for this purpose.[6] Honorius IV did not feel able to withdraw from this undertaking and so he supported it financially and through crusade preaching. The crusade itself was a disaster. Philip III died at Perpignan and his son, Philip the Fair, declined to continue the enterprise. The captive Charles II the Lame was prepared to renounce Sicily to obtain his freedom. The event that contributed most to solve the Sicilian question, however, was the death of Peter III of Aragón on 10 November 1285. He named his oldest son, Alfonso, as his successor in Aragón; his second son, James, in Sicily. It was expected that Honorius IV would lift the excommunication of Alfonso, especially since Edward I of England had intervened and, thanks to him, an armistice had been arranged between France and Aragón. The Pope had ratified this agreement, but he would not consent to the lifting of the censure. He continued obstinately to insist that Sicily belonged to the House of Anjou. When James had himself crowned at Palermo on 2 February 1286, the Pope, far from recognizing him, excommunicated him and his mother Constance. Neither did he accept the treaty whereby Charles the Lame had obtained his freedom by renouncing Sicily and the Calabrian archbishopric of Reggio. Meanwhile, the two regents were governing the remnant of the Kingdom around Naples.

Honorius IV resumed contact with King Rudolf of Germany, in the sense of a renewing of the policy of Gregory X. It was decided that the imperial coronation should take place on 2 February 1287. The embassy of Cardinal John of Tusculum was intended as a preparation for the King's journey to Rome, but it encountered complete defeat at Würzburg in March 1287. The opposition, led by Archbishop Siegfried of Cologne, rejected the Legate's demand for money. It was feared that, after the imperial coronation, Rudolf's son Albert would be made King of the Romans and that the princes' freedom of election would be curtailed. There were rumours of a plan to make the Empire hereditary; the friendship between the Habsburgs and the papacy would allow it to be realized. The Legate had to leave Germany; the imperial coronation was again postponed and did not even take place under the new

[6] See now J. B. Strayer, "The Crusade against Aragon," *Speculum*, 28 (1953), 102–13; *idem*, "The Political Crusades of the Thirteenth Century," in K. M. Setton, *A History of the Crusades*, II, 343–75, especially 367–75.

Pope, Nicholas IV. Rudolf died in 1291 without having worn the imperial crown.

With Nicholas IV (1288–92), who was elected on 22 February 1288, after a rather long vacancy, a Franciscan, formerly Jerome of Ascoli, for the first time succeeded to the papal throne. Under him the Sicilian question continued without a solution and in 1291 Acre, the last Christian outpost in the Holy Land, fell. On 25 July 1287 Charles II the Lame had acquired his freedom again and at Rieti on 29 May 1289 Nicholas crowned him King of Sicily, Calabria, and Apulia. The excommunication of Alfonso of Aragón was lifted when, in a treaty with Charles II and with Philip IV of France, he bound himself not to assist his brother James in Sicily. But Alfonso died on 18 June 1291, thus opening up the whole situation again. For now James was King of both Aragón and Sicily; he appointed his brother Frederick as governor of the island. The Aragonese forced James to accept the Treaty of Figueras with Charles II in December 1293; according to it Sicily was to be returned to the Pope, who could dispose of it only by agreement with Aragón. Frederick was to be compensated elsewhere for the loss of Sicily. The Pope promised to lift James's excommunication and to annul the grant of Aragón to Charles of Valois. It was left to Celestine V to ratify this treaty.

CHAPTER 32

Christian Fanaticism in the Thirteenth Century

The Cathari and Waldensians were defeated by the Church's determined defensive. The crusade, the mendicants' preaching, and the Inquisition had finally overcome this extremely dangerous crisis, even if only by long stages that were marked by losses. In addition to organized heresy with its doctrinal and sectarian opposition to the institutional Church, there also emerged certain movements that advocated devotional practices not in accord with accepted norms. They were resident in those ranks of the mendicants, especially of the Franciscans, that were most responsive to the people, and in the quasi-religious associations among the laity, the Beghards and the Beguines. The basic source of these tendencies was, as it had been from time immemorial, the awareness that one must make one's own the requirements of the *vita apostolica* in order really to take seriously the imitation of Christ. However, the fanatical element of the movement lay rather in its view and purpose not to limit this strict standard only to those charismatically endowed but to prescribe it for all of Christendom. Wherever this standard was lightly esteemed, there was an apostasy from Christianity which had to be condemned and repelled.

And so the demand was often heard that the legal and institutional Church must be left behind, if not superseded, by an *ecclesia spiritualis*, which would be radically serious about the requirements of the Gospel, especially the sermon on the mount. In this demand were encountered the most varied intellectual traditions, among which one of the more recent became especially influential: the apocalyptic theology of history of Joachim, founder and Abbot of San Giovanni at Fiore (d. 1202). According to this tradition, the Age of the Father, the Old Testament, of the carnal man of marriage, was followed by the Age of the Son, the New Testament, of the carnal minded man, especially of clerics, and this was now to be replaced by the Age of the Holy Spirit, the Eternal Gospel, of the spiritual and pneumatic man, who would find the proper form of his existence in monachism. While this idea lacked any anti-hierarchical tone in Joachim, now views were to be propounded which, carried to their ultimate conclusion, aimed at an invisible Church, without hierarchy, Sacraments, and external worship, and in which the spirit of poverty, of peace, and of a spiritual understanding of Scripture was to prevail. The year 1260 was calculated as the time between the Age of the Son and the arrival of that of the Holy Spirit. Joachimite ideas were found especially in broad circles of the Friars Minor, where they were connected with the disputes over the interpretation of the ideal of poverty proper to the order. John of Parma, minister general from 1247 to 1257, was regarded as especially interested in Joachim's ideas. Even if the extreme work of the Paris lector, Gerard of Borgo San Donnino, *Introductorius in evangelium aeternum* (1254), had been published without his knowledge and against his will, its censure by the University of Paris in 1255 and his consequent ambiguous condemnation of Joachim's ideas could not but damage the reputation of the minister general. In 1257 he resigned, but, because of his integrity and the esteem in which he was held in all circles in the Church and the order, he was allowed to name his successor: Saint Bonaventure.[1] The wide circulation of Joachimite ideas, of which, moreover, traces can be found even in Bonaventure's writings, was thereafter promoted also by popular prophecies which appeared in these decades. Even outside the Franciscan Order, they succeeded in fostering in various strata and groups of people an overenthusiasm in religious notions and expectations, they also increased the general disquiet with regard to an official Church that was involved in the power struggles of the time, they incited criticism of her riches, her clerical leadership, her unconcern *vis-à-vis* the spiritual needs of the people.

In the closing decades of the century the Franciscan "Spirituals" became the important spokesmen of the tendency. The beginnings of the Spiritual movement went back to the generation of Saint Francis. At first it had to do

---

[1] H. Denifle, "Das Evangelium aeternum und die Commission zu Anagni," *ALKGMA*, 1 (1885), 49–142; *cf.* also J. Ratzinger, *Die Geschichtstheologie des heiligen Bonaventura* (Munich 1959).

with the consistent realization of the founder's concept of poverty, of his rule, and his testament. But Gregory IX's bull "Quo elongati" of 1230 had denied the testament any legal binding force and had directed the order's development in a more moderate line, which Brother Elias also championed at that time. The stricter disciples of the founder retired, frequently into hermitages, hostile to learning, living for contemplation, avoiding the pastoral apostolate.

Almost reconciled under John of Parma but less pleased with Bonaventure's compromise statutes of 1260 at Narbonne,[2] their fears for the purity of the order's poverty increased when it was rumoured that the Second Council of Lyons intended to do it still greater damage than the previous papal privileges had already done. And so now groups were formed in Provence, where Hugh of Digne (d. 1255)[3] was regarded as their "father," in the Marches of Ancona, where as early as the 1240's Crescentius of Jesi had had difficulties with them, and in Tuscany. From now on they often succumbed to the pressure of the majority in the order, known as the Conventuals. The latter had to be concerned for a uniform interpretation of the ideal of poverty that could be shared by all members of the order. But instead of guaranteeing to the dissidents their own special corporate rights, they took disciplinary measures against them, sought to distribute them among remote houses, and sent them to far-off mission areas; thus the Spirituals in the Marches of Ancona were sent to Cilicia to King Hethum II of Armenia. Their leaders, Peter of Macerata, nicknamed Liberatus, and Angelus of Clareno,[4] the chronicler of the movement, returned in 1293 to Italy, where they joined Jacopone da Todi and Conrad of Offida. Under Celestine V they succeeded in becoming autonomous as the "Pauperes Eremitae Domini Coelestini." But this short-lived arrangement soon fell victim to the general quashing of all of Celestine's administrative measures, which Boniface VIII undertook as soon as he became Pope. The earlier unrest spread, and the measures of the Conventuals became more harsh. Some of the Spirituals fled to Greece.

The group in the Midi found their own spokesman in Peter John Olivi (d. 1298),[5] who as lector at Florence in 1285–89 at the order's house of studies also exercised influence on the Tuscan Spirituals. Together with his pupil and collaborator at Florence, Ubertino da Casale, he managed to give

---

[2] "'Diffinitiones' Capituli Generalis Narbonensis (1260)," ed. F. M. Delorme, AFrH, 3 (1910), 491–504.

[3] Hugh of Digne, "De Finibus Paupertatis," ed. C. Florovsky, AFrH, 5 (1912), 277–90.

[4] L. von Auw, Angelo Clareno et les Spirituels Franciscains (Lausanne 1952).

[5] F. Ehrle, "Petrus Joannis Olivi, sein Leben und seine Schriften," ALKGMA, 3 (1887), 409–552; G. Fussenegger, "'Littera septem sigillorum' contra doctrinam Petri Joannis Olivi edita," AFrH, 47 (1954), 45–53; R. Manselli, La "Lectura super Apocalipsim" di P. di G. Olivi (Rome 1955); L. Hödl, Die Lehre des P. J. Olivi von der Universalgewalt des Papstes (Munich 1958).

the whole movement a theological identity of its own. Many of the Tuscan Spirituals fled to Sicily.

The Spirituals found support in the royal houses of Aragón and Anjou.[6] The influential lay theologian, Arnald of Villanova, also sought to assist them. As the successful personal physician of the Kings and of Boniface VIII, who was himself no friend of the Spirituals, Arnald was able to hold up threatening ecclesiastical measures. Only the Council of Vienne in 1311 and John XXII with his decisions of 1317 and 1318 were able so to confine the living space of the Spiritual movement that only the road to schism and heresy appeared open to it. The conflict over the theory of poverty, which finally emerged from the movement on the theological plane, belongs to the next period of Church History.

The Spiritual movement remained for the most part limited to the order and acted only incidentally on public opinion in the Church. The situation was different with regard to the Apostolics of Gerard Segarelli of Parma,[7] who were constituted from a penitential brotherhood in the Joachimite year 1260. From it proceeded the first flagellant processions, which, full of apocalyptic expectations, carried the summons to penance through city and country. These persons demanded a return to the poverty ideal of the primitive Church and united to this a loud criticism of the wealthy Church of the present, which was acting like a state. Four penitential brothers were burned at Parma in 1294. Gerard Segarelli was imprisoned and in 1300 was also sent to the stake. Leadership was then assumed by Fra Dolcino of Novara, who addressed the faithful in circulars. He proclaimed that the Age of the Spirit had dawned and condemned the Church of the clergy, in which he included even the mendicant friars, because through their possessions they belonged to the carnal Church. Dolcino rejected any subjection to rules that opposed the freedom of the Spirit and demanded apostolic poverty from all. The final age of the world, he said, had begun and people had to hasten it, so to speak, by their actions and contribute to its realization. Dolcino was able to win thousands of adherents. Pursued by the Inquisition, many withdrew into the mountains of northern Lombardy to await the appearance of the Emperor of Peace and of the Angel Pope, from whom they expected help. Against them was organized a crusade, which at Novara in March 1307 brought the movement to a bloody end. One hundred and forty Apostolics were captured and executed along with Fra Dolcino.

[6] M. van Heuckelum, *Spiritualistische Strömungen an den Höfen von Aragón und Anjou während der Höhe des Armutsstreites* (Berlin and Leipzig 1912).
[7] F. Tocco, "Gli Apostolici e Fra Dolcino," *AstIt*, V/19 (1897), 241–75; J. C. de Haan, "De secte der apostolici en haar leiders," *TG*, 42 (1927), 1–31, 144–66; B. Töper, *Die Apostelbrüder und der Aufstand des Dolcino: Städtische Volksbewegungen des 14. Jahrhunderts* (Deutsche Historiker-Gesellschaft 1960, 62–84); E. Anagnine, *Dolcino e il movimento ereticale all'inizio del trecento* (Florence 1964).

Here the cult of poverty and an apocalyptic expectation of a Joachimite hue were associated with dangerous social revolutionary tendencies. One of these Apostolics, Bentivenga of Gubbio, who had become a Franciscan, founded the "Sect of the Spirit of Freedom" in Umbria.[8] His fanatical piety was unmasked as heretical by Saint Clare of Montefalcone in 1306. Ubertino da Casale, prominent among the Spiritual Franciscans, was deputed to interrogate him and was able to convict Bentivenga of heresy. The latter and many of his adherents were condemned at Arezzo in 1307 to perpetual incarceration. They were quietists, who believed themselves to be sinless because all that they did God did in them. They felt bound by no laws of the Church nor by a rule, morality, or conscience. Of course, they did not represent a strictly Joachimite ideology.

From all these trends of fanatical extremism other groups were to develop in the following century, such as the Fraticelli and the adherents of Michael of Cesena.

Subjected together with the Spirituals of the Midi to ecclesiastical disciplinary measures were also the Beguines, who could be regarded as secular followers of the left-wing Franciscans. The Beguines were able to look back to a longer history, not at first affected by the impulse to fanaticism, a history beginning early in the thirteenth century.

There were associations of devout women, virgins and widows, who wished to lead a community life without the vows of religion and established themselves especially in cities. The houses of canonesses were reserved to the nobility, as were also many convents of Benedictine nuns. The reform orders of the twelfth century had at first allowed for the ascetical aspirations of many women by means of their double monasteries, such as Fontevrault and Prémontré. But Prémontré had abandoned the double monastery around 1140 and let the nuns become independent. Cistercian nuns did not appear until late in the twelfth century, because of the aloofness in principle which Cîteaux maintained in regard to the pastoral care of women religious, but then foundations occurred rapidly and everywhere. But whatever the different orders permitted in convents of nuns, it was insufficient by far to take care of the constantly growing number of women who asked for a life according to a religious rule and a common ascetical existence. This female movement, based on economic and religious and mystical motives, almost spontaneously created a form for itself in the Beguine system, whose origins must be sought in the institute of recluses of earlier epochs. The provenance of the name is still unclear, but it is now thought that the gray dress of the sisters spread it. The Humiliati and the Franciscans also wore gray (*bigio*, beige).

---

[8] L. Fumi, *Eretici e ribelli in Umbria* (Todi 1916); L. Oliger, *De secta spiritus libertatis in Umbria saec. XIV (Storia e Letteratura, 3)* (Rome 1943).

The first communities came into being in Flanders and Brabant, under Lambert the Stammerer at Liège (*ca.* 1175), at Mont-Cornillon, at Huy (*ca.* 1182), where Blessed Ivetta was friendly with them, at Willamsbroux near Nivelles (*ca.* 1192) under the influence of Blessed Mary of Oignies, at Nivelles (*ca.* 1207) together with Blessed Ida. These women, like the Cistercian nuns, belonged to the sphere of crusade piety. The spiritual director and biographer of Blessed Mary of Oignies, James of Vitry, an Augustinian canon, then Bishop of Acre, in 1216 obtained from Honorius III a verbal recognition of the new communities, which often took care of a hospital or a leprosary. Thereafter they spread fast and in some cases constituted very large communities. They were in France and Germany, especially on the lower Rhine and in Bavaria, and in almost the whole of Europe. They lived partly by begging, partly by manual labour, and in the course of time on the income from their growing property. Settled, so to speak, between the religious house and the world, they lived under the control of the bishop according to an organization which he had given them or as it had been outlined in the foundation statutes. Varying from the very small house to settlements analogous to cities, the Beguine houses found acceptance in almost all the cities of the countries just mentioned. Without vows, they obliged themselves to daily spiritual exercises, to fasting, and to regular reception of the Sacraments. The uniform gray dress distinguished them from the middle-class women. The government was in the hands of a mistress with her council, while discipline was supervised in a weekly chapter of faults. Procurators or *provisores* often took charge of the economic administration.

The communities of Beguines were often entrusted to the pastoral care of the mendicant orders in Germany and France. If they had their own churches, these orders supplied the rector, if no special chaplain was appointed.

Wherever the pastoral care of Beguines was able thus to move in the proper paths, the institute of Beguines remained free of the suspicion of fanaticism. Nevertheless, after the mid-century the shadows of such a suspicion began to gather around them. The reason for this was probably that at this very time the term Beguine was applied generally to all women and men who devoted themselves to the life of piety outside a type of religious community and gave themselves a special gray dress, as, for example, the Brothers of the New Spirit, male and female recluses, Spirituals who were refugees from their monasteries, and begging and preaching laymen. Since these persons were correctly suspected of fanaticism, through them the very name Beguine acquired a pejorative sound.

While James of Vitry (d. 1240)[9] took the Beguines under his protection even as a Cardinal, — he knew they were called Beguines in Flanders and

[9] James of Vitry, *Lettres*, ed. R. B. Huyghens (Leiden 1960).

Brabant, Papelardes in France, and Bizocche in Italy, — at Paris William of Saint-Amour [10] in his works against the religious orders attacked, among others, also the Beguines. The Franciscan Simon of Tournai warned the Second Council of Lyons of their doings. Even provincial synods began to find fault with them, notably those of Béziers in 1299 and Cologne in 1310. Finally, in 1311 the Council of Vienne issued a prohibition against Beguines [11] but it was only published by John XXII. They were accused of a quietist, pantheistic mysticism and were said to feel themselves above all human and divine laws. Such a prohibition, affecting all without distinction, could of course hardly be enforced, especially as the right boundaries between heretical and orthodox Beguines could be drawn only with difficulty. The honourable and orthodox Beguines, who surely could not have been meant by the prohibition, had to be exempted. The occasion of the prohibition had been, not the Beguines as such, but their sisters in the Midi with their veneration of the Spiritual theologian, Olivi, who had died at Narbonne in 1298. Persons went as pilgrims to his grave, believed they experienced miracles there, and promoted a sort of popular canonization precisely in Beguine circles. The controverted theological evaluation of Olivi's writings affected also the judgment on the Beguines who were his adherents. Olivi's explanation of the Apocalypse, favoured by the fanatics, was subjected to examination by a tribunal and was condemned as heretical, though only by John XXII in 1326. Meanwhile, the fanatical Beguines of the Midi were exposed to the measures of the Inquisition, whose procedures were able to purge them of possible heresy in the course of the first decades of the fourteenth century.

Little has been reported of any persecution of the other French, Netherlandish, and German Beguines at this period.

CHAPTER 33

The Flowering of Scholasticism
and of the Western Universities

The classical period of mediaeval intellectual culture reached its perfection in the thirteenth century. Three factors especially contributed to its construction. The first of these was the making available and the reception of the entire *corpus* of Aristotle by translation, commentary, and assimilation

[10] P. Glorieux, "Le conflit de 1252–57 (à l'université de Paris) à la lumière du Mémoire de Guillaume de Saint-Amour," *RThAM*, 24 (1957), 364–72. Bibliography of William of Saint-Amour in *Glorieux R*, I, nos. 343–46.
[11] "Das Dekret gegen die Beginen," *COD*, 350; in French in J. Lecler, *Vienne (Histoire des Conciles oecuméniques*, 8) (Paris 1964), 195 f.

into Christian philosophy and theology. This took place in confrontation with Arab commentators, Jewish thinkers, and, after 1260, Greek commentators, notably Proclus. The second was the rapidly progressing development of the universities in this century, in particular at Paris, Oxford, and Bologna. Finally, there was the decisive contribution of the mendicant orders, whose members, from the middle of the century, played an outstanding role at Paris and Oxford in the growth of scholarship.

Educational centres of European stature had been formed in the twelfth century, above all at Chartres, Paris, Reims, Laon, Bologna, Salerno, and Toledo. Some of them, however, later lost their importance, as the chief interest of both teachers and students was concentrated on Paris, Oxford, and Bologna. In addition, thanks to princely and papal initiative, there simultaneously appeared *studia* at Naples, founded in 1224 by Frederick II for the Kingdom of Sicily, in Spain, where to Toledo were added Palencia, Léon, and especially Salamanca (1243 and 1254), and finally at the Curia, where in 1244–45 Innocent IV instituted lectures on theology, canon law, and Roman law. Not here, however, but at Paris, Bologna, and Oxford developed the structures that determined the notion of the university of the High Middle Ages.

They were related to and similar to the co-operative organizations formed in the great cities to take care of the social and economic tasks of a population that was constantly undergoing an increasing differentiation of function. Thus at Bologna, where the professors were already integrated into the citizen body, there arose for the students the *universitates* of Lombards, of *ultramontani*, of Romans. City and papal statutes in the course of the thirteenth century regulated the organization of Bologna, where various conflicts between city and student-body had frequently led to emigrations. From 1224 the Holy See managed to establish its control of the university, for which it remained characteristic that the students and not the professors were constituted as gilds. The organization, originally determined by lay persons, was altered by the Holy See in the sense that all, professors and students, clerics and laymen, were strictly subordinated to the jurisdiction of the local bishop, who appointed an archdeacon as chancellor. From 1245 the *universitates* of students could also be incorporated into the city organism. There were now two of them: the Italian or cismontane and the foreign or ultramontane. Each elected its own rector, before whom was made the important oath of obedience, the formality incorporating the student into the *universitas*. Their autonomy was guaranteed by the Holy See.

At Paris the situation developed differently from that at Bologna. Professors and students combined in opposition to the citizens and the local bishop; in 1200 they were exempted by King Philip II Augustus from secular jurisdiction and between 1212 and 1222 also from that of the bishop. The Curia, which, through the Cardinal Legate Robert de Courçon, gave a statute "universis magistris et scolaribus Parisiensibus" in 1215, maintained its supervision of the "university," as the institution was called for the first time in 1219. Originating in the cathedral school of Norte Dame, springing directly from the amalgamation of the communities of professors and students, the University of Paris was complete in its essential characteristics by 1222. Four faculties were to be distinguished: theology, medicine, the liberal arts, and the *Decretum,* that is, canon law. Theology, as the first of them, obtained an autonomous organization in 1219, with its own seal, and the others followed this example. In addition, the university was divided into four nations.[1] The Dominicans settled near the university from 1217, the Franciscans from 1219; in 1224–26 they were more closely linked to it. After a rather long conflict with the chancellor, Philip, and the Bishop, William of Auvergne, as well as with the townspeople, the university left Paris in 1229; its members scattered to Toulouse, Angers, Reims, Orléans, England, Italy, and Spain. By means of the bull "Parens Scientiarum" of 13 April 1231, Gregory IX managed to restore peace and conferred new privileges on the university. During this crisis the position of the theologians belonging to religious orders could be consolidated, so that after 1231 three of the twelve theological chairs were occupied by religious, the cathedral chapter of Notre Dame provided three others, and the remaining six continued to be reserved to diocesan clerics.

Innocent IV confirmed the so-called "foundation bull" issued by Gregory IX in 1231 and in 1245–46 gave the university its own seal and hence full legal existence. The favour and protection of the French Kings enabled it to develop freely. But in the 1250's there occurred a crisis in the theological faculty when the diocesan clergy challenged the teaching of the mendicants. It was ended under Alexander IV in favour of the orders.

Beside Paris, preeminent in theology, and Bologna, which maintained its leadership in law, other universities which received papal privileges in the thirteenth century could play only a far less active role: Padua (1222), Orléans (1229), Angers (1231), and Siena (1246). The medical University of Montpellier also received a statute from the Curia in 1220; it was renewed in 1240. The university established at Toulouse in 1229 during the Albigensian troubles was renewed on the model of Paris in 1245.

The University of Oxford developed in England as the third outstanding higher educational centre alongside Paris and Bologna. Out of the numerous religious houses and particular schools there had arisen there toward the close of the twelfth century an important centre of instruction, where just at that time Aristotelianism was establishing itself. In 1214 the Cardinal Legate

---

[1] French, Picards, Normans, and English; to the English nation belonged also the Germans and Scandinavians; cf. P. Kibre, *The Nations in the Medieval Universities* (Cambridge 1950). Only later was there a separate German nation; cf. P. Perdrizet, *Le Calendrier de la Nation d'Allemagne de l'ancienne Université de Paris* (Strasbourg 1937).

Nicholas of Tusculum settled the conflicts between the town and the institutes of study and granted privileges to the Oxford *studium* just as Robert de Courçon did in 1215 to that of Paris. The incipient university was subjected to the Bishop of Lincoln, who was to direct it through a chancellor, consistently selected from the ranks of the professors of theology. Under the chancellor the university was able slowly to develop its autonomy. The emigration from Paris in 1229–31 brought to the young university a considerable growth, at the invitation of King Henry III. When Robert Grosseteste, who had himself been chancellor, became Bishop of Lincoln in 1235, he further elaborated the chancellor's position. In contradistinction to Paris, at Oxford the chancellor became a member of the university corporation. Oxford received its statutes from Grosseteste in 1252–53. To the efforts of the King and of the successor of Grosseteste at Lincoln to curtail the university's liberties Innocent IV countered with a grant of privileges in 1254 and now named the Bishops of London and Salisbury as the official protectors of the university.

Differing again from Paris, the mendicant orders, above all the Franciscans, had no difficulty in entering the Oxford theological faculty, where they soon occupied a leading position. The number of nations at Oxford, apart from the English, was restricted to two: the Scots or *Boreales* and the Irish or *Hibernenses*.

Cambridge, which had branched off from Oxford in 1209, likewise profited by the Paris exodus of 1229–31. King Henry III especially favoured Cambridge.

Common to all the universities mentioned was a basic structure which recalled their origins in the cathedral schools. First of all there was the chancellor; at Bologna he was a decretist, at Paris and Oxford a theologian, but with authority and possibilities of influence that differed from one place to another. The nations under the direction of elected rectors gained extensive autonomy. At Bologna they even received the oath which was the binding element in all the gilds. At Paris the members of the arts faculty, thanks to their numerical superiority, assumed leadership in the nations. The nations were led by procurators, who in turn decided on the rector; he held office for three months. In 1245 he was head of the university council, which included all the masters, had the right to make its own statutes, and in cases of conflict could appoint arbiters. From the mid-century on the head of the arts faculty was rector of the entire university. The statutes of the arts faculty, regulating the course of instruction and of studies, became a model for all the faculties at all the contemporary universities, except for the faculty of theology, which had its own special regulations. The intellectual connection of the arts with theology was maintained by the circumstance that almost all the theologians had first taught in the arts faculty, which developed in the course of the century into a real faculty of philosophy because literary culture was less and less emphasized and, except at Oxford, the *quadrivium* was also neglected. Since it was less under the magisterial control of the Holy See than were the theologians, it was able, alongside this stronghold of orthodoxy, to exert for the future a decided influence on the development of philosophical movements in the West.

Life at the universities, for which Paris and the Parisian style were always standard, was lived in an ecclesiastical environment, since almost every student was a cleric. And, except at Bologna, the professors had to belong to the clergy. Among masters and students were formed communities that lived together, and, because the students were attached to a specific teacher, there was also a sort of common life within the framework of the *universitas magistrorum et scholarium.*

Instruction was to be imparted basically free of charge, at least in the faculties of the arts and theology. Payment was demanded in the faculties of law and medicine. But gradually it became the custom that fees were required; this can be demonstrated in regard to examination fees, for example. Ecclesiastical benefices were assigned to the masters for their support. Students also, particularly the foreigners, found a similar means of support later.

Financial need and lack of space prevailed, especially at the large university centres, where the numbers were in the thousands; the lack of room applied both to lodgings and to places of instruction. In so far as students did not live in private houses or with teachers they were accommodated in hospitals, which were enlarged for this purpose. But there soon appeared, especially for the poor students, foundations where they could be lodged and take their meals, as, for example, the College of the Eighteen, which Jocius of London, a wealthy Englishman, endowed at Paris. The religious houses included boarding facilities for foreign students, even if they did not belong to the order; their organization served as a model for the rapidly growing number of burses or colleges. Thus in 1257 Robert de Sorbon[2] founded his college, later to become so famous; it was intended for diocesan clerics, who entered it as masters of arts in order to study theology. Such houses were rarer at Bologna, but at Oxford the development was similar to that at Paris. Balliol College was founded at Oxford in 1263, Merton in 1264.

In the thirteenth century, as the monastic schools and those of the canons declined, the universities became the centres of predilection for philosophical and theological scholarship, for scientific medicine, and for the pursuit of both laws. The lively interchange among the faculties was one of the causes of the investigation, becoming more intensive and more methodical from generation to generation, of theoretical as well as of more practical sciences. Exercising an impact in the field of philosophy and, influenced and stimu-

[2] P. Glorieux, *Les origines du Collège de Sorbonne* (Notre Dame, Ind. 1959).

lated by it, of theology in this thirteenth century was the imparting of a stock of ideas, in the centre of which stood the complete *corpus* of Aristotle.

Toledo and Naples were of particular importance in this regard, since both of them lay at the intersection of Christian and Arabic civilization and the Aristotelian legacy was passed on to Western scholarship by means of Arabic and Jewish channels. Authoritative Arabic and Jewish works were translated into Latin at Toledo, which had returned to Christian hands in 1085. Dominic Gundisalvi, John of Spain, Gerard of Cremona, Alfred Sareshel,[3] and Michael the Scot distinguished themselves in this undertaking in the twelfth century, but in the thirteenth they were supplanted by Hermann the German (1240–50), Peter Gallego (d. 1267), and others. The translators wrote their own commentaries too, for example, Gundisalvi's *De divisione philosophiae*, suggested by Alfarabi's *De scientiis*. Michael the Scot treated the same theme. Nicholas of Damascus composed a commentary on the allegedly Aristotelian *De plantis*. But no creative ideas are to be found among these men.

Translation and the pursuit of philosophy likewise characterized the new (1224) University of Naples. Arabs, Jews, and Latins worked together there in harmony. Peter of Ireland commented on Aristotle and Porphyry. Michael the Scot, coming from Spain, became court astrologer in 1220 and as the director of a whole team of co-workers translated the writings of Averroes into Latin. People were still translating here from Arabic and Greek into Latin as late as the time of Manfred (from 1254); for example, William de Luna, Theodore of Antioch, Bartholomew of Messina, John de Dumpno, and others. At the University of the Roman Curia, founded by Innocent IV, Thomas Aquinas, who lectured there from 1259 to 1265 and from 1267 to 1268, met the great translator of Aristotle, his fellow Dominican, William of Moerbeeke.[4] At Oxford the work of translating was fostered by the chancellor, Robert Grosseteste, who himself knew Greek; he interested in it his Franciscan friend, Adam Marsh.

The result of this activity was an almost limitless output of literary works from hitherto inaccessible sources. They included writings of Arabic and Jewish philosophers, who had become acquainted with Aristotle, especially the *Organon*, through the agency of Syrians. In addition, there was a group of commentaries on Aristotle: those by Alexander of Aphrodisias, Porphyry, Themistius, and Ammonius, for the most part Neoplatonists. The Arabs also made use of other Syriac translations: of Theophrastus, Galen, Hippocrates, Euclid, Archimedes. This Aristotelian and Neoplatonic stock of ideas and its literary transmission were independently assimilated by the

---

[3] C. Baeumker, *Die Stellung des Alfred von Sareshel (Alfredus Anglicus) und seine Schrift "De motu cordis" in der Wissenschaft des beginnenden 13. Jahrhunderts* (Munich 1913).
[4] M. Grabmann, *Guglielmo da Moerbeke e le sue traduzioni d'Aristotele* (Rome 1946).

Arab philosophers. Only the most important names can be mentioned here: Alfarabi (d. 950) and Ibn Sina (Avicenna, d. 1037). More Aristotelian than Avicenna was Ibn Rushd (Averroes, d. 1198) of Córdoba. To these must be added the Jewish philosophers, who had already been influenced by the Arabs and made use of an Aristotle infected by Neoplatonism: Solomon Ibn Gebirol (Avencebrol or Avicebron, d. 1070), with his *Fons vitae*, which advocated a pantheistic emanationism, and Moses Maimonides (d. 1204), whom Aquinas highly esteemed and who was dependent on Alfarabi and Avicenna. Like Averroes, these Jewish philosophers lived in Spain. Hence the translators' school at Toledo was so important for their transmission.

But Aristotle came to the Western universities also in direct translations from the Greek. If persons had thus far learned to study an Aristotle who was for the most part understood in a Neoplatonic refraction through the Syriac, Arabic, and Jewish translations, now the genuine Aristotle became known: his hitherto lacking logical treatises — thus far only the so-called Old Logic was known —, his entire metaphysics, ethics, politics, and natural philosophy. And early commentators on Aristotle also found translators: Alexander of Aphrodisias, Simplicius, Eustratius, Aspasius, Michael and John Philoponus, and others. [5]

The scholastic reception of Aristotle has its own history, which of course can be sketched here only in its essential factors. It took place at Oxford with less difficulty than at the University of Paris, where as early as 1210 a provincial council, meeting in Paris, forbade the reading of Aristotle's writings on natural philosophy and their commentaries. The prohibition was repeated in 1215 and extended to the metaphysics, when the legate, Robert de Courçon, gave the university its basic statute. The traditional study of Aristotle was not affected. Perhaps the prohibition is explained by the condemnation, at this same time, of the Neoplatonic-inspired pantheism of Amaury of Bène and David of Dinant. For the Aristotle handed down by the Arabs and Jews was, in fact, of a Neoplatonic colouring. Aristotle was not forbidden at Toulouse, and there, as at Oxford, persons were thereafter preoccupied with the new Aristotle. At Paris, on the other hand, the prohibitions were renewed in 1231 and 1245 and they were mentioned as late as 1263. But they were apparently quickly forgotten, for the reception proceeded apace. Gregory IX had already modified his prohibitions when he entrusted to a commission of theologians the examination of the natural philosophy. Even if this did not meet, people understood the envisaged adjustment as an ecclesiastical permission for the study, especially since only the official, not the private use of Aristotle had been forbidden.

[5] M. Grabmann, *Mittelalterliche lateinische Übersetzungen von Schriften der Aristoteleskommentatoren Johannes Philoponos, Alexander von Aphrodisias und Themistios* (Munich 1929).

In the Paris arts faculty, in any event, persons were keenly interested in the new ideas, whereas in theology this tendency began to make itself felt only around the middle of the century with Albert the Great. At Paris, for the time being, only the *Organon* and the *Ethics* of Aristotle were commented and lectured on, while at Oxford this activity extended also to his natural philosophy and *Metaphysics*. Deserving of special mention are: John Pagus (*ca.* 1230), William of Shyreswood (before 1240), Peter of Spain (before 1246). The last named died as Pope John XXI in 1277; his *Summulae logicales* became the most popular manual of logic at the Western universities.[6] His *Liber de anima* combined Aristotelian with elements recalling Augustine and Avicenna. Among the members of the Paris arts faculty, some of them to become well known theologians, were especially William of Saint-Amour (1236–47),[7] who was to be the sharpest opponent of the theologians of the religious orders in the university crisis of the 1250's, Robert Kilwardby (1237–45), the future Dominican Archbishop of Canterbury,[8] Lambert of Auxerre (until 1250), Nicholas of Paris (until 1263), and a whole group, now anonymous, of their colleagues and students.

Robert Grosseteste translated and commented on Aristotle's *Ethics* at Oxford, while from 1245 the Franciscan Roger Bacon was working on the controverted *libri naturales*. In an effort to overtake Oxford, William of Auvergne, Bishop of Paris, allowed their study at Paris after the death of Gregory IX. Boethius, Avicenna, and Averroes were also esteemed as authorities in philosophy. After 1250 there appeared in the arts faculty the so-called Latin Averroism, a heterodox Aristotelian, under Siger of Brabant. Theologians of all camps strenuously opposed it.

The new philosophy put itself at the service of theology, but without supplanting the Augustinian tradition. At first it was used in an eclectic manner and in the event of conflict the primacy of theology was unreservedly guaranteed. Albert the Great and Thomas Aquinas were the first to rethink Aristotle and to use, very critically of course, the Arabic and Jewish commentaries.

The theology of the early thirteenth century was divided into the conservative wing of the school of Peter Lombard, represented by Peter of

---

[6] J. P. Mullally has edited the *Summulae logicales* of Peter of Spain (Notre Dame, Ind. 1945); *Tractatus Syncategorematum and Selected Anonymous Treatises by Peter of Spain*, translated by J. P. Mullally (Milwaukee 1964).

[7] For William of Saint-Amour see P. Glorieux, "Le conflit de 1252–57 à la lumière du Mémoire de Guillaume de Saint-Amour," *RThAM*, 24 (1957), 364–72 (literature); Y. M. J. Congar, "Aspects ecclésiologiques de la querelle entre mendiants et séculier," *AHD*, 28 (1961), 35–151. There is no real history of the conflict. P. Michaud-Quantin, "Le Droit universitaire dans le conflit Parisien de 1252–57," *Studia Gratiana*, 8 (1962), 577–99.

[8] E. M. F. Sommer-Seckendorff, *Studies in the Life of Robert Kilwardby* (Rome 1937); W. A. Hinnebusch, *The Early English Friars* (Rome 1951), 374–86; A. B. Emden, *A Biographical Register of the University of Oxford to A.D. 1500*, II (Oxford 1958), 1051–69.

Poitiers, lecturing till 1205, Stephen Langton till 1206, Robert de Courçon till 1210, Peter of Capua till 1219, the chancellor Prévotin of Cremona till 1210, and Thomas Gallus of Saint-Victor till 1218, and the progressive wing of the school of Gilbert de la Porrée, represented by Simon of Tournai till 1203, the chancellor Philip till 1236, William of Auxerre till 1228, and William of Auvergne till 1228, when he became Bishop of Paris, dying in 1249. Their extensive writings are in many cases still unpublished and uninvestigated. Included are scriptural commentaries of an increasingly systematic character and commentaries on *The Sentences*, such as those of John of Saint-Gilles (before 1228) and of Hugh of Saint-Cher, a Dominican (1229–30).[9] Theological *summae* were already drafted by Prévotin of Cremona (1206–10), Master Martin, and Godfrey of Poitiers (1213–15), the *Summa aurea* of William of Auxerre (1215–20), the *Summa Duacensis* (*ca.* 1230), the *Summa de Bono* of the chancellor Philip (after 1230), and the *Summa de virtutibus et vitiis* of William of Auvergne (before 1228), as well as his *Magisterium divinale* (1233–40), which includes a critically constructed philosophical system. The *Summa universae theologiae* of the Franciscan Alexander of Hales constituted one climax of this production of theological *summae*. In addition innumerable smaller works of a liturgical, homiletic, and pastoral character, sermons and sermon collections, were composed. Apologetically oriented was the *Summa contra haereticos* of Prévotin (between 1184 and 1210), while controversial theology gave rise to the *Summa contra Catharos et Waldenses* of Moneta of Cremona (d. 1260) and the *Summa de Catharis et Leonists* of Rainer Sacconi (d. 1262).

This wealth of academic and literary production proved the growing importance of the University of Paris, which, by virtue of the activity, shortly to begin, of scholars from the mendicant orders, was to be led to the classic peak of achievement. These scholars succeeded in realizing the long sought synthesis of theology with the new philosophy of the century.

In regard to the Franciscans Martin Grabmann distinguishes three phases. The first was that of Alexander of Hales and the beginnings of the Franciscan school with his pupils, John of Rupella, Odo Rigaldus, and William of Melitona, at Paris. A development of its own must be ascribed to Oxford. These beginnings were carried further under Bonaventure, whose pupils included William de la Mare, John Pecham, Eustace Buisine, and Walter of Bruges, but his greatest student was Matthew of Aquasparta (d. 1302). To a second, somewhat younger generation of Bonaventure's pupils belonged Roger Marston, Richard of Middleton, Guibert of Tournai, and, critically, Peter John Olivi. The transition to the third phase, which centred on Duns Scotus, was constituted by Peter de Trabibus, William of Ware, the minister

[9] *Cf.* J. Fisher, "Hugh of St. Cher and the Development of Mediaeval Theology," *Speculum*, 31 (1956), 57–69.

general Gonsalvus de Vallebona, and Vitalis de Furno. John Duns Scotus himself (*ca.* 1270–1308) stood on the threshold of the new age.

The older Dominican school began with Roland of Cremona (d. 1259) and the well known exegete, Cardinal Hugh of Saint-Cher. To it belonged Peter of Tarentaise (d. 1276 as Pope Innocent V). These scholars still followed the paths of a doctrine that was determined by Augustinianism. The Aristotelian orientation was established by Albertus Magnus (*ca.* 1193–1280). In a comprehensive Aristotelian encyclopedia, which also cited pseudo-Aristotelian works, he laid the ground for a Christian Aristotelianism. Albert obtained the scholastic title of *doctor universalis,* because not only was his knowledge of the sources universal but his scholarship was able to master all fields of philosophy, natural science, and theology. And his influence in the academic world became universal. He commented on all the books of Aristotle, on *The Sentences* of Peter Lombard, on the *De divinis nominibus* of pseudo-Dionysius. His *Summa theologiae* remained unfinished; more famous became the *Summa de creaturis,* which included, among other things, a systematic ethics, a doctrine of the Sacraments, and an eschatology. Many lesser works discussed dogmatic questions of Mariology, the Eucharist, and much else. The earliest pupils of Albert were Hugh Ripelin of Strasbourg and Ulric Engelberti of Strasbourg. Ulric of Strasbourg (d. 1277) created a monumental theological *summa,* called by Grabmann "the greatest and most complete work of German Neoplatonism proceeding from Albert."

Thomas Aquinas (1225–74) ranks as the chief representative of classical scholasticism. He was Albert's pupil at Paris, and followed him to Cologne, where he studied from 1248 to 1252. He himself taught at Paris from 1252 to 1259, then at the University of the Roman Curia from 1259 to 1268, at Paris again from 1268 to 1272, and finally at Naples from 1272 to 1274. He died, *en route* to the Second Council of Lyons, at the Cistercian abbey of Fossanuova near Naples, on 7 March 1274.

His vast literary output can be arranged under six headings. First are the philosophical commentaries on Aristotle's most important works and on the *Liber de causis,* for which William of Moerbeeke supplied him with a reliable text. With these he was able to improve on the inadequate commentaries on Aristotle by Averroes and by Albertus Magnus. The second category includes scriptural commentaries on many books of the Old and the New Testament. His *Catena Aurea* was a collection of patristic texts on the four Gospels, probably intended as a handbook for preachers. Next come theological commentaries on the works of Boethius (*De Trinitate, De hebdomadibus*), pseudo-Dionysius (*De divinis nominibus*), and Peter Lombard (*Liber sententiarum*). The *Scriptum super sententiis* was reckoned among the great works of theological synthesis for which we are indebted to Thomas. The fourth class consists of works of theological synthesis. The *Summa contra gentiles* was begun at Paris in 1258 and completed in Italy under Pope

Urban IV (1261–64). There followed the great and uncompleted *Summa theologica;* Thomas spent seven years on it, and Reginald of Priverno finished it by adding material from the *Scriptum super sententiis.* To his friend and pupil Reginald Thomas dedicated the likewise incomplete *Compendium theologiae.* Next come the notes for academic disputations, the *Quaestiones disputatae* and *Quaestiones quodlibetales.* These provide a mirror of the ideas and controversies of the age. Finally, there are the lesser works, for the most part occasional pieces of the most varied content. Some deal with philosophical questions, such as *De ente et essentia, De aeternitate mundi, De unitate intellectus, De substantiis separatis;* some with theology, including *De articulis fidei et Ecclesiae sacramentis, De regimine Iudaeorum;* some are apologetic: *De rationibus fidei contra Saracenos, Graecos et Armenos* and *Contra errores Graecorum;* and defense of the position of the mendicant orders at the university: *Contra impugnantes Dei cultum, De perfectione vitae spiritualis,* and so forth. Finally, there are works of a devotional, liturgical, canonical, and homiletic content, the most important being the office for the feast of Corpus Christi and the *Expositio de Ave Maria.*

Thomas Aquinas possessed an exhaustive knowledge of the patristic tradition. His exegesis, however, was hindered by his unfamiliarity with Hebrew and Greek. For all his critical method he was, like his contemporaries, tied to the theological acquaintance with the sacred text that the patristic writers and the early scholastics had cultivated, because of the deficiency of his historical horizon, of his knowledge of the auxiliary sciences, and of a technically perfect philology. His definitive achievement lay in the field of speculative theology and of the unique intellectual accomplishment whereby he placed the philosophy of Aristotle's genius at the service of revealed doctrine and of its conceptual presentation. Research during recent decades has especially stressed that Thomas Aquinas was a master of the spiritual life precisely in the scientific dress of his theology.

The point of departure in the method of his speculative theology was, it is true, challenged as early as three years after his death, when Bishop Stephen Tempier of Paris included twenty-one texts from Thomas's works among the 219 condemned propositions of 1277; he thereby rejected the rationalism and naturalism of heterodox Aristotelianism, then a threat at the university. The canonization of Thomas by John XXII in 1323 effaced this shadow from the Church.

The tendency in thought that was really attacked in Bishop Tempier's condemnation was at home in the arts faculty and hence concerned philosophical rather than theological errors. Toward the middle of the century Averroes had supplanted Avicenna in the scholarly world as *the* commentator of Aristotle. The turning of the philosophers to him developed at Paris into a vigorous movement. The doctrine of the eternity of the world, the proposition of the double truth, and monopsychism became characteristic of it. Its leader was Siger of Brabant (1235–84), one of the most important interpreters of Aristotle of that time, independent in judgment and of constructive intellectual powers. He later freed himself from an originally radically Averroistic understanding of Aristotle through the influence of the works of Aquinas and accepted the latter's interpretation of the Stagirite. He abandoned monopsychism and never formally defended the doctrine of the double truth. If he had earlier been a determinist, in his later years he defended the freedom of the will.

Condemned in 1277 along with his doctrines was Boethius of Dacia, in whom was found a more Aristotelian and purely this-worldly paganism. Far more moderate were the masters James of Douai, Raoul the Breton, Peter of Auvergne, Henry of Brussels, and in England Simon of Taversham (d. 1306). This Averroistic movement was felt also at Bologna and Padua.

England's contribution to the history of High Scholasticism matched that of France. Especially in the Franciscan Order were found many scholars of English nationality. One need only recall Alexander of Hales, founder of the Franciscan school at Paris. There and even more at Oxford was established a school of a unique character. Robert Grosseteste, who introduced the Franciscans to Oxford, was also the one who founded that university's fame in science. He was chancellor of the university until his promotion to the see of Lincoln. At first profoundly influenced by mediaeval Augustinianism, he was the first Englishman to adopt Aristotle's philosophical system and sought to assimilate the whole wealth of the onrushing stream of science in the Greek, Arabic, and Jewish tradition. In contradistinction to the Paris scholars he also placed great stress on the cultivating of the sciences of the *quadrivium*, above all mathematics. His scriptural study was bound strictly to the text, his knowledge of Greek being here of use to him, and was critically oriented. On the other hand, like his contemporaries, he was not a humanist. As first regent of the Franciscan house of studies he was succeeded first of all by diocesan priests, Peter, later Bishop of Aberdeen, Roger Welsham, and Thomas of Valais. It was not until 1247 that Franciscans took over the direction of their own house of studies. The first to do so was a close collaborator and friend of Grosseteste, Adam Marsh. His third successor was Thomas of York, whose philosophical *summa,* the *Sapientiale,* became famous. Like Grosseteste he was versed in Arabic and Jewish philosophy. From 1256 Thomas of York directed the Franciscan house of studies at Cambridge. At Oxford he was succeeded by Richard of Cornwall and then John of Wales, who, as author of the *Summa de Poenitentia,* was more outstanding in theology than his predecessors. Following him in the directing of the school was a leading exegete, Thomas Docking of Norfolk.

The greatest name among the English Franciscans was that of Roger Bacon (*ca.* 1214–92). Influenced by Grosseteste, Adam Marsh, Thomas of York, and other Oxford scholars, Bacon himself was not a professor and perhaps not even a priest. He turned from speculation to encyclopedic, comprehensive research in the field of mathematics, natural science, and social science. He pursued positive science not only for its own sake but for the service of theology. Independent and self-willed, intuitively gifted and endowed with critical precision, in his literary works he developed ideas whose significance in intellectual history must be seen not so much in themselves as in their ability to stimulate others. He deplored the separation between speculative thought and experimental science and the uncertainty involved in the uncritical use of traditional texts. An unstable wanderer, he was commissioned by Clement IV to draw up a plan for the reform of ecclesiastical studies; but he made so many enemies that he spent more than ten years, till shortly before his death, under house arrest. His chief work was the *Opus maius,* in which he asked that science be put at the service of practical life. Revolutionary was his demand for the introduction of experiment. In theology he remained bound to the Augustinian tradition.

The great importance of English scholars of the mendicant orders is especially to be seen in the two eminent personalities who successively ruled the archbishopric of Canterbury: the Dominican Robert Kilwardby (*ca.* 1210–79) and the Franciscan John Pecham (*ca.* 1220–92). [10]

After the Paris judgment of 1277, which Pecham also adopted for England, the Thomist school and the Franciscan followers of Saint Bonaventure drew farther apart. The leading English Thomist at Oxford, after Richard Knapwell, was especially Thomas of Sutton. But in intellectual brilliance they were surpassed by the Franciscan Richard of Middleton, who taught at Paris from 1280 to 1295. He is perhaps to be regarded as a precursor of the greatest English theologian, John Duns Scotus (*ca.* 1266–1308), whose beginnings and early death belong in this period. He studied and taught at Oxford and Paris in turn. He was sent to Cologne in 1307, and died there the next year. As a Franciscan he remained attached to the Augustinian tradition, but his eclectic Aristotelianism went far beyond what Bonaventure and Pecham had allowed. The Oxford school gave him his interest in mathematics and in experiment. His keen critical faculty likewise distinguished him from the Augustinian and Thomist-Aristotelian visual range. But he too applied himself to the unity of faith and knowledge, to a synthesis of metaphysics and theology.

In Paris and elsewhere on the continent the great condemnation of Aristotelianism in 1277 meant a splitting of minds. While a certain trend toward a conservative reaction displayed itself, on the whole the development continued on the routes previously pointed out by the great masters of synthesis.

Scholarly life became even more intense and richer and a great number

[10] D. L. Douie, *Archbishop Pecham* (Oxford 1952).

258

of noteworthy teachers and investigators appeared, who devoted themselves to philosophical and theological problems in a personal, independent, and critical method.

Shortly after 1277 appeared the *Correctorium fratris Thomae* of William de la Mare,[11] the manifesto, so to speak, of the neo-Augustinian Franciscan school, in which 117 Thomistic theses were critically examined. Richard of Middleton belonged to this school, even though he approached Thomas in his epistemology. Vitalis de Furno should be mentioned and, even more, William of Ware, one of the teachers of Duns Scotus. Also to be counted in the Franciscan school at Paris was Peter John Olivi (d. 1298), already discussed in connection with the Spiritual movement. However, he did not teach at Paris but, among other places, at Florence. He left very many theological writings. As is well known, the Council of Vienne (1311–12) spoke out against him in favour of the doctrine of the soul as the *forma corporis* of man. In general he remained faithful to his order's traditional intellectual orientation.

In the train of Pecham in his reaction against Thomism was also Henry of Ghent (d. 1293), who showed himself to be a neo-Augustinian in his vigourous dispute with Giles of Rome and Godfrey of Fontaines. He developed a Neoplatonic metaphysics, which was clearly influenced by Avicenna.

Parallel to this neo-Augustinian tendency, represented mostly by Franciscans, there grew up the young Thomist school, whose spokesmen belonged mainly to the Dominican Order. Remarkably enough, Saint Thomas's immediate disciples were not very prominent in it, except for Ptolemy of Lucca in Naples. The most important scholars of the Thomist school were the Augustinian Hermit Giles of Rome (d. 1316), Godfrey of Fontaines (d. 1306), the diocesan priest Peter of Auvergne (d. 1304), and Henry Bate of Malines (d. after 1310).

The thirteenth century can be summarized as an epoch of philosophical and theological culture, and Maurice de Wulf called it the Golden Age of Metaphysics. Through it theology became speculative without losing its contact with Holy Scripture and the patristic tradition. It not only enriched the Greek-Jewish-Arabic legacy; it also made it capable of confronting the world of Judaism and Islam in apologetics.

The literary culture of the twelfth century was replaced by the cultivation of the particular disciplines, which formed their own languages. While the great scholars, especially Bonaventure and Thomas, mastered a distinct

---

[11] *Declarationes Magistri Gulielmi de la Mare O.F.M. de variis sententiis S. Thomae Aquinatis*, ed. F. Pelster (Münster 1956); V. Heynck, "Zur Datierung des 'Correctorium fratris Thomas' Wilhelms de la Mare. Ein unbeachtetes Zeugnis des Petrus Johannis Olivi," *FStud*, 49 (1967), 1–21.

literary style, it did not achieve the rich brilliance and vivacity of the twelfth century.

A certain ambivalence of the age revealed itself in the development of a heterodox Aristotelianism in the arts faculty: the danger of rationalizing naturalism made itself felt. Siger of Brabant became its exponent and against him Bonaventure, Pecham, and Aquinas entered the lists. But Aquinas himself did not escape criticism on the part of almost the entire theological faculty of Paris. By means of his critical study and assimilation of the Aristotelian stock of ideas, especially its concept of knowledge, he had created the first original Christian philosophy, but it was precisely here that, according to his critic, John Pecham, the future dangers lay for theology; he felt that in Thomas there could be detected a surrender to Siger's positions — too far-reaching concessions to a heathen philosophy. And yet from the historical viewpoint the figure of Saint Thomas dominated his century. His work presupposed the exertions of the first century and a half and built on them. The philosophical and theological disputes which filled his lifetime stimulated his thought and promoted its development. The violent reaction against his total view and the sharp criticism of Duns Scotus compelled his pupils and successors to penetrate his work more deeply and make it better understood. The enduring and timeless value of Thomas's synthesis, however, was not to be appreciated fully for centuries. In this sense are to be understood Gilson's words: "This solitary scholar did not write for his own century, but the future was to belong to him."

Chapter 34

The Cardinals and the Curia in the Thirteenth Century

The Emperor Frederick II had addressed the cardinals as "successors of the Apostles" when in 1239 he suggested to them the summoning of a council at which his quarrel with Gregory IX should be arbitrated. And at the end of the century King Philip IV of France used the same phrase in an analogous context. Even if the canonists soon stressed the distinction between a "succession" of that sort and the recognized position of the bishops as *successores apostolorum*, it became clear in other ways how exalted a rank the cardinalate[1] had acquired in the awareness of the age together with the papacy in its rise in esteem. The origins of the cardinalate from the Roman clergy belonged to the remote past. Innocent IV said without affectation that the cardinals

---

[1] S. Kuttner, "Cardinalis, the History of a Canonical Concept," *Tr*, 3 (1945), 129–214; M. Andrieu, "L'origine du titre de cardinal dans l'Église romaine," *MiscMercati*, V (Rome 1946), 113–44.

possessed the authority of senators. As the Pope's advisers and participants in the government of the Church they met under the Pope's presidency in the consistory, which had replaced the Roman synods. They were early called *pars corporis papae*, as the princes of the Empire were regarded as *pars corporis imperatoris*. While the *Descriptio sanctuarii Lateranensis* (*ca.* 1100) still knew fifty-three cardinals, — seven bishops, 28 priests, 18 deacons, — this number fell in the thirteenth century to less than twenty and occasionally to even less than ten. Furthermore, by virtue of the corporative thought of the age, the cardinals appeared ever more clearly as a *collegium* and a corporation.[2] The beginnings of their own financial administration went back to the pontificate of Calixtus II (1119–24). In the thirteenth century it was directed by a Cardinal *Camerlengo*, who should be distinguished from the chief of the papal *Camera*. In 1289 Nicholas IV granted the college one-half of the income of the Holy See. Especially in view of the prolonged vacancies during this period — together they amounted to almost ten years in the thirteenth century — it was not possible to evade the question of what authority pertained to the college in the government of the Church. The leading decretalist, Hostiensis, himself Cardinal Bishop of Ostia and hence *prior et decanus* of the college, held that the college and the Pope constituted a unity, "unum et idem est," and hence it participated in the *plenitudo potestatis*.[3] Others, however, limited the cardinals' proper authority to their right and duty of electing the Pope, while all other authority came to them from the Pope, for they are what they are through the Pope, who named them, bestowed their privileges, assigned their duties, and, if necessary, deprived them of their dignity. As a matter of fact, during the vacancies of the Holy See the cardinals acted so consistently in regard to decisions of law and of administration that they did not lay claim to the papal primatial power. In the consistory they were advisers but not real codetermining participants, even if there was often, though not always, mention in papal charters that decisions were arrived at "de fratrum nostrorum consilio" (or "consensu"). Research is today agreed that neither was the necessity of consultation meant nor did the consent of the cardinals give validity to the papal decrees. The cardinals' signatures on especially solemn papal decrees must be similarly understood. Whatever accrued to the cardinalate in authority and dignity came through a grant by the Pope and was therefore of positive ecclesiastical law. The cardinals received no order and were not necessarily bishops, even though they outranked bishops in the course of time and, like them, had a seat and a vote at councils.

In the thirteenth century, as earlier, the Pope made extensive use of the cardinals in the government of the Church and of the *Patrimonium*, where

[2] For the canonical view of the relationship of Pope and cardinals see B. Tierney, *Foundations of the Conciliar Theory* (Cambridge 1955), 68–84.
[3] Tierney, *op. cit.*, 149–53, gives the opinion of Hostiensis.

they obtained the most important rectorships, that is, the administration of the provinces. When acting as legates they received far-reaching powers, including judicial, and on such occasions appeared in almost papal dress and with papal ceremonial. In 1245 Innocent IV granted them the red hat. At Rome they became a sort of council of state during the Pope's lifetime and they assumed the government after his death.[4] Their honorary rights began to multiply. The Pope was their only judge, and, placed on an equality with the electors in the secular sphere, they ranked immediately after him.

If the cardinals, under the direction of the Pope in the consistory, represented, in a sense, the highest organism for justice and administration in the Church, the Curia developed on its own alongside the college. The departments of the Curia, so far as they were constituted in the thirteenth century, were by no means directed by cardinals, except for the *Penitentiaria*. Perhaps the number of cardinals was too small; some of them were absent from Rome for rather long periods as legates. Perhaps the Popes felt that in this way they could retain the organization of the Curia directly at their own disposal. The exertions of the College of Cardinals to insert itself, on an equal footing and as an essential partner, into the supreme direction of the Church cannot be mistaken in the thirteenth century, even if they only later came to light.

The Curia

The epoch of the great jurist Popes, from Innocent III to Boniface VIII, brought to the elaboration of the Curia[5] a growth and at the same time a simplification. It became the administrative and judicial organ of a spiritual commonwealth, to which the development of canon law, especially through the codifications of the thirteenth century from the decretals of Gregory IX to the *Liber Sextus* of Boniface VIII, had given a uniform order applying to all lands in Christendom. To watch over and perfect it became one of the more essential tasks of the Curia, which thus had to carry out governmental, administrative, and judicial functions. The final decision, of course, lay always with the Pope, who usually reached it in consistory.

The administration fell under the two offices of chancellor and *camerlengo*. Judicial matters were divided between the *Penitentiaria* for the forum of conscience and the *Audientia causarum* or *Audientia Sacri Palatii*, from which was to emerge the *Sacra Rota Romana* from the end of the thirteenth century. Besides these offices, whose activities could not as yet always be clearly distinguished, the papal court also disposed of the *capella*, whose development had been similar to that of its secular counterpart. While

---

[4] G. Le Bras, *Institutions*, I (Paris 1959), 346; *cf.* the entire chapter (340–48).
[5] For the origin of the Curia see *supra*, Chapter 4.

destined for divine worship, the *capellani,* a group that was becoming ever more numerous, had, of course, to be prepared for other duties, in particular diplomatic. Secular dignitaries, officials, and employees took care of the lodging, maintenance, and order of this vast community, whose members were frequently on the road and demanding appropriate provisions.

The Chancery

The name *cancellaria* appeared as early as 1182. Basically, the chancery was supposed to take care of all the correspondence between the Pope and Christendom. However, separate records for the *Penitentiaria* and for the *Camera* soon branched off. From 1187, except for brief intervals, there was no chancellor. Honorius III definitely abolished the office and replaced it with that of vice-chancellor. The vice-chancellor was not a cardinal until the end of the thirteenth century. The organization of the chancery was still in full process of development at this time. Under the vice-chancellor worked the notaries, the *corrector,* the *auditor litterarum contradictarum,* the *abbreviatores,* the *scriptores,* and the *bullatores.* The seal had to be left with the *camerlengo* over the weekend. From around the middle of the thirteenth century the notaries' chancery activity slowly declined, while the vice-chancellor, previously merely *primus inter pares,* increased his authority.

In addition to charters, which corresponded to initiatives of the Pope himself, the chancery especially took care of petitions, *supplicia,* coming in writing to the Curia from everywhere; they dealt with questions from the most varied aspects of ecclesiastical law. They were received and examined in the so-called *Data communis;* the more important were then revised in concise form and submitted to the Pope for a decision. In the event that a favourable decision was there granted, an outline of a letter *(minuta)* was drawn up; a fair copy was made under the supervision of the *corrector* or other officials, such as the vice-chancellor or a notary, and it was sealed by the *bullatores.* If Pope, Curia, or petitioner so desired, the charter was entered in the register and then delivered. If such letters of right or of grace were contradicted and challenged by the parties concerned, the case was sent to the *audientia litterarum contradictarum.* But in the thirteenth century this curial department was not yet fully organized.

The heaviest burden in the chancery lay on the vice-chancellor and his six (at most seven) notaries, who presented the more important petitions to the Pope; later the *referendarius* assumed this function. They had to send back *supplicia* that were improperly composed and expedite those that were granted. Each notary employed his own *abbreviatores* for the drawing up of the drafts of letters. The less the notaries were concerned from around 1250 with the current everyday work, the more the *abbreviatores* came under the direction of the vice-chancellor himself. As earlier, the *camerlengo* continued to be the keeper of the seal. The chancery had close connections with the *Camera;* it obtained its materials, such as parchment, lead, and silk, from the *Camera,* while the *Camera* participated in those charters and *acta* that were concerned with money questions or with the administration of the Papal State. The extant or registered charters do not supply a full picture of the achievements of the chancery, for only a fraction of them was retained or registered. In 1302 the chancery disposed of the material for 11,000 charters but only 1,036 written pieces for that year can be identified.

The *Camera*

The *Camera* provided the financial administration of the Holy See. The Pope had had to assume immense tasks, above all in regard to the organizing of the crusades, in the conflicts between the Holy See and the Empire, and in the matter of subsidies, which proved to be necessary everywhere because of the tensions within Christendom. Furthermore, there was the increasing burden of supporting so expanding an administrative organism as the Curia itself. Hence a special bureaucracy for financial administration became necessary. Cluny was perhaps the model for the origins of the *camera apostolica.* [6] The revenues came from the tax yield of the *Patrimonium,* from the proceeds of Peter's Pence,[7] from the gifts brought by prelates visiting the Curia. From Innocent III these last were converted into fees and specific services. *Servitia communia,*[8] amounting to one-third of a year's income, were payable on the occasion of the nomination and confirmation of bishops and abbots, and the dispatch of chancery *acta* was connected with the payment of various fees. From the crusade tithes there gradually evolved a system for a general taxation of Christendom.

The direction of the *camera* always pertained to a bishop and occasionally even to a cardinal, who should not be confused with the *camerlengo* of the College of Cardinals. Under him were the collectors, sent out to gather on the spot the monies due or, in the case of taxes paid in kind, to convert them into money and to remit them. When, from the middle of the thirteenth century, to the *servitia communia* for the higher benefices were added for the lower benefices the annates,[9] or one's year income, usually paid in kind, the work of the collectors was increased.

[6] J. Sydow, "Cluny und die Anfänge der Apostolischen Kammer," *SM*, 63 (1951), 45–66.
[7] K. Jordan, "Zur päpstlichen Finanzgeschichte im 11. und 12. Jahrhundert," *QFIAB*, 25 (1933 f.), 61–104; C. Daux, *Le Denier de saint Pierre* (Paris 1907).
[8] A. Gottlob, *Die Servitientaxe im 13. Jahrhundert* (Stuttgart 1903).
[9] J. Vincke, "Die Krone von Aragón und die Anfänge der päpstlichen Annaten," *RQ*, 40 (1932), 117–82.

Since there was as yet no distinction between the direction of the papal treasure and that of the Church, such as that between *mensa abbatis* and *mensa conventus* and between *mensa episcopi* and *mensa capituli*, the *camerlengo* was one of the Pope's closest collaborators. His correspondence was recorded since the days of Urban IV in the *camera* register; *camera* clerics took care of the correspondence, examined contracts, and checked the receipts of the collectors. The *camera* had its own judicial officials — *auditor*, fiscal procurator, advocates — as the number of processes increased. For the exchange of money the *camera* made use of the banking firms of Florence, Genoa, and elsewhere, whose agents in Rome were called *mercatores curie romane*. Under the *camerlengo* was the actual administrator of the treasure, *thesaurarius*, who guarded the cash on hand.

Judicial Offices

Whereas in the twelfth century the consistory, presided over by the Pope, was able to settle disputed cases and appeals, in the course of the thirteenth century special offices were constituted, which were not fully established until the fourteenth century. The first was the *Penitentiaria*, for the forum of conscience. For a long time, perhaps from the seventh century, the Pope had made use of the services of a *penitentiarius*, but the latter's activity had grown so extraordinarily by virtue of the frequency and abundance of reservations and dispensations that he had to receive corresponding assistance. Delegations too had so increased since the pontificate of Alexander III (1159–81) that now the Cardinal *Penitentiarius* had to have a staff of coworkers. Thus appeared the *Penitentiaria*,[10] whose structure was organized under Gregory IX (1227–41) and constantly perfected into the fourteenth century.

From the formulary of Thomas of Capua under Honorius III we learn that the *Penitentiaria* absolved from sins and censures that were reserved to the Pope, granted dispensations from irregularities and marriage impediments, could quash illegal and unfair decisions, dispense from vows, commute them, or postpone their fulfillment, dispatched indults, conferred privileges, mitigated penances. The grand *penitentiarius* was the confessor of the cardinals and of prelates staying at the Curia. Under Boniface VIII there were as many as twelve *sub-penitentiarii;* often they were religious of various nations.

The public administration of justice pertained to the *Audientia Sacri Palatii*, from which the *Rota* developed in the fourteenth century. When in

[10] E. Göller, *Die päpstliche Pönitentiarie von ihrem Ursprung bis zu ihrer Umgestaltung unter Pius V.*, I: *Die päpstliche Pönitentiarie bis Eugen IV.* (Rome 1907); T. Majic, "Die Apostolische Pönitentiarie im 14. Jahrhundert," *RQ,* 50 (1955), 129–77.

the course of the twelfth century the legal cases which reached the Curia directly or by means of appeal grew more and more in number, even more *auditores* were commissioned to introduce the processes and lay them before the Pope, together with the cardinals, for decision; sometimes they were themselves authorized to render decisions. *Auditores* were selected from the cardinals, the bishops, and perhaps even from papal *capellani*. Around the middle of the thirteenth century there were general *auditores*, — *auditores generales causarum palatii*, — as many as fourteen under Boniface VIII. They constituted a college: the *Audientia Sacri Palatii*. This was concerned with all civil and penal cases which fell within the competence of the Holy See. The Pope also reserved *causae maiores* and disputes over elections to himself and the cardinals. This papal judicial office only obtained a stable organization in 1331 in the bull "Ratio iuris"; it was later called the *Rota*. [11]

Alongside it worked the so-called *Audientia litterarum contradictarum*, which belonged to the chancery. Authorized by Innocent III, it was concerned with legal documents and with grants of favours by the Curia which had been challenged by opponents of the recipients. In general, it was intended to create order in the extensive legal mechanism of the Curia, to exclude foolish issues from the outset, and to seek an arbitrated compromise before the starting of a process. This could be achieved by revision of records and elimination of bureaucratic chicanery and of delays in trials. While it thus regulated or reformed the course of business in the interests of peace, chancery rules and legal structures were set up and published by the *Audientia publica*. With the increase in the proper legal forms for conducting trials in the thirteenth century the *Audientia litterarum contradictarum* also became interested in the regulating and systematizing of rescripts and the examining of the challenges, especially those that were of a delaying nature. It was supposed to be of assistance to the parties in the selecting of judges.[12]

In addition to the offices of the Curia in the strict sense there appeared the college of papal *capellani*. These devoted themselves not only to the liturgy at the papal court[13] but also to various types of diplomatic and judicial tasks. Already numerous in the twelfth century, their number increased to almost 200 under Innocent IV. At first subdeacons and later also deacons and priests, they came from Roman patrician families and often from the Pope's kindred. They served as *penitentiarii*, distributors of alms, sacristans; they were also chamberlains, treasurers, or lectors in the circle closest to the Pope.

---

[11] E. Schneider, *Die römische Rota* (Paderborn 1914); C. Lefèbvre, "Rote romaine," *DDC*, 7 (1961), 742–71 (bibliography).

[12] G. Mollat, "Contribution à l'histoire judiciaire de l'Église romaine au XIVe siècle," *RHE*, 32 (1936), 877–928.

[13] R. Elze, "Die päpstliche Kapelle im 12. und 13. Jahrhundert," *ZSavRGkan*, 36 (1950), 145–204.

The special palace offices were performed by laymen, and in addition there were the rather numerous personnel of the kitchen, stable, household, police, and messengers.

A mighty mechanism for the business of ecclesiastical law and administration, which of course also had to perform corresponding functions in the government of the Papal State, made it clear toward the end of the thirteenth century how extensive the practical direction of the Church by the Pope had become. Weighed down by all the weaknesses of large bureaucracies, but also distinguished by astonishing achievements in tribunal, *camera,* and chapel, the thirteenth-century Curia was one of the most impressive phenomena of Church life in the High Middle Ages.

CHAPTER 35

Celestine V and Boniface VIII

The Second Council of Lyons in 1274 was, in its achievement if not in its enduring effect, a convincing sign of the still unruffled ecumenical prestige of the papacy, above all of course in the West. The entanglement with Anjou, intensified by the Sicilian Vespers of 1282, compromised the Curia for the future in a way that was as undesired as it was unexpected. All efforts at a settlement collapsed and simultaneously diminished the repute of the Holy See. The rapid succession of brief pontificates made it clear at the same time that even in the College of Cardinals there was no really effective grasp of the threatening situation. The small number of cardinals and their keen partisanship *vis-à-vis* the persons concerned in the Mediterranean tensions prevented agreement on a Pope, who, like Gregory X, coming from outside their numbers, uniting breadth of vision and freedom from factional ties, would have been able to direct the helm toward greater goals. As a matter of fact, the election of 5 July 1294, two years and three months after the death on 4 April 1292 of Nicholas IV, fell on a man who did not belong to the college, where the rivalry of Colonna and Orsini would not allow anyone to obtain the required two-thirds majority. But it was not a happy choice. Piety could certainly be expected in the hermit, Peter of Murrone, and this was probably what motivated the Franciscan Cardinal Latino Malabranca to suggest him. The Pope-elect had been a Benedictine, but later, as a hermit, he had founded an eremitical community, which had been incorporated into the Benedictine Order by Urban IV. The members later called themselves Celestines, from the name which the Pope from their midst had assumed. He only accepted the election under much pressure and despite his own great hesitations. A year earlier the founder, more than eighty-years old, had relinquished to others the direction of his community, whose principal monastery was Santo Spirito near Sulmona. In the Spiritual circles the new Pope was hailed as the "Angel Pope" expected by the Joachimite movement; it was believed that a new era was beginning for the Church. Extraordinary as the election was, the end of the brief pontificate was equally extraordinary: at the end of the same year, Celestine V abdicated.

Charles II the Lame, King of Naples, who had already exercised a determining influence on the conclave, believed himself authorized to exert the decisive impact during the pontificate. He was not only able to prevent the new Pope from transferring his residence to Rome, as the cardinals wanted; he even succeeded in having him take up residence at Naples in the Castel Nuovo, placed at his disposal by the King. Celestine V had been crowned on 29 August 1294 at Aquila in Santa Maria di Collemaggio, a church of his own congregation. Charles II induced him to renew Gregory X's strict rules for the conclave and had himself appointed guardian of the next conclave. The Pope named twelve cardinals. Charles nominated many of them, in particular the seven Frenchmen, four of whom were from Charles's own Kingdom. Two of the cardinals belonged to the Celestine congregation.

Against the opposition of the cardinals the Curia moved from Aquila to Naples, arriving on 5 November. The most important posts were occupied by Charles's creatures, who also succeeded in taking over the key positions in the Papal State. The overhasty measures of the pontificate included the rich grant of privileges to the Celestine congregation, whose confirmation the Pope renewed. The actual administration of the Church fell into hopeless confusion, especially since an insight into the situation was not granted to the Pope and he did not have the strength to exercise supervision. Benefices were given simultaneously to several petitioners. Efforts were made to incorporate the greater abbeys into the Celestine congregation; even Montecassino was threatened. Charles II obtained a ratification of the peace with Aragón and the grant to himself of the tithes from France and Burgundy for four years and from England, Ireland, and Scotland for one year. He was eventually also named Senator of Rome. When the cardinals, to whom Celestine allowed no say, came with their grievances and complaints, the Pope became aware of his very difficult situation. After having consulted with Cardinal Benedict Gaetani, he had it ratified in consistory that abdication was possible. On 10 December he issued a constitution dealing with abdication by a Pope and decreed the legal validity of Gregory X's conclave regulation also for the case of resignation. Then, on 13 December, he laid down his office.

His successor did not permit him to return to his old hermitage, rightly fearing that his own opponents and Celestine's disillusioned friends might exploit the person of the resigned Pope to bring about a schism in the Church. At first, to be sure, Celestine did manage to flee, but he was overtaken and placed in honourable confinement in the Castel Fumone near Ferentino, where he died on 19 May 1296. He was buried in the church where he had been crowned. Clement V canonized him in 1313 under pressure from King Philip the Fair in the course of the struggle over the memory of Boniface VIII. The dream of an Angel Pope had dissolved. Pious asceticism was not enough to qualify one to rule the Universal Church. But in addition Celestine had lacked attributes which would have made possible a fruitful influence to the bearer of the *plenitudo potestatis:* shrewdness, experience, ruling authority, strength, and a statesman's ability to make decisions. All of these qualities were brought to the papacy by Celestine's immediate successor, Boniface VIII.

The conclave following Celestine's abdication began on 23 December — there was a ten days' interval, just as at the death of a Pope. Cardinal Matthew Rosso Orsini was first elected, but he declined. Then Benedict Gaetani was unanimously chosen. Boniface VIII (1294–1303), as he styled himself, came from a Roman family that had branched far out, to Anagni, where he was born, to Pisa, and to Spain. His mother was a niece of Alexander IV, and the mother of Nicholas III was also related to him. He was also connected with the houses of Orsini and Colonna. Born at Anagni around 1240, he was raised by his uncle, the Bishop of Todi, and studied law at Bologna. He became a notary at the Curia and, as secretary, accompanied the future Popes Martin IV and Adrian V on embassies to France and England. He was entrusted with important business at the Curia and, despite the Ghibelline tradition of his family, was oriented toward France, and hence Martin IV created him a Cardinal, first as deacon of San Nicolà and then as priest of San Martino. His legateship in France in 1290–91 became his most important activity. He succeeded in mediating the Treaty of Tarascon with Aragón and in preventing the outbreak of a war with England and restoring good relations between France and the Curia. At the University of Paris he stood up for the rights of the mendicant orders; it had been charged by the diocesan clergy and the University that their excessive privileges disturbed the orderly care of souls in parishes. As a friend of popular piety — he was not a specialist in theology — the Cardinal inclined to the ideal of the mendicant orders. His harsh and intemperate manner of speaking gained him no friends. If, nevertheless, his fellow cardinals elected him, they did so because of the qualities which made him seem suited for the papacy, so seriously compromised by Celestine V: trained intellect, knowledge of the world, experience in business, intrepid boldness, an iron will, and amazing energy.

The new Pope dismissed the curial officials imposed by Charles II and moved to Rome, where he was crowned on 23 January. He had annulled all favours granted by his predecessor; only the prelates appointed by Celestine retained their dignity. All grants of benefices that had not yet been effected and all expectatives were also cancelled. The administration of the Curia's finances was transferred to three Florentine banking firms; hence the *Camera* became only an accounting office, and abuse and suspicion on the part of both payers and receivers were eliminated. The financial administration was tightened and regulated, the returns from public finance increased, and at the end of the pontificate there was an important cash reserve on hand. The city of Rome remained calm under Boniface VIII and the Papal State felt his strong hand. Risings in the Marches could be put down, Orvieto submitted within a year, and only Romagna continued restless. In many places the Pope had himself elected as city lord. The Papal State had not had a more powerful master since Innocent III.

Boniface first tried to solve the problem of Sicily. At the end of 1293 Charles II had arranged by treaty with James of Aragón the evacuation of Calabria and after three years the restoration of Sicily to the Pope; in return James received Charles's daughter as his wife. Sicily would then be given back to Charles. Frederick, who was holding Sicily for James, was to marry Catherine of Courtenay, heiress to the Latin Empire of Constantinople. His advisers, Manfred Lancia, John of Procida, and Roger Loria, made corresponding arrangements with Boniface on 20 June 1295, which included the peace between Charles and James that had been ratified by Celestine V. According to these James would have had to evacuate Calabria, turn over Sicily to the Pope, and receive Charles II's daughter together with a large dowry, Charles of Valois would have renounced Aragón, and the Church would have granted James full pardon. This would have been a satisfactory solution for the Curia, and Boniface set himself energetically to achieve it. But it collapsed on the opposition of France, which refused to allow Catherine of Courtenay to marry, and of Frederick and the Sicilians, who, out of fear of Anjou, elected Frederick as King and had him crowned at Palermo on 26 March 1296. The disillusioned Boniface annulled both the election and the coronation and intended to conquer Sicily with James's assistance. But James procrastinated, negotiated, and demanded Sardinia and Corsica as papal fiefs and corresponding financial help. Meanwhile, from Sicily Frederick conquered Calabria and most of Apulia. Boniface joined James, Naples, and Queen Constance in an alliance against Frederick; a campaign was decided for the summer of 1297.

At the same time a war was in progress between England and France. France was concerned about the English King's fiefs on the continent, Guienne and Gascony. As a Cardinal, Boniface in 1290 had been able to prevent the outbreak of hostilities for some time, but during the long vacancy of the Holy See from 1292 to 1294 war had come. Despite various efforts to gain German and Spanish allies, Edward I was losing. Boniface at once sent legates to Germany, France, and England, but only in Germany was there any willingness to give in. In the summer of 1296 Boniface was asked to mediate, not in his capacity as Pope but personally as an arbiter. Both Kingdoms had demanded taxes from the clergy for the prosecution of the war. Since on the outbreak of war a Pope had not yet been elected, the necessary consent of the Curia, as provided by the Fourth Lateran Council for taxation of the clergy, had not been sought. When at the beginning of 1296 new tithes had been announced for a year, two for the North and four for the South, the clergy, led by the Cistercians, had protested, but the bishops had not. Boniface complied with this protest in the bull "Clericis laicos" of 24 February 1296, which was entered in the chancery register as "Statute on Ecclesiastical Freedom." It renewed the enactment of the Fourth Lateran Council and made it stricter in the sense that any tax not expressly authorized incurred the penalty. Promulgated as a general law, it was directed equally at France and England and intended to make unambiguous a law that had become doubtful. Thereby the Pope intervened as legislator in important areas of the life of the state, which was becoming ever more keenly conscious of its autonomy. In practice kings in their wars would have become dependent on the good will of the Pope, who could permit the paying of war taxes.

Did Boniface intend to further his peace efforts by this decree? In any event, the English clergy refused further contributions, appealing to the bull, and the barons followed their example. There ensued a constitutional conflict, which, as in 1215, ended in 1297 with the submission of the King and the confirmation of Magna Carta. In France the episcopate at first withdrew its consent to the tithe, but at an assembly at Paris in June 1296 it asked the Pope for authorization. At the same time Boniface was asked by both belligerents to mediate personally in the war. Surprisingly, there quickly followed, on 18 August 1296, a prohibition of the export from France of precious metal, money, and bills of exchange. This was explained as an ordinary war measure, but the Pope was the one chiefly affected by it, for his budget was dependent on French dues. He reacted on 20 September with a sharp note to King Philip the Fair. He accused him of violating the liberties of the Church and reminded him that the edict contained nothing new; it authorized the Pope to protect the clergy but by permitting particular taxes it did not exclude support for the King. Boniface had always been particularly friendly to France, but the letter ended with certain threatening admonitions: the Pope would see himself compelled to have recourse to extraordinary means in the event that France did not comply. There then began in France a journalism, probably managed by the court, which discussed in a polemical fashion fundamental questions of the relations between laity and clergy within the Church, understood as Christendom. The French Church, it was said, had special obligations toward the "political" community because of its wealth, which came from the laity, and the penalties threatened by the Curia were felt to be unjust. In the widely circulated *Dialogue Between A Cleric and A Knight*[1] it was admitted that the secular

---

[1] On the "Disputatio inter clericum et militem," see R. Scholz, *Die Publizistik*, 333–52.

was bound to assist the spiritual, but the superiority, deduced from this, of the spiritual power to the secular power was denied. The Church of the clergy was advised to undertake an extensive spiritualizing process: the word and the Sacrament and Sacrifice were her vocation, and she should be concerned for the heavenly rather than the earthly kingdom. The territorial Church was obliged to aid the King, since he was constituted as her protector.

In the course of this polemic the political powers regrouped themselves. Flanders, threatened by France, allied with England. The Burgundian princes again made contact with Germany. An understanding with the Pope rather than a fight against him now seemed to be what was needed by the French crown and its advisers. The non-arrival of the French dues so crippled the Curia's policy, especially that against Sicily, that it too was for an understanding. A Florentine banker, John Francesi, nicknamed Musciatto, undertook to make the contacts. In a letter to the French King, Boniface declared that the bull "Clericis laicos," as a universal law, was not directed specially against him, complained of the export prohibition, and stated that he was prepared to accommodate the King. An accompanying interpretation of the law explained that voluntary contributions by the clergy were not bound by the requirement of authorization and that, in emergencies, when the Pope could not be approached in time, such authorization was to be presumed.

When there arrived a petition from the French episcopate that special contributions be approved, Boniface granted them for one year. The French clergy thereupon expressed themselves in favour of a two-years' tithe to the King. The crown was not satisfied with this consent. An embassy led by Peter Flotte, the chancellor, went to Rome for negotiations, since a favourable situation had arisen there: from May 1297 the Pope was occupied with the revolt of the House of Colonna.

The occasion was supplied by the private property policy of the Pope, who invested his cash resources in land and in so doing conflicted with the interests of the Colonna. The conflict became concrete over the village of Ninfa, adjoining the lordship of Norma, which had already been almost entirely acquired by Boniface. At the same time the Colonna Cardinals, James and Peter, were working against the Pope's Sicilian policy; they had long belonged to the Aragonese faction, but just the same they received an annual contribution from Naples. They had also supported the rebel Frederick. Both points — the property policy of the family and their political outlook — may have motivated the Pope to annul the acquisition of Ninfa by the Colonna and to dislodge them by purchasing the farms there for his own family. The money for the purchase was seized by Stephen Colonna while it was being transported from Anagni to Rome. The indignant Pope demanded the return of the money, the surrender of the culprit, and, as surety for the future, the handing over of the Colonna castles in the Campagna. Word came from the Colonna that they were prepared only to give back the money. When nothing more happened after three days, the Pope struck, moved especially by the fact that the Colonna had joined the Spiritual opposition against him. The Spirituals, to whom as such Boniface was not unfriendly, had been angered by the abdication of "their" Pope, behind which, not entirely without reason, they suspected Cardinal Gaetani. But when their opposition increased, Boniface declared invalid their separation by Celestine from the Conventuals and reincorporated them into the entire Franciscan Order. This intensified their hostility to him. There began a vast campaign of calumny against the Pope, in which all his enemies took part. The opposition developed into a Colonna-led conspiracy against the Pope. This explains the harshness of the action of 9 May 1297. The Colonna sent back the stolen money, but on 10 May Boniface deprived the two cardinals of their rank and excommunicated them. Corresponding penalties were visited on the family and its adherents in the ecclesiastical and secular state.

All this took place *consensu fratrum* but without any judicial procedure and corresponding judgment; this had been reserved, in the event that the cardinals concerned should, as Boniface had demanded, personally arrange for proceedings. The Colonna undertook counter-measures. On the altar at Saint Peter's they laid a solemn protest, in which it was stated that Boniface was not a legitimate Pope; the judgment of a general council was demanded, at which Boniface should be called to account for the murder of his predecessor. On 23 May the Pope renewed his sentence on the Colonna, and on 9 July the Inquisition was directed to begin a process against them and two of their adherents. The resistance of the Colonna to the Pope's measures found support in the French crown. In a comprehensive memorial they summarized all the charges against the Pope and invited the Universal Church — kings, princes, prelates — to have a general council decide on the punishment and removal of the Pope. Copies were sent everywhere. The French embassy, mentioned earlier, was informed of it. The memorial provided it with a favourable point of departure in its negotiations with the Curia. These could be concluded to the advantage of France on 31 July. It was agreed that the bull "Clericis laicos" did not apply to France. The crown was qualified to decide when an emergency existed which made recourse to the Pope pointless. A group of further privileges was added, and the canonization of Louis IX was promised. The extraordinary success of the French agents can only be grasped if one assumes that they had threatened to join the Colonna in the event that the Curia should not return a favourable answer. And despite the restoration of friendly relations with France this shadow remained.

The price of the understanding had to be paid by the Colonna, who now did not find in France the expected support. Peter Flotte held himself aloof from them. The front that had been forming against Boniface fell to pieces.

The cardinals were ready to declare their solidarity with Boniface. The minister general of the Franciscans demanded submission from his subjects. The Dominicans were commanded by their general publicly to recognize Boniface as true Pope. At the same time they were forbidden to join the Colonna. A crusade was preached against the Colonna. It lasted only until October 1298, when their chief fortress, Palestrina, fell and was razed to the ground. The Colonna submitted, but when the two Cardinals were freed only from excommunication and not from the other penalties, they again took up resistance. However, it did not become a reality until they allied with France after the beginning of the new century. The Pope's harsh proceedings against the Colonna very seriously damaged his reputation in the public opinion and led to those slanders that have so darkened his memory in history.

The enterprise against the refractory Frederick of Sicily went on without success throughout 1297 to 1299, since King James of Aragón, despite the great financial assistance he received from the Curia — he had become, among other things, the salaried standard-bearer of the Church, with an annual allowance of 100,000 florins, — made no serious efforts to weaken his brother's position. Not until Boniface began seriously to negotiate with Charles of Valois, the pretender to the throne of Aragón, for help did James finally take action. The outcome was the Aragonese naval victory off Cape Orlanda on 5 July 1299. But the victory was not followed up; Frederick escaped, and it was said that his brother helped him to do so. Boniface was disillusioned and provoked and relations with Aragón were at a breaking point. While Boniface was making peaceful overtures to Sicily through two legates, Naples decided on military measures, but they were thwarted by Frederick's victory at Falconaria on 1 December. The Sicilian problem had to be tackled again, so to speak. But despite efforts to unite Aragón, France, and Naples, in addition to all available Italian resources, such as the cities and the military orders, for it, all was in vain.

In vain also were the Pope's exertions to mediate between Venice and Genoa and to intervene with the English King on behalf of Scotland and in Hungary to secure the succession for the House of Anjou.

Imperial Italy played an important role in his relations with Germany. Boniface was less interested in Lombardy than he was in Tuscany, which he would have liked to incorporate into the Papal State. In this aspiration he was in accord with a traditional claim of the Curia, deriving from the Carolingian promises and the Mathildine Donation. Boniface had close ties with the chief city of Tuscany, Florence. Important Florentine banking houses were in the service of the Curia. In Florence the Blacks and the Whites vied for control of the government; both factions belonged to the wealthy class, which had imposed its rule on the lesser folk. The Pope decided for the Blacks, who included the papal bankers.

Adolf of Nassau had been King of Germany since 5 May 1292. But in the course of the years he had so alienated his electors that in June 1298 he was deposed. Duke Albert of Austria, son of King Rudolf I and centre of the opposition to Adolf, was chosen to succeed him. In the struggle for the crown, Adolf perished on 2 July 1298 in the cavalry battle of Göllheim. The Electors announced Albert's elevation to the Pope and asked him to summon their choice for coronation as Emperor at a suitable opportunity. Boniface stressed his right to examine the fitness of the Emperor-elect and even the legitimacy of a unanimous election. He held himself aloof from Albert, because of his behaviour toward King Adolf, and there ensued years of negotiations, during which the Pope demanded the cession of Tuscany in return for recognition. Since Adolf for his part had been on terms of friendship with England, Albert in opposing him had established good relations with France, and as King he consolidated these by the Friendship Treaty of Quatrevaux in the fall of 1299. In April 1301 the Rhenish Electors revolted against Albert and the Pope supported them. But when the final conflict with France became intensified, Boniface yielded, especially since the King had also defeated the electoral opposition. On 30 April 1303 in the bull "Aeterni Patris" he solemnly recognized Albert as King of Germany and future Emperor. Albert now broke off his alliance with France and bound himself not to appoint an imperial vicar in Lombardy and Tuscany for the next five years without the Pope's consent and after that to name only a vicar acceptable to the Pope. Herein lay a recognition by the Curia that this was imperial property. On 13 July 1303 the King renewed the oath taken by his envoys.[2] This was no formal oath of vassalage but a promise of obedience according to a formula often used at the Curia. The Curia regarded it as an oath of security, such as had been customarily taken in similar cases. It acquired no practical political significance.

The Jubilee of 1300 formed a sort of caesura in the pontificate of Boniface VIII, at least in regard to the relationship with France, which had calmed in this year. Rumours at the end of 1299 had told of ample grants of indulgences which persons could gain at the beginning of the new century in Saint Peter's. And so from the start of the year great crowds of pilgrims arrived in Rome. Only because of these was the Pope induced, after consultation with the cardinals, to issue the bull "Antiquorum habet fidem" on 22 February 1300. Anyone who in this year, a year of jubilee, such as was thereafter to be celebrated every hundredth year, should, after contrite confession, visit the basilicas of the two Princes of the Apostles, — Romans

---

[2] The King promised to protect the Pope and render him loyal obedience; he intended to be "fidelis et oboediens" to him. Cf. Gebhardt-Grundmann, I, 410–12, with a detailed discussion of the promise, "which resembled less the oaths of security made by earlier Emperors than that of the subjects and officials in the Papal State." The text is in MGConst, IV, no. 181.

thirty times, foreign pilgrims fifteen times, — received a plenary indulgence for the temporal punishment due to his sins. Enormous crowds of pilgrims came, attracted by this indulgence, hitherto not granted. A great need for expiation, penance, and conversion seemed to fill Christendom. At Rome arrangements had to be made to take care of the stream of visitors. The pilgrims' offerings were considerable; they profited not the papal coffers but those of the churches visited. For the Pope the jubilee brought a gain in prestige *vis-à-vis* the Western kings with whom he was engaged in a political confrontation. The unchallenged esteem of the Apostolic See and its religious authority found an unexpected confirmation. The self-assurance of Boniface VIII increased. It also led him to disregard a proper judgment of the political reality. This would soon be made crystal clear in the renewal of the conflict with France.

An insignificant incident started it. Bernard Saisset, provost of the collegiate chapter of Saint-Antonin, had become first Bishop of Pamiers, created by Boniface VIII in 1295. The King had not been consulted, nor had the Bishop of Toulouse, from whose diocese Pamiers had partly been carved. As provost the new Bishop had had difficulties with the King on account of the patronage of Pamiers, which he exercised in condominium with the Count of Foix. An understanding had been reached, but when King Philip the Fair again transferred to the Count of Foix the patronage which the crown had temporarily assumed, Bishop Saisset appealed against this to the Pope. Boniface had protested in vain to the King and had then proceeded against the Count with ecclesiastical penalties. Careless remarks by the Bishop that were critical of the King led to Bernard's being cited before the *conseil* after his property had been sequestered on 24 October 1301. He was prosecuted under the direction of the chancellor, Peter Flotte, on charges of defamation of the King, sedition, high treason, simony, and heresy. He was judged guilty and turned over to his metropolitan, the Archbishop of Narbonne, for imprisonment. The Pope was informed of the outcome and asked to depose and punish the Bishop of Pamiers. Without studying the dossier, Boniface demanded the Bishop's release on 5 December 1301. By the bull "Salvator Mundi" he withdrew the privileges granted to the King, because the freedom and immunity of the Church had been violated. In effect, the bull "Clericis laicos" was again made binding for France. The Pope summoned the French episcopate, the deans of the cathedral chapters, and the doctors to a special synod, to be held at Rome on 1 November 1302. The King was also invited. The bull "Ausculta Fili" contained all the grievances of the Church against the crown and its agents. They were to be the object of the discussions at the synod. There was also mention of the unconditional superiority of the papal over every secular power. Hence, involved was, beyond any concern for the question of Pamiers, a confrontation on fundamentals. A notary carried the bulls to Paris. Instead of justifying himself, King Philip had decided to fight. It was forbidden to publish the bull "Ausculta Fili." In its place Peter Flotte circulated a forgery, "Deum Time," in which, over the Pope's name, the content of the suppressed bull was made known in a distorted and sharpened manner. At the same time an alleged reply of the King was sent out with it — "Sciat maxima tua fatuitas." This maintained that in secular matters the King was subject to no one. Thus was French public opinion formed. In order to win the leading circles of the nation, a meeting of the Estates General was summoned to Paris; in addition to the nobility and prelates the cities were invited for the first time. The meeting took place on 12 April 1302. Peter Flotte read "Deum Time" and defended the King's case. The estates were persuaded to defend the King and to write to Rome in this sense. Only a few of the bishops attended, but they conformed after some hesitation. The nobility and the cities received a reply from the cardinals; the episcopate received theirs from the Pope. A consistorial discourse exposed and condemned the intrigues of Peter Flotte. It then declared that the Pope claimed no feudal suzerainty in France but could take the King to task *ratione peccati*. However, he threatened Philip with deposition and repeated the summons to the announced synod.

In spite of a royal prohibition, thirty-nine prelates appeared, but no decrees were issued. The bull "Unam Sanctam" may have been discussed, for it was published soon after, on 18 November 1302.[3] It became the most debated document of this pontificate, perhaps even of the mediaeval papacy in general. There is only one Church, so it explained, outside which there is no salvation, with only one head, who is Christ, and his vicar Peter and Peter's successors. Both swords, the spiritual and the temporal, are in the power of the Church, the spiritual wielded by her, the temporal wielded by the hand of the king but according to the priests' instructions. The spiritual power surpasses every secular power in dignity. The spiritual power can institute the secular[4] and judge it, if it transgresses. The highest spiritual power can be judged only by God. Whoever opposes it resists God. Hence

---

[3] Text in *Denzinger-Schönmetzer* (34th ed. 1967), nos. 870–75, pp. 279–81; see here the critical introduction, which points to a consistorial address by the Pope on 24 June 1302. It makes clear how little it was the Pope's intention to claim a limitless and direct power in the sphere of the secular, that is, of kings: "quasi Nos mandaverimus regi, quod recognosceret regnum a Nobis. Quadraginta anni sunt, quod Nos sumus experti in iure, et scimus, quod duae sunt potestates ordinatae a Deo; quis ergo debet credere vel potest, quod tanta fatuitas, tanta insipientia sit vel fuerit in capite Nostro? Dicimus quod in nullo volumus usurpare iurisdictionem regis, et sic frater noster Portuensis dixit." The Cardinal Bishop of Porto, here referred to, was Matthew of Aquasparta.
[4] The text reads: "Nam Veritate testante, spiritualis potestas terrenam potestatem *instituere* habet et iudicare"; here the word "instituere" can mean both "institute" and "instruct." English trans. in *Church and State through the Centuries*, ed. S. Ehler and B. Morrall (Westminster 1954), 89–92.

it is necessary for the salvation of every man that he be subject to the Roman Pontiff.

None of this was new. The celebrated concluding sentence comes from Thomas Aquinas.[5] The bull's train of thought followed the treatise *De ecclesiastica potestate* by the Augustinian Hermit, Aegidius Romanus (Giles of Rome), which had appeared only shortly before.[6] In 1295 Boniface had promoted this master of theology at Paris, who had become general of his order, to the archiepiscopal see of Bourges. However, not he but the Franciscan Cardinal Matthew of Aquasparta was probably the one who drew up the bull.[7] The violent reaction to this document was directed, not especially against the theological and canonical doctrines of the century just ended which were summarized in it, but against the supposed political program which persons thought they had to see in it. Dogmatic significance attaches only to the concluding sentence, which obtained its importance through its confirmation by the Fifth Lateran Council.[8]

Attempts to reach a compromise with the French King continued even after the promulgation of the bull. Cardinal Le Moine, or John the Monk, was commissioned as legate to lay the Pope's demands before the King. At first Philip refused to commit himself, but then he decided on a more vigorous fight; he would attack the Pope's person, his good name, and the legitimacy of his position. Responsible for this turn was William of Nogaret, who had taken the place of Peter Flotte after the latter had perished in the battle of Courtrai, which France had lost to the Flemings on 11 July 1302. Through Nogaret the Colonna cardinals now gained influence on the further course of events. And the legate, Le Moine, now abandoned the side of the Pope, one of whose most trusted advisers he had been, and treacherously joined the French faction. In the *conseil* on 12 March 1303 Nogaret brought forward the grievances against Boniface VIII, which were substantially the same as the accusations made by the Colonna in their memorials. The King's consent was obtained. There was propaganda for a general council at which the Pope would have to justify himself. Nogaret received authorization for an expedition to Italy. Apparently the plan was to arrest the Pope and take him to France, where it was intended that he should be presented to the projected council.

Boniface considered inadequate the French reply to his demands as made known by Cardinal Le Moine, and on 13 April 1303 he declared the excommunication of the King. The bearer of the document was imprisoned in France, and the information was suppressed. In mid-June Philip again had

---

[5] *Contra errores Graecorum*, ed. P. Mandonnet, *Opuscula omnia*, III (Paris 1927), 325.

[6] Ed. R. Scholz (Weimar 1929).

[7] Thus I. B. Grasso, *Ecclesia et Status: De mutuis officiis et iuribus fontes selecti* (Rome 1939), no. 430.

[8] COD, 620 (Session XI, 19 December 1516).

charges brought against the Pope before the Estates General, this time by William of Plaisians. The King declared the necessity of a council and spoke in favour of convoking one. The consent of the assembly was general, though there was some reservation among the bishops. The record of the discussions was circulated, and meetings to obtain consent were held. Only the Cistercians and a few houses of mendicants refused. Even imprisonment and banishment were resorted to. A great popular gathering at Paris on 24 June 1303 was prepared to give consent, letters were dispatched to foreign princes and to the cardinals, and a messenger even went to the Pope. From Anagni Boniface rejected the charges, issued a series of bulls against Philip and his councillors on 15 August 1303, and finally began work on the bull "Super Petri Solio," in which the solemn excommunication of the King was proclaimed and his subjects were released from their oath of loyalty. It was to be published on 8 September 1303.

On the previous day occurred the well known attack at Anagni, perpetrated by Nogaret in association with Sciarra Colonna, head of that family of enemies of Boniface. The residences of the cardinals and the papal palace were stormed. It was demanded that the Pope should lay down his office, restore offices and possessions to the Colonna, turn over the treasure of the Church to several older cardinals, and submit to imprisonment. Boniface rejected the demand and even offered his life. Nogaret did not permit Sciarra Colonna to go along with this suggestion; he was concerned only for the living Pope, who was to be judged in France. In the city, which at first had aided the conspirators, the mood changed, Boniface was rescued, and the conspirators were driven out. Boniface left insecure Anagni for Rome, and the Orsini undertook to protect him. He arrived there on 25 September but on 12 October he succumbed at the Vatican to his sufferings and the disillusionment of Anagni. He was laid to rest in the chapel of Saint Peter which he had constructed, in a tomb which he had had built by Arnolfo di Cambio in his lifetime.

His political measures turned out for the most part unsuccessfully or critically for the Curia. On the other hand his activity within the Church was to survive the pontificate: first, the publication of the *Liber Sextus*,[9] a supplement to Gregory IX's collection of decretals, then the introduction of order into the chaotic state of affairs in the curial administrative system, brought about in the previous pontificates, and finally the decision in the question of the relations between the mendicant orders and the diocesan clergy in the bull "Super Cathedram" of 18 February 1300.

The mendicants were permitted to preach freely in their own churches and in public squares, but in parish churches only with the permission of the

---

[9] For the legislative work of Boniface VIII see now the detailed study by S. Gagner, *Studien zur Ideengeschichte der Gesetzgebung* (Uppsala 1960), 121–287.

pastor. They had to ask faculties for hearing confessions from the local bishop, and these were limited to the territory of his see. The number of confessors thus licensed was determined by the needs of the diocese. The denial of such faculties by individual bishops could, if necessary, be righted by a papal decision. In regard to reserved cases the mendicants were not to have more authority than the parish priests. The right of burial was conceded them; that is, they were allowed to bury in their churches whoever asked this, but one-fourth of the fees falling due pertained to the proper pastor as his canonical share. This was a carefully weighed regulation, distinguished by impartiality. The respective legal competences were exactly determined. The preeminence of an orderly care of souls was assured, and the orders gave extraordinary assistance which was to be understood as supplementary. No doubt Boniface VIII disappointed the mendicants by this decree, but he was not their enemy; he raised too many members of orders to the episcopate to permit one to believe that. After a brief setback under the Dominican, Benedict XI, who annulled it, the bull was renewed by Clement V and even today it is substantially the law.

In June 1303 the Pope founded a university at Rome, the later Sapienza, as a *studium generale*. He bestowed careful attention on the library and archives of the Vatican. A university was also to come into being at Avignon.

The fate of the Pope was not decided by his death, and the process concerning him did not preoccupy only the succeeding pontificates. It has been said that even today his records are not yet closed. His outstanding juristic and administrative gifts, his energetic direction of the Curia, the intensive work which he demanded of himself and of his co-workers — these remain unchallenged. His broad education and his knowledge of Holy Scripture were famed. But his arrogant bearing, which people labelled pride and contempt, made him no friends. The failures of his political enterprises raised the suspicion of a lack of judgment, which seemed to plague him even in the formulating of his fundamental bulls. His nepotism placed him beside many of his predecessors, but with him everything assumed immoderate forms: he aimed to create for the Gaetani a principality, if not a kingdom even, in Tuscany. As a legislator and judge he remained for all contemporaries a vast and enduringly influential figure, but people were unable to venerate him as the Father of Christendom. The Spirituals continued to be hostile to him because of Celestine, although in the long run his legislation served the mendicants better than the extensive privileges granted by his predecessors. His memory remained overclouded by the unrestrained propaganda of his opponents and the repeated attempts to have him tried posthumously as a heretic. He was not guiltless in regard to some charges, which, however, were completely distorted in the light of an excessive hostility. Things that can more easily be twisted in regard to a fellow citizen are not expected in a Pope: a harsh word, an impatient turn of phrase, violent anger. All things considered, he was an important Pope, worthy to be mentioned together with Innocent III and Innocent IV.

CHAPTER 36

The End of the Crusading Epoch

The fall of Acre in 1291 ended the rule of the crusaders in Syria and Palestine. After the taking of the city in May the Sultan al-Ashraf Khalil, with his Mamelukes, completed the mopping up: Tyre was taken as early as 19 May, Sidon at the end of June, Beirut surrendered in July, and the Templars handed over their remaining strongholds, Château Pèlerin and Tortosa. Nothing was left to the Franks; only the small and waterless island of Ruad, off Tortosa, was retained for twelve more years. One who sees the epoch of the crusades as conditioned by the fate of Frankish rule in the Holy Land must admit that it ended with the definitive collapse of 1291, even though the crusade and the crusading idea did not necessarily disappear then from the awareness and the affairs of Christendom.

There remains the astonishing fact that the conquests of the First Crusade — the Kingdom of Jerusalem and its vassal principalities — could be maintained at all for almost 200 years, even though in a constantly diminishing extent. Pilgrims, merchants, knights, princes, and kings had travelled beyond the sea almost without interruption. The classical crusades were only moments of special energy in this movement. What is most astounding is that in the crusader states, small lordships in the sphere of influence of port cities, the circumstances of government had to be constantly revised and kept in balance in accord with the model of Western feudal relationships, a strong kingship was for the most part lacking, the military orders did not co-operate, and the commercial colonies of Venice, Genoa, and Pisa at Acre, Haifa, Beirut, and Tripolis were basically concerned only for assuring their own mercantile interests. If Islam itself had not been often handicapped by the tensions between Damascus and Cairo, if in the thirteenth century the invasion of the Mongols had not brought the Franks a breathing-space, if help had not poured in from the homeland from decade to decade, the crusader states could hardly have lasted for two centuries. Despite all the disappointments of the past, the thirteenth century also had its crusades.

More than ever, the crusade dominated the program of councils from the Fourth Lateran Council in 1215 to that of Vienne in 1311–12. It had become a virtually essential task of the Popes to be concerned for its continuation, to plan great expeditions, to organize them, to help finance them, and occasionally to assume even their direction. Anxiety over the maintaining of the Latin Empire (1204–61) was drawn into the papal crusade policy, even though it constantly compromised the accumulated effort on behalf of the Holy Land. Despite the fact that, now too, as really unceasingly earlier, the large and the small expeditions usually ended with serious misfortunes, the zeal of the Popes seemed not to flag. The generosity of broad classes of the Christian peoples could be successfully appealed to again and again. They were ready to place money, goods, and men at the service of the crusade, to make heroic efforts, to go to meet that martyrdom which, for the majority of all participants, was still the real reward that awaited them. Even though hopes of adventure, economic expectations, and political motives again and again interfered, what was decisive for most crusaders was, as earlier, the appeal which crusade preaching had directed to them.

At the Fourth Lateran Council in 1215 Innocent III had endeavoured to mobilize all the resources of the West in order to make good the failure of 1204. He died in 1216 during the proximate preparations, and so the implementation of his project had to be left to his successor, Honorius III. The mighty enterprise that was the Fifth Crusade, in which almost all the nations of Christendom took part, with in some cases very large contingents, lasted from 1217 to 1221. The first to set out were King Andrew II of Hungary and Duke Leopold VI of Austria with German nobles and bishops; later came those from the Lower Rhineland and Frisia, under the direction of the successful crusade preacher, Oliver, *scholasticus* of the Cologne cathedral. Then came Flemings, Englishmen, Frenchmen, Scots, and finally Italians from the cities and the knightly class. From 1218 the enterprise was directed by the Cardinal Legate Pelagius. His big success was the taking of Damietta, the key to Egypt, on 5 November 1219. But in August 1221 the legate was responsible for the defeat at Mansurah, which ruined the earlier achievement. The history of this crusade became a tragedy of Christian disunity, of heroic effort, and of diplomatic folly. At times the Sultan al-Kamil had been ready to surrender the entire Holy Land in return for peace, but the obstinate greed for conquest in the Spanish Cardinal Legate led to the breakdown of all offers and hopes. Never again would the century be able to assemble such a mass levy of crusaders.

The often promised and just as often postponed crusade of the Emperor Frederick II — a part of his forces had taken part in the Fifth Crusade — was finally led in 1228 when the Emperor had already incurred excommunication. Negotiations with the Sultan al-Kamil were successful, and Jerusalem, Nazareth, and Bethlehem were restored, together with a corridor to enable pilgrims to reach the coast. A ten-years' armistice was concluded in 1229.

A further territorial gain accrued from the curious double crusade, expressly forbidden by Gregory IX, of Count Theobald of Champagne, King of Navarre, and Earl Richard of Cornwall:[1] Galilee was recovered from

[1] S. Painter, "The Crusades of Theobald of Champagne and Richard of Cornwall (1239 to 1241)," in K. M. Setton, *A History of the Crusades*, II, 463–86.

Damascus. The public crisis between Gregory IX and Frederick II had impeded the preparation and implementation. The two phases of this crusade of 1239–41 followed in such a manner that the two leaders did not meet, but Richard managed to conclude favourably the negotiations prepared by Theobald with the Sultans of Damascus and Cairo. While there was fighting at various times, there were no crucial battles. The model of the Emperor in 1228–29 was decisive.

A few years later, in 1244, all was again lost. Jerusalem fell, this time forever, and the hosts of the military orders and crusaders were overwhelmed at Gaza. The First Council of Lyons in 1245 concerned itself, as expected, with the distress of the Holy Land, but the needs of the Latin Empire obtained preference in the discussions. And, even after the Council, the quarrel with the Emperor Frederick II continued to eclipse all other concerns of Innocent IV.

King Louis IX of France, representing, as it were, a Christendom which was implicated in so many other distractions, assumed the duty of assisting the Holy Land.[2] The expedition, which he carefully prepared for years and on which he set out in 1248, was the last grand-scale crusade of the century. Damietta was captured; then followed, as in 1221, an overwhelming defeat at Mansurah, in which Louis IX was captured. Set free on the payment of a high ransom, he stayed until 1254 in the Holy Land in order to do what he could to regulate the political situation and to unify the rival resources of tradesmen, knights, and orders on the one goal of defense. Only so long as he was there, personally intervening, reconciling, and punishing, was there the appearance of inner peace. It ended as soon as he had departed.

Once more, in 1270, Louis went on crusade. He landed in Tunis, but pestilence and hunger destroyed his army, and the King himself died on 25 August 1270. His brother, Charles of Anjou, arrived in time to liquidate the enterprise in a peace advantageous to his Kingdom of Sicily. Other expeditions of this century were without importance. These were the groups, half pilgrim, half warrior, organized time and again between the classical crusades of the age, which went to the East to fulfill vows or to seek their fortune.

The *reconquista* in the Iberian peninsula[3] had long borne the character of a crusade, so that during the Second Crusade the Frisians *en route* to the

---

[2] J. R. Strayer, "The Crusades of Louis IX," *ibid.*, 487–521. The most important source is Jean de Joinville, *Vie de Saint Louis*, ed. Natalis de Wailly (Paris 1874); the latest edition is that of E. Jarry (Angers 1942); R. Sternfeld, *Ludwigs des Heiligen Kreuzzug nach Tunis (1270) und die Politik Karls I. von Sizilien* (Berlin 1896); F. Jammes, *Saint Louis ou l'esprit de croisade* (Paris 1941); L. Buisson, *König Ludwig IX. der Heilige und das Recht* (Freiburg 1954); T. Michaux, *Die Hauptentscheidungen des 1. Kreuzzugs Ludwigs IX. in ihrer politischen Bedingtheit* (dissertation, Cologne 1954); J. Levron, *Saint Louis ou l'apogée du moyen âge* (Paris 1957).
[3] For the *Reconquista* see J. Goñi Gaztambide, *Historia de la bula de la cruzada en España* (Vitoria 1958, literature).

Holy Land could, with a good conscience, take part in it at Lisbon. From the time of Innocent III the struggles for the conquest of the Baltic area were also endowed with crusade privileges, on the model of the Wend Crusade of 1147–48. At the same time there was added the Albigensian Crusade to overcome the serious threat from the Cathari in the Midi. This crusade turned into a war and finally a merely political affair of the French crown. Here too was obvious that expanding of the idea of the crusade, that giving it a political character, which especially marked it in the thirteenth century. The Stedinger crusade (1232–34) of Archbishop Gerard II of Bremen against peasants on both sides of the lower Weser for non-payment of tithes is an example. [4] Gregory IX issued the requisite bulls and granted the crusaders the "great crusade indulgence." More hotly disputed by contemporaries were the crusades of Innocent IV against the excommunicated and deposed Emperor, in which Germany, Lombardy, and Sicily were summoned to participate. For this Innocent III had already created a precedent with his expedition against Markward of Anweiler in 1199, while on the occasion of the Albigensian War he had developed the theory and practice of the political crusade. But Gregory IX, in the last phase of his quarrel with Frederick II, was the first to permit his legates in Lombardy and Germany to preach the crusade in order to be able to raise troops for the fight against the Emperor. Following his example, Innocent IV, after the First Council of Lyons (1245), had recourse to this means against Frederick II in Germany and Italy. And he also had a crusade preached in Germany against Conrad IV in 1253 and 1254.

Urban IV granted boundless crusade privileges to Charles of Anjou for the latter's struggle to gain the Kingdom of Sicily from Manfred, and in order to finance it and to make up for losses sustained he had the crusade preached in France and Italy. He took similar steps against Byzantium in 1263 and against Manfred's friends in Sardinia. Clement IV continued this policy, notably during the expedition of young Conradin to Italy and the Sicilian Kingdom in 1268.

The Sicilian Vespers of 30 March 1282 made the island a bone of contention between the Houses of Anjou and Aragón. Pope Martin IV, a Frenchman, opposed Aragón and deprived King Peter III of his crown, which was held in fief of the Holy See. Charles of Valois, a son of King Philip III of France, was to receive it and to conquer the Kingdom. The expedition of 1285 was financed and endowed with privileges, just like a crusade.

---

[4] The basic work is H. A. Schumacher, *Die Stedinger* (Bremen 1865); C. Woebken, "Die Schlacht bei Altenesch und ihre Vorgeschichte," *Oldenburger Jbb.*, 37 (1933), 5–35; L. Deike, *Die Entstehung der Grundherrschaft in den Hollerkolonien an der Niederweser* (Bremen 1959).

The last of these political crusades was raised by Boniface VIII in 1298 against the Colonna.

The original idea of the crusade was determined by the wish to defend the Christians of the East, who were hard pressed by Islam. Hence the crusade became a war against Muslims (the "infidel"), wherever Western and Eastern Christianity had their frontiers. If the evangelization by the sword in Central Germany and the Baltic area assumed a crusade character, the enterprise remained basically true to the original notion of military defense of the faith, even though the element of extending the sphere of the faith had been added. Here the unforgotten duty of proclaiming the faith was put forward in forms suitable to the age. Even the political crusades of the thirteenth century, just mentioned, were theoretically justified as struggles for the faith. This was more apparent in the Albigensian Crusades than in those against Frederick II. But here too it must not be overlooked that the concept of heresy at that time included obstinate opponents of the Roman Church.

The crusade organization drawn up by Innocent III stood the test, especially with regard to the preparing of planned journeys. A plenary indulgence, presupposing sincere repentance, confession, and satisfaction, was promised on setting out. Efforts were made to raise money in the form of income taxes, testamentary bequests, and even commutation of crusade vows. From all this developed the crusade taxes, laid first on the clergy, then on the laity also. The deciding of the amount pertained to councils and also to the Pope in agreement with kings and princes. The collecting of these taxes brought into being a real financial organization, which became useful not only to the Curia but also to state administrations. Toward the end of the century, when real crusades to the Holy Land had long since ceased to materialize, the taxes were still repeatedly demanded, especially by King Philip IV of France, and their levying was granted. This preoccupation of the crusade idea with finance contributed greatly to the decay of the notion.

Legates were named and preachers were commissioned specifically for the propaganda preparation of the crusade. The history of preaching was thereby greatly enriched. The Dominican Humbert of Romans created a *summa* of crusade preaching with his treatise *De predicatione crucis* (1268). Its theme was provided by the appeals of the Popes for the liberation of the Holy Land. Entrusted ever more in the thirteenth century to the mendicant orders, this preaching developed into the popular mission in a liturgically oriented *milieu*. The success of this preaching, even though in particular cases it is difficult to show it because of the meagre information in the sources, was sufficiently extensive and profound to cause the flow of pilgrims and fighters to continue without interruption till the end of the real age of the crusades and to revive and deepen the crusade spirituality of both those who undertook the journey and those who remained home.

The growing number of voices expressing disillusionment and doubt, criticism and abhorrence, was basically unable to change much of this. Disillusionment grew by virtue of the failures, especially of the big expeditions, whose returns seemed in no way to correspond to the mighty output in money and manpower. Doubt was expressed chiefly because in these failures people felt they were abandoned by God, whose business they had undertaken to defend in the crusade vow. Criticism was directed not only against poor leadership and the disunity of the political authority in the Holy Land, where there was a readiness to ally with the infidel and thereby the impression was created that in the Holy Land there was at stake not the preservation of the holy places but the constructing of positions of political power. But criticism was also turned on the growing preoccupation of the crusaders with finance and the Curia's share in creating this atmosphere. The more frequently the crusade tithe was diverted from its proper purpose, whether it was devoted to the needs of the Latin Empire or withheld for the political enterprises of the Popes or, finally, was granted in great part to the royal coffers, the less were persons willing to pay it and the more difficult it was to collect it. There was likewise a growing readiness on the part of the Curia to commute the taking of the cross into corresponding sums of money. In the long run this could not but undermine the seriousness of people's willingness to submit to such sacrifices at all.[5]

It is astonishing that the collapse of Frankish rule in the Holy Land still evoked a flood of literary propaganda, as though persons in the West regarded such an outcome as shameful. But at the same time one can see in it an aspect of the reflection that seems to follow every period of emphatic action.[6] No longer the preachers but scholars and writers took the floor. As late as 1291 the Franciscan Fidentius of Padua published his *Liber de Recuperatione Terre Sancte* for Nicholas IV. Evoked by the fall of Acre was the treatise of Thaddeus of Naples, which powerfully indicted the West and summoned Pope, princes, and faithful to save the Holy Land, the inheritance of Christ and of Christians. In 1294 the Genoese Galvano of Levanti, physician at the papal court, dedicated an essay of a similar sort to King Philip IV of France. Special importance belonged to the writings of Raymond Lull (1232–1316), who in many memoranda presented to the Popes practical plans for the fight against Islam. His *Liber de Fine* (1305), with its far-reaching suggestions for strategy, became famous. Two years later the Armenian Prince Hethum, now Premonstratensian prior at Poitiers, published his *Flos Historiarum Terre Orientis*, which recommended a collaboration with the Armenians and the Mongols. For the sphere of French influence the works of the jurist, Peter Dubois, intended as memoranda for

---

[5] On the relationship of crusade and mission see *supra*, Chapter 29.
[6] For what follows *cf.* J. Lecler, *Vienne (Histoire des conciles oecuméniques,* 8) (Paris 1964), 68–76.

the French crown, were particularly influential. In these the crusade appeared chiefly as a means of assuring the hegemony of King Philip the Fair and of ameliorating the royal finances. It was suggested that the Order of the Templars be forbidden, that its property be seized, and that an inheritance tax be imposed on the clergy. Pope Clement V in 1307 had the grand masters of the Templars and the Hospitallers prepare memoranda for him. In 1310 he also received an unsolicited testimonial from William of Nogaret, the chief adviser of the French crown, which, however, had to do mainly with questions of finance. These literary works, partly stimulated by the Curia, partly coming to it from all sides, played an important role in the preparations for the Council of Vienne (1311–12).

It may be held that, with this chiefly meditative pursuit, which was at the same time an examination of conscience and a planning, the strictly classical Age of the Crusade had come to an end, only to make ready the epochs of the late mediaeval expeditions against the infidel.

PART TWO

The Late Middle Ages

The Popes at Avignon

CHAPTER 37

The Situation after the Death of Boniface VIII: Benedict XI and Clement V

When, a few weeks after the outrage at Anagni, Boniface VIII died in Rome, the city and the Papal State were filled with unrest, and the strife between the Gaetani and the Colonna was raging even more violently than before.[1] But the supporters of the dead Pope in the College of Cardinals, led by Matthew Rosso Orsini, succeeded in opening the conclave at Saint Peter's on the expiration of the appointed interval and in rejecting the demand of the deposed Cardinals, James and Peter Colonna, to take part in the election. The French envoys and Nogaret actively supported the Colonna, but King Charles II of Naples used his troops to thwart all attempts to enter the Eternal City by force. Hence, from the outset, the validity of the papal election was placed in doubt.

Despite serious difficulties, due to the existence of two factions of equal strength in the conclave, the election was completed on the first ballot, when the Cardinal Bishop of Ostia, Nicholas Bocassini of Treviso, former master general of the Dominicans, was chosen Pope.[2] But this did not resolve the severe tensions nor close the split between the quarrelling groups. Quite the contrary: the situation required of the new Pope discretion and strength, qualities in which Benedict XI was not especially outstanding. His having begun to reconcile opponents was often construed as weakness. But how would he have been able to act otherwise in view of the excessive influence of France throughout Italy and of the agitation in the Papal State? These, however, were only the external difficulties. Boniface VIII's new style had altered the papacy as an institution and evoked opposition which went far beyond the political sphere, as would become evident in the process against him and the repeated demands for a council. To oblige France as far as possible without total surrender seemed to the new Pope to be politic, but it

[1] H. Finke-M. Gaibrois y Ballesteros, *Roma después de la muerte de Bonifacio VIII* (Madrid 1924).

[2] H. Finke, *Aus den Tagen Bonifaz' VIII.*, 275 ff.; *Haller*, V, 218 f.; A. M. Ferrero, *Benedetto XI papa domenicano* (Rome 1934).

involved great risks. Following the advice of the French envoys, he sent notice of his election, thus far postponed, absolved King Philip IV from all censures he might have incurred, and freed the Colonna Cardinals from the ecclesiastical penalties imposed by Boniface VIII, though without completely restoring their functions, dignities, and possessions. When he was able to leave his restless capital and find more security in stable Perugia, Nogaret and his closest accomplices in the outrage of Anagni were excommunicated. [3]

As a Cardinal, the new Pope had clearly been a success in the capacity of legate and had behaved courageously at Anagni. But he was not quite equal to the demands of his new, burdensome office. If he would do nothing without the cardinals, he was presumably returning to a collegial administration of the Church and thus abandoning the methods of the Gaetani Pope. Insecurity and narrowness are evident in the fact that the three cardinals created by him were Dominicans and in the further fact that he spoke "only to Dominicans and Lombards." [4] When Arnald of Villanova, Boniface VIII's physician and an ardent Spiritual, sent him admonitions and threats in apocalyptic dress, he had this opponent of Thomistic philosophy imprisoned without trial. [5] But Arnald's prophecies were fulfilled. On 7 July 1304, after an eight-months' pontificate, the Pope died at Perugia and was buried there in the church of his order. [6]

In an extremely difficult situation, the cardinals, according to regulations, entered the conclave ten days after the death of the unhappy Benedict XI and in the place where he had died. Contemporaries were, of course, in no position to grasp the full significance of this conclave, which was to be one of the most momentous in Church History, for it was to result in the Avignon residence and eventually in the Great Schism. Hence the history of this conclave has been the object of ever more research. [7] When it opened in the summer of 1304 it comprised nineteen members, eight of whom were religious. In the course of its eleven months four cardinals left because of sickness but

---

[3] By the bull "Flagitiosum Scelus," in Grandjean, *Registre*, no. 1276.

[4] H. Finke, *Acta Aragonensia*, I, 162: "quia vix aperit iste papa os suum nisi ad Predicatores et ad Lombardos."

[5] R. Manselli, "Arnaldo de Villanova e i papi del suo tempo," *Studi Romani*, 7 (1959), 146 ff.

[6] The Aragonese envoys knew nothing about the alleged poisoning (H. Finke, *Acta Aragonensia*, I, 173: "lo papa es mort de disinteria e durali tro en XV dies"). R. Manselli, *op. cit.*, 152, rightly points out that, in the event of poisoning, Arnald of Villanova would probably not have been able to boast of the complete fulfillment of his prophecies.

[7] A list of the sources in *Baluze-Mollat*, II, 31. The most important sources are the reports of the Aragonese envoys in H. Finke, *Acta Aragonensia*, I, 169–95, III, 128–39. Accounts in H. Finke, *Aus den Tagen Bonifaz' VIII.*, 279–90; *Haller*, V, 225–27; 392; C. A. Willemsen, *Kardinal Napoleon Orsini* (Berlin 1927), 13–24; E. Dupré-Theseider, *I papi di Avignone*, 3–8; R. Morghen, "Il conclave di Perugia nel 1305 e la lettera di Dante ai cardinali," *L'Umbria nella storia, nella letteratura, nell'arte* (Bologna 1954), 103–24; *idem*, "La lettera

they remained in the city and were kept informed of the proceedings. Fifteen cardinals took part in the actual election. The two Colonna Cardinals, deposed by Boniface VIII and only partially restored by Benedict XI, were again denied entry. Of the two almost equally strong factions, one demanded the energetic punishment of the criminals of Anagni, not excepting the French King, and the safeguarding of the memory of Boniface VIII, still under attack after his death. The leader of this faction, the worthy Cardinal Dean Matthew Rosso Orsini, was considered its candidate from the start. His nephew, the Cardinal Deacon Napoleone Orsini, leader of the opposing group, regarded respect for French might and hence reconciliation with the Colonna as necessary; in this outlook he was supported by the French King and loaded with gifts of every sort. Common to both factions was the desire, it seems, that the tiara should not go again to so strong a personality as Boniface VIII, for, in disciplining the Colonna, he had obviously carried his independence of the oligarchic college too far. Since the Colonna were also regarded as friendly to reform, the mendicant friars in the Sacred College were on the side of Napoleone Orsini.

After the experiences of past decades, this division in the college could result in a speedy election only by means of a strict enforcement of the prescriptions for the conclave, and at first the municipal council of Perugia was apparently determined on this. But the question of the cardinals' competence, *sede vacante*, to maintain or to alter the rules was at the time a subject of lively discussion. And so before long the originally strict regulations were relaxed and, when the prospects of a quick agreement faded, preparations for the winter were made. Almost every time that the cardinals met for the business of election, — and such gatherings were not numerous, — there were violent quarrels between the two Orsini. Toward Christmas of 1304 it was plain that no member of the college could muster the required two-thirds of the votes and hence it was necessary to seek candidates from the outside more earnestly than ever, while external influences grew stronger or at least became more evident.

Shortly after the beginning of the conclave, in August 1304, the cardinals had sent the Patriarch of Jerusalem to King Charles II of Naples to ask him to come, for he was regarded as *advocatus ecclesiae* and a neutral mediator. When, toward the end of February 1305, he finally arrived, he was enlisted in the French ranks. But he was admitted to the conclave only after a prolonged delay. After a stay of three days with the cardinals and many conversations he was evidently able to accomplish nothing, for the faction

di Dante ai cardinali italiani," *Bollettino dell'Istituto storico italiano per il medio evo e Archivio Muratoriano,* 68 (1956), 1–31; G. Fornaseri, "Il conclave Perugino del 1304–05," *RSTI,* 10 (1956), 321–44, together with supplementary material by R. Morghen, "Ancora sulla lettera di Dante ai cardinali," *Bollettino ... e Archivio Muratoriano,* 70 (1958), 513–19.

of the cardinals favourable to Boniface VIII now regarded him as too biased. At this time there also appeared a French embassy, which, according to its official declarations, was supposed to conduct discussions between the Gaetani and the Colonna for reconciliation and settlement of their differences over their possessions in the southern part of the *campagna*. It lingered in Perugia for several months, and the city officials could not but be concerned with its suspicious behaviour.

In the first weeks of the conclave the name of the Archbishop of Bordeaux, Bertrand de Got, had been brought up by someone of the "Bonifacian" party, possibly by Matthew Rosso Orsini. He was regarded as one to whom the memory of Boniface VIII was sacred and who would not go too far in appeasing the French King. Napoleone Orsini had not forgotten this name; on the contrary, in the utmost secrecy he had got in touch with him, probably through the French embassy that was staying in Perugia. Apparently his inquiries turned out favourably, and the Bonifacians were tricked in a subtly devised scheme after the aged Matthew Rosso had had to leave the conclave because of sickness.[8] In his famous letter to the cardinals Dante reproached the acting leader of the Bonifacians, James Gaetani Stefaneschi of Trastevere, for not having adequately defended the interests of Rome and Italy.[9] By exactly a two-thirds majority Bertrand de Got was elected on the Vigil of Pentecost, 5 June 1305, in spite of the emphatic protest of the remaining five Bonifacians, who then accepted the result.

Following this curious conclave of eleven months, who was the newly elected Pope on whom the direction of the Church was laid in so uneasy a time? Bertrand de Got was from Gascony in southwestern France. His older brother, Bérard, had been Archbishop of Lyons and had been made Cardinal Bishop of Albano by Boniface VIII. Bertrand himself had become Bishop of Comminges in 1295 and Archbishop of Bordeaux in 1299; since 1303 his city had again come under English rule. He could be regarded as an adherent of Boniface VIII, because for a short time he had belonged to the household of Cardinal Francis Gaetani and he had attended the Roman Council of 1302. But Napoleone Orsini knew very well that, in the person of this man, he had provided the French King with a compliant Pope.[10]

The newly elected Pope accepted the notification made to him at the end of June, styled himself Clement V, and prepared for the journey to Rome

---

[8] H. Finke, *Acta Aragonensia*, I, 191 f.: "Ispanus respondit quod placeret sibi, set quod volebat loqui cum domino Napoleone, sic quod iverunt ad locum, ubi deponebant superflua, quia alibi secrete loqui non poterant ... Unde cum scrutinium legeretur per dictum dominum Franciscum et X predicti apparerent concordes, alii inceperunt clamare, quod non poterat fieri, eo quod decepti erant et quod modo patebant consilia latrinarum." D. Mansilla, "El cardenal 'Petrus Hispanus,' obispo de Burgos (1300–03)," *HS*, 9 (1956), 27 ff.
[9] R. Morghen, "La lettera di Dante," *loc. cit.*, 18.
[10] B. Guillemain, *La cour pontificale*, pp. 156 f., footnote 333 (genealogy of Clement V).

via Provence. But then he ordered six cardinals to attend his coronation at Lyons on All Saints.[11] During the solemn coronation procession on 14 November a wall collapsed, killing several persons of high rank; the Pope fell from his horse, and the most expensive jewel in the tiara was lost. People read these happenings as an evil omen.[12]

Now was the time to set out for Italy. Again and again plans for the journey were announced, and it is said that embassies from Rome and Tuscany arrived to expostulate with the new Pope. The Romans' threat, traditionally dated for the end of December 1305, that, because of the Pope's delay, they intended to elevate someone as Emperor, is to be accepted only with reserve.[13] It is not to be doubted that at the beginning of his pontificate and even later Clement did intend to go to Rome. In any case he never considered transferring the seat of the Curia from Rome. His inability to make up his mind during the nine years of his reign was due to his weakness and the ever increasing pressure of the French King. His first creation of cardinals, in December 1305, makes this clear enough: nine, including four nephews, were French and one was English. Thus the Sacred College, long overwhelmingly Italian in composition, had changed its appearance. It abandoned the Roman tradition for the narrowness of a region hitherto hardly noticed. And the Pope was even more confined to his homeland: he continued to be a Bishop of the Midi or, more properly, a Bishop of Gascony. He was not familiar with curial procedure, of which his electors were masters; and at first he was even without the very mechanisms of the Curia.

After his coronation he stayed for quite a long time in his native plains, in Poitiers alone for sixteen months.[14] It was not until 1309 that he went to Avignon, because of its proximity to Vienne, where the Council was soon to meet. Still, Avignon was not his permanent residence. From 1309 till his death he spent most of his time outside the city on the Rhone. French scholars have rightly referred to the absence of a *stabilitas loci* in the thirteenth-century Popes. But there is a difference between the Roman Popes who, when not in Rome, resided in the strongholds of the Papal State — Viterbo, Perugia, Orvieto, Anagni — and Clement V wandering about Gascony and Provence. If he was no Roman Pope, neither was he an Avignon Pope. A sick man, always dependent on place and season, always in search of the spot most advantageous to his health, for weeks at a time he granted no audiences and only the Cardinal-nephews could speak with him. He touchingly endowed his former see of Bordeaux and the churches and chapels

[11] H. Finke, *Acta Aragonensia,* I, 196–98, III, 139; *idem, Gesammelte Aufsätze,* IV (1933), 448.
[12] *Baluze-Mollat,* I, 61.
[13] H. Finke, *Acta Aragonensia,* II, 512.
[14] E.-R. Labande, "Clément V et le Poitou," *Bulletin de la société des antiquaires de l'Ouest,* Series 4, 4 (1957), 11–33, 83–109.

of his homeland with spiritual and secular favours. His army of relatives brazenly exploited their kind uncle, as will be noted elsewhere. The riddle of his personality lies in its hypochondriac nature. Though intelligent to the point of craftiness and at times even obstinate, he was basically a good-natured and vacillating man.[15] This weak personality was forced to deal with men such as Philip the Fair and his councillors. In his relations with France the Pope's dependence was especially clear in two matters: the process against the dead Boniface VIII and that against the Templars.

The Process against the Memory of Boniface VIII

The process instituted by the French king and the crown jurists against Boniface VIII was intimately connected with the very obvious collision of the two powers in the outrage of Anagni.[16] Nogaret, excommunicated by Benedict XI, was especially interested in it and had to be, for his fate — condemnation or rehabilitation — depended on the settlement with the deceased Boniface. Since, according to the general opinion, only a council could judge the Pope, efforts to hold one had been made ever since Anagni. But outside France voices were raised against a defamation of the memory of the great Gaetani Pope. As early as the coronation in Lyons a council and proceedings against Boniface were discussed, and again during the brief meeting of Clement and Philip at Poitiers in April 1307. Several extant memoranda make clear how painstakingly the matter was prepared. For example, it was to be emphatically demanded of the Pope that all measures of Boniface VIII against France and against his assailants at Anagni be annulled, that full compensation be made to the Colonna, that the corpse of the Pope be disinterred, and that the sentences issued by Benedict XI be recalled. Precise directions were even given for the formulating of the bull to be issued by the Pope. If these demands were met, then the case could rest for some time. At the Curia the demands caused consternation. A committee of six cardinals was set up and after much deliberation a bull was sketched, but it was not actually drawn up.[17]

In the long interview between King and Pope, again at Poitiers a year

---

[15] B. Guillemain, *op. cit.*, 114, 129, 151, 174 ff.; J. Bernard, "Le népotisme de Clément V et ses complaisances pour la Gascogne," *Annales du Midi*, 61 (1948 f.), 369–411; R. Gaignard, "Le gouvernement pontifical au travail. L'example des dernières années du règne de Clément V, 1ᵉʳ août 1311–20 avril 1314," *ibid.*, 72 (1960), 169–214. For a complete evaluation, see H. Finke, *Papsttum und Untergang des Templerordens*, I, 97–110; *idem, Aus den Tagen Bonifaz' VIII.*, LXXXIII–IC; *Haller*, V, 295–301.

[16] *Haller*, V, 262–70, 399 ff.; A. Corvi, *Il processo di Bonifacio VIII. Studio critico* (Rome 1948).

[17] R. Holtzmann, *Wilhelm von Nogaret* (Freiburg 1898), 137 ff.; H. Finke, *Papsttum und Untergang des Templerordens*, I, 128–39.

later, the topic of discussion was chiefly the Order of the Templars. As an introduction to the conversations the King had his entire program submitted: permanent settling of the Curia in France, condemnation of the Templars who had been cross-examined in France, holding of the projected general council in France, canonization of Celestine V, condemnation of Boniface VIII, burning of his remains, and absolution of Nogaret.[18] If the Pope at first vigorously refused any procedure against Boniface VIII, a little later he specified that the process should begin in the spring of 1309. But it was still another year before it opened at Avignon. We need not concern ourselves further with the contents of the indictment, since most of it had already been brought forward in the last year of Boniface's reign.[19] Evidently neither side had any interest in a speedy conducting of the trial. The case was discussed in many consistories and again and again adjourned. Several committees were concerned with hearing witnesses of very doubtful provenience; they had been recruited in Italy for the public spectacle. The most dangerous accusation, that of heresy, revealed the political intent of the process: to render the weak Pope pliable for other purposes. It was probably the influential Enguerran de Marigny who proposed the discontinuance of the trial, once the Pope, in the Bull "Rex Gloriae" of 27 April 1311, had acknowledged the King's praiseworthy zeal in his proceedings against Boniface and had absolved Nogaret *ad cautelam*.[20] The cancellation in the official register of the bulls issued by Boniface VIII against France was a serious humiliation. The *factum Bonifacianum* cropped up again at the Council of Vienne but it was only cursorily dealt with.[21]

Ruin of the Templars: The Council of Vienne

The downfall of the Order of Knights Templars was one of the most dramatic happenings in the Church History of the early fourteenth century. To contemporaries the loss of Acre, the last Latin foothold in the Holy Land, in 1291, did not imply the end of the crusades. The idea above all persisted, even though in actual fact it served only as an excuse for prescribing tithes in most states. Even before the pontificate of Clement V the French King had been concerned with the Templars. He had planned the merging

---

[18] H. Finke, *Papsttum und Untergang des Templerordens*, I, 224.

[19] H. Finke, *Aus den Tagen Bonifaz' VIII.*, 227–68.

[20] R. Holtzmann, *op. cit.*, 176–206; J. Favier, *Un conseiller de Philippe le Bel, Enguerran de Marigny* (Paris 1963), 135; F. Merzbacher, *Enguerran de Marigny, Minister Philipps des Schönen von Frankreich: Speculum historiale* (Freiburg and Munich 1965), 479–85.

[21] E. Müller, *Das Konzil von Vienne*, 184–90. The demand for the canonization of Celestine V was a weapon against the memory of Boniface VIII. After long discussion it was finally proclaimed on 5 May 1313.

of all the military religious orders, with himself as grand master, and in Lyons, at the time of the Pope's coronation, he had brought forward his complaints. Complaints were also expressed by others.

The real motive for the prosecution and destruction of the Templars eludes us to a great extent. Certainly the independence of the military orders and their great wealth in landed property and money were irksome to the growing power of the so-called national states. No doubt they were defamed to some degree. Evil rumours were nourished by Esquiu de Floyran, the well-known betrayer of the order, who first denounced it to the King of Aragón and then, with more success, to Philip IV of France, and by the spies introduced into the order by Nogaret. Damaging reports about the order were also carried to the Pope, who became quite worried. But there was general consternation when, early on 13 October 1307, all French Templars were arrested at the King's order and then subjected to strict interrogations by royal officials, who made abundant use of torture. In this way were extorted confessions, the repudiation of which could lead to the pyre, in accord with the procedure of the Inquisition. Somewhat later, inquisitors continued the investigation, while accepting for the most part the numerous confessions already obtained.

What did the tortured Templars admit? Rejection of and spitting on the cross, indecent kissing and exhortations to commit sodomy, and even the adoration of an idol in the ceremony of admission to the order. Matters were further complicated at the end of the month by the confession of the grand master, James de Molay, and his circular to the imprisoned knights, who were also asked to confess.[22] These avowals were handed to the Pope. Impressed by them, he ordered the arrest of the Templars in all countries. In so acting he had no doubt kept in mind that it belonged to the Church and its head to pass judgment on an exempt order of such importance and under so serious an accusation and to control the disposal of its property. But when he had been apprised of the nature of the proceedings and of the repudiation of many of the confessions, he suspended the delegated authority of the bishops and inquisitors in February 1308. Nevertheless, the imprisoned Templars remained under the custody of the King and his officials.

A story from this period relates that the ten cardinals thus far created by Clement came to him to give back their red hats. In accepting them, they said, they had incorrectly thought that, like all previous Popes, he was the lord of the world, superior to the Emperor and to kings; but actually he was the servant of the King of France, who in his arrogance had committed a grave injustice against the renowned order. Incidents in the consistory may have been here fantastically exaggerated, but the report affords a good insight into the tangled situation.[23]

[22] H. Finke, *Acta Aragonensia*, III, 168 ff.
[23] H. Finke, *Papsttum und Untergang des Templerordens*, II, 110 f.; *idem, Gesammelte Aufsätze*, IV (1933), 454, 535.

It was necessary to start again in order to achieve the goal: the extermination of the order. The celebrated meeting at Poitiers in the summer of 1308 followed upon accusations against the Pope as an abettor of heresy, notably at the Estates General of Tours. Accompanied by the delegates of the estates, the King arrived in Poitiers on 26 May and remained there until 20 July. In solemn consistories the Pope was shockingly attacked in speeches outlined by Nogaret and was overwhelmed by threats. And carefully selected Templars repeated their previous confessions in the presence of Pope and Curia. On the other hand, the King did not allow the grand master and the chief officials of the order to come to Poitiers; they were questioned in the vicinity by accommodating cardinals, with, of course, the expected result.

At Poitiers the Pope's will to resist was completely broken. He had to agree to hold a council in France, to open the process against the memory of Boniface VIII, and to lift the suspension of the authority of bishops and inquisitors in regard to the Templars. It seems pretty certain that he gradually came to doubt the order's innocence. And so he cited the Templars before the Council, which was to meet at Vienne on 1 October 1310, and appointed two investigating committees. One of these, a papal commission to deal with the entire order, was to operate in larger areas; the King nominated its members for the investigations, not in France alone, but also abroad. These commissions were to concern themselves with the guilt of the order as such and with its highest ranking dignitaries. The Templars were to be interrogated as individuals in every diocese on more than a hundred questions by means of the episcopal commissions, and the material thus amassed was to be laid before the provincial council. The King also had an influential voice in the composition of the local commissions. Many fragments survive of the activity of these two committees. They give a manifold picture of the proceedings, in which as far as France was concerned the goal was clear: to extort confessions and prevent the repudiation of previous avowals by threat of the stake for the relapsed. When, especially outside France, confessions were slow in coming, the Pope ordered the universal application of torture. Just the same, in many places there were heroic scenes, when whole groups of imprisoned Templars publicly declared their innocence and that of the order. Thereupon, the new Archbishop of Sens, a brother of the almighty royal minister Enguerran de Marigny, in May 1310 sent fifty-four of them to the stake on a single day and later several small groups. Even in the flames they repudiated their previously extorted admissions. Since material was arriving only slowly, the opening of the Council was postponed a year, till 1 October 1311, in order meanwhile to be able to prepare from the urgently requested records summaries for its deliberations.[24]

[24] Synopsis of all the acts of the trial in E. Müller, *op. cit.*, 32 f.; also A. J. Mur, "Aportación al estudio del proceso contra el Temple en Castilla", *Revista de archivos, bibliotecas y museos*, 69 (1961), 47–100.

Outside the Kingdom of Philip the Fair we are especially well informed about the proceedings against the Templars in Aragón. King James II eagerly seized the opportunity to take possession of the order's many strong castles, but in an opaque and not entirely unobjectionable manner. At the news of the start of the prosecution, the Aragonese Templars put their castles in a state of defense, and their resistance was broken only after a long siege and starvation.[25] Occasionally torture was resorted to here also, but recent evidence from Barcelona shows that, despite repeated torture, confessions could not be extracted.[26] In the other countries of Europe, such as Italy, Germany, and England, and especially at its headquarters on Cyprus, the order's innocence was unquestioned, despite the use of torture. Because of his proceedings against the few Templars in his territory the Archbishop of Magdeburg incurred the indignation of the other German bishops. Thus, nothing had been definitively decided when the Council convened at Vienne on 16 October 1311.

The Council had been summoned chiefly because of the affair of the Templars; other tasks mentioned in the bull of convocation — crusade and reform — were only platitudes.[27] The summons was formally directed to all possessed of jurisdiction in the Church, but only those bishops were supposed to come who were specified by name. Indicative of the King's interest in those invited is the list preserved in the royal archives, presumably a rough draft or preliminary step for the later papal list. Whether the King demanded it or it was submitted to him by the Curia *motu proprio* cannot now be determined.[28] Of importance is the summoning of all archbishops, usually with one or two of their suffragans, who should then represent the Universal Church — an idea to be met again at the period of the reform councils. For the strengthening of the Pope's stand it must have been of importance that at least those bishops who were personally invited should actually come. But outside France there was little desire to cooperate in such an affair. The number of participants amounted to about 120 patriarchs, archbishops, bishops and mitred abbots; with the proxies of absent bishops and of chapters and monasteries, the total was around 300.[29]

At the opening session on 16 October, Clement referred to the settlement of the question of the Templars as the chief task. At the Pope's suggestion the Council selected from among its members a large committee, to which the records and summaries were submitted for examination. A smaller

[25] H. Finke, *Papsttum und Untergang des Templerordens*, I, 282–306; idem, *Gesammelte Aufsätze*, IV (1933), 380–91.

[26] A. Mercati, "Interrogatorio di Templari a Barcellona (1311)," *Gesammelte Aufsätze*, IV (1933), 240–51.

[27] E. Müller, *op. cit.*, 13–19.

[28] H. Finke, *Papsttum und Untergang des Templerordens*, II, 303–06; E. Müller, *op. cit.*, 663–70, gives the two lists in parallel columns.

[29] E. Müller, *op. cit.*, 68–84.

working committee saw to the necessary preliminaries. In addition, a committee of cardinals seems to have concerned itself with the special problems of the Templars, and there was frequent discussion of the subject in consistories. The appearance of several Templars before the full committee brought up the question of the order's defense. An oral and written questioning of the members of the committee by the Pope showed that at least four-fifths were in favour of granting the order the possibility of defending itself, to the great chagrin of the Pope and the anxiety of the Council Fathers on account of the King's "intense anger." For Clement, out of regard for the King, had by now apparently decided to dissolve the order in any case. While the Council, awaiting the further development of the case of the Templars, was preoccupied with plans for a crusade and was granting extensive tithing authority to the French King in anticipation of it, secret negotiations were in progress between the Curia and the *conseil;* they represent the climax of the "conciliar activity." The French envoys, headed by Enguerran de Marigny, contrived, presumably by threatening to renew the process against Boniface VIII, to extract from the Pope the suppression of the order by an administrative action, a result probably gratifying to both parties, in view of the mood of the Council. Immediately following, there occurred at Lyons a meeting of the Estates General — the customary means with the customary result. Accompanied by the estates and by his own large retinue, the King then arrived at Vienne on 20 March. Two days later the large committee met — and by a large majority accepted the Pope's proposal that the order should be dissolved by an apostolic decree. Finally, on 3 April, in the Council's second public session, the suppression was announced by the Pope.

Then began the struggle for the Templars' property. Most prelates wanted it to be transferred to a new military order, yet to be founded. But the Pope and the French government, influenced by Marigny, the official expert in this matter, were for assigning it to the Hospitallers. [30] From the Aragonese diplomatic dispatches we are well informed about the discussions concerning the Templars' fortresses. On 2 May, shortly before the close of the Council, the transfer of the Templars' property to the Hospitallers, except in Castile, Aragón, Portugal, and Mallorca, was published.

Several dogmatic discussions were occasioned by the continued discord between the two Franciscan factions. They centred on the person and teaching of Peter John Olivi, whom the so-called Conventuals had long persecuted and whose condemnation they aspired to extort from the Council. It seems that an effort was made to dispose of the difficulties by a suitable compromise. The Constitution "Fidei catholicae fundamento," read in the closing session on 6 May, proclaimed:

[30] J. Favier, *op. cit.*, 143.

The side of Christ was not opened until after the Lord's death. The substance of the rational human soul is, of itself, really the form of the human body. Children and adults obtain in baptism sanctifying grace and the virtues in the same manner.

Since Olivi was not named in the decree, violent quarrels would later arise in regard to the import of these words. But the difficulties could not be eliminated because of the unfavourable state of the transmission of the sources.[31] Furthermore, the quarrels in the Franciscan family over the meaning of *usus pauper* occupied much space. A committee was appointed to settle them, and its testimonial has recently come to light.[32] The controversy ended with the publication of the Apostolic Constitution "Exivi de Paradiso," also in the closing session of the Council. It prudently followed the middle path and gave a detailed explanation of the rule, without touching the dogmatic side of the controversy.

Opinions vary as to whether the Council of Vienne can be termed a "reform council" in the same way as others of the late Middle Ages. The Council does not seem to have been summoned for the sake of reform, but from the start the Pope had asked for testimonials on the subject. Some fragments that have been preserved allow us to infer rather ample matter. For receiving complaints and proposals Clement in the first solemn session appointed a commission of cardinals, which then undertook to edit the many-layered material. Occasionally the Pope personally took part in the discussions. For the most part they were concerned with eliminating the many interferences of the organs of the state in the Church's judicial procedure — these were frequently described in great detail — and also with the degree of exemption of religious, in particular of the mendicants. Since the Council ended right after the settlement of the affair of the Templars, the consultations on reform had to be broken off abruptly. Only a few decrees were ready. These were read on 6 May in the third and final session. A subsequent reading and putting into force at a later time were announced for all reform decisions. A reading actually did take place at a public consistory in the Château Monteux four weeks before the Pope's death. Since certain decrees or outlines of decrees were already in circulation, there was much uncertainty until John XXII brought clarification by officially publishing them and sending them in the usual way to the universities. Thereafter, the decrees, partially revised after the Council, formed part of

---

[31] E. Müller, *op. cit.*, 352–86; J. Koch, "Das Gutachten des Aegidius Romanus über die Lehren des Petrus Johannis Olivi. Eine neue Quelle zum Konzil von Vienne, 1311–12," *Scientia Sacra, Festgabe Kardinal Schulte* (Cologne and Düsseldorf 1935), 142–68; A. Emmen, "Doctrina Petri Johannis Olivi de baptismi parvulorum effectibus," *Antonianum*, 37 (1962), 350–92; *COD, 336 ff.*

[32] G. Fussenegger, "Relatio commissionis in concilio Viennensi institutae ad decretalem 'Exivi de paradiso' praeparandam," *AFrH*, 50 (1957), 145–77.

the *Corpus Iuris Canonici* as the "Clementines." [33] Prominent in the reform material are several testimonials of general importance, which will be mentioned later in another context. Of significance for the missionary work of the late Middle Ages were the decisions issued, at the urging of Raymond Lull, in regard to establishing schools of languages.

In accord with the instructions of the Council, the property of the Templars should have been turned over to the Hospitallers, but the execution of this regulation proceeded very slowly and was dragged out for decades. In France the greatest part of it apparently landed in the King's hands, since he claimed an adequate compensation for having brought the case to a conclusion. The fate of the high dignitaries had been reserved by the Pope to himself. When they were to repeat their confession of guilt in front of Notre-Dame de Paris and accept their sentences of life-imprisonment, the grand master and the grand preceptor of Normandy recovered their sense of duty. They publicly repudiated all confessions and swore to the order's innocence. On the same day both were burned without regard for the Pope.

To determine responsibility for the gruesome fate of so famous an order has again and again been the preoccupation of research and of historical journalism. Today it is generally agreed that the order as a whole was guiltless of the crimes attributed to it. In addition to H. Finke, outstanding specialists in that period, such as G. Mollat and J. Haller, defend the order's innocence and strongly condemn the machinations of Philip the Fair. [34] Still, a legitimate question has been recently posed: To what extent does the enigmatic King bear personal responsibility and could he have possibly acted from pure religious motives? [35] It is true that he was overawed by the grandeur of the French crown and the consciousness of being specially chosen and he was filled with a deep and even fanatical piety, but the means here resorted to cannot be defended even for the Middle Ages. Before the court of history Philip bears the chief responsibility for the ruin and death of the Templars. William de Nogaret's share of guilt is hardly less, for the diabolical nature of the proceedings corresponds in almost every respect to methods otherwise used by him. [36] The estimation of the grand master, James de Molay, varies in the judgment of historians, just as his own conduct on the outbreak of the storm varied. At first he confessed, then he repeatedly retracted his

[33] S. Kuttner, "The Date of the Constitution 'Saepe,' the Vatican Manuscripts and the Roman Edition of the Clementines," *SteT* (1964), 427–52.
[34] H. Finke, *Papsttum und Untergang des Templerordens*, 326–44; G. Mollat, *The Popes at Avignon* (first Harper Torchbook ed., New York 1965), 242–46; *Haller*, V, 395 f.
[35] His exoneration is attempted especially by R. Fawtier, *Histoire du moyen âge*, VI: *L'Europe occidentale de 1270 à 1328* (Paris 1940), 298–302. To a great extent he is followed by C. H. Peyer, "Philipp IV. von Frankreich und Dante," *Dante und die Mächtigen seiner Zeit* (Münchener romantische Arbeiten, 15) (Munich 1960), 58–74.
[36] G. Mollat, *op. cit.*, 245 f.

confessions, and again he confessed. The explanation lies in the frightful pressure brought to bear on him. Whether he was subjected to physical torture is an open question, for the sources still extant following the disappearance of the secret acts are not entirely clear.[37] Perhaps he sought, by means of the scarcely plausible confession of a denial of the cross of Christ at admissions into the order, to come before the Church's tribunal and staked all on the hope of revealing the true state of affairs before the Pope and the cardinals.[38] That he did not succeed in this constitutes his great tragedy and also the serious guilt of the Pope, who, slowly, step by step, allowed the defense of the order to be wrested from him.

Italy and the Papal State

In an effort to justify the stay of Clement V and his successors at Avignon the political situation in Italy and in the Papal State has been depicted in the blackest colours. But it was scarcely worse than it had been in the decades following the downfall of the Hohenstaufen. The House of Anjou was in firm control of the south, except for Sicily, where under Frederick II, of the House of Aragón, a new type of government was developing. And under Robert of Naples the Angevin influence extended far beyond the Papal State into Central and Upper Italy. In addition to Florence, Milan especially had become a power centre of great attraction with an incessant change of conditions and relationships virtually impossible to estimate.[39] This is especially true of the internal life of the numerous cities, of the rapid changes of government and the consequent difficult problem of the exiled. The strongest external influences came from France, but on the other hand the seizure of Corsica and Sardinia stands out in the execution of the investiture of James II of Aragón, arranged by Boniface VIII as far back as 1297.[40]

For the new Pope the situation in the Papal State was, of course, of special importance. For a long time it had not been a real state at all, but a conglomeration of many lordships. There were striking differences between the baronial feudal *Patrimonium,* including Rome, and the Marches of Ancona

[37] The following maintain the use of torture: A. Trunz, *Zur Geschichte des letzten Templermeisters* (Diss. phil., Freiburg 1920), 40, and Posch in *LThK*, V (2nd ed. 1960), 843 f. The contrary is held by: W. Schwarz, "Die Schuld des Jakob von Molay, des letzten Grossmeisters der Templer," *Die Welt als Geschichte,* 17 (1957), 259–79, and H. Finke, *Papsttum und Untergang des Templerordens,* I, 169, 187 f. But Finke is more reserved in *Gesammelte Aufsätze,* IV (1933), 387–91.

[38] This opinion has been recently maintained again by W. Schwarz, *op. cit.,* and is also that of A. Busson, *MIÖG,* 9 (1888), 496–515.

[39] *Storia di Milano,* V (1955).

[40] V. Salavert y Roca, *Cerdeña y la expansión mediterránea de la corona de Aragón,* 2 vols. (Madrid 1956).

and Romagna, with their new *signorie*. [41] Boniface VIII made allowances for this state of affairs in a series of excellent reforms, which, however, were cancelled in the brief reign of his successor. [42] The sequel was revolts lasting for years, and Clement V had to try to crush them. The pacification of the northern parts of the Papal State was one of his principal tasks, and he devoted himself to it with energy and some success. [43] That he first inclined to the Ghibellines, only to rely later almost exclusively on the Guelfs, is a theory that goes too far in simplifying the tides of history. Very damaging to an orderly administration was his unrestrained nepotism in filling the important and lucrative rectorships in the provinces. [44] In the war with Venice over Ferrara, which had long been ruled by the House of Este and which the Pope at a favourable opportunity claimed for the Papal State by virtue of the alleged Donation of Constantine, Clement displayed a really inhuman harshness. He succeeded in acquiring the city and the territory of Ferrara and in humiliating proud Venice, but his achievement was of brief duration. [45]

Clement V and the Empire

After the new Pope had called upon the German King to go on crusade, a solemn embassy was sent to Lyons by Albert I to request his imperial coronation and to ask that the tithes collected in Germany not be spent elsewhere (that is, not in France) and that persons suspected by the King be excluded in the filling of German sees. [46] Like Boniface VIII, Clement could not but see in the Empire and in the German King a support against the overmighty influence of France. But this was possible only so long as France itself did not assume the *Imperium* — an idea toyed with by Philip and his advisers. The question became pressing when in 1308 Albert was assassinated. Now the pressure on the Pope increased greatly, especially during the discussions at Poitiers in the summer of 1308, and it seems that only by some stratagem did he evade an effective direct recommendation of Charles of Valois. [47]

The new King Henry VII, of the House of Luxembourg, brother of

---

[41] D. Waley, "Lo stato papale nel tredicesimo secolo," *RSIt*, 73 (1961), 429–72; G. Marchetti-Longhi, "La carta feudale del Lazio nella mostra permanente del Lazio meridionale in Anagni," *QFIAB*, 36 (1956), 324–27.

[42] M. Seidlmayer, "Papst Bonifaz VIII. und der Kirchenstaat," *HJ*, 60 (1940), 78–87.

[43] A. Eitel, *Der Kirchenstaat unter Klemens V.* (Berlin 1907).

[44] *ALKGMA*, 5 (1889), 141: "per predones potius quam per rectores est spoliata et confusa."

[45] A. Eitel, *op. cit.*, 170–205; H. Finke, *Acta Aragonensia*, II, 641–60; V. Salavert y Roca, "Notas sobre la política italiana de Clemente V y sus repercusiones en Aragón," *Storia e letteratura*, 71 (Rome 1958), 255–98.

[46] *Baluze-Mollat*, I, 66 f.; H. Finke, *Acta Aragonensia*, III, 144.

[47] E. E. Stengel, *Avignon und Rhens*, 1–35.

Archbishop Baldwin of Trier, also came from the French sphere of influence, but, with all his deference to France, he always honourably defended the interests of the Empire.[48] He was able to obtain recognition in the manner of the Habsburg submission of the *Imperium* to the Roman Church. The Pope intended to officiate personally at the imperial coronation, perhaps in 1312,[49] but only after the settling of outstanding ecclesiastical matters, such as the Council of Vienne. However, the Emperor-elect's journey to Rome was decided in the summer of 1309 and began in the autumn of the following year. At first joyfully received in Italy, the German King quickly came of necessity into conflict with the interests of Anjou and hence of France, a situation that could lead to trying developments, especially if the new Emperor should lay claim to the customary imperial rights in Italy. When at last he reached Rome, a part of the city, including Saint Peter's, was occupied by the troops of Robert of Naples. The coronation was performed by three cardinals in the Lateran on 29 June.[50] Meanwhile, the Pope had succumbed to French pressure also in this area. When after his coronation the Emperor moved against Robert of Naples and instituted proceedings against him, the Pope openly espoused the cause of the Guelfs. Once again a great controversy of theory concerning the power of the Emperor and the imperial institution itself began to keep public opinion busy. Expert opinions and memoranda were issued by both sides.[51] Because of his depth of thought, Dante deserves, unchallenged, the first place in these considerations. Having rapturously hailed the King on his journey to the "garden of the Empire," he discussed in the three books *De Monarchia*, which was probably composed at this time, the theological necessity of the *Imperium* and the legitimacy of Rome's claims to the imperial office and then demonstrated the direct dependence of the *Imperium* on God, without any mediation of the Pope. The aim of his great work was to prove the Emperor's independence in the political field.[52] On the other hand, in the Neapolitan opinions the *Imperium*, as *de facto* German, was attacked and repudiated as an institution,

---

[48] F. Schneider, *Kaiser Heinrich VII.* (Stuttgart, 2nd ed. 1943).

[49] W. Bowsky, "Clement V and the Emperor Elect," *Medievalia et Humanistica*, 12 (1958), 52–69.

[50] F. Bock, *Reichsidee und Nationalstaaten*, 125–45; W. M. Bowsky, *Henry VII in Italy* (Lincoln 1960); W. Bowsky, "Florence and Henry of Luxembourg, King of the Romans," *Speculum*, 33 (1958), 177–203; F. J. Heyen, *Kaiser Heinrichs Romfahrt. Die Bilderchronik von Kaiser Heinrich VII. und Kurfürst Balduin von Luxemburg* (Boppard 1964).

[51] *MGConst*, IV, 2; F. Bock, "Kaisertum, Kurie und Nationalstaat," *RQ*, 44 (1936), 110 ff.; M. Seidlmayer, *Geschichte Italiens* (Stuttgart 1962), 202–15.

[52] F. Schneider, *Dante, sein Leben und sein Werk* (Weimar, 5th ed. 1960); the latest comprehensive evaluation of Dante is that in "Alighieri, Dante," *Dizionario biografico degli Italiani*, 2 (Rome 1960), 385–451 (for *De Monarchia*, see 418–20; bibliography, 447 f.). H. Conrad, "Dantes Staatslehre im Spiegel der scholastischen Philosophie seiner Zeit," *Deutsches Dante-Jahrbuch*, 27 (1948), 43–80; M. Seidlmayer, *Dantes Reichs- und Staats-*

and, with many historical citations, proven to be the source of numerous evils.

After the early death of the Emperor at Buonconvento near Siena on 24 August 1313, Clement made his position clear in the famous bull "Pastoralis Cura," written between the fall of 1313 and the spring of 1314, probably with the assistance of Robert of Naples. He carried further the theocracy of Boniface VIII by declaring null the imperial sentence against Robert and claiming for himself the right to name imperial vicars during the vacancy of the Empire. Significant in this decretal is the limitation of the *Imperium* in extent and hence the denial of its universality.[53] Then in 1314 he named Robert as imperial vicar for all of Italy.[54] When, *en route* to his beloved Gascony, Clement died at Roquemaure near Carpentras on 20 April 1314, the unlucky Pope bequeathed an evil legacy to his successor: Rome abandoned, the government of the Church shamefully dependent on France, a College of Cardinals consisting mostly of Frenchmen, and a Curia bloated and plundered by narrow nepotism.

---

lehre (Heidelberg 1952); M. Maccarrone, "Il terzo libro della 'Monarchia'," *Studi Danteschi*, 33 (1955), 5–142; H. Löwe, "Dante und das Kaisertum," *HZ*, 190 (1960), 517–52; Grundmann-Herding-Peyer, *Dante und die Mächtigen seiner Zeit* (Münchener romanistische Arbeiten, 15) (Munich 1960), especially O. Herding, "Über Dantes Monarchia," *ibid.*, 37–57.

[53] Text in *MGConst*, IV, 2, no. 1166; M. Delle Piane, "Intorno ad una bolla papale, la 'Pastoralis cura' di Clemente V," *Rivista di storia del diritto italiano*, 31 (1958), 23–56. A recently discovered view of the Ghibelline position in K. Pivec - H. Heimpel, "Neue Forschungen zu Dietrich von Niem," *NAG* (1951), no. 4, pp. 97–122; K. Hitzfeld, "Die letzte Gesandtschaft Heinrichs VII. nach Avignon und ihre Folgen," *HJ*, 83 (1964), 43–53.

[54] F. Baethgen, "Der Anspruch des Papsttums auf das Reichsvikariat," *Mediaevalia*, Teil I, Schriften der Monumenta Germaniae, 17/I (1960), 159–68.

CHAPTER 38

From John XXII to Clement VI

John XXII (1316–34)

The difficult situation of the cardinals at Carpentras was due to the factions within the college — ten or eleven Gascons, six other French or Provençaux, and seven Italians. The creations of Clement V had contributed not only an excessive growth of French influence in general, but so strong a group of relatives and tightly knit countrymen as had never existed previously. Scarcely had the business of the election got under way before the conclave was blown apart by the adherents of Clement V, who assaulted the Italian curialists and threatened the Italian cardinals. The Italians had great difficulty in escaping from the city. Not until two years later was it possible to bring the cardinals together again at Lyons, where the Count of Poitiers, brother of the French King, contrary to his oath to assure freedom of movement, locked them up in the Dominican monastery and gave them the names of four candidates. After weeks of efforts to reach an agreement, it was once again Napoleone Orsini who brought three of his countrymen over to the Gascon faction and thereby determined the election.

On 7 August 1316 accord was reached on the Cardinal Bishop of Ostia, James Duèse of Cahors, seventy-two years old and seemingly in poor health.[1] Throughout his life he remained closely bound to his restricted homeland, as his unbounded preference for Cahorsins shows. He had become Bishop of Fréjus in 1300, was chancellor of Charles II of Naples from 1308 to 1310, was made Bishop of Avignon in 1310, and received the red hat in 1312. Of vast experience in all questions of politics and administration, he found the papal Curia in utter chaos, as a result of the weak, not to mention confused, government of his predecessor and of the two-years' vacancy. His fear of assassination seems to imply a strong opposition to his election.[2] His coronation, performed at Lyons on 5 September, was more solemn than was customary and was attended by the French King. The new Pope arrived in Avignon in October. At first he resided in the Dominican monastery and later in the episcopal palace, after elevating the former Bishop to the cardinalate and arranging for an administrator to manage the diocese.[3]

With good reason qualified judges have termed this period the age of the avowedly political papacy, adding that little time for things purely religious

---

[1] On the election of John XXII see *Haller*, V, 302 ff., 405 ff. (with bibliography). The chief source is a report to the King of Aragón in H. Finke, *Aus den Tagen Bonifaz' VIII.* (Münster 1902), LXVII f.

[2] H. Finke, *Acta Aragonensia*, III, 336.

[3] L. H. Labande, *Le palais des papes*, 18 f.

was left to the Popes.[4] With the election of John XXII the choice was made for the priority of politics over every other point of view. And on that, as would become apparent, depended the decision whether a return to Rome was seriously considered or whether persons were willing or forced to continue the provisional arrangement bequeathed by Clement V. If Clement was always in need of being pushed, John brought an entirely different sort of personality to the government, which successfully influenced the course of history during his long pontificate. Certainly the new Pope did not from the first exclude a return of the Curia to Rome or Italy; he repeatedly expressed the desire, even before the close of the year in which he had been elected, to go to Rome. But, captivated by the notion of a Guelf-French Italy, he regarded a return as possible only after this aim had been realized. The longer the delay lasted, the more serious became the psychological difficulties confronting a transfer of the Holy See. As would later appear, the situation in Italy could have been corrected only by a Pope functioning in the Papal State.[5]

At the very centre of this pontificate, too, loomed always its relationship with France and its Kings and with the Angevin Dynasty that dominated South and Central Italy. Efforts to settle France's long war in Flanders and quarrel with England and the dubious agreement with Aragón in regard to the occupation of Sardinia were motivated by the desire for a stronger France, necessary if the Pope was to realize his contemplated goals.[6] This end was served also by the numerous but not always satisfactory interventions in French dynastic matters, in questions of administration, and by the profuse grants of Church tithes and subsidies that were dubiously accounted for. The aim was obvious: the continuation of the curial policy, followed from the latter half of the thirteenth century, of consolidating Angevin power throughout Italy and, correspondingly, of routing and eliminating the *Imperium* and Frederick of Sicily. If we want to employ the then current terms for the political factions — Guelfs and Ghibellines — John XXII was certainly the Guelf chief, far more effectively than was Robert of Naples, whose attitude and activity did not always meet with the Pope's approval.[7]

The situation in the Empire was not unfavourable to the new Pope. The premature death of Henry VII at Buonconvento was followed by a double election, with Louis the Bavarian and Frederick of Habsburg claiming the throne. Both applied to the Pope, who treated both as Kings-elect and claimed the right to give the decision. His first measures in Italy were based on his duty

[4] H. Finke, *op. cit.*, I, pp. XVI f.
[5] On the return to Rome see H. Finke, *op. cit.*, I, 217; E. Dupré-Theseider, *I papi di Avignone*, 48 ff.; F. Bock, "Roma al tempo di Roberto d'Angiò," *AS Romana*, 65 (1942), 171, 187.
[6] Abundant material in H. Finke, *Acta Aragonensia*, I–III, and the appendices.
[7] G. Tabacco, *La casa di Francia*, 129 ff.

to mediate a general peace, but before long the Pope referred in a constitution to the claim made by his predecessor to act as imperial vicar and forbade the vicars appointed by the late Henry VII to exercise their functions. He then made Robert of Naples Senator of Rome and Imperial Vicar of all Italy.[8]

Matters did not remain in the realm of theory. There now began strong measures against all who were not in agreement with the papal policy, in the form of canonical Inquisition processes with various degrees of penalties, including the branding of persons as heretics and the laying of interdict on cities and territories.[9] A relative of the Pope, Cardinal Bertrand du Poujet, appointed legate for Lombardy in 1319, entered upon his assignment in the summer of the next year.[10] Until his unhappy departure in 1334, he had as his task to topple the tyrants, a term used by the Pope to denote all non-Guelfs. The wars now erupting dragged themselves out for years, with rapidly changing political groupings but without any real decision.[11] Of particular importance were the interventions of French troops in North Italy. Moreover, vessels which had been provided for the crusade participated in the wars. Though the French government regarded a change in the political views of the Visconti as possible and worth seeking, the Pope inexorably demanded the forcible overthrow of their authority in Milan and Lombardy. He went so far as to grant the crusade indulgence "contra hereticos et rebelles partium Italiae." All bishops were required to proclaim it and to provide separate collection boxes for this purpose.[12] The cardinals were apparently not consulted about these measures and not all of them approved.[13] It is hard to determine how seriously John XXII took the idea of a genuine crusade, but it is difficult to avoid the impression that to a great extent he used it as a pretext for strengthening the papal finances and French predominance. For such an undertaking was possible only under the leadership of the French King, and Philip VI seems to have been well disposed.[14]

---

[8] F. Baethgen, *Der Anspruch des Papsttums auf das Reichsvikariat*, 169; G. Mollat, *The Popes at Avignon*, 80; F. Bock, "Kaisertum, Kurie und Nationalstaat," *RQ*, 44 (1936), 184 ff.; C. Erdmann, *Vatikanische Analekten*, 44.

[9] On the gist of the procedures see F. Bock, *Reichsidee*, 181 ff.; on individual procedures see *idem*, "Studien zum politischen Inquisitionsprozess," *QFIAB*, 26 (1935 f.), 21–142; also, *idem*, "Processi di Giovanni XXII contro i ghibellini italiani," *ASRomana*, 63 (1940), 143; *Storia di Milano*, V (1955), 148–54.

[10] F. Bock, "Kaisertum, Kurie und Nationalstaat," *loc. cit.*, 188 ff.; *DHGE*, 8 (1935), 1068–74 (Mollat).

[11] *Storia di Milano*, V, 131 ff.

[12] F. Bock, "Studien zum politischen Inquisitionsprozess," *loc. cit.*, 48 f.; P. Gasnault, "La perception dans le royaume de France, du subside sollicité par Jean XXII 'contra haereticos et rebelles partium Italiae,'" *MAH*, 69 (1957), 273–319.

[13] H. Finke, *Acta Aragonensia*, I, 377.

[14] F. Bock, *Reichsidee*, 339 f.; G. Dürrholder, *Die Kreuzzugspolitik unter Papst Johann XXII.* (diss., Strasbourg 1913); G. Tabacco, *op. cit.*, 213 ff.; J. Goñi Gaztambide, *Historia de la bula de la cruzada en España* (Vitoria 1958), 282 ff.; *Runciman*, III, 472: "till

It was quite extraordinary to find one of the German claimants, Frederick of Habsburg, on the side of the Guelfs in Italy. In 1322 his brother Henry appeared with an army before Brescia to support this gravely threatened Guelf city, but then, to the great annoyance of the Pope, he withdrew, presumably influenced by the diplomacy of the Visconti, who pointed out to Frederick the consequences for the *Imperium* of such action.[15] Far more portentous and decisive for events in Italy till the end of the pontificate was the intervention of Louis the Bavarian after the battle of Mühldorf in 1322, which was supposed to have established him as sole King. But the Pope in no way changed his earlier alleged neutrality; so far as he was concerned, Louis was still only King-elect. Since the King, now triumphant in Germany, laid claim to the customary royal rights, which also covered Italy in varying degrees, there once more broke out a bitter war between *Imperium* and *Sacerdotium,* but now the *Sacerdotium,* no longer in Rome, was in the immediate vicinity of France and strongly dependent on it. Approached for help by the Ghibellines, King Louis in the spring of 1323 dispatched a delegation to Italy. Having first bound several wavering Ghibelline leaders by oath, it contributed decisively to the relief of Milan, besieged by the legate's army. Thereby were ruined the Pope's prospects for an imminent victory over the Visconti.[16] Hence his violent wrath and his proceedings against Louis from the autumn of 1323, despite the strong opposition of some of the cardinals, are understandable.[17] Following the Italian model, the German King was now warned, then cited and entangled in the procedure of canonical trials with the aim of excluding him from the throne and of introducing another, perhaps French, candidacy.[18]

Only after long hesitation did Louis decide to resist. First at Nürnberg in December 1323, and then, following his excommunication in March 1324, at Sachsenhausen near Frankfurt in May, in the Chapel of the Teutonic Knights, Louis lodged an appeal against the Pope's rebukes and sentences.[19] He first protested against the reproach of illegally bearing the royal title and exercising the royal rights and then against the charge of patronizing heretics, and concluded with the request for the convoking of a general council. More calculated for a public reaction against the adroitly publicized papal proceedings was the so-called Declaration of Sachsenhausen, which charged the Pope with a prejudiced recourse to ecclesiastical censures for the

at last the Crusade came to mean any war against the enemies of Papal policy, and all the spiritual paraphernalia of indulgences and heavenly rewards was used to support the lay ambitions of the Papal See."

[15] F. Bock, "Kaisertum, Kurie und Nationalstaat," *loc. cit.,* 195–203.

[16] F. Bock, "Studien zum politischen Inquisitionsprozess," *loc. cit.,* 53 ff.

[17] H. Finke, *Acta Aragonensia,* I, 391 ff. "Per Deum! Et furiam invenient et iterum furiam invenient" (*ibid.,* 395).

[18] F. Bock, *Reichsidee,* 212 ff.; G. Tabacco, *op. cit.,* 337 ff.

[19] F. Bock, *Reichsidee,* 201 ff.

struggle against his political opponents and in particular branded as clear heresy John's stand in regard to the Spirituals' ideal of poverty. Here were the accusations of heresy, familiar since the days of Philip the Fair, for which even a Pope could be prosecuted by the whole Church at a council. Recent studies establish strong resemblances to the Ghibelline stock of ideas in the content and formulation of the Declaration. The extent of Franciscan participation cannot as yet be exactly determined. [20]

The conflict became more acute when Louis, invited by Ghibelline circles, began in 1327 to intervene personally in Italy. In many respects his journey to Rome differed from previous journeys of German kings and emperors. He did indeed go to Rome but found there no ecclesiastical dignitaries who would officiate at his coronation. Appealing to the imperial idea of antiquity, old Sciarra Colonna conferred the crown on him in the Lateran. More serious, and certainly a political blunder, was the setting up of an Antipope in the person of the Franciscan, Peter di Corvaro, who called himself Nicholas V. Of no great personal significance and merely a tool of an inept policy, he quickly disappeared after the Emperor's departure from Italy and at Avignon made his peace with the very accommodating Pope. [21] On the other hand, the Franciscan superiors who had fled from Avignon and joined Louis at Pisa were of great assistance in the literary conflict with the Curia. [22] The Pope's reaction was not confined to a renewal and intensification of the processes. As he had earlier done, now again he urged the deposition of Louis, but a new election, suggested by him and agreed to by some of the Electors, did not take place. [23] By means of a fictitious plan of abdication Louis

---

[20] *MGConst*, V (1909–13), 722 ff. On the content of the declarations see F. Bock, *Reichsidee*, 201 ff.; on the textual problem, *idem*, "Die Appellationsschriften König Ludwigs IV. in den Jahren 1323/24," *DA*, 4 (1940), 179–205; on the authors, *idem*, "Politik und kanonischer Prozess zur Zeit Johanns XXII.," *ZBLG*, 22 (1959), 1–12, in which the participation of Michael of Cesena is made probable; K. Bosl, "Der geistige Widerstand am Hofe Ludwigs des Bayern gegen die Kurie. Die politische Ideenwelt um die Wende vom 13./14. Jh. und ihr historisches Milieu in Europa," *Vorträge und Forschungen*, 9 (Constance 1965), 99–118.

[21] On the journey to Rome see H. Otto, "Zur italienischen Politik Johanns XXII.," *QFIAB*, 14 (1911), 140–265; F. Bock, *Reichsidee*, 225–85.

[22] F. Bock, *Reichsidee*, 321–26; H. Kämpf, "Die Codices latini 4008–10 der Vatikanischen Bibliothek," *QFIAB*, 26 (1935 f.), 143–70 (Cod. Vat. Lat. 4009 contains documents in the hand of Michael of Cesena); H. S. Offler, "Meinungsverschiedenheiten am Hof Ludwigs des Bayern im Herbst 1331," *DA*, 11 (1954), 191–206; K. Bosl, "Die 'geistliche Hofakademie' Kaiser Ludwigs des Bayern im alten Franziskanerkloster zu München," *Der Mönch im Wappen. Aus Geschichte und Gegenwart des katholischen München* (Munich 1960), pp. 97–129; F. Hofmann, *Der Anteil der Minoriten am Kampf Ludwigs des Bayern gegen Johann XXII. unter besonderer Berücksichtigung des Wilhelm von Ockham* (diss. phil., Münster 1959); H. J. Becker, "Zwei unbekannte kanonistische Schriften des Bonagratia von Bergamo in Cod. Vat. Lat. 4009," *QFIAB*, 46 (1966), 219–76 (literature).

[23] E. E. Stengel, *Avignon und Rhens*, 36–59; G. Tabacco, *op. cit.*, 341 ff.

contrived to master the difficulties in both Germany and Italy, though, after his departure from Italy, the Visconti drew near to the Pope.

But the last years of John XXII saw new complications. In 1331 there appeared in Lombardy the young King John of Bohemia, son of the Emperor Henry VII. Feigning an understanding with Emperor and Pope — *rex pacificus, filius ecclesiae, et vicarius imperii* — he apparently intended to establish his own rule. The Pope also considered the French King's plan of holding Lombardy in fief from the Holy See in order thus to exclude the German Kings from Italy for good. And in his last year John even thought of going to Bologna, but not as a result of any accord with France. All these projects collapsed when in 1333 Guelfs and Ghibellines allied against foreign domination and forced the Bohemian King to withdraw and the papal legate to flee from Italy.[24] The enormous sums which John sacrificed from the Church's treasury on his Italian schemes were squandered for nothing.[25]

The Pope's harsh stand in the controversy over poverty not only exasperated the Spirituals and made him implacable enemies but likewise incensed wide circles of ecclesiastics and lay persons against him, notably King Robert of Naples and Queen Sancia.[26] Grave dissensions ruined hitherto intimate relations, especially when differing political views arose in regard to domination in North Italy. In addition, the Pope became embroiled with a part of the Sacred College, which, led by Napoleone Orsini, tried earnestly to have a general council put him on trial and got into contact with the Emperor Louis and the German bishops.[27] Toward the close of his pontificate the Pope even gave scandal in the purely dogmatic field by defending in his preaching a quite unusual view of the beatific vision but one not unknown to early Christian thinking: that the souls of the just do not enjoy the full vision of God immediately after death but only after the general judgment. The ensuing controversy affected a large audience, and the greater number of theologians opposed John. These problems were discussed in many meetings and extensive disputations, and a series of expert opinions were handed down. In Paris the government unequivocally opposed the Pope and threatened to prosecute him for heresy. On the eve of his death he is said to have abandoned his peculiar opinion.[28]

---

[24] G. Tabacco, *op. cit.*, 297 ff.; A. Mercati, "Dall'archivio Vaticano I. Proposte di Giovanni, il francofilo re di Boemia, a Giovanni XXII," *MAH*, 61 (1949), 195–209; C. Dumontel, "L'impresa italiana di Giovanni di Lussemburgo re di Boemia," *Pubblicazioni della facoltà di lettere e filosofia*, IV, 3 (Turin 1952).

[25] E. Göller, *Die Einnahmen der apostolischen Kammer unter Johann XXII.* (Paderborn 1910), 133.*

[26] Literature on the poverty controversy in Chapter 43.

[27] O. Bornhak, *Staatskirchliche Anschauungen und Handlungen am Hofe Ludwigs des Bayern*, 37 ff.

[28] G. Hoffmann, *Der Streit über die sel. Schau Gottes, 1313–38* (Leipzig 1917); D. Douie, "John XXII and the Beatific Vision," *Dominican Studies*, 3 (1950), 154–74;

It has long been known that the Pope liked to preach and often did so in the presence of cardinals, bishops, and curial prelates, using this opportunity to make known his theological views and positions, which were further publicized by official transcripts. It has recently been shown that he carefully studied collections of sermons and annotated them for his own use. And we know of more than thirty of his sermons, some *verbatim*, others in outline. As regards content, they deal mostly with the Blessed Virgin, including unambiguous remarks against the Immaculate Conception, and with political views, as is to be expected from the greatest politician in Avignon. Many extant codices of his personal library and of the papal library prove him to have been an attentive reader, as the marginal notes on requested expert opinions indicate. They also reveal a thorough knowledge of the theology of Thomas Aquinas, in preparation for his canonization. On the whole, the Pope favoured the collecting of material and possessed many such *tabulae*. Probably most important in his eyes were legal questions, and a group of these in his own hand has survived.[29] While in general the only fourteenth-century papal autographs that we have are the notes of approval on the few extant original petitions, the scarcely legible hand of John XXII has been preserved in many places, for example, in his outlines for political writings of great importance. They show the Pope at work, the repeated efforts of the aged and trembling hand for a new wording; he even took part personally in the composing of weighty political *cedulae*, using a cipher.[30]

If any Pope deserves the label of politician, it is John XXII. In the years when his own views were being formed and were acquiring their constituents, he was at the Angevin court in Naples. Is he to be blamed for never having given up the there dominant Guelf doctrines? As Pope, he certainly ought to have acted differently, but the question remains whether he could have. Thus he established the Angevin political style even for his successors and thereby caused untold harm. For achieving his ends he ruthlessly made use of all the means at his disposal as Pope. He stubbornly continued along the road taken by Innocent IV and Boniface VIII in the high-handed setting up

M. Prados, *El papa Juan XXII y las controversias sobre la visión beatífica* (Granada 1959); A. Maier, "Die Pariser Disputation des Geraldus Odonis über die Visio beatifica Dei," *Archivio italiano per la storia della pietà*, 4 (1965), 213–51; F. Wetter, "Die Lehre Benedikts XII. vom intensiven Wachstum der Gottesschau," *AnGr*, 92 (Rome 1958), with the literature.

[29] A. Maier, "Zwei Vatikanische Handschriften und ihre Besitzer," *RSTI*, 12 (1958), 262–80; E. Pásztor, "Una raccolta di sermoni di Giovanni XXII," *Bollettino dell'Archivio paleografico italiano*, Nuova serie, 2–3 (1956), parte II, 265–89; A. Maier, "Annotazioni autografe di Giovanni XXII in codici Vaticani," *RSTI*, 6 (1952), 317–32; T. Käppeli, "Predigten am päpstlichen Hof von Avignon," *AFP*, 19 (1949), 388–93.

[30] F. Bock, "Die Geheimschrift in der Kanzlei Johanns XXII.," *RQ*, 42 (1934), 279–303; A. Mercati, "Dagli Instrumenta Miscellanea dell'archivio segreto Vaticano," *QFIAB*, 27 (1936 f.), 137–67.

of new rights and through his decretals became the prototype of the brutally political Pope.[31] The rights claimed by the Curia from the thirteenth century in the matter of matrimonial dispensations were exploited by John XXII in a completely biased manner for his political goals, the advice of the cardinals being sought only to cover up a refusal.[32] The imposition of ecclesiastical censures on purely political grounds and the arbitrary granting or refusing of dispensations were garnished as *necessitas et utilitas ecclesiae* or *utilitas publica,* in an arrogant identification of his politics with the Church, of the hierarchy with religion. His irresponsible dealing with benefices and with the Church's financial system for the completion of the administrative primacy will be examined later. His pontificate was the climax of the hierocratic system. Whoever regards this as something positive can admire in John XXII one of the most important of the Popes.[33]

Benedict XII (1334–42)

The conclave, meeting in the episcopal palace at Avignon at the appointed time after the death of John XXII, faced not only personal but also great material decisions. On it depended a return to Rome or a staying on for the time being at Avignon. It is perhaps an exaggeration that the Cardinal of Comminges declined to give his word that he would not go to Rome and therefore was not elected, but the story throws a penetrating light on the situation. The quickly accomplished election of the "White Cardinal" on 20 December 1334 is said to have caused surprise. Perhaps, following the anxiety caused by the *dilettante* theologian, a real specialist was desired, and such was James Fournier, who became Benedict XII. As a youth he had entered the Cistercian Order, in which his uncle was an abbot, and in 1311 he became his successor at Fontfroide. In 1317 he was Bishop of Pamiers, in 1326 of Mirepoix, and in 1327 a Cardinal. In Paris he had engaged in profound studies and had earned the degree of master in theology. As Bishop and even as Cardinal he paid special attention to the fight against heresy.[34] Significant also was his activity as a theological expert. Our present knowledge of his views in the process against the *postille* on the Apocalypse of Peter John Olivi,[35] against William of Ockham and Master Eckhart, has

[31] H. Finke, *Acta Aragonensia*, I, 231, 395.

[32] A. Esch, "Die Ehedispense Johanns XXII. und ihre Beziehung zur Politik," *HStud*, 183 (Berlin 1929); H. Finke, *Acta Aragonensia*, I, 409, 415.

[33] Characterization in H. Finke, *Acta Aragonensia*, I, 216, 395, 414 f., III, 315, 342, 351 f.; J. Haller, *Papsttum und Kirchenreform*, 90 ff.; G. Tabacco, *op. cit.*, 334 ff.; F. Bock, *Reichsidee*, 171 f., 364 ff.

[34] J. Duvernoy, *Le registre d'inquisition de Jacques Fournier évêque de Pamiers, Benoît XII* (Toulouse 1964).

[35] R. Manselli, *La "lectura super apocalipsim" di Pietro di Giovanni Olivi* (Rome 1955).

been extended by new discoveries.[36] He took a stand early in the dispute over the beatific vision. John XXII entrusted him with a study of the question, the result of which is found in a large unprinted work.[37] He presided at the trial of the Dominican Thomas Waleys.[38] This thorough familiarity with problems facilitated for him as Pope the settling and provisional ending of the discussions in the usual manner.[39]

Difficult to assess is his position in regard to the return of the Curia to Rome, in particular whether he was really in earnest when he held out to the envoys of the Roman people the prospect of a speedy return and yet in the first months of his pontificate undertook the building of the great palace at Avignon. Thereby an important decision had in effect been made and no more thought was given to a departure for Italy. Rather detailed reports give information about the exertions for order in the Papal State. Archbishop Bertrand of Embrun, sent to Central Italy by John XXII, continued his activity under Benedict until 1337. He was followed by John de Amelio as reformator generalis, who is known chiefly for his having transported the papal archives to Avignon. Repeated peace edicts endeavoured to check the quarrels in Rome between Colonna and Orsini over the Tiber bridges and fortresses in the city.[40] It is false to say that the Pope could not return because of the anarchy in Italy and Rome. The disorders continued precisely because the Curia did not combat them on the spot.

Benedict too had to travel the way of dependence on France, marked out by John XXII. His great reserve in the granting of tithes for the crusade or his reclamations because of the non-fulfillment of promises made no difference. After long negotiations on this subject and a visit of the French King Philip VI to Avignon, the Pope gave in. The French Church was again and again seriously burdened for the political needs of the government, a situation that repeatedly gained for the Curia the reproach of partiality as the war against England got under way. Furthermore, Avignon's intelligence service was at the disposal of the French King. In an effort to mediate peace the Pope sent two cardinals to England, but they obtained only transitory

[36] J. Koch, "Der Kardinal Jacques Fournier (Benedikt XII.) als Gutachter in theologischen Prozessen," Die Kirche und ihre Ämter und Stände (Cologne 1960), 441–52.

[37] F. Wetter, "Die Lehre Benedikts XII. vom intensiven Wachstum der Gottesschau," AnGr, 92 (Rome 1958).

[38] T. Käppeli, Le procès contre Thomas Waleys O.P. (Rome 1936).

[39] Constitution "Benedictus Deus" of 29 January 1336.

[40] H. Otto, "Benedikt XII. als 'Reformer' des Kirchenstaates," RQ, 36 (1928), 59–110; A. Mercati, "Nell'Urbe dalla fine di settembre 1337 al 21 gennaio 1338", Misc Hist Pont, 10 (1945), 1–84; G. Mollat, "Construction d'une forteresse à Bénévent sous les pontificats de Jean XXII et de Benoît XII," MAH, 62 (1950), 149–64; G. Tabacco, "La tradizione guelfa in Italia durante il pontificato di Benedetto XII," Studi di storia medievale e moderna (Rome 1958), 95–148.

results. [41] To the people of northern France, severely tried by the war of devastation in 1339–40, the Pope sent generous financial help. [42] Throughout his pontificate Benedict was unable to free himself from the strong bonds linking him to French policy.

Peaceable remarks at the beginning of his reign awakened the hope of a settlement of the strife with the *Imperium*. In any event, as early as the spring of 1335 the Emperor got into contact with the Curia in order to ascertain the conditions for a peaceable solution of the affair, which was having a progressively worse effect on public opinion. We are rather exactly informed about these negotiations by the preservation of a portion of the detailed formulations within the frame of the canonical process, the so-called procurations. [43] Despite much yielding on the part of the imperial envoys no agreement was reached, for it was not in accord with the political line of Philip VI, who was kept abreast of the complicated discussions by the Pope in all details. [44] On the whole, Benedict was even more subservient to French policy than his predecessor had been. And so there had to be a new break, after the imploring speeches of the envoys in consistory, sharply condemning the policy of John XXII, had failed to accomplish anything. [45]

But the attitude in Germany was now quite different from what it had been under Benedict's predecessor. Many Imperial Estates — Electors, nobility, the higher clergy, and especially the cities — were alienated by this policy of the Curia. [46] The desertion of the papally provided Archbishop of Mainz, Henry von Virneburg, was of great advantage to the Emperor's cause. At the end of March 1338 a synod of the province of Mainz at Speyer rallied many bishops around the Emperor and interceded in his behalf with the Curia, only to receive the reply that the Pope was unwilling to throw his cardinals to bears and lions. [47] Important rallies rapidly followed one

[41] F. Trautz, *Die Könige von England und das Reich 1272–1377* (Heidelberg 1961), 263 f.

[42] L. Carolus-Barré, "Benoît XII et la mission charitable de Bertrand Carit dans les pays dévastés du nord de la France, Cambrésis, Vermandois, Thiérache 1340," *MAH*, 62 (1950), 165–232.

[43] F. Bock, *Reichsidee*, 367 ff.; *idem*, "Die Prokuratorien Kaiser Ludwigs IV. an Papst Benedikt XII.," *QFIAB*, 25 (1933 f.), 251–91; H. S. Offler, "Über die Prokuratorien Ludwigs des Bayern für die römische Kurie," *DA*, 8 (1951), 461–87.

[44] F. Bock, *Reichsidee*, 409; F. Trautz, *op. cit.*, 264.

[45] F. Pelster, "Die zweite Rede Markwarts von Randeck für die Aussöhnung des Papstes mit Ludwig dem Bayern," *HJ*, 60 (1940), 88–114.

[46] Konrad von Megenberg, *Planctus ecclesiae in Germaniam*, ed. by R. Scholz, MG Staatsschriften des späteren Mittelalters, II, 1, 1941. Latin-German edition prepared by H. Kusch, Leipziger Übersetzungen und Abhandlungen zum Mittelalter, series A, vol. 1 (Berlin 1956). *Kaiser, Volk und Avignon. Quellen zur antikurialen Bewegung in Deutschland in der ersten Hälfte des 14. Jahrhunderts*, ed. and trans. by O. Berthold, Leipziger Übersetzungen, series A, vol. 3 (Berlin 1960).

[47] E. E. Stengel, *Nova Alamanniae*, 352 f.: "Papa dixit, quod suos cardinales nollebat ursis et leonibus destinare."

another this same year. In May at the first Diet of Frankfurt was published the celebrated manifesto "Fidem Catholicam," produced with the vigourous co-operation of the Franciscan court theologians.[48] It solemnly proclaimed that the imperial authority derives directly from God and not from the Pope, and that the Emperor-elect, even without having been crowned, can rule the Empire. Accordingly, John XXII's institutive proceedings were unjust and must not be obeyed. The Empire itself took its stand in the declarations made by the Electors around the royal throne in Rhense, where, after uniting in the Electoral Union for the protection of their traditional rights, they made the following proclamation with legal force: the one elected King of the Romans by the Electors, or by a majority of them, needs no nomination, approbation, confirmation, consent, or authorization of the Apostolic See for administering the property and rights of the Empire or for assuming the royal title.[49] A second Diet of Frankfurt in August of the same year produced the imperial law "Licet Iuris," which, expanding the Rhense decrees, conceded also the imperial dignity to the one properly elected, without the need of any approval or confirmation by the Pope.[50] The Franciscans of the "Munich Academy" had shared in the preparation of these momentous proclamations by numerous opinions and day-to-day consultation.[51] There immediately followed, in September, the Diet of Koblenz, where the alliance with King Edward III of England was concluded, despite the opposition of the Curia. Five imperial laws prescribed the implementation of the great decrees of this year.[52]

In the face of this unexpected development in the Empire, the Pope, in the interests of France, sought to resume and drag out the discontinued negotiations and especially to dissuade the English King from the German alliance.[53] Anti-curial feeling in Germany was growing, and the announcement of trials and observance of censures imposed were almost out of the question. In the spring of 1339, again at a Diet of Frankfurt, the Electors, in

---

[48] Text and German translation in *Kaiser, Volk und Avignon*, 248–71; H. J. Becker, *op. cit.*, 246 ff.

[49] E. E. Stengel, *Avignon und Rhens*, 112–53; *idem, Baldewin von Luxemburg. Ein grenzdeutscher Staatsmann des 14. Jh.*, 207 f.; F. Bock, *Reichsidee*, 398 ff.; *Kaiser, Volk und Avignon*, 274 f.

[50] Text and German translation in *Kaiser, Volk und Avignon*, 282–85; H. Lieberich, "Kaiser Ludwig der Baier als Gesetzgeber," *ZSavRGgerm*, 76 (1959), 173–245.

[51] C. Schmitt, *Benoît XII et l'ordre des frères mineurs*, 197–249; K. Bosl, "Die 'geistliche Hofakademie' Kaiser Ludwigs des Bayern im alten Franziskanerkloster zu München," *loc. cit.*

[52] F. Bock, *Reichsidee*, 436; F. Trautz, *op. cit.*, 361; F. Bock, "Das deutsch-englische Bündnis von 1335–1342, I, Quellen," *Quellen und Erörterungen zur bayerischen Geschichte*, NF, XII (Munich 1956).

[53] For the mission of Arnald de Verdalla see E. E. Stengel, *Avignon und Rhens*, 170 ff.; F. Bock, *Reichsidee*, 443 ff.

a new proclamation, went beyond the Rhense formulation and uncon-
ditionally acknowledged Louis's imperial dignity.[54] Even present was
Archbishop Baldwin of Trier, known for his ambiguous policies; from his
chancery are preserved reflections on the war of the Empire against France
and its effect on Avignon.[55] Louis's eventual withdrawal from the English
alliance and his *rapprochement* with France hardly changed the situation.
Even the unfortunate matrimonial barter with Margaret Maultasch over
Tirol did not gravely damage the Emperor's position. The ecclesiastical
anarchy grew worse than before. Differing from the tactically more clever
John XXII, Benedict scarcely allowed any suspension of the interdict. And
so now, to a far greater degree than before, there was recourse to self-defense,
to the very great prejudice of the ecclesiastical authority. The state of affairs
is described in chronicles of that age, for example in those of John of Winterthur, Matthias of Neuenburg, and the Constance Canon Henry of Diesen-
hofen. And in his exhortation to Charles IV the Dominican John of Dambach
sketches a shocking picture in an effort to induce the King to negotiate with
Rome for the purpose of obtaining general absolution for all territories
affected by censure — not only in Germany — and a definite clarification of
who is to be regarded as *vitandus*.[56]

Benedict XII is reckoned among the reform Popes, not because of the
customary statements on the subject at the outset of his pontificate but
because he actually started a comprehensive reform activity. A few days
after his coronation he sent back to their benefices all ecclesiastics who could
not satisfactorily justify their sojourn at the Curia.[57] In the government of
the Curia he took up and extended the principles of his predecessor but
differed from him in a strict control of the full authority to issue decrees in
order to avoid the many abuses that had crept in. He abolished the unfortunate and odious system of expectatives and the *commenda* for high ecclesiastical dignitaries other than cardinals. The examination he introduced
to determine the suitability of petitioners for benefices was well meant but
in practice it was ineffectual. Contrary to the prodigality of his predecessor,
he was sparing in the granting of dispensations.[58]

The religious orders were the special concern of the Pope, who as a Cardinal had continued to wear his Cistercian habit, and his most important and
most thorough reform measures were devoted to them, but not to their great
joy. In the bull "Fulgens sicut Stella" he began with his own order, which

[54] E. E. Stengel, *Avignon und Rhens*, 174 ff.; F. Bock, *Reichsidee*, 451 f.
[55] On the role of Baldwin of Luxembourg, see E. E. Stengel, *Baldwin von Luxemburg*,
207–14; F. Bock, *Reichsidee*, 398–405.
[56] A. Auer, "Eine verschollene Denkschrift über das grosse Interdikt des 14. Jh.," *HJ*, 46
(1926), 532–49.
[57] *Baluze-Mollat*, I, 217.
[58] Examples and further details in Chapter 40.

had already preoccupied John XXII. The bull for the reform of the Benedictines, "Summi Magistri," whose importance was for long a subject of controversy, has recently been judged more soberly. The Dominicans very skillfully contrived to escape the Pope's zeal for reform. On the other hand, the bull "Redemptor Noster" for the Franciscans, drawn up in an authoritarian tone, produced great alarm, above all because of the unprecedented character of the Pope's stand, which displayed no particular regard for the order's tradition and insufficient insight into its internal difficulties and a situation that had been exacerbated by John XXII's rough dealings with the Spirituals. Prepared by a commission of specialists — including not only cardinals and bishops but expert theologians, — it was felt by many contemporaries to be too monastic because of its regulation of even small details and it was cancelled in part by Clement VI. Incorrect is the widespread view that, after the death of its author, the reform bull was rejected by the general chapter at Marseilles in 1343. Many of its prescriptions, changed in their wording, were preserved essentially in the statutes of the order or were of significance for all religious orders, such as the directions in regard to the fostering of studies and the central training of the novices.[59]

Estimates of Benedict XII's personality vary.[60] No one denies that he was inspired by lofty motives. His manner of life seems to have been unpretentious, and the words *bibamus papaliter,* attributed to him, are found in only one of his eight *vitae,* but the seventh *vita* expresses itself in similar vein. Very likely these reproaches emanated from hostile Franciscan circles.[61] In his first *"sine nomine"* letter Petrarch judges him quite severely, characterizing him as a totally unfit, drowsy, and drunken helmsman of the ship of the Church.[62] He is alluding especially to Benedict's continued stay at Avignon, his momentous erecting of the palace, his dependence on the French government, and his scarcely flexible, often even unwise policy. In regard to theology he was rightly considered scholarly but of inquisitorial harshness.[63] Ockham may be exaggerating when he characterizes him as master over the faith, even against the authority of Scripture.[64] He unflinchingly fostered the growth of papal power in the government of the Church — a spiritual autocrat but a firm preserver of legality.

---

[59] C. Schmitt, *op. cit.*

[60] Most recent characterization in B. Guillemain, *La cour pontificale,* 134 ff.

[61] *Baluze-Mollat,* I, 236 f., 234.

[62] P. Piur, "Petrarcas 'Buch ohne Namen' und die päpstliche Kurie," *DVfLG,* series 6 (Halle 1925), 165 f., 317–24. But John E. Wrigley, "A Papal Secret Known to Petrarch," *Speculum,* XXXIX (1964), 613–34, shows that Clement VI better fits what Petrarch has to say (translator).

[63] *Baluze-Mollat,* I, 223: "hic iustus et durus erat"; 232: "hic fuit homo durus et constans."

[64] "Tractatus contra Benedictum," *Opera Politica,* III (1956), 244 f.

King Philip VI of France sent his son, the Duke of Normandy, to Avignon for the election of a successor to Benedict XII. A direct influence on the election of Peter Roger cannot be proved, but certainly a candidate unacceptable to France could have been stopped. [65] The election of the Cardinal from the Limousin took place on 7 May 1342, his coronation on 19 May.

At an early age he had become a Benedictine at La Chaise-Dieu, and extended studies at Paris had equipped him with a broad education. Known early for his oratorical gifts, he was soon regarded as one of the best speakers of his time, but this reputation refers to form rather than to content. Many testimonies are extant in regard to his course of studies and his literary activity. Hundreds of "pages in his autograph" fill in details of the picture of Clement VI, something true of hardly any other person of the age. [66] After a brief period as Abbot of Fécamp, he became Bishop of Arras, Archbishop of Sens, and finally, as a royal councillor, he obtained the wealthiest of all French benefices, the archbishopric of Rouen. Thanks to his gifts in speech and diplomacy he was entrusted by the government with numerous tasks, he was the spokesman of the episcopate in the negotiations over nominations to and taxation of benefices, and he was the official preacher of the crusade, once again in prospect. Created a Cardinal in 1338, he soon occupied an important position at the Curia.

Even more than his predecessors at Avignon, Clement VI was a French Pope, and, altogether apart from the intensification of the opposition between England and France at the beginning of his pontificate, a return of the papacy to Rome was not to be expected from him. Like his predecessors, he exerted himself, chiefly in the interests of France, for a settlement of the conflict. He was unable to prevent military engagements, but through his legates he played a decisive role in achieving the truce of Malestroit in 1343; the long negotiations were conducted at Avignon. By means of loans, grants of tithes and subsidies, and the making over of crusade contributions, occasionally in very great amounts, he embraced the French cause. [67] The very active relations between Clement and King Philip retained a personal stamp. Most of the harshness in the disputes over the freedom and privileges of the Church and most of the success were on the side of the royal government.

In this state of affairs a reconciliation with Louis the Bavarian was unthinkable, unless he totally renounced his rights as recognized by Electors

---

[65] The seven *vitae* in *Baluze-Mollat*, I, are rather colourless.
[66] A. Maier, "Der literarische Nachlass des Petrus Rogerii (Clemens VI.) in der Borghesiana," *RThAM*, 15 (1948), 332–56, 16 (1949), 72–98; J. Barbet, *François de Meyronnes-Pière Roger. Disputatio 1320–21* (Paris 1961).
[67] F. Trautz, *op. cit.*, 317–19.

and Empire. Apparently Clement's demands on the Emperor were not made more severe, as was once generally held. The evidence for this is a recently published talk delivered by the Pope on Holy Thursday of 1343.[68] On the other hand, he was deeply interested in the deposition of Louis and the holding of a new election in Germany after there had been a rumour that Louis was planning a new journey to Rome. In 1346 the papal-Luxembourg party contrived to have the young Bohemian King Charles elected by a part of Electoral College. Louis's death in the following year soon brought general recognition of Charles IV. His subservience to the Curia gained him the nickname of the "Priests' King," but not quite fairly. Naturally, at the beginning of the negotiations he abandoned the prevailing attitude in regard to papal claims to approve the election and made very extensive concessions. Then he slowly but consistently took them back by means of a very cunning diplomacy.[69] This development in Germany was made possible by the course of the war with England, which was unfavourable to France, and by events in Italy.

In Italy Clement at first followed the method of negotiations with varying success. When the warlike Archbishop and *Signore* of Milan, John Visconti, invaded Piedmont and was threatening Provence, Clement too passed to the offensive. In the struggle for the possession of Bologna, however, he was the loser in dealing with the more cunning Visconti. His asking the aid of Charles IV and urging the formation of an Italian league against Milan were of as little advantage as were ecclesiastical procedures and censures. In a treaty concluded after stubborn bargaining the Visconti submitted to the Pope but received Bologna from him in fief for twelve years — and was the real winner.[70]

In the pontificate of Clement VI occurred an event important not alone for Rome and Italy but for the history of ideals in the Middle Ages: the appearance of Cola di Rienzo, tribune of the people. A few months after the Pope's election there arrived in Avignon a large Roman embassy to offer him, as a private person according to the established custom, the highest offices in the city and to ask the reduction of the jubilee from every one-hundredth to every fiftieth year. The proferred dignities were accepted in a most solemn manner and the grant of the jubilee for 1350 was proclaimed in a public consistory in 1343.[71] Present was a man whose character has been much discussed — and variously interpreted as psychopath or actor or cultured

[68] H. S. Offler, "Über die Prokuratorien Ludwigs des Bayern für die römische Kurie," *DA*, 8 (1951), 477, 480; *idem*, "A Political 'collatio' of Pope Clement VI, O.S.B.", *RBén*, 65 (1955), 126–44.

[69] E. E. Stengel, *Avignon und Rhens*, 206–08.

[70] *Storia di Milano*, V, 306–54.

[71] H. Schröder, "Die Protokollbücher der päpstlichen Kammerkleriker 1329–47," *AKG*, 27 (1937), 228.

though fantastic renewer of Rome's past greatness.[72] At first closely linked to the papal vicar, on Pentecost 1347 Cola di Rienzo took over the administration of the city amid exotic rites. He then planned further: the sovereignty of the Roman People after the suppression of barons and foreign mercenaries, independence of Pope and Emperor, unification of all inhabitants of the peninsula under a ruler of Italian blood. He came to grief in the seventh month of his tribuneship after the Curia had recognized the dangerous nature of his program, and in Rome and the Papal State the old chaos soon returned. However, the Jubilee of 1350 could be celebrated without too great difficulties, with a large influx of pilgrims and considerable revenues for the city.[73]

The news of the purchase of Avignon and of the Comtat Venaissin from Queen Joanna I of Naples by Clement in 1348 and the magnificent construction of the *palais des papes* disappointed all Italian hopes of a return of the Curia. The death in 1343 of King Robert of Naples was followed by a seriously troubled state of affairs during the long reign of his granddaughter, Joanna I. Her first husband, Andrew of Hungary, was not acceptable to the Curia, and the papal legate received orders to crown only the Queen. This is understandable, for a future occupation of South Italy by an outside power was contrary to the interests of the Papal State. The murder of Andrew was followed by an expedition for revenge led by his brother, King Louis I of Hungary. As a result, Joanna, who had meanwhile married Louis of Taranto, fled to Avignon. Her return was made possible by a great Italian league in which the Pope took part.[74] Louis of Taranto repeatedly attacked Aragonese Sicily, and the Pope sought to mediate. But his peace efforts in the war between Aragón and Mallorca and in that between Aragón and Genoa were equally fruitless. On the other hand, despite great difficulties, the marriage of the King of Castile with the daughter of the Duke of Bourbon, urged by French policy and hence also by the Pope, materialized. It is probably an exaggeration to say that interest in the East contributed much to the Western policy of Clement VI.[75]

Clement ranks as the most splendid representative of the Avignon regime, if by this expression are understood grand-scale expenditures, a court of princely luxury, and unbridled favouritism of relatives and countrymen. With him begins the age of three Limousin Popes, who gave to the papacy a South French stamp even stronger than had been the case in the first half

---

[72] P. Piur, *Cola di Rienzo, Darstellung seines Lebens und seines Geistes* (Vienna 1931); E. Dupré-Theseider, *Roma dalla comune di popolo alla signoria pontificia*, 517–608.

[73] P. Brezzi, *Storia degli anni santi* (Milan 1949), 43–62.

[74] E. G. Léonard, *Histoire de Jeanne Ière reine de Naples* (Paris 1932–37).

[75] F. Giunta, "Sulla politica orientale di Clemente VI," *Studi di storia medievale e moderna in onore di Ettore Rotta*, Biblioteca storica, 3 (Rome 1958), 149–62.

of the century.[76] Under Clement the Curia was scarcely to be distinguished from a secular court. He delighted to display his sovereign power through a gorgeous retinue, quite in accord with the saying ascribed to him — that his predecessors had not known how to be Popes.[77] For the honour of his name, no petitioner should go away discontented. The consequences in finance and administration are treated elsewhere. Charges against his morals are not explained away by recent attenuations.[78] Not a man of great determination and stern accomplishment, he endeavoured to master difficulties by wily diplomacy in the sense of temporizing. His pontificate bore a worldly character and even contemporaries saw divine judgment in the Black Death that fell upon all of Europe in 1347 to 1352.

CHAPTER 39

From Innocent VI to Gregory XI

Innocent VI (1352–62)

The conclave following the death of Clement VI, in which twenty-five cardinals took part, lasted only two days. Hence there was no need to have recourse to the mitigation of the strict prescriptions for the conclave, enacted the previous year by the deceased Pope.[1] It seems scarcely credible that the election of the Prior General of the Carthusians, ignorant of the ways of the world, was only prevented by the worldly-wise Cardinal Talleyrand de Périgord.[2] More important is the information concerning the first known election capitulation, which was intended to assure the growing influence of the College of Cardinals in the government of the Church and was sworn to by all the cardinals, in some cases with reservations. According to it, the Pope could create no more cardinals until their number had dropped to sixteen and there could be no more than twenty of them. The Pope was bound in this matter by the consent of all or at least of two-thirds of the

[76] B. Guillemain, *La cour pontificale*, 137–40.

[77] H. Schröder, *loc. cit.*, 179–92. Philip Hughes, *A History of the Church*, III (New York 1947), 143, calls Clement VI "as near an approach to Aristotle's magnificent man as the order of St. Benedict has ever known" (translator).

[78] G. Mollat, "Clément VI et la vicomtesse de Turenne," *MAH*, 73 (1961), 375–89; also, P. Piur, "Petrarcas 'Buch ohne Namen' und die päpstliche Kurie," *loc. cit.*, 349, 376 f.; J. E. Wrigley, "A rehabilitation of Clement VI. Sine nomine 13 and the kingdom of Naples," *Archivum historiae pontificiae*, 3 (1966), 127–38.

[1] *Clément VI. Lettres se rapportant à la France*, no. 5137 (6 December 1351).

[2] N. P. Zacour, "Talleyrand the Cardinal of Périgord, 1301–64," *Transactions of the American Philosophical Society*, new series, vol. 50, part 7 (1960), 21 ff.

cardinals; such consent was also required for any procedure against individual cardinals and for the alienation of any part of the Papal State. The revenues allotted by Nicholas IV to the College were to be guaranteed. The consent of the cardinals was to be obtained in filling the higher administrative posts, in granting tithes and subsidies to kings and princes, and in demanding tithes for the benefit of the *Camera Apostolica*. The Pope was not to hinder the cardinals' free expression of opinion. As was to be expected, half a year after his election the new Pope, following consultation with some of the cardinals and with legal experts, declared this capitulation null, as being incompatible with the *plenitudo potestatis*.[3]

The choice of the conclave, Stephen Aubert, from the Limousin, had studied canon law and had become Bishop of Noyon and Clermont. In 1342 his countryman, Clement VI, made him a Cardinal and later Bishop of Ostia and grand penitentiary.[4] Judged by the brilliant show of the previous pontificate, he was considered a "rough Pope," and his health was not too good. If he began at once with reforming the papal court, sent many curialists back to their benefices, reduced the size of his retinue, and intended to be a thrifty steward of ecclesiastical property, still his reform endeavours have often been exaggerated by comparing him with his predecessor. His reforms affected the orders also, especially the mendicants and the Hospitallers. He was clearly unlucky in his Eastern policy. He sought to aid Smyrna in its affliction and untiringly endeavoured to make peace between the warring maritime cities of Genoa and Venice, but he was very niggardly in his financial assistance and regarded the indispensable union with the Eastern Church as possible only in a total subjection to the papacy and the Western Church.[5] If his attitude to the question of the so often projected crusade was lacking in grandeur, his undertakings in Italy were all the more successful, and they were his real preoccupation.

Since the mid-century the idea of a return to Rome had acquired momentum, stimulated by the deteriorating situation in the Papal State and throughout Italy as well as by the serious threat posed by wandering mercenary bands to the hitherto so peaceful stay in Provence. For protection from surprise attacks and plundering, Avignon was surrounded from 1357 by strong walls and fortifications covering a wide area, and even clerics were called upon for contributions and services. As a rule it was possible to induce the companies to depart on payment of blackmail or to hire them for the papal armies in Italy.[6] Soon after his election the Pope had decided to

---

[3] *Innocent VI. Lettres secrètes et curiales*, no. 435 (6 July 1353); on this point see W. Ullmann, "The Legal Validity of the Papal Electoral Pacts," *EIC*, 12 (1956), 246–78.
[4] B. Guillemain, *La cour pontificale*, 140 f.; Innocent's genealogy, *ibid.*, 161, footnote 356.
[5] F. Giunta, "Sulla politica orientale di Innocenzo VI," *Storia e letteratura*, 71 (1958), 305–20.
[6] B. Guillemain, *op. cit.*, 615–25.

send there a vigorous personality, and he did so in selecting the former Archbishop of Toledo, now Cardinal of San Clemente, Gil de Albornoz.

Provided with almost unlimited authority, the Cardinal set out in August 1353.[7] He was to spend thirteen years in Italy, with a brief interruption, and, in spite of the Pope's lack of political judgment and the Curia's failure to supply funds, to become the second founder of the Papal State. He began the work of reconstruction in the *Patrimonium* proper, and at first had to deal with the most detested opponent of papal authority, the Prefect di Vico, labelled by the Pope *abominationis ydolum*.[8]

Cola di Rienzo had set out for Italy close on the heels of the Cardinal Legate.[9] Following his deposition from his six-months' tribuneship in December 1347, Rienzo had stayed in the Papal State and the Kingdom of Naples, usually in hiding with the Fraticelli of Monte Majella, before seeking out Charles IV at Prague in July 1350. He was there imprisoned and in the summer of 1352 turned over to the Curia, where, as a prisoner in the papal palace, he survived a trial. Innocent VI evidently placed his hopes for the pacification of the Eternal City on Rienzo's appearance as Senator, especially since repeated requests for the tribune's return came to the Curia from Perugia and Rome. After much hesitation Albornoz also let him have his way, but following a second tribuneship of only nine weeks, Rienzo met an inglorious end.[10]

Once the *Patrimonium* had been gained, Albornoz devoted himself to the Duchy of Spoleto and then to the Marches of Ancona and Romagna, where success was possible only after years of effort. Through the intrigues of the Visconti the legate even had to withdraw from Italy for a while, but after the renewal of his commission he won back for the Papal State the important city of Bologna. If the papacy could now be restored from Avignon to Rome, this was due to the military and administrative gifts of the Cardinal. The *Constitutiones Aegidianae,* or *Liber constitutionum sanctae matris ecclesiae,* published at the Parliament of Fano in 1357, provided a sure legal basis for administration, while the many fortifications erected at his orders were adequate strongholds for suppressing local risings. The Spanish College that he established at Bologna testifies to his interest in learning. According to all information, however, he never set foot in the Eternal City.[11] But the prematurely aged, sickly, and indecisive Pope could no longer realize his often expressed desire to go to Rome. He died at Avignon on 12 September 1362.

[7] *Innocent VI. Lettres secrètes et curiales,* no. 352–432 (30 June 1353). For Albornoz see *Dizionario biografico degli Italiani,* II (Rome 1960), 45–53 (with copious bibliography); "Il card. Albornoz nel VI centenario delle 'Constitutiones' 1357–1957," *Studia Picena,* 27 (1959); J. Glénisson-G. Mollat, *Gil Albornoz et Androin de la Roche 1353/67* (Paris 1964).
[8] *Innocent VI. Lettres secrètes et curiales,* no. 887.
[9] *Ibid.,* nos. 559, 563, 564, 566, 568.
[10] P. Piur, *Cola di Rienzo* (Vienna 1931), 195–216.
[11] V. Fanelli, "Roma e il cardinale Albornoz," *Studi Romani,* 6 (1958), 413–21.

The factional division in the Sacred College was apparently so complicated that the candidacy of a cardinal seemed hopeless. There is a probably not too reliable report of the election of Cardinal Hugh Roger, brother of Clement VI, who, however, did not accept. And there was talk of seeking to come to an agreement by compromise. William d'Aigrefeuille seems to have directed the attention of the electors to the Abbot of Saint-Victor de Marseille, who was thereupon chosen after a conclave of five days.[12] Since at the moment he was acting as legate in Naples, it was necessary to recall him before obtaining his consent to the election and publishing the result.

William Grimoard, from the vicinity of Avignon, was regarded as a fine canonist. He had been a professor at Montpellier and Avignon and shortly before his election had become Abbot of Saint-Victor.[13] The new Pope retained his monastic habit and even more so his monastic way of life. He understood the importance of studies, which he promoted by founding colleges and burses, while a large number of students were indebted to him, even for information. It should cause no surprise that he took steps against the luxury of the papal court and sent many curialists packing.[14] As a monk and never a cardinal, he found it difficult to maintain a frank relationship with the self-assured College of Cardinals and was often insecure *vis-à-vis* the great lords. This explains his frequently abrupt expressions and measures, for example, the creation of young William d'Aigrefeuille at Marseilles immediately before the departure for Italy. To the remonstrances of several members of the Sacred College he rejoined that he had even more cardinals in his capuche.[15] A man of a deep interior life and somewhat ignorant of the world, he did not always see through the diplomatic game and, curiously enough, fell prey to the allurement of political power. His predecessor had already had to deal with the wandering mercenary companies. Urban was deadly serious in seeking to end the scourge; but his burning appeals against them went abroad without great success and his efforts to divert these certainly experienced fighters to the crusade or to the East in general were in vain. There were also voices which did not expect much of such "crusaders."[16]

---

[12] N. P. Zacour, *op. cit.*, 64 f.

[13] B. Guillemain, *op. cit.*, 142 ff.; genealogy of the Grimoard family, *ibid.*, 164, footnote 375.

[14] *Baluze-Mollat*, I, 376 ff.

[15] *Baluze-Mollat*, I, 403; G. Pirchan, *Italien und Kaiser Karl IV. in der Zeit seiner zweiten Romfahrt*, II (Prague 1930), 159*–62*.

[16] A. Theiner, *Codex dipl. dom. temp.*, II, no. 410; *Baluze-Mollat*, I, 352, 357; P. Piur, "Petrarcas 'Buch ohne Namen' und die päpstliche Kurie," *loc. cit.*, 97 ff.; A. Cretoni, "Il Petrarca e Urbano V," *Studi Romani*, 9 (1961), 629–46.

At the beginning of Urban's reign the situation in Italy was not unfavourable, but only because of Albornoz, whom he confirmed in office. As Abbot of Marseilles and even earlier he had known the state of Italian affairs to some extent from several missions and he had personal experience of the despotic rule of the Visconti. Hence he immediately resumed the proceedings against Bernabò Visconti, uttered all possible condemnatory sentences against him in March 1363, and summoned a crusade against him. [17] It quickly became clear to him that only in Italy could he realize his great plans — elimination of the mercenary companies, crusade, union with the Greek Church, — once Italy had been pacified and all the forces of the peninsula brought together. Thus he made a change of policy, contrary to that followed by the great soldier and politician Albornoz.

The new policy involved secret negotiations with the Visconti behind the back of the Cardinal Legate and the appointment of Cardinal Androin, former Abbot of Cluny, an opponent of Albornoz and friend of the Milanese. The resulting peace with the Visconti burdened the Church with enormous payments to Bernabò for the evacuation of Bologna and was felt even by contemporaries to be pernicious and unworthy. The next task — a league to expel or exterminate the mercenaries — was also unsatisfactorily executed, for it forbade only future arrangements with them, and furthermore Florence held aloof. A meeting of Pope and Emperor at Avignon in the spring of 1365 was intended to further the achieving of the goals and, by means of an imperial journey to Rome, to assure the return of the Curia. Urban, however, quickly adopted the plan of going to the Eternal City without the Emperor. Objections to the Pope's intended journey to Italy came from all sides — from France and from the College of Cardinals — but he could not be dissuaded. After changing the date of departure several times he left Avignon on 30 April 1367 and on 4 June landed at Corneto in the Papal State, to be welcomed by the one who had restored his principality. After a brief rest the Pope proceeded to the security of Viterbo in preparation for entering Rome, with a strong military escort, on 16 October. [18] Earlier, on 23 August, had occurred the death of the great Cardinal who had so often been permitted to experience the gratitude of the prince.

In Italy the Pope's political aims quickly changed. [19] In an extensive league of the Curia with the smaller Lombard states the Visconti was defied. The Emperor, the Queen of Naples, and even several cities of Tuscany joined, but not Florence. It would be an exaggeration to say that the otherworldly monk had now become a politician, but he did not want to tolerate any great

---

[17] *Storia di Milano*, V, 420 ff.; *Urbain V. Lettres secrètes et curiales*, no. 414.

[18] *Baluze-Mollat*, IV, 131–37: "Iter italicum Urbani V Romani Pontificis."

[19] G. Pirchan, *Italien und Kaiser Karl IV. in der Zeit seiner zweiten Romfahrt*, 2 vols. (Prague 1930), with abundant literature.

power besides his own on Italian soil. This was no secret from Florentine diplomacy, which for that reason was not especially happy over the Pope's return. The Visconti tried to meet the threatening danger by an attack on the important territory of Mantua. Since, despite the concentration of a large army, the league had no successes in the field, the Emperor, who had meanwhile come to Italy, contrived to establish peace in accord with his policy of compensations, even against the real aims of the Pope, who had sought the complete subjugation of the Visconti.

The Pope, finally residing in Rome after many decades, devoted special attention to the repair and adornment of the Roman churches, especially the Vatican and Lateran basilicas. In the summer of 1368 he went to Viterbo and then for several months of that and the following years he stayed in the higher altitude of Montefiascone on the Lake of Bolsena.[20] In October the Emperor came to Rome, where his Queen received the imperial crown. There were long discussions of the political situation in North and Central Italy. The Pope's intention of exercising greater influence in Tuscany was only reluctantly encouraged by the Emperor and it was observed by Florence with much anxiety. In general, in conformity with the Emperor's policy, the delineation of the power system continued as it had been since the middle of the century. For the Pope this was a great disappointment, and gradually he became obsessed with the notion of a return to Provence.

The great creation of cardinals at Montefiascone in September 1368 was a bad omen: five Frenchmen, one Englishman, one Italian. Disorders in Rome and Viterbo, the hostile attitude of Perugia and of the Visconti, the disintegration of the papal league, and the recent flaring of the Hundred Years' War were assigned as reasons for this change. In vain did Catherine of Siena, Birgitta of Sweden, and Peter of Aragón — all of them regarded as supernaturally gifted — advise against it. French influences, above all that of the cardinals, were stronger, and the miscarriage of the Pope's political plans was the chief motive for his giving in. "The Holy Spirit led me here, and now he is leading me back for the honour of the Church." Thus he may have reassured himself, but to contemporaries it was a terrible disillusion-ment and, as became clear later, a serious mistake and a measure very difficult to understand.[21] Urban left Italy on 5 September 1370 and on the twenty-seventh of the month reentered Avignon. He was not long to enjoy that city's jubilation, for on 19 December he died. Not until five centuries later was he beatified.

---

[20] M. Antonelli, "La dimora estiva in Italia di Urbano V," *ASRomana*, 65 (1942), 153–61.
[21] *Baluze-Mollat*, IV, 136: "Sanctus Spiritus duxit me ad partes istas, et reducet me ad alias ad honorem sancte Ecclesie."

The conclave, which began on 29 December with seventeen cardinals, ended the following morning with the election of Cardinal Peter Roger, nephew of Clement VI. Gregory XI was crowned on 5 January 1371 and, in contrast to his predecessor, appeared on horseback in a colourful procession in Avignon. [22] Thus the so-called Limousin faction had provided its third Pope. [23] Elected at the age of forty-two, Gregory had been in the Curia for more than twenty years and so had ample opportunity of training and activity in ecclesiastical policies. When only nineteen, he had been made a Cardinal-Deacon by his uncle in 1348, but he continued his studies and acquired a solid and comprehensive education. [24] As Pope he too remained strongly attached to family and homeland. Of the twenty-one cardinals he created, eight were from his own land; there were eight other Frenchmen, two Italians, and one each from Geneva, Castile, and Aragón. [25]

Judgments of his personality and character vary greatly. In poor health and very sensitive, he is said to have been an indecisive brooder, a weak and easily influenced man, who liked especially to seek the solution of difficult problems in mystical enlightenment. All this was certainly present in this rich personality, but there were also other traits, including tenacity and energy and even unrelenting severity, as in his procedures against Milan and Florence, which can hardly be understood from a religious viewpoint. [26]

Gregory was experienced enough to comprehend, from the beginning of his pontificate, the necessity of the papacy's return to Rome, whether the report that he had earlier made a vow in this regard is true or not. But the abortive effort of his predecessor was an oppressive legacy. This catastrophe could always be brought up by the many, far too many, who held out for remaining at Avignon. But to the reasons hitherto in favour of Rome was now added the growing insecurity in the Midi because of the Hundred Years' War, and from 1372 official announcements of the impending journey to Rome were multiplied. But first the situation in North Italy had to be clarified. Gregory soon was resolved to make a clean sweep of the Visconti, as the chief enemies of the Papal State. [27] A great league against Milan was

---

[22] Account of the election in *Gregoire XI. Lettres secrètes et curiales relatives à la France*, no. 1 (no date); G. Mollat, "Relations politiques de Grégoire XI avec les Siennois et les Florentins," *MAH*, 68 (1956), 335–76.

[23] B. Guillemain, *op. cit.*, 144–48; genealogy, *ibid.*, 160, footnote 345.

[24] The contention that, after his elevation, he pursued studies at Perugia (G. Mollat, *The Popes at Avignon*, 59, and B. Guillemain, *op. cit.*, 118 ff.) does not seem to follow from *Baluze-Mollat*, I, 460.

[25] B. Guillemain, *op. cit.*, 187.

[26] E. Dupré-Theseider, *I papi di Avignone*, 193–99; G. Mollat, "Grégoire XI et sa légende," *RHE*, 49 (1954), 873–77; A. Segre, *I dispacci di Cristoforo da Piacenza*, 89.

[27] *Cristoforo da Piacenza*, 40: "valde animosus ad guerram"

formed in August 1371, a new cardinal legate proceeded to Lombardy, and Amadeus VI of Savoy assumed command of the troops, which were to be reinforced by a contingent from France under the Pope's brother, the Viscount of Turenne.

The institution of processes against the Visconti was proclaimed at the beginning of 1373 and then a crusade was preached against them. Considerable sums were demanded of cardinals and curialists, and contributions were imposed on all countries. Milanese envoys, whose instructions were intercepted, tried negotiations in vain; even the intercession of the Duke of Anjou was futile, and most of the cardinals were not in favour of yielding.[28] The journey to Italy now seemed to the Pope necessary for the destruction of the Visconti, and the spring of 1375 was considered. Many cardinals arranged lodging for themselves in Rome, the Pope's *magister hospitii* was sent there, and galleys were requested from Venice and Naples for September.[29] The Pope's tenacity attracted general attention, as when, in the consistory of 7 February 1375, the Duke of Anjou in a powerful speech advanced ten reasons why the Curia should remain at Avignon. The reply, made by Cardinal James Orsini, referred emphatically to the Papal State as the Pope's country and maintained that its confused situation was due to its sovereign's tarrying abroad.[30] Even the pleas of the Pope's closest relatives and of the people of Avignon were ineffectual; but the date of departure was postponed in August until Easter of 1376.[31]

Earlier, in June 1375, the Curia had been obliged to make peace with Milan because of the defection of several of its allies, but presumably the Pope did not regard it as a real peace. No good was to be expected of the league made between Milan and Florence in the summer of the same year. Florence succeeded in gaining many cities of Tuscany and parts of the Papal State and in inciting revolt against papal rule, for the extravagant demands for subsidies had contributed seriously to a lowering of morale.[32] In addition to Viterbo, Perugia, and Città di Castello, many other cities and territories were in open revolt. Nevertheless, the Pope held to his plan and, as he put it, if at least a foot of ground in his state was left, he intended to be in Italy in the spring.[33] Therefore, extensive preparations were made, mercenary captains were hired, long consistories were held, and all-out war against Florence was decided. The preparations included the issuing of a bull on

[28] *Ibid.*, 56: "nullo modo sperandum est de pace vivente isto papa."

[29] *Ibid.*, 74: "prima die septembris intrabit mare et ibit infallibiliter ad urbem, nisi mors ipsum impediat."

[30] *Ibid.*, 71.

[31] *Ibid.*, 76; G. Mollat, "Relations politiques de Grégoire XI," *loc. cit.*, 369.

[32] J. Glénisson, "Les origines de la révolte de l'état pontifical en 1375," *RSTI*, 5 (1951), 145–68.

[33] *Cristoforo da Piacenza*, 83.

annates, pawning of papal treasures, and extensive striking of coins in Avignon.[34] In the summer the direst threats were directed at Florence: interdict, prohibition of clerics' staying there, suppression of the episcopal see and deprivation of civil rights, confiscation of all property of Florentine citizens in foreign lands, and hence the paralyzing of commerce.[35] Meanwhile, *taxatores domorum* and the papal *capella* set out for Rome. The final strong exertions of the cardinals, the Dukes of Anjou and Burgundy, and the Pope's relatives, who appeared in black as a sign of grief, were unable at the last moment to dissuade Gregory from his purpose. On 13 September he left Avignon forever.[36]

The question of the influence of Saint Catherine of Siena on Gregory's return to Rome has received answers greatly differing from one another. Caterina di Jacopo Benincasa was active as intermediary between Florence and the Pope, though with no official commission from the city on the Arno. From the middle of June 1376 she spent three months at Avignon and presumably she conferred with the Pope. Without falling into the too common error of overestimating her importance in the politics of her time, it may perhaps be said that, by her repeated written admonitions to Gregory, who often wavered and was seeking a sign from heaven, she confirmed him in his resolve. In this matter she was more successful than in her propaganda for the crusade. But the total silence of the envoys of Mantua and Siena, reporting from Avignon, in regard to her activity is striking.[37]

On 2 October 1376 the papal fleet at Marseilles put to sea, but persistent storms forced frequent landings, and it was not until 6 December that Gregory reached the Papal State at Corneto. With thirteen cardinals he made

---

[34] *Ibid.*, 86 f.; H. Hoberg, *Die Inventare des päpstlichen Schatzes in Avignon* (Rome 1944), 535 ff.

[35] G. Mollat, "Préliminaires de la guerre des otto santi (1371–75)," *Académie des inscriptions et belles lettres, comptes rendus des séances* (1955), 113–17; G. A. Brucker, *Florentine Politics and Society 1343–78* (Princeton 1962), with all the literature; M. B. Becker, "Church and State in Florence on the Eve of the Renaissance 1343–82," *Speculum*, 37 (1962), 509–27.

[36] *Cristoforo da Piacenza*, 94 f., G. Mollat, "Relations politiques de Grégoire XI," *loc. cit.*, 371–74.

[37] E. Sommer von Seckendorff, *Die kirchenpolitische Tätigkeit der hl. Katharina von Siena unter Papst Gregor XI. 1371–78* (Berlin-Leipzig 1917); R. Fawtier, *Sainte Catherine de Sienne, Essai de critique des sources*, I (Rome 1921), II (Rome 1930); E. Dupré-Theseider, *Epistolario di santa Caterina da Siena*, I (Rome 1940); Catherine of Siena, *Politische Briefe. Übertragung und Einführung* by F. Strobel (Einsiedeln and Cologne 1944); R. Fawtier-L. Canet, *La double expérience de Catherine Benincasa (sainte Catherine de Sienne)* (Paris 1948); A. Levasti, *Santa Caterina da Siena* (Turin 1947); I. Taurisano, *Santa Caterina da Siena* (Rome 1948); E. Dupré-Theseider, "La duplice esperienza di s. Caterina da Siena," *RSIt*, 62 (1950), 533–74; L. Zanini, "Bibliografia analitica di santa Caterina da Siena 1901 al 1950," *Pubblicazioni dell'università cattolica del s. Cuore*, 58 (1956), 325–74, 62 (1958), 265–367 (thus far 670 of 1044 projected numbers).

his solemn entry into Rome on 17 January 1377.[38] It was high time. Revolts and general unrest had reached dangerous proportions. Hatred against the foreign governors and their fortresses had broken out with unlooked-for violence, nourished by the probably exaggerated dread of the establishing of an Angevin State in Lombardy and Tuscany. The possibility of the loss of the entire Papal State and Rome and even of an ecclesiastical schism in this very papacy was not out of the question. The worst, then, could at least be prevented. Florence, affected less in the spiritual than in the commercial sphere, utilized the mediation of Milan, and the Pope followed suit. A great congress was summoned to Sarzana for February 1378. But before it had completed its work death overtook the Pope on 27 March, and the conclusion of peace with Florence and Milan was reserved for his successor in Rome, Urban VI.

CHAPTER 40

The Curia at Avignon

Avignon, on the banks of the Rhone in Provence, occasioned the expression "Babylonian Exile." For almost seventy years it was the papal residence, though the seat of the papacy was never transferred there. The term "Babylonian Exile" refers to the desolation of Rome and implies an accusation, but recent investigations of the Avignon period have produced a certain mitigation of earlier judgments.[1] In the immediate vicinity of the French Kingdom as it then existed, the city, by its size and favourable location, afforded a respectable site for a court. And, following the purchase of the city and of the surrounding territory by Clement VI in 1348, Avignon was considered a part of the Papal State.

The *palais des papes* was erected over a period of two decades at the midcentury. Begun by Benedict XII soon after his election, at first a gloomy, monastery-like fortress, it was completed by Clement VI as a princely palace. The mighty exterior was designed by French architects; the interior was decorated mostly by Italian artists.[2] The cardinals and the high curial

---

[38] *Baluze-Mollat*, I, 440 f.; P. Ronzy, *Le voyage de Grégoire XI ramenant la papauté d'Avignon à Rome (1376–77)*, suivi du texte latin et la traduction française de l'Itinerarium Gregorii XI de Pierre Ameilh (Florence 1952); also, *Baluze-Mollat*, II, 714. Relations between Pope and Emperor were strained because of the election of Wenceslas as German King; *cf.* H. Helbling, *Saeculum Humanum* (Naples 1958), 148–68 (Niccolò dei Beccari to Charles IV); R. Folz, "Der Brief des italienischen Humanisten Niccolò dei Beccari an Karl IV.," *HJ*, 82 (1963), 148–62.

[1] B. Guillemain, "Punti di vista sul papato Avignonese," *AstIt*, 111 (1953), 181–206.

[2] The best account is still L. H. Labande, *Le palais des papes et les monuments d'Avignon au XIVe siècle*, 2 vols. (Marseilles 1925), with its copious bibliography; A. Pelzer, *Ad-*

officials and their offices were at first lodged in leased or sequestered houses.[3] But there was soon much constructing of palaces, monasteries, hospitals, hospices, business houses, and the now greatly expanded city was protected and defended by a powerful ring of walls. The summer heat could be easily endured in the neighbourhood, famed for its natural beauty, as in John XXII's summer residences at Pont-Sorgue and Châteauneuf-du-Pape. Close by, on the other side of the Rhone, Villeneuve-lès-Avignon offered Pope and cardinals a pleasant and secure abode.

The large incomes of the cardinals were used not only for maintaining princely courts but for art and learning and the building and adorning of churches and chapels in Avignon. The account books of the *Camera Apostolica* occasionally provide glimpses of the carefree life and bustle at this ecclesiastical court. If the extent or excess of the princely household depended on the personality of the reigning Pope, in any event there gradually developed an elegant, even magnificent, style, which was at its best in the great Church solemnities, in consistories, and in the reception of numerous kings, princes, and ambassadors. For the city of Avignon the papal stay meant great structural changes, a large increase in population, an extraordinary stimulus to commerce, and a cosmopolitan mode of life.

In it the Papal Curia constituted a special state in stark contrast to the city population, despite common interests and mutual influence. There was a Curia in the sense of a princely court at Rome already in the High Middle Ages; the household of Boniface VIII is known in detail. But now it was further enlarged and, more important, we have exact information about it. At first Italians still predominated in the higher posts and offices, but the middle and lower personnel were at once recruited from countrymen of the reigning Pope.[4] Thus, Clement V enlisted a sort of bodyguard from his immediate homeland. The systematizing mind of John XXII applied itself even to the household and regulated everything more exactly, but his prescriptions were again and again modified by his successors. More than in the case of other princely courts, a change of pontificate involved a change of personnel and practice, even in the operation of the offices. But in general the style of the *officiales curie* strongly resembled that of the French royal court.[5]

denda et Emendanda ad F. Ehrle historiae bibl. Rom. Pont., tomus I (Rome 1947), 167–78; E. Castelnuovo, *Un pittore italiano alla corte di Avignone, Matteo Giovanetti e la pittura in Provenza nel secolo XIV* (Turin 1962); F. Enaud, "Les fresques de Simone Martini à Avignon," *Les monuments hist. de la France*, 9 (1963), 115–71.

[3] For housing at the Curia and especially in Avignon see P. M. Baumgarten, *Aus Kanzlei und Kammer* (Freiburg 1907), 54 ff.

[4] G. Mollat, "Clément VI et le Limousin," *Journal des Savants* (1959), 16–27; B. Guillemain, "Les Français du Midi à la cour pontificale d'Avignon," *Annales du Midi*, 74 (1962), 29–38.

[5] B. Guillemain, "Les carrières des officiers pontificaux au XIVe siècle," *MA*, 69 (1963), 565–81.

The management of the Apostolic Palace was the charge of the *Magister hospitii papae*. *Clerici capelle* and *cantores* took care of the liturgical rites in the papal *capella*. The *capellani commensales*, whose duties were not always strictly defined, were influential persons, who were frequently promoted to episcopal sees. In immediate attendance on the Pope were the *cubicularii*, among whom physicians were specified, and the *Magister sacri palatii*, usually a Dominican. The division of the household administration into four basic functions — kitchen, food, drink, stable — was already old. They were retained, even though circumstances changed and new divisions were created, such as the *magister aquae, magister cere,* and *magister folrarie.* Even in periods of severe financial strain the office of almoner *(panhota)* got large contributions from the papal chest for feeding and clothing many hundreds of poor persons. All these functions were performed by clerics, even though lay persons could have done as well or better. In addition, there was a lay personnel of probably the same number: porters *(hostiarii maiores et minores)*, soldiers and police *(servientes armorum)*, and a sort of Noble Guard *(scutiferi* and *domicelli)*. Some 500 persons were employed in the household.[6] Many offices were life-grants, while others, especially those in closest touch with the Pope, ended at his death. Only a portion of these courtiers were *familiares* of the Pope; this title was regarded as a distinction and it was also useful for obtaining benefices. To satisfy the conceit of many ecclesiastics there was an increasing number of honorary nominations as papal chaplains — for the period from John XXII to Benedict XIII the number is estimated as 3,000.[7]

The French orientation is seen clearest in the College of Cardinals.[8] Shortly after his coronation at Lyons, Clement V created ten new cardinals — nine Frenchmen and one Englishman. The ratio of preponderance was thereby decisively shifted to the disadvantage of the Italians and so it remained. In his three promotions Clement V created twenty-four cardinals. Of twenty South French thirteen were from his native Gascony; three of the others were from northern France, one from England, none from Italy or the Empire. Matters were similar in the succeeding pontificates. From 1316 to 1375 the figures were: ninety French, fourteen Italians, five Spaniards, one Englishman. Particularly obtrusive in all the Avignon pontificates, except that of Benedict XII, were relatives and countrymen from Gascony, Quercy, and the Limousin. A representation of the Universal Church was out of the question; the influence of the French crown was constant and unabated, and

---

[6] G. Mollat, "Règlement d'Urbain V sur les insignes des sergents d'armes des portiers et des courriers de la cour pontificale," *SteT,* 235 (1964), 165–69.

[7] B. Guillemain, "Les chapelains d'honneur des papes d'Avignon," *MAH,* 64 (1952), 217–38.

[8] G. Mollat, "Contribution à l'histoire du sacré collège de Clément V à Eugène IV," *RHE,* 46 (1951), 22–112, 566–94; H. Hofmann, *Kardinalat und kuriale Politik in der ersten Hälfte des 14. Jahrhunderts* (diss. phil., Leipzig 1935).

several members of the Sacred College had formerly been in the service of that crown. In the Avignon period the revenues of the College were considerable, especially those accruing from prodigal gifts at papal elections and from numerous benefices, but on the outbreak of the Great Schism they declined.

Participation of the cardinals in the government of the Church was manifested principally in the consistory, in judicial commissions, and in legations. Several examples are known of open expression of opinions in consistory, as well as of weak giving in. The effort of the conclave of 1352 to bind the future Pope in law to the demands of the College, by means of a written election capitulation, failed in part. However, in general the Pope's freedom of action was restricted by the College of Cardinals. The number of cardinals stayed at about twenty. Most of them maintained a large house with a numerous retinue and dependents, and the Popes quite often had to urge them to moderation. The extant last wills of several cardinals show that they had the disposal of great wealth. Especially well known figures who held the cardinalatial dignity for decades were Napoleone Orsini,[9] James Stephaneschi,[10] William de Longis,[11] and Talleyrand de Périgord.[12]

The term "Avignon Papacy" connotes also the centralized system of Church government, which was decidedly different from the previous regime and created new forms in the ecclesiastical constitution and the papal system of finance and an unqualified Church bureaucracy. Together with the excessive favouring of countrymen and relatives in the conferring of benefices, it evoked strong criticism then and later and became an important ingredient of the *gravamina* for several centuries. In spite of all reform efforts, important elements of this papal absolutism are still in force.

The juridical basis for the *plenitudo administrationis* had been laid in the thirteenth century. The Popes at Avignon accepted it and developed it in masterful fashion in the so-called reservations. If the notion of "vacant at the Curia" was extended by Boniface VIII to mean a distance of two days' journey from Rome, Clement V extended the reservation to the benefices of bishops who had been consecrated at the Curia or whose resignation, transfer, or exchange of benefice had taken place at the Curia. John XXII went still further in his Constitution "Ex Debito" of 1316, by including under a vacancy at the Curia the deposition of a benefice holder, the annulment of an election, the rejection of a postulation, and resignation into the hands of

[9] C. A. Willemsen, *Kardinal Napoleon Orsini 1263–1342* (Berlin 1927).

[10] A. Frugoni, "La figura e l'opera del cardinale Jacopo Stefaneschi, 1270–1343," *Atti della Accademia nazionale dei Lincei*, serie ottava, Rendiconti classe scienze morali, storiche e filologiche, 5 (1950).

[11] G. Marchetti Longhi, *Il cardinale Guglielmo de Longis di Adraria di Bergamo* (Rome 1962).

[12] N. P. Zacour, "Talleyrand the Cardinal of Périgord, 1301–64," *Transactions of the American Philosophical Society,* new series, vol. 50, part 7 (1960).

the Pope; also comprised were the benefices of cardinals and of almost all curial officials. Furthermore, probably for political reasons chiefly, the more important benefices in the Papal State and in Central and North Italy were reserved for two years and this term was again and again extended. A year later, in his Constitution "Execrabilis," the Pope turned to the subject of pluralism. For the future it was permitted only to retain one benefice having the care of souls and one other without it; all others were to be resigned to the bishops, but the benefices thus vacated were all reserved to the Holy See. Benedict XII's Constitution "Ad Regimen" of 1335 comprised all previous reservations and some new ones. It should come as no surprise, then, that, with such precedents, Urban V in 1363 reserved to the Holy See the filling of all patriarchal and episcopal sees and of all monasteries of men and women of a specified income level. Thereby was attained in theory the complete bureaucratic supremacy of the Curia. [13]

The implementation of these important constitutions required numerous offices and a powerful civil service. [14] The Apostolic Chancery was responsible for the technical aspect. Its chief, the vice-chancellor, belonged to the College of Cardinals. The regulations and rules of the chancery determined even the details of its routine. Its personnel comprised *notarii, referendarii, abbreviatores, scriptores, correctores, registratores, bullatores,* and the *auditor litterarum contradictarum.* Procurators and agents managed the business of their clients, for they alone were at home with the extremely complicated routine.

Ordinarily, every piece of business, and especially questions of benefices, began with the submitting of a petition which, according to the degree of its importance, had to be referred to the Pope, the vice-chancellor, or one of the *referendarii* for approval (signature). Then followed the dating, which was decisive for all that followed. The majority of approved petitions were, probably from the time of Benedict XII, registered for easier verification. After the perhaps necessary examination of the candidate, the petition proceeded to the *abbreviatores,* who prepared the rough draft. Then followed the fair copy, the assessing of the fee, the placing of the seal, the posting in the *registrum* of bulls, the making of the payments due to the *Camera*

[13] E. Göller, *Die Einnahmen Johanns XXII.,* 93; *Rep Germ,* I (1916); Barraclough, *Papal Provisions;* B. Guillemain, *La politique bénéficiale du pape Benoît XII, 1334–1342* (Paris 1952); C. J. Godfrey, "Pluralists in the Province of Canterbury in 1366," *JEH,* 11 (1960), 23–40; D. E. R. Watt, "University Clerks and Rolls of Petitions for Benefices," *Speculum,* 34 (1959), 213–29; G. Brucker, "An unpublished Source on the Avignonese Papacy. The letters of Francisco Bruni," *Tr,* 19 (1963), 351–70.

[14] E. von Ottenthal, *Die päpstlichen Kanzleiregeln von Johannes XXII. bis Nicolaus V.* (Innsbruck 1888); M. Tangl, *Die päpstlichen Kanzleiordnungen von 1200–1500* (Innsbruck 1894); F. Bock, "Einführung in das Registerwesen des avignonesischen Papsttums," *QFIAB,* 21 (1941); P. Herde, *Beiträge zum päpstlichen Kanzlei- und Urkundenwesen im 13. Jahrhundert* (Munich 1961).

Apostolica, the appointing of executors to carry out the papal directive. The formal part was now completed.

But it was seldom that a papal order realized its goal at once. The case was relatively simple if a benefice was vacant because of the death of the previous incumbent, but there were ordinarily several persons seeking it. The usual reasons for the vacancy of a benefice were different: resignation, acquiring of another benefice, failure to obtain ordination in benefices involving the care of souls, marriage of a cleric in minor orders, illegitimate birth, lack of the required age, bodily defects, pluralism without a proper dispensation. If difficulties arose, a suit was instituted before the *auditores sacri palatii* (the *Rota*), again beginning with the filing of a petition and including many steps and much time, and even then often unsuccessfully.[15] All these proceedings involved fees, perquisites, and considerable gratuities.

In spite of many losses, the series of registers of the Vatican Archives for the fourteenth century include hundreds of thousands of such documents — for example, for John XXII about 65,000 in the local registers alone, for Clement VI about 90,000, for Innocent VI 30,000, for Urban V 25,000, for Gregory XI 35,000. The enormous quantity of written documents proceeding from the Curia, especially the routine affairs of the Apostolic Chancery, posed serious problems in regard to their dispatch. A great part, possibly half, was taken along by the petitioners themselves; a further considerable percentage by persons traveling from Avignon to the areas in question. Neither sort went at the expense of the Curia. Much was conveyed by means of the world-wide business connections of banking firms which had an establishment in Avignon.

Only in regard to especially important documents, chiefly political and urgent, was recourse had to the Pope's *cursores* or to high ecclesiastics or religious, chiefly Dominicans. The *cursores papae* were employed for ceremonial summonses rather than for ordinary carrying. In the Avignon period there were on the average about fifty of them, gathered into a sort of college under the *magister cursorum* and enjoying a position of trust. They belonged to the higher ranks of the curial personnel and to the more stable element around the Pope, especially when of advanced age. They made purchases for the papal palace and its kitchen and cellar. In addition to these *cursores papae* there were also *cursores curiam sequentes,* who for the most part had connections with the *mercatores curie* and acted as a sort of postal service. Weighty political communications were often prepared in duplicate and forwarded separately. The use of ciphers, usually as *cedulae interclusae,* was resorted to in the interests of secrecy; such documents were often written by

---

[15] W. Engel, "Würzburg und Avignon. Kurienprozesse des Würzburger Domkapitels im 14. Jahrhundert," *ZSavRGkan,* 35 (1948), 150–200; J. Reetz, "Kuriales Prozesswesen um 1340. Nachrichten aus Avignonesischen Akten in Hamburg," *ADipl,* 9/10 (1963 f.), 395–414.

the Pope personally or by the *camerlengo* and, it seems, were rarely registered. Moreover, messages were frequently delivered to the Curia by word of mouth, guaranteed by the proper credentials.[16]

The most important administrative body was the *Camera Apostolica.*[17] It was presided over by the *camerlengo,* usually an archbishop, who in the past had been employed in the Curia and as collector outside. The *camerlengo* and a small staff of cameral clerks and secretaries took care of political correspondence, and the personnel of the papal court took the oath of office in his presence. We know relatively little about the *Camera's* secret policies but a great deal about its administration of finance. The ledgers were the "Introitus et Exitus," that is, income and expenditure, and the accounts of the collectors, who, as *nuntii et collectores,* collected throughout Christendom the moneys owed to the *Camera.*[18] In addition, there was a whole series of special registers for tithes, revenues of vacant benefices (*fructus medii temporis*), procurations, payments due, and payments received. The register of division dealt with the receipts from *servitia,* visitations, and *census,* which since the thirteenth century had been divided equally between Pope and cardinals.

The most important types of income were *servitia,* annates, tithes, subsidies, and *spolia.* Since the High Middle Ages Pope and cardinals had received an increasing amount of money gifts, which were gradually stabilized and regarded as of obligation. Registers of *servitia* due are extant from 1295. Bishoprics and monasteries having an annual income of more than 100 gold florins were bound to the *servitium* on the occasion of a nomination made by the Curia. This amounted to one-third of the first year's income and could be required only once in a year. The methodical development of the system of reservations constantly increased the number of those thus obliged, and from the middle of the fourteenth century almost all consistorial benefices were included. One half of the *servitium* went to the Pope, the other to the College of Cardinals; the cardinals present in consistory at the conferring of the benefice received equal shares. Likewise, five *servitia minuta,* in the amount of five cardinalatial shares, were assigned to the curial officials,

---

[16] Y. Renouard, "Comment les papes d'Avignon expédiaient leur courrier," *RH,* 180 (1937), 1–29; G. Mollat, "Correspondance de Clément VI par cédules," *Bollettino dell'Archivio paleografico italiano,* nuova serie, II–III (1956 f.), parte II, 175–78.

[17] P. M. Baumgarten, *Aus Kanzlei und Kammer* (Freiburg 1907); *idem, Von der apostolischen Kanzlei* (Cologne 1908); G. Mollat, "Contributions à l'histoire de la chambre apostolique au XIVᵉ siècle," *RHE,* 45 (1950), 82–94; P. Gasnault, "Notes et documents sur la chambre apostolique à l'époque d'Urbain V," *MAH,* 70 (1958), 367–94. List of *camerlenghi* and treasurers in K. H. Schäfer, *Die Ausgaben der apostolischen Kammer unter Johann XXII.,* 5–7.

[18] J. P. Kirsch, *Die päpstlichen Kollektorien in Deutschland während des 14. Jahrhunderts* (Paderborn 1894); J. Favier, "Le niveau de vie d'un collecteur et d'un souscollecteur apostolique à la fin du XIVᵉ siècle," *Annales du Midi,* 75 (1963), 31–48.

in accord with a complicated method. The registers of dues at first served for the determining of the amount of the income, but from the end of the century this was taken care of by the *Liber Taxarum* of the *Camera Apostolica*.[19]

Annates first made their appearance at the Curia when in 1306 Clement V demanded the first year's income of all benefices, vacant or to be vacated, in England, Scotland, and Ireland, without regard to the type of nomination. He based this on the classical statement: *quia quod postulat inferior, potest etiam superior*. The Council of Vienne raised strong opposition and demanded a sufficient income for the one who obtained the benefice. John XXII also prescribed annates, sometimes for almost all of Europe, at other times for several ecclesiastical provinces or countries. In 1326 he decreed that annates were due from all benefices vacated at the Curia and continually repeated these reservations. The amount of annates fluctuated in the fourteenth century but for the most part corresponded to the assessment of tithes. "Annata, seu medii fructus primi anni," was a favourite definition from the end of the century. Considered bound to annates were benefices with an income in excess of twenty-four gold florins. Since annates went to the papal treasury in their entirety, they constituted the surest source of income and in most cases equalled the *servitia* in their amount.[20]

Compared with the previous century, the proceeds from the still frequently demanded tithes had greatly decreased.[21] The great crusade tithes of the Second Council of Lyons and those of Boniface VIII had still not been entirely paid and settled when the Council of Vienne demanded from all Christendom another crusade tithe for six years. John XXII did the same at the end of his pontificate, but Benedict XII countermanded the tithe and ordered the return of the money already collected. Clement VI, Innocent VI, and Urban V again prescribed general tithes but without much success. In the course of the century demands for tithes were very frequently made in particular territories but the proceeds had to be shared with the local lords. The Kings of France received most of the crusade tithes, without having to account for them or pay them back when no crusade materialized.

Originally a spontaneous donation in return for a specific thing, the

[19] E. Göller, *Die Einnahmen der apostolischen Kammer unter Johann XXII.*, 20*-52*; idem, "Der liber taxarum der päpstlichen Kammer," *QFIAB*, 8 (1905), 113–73, 305–43; H. Hoberg, "Taxae de communibus servitiis ex libris obligationum ab anno 1295 usque ad annum 1455 confectis," *SteT*, 144 (1949); J. Favier, "Temporels ecclésiastiques et taxation fiscale, le poids de la fiscalité pontificale au XIVe siècle," *Journal des Savants* (1964), 102–27.
[20] J. P. Kirsch, *Die päpstlichen Annaten in Deutschland während des 14. Jahrhunderts* (Paderborn 1903); F. Baix, *La chambre apostolique et les "Libri annatarum" de Martin V, 1417–1431*, première partie (1947), with full details of the literature.
[21] E. Hennig, *Die päpstlichen Zehnten aus Deutschland im Zeitalter des avignonesischen Papsttums und während des Grossen Schismas* (Halle 1909).

subsidium caritativum was regulated in the fourteenth century in regard to the amount and made obligatory. For the most part it was collected in locally restricted areas, chiefly for the unending wars in Italy. A *subsidium* demanded in French bishoprics by John XXII brought in between 200,000 and 300,000 florins.[22] Seizure of the estates *(spolia)* of cardinals and higher prelates who had died at the Curia was an old practice, but from the fourteenth century it was demanded on the basis of special reservations until finally Urban V reserved to himself the estates of all bishops, abbots, deans, provosts, and rectors.

The direction of the treasury at the Curia was the duty of the *thesaurarius,* whose office was sometimes shared by two men. Working closely with the treasurer were the *depositarii,* the representatives of the banking firms which gave credit and made loans and saw to the transfer of money. In spite of the imposing mass of account books for the fourteenth century, the question rises whether they afford a complete picture of the Curia's conduct of finances and its background. Lately the opinion has been maintained that they do not represent a balance but rather serve as receipts for sums paid in and as vouchers to the credit of the acting officials; hence, basically they noted only that which had to be ascertained.[23] In any case, in addition to the ordinary administration there were secret funds, which were also called the Pope's privy purse. Clement V had a *liber tam de secretis receptis quam expensis* and records of *dona data domino* and *servitia secreta,* which he had destroyed shortly before his death. For the war in Lombardy John XXII contributed more than 400,000 gold florins "ex coffinis suis," "de bursa sua."

It has been estimated that John XXII had an average annual income of 230,000 gold florins, Benedict XII 165,000, Clement VI 190,000, Innocent VI 250,000, Urban V 260,000, and Gregory XI 480,000. The finances of Clement V are the least clear. Of course, he had received out of the treasure left in Perugia by Boniface VIII and Benedict XI only what he was able to have sent to Lyons for his coronation. Shipments arranged later were plundered at Lucca and Assisi. Just the same he left large sums of money — not to the Church but to his relatives. The treasure amassed by John XXII amounted to about 1,000,000 gold florins; that of the frugal Benedict XII to about 1,500,000. On the other hand, at the death of the very hospitable and generous Clement VI only a small estate remained. The treasure was stored in the mighty fortress at Avignon in secure vaults of the great towers close to the papal bedrooms. Inventories surviving from this period list many coffers of gold and silver coins, then gold and silver vessels and *objets*

---

[22] P. Gasnault, "La perception, dans le royaume de France, du subside solicité par Jean XXII 'contra haereticos et rebelles partium Italiae,'" *MAH,* 69 (1957), 273–319.

[23] J. Favier, "Introitus et Exitus sous Clément VII et Benoît XIII, problèmes de diplomatique et d'interprétation," *Bollettino dell'Archivio paleografico italiano,* new series, II–III (1956 f.), part I, 285–94.

d'art, many expensive gold rings with precious stones, probably accruing for the most part from the *spolia* of cardinals and bishops, costly fabrics, mitres, and books. Cash in the treasure grew steadily less from the mid-century, and frequently valuables of precious metals had to be converted into coin to defray the expenses of the wars in Italy.[24]

In the ledgers of the central administration expenses were classified under the following heads: kitchen, food, drink, stables, clothing and fabrics, *objets d'art* and finery, library, construction, the official seal, extraordinary wages and armaments, *pro cera et quibusdam aliis* (chiefly war expenses), salaries, real estate and houses, alms, and miscellaneous. The average annual expenses of John XXII were computed as 233,000 gold florins, of Benedict XII 96,000, of Clement VI 165,000, of Innocent VI 260,000, of Urban V 300,000, and of Gregory XI 480,000. But it is to be noted that we are insufficiently informed about extraordinary revenues and expenditures. The wars in Italy consumed vast sums — sixty-three percent of the expenses in the pontificate of John XXII and then especially in those of Innocent VI and Gregory XI. Between ten and twenty per cent went for the salaries of officials, and to these must be added the expenses for the maintenance of the court and the curialists. The household of the Popes at Avignon was furnished essentially by the local area, but expenditures for imported luxuries still accounted for from five to ten percent of the annual budget, and the expenses for Clement VI's coronation banquet amounted to over 15,000 gold florins.

Unlike the government of individual states, the Curia had a thoroughly international character with a ceaseless coming and going, to and from all parts of Christendom. And these transactions had been developed since the thirteenth century largely out of great business undertakings, but only on the part of those who had close political connections with the Curia, especially the Florentine wholesale merchants: Bardi, Peruzzi, Acciaiuoli, Bonacorsi, and Alberti. Only Clement V, immediately after his election, broke off all relations with banks and had the money administered by clerics and deposited in monasteries. In view of his personality this is not surprising. Though the rapid development of the curial financial system really began in his pontificate, his inconstant nature and his prolonged wanderings rendered banks out of the question as institutes of credit. But later Avignon became a first-class commercial centre as probably the third city in size at that time, with some 30,000 inhabitants, where most of the great commercial houses set up offices. After the collapse of Florentine high finance around the middle of the century other banking houses, including Italian firms with Guelf sympathies, were temporarily made use of until it was possible to resume business with the Florentine bankers. Not only money transactions in the

[24] H. Hoberg, "Die Inventare des päpstlichen Schatzes in Avignon, 1314–76," *SteT*, 111 (1944); P. Guidi, "Inventari di libri nelle serie dell'Archivio Vaticano, 1287–1459," *SteT*, 135 (1948).

strict sense were handled by the commercial houses. They were also forwarding agents for the mails and were known as suppliers of commodities and news.[25] Under John XXII and Benedict XII income exceeded expenditures and made possible the investing of the reserve, which had to be drawn upon for the higher expenses under Clement VI and Innocent VI. Urban V and Gregory XI contrived to keep abreast of continually mounting expenditures only by means of loans. Though the revenues of the Curia were smaller in comparison with those of the Kings of France, England, and Naples, they were nevertheless always imposing sums.

It is difficult to resist the impression that at Avignon the Curia felt free to dispose at its discretion of the money gathered from the whole Christian world. Clement V especially, *pastor senza legge*, was outstanding for such caprice. Even the incomplete financial data of his pontificate show clearly that he dealt irresponsibly with the Church's material treasure. Of the 1,000,000 gold florins at his disposal at the close of his reign more than 800,000 went to a nephew, the Viscount of Lomagne, for whom he had already purchased the Château Monteux for the custody of his money and treasure. To the Kings of France and England he made over huge sums in tithes with no obligation of accounting for them. John XXII, elected after a vacancy of two years, received only 70,000 gold florins, half of which was the share of the College of Cardinals. The suit instituted by John XXII, after much patient waiting, against the heirs of Clement V lasted for years, but the Pope was able to recover 150,000 gold florins.[26]

This state of affairs did not escape criticism from those affected. The Council of Vienne summed up much that earlier had been expressed only by complaining voices. Throughout the century, especially during the Great Schism, bishops and abbots and even entire ecclesiastical provinces sought to defend themselves against being rendered impotent by the Curia. Above all, the unceasing and inconsiderate demands for money and the defective administration of the systems of benefices and finances gave scandal. It is true that the initiative did not always lie with the Curia, yet it did bear the responsibility when it yielded to the often very importunate and menacing wishes of kings and princes in nominations to offices and in demands for tithes. Every possibility for the obtaining of money was exploited ruthlessly. For example, benefices often remained vacant for a year or longer to enable the Curia to acquire the revenues during this period; or high-ranking prelates had to assume all the still unpaid *servitia* of their predecessors. Particularly

---

[25] Y. Renouard, "La consommation des grands vins du Bourbonnais et de Bourgogne à la cour pontificale d'Avignon," *Annales de Bourgogne*, 24 (1952), 221–44; R. Delort, "Note sur les achats de draps et d'étoffes effectués par la chambre apostolique des papes d'Avignon (1316–1417)," *MAH*, 74 (1962), 215–88.

[26] F. Ehrle, "Der Nachlass Clemens' V. und der in Betreff desselben von Johann XXII. (1318–34) geführte Prozess," *ALKGMA*, 5 (1889), 1–158.

irresponsible was the manipulation of ecclesiastical censures when payments promised under oath were not made on time. The infliction of suspension, excommunication, and interdict followed automatically. Thus on 5 July 1328 it was announced that one patriarch, five archbishops, thirty bishops, and forty-six abbots had incurred suspension, excommunication, and interdict for non-payment of *servitia*. In three charters of the *Camera Apostolica* between 1365 and 1368 seven archbishops, forty-nine bishops, 123 abbots, and two archimandrites in France and Spain are listed as under censure or guilty of perjury.[27]

The unclerical management of the Avignon government, which was continued and multiplied during the Great Schism in two and then in three obediences, led to a serious decline of confidence in the Curia and in ecclesiastical authority.[28] Thus the bitter reproaches hurled at Popes and cardinals during the Schism and the obstinate struggle for a true reform of the Church at Constance and Basel become intelligible. For, if not directly simoniacal, these money transactions were at least incompatible with the predominantly spiritual character of the papacy and introduced a dangerous secularization of the highest Church posts. Did John XXII perhaps feel this when, a few hours before his death, he annulled all reservations?

CHAPTER 41

Nominalism:
The Universities Between Via Antiqua and Via Moderna

The beginning of the fourteenth century marked a turning point in philosophy and theology. In general this can be characterized as the dissolution of the universalism and objectivism which had found their imposing expression in the *summae* of High Scholasticism. The philosophical and theological syntheses were supplanted by the critical investigation of individual problems. If everything had hitherto been referred to the universal in which individual things participated, interest was now concentrated rather on the concrete thing; it is perceptible directly and does not stand in need of the roundabout recourse to the universal. The individual was more strongly stressed, and the perceiving subject became its own object to a much greater extent. Precedence was given to reasoning and, in contradistinction to doctrinal authority and tradition, the right of criticism was claimed more than hitherto. Epistemology

[27] E. Göller, *Die Einnahmen der apostolischen Kammer unter Johann XXII.*, 45* f.; P. M. Baumgarten, *Untersuchungen und Urkunden über die Camera collegii cardinalium* (Leipzig 1898), CLXXVII–CLXXXV; P. M. Baumgarten, "Exkommunikation von Prälaten im Jahre 1390 wegen Nichtzahlung der Servitien," *RQ*, 22 (1908), 47–55.
[28] A. Esch, "Bankiers der Kirche im Grossen Schisma," *QFIAB*, 46 (1966), 277–398.

and formal logic thus attained to greater importance. In fact, the great achievements of the century lay in the field of logic. Recognition of this fact is not incompatible with the view that this shift from metaphysics to logic implies the dissolution of the Middle Ages.

After Duns Scotus, the critical attitude was especially clear in the Dominican Durandus of Saint-Pourçain (d. 1334) and the Franciscan Peter Aureoli (d. 1322), both of whom turned against the great authorities of their respective orders, Thomas Aquinas (d. 1274) and Duns Scotus (d. 1308). For human authority should be given little weight in comparison with clear rational knowledge. For it no principle of individuation is needed to bring the individual into existence, no species to recognize it. Peter Aureoli distinguished the thing *in rerum natura* and the thing in so far as it is grasped by our intellect (*res apparens in intellectu*). The universal concept is the product of our cognition (conceptualism).

What was, so to speak, in the air and was variously advertising its presence received its definite impetus, and the form that would characterize the future, in William of Ockham. We are accustomed to label the attitude brought about by him as nominalism, but it is much disputed whether Ockham was a nominalist.[1] A crass nominalism, such as Anselm of Canterbury (d. 1109) attributed to Roscelin of Compiègne (*ca.* 1050–1120), was hardly thinkable in the fourteenth century. The great tradition of the thirteenth century had left an imprint which was too deep and strong to allow it.[2] More important is the fact that, in the term nominalism, the epistemological aspect, that is, the controversy over universals, is too much in the foreground, whereas the mentality characterizing it operated with even more serious consequences in metaphysics, ethics, and sociology, and was even more destructive in theology than in philosophy. To speak simply of Ockhamism is equally not permissible, for a certain nominalist trend was inherent in all theology in the fourteenth and fifteenth centuries and characterized not only Ockham's pupils but also many a theologian actually belonging to the schools of Thomas Aquinas and Duns Scotus. Thus, characteristic views of Ockham, such as those of the sovereign omnipotence of God, the acceptance of man, or the act of natural and of supernatural love, were expressed before him and in an even more extreme form by contemporaries, such as the Dominican Peter de Palude (*ca.* 1280–1342) or Scotus's pupil, John de Bassolis (d. 1347).[3]

---

[1] P. Böhner, "The Realistic Conceptualism of William Ockham," *Traditio*, 4 (1946), 307–35; G. Martin, "Ist Ockhams Relationstheorie Nominalismus?", *FStud*, 32 (1950), 31–49; E. Hochstetter, "Nominalismus?", *FStudies*, 9 (1949), 370–403; H. Oberman, "The Theology of Nominalism," *Harvard Theological Review*, 53, 47—79.

[2] *Cf.* Maurice De Wulf, *History of Medieval Philosophy* (London, 3rd. ed. 1909), 425 f.

[3] W. Dettloff, *Die Entwicklung der Akzeptations- und Verdienstlehre von Duns Scotus bis Luther* (Münster 1963), 289 f.

The nominalism of the fourteenth century is described correctly but not adequately, by designating "as its essence an unrestrained craving for novelty allied to a strong inclination toward a purely skeptical and destructive criticism." [4] This description is too formal and too unsatisfactory in regard to content. For the epistemological starting point of nominalism, which implied a separation of thought and essence, affected all other fields much more directly than at first it seemed to. The often presumptuous speculation with its subtle and hair-splitting questions, which characterized the thinking of the age, was the result of a science which was concerned only with ideas, not with essence. The more the ideas lost ontological significance, the more easily could they be manipulated and the less persons felt the obligation of examining the results of thought in the reality. The separation of thought and essence led in theology to a preference for the investigation of all imaginable possibilities on the basis of the *potentia dei absoluta* and to a neglect of the way of salvation, which was effectively pointed out and binding in the sources of revelation. If the genuine symbolic nature of word and idea was surrendered, soon there was no further place whatsoever for symbols. Thus the approach to a deeper understanding of the Sacraments was barred. In ethics a radical separation of essence and duty and the allied formalism and voluntarism indicated the main feature of nominalism. And in Church-State quarrels criticism would often have been less immoderate, claims would have been championed with less exaggeration, if reality had been kept in mind to a greater degree. [5]

William of Ockham represents in its original radicalism that which characterized the two following centuries but which, as they ran their course, was variously covered over or set straight by the traditional theology of the schools. Born in England around 1285, he became a Franciscan and in 1306 was ordained a subdeacon. [6] In regard to his higher studies at Oxford we can determine only that around 1317–18 he prepared an *ordinatio* on the first book of *The Sentences* and in 1318–20 lectured on *The Sentences;* [7] the commentaries on Books II–IV are preserved. As *baccalaureus formatus* he had fulfilled the requirements for *magister regens* but never took the degree and hence found his way into history as *venerabilis inceptor*. His career was interrupted when his philosophical and theological teaching became the subject of a violent controversy at Oxford. John Lutterell, chancellor of the University, sought to end Ockham's teaching by disciplinary measures.

---

[4] F. Ehrle, *Die Scholastik und ihre Aufgaben in unserer Zeit* (Freiburg, 2nd ed. 1933), 21.

[5] E. Iserloh, *Gnade und Eucharistie*, 3.

[6] According to a document discovered by C. Walmesley. *Cf. Guillelmi de Ockham Opera Politica,* ed. by J. G. Sikes (Manchester 1940), 288.

[7] C. K. Brampton, "The Probable Date of Ockham's Lectura Sententiarum," *AFrH*, 55 (1962), 367–74, decides for 1318.

Perhaps out of concern for their academic freedom, the professors induced the Bishop to deprive Lutterell of the chancellorship. Then, in an extensive polemical treatise Lutterell in 1323 accused Ockham to the Curia at Avignon of heretical or at least dangerous doctrines. Proceeding from the scriptural text, "see to it that no one deceives you by philosophy and vain deceit" (Col. 2:8), Lutterell charged Ockham with misuse of logic. In so doing he himself employed logic as an instrument of theological proof, aware that this was regarded as a peculiarity of English theologians.[8] His charges in regard to content were especially directed against immoderate speculation *de potentia dei absoluta* in Ockham's teaching on the Eucharist, man's acceptance, and grace.

Pope John XXII summoned the *venerabilis inceptor*. He appeared at Avignon in 1324 and had to defend himself before a commission, which filed two expert opinions against him. Apparently, however, the judges, including so controversial a figure as Durandus, could not agree, and the case was drawn out. By his flight on 26–27 May 1328 to Louis the Bavarian at Pisa, along with Michael of Cesena and Bonagrazia of Bergamo, who were being detained at Avignon because of the poverty controversy, Ockham escaped the court. No condemnation of his philosophical and theological views would be forthcoming, for thereafter the question of poverty and the quarrel between Louis the Bavarian and John XXII claimed the Curia's interest. And Ockham's writings would now be exclusively preoccupied with these matters until his death at Munich in 1349 or 1347.[9] He was never reconciled with the Curia. Thus the philosophical and theological works of the *venerabilis inceptor* all appeared before 1324 or, at the latest, 1328.[10] In addition to the commentary on *The Sentences,* or rather the *Quaestiones on the Sentences of Peter Lombard,* and the *Quotlibeta septem,* there were the *Summa logicae,* the exposition of the logical treatises of Aristotle, published in 1496 as the *Expositio aurea,* the writings on physics,[11] and several smaller treatises, including two *De sacramento altaris* or *De corpore Christi.*

---

[8] In the *Epistula de Visione* he wrote: "Sed mihi opponitis quod nobis Anglicis frequenter hic opponunt: Ecce secundum logicum respondisti. Tolle, tolle! Secundum theologiam responde!" In F. Hoffmann, *Die Schriften des Oxforder Kanzlers Joh. Lutterell* (Leipzig 1959), 117, no. 20.

[9] Against the sources, including the grave inscription, R. Höhne, "Wilhelm Ockham in München," *FStud,* 32 (1950), 142–55, accepts 1349 as the year of his death; C. K. Brampton, "Traditions Relating to the Death of William of Ockham," *AFrH,* 53 (1960), 442–49, clings to 1347.

[10] E. Iserloh, "Um die Echtheit des 'Centiloquium,'" *Gregorianum,* 30 (1949), 78–103, 309–46, and especially page 102; A. Maier, "Zu einigen Problemen der Ockhamforschung," *AFrH,* 46 (1953), 161–94, especially page 163.

[11] *Summulae in libros Physicorum; Expositio super libros Physicorum; Quaestiones super libros Physicorum.*

According to Ockham we have a direct intuitive knowledge of the particular thing. As soon as we make statements we make use of ideas which our mind forms. No universality in things, no universal nature corresponds to universal concepts. At first Ockham looked upon universal ideas as mere figments of thought (ficta, figmenta), but later he identified them with the act of knowing. In the passive intellect the particular thing produces an image similar to itself. The universal is the things imagined and inheres in the soul as its subject. Thus ideas are based on the reality, not of universal substances, but of the particular things. There is no need of a third element, of a means of knowing between subject and intellect and it is precisely in the fact of the passivity of the intellect that the objectivity of knowing is assured.

In his teaching on God Ockham especially stresses God's freedom and omnipotence. He can do whatever does not involve a contradiction. God's will is bound neither externally nor internally. He acts when and as he will. The almighty divine will suffices to explain the *de facto* situation. The good is what God ordains, and even in regard to the order established by him he is entirely free. He could annul the commandments and command theft, unchastity, even hatred of himself. In the *Centiloquium*, a collection of 100 very pointed theses, whose authenticity is today disputed by Ockham's admirers, objection is made to a divine command to hate God as being incompatible with the principle of contradiction, for one who, at God's command, hated him would be loving him by fulfilling his command. Obedience to a divine command and hatred of God are mutually exclusive (*Cl.* 5 and 7).

If God's own action is subject to no necessity, it was the more repugnant to Ockham to assume that God should in any way be bound by man's being and conduct. Even if he strongly emphasized the freedom of man and was confident of man's natural capability, — for example, that man can of himself love God above all things, — in doubt he would always decide in favour of the sovereignty of God. God can save a man in sin and condemn a person in the state of grace. More than once Ockham used the following example for the transition *a contradictorio in contradictorium* by the mere lapse of time: God can decide that all who today are at a specified place will be damned and that all who are there tomorrow will be saved. Now if anyone stays there two days, he who was yesterday rejected is today accepted into favour, without himself or anything in him having been changed (*IV Sent.*, q. 4, L ad 2).

But God has bound himself by his dispositions, which he observes and which acquire their necessity for man from God's *fiat*. What God can do in the abstract, he cannot do in consequence of the order decreed by him; what he can do *de potentia sua absoluta*, he cannot do *de potentia sua ordinata*. In the effort to make clear the contingency of the actual order, Ockham found delight in showing the possibilities which exist on the basis on the *potentia absoluta dei* and deducing further possibilities from them. In these daring speculations concerning *potentia dei absoluta,* which often went beyond the limits of what could be tolerated, he developed a theology of the "as if" and lost sight of the way of salvation actually traced out by God. Moreover, no attempt was made to establish this way of salvation nor to inquire reverently into the wisdom of the ways of God. The presentation of sacred history gave way to the discussion of mere possibility, and theology became a practising ground for logical and dialectical dexterity.

It is in keeping with this attitude that Ockham preferred extreme cases or exceptions and deduced further possibilities. Since God can produce directly whatever he can produce by secondary causes, it can, for example, not be proved that something was produced by a particular secondary cause. Only a *post hoc* but no *propter hoc* can be established. For example, from the fact that, on being brought into contact with fire, something burns, it cannot be proved that fire was the cause of the burning. For God can arrange precisely that, whenever anything is brought into contact with fire, he alone produces the burning, just as he has arranged in regard to the Church that at the uttering of specified words grace is effected in the soul (*II Sent.,* q. 5, R).

Hence one can speak of a causality of the Sacraments only in so far as the sign is a mere condition of the direct action of God. Furthermore, these signs were established quite arbitrarily. God could link the grace of baptism to contact with a piece of wood and determine that confirmation should be conferred with baptismal water (*IV Sent.,* q. 1, G).

The reaching of conclusions by means of exceptions becomes especially clear in Ockham's teaching on the Eucharist, which he restricts to the doctrine of transubstantiation, in fact to the discussion of questions of natural philosophy, such as the relationship of substance and quantity. Ockham would prefer the coexistence of the bread and the body of Christ, for this doctrine in his view opposed neither reason nor Scripture. In fact, he held, it was *rationabilior* and easier to reconcile with the principle of economy, according to which as few miracles as possible were to be posited. For then the greatest difficulty would disappear: the existence of accidents without a supporting substance (*IV Sent.,* q. 6, D). But since the judgment of the Church requires it, Ockham clung to transubstantiation. The accompanying miracle of the continued existence of the accidents after the destruction of the substance became for him the chief proof that corporeal substance is extended in itself and has no need of a really distinct accident of quantity. For if, so he argues, God can permit accidents to exist of themselves, then he can also certainly destroy them and preserve the substance without any local motion of its parts. But then substance would be extended without quantity (*De sacramento altaris,* cap. 25). Furthermore, if God can destroy the accidents of the bread and preserve the body of Christ, the latter must be in the place directly and not by means of the species (*IV Sent.,* q. 4, N, Resp. ad 2 dubium).

Another case of the suspension of the *causa secunda,* namely that God produces in me the intuitive knowledge of something non-existent, became the point of departure for the proof of the possibility of seeing Christ in the Sacrament in a natural manner (*IV Sent.,* q. 5, D).

For Ockham there was no basic distinction between a natural and a supernatural act; they are "eiusdem rationis" (*I Sent.,* d. 17, q. 1, K). By purely natural power man can love God above all things. In this and in his extravagant speculation to the effect that, in the abstract, habitual grace is not necessary for salvation, Ockham incurs the suspicion of Pelagianism. On the other hand, he claimed to be protected from any Pelagian tenet because, according to him, God is independent of every created thing, is no one's debtor, and nothing in man, neither anything good nor anything evil, and no supernatural form inhering in the soul can compel God to save or to damn anyone (*I Sent.,* d. 17, q. 1, M; q. 2, E; *III Sent.,* q. 5, L; *Quotl.,* VI, q. 1). No act is meritorious because of any quality proper to it, even though it may have been produced by God; it is meritorious only on the basis of divine acceptance.[12] Only a theologian who had lost sight of Scripture and a nominalist who no longer asked what intrinsic value there is in a concept could so entirely disregard the objective and subjective importance of *caritas* and regard as possible the simultaneous existence of the state of sin and infused love. Conversely, only such a person could so completely tear asunder habitual grace, or love and beatitude, and no longer realize that one who participates in the divine life, and is not just called a child of God but is one (1 Jn. 3:1), is included in the love with which God necessarily loves himself. For Ockham grace is not a power which is communicated to man, renews him, and qualifies him for meritorious actions, but God's indulgence, whereby he accepts man or not, as he pleases.[13]

Hence the importance of Ockham and his impact on future generations lie not so much in his particular teaching, daringly formulated rather than really original, as in the nature of his theological speculation. The significant and passionate logician failed to place his skill at the service of theology. Instead, theology furnished the occasion for showing off his acrobatics in logic. An inner relationship to the subject was wanting. Theology was no longer the doctrine of salvation, and the theologian could the more easily

---

[12] "...solum [actus] est meritorius per potentiam dei absolutam acceptantem" (*Quotl.,* VI, q. 1); "...ut deus per nullam rem possit necessitari ad conferendum unicuique vitam aeternam et sic ista [propria] opinio maxime recedit ab errore Pelagii" (*I Sent.,* d. 17, q. 1, L quanto); *cf.* E. Iserloh, *Gnade und Eucharistie,* 127.

[13] W. Dettloff, *Die Entwicklung der Akzeptations- und Verdienstlehre,* asserts against me that one cannot rightly claim that Ockham understood grace merely as the good pleasure or favour of God (271 f., 284, 286). I have not denied but rather have demonstrated in detail (*Gnade und Eucharistie,* 104–26) that Ockham regarded habitual grace as necessary in the existing order. But that is a Church doctrine accepted by him; as Dettloff himself repeatedly stresses, it is of no great weight with Ockham.

abandon himself to daring speculations, the less he regarded his salvation as at stake in his theological endeavours.[14]

In Ockham's own lifetime a school of thought was attributed to him which quickly captivated the universities, Paris at their head; but this school of thought was likewise quite early violently attacked as an innovation. Its adherents were called *nominales* or *moderni* in contradistinction to the *reales,* and the method they represented was called *via moderna.* Immediate disciples of Ockham were Adam Wodham (d. 1358) and John Buridan (d. after 1358). The latter maintained a moderate attitude and, as rector of the University of Paris, even signed a condemnation "of the new teachings of certain Ockhamists" in 1340. He was especially preoccupied with the Ockhamist logic and took up the new efforts for a natural science. The Dominican Robert Holkot (d. 1349), on the other hand, became prominent under the spell of Ockham for his extreme radicalism in the use of nominalist principles and delighted in oversubtle formulations. He questioned the validity of Aristotelian logic in the realm of faith and regarded the existing order as based solely on God's free determination.

Around the middle of the fourteenth century the Ockhamist method had established itself at the University of Paris. As early as 1339 and 1340 the faculty of arts was induced to proceed against abuses of Ockhamism,[15] and the Parisian masters, Nicholas of Autrecourt (d. after 1350) and John of Mirecourt, were personally condemned. The first named became in 1340 the subject of a process at Avignon, which ended in 1346 with the condemnation of sixty propositions. He was especially charged with denying the principle of causality.[16] At the same time a papal bull was directed against the luxuriant growth of disputations in formal logic. Theologians were exhorted to keep to the texts of the old masters and not to neglect the Bible and the Fathers in favour of entirely useless philosophical questions, subtle disputations, and suspected doctrinal views.[17]

The Cistercian John of Mirecourt was denounced for sixty-three suspected propositions in his commentary on *The Sentences.* Despite his written justification, forty-one of his theses were condemned at Paris in 1347 because of their exaggeration of God's arbitrariness and the dangerous consequences resulting for ethics.[18]

---

[14] According to W. Dettloff, *op. cit.,* 290, the negative importance of Ockham lies in this, "that he displays a marked preference for daring theses but hardly any grasp of the subjects of his speculations, neither of God nor of grace nor of the divine economy of salvation." Can there be a more devastating judgment on a theologian? Why, then, his criticism (*op. cit.,* 288) of my evaluation of Ockham?

[15] Denifle-Chatelain, *Chartularium Universitatis Parisiensis,* II (Paris 1891), nos. 1023, 1042; for the explanation *cf.* E. Iserloh, *Gnade und Eucharistie,* 6 f.

[16] Denifle-Chatelain, *op. cit.,* II, 576–87; *Denzinger-Schönmetzer,* nos. 1028–49.

[17] Denifle-Chatelain, *op. cit.,* II, 587, no. 1125.

[18] *Ibid.,* II, 610–14.

Nominalist tendencies in epistemology and harsh anti-Pelagianism in the doctrine of grace characterized Gregory of Rimini, general of the Augustinians, who died at Vienna in 1358. He had studied and taught at Paris, where he became a master in 1345. In the doctrine of acceptance he showed his dependence on Ockham, whose optimism, however, in regard to naturally good works he did not share. Here, as in the doctrine of original sin, he was fascinated by the "founder" of his order, Saint Augustine. Without a special divine aid man cannot overcome temptation to sin, do any naturally good work, or even know what constitutes a morally good life.[19]

Already from the middle of the fourteenth century onwards, the originally excessive radicalism gave way to a more moderate view. Characteristic of the second half of the century, the epoch of the establishing of universities in Germany,[20] were German theologians, such as Marsilius of Inghen (d. 1396) at Heidelberg, Henry Heinbuche of Langenstein (d. 1397) and Henry Totting of Oyta (d. 1396), both of whom eventually taught at Vienna, and their pupil and successor, Nicholas of Dinkelsbühl (d. 1433). They were eclectics, who "were able to deflect the pernicious tendency of nominalism and, almost unnoticed, to regain the connection with the scholastic traditions."[21] And such a series of important theologians is found in this period that one can refer to it as the climax of nominalist-influenced scholasticism, "a climax the more important in that it was followed only by extracts and epitomes in the fifteenth century, which turned into current coin the achievements of the fourteenth century."[22]

In addition, the fifteenth century was, in Harnack's term, decidedly "untheological." Edifying writings, practical moral instruction, and the treatment of rubrical and canonical questions became predominant. Characteristic of this change was the transition at Paris from Peter d'Ailly (d. 1420), a leading representative of "undiluted Ockhamism," to his pupil, John Gerson (d. 1429), who in 1395 succeeded him as chancellor of the University. "It was this nominalist, with his edifyingly scholarly writings, his combination of mystical, Ockhamist, and Thomistic ideas, who became the prototype of an extensive, half-popular, syncretistically inclined theological literature, which was characteristic of the whole fifteenth century."[23] He directed sharp criticism at theological scholarship, with its sophistical-logical ballast, and attacked those who dealt with useless and sterile doctrines while neglecting the truths necessary for salvation and scorning Scripture. He

---

[19] II *Sent.*, d. 26–28; P. Vignaux, *Justification et prédestination* (Paris 1934), 154 ff.; W. Dettloff, *Die Entwicklung der Akzeptations- und Verdienstlehre*, 320; *ECatt*, VI, 1156 f.

[20] Prague, 1348; Vienna, 1365; Heidelberg, 1386; Cologne, 1388; Erfurt, 1392; Leipzig, 1409.

[21] A. Lang, *Heinrich Totting von Oyta* (Münster 1937), 244.

[22] F. Ehrle, *Der Sentenzenkommentar Peters von Candia* (Münster 1925), 78.

[23] G. Ritter, *Studien zur Spätscholastik*, II (Heidelberg 1922), 133.

assailed the one-sided preoccupation with the first book of *The Sentences,* which offered more scope for interest in logic and purely formal theologizing, and demanded full treatment of the second to fourth books with the mysteries of salvation history.[24] Considering the need of the age and the danger to souls, it was wrong, he said, to take delight in playing with or even indulging in reveries of superfluous things. No one should deem it beneath him to instruct the uneducated simple people in the faith. It was no mere chance that this nominalist, strictly geared to practice, who stressed the preeminence of mystical over scholastic theology but also warned against the dangers of a too presumptuous mysticism, stood up for the *devotio moderna* at the Council of Constance.

Characteristic of his century was the great compiler, Dionysius the Carthusian (*ca.* 1402–71) from Rijkel in Belgian Limburg. The mere size of his output — the modern edition comprises forty-four bulky volumes — shows him to have been every bit as diligent as he was unoriginal. With great ardour he gathered the fruits of the works of the great philosophers, Fathers, and scholastics and aspired to render them useful for practical piety. Besides a detailed commentary on the Bible (Volumes 1–14) and theological works, he left a large number of sermons (Volumes 29–32) and treatises (Volumes 33–41), which deal especially with questions of the spiritual life, asceticism, and mysticism. In this field he exerted a great influence going beyond his age and the Low Countries. In keeping with his education at Cologne and the fact that he copied and commented on the great men of the past, he is to be assigned to the *via antiqua;* but on the other hand, his work also indicates how party lines became more and more obscured in the fifteenth century.

At the universities, of course, the conflict between the two "ways" was prolonged throughout the fifteenth century. In the course of these developments the *via antiqua* recovered ground. For example, at the University of Cologne, founded in 1388, both ways were allowed by the statutes, but at first nominalism predominated. As early as 1414 the faculty of arts had to resist the efforts of the *antiqui* to suppress the modern methods.[25] But, soon after, the adherents of the *via antiqua* acquired the ascendancy. In 1425 the Electors urged the city of Cologne to reintroduce the modern methods at the University. They regarded Thomas, Albert, and the other teachers of the old school as profound but too difficult for the students, who would be seduced by a lack of understanding into errors and heresies, as the chaos at Prague testified.[26] Tactfully but decisively the University refused, and under men like Henry of Gorkum (d. 1431) became the forerunner of a Thomistic

---

[24] *Epistula secunda de reformatione theologiae ad studentes collegii Navarrici, Opera omnia,* ed. by Du Pin, I (Antwerp 1706), 123.

[25] A. G. Weiler, *Heinrich von Gorkum* (Hilversum and Einsiedeln 1962), 57 f.

[26] F. Ehrle, *op. cit.,* 355–58.

renaissance, which gradually replaced *The Sentences* of Peter Lombard with the *Summa theologiae* as the textbook. In his *Compendium Summae theologiae Sancti Thomae*, printed in 1473, Henry of Gorkum gave an excellent summary of its arrangement and content.[27] Quarrels in the camp of the realists produced temporarily at Cologne a third doctrinal school, the Albertists, whose chief representative was Heymeric van de Velde (de Campo; d. 1460), a pupil of the Parisian master John de Nova Domo. The Albertists denied the real distinction between essence and being and maintained a Neoplatonic dynamic notion of being.[28]

Vienna and Erfurt were the only German universities that were exclusively nominalist. Others had been so at first but later opened their doors to the realists. At Heidelberg, where the realist John Wenck (d. 1460), rector in 1435, 1444, and 1451, demanded a sober biblical theology, free from all sophisms and inventions of human ingenuity, the Elector Palatine in 1452 decreed the admission of the *via antiqua* and the equalization of the two ways. This was achieved at Basel in 1464, but at Freiburg not util 1484.[29]

Like Cologne, the Universities of Cracow, Leipzig, Greifswald, Ingolstadt, Tübingen, and Wittenberg gave equality to both ways. If the arts faculty was nominalist, then the theological faculty did not have to be. Here the pressure of tradition was stronger and the influence of professors bound by the school of their order operated in many ways. Indeed, "many teachers who were devoted to the innovation in logic remained conservative in theology."[30] At Paris the conflict of the ways led toward the close of the fifteenth century to the prohibition of nominalists. By a royal decree of 1 March 1474 they were banished from the University and the confiscation of their writings was ordered. However, these measures were annulled in 1481.

In the course of time the originally basic philosophical opposition in epistemology, especially in the solution of the problem of universals, played a more subordinate role, which in many ways was merely artificially maintained. More important were differences in the content of instruction and in the method followed. In the faculties of a nominalist hue more value was set on "terminist" logic. Following the *Summulae* of Peter of Spain (d. 1277), presented in the revision of John Buridan, this logic regarded the concept rather than the judgment as the central point of reflection and in the exposition of a text was not content with presenting the actual content but

---

[27] M. Grabmann, "Hilfsmittel des Thomasstudiums aus alter Zeit," *Mittelalterliches Geistesleben,* II (Munich 1956), 440–43.
[28] G. Meerssemann, *Geschichte des Albertismus,* 2 vols. (Paris 1933; Rome 1935); R. Haubst, *Studien zu Nikolaus von Kues und Johannes Wenck* (Münster 1955).
[29] Cf. J. J. Bauer, *Zur Frühgeschichte der Theol. Fakultät der Univ. Freiburg (1460–1620)* (Freiburg 1957), 118 ff.
[30] A. Lang, *op. cit.,* 159.

was more logically concerned with the terms employed. "Nos imus ad res, de terminis non curamus" was a favourite slogan of the realists against the "terminists."

The *via antiqua* brought the text of Aristotle, of Peter Lombard, or of Aquinas again into the foreground and was content with an exegesis or paraphrase instead of debating in subtle details special problems in the questions on the text. If the *moderni* could be accused of sophistry and a craze for novelty at any price, the *antiqui* could be reproached for having renounced independent study of the thought contained in the "ancients" and for failure to develop ideas of their own. The orientation to the text and the simplification of theological teaching methods were not the exclusive property of the *via antiqua;* at the middle of the fifteenth century they were shared also by humanism and the Church reform efforts of the age and to some extent by the *devotio moderna.* In any event, humanism did not level its criticism at a scholasticism characterized by special radicalism and the subtlety of its theses — in this respect the climax had been reached *ca.* 1350. Rather, it attacked a school theology already groaning "under the weight of the literary tradition which in the course of the centuries had accumulated an immense mass of 'authorities,' opinions, and controversies, whose eternal ruminations, comparisons, and manipulations for new, and yet basically old, 'conclusions' [had] become an unending business." [31]

CHAPTER 42

Concept of the Church and Idea of the State in the
Polemics of the Fourteenth Century:
The Laicized State in Marsilius of Padua

The claims of Boniface VIII and John XXII to authority in the secular domain were excessive and not in accord with the doctrine of the two powers developed from the time of Pope Gelasius I (492–96) and still accepted by Innocent III. According to this theory, the ecclesiastical and secular powers are mutually independent but related to each other; the spiritual power is nobler but it is not possessed of superior authority. The pretensions of Boniface VIII and John XXII were likewise historically obsolete, for the West had achieved maturity and the age of a universalism and clericalism occasioned by the situation was past. In 1286 the Dominican John Balbi of Genoa (d. 1298) in his lexicon of the liberal arts could still define the layman

[31] G. Ritter, *op. cit.,* II, 98.

as *extraneus a scientia litterarum*, lacking in a literary education.[1] In the meantime, in that very thirteenth century, a far-reaching process of individualization was under way; the individual had been discovered in the universal, and vast intellectual, artistic, and religious forces had been released. Related to this were the awakening of a responsible laity, the growth of cities, and the formation of national states. There was no longer a question solely of the relations of Emperor and Pope, but of the clerical and lay community and the place of man, who was both believer and citizen, in them.

The question was to what extent the Church was able to yield to the new claims and how far her religious nature was adequate to bind these driving forces individually and collectively to her own centre. Mere resistance was no solution; an exaggeration of her own position was bound to produce a contrary effect. Statements such as Boniface VIII employed in the introduction to the bull "Clericis Laicos" (1296), "that the laity are hostile to the clergy is proved abundantly by antiquity and is clearly taught by the experiences of the present," did not do justice to reality. It was to be feared that developments, in themselves legitimate, which the Church failed to take promptly into account and in fact opposed, would forcibly find a place for themselves. In this respect the arrest of Boniface VIII at Anagni in 1303, in which the national state and the lay world represented by Nogaret and Sciarra Colonna acted jointly, was a warning signal. If Popes offered the political forces a legitimate ground for resisting them on account of obsolete and exaggerated claims, then it was obvious that the fight would soon be directed against the papacy itself. This struggle was not merely literary, but it was to a great extent prepared and waged by polemical writings and bulky treatises.

On behalf of Pope and Curia the polemic was especially conducted by the Augustinians Aegidius Romanus (1243/47–1316) in *De ecclesiastica potestate* (1302), James of Viterbo (d. 1308) in *De regimine christiano* (1302), and Augustinus Triumphus (1243–1328) in *Summa de potestate ecclesiastica* (1320).

According to Aegidius Romanus, or Giles of Rome, the Church has universal dominion. If she does not ordinarily exercise this directly over worldly things, no fundamental limitation is to be inferred from this fact. At any time she could monopolize secular dominion.[2] In ordinary circumstances, in accord with 2 Timothy 2:4, the sword is to be wielded, not by the Church, but for her and at her bidding (III, 11, p. 205). Outside the Church there exists no right in the full sense. Only baptism makes one a lawful ruler and owner of earthly things. Outside the Church no one can

---

[1] *Summa quae vocatur Catholicon* (ed. Nürnberg 1486), fol. ee, I, ra.
[2] *De ecclesiastica potestate*, Liber III, c. 2, ed. R. Scholz, 149; III, 4, *ibid.*, 161–64.

possess in full right a field or vineyard or anything else (III, 11, p. 201). In brief, "the secular power is established through the ecclesiastical and by the Church and for the attaining of the Church's ends."[3]

The work of Aegidius Romanus acquired a far-reaching importance, since it served as the basis of the bull "Unam Sanctam." James of Viterbo did not adopt these extravagant theses of his confrère in *De regimine christiano*, despite his effort to justify the policy of Boniface VIII. In his eyes the secular power does not stand in need of any consecration by the Church to gain legitimacy. It is certainly formed and perfected by the spiritual power.[4] But if the spiritual power is the form of the secular power, as light is the form of colour, then, despite all of James's efforts to maintain the legitimacy of the secular power according to natural law, the door is opened to unilaterally curialist conclusions.

In addition, it is to be realized that we are at the beginning of the fourteenth century, when formal logic acquired a leading role. An excessive confidence in the accuracy of their logic induced the two Augustinians, like many of their contemporaries, to push to extremes, even to "absurd conclusions,"[5] hitherto current axioms, which had been prudently and carefully applied earlier with regard to a living reality, and then not even to test the result of thought by the reality. This is to be regarded also as nominalism, or at least as conceptualism. Major terms of this sort were, for example, the principle of the subordination of the imperfect to the perfect, of the body to the soul, of the temporal to the eternal, of the secular power to the spiritual power, and of the unity of social life. The comparison of secular and spiritual powers to body and soul acquired an entirely different impact after the decision by the Council of Vienne (1311–12) that the soul is the single immediate essential form of the body. For in accord with this the secular power would be an authentic power only through the spiritual power. Thus the same image could acquire in the fourteenth century a significance entirely different from what it had in Augustine, for example, or in the eleventh century. From the "one Lord . . . one God" of Ephesians 4:5, James of Viterbo deduced "unus princeps, unus principatus, unus rector, una res publica,"[6] and Aegidius Romanus concluded:

---

[3] "Bene itaque dictum est, quod terrena potestas est per ecclesiasticam et ab ecclesiastica et in opus ecclesiasticae constituta" (II, 5, p. 59).

[4] "Institutio potestatis temporalis materialiter et inchoative habet esse a naturali hominum inclinatione, ac per hoc a Deo inquantum opus naturae est opus Dei, perfective autem et formaliter habet esse a potestate spirituali quae a Deo speciali modo derivatur. Nam gratia non tollit naturam sed perficit eam et format et similiter, id quod est gratiae non tollit id quod est naturae, sed id format et perficit" (II, 7, ed. Arquillière, 232).

[5] R. Scholz, Introduction to *De ecclesiastica potestate*, p. x; G. de Lagarde, *La naissance de l'esprit laïque au declin du Moyen Age*, I (Louvain-Paris, 3rd ed. 1956), 196.

[6] *De regimine christiano*, I, 3, p. 118.

In the Church Militant there can be only one source of power, only one head, which possesses the fulness of power . . . and both swords, without which its power would not be complete. From this source all other powers are derived.[7]

In opposition to Aegidius Romanus, Augustinus Triumphus in *Summa de potestate ecclesiastica* stressed the independence of the natural order. But it is oriented to the order of grace and is enlisted in its service. The Pope does not establish the secular power but involves it in the economy of salvation by virtue of his spiritual power. However, he can do so only on the basis of the relationship of the princes or citizens concerned to the Church. The state as such does not become a part of the Church, but, to the extent that its members belong to the Church and render the Church's standards operative in it, it becomes a social structure in the *populus christianus*. In the worldly sense the king has no superior (q. 45, 1 ad 2), but only in so far as his power as a Christian authority is an integral part in the economy of salvation. This latter is Augustinus Triumphus's real concern, and his papalist claims are to be understood from this point of departure. It is a question of the "inclusion of the secular order in the economy of salvation and of the proper permeation of the world by the redemption."[8]

The extreme formulation of the curial viewpoint encouraged the development of the contrary doctrine of the independence of the state and of its claims to direct the Church. Of the writings of the legists, that is, of those who sought to shore up the position of the French King, the most important are: *Disputatio inter clericum et militem*,[9] the treatises *Antequam essent clerici*[10] and *Rex pacificus*,[11] and, as the voice of moderation, the *Quaestio in utramque partem*.[12] The legists likewise proceeded from the oneness of power and in this they were supported by Roman Law. The power attributed by it to the Emperor they ascribed to the King of France, who "is Emperor in his Kingdom."[13] The supreme power of emperor or king respectively is inalienable. Therefore, the Donation of Constantine is to be regarded as unauthentic and the privileges of the clergy in regard to taxation and courts are to be abolished. The clergy, who "have become fat and obese because of the piety of princes," must have their recompense. But if the laity place the

---

[7] *De ecclesiastica potestate*, III, 2, p. 152; *cf.* the bull "Unam Sanctam": ". . . Unum caput, non duo capita, quasi monstrum . . . Uterque ergo [gladius] est in potestate ecclesiae."

[8] W. Kölmel, "Einheit und Zweiheit der Gewalt," *HJ*, 82 (1963), 143.

[9] Ed. M. Goldast, *Monarchia*, I (Hanover 1612), 13–18; *cf.* R. Scholz, *Publizistik* (Stuttgart 1903), pp. 333–52; J. Rivière, *Le problème* (Paris 1926), pp. 253–62.

[10] Text under a wrong title in P. Dupuy, *Histoire du différend d'entre le pape Boniface VIII et Philippe le Bel* (Paris 1955), 21–23.

[11] P. Dupuy, *op. cit.*, 262–71; *cf.* J. Rivière, *op. cit.*, 135–37, 262–71; R. Scholz, *Publizistik*, 252–75.

[12] M. Goldast, *Monarchia*, II (Frankfurt 1614), 95–107; R. Scholz, *Publizistik*, 224–51.

[13] *Quaestio in utramque partem*, M. Goldast, *Monarchia*, II, 98.

means at their disposal, then the laity must be permitted to supervise them to see whether such means are used properly. As a matter of principle they state that "Holy Mother Church consists not only of clerics but also of lay persons."[14] Did Christ not die for all the faithful? Among the laity the French King performs a special function, for according to Peter Dubois, he is "the most Christian King, the defender of the Church," and France is the *directrix veritatis*.[15]

If the Pope has an indirect power in the temporal sphere, then, according to John of Paris (d. 1306), an advocate of the doctrine of the two powers, the king has the same in the spiritual domain. He can "indirectly" excommunicate an unworthy Pope and *per accidens* depose him, by himself or through the cardinals.[16]

Laity and state emerged from these disputes with a more vivid sense of their independence and a growing awareness of their rights and duties, even with regard to the spiritual. Whereas the defenders of the Curia, frequently in a most presumptuous manner, advocated an abstract system that did not correspond to the Church's past nor take account of her future, and thus missed the reality and the opportune moment, the representatives of the state registered such elementary rights as sovereignty over property and persons, judicial supremacy, autonomy in legislation, and a certain control of the intellectual life of the nation.[17] Though individual demands may have been expressed obscurely and exaggerated, a justified concern was present in them and the future was to belong to it.

Marsilius of Padua

The struggle of the legists, in the name of princes and cities, for the autonomy and independence of the secular power against encroachments of the spiritual did not terminate in a separation of Church and State in the modern sense but rather in a State Church or at least an extensive control of Church life by the secular power. In the *Defensor pacis* of Marsilius of Padua this attitude led to the total destruction of the ecclesiastical power and the total control of all aspects of life, including the Church, by the purely secular laicized state, so called because in final analysis deprived of authoritative values.

It is assumed that Marsilius was born at Padua between 1275 and 1280

---

[14] *Antequam essent clerici*, ed. P. Dupuy, *op. cit.*, 21 f.
[15] The King himself said in 1303: "Cum in talibus et similibus casibus semper directrix veritatis exstiterit regia domus nostra"; *cf.* P. Dupuy, *op. cit.*, 124 f.; G. de Lagarde, *op. cit.*, I, 207.
[16] *De potestate regia et papali*, c. 13, ed. J. Leclercq (Paris 1942), 214.
[17] G. de Lagarde, *op. cit.*, I, 210.

and there began his studies. The first certain date is that of his rectorship as master of arts from December 1312 to March 1313 at the University of Paris. As a partisan of the Ghibellines he seems to have taken part in the Italian factional strife from around 1314, and he carried out diplomatic tasks for Can Grande della Scala and Matthew Visconti. Between times he tried to obtain a benefice at the Avignon Curia. From 1320 he again concentrated on study at Paris in natural philosophy, medicine, and perhaps theology. Here he was intimately associated with the leader of the Parisian Averroists, John of Jandun (d. 1328), who probably inspired the *Defensor pacis* but cannot be called its coauthor.[18] Marsilius completed this, his chief work, in June 1324, shortly after the Sachsenhausen Declaration of Louis the Bavarian. This great book was probably intended from the outset to play a role in the antipapal activity to which had rallied Ghibellines, cardinals of the opposition, and Spirituals.[19] But it was not until 1326 that Marsilius fled with John of Jandun to the court of Louis the Bavarian in Germany, probably because his authorship had become known. At first Louis apparently did not want to compromise his case with the work of these men, who were to be condemned as heretics on 3 April 1327.[20] But during the Emperor's journey to Rome (1327–29) Marsilius and his friend were the influential advisers. Events such as the imperial coronation in the name of the Roman people and the installing of the Antipope appear to be the realization of the basic ideas of *Defensor pacis*.[21] Following the collapse of the Emperor's Italian policy, Marsilius lived at Munich as a physician. His influence seems to have been insignificant in comparison with that of the more moderate William of Ockham and the other Franciscans. At this time he wrote the *Tractatus de translatione Romani imperii*, the opinion on *The Imperial Jurisdiction in Matrimonial Cases*, and the *Defensor minor* (1342). His death must have occurred soon after the appearance of the last named work, for on 10 April 1343 Clement VI referred to him as lately deceased.

According to the *Defensor pacis*, peace, the principle of order in the state and the basic presupposition for human happiness, is greatly disturbed. In an effort to inquire into the causes of this and to indicate the fundamental principles for the assuring of peace, Marsilius develops his theory of state and society. In this he is guided by his experiences in the North Italian city states, the writings of the French legists, and the Averroist interpretation of the Aristotelian political doctrine. According to him the fundamental evil is the papal pretension to the fulness of power, to a *vis coactiva* over Church,

---

[18] Ed. R. Scholz, li ff.; A. Gerwirth, "John of Jandun and the Defensor pacis," *Speculum*, 23 (1948), 167–72.

[19] Ed. R. Scholz, lvii.

[20] Bull "Licet iuxta;" *MGConst*, 6, 1, 265, no. 361.

[21] O. Bornhak, *Staatskirchliche Anschauungen und Handlungen am Hofe Kaiser Ludwigs des Bayern* (Weimar 1933).

princes, and kingdoms; as a matter of fact, that, in addition to the state, another principle of power should claim the right to exist. Opposing this, Marsilius stresses the unity of power. "The multiplicity of sovereign powers ... is the root and origin of corruption" (II, 23, 11; *cf.* I, 17, 1–9).

The state is the union of men for the sake of a satisfying existence (*sufficienter vivere*, I, 5, 5). What the individual cannot do, the state accomplishes in its various professions. Among these is included also the priesthood, for the state must assure the earthly and the supernatural welfare of man. "The legislator or the first and specific efficient cause of law is the people or the totality of citizens or a majority of them" (I, 12, 3). The people, as *legislator humanus*, commits the exercise of power to a ruler *(princeps)*, who has to preserve and guarantee peace, which makes possible the good life for the citizens.

Every other power, and hence that of the Church, is delegated. Inasmuch as priests and bishops exercise power, they receive it from the believing human legislator, that is, from the lay hand. The Church is "the totality of the faithful, who believe in Christ's name and invoke him" (II, 2, 3).

> Therefore all Christ's faithful are churchmen *(viri ecclesiastici)* in the truest and most proper meaning and must be so called, priests and those not priests, for Christ has acquired and redeemed all by his blood ...; hence bishops or priests and deacons are not exclusively the Church, which is the bride of Christ (II, 2, 3).

The priesthood is a divine institution. "Christ gave priestly power to the Apostles and he still gives it today, whenever one of them invests his successors with full powers through the imposition of hands" (II, 15, 3). "This power, inseparable from the priest as priest, ... this priestly character is possessed by all priests in the same manner, and neither the Bishop of Rome nor any other possesses any more comprehensive power than any so-called simple priest" (II, 15, 4; *ibid.*, 15, 5, 7). Hence the hierarchy is of human law; "not God directly but the human will and mind" (I, 19, 8; II, 15, 6) created it for the sake of order, "like the other offices of the state." The attempt to deduce a special dignity of the Bishop of Rome from the Petrine succession runs aground on the impossibility of proving Peter's being in Rome (II, 16, 15). No real external power is, however, given along with the priestly character bestowed by God. In confession the priest can merely "declare to whom God has retained or pardoned sins" (II, 6, 7). He has no *vis coactiva*, for offenses against the divine law are not punished in this world (II, 9, 3–10; III, 2, 3), unless they are also forbidden by human law. But then it is the business of the state to prosecute and excommunicate the heretic. At the most the priest is called upon as a specialist for an opinion.

In disputes over doctrinal questions or uncertainties as to the meaning of a scriptural passage the decision pertains "to a council of all the faithful or of their delegates" (II, 18, 8). As the rule of faith Marsilius laid down:

"Only the divine or canonical Scripture and every interpretation that is convincingly deduced from it and that which is handed down by a general council is true; it is necessary for eternal salvation to believe these" (III, 2, 1). But the council is not an autonomous body beside the state; on the contrary, it is instituted in it, so to speak, as an organ for definite questions. Only "the believing human legislator or the one who rules through it by proper authority" has the power "to convoke or direct a council, to choose and determine suitable persons for it, command the observance of the conciliar decrees, and punish transgressors" (II, 21, 1; II, 18, 8). The decisions of the council have their truth from the Holy Spirit, "but from the human legislator the authority which enforces their acceptance and their propagation by priests" (II, 19, 3). If, "by a council or the believing human lawgiver," a bishop or a church is appointed as head and ruler of the others, then this bishop together with the college of priests assigned to him by the legislator, can, in case of necessity, ask for the summoning of a council (II, 22, 6).

Accordingly, there exist no clerical person and no college which were not delegated by the *legislator humanus,* that is, by the totality of citizens. The frequently recurring phrase, *concilium generale vel fidelis legislator humanus,* shows to what an extent *universitas fidelium* and *universitas civium* are identical for Marsilius and that the council is not a separate entity. For Marsilius, the Church is directed neither monarchically by a Pope nor collegially by the episcopate nor democratically by a council. She is also not purely spiritualized but fully disintegrated. She is devoid of any character as a society and has become a mere function of the state. From this arise two difficulties. For Marsilius the universal state is not the ideal; in his view peace and the public welfare are better guaranteed in several states (*cf.* for example, II, 28, 15). But if the *universitas civium* and the *universitas fidelium* are to him identical, then the council, which is conceived as a universal institution, must have its counterpart in a realm which unites all Christendom and in which the conciliar decrees have the force of law. Can the prince of a national state be the "believing human lawgiver, who recognizes no higher power," [22] or is an emperor or a world state still postulated? Marsilius ignores this question. But he does not wish to pass over the second question in silence (II, 22, 12). If the believing human lawgiver alone renders the Church capable of functioning, if he summons the council, appoints priests, looks after worship, and so forth, who assumes these tasks when believers are subjects of unbelieving lawgivers? In the age of the persecutions, so Marsilius claims, the Church was charismatically guided. Believers were prepared to obey the bishops, and in particular the Roman Bishops, who

---

[22] "... fidelis legislator humanus superiore carens" (II, 19, 3, p. 386). *Cf.* R. Scholz, "Marsilius und die Genesis des modernen Staatsbewusstseins," *HZ,* 156 (1937), 88–103 (especially page 102).

excelled in love of God and exemplary poverty, in order to preserve the unity of faith and peace. For this could "be achieved neither by coercive power nor in any more appropriate manner, because the human legislator was at that time almost everywhere an unbeliever" (II, 25, 3). Hence, the Primitive Church was a state of emergency, which was only ended by Constantine.

On 23 October 1327 five propositions of the *Defensor pacis* were condemned as heretical: 1. That Christ by paying the tribute money intended to testify to his subordination to the secular power. 2. That Peter had no more authority than the other Apostles. 3. That the Emperor can appoint, depose, and punish the Pope. 4. That all priests are equal in degree. 5. That priests have no penal authority of themselves but only by grant of the Emperor.[23] Despite this condemnation the book and its ideas continued to be influential. Louis the Bavarian had it read to himself[24] and his Italian policy determined by it. However, a moderating tone gained ground at the court of Munich with the Franciscans Michael of Cesena and Ockham. And the German jurists who were fighting for the independence of the German kingship, for example Lupold of Bebenburg (d. 1363) and Conrad of Mengenberg (d. 1374), did not share Marsilius's radical principles on the relations of Church and state. In the fifteenth-century struggles over the constitution of the Church the *Defensor pacis* again became influential. While the heretic and determined foe of the papacy was rejected and his doctrine of the laicized state was not accepted, his historical and moral criticism of the abuses in the Church were. This is true of Dietrich of Niem (d. 1418) in his *De modis uniendi et reformandi ecclesiam in concilio universali* (1410)[25] and of Nicholas of Cusa (d. 1464) in his great reform treatise *De Concordantia Catholica* (1432–33).[26] In summary it can be stated that the *Defensor pacis* was too radical to exert an immediate influence, but indirectly it had a great and far-reaching effect.

William of Ockham

It was not until his Munich period that William of Ockham was concerned with the poverty dispute and the relations between the spiritual and the secular powers. His philosophical and theological works appeared before

[23] D (32nd ed. 1963), nos. 941–46.

[24] *Compendium maius*, R. Scholz, *Streitschriften*, II, 184.

[25] *Cf.* Dietrich of Niem, *Dialog über Union und Reform der Kirche 1410*, ed. by H. Heimpel (Leipzig and Berlin); H. Heimpel, *Studien zur Kirchen- und Reichsreform des 15. Jahrhunderts*, Part I, "Eine unbekannte Schrift Dietrichs von Niem über die Berufung der Generalkonzilien (1413/14)," (Heidelberg 1929); *idem*, *Dietrich von Niem* (Münster 1932).

[26] R. Scholz, "Marsilius von Padua und Deutschland," *Marsilio da Padova. Studi Raccolti*, ed. by A. Cecchini et al., 3–35.

his flight from Avignon in 1328; his fifteen ecclesiastico-political writings,[27] without exception, after it. "Emperor, protect me with your sword; then I will defend you with my pen," he is alleged to have said as a refugee in the train of Louis the Bavarian.[28]

The Pope had already taken a final stand in the poverty dispute with "Quia Vir Reprobus" (1329),[29] the *Defensor pacis* had appeared, and the decisive events had taken place during Louis the Bavarian's journey to Rome — the imperial coronation and the appointment of the Antipope — when Ockham intervened in the discussion in 1333–34 with his *Opus nonaginta dierum*, so called because he claims to have composed the voluminous work in ninety days. Ockham could merely establish and defend what was already an accomplished fact. He was and continued to be a philosophical and theological thinker, accustomed to pursue questions to their ultimate possibilities in a critical and biased speculation and as far as possible to go back to principles and sources. Although he was unable to deny his own opposing stand and its origin in the polemics of the day, he did not get stuck in them.

The great ecclesiastico-political writings, the *Opus nonaginta dierum* (1333–34), his extensive but still incomplete principal work, *Dialogus inter magistrum et discipulum de imperatorum et pontificum potestate* (1333–38), and the *Super potestate summi pontificis octo quaestiones* present the difficulty that the author does not clearly come forth with his own opinion but lets the several sides speak and refers to himself only as the narrator. For the sake of the disputation, a sort of school exercise, he can expound the most audacious theses without identifying himself with them and he cannot be tied down to them.[30] As evidence for Ockham's view these writings can be used only with caution. He expressed himself more directly, in a more exact form, and, as to content, more clearly and more moderately in the *Breviloquium de principatu tyrannico super divina et humana* (1342) and in *De imperatorum et pontificum potestate* (1347), the final and comprehensive exposition of his views on Church politics.

As with his image of God and man, Ockham's doctrine of state and

---

[27] According to the count of R. Scholz, who cites the second and third parts of the *Dialogus* separately, there are seventeen; cf. *Breviloquium*, p. 7, footnote 1, with the indication of the editions.

[28] John Trithemius (d. 1516), *De scriptoribus ecclesiasticis* (Cologne 1546), 233.

[29] *Bull Fr*, V, no. 820, 408–49.

[30] In the *Dialogus* the "pupil" says: "Neque asserendo neque dubitando aliquid sis dicturus sed solummodo recitando, sicut pro toto isto Dialogo peractum est inter nos" (Goldast, *Monarchia*, II, 771) or "Nolo, ut quod tenes in mente, reveles, sed responsiones aliquas, quae cogitari vel teneri potuerint a quocunque, non differas recitare" (*ibid.*, 504). On the other hand Ockham observes in the *Breviloquium*: "Porro, quia in hoc opere non tantummodo recitando, sicut in praedicto dialogo et quibusdam aliis operibus, sed in aliqua asserendo constanter, aliqua absque assertione temeraria opinando, verborum faleras relinquendo procedam. . ." (ed. R. Scholz, 40).

Church and of their mutual relations is determined by freedom — the freedom of the individual in Church and state and the freedom of the secular ruler *vis-à-vis* the Pope. The principle of economy of his philosophy attests the sociological doctrine that no more obligations and norms should be permitted than the public welfare requires. In particular it is important to safeguard freedom against "the Church of Avignon, which stubbornly maintains errors, indeed manifest heresies, . . . and is currently guilty of the gravest injustices against the rights and the liberties of the faithful, great and small, lay and cleric . . ." [31]

Opposing the monism of both the curialists and Marsilius of Padua, Ockham defends a theory of the two powers, in which both powers are mutually complementary, are even "allied in a mutual dependence." [32] Apart from the divine law, Emperor and Pope in their respective spheres have no such absolute power that it could not be limited by the freedom of the individual and by the public welfare. Ockham firmly emphasizes the independent status of the secular power. There was a lawful worldly order before Christ and before the Church. The Empire was not first made legitimate by the baptism of Constantine; the pagan Roman Empire already had real jurisdiction and hence was acknowledged by Christ and the Apostles (*Breviloquium*, IV, 10; III, 2). Like private ownership, the political order also, "the power to appoint rulers who have secular powers of government," is derived from the divine arrangement. After the fall the liberty of the primeval condition, like the absence of ownership, could not be maintained any longer, and for the sake of *bene et politice vivere* governmental power was necessary (*Brev.*, III, 7). And though this is transmitted by means of men, it comes from God. "All mortals who were born free and have not been subjected to another by human law derive from God and nature the right freely to elect a ruler" (*Brev.*, IV, 10). If peoples are forcibly subjugated, dominion becomes legitimate only through their inner assent. Ockham is unable to say when such was the case, for example in the Roman Empire. Anyhow it is true that "the power to make laws and establish human rights lay first and originally in the people, who transferred it to the Emperor" (*Brev.*, III, 14). But the transmission of power by the totality of the citizens does not include the right to terminate allegiance. And if the authority of princes is termed dominative, in contrast to the ministerial office of the Pope (*De potestate*, c. 6 and 7), it is still not unlimited. It finds its limits in the liberties of man, which are of an earlier origin than the state, and in the public welfare, for which authority is instituted (*Brev.*, II, 5).

The Church is the community of all the faithful. To the nominalist, who does not recognize the relation as real and for whom the totality is only the

---

[31] *De imperatorum et pontificum potestate*, c. 1, ed. R. Scholz, 454.
[32] W. Kölmel, *W. Ockham und seine kirchenpolitischen Schriften*, 223.

sum of its parts, the Church is a multiplicity of individuals. In fact, she is a phantom and a chimera. To be exact, just as there is not an order apart from the Franciscans subject to the law of poverty but only a *persona repraesentata*, which possesses a *ius utendi*, so it is a fiction to speak of the Church as a legal person. [33] As the community of the faithful, she has, according to Christ's will, a monarchical form of government. He appointed Peter as his vicar. Differing from Marsilius of Padua, Ockham concedes to the Pope real power transmitted by Christ. "Christ would not have taken sufficient care of the Church and would have neglected something necessary" (*De potestate*, c. 8), if he had not given her in the Pope the principal who should see to all things necessary for the salvation of the faithful and guide them. But Christ did not invest Peter with full power, either in the secular or in the spiritual sphere (*De potestate*, c. 2). It is entirely clear that he did not give him absolute power *in temporalibus*, for otherwise he would have made slaves of all and there would no longer be any "evangelical liberty" (*De potestate*, c. 1). But the spiritual power also has its limits. Ockham speaks of the "ancient boundaries" (*De potestate*, c. 15, 1) to which the Church of Avignon should be again reduced. The Pope is not allowed to command everything which is not contrary to the divine precept and natural law (*De potestate*, c. 1). For example, he is bound to respect the legitimate titles of kings, whether Christian or non-Christian. Furthermore, liberty must not be unnecessarily restricted. The Pope's full authority extends only to what is necessary for the salvation of souls and the guidance of the faithful. "All else, even though it be spiritual, he must not command, lest the law of the Gospel become a law of slavery" (*De potestate*, c. 10; *Brev.*, II, 4). The Pope's power is one, not of dominion, but of service. [34]

Despite the rigorous inclination to confine the Pope within his limits, Ockham foresees the case in which he directly assumes secular duties. In an emergency, when the proper authorities fail or break down, the Pope may and should intervene in worldly affairs for the sake of the common welfare. [35] Without using the expression, Ockham is thereby championing the theory of the *potestas indirecta in temporalibus*. There are no rules for such a case. The greatest discretion is indicated and the counsel of experienced and impartial men is necessary (*De potestate*, c. 13).

Eminent as is the Pope's dignity as Christ's deputy, above him is the *Ec-*

---

[33] "... hoc dicunt fantastice dictum: quia ordo est verae personae, sicut ecclesia est verae personae" (*Opus nonaginta dierum*, c. 62, Goldast, *Monarchia*, II, 1108).

[34] "... principatus non dominativus, sed ministrativus" (*De potestate*, c. 6); "Papa autem est pater fidelium, et principatus eius non assimilatur principatui despotico, sed paterno; ergo non habet talem plenitudinem potestatis" (*Breviloquium*, II, 6).

[35] "In casu autem necessitatis ... quando omnes alii, ad quos spectarent, deficerent, posset et deberet temporalibus se immiscere" (*De potestate*, c. 10; *cf. Dialogus*, III, 1, 1, c. 16, Goldast, *Monarchia*, II, 785 f.).

clesia Universalis. Not to be identified with the contingent aspect of *Ecclesia Romana* or *Avionica,* she will never fall into error. But every individual in her can err, Pope as well as layman. Even a council is not protected from error. This *Ecclesia Universalis,* guided and kept free of error by the Holy Spirit, could eventually be represented in an individual man, a woman, or even in children under age. [36] Accordingly, Ockham cannot, without more ado, be termed a precursor of conciliarism. He did not himself travel the road of the council and in his writings, except for the *Dialogus,* the council plays no special role. In any event, it cannot be an absolute standard in matters of faith. Final resort is Holy Scripture and reason. Pope, clergy, and council must answer to them. [37]

If in *De corpore Christi (ca.* 1323) Ockham had asserted that his faith was that of the Roman Church, that he intended to maintain only what she taught and observed, [38] still in the *Breviloquium* he is unwilling to submit to anyone's correction whatever is made certain by Scripture, by rational insight, or in some other way. [39] In his last work, *De imperatorum et pontificum potestate,* he appeals to the public, because there could no longer be any question of the Pope as a judge and the "Church of Avignon" had succumbed to the greatest heresies. He does not want to submit to the majority but only to rational insight and the clear testimony of Scripture. The crowd, he said, has quite often erred and more than once in the history of the Church truth has been found in an individual (c. 1). Here Ockham is that individual. But it can also be the Emperor. In a state of emergency in the Church the Emperor can intervene in the spiritual realm, just as the Pope in cases of necessity can intervene in the temporal. For example, the Emperor can convoke a council or even depose the Pope. But he can do so, not by virtue of his office, but only as a believing member of the Church (*De potestate,* c. 12). For if the clergy fail, the laity bear responsibility for the Church. But there is no tribunal to decide when they must intervene on behalf of the faith and of the public good.

---

[36] "Fides etiam beati Petri, pro qua Christus rogavit, nequaquam deficeret, quia reperiretur in parvulis. Parvuli enim habent habitum fidei; ergo errante tota multitudine Christianorum usum rationis habentium, possunt salvari promissiones Christi per parvulos baptizatos; ergo temerarium est asserere, quod numquam tota multitudo Christianorum usum rationis habentium contra fidem errabit" (*Dialogus,* I, 5, c. 35, Goldast, *Monarchia,* II, 506); *cf.* G. de Lagarde, *op. cit.,* V (1963), 151.

[37] G. de Lagarde, *op. cit.,* V, 53–86; Ockham is no conciliarist nor does the principle of popular sovereignty dominate his ecclesiology, as Seeberg, III (Darmstadt, 5th ed., 1963), 589, maintains.

[38] ". . . me nihil asserturum nisi quod Romana tenet et docet ecclesia" (prologue); "Quicquid enim Romana ecclesia credit hoc solum et non aliud vel explicite vel implicite credo" (c. 1; ed. Strasbourg 1491, fol. C, I, ra.); G. de Lagarde, *op. cit.,* V, 139.

[39] "Quae autem per scripturas sacras vel per rationem evidentem aut quocumque modo sunt certa, nullius correctioni subicio" (prologue, ed. R. Scholz, 40).

In case of necessity the Emperor may, on his own authority, requisition Church property for worldly tasks.[40] Ockham distinguishes between the temporal property necessary for the support of clerics — this belongs to the Church *iure divino* — and whatever, over and beyond this, is entrusted to the Church *iure humano*, from the generosity of kings and laity, *ad pias causas:* care of the poor and strangers, construction of churches, and so forth. The donor can determine the use, and the Pope has no authority over this. On the other hand, the King can dispose of the Church property donated by himself or his predecessors without consulting the Pope. He can "on his own authority in case of need demand subsidies from the churches for pious ends" (*De potestate*, c. 24). According to the treatise *An rex Angliae*, among these *piae causae* is included the defense of the country, for the welfare of the father-land is superior to that of its poor. Now the clergy must make the goods of the Church available for the poor and hence all the more for the defense of the fatherland.[41] It is more religious to defend the fatherland than to care for the poor. Urgent cases in which it is even unlawful to ask the Pope or to observe his prohibition include danger to the King's life, his capture, the release of prisoners, and bridge-building.[42]

Ockham's efforts for a definition of the competence of the secular and spiritual powers are noteworthy. In emphasizing their mutual independence in reciprocal assistance he could have prepared for an adjustment in accord with reality. But his polemical stand in the struggle for the Emperor's rights against the Curia and the opinion he championed in the poverty dispute, according to which the Church, emulating Christ's poverty and powerlessness, should, as far as possible, renounce all functions in the world, caused him to underestimate the danger of state absolutism and so to expand the absolute powers of the secular authority that he promoted an *étatisme*. He stressed the liberty of the individual and of princes, but on the other hand did not even concede to the Pope the defense of the liberty of the Church as a justi-fication of his actions, "for the liberty of the Church and her honour in this world are to be reckoned among the least important goods" (*De potestate*, c. 23). "*Libertas evangelica* comes to a halt in a certain sense before the thrones of kings in the service of their expansion of power."[43]

---

[40] *De potestate*, c. 24; *cf.* the treatise *An rex Angliae pro succursu guerrae possit recipere bona ecclesiarum*, R. Scholz, II, 432–53.
[41] *An rex Angliae*, c. 8; R. Scholz, II, 444.
[42] *Ibid.*, c. 11.
[43] W. Kölmel, *W. Ockham und seine kirchenpolitischen Schriften*, 150 f.

CHAPTER 43

The Spiritual Movement and the Poverty Dispute

In the very lifetime of Saint Francis there had begun among his friars a vehement struggle over the ideal of absolute poverty. In it victory had soon gone to the circles which, because of the necessity resulting from the order's world-wide expansion and in the interests of a fruitful care of souls, modified the saint's ideal by means of papal privileges and interpretations of the rule to such an extent that absolute poverty was abandoned. In 1245 Innocent IV (1243–54) had declared[1] the movable and immovable property of the Franciscans to be the property of the Roman Church, and in 1247 he had allowed them procurators who could take care of legitimate business affairs according to the will of the friars, that is, "they are permitted to collect, sell, exchange, alienate, trade, spend, ... and use for the needs of the friars."[2] If this development was necessary, it was also ominous and the source of criticism and unrest that officially the founder's ideal was adhered to and the order claimed to practice the poverty desired by Francis. It was only a matter of time until the friars would be reproached on the ground that their poverty was a legal fiction.

Around the same time, at the middle of the thirteenth century, the spiritualism of Joachim of Fiore (d. 1202) gained a foothold in Franciscan circles. Gerard of Borgo San Donnino (d. 1276) in his *Liber Introductorius* (1254) published the three chief writings of the Calabrian Abbot as the "Eternal Gospel," which was supposed to be preached by the Franciscan Order from 1260 in place of the old Gospel. The order, he said, was the prophesied Spiritual Church, which would replace the property-holding Priestly Church. Pope Alexander IV had the *Introductorius* burned in 1255, and Gerard was imprisoned. But his opponent, the Master William of Saint-Amour, who had attacked the mendicant orders as such in the controversy at the University of Paris and had condemned poverty as morally evil, was also condemned by the Pope in 1256. Saint Bonaventure, minister general of the order from 1257 to shortly before his death in 1274, had thus to defend Franciscan poverty *(Quaestio de paupertate)* and at the same time to fight the Joachimite apocalyptic currents in the order. He sought to save the ideal of poverty and to restrict the use of property as much as possible. In accordance with Bonaventure's ideas, Pope Nicholas III (1277–80) issued an authentic explanation of the rule in the Constitution "Exiit qui seminat" of 14 August 1279.[3] It stressed the sanctity of evangelical poverty and the

---

[1] "Ordinem vestrum" of 14 November 1245, in *Bull Fr*, I, no. 114, p. 401.
[2] "Quanto studiosius" of 19 August 1247, in *Bull Fr*, I, no. 235, p. 487.
[3] *Bull Fr*, III, no. 127, p. 404.

obligation to its observance on the basis of the rule, but, by distinguishing between property or the right of usufruct and simple use (*usus moderatus*), enabled the Franciscans to retain their houses and the use of their properties. As a result the stricter element was rendered all the more unhappy, for even this modified ideal of poverty was not observed by a great part of the order and since the death of Bonaventure a decline of discipline was becoming widespread. Hence the dispute over poverty continued.

Spokesman was Peter John Olivi (d. 1298). The point in controversy was not whether there could be property or not, but the restricted use of earthly goods, the question whether an *usus pauper* was desirable and whether it was implied in the order's vow. Olivi gave his support for it and demanded this "use of things in a spirit of poverty" even by bishops belonging to the order. Renunciation of earthly possessions without a real life of the poor was, he said, similar to matter without form and brought the members of the order the scorn of the world.[4] Olivi had to vindicate himself at the general chapter in Montpellier (1287). Nevertheless, in Provence and in Italy a growing circle of zealots for poverty was forming around him. People were beginning to call them the "Spirituals" in contradistinction to the "Conventuals," who tried to adapt themselves to the situation and to achieve a mitigation based on the interpretations of the rule by Gregory IX and Nicholas III. The Conventuals were thereafter in a difficult position because all abuses were laid at their door and they were held responsible for the decline of fidelity to the rule, although they also struggled against it.

With the pontificate of Celestine V (1294) the Spirituals felt they had achieved their goal. He permitted a group of them under Angelus of Clareno and Peter of Macerata ("Liberatus") to live the rule in its full austerity according to the last will of Saint Francis, as a special branch of the order. Great was their disappointment when this "Angel Pope" gave way to the totally different Boniface VIII. Ubertino da Casale, who became leader of the Spirituals after Olivi's death in 1298, later branded the new Pope as the beast of the Apocalypse, the "mystical Antichrist." Boniface abolished the privilege of exemption granted by Celestine and in 1295 deposed the general, Raymond Gaufridi (d. 1310), who was friendly to the Spirituals.

The quarrel in the order continued. The harsh proceedings of the Conventuals, under the general Gonsalvo de Valboa (1304–13), against the Spirituals and the latters' charges against their persecutors and the presence of their influential patrons among princes and cardinals made it impossible for Clement V not to concern himself with the poverty question. As spokesman of the Spirituals at the Avignon Curia, Ubertino da Casale in his memorandum "Sanctitas Vestra"[5] at the end of 1309 emphasized that the

[4] Qu. 9 of the poverty treatise of summer 1279, ed. by F. Ehrle, *ALKGMA*, III (1887), 507–14 (especially page 508). Similarly in the treatise "De Usu Paupere," *ibid.*, 514–17.

[5] Ed. by F. Ehrle, *ALKGMA*, III (1887), 51–89.

order had declined profoundly because of various offenses against the letter and the spirit of the rule, particularly the view that the *usus pauper* was not binding on the basis of the vow of poverty. He asked the Pope that those who wished to practise poverty in all strictness should be allowed to live in peace and that the others should at least abide by the papal interpretations of the rule. Ubertino therefore urged the separation of the Spirituals from the Conventuals.

In view of the favourable attitude toward the Spirituals at the Curia and the not unjustified reproach of laxity in the observance of the rule, the Conventuals were now hard pressed. In a counterattack they accused Peter John Olivi, already twelve years dead, of heresy and the Spirituals of fostering his heretical doctrines. The Pope wanted to have these questions, for the most part purely dogmatic, discussed by the approaching Council. Thus the poverty dispute came before the Council of Vienne (1311–12), which on 5 May 1312 decided in general in favour of the stricter view. According to the bull "Exivi de Paradiso,"[6] the precepts of the rule were binding under serious sin. Prescriptions which were regarded as equivalent to such precepts were individually specified. "The friars, by virtue of their profession, are obliged to a truly poor use (*ad arctos usus seu pauperes*) in those things which are expressly specified as such in the rule." Individually and as a community they were not capable of receiving inheritances, they were not permitted to bring suit, possess vineyards, or build storehouses, and they were to be content with unpretentious churches and monasteries. The bull intended to provide a practical decision. The effort to connect the friars' poverty with the dogmatic question of the import of Christ's poverty and to brand the opposing view as heretical, according to whether one regarded the *usus pauper* as included in the vow of evangelical poverty or not, was expressly designated as "presumptuous and insolent."[7] The bull said nothing about a return of the Spirituals to their original convents under obedience to the superiors of the order.

This omission led to new difficulties. Michael of Cesena, elected minister general in 1316, tried, with the assistance of John XXII, to reduce to obedience high-handed and refractory Spirituals in Tuscany and Provence. The Pope summoned a number of them to Avignon and in the Constitution "Quorumdam Exigit" of 7 October 1317[8] forbade the Spirituals all unauthorized actions. He stated that obedience was superior to poverty and

---

[6] 6 May 1312, in *Bull Fr*, no. 195, pp. 80–86; G. Fussenegger, "Ratio commissionis in Concilio Viennensi institutae ad decretalem 'Exivi de Paradiso' praeparandam," *AFrH*, 50 (1957), 145–77.

[7] "Dicere autem, sicut aliqui asserere perhibentur, quod haereticum sit, tenere usum pauperem includi vel non includi sub voto evangelicae paupertatis, praesumptuosum et temerarium iudicamus" (*ibid.*, 85).

[8] *Bull Fr*, V, no. 289, pp. 128–30.

that the superiors of the order had the final say in regard to clothing and stocks of provisions. Obstinate Spirituals were handed over to the Inquisition and on 7 May 1318 four of them were burned at Marseilles. In other writings John XXII again dealt with the Spirituals, whom he labelled *fraticelli*, and deprived them of their own monasteries, among other things.

But soon the Pope was destined to oppose the entire order and even to discipline men who, like Bonagrazia of Bergamo and Michael of Cesena, were hitherto the opponents of the Spirituals. In this conflict, the dispute over the theory of poverty, the question at issue was whether Christ and the Apostles, individually or as a group, had possessed property. Thus the poverty dispute affected all Christendom much more deeply and acquired a direct bearing on the relationship, then a subject of controversy, between the spiritual and the secular powers. If Christ as man had renounced property and the exercise of authority over men and things and had subjected himself to Caesar, then this had to have consequences for his vicar on earth and for all who exercised spiritual authority in his name. It was further controverted whether private ownership had come into existence only as a result of the fall or was in accord with a divine ordinance from the very beginning.

The Dominican John of Belna, as inquisitor, had declared as heretical in a trial of Beghards the proposition that Christ possessed absolutely nothing. The Franciscan Berengar of Perpignan protested against this decision, citing Nicholas III. Thus the question came before the papal tribunal. When in the bull "Quia Nonnumquam" of 26 March 1322[9] John XXII annulled Nicholas III's prohibition of discussing "Exiit qui seminat," the Franciscans became afraid that he would decide the question according to the interpretation of the Dominicans. The general chapter at Perugia, under the direction of Michael of Cesena, anticipated such a papal decision by declaring in an encyclical of 6 June 1322 to all Christendom that "it is sound, Catholic, and orthodox teaching that Christ and the Apostles owned nothing as their own." In doing so it cited Nicholas III, Clement V, and even John XXII himself.

The indignant Pope's first reaction was to renounce ownership of the order's property and forbid the naming of procurators.[10] Bonagrazia of Bergamo was imprisoned for protesting this measure. In the bull "Cum inter Nonnullos" of 12 November 1323[11] John XXII declared heretical the assertion that Christ and the Apostles had possessed neither as individuals nor as a group. The entire order was enraged, and some of the members labelled the Pope a heretic. The situation became all the more inflamed when Louis the Bavarian adopted this charge in his Declaration of Sachsenhausen

---

[9] *Ibid.*, no. 464, pp. 224 f.
[10] Constitution "Ad Conditorem canonum" of 8 December 1322, in *Bull Fr*, V, no. 486, pp. 233–46.
[11] *Bull Fr*, V, no. 518, pp. 256–59.

on 22 May 1324.[12] However, the majority of the Franciscans returned to loyalty and the Pentecost Chapter at Lyons in 1325, under Michael of Cesena appealed for respect for the papal decrees. But the Pope apparently did not feel sure of the attitude of the minister general. He summoned him to Avignon in 1327[13] and, not finding him submissive, detained him there. He did not permit him to take part in the Pentecost Chapter at Bologna in 1328[14] but was unable to obtain the election of another minister general there. During the night of 26–27 May, 1328, Michael of Cesena succeeded in escaping from Avignon together with Bonagrazia of Bergamo and William of Ockham. The last named had had to defend his philosophical and theological teachings at the Curia. At Pisa they joined Louis the Bavarian, in whose retinue was already Marsilius of Padua. Thus Louis's quarrel acquired much more an ideological character through becoming involved with the poverty dispute.[15]

Michael of Cesena preached against John XXII and from Pisa released voluminous and scholarly appeals against the Pope, who on 6 June 1328 had deposed[16] and on 20 April 1329 had excommunicated[17] him along with his companions. In the bull "Quia Vir Reprobus" of 16 November 1329 John XXII gave a definitive expression of his views against Michael of Cesena. He stressed that Christ had had a *dominium* over worldly goods. Even in Paradise property was assigned by God to our first parents; it was not a mere human institution after the fall. At that time it required only a regulation by positive law.[18] A general chapter at Paris declared the deposition of Michael of Cesena legitimate and elected Geraldus Oddonis as his successor.

Geraldus wanted to dispense from the prohibition of money and other precepts of the rule. Hence both he and the Avignon Curia were bitterly reproached by Michael of Cesena during the rest of his life in numerous polemical pamphlets, in which he had the assistance of Bonagrazia of Bergamo and William of Ockham.[19]

---

[12] Text ed. by J. Schwalm, in *MGConst*, V, no. 909, pp. 722–44, no. 910, pp. 745–54.

[13] "Cum pro certis" of 8 June 1327, in *Bull Fr*, V, no. 667, pp. 325 f.

[14] *Bull Fr*, V, no. 706, p. 343, footnote to the register.

[15] K. Bosl, "Die 'Geistliche Hofakademie' Kaiser Ludwigs des Bayern im alten Franziskanerkloster zu München," *Der Mönch im Wappen* (Munich 1960), 97–129; cf., however, H. S. Offler, "Meinungsverschiedenheiten am Hofe Ludwigs des Bayern," *DA*, 11 (1954), 193, footnote 5.

[16] *Bull Fr*, V, no. 714, pp. 346–49.

[17] *Ibid.*, no. 786, pp. 383 f.

[18] *Bull Fr*, V, no. 820, pp. 439 ff.; cf. Michael's appeal of 26 March 1330 (*Bull Fr*, V, no. 820, 426 f., footnote) and his letters to the order of 24 January 1331 (*ibid.*, pp. 427–38, footnote) and 25 March (*ibid.*, pp. 497–500, footnote 7).

[19] Cf. the writings reproduced in M. Goldast, *Monarchia S. Romani Imperii*, II (Frankfurt 1614), 1236–1361: *Tractatus contra errores Johannis XXII* (1331), *Litterae deprecatoriae*, and *Littera ad omnes fratres Ordinis* (1333).

In his *Literas plurium*, which he sent to the general chapter at Perpignan, Michael declared that he was an orthodox Franciscan and the legitimate general and that John XXII was a heretic. Unfortunately, the Pope was destined to provide further substance for this charge in his teachings on the beatific vision. The chapter expelled from the order the Franciscans at the court of Munich. There they were more and more involved in the ecclesiastico-political struggle and became champions of the lay power against the Avignon papacy. Thus, almost exactly a century after its establishment, a part of the Franciscan Order became the chief prop of resistance to the Holy See. They were fighting with justification against the worldly and un-Christian spirit which was widespread at the Curia as well as in their order, but their struggle was in many ways a mockery of the ideal which they claimed they were renewing.

> Those men did not have the power to defend this ideal as Francis had done: silently, patiently, obediently. In their religious fanaticism they proceeded into active rebellion. [20]

The poverty dispute itself, the further decline of the ideal of poverty, and the universal abuses evident in Christendom, such as the prolonged interdict occasioned by the quarrel between Pope and Emperor, the Hundred Years' War (1337–1453), and the Western Schism produced a further decay of the order. The endeavour to supply as quickly as possible for the inroads of the plague (1348–52) — it is said that two-thirds of the members of the order fell victim to the Black Death — did nothing to advance religious discipline. But it is a testimony to the vitality of the order and the strength of its ideal that, in an effort to correct evils, reform circles were established again and again and in all the provinces. Thus there occurred in the second half of the fourteenth century and in the fifteenth the Observant movement, which led to the dividing of the order into Observants and Conventuals. While the former clung to the non-possession of property even by the community and wanted to renounce any regular income and real estate, the latter accepted common property, income, and estates.

The Council of Constance (1414–18) granted to the Observants of France their own provincial vicars and a vicar general. Continuing efforts to reform the order as a whole and thus to preserve its unity were futile. Saints Bernardine of Siena (d. 1444) and John of Capestrano (d. 1456) laboured for this purpose in Italy. In 1443 Pope Eugene IV gave the Observants two vicars general, one for their cismontane and one for their transmontane communities, and their own chapter. In 1446, at the suggestion of John Capestrano, he made the position of these vicars general so independent of the minister general that in actuality the Observants had become independent, even though the legal connection was still maintained. The complete

[20] J. Lortz, *Der unvergleichliche Heilige* (Düsseldorf 1952), 24.

division of the order occurred in 1517 when the Observants already constituted a majority. At the general chapter Leo X excluded the Conventuals
from the election of the minister general and united all branches of the
Observants as the *Ordo Fratrum Minorum Regularis Observantiae*. The
new arrangement was confirmed in the bull "Ite et vos in vineam" of 29 May
1517, and on 1 June a new minister general was elected, to whom the minister
general hitherto in office had to surrender the seal of the order. The Conventuals elected their own general, who, at the command of the Pope, had
to assume the title of master general.

Chapter 44

The German Mystics

In the scholasticism of the thirteenth century speculative discursive theology,
which Bernard of Clairvaux had felt called upon to assail as arrogant learning (*stultilogia*) in Peter Abelard, had carried off the victory. Just the same
the tide of the theology of practical acquisition and prayerful achievement
(*théologie monastique*), advocated by Bernard, never ceased.[1] Neoplatonism
too continued to exert its influence beside and within the Aristotelian trend
of thought. Indicative of Neoplatonism's increased influence at the close of
the thirteenth century is the translation of the *Institutio theologica* of Proclus
(d. 485) by William of Moerbeeke in 1264.[2]

In addition, the increasing coming of age of the laity brought along a
great yearning for education and a religious interest which had to be met
more fully and more deeply. In particular, women made widows as a
consequence of the crusades, other wars, and plague, and unmarried women
longed for religious and theological instruction. Many religious houses for
women were founded in the thirteenth century, especially for Dominican
nuns. In Strasbourg alone there were seven. Decrees of Pope Clement IV in
1267 and of the German provincial, Hermann of Minden, in 1286–87,
entrusted Dominican friars, especially lectors and masters,[3] with the care of
souls in the order's houses of women. Thus was called into being a more
practical theology, cultivating the spirituality of the heart and leading

---

[1] *Cf.* J. Leclercq, *The Love of Learning and the Desire for God* (New York 1961).

[2] *Cf.* Grabmann, *MGL*, II, 413–23.

[3] Text in Denifle, *ALKGMA*, II, 649 f., who, however, according to H. C. Scheeben ("Zur
Biographie Johannes Taulers," *Johannes Tauler, Gedenkschrift zum 600. Todestag,* ed. by
E. Filthaut [Essen 1961], 25 f.), understands too narrowly the *fratres docti* in the decree
of Hermann of Minden. Scheeben holds it is a question not of masters and lectors, not
even of scholars, but of capable and experienced preachers.

directly to union with God. Naturally, it was expressed in the German tongue. The presupposition for the rise of German mysticism was, then, the "combination of Dominican theology and pastoral care, vernacular preaching, feminine piety, and Germany's special position in the religious movements of the thirteenth and fourteenth centuries." [4] It presented itself as a doctrine of the experimental knowledge of God in the soul, as a guide to this, and as a witness of the mystical experience itself. We must not understand too narrowly the circle of persons termed mystics. In the fourteenth century we may include among them not only those favoured with extraordinary gifts and visions but all who wrote on piety in the vernacular.

The Dominican Henry of Halle collected from 1250 the notes of Mechtilde of Magdeburg (ca. 1212–85 or 1294), who, after a penitential life of more than thirty years as a Beguine, spent her last days in the Cistercian convent of Helfta. This collection, *Das fliessende Licht der Gottheit* (*The Streaming Light of the Godhead*), is the first great mystical work in German. Its Low German original is lost and has come down to us only in a free Latin translation and in the High German text of Henry of Nördlingen (d. after 1379). In daring but fervent images, determined by the *Minnesang*, Mechtilde beholds in her meditations, sayings, and verses the birth of the soul from God the Father, beyond the whole world and all time. The supernatural union with God is thus the vital element, the true "nature" of the soul (I, 44). Christ is the bridegroom destined for it, to whom it surrenders itself without disguising or reserving anything, and the Holy Spirit is the "lavish outpouring of the Father and the Son" (VI, 32), "the blessed gushing fountain of love" (VII, 24). The soul living in the streaming light of divine grace breaks out of its bounds, belongs to Christendom and to the world, lives and suffers for them. Unlike the Neoplatonic formula of purgative, illuminative, and unitive ways, for Mechtilde love is fulfilled in this earthly life in suffering, in patient longing, even in descent with Christ into hell. "It is the nature of love that it first proceeds in sweetness, then becomes rich in perception, and, thirdly, becomes desirous of and eager for abandonment" (IV, 20).

Under the influence of Mechtilde of Magdeburg at Helfta were Mechtilde of Hackeborn (1241–99), author of the *Liber specialis gratiae*, and Gertrude the Great (1256–1302), who wrote the *Legatus divinae pietatis* and *Exercitia spiritualia*. Gertrude's visions, written down in German and Latin, deal especially with the Eucharist and the Sacred Heart in connection with the liturgy. She is regarded as the herald of devotion to the Sacred Heart in the Middle Ages.

In Italy Angela of Foligno (1249–1309), who as a Franciscan tertiary led an austere penitential life in poverty and prayer, had mystical experiences

---

[4] H. Grundmann, *Religiöse Bewegungen im Mittelalter* (Darmstadt, 2nd ed. 1961), 527.

which her confessor wrote down in the *Book of Visions and Instructions* as dictated by her.

Among the Dominicans who combined the intellectual treasures of scholasticism with strongly Neoplatonic elements to render it fruitful for mystical piety and communicated it to nuns were John and Gerard Sterngassen[5] and Ulric of Strasbourg (d. 1277), the last named being the author of *De summo bono,* and, above all, Dietrich of Freiberg (d. after 1310). His mystical sermons, praised by contemporaries, have not been preserved, but they were probably treatments of metaphysics and cosmology. He stressed the great importance of experience in natural science and wrote *De iride et radialibus impressionibus* with an explanation of the rainbow, but otherwise he was under the spell of Neoplatonism. He explains the *emanatio* as creation, to which corresponds the *reversio* to the One. He identifies the *intellectus agens* with the Augustinian *memoria interior,* the *abditum mentis,* the basis of the soul, the heart of the soul, the divinely formed in man, in which truth is present. Dietrich of Freiberg exerted a great influence on Master Eckhart, Berthold of Moosburg, and John Tauler.

Master Eckhart

Master Eckhart was the most important and most daring representative of speculative German mysticism. He was German in the deep fervour of his thought, in the radicalism, even extravagance, with which he sought to carry his speculations to their ultimate consequences, even to paradox, and in the vigorous style with which he was able to express them in German. Born at Hochheim in Thuringia around 1260, he became a Dominican and, following studies at Cologne and Paris, was made, while still young, prior at Erfurt and vicar of the provincial, Dietrich of Freiberg, for Thuringia. As such he delivered to the young members of the order the *Reden der Unterscheidung (Discourses on Discrimination).* In these he outlined the criteria of genuine piety and taught "the total divesting of self for God" in obedience. Thus was sounded the keynote of his later preaching: solitude as the prerequisite of union with God. In 1302 he became master of theology at Paris, and, after the division of the German province, provincial of the new Saxon province (1303–11), with forty-seven houses of friars and more than seventy of nuns. In addition, he became vicar general of the Bohemian province in 1307. When Eckhart's election as provincial of the South German province was annulled, the general sent him to Paris as master for the school years 1311–12 and 1312–13. From 1314 he was at Strasbourg, his headquarters

---

[5] *Grabmann, MGL,* I, 392–404; N. Appel, *Gerhard von Sterngassen und sein Pratum animarum* (Diss. theol., Bonn 1934).

for supervising the spiritual care of the convents of nuns in Alsace and Switzerland until 1322. During the last five years or so of his life he was director of studies at the house in Cologne and a zealous preacher.

Transcripts of his German sermons provided the material which induced Archbishop Henry von Virneburg to institute a process in 1326 because of the propagation of false teaching. Eckhart declared on 26 September 1326 that the archiepiscopal court had no jurisdiction over him as a Dominican and a master, but he nevertheless answered the charge in an "essay of vindication." On 13 February 1327, in the church of the Dominicans, he protested his orthodoxy and his readiness to repudiate ascertained errors. In spite of the rejection of his appeal on 22 February 1327, the case was referred to Avignon, where he personally undertook his defense. It was only after his death, which occurred before 30 April 1328, that seventeen propositions were condemned as heretical and eleven declared suspect in the bull "In agro Dominico," issued by John XXII on 27 March 1329. Only the third part of the projected *Opus tripartitum* was finished: scriptural exegesis — Genesis, Exodus, Wisdom, and Saint John's Gospel (Lat. WW, I–III) — and sermons on biblical texts (IV). More controversial, but also more influential, were his German writings: *Reden der Unterscheidung, Buch der göttlichen Tröstungen (Book of the Divine Consolations)*, with the sermon "Von dem edeln Menschen" ("On the Noble Man"), and some 160 sermons which have been handed down only in transcripts; it is difficult to prove that all are genuine.

With a grandiose partiality Eckhart repeats some fundamental notions of God as the basis of all being, of the birth of the Son from the Father in the spark of the soul, and of solitude of soul whereby it is able to contain God.

> When I preach, I am accustomed to speak, first, of solitude and that man should be devoid of self and of all things; second, that one should be re-formed into the one good, which is God; third, that one should be aware of the great nobility with which God invests the soul in order that man may thereby enter into the wonderful life of God; fourth of the purity of the divine nature (F. Pfeiffer, *Deutsche Mystiker* [= Pf.], 91).

Proceeding from the scriptural texts, "I am who am" (Exodus 3:14) and "In the beginning was the Word" (John 1:1), Eckhart stresses perceiving as the basis of God's existence. If existence follows the divine perceiving, God is something higher than existence. "And hence whatever is always in God is above existence itself and is exclusively perception" (Lat. WW, V, 44). Thus Eckhart is able to say "that in God non-existence is still existence," for he is the source of all existence. "Accordingly, existence is not within God's province, unless you should wish to term such purity existence." That which perceives this knowing, supporting and embracing all existence, is its own self, which the Father beholds and expresses in his Word, the Son. At the same time he comprehends in it all ways in which creatures can portray his essence. "The Father perceives nothing except this same Word and himself and the whole divine nature and all things in this same Word, and whatever he perceives in it is equal to the Word and is the same Word by nature in truth" (Pf., 290; J. Quint, *Meister Eckhart* [= Qu.], 25).

Thus Eckhart endeavours to safeguard God's distinction from the world and at the same time to make clear his presence in the world. God calls creatures to himself out of nothing, and hence they obtain and have existence in him and only in an enduring relationship to him. Because their being depends on God's presence, they are nothing if left to themselves. Thus Eckhart can say in exaggeration that all creatures "are pure nothingness" (Germ. WW, I, 80). But if the existence of creatures depends on God's presence, then there must be a point of contact with him. In man this is located in the depths of the spiritual soul in the state of grace. Here man is responsive not only to God's action but to God himself.

> I have a power in my soul which is fully responsive to God (Qu. 323). God is in all things; but ... nowhere so really as ... in the innermost part and the highest part of the soul (Qu. 356). It is the castle which Jesus enters, more according to his existence than according to his activity: by giving to the soul a divine and godlike existence through grace, which is oriented to essence and existence, according to the text: By the grace of God I am what I am ...[6] God has no more fitting abode than a pure heart and a pure soul; there the Father brings forth his Son, as he brought him forth in eternity, neither more nor less (Qu. 175).

Hence on man is enjoined the duty of becoming "God's son by grace."[7] "The image of God, the Son of God is in the soul as a living fountain." It must be freed of all concealing layers. Man must separate himself from all that is not God, especially from his own will. "That is pure which is detached and separated from all creatures, for all creatures defile, since they are nothingness" (Qu. 175). Man is he "who submits himself to God with all that he is and has, obeys him, and gazes upward at God" (Qu. 145). In keeping with the Gospel (Mark 8:35, and elsewhere), man must practise humility, poverty, resignation, seclusion, and self-denial in order to become free for the encounter with God in the depth of the soul. He must progress from distraction to recollection, from diversity to unity.

> Hence I say: If man renounces himself and all created things — to the extent that you do so, you will be united and blessed in the soul's little spark, which knows neither time nor place. This spark rejects all creatures and wants nothing but God, revealed as he is in himself (Qu. 315f.).

[6] "Rechtfertigungsschrift," ed. by A. Daniels, *BGPhMA*, 23 (1923), 60; O. Karrer-H. Piesch, 129; G. Théry, 258.
[7] *Buch der göttlichen Tröstung*, Germ. WW, V, 37 f.

Though mystical union in the depth of the soul is the highest stage that man can attain to, he is not permitted to remain satisfied with it. No creature can be man's beatitude and perfection, and so he must keep himself aloof from finite being in order to permit himself to be seized upon by God. But once man has become aware of God, then he can rightly know and love his fellowmen and things. In fact, whoever is most intimately united to God, "whoever does right," finds God in all things and deeds. "Such a man bears God in all his works and in all places" (Qu. 59). "Whoever thus has God in his existence understands God as God, and God radiates on him in all things; for in all things there is for him the taste of God, and the image of God becomes visible to him in all things" (Qu. 60). Virginity must be realized in the fecundity of woman. "It is good that man receives God in himself and in this receptiveness he is a virgin; but for God to become fruitful in him is better, for to become fruitful with the gift is the only gratitude for the gift, and the spirit lies in gratitude returned ..." (Germ. WW, I, 27). Contemplation and the active life thus call for each other. Mary at the Lord's feet was only at the beginning.

> For when she was [still] sitting at our Lord's feet, she was not [yet the true] Mary; she may have been in name but not [yet] in her being. For she [still] sat in pleasant feeling and sweet sensation and was being taken in hand and was [now] learning life. But Martha was fully real there (Qu. 288).

> If a man were in ecstasy as was Saint Paul and knew of a sick man who wanted a bit of broth from him, I would deem it far better for you to surrender the ecstasy out of love and serve the needy one in greater love (Qu. 76).

The condemned propositions extracted from Master Eckhart's works, in so far as they clearly reflect his views, can be shown to be orthodox in the context of his doctrine. We must also bear in mind the difficulty of the mystic, who must express subtle knowledge and experiences of the spiritual life in human speech, particularly in a vernacular hardly developed for this. Yet, the charge of "having propounded many doctrinal propositions which laid a smoke screen over the true faith in many hearts, which he taught above all in his sermons to simple people, and which he also put in writing,"[8] is not wholly wrong. The cause here lay in his boundless and ever more extravagant eagerness to express himself even to excess and in paradox, which in his exalted solitude saw no need to have regard for the many who did not understand him, who in fact could not but misunderstand him. "If, however, there is anyone who understands this word incorrectly, what can be done by one who correctly utters this word which is correct?" (Qu. 139). But if truth is to be expressed in love (Ephesians 4:15), the theologian, and in particular

---

[8] John XXII, bull "In Agro Dominico," ALKGMA, II (1888), 636.

the preacher, must be guided by a pastoral consideration. It was also dangerous that Eckhart in his speculation on the Logos lost sight of the historical Christ and did not accept the literal sense of Scripture as his standard, while the Church and the Sacraments, though not denied, were not given their proper place. At that very time the Church was concerned with rejecting the extravagances of the nominalists. It is significant of the risks to which theology was then exposed that William of Ockham, who had to justify himself at the papal tribunal in Avignon at the same time that Eckhart did, for his part regarded the views of the Dominican as absurd. [9]

John Tauler

Master Eckhart's most important disciples were John Tauler (*ca.* 1300–61) and Henry Suso (1295–1366). While avoiding bold formulation, they aimed to make clear the orthodoxy of Eckhart's ideas and to prevent their being misused by enthusiasts.

The claim that John Tauler heard the lectures of Master Eckhart and of Nicholas of Strasbourg along with Suso at Cologne in 1325–29 is not confirmed by the sources. On the contrary, Tauler was probably never a lecturer and hence it is unlikely that he attended the *Studium generale* at Cologne. [10] He probably studied at Strasbourg or elsewhere in southern Germany. He may have known of Eckhart through his writings, which were available to him in 1339 at Cologne or Strasbourg. Perhaps he met the master personally when the latter was on the upper Rhine carrying out his function in the order. From 1330 Tauler was a preacher in Strasbourg, his native city. In the conflict between Louis the Bavarian and John XXII the city sided with the Emperor and hence lay under interdict from 1329 to 1353. When the conflict reached its critical stage and Louis ordered the public celebration of Mass, Tauler and his community withdrew to Basel in 1338–39. Here he was in touch with Henry of Nördlingen and the "friends of God." He spent some time in Cologne in 1339 and 1346. In 1342 he must have returned with his community from Basel to Strasbourg, where thereafter he was chiefly concerned with popular preaching and the spiritual care of nuns and Beguines. He died at Strasbourg on 16 June 1361.

There is still no critical edition of Tauler's works. Only his German sermons are undeniably authentic, and only about eighty of the 144 ascribed to him. His mysticism is based on Eckhart's speculations but it has a more ethical and psychological orientation, is far more practically concerned for

[9] *Dialogue*, III, 2, 2, c. 8, ed. M. Goldast, *Monarchia Sacri imperii*, II (Frankfurt 1614), 909.
[10] H. C. Scheeben regards "it as out of the question that he studied at Cologne" ("Zur Biographie Taulers," *loc. cit.*, 23).

day-to-day living, and places more strongly in the foreground the exertion of the will in the purgative way. In Tauler the divine birth is not so much a participation in the divine knowing as an assimilation to the divine will after the example of the suffering and life of Christ. Tauler, the practical mystic, pastor of souls, and cheerful master, gained through his preaching enthusiastic listeners in the circles of the "friends of God."

> You know there is many a woman in the world who has a husband and children and many a man makes shoes, and they seek God [in their work] and try in this way to feed themselves and their children. And many a poor man in the village carts manure and earns his morsel of bread in hard and bitter work. And it may be that all these manage a hundred times better while following [God's] call unpretentiously ... These men live humbly and in the fear of God in their poverty, and follow the call in simplicity ... The most sublime, the supreme way of [God's] call consists in following, outwardly and inwardly, the loving example of his beloved Son, actively and passively, with the aid of images or in contemplation apart from all images. And whoever imitates this [model], with pure heart and totally, will attain to the highest and sublimest goal. [11]

Tauler frequently admonishes that contemplation should be rendered effective in active love. The active life, then, is not merely a preparation for the contemplative life but just as much its fruit.

> You should know that, if I were not a priest and did not live in an order, I would regard it as a great thing to be able to make shoes and I would do it better than anything else and would be happy to earn my bread with my hands ... I know one of the most honoured friends of God. He has been a farmer all his days, more than forty years, and that is what he still is. He once asked our Lord whether he should stop work and go to the church. But the Lord said: No, he should not do that; he should earn his bread in the sweat of his brow in honour of the Lord's precious blood. [12]

Henry Suso

If daring and lonely speculation was characteristic of Eckhart and practical ethical striving of Tauler, Henry Suso was noteworthy for the warmth and depth of his feeling. He was born around 1295 at Constance of a knightly family. Having become a Dominican at the age of thirteen, he studied at the house in Constance and then around 1322 was sent to the *Studium generale* at Cologne. Here he was an enthusiastic disciple of Eckhart and was

[11] Ed. F. Vetter, *Predigt*, no. 53, p. 243; G. Hofman, no. 65, p. 507.
[12] Ed. F. Vetter, no. 42, p. 179; G. Hofman, no. 47, pp. 361, 364.

with him during his trial. From around 1327 he acted as lecturer at Constance, but around 1330 he was reprimanded for his association with Eckhart. Hence he did not continue his academic career but devoted himself entirely to the care of souls, chiefly in the houses of nuns on the upper Rhine and in Switzerland. He was in contact with the "friends of God" and engaged in a lively correspondence with them and with his spiritual women disciples, especially Elsbeth Stagel, who edited his autobiography. In the *Büchlein der Wahrheit (Little Book of Truth)* Suso defended Eckhart's mysticism and sought to protect it against misunderstandings. In the *Büchlein der ewigen Weisheit (Little Book of Eternal Wisdom)*, and its expanded and widely disseminated Latin version, the *Horologium Sapientiae,* Suso provided a practical mysticism of the following of the suffering Christ and union with his Mother beneath the Cross. He expresses his mystical doctrine in the words: "A detached man must put off the image of the creature, be formed into the image of Christ, and be further formed into the image of the Godhead." [13] Thus Suso was in the school of Eckhart. But in the manner of his mystical way, with its orientation to the tangible events and situations of the life of Christ, accessible to contemplation and actual imitation, he is far removed from his master. This moulding and this very detailed description of sacred history call directly for artistic representation. Thus Suso's mysticism stands in an especially close, perhaps reciprocal, relation to the pictorial art of his age. [14] As the minnesinger and poet among the mystics, he combined sensitivity and warmth of feeling with chivalrous magnanimity. This investing of the "mystical devotion to God with the symbolism of courtly love," to use the words of Kunisch, caused him to stress clearly the relation to the beloved "thou" and preserved him from a pantheistic misunderstanding.

Mysticism was not confined to the few great masters from the ranks of the Dominicans. But the diocesan priest Henry of Nördlingen (d. after 1379) lacked their independence and depth. His significance lay in his tireless activity in many places, as leader and adviser of the "friends of God" in the world and in the cloister, for the spread of the notions and practice of the mystical life. His correspondence with Margaret Ebner (d. 1351) and her circle is the oldest extant collection of letters in German. It affords a glimpse into the life of the mystical circles of the fourteenth century.

Strong reminiscences of the mystics appear in sermon material relating to the lives of the saints which the layman Hermann of Fritzlar put in writing in 1343–49. A far-reaching influence, extending to the *Exercises* of Saint Ignatius Loyola and to Saint Teresa of Ávila, was exercised by Ludolf

---

[13] Suso's *Life,* chapter 49, ed. K. Bihlmeyer, 168; N. Heller, 155.
[14] *Cf.* the references of K. Bihlmeyer in his edition of Suso, 45–62, and U. Weymann, *Die Seusische Mystik und ihre Wirkung auf die bildende Kunst* (Berlin 1938).

of Saxony (d. 1378) in his *Meditationes vitae Christi,* a *summa* of the life of Jesus with expositions by the Fathers, meditations, and exhortations.[15]

The "Engelberg Preacher," an unknown diocesan or religious priest, whose identification with Bartholomew Friedauer is disputed, shows far more of Tauler's than of Eckhart's influence in his lively style.[16]

John van Ruysbroeck

In the area of the Netherlands and Flanders German mysticism reached its peak in John van Ruysbroeck (Ruusbroec). He was born in 1293 in the village of Ruysbroeck between Brussels and Hal. After his ordination in 1318 he acted as vicar of Saint Gudula at Brussels, but at the age of fifty (1343) he withdrew with some like-minded canons into the solitude of Groenendael. They lived here as a community of hermits until 1350 when they adopted the rule of the Augustinian canons. Ruysbroeck became prior of the new monastery. He was in close relationship with mystics and reform circles, and Gerard Groote and perhaps also Tauler came to see him. He died in 1381 at the age of eighty-eight.

His eleven authenticated writings were composed in great part while he was still a diocesan priest. The urban population of the economically and culturally highly developed Netherlands was prepared for a deeper religious life in keeping with its greater maturity and independence and set higher standards for itself as well as for preaching and pastoral care. This is evident in the numerous communities of Beguines and Beghards. Men and women of deep religious sensitivity but of insufficient theological training were exposed to the danger of falling victim to an unenlightened heretical exuberance in their mystical religious aspirations. If in addition it was not always easy to distinguish between genuine religious striving and experience and an ecstatic pseudo-mysticism, it was especially hard to determine the boundaries between, on the one hand, Beguines and Beghards, who, unlike the orders, were not clearly indicated by organization and theological education, and, on the other, such heretical groups as the "Brothers and Sisters of the Free Spirit." Time and again the former had been confused with these sectaries, who subscribed to a monistic pantheism, aimed to participate in the vision of God even in this world by being merged into the universal oneness of God, and fancied themselves to be above all laws and sinless. Closely connected with them was the visionary Blommaerdine (d. 1336), who in Ruysbroeck's

---

[15] N. Paulus, *AElsKG,* 2 (1927), 207–22; M. I. Bodenstedt, *The Vita Christi of Ludolf the Carthusian* (Diss., Washington 1944, with the literature).

[16] S. Beck, *Untersuchungen zum Engelberger Prediger* (Fribourg 1952); W. Muschg, *Die Mystik in der Schweiz* (Frauenfeld and Leipzig 1935), 310–32.

day caused a great stir at Brussels through her teaching and writing and was idolized by her followers.

The young vicar of Saint Gudula sought by his writings to satisfy the genuine hunger for spiritual guidance and at the same time to counteract Blommaerdine's false mysticism. Hence in 1330 he wrote his treatise *Von dem Reich der Liebenden (The Kingdom of Lovers)* and soon after his most admired work, *Zierde der geistlichen Hochzeit (The Spiritual Espousals).* To this period of his pastoral activity at Brussels belong also the works *Vom glänzenden Stein (On the Sparkling Stone), Von den vier Versuchungen (The Four Temptations),* and *Vom Christenglauben (On the Christian Faith),* an explanation of the creed for the use of priests. The very large *Buch von den geistlichen Tabernakeln (Book of the Spiritual Tabernacles)* was completed at Groenendael. It was strongly critical of the Church and clergy of the day. *Von den sieben Einschliessungen (On the Seven Enclosures)* was intended for nuns. In the *Spiegel der ewigen Seligkeit (Mirror of Eternal Happiness)* Ruysbroeck provides a comprehensive instruction in the spiritual life. The *Buch von den sieben Stufen auf der Treppe geistlicher Minne (Book of the Seven Steps on the Ladder of Spiritual Love)* strongly emphasizes asceticism, while *Das Buch von den zwölf Beginen (Book of the Twelve Beguines)* is a collection of pious meditations. In order to counteract all misunderstandings, Ruysbroeck, when almost seventy, once more took up his pen and, at the request of friends, gave a condensed explanation of his doctrine in *Samuel oder das Buch von der höchsten Wahrheit (Samuel or the Book of the Sovereign Truth).*

The starting point and the final goal of Ruysbroeck's mysticism is God, one and three-in-one. His idea of the world and of man and even more his doctrine of grace and the spiritual and mystical life are oriented to the Trinity. God's being exceeds all limits, is *wijselos,* is "inaccessible height, abysmal depth, incomprehensible breadth, eternal length, a gloomy silence, a sumptuous desert." [17] But his nature

> is fecund. Hence it does not remain in the oneness of fatherhood but must generate unceasingly the Eternal Wisdom, the Son of the Father . . . Since the Father beholds his Son, the Eternal Wisdom, and all things in this same Wisdom, he was born and is a different person from the Father.

However, this self-contemplation of Father and Son is at the same time a mutual affirmation of self, is love. From the fact

> that the Son is born as a different person from the Father, since the Father beholds him as born and all things in him and with him, as a life of all things, and that the Son in turn beholds the Father as giving birth and fecund and himself and all things in the Father, proceeds a love,

---

[17] *Zierde der geistlichen Hochzeit,* II, 38; WW, I, 181.

which is the Holy Spirit and the bond from Father to Son and from Son to Father. This giving birth and returning to unity is the work of the Trinity — unity of nature, trinity of persons. [18]

This union of fruitfulness of nature and singleness of essence, of becoming and being, of activity and blessed enjoyment, of overflow into multiplicity and discharge into oneness, of beginning and completion, is the goal of the mystical life.

> The Holy Trinity has created us according to this eternal image and this parable. Hence God intends that we move out of ourselves in this divine light and seek to attain supernaturally to this image, which is our real life, and possess it with him, working and enjoying in everlasting blessedness. [19]

As image, as mirror of the Triune God,

> the substance of our soul [has] three properties, which according to their nature are one. The first property is the formless and essential nakedness (blooetheit) whereby we are like the Father and his divine nature and united with him. The second property can be called the higher reason of the soul. It is a reflecting clarity in which we receive God's Son, the Eternal Truth. In the clarity we are like him, in receiving him we are one with him. The third property we call the spark of the soul; it is a natural inclination of the soul for its origin, in which we receive the Holy Spirit, the love of God. In the inclining we are like the Holy Spirit, in the receiving we become one spirit and one love with God. [20]

These three properties are at the same time the organs of the efficacy of the divine persons on the soul. We are created "to" the image of God, that is, the essence of the image is both giving and surrendering. "God has created us that we may find, know, and possess this image in our being and in the purity of the depth of our soul (in puerheit onser ghedachten)." [21] In the spark of the soul God touches man, so that man feels himself drawn by God and begins his return to the purity and oneness of the spirit. This return to God in grace and the virtues, in the contemplative life and moral exertion, follows in three stages, the "active," the "intimate," and the "contemplative" life. These stages roughly correspond to the three ways of mysticism in general, and hence in Ruysbroeck the practical and personal feature is especially stressed.

In the "active" life there is question not so much of acquiring and practising various virtues as of the "advent of Christ," to whom the pious person

---

[18] *Ibid.*, WW, I, 60 f.
[19] *Ibid.*, III, 5; WW, I, 245.
[20] *Spiegel des ewigen Heiles*, c. 8; WW, III, 167 f.
[21] *Sieben Stufen der Liebe*, c. 13; WW, III, 264.

is betrothed, and of union with and likeness to the manner and work of Christ.

The aim and end of the "intimate" exercise is the mystical recognition of the bridegroom as he is in himself and the mystical union with him in the depth of the soul, which is made ready by the grace of God and the virtuous deeds of the "active life." [22]

Likeness to and union with the Son leads to the Father, the source of the Godhead. Just as the Son proceeds from the Father in the eternal birth and flows back in love to unity, so does he speak to the soul united to him: "Follow me to my Father." [23] Hence all holiness and beatitude consist in our being led to the Father, that is, to repose in the essential oneness. [24] But as God, by virtue of his unity, abides in blessed repose and, by virtue of his trinity, works in active love, so the loving soul in the "God-seeing life" is one with God in repose and like him in works of love. [25] In connection with Psalm 41:8 it is said:

And the abyss [of God] calls to the abyss . . . This calling is an outpouring of the essential light, and this essential light causes us to lose ourselves in the embrace of an unfathomable love and to escape into the wild darkness of the Godhead. And hence, one with God's spirit in a direct union, we can meet God through God; [26] that is, like God and made in his image by God himself, by union and likeness with the Holy Spirit, the Son, and the Father, we can now take possession of God also in his oneness and repose, and hence of the divine nature as such. [27]

To this contemplation, this nearness of the depths of the soul with the depths of the Godhead,

no one can attain by means of learning and cleverness nor by any sort of practice. But only he whom God wishes to make one with his Spirit and to illuminate with himself can seize upon God in contemplation — no one else. [28]

This doctrine of God-seeing love in the third book of *The Spiritual Espousals*, according to which "the soul receives the clarity which is God" and "it becomes itself the clarity which it receives," [29] and similar pantheistic-sounding sentences were attacked by John Gerson soon after 1400. [30] But

---

[22] G. Dolezich, *Die Mystik Johannes van Ruysbroecks*, 92.
[23] *Zierde der geistlichen Hochzeit*, II, 65; WW, I, 213.
[24] *Ibid.*, II, 60; WW, I, 207.
[25] *Ibid.*, II, 66; WW, I, 216.
[26] *Ibid.*, II, 70; WW, I, 223.
[27] G. Dolezich, *op. cit.*, 115.
[28] *Zierde der geistlichen Hochzeit*, III, 1; WW, I, 239.
[29] WW, I, 242.
[30] "Epistola . . . ad Fr. Bartholomaeum Carthusiensem," *Opera Omnia*, ed. Du Pin, I (Antwerp 1706), 59–63, and A. Combes, *Essai sur la critique de Ruysbroeck par Gerson*,

from the first Ruysbroeck anticipated reproaches of this sort, by often emphasizing in his later writings, as protection against misinterpretations, that this oneness of being with God must be understood as

> one with him in his love but not in his nature. For otherwise we would be God, annihilated in ourselves, which is impossible. [31] Indeed, we are further formed by the Spirit of God, as iron by fire, so that, as far as there is iron, there is also fire, but the fire does not become iron and the iron does not become fire. [32]

The relationship of this mystical speculation to Master Eckhart is easy to establish. But whether there is a direct dependence, or the resemblance to the common sources, such as Dionysius the Areopagite, the Victorines, and others, is sufficient explanation, is difficult to say. The style of the Fleming is more intense in feeling, bolder, and more down to earth, and he is also more concerned with actually living the truths contemplated. But his mystical doctrine is less oriented to actual realization and verification in daily life than was that of the great Rhenish mystics. And a quietistic trend is unmistakable.

To what extent mysticism, as a movement of renewal, embraced large circles appears from numerous memoirs and *vitae* from the monasteries of women of the period. The most precious of these accounts of mystically gifted nuns are those of the sisters of Töss near Winterthur by Suso's friend, Elsbeth Stagel (d. *ca*. 1350–60), and of the nuns of Engelthal, which Christine Ebner (d. 1336) relates in the *Büchlein von der Gnadenüberlast (Little Book of Overflowing Grace)*.

Naturally, the powerful spread of mysticism contained the danger of superficiality and falsification. The larger the circle in search of mystical experience became, and the more mysticism became a form of religious existence which people wanted to teach and learn, so much the sooner did vision become the rule, individual experience become the fashion, and eventually there resulted a craze to imitate, sterile reflection, and exaggerated analysis of occurrences within the soul. Lack of self-criticism and self-discipline then led easily to sensuous emotional excesses, to self-deception, and to extravagances in poor taste. John Gerson (d. 1429) came out against such aberrations in the mysticism of his time. In his chief work, *De mystica theologia* (1408), [33] he gave to mystical theology preeminence over scholastic theology and termed it the source of the complete knowledge of God. But he

---

I (Paris 1945), 615–35. Defense by John von Schoenhoven (d. 1432) in Du Pin, I, 63–78; A. Combes, *Essai*, I, 716–71.

[31] *Spiegel des ewigen Heiles*, c. 24; WW, III, 219; cf. c. 25, WW, III, 216 f.

[32] *Von den zwölf Beginen*, c. 14; WW, IV, 26; *Buch von der höchsten Wahrheit*, c. 8; WW, III, 286 f.

[33] Ed. A. Combes (Lugano 1958).

warned against a deviation of mystical love into sensuality and feasting on sweetness and showed the way to a practical piety. [34]

How men who were concerned for miracles and extraordinary mystical occurrences but were lacking in really mystical gifts seized upon mystification in order to reassure themselves and to emphasize their claim before others is made clear in the figure of the layman Rulman Merswin (1307–82). With the consent of his second wife, this distinguished Strasbourg merchant and banker renounced the world at the age of forty, got into contact with Tauler, Henry of Nördlingen, Margaret Ebner, and other "friends of God," and in 1367 acquired from the Benedictines the monastery on the Grünenwörth near Strasbourg to lead a retired life there with others of like mind. Even after the transfer of this foundation of his to the Hospitallers in 1371 he secured for himself a determining influence, in fact the actual direction. He passed himself off as the middleman of a secret "great friend of God from the up-country." After his death in 1382 a number of writings in his hand were found, treatises and letters, which were attributed to the mythical "friend of God from the up-country." In a tedious style, rich in pious platitudes, their author indulges in complaints over the maladies of Christendom and extols in stories of conversions the mode of life of the "friends of God," in proper contrast to the lives of the clergy. After long and heated discussion there is today agreement that the figure of the "friend of God from the up-country" is a fiction and that these writings are fabrications of Merswin himself (Denifle, Strauch, Oehl) or at least of his confidant, the Hospitaller priest, Nicholas of Louvain (Rieder). They were intended to procure for Merswin greater esteem and assure the form desired by him for his foundation or give it permanence.

The mystical and ascetical writings of the Benedictine, John of Kastl (d. ca. 1410), a reform abbey in the Upper Palatinate, extended into the fifteenth century. Martin Grabmann proved that the widely known De adhaerendo Deo, [35] attributed to Albertus Magnus, was John's work. [36]

Of the Dominicans who kept up with the spiritual legacy of their order in the fifteenth century, John Nider (d. 1438) is especially noteworthy. [37] In his writings, for example Vierundzwanzig guldin Harfen (Twenty-Four

---

[34] De distinctione verarum visionum a falsis, ed. Du Pin, I, 43–59; "potest fieri, ut amor a spiritu incipiat, sed vehementer formidandum est, ne per blanditias sensim carne consumatur" (ibid., 55).

[35] German translation, ed. by W. Oehl, Dokumente der Religion, II (Paderborn 1923).

[36] Grabmann, MGL, I, 489–524; for all of Kastl's works see J. Sudbrack, Die geistliche Theologie des Johannes von Kastl, 2 vols. (Münster 1967).

[37] K. Schieler, Magister Johannes Nider aus dem Orden der Predigerbrüder (Mainz 1885); J. Geiraths, "Nider Johannes und die Mystik," DTh, 321–46; idem, "Johannes Tauler und die Frömmigkeitshaltung des 15. Jahrhunderts," Johannes Tauler, Gedenkschrift zum 600. Todestag, 422–34.

Golden Harps), published at Strasbourg in 1493, and *Formicarius* (Strasbourg 1517), are found many phrases and ideas from fourteenth-century mysticism and resemblances to Henry Suso and John Tauler especially. But precisely because of the far-reaching agreement, the quite different attitude of the fifteenth century and the change in meaning of basic ideas become especially clear. Mystical speculation has yielded to guidance for pious living, determined by the care of souls. This turning to the ethical, the practical, and the concrete, joined to a stricter withdrawal from the world, is characteristic of the fifteenth century in general.

In the first half of the century a so far unknown "priest and guardian of the Teutonic Knights at Frankfurt," as the introduction styles him,[38] provided in his *German Theology* a "summary of the intellectual output of German mysticism" (J. Bernhart). Prudent in speculation, he was, like Tauler, concerned for the practical and pastoral. He would like, as a defense against "unauthentic, false, free spirits, who are harmful to Holy Church," to lead to the true and proper "friendship of God." In this book, which Luther edited for publication in 1516 and 1518, German mysticism acquired a direct influence on the reformer and on Lutheranism.

In mysticism we have before us a first initial effort of some importance toward a German theology, that is, the attempt to penetrate revelation on the part of German thinkers and with the possibilities of the German tongue. This endeavour did not get beyond the first starts, imposing as they are. Eckart was condemned; Tauler was slandered in connection with the Reformation and in 1559 put on the Index.[39] Then the stream of German mysticism was sealed off, at least within the Catholic Church, and the chasm between spirituality and theology in the West became deeper still. At the Council of Trent and thereafter theology acquired an exclusively Romance colouring, and in it and in the liturgy the Latin language virtually took on the character of orthodoxy.

[38] R. Haubst, *Scholastik,* 33 (1958), 375–98, holds that John of Frankfurt is to be considered the probable author of "Eyn deutsch Theologia." John was professor of theology at Heidelberg and preacher at the Holy Spirit Monastery. He died in 1440. Accordingly, the "Theologia Deutsch" must have originated between 1420 and 1440.

[39] The revised edition of Tauler's works, in Dutch, that appeared at Frankfurt in 1565 was placed on the Antwerp appendix to the Trent Index of 1570. From there it was adopted in the Index of the Spanish Inquisitor General, Quiroga (1583/84) and then in the Roman Index of Sixtus V in 1590; this last forbade "Jo. Taulerii Sermones et Institutio passionis Domini, donec corrigatur." Cf. H. Reusch, *Der Index der verbotenen Bücher,* I (Bonn 1883), 523; *idem, Die Indices librorum prohibitorum des 16. Jh.* (Tübingen 1886), 317. The Jesuit general, E. Mercurian (1573–80), forbade his subjects to read the works of Tauler and other mystics. The Belgian Capuchins followed this example.

CHAPTER 45

Missionary Work of the Mendicants outside Europe

It was especially the two great mendicant orders, Dominicans and Franciscans, who were most responsible for carrying missionary work beyond Europe. As the first founder of an order, Francis of Assisi devoted to the missions a special chapter in his "Regula prima." [1] Dominic "only gradually advanced into the great commitment of a world-embracing action" (Altaner), but the Preaching Friars were sent forth to evangelize not much later than the Friars Minor (1217–18). At first the mendicants apparently played no particular role in the deliberations of the Curia. Unlike that of the Trinitarians in 1199, [2] their founding was not made known to the Sultan of Morocco. And in his general bull on the missions [3] Honorius III was still counting especially on the Cistercians for the evangelization of the pagans, even though his predecessor in 1212 had had to remind the general chapter not to impede individual monasteries in their mission activity. [4] As late as 1219 an Hospitaller was dispatched with a message from the Pope to the *Miromomelinus* (for the Arabic *Emir-el-mumenin*, "the ruler of the believers"). [5]

When in 1219–20 Francis of Assisi proceeded to the camp of the Sultan of Egypt in order to preach Christianity to him, [6] his action stimulated the emergence of the realization, slowly awakening during the crusades, that Christianity should not be spread by force of arms but only by preaching and love. At any rate, the missionary concept moved on equal terms alongside the crusading idea, even though it still needed a long time before its implications were fully clarified. Thus Roger Bacon (d. 1294) represented the view that it is better to convert infidels by means of knowledge and wisdom than by wars, whereas his confrère, Duns Scotus (d. 1308), demanded the severest punishment of idolators and allowed princes the right to spread God's Kingdom by force. In his *Defensor pacis* (1324) Marsilius of Padua taught that the Church has no coercive power against heretics and infidels, but the Council of Basel still held that Jews could be compelled to listen to Christian sermons.

Like theory, practice oscillated between the extremes. The mendicant orders offered their services not only for evangelization but for crusade

---

[1] O. van der Vat, *Die Anfänge der Franziskanermissionen im nahen Orient und in den mohammedanischen Ländern während des 13. Jahrhunderts*, 9–25.

[2] *PL*, 214, 544.

[3] "Ne si secus" (25 March 1221), in *Potthast R*, 6599; *Streit*, XV, 50; *cf.* Altaner, *Die Dominikanermissionen des 13. Jahrhunderts*, 1 f.

[4] *Potthast R*, 4573.

[5] *Streit*, XV, 24; *Potthast R*, 6121.

[6] *Golubovich*, I, 1–104; *Streit*, XV, 41.

preaching as well. Again and again events tempted Christendom to take up the sword. The victory of Alfonso VIII of Castile over the Muslims at Las Navas de Tolosa in 1212 was an inducement to transfer the war to African soil, and Honorius III granted the same indulgences as for a crusade.[7] And the appearance of the Mongols raised the hope of finding in them allies against the Muslims. People regarded their Khans as successors of Prester John, whose image had excited the West for centuries.[8] This legend was in circulation long before the time of Otto of Freising (Chronicon, VII, 33). An Ethiopian priest-king, John, was known to Italian seafarers before the crusades.[9] Deficient geographical data — Ethiopia was identified with India — explain why the rumour of a Christian king in Ethiopia could be confused with the news of the victory of a Christian Kerait prince over the Muslim Khwarazmians in 1141. (When, later, the error was realized, people looked for Prester John in Africa again into the sixteenth century.)

Against public opinion, the mendicant orders gave preference to the missions. It is true that in North Africa and the Near East their activity was missionary in intention rather than in reality. For in North Africa it was restricted to caring for the needs of Christian merchants, mercenaries, and slaves. Neither the Popes nor the Christian commercial city states could obtain from the sultans more than freedom of worship for Christians.[10] Preaching to Muslims remained forbidden, and when the preachers violated the prohibition they risked their lives, as did the first Franciscan martyrs in Morocco, who even felt that they could preach as they did in Italy and harshly refuted the teachings of Islam.[11] A like fate befell the Franciscans at Tunis in 1225 and at Ceuta in 1227. Still, the two sees of Morocco and Fez could be erected in North Africa.[12]

In the Near East the mendicants were chiefly interested in bringing back the schismatics and they were so successful that Gregory IX in 1238 admitted that it is just as good to lead unbelievers to the praise of God as to overcome them by armed force. This activity among schismatic Christians[13] was regarded as preliminary to missions among Muslims, and the Popes supported the mendicants in this view. They even gave them letters for the sultans in

---

[7] Streit, XV, 21.

[8] F. Zarnke, "Der Priesterkönig Johannes," AGL, philos.-hist. Kl, 7 (1879), 827–1030, 8 (1883), 1–186; R. Hennig, Terrae incognitae, II (Leiden 1937), 361–76.

[9] R. Lefèvre, "Riflessi etiopici nella cultura del Medioevo e del Rinascimento I," Annali Lateranensi, 8 (Rome 1944), 9–89.

[10] T. Grentrup, "Das Missionsprotektorat in den mohammedanischen Staaten Nordafrikas vom 12.–15. Jh.," ZMR, 8 (1918), 88–96; idem, Jus missionarium, I (Steyl 1925), 361–69.

[11] H. Koehler, L'Église chrétienne du Maroc et la mission franciscaine 1221–1790 (Paris 1934), 22 f.

[12] A. López, Obispos en el África septentrional (Tangiers 1941).

[13] This explains the term Eastern "mission."

which the Christian faith and its messengers were commended. We thus hear of mission journeys to Aleppo, Damascus, Cairo, and Iconium. That successes were not lacking is certified by William of Tripolis, who claims to have baptized more than a thousand Saracens in his lifetime.[14]

Such numerical data are unusual. William based them on an indication of his method: he had obtained his successes "by the simple Word of God, without philosophical arguments and without force of arms." This allusion was not unintentional, and it contradicted the prevailing opinion that Muslims could not be converted. The mission work of the mendicants among them made it clear that the reasons for the sterility of efforts thus far made were to be sought not only on the side of Islam but equally in the missionaries. Since a command of languages is the first requirement for properly facing the missionary project, the mendicants, and in particular the Dominicans, established their own schools of languages and eagerly pursued Islamic studies.[15] Such language schools were in existence in the Holy Land from 1237, and in 1250 the *Studium Arabicum* was founded at Tunis at the suggestion of Saint Raymond of Peñaforte. Following the unfortunate outcome of the last crusade, schools of Arabic and Hebrew were opened in Spain. Prominent as writers were the Dominicans William of Tripolis (*Tractatus de statu Saracenorum*, 1273), Raymond Martí (*Pugio fidei contra Mauros et Iudaeos*, 1278), Ricoldo da Monte Croce (*Contra legem Saracenorum*, better known as *Confutatio Alcorani*), and others. In this connection can be mentioned Aquinas's *Summa contra gentiles*.[16] Among the Franciscans Raymond Lull (1234–1315)[17] is especially deserving of mention. Through various memoranda to the Popes, the King of France, and the University of Paris, he exerted himself to appeal to the conscience of Christendom and to draw attention to the duty to the missions. Besides the erecting of mission colleges, he suggested the founding of a supreme missionary authority, which, directed by a cardinal, should co-ordinate the mission efforts of the various orders. At his request the Council of Vienne in 1312 prescribed the setting up of two chairs of oriental languages in the most important universities.[18] But the

---

[14] *Tractatus de statu Saracenorum* (1273), conclusion.

[15] *Cf.* the works of B. Altaner, *ZMR*, 21 (1931), 113–26, 23 (1933), 233–41, 26 (1936), 165–71; *BZ*, 21 (1933 f.), 288–308; *ZKG*, 53 (1934), 469–79, 55 (1936), 83–126; *OrChrP*, 2 (1936), 437–52.

[16] M. Grabmann, "Die Missionsidee der Dominikanertheologen des 13. Jahrhunderts," *ZMR*, 1 (1911), 137–46; B. Altaner, "Zur Geschichte der anti-islamischen Polemik während des 13. und 14. Jh.," *HJ*, 56 (1936), 227–333.

[17] R. Sugranyes de Franch, *Raymond Lulle, Docteur des Missions* (Schöneck-Beckenried 1954) (literature).

[18] B. Altaner, "Raymundus Lullus und der Sprachenkanon (can. 11) des Konzils von Vienne (1312)," *HJ*, 53 (1933), 190–319; *idem*, "Die Durchführung des Vienner Konzilsbeschlusses über die Errichtung von Lehrstühlen für orientalische Sprachen," *ZKG*, 52 (1933), 226–36. *Cf. Conciliorum Oecumenicorum Decreta* (2nd ed., 1962), 355 f., 459.

decree was not implemented. Once again, in 1434 the Council of Basel called attention to it, but to no purpose.

The appearance of the Mongols in Eastern and Central Europe contributed directly to the expansion of mission work outside Europe. At first consideration was given to meeting them also with crusade methods. But once the gravest danger seemed to have been warded off from the West – after their victory at Liegnitz in 1241 the Mongols returned to Central Asia to arrange the succession to the khanate, — other ways of reaching them were sought. The finding of a *remedium contra Tartaros* was for Innocent IV one of the motives for summoning the First Council of Lyons.[19] Even though, shortly before, the Mongols had been regarded as fiends — "Tartari, imo Tartarei!"[20] — now they were sought as allies against the Muslims. To this end the Pope sent the Franciscans Lawrence of Portugal and John of Piano di Carpine to the Mongols before the opening of the Council. Lawrence's task was purely missionary; his instructions contained only a catechetical exposition of the Christian faith. Other embassies were more of a diplomatic nature. John was supposed to urge peace, while two Dominicans, Ascellin (or Anselm) and Andrew of Longjumeau, were to prepare the desired alliance against the Muslims. But the journeys produced no tangible results, even though embassies were dispatched by the Mongols to the Pope and to Louis IX. Among those who set out for the Mongols in the course of the following years, the most important was William of Ruysbroeck, who reached Karakorum and left a detailed account of his travels, which is generally reliable and valuable.[21] The missionary aims of all these journeys are unmistakable,[22] but in the final analysis they were not the appropriate means of effecting lasting conversions. Even Innocent IV seems to have been convinced of the fruitlessness of these endeavours. William of Ruysbroeck had not yet returned when the Dominicans and the Franciscans, with papal encouragement, undertook direct missionary work. To what extent the mendicant friars were regarded as the real representatives of the Church's missionary work is shown by the resolution of the Cistercian general chapter to ask prayers for the heralds of the faith who were going to the Tartars. Not incorrectly has this directive been termed "the order's charter of resignation of its missionary activity."[23]

Of special importance for the effectiveness of the mendicant orders was

[19] *Potthast R*, 11493; *Hefele*, V, 981–1002.

[20] Frederick II to Edward of England, in Matthew Paris, *Historia Anglorum*, II (London 1886), 820, quoted in *Streit*, IV, 1.

[21] *Sinica Franciscana* [= *SF*], I, 164–332.

[22] C. Schollmeyer, "Die missionarische Sendung des Fr. Wilhelm von Rubruk," *OstKSt*, 5 (1955), 138–46; *cf. ZMR*, 40 (1956), 200–05.

[23] B. Altaner, *Dominikanermissionen*, 2, following F. Winter, *Die Cistercienser des nördlichen Deutschlands bis zum Auftreten der Bettelorden*, I (Gotha 1868), 294.

the jurisdictional organization of their mission work. Not only did the authority to dispose of the individual friars no longer lie with the respective superiors of the several houses but rather with the generals of the orders; the friars who chose the missionary vocation themselves constituted special missionary communities within their order. Even so, the ecclesiastical mission was received, not by these groups but by the order as such. The general handed over the mission by appointing prefects or vicars, who, at the orders of the general and as his representatives, were to supervise its implementation. Hence, unlike the later vicars apostolic, these prefects or vicars were not ecclesiastical authorities but religious officials. This arrangement is especially striking among the Franciscans. Their mission fields were divided into six vicariates: those of Tataria Aquilonaris, Tataria Orientis, and Cathay, embracing the lands of the Mongols, the Vicaria Marocchii for North Africa, and those of Bosnia and Russia for Southern and Eastern Europe. The Dominicans adhered in their mission territories to their familiar division into provinces. But toward the close of the thirteenth century there arose the *Societas fratrum peregrinantium propter Christum in gentes,*[24] which seems to have included chiefly the Dominicans working in the Orient. The first documented information about it is from 1304. A similar missionary society of Friars Minor is first referred to under Urban V. Little is known of its organization, except that a home missionary society, the Confraternity of Saint Francis, was attached to it, which supported especially the Franciscans in Eastern Europe.[25] It was approved by Martin V in 1421.

Activity among the unfamiliar peoples of Eastern Europe must be regarded as the starting point for the mission in the interior of Asia. As early as 1211 King Andrew II of Hungary had called upon the Teutonic Knights for protection from the invading Cumans. Their successes justified the establishment of a special Cuman bishopric. When, as a consequence of conflicts with the King, the Knights left Hungary, the Dominicans took their place. They were able to push forward to the Dnieper and to convert the Cuman Prince Bortz, who was baptized by the Archbishop of Esztergom in 1227. The Dominican Theoderic was consecrated Bishop of the Cumans, his bishopric being directly subject to the Holy See. Several thousand Cumans must have embraced the faith, but the Mongol fury completely wiped out the mission. Ninety missionaries were killed, and the Cumans were scattered throughout the Balkans.

It was not until 1253, after the diplomatic visits to the Mongols, that the missionary journeys to Eastern Europe were resumed. The first quarter-century of this new start is shrouded in darkness and only in 1278 do we discover efforts to reestablish the Cuman bishopric in connection with an

---

[24] R. Loenertz, *Société des Frères Pérégrinants* (Rome 1937).
[25] A. Groeteken, "Eine mittelalterliche Missionsgesellschaft," *ZMR*, 1 (1911), 1–13.

account of the Franciscan missionaries working in Qipčaq, the Khanate of the Golden Horde.[26] In 1287 we hear of several Franciscan houses in the Crimea and in Sarai, the capital of Qipčaq.[27] The Franciscans succeeded in baptizing the "Empress" Yailaq and eventually even the Khan Toqtai (1300–12) and several members of his household.[28] Around 1320 Franciscans were working even among the Bashkirs,[29] but unfortunately the conversion of the Khan Uzbek (1312–40) to Islam soon forced the greatest part of the Golden Horde to embrace the religion of The Prophet. At the beginning of his reign the Vicariate of Tataria Aquilonaris counted seventeen settlements and between 1318 and 1321 Sarai became the see of a Latin bishop.

Political events contributed substantially to the development of the mission in Tataria Orientis, where the Mongols' originally hostile attitude to Islam roused great hopes. The incentive was provided by the taking of Baghdad in 1258 by Hulagu, a brother of the Great Khan Mangu. The Abbasid Caliphate in Persia came to an end, and Hulagu established the dynasty of the Il-khans (1256–1335). His empire embraced Iran, parts of Turkestan, Armenia, and eastern Anatolia, and Azerbaijan and Iraq. His warfare was aimed chiefly at the Mameluks of Egypt. Thus he established numerous contacts with the Christians of Syria and as a consequence there were missionary undertakings in the empire of the Il-khans and the neighboring lands. Christian Mongol princesses, such as Soyorgatani Baigi, mother of Mangu, Kublai, and Hulagu, and Hulagu's wife, Dokuz Khatun, played a prominent role in all this.

Less stress was laid on the conversion of Muslims and pagans than on reunion with the Nestorian Church, which had benefited by Mongol toleration to reorganize itself in Asia. Efforts for union reached their climax when in 1287 the Catholicos Jahballahā III of Baghdad (1281–1317), an Ongüt, sent his confidant, the Uigur Bar-Sauma, to Rome.[30] Bar-Sauma had no scruples about recognizing the papal primacy and in 1304 Jahballahā followed suit. But matters proceeded no further. Under the Il-khan Gazan (1295–1305) Islam gained the upper hand and the conflicts between Shi'ites and Sunnites contributed to the decline of the Il-khan empire. From 1295 the preaching of the faith to Muslims caused persecutions and bloody martyrdoms. But the fact remains that in 1314 Dominicans and Franciscans each had fifteen monasteries in these areas.

Greater significance attaches to the missionary work on the farthest edge of the then known world, in China. The earliest contacts with the Mongol

[26] *Streit*, IV, 48.
[27] *ibid.*, 50.
[28] *Golubovich*, III, 170–77.
[29] *Streit*, IV, 130.
[30] J. B. Chabot, *Histoire du Patriarche Mar Jabalaha III et du Moine Bar Çauma* (Paris 1895).

dynasty in China were made by Venetian merchants, the Polos, in 1261–69. They delivered to the Pope a message from the Great Khan Kublai (1260–94), in which he asked for 100 missionaries. But two expeditions sent by the papacy did not reach their goal. The first to arrive in China was the Franciscan John of Montecorvino,[31] dispatched by Nicholas IV in 1289. He was the first to select, not the land route through the interior of Asia, but the sea route from the Persian Gulf. He delivered the papal letter to Kublai's successor Timur (Ch'eng-tsung, 1294–1307) and then began his apostolate, first among the Nestorian Ongüt in Northern Tenduc. He was able to bring their King George into union with Rome and in the latter's capital built a church,[32] where the Latin Mass was celebrated in the Mongol tongue. Unfortunately, George died in 1298 and the strong opposition of the Nestorians induced John to seek out Khanbaliq, "City of the Khan," later Peking, where he began missionary work in the proper sense. After some setbacks he was able to establish a numerous community of Mongols and Chinese. In a letter of 1305[33] he recounted his successes and asked for assistance. In regard to mission procedure the letter is unusually rich in information. John emphasized catechetical and liturgical formation and excelled in intelligent and generous adaptation. His achievements induced Clement V to name John Archbishop of Peking in 1307, with Khanbaliq as metropolitan see for all the Mongol missions.[34] Six bishops were sent by the Pope to China to consecrate John and then to be assigned by him to the suffragan sees of Zaitun (Fukien), Almaligh (Jagatai), Kaffa, Sarai, Tana, and Kumuk (Qipčaq). John directed the mission until 1328. At his death Catholic Christianity in China counted some 30,000 faithful, including about 15,000 Alans, whom the Mongols had transferred from the Caucasus to China. (The first Chinese plenary council, held at Shanghai in 1924, proposed the beatification of John of Montecorvino.)

John's accomplishments stand out in even greater relief when it is remembered that for years he worked alone. It was not till 1303 that he obtained an assistant in Arnold of Cologne,[35] the first German missionary in China. When John was appointed Archbishop, many mendicant friars tried to hurry to his aid, but how many of them reached their goal is not known. Still, there must have been several monasteries in China. An amazing account of this period is given by the Franciscan Odoric of Pordenone, who

---

[31] A. van der Wyngaert, *Jean de Mont Corvin* (Lille 1924); J. de Ghellinck in *RHM*, 5 (1928), 506–44.
[32] Namio Egami, "Olon-süme et la découverte de l'église catholique romaine de Jean de Montcorvin," *JA*, 240 (1952), 154–67.
[33] *SF*, I, 345–51.
[34] *Streit*, IV, 97–100.
[35] *ibid.*, 107.

spent three years in Khanbaliq and then took the land route back to Europe *via* Tibet. [36]

In the meantime Pope John XXII had reorganized Church affairs in Asia. [37] In 1318 he erected the province of Sultaniyah, to which he assigned six suffragan sees, entrusting them to the Dominicans. [38] His principal concern here was the promoting of reunion with the schismatic Armenians. Monks of the monastery of Qrna, having returned to Rome in a body, formed a special community and, with reference to their aim, called themselves the *Fratres Unitores.* [39] They were loosely connected with the Order of Preachers and existed into the eighteenth century.

To the province of Sultaniyah belonged two sees located outside the area just referred to. One was Samarkand, in the province of Sogdiana in the Khanate of Jagatai; its first bishop was the Dominican Thomas Mancasole of Piacenza. [40] The other was Quilon (Kollam) in South India, which owed its origin to the circumstance that missionaries *en route* by sea to China transferred here to Chinese junks. The interval was filled with missionary work. First Bishop of Quilon was the Dominican Jordan Cathala of Sévérac, [41] who gave up his journey to China and remained in India when his four Franciscan traveling companions were martyred by fanatical Muslims at Tana (near modern Bombay). [42] From Quilon arose the first connections with Ethiopia, and the Dominican William Adam may have reached East Africa south of the equator. [43]

Our last detailed information about the two provinces of Sultaniyah and Khanbaliq is provided by the report of the journey of the Papal Legate John de Marignolli of Florence, [44] who visited all of Asiatic Christendom between 1338 and 1353. Then disaster overtook the late mediaeval missionary work. The Black Death, which in 1348 carried off almost all the missionaries in Persia, on its progress through Europe also depopulated the monasteries of the homeland so that it became impossible to supply the required number of apostles for distant lands. To this was added the unceasing Islamization of the Mongols, forcibly completed under Timur-Leng (1336–1405). The religious toleration practised by the Mongols was succeeded by intolerant Sunnite fanaticism, which met all missionary endeavours with bitter hostility.

[36] *SF*, I, 411–95.
[37] A. Fliche, "L'action missionnaire du Pape Jean XXII," *Bulletin des Missions,* 22 (Bruges 1948), 1–8.
[38] *Streit*, IV, 121 f.
[39] *Cf.* the series of articles by M. A. van den Oudenrijn in *Het Missiewerk,* 17–19 (Nijmegen 1935 f.–1937 f.).
[40] *Streit*, IV, 166.
[41] *ibid.,* 167 f.
[42] *ibid.,* 132–35.
[43] R. Hennig, *Terrae incognitae,* III (Leiden 1938), 144–47.
[44] *SF,* I, 524–60.

In addition, all travel was prevented by the wars with which Timur-Leng filled Asia for a whole generation.

For the Church in China matters were decided when in 1368 the Mongol Dynasty was overthrown by the nationalistic Ming. Until the beginning of the fifteenth century occasional reports concerning Christianity in China are found, but thereafter the final remnants seem to have perished. In 1410 the archbishopric of Sultaniyah was united with Khanbaliq, but in 1473 the Venetian Contarini found there neither churches nor Christians.

Success had been achieved neither in direct missionary work among the Muslims of North Africa nor in the endeavour to gain the Mongols as allies against Islam. On the contrary, the barrier which Islam had erected between Europe and Africa had been extended from the Near East into Central Asia when the Mongols turned to Islam. More than ever Christendom was eager to breach this barrier, and to do so became the goal of a community of Portuguese Knights who had united after the suppression of the Templars and in 1319 had been recognized by John XXII as the "Militia Iesu Christi."[45] The bull "Ad ea ex quibus cultus"[46] is not only the Magna Carta of the Order of the Knights of Christ. It is equally the basis for Portugal's colonial expansion, for ecclesiastical jurisdiction in the conquered territories, and for the future Portuguese royal *padroado* in the missions.

In contrast to the other military orders, the Order of Christ had to conduct the war against the Muslims chiefly on the sea. Since Southern Spain was still under the rule of the Moors, it was important to gain a foothold in North Africa and attack the enemy from the rear. This tactical idea was maintained when Prince Henry the Navigator (1394–1460), after the victory of Ceuta (1415), laid the ground for the Portuguese voyages of discovery. The Holy See did everything possible to promote these undertakings.[47] In 1418 Martin V summoned all of Portugal to the crusade against the Muslims and to the spread of the faith.[48] In 1443 Eugene IV awarded all islands, conquered or to be conquered (!), to the Order of Christ.[49] In the bull "Romanus Pontifex"[50] Nicholas V gave voice to the expectations of all Christendom: that the voyages of discovery on the African coast should

---

[45] A. Jann, *Die katholischen Missionen in Indien, China und Japan* (Paderborn 1915), 1–63.

[46] *Streit*, XV, 271.

[47] Sixty-nine papal bulls are known between 1415 and 1500; *cf.* C. M. de Witte, "Les Bulles pontificales et l'expansion portugaise au XV⁰ siècle," *RHE*, 48 (1953), 683–718, 49 (1954), 438–61, 51 (1956), 413–53, 809–56, 53 (1958), 4–46, 440–471; F. Mateos, "Bulas portuguesas y españoles sobre descubrimientos geográficos," *Missionalia Hispanica*, 19 (Madrid 1962), 5–34, 129–68.

[48] *Streit*, XV, 373; J. Goñi Gaztambide, *Historia de la Bula de la Cruzada en España* (Vitoria 1958).

[49] *Streit*, XV, 460.

[50] 8 January 1455; *cf. Streit*, XV, 512–14.

help to find the sea-route to India, to enter into an alliance with the Saint Thomas Christians living there, and to lay hold of the Muslims from behind. The bull awarded Portugal a monopoly of conquest and trade on all seas and islands. In return, Portugal had to do all in its power for the spread of the faith. A protest by Castile was rejected by Calixtus III in 1456 and quasi-episcopal jurisdiction over all lands still to be conquered was given to the Order of Christ in perpetuity.[51] This was to be of exceptional significance for evangelization in the following epoch, since all authority granted for the mission was to be regarded only as delegated authority. The vicars and prefects of the contemporary sources were not ecclesiastical officials but deputies of the Order of Christ. This meant also that missionary activity could develop only on the Portuguese firing line.

[51] *Streit*, XV, 523; F. Pérez Embid, *Los descubrimientos en el Atlántico y la rivalidad castellano-portuguesa hasta el Tratado de Tordesillas* (Seville 1948).

The Western Schism and the Councils

CHAPTER 46

The Western Schism to the Council of Pisa

The premature death of Gregory XI placed the Church in a difficult situation. The Curia, back in Rome, and in particular the many French cardinals were not yet acclimated to Italy, and six cardinals were still at Avignon. The anxiety of the Romans lest they might again lose the recently recovered papacy makes it easy to understand their exertions to obtain a Roman or at least an Italian as the new Pope. These exertions were not confined to requests and expostulations; they took on the forms of violence.

Even during the obsequies for Gregory XI there were riots in the city, and after the sealing off of the conclave in the Vatican Palace on the evening of 7 April 1378 the excitement and pressure increased notably. Thousands of Romans noisily demanded someone from Rome or at least a native of Italy as Pope. It was only with great effort that armed bands could be removed from the area of the conclave. On the same evening the desire for an Italian Pope was presented to the sixteen cardinals — eleven French, four Italians, and one Spaniard — by the heads of the urban "regions." The cardinals gave them an evasive reply.

Even apart from these external troubles, the usual factional groupings gave reason to expect that the course of the business would be unpleasant. The strongest faction comprised the so-called Limousins, who were interested in continuing the tradition of the three recent Limousin Popes. Opposed to them was the small so-called French faction, determined to thwart this project at any cost. With this in mind, outside candidates had already been mentioned, including the Archbishop of Bari, Bartholomew Prignano, regent of the papal chancery, since the actual vice-chancellor was still at Avignon. He may have seemed acceptable to both French and Italians, for he came from Angevin Naples and had spent many years at Avignon.

A proper election procedure soon proved to be impossible. The very next morning, following a restless night, the disturbances were renewed. Again and again the guardian of the conclave, the Bishop of Marseilles, had to send for the seniors of the three orders of cardinals to have them calm the mob by holding out the prospect of a Roman or an Italian Pope in the course of the day. In the early morning a part of the cardinals decided to vote for Prignano. Whether this was with a general reservation is not entirely certain, but it is attested for a few cardinals. In the afternoon, some, but not all, of the cardinals sought to repeat the voting in regard to Prignano and to question the candidate, who had meanwhile been sent for, as to his acceptance of the election. But they were unable to finish, for then ensued an invasion of the conclave. It was calmed for the moment when it was declared that the aged Roman Cardinal Tebaldeschi had been elected. Despite his resistance he was enthroned before the altar of the chapel by the mob. The other cardinals profited by the break to flee, six to Castel Sant'Angelo, the others to their residences or outside Rome. On the next afternoon twelve cardinals returned voluntarily or were called to the Vatican to complete the election procedure.

The real problem begins after this very dubious election, since the cardinals took part in the enthronement, treated Urban VI (1378–89) as Pope, at least outwardly, presented their petitions to him, and sent notification of the election to the princes. Thereby, so one often reads, tacit consent was given and the cardinals lost their right of protest against "pressure" in the election.

The elucidation and evaluation of the events in Rome in the weeks from the election to the open defection of the cardinals in June are among the most difficult problems of late mediaeval Church History. Among the many double papal elections of the Middle Ages, that of 1378 occupies a special position, because a quick political decision did not liquidate the theoretical considerations, as had frequently been the case previously. There was no lack of endeavours to dissipate the uncertainty as to the legitimate Pope. No other occurrence of this period left behind such an amount of written material; in no other burning question were so many inquiries instituted and so many witnesses called.

Consideration must be given above all to the collection of about sixty manuscripts preserved in the Vatican archives under the title *Libri de schismate*. This comprises a many-layered material, which goes from the beginning of the Schism to the turn of the century and was compiled by a loyal adherent of Benedict XIII, Martin de Zalva, Bishop of Pamplona and Cardinal. Later it passed into the possession of Benedict XIII, who had a *tabula* prepared for ready use. Hence the collection served the practical purpose of defending legitimacy, but it was more far-reaching and took the opposing side into full consideration. It is a kind of source-material which is otherwise hardly to be found in such an intact state among medieval documents, and makes us regret the loss of other source-material of equal value. It has often been utilized, and is the basis of a variety of interpretations, especially by Raynald and Baluze and, more reliably, by Gayet, Ehrle, Valois, and finally by Seidlmayer and Přerovský.[1]

A substantial portion of these *Libri de schismate* consists of the testimony of witnesses concerning the origin of the Schism, especially the election of Urban VI and the ensuing weeks until the election of Clement VII. Hence they are at first concerned with the so-called *factum*. In general, the persons interrogated decided, according to the two obediences, in the contemporary terminology, for the *primus electus* or the *secundus electus,* but they were not merely partisan and made many neutral declarations concerning the events.

The first really important hearings took place in Rome in March 1379 and were in favour of Urban. A second hearing was arranged at Barcelona in May and September 1379 by the royal council, and it supported Clement. The twenty-three witnesses interrogated at Rome in November 1379 decided for Urban. We are best informed about such efforts in the Iberian peninsula, and in most detail for Castile, where King Henry II was kept very well informed by his envoys then staying in Italy; in view of the difficult circumstances the strictest secrecy and the utmost circumspection were maintained. Then, by order of the new King John I, extensive hearings were conducted at Avignon in May 1380 and at Rome in the following July as the basis for the great judicial procedure at Medina del Campo from November 1380 to May 1381; further written material was submitted here and oral testimony received. More than 100 declarations of all tendencies were here considered and, after months of deliberations, they resulted in the Kingdom's deciding for Clement VII.[2] Much later, in the summer of 1386, the King of Aragón had forty more persons questioned at Avignon, and, as expected, they pronounced in favour of the Pope there resident. These late declarations also, despite the great lapse of time and the consolidation of the obediences, are not without value, but the organization of the process in Castile excels all the others.

What, then, is the result of these efforts to ascertain the *factum?* This *dubium in facto* was examined from all points of view with the aim of investigating the events in Urban's election down to the least detail and, as far as possible, the intention of the electors. The opinion of the election is virtually unanimous. The election was not free but resulted from *impressio,* from *metus qui cadit in constantem virum,* neither absolutely valid nor

---

[1] M. Seidlmayer, "Die spanischen 'Libri de schismate' des Vatikanischen Archivs," *Gesammelte Aufsätze zur Kulturgeschichte Spaniens,* 8 (1940), 199–262.

[2] Paris, Bibliothèque Nationale, Cod. Lat. 11745; on the manuscript see *Baluze-Mollat,* II, 800–12; N. Del Re, "Il 'consilium pro Urbano VI' di Bartolomeo da Saliceto (Vat. lat. 5608)," *Collectanea Vaticana in honorem Anselmi M. card. Albareda,* I, SteT, 219 (1962), 213–63; L. Saggi, "Bartolomeo Peyroni O.Carm., vescovo di Elne, e la sua testimonianza circa il conclave del 1378," *AHPont,* 4 (1966), 59–77.

absolutely null, but in any event controvertible. If an effort is made to form a picture out of this thicket of numberless declarations (*depositiones*), it does not favour Urban, not merely in view of the events of the election and his personality but also in regard to the period immediately after the election.

The first reports reaching the outside carried chiefly only the news of the completion of the election and with it the acceptance or recognition of the one elected. But, before long, details of the happenings in Rome were known in various places, and these urged caution if not reserve in regard to recognizing the new Pope. At Rome itself, two days after the election, doubts as to its validity were expressed in a sermon at Ara Coeli.[3] And official letters sent by cardinals to princes, whose wording was occasionally approved by the new Pope, were accompanied by secret messages which read differently from the official text.[4] Everything now depended on how the new Pope conducted himself and whether the defects in the election could be eliminated by actual subsequent consent.

But matters did not turn out that way at all. Soon there were quarrels and collisions with the envoys of princes, with cardinals, bishops, and curial functionaries, and politically very unwise behaviour toward such persons as Queen Joanna I of Naples and the German King Wenceslas. Furthermore, basic reforms were at once announced — to begin with the cardinals. It was not so much the question of reform that was important but rather of the unfortunate style and method of an authoritarian, dictatorial government by a hitherto subordinate curial *archiepiscopellus,* as one cardinal called him to his face,[5] of a morbidly exalted notion of his new office, no longer corresponding to the actual status of the papacy, and of an offensive arrogance gushing from this. All this confirms the impression of a pathological personality.[6] Not long ago this *incapacità* was profoundly investigated. The outcome was an interesting and subtle question: Can the cardinals retract their vote if they notice that the one elected by them is unable to carry out his function in a reasonable manner; in other words, that a grave mistake has been made in regard to the person and his qualities?

What had previously been active only in the background and had been expressed only with the utmost caution quickly put in an appearance after the beginning of the summer *villeggiatura.* In quick succession the cardinals left Rome in June with the Pope's permission and came together at Anagni.

[3] O. Přerovský, *L'elezione di Urbano VI,* 42.
[4] M. Seidlmayer, *Die Anfänge des grossen abendländischen Schismas,* 243, 288, 332.
[5] *Ibid.,* 280.
[6] O. Přerovský, *op. cit.,* 65 ff., 182 ff. Particulars in M. Seidlmayer, Anfänge, 8–18. A member of the Consiglio of Florence said: "Singulariter et precipue seipsum destruit" (*Archivio storico per le provincie Napoletane,* 45 [1920], 40).

The Curia had been transferred there and the Pope intended to follow. Now voices were multiplied, speaking of an invalid election, of new discussions to take place at Anagni, of a second election under normal circumstances, and also of a council and of a sort of tutelage for the not completely qualified Pope. These voices did not remain concealed from Urban; even cardinals now made known to him their misgivings. Though he was not fully aware of the gravity of the situation, he put off going to Anagni and at the end of July went to Tivoli. Shortly before this there had appeared in Rome an official representative of the cardinals assembled at Anagni to make known to him their opinion: that he had no right to the papal dignity and would either be reelected or otherwise provided for.

The three Italian cardinals, still in Rome and as yet undecided, were thereupon sent by Urban to Anagni with compliant proposals that betrayed weakness. But before long he returned to his usual obstinacy and rejected the considerations put forth by a new embassy from the cardinals as well as those of the Italian cardinals, who returned to him at Tivoli. He would not consent to one or more coadjutors who would cover up his incapacity, but demanded unconditional recognition of the validity of his election. In the very lively exchange of proposals throughout July a council occupied a special place. The chief advocates of this idea were the Italians, and, above all, Orsini.[7] The declaration of the French cardinals of 20 July with regard to the nullity of the election and hence of the vacancy of the see rendered further negotiations complicated, while the three Italians, who continued to regard a council as the final remedy, did not return to the Pope again but maintained relations only in writing. Submission on Urban's part was less and less to be looked for.

Decisive discussions among all the cardinals took place in mid-September at Fondi. Once again the Italians referred to a council, which need not include all bishops but could consist of representatives of each province. Venice, Pisa, and Naples were suggested, or even the Piedmontese area because of its proximity to France. These considerations foundered on the difficulties attendant upon the convocation and the interim administration, and it required decades of discussions before the matter was clarified.

These consultations at Fondi concluded with a new election. Presumably, the Italians had been given reason for hope and so they took part in the conclave of 20 September. None of them, however, was elected, but instead Cardinal Robert of Geneva, who had long been considered. If one so desired, one could see in him a neutral, between France and Italy. He was elected on 20 September, the election was proclaimed on the twenty-first, and on 31 October he was crowned as Clement VII (1378—1394). The Schism was a reality.

[7] M. Seidlmayer, *Anfänge*, 179 ff.

A careful weighing of all the facts gives the impression that Urban's election can by no means, and the so-called tacit consent only in a highly questionable manner, support the legitimacy of the beginnings of his pontificate; his *incapacità* was too notorious. The cautious judgment of Valois is, from the historical viewpoint, still probably the correct stand, and so eminent a specialist of our own day as G. Mollat has adopted this opinion.[8] Decisions as the Schism began, however, were made at first on political grounds.

As regards the Curia and its staff, Robert's election was for the most part hailed. Whoever could escape from Rome did so, along with official books, registers, and the impressions for the seals. The highest ranking officials of the curial administration went over to Clement VII and hence Urban's position appeared very precarious. Both claimants endeavoured by means of numerous letters and embassies to kings, princes, bishops, universities, and cities to prove their legitimacy and to acquire recognition. At first the political climate seemed to favour Clement, but he was unable to take possession of Rome and of Urban's person. On the contrary, following the victory of Urban's mercenaries near Marino on 29 April 1379 and his acquiring of Castel Sant'Angelo, Clement had to withdraw from Italy, in spite of the support of the Queen of Naples, and retire to Avignon in May 1381. From this last point persons have rashly inferred a close understanding with the French King at the time of the events in Anagni and Fondi. But at the start France seems to have held back, even if its sympathies were with Clement.[9]

For Urban it was important to organize a new Curia. He began with the promotion of twenty-nine cardinals but not all those selected accepted. Urban was almost universally recognized in Italy, with its many large and small lordships. To be sure, there was much vacillating and changing, always in accord with high politics, and neutrality was not rare. When a quick decision between the *primus electus* and the *secundus electus* and the holding of a council did not materialize, the Great Schism began to come clearly into view. It was consummated mainly under political aspects. On Urban's side, in addition to Italy, were ranged especially the Empire and King Wenceslas, the eastern and Nordic countries and Hungary, and, of the western states, England, the enemy of France. After a brief neutrality France became Clement VII's chief support, along with its dependent territories, Burgundy, Savoy, and Naples, and Scotland, the foe of England.

There were likewise political areas where a decision for one claimant or the other did not occur so rapidly. Since the call for a council, raised early, could not be realized, or at least not soon, efforts were made to form a judgment on the basis of the most exact possible examination of the facts.

[8] *DHGE*, 12 (1953), 1166 f.
[9] M. Seidlmayer, *Anfänge*, 19, 69. For Clement VII see *DHGE*, 12 (1953), 1162–75.

The careful endeavours in Castile have already been mentioned; they resulted in the recognition of Clement VII in 1380. More so than in previous schisms an attitude of reserve appeared, the so-called indifference, which does not mean unconcern or a lack of interest, but a neutral waiting for a universally acceptable solution of the extremely difficult canonical questions. Meanwhile, the administration of Church benefices and finances in the "indifferent" territories required a competent authority. It was not merely financial aspects which led in Aragón especially to the organizing of a royal *Camera Apostolica;* in many places a similar expedient was resorted to. Aragón was rather for Urban, but when Peter de Luna came to the Kingdom as Cardinal Legate there was soon a change of atmosphere. However it was almost ten years before the new King John I decided for the Avignon obedience.[10] But Aragonese Sicily was subject to Rome. Portugal at first remained passive, but declared for Avignon in 1380, changed to Urban in 1381, returned to Clement in 1382, and went over definitely to Urban in 1385.[11] The King of Navarre did not declare for the Avignon obedience until 1390, after a long "indifferent" period.[12] More so than in these large states there were difficulties on the frontiers of the obediences, where the Schism often assumed bizarre forms, above all on the western boundary of the Empire, which did not even present a stable line and hence produced frequent changes.

At the beginning of the Schism Clement displayed a feverish activity in an effort to secure influence in Germany, an area lacking a strong central power. Many provisions, expectatives, and interventions in disputed cases have come down to us but we do not always know the outcome. Still, the material made available by E. Göller shows a great uncertainty in the

---

[10] M. Seidlmayer, *Anfänge,* 65–118; *idem,* "Peter de Luna (Benedikt XIII.) und die Entstehung des grossen abendländischen Schismas," *Gesammelte Aufsätze zur Kulturgeschichte Spaniens,* 4 (1933), 206–47; J. Zunzunegui, "La legación en España del Card. Pedro de Luna 1379–90," *Miscellanea Hist. Pont.,* 7 (1943), 83–137; J. Vincke, "Der König von Aragón und die Camera apostolica in den Anfängen des Grossen Schismas," *Gesammelte Aufsätze zur Kulturgeschichte Spaniens,* 7 (1938), 84–126; *idem,* "Die Berufung an den römischen Stuhl während der 'Indifferenz' König Peters IV. von Aragón," *ibid.,* 8 (1940), 263–79; *idem,* "Die Krone von Aragón und das grosse abendländische Schisma," *Staatl. Akademie zu Braunsberg,* Personal- und Vorlesungsverzeichnis, summer semester 1944; A. Boscolo, *Medio evo Aragonese,* chapter "Isole mediterranee, chiesa e Aragona durante lo scisma d'occidente," (Padua 1958); J. Morera Sabater, "Una curiosa correspondencia del año 1386 relativa al cisma de Occidente," *Ges. Aufsätze zur Kulturgesch. Spaniens,* 22 (1965), 202–16.

[11] M. Seidlmayer, *Anfänge,* 24; J. C. Baptista, "Portugal e o cisma de occidente," *Lusitania sacra,* 1 (1956), 65–203.

[12] J. Zunzunegui, *El reino de Navarra y su obispado de Pamplona durante la primera época del cisma de occidente. Pontificado de Clemente VII de Aviñón 1378–94* (San Sebastián 1942).

delimitation of the obediences and indicates numerous adherents of the Avignon claimant in all German bishoprics. The upper Rhine sees of Constance, Basel and Strasbourg, Duke Leopold of Austria, Count Eberhard of Wirtemberg, Margrave Bernard of Baden, and lower Rhine princes and cities inclined to Clement.[13] But apart from the borderlands, the Roman obedience clearly consolidated itself in the Empire, chiefly through the activity of King Wenceslas and the Urbanist alliance brought about by the efforts of the Count Palatine Rupert I, as well as by the successful legation of Cardinal Pileo da Prata. But not even all the German bishops entered the Urbanist alliance; in spite of the prevailing sympathy for Urban, imperial unanimity was unthinkable.[14]

The split also affected the centrally organized religious orders, which soon had a duplication of superiors and of general chapters. For the same reason there was schism in the cathedral and collegiate chapters, and dissension even invaded families, though, of course, we do not know much about the distress of consciences. Much is made of the fact that on both sides saints ardently defended the Pope they recognized at a given moment. That is of no particular importance and is only further proof that there was no universally recognized Pope, no *papa indubitatus*. Revealing is the attitude of the influential and scholarly Archbishop Peter Tenorio of Toledo, who in the Canon of the Mass replaced the name of the Pope with the phrase *pro illo qui est verus papa*.[15] It is useless to argue whether in the decisions for one or the other claimant more weight should be attributed to the political or the religious aspect. Even in predominantly theological considerations there was need of political measures for making convictions prevail. There were, to be sure, even clerics who, in order to acquire benefices, addressed themselves to both Curias, but the change of high ranking personalities from one obedience to the other depended most of all on political circumstances, just as the opinions of experts were guided by the political situation of the moment. Examples of renunciation of obedience are the Franciscan Cardinal Leonard Giffoni and Pileo da Prata, called the Cardinal of the Three

---

[13] E. Göller, *RepGerm*, I (Berlin 1916), 99*–170*; C. Schmitt, "Le parti clémentiste dans la province franciscaine de Strasbourg," *AFrH*, 55 (1962), 82–102; K. Schönenberger, *Das Bistum Konstanz während des Grossen Schismas* (Fribourg 1926); *idem, Das Bistum Basel während des grossen Schismas* (Basel 1928); J. Rott, "Le grand schisme d'occident et la diocèse de Strasbourg," *MAH*, 52 (1935), 366–95; A. Largiadèr, "Zum Grossen abendländischen Schisma von 1378 bis 1415," *Mélanges offerts à M. Paul-E. Martin* (Geneva 1961), 199 to 212; G. A. von Asseldonk, *De Nederlanden en het western schisma tot 1398* (Utrecht 1955); J. Paquet, "Le Schisme d'Occident à Louvain, Bruxelles et Anvers," *RHE*, 59 (1964), 401–36.

[14] H. Weigel, "Männer um König Wenzel. Das Problem der Reichspolitik 1379–1384," *DA*, 5 (1942), 112–77; *idem*, "König Wenzels persönliche Politik. Reich und Hausmacht 1384–1389," *DA*, 7 (1944), 133–99; P. Stacul, *Il cardinale Pileo da Prata* (Rome 1957).

[15] F. Ehrle, *Martin de Alpartils cronica actitatorum* (Paderborn 1896), 519.

Hats.[16] Only in the field of international finance was there little evidence of the split in Christendom, since most banks served both obediences.[17]

Clement VII, an extremely able politician, was not content with drawing up the Mass *De schismate tollendo* and arranging processions for ending the evil; he stubbornly strove for the *via facti*. Even before leaving Italy he had invested Louis I of Anjou with a large slice of the northern part of the Papal State by bulls issued at Sperlonga in April 1381, thereby proposing a Kingdom of Adria. In this way Italy would have come entirely under French rule or influence. But Louis was unable to make headway against Charles of Durazzo.[18] Here again it was high politics that impeded the realization of the *via facti*, above all the opposition between England and France, which had its effect also on the situation in Italy.

At scarcely any other period of the peninsula's history was it so confused and were alliances and treaties so fragile. This was the age of the greatest ascendancy of the Visconti at Milan, especially under Gian Galeazzo. He was opposed by Florence, which had the greatest reasons for fear, whereas Venice held aloof. Virtually all undertakings of the Italian *signorie* took place under the proud banner of *Italianità*, but in reality this mostly constituted the trimmings for selfish political ends. But interventions by France and the German King had to be avoided if a balance of power was to be maintained.

The two papal claimants were to a great extent mere figures in the high politics of Europe and of the small Italian states. Again and again one comes across a readiness to switch obediences at a favourable opportunity. But the situation existing shortly after the outbreak of the Schism was maintained for a long time. Because of his unfortunate policy Urban VI repeatedly ran into difficulties, for example, when he fell out, first with Queen Joanna I of Naples, and then also with his protector, Charles of Durazzo. His expedition to Naples, undertaken from considerations of nepotism in addition to other reasons, ended with his being detained at Nocera. He escaped to Genoa only by great exertions and there had some discontented cardinals cruelly

---

[16] C. Schmitt, "La position du card. Léonard de Giffoni O.F.M. dans le conflit du Grand Schisme d'Occident," *AFrH*, 50 (1957), 273–331, 51 (1958), 25–72, 410–72; P. Stacul, *op. cit.* More examples of the uncertainty in F. Babudri, "Lo scisma d'occidente e i suoi riflessi sulla chiesa di Brindisi," *Archivio storico Pugliese*, 8 (1955), 85–120; *idem*, "Oria e lo scisma d'Occidente," *ibid.*, 9 (1956), 145–53; G. G. Meersssemann, "Études sur l'ordre des frères Prêcheurs au début du Grand Schisme," *AFP*, 25 (1955), 213–57, 26 (1956), 192–248, 27 (1957), 170–99.

[17] A. Esch, "Bankiers der Kirche im Grossen Schisma," *QFIAB*, 46 (1966), 369 ff.

[18] M. De Boüard, *La France et l'Italie au temps du grand schisme d'occident* (Paris 1936), 38–41; P. Brezzi, "Lo scisma d'occidente come problema italiano," *ADRomana*, 67 (1944), 404; J. Zunzunegui, "Las cuentas de las galeras enviadas por Juan I de Castilla en favor de Clemente VII de Aviñón," *Anthologica Annua*, 5 (1957), 595–652.

executed. After a long absence he returned to Rome in 1388 and died there a year later. [19]

When the prescribed interval after Urban's death had ended, the conclave began at Rome without any serious consideration of postponing an election. Neither Poncello Orsini nor Angelus Acciaiuoli — the latter supported with all the means available to Florence — could achieve two-thirds of the votes, and, after a few days, agreement was reached on the still youthful Neapolitan Cardinal Peter Tomacelli, who became Boniface IX (1389–1404). [20] He at once turned against Louis II of Anjou and hence against France, from where loomed the gravest danger in the repeatedly projected campaigns into Italy, now in agreement with Milan, now with Florence. Many cities in the north of the Papal State were openly sympathetic toward Avignon, and even Viterbo was for a while Clementine. [21] But Boniface IX contrived to establish himself in Rome and then in the Papal State. His pontificate was without great significance in the general field of politics. Much as he frequently and willingly had recourse to arguments common to Italians, a large or decisive role in the maintenance of the balance of power can probably not be ascribed to him. [22] A very grave situation seemed to be created when in 1392–93 the former project of a Kingdom of Adria was revived by France. But this time Clement VII, with regard for the cardinals, was not so eager to accept it, though he did offer to invest the Duke of Orléans with the Marches of Ancona, Romagna, Ferrara, Ravenna, Bologna, Perugia, and Todi. However, he died on 16 September 1394, during the negotiations, and the plans were not pursued further. [23]

Two weeks after the death of Clement VII, the Avignon College of Cardinals elected a successor on 28 September 1394, even though the desire of the French government that there be no election immediately had been made known to the cardinals while still in conclave by protagonists of the *via cessionis*. Peter de Luna, now elected and styling himself Benedict XIII (1394–1423), was certainly the most outstanding figure in the Avignon College and fully conversant with all the theological and canonical problems of the Schism. With most of his colleagues in the conclave he had signed under oath a statement that he would devote himself to union with all zeal and would even abdicate in the event that the cardinals should regard this as necessary. [24] This *via cessionis* had for years been prominent in discussions

[19] Theodorici de Nyem, *De schismate*, 78–123; *Cosmidromius* Gobelini Person, 97–126.

[20] *DHGE*, 8 (1935), 909–22 (E. Vansteenberghe).

[21] P. Stacul, *op. cit.*, 195 ff.

[22] P. Brezzi, "Lo scisma d'occidente," lays special emphasis on the importance of Boniface IX in Italian policy.

[23] *Storia di Milano*, VI (1955), 6–9.

[24] For Benedict XIII see *DHGE*, 8 (1935), 135–63 (Jadin); the statement is in F. Ehrle, "Afterconcil," *ALKGMA*, V (1889), 403, and *Baluze-Mollat*, I, 541 f.; F. Ehrle, *Alpartil*,

and considerations for the ending of the Schism. It had been frequently brought up under Clement VII and possessed a notable majority in both Colleges of Cardinals.

In many respects Benedict XIII was the heir of the policy of Clement VII, such as in his confidence in the *via facti*, that is, the settling of the question in a practical manner by a campaign in Italy. But Benedict displayed an incomparably greater energy and diplomatic skill. In his first close contacts with the court of Paris for the liquidation of the Schism in October 1394 he was very courteous, but in January 1395 he precisely stated his views and later rejected the decrees of the first Council of Paris, held in the spring.

After there had been discussions at Paris for years on the ways of restoring unity, there began also at Avignon a feverish activity in this direction. An abundance of suggestions is mentioned; committees of cardinals were busy with them, and the cardinals set forth their individual views in writing. Opinions and pamphlets circulated, predominantly in the sense of the *via discussionis (conventionis, compromissi, iustitiae)*, but also of the *via cessionis* as a last resort.[25] Meanwhile, the so-called first Council of Paris (3–8 February 1395), under the influence of a few cardinals and of the extreme factions at the University, had declared abdication to be the only way to be adopted. This was contrary to the moderate proposals of d'Ailly, who returned from an embassy to the Pope, and it was adopted in a not entirely clear voting procedure.[26] Then in the summer of 1395 (22 May–9 July) there appeared at Avignon a "high embassy," consisting of the King's uncles, the Dukes of Berry and Burgundy, and his brother, the Duke of Orléans, with many experts and delegates of the University. In several audiences they made known to the Pope the King's vigorously formulated desire but were able, of course, to obtain from Benedict only an evasive reply which rejected the *via cessionis*. The embassy had more success with the cardinals, most of whom in personal interviews consented to the *via cessionis*.[27] The government at Paris exerted itself in numerous embassies to the German princes and to Kings Wenceslas and Sigismund, to King Richard II of England, and to Spain to gain support for this plan.[28]

A second synod of the French clergy at Paris, from 16 August to 15 September, was again preoccupied with the unsatisfactory situation. In accord

217; F. Stegmüller, "Die Consolatio Theologiae des Papstes Pedro de Luna (Benedikt XIII.)," *Ges. Aufsätze zur Kulturgesch. Spaniens*, 21 (1963), 209–15.
[25] F. Ehrle, "Afterconcil," *ALKGMA*, V (1889), 406 f.; *idem*, "Neue Materialien," *ALKGMA*, VI (1892), 148–62; *idem*, Alpartil, 14, 439–61; C. Schmitt, *op. cit.*
[26] N. Valois, *La France et le grand schisme d'occident*, III, 27–44; F. Ehrle, *Alpartil*, 468–74.
[27] *Martène C*, VII, 466–72; N. Valois, *op. cit.*, III, 44–67; F. Ehrle, *"Afterconcil,"* *ALKGMA*, V (1889), 408–21; *idem*, *Alpartil*, 14 f., 449 f.
[28] F. Ehrle, "Neue Materialien," *ALKGMA*, VI (1892), 200 f.

with the royal instructions the deliberations were to deal, no longer with the *via cessionis,* but only with the best method of realizing it. The majority favoured a withdrawal of obedience, but one more admonition should be directed to the Pope before suitable measures were taken.[29] Meanwhile, he had not been idle. He eagerly sought to promote the *via conventionis* by negotiations with the Roman claimant and even more to effect the elimination of his rival by the *via facti.* Already in 1395 embassies had proceeded from Avignon to Rome and one from the Roman claimant to Avignon. Benedict's envoy, the Bishop of Elne, did not succeed in getting to Rome *via* the territory of the Count of Fondi and Marino, which belonged to the latter, but he was able to bring about a dangerous conspiracy against Boniface IX. The Bishop of Tarazona, received at Rome as Benedict's ambassador in the summer of 1396, had very interesting discussions with Boniface and a few cardinals, including the events in the election of Urban VI, in which he had taken part as a conclavist. The repeated offers for an encounter of the two rivals or at least for negotiations by plenipotentiaries were repulsed by Boniface.[30] Concerning the activity of the envoys he sent to Avignon the same year we have no more precise information than that they reported on the imminent *démarche* of the French government and advised against concessions. Boniface's apprehensions were not unfounded, for Benedict had many adherents in Italy and enjoyed much sympathy even in Rome. Several mercenary captains were in his service in the northern part of the *Patrimonium,* and for many years he maintained a strong garrison in the fortress of Soriano to the east of Viterbo. The possibility of an occupation of Civitavecchia in a plot with Roman circles and the Count of Fondi was left untried by Benedict in the summer of 1396.[31]

En route from Sicily to Aragón, King Martin I had visited Benedict at Avignon and had been won to his policy. Hence he participated in Benedict's efforts to enter into serious discussions with his rival or to reach a decision by the *via facti.* The Aragonese King, loyal to Benedict, wanted to gain also the King of Castile for this policy, but without success, since political developments bound Castile ever more strongly to France.[32] And in the meantime France had succeeded in finding sympathy for the *via cessionis* in England, hitherto belonging to the Roman obedience. To what degree politics decided ecclesiastical questions is evident from this procedure of England, which resulted automatically from its *rapprochement* with France.

[29] N. Valois, *op. cit.,* III, 104–23; F. Ehrle, "Neue Materialien," *ALKGMA,* VI (1892), 193–241; *idem, Alpartil,* 475–91.
[30] F. Ehrle, "Neue Materialien," *ALKGMA,* VI (1892), 162, 193; *idem, Alpartil,* 19–23; N. Valois, *op. cit.,* III, 88–96.
[31] F. Ehrle, "Neue Materialien," *ALKGMA,* VII (1900), 9–13; *idem, Alpartil,* 23–25, 533–41.
[32] F. Ehrle, "Neue Materialien," *ALKGMA,* VII (1900), 1–15; *idem, Alpartil,* 252–66, 509–20.

Envoys of the Kings of England, France, and Castile went to Avignon and Rome but could accomplish nothing definite.[33]

Of great importance for theory and practice was the third Council of Paris, which sat from the middle of May till the beginning of August 1398 and decreed the withdrawal of obedience. Estimates of it differ greatly, but two notions seem especially pertinent. By being deprived of his income from France the Pope should be forced to resign and on this pretext the influence of the government in the administration of the French Church, naturally including the financial aspect, should be further strengthened. The result of the voting — 247 to thirty-four or thirty-eight — is incorrectly represented as falsified by the government. And the deliberations were much more solid than has hitherto been supposed, even if many of the questions that came up, notably in regard to implementation in practice, had to remain unsettled.[34] The decree of withdrawal was dated 27 July, and on the following day it was solemnly published by the King. In the next weeks instructions were issued to the officials. Almost no one in the Kingdom resisted the decrees of the synod, and at Avignon itself eighteen cardinals, one after another, abandoned the Pope and betook themselves to French territory at Villeneuve-lès-Avignon. There they made preparations for impeding Benedict in the exercise of his office and for getting him into their power if possible.

Thus began the memorable siege of the papal palace, which the Pope had some time before converted into a fortress, well provided with all war equipment. The shelling and assaults made in the fall of 1398 by the troops of the mercenary Captain Boucicaut, engaged by the cardinals, were at first without effect. Though a fleet sent by the King of Aragón was unable to get as far as Avignon, there ensued a truce in May 1399 and the departure of the greater part of the garrison. However, Benedict was isolated in the palace by a zone of stockades until 1403 and only scantily supplied, despite several safe-conducts which the Duke of Orléans had secured from the King. By secret protests in the summer of 1399 Benedict had in law repudiated all concessions wrung from him.[35] On 12 March 1403 he made a fantastic escape from the papal palace down the Rhone to the Château-Renard in the territory of the Count of Provence. With this there began a new episode in the troubled history of the Western Schism.

[33] E. Perroy, *L'Angleterre et le grand schisme d'occident* (Paris 1933), 352–87.

[34] N. Valois, *op. cit.*, III, 150–82; F. Ehrle, "Neue Materialien," *ALKGMA*, VI (1892), 115–49; J. Haller, *Papsttum und Kirchenreform* (Berlin 1903), 228–37, 535–43; G. Barraclough, "Un document sur la soustraction d'obédience en 1398," *RHE*, 30 (1934), 101–15; G. Mollat, "L'application en France de la soustraction d'obédience à Benoît XIII jusqu'au concile de Pise," *RMA*, 1 (1945), 149–63.

[35] F. Ehrle, "Afterconcil," *ALKGMA*, V (1889), 425–29; *idem*, "Neue Materialien," *ALKGMA*, VI (1892), 302–08; *idem, Alpartil*, 38–81, 213–17; G. Mollat, "Épisodes du siège du palais des papes au temps de Benoît XIII, 1398–1399", *RHE*, 23 (1927), 489–501; J. Rius Serra, "Galeres catalanes al servei de Benet XIII," *AST*, 11 (1935), 333–41.

An almost incalculable number of discussions and embassies had prepared, accompanied, and effected this result. Even during the siege Benedict was in contact with the disloyal cardinals and Paris.[36] There the difficulties attendant upon the withdrawal had become greater and greater in the administration of benefices and in the Church's financial system. If the bishops had expected more independence by virtue of the "liberties of the Gallican Church," they felt greatly deceived. The court and the government took the place of the papal Curia. Wide circles doubted the legitimacy of the proceedings against one who till now had been defended as the only lawful Pope, and his inflexibility created a profound impression. Apparently he was not to be subdued by military measures. Withdrawal by the government and siege by the College of Cardinals were not regarded as legitimate means for liquidating the unsatisfactory state of things. For this a judgment of the Church, and hence a council, was qualified. And representatives of the French government discussed such a council at Metz and Mainz with Rupert of the Palatinate, elected King of Germany on the deposition of Wenceslas.[37]

Provence had returned to Benedict in 1402 and in Paris Castile was working for a restitution of obedience as the best way out of the hopeless situation. To Château-Renard went the cardinals, to obtain reconciliation with Benedict. Then faithless Avignon also submitted to the now liberated Pope. Two cardinals proceeded to Paris to expedite the matter of obedience, and on 28 May it was decreed by the King under the influence of the Duke of Orléans. But still certain concessions on Benedict's part had to be discussed with the Duke at Tarascon. Absolution was granted to the King *ad cautelam* and the new peace was sealed by a compact of the Pope with the King, the Queen, and the Duke.[38]

Soon after his liberation, Benedict sent important proposals to Rome: 1) for a meeting of the two rivals on the borders of their respective obediences or in Italy, for example in the territory of Genoa; 2) for negotiations by plenipotentiaries in the event that the claimants could not meet personally; 3) for resignation. All of this was rejected by Boniface with subterfuges and feeble arguments.[39] Even considering the tendencies of the reports that have

---

[36] F. Ehrle, "Afterconcil," *ALKGMA*, V (1889), 425–87.

[37] A. Mercati, "Dall'archivio vaticano II. Un'ignota missione francese nel 1401 presso Roberto del Palatinato eletto re dei Romani," *MAH*, 61 (1949), 209–25; H. Finke, "Zur Korrespondenz der deutschen Könige und Fürsten mit den Herrschern Aragóns im 14. und 15. Jahrhundert," *Gesammelte Aufsätze zur Kulturgeschichte Spaniens*, 5 (1935), 458–505; also important in regard to Aragonese efforts to gain King Wenceslas for Avignon, and likewise Rupert.

[38] F. Ehrle, "Neue Materialien," *ALKGMA*, VII (1900), 278–310; J. Schoos, "Der Machtkampf zwischen Burgund und Orléans unter den Herzögen Philipp dem Kühnen, Johann ohne Furcht von Burgund und Ludwig von Orléans," *Publications de la section historique de l'Institut G.-D. de Luxembourg*, 75 (Luxembourg 1956).

[39] F. Ehrle, "Afterconcil," *ALKGMA*, VII (1900), 580–84; *idem*, *Alpartil*, 147 f.

come down to us in a biased form, Boniface does not cut a fine figure. His death, occurring while the Avignon envoys were in Rome, interrupted the contact, and the new Pope Innocent VII, Cosimo Migliorati (1404–06), did not take part in discussions.

In consultations at Villafranca near Nice in 1405 with King Martin I of Sicily, Louis II of Anjou, claimant to the Kingdom of Naples, and Duke Louis of Bourbon, Benedict made known the plan of a great expedition to Italy. But the project did not materialize, for both the King of Aragón and the French government refused consent. However, Benedict stubbornly pursued his projects in missions to Sicily and to many Italian cities and lordships. He gained for his obedience a great part of the Riviera with Genoa, which was then ruled by Marshal Boucicaut, and proceeded as far as Genoa, but was then forced by the outbreak of an epidemic to return to Marseilles. In Paris this move into Italy was regarded with a certain amount of fear that the Pope, if successful in his Italian schemes, might be able to reside in Rome. [40]

The death of Innocent VII in 1406 seemed to open up another solution when Benedict asked the Roman cardinals not to proceed to an election. But before his envoys arrived the new Pope had been elected: the Venetian Angelus Correr, who became Gregory XII (1406–15). Just as earlier at the election of Benedict XIII at Avignon, now too each cardinal had bound himself, in the event of his election, to resign if the same thing were to happen on the opposing side; specific regulations concerned the naming of new cardinals in order to maintain both colleges at numerical equality. This was a step in the direction of a meeting of the two rivals or at least of the two Colleges of Cardinals.

During the night following his election Gregory had solemnly accepted these stipulations and in numerous letters to kings, princes, and cities he had proclaimed his willingness to resign. [41] Then on 21 April 1407 was signed the Treaty of Marseilles, in which, as its principal item, the meeting of the claimants at Savona near Genoa on Michaelmas was agreed to. [42] But from now on Gregory's behaviour is difficult to understand and so far there has been no satisfactory explanation. His postponing the fulfillment of the treaty, in fact his downright refusal to do so, has been interpreted as due to the unfortunate influence of his nephews. But the danger of his position was sufficiently well known to him and his fear of a trap was not entirely groundless. His words and deeds, however, hardly display greatness in comparison with the dignified, learned, and very skilfull diplomatic procedure

---

[40] F. Ehrle, *Alpartil*, 149 f.

[41] J. Vincke, *Schriftstücke zum Pisaner Konzil*, 27–29.

[42] Hefele-Knöpfler, VI (1900), 890 f.; F. Ehrle, "Afterconcil," *ALKGMA*, VII (1900), 594–623; *idem, Alpartil*, 160 f.

of Benedict, who was apparently more profoundly convinced of his legitimacy and of the success of his plans. To be sure, despite a vacillating obedience in France, Benedict was in a far better situation than Gregory. The King of Aragón, with his considerable strength in the Mediterranean, clung loyally to him, and in the Midi he had many adherents. An embassy from the French government, led by the Patriarch Cramaud, was supposed to have Benedict confirm by a bull his readiness to yield and obtain from him a decree that after his death the cardinals must not proceed to a new election but should bring about a reunion with the cardinals of the Roman claimant in order to elect a new Pope by common action in the given situation — a proposal such as was later realized at Pisa. Benedict was ready only with proposals to the cardinals. In the reports of the negotiations the mutual regard of the two rivals is astonishing and perhaps implies secret arrangements; such at least was the reproach often hurled at both pretenders at the Council of Pisa. [43]

Not until the beginning of August did Gregory quit Rome, indecisive and already too late to reach Savona at the date agreed upon. He was with his Curia at Siena from the beginning of September till January 1408. The advance of King Ladislas of Naples on Rome created for Gregory a really threatening situation, for then the Romans themselves applied to Benedict for subsidies. The fleet that had put to sea on his orders arrived too late to prevent the capture of Rome, and it probably had other assignments than merely that of supplying the Romans with money. [44] In conformity with the stipulations of the Treaty of Marseilles, Benedict set out, arrived at Savona before the appointed day, and left half the city for Gregory. From the latter came messages with excuses and requests for another place of meeting. Meanwhile, Benedict sailed with his galleys to Portovenere, while Gregory appeared at Lucca at the end of January 1408. Negotiations were drawn out for months, and French delegations of various tendencies visited both rivals. It is downright tragic to observe how the two claimants got within a few leagues of each other and then neither met in person nor effected an agreement through deputies. As other places of meeting were mentioned Portovenere, Pietrasanta, Carrara, Lucca, Livorno, and finally Pisa and Livorno.

The negotiations, unceasing and unsuccessful, dragged themselves out but then came to a sudden end with the defection of Gregory's cardinals and the simultaneous renewal of proceedings against Benedict by France. Gregory's cardinals had long been unhappy over his delaying tactics. The creation of four new cardinals was regarded as a violation of his election commitments and induced most of his cardinals to abandon him and to flee to Pisa

[43] F. Ehrle, *Alpartil*, 161, 163; A. Bossuat, "Une relation inédite de l'ambassade française au pape Benoît XIII en 1407," *MA*, 55 (1949), 77–101.
[44] F. Ehrle, *Alpartil*, 541–45.

in May 1408. Gregory thereupon withdrew to Siena and the meeting of the rivals suffered shipwreck. Wide circles in Christendom had familiarized themselves with the notion of neutrality and council. And so, after their departure from Lucca, the cardinals of the Roman obedience at once appealed to a council, but without destroying all bridges to their Pope. Relations with Benedict's cardinals now became more intense, especially after the new withdrawal of obedience by France. The assassination of the Duke of Orléans in 1407 had deprived Benedict of his strongest supporter. When in the spring of 1408 France resumed its neutrality, Benedict replied in April with the publication of the long ready bull of excommunication. It seems that the French envoys, led by the Patriarch Cramaud, intended to seize Benedict's person. Benedict then decided to leave Portovenere, after he had summoned a council to meet at Perpignan on the coming All Saints' Day. On 15 July his fleet put to sea and, after some unfriendly treatment at the Riviera ports, made its way to Perpignan at the end of the month. Most of his cardinals had not followed him and in August they joined Gregory's cardinals. [45]

When all of Gregory's attempts for a resumption of negotiations had collapsed, his rebel cardinals had resolved, probably as early as the beginning of June, on a council which they would summon. February of 1409 was proposed as the date; the territory of the Margrave of Este or the Principality of Montferrat, as the place. But once Florence had disavowed Gregory, Pisa was decided on as the place of the council. Publicity for the council was undertaken in the grand manner. Thousands of documents were sent to princes, the hierarchy, and cities. Each College of Cardinals sent out its own propaganda missions. [46]

Meanwhile, Benedict's council got under way at Perpignan in November 1408; it was mainly occupied with the reading of the *informatio seriosa,* a detailed exposition of Benedict's efforts for unity. Though drawn up in accord with his viewpoint, it is, by reason of the vast number of documents, one of the most precious sources of the period. The Council of Perpignan was well attended from Spain and the Midi; besides numerous bishops, there were more than 120 abbots or their proxies, superiors of religious houses, and representatives of cathedral chapters, universities, and the military orders. In spite of all the admonitions to the Pope to resign, the only tangible result was the dispatch of an embassy to the Council of Pisa. Then, on 26 March 1409, the session was interrupted and again and again prorogued into 1416. [47]

---

[45] F. Ehrle, "Afterconcil," *ALKGMA,* VII (1900), 623–52; *idem, Alpartil,* 165–69.

[46] J. Vincke, *Briefe zum Pisaner Konzil,* 216–38.

[47] F. Ehrle, "Afterconcil," *ALKGMA,* VII (1900), 652–94 (lists of participants, 669–91). A further tradition of the *informatio seriosa* in *Baluze-Mollat,* IV, 391–408; F. Ehrle, *Alpartil,* 173–91.

The exertions of the united College of Cardinals for a good attendance at the announced Council were a complete success. In addition to twenty-four cardinals and four patriarchs, there were more than eighty archbishops and bishops, an equal number of abbots, the proxies of more than 100 bishops and over 200 abbots, many deputies of princes and universities, the generals of the important orders, and numerous doctors of theology and canon law.[48] Pointedly absent were the German King Rupert and the kingdoms of the Iberian peninsula. On 25 March the Council was opened with the traditional solemnities in the cathedral of Pisa.

In view of the fact that the cardinals rather than the papal rivals had convoked the Council, the external conduct of business naturally differed from preceding mediaeval councils. Furthermore, the purpose of the gathering was to institute proceedings against both *pro papa se gerentibus* and thus the trial formalities were in the foreground. This was evident right after the opening, with the appointing of the officials: two marshals, two auditors, four advocates, four procurators, and twelve notaries. Most often mentioned was the consistorial advocate, Simon of Perugia, who had charge of the technicalities in almost all of the sessions. Documents were prepared at need by the notaries. The question of the Council's presidency was solved in a very different manner. The College of Cardinals in its entirety was regarded as holding this office, but this was not emphasized. As representative of the College, Malesec, the ranking Cardinal Bishop, received the oaths of the officials appointed by the full Council and proposed the introduction of the process against the two pretenders. But the most important personality was the leader of the French delegation, Simon de Cramaud, Patriarch of Alexandria, who was often attended by two other patriarchs in his official appearances. After the papal election it goes without saying that the new Pope assumed the direction of the Council.

The assembly completed its work in twenty-two sessions, usually following close upon one another. In preparing for them the members met in what they called "nations" — German, French, English, Italian, and a small Provençal "nation" — while the cardinals met as a college, frequently with representatives of the "nations."[49] At the first session, on 26 March, the Cardinal of Milan delivered the opening sermon, which propounded

---

[48] *Hefele-Leclercq*, VII, 1 (1916); *Mansi*, XXVI, 1193–1256, XXVII, 331–56 (with important additions); J. Vincke, *Schriftstücke zum Pisaner Konzil*, 178–205; Graziano di S. Teresa, "Un nuovo elenco dei participanti al concilio di Pisa," *ECarm*, 16 (1965), 384–411.
[49] F. Stuhr, *Die Organisation und Geschäftsordnung des Pisaner und Konstanzer Konzils* (Diss., Berlin 1891); L. Schmitz, "Zur Geschichte des Konzils von Pisa 1409," *RQ*, 9 (1895), 351–75; H. Finke, "Die Nation in den spätmittelalterlichen allgemeinen Konzilien," *HJ*, 57 (1937), 327 f.

sixteen important propositions on the cardinals' right to convoke the Council in view of the refusal of the papal rivals — theses which reproduced what had been held and taught by a great many theologians and canonists, for years and decades now, as the correct doctrine of the constitution of the Church.[50]

The Council's principal task, the process against the two pretenders, was provided for by the appointment of an investigating committee, which was resolved in the seventh session, on 4 May, at the suggestion of the "nations" and of the envoys of princes, prelates and universities.[51] But before the process began there arrived envoys of the German King Rupert, a loyal adherent of the Roman obedience, who protested both in lengthy speeches and in writing and at once left the city. Later appeared envoys of King Martin of Aragón and of Benedict XIII, who were also heard.[52] The process displayed the usual involved and cumbersome methods with which we are already acquainted from the endless interrogations at Medina del Campo and which we shall likewise encounter in the proceedings against John XXIII at Constance. The thirty-seven articles of accusation against both claimants were publicly read at the fifth session, on 24 April, and the introduction of the process was moved. Later, further articles were added. On 4 May, in the seventh session, the proposed committee was approved by the Council. It consisted of two cardinals, four representatives of the German nation, five of the French, one of the English, five of the Italian, and one of the Provençal.

As early as 7 May occurred the public citation of the witnesses, who were sworn by the committee on 9 May in the sacristy of the Carmelite church. At first there were sixty-six witnesses, and later eleven more. The hearing of the witnesses began on the same day; a total of sixty-two witnesses were interrogated on the chief points. In a laborious procedure the articles with their subdivisions were read aloud to them word for word. The committee did its work in several groups. The hearings were often in the residence of one of the cardinals of the committee, and the cardinals themselves, almost all of whom testified, could do so in their dwellings. Several gave their information in writing, such as Cardinals Brancaccio and Orsini — the latter likewise made written depositions at Constance — and the most prominent figure at the Council, Simon, Patriarch of Alexandria. In addition, many documents were submitted as corroborative evidence.

On 22 May the Archbishop of Pisa began his report on the result of the

---

[50] *Mansi*, XXVII, 118 ff.; these theses are in J. Vincke, *Acta concilii Pisani*, 91 ff. The second declaration of legitimacy on 10 May in the eighth session had been brought about by a motion on 24 April in the fifth session; *cf.* J. Vincke, *Acta concilii Pisani*, 133, 149 f.

[51] J. Vincke, *Acta concilii Pisani*, 140–43.

[52] *Ibid.*, 129–36, 305–07.

inquiries. Since such processes pursued a definite goal, in this case the deposition of both rivals, their lack of an intention to resign was especially emphasized — matters which had been long known and whose notoriety was to be made clear and stressed. Of course, in this process, as in that against John XXIII at Constance, a great deal of gossip was in circulation and some common views or impressions were transmitted only by hearsay. But among the witnesses were many prominent men, persons in high positions of responsibility at both Curias, who reported things in which they had participated. Above all, many of the things now brought forward belonged to the quite recent past, and so were different from a part of the investigations into the events of 1378.

The long duration of the Schism, notwithstanding many attempts at a settlement, was blamed, perhaps too much, on the individual papal claimants, and the confusion of the situation was treated too lightly. Too little account was also taken of the psychological state of the respective Popes, who, as Cardinals in conclave, had, like their colleagues, sworn to resign, but of course in regard to this serious step wanted to wait for the most favourable moment. Quite apart from this was the fact that the personal conviction of legitimacy could only make resignation very painful.

Benedict, of course, never seriously considered abdication, though as a Cardinal he had been energetically in favour of it and in the conclave had obliged himself to it under oath. But it is reported that in the first year of his pontificate he had stated that he would rather have himself burned than resign. It was claimed that he dismissed all advocates of the *via cessionis* and advanced those who said what he wanted to hear. The *Magister sacri palatii*, who in a Good Friday sermon urged him to resign, was removed from office and imprisoned for two years. Witnesses claimed to have seen the authentic documents in which, following the withdrawal of obedience, he had declared his readiness to resign, but he had not made good his promise. He imprisoned officials who refused to draw up documents according to his wish by expunging the article on resignation in the negotiations with the Roman cardinals after the death of Boniface IX. To Gregory's clear offer to resign he returned evasive replies. At Portovenere he was said to have first agreed to the plan for a general council, then to have rejected it, only to retire to Perpignan and summon a council there. There were many specific charges: acts of violence, execution of clerics in major orders, arrest of priests and of superiors of orders for service on his galleys, favouring of heretics, and of course magic, which finds a place in all the contemporary trial material.

And Gregory XII was no different. He once planned to go on foot to Paris, if thereby the Schism could be settled, and then he took it amiss when his advisers suggested the land route to Savona in the event that vessels were not at his disposal. A long list of omissions and intrigues was laid to his charge. In place of Charles Malatesta it was Gregory's nephew Anthony who was sent to Benedict; he alone was provided with the secret instructions, and the other envoys were duped. Time and again Gregory mentally disavowed Savona, despite the opinions given by the cardinals. In a public consistory at Lucca he termed the *via cessionis* "diabolica et damnata," branded it as heretical, and said, "I intend to die as Pope." Advocates of resignation were also ill-treated and imprisoned by him. At Lucca he made arrangements to put the cardinals in irons and was only prevented by the *signore*. The Cardinal of Liège, who had fled from Lucca, was to be brought back dead or alive. Money and valuables of churches and parts of the Papal State went to his nephews.

All these charges probably have an historically true basic element, but they must have been often exaggerated in the drawing up of the accusations and in the depositions of the witnesses. Quite rightly did Gregory's confidant, Cardinal Dominici, complain later in his behalf. Some things were pure fabrications, others were reported inexactly, torn from their context, and thus altered.[53] On one very weighty point, the so-called *collusio*, or secret dealings and understandings between the two rivals, full clarity will never be obtained. The many secret conferences in the dead of night in the rooms of the claimants or in the cathedral sacristy at Siena between Gregory's nephews and Benedict's envoy supplied plenty of material for fantastic conjectures. But what Leonard Bruni, Gregory's secretary and a renowned humanist, was able to report is of interest. According to him, it had been planned to imprison the cardinals, bar them from the election, and entrust it to a committee of four, composed of two representatives of each obedience. The Cardinal of San Marco, who remained even longer with Gregory and did not go to Pisa for the conclave until 16 June, contributed to the record in writing on 5 August that Gregory had later regretted not having accepted the offer; he entertained the really childish idea that he would have delegated his nephews, who were accustomed to privation, and they, having been inclosed with the other two, would have compelled them by hunger to give in and hence to elect him.

A quick winding up of the hearings was agreed to by the Council because of the threat from King Ladislas and on 1 June the accepting of reports ceased, while copies were made accessible for further information. Meanwhile, the two papal claimants had been repeatedly cited by the Council and on several occasions solemn deputations proceeded to the doors of the cathedral to call in a loud voice the pretenders or their representatives — everything according to the precise rules of trial procedure. Then the process was quickly concluded and in the fifteenth session, on 5 June, the judgment was publicly read by the Patriarch of Alexandria, sitting as judge

[53] H. Finke, *Acta concilii Const.*, I (Münster 1896), 273 f.

and attended by the Patriarchs of Antioch and Jerusalem. Gregory XII and Benedict XIII were cast out of the Church as notorious schismatics, promoters of schism, and notorious and obdurate heretics and perjurors, obedience was withdrawn from them, and the vacancy of the Holy See was confirmed.[54] The sentence was signed by almost all members of the Council; the list of signatures comprises 213 entries, including twenty-four cardinals.[55]

At once preparations were made for the conclave. Part of its task should be to bind the future Pope to a wise and adequate reform of the Church at this very Council. Apparently an agreement had been made among the cardinals that for the validity of the election at least two-thirds of the votes of the cardinals of each obedience were necessary. The conclave began on 15 June in the archiepiscopal palace and ended on 26 June with the unanimous election of the Cardinal of Milan, Peter Philarghi, who called himself Alexander V (1409–10). The electoral protocol, with the signatures of all the cardinals, was read in the next session.[56]

Peter Philarghi, born in northern Crete of Greek parents and educated by Franciscans, had entered the Franciscan Order. He soon went to Italy, then to Oxford for study, and later to Paris and Pavia. To this period belong his widely known commentary on *The Sentences* and his reputation as a humanist. Galeazzo Visconti arranged his promotion to the sees of Piacenza, Vicenza, and Novara in succession. From 1392 he carried out diplomatic missions for the Visconti and in 1395 procured the ducal title for him from King Wenceslas. In 1402 he became Archbishop of Milan, in 1405 a Cardinal and Legate in North Italy.[57] He had taken a prominent part in arranging the Council of Pisa, and his election as Pope had been strongly promoted by Cardinal Baldassarre Cossa.[58] Though the French court had relinquished its demand for a French candidate and for residence at Avignon, the new Pope owed his elevation to France.[59] After his coronation on 7 July the Council quickly finished its business. And first of all, the Pope confirmed in favour of the adherents of the Council all measures taken during the Schism in the administration of benefices. A reform committee did not actually take up any business; for this purpose a new council was announced for 1412 and provincial and diocesan synods were directed to prepare for it. The Council ended on 7 August.[60]

[54] J. Vincke, *Acta concilii Pisani*, 295–98.
[55] J. Vincke, *Schriftstücke zum Pisaner Konzil*, 177–205.
[56] J. Vincke, *Acta concilii Pisani*, 309–14.
[57] *Dizionario biografico degli Italiani*, II (1960), 193–96; G. D. Oltrona Visconti, "Ancora sui natali di Pietro Filargo, vescovo di Novara poi papa Alessandro V," *Bollettino storico per la provincia di Novara*, 51 (1960), 119–29.
[58] *Duchesne LP*, II, 511 f.
[59] J. Vincke, *Schriftstücke zum Pisaner Konzil*, 176 f.
[60] J. Vincke, "Zu den Konzilien in Perpignan und Pisa. 2. Ein auf dem Konzil von Pisa diskutierter Reformvorschlag, Pisa etwa Mitte Juli 1409," *RQ*, 50 (1955), 91–94.

An assessment of the Council of Pisa depends upon whether one adheres to the contemporary viewpoint or considers the matter in the light of later developments. According to the second alternative, Pisa was a failure, it is stigmatized as a pseudo-council or rump council, and it is denied the rank of a general council. [61] But when judged by the views of contemporaries it cannot be denied recognition as a general council. Even in regard to the participants, it surpassed in numbers and especially in the question of representing the Universal Church in the Lateran Councils, except the fourth, that of Vienne, and the first two periods of Trent. Since it dealt primarily with a process against the two claimants to the papacy, there were few theological discussions and scarcely anything to record in regard to the theory of Conciliarism. Conciliar notions were first expressed in their entirety at Constance. But Pisa had taken the road to the complete liquidation of the Schism with much success, and without this Council the happy ending of the division can hardly be imagined.

The Conciliar Idea

More recent research has contributed substantially to our understanding of the importance of the general council in the central and late Middle Ages. But it was already known that the general council occupied an important place in the constitution of the Church at that time. It is true that the varied concepts of the external structure and the distribution of powers were hardly ever presented in a compact system, but were widely scattered in the glosses of decretists and decretalists. That is why very contradictory theses are often to be met in the same author. Ockham and Marsilius of Padua no longer rank as the only ancestors of what is called Conciliarism. Theories labelled with the catchwords "papalism," "conciliarism," "corporation system," "oligarchy," can be detected everywhere. Less happy were the efforts to establish a biblical basis for the theory of the moment, but this did not hinder their having a historical reality of tremendous influence.

Following the outbreak of the Western Schism and the first unsuccessful efforts to end it, it was natural to look about for a fundamental remedy for the now disjointed *corpus politicum* of the Church. Then the conciliar idea suggested itself as an aid. In an almost limitless profusion of still mostly unprinted treatises and testimonials the council was again and again recommended as the saviour in the emergency. But it should finally be admitted that most of the testimonials, memoranda, and theological treatises were predominantly political in character and, despite all the scholarly embellishments,

[61] *Pastor,* I (St. Louis, 2nd ed. 1899) 178–91. Likewise in the more recent literature, for example A. Favale, *I concili ecumenici* (Turin 1962).

423

had to conform to their current sphere of influence. First of all, the Italian cardinals demanded the convoking of a council, before which Urban VI should appear, and then also Clement VII after his election at Fondi. Even Peter de Luna, who later as Benedict XIII was bluntly to reject a council as a means of uniting the two or later the three obediences, is said to have desired a council at the beginning of the Schism. The conciliar idea encountered powerful opposition from Clement VII's cardinals, especially from the important jurists Flandrin and Amelii. But there were demands for a council in Castile and Aragón, notably by the forceful inquisitor Nicholas Eymerich and the fiery Vincent Ferrer. Best known are the treatises *Epistola pacis* (May 1379) and *Epistola concilii pacis* (summer of 1381) of the Paris professor, Henry von Langenstein, and the opinions of the provost of the Worms cathedral, Conrad von Gelnhausen, expressed in *Epistola brevis* (August 1379) and *Epistola concordiae* (May 1380).

At the basis of the conciliar idea, which found at times stronger and at times weaker expression, according to the political situation, lay the concept that the Pope is not the absolute master of the Church. In normal conditions he or the *Ecclesia Romana* in the narrower sense governs the visible Church. But in special cases — schism, heresy, "contra bonum commune ecclesiae" — the Universal Church comes to the fore — *ecclesia universalis, congregatio fidelium, corpus Christi mysticum* — in accord with the frequently recurring proposition: "quod omnes tangit, ab omnibus approbari debet" or "maior est auctoritas totius orbis quam urbis alicuius." [62] According to this opinion, the power of the whole Church is greater, and she alone is infallible. Numerous concepts sought to clarify the complicated problem of the *plenitudo potestatis, potestas actualis* and *habitualis*. The favourite set of terms, *potestas — exercitium*, generally meant that the *exercitium*, the *potestas actualis*, is ordinarily vested in the Pope and Curia — *minister, dispensator, procurator, caput ministeriale* — but in emergencies the greater *potestas, habitualis* of the Universal Church is actualized in the council as the great regulator.

The emphasis on the extremes, papalism — conciliarism, which was up to this time often the favourite approach, caused the broad middle course to fade into the background. According to it the Pope's will is not the supreme law of the Church; or, the Pope is really the Church, but his power is hemmed in by the higher power of the Universal Church. But this is not to be understood in the sense that he has nothing further to say and has only to execute the conciliar decrees. From this body of theories the proper means had to be selected and applied on the occasion of the first great practical case, the double election of 1378 and the subsequent years, in the

---

[62] A. Marongiu, "Il principio della democrazia e del consenso (Quod omnes tangit, ab omnibus approbari debet)," *StG*, 8 (1962), 553–75.

event that a quick political solution should prove to be impossible. There was no doubt that the Pope or, now, the two claimants could be examined by the Universal Church in regard to legitimacy. But who sets the Universal Church in motion? Who acts for her? How will she appear and act? The hoped for convocation of a council by Urban VI, or by Urban VI together with Clement VII, was unfulfilled.

Among the views on the distribution of powers in the Church a very great importance was attributed to the College of Cardinals, at least at the beginning of the Schism, when there was question of finding a supreme authority for judging the legitimacy of the elections. In the great and, despite their length, important treatises of the cardinals of Clement VII, the College itself was the competent judge of the papal election. The comparison of the bishop and his chapter and the widely held opinion that the cardinals, and not the bishops, are the successors of the Apostles served as the basis for this view. [63] The authority to convoke the council had occasionally been attributed also to the patriarchs and, to a much greater degree, to the princes, especially to the Emperor or the King of the Romans. Just as the secular princes must force the cardinals to elect a Pope, so in a case of schism they must force the Church to hold a council. [64] Various kinds of councils are to be distinguished here: a general council in each obedience or the *conventio universalis utriusque partis* or the *congregatio universalis* under the direction of the College of Cardinals. And the idea of a council made up of cardinals alone was mentioned more than once, as was also one consisting of a few but well chosen representatives of all ecclesiastical provinces.

Furthermore, there was need of a council for the already long overdue reform of the Church. As early as the Council of Vienne Durandus the Younger had demanded the holding of a general council every ten years. It became an increasingly universal conviction that reform could not be realized without a council.

And so there was a variety of opinions in regard to the council and the constitution of the Church. Therefore, it will not do to speak of an exclusively correct "divinely willed monarchical structure" of the Church in the late Middle Ages.

---

[63] O. Přerovský, "Le idee oligarchiche nei diffensori di Clemente VII," *Salesianum,* 22 (1960), 383–409.

[64] H. Heimpel, "Studien zur Kirchen- und Reichsreform. Eine unbekannte Schrift Dietrichs von Niem über die Berufung der Generalkonzilien 1413/1414," *SAH,* 1929, 1. Abhandlung.

CHAPTER 47

The Devotio Moderna

Devotio moderna is the descriptive term, occurring already in Thomas à Kempis (1380–1471) and John Busch (1399–1479),[1] for the spiritual movement which began in the Low Countries at the end of the fourteenth century and spread throughout Europe, especially Germany, during the fifteenth century. This form of piety was "modern" in its orientation to practical experience, in its activation of the affective powers, and in its instruction for self-control. It "would rather feel compunction than know its definition" (*Imitation of Christ*, I, 1, 9). In this empirical trait the *devotio moderna* takes its stand in the *via moderna* of late scholastic nominalism. But simultaneously disgust with nominalism's extravagant speculation, unrelated to life, led in the *devoti* to an estrangement from theology in favour of virtue made good in humdrum day- to-day living.

> Of what use is it to discourse loftily on the Trinity, if you lack humility and hence displease the Trinity? Truly, lofty words do not make one holy and righteous, but a virtuous life makes one dear to God (*Imitation*, I, 1, 7 f.).

With this in itself sound and justified criticism of a decadent scholasticism was opened up a chasm between theology and piety in the Western Church.[2] The devout even rejected the speculative mysticism of a Master Eckhart and sought intimacy with God on the path of active penance and love. However, the ideas of the great mystics were variously utilized and made productive in circles which had no access to lofty speculations.

Gerard Groote

The father of the new devotion was Gerard Groote (1340–84). Born at Deventer in 1340, the son of a draper patrician, he became a rich orphan at the age of ten, as a result of the plague. He soon found the Latin school of his native town inadequate and in 1355 went to the University of Paris, where in 1358 he became master of arts. The study of law, medicine, and theology was now open to him. In his eager thirst for knowledge and in his own impetuous manner he seems to have devoted himself to all three and in addition to have occupied himself with magic. But he concentrated on canon law. As a student, fond of all intellectual as well as sensual delights, and in diplomatic missions he spent time not only at Paris but at Prague, Cologne,

---

[1] *Cf.* the title of Part II of the *Chronicon Windeshemense:* "Liber de origine devotionis modernae" (ed. K. Grube, 245–375).

[2] F. Vandenbroucke, "Le divorce entre théologie et mystique," *NRTh*, 82 (1950), 372–89.

Avignon, and Aachen. At Aachen he sought a canonry in 1362 and obtained one in 1370; he acquired other benefices at Soest, Nordmünster, and Utrecht. But even these honours and successes were as little satisfying to him as had been his restless studying and life previously. "There is no happiness in it," observed his biographer, Peter Horn.[3]

An encounter after 1370[4] with his friend of student days, Henry Eger of Kalkar (1328–1408), prior of the Carthusian monastery of Monnikhuizen near Arnheim, produced a profound change. The Carthusian showed him the way to a spiritual life. As a consequence, he spent a few years in Eger's monastery, where, as a *donatus*, or brother without vows, he laid the foundations of the new devotion in useful work and reading, especially the mystics Hugh of Saint-Victor, Henry Suso, Gertrude of Helfta, Master Eckhart, Ludolf of Saxony, and John Ruysbroeck. But in the long run his way to becoming one with God was to include the active life in the world; for him self-sanctification was to be connected with the service of his fellowmen. "It would be wrong, for the sake even of contemplative prayer, devotion, and righteousness, to disregard what cannot be done by another and the good of your neighbour, which is pleasing to God," he wrote in his notes "Resolutions and Intentions, Not Vows."[5]

Gerard Groote resigned his benefices and made over his town house at Deventer in September 1374 to some pious, God-seeking ladies, who aimed to lead a quasi-monastic life under a superioress and also support themselves by the labour of their hands. Groote did not give away all his property, but retained what he needed, including two rooms in this house, and from here he tended to his foundation. To this community, the nucleus of the Sisters of the Common Life, he gave in 1379 an organization or, in a sense, a rule.[6] Particularly in such a loosely constructed community it was important to assure discipline and orthodoxy and to protect the members from being mistaken for the "Brothers of the Free Spirit" and other enthusiasts.

At the same time a similar community of brothers was formed at Deventer in the vicarage of Florens Radewijns (1350–1400). After studying in Prague, the latter had been converted in 1380–81 as a result of a sermon by Gerard Groote. He was the only one to whom the master suggested ordination to the priesthood; he sent him for this purpose to Worms in order to find a

---

[3] *Vita Magistri Gerardi Magni,* ch. 1, ed. W. J. Kühler, *NAKG,* 6 (1909), 333.

[4] According to R. Post ("Wanneer heeft G. Groote zich bekeerd?" *StC,* 17 [1941], 293 to 312), his conversion occurred in 1374 or at the earliest in 1372 and the period of his stay at Monnikhuizen from 1376 to 1379 (R. Post, "H. Eger von Kalkar en Gerd Groote," *StC,* 21 [1946], 88–92; *idem, De Moderne Devotie,* 12). According to J. van Ginneken (*Geert Groote's Levensbeeld,* 134), the conversion began soon after 1370, and Gerard Groote spent the next years to 1373 in the monastery, leaving when H. Eger ceased to be superior there.

[5] Transmitted by Thomas à Kempis, *Opera,* ed. J. Pohl, VII (1929), 87–97 (especially page 97).

[6] R. Post, "De statuten van het Mr.-Geertshuis te Deventer," *AGAU,* 71 (1952), 1—46.

bishop with clean hands.[7] Groote himself received only the diaconate (*ca.* 1379) in order to be able to preach in public. He shrank from the priesthood because of his unworthiness and in view of the simony and concubinage prevailing among the priests of his day. As a preacher of penance he led a strong fight against superficial piety, the immorality of the cities, the heretical movements — Bartholomew of Dordrecht and the Brothers of the Free Spirit, — against simony and concubinage in the clergy, and against the disregard of the vow of poverty by religious *(proprietarii)*. When in 1379 Florens of Wewelinghoven became Bishop of Utrecht, Groote at first obtained his support. He received a personal license to preach and was appointed synodal preacher, and as such, on 14 August 1383,[8] delivered his *Sermo de focaristis*. In the form of a pamphlet, it became his most widely known work. Together with the Prague canonist, Conrad of Soltau (d. 1407), he held it to be a mortal sin to attend the Mass of a notorious concubinary, even if a bishop allowed such a priest to celebrate Mass. The opposition of the clerics concerned and of the mendicant orders, which saw themselves threatened by the rejection of begging and by the new way of life of the brothers and sisters, became so stiff that the Bishop had second thoughts. Apart from his rigorism of manner, no charges could be brought against Groote and so he was indirectly silenced by a prohibition against preaching by deacons. This was sufficient to bring down on the master and his brethren the stigma of heresy. Groote had a *protestatio fidei* posted on church doors at Deventer and Zwolle and asked Pope Urban VI for a personal license to preach. Until it was granted he could only live according to his sermon on painful obedience (*Imitation,* III, 19; III, 49, 18–27). He induced Florens to stay at Deventer[9] and thus prevented a dispersal of his community of brothers.

Groote died of the plague on 20 August 1384, without having been rehabilitated. The new devotion that he had established was developed in the communities of brothers and sisters of the Common Life and in the Augustinian Canons of the Windesheim Congregation. He gave their spirituality its characteristic stamp. But his austerity, inclining to rigorism, was of less significance than his practical style and his following of Christ in daily life, determined by the unremitting contemplation of the life and sufferings of Jesus.

---

[7] Rudolf Dier van Muiden, *Scriptum de magistro Gherardo Groote:* "Dominus Florentius ... quem magister Gherardus fecit ordinari presbyterum, mittens eum ad episcopum Wormatiensem, credo ad vitandam symoniam ..." (ed. G. Dumbar, *Analecta,* I, 7).

[8] According to J. van Ginneken, *Geert Groote's Levensbeeld,* 305. But S. Axters, III, 39, assigns the sermon to 14 August 1381; R. Post, *Kerkgeschiedenis,* I, 294, to 14 May 1381. Probably Gerard Groote delivered two synodal sermons, the first in connection with Bernard's "Sermon on Acts 9:4," as John Busch reports (ed. K. Grube, 252).

[9] Ep. 62, *De patientia,* ed. W. Mulder, 232–43.

The Brotherhood of the Common Life was already so firmly established by the death of Gerard Groote that its continued existence was assured and its further growth made good progress. In the spirit of their master, who rejected begging and regarded manual labor as an aid to virtue, the brothers, following the example of Saint Paul, earned their common livelihood — in their case, by copying and binding books. [10] Hence they had at the same time the opportunity for spiritual reading, did not have to leave the community or the house, and contributed to the spread of Christian doctrine and education. However, there was not much possibility of exterior apostolic work. Perhaps that is why Gerard Groote in 1383 had accepted an endowment for the support of two or three priests who would be active in the care of souls. Otherwise, the seeking of the priesthood was regarded at first as contrary to humility. Much as it was desired to promote the salvation of others, the brothers were glad to be able to devote themselves more freely to their own perfection without the burden of the priesthood. They aspired to help their fellowmen by prayer, silent example, and encouragement. [11]

Spiritual reading, chiefly of Scripture, meditation, and prayer occupied their day in addition to manual labour. Fraternal correction and common examination of conscience were intended to aid in observance of the rule and to foster humility. Radewijns advised his disciples: "Persevere in humble simplicity, and Christ will be with you." [12] The following of the humble Christ was the central idea of their piety. In the midst of the late mediaeval urban middle class they wanted to live the life of the fathers of the desert in prayer and work. [13] Differing from the Beguines and the Beghards, the Brothers and Sisters of the Common Life had all property in common. Middle-class is the prosaic, calculating characteristic of this piety, its systematic and methodical struggle against faults, and its strong consciousness. Everything that exceeded a sound golden mean was regarded with suspicion. There was a preference for reaching not so high, but for persevering. An

---

[10] "Volo enim, quod, qui gratiam habent laborandi, laborent manibus suis... labor mirabiliter homini necessarius est et reductivus mentis ad mundici[ti]am et diminuendam immundici[ti]am" (*Ep.* 32), ed. W. Mulder, 138.

[11] *Vita Florentii:* "...ut non tantummodo sibi, sed et proximis suis proficerent ad salutem" (J. Pohl, VII, 133). "Tertia temptatio est, quando clericus et litteratus anhelat ad sacros ordines et praelaturam aut aliquam dignitatem" (*ibid.*, 184). "Nam nisi iussus et compulsus pro communi utilitate, nemo hoc acceptare audebat: quia omnes altiorem statum fugiebant et in humiliori loco et officio minori manere eligebant. Unde dominus Florentius qui erat gemma sacerdotum fertur aliquando dixisse. Si non essem sacerdos, nec curam aliorum haberem, tunc possem me perfecte emendare" (*ibid.*, 291).

[12] J. Pohl, VII, 190.

[13] F. Radewijns, *Tractatus devotus*, ed. M. Goossens (Haarlem and Amsterdam 1954), 331; *Imitatio*, I, 18, 6.

abundance of ideal programs which had remained unrealized were in clear view in late mediaeval religious life. Following the example of their master's "Resolutions and Intentions," many brothers drew up their own rule of life and wrote spiritual diaries with the results of their edifying reading *(rapiaria)*. A great part of the devout literature was composed or compiled as such, in the first place for edification, or consisted of letters intended to introduce others to the spiritual life.

From the *Exercitium* of John Kessel (d. 1398), a lay member of the Deventer community, which comprised four priests, eight clerics, and a few lay brothers, we can obtain a picture of the order of the day. The day began with meditation at 3: 00 A.M., followed by Matins and scriptural reading. To guard against drowsiness it was recommended that the brothers make notes. At 5: 00 o'clock each went to his work, which lasted until the bells of the parish church rang for Mass. On the way the brothers prayed the psalms of Terce; returning, those of Sext. During Mass they were to meditate on the life and sufferings of Christ. Back home, they resumed their work. The common meal was not eaten before 10: 00 o'clock, accompanied by reading. Then each retired to his cell until None. The time between None and Vespers was again devoted to work, and after Vespers there was meditation. The work that followed until Compline was interrupted by the common supper, the second meal. The day ended at 8: 00 o'clock with the examination of conscience, in which each jotted down the day's faults. Bedtime was at 9: 00 P.M. [14] unless, in conformity with the example of the desert fathers, they engaged at night in spiritual discourses. [15] According to Thomas à Kempis, the model of this life was the fraternal community of the Primitive Church. [16]

The *devoti* had no regard for the beauty of creation. There are no traces of a Christian humanism in their spirituality, at least in the earliest period, even though by study and the diffusion of the Bible and the Fathers they did foster the new trends in education.

With reference to the saying attributed to John Gerson, "if the Church must be reformed, this cannot happen with greater ease than through men who have been prepared for it in the flower of youth by good morals and the practice of virtue," [17] the apostolic work of the Brothers of the Common Life was oriented to the young student. To be sure, they did not themselves found and accept schools but they devoted themselves to the religious education of pupils apart from their formal lessons. [18] Nevertheless, they

[14] J. Pohl, VII, 309–12; R. Post, *De Moderne Devotie*, 41.

[15] J. Pohl, VII, 238 f.

[16] "Secundum primitivae ecclesiae formam, et sanctorum patrum laudabilem consuetudinem ab apostolis introductam" (J. Pohl, VII, 486).

[17] G. Dumbar, *Analecta*, I, 184; C. van der Wansem, *Broederschap*, 126.

[18] R. Post, *Scholen en Onderwijs in Nederland gedurende de Middeleeuwen* (1954).

acquired an influence on the educational system of the age. Gerard Groote was a friend of the headmasters at Deventer, Kampen, and Zwolle. It was not until the second half of the fifteenth century that the Brothers of the Common Life participated directly in education in a few cities, such as Utrecht, Liège, and Groningen and, in Germany, Magdeburg and Trier.

If any of their pupils were thinking of the priesthood or the religious state or were suited for them, they were admitted into their houses. Others they lodged with reliable townsmen. They gathered the pupils for spiritual conferences *(collationes)* and were at their disposal for discussions and confession.[19] When in 1391 the brothers at Deventer were able to acquire a larger house of their own, they adapted the one hitherto used as a house for the pupils. The brothers' house at Deventer under the direction of Florens Radewijns became a model for many others but it can hardly be said to have contributed directly to their establishment. In fact, it was still without ecclesiastical approbation. In Kampen and Zwolle citizens affected by Gerard Groote's sermons founded similar religious houses. In 1394 Florens sent Gerard Scadde to Zwolle as rector. Under its second rector, Dirc van Herxen (1381–1457), the "father of all the *devoti*," this house acquired great prominence and after 1420 was the site of the annual chapter. Other communities arose at Almelo, Hoorn, and Amersfoort. In addition, there were houses of sisters at Deventer, Zwolle, Delft, Amersfoort, Hoorn, Hasselt, Leiden, Rhenen, and Utrecht.

But the ecclesiastical status of the new communities was still not settled. The brothers were not an order — the Lateran Council of 1215 had forbidden the founding of new orders — but they lived a quasi-monastic life. They had no vows but they observed the evangelical counsels, and they earned their livelihood by the work of their hands. Learned treatises, ill-disposed and well-disposed, on the lawfulness of this way of life went to and fro. The most important product of the dispute was the *Libellum super modo vivendi hominum simul commorantium*[20] of Gerard Zerbolt van Zutphen (1367–98), who sought to prove that, despite the deviation from the traditional form of monastic observance, the life of the brothers was a school of perfection. It was only in 1401, after the death of Florens Radewijns (24 March 1400), when the direction of the house had passed to Emil van Buren, that the long sought confirmation of the Brotherhood of the Common Life was forthcoming in an apostolic mandate obtained by the Bishop of Utrecht, Frederick von Blankenheim.[21] The brothers were permitted to

---

[19] *Cf.* the pedagogical treatises of Dirc van Herxen; for example, *Tractatus de iuvenibus trahendis ad Christum* (see under footnote 38).

[20] Ed. by A. Hyma, *AGAU*, 52 (1926), 1–100.

[21] Text in J. Hofmann, "De broeders van het Gemene Leven en de Windesheimse kloostervereinigung," *AGAU*, 2 (1875), 229–36, and P. Frédéricq, *Corpus documentorum inquisitionis haereticae pravitatis Nederlandicae*, II (Ghent and The Hague 1896), 190–93.

maintain their common meals, to make common property out of their possessions and the proceeds from their work, and perform pious exercises together, but they could not found a new order or adopt a new habit.

The Windesheim Congregation

In addition to the association of the Brothers of the Common Life, which represented something new between cloister and world, the *devotio moderna* led to a monastic reform movement. If we can rely on Thomas à Kempis, Gerard Groote, following his visit to Ruysbroeck at Groenendael, had already given thought to the establishment of a cloister for canons for such of the brothers as inclined to the monastic life.[22] As a matter of fact, in 1382 he recommended Berthold ten Have, of the Deventer house, to the provost of Emstein for reception into that community. In view of the difficulties of 1383–84 it was natural to seek support in one of the old orders and to assure the continuance of the movement of the *devoti* by means of a monastery. Accordingly, John Busch relates in the *Windesheim Chronicle* that Groote, on his death bed, recommended to his brothers the founding of a monastery in which all the brothers and sisters could find refuge, aid, and protection.[23] The so-called Augustinian rule presented itself as the most appropriate for this purpose. Certain as it is that Gerard Groote, Florens Radewijns, and other brothers purposely rejected the official monastic form of life for themselves and aimed at closer contact with the world, apparently there were also among their pupils some who felt themselves called to the religious state. For many the brothers' houses became places of preparation for the cloister. This prevents us from regarding the criticism levelled by Gerard Groote and his pupils at religious who did not take their vows seriously as a fundamental rejection of the monastic life, or, as it were, an anticipation of the Reformation.

To provide models of true claustral life and also to preserve the special character of their own form of life, it was natural to found a monastery for the brothers with an inclination to the religious state. Within its shelter they could assure protection for the real offshoot of the *devotio moderna*, in still so precarious a situation in regard to canon law and the recipient of so much enmity.

And so from Deventer occurred the founding of the Canons of Windesheim near Zwolle. On 17 October 1387 the church was consecrated and six

---

[22] *Vita Gerardi*, chapter 15, ed. J. Pohl, VII, 77 f.

[23] "Verumtamen aliqui vestrum ordinem ab ecclesia approbatum debent assumere, ad quos omnes devoti utriusque sexus in cunctis suis necessitatibus securum habere debent recursum consilium et auxilium defensionisque presidium petentes receptari" (*Chronicon Windeshemense*, II, c. 5, ed. K. Grube, 263).

pupils of Gerard Groote made their vows. Previously they had familiarized themselves with the traditions of the Augustinians at the monastery of Emstein, founded from Groenendael in 1382, where at the same time they had come into contact with the spirituality of John Ruysbroeck. Before long, in 1392, two more monasteries were founded, at Marienborn near Arnheim and at Neulicht near Hoorn. With these and Emstein Windesheim established a congregation under the "Prior Superior," John Vos van Heusden (1391 to 1424), in 1395. By 1407 twelve monasteries belonged to it, including Agnetenberg, of which Thomas à Kempis was a member. Union with the chapters of Groenendael (1417) and Neuss (1430) brought a great increase in numbers. By 1500 this number was to grow to eighty-seven houses. The spirit was purely contemplative. The very location of Windesheim and other houses outside cities indicates that they were not adapted to pastoral work, and in the statutes from the pre-Reformation period we find no reference to apostolic or educational activity, apart from the copying of books and monastic reform.

The last mentioned became the specific historical achievement of the Windesheim Congregation in the fifteenth century. In 1435 the Council of Basel entrusted Windesheim with the reform of the German Augustinian monasteries. On this mission the later chronicler of the Congregation, John Busch (d. 1479/80),[24] came to Wittenburg, west of Hildesheim, in 1437 as subprior, reformed Sylte, and in 1447 became provost of Neuwerk near Halle. In 1451 the papal legate, Cardinal Nicholas of Cusa, named him visitor of the Augustinian monasteries of Saxony and Thuringia. On his visitations Busch unhesitatingly made use of the secular arm against the refractory. Superiors were deposed and religious were expelled or transferred. This was not only done to insure new respect for the vows or to enjoin inclosure again, but even, when the introduction of the Windesheim usages was involved, the adopting of a certain habit or a method of chanting.

If in persons like John Busch we note the absence of proper religious depth, and if external fidelity to the rule apparently replaced the pious sentiment which characterized men like John Vos and his successor, Willem Vornken (1425–54), still the Windesheim Congregation, even in the latter half of the century, represents a flourishing and vigorous monastic life, which acted as a model for other communities.

The monasteries, gathered into so compact a congregation, were naturally much stronger and more secure in regard to their institutions than the less firmly united houses of the brothers. Entirely on their own, they moved into the foreground, assumed leadership, and represented themselves in literature, with Thomas à Kempis and John Busch, as the true heirs of Gerard Groote.

---

[24] Cf. K. Grube, *Des Augustinerpropstes Johannes Busch Chronicon Windeshemense und Liber de reformatione monasteriorum* (Halle 1886).

On the other hand they afforded support and protection to the communities of the brothers. Thus, on 19 March 1395, the superiors of the monasteries of the Windesheim Congregation issued a solemn declaration on the orthodoxy and proper manner of life of the Deventer brothers.[25]

The Brothers of the Common Life in Germany

The "Brother Movement" in Germany also originated at Deventer. In April 1400, soon after the death of Florens Radewijns, Henry von Ahaus d. 1439), vicar of the Münster cathedral, visited Deventer. He was deeply impressed by the primitive Christian spirit in the house and shared its life for more than a year. Having returned home, he founded at Münster on 26 October 1401 the first house of the Brothers of the Common Life. According to the foundation charter, "two or more priests, with a few clerics and one or more lay brothers" should live in it permanently with common ownership of books and other property; they should be such as "were unable to enter an order because of some impediment or did not regard that as their vocation, but, remaining in the house to the end and living in humility, chastity, and the other virtues, were desirous of serving God and assisting one another in a common life."[26] Henry seems not to have been the rector at first of this still loosely organized community. It took him perhaps fifteen years to consolidate the house in the Deventer spirit and to overcome the opposition of the "rude and uncouth Westphalians" ("groven ende onbesnedenen Westphalen"). But in the later fifteenth century Westphalians were the chief representatives of the German aspect of the movement. At that time they were found in all the houses of western and central Germany.

Henry von Ahaus founded another house at Cologne in 1416, which he directed for three years until his return to Münster in 1419. Shortly before his death he founded one at Wesel in 1435. In addition, there were houses of sisters at Borken, Coesfeld, Wesel, Dinslaken, Lippstadt, Schüttorf, and Münster. Henry von Ahaus was not satisfied with the founding of individual houses. It was important to assure their existence and to maintain the proper spirit in them. To these ends he worked for a union *(confederatio)* among the houses, and in 1425 it was realized in the case of Münster and Cologne. From it developed the so-called Münster Colloquy of 1431. Every year, on the Wednesday preceding "Cantate" Sunday (the fourth Sunday after Easter), the superiors of the houses of brothers and sisters in northwest Germany were to meet at Münster to discuss common affairs, such as the

---

[25] J. Hofmann, *AGAU*, 2 (1875), 225–29; P. Frédéricq, *Corpus documentorum*, II, 156–58; E. Barnikol, *Studien*, 158 f.

[26] K. Löffler, *Heinrich von Ahaus*, 793.

installing of rectors, the appointing of confessors and visitors, new foundations, and so forth. The connection with the brothers in the Netherlands was
maintained by the interchange with the Zwolle Colloquy of two representatives of each group. Later attempts of the Münster house to establish its
position of supremacy as the regular place for holding the colloquy in order
to effect a stricter organization and a uniform observance in the twenty-six
German houses foundered on the resistance of the other houses, notably
Hildesheim. From 1479 Hildesheim instituted a colloquy of its own with
Kassel and Magdeburg. Aspirations for union finally led in 1499, under the
influence of Jasper (d. 1502), rector of Deventer, to a general chapter.
Whether the general statutes were actually adopted here and the union
thereupon came into being is uncertain.

The growth of the Brothers of the Common Life in Germany presents
itself in four centres, which are to some degree definable in time and
geography.

1. The West German or Münster circle, with houses at Münster (1401),
Cologne (1416), and Wesel (1435). Not established by Münster, but closely
connected with it, were Osterberg near Tecklenburg (1409–27), Osnabrück
(1410–30?), and Herford (1426). Later Rostock (1462) and Marburg (1477)
were founded from Münster, and Emmerich (1467) from Deventer.

2. The Hildesheim circle, with the central German, chiefly Hessian,
houses: Hildesheim (1440), Kassel (1455), Kulm (1472), Magdeburg (1482),
Berlikum in Friesland (1483), and Merseburg (1503). Of these, Kulm and
Berlikum, like Emmerich, were at first oriented to Holland.

3. The Middle Rhine circle, proceeding from Cologne: Marienthal in the
Rheingau (1463), Wiesbaden (1465, but it probably never actually came into
existence), Königstein (1466), Butzbach in South Hesse (1468), Wolf on the
Moselle (1478), and Trier (1499).

From 1471 these Middle Rhine foundations formed, against Münster, a
special union with its own general chapter, which in 1477 was joined also
by the Württemberg houses. The communities of this "South German"
union strongly resembled the communities of canons. Their members were
"Canons of the Common Life" and the term was not a camouflage. They
were headed by provosts; Gabriel Biel, for example, was provost of Butzbach
in 1477 and of Urach in 1479.

4. The Württemberg circle. From Butzbach, Gabriel Biel (d. 1495) founded
Urach in 1477 on the initiative of Count Eberhard the Bearded. Then arose
Herrenberg (1481), Tübingen (1482), Dettingen (1482), Dachenhausen
(1486), and Einsiedel in the Schönbuch (1491). Gabriel Biel exerted the
decisive influence in the establishing and in the internal and external organization of the Württemberg houses. And even when he was no longer provost
of Urach, this house occupied a leading position among those of Württemberg.

To these twenty-six German houses of the brothers are to be added the even more numerous houses of sisters, which were under the pastoral care of the brothers. Because of their cowl, the brothers were often referred to as Kogelherren or Kugelherren or, in Württemberg, as Kapuziaten or Kappen-herren.

Opposition: Matthew Grabow

The new form of life, between world and cloister, encountered various kinds of lack of understanding and opposition. These came from the old orders, especially the mendicants, who felt themselves under criticism or even defamed because of the rejection of begging; from the diocesan clergy, who at times were unwilling to relinquish to the brothers the care of souls in the sisters' houses; and from trade circles, who saw an unwanted competition in the brothers and sisters who lived from the proceeds of their labour.

Offense was also given by the translating of the Bible into the vernacular and the using of such versions in the houses of the brothers and sisters. Gerard Groote had spent the last days of his life in translating parts of the breviary in order to make possible for the sisters and others who were uneducated a meaningful participation in the liturgy. At the monastery of Windesheim there was a special *Librarius teutonicorum librorum*.[27] To what extent the *devoti* thus fell under suspicion is clear from the *apologiae* attributed to Gerard Zerbolt van Zutphen (d. 1398), *De libris teutonicalibus* and *De Precibus vernaculis*, or the opinion handed down by Abbot Arnold, of the Dutch Benedictine monastery of Dickeninge, on 2 December 1397, in favour of the brothers. In it the question, is it lawful to read and to have books of the Bible in the vernacular, was answered in the affirmative.[28]

The opposition to the Brothers and Sisters of the Common Life found expression in principle in the work of the Dominican Matthew Grabow. A member of the friary at Wismar, he was a lector in theology at Groningen and in 1400 is mentioned as inquisitor. He delivered to the parish priest of Deventer a treatise against the brothers, of which only the conclusions are extant.[29] The brothers defended themselves in a counter-complaint to the Bishop of Utrecht, who condemned Grabow. He thereupon brought the case before the Council of Constance. Here Peter d'Ailly and John Gerson attacked his thesis, that no one can meritoriously or even sincerely observe the universal counsels of obedience, poverty, and chastity if he remains outside the true and recognized religious orders. Appealing to Thomas Aquinas, Grabow held that the renunciation of all ownership in the world

[27] *Chronicon Windeshemense*, ed. K. Grube, 125.
[28] L. Korth, "Die ältesten Gutachten über die Brüder vom gemeinsamen Leben," *Mitteilungen aus dem Stadtarchiv Köln*, 13 (1887), 1–27 (especially pages 14 f.).
[29] "Conclusiones contra devotarios extra congregationem approbatam viventes."

was sin and murder. In 1419 his theses were repudiated by Martin V at Florence, his writings were consigned to the flames, and he was himself condemned to imprisonment. Despite his abjuration,[30] he was still confined in Castel Sant'Angelo as late as May 1421.

How difficult it was to understand the special character of the Brothers of the Common Life and how natural to count them among the traditional orders or how necessarily they had to sail under the "standard of a false canon law"[31] in order to obtain recognition is evident from the bull of 18 April 1439, in which Eugene IV granted papal confirmation to the houses in Münster, Cologne, and Wesel.[32] In this the houses are declared to be monasteries of canons, the brothers become canons, their rector a provost.

In view of similar misconceptions or centralizing tendencies and out of an anxiety to maintain their original character, Peter Dieburg (d. 1494), superior and chronicler of the Hildesheim house, declared on 13 May 1490 in a letter to the rector of Münster: "We are not religious; our endeavour and purpose is to live piously in the world."[33]

It is with reference to such manifold difficulties that the repeated efforts of the brothers for express sanction of their manner of life by the competent authorities and the custom of placing at the head of their lists of benefactors princes of the Church who had approved their house are to be understood.

Literature and Spirituality

The *devotio moderna* produced no great theologians. It aimed to avoid theological disputations, held speculation in no esteem, and even in regard to mysticism was on the whole reserved. Its significance lay in the practice of the spiritual life, and its literary output served this end. The communicating of one's spiritual practical experience in letters, diaries, or rules of life for the guidance of others occupied a large place. There were also *rapiaria* and idealizing biographies of the founders, whom the brothers wished to emulate in the following of Christ.[34] In addition to Scripture and the Fathers, especially Augustine, Gregory the Great, pseudo-Dionysius, and John Cas-

---

[30] Thus S. Wachter, "Matthäus Grabow, ein Gegner der Brüder vom gemeinsamen Lehen", *Festschrift zum 50jährigen Bestandsjubiläum des Missionshauses St. Gabriel* (Vienna-Mödling 1939), 289–376, especially 348–51 and 362, against H. Keussen, "Der Dominikaner Matthäus Grabow," *Mitteilungen aus dem Stadtarchiv Köln*, 19 (1890), 103.

[31] E. Barnikol, *Studien*, 32.

[32] Document no. 1729 of the Münster diocesan archives, Abt. Generalvikariat (Fraterhaus).

[33] "Non sumus religiosi, sed in saeculo religiose vivere nitimur et volumus" (H. Doebner, *Annalen*, 113).

[34] *Cf.* Thomas a Kempis, *Dialogi noviciorum*, ed. J. Pohl, VII, 1–329; Rudolf Dier (d. 1458), *Scriptum de magistro G. G., domino Florencio et multis aliis devotis*, ed. G. Dumbar, *Analecta*, I, 1–11; John Busch, *Liber de viris illustribus* in *Chronicon Windeshemense*, ed.

sian *(Collationes)*, the *devoti* preferred as the sources of their spirituality the works of Bernard of Clairvaux (d. 1153), the Franciscans Bonaventure (d. 1274), especially his *De triplici via*, and David of Augsburg (d. 1272), in particular his *Profectus religiosorum* and *Speculum monachorum*, Henry Suso, and the *Life of Christ* by Ludolf of Saxony (d. 1378).[35]

The centre and root of the *devotio moderna* was the Christ of history. "Our first effort should be to become absorbed into the life of Jesus" *(Imitation*, I, 1, 3). "The life of our Lord Jesus Christ, which he has held up as an example to us, is the source of all virtues and the model of all sanctity," declares the *Epistola* attributed to John Vos van Heusden.

The aim was to nourish oneself by meditation "on the soul's true food of the most holy life of our Lord Jesus Christ." It is above all important to imitate his humility, his obedience in the degradation of his Passion.[36] The imitation of the humanity of Christ gives access to his divinity.[37] One should want "to know Jesus from within." Florens Radewijns' books, *Omnes, inquit, artes* and *Multum valet,* provide a series of meditations on Christ. Especially worthy of mention are the *Devota exercitia passionis* of Dirc van Herxen (d. 1457). In *De duplici modo se exercendi* he is said to have composed a plan of meditations for individual days and hours.

This attention to systematic meditation and the development of its method characterized the *devotio moderna.* In it were sought, not transporting ecstasy nor even mystical union, but rather the simple narrating and experiencing in loving contemplation of the life of Christ and the sorrows and joys of his Mother. Gerard Zerbolt van Zutphen (d. 1398), the most prolific author among the Brothers of the Common Life, in *De spiritualibus ascensionibus* provided guidance in reflecting on what had been heard and read and in applying it to one's own life in the practice of love and humility. He arranged in detail the subject and time of the meditation.

The special care of the *devoti* for the young was expressed in the four pedagogical writings of Dirc van Herxen: *Tractatus de iuvenibus trahendis ad Christum, De innocentia servanda, Libellus de parvulis trahendis ad Christum,* and *Libellus de laudabili studio eorum trahentium.* The first two

---

K. Grube; *Vita Johannis Brinckerinck, NAKG,* NS, 1 (1900), 314–54. Likewise, the "Frensweger Handschrift" (Univ. Utrecht, Ms 8, L. 16, ed. by W. Jappe Albertz and A. L. Hulshoff [Leiden 1958]) contains mostly biographies of *devoti.*

[35] *Cf.* Gerard Groote, *De sacris libris studiendis,* ed. J. Pohl, VII, 97 f.; a similar list of books is provided by Florens Radewijns (*Collationes Brugenses,* 14 [1909], 89) and John Mombaer in the *Rosetum* (P. Debongnie, *Jean Mombaer* [Louvain 1928], 320–31).

[36] J. Mak, "Christus bij de moderne devoten," *OGE,* 9 (1935), 105–66. *Cf.* John Busch, *Chronicon Windeshemense,* chapter 4: "... Super fundamentum sancte paupertatis, verecunde simplicitatis ac profunde humilitatis originaliter se fundabant" (ed. K. Grube, 15).

[37] G. Groote, *Ep.* 9, ed. W. Mulder, 31; *cf.* the *Rosetum* of John Mombaer: "Est enim meditatio humanitatis sc[h]ala qua pervenitur ad contemplationem divinitatis" (ed. Basel 1504), 135.

are addressed to the young to induce them to seek Christ and preserve virtue. The last two are intended rather for their instructors. [38]

Of the Windesheim canons, in addition to John Vos (d. 1424) and Thomas à Kempis (d. 1471), mention should be made of Hendrik Mande (d. 1431), with his twelve works in the Dutch language which are heavily indebted to Ruysbroeck, and of Gerlach Peters (d. 1411). The last named developed a strongly emotional, practical, Christ-oriented piety in his *Breviloquium*, in two letters to his sister, and especially in his *Soliloquium*. This spiritual literature of the *devotio moderna* originated for the most part in the communities, was destined for their aims, for example, biographies for reading matter during the common meals, and was regarded as their common property. Hence our notion of authorship cannot in numerous cases be applied to it strictly. This explains the anonymity of so much of the literature and probably also the fact that even in regard to works so well known and influential as the *Imitation of Christ* and the *Epistola de vita et passione Christi* the authorship is disputed.

The Letter on the Life and Passion of our Lord Jesus Christ and other devout exercises, according to which the brothers and laymen at Windesheim are accustomed to arrange their exercises has come down to us in a Latin translation as Part III of the *Chronicon Windeshemense* of John Busch. [39] John Vos, the "Prior Superior" of the Windesheim Congregation, was long considered to be its author. In any event, he recommended the letter to the *devoti* entrusted to him and based his own exercises on it. The *Epistola* is intended as a handy guide for the weekly religious exercises of persons practising this devotion. The material for meditation is arranged for the week. Three meditations are provided for each day. In the first, one considers a mystery from the youth of our Lord; in the second, from his passion and death; while in the third attention is centred on a saint.

> What is sweeter, more comforting, more pleasing to God, more salutary for the simple dove than to dwell devoutly in the cleft of a rock, that is, in the wounds of our Lord Jesus Christ? May your sweet Lord and lovable bridegroom grant you the favour not merely to dwell there daily and to repose in joy but also to die daily, while still alive, in the same love with which he accepted wounds and death. [40]

[38] P. H. J. Knierim, *Dirc van Herxen*, 105–12.

[39] Ed. K. Grube, 226–44. The original text of the *Epistola* has recently been edited by C. de Bruin, "De Dietse oertekst van de anonieme 'Epistola de vita et passione domini nostri Jesu Christi et aliis devotis exercitiis,'" *NAKG*, 34 (1944 f.), 8–23. On the question of authorship see J. G. R. Acquoy "Is de Windesheimsche prior Joh. van Heusden de schrijver van de 'Epistola de vita...,'" *Handelingen en Mededeelingen van de Maatschappij der Nederlandsche Letterkunde te Leiden, 1891–1892* (Leiden 1892), 95–97 (especially page 96). S. van der Woude, *Joh. Busch Windesheimer kloosterreformator en kroniekschrijver* (Edam 1947), 150.

[40] Ed. K. Grube, 242; *cf. Imitatio*, II, 1, 21 f.

Here is indicated the same *via regia* of meditation on and following of the passion of Christ as in *The Imitation of Christ*.

The Imitation, comprising since 1427 four perhaps originally independent works, is not only the best known book of the *devotio moderna* but, after the Bible, of world literature in general. We know 700 manuscripts of it alone — of Book I from 1424, of Books I–IV from 1427. It has been translated into ninety-five languages and has gone through more than 3,000 editions. It has come down anonymously. In the 1441 autograph (MS 5855 to 5861 of the Bibliothèque Royale of Brussels) Thomas à Kempis designates himself merely as scribe and in the same words with which he ends a Bible manuscript that he prepared.

Contrary to the intention of the author (*cf.* I, 5, 6) there began in the fifteenth century a violent dispute, even involving politics, over the authorship. More than thirty-five names, including Bernard of Clairvaux, Bonaventure, Ludolf of Saxony, John Tauler, Henry Suso, Dionysius the Carthusian, and John Gerson were brought on the field. Favourites in this dispute, exacerbated by national feeling and rivalry of religious orders, were for centuries, besides Thomas à Kempis, a Benedictine Abbot John Gersen, who allegedly lived in the thirteenth century at Vercelli in North Italy, and John Gerson (d. 1429), the defender of the Brothers of the Common Life at the Council of Constance. But language and spirituality point to the Low Countries and today almost all scholars agree that the author of *The Imitation of Christ* is to be sought in the ranks of the *devotio moderna*. There is also agreement that Thomas à Kempis was the last to take the work in hand. To what extent Gerard Groote had anything to do with the wording is less clear. Did he merely inspire it or can he be called the author of a first draft which would then have been revised by others, last of all by Thomas à Kempis? The question of authorship is of significance only to the extent that it is not unimportant for an evaluation to ascertain whether the author was a worldly-wise and active man like Gerard Groote, who had experienced the temptations of the world in his own body and was calling for renunciation of the world, or an awkward, introverted, pious man, ill at ease in the world, who like Thomas à Kempis had proved to be useless in practical business and for whom activity in the world was never a serious temptation. More important is the question of the content and spirituality of the work. It offers no systematic doctrine of piety or even of the mystical life. It is rather a spiritual diary or, better, a collection of pithy sayings about the spiritual life, a so-called *rapiarium*. The author seems to have written it over a somewhat long period of time, chapter by chapter, without being particularly concerned for their coherence and logical order.

Book I aims to lead to humility and inner peace through contempt of the world and of vain knowledge, through self-control and contrition of heart. A glimpse of death and judgment is intended as a further aid. Book II shows how we "must enter the kingdom of God through much affliction" (II, 12, 62). This kingdom of God is within us; hence the admonition, "Despise what is external, surrender yourself to what is within, and you will see the kingdom of God grow in you" (II, 1, 2). The devout man feels that he is unjustly treated by men; he is disappointed in them. He finds comfort in the friendship of Christ (II, 8, 18 ff.). For the sake of this friendship sufferings are glorified (II, 3, 19), cheerlessness and loneliness are accepted (II, 9), the cross is loved. But, despite all longing for inner consolation, the devout man of *The Imitation* knows also that mature love for Christ proves itself in cheerlessness, when one perseveres with Jesus in the abandonment of the cross (II, 11, 1–11).

Books III and IV are in the form of a conversation which the Lord has with his servant, Christ with his disciple. If the human will is stressed in Book I, grace is predominant in Book III. Man of himself has nothing that is good (III, 49). The more he is stripped (III, 37, 6, 16) and abandons himself (III, 37, 17 ff.; 42, 9; 49, 9 ff.; 54), he acquires true liberty in grace. Book IV presents "pious exhortations for holy communion" in three exercises (chapters 1–5, 6–11, 12–18). *The Imitation*, like mysticism, wants to lead to union with God (III, 31, 5 ff.). But this union is genuine and real only if it grows out of virtue (II, 10, 5 f.) and it does not absolve from persevering moral effort. The unassailed, peaceful possession of God is reserved for the next world; here the *militia Christi* is our portion (III, 25, 8; 6, 27). In this struggle Christ under his cross is both model and help (III, 56, 28). Seeking God's will and concern for a pure conscience take precedence over contemplation in this world (I, 3, 23; 20, 14). In addition to this strongly ethical orientation, the mysticism of *The Imitation* is dominated by the opposition between the spiritual and the material, the internal and the external.

> Be intent on setting your heart free from an inclination to the visible and raising it to the invisible. Whoever follows his senses stains his conscience and loses God's grace (I, 1, 20).

For the sake of this inner life, external exercises of piety are underestimated, and pilgrimages and the cult of relics are criticized (I, 11, 13; 23, 25; III, 58, 9 f.; IV, 1, 38 f.). By virtue of this criticism of the externalization of late mediaeval piety through the multiplying of external forms at the expense of depth and the mean, by virtue of this struggle against a piety of good works and for a better inner righteousness, *The Imitation* is in the lineage of both the Catholic Reform and the Reformation of the sixteenth century.

But because its intensification of inner feeling was connected with a disregard for the mystery of creation as well as of the Incarnation, the piety of *The Imitation* threatened to lose its context to the world. In contradistinction to German mysticism, the "imitation of Christ" did not see that the dignity of things is based on creation. They are experienced only as seductive glamour and not as symbols pointing to God. The world is fit only to impede the glimpse of God. "If you look at creation, the creator withdraws from you" (II, 42, 10).

The idea of the "following of Christ" does not become the prevailing viewpoint. Above all, union with Christ is not seen in its essentially sacramental basis. It is confined to the example of the historical Christ, whose sufferings bring us comfort and strength. There is no mention of the mediatorship of the God-Man, of "through Christ in the Holy Spirit to the Father." Hence the mystery of the Church is not envisaged, let alone seen as the basis and subject of piety. [41] *The Imitation* can be termed Christocentric at the most in regard to the individual, but he does not perceive that his love of God can be full only when it extends to love of neighbour and apostolate. A synthesis of self-sanctification and apostolate is not to be found, and even the missionary obligation of the pious person plays no role. What is important is flight from the world; the strength is lacking to bring the world back to Christ and to exorcise the danger of secularization.

Toward the close of the century one encounters a union of mysticism, humanism, and *devotio moderna* in one of the Münster brothers, John Veghe (d. 1504). After a short time at Rostock, he became rector of the brothers' house at Münster in 1475 and in 1481 of the local Niesink convent of the Sisters of the Common Life. In his Low German treatises, *Gheystlike jagd, Lectulus noster floridus,* and *Wyngaerden der sele,* and his sermons or conferences, twenty-four transcripts of which are extant in Low German, he offers, in connection with the Canticle of Canticles, a mysticism directed to practical ends and thus makes the teaching of the mystics fruitful for the various levels of Sisters of the Common Life. All are called to be God's brides. "God has created mankind that he may make use of it." This union with God, the participation in the divine joys, begins already in this life but finds its fulfillment only in the next. Man must exert himself to achieve it. This blessed union of man with God in love is explained by Veghe under the symbol of sacramental communion and of the union of spouses.

The last important spiritual writer from the Windesheim circle was John Mombaer (Johannes Mauburnus). Born at Brussels around 1460, around 1480 he became a canon at Sankt Agnetenberg. Important and entirely too little esteemed is his significance as a monastic reformer in France at the end of the century. There he became Abbot of Livry in 1501, but he died at Paris soon after, possibly on 29 December of the same year. Like Wessel Gansfort (d. 1489) and following his example, Mombaer wanted to indicate ways to the interior life, especially to devotion during the canonical hours,

---

[41] *Cf.* E. Iserloh, "Die Kirchenfrömmigkeit in der Imitatio Christi," *Sentire Ecclesiam* (Freiburg 1961), 251–67.

at the reception of holy communion, and in meditation — in other words, the most important spiritual exercises of the *devoti*. But in so doing he developed the method of the spiritual life to such a degree that the danger of mechanical routine, which he, like the *devotio moderna* in general, aimed to combat, became acute again in a new form. In the *Venatorium sanctorum ordinis canonicorum regularium* he defended the customs of his order, while in the *Rosetum exercitiorum spiritualium et sacrarum meditationum* (Zwolle [?] 1494; Basel 1504; Paris 1510) he provided a *summa* of the spiritual doctrine and practice of the *devotio moderna*. A sort of *rapiarium*, the *Rosetum* gives an abundance of the spiritual experiences of the writer and his circle and the fruits of an uncommonly wide acquaintance with religious literature.

As an aid to the memory the rules of meditation and its content were put in verse. These were arranged in groups of seven for the days of the week or the seven canonical hours or in "rosaries" of 150 points. To aid the canons in a devout chanting of the psalms during the Office, Mombaer gave them, in the *Chiropsalterium*, a further mnemonic aid.

Through the *Rosetum*, the *devotio moderna* acquired a stronger influence in France and, *via* France, in Spain, for example, on Abbot García Jiménez de Cisneros (d. 1510) of Montserrat. His writings, which aimed to provide a help for the interior performance of the choral liturgy *(Directorium horarum canonicarum*, Montserrat 1500) and for meditation (*Exercitatorium spirituale*, Montserrat 1500), are strongly dependent on the *Rosetum*. Whether Ignatius Loyola obtained the stimulus for his method of meditation through this Benedictine Abbot or directly from John Mombaer cannot be definitely determined. In any case, at Manresa he had *The Imitation of Christ* at his side and thereafter is said to have preferred it to any other devotional book. [42] Thus was established the direct connection of the *devotio moderna* with the Catholic Reform of the sixteenth century.

CHAPTER 48

The Nationalist Heresies: Wyclif and Hus

Ideas regarded as heretical, which were maintained in England and Bohemia toward the end of the fourteenth and at the beginning of the fifteenth century, acquired a universal importance because they expressed revolutionary views in the quarrels over the constitution, structure, and life of the Church.

John Wyclif, born near York around 1330, spent most of his life at Oxford

---

[42] "Tagebuch des Pater Gonçalves," *Monumenta Ignatiana*, IV, I (Rome 1944), 200.

as master of theology following his studies at that University and held several lucrative benefices. While he has until now been regarded chiefly as a philosopher and politician, numerous recent studies point up his interest as primarily theological and especially biblical. Though he has often been referred to as a nominalist, an emphasis on his extreme realism seems to correspond better to reality.[1] Detailed commentaries on Holy Scripture and the treatise *De veritate sacrae scripturae* gained him the title *Doctor evangelicus*. After he had become professor of theology, he composed a sort of theological *summa* in several treatises: *De dominio divino, De civili dominio, De officio regis, De ecclesia*. Moved by the deplorable situation of ecclesiastical administration and by the insecurity consequent upon the outbreak of the Western Schism, he now came forward as a reformer of more aggressiveness than had been indicated in his biblical exegesis. His theses, regarded as dangerous, gave the competent ecclesiastical authority the excuse to intervene, especially since denunciations came from several quarters. An interrogation before the Bishop of London at Saint Paul's in February 1377 took him to task for nineteen articles extracted from *De civili dominio*, but his patron, the Duke of Lancaster, prevented any severe action.[2] Likewise fruitless were the bulls sent by Gregory XI in May of the same year to the King, the bishops, and the University of Oxford.[3] The next year a hearing at Lambeth before several bishops obtained from Wyclif a partial recantation or at least an evasive interpretation of the nineteen articles.[4] His Eucharistic theory of *remanentia* in his *De Eucharistia* was attacked by the mendicant friars, the Chancellor of Oxford, and a part of the masters; against them he drew up a *Confessio*.[5] He took no direct part in the disturbances of 1381 and spoke out against the insurgents. In May 1382 Archbishop Courtenay of Canterbury (1381–96) convoked a provincial council at the Dominican house in London — the "Earthquake Synod." In prolonged discussions twenty-four propositions were branded, some as heretical, some as erroneous,[6] and a synod at Oxford in November of the same year approved these proceedings.[7] Wyclif had to give up his teaching position and retired to his parish of Lutterworth, where he remained unmolested until his death on 31 December 1384. To this period belong a group of important writings, such as the *Trialogus*. When Urban VI cited

---

[1] R. Kalivoda, "Johannes Wyclifs Metaphysik des extremen Realismus und ihre Bedeutung im Endstadium der mittelalterlichen Philosophie," *Miscellanea Mediaevalia*, 2 (Berlin 1963), 716–23.

[2] J. H. Dahmus, *The Prosecution of John Wyclif* (New Haven 1952), 7–34.

[3] The five papal bulls, with English translation, in Dahmus, *op. cit.*, 39–49; the bull to the University of Oxford in *Fasciculi zizaniorum*, 242 ff., with the date 31 May 1377.

[4] Dahmus, *op. cit.*, 35–73.

[5] *Fasciculi zizaniorum*, 105 f.

[6] *Mansi*, XXVI, 695–722; Dahmus, *op. cit.*, 89–128; *Fasciculi zizaniorum*, 277–82.

[7] *Mansi*, XXVI, 811–20; Dahmus, *op. cit.*, 136 f.

him to the Curia he replied in a work that was hardly submissive[8] and then in his *De citationibus frivolis.*

Wyclif's criticism of Church and theology soon found a response in wide circles and imitation through the so-called "Poor Priests." Recently, however, their connection with Wyclif and their importance and diffusion are less emphasized than they were in earlier presentations. After Wyclif's adherents at the University of Oxford had been expelled by the Archbishop and the state officials or had submitted, a cruder Wyclifism remained active in the middle and lower strata of the population for several decades more. They went into the catalogue of heretics under the old label "Lollards," and the translation of the Vulgate into the vernacular, suggested by Wyclif, was called the "Lollard Bible."[9] Energetic steps were taken by state and Church to prevent the survival of Wyclif's doctrines. Thus in 1397 Archbishop Arundel (1396–1414) at a provincial synod condemned eighteen propositions from the *Trialogus.* At the beginning of the fifteenth century the German master, John Hübner, at Prague added twenty-one other propositions to the twenty-four that had been condemned at London in 1382.[10] In Bohemia in 1412 the defending of these forty-five articles and of seven others was forbidden, theological censures being added to each article.[11] And at Oxford in 1411 the Archbishop, after a visitation of the University, obtained the compiling of a list of 267 false opinions of Wyclif; he then transmitted this to Rome. The at first strong opposition to the visitation was less an advocacy of Wyclif than a protest in favour of the University's freedom. At Rome on 10 February 1413 John XXIII's bull of 2 February was published in the single solemn session of the Council of Rome. This contained the condemnation of all Wyclif's writings, especially the *Dialogus* and the *Trialogus,* and also the demand that anyone who intended to defend Wyclif's memory had to appear at the papal court within nine months.[12] At Constance, right after the opening of the Council in 1414, persons were also concerned with Wyclif and Hus.[13] On 4 May 1415, in the eighth session, the Council condemned the forty-five propositions after they had been examined in

---

[8] *Fasciculi zizaniorum,* 341 f.

[9] K. B. McFarlane, *John Wycliffe and the Beginnings of English Nonconformity* (London 1952); M. E. Aston, "Lollardy and Sedition 1381–1431," *Past and Present,* 17 (1960), 1–44; M. Deanesly, *The Lollard Bible* (Cambridge 1920).

[10] F. Palacký, *Documenta Mag. Joannis Hus vitam, doctrinam, causam in Constantiensi concilio actam et controversias de religione in Bohemia annis 1403–1418 motas illustrantia* (Prague 1869, reprinted Osnabrück 1966), 327–31.

[11] *Ibid.,* 451–57; also in M. Spinka, *John Hus' Concept of the Church* (Princeton 1966), 397–400.

[12] H. Finke, *Acta concillii Constanciensis,* I, 123 f., 162 f., IV, 643; *Calendar of entries in the Papal registers relating to Great Britain and Ireland. Papal letters,* VI (London 1904), 174, 343 f.

[13] H. Finke, *op. cit.,* IV, 17.

detail in expert opinions;[14] discussion was also begun on the 260 theses which had been condemned by Oxford University but it was then postponed. There followed the decree that Wyclif's remains were to be removed from consecrated ground. In the twelfth session, on 29 May, there was discussion of 266 articles of Wyclif[15] and on 6 July the fifteenth session confirmed the verdict of the Roman Synod after fifty-eight of the 260 articles had been read.[16] While yet at Constance the new Pope, Martin V, issued a series of decrees on the religious situation in Bohemia, which included an enumeration of Wyclif's forty-five articles and thirty articles of John Hus; these too were condemned in the fifteenth session. Also issued was a questionnaire with thirty-nine questions, which were to be presented to suspected persons.[17] He addressed himself to England in repeated documents and demanded the destruction of Wyclif's writings and the suppression of his errors. Finally, in December 1427 the Bishop of Lincoln was commanded to have Wyclif's remains disinterred and burned; this was carried out.[18]

An evaluation of Wyclif's personality was from the start a cause of dispute, since his strictly scholastic style, a certain obscurity in his caustic criticism, and the frequent repetition of his pet ideas impeded the study of his writings. If he was long regarded as a typical "pre-reformer," today persons incline rather to include him in the front ranks of the reformers. It must be said, however, that he did not rest content with a criticism of external and superficial things, such as the veneration of relics and saints, auricular confession, purgatory, indulgences, and monasticism, but, proceeding from the *lex Dei* in Scripture, attacked the theological bases of the mediaeval Church and hence was regarded as one of the worst enemies of the hierarchy. As an extreme Augustinian he represented in a radical manner a Church of the predestined in which there was no room for the hierarchy and ecclesiastical property in their contemporary form; to the Church of his day — *lex ecclesiae, epistulae papales* — he opposed the ancient Church in his indictment. If the papal bulls compared him to Ockham and Marsilius of Padua, this probably referred less to his philosophy than to the practical danger he implied for the structure of the late mediaeval Church. The frequently defended view that he was especially favoured or even protected

---

[14] H. von der Hardt, *Magnum oecumenicum Constantiense concilium*, III (Frankfurt 1698), 168–211 ("Theologorum Constantiensium brevis censura XLV articulorum Wiclefi"), 212–335 ("Theologorum Constantiensis concilii diffusa condemnatio XLV articulorum Wiclefi").

[15] H. Finke, *op. cit.*, II, 362.

[16] The numerical data in regard to the Oxford articles fluctuate between 260 and 266: *Acta concilii Constanciensis*, II, 34, 40, 48. The fifty-eight articles that were read are in *Mansi*, XXVII, 748–52, and *COD*, 398–402.

[17] "Inter cunctas" of 22 February 1418, in *Hefele-Leclercq*, VII, 511–28.

[18] *Calendar of entries. Papal letters*, VII (London 1906), 21–23.

by the English government because of his hostile attitude to Rome and the bishops has justifiably been contradicted.[19] New interpretations of his Eucharistic doctrine have also made their appearance. Many aspects of his teaching and the meaning of his enigmatic personality thus need a thorough and unpolemical clarification.

A powerful reform movement was in progress in Bohemia from the middle of the fourteenth century, even before Wyclif's ideas became known and obtained a wide circulation there. As everywhere else, the usual reproaches were directed against the wealth and privileges of the clergy. Protagonists of such reform ideas were quite numerous among the theological masters of the University. Hence it is not difficult to understand that Wyclif's doctrines and writings fell on a well prepared soil. Through the marriage of Anne, sister of King Wenceslas IV of Bohemia, to King Richard II of England intellectual interchange, especially through the activity of Bohemians studying at Oxford, became very lively. It is significant that more manuscripts of Wyclif are found in Bohemia than in England.

Into this situation, politically excited by the opposition between Germans and Czechs, came John Hus, who was born around 1370. He had obtained the master's degree in the Prague arts faculty and, after receiving the priesthood in 1400, devoted himself to the study of theology. The period up to his public appearance is obscure. His scholarship and theological originality are controverted, as is also his whole character, especially since it became involved in the Bohemian nationalist movement and, most recently, in the Marxist interpretation of history. In the first years of the new century he appeared as one friend of reform among many. Appointed by the Archbishop of Prague as synodal preacher, he began with remarkable asperity to denounce the vices of the clergy and in the Bethlehem Chapel, established for vernacular preaching by some lay enthusiasts for reform, he addressed the ordinary people. Earlier research pointed to his far-reaching dependence, both as to content and as to text, on Wyclif and accordingly greatly restricted Hus's originality. But his independent elaboration and politically shrewd use of Wyclif's ideas, expressed by the Englishman in ponderously scholastic fashion, is justly stressed.[20] He rejected the wholesale condemnation of Wyclif, since, he said, there was much that was orthodox in his formulations. He played no leading role in the decree of Kutná Hora, which in 1409 annulled the previous privileges of the German nation at the University.[21] Minor collisions with the Archbishop and the University were followed by

---

[19] J. H. Dahmus, "John Wyclif and the English Government," *Speculum*, 35 (1960), 51–68; L. J. Daly, "Walter Burley and John Wyclif on Some Aspects of Kingship," *SteT*, 234 (1964), 163–84.

[20] P. De Vooght, *L'hérésie de Jean Hus*, 75 ff.; J. Kejř, *Zur Entstehungsgeschichte des Hussitentums*, 52; G. A. Benrath, *Wyclif und Hus*, 197 f.

[21] F. Seibt, *Hussitica*, 65–77.

a process against Wyclif's adherents, instituted by the Prague curia in accord with the instructions of Alexander V, the public burning of his writings, and the forbidding of preaching in private chapels. The result was an open break and Hus's excommunication. As he had done earlier, he now appealed to the new Pope, John XXIII. The matter was turned over to Cardinal Colonna for consideration and decision; he approved the Archbishop's measures and sent Hus an invitation to appear at the Curia; he rejected the excuses submitted by proxies and in February 1411 excommunicated Hus. Before long an interdict was laid on Prague. The Pope, however, named a new commission of four cardinals, but only Cardinal Brancaccio busied himself with the affair. King Wenceslas now intervened more forcefully in the disputes in order to put an end to the unrest and, in the expectation of recovering the imperial dignity, to present his Kingdom as free from heresies. But then Hus's preaching in the summer of 1412 against the crusade indulgence which John XXIII had offered because of King Ladislas of Naples brought the strife to a climax. A great part of the clergy, many masters of the University, and finally even the King withdrew their earlier support. Cardinal Brancaccio renewed Hus's excommunication and threatened his followers with excommunication and interdict. Hus had to leave the city and stayed with friendly Bohemian nobles. At this time he composed a work entitled *De ecclesia*. In this unsystematic polemic, which also borrowed from Wyclif, against the Prague theological faculty the Englishman's notion of the Church as the community of the predestined was very prominent, and hence the prevailing structure of the hierarchical Church and the obedience due to her were brought into question. It is not surprising, then, that there was a powerful opposition to it and that most of the points of the indictment could be taken from this document. The situation in the Bohemian Kingdom was now so tense that even King Sigismund, as heir of Bohemia, looked to the coming Council for the solution of the political and ecclesiastical difficulties and suggested to Hus that he appear there.

CHAPTER 49

The Council of Constance: Martin V

The Council of Constance (1414–18)

In spite of the great successes of the Council of Pisa union had not yet been entirely achieved, especially in the obedience of Benedict XIII in the Iberian peninsula. Once again politics determined the further development of ecclesiastical matters. The fate of the envisaged synod hung upon the attitude of the European states.

The extremely complicated prehistory of the Council of Constance is best grasped in the activity of the German King Sigismund. Already as King of Hungary he had early taken the part of the Council of Pisa and its Popes, Alexander V and John XXIII. Since his unanimous election as German King in June 1411, his actions and influence had concentrated especially on the unity of Christendom.[1] It was clear to him from the start that, despite the extensive Pisan obedience, only a radical solution, namely the withdrawal of all three pretenders, could lead to the desired goal. For no success attended the Council of Cividale, held by Gregory XII in the summer of 1409. It was opened on 6 June and, after eight or nine sessions, was secretly abandoned by the Pope on 6 September. The attendance was slight, for the greatest part of the Italian bishops responded to the summons to Pisa. It was further impeded by the Patriarch of Aquileia, who supported Pisa, and in comparison with Benedict XIII's Council of Perpignan it ended wretchedly.[2] The diffi‑culties connected with union lay chiefly in the political field. So long as John XXIII, elected at Bologna in 1410 as successor of Alexander V, was able to maintain himself in Italy, any rapid progress on the road to union was out of the question. This crafty man, who was not particularly choosy about means, succeeded in establishing himself in Rome through the instru‑mentality of Louis of Anjou and in expelling the Pope of the Roman obedience from South Italy. Thus Gregory XII had only a few adherents in the lordship of Prince Charles Malatesta of Rimini and, in Germany, in the territory of the Count Palatine of the Rhine and in the dioceses of Trier, Worms, Speyer, and Verden.

In conformity with the decrees of Pisa, John XXIII summoned a council to meet at Rome on 1 April 1412. But this was announcement rather than fulfillment, although the peace made with Ladislas of Naples in June 1412 introduced a brief interval of peace in Italy's agitated political situation. Especially France, but also Italian circles, Malatesta in particular, displayed great interest in the meeting; the Pope was less interested. After the opening on 14 April there took place, apart from several rather insignificant sittings, only one solemn session, in which occurred the condemnation of Wyclif's propositions. When in March 1413 this gathering was adjourned, a new council was simultaneously announced but without any mention of where it would meet. As early as June, however, the Pope, again seriously menaced by Ladislas, had to abandon Rome in great haste. He found shelter outside the gates of Florence, while his Curia was lodged in the city.

---

[1] J. Leuschner, "Zur Wahlpolitik im Jahre 1410," *DA*, 11 (1955), 506–33; A. Gerlich, *Habsburg-Luxemburg-Wittelsbach im Kampf um die deutsche Königskrone. Studien zur Vorgeschichte des Königtums Ruprechts von der Pfalz* (Wiesbaden 1960).

[2] L. Schmitz, "Die Quellen zur Geschichte des Konzils von Cividale 1409," *RQ*, 8 (1894), 217–58; J. Petersohn, "Papst Gregors XII. Flucht aus Cividale (1409) und die Sicherstellung des päpstlichen Paramentenschatzes," *ibid.*, 58 (1963), 51–70.

Now Sigismund's hour had arrived. The developments in Central Italy caused John to look around for a protector, since Ladislas was beginning to push northward *via* Rome, and even Florence decided to seek a *rapprochement* with the King of Naples. It would be incorrect to regard Sigismund as the sole saviour of this emergency, but in regard to the place for the council the German King obtained the upper hand. After lengthy consultations with his Curia, John XXIII at the end of July 1413 announced the dispatch of cardinals for negotiations in regard to the time and place of the future council. Cardinals de Chalant and Zabarella were thereupon commissioned. Also envisaged was a meeting with the King at Genoa or Nice. But then the cardinals met with the King at Viggiù near Como from 13 to 31 October. The outcome of these detailed conversations was the announcement by Sigismund on 30 October of a council which was to meet on 1 November 1414, at Constance, as Sigismund had proposed. On 31 October a notarial instrument dealing with this agreement was prepared, and a meeting of the Pope with Sigismund at Lodi within forty days was decided upon. Negotiations began there on 25 November and lasted throughout December; then they were continued in Cremona until the middle of January. On 9 December the Pope issued the bull convoking the council to Constance. Thus, from the political viewpoint, Sigismund had quite rightly sided with the Pope with the largest obedience and for a long time had seemingly avoided any connection with Gregory XII, even inviting him to Constance very late. For a capitulation could more easily be obtained from the Roman Pope, either by kindness or by force.

In contrast to Gregory XII, Benedict XIII was a dangerous rival; his obedience was still solid and he was planning to enlarge it and even to invade Italy, with the assistance of King Ferdinand I of Aragón, who wanted to marry his second son, John, to the heiress of Naples, Ladislas's sister Joanna. And so the intermediaries sent by Sigismund, by the French King, and by John XXIII to the Iberian peninsula at first had a difficult time. Only the Aragonese King's eagerness for union brought about the great gathering at Morella on the frontier between Catalonia and Valencia. The participants were Benedict XIII, Ferdinand of Aragón, and envoys of the Kings of Castile, France, and Germany. In the discussions, lasting from June to September 1414, Benedict and his Spanish obedience showed themselves to be unprepared to yield, despite many obliging words. Nevertheless, envoys of the Pope and of the King of Aragón were sent to Sigismund with the suggestion of a meeting of Benedict and Ferdinand with the German King. The previous crude refusal was now succeeded by a close contact and as a result very much was gained. Following these circumspect preparatory steps, everything now depended on whether the states, especially the great powers, would really take part in the Council. For this Sigismund had to display all his mastery of politics and diplomacy. The greatest difficulty was the war, or at least the hostility, between England and France, together with the changing and uncertain attitude of Burgundy. Even before issuing the official invitation to the Council, Sigismund had simultaneously conducted negotiations for an alliance with England and France; then, in June 1414, he had signed with France the secret Treaty of Trino, directed less against England than against Burgundy. The usual rapid change in the coalitions at this period was already apparent in September in France's *rapprochement* with Burgundy in the Peace of Arras. Although the negotiations and the plans for an alliance with England were more in keeping with Sigismund's policy, here too the idea of the Council held the first place. Accordingly, it was a question of preventing the outbreak of hostilities until the Council could get under way and then of preventing the forsaking of the Council by the powers. Sigismund's diplomacy and his temporizing were successful in both matters and so to him belongs the chief merit for having brought the Council into being and for its accomplishments.[3] His policy before the Council was as important as that at the Council. The Council of Constance was essentially a political event and can be understood and appreciated only from this viewpoint.

It was due to the powerful pressure from the cardinals that, after the sudden death of King Ladislas of Naples on 6 August 1414, John XXIII did not devote himself to winning back the Papal State but set out for Constance. In order to safeguard himself, he allied with Duke Frederick of Habsburg and with the Margrave of Baden. He entered Constance on 28 October and on 5 November solemnly opened the Council. At first the number of participants was slight, because many wanted to see whether the Council would meet at all. The German King arrived at Constance on Christmas, and with the new year, 1415, the attendance rapidly grew: cardinals, archbishops and bishops, abbots, generals of orders, the grand masters of the military orders, many proxies of the higher clergy, deputies of chapters, professors of theology and of canon law, envoys of kings, princes, free cities, cities, and, not least, universities. The lay element was very strongly represented, especially the German princes, counts, and other nobles. Another class appeared in large numbers at a general council for the first time since Pisa: the scholars, for since the High Middle Ages the universities, Paris at their head, had assumed the tasks of the *magisterium ordinarium*. Many thousands gathered in the city of the Council, even if the numerical data given by the Constance chronicler, Ulric Richental, in his work, which is so significant for cultural history, are exaggerated. By virtue of John XXIII's creations the College of Cardinals displayed a group of outstanding personalities, as did also the body of curialists. Present at this greatest congress

---

[3] E. Göller, *König Sigismunds Kirchenpolitik*, 166; H. Finke, *Acta conc. Constanc.*, I, 170; H. Heimpel, *Aus der Kanzlei*, 136.

of the Middle Ages was the whole of contemporary Christendom, including the Eastern Church. The importance of this gathering of peoples for the spread of humanism can scarcely be overestimated. A new style made its appearance in sermons, treatises, and especially pamphlets. All the weighty questions of the age were treated at the Council. In its three-and-one-half years there occurred forty-five solemn sessions and hundreds of general congregations and meetings of the nations and of the various committees. The Popes, John XXIII and then Martin V, presided over the Council. From the spring of 1415 voting in the solemn sessions was by nations, the College of Cardinals occupying the position of a nation. In the nations themselves, following the precedent of Pisa, voting was by heads.[4]

By contemporaries themselves the tasks of the Council were designated pointedly in the brief summation: *causa unionis, reformationis, fidei*. All three tasks continuously occupied the Council, sometimes in the foreground of the discussions, sometimes only in committees, depending on the political situation. Unquestionably, the restoration of unity was the most important and most pressing task. The difficult struggle for it was not lacking in drama. John XXIII and his large Italian retinue came to Constance with the intention of having the Pisan decrees against Gregory XII and Benedict XIII confirmed and then of dissolving the Council. This would have been significant only if all states would have complied with this decree, but this was not to be expected. Although the legitimacy of the Council of Pisa and of the election of John XXIII was recognized almost unanimously, only the resignation of the Pisan Pope also and of the two deposed at Pisa seemed to give hope of success. This was also Sigismund's plan and that of most of the nations. The Council's journalists pressed for the Pope's resignation with menacing accusations. John finally yielded to the pressure and held out the prospect of abandoning his claims, but he bargained for a week about the proper formulation. Then, in the night of 20—21 March 1415, he left the city secretly and in disguise and, under the protection of Frederick of Habsburg, went to Schaffhausen; from there he fled to Freiburg and to the Rhine, where, on the other side, Burgundian knights were awaiting him. He intended that his flight should disrupt the Council, but the German King kept it together with all the means at his disposal. In these fateful days, when the existence or non-existence of the Council and hence of union was at stake, the assembly, in the fifth session on 6 April, promulgated the decrees, later so controversial, on the superior power of the general council in the Church.[5]

---

[4] H. Finke, "Die Nation in den spätmittelalterlichen allgemeinen Konzilien," *HJ*, 57 (1937).

[5] *Conciliorum oecumenicorum decreta*, 385: "Haec sancta synodus Constantiensis generale concilium faciens, pro exstirpatione praesentis schismatis, et unione ac reformatione ecclesiae Dei in capite et membris fienda, ad laudem omnipotentis Dei in Spiritu sancto legitime congregata, ad consequendum facilius, securius, uberius et liberius unionem ac reformationem ecclesiae Dei ordinat, diffinit, statuit, decernit et declarat, ut sequitur. Et primo de-

It then instituted the process against the fugitive Pope. He was brought back as a prisoner and deposed on 29 May in the twelfth solemn session. He accepted the Council's sentence, but until 1419 he remained in the custody of the Count Palatine of the Rhine.

The proceedings against John XXIII belong in the series of famed papal processes of the Middle Ages. From the many abominations noised about in the Council seventy indictments were compiled in all haste, and in barely two weeks numerous interrogations of cardinals, bishops and high ranking prelates of the Curia took place. Some of the officials and notaries employed in the process had had a similar experience at Pisa. Out of the official records of the indictment and of the interrogations, as well as from the libels of the German curialist, Dietrich von Niem, emerges a dreadful picture of the Pope, from his youth and through his clerical and curial career up to the cardinalate and the papacy. He was accused of immorality of the worst sort, of having poisoned his predecessor, Alexander V, of having squandered the property of the Church and of the Papal State, of simony, and of intolerable avarice in appointing to benefices. As was customary in such processes, some articles referred to facts already well known, which were supposed to be attested by as many witnesses as possible. Much else was reported only by hearsay. Even if some points were then dropped, still the defamation was general and uncontested, and that is what especially mattered.[6]

What is to be thought of this trial and the shocking accusations? First of all, the desired goal of a quick elimination of the Pope stands out clearly in the hasty and perhaps even precipitate procedure. A qualified specialist in this period puts it thus:

> He was no better and no worse than his contemporaries... But when at the Council of Constance he had to be sacrificed to the aspirations of the Christian nations after unity, all the guilt and sins of the age were heaped on his head, so that he could be deposed from his position with an appearance of legality. Thus he had to be tossed out of Peter's bark and a faithful and skilled pilot had to be installed in his place.[7]

clarat, quod ipsa in Spiritu sancto legitime congregata, generale concilium faciens, et ecclesiam catholicam militantem repraesentans, potestatem a Christo immediate habet, cui quilibet cuiuscumque status vel dignitatis, etiam si papalis exsistat, obedire tenetur in his quae pertinent ad fidem et exstirpationem dicti schismatis, ac generalem reformationem dictae ecclesiae Dei in capite et membris. Item declarat, quod quicumque cuiuscumque conditionis, status, dignitatis, etiam si papalis exsistat, qui mandatis, statutis seu ordinationibus, aut praeceptis huius sacrae synodi et cuiuscumque alterius concilii generalis legitime congregati, super praemissis, seu ad ea pertinentibus, factis, vel faciendis, obedire contumaciter contempserit, nisi resipuerit, condignae poenitentiae subiiciatur, et debite puniatur, etiam ad alia iuris subsidia, si opus fuerit, recurrendo."

[6] H. Finke, *Acta conc. Constanc.*, III, 11–29, 157–209, IV, 758–891.

[7] G. Erler, *Dietrich von Nieheim* (Leipzig 1887), 341, 384.

But this judgment is certainly too favourable. Still, much was charged to him for which his predecessors and the system were responsible. Deposition followed because of "unworthy life, notorious simony, incorrigibility, misgovernment of the Church, fostering of the Schism, and much scandal given to the Church." Hence he was regarded as an unworthy but not as an unlawful Pope.

Envoys of Gregory XII had arrived in Constance very soon after the opening of the Council. It was more than a trifling incident that the arms of their Pope, displayed at their lodgings, were torn down. It gave rise to a spirited discussion about the retirement of all three claimants in a kind of cancellation of the Pisan sentences. But then Gregory would be unable to come to a synod convoked by John XXIII; rather, he must summon it himself. This was granted to him. In the fourteenth solemn session, 4 July, his Cardinal John Dominici convoked the Council, whereupon Charles Malatesta announced Gregory's resignation. The Council appointed him Cardinal Bishop of Porto and Legate of the Marches of Ancona.

All these events lay within the bounds prescribed by politics. Following the now realized union of the Roman and Pisan obediences, there still remained the definitive elimination of Benedict XIII and the winning of his adherents in Spain and the Midi. Here too the Council wanted to complete the job before proceeding to the election of a new Pope.

Quite soon after the opening of the Council, envoys of Benedict XIII and of King Ferdinand of Aragón had appeared in Constance. They held out the prospect of a meeting with Sigismund at Nice. But it was not until July that a large delegation from the Council, Sigismund at its head, set out for Perpignan. Long and stubborn negotiations were unable to move Benedict to retire, but the kingdoms of the Iberian peninsula were won for the Council in the Treaty of Narbonne of 13 December 1415. The form of a reciprocal invitation betrays the primacy of politics here too. Thereby the Council, which had already been in session at Constance for more than a year, was to become a lawfully convoked Church gathering also for the former obedience of Benedict XIII. Even so, it was almost two years before all the Spanish states were represented at the Council as the fifth nation. The withdrawal of obedience also proceeded slowly and it was only in the thirty-seventh session, on 26 July 1417, that Benedict XIII was deposed, following a detailed process in which ninety charges figured. Till his death in 1423 the aged Pope, in his fortress of Peñíscola near Tortosa, regarded himself as the only legitimate successor of Peter.

The political amalgamation of all the former obediences finally opened up the way for the election of a new Pope. In the long and bitter debates of the summer of 1417 the point at issue was the priority of the papal election or of reform. Both viewpoints are understandable, even though the subsequent course of history may gain more sympathy for the call to reform. The form of the election was already the subject of detailed discussions. It had been said for some time that, in the event of the vacancy of the Holy See during a council, this council should certainly take part in the election of the new Pope. In view of the political structure of the Council of Constance, the cardinals were in no sense considered as the sole papal electors. The College had already made concessions in this regard in the deposition of John XXIII and in the resignation of Gregory XII, but it now sought to recover as much influence as possible. And so at Pentecost 1417 it submitted the celebrated *cedula* "Ad laudem," which, by way of exception, proposed the admission of representatives of the individual nations, with the proviso that, in comparison with the College of Cardinals, they must constitute a minority. Two-thirds of the votes in each of the two groups would be required for the validity of the election. Meanwhile, the German King succeeded in achieving the deposition of Benedict XIII and in assuring Church reform by a conciliar decree to the effect that what had so far been accomplished in regard to reform would be promulgated in a decree and the future Pope would be obliged to further reform before the close of the Council. This much had been achieved when the French nation submitted its new proposal for conducting the papal election. The new Pope, as the Pope of the now reunited Universal Church, should be elected by the College of Cardinals and six representatives of each of the five nations. His position would be politically unassailable, for the customary two-thirds would be required not only from the College of Cardinals but also from the representatives of each individual nation. The election thus carried out would be assured against any later objection. And so it was decided. This method of election was decreed in the fortieth session, on 30 October, and the opening of the conclave was set for within ten days.

In rapid succession occurred the selecting of the deputies in the nations, — not always without difficulties, — the appointing of the guardians of the conclave, the preparing and sealing off of the place of the election in the Merchants' Hall on the lake. The electors entered the conclave on 8 November and on the following day they began the deliberations. Faithful to the political mandate, the election could not be secret. On the reading of the ballots aloud, each elector was carefully asked whether it was his ballot and whether he wished to vote thus.

The first voting took place on 10 November, the votes being rather widely scattered. In the afternoon it was decided to allow the customary *accessus*, but only in writing. The decision was reached as early as 11 November. Serious candidates were the Cardinals of Ostia and Saluzzo, Colonna, and the Bishop of Geneva. If Colonna obtained only eight votes from the cardinals, he also had votes from each nation and the required number from the Italians and the English. While the *accessus* was taking place, the daily procession came to the conclave and sang the "Veni Creator Spiritus." Even the dull chroniclers mention the emotions thereby produced and the admonition to unity. Before noon Cardinal Oddo Colonna obtained two-thirds of the votes of the cardinals and of the delegates of each nation, accepted the election, and took the name of Martin V in honour of the saint of the day. No one had expected so quick an election, considering the extremely difficult mode of election. All the greater, then, was the general rejoicing in the conciliar city. Following his ordination to the priesthood, the new Pope was consecrated a Bishop and crowned on 21 November. From now on the Council was under his direction.

To the area of the *causa fidei* belong the controversial granting of the chalice to the laity, the attitude toward Hus and Wyclif, the question of the lawfulness of tyrannicide, and the dispute between the Teutonic Order and Poland.

The method of administering communion, actually a question of liturgical practice, acquired the greatest political importance because of special circumstances. Well into the High Middle Ages the Eucharist was ordinarily administered to the faithful under both species, but from about the middle of the thirteenth century for the most part under the species of bread. Apparently the introduction of communion *sub utraque* in Bohemia can be dated rather exactly to the autumn of 1414 and can be ascribed chiefly to the Prague master, James of Mies.[8] Hus was not involved. But on being questioned by his followers in his first weeks at Constance, he expressed himself prudently in favour of it in the pamphlet "De sanguine Christi sub specie vini a laicis sumendo." Later he came out publicly for it.

The treatment of this question proceeded together with the process against Hus. Reports on the granting of the chalice in Bohemia had piled up and the Council occupied itself with the question in the spring of 1415. On 15 June, in the thirteenth session, the lay chalice was forbidden by a synodal decree. When the report of this reached Bohemia together with the news of the condemnation and execution of Hus, the really disciplinary question of the chalice became a prominent sign of opposition and also, for wide circles, an intelligible symbol of the Hussite Revolt. After long negotiations and internal discussions the University of Prague — now the highest ecclesiastical tribunal in Bohemia — approved the lay chalice in the spring of 1417. This decision, together with an extensive historical demonstration of communion under both species, was transmitted to the Council through the good offices of King Sigismund. This was, then, an effort to induce the Council to a reexamination of the decision already rendered. But it took place only by means of the obtaining of further testimonials, for example, from Gerson and Nicholas von Dinkelsbühl, and these were naturally in

[8] F. Seibt, "Die revelatio des Jacobellus von Mies über die Kelchkommunion," *DA,* 22 (1966), 618–24.

conformity with the conciliar decree. This negative attitude was then confirmed by the bulls "Inter Cunctas" and "In Eminentis" of the new Pope on 22 February 1418. It took the frightful experiences of the Hussite wars to bring the Council of Basel to an accommodation.

The Bohemian reformer, John Hus, set out on 11 October 1414 and arrived at Constance on 3 November. The journey passed without incident, even though Hus had not yet received the royal safe-conduct. From the outset he did not find the atmosphere favourable at Constance. His chief Bohemian opponents, Stephen Paletsch and Michael de Causis, referred with great prudence to the presence of one who had been excommunicated and was suspect of heresy. Cardinals Colonna, Zabarella, and Stefaneschi and curial *auditores* had already been concerned with Hus for years and had laid censures on him. To Gerson and many doctors of Paris he was a dangerous heretic, against whom measures had to be taken. Out of regard for the King, John XXIII was mild, lifted the censures, and allowed Hus to celebrate Mass. But already at the end of November, despite energetic protests by the knights who were guarding him under the King's commission and despite an appeal to the royal safe-conduct, he was imprisoned. Attempts to treat his case in a small committee and to settle it there were frustrated by his demand to speak before the whole Council. The committee appointed on 4 December to handle his case consisted of the Patriarch of Antioch and the Bishops of Castellammare and Lebus. It set to work at once, relying on the often dubious charges of his Bohemian adversaries; many of these articles were later rejected by the committee. Until John XXIII's flight Hus was in custody in the Dominican monastery on the island, busy with replies to the questions of the members of the committee.[9] After the Pope's escape, the Bishop of Constance had to take charge of the prisoner; he let him stay at his castle of Gottlieben.

The King's demand that Hus be given a public hearing was complied with at the beginning of June. On 5, 7, and 8 June he stood before numerous prelates and theologians in the Franciscan refectory. While the first session was stormy, the two others were devoted to the quiet interrogation of the master. Hus rejected many articles that were falsely attributed to him, especially in regard to the Eucharist, but without much success, for, now just as earlier, he was regarded as Wyclifite. This was all the more unfortunate, since shortly before, in the eighth session on 4 May, the forty-five articles of Wyclif, his writings, and an additional 260 articles, earlier condemned by the University of Oxford, were again condemned. Hus refused to accept the judgment of the Council, and the King's kind exhortations

---

[9] On his attitude to the forty-five articles of Wyclif that were submitted to him *cf.* A. Molnár, "Les réponses de Jean Huss aux quarante-cinq articles," *RThAM*, 31 (1964), 85–99.

were unsuccessful. Thus his fate was sealed, despite many efforts to get him to change his mind.

The decision was reached in the fifteenth session on 6 July, before the King's departure for Perpignan. Several previous attempts to save him foundered on his opposition. On the very eve of the session Cardinals d'Ailly and Zabarella, with many prelates and doctors from all the nations, submitted to him a very moderate formula of abjuration, but Hus rejected it. That evening there arrived, by order of the King, Duke Louis of Bavaria and the Count Palatine, with the Bohemian knights who were his friends, to persuade him to yield, but in vain. And so fate took its course. After the Mass preceding the solemn session, Hus was led into the cathedral to hear the reading of the indictment and the sentence. Again and again he interrupted the solemn action with challenges, protests, and prayers, but he gave no sign of submission. Two sentences had been prepared, one for the case of his recantation, the other for that of his persisting in his previous attitude. It was the second that was read. Hus was immediately degraded and surrendered to the secular arm, and the judgment was thereupon executed by burning. Hus died a martyr to his convictions.

The position of the German King has often been investigated and usually blamed.[10] There is no doubt that he intended by means of the Council and the anticipated justification of John Hus to master the difficulties in Bohemia. He had probably not given a thought to an unfortunate outcome and had long sought earnestly to prevent one. He thus protested energetically against the imprisonment and forced the three great interrogations and the submitting of the authentic and unfalsified writings of the master. It was some time before he became convinced of heresy, and still longer in regard to dangerous fanaticism. Only for a time was it possible to insist, against the verdict of the Council, on the promised safe-conduct. He could not and would not protect a heretic, as a testimonial of Dietrich von Niem shows.[11]

---

[10] The safe-conduct consisted of: 1) a personal escort, appointed already in the spring of 1414, of two Bohemian nobles delegated by the King; 2) a letter of safe-conduct drawn up in Latin and German. Only the Latin version, dated 28 October 1414, is extant (F. Palacký, *Documenta*, 237 f.). Hus undertook the journey to Constance without the letter of safe-conduct, as he himself repeatedly wrote to Prague, but under the protection of the two Bohemian knights. Apparently no special safe-conduct was supplied to Hus by Pope or Council, but at first he was under the general safe-conduct of persons going to the Council. Opinions differ as to the import of the royal safe-conduct. The letter was probably no more than an ordinary passport. But from the sharp reaction of the knights accompanying Hus and the repeated protests of many Bohemian nobles it may be surmised that Sigismund had given extensive assurances of a safe return-journey. *Cf.* A. Hall, *Siegmund und Hus* (Diss. phil., Freiburg 1912); H. Finke, *Acta conc. Constanc.*, IV, 495.

[11] H. Heimpel, *Dietrich von Niem*, 343–49; also, H. Finke, *Acta conc. Constanc.*, IV, 662 f.

The figure and the fate of the Bohemian master have found many interpretations — nationalist, heretic, martyr for freedom of conscience, to name only the most important. That he went voluntarily to Constance attests his courage, but also a remarkable misunderstanding of his situation. He came, not as a free participant in the Council, but as one accused and excommunicated, who was to answer before it. If he was willing to be taught by discussion and to be convinced of the incorrectness of his theses, he confused the sovereign authority of the General Council with a scholastic disputation. Especially unfortunate for him were the insurrection in his homeland, which was blamed on him, and the spiteful attacks of his countrymen. Until the bitter end he rejected the misinterpretation of his intentions by the Council. He said that he had not defended the greatest part of the articles attributed to him, or not as they appeared, and that hence he could not abjure them. Recently the exhaustive research of P. De Vooght, based on the sources, has prepared the way for a substantially milder evaluation, not to say rehabilitation. Accordingly, caution is called for in regard to all the earlier claims, both at Constance and in later historians, of a strong dependence on Wyclif. Erroneous theological views are to be found only in the notion of the Church and in the doctrine of the papacy. Not only misunderstandings in terminology but two different ideas confronted each other. Hus exhibited rather an ethical and spiritual understanding of the Church, of a strong Augustinian stamp, whereas the juristic and institutional element prevailed among the Council Fathers. A tragic fate obscures the indomitable but enigmatic personality of the Bohemian reformer.

A year after Hus's death, Jerome of Prague also had to mount the pyre at Constance. Less a theologian than his master, on many academic travels he acquired a comprehensive knowledge of philosophy and brought Wyclif's works from Oxford to Bohemia and Poland. His propaganda activities got him into various difficulties, and he was expelled from universities or took to flight. As a Czech nationalist and patriot he defended Hus at Constance but left the city, was arrested *en route* to Bohemia, and was brought back to the Council. After a first submission he disavowed his action and was burned on 30 May 1416.[12]

In the area of the *causa fidei* the question of the lawfulness of tyrannicide occupied the Council the longest and agitated it the most. To begin with, it concerned a problem of urgent political relevance. The occasion went back some years, to the assassination of Duke Louis of Orléans, brother of the French King Charles VI, in the fall of 1407 at the instigation of John the Fearless, Duke of Burgundy. In the following spring the Parisian master, John Petit, a Franciscan, justified this deed in the presence of the court and

---

[12] S. Šmahel, "Leben und Werke des Magisters Hieronymus von Prag. Forschung ohne Probleme und Perspektiven?" *Historica,* 13 (1966), 81–111.

of an illustrious gathering in his famous, and soon to be infamous, *Iustificatio ducis Burgundiae*. When there occurred a change in France's internal politics a synod at Paris and the Bishop of Paris, at Gerson's urging, condemned the *Iustificatio* in the spring of 1414, whereupon the Duke of Burgundy appealed to John XXIII at the beginning of March. The Pope entrusted the case to Cardinals Orsini and Zabarella and the Cardinal of Aquileia. Since there was no immediate decision, this matter also came before the Council. Here too it was unable to achieve a quick settlement, since too much regard had to be taken for political considerations and it was not permitted to endanger the chief business, that of union.

And so the problem was not brought up until after the deposition of John XXIII. It is true that the commission of cardinals, instituted earlier, was still competent, but soon the committee on the faith became interested. The result was the condemnation of the thesis "Quilibet tyrannus" in a general form, with no mention of John Petit, in the decree of the fifteenth session, 6 July 1415. The struggle of the two factions continued during the preparation of this decree and, even more, afterwards until the end of the Council. The Burgundian party and its leader, Bishop Martin Porré of Arras, took a firm stand against attributing the controverted extracts to Petit and against including him with the condemned theses. On the other side Gerson had for years taken the lead in numerous treatises and memoranda to the committee on the faith, demanding the condemnation of Petit's theses.

The majority of the testimonials requested by the committee and still known to us belong to the period from the autumn of 1415 to the spring of 1416. However, in a question of such political significance and such dogmatic importance, it is remarkable that a strong majority opposed Gerson: sixty-one opinions against condemnation and only twenty-six for it.[13] Of course it would have been best, so many felt, if a decision were postponed to the next council. The annulment of the Parisian verdict, pronounced by the committee of three cardinals on 15 January 1416, was in accord with this frame of mind. Hence the outcome was a retreat, without any direct approval of either side. This, however, only gave rise to new exertions for a clear verdict by the Council, but neither the Council nor the new Pope was able to render one. The difficulties were not only political. The fundamental texts were disputed at Constance, just as they had been earlier at Paris. The particular case defended by Petit had been made into a universal in order thereby to arrive more easily at a condemnation and still to spare the Duke of Burgundy. If by "tyrant" Petit apparently understood only a traitor, then in addition there was a widely divergent terminology. Not

---

[13] On the treatises see H. Heimpel, "Dietrich von Niems Gutachten gegen die Sätze Jean Petits vom erlaubten Tyrannenmord 28. Juni (1415)," *Studien zur Kirchen- und Reichsreform*, 62–64.

without significance for the obstinacy of the conflict was the peculiar development of the French notion of kingship. Viewed from without, it is especially striking how very useful the scholastic form of politics had become in the endless controversy in word and writing, how it believed it could prove all things and everything. The testimonials were often of political rather than dogmatic relevance — a thing already familiar from the beginning of the Schism.

The quarrel between the Teutonic Order and Poland also led to a dispute over principles. The Peace of Toruń (1411) was followed in 1414 by a new conflict, which was temporarily ended by the armistice of Strasbourg. As in all great and undecided questions, here too the Council was supposed to be the final and highest court, especially since the attack on the order and its justification of its existence had been introduced on a broad theoretical front by Paul Wladimiri, a member of the Polish delegation at the Council, shortly after the opening. As in the case of the other business, here too a series of testimonials was submitted by the parties and called for by the officials. Just the same, the order's procurator, Peter of Wormdith, obtained the confirmation of its most important privileges by the Council and thus recognition of its past and future activity. The quarrel was aggravated by the *Satyra* of the Prussian Dominican, John Falkenberg, which was very hostile to the Polish King and nation. All motions by the Polish delegation, which also enjoyed Sigismund's support toward the close of the Council, for the condemnation of the Falkenberg theses as heretical were fruitless. The matter was often discussed in the committees and in the nations, but no conciliar decree materialized, not even when the Poles, in the last solemn session on 22 April, directly before the announcement of the ending of the Council, sought tempestuously to force one from the Council or the new Pope. Falkenberg himself, whose writings were condemned as dangerous and to be burned but not directly as heretical by a committee of cardinals appointed by Martin V, remained in the custody of the Curia until he recanted in 1424.

To the subjects treated at Constance in regard to faith belonged also the case of another Dominican, Matthew Grabow, a native of Wismar. He was active in Utrecht and had repeatedly lodged serious charges against the Brothers of the Common Life and all similar groups. He appeared before the Council with his accusations but was forced into the defensive by the accused and had to remain at the Council to justify himself. He submitted his views to the new Pope, but they were rejected by several who studied them, including d'Ailly and Gerson, and branded as heretical. By order of the Pope the Cardinal of Verona and, after the latter's death, the Cardinal of Aquileia had to deal with the matter. However, it was not settled at Constance but during Martin V's long stay at Florence. Condemned on 6 May 1419, Grabow recanted on 22 October. He was taken to Rome with

Falkenberg and was long detained in Castel Sant'Angelo. Nothing is known of his later fate, but he is said to have died in prison. [14]

If reunion was certainly the most important, even though a strictly limited, task of the Council, the reform of the Church or at least of the Curia was the broadest program. It was the special theme of the late Middle Ages and not merely a vague or mystical notion. For, according to the idea of contemporaries, unity could be assured only by the long demanded and desired reform. The notions of council and reform were inseparably linked in the fourteenth and fifteenth centuries, and, following the achieving of reform, even reunion with the Greek Church was supposed to take place.

This reform was no revolution but a restoration of the old order. But no reform without a council. This proposition was realized in a fateful manner. Reform of the Church seemed possible only if the general council was regarded as the fundamentally sovereign organ of the Church. The great memoranda represented this standpoint almost unequivocally. If at the Council of Vienne Durandus the Younger had already demanded the holding of general councils at least every ten years, this thesis was vigorously taken up at the beginning of the Schism and continued into the fifteenth century, especially around the turn of the century and between the Councils of Pisa, Constance, and Basel. There were many proposals in regard to the interval between councils: every five, seven, ten, thirty, or even fifty years. Every Pope should hold one at least once in his pontificate. The Universal Church, all the provinces, should be represented, and because of the ignorance of many bishops the attendance of *periti* was necessary. At each council the date for the next was to be determined, so that the Pope could not change or transfer place or date. The council alone, but not the Pope, could dispense from the conciliar decrees. Apart from the proposals for the improvement of morals, especially those of the clergy, at the next council after Pisa a revision of Holy Scripture and of canon law should be undertaken and brief summaries of the doctrine of faith and morals should be approved and distributed to all metropolitans and bishops. What were lacking were theologians; there were too many jurists and canonists at councils. It was due to the previous refusal of reform and to the simony of the Roman Curia that heresies had arisen, especially in England and Bohemia. Regarded almost universally as causes of abuses and of the Schism were the failure to hold general councils, the forsaking of the old canons and of a more synodal constitution of the Church, and the exaggerated growth of papal power. Reference was made again and again to the old rules, which had been abandoned to the benefit of a growth of juristic

[14] S. Wachter, "Matthäus Grabow, ein Gegner der Brüder vom gemeinsamen Leben," *St. Gabrieler Studien*, 8 (1939), 289–376; see also Chapter 47.

abuses and had contributed to the hypertrophous development of the curial system. The luxury of the papal court, of the cardinals and curialists, of bishops and prelates was a favourite theme of reform writings and reform preachers, but only the external aspects were dealt with. The system of benefices and of finance, reservations and provisions, as the effluence of a falsely understood *plenitudo potestatis,* must be regarded as the basic evil. A reform writing of 1406 says:

> The *plenitudo potestatis* resides only in God — not in an individual man, not even in the Pope. The Pope has no absolute and full authority; he is not allowed to call himself *summus pontifex* but only *primae sedis episcopus.* His reserving all the business of his subjects to himself, his conferring of dignities and benefices, is a recent invention of the Latin Church and contrary to the canons ... Since Clement V three great evils have prevailed: Curia, *Camera,* and *potestas plenaria.* Since then all churches have been tributary. Tithes, *subsidia,* procurations, reservations, accumulation of benefices, exemptions, the arbitrary sale of plenary indulgence to the rich, provisions, commutation of penances for money payments — all this in the hands of a single man! Only Christ and the Universal Church in a general council are permitted to have such power. [15]

And in Dietrich von Niem's work, which summarized all reform proposals, there occurs in several places the statement, short and to the point: "concilium ergo generale ... limitet ac terminet potestatem coactivam et usurpatam papalem." [16] This meant the abolition or at least an extensive curtailing of expectatives, reservations, dispensations, exemptions, the *commenda,* annates, tithes, *subsidia,* and *spolia* in order to avoid simony and the simplification of the curial administration and of the chancery rules. Reform must begin at the top, for now there is no longer the *servus servorum Dei* but rather the *dominus dominorum.*

This brief glance at the universal desire for reform is necessary for an understanding of the Constance reform. The desire for reform was expressed previous to the Council in the *De squaloribus Romanae curiae (ca.* 1404) of Matthew of Cracow, Bishop of Worms, in the *Aureum speculum de titulis beneficiorum,* in the reform work, already mentioned, of the Bishop of Senez *(ca.* 1406), in the pamphlet *De ruina et reparatione ecclesiae* by

---

[15] R. Scholz, "Eine Geschichte und Kritik der Kirchenverfassung vom Jahre 1406. Nach einer ungedruckten Reformschrift." *Papsttum und Kaisertum, Paul Kehr zum 65. Geburtstag* (Munich 1926), 609, 616.

[16] Dietrich von Niem, *De Modis* (ed. H. Heimpel), 43, 47; 46: "Ideo sacrum universale concilium reducat et reformet ecclesiam universalem in iure antiquo et abusivam papalem in decreto et decretalibus, Sexto et Clementinis nec non extravagantibus papalibus pretensam limitet potestatem."

Nicholas of Clémanges, in Andrew of Escobar, in the *Capitula agendorum,* and in the pamphlet *De materia concilii generalis* by Cardinal d'Ailly. At the Council itself it was heard in numerous sermons and motions, above all in the *Avisamenta* of Dietrich von Niem and in Gerson's treatises *Tractatus de simonia* and *Ad reformationem contra simoniam.*[17]

Reform writings also criticized the form of the papal election. Not only the cardinals should have a vote; in alternate elections there should be another electoral college, to be determined by the Council. The Pope must not be always chosen from the same nation; and under no circumstances might two Popes in succession come from the same nation. It would be best to alternate between cisalpine and transalpine candidates. Intimately connected with the preceding was the reform of the College of Cardinals, which, according to some very critical voices, should be entirely abolished. The cardinals should not always come from the same country but from the various ecclesiastical provinces; from no nation should there be enough to give it a majority of the votes. The number of cardinals should be decreased, so that there should be, for example, between eighteen and twenty-four and never more than thirty. Their creation should take place by means of a vote in consistory, and for the future they should no longer obtain the *commenda* but only minor benefices. The income allowed them fluctuated between three and four thousand gold florins.

The Council of Constance was very much preoccupied with this reform program, only selections from which are here given, and the old and often repeated assertion that it did little for the reform of the Church is completely unjustified. Three commissions and, according to need, a group of smaller committees were instituted for handling reform questions. They corresponded to the momentary political situation of the Council. The first commission, with eight members from each of the four nations and three cardinals, met from August 1415 to the summer of 1417. The second, consisting of five delegates of each of the five nations, could function only from the summer of 1417 to the election of the new Pope in the fall of that year. Following the election of Martin V, in the same month of November a

---

[17] For the reform literature *cf.* the general survey in *Fliche-Martin,* 14, 892; J. Haller, *Papsttum und Kirchenreform.* On the Bishop of Senez, Scholz, *op. cit. (supra,* footnote 15). On Nicholas of Clémanges, *LThK,* VII (2nd ed. 1962), 983 f., and the edition of A. Coville, *Le traité de la ruine de l'église de Nicolas de Clamanges* (Paris 1936). On Andrew of Escobar see E. Candal, *Concilium Florentinum, Documenta et scriptores,* series B, vol. IV, fasc. I (1952), XVIII–LXXVII, and V. Beltrán de Heredia in *CTom,* 80 (1953), 335–40; A. D. De Sousa Costa, *Tribulações de Mestre André Dias, apreciado poligrafo de Quatrocentos* (1964). The "Capitula agendorum" are in H. Finke, *Acta conc. Constanc.,* IV, 539–83. The *Tractatus de materia concilii generalis* in B. Meller, *Studien zur Erkenntnislehre des Peter von Ailly,* 289–336, is incomplete; complete edition in F. Oakley, *The Political Thought of Pierre d'Ailly,* 244–342. Gerson's writings in Jean Gerson, *Œuvres complètes,* VI (1965), 167–74, 179–81.

third commission was instituted, comprising six representatives of each of the five nations and six cardinals.

Out of the wealth of reform proposals, what was decreed by the Council? Here, more than in the other tasks of the Council, general politics were the determining factor. When, following thorough preliminary work by the first and second reform commissions, much material was ready for formulation and voting, the reform got bogged down in the so-called "priority controversy" in the summer of 1417.

It is entirely understandable that at last, following the deposition of Benedict XIII, persons wanted to proceed to the election of a new Pope, especially since the Council was already in its third year. Equally understandable are the exertions of Sigismund and his adherents somehow to bring reform to a conclusion, since only through reform did it seem possible to avoid a new schism. The outcome was a compromise: the reform articles already approved by all the nations were to be published by a conciliar decree and put into effect before the papal election. This was done on 9 October 1417, in the thirty-ninth session.

The following points were covered: *De conciliis generalibus. Provisio adversus futura schismata praecavenda. De professione facienda per papam. Ne praelati transferantur inviti. De spoliis et procurationibus.* In the five decrees under these headings were contained these regulations: the holding of a general council, at first after five, then after seven, and thereafter every ten years; precautions against the future occurrence of a schism; the making of a profession of faith by every newly elected Pope; the non-transferability of the higher clergy; and the suppression of *spolia* and procurations. Moreover, in the compromise the future Pope, soon to be elected, was obliged to Church reform "in capite et curia Romana" at this very Council.

On 30 October, in the fortieth session, the Council decreed the implementation of these stipulations and specified the details in eighteen subtitles: *De numero, qualitate et natione dominorum cardinalium. De reservationibus sedis apostolicae. De annatis, communibus servitiis et minutis. De collationibus beneficiorum. De causis in Romana curia tractandis vel non. De appellationibus ad Romanam curiam. De officiis cancellariae et poenitentiariae. De exemtionibus et incorporationibus tempore schismatis factis. De commendis. De confirmationibus electionum. De fructibus medii temporis. De non alienandis bonis Romanae Ecclesiae et aliarum ecclesiarum. Propter quae et quomodo papa possit corrigi vel deponi. De extirpatione simoniae. De dispensationibus. De provisione papae et cardinalium. De indulgentiis. De decimis.*

The activity of the third reform commission was under omens different from those of its predecessors, since now the Pope also had something to say. In conformity with the obligation imposed on him, he treated with the commission and the individual nations. The difficulty of adjusting general decrees to the peculiar wishes of the nations was solved in such a way that seven reform decrees were promulgated by the Council in the Pope's name in the forty-third session on 21 March 1418. These were the reform articles that had found general acceptance: *De exemtionibus, De unionibus et incorporationibus, De fructibus medii temporis, De simonia, De dispensationibus, De decimis et aliis oneribus,* and *De vita et honestate clericorum.* In addition, the concordats agreed upon by the Pope with the individual nations but not yet formally concluded were read at this time.

The reform decrees were approved *conciliariter,* the concordats *nationaliter,* and the execution of the version agreeable to the Pope was certified. The separate arrangements with the five nations were drawn up in three versions, with the German, the English, and the three Romance nations. All except the English concordat were concluded for a period of five years, namely until the next council, at Pavia, which was to continue the work of reform.[18] Already in the autumn of 1416 the Bishop of Lodi had demanded that, in order to continue the reform discussion and to prepare for the next council, a commission, to be set up now, should obtain opinions from the universities on important questions; the representatives of the universities should then report at the next council.[19] Naturally, not all reform aspirations were fulfilled by the decrees and the concordats, but the Council had done good work. However, very much or everything depended on the attitude of the new Pope and his successors to the decree "Frequens."

The importance of the Council of Constance has been variously estimated down to the present, and the evaluation extends from full or partial recognition to rejection. The Council of Constance, like that of Basel, was not contained in the enumeration of the general councils current from Bellarmine on. This computation sprang, not from scholarship, but from a preponderantly apologetic effort and hence it has little claim to objectivity. Constance and Basel belonged to the group of synods that were only partially to be recognized, because they did not correspond to the canon provided for an evaluation of the past. But a part of the decrees of Constance are contained in the fourth volume of the *Editio Romana* (1612), the official Roman edition which was prepared in a congregation set up for this express purpose.[20] This onesided viewpoint and the effort to decide historical facts by ecclesiastical authority were opposed by scholars who were less apologetically oriented.[21] The evaluation depends especially on the attitude to the so-called "decree on

[18] *Raccolta di concordati su materie ecclesiastiche,* ed. A. Mercati (Rome 1919), pp. 144–68.
[19] H. Finke, *Acta conc. Constanc.,* IV, 712 f.
[20] V. Peri, "Il numero dei concili ecumenici nella tradizione cattolica moderna," *Aevum,* 37 (1963), 430–501; K. A. Fink, "Konziliengeschichtsschreibung im Wandel?" *Theologie im Wandel: Festschrift zum 150jährigen Jubiläum der kath.-theol. Fakultät der Universität Tübingen* (Munich 1967), 179–89.
[21] K. A. Fink, "Zur Beurteilung des Grossen abendländischen Schismas," *ZKG,* 73 (1962).

superiority" of the fifth session.[22] It would be preferable now not to gauge this decree by the constitutions of Vatican I, but rather to proceed in the opposite direction and thereby to do justice to the historical development.[23] Then the question withdraws behind the perhaps necessary and express approval of the decrees by Martin V and Eugene IV.[24] That the new Pope exerted himself to maintain the position gained in the thirteenth and fourteenth centuries is understandable,[25] but his strivings found a limit in the almost universal teaching of the theological world on the higher power of the general council. It would be incorrect to accept only the extreme tendencies as the expression of the time; different views stood beside one another. But there is no doubt that the higher position of the general council had already been represented for a long time and by a much larger portion of theologians. The flight of John XXIII was only the occasion for actualizing and confirming, at this very moment, the previously more habitual power of the council. Everything connected with reform — "without a council, no reform" — points in this direction, especially the decree "Frequens." From

[22] It is advisable to speak of the decree of the fifth session instead of the decree "Haec sancta." About a dozen decrees of Constance begin with "Haec sancta"; they have not in general been transmitted accurately in regard to the opening words.

[23] Cf. H. Riedlinger, "Hermeneutische Überlegungen zu den Konstanzer Dekreten," in Franzen-Müller, Das Konzil von Konstanz, 214–38; August Franzen, "The Council of Constance: Present State of The Problem," Concilium, 7, Historical Problems of Church Renewal (Glen Rock, N. J. 1965), 29–68; A. Franzen, "Das Konstanzer Konzil. Probleme, Aufgaben und Stand der Konzilsforschung," Concilium, 1 (1965), 555–74; P. De Vooght, Les Pouvoirs du concile et l'autorité du pape au concile de Constance (Paris 1965); W. Brandmüller, "Besitzt das Konstanzer Dekret Haec sancta dogmatische Verbindlichkeit?" RQ, 62 (1967), 1–17; B. Tierney, "Hermeneutics and History. The Problem of Haec sancta," Festschrift für Bertie Wilkinson (Toronto 1967); J. Gill, "Il decreto Haec Sancta Synodus del Concilio di Costanza," RSTI, 21 (1967), 123–30; R. Bäumer, "Die Interpretation und Verbindlichkeit der Konstanzer Dekrete," ThPQ, 116 (1968), 44–52; I. H. Pichler, Die Verbindlichkeit der Konstanzer Dekrete (Vienna 1967).

[24] On the actual recognition see K. A. Fink, Die konziliare Idee im späten Mittelalter. Vorträge und Forschungen, 9 (Constance 1965); P. De Vooght, Les Pouvoirs, 55–80.

[25] Here belongs the evaluation of Martin V's intended prohibition of an appeal from the Pope to the council in connection with the appeal lodged by the Poles. In the final session the Pope had refused to allow the condemnation of Falkenberg by a conciliar decree, since the matter had been dealt with nationaliter rather than conciliariter. Thereupon the Poles appealed to the next council. In consistory the Pope caused the reading of the sketch of a bull with a prohibition of such appeals, but the bull was not published. Gerson sharply attacked the Pope's contemplated step (Œuvres complètes, 6 [1965], 283–90). Several authors consider the question as pertaining only to the Poles' conflict with the Pope. But R. Bäumer, "Das Verbot der Konzilsappellation Martins V. in Konstanz," in Franzen-Müller, Das Konzil von Konstanz, 187–213, maintains, with copious recourse to the literature, the universal validity of the prohibition. No matter how this question is decided, it in no way alters the fact that quite different views were then defended and that the later prohibitions by Pius II and Julius II were vain, because in them persons rightly saw only a partisan stand.

the viewpoint of the contemporary political and intellectual situation, the Council of Constance in its entirety must be regarded as ecumenical and its decrees as universally binding.

Martin V (1417–31)

The first and only Pope from the Colonna family was a Roman in the full sense of the word. Always at the Curia, as a Cardinal from 1405, under Popes Boniface IX, Innocent VII, and Gregory XII he had abundant opportunity to become conversant with the confused situation in political and ecclesiastical life. But the stayed aloof from it, except in the preparations for the Council of Pisa, when he displayed great zeal to make it possible. He went to Constance with John XXIII, stayed with the refugee Pope for a short time, and then returned to the Council. Busy on many committees, he was not very prominent to outsiders and in the conclave he was regarded as one who, while perhaps having few friends, had scarcely an enemy; hence he was a genuine compromise candidate. With his election the Council acquired a new appearance, for, in accord with tradition, the Pope assumed its direction. This was very difficult, however, since it was not easy to distinguish what was the Council's business and what pertained to the Pope and his Curia.

The Pope proceeded at once to construct a Curia. Enough persons from the three now reunited obediences were at his disposal but not much money. Furthermore, in keeping with the conciliar decrees, the number of officials had to be reduced. The new curialists came predominantly from the Avignon obedience, which had the advantage of a longer and less interrupted tradition. As has already been said, the reform, discussed at length and in detail, was settled to a certain extent when the generally accepted motions were enacted as decrees and the more special questions were adjusted in the concordats with the nations. The announcements of the election were received in a friendly manner for the most part, though in some cases their reception left something to be desired. In a skilful, reserved, and apparently accommodating manner Martin V had achieved a great deal without any great conflicts. The general exhaustion of the Council did the rest, so that some still unsettled questions could be postponed until the next council, to meet in five years. Until then, therefore, the Pope was able to save a considerable part of his current rights and revenues. His task was now to salvage as much as possible from the new situation, and for this he needed a certain independence in ecclesiastical and political matters.

But how was this to be achieved? From the political viewpoint, Martin V was the right man for the papacy. Since he was regarded as Pope of the Germans and the English, he had to repulse all of Sigismund's efforts to keep him in imperial territory for a while. From the start of his pontificate he pushed for a return to Rome; Avignon was for him out of the question, though persons there were expecting him. He felt that only in Rome could he escape the often overwhelming influence of the states and the predominance of the Council. In addition, for a merely relative independence a financial basis was required, and only one territory offered it. But almost insuperable obstacles stood in the way of a quick return to Rome. During the Schism and especially since the death of Boniface IX the Papal State had fallen into a critical situation. One could hardly speak any more of the Papal State, for the real lords were King Ladislas of Naples up to the opening of the Council of Constance and then, during it, the first great *condottiere*, Braccio of Montone, who ruled all of Central Italy and was subjugating more and more territories. If the Legate appointed by the Council was seemingly the ruler in Rome under Neapolitan influence, in reality the local powers ruled there, just as in the many smaller states and territories. Toward the end of the Council and at the beginning of Martin V's pontificate there loomed the possibility of an invasion of South Italy by Benedict XIII.

Together with the establishing of a Curia and the sending of cardinal legates to Aragón and France, Martin's first instructions had to do with the situation of the Papal State, where he appointed rectors and officials. The Council and the new Pope had issued decrees on the administration of the Papal State, the recovery of the lost territories, and the duration of the vicariates.[26] The goal — the reestablishment of papal sovereignty — was clear, but it was difficult to realize, especially from afar. Hence, for all his seeming patience, Martin worked for the quick liquidation of the Council and his departure from Constance. There began at once a vigorous diplomatic activity, which was to last throughout the pontificate. In view of the rapidly changing balance of power in Europe and especially in Italy at that time, this meant a ceaseless tension, which filled the entire reign.

The first task was to clear the road to Italy. When on 16 May 1418 Martin V left Constance and went through western Switzerland toward Geneva, the remainder of his route was not yet visible; at Avignon it was expected that he would come there. After a stay of several weeks at Geneva and some lively political activity, at the beginning of September the Curia proceeded *via* the Mont-Cenis to Upper Italy, where stops of several days were made at Turin, Pavia, and Milan. For more than three months at Mantua it was not clear whether the route to Rome should be selected *via* Pisa or Florence, since rebellious Bologna was unwilling to receive the Pope. By way of Ferrara, Ravenna, and Forlì the procession moved to Florence, where the Pope had to wait for almost one and a half years before he could finally

[26] B. Hübler, *Die Constanzer Reform und die Concordate von 1418* (Leipzig 1867), 39, 99, 144, 238.

enter the Eternal City on 28 September 1420. These details should make clear how difficult was the new Pope's situation.

The chief difficulty was the *condottiere* in the grand style, Braccio of Montone, with his supremacy in Perugia and far beyond Umbria; a great part of the Papal State had become financially subject to him. That the Colonna Pope could only take a dim view of Braccio's "state" was clear to the *condottiere*, and so recognition came only reluctantly in the areas dependent upon him. While still at Constance the Pope began the process of isolating Braccio by making contact with Milan, Florence, Naples, and many smaller *signorie*. From the outset he decided to get rid of the dangerous *condottiere* by military action, especially when the first negotiations were not very favourable. Only the extensive promises which Martin had to make at Florence in February 1420 opened the road to Rome.[27] But they implied no more than an armistice, and the great confrontation was yet to come. Uprisings at Bologna, which Martin suppressed with armed force, and the struggle for Naples postponed the reckoning with Braccio. It occurred in May 1424, when Braccio was defeated and found death at the siege of Aquila. The Pope at last had a free hand in domestic matters and could turn with more success to the recovery and reorganization of his state.

His relationship with Naples was of great importance.[28] In order to bring about the evacuation of Rome, which was occupied by Neapolitan troops, the Pope made great concessions in this regard too while still at Constance, including even the coronation of Queen Joanna II. Domestic difficulties in the Kingdom induced the Curia to turn again to the French House of Anjou and to enfeoff Louis III with the crown of Naples and the right to the succession after the Queen's death. But this led to a countermeasure when Joanna adopted the young King of Aragón, Alfonso V, who presented a danger to the Curia. Then Braccio went over to the Aragonese faction. When in the summer of 1421 Alfonso entered Naples, the situation became very critical for the Pope and for a Papal State that was in process of reconstruction. Whatever money could be raised was diverted to the levying of great military companies, for the Pope was firmly determined to take up the struggle. The strength of his forces saved him from defeat in the field and, through the good offices of Florentine envoys, there occurred in the fall of 1421 an armistice, which was followed by further negotiations. In the spring of 1424 the King of Aragón left Naples, only to return with more luck under Martin's successor. The Pope had succeeded in keeping the Aragonese great power away from Italy and the Papal State.

In addition to diplomacy, of which the Pope was a real master, he also displayed, as we have seen, an occasional resort to force, as in Bologna's

[27] Text of the treaty in Valentini, "Lo stato di Braccio," *ASRomana*, 52 (1931), 121–28 (the offprint).
[28] K. A. Fink, *Martin V. und Aragón* (Berlin 1938), 60–112.

first great revolt in 1420 and in the second, which involved all of Upper Italy in 1428–29. By means of a considerable military levy he compelled the refractory city to yield and thus retained the important northern pillar of his state.[29] This state was not a centrally administered territory in the modern sense. A variety of bonds held it together: direct subjection to the Curia by means of legates, governors, and rectors, and short-term enfeoffments with vicariates. The decisive factor, however, was that the finances of these areas were largely at the disposal of the Curia. To the extent that the sources provide reliable information, two-thirds of the income of the pontificate came from the Papal State — and were in turn expended on it. Because of the importance of finance, the *Camera Apostolica* was the highest administrative department of the Papal State. Rome, formerly so restless, was under the Pope's absolute rule from the time of his entry there, even though the forms of administration might appear otherwise. In return, the dilapidated city was splendidly renovated, especially the great basilicas, streets, and bridges and the fortifications of the city and its immediate vicinity. It goes without saying that the Colonna family in its many offshoots was much used in the administration of the Papal State. Considering the uncommonly difficult situation in which the Pope found himself after his return from the Council, he needed absolutely trustworthy people if he was to realize his plans. But this nepotism and its attendant enrichment went too far, led to conflicts with other great families, especially the Orsini, and was the motive for reprisals after the Pope's death.

Thus far we have spoken only of political enterprises which served for the restoring of the Curia's secular power. What about the spiritual power, the relationship to Church and council? In many respects the Council of Constance had sketched the further development, but the details were not yet visible. Following the achievements thus far it was natural that here too the Pope would take matters into his own hands in the sense of restoration — nothing less could be expected of a Colonna. This was obvious in the prudent but unambiguous efforts at the close of the Council. In the limits drawn by the conciliar decrees he tried to regain as much as possible in rights before the new general council, to be convoked in about five years, could undertake new measures. The customary chancery rules were published at Geneva with the traditional dating from the day of coronation. But a beginning had already been made at Constance with the granting of expectatives. In this context belong also the less well known reform proposals of two commissions of cardinals; for the most part they were rejected by the Pope. They were made before the Councils of Pavia and Basel, probably to anticipate the tumultuous reform desires that were to be expected.[30] If Martin V

[29] *Idem,* "Martin V. und Bologna," *QfdAB,* 23 (1931 f.), 182–217; also B. Partner, *The Papal State under Martin V* (London 1958), 92.
[30] J. Haller, *Concilium Basiliense,* I (1896), 107–10, 163–83.

was not a friend of conciliar reform which might lay a hand on the organization that he was defending, he did everything to guide the implementation of the rights pertaining to him in orderly paths; hence a reform of administration. He honestly exerted himself to see to it that the cardinal legate in Germany observed the principles communicated to him in regard to the filling of benefices. [31] This is apparent in several reform decrees for the curialists and the curial offices and can be demonstrated from the numerous volumes of registers of his pontificate. On the expiration of the concordats after five years he reverted without more ado to the old system of reservations and provisions in so far as no general decrees of the Council stood in the way and the countries concerned were agreeable. Thus the revenues of the *Camera Apostolica* from *servitia* and annates were not inconsiderable.

With regard to the Council he observed the decree "Frequens," even though he was reluctant and was forced by public opinion. Accordingly, the Council that was due to take place in five years was summoned to Pavia but it was soon transferred to Siena. The attendance was quite small and the political situation was extremely dangerous. It cannot now be determined whether the Pope seriously intended to go to the Council. The fear that, in the midst of the Neapolitan conflict, it would be used by the King of Aragón as a means of pressure was certainly not unfounded. Determined not to tolerate any revival of the Council at the height of the crisis with Braccio, he proceeded to dissolve it before it could show its possibilities. Decrees on lessening the Curia's income were at this point unacceptable to him. Hence all conciliar discussions were deferred for seven more years, since the letter of "Frequens" had been sufficiently respected. [32] Shortly before his death Martin summoned, but not voluntarily, the Council of Basel and appointed Cardinal Julian Cesarini as president with authority to dissolve it. Hence it came about that a continuous curial administration was and is more than a match for a council meeting only at infrequent intervals. The Pope greatly exploited this advantage. It makes little sense to deduce from this procedure a theological concept, just as it would seem hopeless to include Martin in one of many tendencies and to label him, for example, a moderate conciliarist. He was only a politician, though a great politician with a bent for power, and such was what the Church and the Curia needed in order to be able to

---

[31] K. A. Fink, "Die politische Korrespondenz Martins V. nach den Brevenregistern," *QFIAB*, 25 (1933 f.), 184, no. 33: "[circumspectio tua] que animum et propositum nostrum novit et quanto studio laboremus Romanam curiam a priorum temporum immoderata licentia et consuetudine revocare; quod enim de firmitate nostra loquuntur dicant ut velint; nos vero non intelligimus, ubi possint ostendere aliquid nostra scientia atque consensu iniuste aut turpiter factum esse"; 185, no. 37: "quia intentio nostra est, ut omnia cum equitate et iustitia disponantur, ut nemo iuste querele causam habere possit."

[32] W. J. Koudelka, "Eine neue Quelle zur Generalsynode von Siena 1423–1424," *ZKG*, 74 (1963), 244–64.

exist again, in the old style, after the confusion of the Western Schism and the Council of Constance. A man of very simple life, he used all the means which his state and the government of the Universal Church offered him for reestablishing the Papal State, whose third founder he is rightly called.[33] If his sepulchral inscription in the Lateran extols him as *temporum suorum felicitas,* this may be correct for Rome and the Papal State. When he died on 20 February 1431 he left to his successor, despite all the tensions, a state in relatively good order and hence a basis on which the Roman Curia could look forward to further political and conciliar developments more calmly than had been possible hitherto. But it is not permissible to conclude, as has often been done, that this was right and divinely willed.

CHAPTER 50

Eugene IV and
The Council of Basel-Ferrara-Florence

While Martin V at his death on 20 February 1431 had left a Papal State that was in a peaceful condition, still the conclave that met to choose his successor heralded new difficulties. The cardinals gathered in Santa Maria *sopra Minerva,* but not all of them were present. Despite the binding instructions of the Colonna Pope, the majority prevented Dominic Capranica, who had not yet been proclaimed, from taking part in the election, which on 3 March fell on Gabriel Condulmer, a Venetian and nephew of Gregory XII. He called himself Eugene IV (1431–47); his pontificate was not one of the happiest. Since the cardinals had been dissatisfied with Martin V's authoritarian administration, an election capitulation had been decided upon and signed by all the cardinals. It demanded not so much a change in the constitution of the Church, as has often been said, as it did an implementation of the Council of Constance. In it were unequivocally expressed the aspirations of the College of Cardinals for a share in the government of the Church. But current demands were just as clearly registered: reform of the Curia in head and members; general reform at a general council; consent of the College for a transfer of the Curia; observance of the rules issued at Constance in regard to the nomination of cardinals; a sharing by the College in the income, in accord with the arrangements of Nicholas IV, and in the

---

[33] H. Zimmermann, "Thomas Ebendorfers Schismentraktat," *AÖG,* 120. Band, 2. Heft (1954). Here, pages 71–74, the Pope is represented as primitively greedy and in general is badly treated, but the matters are reported only from hearsay and do not stand firm against examination.

government of the Papal State; no proceeding against the person and property of a cardinal without the consent of the majority; and, whenever the formula "de fratrum nostrorum consilio" was in a decree, the listing by name of the consenting cardinals. This election capitulation was again sworn to by Eugene IV after his election and confirmed by apostolic constitutions after his coronation.[1]

Martin V had been skillful as a politician and as ruler of the Papal State. His successor, Eugene IV, a former canon regular, was to an equal degree incompetent. His rash proceedings against the Colonna produced long lasting troubles in all parts of the Papal State. Risings in individual provinces and in Rome itself could be put down only by great exertions. In 1434 the Pope had to flee from the Eternal City; he found refuge at Florence and then at Bologna. He was not able to return to Rome until 1443.

The pontificate of Eugene IV was entirely overshadowed by the Council of Basel. The date of its opening had been determined by Martin V, and the new Pope at once confirmed the appointment of the Cardinal Legate in Germany, Julian Cesarini, as legate and president of the Council. Since Cesarini was still involved in the anti-Hussite campaign, he had the Council opened at Basel on 23 July 1431 by his vicars, John of Ragusa and John of Palomar. The number of those present was still quite meagre when Cesarini reached Basel in September. Contrary to the election capitulation that he had sworn to observe, Eugene IV opposed the Council from the start. Following the example of Martin V, who had managed to dissolve the previous Council of Siena, Eugene, through his unsure, vacillating, and even dishonest conduct, led himself, the Curia, and all of Christendom into the worst difficulties.

In the bull "Quoniam alto" of 12 November 1431, which only ten cardinals signed, he dissolved the Council and summoned a new synod, which was supposed to meet in Bologna eighteen months later. The legate was ordered to carry out the dissolution and depart. But before anything could be done at Basel, the Pope, at the consistory of 18 December, published the bull of dissolution, even though some of the cardinals were not in agreement with this procedure and challenged the Pope's right to dissolve a legitimately meeting Council. Meanwhile, the first solemn session had taken place at Basel on 14 December, with the reading of the decree "Frequens" and of the bull of convocation. The legate declined the mandate committed to him, and so a member of the household of the Bishop of Parenzo, who had brought the bull, intended to publish it on 13 January. He was prevented by an exodus on the part of the Fathers. The Council organized itself in the second

---

[1] J. Lulvès, "Päpstliche Wahlkapitulationen," QFIAB, 12 (1909), 212–35; W. Ullmann, The Legal Validity of the Papal Electoral Pacts," ECI, 12 (1956), 246–78; W. Brandmüller, "Der Übergang vom Pontifikat Martins V. zu Eugen IV.," QFIAB, 47 (1967), 596–629.

session, held on 15 February 1432, following the pattern of the Council of Constance and the decree "Frequens." The Pope was pressed to withdraw the dissolution and it was demanded that he and the cardinals must appear at Basel.

To appreciate the situation it is important to note that the majority of the cardinals adhered to the Council; only six out of twenty-one were on the Pope's side. From then on Pope and Council were hostile to each other, and, as at Constance, the future fate of the Synod depended essentially on the politics of the various states. On the Council's side were at first the King of the Romans, France, England, Scotland, Castile, Burgundy, and Milan. At this time the Pope could count on only Venice and Florence as loyal adherents. But the attitude of the powers to the Council continually changed. During the tedious negotiations with the Pope the Council, now better attended, arranged its own organization and personnel. As at Constance, it was desired also at Basel to organize by nations, but the very uneven participation — the Germans and the French were the strongest in representation – compelled the setting up of permanent committees, the so-called "deputations," with the College of Twelve as the group of presidents. The political situation, above all the unrest in the Papal State, forced the Pope to give in, although King Sigismund of Germany, because of his impending coronation as Emperor, gave him assistance and restrained the Council from precipitate measures. Since a new schism was becoming a distinct possibility, most states advised yielding and compromise. The Council was unmoved, and the Pope had to agree entirely with Cesarini's proposals and, in the withdrawal of the bull of dissolution, required by the Cardinal President, substitute "decernimus et declaramus," in speaking of the legitimate continuance of the synod, for his own formula, "volumus et contentamur." This he did in the bull "Dudum sacrum" of 15 December 1433. The presidents sent by the Pope were admitted only with great restrictions and took the required oath to the decrees of Constance.[2] The long and unpleasant jockeying had led to an armistice rather than to peace; it had also led to a hardening of positions, in particular on the part of the Council Fathers. The Pope was mostly to blame for the situation that had arisen.

The question of union with the Greek Church decided the contest between Council and Pope. Martin V had reached an agreement with the Byzantine court relevant to a council in the West, and in the first year of his pontificate Eugene IV obtained assurances of Greek attendance at a Western council, for example in Bologna. Aware of the political importance for whichever succeeded in restoring union between the separated Churches, both Pope and Council took great pains in regard to the Greeks. From the spring of 1433 embassies of the Council as well as of the Pope went to Constantinople, and

[2] J. Haller, *Conc. Basil.*, I, 22 f.

Greek envoys travelled to the West. The means resorted to in order to gain the Byzantine Emperor and to outdo the other side were not exactly edifying. Conflict over the meeting place of the union council went on for years. While the Pope and most Greeks favoured, apart from Constantinople, a city in Italy, the Council for obvious reasons insisted on Basel itself, Avignon, or Savoy. The final voting produced a schism. More than two-thirds of the members held to the proposal of the Council. Despite many efforts for an understanding, a memorable scene took place on 7 May 1437: each group promulgated its decision in the Basel cathedral, but only that of the majority was sealed. Nevertheless, the Pope, in the bull "Salvatoris et Dei nostri" of 30 May 1437, confirmed the minority decision, and, after long debates and recourse to not unobjectionable means, his envoys at Constantinople succeeded in winning the Greeks for the minority and hence for the holding of the council in Italy. On 18 September 1437, in the bull "Doctoris gentium," recognizing the minority as the *pars sanior*, Eugene IV transferred the Council to Ferrara. Thus ended the first phase of the Council of Basel. The question of what it achieved naturally presents itself.

The repeated defeats of the anti-Hussite crusade armies suggested the idea of negotiations. Hence it is not surprising that after the defeat at Domažlice in August 1431 the Cardinal Legate and one so familiar with the Hussite danger as John of Ragusa pressed for an invitation to the leaders of the Hussite factions. As early as 15 November 1431, and hence shortly after the opening of the Council, there was issued a message to appear in Basel. Many discussions relevant to safety and free discussion led to the very accomodating letter of safe-conduct of 20 June 1432, in the fourth session. An imposing embassy of some 300 persons appeared on 4 January 1433 and, after the customary formal greetings, the discussions got under way between Rokycana and Procop for the Hussites and John of Ragusa, Henry Kalteisen, Aegidius Charlier, and John of Palomar. The Bohemians left Basel on 14 April, but the negotiations were continued at Prague and led to agreement on the four articles of Prague, which had in the meantime been frequently modified, concerning the chalice for the laity, free preaching, the punishment of those guilty of serious sins, and a far-reaching renunciation of ecclesiastical property. This agreement, the so-called Prague *Compactata*, was promulgated on 5 July 1436 in the presence of the Emperor at the Diet of Iglau, and was ratified by the Council of Basel on 15 January 1437. The *Compactata* were not ratified by the Curia and were annulled in 1462. But this settlement of the Bohemian affair was a great success for the Council. If there could have been an accommodation at Constance in regard to the chalice, Christendom would probably have been spared much anguish.

Despite some accomplishments, the reform of the Church could not be brought to a conclusion at Constance. A glance at the enormous reform literature makes this clear, and the decree "Frequens" had been issued for the very purpose of assuring the reform. And there have come down proposals which envisaged the thorough study of specific matters, such as union with the Greeks, by commissions of cardinals and university professors in the interval till the next council.[3] Since the Council of Siena, where the reform proposals had hardly been considered, had been dissolved, persons were looking to Basel for decisive progress. As was the case with the Council of Constance, three tasks were assigned to that of Basel in Martin V's bull of convocation of 1 February 1431: concern for the Christian faith, the restoration of peace in Christendom, and the reform of the Church. It is beyond doubt that the last of these was regarded as the most important.[4] If, later, the conflict with Eugene IV dominated any estimation and evaluation of the Council, reform must still be considered the real and most significant achievement of the Synod. But with the treatment of reform there began the breach which lasted throughout the Council and led for some time to schism.

Soon after the opening of the Council a reform commission of twenty-four members was set up. The well known eighteen articles of the Constance reform demand had been discussed and passed only in part. This work was now resumed at Basel, but it required a long time before any order could be discerned in the reform motions, while again and again the effort for reform was interrupted by the conflict with Pope and Curia.

Following the expiration of the concordats and the disappointing outcome of the Council of Siena, the filling of the higher benefices was once more an open question. In addition, a group of proposals and memoranda were soon presented to the Council with the aim of completely eliminating papal reservations. This was a theme that had been for decades at the very centre of *reformatio capitis et curiae Romanae* and was intended to lead back to the ancient law. The French and the Germans were the ones chiefly interested in the total eradication of the papal right of collation, while the English, Italians, and Spaniards were of the contrary opinion, since their governments were able to protect them from the clutches of the Curia. The so-called election decree, published on 13 July 1433, in the twelfth solemn session, is rightly termed moderate. It abolished general and specific reservations of bishoprics and monasteries and prescribed election by the qualified bodies according to earlier usage. The Pope could decide otherwise only in exceptional cases and with a precise listing of his reasons. Upon assuming office each Pope had to bind himself under oath to observe the decree. Since Eugene IV paid no heed, even though his presidents had declared that the Pope was prepared to accept every reform measure of the Council, a more

[3] H. Finke, *Acta conc. Const.*, IV, IV, 712 f.
[4] *Mon. conc. general.*, II, 700: "... ad reformacionem faciendam principaliter fuerat congregata."

precise version of the decree was substituted in the twenty-third session, in March 1436.

The question of the payments made to the Curia, summarized under the term "annates," had also to begin over again. Here too there was a two-way split: Germans and French opposed annates, while Spaniards and Italians were uninterested, because they were in a position not to be molested, or at least not seriously, by curial demands and in the prospective event of a general taxation of ecclesiastical benefices for the benefit of the Curia they were afraid of being required to pay. The outcome was tedious consultations and many proposals, in which the question of indemnification of the Curia for the loss of annates occupied an important place. In view of the Pope's very difficult, even if not unmerited, situation this was understandable. The discussion was heightened and also prolonged by the preparation of a fundamental decree on simony with the decisive participation of the Cardinal Legate. The decree on annates, of the twenty-first session on 9 June 1435, peremptorily forbade all payments at the filling of benefices by either the Curia or the ordinaries. Thus was the late mediaeval development ended and, above all, a serious blow was given to the Curia. Nevertheless, it is noteworthy that Cesarini himself, as the expert on sentiment beyond the Alps, spoke very energetically in favour of the decree.

Long in need of reform was the curial system of procedures, which had assumed a downright colossal magnitude. Since not much had been accomplished in this area at Constance, the old demands for limiting the Roman jurisdiction in favour of the ordinary courts were renewed at Basel. In several decrees of the Council there was enacted a restriction to *causae maiores* as in the old law, appeals were curtailed, and precautions were taken against the harassing of occupants of benefices.

Of special importance in the reform of the Curia were the decrees on the papal election and the College of Cardinals. If one were unable to go back to the reform proposals before, during, and after the Council of Constance, the Basel decrees would have to be regarded as far-reaching. Precisely considered, they were a balanced product of earlier reform literature and searching consultation. Whereas the election of the Pope of unity at Constance took place outside what had hitherto been customary and the prescriptions laid down by conciliar decrees and papal directives for their implementation, the Council of Basel reverted to the old practice, allotting the election once again to the cardinals alone, despite many contrary voices. New, however, was the rule in regard to voting: that at most three candidates might be named; if more than one candidate was written on the ballot, one of those named had to be a non-cardinal. In this way the much complained of inbreeding in the College would be at least theoretically limited.

To what extent Basel was strictly a continuation of Constance appears above all in the oath to be taken by the newly elected Pope. The proposals at Constance required, besides the making of the so-called profession of faith of Boniface VIII, a whole series of promises relating to the government of the Church and of the Papal State. There is no question that here the College of Cardinals was keenly interested in the formulating of the oath, and the election capitulation of 1431 points in the same direction. The Pope's oath as prescribed by the Council of Basel retained completely the brief version used at Constance except that, understandably, it included also the General Councils of Constance and Basel and their decrees, especially in regard to the observance of the decree "Frequens." From the experiences of the fourteenth century and of the most recent decades there proceeded the listing of guidelines for the carrying out of their functions by the Popes.

The decrees of the twenty-third session *de numero et qualitate cardinalium* likewise adhered closely to the Constance proposals, reform acts, and concordats. The number of cardinals was to be at most twenty-four and they were to be doctors of theology or of canon or civil law. The Constance prescriptions that cardinals must no longer be elevated merely by oral expression of opinion were extended at Basel to include the requirement of a written consent of a majority of the College. The so difficult and much discussed problem of the representation of all countries in the Senate of the Church was prudently decided in the sense that no nation might have more than one-third of the cardinals at any one time.

Ferrara and Florence

The Council that Eugene IV had summoned to Ferrara was opened in January 1438, though without the Greeks. They only arrived at Ferrara at the beginning of March. Having reached Venice at the beginning of February, they had finally decided, on the advice of the Doge, to attend the Pope's Council. While the Curia pressed for quick action, the Greeks worked for delay in order to await the Western princes or their envoys. And so an interval of four months was first agreed upon. The hopes of the Pope and of the Byzantine Emperor John VIII for representatives of the Western states were not realized; only the Angevins and the Duke of Burgundy sent official envoys. In June began the theological discussions. The forms of the discussions were quite varied. There were few general sessions; for the most part the work was done in committee discussions, in which prepared *cedulae* were debated by experts of both groups, often in a very sharp fashion. Joseph II, Patriarch of Constantinople, was favourable to union but he died before the publication of the union decree at Florence.

Because of an alleged danger of pestilence, but really for financial reasons, the Synod was transferred to Florence in January 1439. The expenses of the conciliar meetings were a burden on the Curia. After long and fruitful discussions, conversations between Emperor and Pope, and repeated threats of departure by the Greeks, there finally took place on 6 July 1439 the promulgation in both languages and signing of the union decree "Laetentur coeli." [5] Soon after the Greeks left, and on the very return voyage many of those among them who had taken part in the Council withdrew their consent. The union was scarcely acknowledged in the East, even though other smaller groups of Oriental Christians — Armenians, Copts, Syrians, Chaldees, and Maronites — reached an understanding with the Curia. [6] On the Pope's return to Rome in 1443 the Council was transferred to the Lateran; it quickly declined in importance and was never officially concluded.

The points of theological controversy were the *Filioque,* purgatory, the matter and form of the Eucharist, and the interpretation of the papal primacy. For the Greeks the *Filioque* was the most important and really decisive point. Nevertheless, the theological conversations first took up the doctrine of purgatory; there were long discussions on it at Ferrara and Florence. The Greeks especially took issue with the Latin notion of a purifying fire, since Scripture and the Fathers had nothing to say about it. The union decree evaded an exact definition and confined itself to the statement that the souls in question had to undergo a cleansing penalty after death: "penis purgatoriis post mortem purgari."

The question longest discussed was the *Filioque,* which had been inserted into the Nicene Creed in the early Middle Ages. The debates began at Ferrara in September and were prolonged until December without success; then they were resumed in Florence at the beginning of March 1439 and were concluded in June. The Greeks took as their point of departure the decree of the Third Ecumenical Council at Ephesus, according to which the creed was not to be altered by additions; in the *Filioque* they saw a modification in content. In the long and bitter discussions, which included frequent interventions by the Emperor, the difference in the development of the two halves of the Church was clearly exposed. The Greeks especially rejected the scholastic deductions of the Western theologians. It was easier to convince them on the basis of patristic theology that the addition they so disliked had a certain basis in the Eastern and Western Fathers. But since they regarded the *Filioque* as the cause of the Schism, their resistance was stubborn. Again and again they said they would sooner depart than yield. The axiom, theologically doubtful but enthusiastically hailed as a way out, that "between the Western and Eastern Fathers there can be no contradiction, since they are all illuminated by the Holy Spirit," quickly produced agreement but no solution of the theological question. In the decree of union the accord and the permissibility of the

---

[5] Text of the decrees of union in *Conciliorum oecumenicorum decreta* (Freiburg 1962), 499–567.
[6] For the fate of the union, see Chapter 51.

accepting of the *Filioque* into the creed were defined with many words but it was not said who could lawfully make such an addition, and the Greeks were not obliged to insert the Western addition.

There were likewise grave difficulties in the discussions on the Eucharist, although there seemed to be reasonably close agreement as to essentials. A compromise got around the difficulties by recognizing unleavened and leavened bread as the matter but there was no decision relevant to the form, that is, to the words of consecration and the *epiclesis*.

The papal primacy came up as the final topic of discussion at the demand of the Latins and especially of Eugene IV, but too hastily. The Emperor opposed the discussion but in the interests of union he had to exert considerable pressure on the Greek participants. The Greeks regarded as the highest tribunal in the constitution of the Church the pentarchy, the traditional Five Patriarchates of Rome, Constantinople, Alexandria, Antioch, and Jerusalem. They were fully prepared to concede to the Patriarch of Old Rome the privileges he had enjoyed before the outbreak of the Schism. There could be no question of a primacy of jurisdiction. But in barely three weeks the Greeks were compelled to yield on a broad front. However, this was not a genuine solution, as the various possibilities of interpretation showed and still show.

Even if the importance of the dogmatic discussions and decisions must not be detracted from, still it must be noted that they took place in a politically conditioned climate and that the participants kept fully concrete political goals before their eyes. Pope and Emperor needed the union. The Emperor wanted the military assistance of the West in exchange for the slightest possible dogmatic concessions; the Pope wanted aid against Basel and hence demanded recognition of the primacy. The confrontation between the Curia and the Council of Basel was also of great influence on Ferrara-Florence. It seems as though the Council of Basel was expecting from the Greeks' concept of the ancient councils a support for its own conciliar theory. Both at Basel and in the papal camp persons entertained ideas in regard to the Byzantine Church that were erroneous because they were preponderantly idealistic. But the Pope and Curia displayed greater skill, made many otherwise unusual concessions, and played off union against Basel. The title of the tendentious work by Syropoulus, *Vera historia unionis non verae*, in many respects hit the nail on the head. More important than the subsequent "union" was the exposition of standpoints and the constant referring by the Greeks to Scripture and the Fathers as the unique source *vis-à-vis* the Latins' deductive theology. Although Greeks and Westerners regarded one another as schismatics, if not as heretics also, there were no abjurations at the end.

It goes without saying that the ecumenical character of the Council of Ferrara-Florence was accepted on account of the personal attendance of

Pope and Emperor. But it must be noted that relatively few bishops, and those almost entirely Italians, represented the Latin Church. The few bishops from France were also partly Italians or not in possession of their dioceses. In addition there were three Spaniards, two Irish, and one bishop each from Portugal and Poland, but none from the Empire and from England. Furthermore, several bishops were at the Curia as *electi*.[7] Of the states only Burgundy and the Angevins had sent an official embassy to the Council. And so there could be no question of a representation of the Universal Church or of the European states, and that at a time when Basel again obtained recognition from numerous quarters.

The position of France in regard to Basel was important for the reason that most of the participants and the most influential personalities came from France, and from them came, to a great extent, the proposals for the reform discussions. Even if one admits annoyance over the loss of the papacy after the Council of Constance as a powerful stimulus to the anti-curial policy, without the Neapolitan question the changing attitude of the French King would be inexplicable. If France had favoured a transfer to a French city, the *rapprochement* with the Curia began in 1435 when Eugene IV made the enfeoffment of René of Anjou as King of Naples dependent on his abandoning the Council of Basel. But the Pragmatic Sanction of Bourges in 1438 was the reply to the miscarriage of this plan. In this the French Church in twenty-three articles adopted, with some modifications, the reform decrees of Basel, in particular "Frequens" and the decrees on the authority of the Council: the election decree, that on the abolition of annates, and a group of prescriptions on reform of the liturgy and of the clergy. But the suspension of the Pope was not recognized and relations with the Curia were not broken off; in fact, a few years later they were again rather lively. But attendance at the Council of Ferrara was not permitted; on the other hand, while France had no share in the deposition of Eugene IV, any molestation of the Council at Basel was forbidden.

At first Aragón was represented at Basel only by one envoy as an observer. It was not until the death of Joanna II of Naples in 1435 had opened the question of the succession and Alfonso V of Aragón, after the battle of the Pontiae Islands, had become first the prisoner and then the ally of Milan that a rather large embassy arrived at the Council. Since the Pope apparently wanted to confiscate the escheated fief and incorporate it into the Papal State, the task of the Aragonese embassy consisted chiefly in inciting the Council to sharp measures against the Curia. When the effort, sanctioned by the Council, to deprive the Pope of the Papal State misfired, the Aragonese

---

[7] Signatures of the union decree in *Conc. Flor. Documenta et scriptores*, series A, *Epistolae*, II (1944), 68–79, and series B, II, 1 (1942), 115–20. See also A. Mercati, "Il decreto d'unione del 6 luglio 1439 nell'Archivio segreto Vaticano," *OrChrP*, 11 (1945), 5–44.

at Basel at least worked eagerly for the trial, suspension, and deposition of Eugene. Only thus can one understand the frequently changed roles of the French and Aragonese embassies, both of which sought to achieve a decision for their respective sides by supporting the Council against the Pope.[8]

The policy of Castile was strictly dependent on France. John II inclined to the Council but no embassy went to Basel until 1434. In the struggle with England for the place after the French in June 1434 Castile was victorious. From 1437 Castile's attitude was one of reserve, although the Fathers at Basel went to great pains to be accommodating. The envoys left the city in 1438 and, after visiting the new German King Albert II at Breslau and attending the Diet of Princes at Mainz in 1439, returned home. Thereafter Castile was on the side of Eugene IV.[9]

Philip the Good, Duke of Burgundy, was for a long time neutral. He made promises to both sides and obtained the approval of the Treaty of Arras from both Eugene and the Council of Basel. From 1435 he inclined to the Curia, recalled his embassy from Basel, and was represented at the Council of Ferrara. But his policy was always very cautious.

England did not play a decisive role in the history of the Council of Basel. Its championing of the Curia was to a great extent determined by opposition to France, even though the Fathers at Basel tried again and again to draw the English King to their side. Yielding to the insistence of the Council, a small but highly qualified embassy appeared at Basel in 1433, probably chiefly motivated by the hope of bringing back the Hussites to the Church. However, the envoys did not permit themselves to be incorporated and demanded an organization by nations, as at Constance. A second embassy came in 1434 to discuss peace with France. English prestige suffered a severe blow at Basel in the strife with Castile over precedence. The deposition of Eugene IV and the election of Felix V were not recognized in England. What France and Germany adopted of the reform decrees the English King had long ago attended to on his own.[10]

And so from 1438 there faced each other two mutually hostile general

---

[8] E. Dupré-Theseider, *La politica italiana di Alfonso d'Aragona* (Bologna 1956); G. F. Ryder, "La politica italiana di Alfonso d'Aragona 1442–58," *Archivio storico per le province Napoletane*, N. S., 38 (1959), 45–106; A. Javierre Mur, "Aportación documental a las relaciones entre Alfonso V de Aragón y el ducado de Milán," *IV congreso de historia de la corona de Aragón. Actas y comunicaciones*, I (Palma de Mallorca 1959); *Dizionario biografico degli Italiani*, II (1960), 323–31 (with the literature); W. Küchler, "Alfons V. von Aragón und das Basler Konzil," *Ges. Aufsätze zur Kulturgesch. Spaniens*, 23 (1967), 131–46.

[9] L. Suárez Fernández, *Castilla, el cisma y la crisis conciliar 1378–1440* (Madrid 1960), 112, documents, 347–438; V. Laurent, "Les ambassadeurs du roi de Castille au concile de Bâle et le patriarche Joseph II février 1438," *RÉB*, 18 (1960), 136–44.

[10] J. Haller, *Piero da Monte* (Rome 1941), 43 ff.; A. N. E. D. Schofield, "The First English Delegation to the Council of Basel," *JEH*, 12 (1961), 167–96.

councils, and each was exerting itself to obtain recognition by the states. If the Western Schism had to do with the *papa indubitatus,* so now the problem was the *concilium indubitatum.* Since the Council of Basel was meeting in Germany, the attitude of the German King and of the German Church was not unimportant. Until his death in 1437 the Emperor Sigismund worked constantly for an adjustment between Pope and Council, though his sympathies lay rather with the Council.

After his disappearance the ecclesiastical question was treated at numberless diets, but, despite detailed discussion by representatives of both sides, it remained undecided. The indecision found expression in what was called neutrality, which was extended from meeting to meeting. The proclamation of neutrality was intended especially as a protection against the censures of both Pope and Council and a means of preventing unrest among the faithful and of assuring the possession of benefices. The Mainz *instrumentum acceptationis* of 1439, in which, following the French model, the Council's reform decrees were declared valid with certain modifications, was a taking of a stand for the Council and its teaching but without an adopting of the Council's policy. Since, as earlier, both the Curia and the Council were applied to by the higher and the lower clergy, there could be no question of strict neutrality. Thus the representation of German sees at Basel reached its high point around 1440, while suits at the Curia strongly declined. The ecclesiastical Electors of Mainz and Cologne supported Basel and were unsuccessfully deposed by the Curia in 1446. An escape from the complicated situation seemed to be offered by the plan for a new, third council, which was eagerly defended in Germany; but, despite a seeming willingness, it was rejected by the Curia. Since the Council, in contrast to the Pope, possessed no real power, its importance steadily declined. No change was made by the promulgation on 16 May 1439, in the thirty-third session, of earlier formulated propositions as *veritates catholicae:* The proposition concerning the power of the Council over the Pope and every other person among the faithful is a truth of the Catholic faith; the proposition that the Pope cannot dissolve a general council without its consent is a truth of the Catholic faith; whoever obstinately opposes these truths in word, deed, and writing is to be regarded as a heretic.

The Council of Basel deposed Eugene IV in June 1439. In November it elected as Pope Duke Amadeus VIII of Savoy, who styled himself Felix V (1439–49). He was able to obtain recognition only in a very restricted area.[11] The Council continued at Basel until 1447, when it was transferred to Lausanne.[12] The greatest danger for the Curia was over when King

---

[11] On Felix V, see *Dizionario biografico degli Italiani,* II (1960), 749–53 (with the literature).
[12] *Deutsche Reichstagsakten,* 17 (1963), 624 f.

Alfonso V of Aragón, after conquering Naples, went over to the Pope in 1443 in exchange for far-reaching concessions and recalled his bishops from Basel. And the new German King, Frederick III, let himself be won over by the promise of the imperial crown and much ecclesiastical patronage. It was more difficult to reach an agreement with the Electors, the real imperial government. Their demand for the reinstatement of the Archbishops of Mainz and Cologne, recognition of the Basel reforms and of the decrees of Constance and Basel, and the convocation of a third council was accepted in the Concordat of the Princes in 1447 in a veiled form that still remains obscure. To the same twilight belongs the secret document signed by Eugene IV three weeks before his death, according to which he did not intend to approve anything that was contrary to the faith of the Fathers or was to the detriment of the Holy See.

Eugene died on 23 February 1447, just after envoys of the German King and of some German princes had taken the oath of obedience to him. His successor, Nicholas V (1447–55), at once ratified the settlement with the German Church. More adroit than his predecessor, he reached an agreement with Frederick III in the so-called Concordat of Vienna and was able to effect considerable modifications in the Basel reforms. Negotiations for the ending of the schism were conducted by France as early as 1447, first at Bourges, then at Lyons and at the Curia. But it was only in 1449 that it was possible to induce Felix V to retire and the Council of Basel to decree its own dissolution after it had been allowed to elect Nicholas V. Without any condemnation of the theological views, the mutual censures and processes were annulled, the possession of benefices was confirmed, some of the cardinals of the Basel obedience were admitted into the Roman College of Cardinals, and Felix V was allowed to exercise papal rights in his former obedience.

The great quarrel was thereby ended for the moment, not by a theological solution of the vexing questions but under political auspices. The difficulty and also the political importance of the long struggle clearly revealed themselves in a group of personalities. If on the side of the Council of Basel there unflinchingly stood men such as Cardinal Louis d'Aleman, John of Segovia, Nicholas of Tudeschi, Archbishop of Palermo, John Schele, Bishop of Lübeck and royal envoy, Henry Toke, Thomas Ebendorfer, John of Ragusa, and Peter of Rosenheim, just as firm on the other side were John of Torquemada, John of Palomar, and Ambrose Traversari.[13] The often recurring

<hr/>

[13] G. Pérouse, *Le cardinal Louis d'Aleman, président du concile de Bâle, et la fin du grand schisme* (Paris 1904); *Dizionario biografico degli Italiani*, II (1960), 145–47 (with the literature); H. Ammon, *Johannes Schele, Bischof von Lübeck, auf dem Basler Konzil* (Diss. phil., Erlangen 1931); A. Lhotsky, *Thomas Ebendorfer, ein österreichischer Geschichtsschreiber, Theologe und Diplomat des 15. Jahrhunderts* (Stuttgart 1957); W. Jaroschka, "Thomas Ebendorfer als Theoretiker des Konziliarismus," *MIÖG*, 71 (1963), 87–98; H. Schmidinger,

switching of loyalty and of faction, the fear of being caught, despite precautions, between the two millstones, depended on so many factors that one should not, without more ado, speak of opportunism. As clearly classical examples could be mentioned Julian Cesarini, Nicholas of Cusa, and Aeneas Silvius Piccolomini.[14]

From the political viewpoint the Council of Basel, a gathering of solely intellectual power, was more dependent than the Roman Pontiff on the princes, who sought to extract as much as possible from both sides. Not only were political disputes brought before the Council, but in its competition with the Pope the Council sought political successes by mediating peace or, especially clearly, by arranging union with the Greeks. Always dependent on the good will of the secular lords, great and small, the Council had to move very circumspectly in its administration. A good example is the wearisome struggle over the see of Trier.[15] Reform questions were important at Basel because of the time limit in the Constance concordats. The real difficulties appeared much more clearly than at Constance in the long drawn out discussions: the very different situation in individual states and territories, which called for a practical solution. The discussions and treatises, though theologically and philosophically sound, could change nothing there, since the envoys and proxies had to uphold the changing policies of their lords and did so with great skill. It is to be regretted that the carefully considered and moderately formulated reform became an object of political transaction. In this controversy, conducted by both sides with distasteful means, the Curia managed to a very great extent to rescue its situation. This was a considerable political achievement, but far removed from a genuine reform will. It purchased its own recognition by means of great compromises and withdrew into the Papal State as one of the *cinque principati* of Italy. In this way its world-wide impact was powerfully obstructed and reform was frustrated. It is a failure to grasp the spirit of the age when the conciliar idea is regarded as something false and there is talk of Basel's radicalism. But one must distinguish between adhering to the Council of Basel and defending the conciliar idea. The Council of Constance presented so many complications to the Roman *Congregatio super editione conciliorum generalium*

[footnote] "Begegnungen Thomas Ebendorfers auf dem Konzil von Basel," *Festschrift O. Vasella* (Fribourg 1964), 171–97; A. Krchnák, *De vita et operibus Joannis de Ragusio, Lateranum*, N. S., 26 (Rome 1961); F. Thoma, "Petrus von Rosenheim," *Das bayerische Inn-Oberland*, 32 (1962), 97–164; C. Somigli, *Un amico dei Greci: Ambrogio Traversari* (Arezzo 1964).

[14] P. Becker, *Giuliano Cesarini* (diss. phil., Münster 1935); J. Gill, *Personalities of the Council of Florence*, 95–104 (Cesarini). For Nicholas of Cusa, see *infra*, Chapter 59. B. Widmer, *Enea Silvio Piccolomini in der sittlichen und politischen Entscheidung* (Basel 1963); L. M. Veit, "Pensiero e vita religiosa di Enea Silvio Piccolomini prima della sua consecrazione episcopale," *Analecta Gregoriana*, 139 (Rome 1964). For other literature, see *infra*, Chapter 56.

[15] E. Meuthen, *Das Trierer Schisma von 1430 auf dem Basler Konzil* (Münster 1964).

that the congregation decided to remove the Council of Basel from the list of general councils. Such a procedure attests, not a scholarly outlook, but bias.[16]

The person of Eugene IV must be evaluated in the same manner. Judgments by contemporaries were in general quite reserved. He was blamed for the harshness of his procedures, his quick recourse to force, and the incessant stressing of his position as ruler of the Church. If, as J. Haller says, we do not encounter "in the annals of this Venetian Pope anything out of the Piombi of his native city," there was still enough of what was unseemly for the Pope and Curia. De Vooght has rightly pointed to his insecurity, the vacillation of his teaching and policies.[17] While, with Pastor and Gill, one may be happy to regard him as the papacy's saviour from the danger of "conciliarism," the failure of reform is also his responsibility, for it had become all too clear that without a council there could be no reform. From the viewpoint of Church history the decisive turning from the Middle Ages to modern times occurs around the middle of the fifteenth century. Rome had prevented reform and in return soon received the Reformation.

[16] V. Peri, "Il numero dei concili ecumenici nella tradizione cattolica moderna," *Aevum*, 37 (1963), 430–501; C. Leonardi, "Per la storia dell'edizione Romana dei concili ecumenici 1608–12," *SteT*, 236 (1964), 595; K. A. Fink, "Konziliengeschichtsschreibung im Wandel?" *Theologie im Wandel. Festschrift zum 150jährigen Jubiläum der kath.-theol. Fakultät der Universität Tübingen* (Munich 1967), 179–89.

[17] D. Caccamo, "Eugenio IV e la crociata di Varna," *ADRomana*, 79 (1956), 54 ff.; P. De Vooght, *Les pouvoirs du concile et l'autorité du pape* (Paris 1965), 81–103. In the funeral oration Aeneas Silvius Piccolomini stated: "Alti cordis fuit. Sed nullum in eo magis vitium fuit, nisi quia sine mensura erat, et non quod potuit, sed quod voluit aggressus est" *(Muratori*, III, 2, 861).

The Byzantine Church: The Age of Palamism

CHAPTER 51

From the Second Council of Lyons to the Council of Ferrara-Florence

Probably at no other period were relations between the Orthodox Church of the Byzantine Empire and the papacy in so deplorable a state as during the long reign of the Byzantine Emperor Andronicus II (1282–1328). The great gamble of his father, Michael VIII, to assert power *vis-à-vis* Charles of Anjou depended on his playing with high stakes — the policy of reunion, — even if one is not justified in denying an inner sympathy on the part of the Emperor, who had grown up in an atmosphere favourable to union. With Michael's death in 1282 the game ended for a long time, for his successor did not have to play.[1] The Sicilian Vespers[2] had relieved the Empire for years to come from a severe direct pressure. And so Andronicus annulled the union, even though he had subscribed to it under oath as recently as 1279. His decision was, to be sure, no mere caprice. Michael VIII, who had concluded the Union of Lyons on his own, had never contrived to break popular resistance. Part of the higher clergy had adopted a passive attitude, and the Patriarch John XI Beccus, favourable to the union and a theologian of importance, had known how to remove many obstacles. But all the more obstinate was the opposition from monastic circles, whose influence prevailed not only with the people in the streets but to a degree even with members of the imperial family. Furthermore, the Popes plainly cherished false views of the Emperor's real power and in their demands actually recognized and furthered that very Caesaropapism which the union was supposed to eliminate. They showed little understanding of the Emperor's difficult position, often perceived bad will in circumstances in which Michael was compelled to hesitate and to resort to tactics, and failed to make themselves clear in their ritual demands on the Greeks, until finally Pope Martin IV, completely under the influence of the House of Anjou, excommunicated Michael and his associates for schism and heresy.

For the Emperor the situation was all the more dangerous in that the

---

[1] Cf. F. Dölger, *Regesten der Kaiserurkunden des oströmischen Reiches,* IV (Munich 1960); hereafter, Dölger, *Reg.*

[2] Steven Runciman, *The Sicilian Vespers* (Cambridge 1958).

opposition to the union was secretly associated with repudiation of the legitimacy of the imperial house. When he seized the throne, Michael VIII had first reduced the lawful heir, John IV Lascaris, to second place and then, by blinding him, had disqualified him for the imperial office. Arsenius, then Patriarch (1255–60 and 1261–63), at first assumed a vacillating attitude to the situation. But under pressure from a strong opposition in Asia Minor to the Palaeologi and in favour of the Lascarid, he finally became the leader, at least passively, of this very group. There was formed the Arsenite faction[3] with no real program except to keep faith with Arsenius and to reject all new patriarchs. But it replenished its members with dangerous and nameless forces — the higher clergy were almost totally absent from the ranks of the Arsenites — whose hunger for position was insatiable and who knew no scruples in the choice of means. This was a symptom of the restratification of Byzantine society which came to light as a consequence of the impoverishment of the Empire on the one hand and of the related disintegration of the central imperial power on the other. The theory of the Emperor as master of the Church remained unquestioned in official circles, the practice of communication between palace and *patriarchium* was unchanged, but both Emperor and bishops had to admit in the end their powerlessness against pressure from the masses led by the monks. It is a characteristic of the new Emperor's insight that he gave the Arsenite problem his full attention. He made several attempts to induce the faction to a more reasonable attitude but they always collapsed on the fundamental point that the demands of the Arsenites would have thrown the entire hierarchy into chaos. Not for some decades were they inclined to make peace. In 1310 the schism was ended by a detailed pact, sealed by a macabre scene in Hagia Sophia, in which the corpse of the Patriarch Arsenius, a bull of absolution in his hand, freed his opponents from anathema.[4]

Meanwhile, affairs in the West had worked to the benefit of the Byzantines. The Popes were still trying to keep alive the crusading idea, and again and again the planning of the crusade advocated by them was directed against Constantinople for the restoration of the destroyed Latin Empire. And there was no dearth of French princes, who, as heirs of the dethroned Emperors of Constantinople, placed themselves at the service of such ideas with purposeful interest. But the preaching of the crusade evoked no response. Acre, the last foothold of productive activity in Syria, fell in 1291. The commercial interests of the Italian cities were more concerned with the *status quo* than with the risks of a campaign. The indulgence found

---

[3] On the Arsenite schism see I. Sykutres, in Ἑλληνικά, 2 (1929), 267–332, 3 (1930), 15–44, 5 (1932), 107–26 (Greek); summarized in V. Laurent, "Les grandes crises religieuses à Byzance. La fin du schisme arsénite," *Bulletin Sect. Hist. Académie Roumaine*, 26/2 (Bucharest 1945), 225–313.

[4] Dölger, *Reg*, 2321 and 2323.

hardly any response, and the Western kings were too much engrossed in the consolidation of their national states to listen with both ears to the preaching of the Pope and his legates. Theorists, it is true, were not satisfied. Men like Raymond Lull, William d'Adam, and Peter Dubois squarely faced the possibilities of a crusade in very well informed tracts, but the meagre success they achieved belied even this recital of the situation.[5] If the expedition planned by Charles of Valois, who through his marriage to Catherine of Courtenay had become pretender to the throne of the Latin Empire, had already come to a standstill in Tuscany (1302) and the greatest part of the crusade obol had made its way into the pockets of Frederick the Handsome, the first Avignon Pope, Clement V (1305–14), had no greater success to record. He did indeed renew the excommunication of Andronicus and grant the Holy Land indulgences to armies, that would proceed against Constantinople, but the "prince without a principality," Charles of Valois, did not get out of Italy despite an alliance with the Kral of Serbia, Stephen Urosh II, and the latter's offer of union with Rome and even though the Catalan Company had sworn loyalty to him. His captain general, Theobald of Cépoy, took the island of Euboea but before long the Catalans made themselves independent. They contributed at least as much to the weakening of Frankish might in Greece as to the weakening of Byzantine power, and Theobald had to return to the West empty-handed in 1309–10.[6] Charles had overplayed his hand. Other undertakings, led by Philip of Taranto, one of Charles the Lame's sons, who maintained hereditary claims in Epirus, had been started as early as 1306, but it was not until 1323, after numerous failures, that he contrived a real expedition. But it was never to reach Constantinople. In these and similar undertakings, which served, not the crusading idea, but the dynastic policies of *la France outremer*, Andronicus could wait calmly for the opposing forces in Achaia to dissipate themselves. The danger again assumed a serious nature with the more extensive plans of Charles IV of France (1322–28) in favour of the Kingdom of Armenia. That this expedition could have been diverted to Constantinople was not to be denied. And so Andronicus reverted to his father's policy, proposing negotiations for union. But with the fading of the danger and because of the civil war between Andronicus and his grandson they were soon shelved.[7]

Meanwhile, circumstances occurred which forced upon the Curia a reorientation of its reunion policy and, in fact, caused all interested Western powers to look for an entirely new approach in the Eastern policy. It suffices

---

[5] Steven Runciman, *A History of the Crusades*, III, 432 f.

[6] H. Moranville, "Les projets de Charles de Valois sur l'empire de Constantinople," *BÉCh*, 51 (1890), 63 ff.; J. Petit, *Charles de Valois* (Paris 1900).

[7] Dölger, *Reg*, 2492, 2556, 2557; H. Omont, "Projet de réunion des églises grecque et latine sous Charles le Bel en 1327," *BÉCh*, 53 (1892), 254–57; G. Dürrholder, *Die Kreuzzugspolitik unter Papst Johannes XXII.* (Freiburg 1913).

to mention the key phrase, "the Turkish danger," to indicate a factor which remained in the foreground of Church History for the next four centuries. [8]

The capture of Constantinople by the Byzantines in 1261 and the return of the imperial court had again necessarily shifted the emphasis in Byzantine policy much more sharply toward the West. After the reconquest there were not sufficient forces to keep a determined and watchful eye on the East at the same time. Asia Minor was neglected, the frontiers were left exposed. The welfare of the eastern provinces, energetically promoted by the Emperor John III Vatatzes (1222–54) especially, yielded to general decline, and the Lascarid legitimists reduced the provinces to disorder. Danger from the Seljuks was no longer serious, since their power had been broken by the Mongols in 1243. But a result of this event was the rise on the edges of the Seljuk empire of Turkish tribes which made themselves independent and on their own not only threatened the dominions of the Sultan but also pressed against the inadequately tended frontiers of the Byzantine Empire. One of the leaders of these various tribes was Osman, son of Ertogrul, founder of the Ottoman State. Like an avalanche, Ottomans and Seljuks fell upon the Byzantine provinces in Asia Minor. Around 1300 virtually all of the countryside had become Turkish and it was not long before the famous old metropolises of Asia Minor fell to them: Prusa in 1326, Nicaea in 1331, Nicomedia in 1337. Meanwhile there occurred the first offensives against the Aegean islands, Thrace, and the environs of Constantinople. At first only desultory raids, these expeditions were soon systematically managed, and in 1354 Kallipolis (Gallipoli), the key to the Dardanelles, became a firm Turkish foothold in Europe. Adrianople (Edirne) became Turkish in 1362, and there, around 1365, the Ottoman Sultan established his capital, about 100 kilometres to the rear of Constantinople.

Since the Arab attack in the seventh century no invasion had brought greater losses to the Church than that of the Ottomans. In the earlier onset Syria, Palestine, Egypt, and Africa had been lost and the Christian communities in those lands could maintain themselves only in precarious circumstances. But now the ancient Christian metropolises of Asia Minor were swallowed in the Islamic desert and before long the Balkans would share their fate. In these circumstances the political problem of the Western powers was not so much to reestablish the Latin Empire, for which it was difficult to find a serious aspirant, but rather to defend Europe from the infidels in union with the beleaguered Greeks. Such an association would inevitably involve discussion of Church union, but now with far less political justification. And for the Greeks the difficulty no longer consisted in

[8] *Cf.* W. L. Langer - R. P. Blake, "The Rise of the Ottoman Turks and its Historical Background," *AHR*, 37 (1932), 468–505; P. Wittek, *The Rise of the Ottoman Empire* (London 1938); G. Georgiades Arnakes, Οἱ πρῶτοι Ὀθομανοί (Athens 1947); N. Jorga, "Latins et Grecs d'Orient et l'établissement des Turcs en Europe 1342–1362," *ByZ*, 15 (1906), 179–222.

keeping the Latins out of the Sea of Marmora but in gaining them as auxiliaries, even at the price of union. So long as the danger was only dimly in the consciousness of the West, it was felt that the idea of union could not be disregarded, and political circles in the Byzantine Empire reckoned with this condition. But they also recalled the Second Council of Lyons, which was rejected in the East mostly because it had been attended only by delegates of the Emperor, not by any of the Orthodox Church. And so this time the East insisted on a truly ecumenical council, a suggestion now more strongly supported in the West, not at first by the Popes but by those circles representing the conciliar movement. Unfortunately, the problem of union thereby became a political question between papacy and conciliarism. [9]

Despite everything, the difficulties remained almost insuperable. To a great extent they were psychological. The East until now knew Westerners either as conquerors who, with a cross on their shoulders, wanted to establish a domain of their own and for whom the problems of Church union, if they were important at all, were to be solved in the manner of conquerors, or as mercenaries, adventurers, and traders, who with skill and money had deprived the Byzantines of all positions of commerce and trade. [10] The intellectual forces of the West were virtually unknown to the East until the middle of the fourteenth century. Potentially effective influences, such as the activity of the Franciscans and the Dominicans, were unrealized because of reciprocal charges of heresy. And the information that the West had concerning the East derived almost exclusively from those who represented the West in the East. Relations thus revolved on a not very high plane. The standard bearers of Orthodox theology compiled long lists of heresies which were prevalent in the West and multiplied them further by several enticing new numbers, such as the questions of the *epiclesis* and purgatory. With equal ardour their Western counterparts made the Greeks responsible for dozens of heresies, and no one can explain how Guy Terrena of Perpignan (d. 1342), for example, arrived at his catalogue of twenty-five Greek heresies in his *Summa de haeresibus*, unless the fact is taken into consideration that, for the Latin, the Greek had become the prototype of heretic.

The amazing thing in all this is that the Union of Florence was eventually achieved. To be sure, it took a whole century. The initial stage is best indicated by the mission of the Calabrian Orthodox monk and later convert, Barlaam, to the court of Avignon in 1339. [11] He suggested to Pope Benedict XII

---

[9] *Cf.* G. Hofmann, "Papato, Conciliarismo, Patriarcato," *Miscell. Hist. Pont.*, 2 (1940), 1–82.

[10] Especially informative is the judgment in Demetrios Kydones, *Autobiographie*, German version of H. G. Beck in *OstKSt*, 1 (1952) 208–25, 264–82.

[11] *PG*, 151, 1331–42; C. Giannelli, "Un progetto di Barlaam Calabro per l'unione delle chiese," *MiscMercati*, III (1946), 157–208; J. Meyendorff, "Un mauvais théologien de l'unité au XIV⁰ siècle," *L'Église et les églises*, II (Chevetogne 1954), 47–64.

the alternatives of convincing either only the learned Byzantine theologians of the truth of Latin doctrine or of convincing both people and theologians. The former, he thought, would not be difficult, for the experts would quickly reach an understanding, but on their return home they would be exposed to a strong opposition which would exploit the ever effective argument: "Let us not be robbed of the faith we have inherited from the Fathers!" But if union of East and West were to take place at a truly ecumenical council, attended by accredited representatives of all the patriarchates, the Greek people, with their tremendous regard for an ecumenical council, would also accept it. The contrary argument of the cardinals, that truths once defined do not admit of further discussion, was countered by Barlaam with the point that even an established truth can stand clarification. If this argument found little support, even less did Barlaam's claim that military aid for Constantinople must precede union and that only such a favour would render union palatable to the Greek people. The Pope had the cardinals answer this: Quite the contrary! If the aid brought success, the Greeks would quickly be no longer willing to hear of a union.

Thus Barlaam, who amazingly foresaw much of what would eventually happen, failed, but behind his mission stood the grand chamberlain John Cantacuzene, who, as the Emperor John VI (1347–54), further pursued his lofty goal. Around 1350 one embassy after another set out for Avignon. The council, according to the Emperor's wish, ought to meet at a place equally distant from Rome and Constantinople. Pope Clement VI was not at first opposed to the idea, but eventually the plan miscarried and in this connection the rebellion of Cola di Rienzo and the war between France and England were certainly not decisive. However, Cantacuzene did not cease his exertions and his successor, John V Palaeologus (1354–91), walked in his footsteps, though probably without much genuine dedication. New discussions took place in 1367, with the co-operation of the former Emperor Cantacuzene, the Latin Archbishop Paul, papal legate and titular Patriarch of Constantinople. The outcome appeared favourable, and even the Patriarch Philotheus Coccinus of Constantinople (1353–54 and 1364–76) seems to have accepted it. In any event, the first moves for convoking the council were made. [12] But, unfortunately, John V had in the meantime decided, like Michael VIII, to go it alone. In 1369 he became a Catholic at Rome, a step

[12] J. Gay, *Le pape Clément VI et les affaires d'Orient* (Paris 1904); R. J. Loenertz, "Ambassadeurs grecs auprès du pape Clément VI (1348)" *OrChrP*, 19 (1953), 178–96; J. Darrouzès, "Conférence sur la primauté du pape à Constantinople en 1357," *RÉB*, 19 (1961), 76–109; J. Meyendorff, "Jean-Joasaph Cantacuzène et le projet de concile œcuménique en 1367," *Akten XI. Internat. Byzant.-Kongr.* (Munich 1960), 363–69; *idem*, "Projet de concile œcuménique en 1367. Un dialogue inédit entre Jean Cantacuzène et le légat Paul," *DOP*, 14 (1960), 149–77.

which certainly enhanced the Pope's prestige in regained Rome but without significance in the overall picture of the relations between the Churches, if indeed, as it is described, it could have had any significance.[13] In an encyclical to the Churches the Pope once more rejected the idea of a council on the ground that it was absurd to make defined truths a subject of controversy again.[14]

But before long the Western Schism and the resulting Conciliar Movement produced a change along the entire front. Now the West almost forced a council upon the East and the retarding factor was the Byzantine Emperor Manuel II Palaeologus (1391–1425). A genuinely religious man, he knew exactly how difficult, if not impossible, it would be to make union palatable to his people. A miscarriage would aggravate the schism and deliver Byzantium to the mercy of the Turks, whereas the threat of union would continue to be a means of impressing the Turks.[15] Hence the Emperor was determined *a priori* not to draw the final conclusion from the union discussions but to seek the Empire's safety in the purely political sphere. But meanwhile the situation had become still more threatening and he may have hoped that it would open the eyes of the Western princes. Bulgaria became a vassal state of the Turks in 1371. In 1389 occurred the celebrated First Battle of Kossovo, which made the Turks masters of the entire Balkan peninsula. The remnant of the crusading states in Greece had long been dependent on the favour of the Turkish overlord. Theological prolegomena were now too late. Still, chiefly on the initiative of the French King Charles VI and of King Sigismund of Hungary, an army of crusaders was actually assembled, but the Battle of Nicopolis on 26 September 1396 was a Turkish victory and proved, to quote Runciman, "that the Crusaders had learned nothing in all the centuries."[16]

In these circumstances the Byzantine Emperor Manuel made a desperate attempt to arouse the Christian West to a new expedition by means of a personal visit to Western Europe, which took him *via* Venice to Paris and as far as London. But in spite of the brilliant reception everywhere accorded him, the actual result was at most a vague promise here and there.[17] That Byzantium did not then become the spoil of the Turks was due solely to the

[13] O. Halecki, *Un empereur de Byzance à Rome* (Warsaw 1930).

[14] Raynaldus, *Annales eccl.*, 1370, no. 3.

[15] This may have been the content of Manuel's "testament" to his son, John VIII, reported by Sphrantzes, *Chron. maius*, II, 13 (*PG*, 156, 784 f.).

[16] A. S. Atiya, *The Crusade of Nicopolis* (London 1934); *Runciman*, III, 460.

[17] A. A. Vasil'ev, "Putešestvie vizantijskogo imperatora Manuila II Paleologa po zapadnoj Evrope," *Zurnal Ministerstva Narod. Prosv.*, NS, 39 (1912), 41–78, 260–304; M. Jugie, "Le voyage de l'empereur Manuel Paléologue en occident," *ÉO*, 15 (1912), 322–32; G. Schlumberger, "Un empereur de Byzance à Paris et à Londres," *Byzance et croisades* (Paris 1927), 87–147, 361 f.; M. A. Andreeva, "Zur Reise Manuels II. nach Westeuropa," *ByZ*, 34 (1934), 37–47, 351.

fact that at that very moment (1402) the Mongols under the Khan Timur-Leng decisively defeated the Ottoman Sultan Bajazet at the Battle of Ankara and thereby gave the Empire a breathing spell.

The project of a union of the Churches was now more animated in the West than in the East. Manuel was invited by the cardinals to send delegates to the Council of Pisa (1409). The Emperor Sigismund informed his colleague in Constantinople that the Council of Constance (1414–18) aimed "contra infideles paganos et praecipue Turcos remedia vobisque et predicte civitati Constantinopolitane ... providere" and invited him to send representatives. [18] Manuel complied, but his highly esteemed agent, Manuel Chrysoloras, died at the Council in 1415 [19] and since the Synod soon realized the impracticability of its too detailed program the reductio Graecorum was put on the waiting list.

But in the interval new imperial envoys had arrived. They submitted thirty-six articles in which the Greeks had specified their notions of the preparations for union. [20] The embassy seems to have been optimistic in all regards. To its superiors it painted in glowing colours the readiness of the Council and of the Curia to meet every advance half-way and with the same palette depicted the inclination of the East to return to Rome's obedience in both faith and ritual. It must have been these brilliant hues that induced the new Pope, Martin V, to agree to the Greeks' demand that he be represented at a union council to be convoked to Constantinople by the Emperor, just because in such a council he apparently saw nothing more than the solemn framework for the ratification of a unity already established de facto. Cardinal Fonseca was supposed to represent the Pope at this ceremony. But the realization was slowed down, because in the thirty-six articles it was stipulated that the Pope should finance the undertaking and at the moment he did not have the necessary means. And once the papal till had been replenished, a Turkish attack on Constantinople thwarted the projected meeting (1422). Hence Martin V first sent a nuncio to Constantinople, the Franciscan Anthony da Massa, to make the preparations. At that time, however, it soon became clear how misleading had been the optimism of the Byzantine envoys. The Greeks were far from agreeing to an unscrutinized union and had no intention of viewing an ecumenical council as a mere backdrop for submission. The Emperor flatly disavowed his envoys and demanded a council at which the disagreements between the Churches should be taken up point by point. [21] Thereupon, quite under-

[18] H. Finke, *Acta conc. Constanc.*, I (Münster 1896), 491.
[19] About him *cf.* G. Cammelli, *Manuele Crisolora* (Florence 1941).
[20] The chiefs of the embassy were Nicholas Eudaimonoioannes and Joseph Bladynteros. The articles are not extant.
[21] Da Massa's report is given in Raynaldus, *Annales eccl.*, 1422, nos. 5–15, and *Mansi*, XXVIII, 1063–68. Other documents (Greek translation and the position of the Byzantine

standably, the Pope's readiness for what was basically a Greek Council at Constantinople with a single representative of the Latin Church quickly disappeared.

Just the same, the way was opened for a compromise. Martin V, however, died and his successor, Eugene IV, had his hands full in dealing with conciliarism, which now exploded at the Council of Basel. But eventually it was this very power struggle — *risit Oriens*, remarked Aeneas Sylvius of this favourable moment — that brought the idea of union to maturity. For both sides the gaining of the Greeks could only mean a powerful rise in prestige and so both sides wooed them. All cities that were adequate were suggested as the meeting place; Constantinople was repeatedly considered, as were Vienna and Buda and finally preference was given to Avignon or Florence or Ferrara. Even just before the departure of the Greeks it was not clear whether they would board the squadron sent by the Council of Basel or that sent by the Pope, and when at last they reached Venice in the papal flotilla it was even then probably only the political advice of the Most Serene Republic that definitely induced them to go to Ferrara.[22]

The story of the Council of Ferrara-Florence (1438–39) is related elsewhere.[23] For an appreciation of the fate of the union in the East only what follows need be noted here. Since the victory of Eugene IV over his opponents at Basel, far from being achieved at the beginning of the Council, needed a real union to crown it, the Pope was prepared for every imaginable concession. The Synod was a papal epic *par excellence*. Any forced union, any lack of freedom of debate, even any cutting short of disputes by means of dictation from Rome was out of the question. It was the sort of council the Greeks had always wanted.[24] But the pressure of political circumstances? With this the Emperor John VIII (1425–48) had primarily to reckon. He took part in the Council in person and switched signals on several occasions. But one almost feels that, the longer the Council lasted, the more precisely he got to know the Pope's financial difficulties and mortgaging, and the more disillusioned he must have become because of the slight participation of the secular princes, so much the less was he convinced of the political success of a Church union. Even at the very end he hinted

---

synod) in V. Laurent, "Les neufs articles du Pape Martin V et la réponse inédite du patriarche de Constantinople Joseph II," *RÉB*, 20 (1962), 5–60.

[22] J. Zhishman, *Die Unionsverhandlungen zwischen der orientalischen und römischen Kirche seit dem Anfang des 15. Jh. bis zum Conzil von Ferrara* (Vienna 1858); M.-H. Laurent, "L'activité d'André Chrysoberges O.P. sous le pontificat de Martin V," *ÉO*, 34 (1935), 414–38; A. N. Diamantopulos, 'Απόπειραι πρὸς ἕνωσιν τῶν ἐκκλησιῶν κατὰ τὸν ιε' αἰῶνα (Athens 1924).

[23] See *supra*, Chapter 50.

[24] *Cf.* especially J. Gill, "Greeks and Latins in a Common Council," *OrChrP*, 25 (1959), 265–87, and B. Schultze, "Das letzte ökumenische Einigungskonzil theologisch gesehen," *OrChP*, 25 (1959), 288–309.

at his readiness to return to Constantinople without a settlement. And his later attitude does not give the lie to this impression. At last, on 6 July 1439, the union was promulgated in the decree "Laetentur Caeli"[25] and all the Greeks who were entitled to do so signed it, except the Metropolitan Mark Eugenicus of Ephesus. The signatures were not coerced and were probably sincere.

Nevertheless it is impossible to maintain that one side had convinced the other by arguments. If, for example, both *a filio* and *per filium* were considered valid and accepted as expressing one and the same dogmatic truth, this happened not from philological and primarily also not from dogmatic considerations, but because both formulations were found in recognized Fathers and because all held to the axiom that the Fathers of the Church, being inspired, could not err and accordingly the different formulations had to mean the same thing. Even Mark Eugenicus could not escape this argument, and hence he again and again hinted that the writings of the Latins were probably falsified. Thus, except for men like Bessarion of Nicaea and Isidore of Kiev, the Greeks were coerced by the possibility of union to a "notional assent," but they were unenthusiastic over the achievement of union, because the last inner resistances had by no means been broken — a mood that could not long withstand the cool reception that was theirs at Constantinople in February 1440. More serious was the fact that the Emperor himself died in 1448 without having been able to decide to promulgate the union,[26] although both successors of the Patriarch Joseph II,[27] who had died at Florence, Metrophanes II (1440–43) and Gregory III (1443–51), constantly urged him to do so.

Yet the achieving of union had, in the meantime, brought about even political consequences. As seldom before, it now seemed possible to end Turkish rule in the Balkans. A joint expedition of Hungarian, Venetian, and papal forces, combined with a Byzantine shielding maneuver, was to force the issue. But the Battle of Varna (1444) ended as one more defeat. The union had not fulfilled its political aim.[28] The new, and last, Byzantine Emperor, Constantine XI Dragases (1448–53), a man of political ability, saw in the union, in spite of everything, a better basis of further exertions for the defense of Constantinople than had been the case with the delaying tactics of his dead brother, John VIII. At first there were severe tensions, as a result of which the Patriarch Gregory III abandoned his see and went into voluntary exile in Rome, but finally, on 12 December 1452, a solemn

---

[25] The original is in the Laurenziana in Florence; *cf.* A. Mercati, "Il decreto d'unione del 6 luglio 1439 nell'Archivio Segreto Vaticano," *OrChrP*, 11 (1945), 5–44.
[26] J. Gill, "John VIII Palaeologus. A Character Study," *Silloge Bizantina in onore di S. G. Mercati* (Rome 1957), 152–70.
[27] J. Gill, "Joseph II, Patriarch of Constantinople, " *OrChrP*, 21 (1955), 79–101.
[28] O. Halecki, *The Crusade of Varna* (New York 1943).

liturgy with a commemoration of the Pope could be celebrated in Hagia Sophia, and during it the decree "Laetentur Caeli" was promulgated.[29] But this had no effect on the fate of Constantinople. And the first Patriarch under Muslim rule, Gennadius Scholarius, governed the remnant of his church as though the act of 1452 had never taken place.

CHAPTER 52

Hesychasm and Palamism

Once again, before the history of the Byzantine Empire came to an end, the structure of the Imperial Church was convulsed by a quarrel that recalls the iconoclast strife of the eighth and ninth centuries. It was a dispute in regard to a mysticism, fought out on dogmatic grounds. Hesychasm may be understood as Byzantine mysticism in its entirety, with its striving for *apatheia* (resignation) and peace of soul. By reason of expediency in regard to terminology, however, it is best to restrict the term Hesychasm to one facet of this mysticism, which cannot be separated from the whole but shows specific trends.[1] In the classical threefold ascent to God — practice (asceticism), "natural theology" (comprehension by means of meditation and contemplation of the ultimate cause of things and of their history in God), and *theoria* or *theologia* (union with God) — the emphasis shifts slowly but constantly. The great ascetical subject of "practice" is displaced, not completely but nevertheless energetically, by a psycho-physical technique of recollection and prayer. The rhythmic repetition, carried out in a Yogi-like position, of a prayer formula — the "monologue" usually called the "Prayer of Jesus" today[2] — has the task of completely "emptying" the mind, of transcending not only every meditative representation of the imagination but also every λογισμός, every formation of concepts, to arrive at full "nakedness" of mind upon which shines the vision of the Godhead in light, a vision which seizes upon the whole man and comes to rest in an undefined sphere between corporal visibility and invisibility. That which the classical

---

[29] The "acts" of a synod in Constantinople in 1450, in which the union is supposed to have been solemnly repudiated, are a forgery. *Cf.* Chr. Papaioannou, 'Εκκλησ. 'Αλήθεια 15 (1895–96), 16 (1896–97), in several sequences, and S. Petrides, *ÉO*, 14 (1911), 204–07.

[1] *Cf.* I. Hausherr, "Les grands courants de la spiritualité orientale," *OrChrP*, 1 (1935), 114–38.

[2] *Cf.* I. Hausherr, *Noms du Christ et voies d'oraison* (Rome 1960); J. Brian-Chaninov, *On the Prayer of Jesus* (London 1952); B. Schultze, "Untersuchungen über das Jesusgebet," *OrChrP*, 18 (1952), 319–43; G. Wunderle, *Zur Psychologie des hesychastischen Gebets* (Würzburg 1949).

Byzantine mystics, and especially Maximus Confessor, had cultivated, "natural theology," declines more and more in importance, even if it is dragged into the terminology.[3] There thus disappears one of the chief connections between mysticism and Christian humanism, because this natural theology was the sphere of a spiritualized universal sympathy, a universal embrace, a universal emotion. The Hesychasts' impatience could not endure stopping at this level.

The age of the first Emperors of the House of Palaeologus was the period of the triumphant progress of this method of prayer, which possessed the inherent desire to establish itself absolutely. There appeared treatises explaining, revealing, and concealing this method, for example, by Nicephorus,[4] a monk of Mount Athos and contemporary of Michael VIII, and especially by Gregory Sinaites, known as the father of this mysticism, though he was certainly its most cautious theorist.[5] The masters gained disciples. Political difficulties on Athos — raids by the Turks, arguments with the Serbs, and so forth — again and again led masters and disciples to more distant surroundings, especially to Thessalonica. Devout circles were formed, in which the Hesychasts passed on their method, and quarrels with the still active Bogomilism intruded themselves. The more this mysticism spread, naturally the more it was exposed to misinterpretation and misuse. The terminology of the masters, going back to Simeon the New Theologian[6] and even to a Messalian origin, in regard to the vision of light strongly scintillated between metaphor and matter and thus gave support to those who were inclined, contrary to the counsels of Gregory Sinaites, to identify every light experience and every by-product of their rigorous psychotechnique with a specific grace of God and his own proper light.

Conflict was not long in coming.[7] It found its occasion at last in the susceptible vanity of the protagonists. The monk Barlaam of Calabria, born in Orthodoxy and raised a Greek, but even so hailing from the "Latinizing" fringes of the Empire — this was one of the chief reasons for the antipathy that he encountered everywhere — had energetically defended the Byzantine view in his treatises on the procession of the Holy Spirit, but a monk of

---

[3] I. Hausherr, "A propos de spiritualité hésychaste," *OrChrP*, 3 (1935), 260–72.

[4] *PG*, 147, 945–66. Older is the most celebrated of the methods, attributed to Simeon the New Theologian; see I. Hausherr (ed.), *La méthode d'oraison hésychaste* (Rome 1927), with French translation and commentary; cf. also M. Jugie, "Les origines de la méthode d'oraison des hésychastes," *ÉO*, 30 (1931), 179–85.

[5] His works in *PG*, 150, 1240–1345.

[6] K. Holl, *Enthusiasmus und Bussgewalt* (Leipzig 1898) is still the best work on him; cf. also the long introduction in I. Hausherr and G. Horn, *Un grand mystique byzantin: Vie de Syméon le Nouveau Théologien* (Rome 1928).

[7] Cf. especially J. Meyendorff, "L'origine de la controverse palamite," *Théologie*, 25 (1954), 602–27; *idem*, "Les débuts de la controverse hésychaste," *Byzantion*, 23 (1953), 87–120.

Athos, Gregory Palamas, took exception to the form of his syllogistic reasoning. Barlaam, easily offended and greatly infatuated with his Aristotelian education, thereupon attacked Palamas's method of argument — perhaps, in the situation, not without reason. The quarrel rapidly and noticeably became envenomed and Palamas soon fell back upon a fundamentally anti-dialectical procedure, that is, to a type of theology that is no longer rational but purely mystical in nature. Thereupon, Barlaam felt obliged to throw light on his opponent's intellectual background and in so doing he quickly met something of which he had hitherto been unaware — Hesychasm, of which Palamas was an ardent protagonist. He was told by Hesychasts — by immature pupils, so the Palamites later claimed — that they were in possession of an infallible method which helped them to see with bodily eyes that uncreated light which suffused Jesus on Mount Tabor and is identical with the divinity itself. They told him about their exercises of concentration and their technique of prayer — and soon Barlaam knew enough. In the Hesychasts he saw a return of the old Messalians, people who apparently sought the seat of the soul somewhere in the region of the navel — that is why he gave them the derisive label of "Omphalopsychists," — above all, men who either materialized God in order to see him or introduced an unlawful distinction between God's essence and operations.

A friend of both Barlaam and Palamas, the Athos monk Gregory Akindynos, warned the Calabrian against rash attacks on the sacrosanct Athonian monachism but Barlaam refused to be deterred any longer and from 1338 proceeded to denounce this mysticism in treatises and at a synod in Constantinople. Palamas took this deeply to heart and in a steadily rising spiral developed an anti-Barlaamite pamphlet literature, the essence of a theology that was fittingly termed "Palamism." At intervals this theology also had recourse to syllogisms but fundamentally it recognized as the basis of theology only the tradition of the Fathers and the personal mystical inspiration of the theologian. Central, precisely in order to safeguard the light visions of the Hesychasts, is the real distinction between God's completely inaccessible essence, invisible even to the blessed in heaven, and his operations, the chief of which is *gratia increata* and to which belongs the light of Tabor, identical with it. Nothing was farther from Palamas's thought than to introduce a "division" in God but he merely succeeded in establishing an antinomy between unity and real distinction. The attempt to trace this doctrine to the patristic tradition was based, at least as regards the much quoted Maximus Confessor,[8] on a misinterpretation, even if occasionally the strongly rhetorical and emphatic diction of Orthodox preachers and hymnographers can be properly bent in favour of Palamas without too great

---

[8] E. v. Ivánka, "Palamismus und Vätertradition," *L'Église et les églises,* II (Chevetogne 1954), 29–46.

difficulties. But his adherents were basically by no means hesitant to waive the proofs from tradition and to expound their theology as something new: a legitimate continuation of the New Testament revelation through their inspired master.

Barlaam submitted his writings to the Patriarch John XIV Calecas (1334 to 1347), a theologically indecisive and politically wavering prelate, who doubtless found Palamas's theology intrinsically foreign, although he was not favourably disposed toward Barlaam. He wanted to dispose of the quarrel and understood exactly how dangerous it would be to run afoul of the Athonians. Monachism had indeed become a dread power, especially since the Second Council of Lyons and the abortive union, and in comparison with it the union of patriarchal and imperial authority counted for rather little. Meanwhile, inspired by Palamas himself, a large majority of the Athonians had issued a *tomos,* a dogmatic manifesto, which set forth the basic tenets of the Palamite doctrine as the original proper ingredient of Orthodoxy and anathematized Barlaam as a heretic.[9] The matter pressed for a decision.

Details of the two synods held in Constantinople in June and August 1341 escape us, for the evaluation of the extant official documents will remain disputed. The first session took place on 10 June in Hagia Sophia, with the Emperor Andronicus III (1328–41) presiding. Barlaam was not permitted to advance his dogmatic contentions, since, as he was told, this was the affair of the hierarchy. Palamas, on the other hand, was absolved of the charge of ditheism, the doctrine of the real distinction between God's essence and operation was considered rather *en passant* than expressly, and the reproaches levelled at the Hesychasts' method of prayer were rejected. The questions were in no sense probed by the members of the synod, but Barlaam observed that he could count on no sympathy and submitted to the prohibition of again attacking Palamas and the mystics. Thereupon the session ended, and the Emperor died a few days later. Barlaam now felt no longer bound by his promise, but he returned to the West and eventually became a Catholic and Bishop of Gerace. He died in 1350.

A new opponent, who remained behind, was Gregory Akindynos. He had not become disloyal to the monastic ideals of the Athonians but he now rejected the theological argumentation of his friend Palamas. The synod again met, presided over by the grand chamberlain John Cantacuzene, a member of the Council of Regency for the Emperor John V Palaeologus, who was under age. But political complications began to play a role. In the Council of Regency the Patriarch and the grand chamberlain were struggling for the decisive influence, and above them both stood the widowed Empress, Anne of Savoy. This rivalry, rather than any particular internal affinity,

---

[9] The so-called Τόμος ἁγιορειτικός in *PG,* 150, 1225–36.

may have been the reason why Cantacuzene now resolutely embraced the Palamite faction *vis-à-vis* the half-hearted Patriarch. And thus Palamism was dragged into the conflict about to explode between Cantacuzene and the Palaeologi and at the same time into the corresponding social struggles in the Empire; yet no inner connection can be established. At any rate, Akindynos was condemned (August 1341). Then the synodal decree *(tomos)* [10] of both sessions was to be prepared, but the Patriarch refused to participate unless action was limited to a *tomos* which would ignore the August session, over which, in his opinion, Cantacuzene had unlawfully presided, and the condemnation of Akindynos. The *tomos* was drawn up anyhow, but displayed great restraint. It was not really a far-reaching decision, but merely a prohibition of further discussion of the subject. The struggle in the Council of Regency continued to smoulder, and the Patriarch joined with Alexius Apokaukos in an effort to hamstring Cantacuzene. When a campaign kept the grand chamberlain away from the capital, Apokaukos and the Patriarch finally usurped power. Palamas had reason to fear that in these circumstances the successes of 1341 would be lost to him, and so he definitely joined the faction of Cantacuzene, who thereupon had himself acclaimed as Emperor on 26 October 1341. He obviously found in the Palamites a suitable instrument for his plans and thereafter energetically favoured them, though he had originally supported Barlaam.

Palamas continued to develop his theories in writings, thereby affording the Patriarch an opportunity to charge him with violating the *tomos* of 1341. On the other hand, he allowed Akindynos more and more leeway for his attack on Palamas. At several conferences in 1342 and 1344 the writings of Palamas, who was arrested at the behest of Calecas, were condemned and he was personally anathematized. But the Patriarch's days were numbered. Cantacuzene approached the capital in a menacing mood, and Anne of Savoy considered sacrificing the Patriarch and reaching an amicable settlement with Cantacuzene. Only in this way could the Palamites be won over and the Dynasty of Palaeologus saved. Since Calecas had meanwhile raised Akindynos, who had earlier been condemned, to the diaconate, there was at hand a canonical reason for deposing him. This took place the day before Cantacuzene triumphantly forced his way into the capital on 2 February 1347 and was crowned Emperor. [11] At once Palamas was set free and Akindynos was excommunicated. Isidore, former Bishop of Monembasia, a staunch Palamite, was chosen Patriarch (1347–50).

Still, the victory of Palamism was not yet assured. The opposition was

---

[10] PG, 151, 679–92, and Miklosich-Müller, *Acta et diplomata graeca medii aevi*, I (Vienna 1860), 202–16.

[11] J. Meyendorff, "Le tome synodal de 1347," *Zbornik radova Vizant. Inst.*, 8 (1963), 209–27; cf. also G. T. Dennis in *JÖByzG*, 9 (1900), 51–55, and P. Wirth in *ByZ*, 56 (1963), 16–23.

active. Not a few prelates and clerics regarded the theology of Palamas as merely an unlawful *neoterismos,* and not a few monks were unwilling to be identified with the behaviour of the Hesychasts. One may suspect that this was the position of the cenobites, to whom it was clear that Hesychasm implied the destruction of the cenobitic ideal. And finally, the opposition had its chief centre in the intellectuals and humanists of the capital. These circles must not for that reason be charged with "agnosticism." They were as orthodox as their opponents claimed to be, but in Hesychasm and Palamism they saw threats to far too many values which had hitherto flourished peacefully in the shadow of Orthodoxy. [12] Thus all questions were supposed to be settled at a general synod which met on 28 May 1351 in the imperial palace. John VI Cantacuzene presided. He had probably gone to great pains to see to it that the opposition was only meagerly represented. Its leadership had meanwhile been assumed by the historian and polyhistor, Nicephorus Gregoras. The opposition was heard, but there is no doubt that it presented its case clumsily and failed to concentrate on the essentials of the dispute. Finally, at the fifth session, all were excommunicated who refused to recognize the orthodoxy of the Palamite doctrine. A long synodal *tomos* was drawn up, which contained an account of the proceedings and the dogmatic decisions. On 15 August it was published over the signatures of the Emperor John Cantacuzene and the Patriarch, and later that of the coemperor, John V Palaeologus, was added. [13] One further solemn act occurred. In the *synodicon* for the annual celebration of the Sunday of Orthodoxy new anathemas were inserted against all who opposed the teachings of Palamas. [14] It was the greatest triumph which Palamas, who had in the interval become Metropolitan of Thessalonica, could have hoped for. Hardly ever had Orthodoxy so identified its doctrine with a single person as it did in this case. And hardly ever had it put its fundamental principle of traditionalism to so severe a test as now. No change in the situation occurred when Cantacuzene, the protector of the Palamites, had to give place to the legitimate Palaeologus in 1354. John V could scarcely afford to antagonize the large Palamite party by an opposing religious policy and besides he was apparently uninterested in theology. Furthermore, Cantacuzene, as earlier, was still a towering personage, whom John V could not ignore. Hence the Palamite hierarchy, headed by the Patriarch Philotheus Coccinus (1353–54 and 1364–76), [15] had a free hand.

[12] *Cf.* especially, H. G. Beck, "Humanismus und Palamismus," *XIIᵉ Congrès Intern. des Études byzantines,* Ohrid 1961, Rapports III (Belgrade 1961), 63–82.
[13] *PG,* 151, 717–63, and *Mansi,* XXVI, 127–99; F. Dölger, "Ein byzantinisches Staatsdokument in der Universitätsbibliothek Basel," *HJ,* 72 (1953), 205–21; also E. Honigmann, *ByZ,* 47 (1954), 104–15, and R. J. Loenertz, *ByZ,* 47 (1954), 116.
[14] F. Uspenskij, *Sinodik v nedělju pravoslavija* (Odessa 1893), 30–38.
[15] On Philotheus, see V. Laurent, *DThC,* XII/2, 1498–1509.

In no sense was Palamism, as has been said repeatedly, the result of a conflict between Latin scholasticism — Barlaam was not a Latin scholastic — and Greek patristic thought. Its victory was easy for the very reason that its strongest opponents, Barlaam and Akindynos, were quickly reduced to silence and thereafter the opposition lacked qualified leaders. The situation did not change until, through the translations of Demetrius Kydones and his brother Prochorus, the writings of Thomas Aquinas and other scholastics became known in Byzantium and exercised an influence. Aquinas's rigid theology provided the opponents of Palamas with strong weapons not available in the limited arsenal of fourteenth-century Byzantine theology. It is true that Prochorus Kydones, a monk of Athos, did not escape excommunication at the hands of the Patriarch Philotheus (1368), but from the *tomos*[16] condemning him it is evident how far Prochorus had driven his opponents into a corner, and from the writings of Demetrius Kydones it appears that the victory was not achieved by the Palamite doctrine exclusively. Other theologians, John Kyparissiotes and especially Manuel Calecas, stiffened the opposition. Then the Palamites themselves abandoned certain daring formulations — even Cantacuzene, who had meanwhile become a theological author in his monastic retreat. The light of Tabor played an ever less prominent role, the teaching on the distinction was made more refined, and scholars have referred to a *palamisme mitigé* among the later Palamites. Furthermore, a man such as Cantacuzene, even as a monk still a politician, clearly perceived the urgency of Church reunion and was smart enough not to aggravate further the points of controversy between East and West by anything so serious as the Palamite teaching on God. Thus intransigent Palamism was recalled from the front line of battle and intentionally kept outside the negotiations with Rome, especially at the Council of Ferrara-Florence.[17]

But the mystics, including the Hesychasts in the strict sense, had fundamentally no need of the support of Palamism. Palamism proper almost completely died out for centuries around the middle of the fifteenth century, while mysticism, the source for its rise, continued on undisturbed.

A comprehensive evaluation of the movement is difficult to reach, since as yet too few sources have been edited and published and we are only meagerly informed about its sociological stratification. Palamas undoubtedly had recourse to an ancient basic concern of Eastern theology and in addition possessed a refined sensitivity to the limits of theological testimony. But neither he nor his age was in a position to grasp mystical facts of a parapsychological nature and reduce them to their contingency. His mistake was to have ignored — or not to have taken seriously enough — the warnings of

---

[16] *PG*, 151, 693–716. The synod canonized Palamas, who had died in 1359.
[17] *Cf.* J. Gill, *The Council of Florence* (Cambridge 1961), 205 f. and 267.

the classical Byzantine mystics against such phenomena. And his mystical polemic urge kept him from appreciating the proper scope of a rational theology. That he decisively influenced Orthodox theology, that he again opened up recourse to the mystical sources and heightened the skepticism in regard to rational theology cannot be denied. He gave to Orthodoxy a colouring which has become integral to it.

CHAPTER 53

Intellectual Life in the Late Mediaeval Byzantine Church

The great doctrinal controversy over union of the Churches in the second half of the thirteenth century had summoned theologians of all trends and shades to the battle field and had finally exhausted them. Thus at the beginning of the fourteenth century there was everywhere an unmistakable lack of interest in dogmatic questions and several contemporary representatives of the Byzantine intelligentsia made no secret of this. On the other hand, these decades were a great and auspicious age of Christian humanism in Byzantium. It was not only that in this period the output of studies dealing with ancient authors was especially large, as evidenced by the manuscripts extant. This was no mere accident but an expression of the pains taken by the intellectuals. Far more significant is the fact that the pagan cultural tradition was now interpreted and made available in terms of Christian standards by means of new ideas, a new receptiveness, and new theological categories. In other words, the mere acknowledgment of these treasures, their existence in mutual isolation, gave way to a synthesis, however risky this may have been in individual cases. For the first time in Byzantine intellectual history even churchmen no longer regarded the legacy of antiquity as mere decoration in comparison with the strictly Christian inheritance, something merely tolerated for possible use. This was the age when the term "Hellene" no longer referred almost exclusively, as earlier, to pagans but was used proudly by the "Romaioi" as an expression of their history and of their zeal for education.[1]

Many names could be given. Let it suffice, however, to treat of Maximus Planudes, Theodore Metochites, and Nicephorus Gregoras, while mentioning at least some others in passing. Their activity was versatile, each was some-

---

[1] *Cf.* D. S. Balanos, "Kirche und Nation in der orthodoxen Kirche," *ZKG,* 57 (1938), 554–65; F. Dölger, *Rom in der Gedankenwelt der Byzantiner: Byzanz und die europäische Staatenwelt* (Ettal 1953), 70–115; S. Runciman, "Byzantine and Hellene in the Fourteenth Century," Τόμος Κωνσταντίνου Ἀρμενοπούλου (Thessalonica 1952), 27–31; K. Lechner, *Hellenen und Barbaren* (Munich 1954).

thing of a polyhistor, and as a group they formed a not unimportant class of sensitive humanists, who, guided by Christian categories of thought, allowed the abundance of the legacy to take its effect on themselves, not, however, forcing a compromise but striving for it by means of a calm development — *viatores in hoc saeculo*.

With Maximus Planudes (d. *ca.* 1305)[2] we are not merely in the very midst of the best period of the transmission of classical literature but likewise at the start of a vast extension of the content and horizon of culture, achieved by the reception of the Latin heritage also. Planudes translated into Greek not only the *Somnium Scipionis*, not only Ovid and Macrobius, but Boethius's *De consolatione Philosophiae* and Augustine's *De Trinitate*. It is revealing that the last mentioned translation had no direct connection with the theological controversies of the day but, together with the other translations, was an expression of a happy curiosity, stirred by a universal interest in the good and the beautiful, even though this emanated from a "Church" which till then had been faced as something foreign.

Nicephorus Chumnus (*ca.* 1250–1327),[3] for years imperial chancellor and high court dignitary, frequently wrote, it is true, against Plato's seductive tricks and regarded Aristotle as the genuine philosopher of humanism; but this was more a warning against those doctrines of Platonism and Neoplatonism that were irreconcilable with Christianity than a war against Platonism as such. He too lived to a great extent on the heritage of antiquity, even though he was certainly prudent and petulantly guarded. And in fact the many controversies in which he found himself involved because of his writings[4] show how actively problems engaged the minds of the age. His chief opponent, Theodore Metochites (*ca.* 1260–1332),[5] belonged, like Chumnus, to the lay class which was the backbone of public service and of culture. He too made his career at the court of the Emperor Andronicus II and rose to the highest dignity, that of *megas logothetes*. No systematizer, his thought unfolded itself in the *aperçu*, his literary form was the essay. More than is true of the other Byzantines, his literary output was marked by the prevailing internal insecurity and frequently he could not offer more than to set one solution in opposition to the others. The problematic order of precedence between *vita activa* and *vita contemplativa* permeated his entire

[2] C. Wendel, "Maximos Planudes," *Pauly-Wissowa*, XX/2, 2202–53; A. Pertusi, "La fortuna di Boezio a Bisanzio," *APhilHistOS*, 11 (1951), 301–22; M. Gigante, "La cultura latina a Bisanzio nel secolo XIII," *La Parola del Passato*, 82 (1962), 32–51.

[3] J. Verpeaux, *Nicéphore Choumnos, homme d'État et humaniste byzantin* (Paris 1959).

[4] I. Ševčenko, *Études sur la polémique entre Théodore Métochite et Nicéphore Choumnos* (Brussels 1962).

[5] H. G. Beck, *Theodoros Metochites: Die Krise des byzantinischen Weltbildes im 14. Jh.* (Munich 1952); H. Hunger, "Theodoros Metochites als Vorläufer des Humanismus in Byzanz," *ByZ*, 45 (1952), 4–19.

creative activity and obviously his very existence, to the prejudice of the policy of his Emperor, for which he must bear responsibility to a great extent — a central problem of any intellectual history, but an absolutely elementary problem of Greek Orthodoxy. His views on the value and prestige of practice were more progressive than those of his contemporaries and, without even making mention of it, he had attained, better than they, to the proper balance postulated by Christianity, not least because he left the balance there, exposed and with all its susceptibility. He was not a theologian, but he did theolgy a service precisely because he did not presume to force this system of thought into the theological categories of his Church, to which he was devoted. In view of the nature of this terminology, such a situation would have involved the collapse of the desired intellectual progress *a priori*.

Metochites refers again and again gratefully and respectfully to the monk Joseph, known as the Philosopher (*ca.* 1280–*ca.* 1330),[6] author of a broadly planned "Encyclopedia." In this work he gave full recognition to the individual fields of knowledge, but then in treating of the four cardinal virtues he directed these fields to the contemplation of God and of the Trinity.

Metochites's pupil, Nicephorus Gregoras (1295–*ca.* 1360),[7] belonged to the period when the halcyon days of Byzantine intellectual history were already over. He is first and by predilection the historian of his age. And if he was not at his best as protagonist of the anti-Palamites, he nevertheless proved himself to be a humanist who, in defense of his intellectual ideals, entered the arena against Palamite intransigence. Particularly, his rich output in hagiography demonstrates that these humanists wanted to operate within the Church and using the Church's means.

But if the great generation of humanists was buried with him, this was surely not due primarily to the victory of Palamism. Equally responsible was the hopeless situation of the Empire: civil strife, social revolution, and the steadily increasing danger from the Turks. The intellectual forces were, it is true, powerfully engaged by the Palamite controversy. But in the very midst of this struggle occurred an event of far-reaching importance: the translating of Latin theologians into Greek. In this respect *facile princeps* was Demetrius Kydones (*ca.* 1324–*ca.* 1398),[8] a highly cultured citizen of Thessalonica, for many years chancellor of Emperors and the leading

---

[6] *Cf.* G. Vitelli, "Indice de' codici greci Riccardiani," *Studi Ital. di Filol. Class.*, 2 (1894), 490–92; M. Treu, "Der Philosoph Joseph," *ByZ*, 8 (1899), 1–64; N. Terzaghi, *Studi Ital. di Filol. Class.*, 10 (1902), 121–32.

[7] R. Guilland, *Essai sur Nicéphore Grégoras. L'homme et l'oeuvre* (Paris 1927).

[8] M. Jugie, "Démétrius Cydonès et la théologie latine à Byzance aux XIVᵉ et XVᵉ siècles," *ÉO*, 27 (1928), 385–402; M. Rackl, "Demetrius Kydones als Verteidiger und Übersetzer des hl. Thomas von Aquin," *Katholik*, 95, I (1915), 21–40; *idem*, "Die ungedruckte Vertei-

personality of the second half of the century. Dependent in the foreign ministry on the inadequate knowledge of Latin possessed by his interpreters, he decided to learn Latin himself and studied under a Dominican, who made him thoroughly familiar first of all with the *Summa contra Gentiles*. Struck by the lucidity of this Latin, he set about translating it and on 24 December 1354 completed the task in an equally lucid classical Greek. Then he took up parts of the *Summa theologica,* besides the brief *Ad cantorem Antiochenum* and other short works. Delight led him on to Augustine, Anselm of Canterbury, Peter of Poitiers, and Ricoldo da Monte Croce. At first Kydones had no theological aim in mind. And when people discovered the treasures of Greek thought in Latin dress, the translations were a huge success. John Cantacuzene, Neilus Kabasilas, [9] and others were enraptured.

But it was not long before the theological content was discovered, before advocates of union ascertained how valuable an alliance they had found and enemies of union how difficult it would probably be to argue against them. The translations thus intensified the Byzantine discord — from the time of the Second Council of Lyons there had been a not insignificant group of "Latinophrones" — and the controversy could only become worse. The wealth of Latin scholasticism now saw service in the conflict with the Palamites, and Demetrius bore the entire brunt. While it is true that he was not personally attacked, he had to look on while his brother Prochorus, who had shared the work of translating and was the first to draw the theological conclusions, was accused of heresy, while his many other students, several of whom thus found the way to the Catholic faith, had to go into exile, and he himself was driven into an increasing isolation. His autobiographical writings [10] are the deeply human expression of the intellectual situation in dying Byzantium.

In John Kyparissiotes, one of the most important of the anti-Palamites, an acquaintance with the Kydones translations probably exerted very little influence. But Manuel Calecas (d. 1410), [11] a pupil of Kydones, followed in the steps of his master and composed a brief *Summa* of the faith, in which Augustine and Aquinas obtain full recognition. It is significant for the extent of the interchange that Ambrose Traversari now translated his work against the heresies of the Greeks into Latin, just as it is no longer a matter for surprise that Calecas died a Dominican after imitating Kydones by

digungsschrift des Demetrius Kydones für Thomas von Aquin," *DTh,* 7 (1920), 303–17; H. G. Beck, "Der Kampf um den thomistischen Theologiebegriff in Byzanz," *DTh,* 13 (1935), 1–22.

[9] *Beck,* 727 f.

[10] H. G. Beck, "Die 'Apologia pro vita sua'," *OstKSt,* 1 (1952), 208–25, 264–82 (German translation).

[11] R. J. Loenertz, "Manuel Calécas, sa vie et ses œuvres," *AFP,* 17 (1947), 195–207; *Beck,* 740 f.

translating Anselm, Aquinas, and other Latin writers. Still to be mentioned are the brothers Chrysoberges. Of these, Maximus (d. *ca.* 1429),[12] a pupil of Kydones, also became a Catholic and a Dominican; Andrew (d. 1456)[13] was interpreter of the Greek envoys sent to Pope Martin V, worked tirelessly for union, acted as papal nuncio to the Emperor John VIII, and finally became Archbishop of Nicosia on Cyprus. And by no means least of the pupils of Kydones was the famed humanist Manuel Chrysoloras (d. 1415), the first teacher of Greek in Florence.

Opposition to the Kydones translations grew slowly. The most striking example is provided by Neilus Kabasilas, Metropolitan of Thessalonica (d. *ca.* 1363), Kydones's deeply revered teacher. On the appearance of the first translations of Aquinas he had nothing but praise for his pupil's achievement. But when he recognized that here was an arsenal which the Byzantines could match only with great difficulty, he tried to dissuade Kydones from his undertaking. In this effort he brought forward the patriotic argument that would become increasingly decisive in the course of the next years: Whatever may be thought about the opinion of the Latins, one must not on their account sacrifice the teaching inherited from one's ancestors; "it is not safe to take up arms against Emperor, Patriarch, and people." When this argument proved unavailing, Kabasilas undertook to compose a voluminous refutation of Aquinas, which included a sharp attack on the scholastic method altogether.[14] Other treatises followed, from the pens of Joseph Philagrius, Angelus Panaretus, George Boilas, and Angelus Aeidarus. Demetrius Chrysoloras, friend of the Emperor Manuel II, wrote a dialogue in which he had Thomas Aquinas, Neilus Kabasilas, Kydones, and himself take part.

The sequel to all this was a great uneasiness. Some simply rejected the scholastic method.

> Go ahead and use your syllogisms and unsheathe them against us. . . . If I so wished, I could hold far better syllogisms against your sophistic considerations. But I do not care to. I obtain proofs from the Fathers and their writings. You come with Aristotle and Plato; I oppose you with the Galilean fishers and their candid word. The cross has not yet lost its power, even though for some it is regarded as folly to preach it (Simeon of Thessalonica).[15]

Others suffered greatly from the inferior state of theological refinement in

---

[12] *Beck,* 742; R. J. Loenertz, *Correspondance de Manuel Calécas* (Città del Vaticano 1950), 57–63.

[13] R. J. Loenertz, "Les dominicains byzantins Théodore et André Chrysobergès," *AFP,* 9 (1939), 5–61, 128–83; M.-H. Laurent, "L'activité d'André Chrysobergès," *ÉO,* 34 (1935), 414–38.

[14] Partially edited by E. Candal, *Nilus Cabasilas et theologia s. Thomae* (Città del Vaticano 1945).

[15] *PG,* 145, 140.

Byzantium and reproached their fellow countrymen for this. George Scholarius, for example, did so expressly at the Council of Florence:

> There are people with no qualifications who want to compete with the Latins in theology and philosophy. For among us matters are not at their best. A person can attain to the highest posts even if he knows just enough theology not to give the impression of a complete lack of education. You see, classrooms are lacking, zeal for study has disappeared, and what does take place is subject to the circumstances.[16]

And even Syropulus, the antiunion historian of the Council of Florence, wrote incidentally:

> I know our prelates. Except for one or two, of what worth are they? I have no desire to follow persons whose theology cannot produce anything better.[17]

Kydones himself expressed the uneasiness of the opposite side:

> We exhaust ourselves with these quarrels and make it clear to the others that they should keep at a distance so that they will not be infected by contact with us... Is there anything imposing about our Empire — the only thing we can do is to complain![18]

If intellectual life in the Byzantine Empire had more and more to suffer from the growing malice of external circumstances, this situation was still unable to cripple its intellectual powers, and it may be emphasized that in this very period churchmen gave increasing thought to their social tasks. In this connection, for example, should be mentioned the preaching activity of the Metropolitan Isidore Glabas of Thessalonica (1380–96) in the face of the political difficulties of his flock. Most important were the social and ethical treatises of the great mystic Nicholas Kabasilas (d. before 1391),[19] nephew of Neilus Kabasilas. He preached against usury and exerted himself at the imperial court for a more equitable system of taxation. In a long squib he also attacked the judicial deterioration evident in state and Church.[20] Also to be mentioned is Joseph Bryennius (d. *ca.* 1431),[21] who, as a missionary of Orthodoxy on Crete and Cyprus, not only energetically

---

[16] L. Petit - M. Jugie - X. A. Siderides, *Œuvres complètes de Georges (Gennade) Scholarios,* I (Paris 1928), 299.

[17] S. Syropulus, *Vera historia unionis non verae* (The Hague 1660). 274.

[18] G. Mercati, *Notizie,* 374–76.

[19] His chief works are *Explanation of the Liturgy* (PG, 150, 368–492) and *On the Life in Christ (PG,* 150, 493–725); *cf. Beck,* 780–83; M. Lot-Borodine, *Un maître de la spiritualité byzantine au XIVe siècle: Nicolas Cabasilas* (Paris 1958).

[20] Against usury in *PG,* 150, 727–50; on taxation in R. Guilland (ed.), Εἰς μνήμην Σπ. Λάμπρου (Athens 1933), 269–77; on the deterioration in state and Church in I. Ševčenko (ed.), "Nicolas Cabasilas' 'Anti-Zealot' Discourse," *DOP,* 11 (1957), 81–171.

[21] N. Tomadakes, Ὁ Ἰωσὴφ Βρυέννιος (Athens 1947); *idem,* Σύλλαβος βυζαντινῶν μελετῶν καὶ κειμένων (Athens 1961), 491–611.

defended Orthodox doctrine against the Latins but just as zealously lashed out against the moral degeneration of clergy and people, so that the nickname "terror of priests" stuck to him. The abridged collection of his missionary sermons is one of the most eloquent sources for the cultural history of the age. [22]

Even in the domain of mysticism neither the Palamite controversy nor Hesychasm held a monopoly. In fact, it really seems as though the oversimplification of Hesychasm and Palamism evoked a reaction connected with the name of Nicholas Kabasilas. [23] This lay theologian did on occasion display a curt and scanty respect for Palamism, but his system sprang from an entirely different soil. His aim too was participation in God and deification, but the road leading to this included everything that fared badly with the Hesychasts, not only "natural theology," that is, mystical absorption in the world of creation, but especially the liturgy and not least an active mystical union with Christ. Meditation on the life of Christ, the imaginative submersion into his teaching, life, and example in a Franciscan fervour, the conscious contemplative junction with all phases of the liturgical celebration — all these elements clearly made his mysticism appear as necessarily antipodean to the Hesychasts' abrupt seeking of God. It preserved both the human nature of Christ and Christian humanism.

The Empire's closing decades encroached day by day upon the foundations of its intellectual life without bringing it to destruction. The intensified controversy with the West brought ever new impulses, and the gravest danger finally induced recourse to desperate means. Three representatives of this period brought this into clear awareness: Bessarion of Nicaea, George Scholarius, and George Gemistus Plethon.

Bessarion (ca. 1403–72) [24] was the Byzantine who, in exile, did most, next to Plethon, to keep alive the intellectual treasure of his nation. His development from the convinced Orthodox to the Catholic and the Cardinal was accomplished without any break, in a healthy, slow movement, and because his breadth of knowledge was already that of a Renaissance-type. Pupil and intimate of the paganizing Plethon, his heart was centred on Church union not only for political but for theological and religious reasons. His intellect submitted to the Latin arguments, but even as a Cardinal he never forgot the distress and the need of his homeland. His work *Contra calumniatores Platonis* attempted to do for Plato nothing less than what Albertus Magnus and Thomas Aquinas had actually done centuries earlier for Aristotle.

George Scholarius (ca. 1405–ca. 1472) [25] went the opposite way. Active

---

[22] Volume III of the edition printed in Leipzig in 1784.

[23] See footnote 19.

[24] L. Mohler, *Kardinal Bessarion als Theologe, Humanist und Staatsmann* (Paderborn 1923); *idem, Aus Bessarions Gelehrtenkreis* (Paderborn 1942); *idem, In Calumniatores Platonis* (Paderborn 1927).

[25] The extensive edition of his works, L. Petit - M. Jugie - X. A. Siderides, *Œuvres complètes*

first as a teacher and a lawyer, he soon became an imperial supreme judge and councillor and in this capacity accompanied John VIII to Florence. In their fulness his literary works show what the Byzantine mind was still capable of. Aquinas was scarcely less important to him than to Kydones. He translated the *De ente et essentia* and epitomized the *Summa contra Gentiles* and parts of the *Summa theologica,* he wrote the most distinguished Byzantine treatises on divine providence and predestination, and attacked simony, Judaism, and atheism. His formation was solid and he deplored nothing so much as the intellectual decay of his country. The sarcasm to which he gave vent at the Council of Florence was not directed against the Latins. He said that some persons had come to Florence convinced that they would have an easy time with the ignorance of the Latins, but matters had actually turned out quite differently. The Latins had brilliantly defended their faith; the Greeks could contribute only words which were without any importance. Why, then, should they not simply yield and conclude the union? And yet, at the death of Mark Eugenicus in 1445, this same Scholarius assumed the leadership of the antiunionists. His desperate patriotism clung to the "faith of the Fathers" as to the only thing left to the Byzantines, and his old love of Aquinas caused him now to exclaim, "O Thomas, if only you had been a Greek!"

The most singular road of all was that travelled by George Gemistus Plethon (d. 1452).[26] He belonged to one of those families which by custom held the high patriarchal posts at Hagia Sophia. He had to leave Constantinople quite early because of ideas which he had spread among his pupils, but he found refuge at the court of the Despots in Mistra, where Hellenism could still breathe somewhat freely. No less than Scholarius did he suffer from the misfortunes of his homeland, but, born reformer that he was, he thought to find in Hellenic antiquity enough material for a religious and political rebirth of the Greeks. Thus the road led him away from Christianity, especially from the monastic Byzantine Christianity of his day, to a Plato interpreted from the point of view of politics and reform. His aim was to establish a new state on the Platonic model, his central idea was that of fate, a *heimarmene,* which controls the hierarchy of gods and from which he expected a strengthening of the self-consciousness of his fellow-countrymen similar to that of the Muslims in regard to kismet. All this was no frivolous ideas with which he toyed in the comfort of Mistra but a serious and carefully planned reform project. We know that Plethon was not alone; he was able to gather around him a not unimportant circle of enthusiastic disciples.

de Georges (Gennade) Scholarios, I–VII (Paris 1928–36), gives for each separate part a topical introduction and biographical notes. *Cf.* also S. Salaville, "Un thomiste à Byzance au XVᵉ siècle," *ÉO,* 23 (1924), 129–36; *idem,* "Georges Scholarios et St. Thomas d'Aquin," *Mélanges Mandonnet,* I (Paris 1930), 423–40.

[26] F. Masai, *Plethon et le platonisme de Mistra* (Paris 1956).

Furthermore, similar paganizing tendencies were to be observed in other parts of the Empire. They had no future, but they are of historical interest because they drew an arc whose ends often moved apart only in appearance throughout the Byzantine centuries.

CHAPTER 54

Patriarchate — Emperor and Church — Missions — Monasticism

The collapse of the Empire, in progress during the fourteenth and fifteenth centuries, involved frightful losses for the Orthodox Church.[1] Not every Seljuk or Ottoman conquest of a strip of territory meant the annihilation of Orthodoxy and the elimination of Church government, but the unceasing raids of undisciplined tribes and the changing religious policy of the conquerors produced great insecurity and complete impoverishment. We constantly hear of complaints that now even great and wealthy ancient cities were no longer able to maintain a cleric, let alone a bishop. From time immemorial the Greek metropolitans had preferred residence in the capital rather than in their own provinces. What had once been a pretext had now become a necessity. In the *Notitiae episcopatuum*, which in their several revisions reflect the actual importance of the sees, we learn how one after another of the metropolitan sees of Asia Minor had to be transferred to dioceses that had not been especially important earlier but were more fortunately located. *De facto*, however, the synod at Constantinople for the most part had no alternative but to unite two or more bishoprics under one bishop, even if they were far apart, so that the more abundant resources of the one might provide for the administration of the other. These grants and combinations, regarded as temporary, fill the patriarchal registers of the age. The ruin of the churches in the conquered territory could thereby be arrested for a while, but in many cases the course of events could be retarded no longer. In addition, some communities made use of the political advantages connected with accepting Turkish rule and, not infrequently, even of Islam, or at least they made accomodations in the externals of their religious life — a state of things rejected with horror by the Orthodox. Even clergy and bishops who remained behind adapted themselves to circumstances here and there, and thus the total picture of the Orthodox Church in Asia Minor grew ever more bleak.

[1] On the expulsion of the Greeks from Asia Minor, see K. Amantos, Ὁ ἑλληνισμὸς τῆς Μ. Ἀσίας κατὰ τὸν μεσαιῶνα (Athens 1919); A. Wächter, *Der Verfall des Griechentums in Kleinasien im XIV. Jh.* (Jena 1903); I. K. Bogiatzides, Ἱστορικαὶ μελέται (Thessalonica 1933), 1–60; P. Wittek, *Das Fürstentum Mentesche* (Istanbul 1934).

In a great part of the interior of Asia Minor celebrated metropolises such as Sebaste, Euchaita, Iconium, Mocissus, and Nazianzus were without their own bishop for decades. Impossible though it was, their administration was entrusted to a single person, the Metropolitan of Caesarea in Cappadocia. This happened in 1327, and by 1365 the situation was virtually unchanged.[2] Better off were the cities on the northern fringes of Asia Minor, in particular Trebizond, which was actually under the protection of an Emperor of its own, and Amaseia and Sinope in Helenopontus. But here also long vacancies of sees occurred again and again. Special efforts were made to keep the ancient apostolic see of Ephesus alive. This bishopric contrived to have a bishop throughout almost the entire fourteenth century but only by amalgamating most of the sees of its former extensive province, which for decades and even centuries had been autonomous metropolitan or archiepiscopal sees.[3] The destruction of Christianity in Sardis must have begun as early as the beginning of the fourteenth century, for around the mid-century Philadelphia, the last Byzantine stronghold in Asia Minor, took its place, at first temporarily but in 1369 definitively.[4] Likewise, at the very beginning of the century Smyrna had to be governed for a time from the Island of Chios. In 1347 a crusading army occupied the city and established a Latin hierarchy. Then, sometime later, a Greek metropolitan could have been installed again, but no person could make up his mind to accept the office.[5] The Bithynian countryside came into Ottoman possession early in the century, but the most important cities held out until the beginning of the fourth decade. At the same time the inhabitants of Nicaea seem to have gone over to Islam in large numbers. In 1338 the Patriarch offered to accept them back into the Church if they were repentant. He even went so far as to dispense them from the public exercise and the public profession of Christianity in so far as fear of the Turks made such behaviour seem necessary — something unique in Orthodoxy.[6]

The Patriarch was scarcely in a position to support the needy churches financially. Hagia Sophia had, as a result of the Fourth Crusade, lost most of its real estate and had been given back only a small amount since 1261. In 1324 the metropolitan and archiepiscopal sees, Monembasia at their head, pledged themselves to support the Patriarch by special contributions.[7] The more the metropolitan sees themselves now ran into difficulties, the less effective was this resolution. As early as 1381 the complaint was heard that

---

[2] Miklosich-Müller, *Acta et diplomata graeca medii aevi*, I (Vienna 1860), 143 ff., 468 ff.
[3] *Ibid.*, II, 103 ff.
[4] *Ibid.*, I, 270, 509.
[5] *Ibid.*, I, 447.
[6] *Ibid.*, I, 183.
[7] *Ibid.*, I, 126–29.

no metropolitan see of the Orthodox Church was poorer than the "Great Church." [8]

But despite everything, to the last Constantinople did not fail to recall emphatically the territorial, juridical, and spiritual rank of its Church.

The smaller the actual extent of the patriarchate grew and the more vigorous the dispute over the Roman primacy became, the more strongly did Constantinople move toward a concept of centralization that was nourished by reflection on the universal primacy of its own church. On this point too the patriarchal records of the age are clear. The concept of a pentarchy, that is, the idea that the essence of the constitution of the Church consists of a loose co-operation of five actually autocephalous patriarchates, is found not only in the middle but also in the late Byzantine age. [9] But more and more the Patriarchs of Constantinople stressed their special position, using for this purpose a papal vocabulary, so to speak. The Church of Christ has its head in Constantinople, the foundation of Andrew, the "first called." The Bishop of Constantinople is "the common father of all Christians on earth"; the metropolitans are his vicars. Every Christian has the right to appeal to him. He is also the "universal teacher" of the world and vicar of Christ, on whose throne he sits. [10]

In all this, his relationship to the Emperor had scarcely changed in theory. *In hoc discrimine rerum* the two powers were more than ever bound to work together. Perhaps the practical experience gained from the Second Council of Lyons, in which the Emperor had achieved union without the participation of the hierarchy as such, made it more and more clear to him that in fundamental ecclesiastical matters he must rely ever more strongly on the Patriarch and his synod. As people became more familiar with the situation in the West, the more they adjusted themselves in the discussions to the Western body of ideas on the relations between Church and state. The best example of this is the attitude of the Emperor John VIII at the Council of Ferrara-Florence. While never letting the control of the conduct of negotiations out of his own hands, he allowed the Patriarch and the bishops more freedom in the theological discussion than any of his predecessors had and did not object when churchmen insisted on the independence of their authority. Nevertheless, to Pope Eugene IV the position of the Church *vis-à-vis* the Emperor seemed deplorable, and the Patriarch Joseph II had hopes of strengthening the Church's liberty with the Pope's assistance by establishing the union. [11] Likewise, in bishops and high Church officials, such as Simeon of Thessalonica and Silvester Syropulus, resentment over the Church's lack of freedom increasingly made itself felt. Moreover, the Church

---

[8] *Ibid.*, II, 35.
[9] See *Beck*, 33 f.
[10] Evidence in *Beck*, 35.
[11] S. Syropulus, *Vera historia unionis non verae* (The Hague 1660), 92, 100.

had to acknowledge in writing this absence of freedom in this very period. The Emperor John V demanded of the patriarchal synod between 1380 and 1382 a decree which sanctioned the principal rights thus far exercised by him in matters of Church government. [12] The crucial point was, of course, that now, contrary to the legalist theories of the past, the Emperor's rights were specified as a privilege granted by the Church rather than as innate rights, but the irony that the Emperor could compel such a grant of privilege shows the real distribution of powers. But it can be said that, obstinately as the Emperors clung to their rights over Church government, they more and more yielded the rights hitherto made use of in matters of faith and dogma, guaranteed by the proviso of 1380–82 that the synod and the Patriarch could not excommunicate the Emperor and court.

Once again it should be stressed that, in spite of all the dissentient voices which imperial interference evoked at this time, the situation of Church and state required the avoidance of conflict as far as possible. A separation of powers would have seriously affected both of them. We sense the Patriarch's anxiety in regard to developments in Russia, where voices were heard which, while desiring to maintain ecclesiastical union with the patriarchate of Constantinople, rejected the legal connection between Church and Empire. In 1393 the Patriarch Anthony wrote anxiously to the Grand Duke Vasilij:

> You say: We have a Church, but we accept no Emperor. But that is out of order. The sacred Emperors occupy an important place in the Church, for from the very beginning they have supported and maintained Christian life in the entire world. Christians cannot possibly have a Church without an Emperor. Both are most intimately united and cannot be separated! [13]

But even this fervent stand could not halt the Russian development. And from the moment that there was no longer a Byzantine Emperor Moscow would seek and realize ecclesiastical autonomy.

The activity of the patriarchs at this period did not envisage merely the prestige of their own position. It also followed attentively the consolidation and extension of Orthodoxy wherever there remained such a possibility. At times it seemed that parts of the Mongol dominion, which extended far into former imperial territory, might become Christian. The Mongols of Persia, in particular, were inclined toward Christianity, especially in its Nestorian form, from the time of the Khan Hulagu (1256–65). The Orthodox benefited from this toleration, and at the beginning of the fourteenth century Constantinople could even send Gregory Chioniades to Tabriz as Bishop. [14] Even if

[12] V. Laurent, "Les droits de l'empereur en matière ecclésiastique," *RÉB*, 13 (1955), 5–20.
[13] Miklosich-Müller, *op. cit.*, II, 191.
[14] J. B. Papadopulos, "Une lettre de Grégoire Chioniadès, évêque de Tabris," *Mélanges Ch. Diehl*, I (Paris 1930), 257–62, cf. also R. Grousset, *L'empire des steppes* (Paris 1952), 420 ff.

this success was not lasting — Chioniades seems soon to have been imprisoned — the Patriarch applied himself all the more energetically to that former imperial territory where the weakening and incipient collapse of Latin rule gave great hopes to Orthodoxy, especially Crete, Cyprus, and the Peloponnesus.

On Crete the Greek Church was nominally united to the Latin Church,[15] but the Venetians would not allow a Greek bishop on the island. The direction of the Greeks was in the hands of the archpriest (protopapas) of Chandax, who was responsible to the Latin Archbishop of the island. No ecclesiastical relations with Constantinople were permitted and, after being examined by the Latin bishops of Crete, Greek clerics were ordained by Greek bishops of the Venetian possessions, Modon and Croton, in the Peloponnesus. Just the same, Orthodoxy maintained an uninterrupted existence and even contrived to gain not a few Venetian colonists in the interior of the island. Constantinople again and again undertook efforts for direct influence. Thus the mission of Bishop Anthimus to Crete in the second half of the fourteenth century was probably connected with the Greek rising against the Most Serene Republic in the sixties.[16] And soon afterwards Joseph Bryennius (d. ca. 1430) went to Crete for twenty years,[17] doubtless at the order of the Patriarch, though this was not stated publicly. At that time Crete was the refuge of a number of Catholic converts who had left Constantinople, and Bryennius exerted himself to check their influence as well as to encourage the Orthodox, especially monks and clerics, in their moral life, which, in the twilight zone between the two confessions, apparently needed a vigorous strengthening. Orthodox circles not in sympathy with his moral earnestness seem to have obtained his expulsion.

The situation of the Orthodox Church on Cyprus was desperate.[18] It managed as well as it could under the legal provisions of the Bulla Cypria of Pope Alexander IV of 1260. There were four Greek bishops but each had his Latin counterpart and the one metropolitan was the Latin Archbishop. A newly elected bishop was examined and approved by the Latin hierarchy and had to take an oath of loyalty to the Pope. Diputes between Orthodox clerics were decided by an Orthodox court but had to be reported to the Latins, while mixed cases fell exclusively under the canonical judgment

---

[15] N. B. Tomadakes, "Ὀρθόδοξοι ἀρχιερεῖς ἐν Κρήτῃ ἐπὶ Ἐνετοκρατίας", Ὀρθοδοξία 27 (1952), 63–75; idem, "Οἱ ὀρθόδοξοι παπάδες ἐπὶ Ἐνετοκρατίας", Κρητικὰ Χρονικά 13 (1959), 39–72; G. Hofmann, "Wie stand es um die Frage der Kirchenunion auf Kreta im XV. Jh.?" OrChrP, 10 (1944), 91–115; idem, "Nuove fonti per la storia profana ed ecclesiastica di Creta nella prima metà del secolo XV," Ἑλληνικά, Παράρτημα 9 (1955), 462–69; M. J. Manusakas, "Μέτρα τῆς Βενετίας ἔναντι τῆς ἐν Κρήτῃ ἐπιρροῆς τοῦ πατριαρχείου Κωνσταντινουπόλεως", Ἐπετηρίς 30 (1960), 85–144.

[16] See I. Dyobuniotes, Ἐπετηρὶς Ἑταιρ. Βυζαντ. Σπουδῶν 8 (1931), 30–41, 9 (1932), 53–55.

[17] For Bryennius, see supra, Chapter 53, footnotes 21 and 22.

[18] G. Hill, A History of Cyprus, II (Cambridge 1948).

of the Latin hierarchy. Thus the Greeks on the island were not only fully dependent on the Latins but were held in contempt by the Orthodox world, and especially by the patriarchate. Under these circumstances the Greek bishops at the beginning of the fifteenth century resolved, though not unanimously, to become again subject to Constantinople. Joseph Bryennius, acting again as the Patriarch's deputy, went to the island and held a synod. [19] His instructions demanded that the Cypriot bishops should renounce obedience to the Pope and discontinue their collaboration with the Latin bishops. When the bishops, from fear of their masters, proposed a secret understanding with the Patriarch with no change in externals, Bryennius recommended that the synod renounce the union.

In the Peloponnesus Orthodoxy made real progress. [20] The successful campaigns of the Despots of Mistra enabled the Greek hierarchy to take effective possession of several of the great ancient metropolitan sees such as Patras and Corinth. The reorganization of the church of Patras had been under way for decades when the city again became Greek in 1429–30. In the meantime the Metropolitan was forced to rule the see from the Mega Spelaion Monastery. Corinth became Greek once more in 1395. The restoration of the metropolis around the middle of the fourteenth century did not fail to bring about serious disputes over rank with Monembasia, which in the interval had become important and now energetically resisted the ancient privileges of the first see in the Peloponnesus. Mistra too, in the course of these decades, presented itself as a new centre of Orthodoxy with full external splendour. Here lived the Bishop of Sparta; here sprang up new churches and monasteries. Around 1300 arose the imperial Brontochion Monastery, the Zoodotu Monastery, and the Pantanassa. In the other districts of the Despotate also a new surge of monastic foundation is established, as in Monembasia, Messene, Kernitza, and elsewhere. Mistra was also the stage of a brisk intellectual life in which theology played a role and of a rising Greek nationalism with regenerative strength — until Muhammad the Conqueror brought it to an end.

The victory of the Palamite theology in the fourteenth century was at the same time a victory of Hesychast monachism and, *a potiori*, a victory of Byzantine monachism in general. The controversy, it is true, showed that this monasticism was even at that time a sort of sacrosanct national institution and that the condemnations then uttered were often based, not on an exact analysis of the theological views of the anti-Palamites, but simply on the fact of *crimen laesae religionis*. But anti-Palamism, notably as expounded by Barlaam, but also by Gregoras, was precisely an attack, though the final one, on Athos. Simultaneously the victory meant an enhanced political

---

[19] Acts edited by A. Papadopulos-Kerameus, "'Ο ἐν Κω/πόλει Φιλολ. Σύλλογος", Παράρτημα to Volume 17 (1886), 48–51.

[20] *Cf.* D. A. Zakythinos, *Le despotat grec de Morée*, II (Athens 1953), 270 ff.

influence, if such were possible. This development had been in the making for many decades. In places where the Greek hierarchy had been expelled by the Latin conquerors, the Greek monks frequently remained. For within the Byzantine Empire they had been cultivating their ideals in a substantially greater independence of externally monastic ways of life than was the case, for example, in the contemporary West. Hence, in the occupied part of their homeland they could easily submerge themselves in order to supervise the resistance to Latin rule in administrative and Church matters, as leaders and advisors of the people. And they carried the resistance into the interior of the Empire, against the Emperor or the higher clergy and Patriarch, as often as there appeared an inclination to come to an agreement with the Western Church. They often claimed themselves to be the heroes of Orthodoxy and were able to do so the more easily because they frequently lacked any education, including theological knowledge. The esteem the monks enjoyed did not preserve them from severe ridicule and satire. Both were basically innocuous and played merely that compensatory role to be observed in every strongly clericalized culture. The prestige of the monks was shored up by the great landed wealth and small farms, accruing for years to most of the monasteries from pious donations, demonstrations of imperial favour, solicited patronage, and clever economic policy. However, the economic position of the Emperor and the higher nobility was, in the fourteenth and fifteenth centuries, no longer such that the number of great monasteries could be substantially increased. What foundations there were seem to have been all of quite modest proportions.

In the fourteenth century occurred the chief phase of that development which gradually led to the victory of *idiorrhythmia* in the older monasteries. [21] This word had long formed part of the terminology of asceticism and meant self-will bound by no yoke of obedience — always an evil. In this later period the idea retained this meaning, judged now favourably, now unfavourably, while acquiring also in the strict sense the meaning of a form of monastic life resulting from the decay of the *koinobion*. The great monastic family broke up into very small groups, which, apart from the general outlines of the monastic ideal, regulated their own life, acquired property, bequeathed it, and scarcely needed an abbot. In his place soon appeared the so-called *epitropia*, a directing committee made up of representatives of these tiny communities and headed by a person soon called the *dikaios*, who was only *primus inter pares*. In legal literature this situation is first found in the *typikon* which the Emperor Manuel II issued for Athos in 1394. [22] The

[21] P. Meyer, *Die Haupturkunden für die Geschichte der Athosklöster* (Leipzig 1894); *idem*, "Beiträge zur Kenntnis der neueren Geschichte und des gegenwärtigen Zustandes der Athos-Klöster," *ZKG*, 11 (1890), 395 ff.; P. de Meester, *De monachico statu juxta disciplinam byzantinam* (Città del Vaticano 1942), 78–80, 380 f., and *passim*.

[22] Meyer, *op. cit.*, 195–203.

text rejects this manner of life but with so little emphasis as to arouse the suspicion that the author entertained very little hope.

The most varied theories have been advanced to acccount for the origin of this manner of life, but not to be overlooked are the facts that strict cenobitism always encountered resistance in Byzantium and that neither the Emperor Justinian nor Athanasius of Athos ventured to rule out some forms of anchoritism. The numerous monastic *vitae* indicate again and again that the actual state of affairs far exceeded what legislators allowed. And the growth of the Hesychast mysticism could not but directly favour the tendency toward *idiorrhythmia*. Just as the liturgy, the "psalmody", played at most a nominal role in the life of the Hesychasts, and was actually rejected by many enthusiasts, so could a small group of Hesychasts break up the cenobitic life altogether. Their mysticism was incompatible with the formation of larger groups in which the idea of the community ought to be predominant. Hardly had Byzantium fallen when voices multiplied in rejecting *idiorrhythmia*, and they were episcopal voices, but it seems that no one grasped the connection between Hesychasm and *idiorrhythmia*.

But there was one voice in late Byzantium which wanted to make a clean sweep of this and every kind of monasticism, the voice, however, of an outsider, Gemistus Plethon. His reform writings, dedicated to the Palaeologi, were meant to reorganize the Byzantine State.[23] To the monks, "who on the pretext of spiritual contemplation lay claim to a rich share of state property," he denied any right to it, "because they contribute nothing to the common welfare." They should work for their own support rather than extort it from others. "If the state's total income scarcely suffices to defray the expenses of defense, what will be left if a swarm of drones has to be fed, of whom some allegedly devote themselves to spiritual contemplation and others are idle."

Whatever may be thought of this judgment, monasticism was not at its best in Byzantium's final age. Flexible criteria must be sought in determining the social contribution of the Byzantine or any other monasticism to the life of people and state. But whenever Byzantine monachism intervened in Church-State questions of the time, it did so stubbornly and intransigently, with the result that, from the start, legitimate reflection, rational absorption in the question, and a balanced judgment were all lacking.[24]

---

[23] S. Lampros, Παλαιολόγεια καὶ Πελοποννησιακά III (Athens 1926), 257.

[24] Also an Orthodox voice: D. Savramis, *Zur Soziologie des byzantinischen Mönchtums* (Leiden and Cologne 1962), especially pages 92 f.: "The individual morality of Byzantine monks never achieved an adjustment with social morality ... Their conservative spirit shielded the Greek world from negative Western influences but likewise contributed to the fact that the positive Western influences have always encountered a hostile resistance in the East."

From the Middle Ages to the Reformation

CHAPTER 55

Renaissance and Humanism

The events of the mid-fifteenth century — the end of the Council of Basel, the reassurance appearing in the European states, especially in Germany, as a result of Nicholas V's willingness to oblige, the restoration of the Papal State, with the abandoning of a genuine reform of Church and Curia, — point to a decisive turning point in the history of the Church. The age now getting under way, that of the Renaissance and of the Renaissance papacy, led rapidly from the Early to the High Renaissance. This revolutionary change on a vast scale was attended by phenomena of critical importance and has been variously estimated in presentations of Church History.

The investigation of the Renaissance and of humanism has made tremendous progress in recent decades, with a quantity of studies that can scarcely be mastered and its own periodicals and series of publications. They are devoted to an exposition of an extremely lively century, especially in regard to philology and the history of art, civilization, and government. All these questions must be left to one side here, and only ecclesiastical matters, especially the development of the papacy, will receive consideration. From the time that Pastor chose to speak of "good" and of "evil" humanists the problem of the religious and ecclesiastical character of the humanists and other leading figures of the Renaissance has never come to rest. If on the one side Toffanin, for example, probably overstressed their faith, on the other hand we hardly have a right to speak of their widespread paganism. [1]

The beginnings of the Renaissance and of humanism as literary movements are variously stated; in the designations of a Christian or un-Christian

---

[1] G. Toffanin, *La religione degli Umanisti* (Bologna 1950); C. Trinkhaus, "Humanist Treatise on the Status of the Religious: Petrarch, Salutati, Valla," *Studies in the Renaissance*, 11 (1964), 7–45; C. Angeleri, *Il Problema religioso del Rinascimento, Storia della Critica e Bibliografia* (Florence 1952); M. Seidlmayer, "Religiös-ethische Probleme des italienischen Humanismus," *Wege und Wandlungen des Humanismus* (Göttingen 1965), 273–94; a survey of the ideas of the Renaissance in E. Hassinger, *Das Werden des neuzeitlichen Europa* (Braunschweig 1959), 23–50.

Renaissance of believing or unbelieving humanists the evaluation fluctuates from a condemnation as being anti-Christian to the notion of a reform movement. The turning from Aristotle and the late Scholasticism and the trend to Plato and Augustinianism could in many respects signify a renewal. The Renaissance of classical studies was at first a predominantly Italian affair. From Florence, Rome, and the petty princely courts of fifteenth-century Italy it became, in its radiation over all Europe, a new bond, which might have substituted for the bond of the Christian Empire that had weakened as a consequence of the rise of national states.

The humanist movement in Italy was strongly fostered by Greek scholars who came to the West around the turn of the fourteenth century, at the time of the reform councils, and after the fall of Constantinople: Chrysoloras, Gemistus Plethon, Bessarion, and others. But so-called Christian humanism acquired its special importance from figures such as Lawrence Valla, Marsilius Ficinus, Pico della Mirandola, and the Platonic Academy at Florence. Lawrence Valla (1407–57), a Roman by birth, was active at Pavia for some years until a quarrel with local jurists forced him to leave. He then spent eleven years at the court of the great patron of humanists, King Alfonso the Magnanimous of Naples, and during the pontificate of Nicholas V returned to Rome. The most richly endowed of the Italian humanists of the first half of the fifteenth century, he was not satisfied with the philological discussion of texts already known or recently discovered but drew conclusions in the philosophical and theological sphere. He became especially well known for his acrid and clever attacks, based on Nicholas of Cusa, on the *Donation of Constantine, De falso credita et ementita Constantini donatione declamatio* (1440), with its demand for the renunciation of the papacy's secular power. If this frontal attack on the Roman Church in her contemporary structure can be brought into connection with the Neapolitan King's war against Pope Eugene IV, the *Declamatio* also expresses a great understanding of the religious concerns of the reform synods, above all of the Council of Basel.[2] The denunciation, usual among the humanists, of the avarice of the clergy and the duplicity and wickedness of the monks proceeded in Valla's *De voluptate, De vero bono*, and *De professione religiosorum* from a deep layer of genuine religious feeling and true Christianity.[3] Like Nicholas of Cusa, he wanted religious peace, *pax fidei*, in the one religion, even though this religion might be characterized by different rites. From the many philological disputes grew a critical historical sense, which turned away from the

[2] G. Antonazzi, "Lorenzo Valla e la Donazione di Costantino nel secolo XV con un testo inedito di Antonio Cortesi," *RSTI*, 4 (1950), 186–234.

[3] G. Radetti, "La Religione di Lorenzo Valla," *Medioevo e Rinascimento*, 2 (Florence 1955), 595–620; G. Zippel, "La defensio 'Quaestionum in philosophia' di L. Valla, e un noto processo dell'Inquisizione Napoletana," *Bullettino dell'Istituto storico Italiano per il Medio Evo*, 69 (1957), 319–47.

traditional scholastic theology, led back to Saint Paul and the Church Fathers, understood the new religious needs of its time of change, and also extended to the noblest Christian transmission, the New Testament. The comparison of the Vulgate with the Greek text in the *Collatio Novi Testamenti* of 1444 yielded a wealth of new theological knowledge and questions, which were to exert an influence for a long time. The *Annotationes*, first published by Erasmus in 1505, went through numerous editions and were of great influence on the biblical criticism of the sixteenth century. Of course, they encountered strong resistance and were placed on the Index by Paul IV in 1559; the other works were consigned there in 1590.[4] But by then they had made their impact, brought about a new type of discussion, and awakened a zest for life that was opposed to the *miseria humanae conditionis* of the Middle Ages.

But, despite the exertions of Nicholas V and the grand-scale patronage of humanists by Sixtus IV, Rome did not continue to be the centre of humanism and of the Renaissance, at least not in the purely intellectual field. At Florence Christian humanism came to full development as Platonism. Even the first half of the fifteenth century witnessed a lively scholarly activity in the city on the Arno with Coluccio Salutati, Poggio Bracciolini, Leonard Bruni, and others. At first, it is true, Aristotle was still reckoned as the real teacher; he was explained especially by John Argyropulos, who had fled to Italy and been given a position at the Florentine studio. The Academy, fostered by Cosimo de' Medici, arose soon after the mid-century and at once devoted itself almost exclusively to Platonism.[5] Even though Plato's writings had already been translated into Latin,[6] there now came to the Academy, especially through Marsilius Ficinus (1433–99), a philosophizing philologist who had pledged himself in the entirety of his teaching and manner of life to the Athenian philosopher. Besides the translation of almost all the writings of Plato and of the Neoplatonists there appeared his chief work, *Theologia Platonica seu de animorum immortalitate* (1469–74). Hence the interest of this Academy embraced not only Plato in the stricter sense but the intellectual currents of antiquity and late antiquity that he had stimulated and was not restricted to philosophy properly speaking. "Platonism meant rather a manner of speaking and a relish than fixed doctrines; finally, if one wills, a mode which in various ways penetrated everywhere, into literature, the representational arts, the sciences, morals, and customs. Hence it is possible to understand its unique importance and the difficulty of determining its

[4] A. Morisi, "A proposito di due Redazioni della Collatio Novi Testamenti di L. Valla," *ibid.*, 78 (1967), 346–81.

[5] V. R. Giustiniani, *Alamanno Rinuccini 1426–1499* (Cologne and Graz 1965), 19 f.

[6] E. Garin, "Ricerche sulle Traduzioni di Platone nella prima metà del sec. XV," *Medioevo e Rinascimento*, 1 (Florence 1955), 339–74.

image" (Garin). According to the general view, the Florentine Academy reached its high point under Ficinus's pupil, John Pico della Mirandola (1463–94), who in his brief career sought to combine the religious traditions of all peoples and to use them for an understanding of the Christian religion; this was the aim of his *Heptaplus* and *De ente et uno*. Best known was the discourse on human dignity, *De hominis dignitate,* with which he intended to inaugurate the congress that he had planned for 1486 in Rome for a disputation on 900 theses.[7] The esoteric, the hermetic, the Cabala, and the Areopagite played a big role in his train of thought. His non-dogmatic outlook, which frequently rejected the Church's teaching authority, gained him the reputation of being a syncretist and a man living outside the Church, but this is probably refuted by his close relations with Savonarola. Here, as elsewhere in this period, it should be noted that paganizing formulations of Christian truths sought especially to provide proof of a classical education and not to act as a religious profession of the ancient gods. As regards radiation and continued influence, he was the most important figure in Christian humanism. To see in him and his incisive questions to the mediaeval Church and theology a precursor of the sixteenth-century reformers does not in any sense deprive him of his religious stature and Christian uniqueness.

Irrespective of this religious striving, which must be taken seriously, at Rome the Papal State more than ever appeared as the representative of the Church. The Pope thus became chiefly the ruler of a territory which, like the other Italian states, was developing from a feudal state into a *signoria* but with considerable differences from the Italian and foreign dynasties. While it is true that *condottieri* often obtained permanent princely rank, at the Curia it usually happened that the death of the reigning Pope produced a new faction; hence the too frequent changes of political orientation and the so much deplored but mostly misunderstood nepotism. In the nationalist Italian view it was the duty even of the Papal State to keep the great European powers, especially France and Spain, out of the peninsula or not to tolerate an increase of their existing territories. This became particularly clear in the pontificates of Alexander VI and Julius II. Within Italy itself it was important to maintain the balance of power of the *cinque principati* that had been achieved by the Peace of Lodi in 1454. And so the Papal State was compelled to co-operate in this subtle diplomatic game with its ceaseless change of treaties and alliances in the hope of outwitting the partners of the moment. In addition the Curia had at its disposal a superior weapon, that of ecclesiastical censures, which, employed rapidly and ruthlessly, probably caused little spiritual harm. But, even as spiritual weapons, they could be quite effective in the temporal sphere, if the laying

[7] Giovanni Pico della Mirandola, *Über die Würde des Menschen, ausgewählt und übertragen von H. W. Rüssel* (Amsterdam 1940).

of an interdict led to an interruption of commerce and a seizure of the property of outsiders by competitors.

The enemy from the East, the Turks, kept the Popes preoccupied and it is misleading to speak of a "collaboration of the Popes with the Turks." [8] More than all other powers, the Curia sought to halt the advance of the Christians' born enemy, though not always with the utmost exertion. The old crusading spirit had died out in the age of the nationalist states and no one could fan it to new life.

In comparison with politics the papacy's proper religious tasks retired shockingly into the background. If since the fourteenth century the autonomy of the states with regard to the Church had powerfully increased, in the following century the celebrated phrase, "superiorem non recognoscens," achieved its complete practical form and implementation in England, France, Spain, Venice, Milan, Florence, Naples, and some German territories. Since the greatest part of the revenues now came from Rome and the Papal State, this situation could be endured and it made the Curia quite independent, but with regard to the so-called spiritual income there was still question of large sums. These spiritual revenues consisted chiefly of *servitia* and annates, though these were greatly reduced in comparison with the age of the reform councils. The falling off of many sources of income from the Universal Church forced the reorganization of the fee-system and of the *Dataria*, now functioning as the most important financial department, with its often quite dubious compositions. Through the higher assessment of vacant benefices and the increasing of the fees for dispensations further gains could be made in extraordinary cases. The great multiplication of marketable posts, *officia vacabilia*, which were to be regarded as a sort of state loan, endeavoured to keep the mounting debt balanced. In the pontificate of Leo X there were about 2,000 marketable posts with a capital value of about $2^1/_2$ million gold florins and an interest of 300,000 gold florins. A real reform of the curial administration was rendered impossible by this system. Statements concerning the Curia's financial administration differ considerably from pontificate to pontificate and were always dependent on the political situation, and the same is true of the income from the Papal State. But these last always constituted more than half of the total yield of money. The alum mines discovered at Tolfa in the pontificate of Pius II were an unexpected and copiously flowing source; as a monopoly industry they brought in important sums and were supposed to be applied to the Turkish war. We know very little about the secret funds that were always available. Since the costs of the building activity and especially of the even more

---

[8] H. Pfeffermann, *Die Zusammenarbeit der Renaissancepäpste mit den Türken* (Winterthur 1946).

expensive political and military enterprises were often defrayed from them, they must have been considerable.[9]

As an Italian princely court, the Curia had its full share in the so-called Renaissance culture. Because of the extravagant display, the papal household became a very costly business, with the usual expenditures on building, works of art, books, music, the theatre, and gorgeous festivities, with the salaries for the large number of *curiales,* who also obtained part of their support from benefices. This tendency toward display was a universal phenomenon of the age, but it must be asked whether it was lawful for the Renaissance Popes to conform to a characteristic of the time in such a degree.[10]

The College of Cardinals occupied a special position. The Western Schism and the reform councils had greatly tarnished its reputation, but the much demanded reform did not materialize, despite numerous splendid reform drafts. The return of the Holy See to the Papal State, made by Martin V, also assured the existence of the College of Cardinals in its traditional form, even if now and then, under pressure from foreign powers, persons less suited to the tastes of the College had to be accepted. The outlook of the College as a corporation was reflected in the election capitulations, which, while they have not come down to us for every conclave, can always be assumed. If they were perhaps not always fixed in writing, they were at least secret oral agreements. They were concerned first of all with the safeguarding of real or alleged rights of the College against encroachment at the hands of the new Pope. In order to enhance the influence of the individual cardinals it was necessary to keep the number of cardinals as low as possible and so the creation of new members had to be subjected to the consent of the College. Related to this was the guaranteeing of corresponding revenues for the princely mode of life which was considered to be appropriate. In the text of the decrees and arrangements of the Council of Constance these ideas constantly recur: the obliging of the future Pope to summon a crusade against the Turks; reform of the Curia, which, taken up three months after the coronation, must be carried through and observed for the future; the holding of a general council within the space of three years or "quam primum commode fieri potest"; at it the summons to the crusade must be given and the reform of the Universal Church introduced; the number of cardinals must not exceed twenty-four, only one of them could be a relative of the Pope, each creation must have obtained the consent of two-thirds of the College, the nominees must be more than thirty years old,

---

[9] W. von Hofmann, *Forschungen zur Geschichte der kurialen Behörden vom Schisma bis zur Reformation,* 2 vols. (Rome 1913 f.); P. Partner, "The 'Budget' of the Roman Church in the Renaissance Period," *Italian Renaissance Studies,* ed. by E. F. Jacob (London 1960), 256–78.

[10] On Renaissance display cf. *Les Fêtes de la Renaissance,* I (Paris 1956), ed. by J. Jacquot.

the incomes and possessions of the cardinals and their share in the administration of the Papal State must be guaranteed; war or alliance with foreign princes for war against another prince must have the consent of two-thirds of the College; the most important fortresses of the Papal State, especially the Castel Sant'Angelo, must be commanded, not by relatives of the Pope, but only by ecclesiastics, and by these for no longer than two years. Of great importance could have been the concluding decrees, if they had been observed: that the capitulations were to be read in the first consistory of every month, and later of each quarter of the year, in the presence of the Pope, and the cardinals were to ascertain twice a year, on 1 November and 1 May, whether the stipulations were being observed by the Pope; if they were not, he was to be remonstrated with to a third time. No further sanctions were mentioned, but it is clear that then a council could take cognizance of the matter. [11]

More recent research has shown that the income was subject to severe fluctuations, that there were rich and poor cardinals, that benefices and the *commenda,* protectorates and pensions often did not suffice to assure the income of four to six thousand gold florins that was considered necessary. In such cases the Pope was supposed to grant monthly subsidies of from one to two hundred gold florins from the resources of the Church and of the Papal State. But because of a decline in papal cash such allowances often had to be discontinued. [12] In this connection it can be asked whether it was necessary to support an entourage of hundreds of persons, to ride to the Vatican with a large retinue, to build huge palaces or palatial fortresses, and to organize noisy festivities.

The election capitulations contained also a group of general commitments, which in time were often included in a merely schematic way and placed at the beginning: Turkish war, reform of the Curia, calling of a general council within a short time. But it is a serious mistake to speak of a collapse of the conciliar idea. To be sure, because of the successfully managed restoration of the Papal State the Curia was able to a great extent to evade the danger of the conciliar discussion and to thwart the summoning of a general council as threatened by the states from mostly political considerations. But the conciliar idea was still alive within the ecclesiastical sphere itself; several of the prohibitions issued by the Curia against appealing from the Pope to a general council were interpreted only as the opinion of a faction. Renowned canonists stressed the superiority of the council, at least in some important cases, into the sixteenth century. Through the

[11] J. Lulvès, "Päpstliche Wahlkapitulationen. Ein Beitrag zur Entwicklungsgeschichte des Kardinalats," *QFIAB,* 12 (1909), 212–35; *idem,* "Die Machtbestrebungen des Kardinalkollegiums gegenüber dem Papsttum," *MIÖG,* 35 (1914), 455–83.
[12] D. S. Chambers, "The Economic Predicament of Renaissance Cardinals," *Studies in Medieval and Renaissance History,* III (1966), 289–313.

Reformation the conciliar idea obtained a different ecclesiastical and political importance. [13]

A special source of irritation was the persistent disregarding of the undisputed decree of the Council of Constance on the periodic holding of general councils, the celebrated decree "Frequens," according to which a council should have been summoned every ten years from the middle of the fifteenth century at the latest. Even Popes saw in the neglect of this conciliar decree the real cause of the crisis in the Church and of the secularization of the Curia. If the age of the Renaissance is weighed from religious and ecclesiastical viewpoints, one cannot but agree.

CHAPTER 56

The Popes of the Early Renaissance

Nicholas V (1447–55)

When Eugene IV died on 23 February 1447, he left a heavy legacy. While a group of questions had been settled in a manner satisfactory to the Curia shortly before his death, there was still needed a person of moderate views to bring about a suitable adjustment. The conclave again met in Santa Maria *sopra Minerva;* whether an election capitulation was drawn up or that of 1431 was renewed is unknown. The traditional strife between Colonna and Orsini prevented the election of Prospero Colonna, who lacked only two votes for the necessary two-thirds majority. To his own and the general surprise Thomas Parentucelli, the Cardinal of Bologna, was elected in a compromise solution; [1] he had been a member of the Sacred College only a few months.

A native of Sarzana and the son of a physician, after studies pursued amid severe privations he was long in the entourage of the famed Cardinal Albergati. After his patron's death he stayed on at the Curia and in 1444 became Bishop of Bologna, but, because of political troubles, he was unable to enter upon his duties. He was esteemed as highly educated without being a real scholar, as a friend of humanists and of humanistic studies, and, above all, as a lover of peace. The Church and the Roman Curia needed such a man in order to make good the blunders of Eugene IV.

---

[13] Jedin, I, 1–92 (English translation, I, 5–116); J. Klotzner, *Kardinal Dominikus Jacobazzi und sein Konzilswerk* (Rome 1948); O. de la Brosse, *Le Pape et le Concile. La comparaison de leurs pouvoirs à la veille de la Réforme* (Paris 1965).

[1] Sources for the conclave in *Pastor*, II, 6–12.

In Rome and the Papal State he began with pacification and in a short time succeeded in calming the quarreling factions and in winning back a number of cities, among them the important town of Jesi, which he repurchased from Sforza.[2] The political situation in Italy was upset some months after the Pope's election by the death of Philip Mary Visconti, Duke of Milan, in August 1447. The question of the succession was of the greatest importance for all Italy, even the Papal State, since, in addition to France and Naples, Venice and the *condottiere* Francis Sforza laid claim to it. At first, it is true, there occurred the proclamation of the short-lived Ambrosian Republic (1447–50).[3] France and Naples, as foreign powers, would have been in a position to wreck the laboriously achieved balance of power, and especially in the case of Aragonese Naples the Papal State would have been encircled in north and south. The question whether Visconti had actually made King Alfonso of Naples his heir in his last will was long controverted but now it must apparently be answered in the affirmative.[4] In an effort to forestall a French seizure and to challenge Sforza's usurpation, Venice and Naples began war against Milan. The Pope remained prudently aloof, but from the start he was on Sforza's side because only thus could the *status quo* be to some degree maintained. The situation became dangerous when the alliance of Milan and Florence asked French support. And so in 1453 the Pope summoned a congress to Rome for the settling of the smouldering crisis and the pacification of Italy, since, with the fall of Constantinople, it was important to husband all resources. The meeting's lack of success must not be charged to Nicholas alone.[5] At length, secret negotiations between Venice and Milan led to the Peace of Lodi, 9 April 1454; Florence also joined, after long hesitation, and later so did the Neapolitan King, though with some reservations.[6] Despite his annoyance that he had thus far been ignored, the Pope in February 1455 adhered to the comprehensive treaty as *Protector et Custos*.[7]

[2] Pleyer, *Die Politik Nikolaus' V.*, 46–54.

[3] *Storia di Milano*, VI (1955), 387–448.

[4] A. J. Mur, *Aportación documental a las relaciones entre Alfonso V de Aragón y el ducado de Milán (IV Congreso de historia de la Corona de Aragón). Actas y comunicaciones*, I (Palma de Mallorca 1959); *idem*, "Alfonso V de Aragón y la República Ambrosiana 1447–1450," *Boletín de la real Academia de la historia*, Madrid, 156 (1965), 191–269; A. F. C. Ryder, "Alfonso d'Aragona e l'Avvento di Francesco Sforza al ducato di Milano," *Archivio storico per le province Napoletane*, 80 (1962), 9–46; on Alfonso of Aragón see *Dizionario biografico degli Italiani*, II (1960), 323–31 (with bibliography); A. Boscolo, "Ferdinando I e Alfonso il Magnanimo nella storiografia," *Medio Evo Aragonese* (Padua 1958).

[5] Pleyer, *op. cit.*

[6] F. Antonini, "La pace di Lodi ed i segreti maneggi che la prepararono," *Archivio storico Lombardo*, 57 (1930), 231–96.

[7] A. Theiner, *Cod. diplom. dom. temp.*, III, 379–86; *Storia di Milano*, VII, 56–81; G. Soranzo, *La Lega Italica 1454–1455* (Milan 1924); *idem*, "Studi e Discussioni su la Lega

The Treaty of Lodi was intended to assure the inner peace of Italy in accord with the current state of territorial holdings and to protect the peninsula from outside interference. Fixed troop contingents, the creating of courts of arbitration, the peaceful settling of all conflicts, and the avoiding of foreign intervention were the chief points of the treaty, which appears so modern. In the midst of this political tangle occurred the journey to Rome of the German King, Frederick III, for his imperial coronation in 1452. It had only a slight impact on the Italian situation, and the Pope's fears proved to be groundless. [8] The end of the Council of Basel, the agreements with the German Electors, and the Concordat of Vienna have already been discussed. In these Nicholas V showed himself to be a good politician, to whom what especially mattered was peace and who, to achieve this goal, made great concessions. And so in 1450 he could solemnly celebrate the year of jubilee and display the Pope's spiritual power to the Christians who flocked to Rome in great numbers.

How complicated the situation at Rome still was appears in Stephen Porcaro's conspiracy. This native Roman, a spiritual descendant of Cola di Rienzo in his ideas of ancient Rome and, for this reason, an enemy of ecclesiastical rule, had occupied a series of high administrative posts in the Papal State and had been relegated to Bologna because of an insurrection. He returned secretly to Rome and, with his band of conspirators, planned for 6 January 1453 an attack on the Vatican and the Pope. The miscarriage of the romantic undertaking led to his execution. Because of the jubilee the Pope inaugurated a series of important reforms and measures, which began to alter the structural appearance of mediaeval Rome, but only a small part of his great project for the papal city could be realized because of the brevity of his pontificate and the vastness of his plans. He regarded especially the Leonine City and the Vatican palace as a gigantic centre of resistance against dangerous uprisings; from it unrest could be controlled and its inner area could be adorned according to the new methods. [9] To Nicholas goes back also the grandiose plan of replacing the ancient and dilapidated basilica of Constantine by a new construction of splendid proportions.

Ample justice has been done to this Pope's concern for humanistic studies. At his court he gathered hundreds of scholars, who were especially to devote themselves to the translating of Greek authors into Latin. This undertaking was promoted by the many Greeks who fled to the West after the fall of

Italica del 1454–1455," *Studi storici in onore di G. Volpe* (Florence 1958), 969–95; V. Ilardi, "The Italian League, Francesco Sforza, and Charles VII (1454–1461)," *Studies in the Renaissance. Publications of the Renaissance Society of America,* New York, VI (1959), 129–66.

[8] H. Quirin, "König Friedrich III. in Siena, 1452," *Aus Reichstagen des 15. und 16. Jahrhunderts* (Göttingen 1958), 24–79, gives a good survey.

[9] A. M. Frutaz, *Il Torrione di Niccolò V in Vaticano* (Vatican City 1956; bibliography).

Constantinople. In this regard Nicholas and King Alfonso of Naples rank as the greatest Maecenases of their century. The Vatican Library can look to Nicholas as its real founder. He avoided no expense for the purchase of manuscripts, and in a short time his collection became Italy's greatest treasury of books. It was pointed out to him that he might have used this money better for the defense of the East. [10] But he tried again and again to bring about a union of princes for resistance to the ceaseless advance of the Crescent. The realization of this goal was denied him and most of his successors. An obstacle was the priority which was attributed to Church union. [11] The Pope never failed to supply money for the support of the Hungarians and of the heroic Skanderbeg. But a great part of the crusade contributions remained in the hands of the Western princes and was spent in civil strife.

Nicholas was greatly hindered in the last year of his pontificate by a chronic illness. With him died the first Renaissance Pope, but he was a Renaissance Pope in the best sense.

Calixtus III (1455–58)

Nicholas V died during the night of 24–25 March 1455. The next conclave was again overshadowed by the rivalry of Colonna and Orsini but it could be held in the Vatican. Its outcome was totally unexpected. The seventy-seven-year-old Catalan Cardinal, Alfonso Borgia, obviously a compromise and intended as a "caretaker" Pope, was elected; he called himself Calixtus III. As a young professor at Lérida he had been regarded as an eminent jurist and especially as an outstanding canonist and he had distinguished himself at the court of Alfonso V of Aragón through his management of affairs and his diplomatic skill. He had contributed decisively to the settling of the Western Schism and was rewarded by the Aragonese King with the wealthy see of Valencia. [12] He later brought about the reconciliation of his King, who had meanwhile conquered Naples, with Pope Eugene IV — an accomplishment that greatly weakened the Council of Basel and caused its collapse and enabled the Pope, then an exile in Florence, to return to Rome. In return Borgia was admitted to the College of Cardinals in 1444.

The chief activity of the new Pope, who reigned only three years, was devoted to the crusade. With an energy amazing in a man of his advanced age he tirelessly directed all his thoughts and endeavours to this duty. Well known is the vow he made on assuming office: not to rest until he had taken

10 Pleyer, *op. cit.*, 108–18.
11 *Cf.* Chapter 51.
12 K. A. Fink, *Martin V. und Aragón* (Berlin 1938; reprint, Vaduz 1965), 113–41.

Constantinople from the enemy of the Christian faith, had liberated the imprisoned Christians, and had exalted the faith. Resounding appeals, the dispatch of legates to the most important countries and to threatened frontiers, and the proclamation of ample indulgences for all participants in the campaign against the Turks are always recorded. In particular he himself began preparations. Thus at Rome the keels of large vessels were laid on the Ripa and the matter was entrusted to a commission of competent cardinals. [13] Great sums of money were constantly sent to the Balkans, Hungary, and Albania, and many gold and silver works of art from the papal treasure ended up in the furnace. Two such important figures as Cardinal Caravajal [14] and John of Capestrano [15] carried the Pope's enterprising spirit into the various lands, but the response to their ardent preaching was for the most part inadequate or only ephemeral. The Pope was permitted to experience one great success: the relief of the Serbian capital, Belgrade, which was besieged by Muhammad II with a great army and was close to falling. Significant for the crisis of Christian awareness is the fact that in this case and elsewhere Christians, and not under compulsion, served in the Turkish army and that the cannon-founders, the cannoneers, and the builders of siege machines were almost always Westerners; there is no need to mention the secret intrigues of the Italian port cities at the Sultan's court. In July 1456 a motley army led by John Hunyadi and John of Capestrano succeeded in breaking the ring around the besieged stronghold and in forcing the Sultan to a retreat that resembled flight. [16] This really great success was much exaggerated and was not exploited, even though the Pope through legates called for a decisive struggle. Internal unrest in Hungary stood in the way and, since John Hunyadi and John of Capestrano died in the following weeks, the decisive momentum was lacking. Likewise in the summer of 1456 a papal squadron under the command of the Cardinal Patriarch of Aquileia, Louis Trevisan, Cardinal *Camerlengo*, was able to enter the Aegean Sea in order to display there the Christian standard, but the enterprise had no enduring success. [17] And, over and above his military plans, the Pope showed a warm, though perhaps not always enlightened, interest in Christians under Turkish rule and in reunion with the remnants of Eastern Christendom. [18]

His relations with his former master, King Alfonso V of Aragón and

[13] P. Paschini, "La flotta di Callisto III," *ASRomana*, 53–55 (1930–32), 177–254.

[14] A. Strnad, "Francesco Todeschini-Piccolomini," *RömHM*, 124, footnote 62.

[15] J. Hofer, *Johannes Kapistran. Ein Leben im Kampf um die Reform der Kirche.* New edition by O. Bonmann, 2 vols. (Rome 1966).

[16] Babinger, *Mehmed der Eroberer*, 146–51.

[17] P. Paschini, *Ludovico cardinal Camerlengo † 1465, Lateranum*, N. S., V, 1 (Rome 1939).

[18] G. Hofmann, "Papst Kalixt III. und die Frage der Kircheneinheit im Osten," *SteT*, 123 (1946), 209–37.

Naples, were from the first not good and they grew increasingly worse, for the King did not share the Pope's zeal or in any event pursued other goals in the East. Alfonso died a few weeks before Calixtus, who rejected the succession of the King's natural son, Ferrante. It was said that he intended to confiscate the Kingdom as a fief of the Holy See in order to confer it on his nephew, Peter Louis. In any event, the last named was enfeoffed with Benevento and Terracina in the last days of the dying Pope. Against the *condottiere,* Piccinino, who had been rendered unemployed by the Peace of Lodi and intended to pursue his calling before Siena, Calixtus sent an army and thereby preserved peace in the peninsula. To be on the safe side, he garrisoned most of the castles and strongholds of the Papal State with Catalan commanders, while his nephew, Peter Louis, became Captain General of the Church and governor of Sant'Angelo. Peter Louis was a younger brother of Rodrigo Borgia, whom the Pope had admitted along with another nephew into the Sacred College in February 1456.

In comparison with his predecessor and his successor, the first Borgia Pope seems not to have been devoted to the Muses, but he was not uneducated.[19] His interest and his passion concerned other things, which he regarded as more important, and for them he unsparingly employed the energy left to his old age.

Pius II (1458–64)

The death of Calixtus III was followed by a prosecution of the Catalans who occupied many posts in Rome and the Papal State. After the death, shortly before, of the most promising candidate, Cardinal Dominic Capranica, the conclave was from the start overshadowed by the French Cardinal d'Estouteville, who was able to gain a considerable number of votes because of his enormous wealth.[20] By contrast the candidate of the other Italians, Aeneas Silvius Piccolomini, Cardinal of Siena, could offer only his education and experience; but he was a widely travelled man and knew most of the European countries from many political tasks he had performed for the Council of Basel, the Emperor, and later the Roman Curia. After a short but tense course of balloting he was elected on 19 August 1458 and took the name Pius II, not from religious but from classical considerations. An election capitulation that was in some respects borrowed from that of 1431 was decided on and sworn to in the conclave. First came the obligation to continue the Turkish war and the reform of the Roman Curia. There followed decrees on the share of the cardinals in important ecclesiasti-

---

[19] F. Martorell, "Un inventario della biblioteca di Callisto III," *SteT*, 41 (1924), 166–91.
[20] The most important source is the report in the *Commentarii* (ed. Cugnoni, 185), where the discussions "apud latrinas" are again mentioned.

cal measures and in the filling of the higher benefices, a sort of coregency in the administration of the Papal State, and an adequate maintaining and observing of the Constance decrees on the naming of new cardinals. Once a year the College was to meet and to examine whether the Pope had observed the election capitulation and, if necessary, to admonish him. Before the proclamation of the election the newly chosen Pope had to confirm the election capitulation and later have a bull issued on this matter. All of this Pius did. [21]

The previous career of the humanist Pope had long interested his contemporaries. In the retinue of Cardinal Capranica, who was seeking justice at Basel, and later as secretary of the Pope set up by the Council of Basel, he came forward as champion of the conciliar idea and was repeatedly sent by the Council to several European states and to German diets; then he passed over to the imperial chancery and, at the opportune moment, to the Curia. He successfully conducted the negotiations for the ending of the Electors' neutrality and was rewarded with the bishoprics of Trieste, Ermland, and Siena. In 1456 he was created a Cardinal. In general, his election to the papacy was well received.

On the very first day of his pontificate he made it clear that he intended to adopt and to intensify his predecessor's zeal for the crusade. Scarcely a month after his coronation he summoned a European Congress to Mantua or Udine for the following summer and issued a crusade bull that, with regard to style, was unusually impressive. From his youth he had been conversant with questions relating to the Turkish war and in powerful discourses before Pope and Emperor and at German diets he had called for a struggle against the infidel. But, for all his knowledge of the political situation in Italy and the rest of Europe, he probably did not reckon with the great disappointment that was in store for him at Mantua. Venice had rejected Udine as the place of meeting. At Rome persons tried to detain the Pope with the gloomiest predictions, but no remonstrances, even in regard to his weak state of health, were able to divert him from his plan. First, however, the political tension had to be relaxed. [22]

Entering upon his pontificate, Pius II adopted the violent hostility of the Curia for Ferrante of Naples, natural son of the conqueror of Naples, King Alfonso V of Aragón. This claimant, not yet fully recognized in his Kingdom, was especially supported by Francis Sforza, Duke of Milan, from quite obvious reasons, for by conquering that realm France could not but threaten Milan also. The new Pope was now faced with the choice of Sforza and Ferrante or France; he decided for the Italian solution and the keeping of the foreigner at a distance. For this reason he has been praised for his Italian

---

[21] J. Lulvès, "Päpstliche Wahlkapitulationen, " *QFIAB*, 12 (1909), 216 f.
[22] Babinger, *op. cit.*, 178 ff.

nationalist spirit, but his decision was a political act, springing from the justified fear of the hemming in of the Papal State. His attitude was also in conformity with the Peace of Lodi, which had achieved a balance of power in the Italian peninsula. And so, under strong pressure from Sforza, the Pope chose Ferrante and arranged his enfeoffment and coronation and the engagement of the papal nephew, Anthony Piccolomini, to a natural daughter of the new King. This decision was of great importance and, despite frequent vacillation in extremely critical situations, Pius remained faithful to it throughout his pontificate. It brought him first of all a diminution of the danger to the Papal State from the enterprising *condottiere*, Piccinino, but at the same time it also involved the bitter opposition of the French Kings, Charles VII and Louis XI.[23]

As early as the end of January 1459 the Pope left Rome for Mantua; Nicholas of Cusa remained behind as *Legatus Urbis*. The party moved slowly through the Papal State. Pius spent two months in his native Siena; there was a longer stay at Florence and a somewhat shorter one in unruly Bologna.[24] He entered the city of the Gonzaga on 27 May and on 1 June opened the Congress. One disappointment after another awaited him. Months later no prince had appeared, and only a few envoys gradually arrived for the Congress; the first session could not be held until the end of September. Again and again the Pope sent earnest appeals to the Italian and foreign princes to meet in view of the threatening peril. But the Emperor and the King of France had already declined, and the Duke of Burgundy, who was supposed to assume the leadership, then went back on his crusade vow. Of the Italian powers none thought seriously of taking part, and even the collecting of the tithe from the clergy, the twentieth from the Jews, and the thirtieth from the laity, agreed to in the face of great opposition, was rejected in most countries and city states. The attitude of Venice was generally blamed and branded as treason against Christian interests. After long hesitation and repeated unambiguous demands envoys of the Most Serene Republic came to Mantua. Shortly before Venice had made peace with the Sultan. The excuses offered by Picotti for the delay are really striking.[25] Without the Venetian fleet an undertaking of any magnitude was unthinkable, but Venice was the most seriously threatened, especially in its trade, which was after all the backbone of the state, and in its Greek possessions. If it were to begin the war alone, it would have to face the vengeance of the Sultan alone. Hence, while the policy of sensible reserve was not very heroic, it did cor-

---

[23] G. Peyronnet, "La politica italiana di Luigi Delfino di Francia," *RSIt*, 64 (1952), 19–44.
[24] G. B. Mannucci, "Il viaggio di Pio II da Roma a Mantova 22 gennaio – 27 maggio 1459," *Bullettino Senese di storia patria*, N. S., 12 (1941), 62–65; other literature in Strnad, *loc. cit.*, 162, footnote 42.
[25] Picotti, *La dieta di Mantova*, 387–94.

respond to the political situation. And, despite his alliance with the Pope, Francis Sforza, Duke, or "Tyrant," of Milan, continued his double-dealing. He finally appeared in Mantua in September and made great promises. In his case the fear of a French invasion of his territory was understandable. Florence was entirely uncooperative, Genoa had come under French rule, and Naples was justified by its really difficult situation. The Italian states took a realistic view: one feared another, and before a genuine reconciliation the risk of a crusade was too great. "The Mantua Congress did not fail because Venice spitefully wrecked it, but because they were all dispirited and, even worse, insincere."[26] France, once the proud champion of the crusade idea, refused any cooperation with the Pope, his Congress, and his eloquent and fervent appeals. As earlier and as in the succeeding decades, it was a question of Naples, of the expulsion of the Aragonese and the restoration of the Angevin. When at length French envoys came to Mantua they first demanded the investiture of John of Anjou before there was any discussion of the crusade. During the Congress itself a squadron, prepared in Genoa for the crusade voyage, set sail with the French King's permission for the conquest of the Neapolitan Kingdom. And so the Congress moved slowly to its conclusion without any visible success. Nevertheless, the papacy had sought to place itself at the head of Europe and had registered its claim to leadership.

After his return from the Congress of Mantua Pius II found himself involved in the usual disputes with unruly *signori* and Roman barons. Sigismund Malatesta of Rimini, who has been too unfavourably judged by Pastor, rebelled against the papal temporal authority and could be subdued only with difficulty; in this quarrel considerations of nepotism played a decisive role, for a part of the holdings of the Malatesta was intended for the nephew Anthony.[27] With the Pope's aid Ferrante finally established himself at Naples and compelled the Angevin to withdraw, but Pius now had to experience the hostility of Louis XI of France. As dauphin Louis had opposed his father and had to flee to Burgundy; he there promised the Pope that he would annul the Pragmatic Sanction of Bourges when he succeeded to the throne. The annulment actually took place in the autumn of 1461. But it was purchased by the creation of two French cardinals and was intended to win the Pope from his alliance with Ferrante. It was reintroduced in practice by a royal ordinance.

His anxiety for the Papal State and his involvement in Italian politics did not cause the Pope to forget the chief task of his pontificate: the crusade. He again appealed for a crusade in October 1463 and appointed Ancona as the place of gathering in the next summer. Despite his poor state of health,

---

[26] H. Kretschmayr, *Geschichte von Venedig*, II (Gotha 1920), 369.
[27] G. Soranzo, *Pio II e la politica italiana contro i Malatesta* (Padua 1911).

he said that he would himself take part. His appeal found a response among the lower classes throughout Europe. They set out for Ancona in considerable numbers but soon had to turn back. There was no response from the princes, on whom the matter chiefly depended. At Venice the Council had to force the reluctant Doge to give up his opposition and set sail with the fleet. Meanwhile, on 18 June 1464 the seriously ill Pope left the Eternal City and, with many cardinals and curialists, made his way to Ancona. To his great disappointment he found there only a few crusaders and eagerly awaited the arrival of the Venetian galleys. As they came in sight, he died on 14 August and the great enterprise was ruined.

In the period beginning with the autumn of 1461 occurred the work on a remarkable document by the Pope: the so-called letter to Muhammad II. The content and fate of this long treatise are still a puzzle. What could have motivated the Pope to compose, in addition to a detailed refutation of the Koran, an exposition of Christian truth and to urge the Sultan to convert to Christianity and, on his reception of baptism (*pauxillum aquae*), to offer him the crown of the Eastern Empire? Presumably, the "letter" was never sent and never reached the addressee. If Nicholas of Cusa's treatise *Cribratio Alchorani* has hitherto been regarded as the important model, now the preference is given to Torquemada's *Contra principales errores perfidi Machometi,* which appeared between October 1458 and January 1459. In an age when, despite the insecurity, a crusade summons could still be expected to have an impact, the Pope in his vision of Europe moved into the regions of Utopia and of illusion and sketched a grand-scale picture and program of the universalism that haunted him. The letter to Muhammad is an extremely important document for an explanation of the personality of Pius II. [28]

In the pontificate of Pius II began the long quarrel with Bohemia and its King, George of Podiebrad. [29] As always, this struggle was dependent on the political situation in Italy, the Empire, Poland, and Hungary. When in 1458 Podiebrad obtained the Bohemian royal crown, he took in the presence of the two Hungarian bishops who crowned him and of a small group of witnesses an oath, whose not entirely clear text apparently denied the further validity of the *Compactata* of Prague, which had granted free preaching, the lay chalice, the abolition of the temporal authority of the clergy, and the

[28] G. Toffanin, *Introduzione a Pio II (Enea Silvio Piccolomini), Lettera a Maometto* (Naples 1955); F. Gaeta, "Sulla 'Lettera a Maometto' di Pio II," *Bullettino dell'Istituto storico italiano per il medio evo e Archivio Muratoriano,* 77 (1965), 127–227 (with bibliography), 195–227 (edition of the autograph sketch of Part I, according to *Cod. Vat. Regin. lat.,* 1995); Babinger, *op. cit.,* 211 ff.

[29] *Handbuch der Geschichte der böhmischen Länder,* I (1967), 537–61, with very copious bibliography; A. Strnad, "Die Breslauer Bürgerschaft und das Königtum Georg Podiebrads," *Zeitschrift für Ostforschung,* 14 (1965), 401–35, 601–40; R. Kalivoda, "Die hussitische Revolution und die Podiebrader Epoche," *Cultus Pacis,* 167–78.

punishment of mortal sin.[30] In view of the religious situation in Bohemia and Moravia this promise could hardly be kept. And when Podiebrad in 1462 applied for the confirmation of the *Compactata*, the Curia annulled them. But since they had been agreed to by the Council of Basel, no further confirmation was needed. Thus was the break made complete and shortly before the Pope's death the King was cited to Rome.

In 1462–64 Podiebrad came forward with a great project, which Pastor disposes of too quickly in his *History of the Popes*. In the twenty-three chapters of the text, that has now been published according to a good Warsaw source, it was proposed that a sort of European League of Nations, under the motto *Pax et Iustitia*, should be formed for a successful attack on the Turks. It is clear that in this plan the initiative was to be removed from the two swords, the Pope and the Emperor, precisely because the text exhibits a form that frequently recalls curial documents. Beside the program of Pius II there now stood a great vision of a united and pacified Europe, with a board of directors consisting of representatives of the league — *congregatio, pax, unio, fraternitas, amicitia* — which was to have its seat, for periods of five years each, first at Basel, then in France, and next in Italy. However, the noteworthy project was denied any great political impact.[31] Gregory Heimburg, well known as a bitter enemy of the Curia, was active as advisor and envoy in the quarrel with the Pope, especially in the next pontificate; he also played an important role in the revolt of Dieter von Isenburg, Archbishop of Mainz.[32]

Pius II is justly regarded as a reform-minded Pope. More than any other Pope of his century he had the opportunity to become acquainted with the *gravamina* against the Curia in all of Europe and to inform himself on the anti-curial sentiment. He had viewed the reform work of the Council of Basel from close at hand and had worked eagerly for its implementation. Right after his election he began comprehensive preparations for general reform and for the reform of the Roman Curia, called for expert opinions, and worked hard on the drawing up of a great reform bull, which, however, did not succeed in being promulgated in his lifetime. In it he did not exhibit

---

[30] The text of the oath of 6 May 1458 is preserved in Vat. Archiv AA Arm., I–XVIII, no. 639, in a notarial instrument of 10 November 1466, which King Matthias of Hungary sent to the Curia; printed in A. Theiner, *Vetera Monumenta historica Hungariam sacram illustrantia*, II (1860), no. DLXXX.

[31] V. Vaněček, "Eine Weltfriedensorganisation nach den Vorschlägen des böhmischen Königs Georg von Podiebrad und nach den Ideen des Johannes Amos Comenius," *SAB*, Kl. für Philosophie, Geschichte, Staats-, Rechts- und Wirtschaftswissenschaften, 1962, no. 3 (Berlin 1963); *The Universal Peace Organization of King George of Bohemia. A Fifteenth Century Plan for World Peace 1462/1464* (Prague 1964); *Cultus Pacis. Études et Documents du "Symposium Pragense Cultus Pacis generalis 1464–1964." Commemoratio pacis generalis ante quingentos annos a Georgio Bohemiae rege propositae* (Prague 1966).

[32] P. Joachimsen, *Gregor Heimburg* (Bamberg 1891).

any great difference from his predecessors and successors, but he cannot be denied the genuine reform will which was quite often lacking in other Popes. His ideas of reform, especially in regard to the constitution of the Church, had changed very much since the Council of Basel, and it was only natural that as Pope he no longer defended views pertaining to the conciliar theory but rather intended to maintain his primatial prerogatives. In this context belongs his prohibition of appealing to a council in the bull "Execrabilis," a measure which was intended to control the widespread practice, even approved by canonists, of appealing to a council against the Pope. But the prohibition meant only the reaction of a party, and no one who intended to appeal felt himself bound by it, even in the succeeding period. And the question was not settled by the bull, despite what one often finds in print.

In the outline for the bull "Pastor aeternus" the two still extant testimonials of Dominic de' Domenichi and Nicholas of Cusa were abundantly used, as were passages from earlier election capitulations and especially from the reform ordinances of the Councils of Constance and Basel and the reform decrees since Martin V. The sketch dealt thoroughly with the office and person of the Pope and with his Curia. The cardinals, as the most important rank in the Church, were treated in special depth, and then the individual offices or posts in the Curia: the grand *penitentiarius*, vice-chancellor, protonotaries, *referendarii*, chamberlains, auditors of the *Rota,* papal subdeacons, advocates, secretaries, *cubicularii,* and subordinate court positions. The conclusion consisted of general regulations on the curialists' manner of life, on pluralism, and on the appointing of three *officiales honestatis* to supervise the rules that had been issued. This projected reform bull was very much in accord with the concerns of the age, but, like almost all the reform demands of the fifteenth century, it remained merely a sketch. [33] Reforms affected also the City of Rome and its administration and the Papal State. To safeguard his position Pius II was forced to admit several relatives to the College of Cardinals and to confide important posts to Sienese fellow countrymen.

Hardly any other Pope has so engaged the attention of historians and of others as has Pius II, chiefly because until the most recent period we do not know as much about the personal lives of the Popes as we do about his. A group of treatises, poems, numerous letters, reports, and the *Commentarii* afford a good insight into the interior of this man, who was not only a patron of humanism, as was Nicholas V, but was himself a humanist as this word was understood in the fifteenth century. Since the one-sided and almost always unfavourable presentation by Voigt many interpretations have appeared, and in our own day his picture has been drawn in a more

---

[33] R. Haubst, "Der Reformentwurf Pius' II.," *RQ,* 49 (1954), 188–242; E. Iserloh, *Reform der Kirche bei Nikolaus von Kues* (Wiesbaden 1965), and Chapter 59 *infra.*

friendly manner, often inclining to the opposite extreme. A man of broad, though not always deep, scholarship, with an eye alert for nature, beauty, and form, he was able to do justice to the demands and expectations of his time and had in his heart "room for varied strata and ideas." Thus his passage from the Council of Basel and its Pope to the other camp was not accomplished without its guarantee. But behind all the vicissitudes of this interesting life there stood, especially in its maturer years, a manifestation of unity, a grandly conceived universalism, which reached full stature in the idea and project of the crusade. In this lay the distinction from his predecessor's *reconquista* concept. With the strength of his intellect and the fluency of his linguistic formation he proclaimed a united Christian Europe and the superiority of its culture, and yet he was aware that his message was utopian, he knew from bitter experience that his lofty plans and soliloquies were bound by the realities of the Italian and European political systems, by which they were decisively checked. His passing at Ancona was the tragic end of a magnanimous soul.

Paul II (1464–71)

The preparations for choosing a successor to Pius II began in Ancona. Before his death the Pope had decreed that the new election should occur in the place where he died. But the conclave met in Rome and, after some negotiations, in the Vatican. On the first ballot the Venetian Cardinal Peter Barbo, a nephew of Eugene IV, obtained the required majority; after toying with the idea of calling himself Formosus II or Mark II, he assumed the name Paul II. Once again the election was preceded by the drawing up of a capitulation, which to a great extent utilized the text of the previous capitulation, but, because of the experience with Pius II, it included more detailed regulations. [34] Its content is, in short, as follows: continuation of the Turkish war and use of the great alum mines discovered near Tolfa under Pius II for the expenses of the crusade, reform of the Curia within three months of the assumption of the papacy and continuation of the general reform, keeping the chancery fees in line with the prescriptions of the chancery rules of John XXII, keeping the Curia at Rome instead of moving about from place to place, no nomination of cardinals because of requests from outside, respect for the number of twenty-four cardinals as laid down at Constance, observance of the other decrees of Constance, the summoning of a council within the next three years, the paying of 100 florins monthly to cardinals who did not have an annual income of 4,000 florins, filling of the higher benefices only in consistory, the granting of presentations or nominations to benefices

[34] *Pastor*, IV, 9 f., 20 ff.; J. Lulvès, *loc. cit.*, 217 f.; *Storia di Milano*, VII (1956), 202, footnote 4, gives an Italian version in twenty-two chapters, from the end of August 1464.

only with the consent of a majority of the Sacred College, the prosecuting of cardinals only with the consent of a majority, obligatory consultation in regard to enfeoffments in the Papal State, renunciation of the exercise of *ius spolii* at the deaths of cardinals, express consent of the College for military enterprises, no changing of the amount of taxes and no deals with princes on the taxation of the clergy, the taking of an oath by officials of the Papal State to relinquish their posts *sede vacante,* and the prohibiting of relatives of the Pope from governing strongholds in the Papal State: Civitavecchia, Tivoli, Narni, Spoleto, Soriano, Viterbo, Roccacontrada, and Fano. No bull contradicting these regulations was to be drawn up. These chapters were to be read in the first consistory of every month, and the cardinals were to investigate twice a year how they were being observed. The new Pope was required to ratify the chapters before the election was promulgated. Pastor's estimation of the election capitulation is unfounded, especially in regard to the regulation concerning the government of the Papal State. The prompt observance of the reform prescriptions would have been able to put a halt to the excesses of the period of the so-called Renaissance papacy. The Pope, authoritarian and suspicious by nature, immediately declined to acknowledge the election capitulation, even though he had sworn to observe it. It is clear that the requested testimonials turned out to favour him, but the problem was not and is not thereby solved. The election capitulation, as later altered in some decisive points, was recognized under strong pressure by most of the cardinals, but confidence in the Pope's loyalty had disappeared.

Certainly it was difficult to be the successor of Aeneas Silvius Piccolomini, and the judgments of the envoys on the new Pope were not exactly friendly in regard to his intelligence and manners. He had been admitted to the Sacred College by his uncle, Eugene IV, when he was only twenty-three and was still lacking in personal merit. As is often true of those of mediocre talents, he tried to get his way by force and hence was feared rather than loved. On the other hand he exerted himself to win the lesser folk by splendid entertainments. As a Cardinal, he had used his immense wealth to begin constructing the huge Palazzo Venezia and planned great collections. He was not uneducated but he was likewise not a narrowly literary type. An aesthete and bibliophile, he pursued predominantly antiquarian interests and laid great stress on magnificent display. He issued a series of practical rules for the administration and care of Rome and the Papal State.

An insuperable distrust of humanists and literary men brought him into a serious conflict with the then modern educational level and damaged his memory. He abruptly abolished the seventy posts of *abbreviator* which Pius II had created as marketable offices; he thereby made bitter enemies out of a large number of humanists. When their spokesman, Bartholomew Platina, protested in violent turns of expression and threatened to appeal to a council, he was consigned to Sant'Angelo and tortured. Paul, probably incorrectly, regarded the so-called Roman Academy of Pomponius Laetus, with its antiquarian democratic ceremonial, as a band of heathen conspirators and resorted to measures which bore no relationship to the situation. The forbidding of the ancient classical authors in the schools likewise did not contribute to his posthumous fame.

As sometimes happens, there occurred at the change of pontificate also a change in the leading personalities and in politics. While in ecclesiastical matters Paul II did not enjoy good relations with his native city, he was at first devoted to it and also to Florence in Italian politics and abandoned the former close connection with Milan and Naples. The death in 1466 of Francis Sforza brought a new uncertainty into the well known instability of the Italian leagues. His son, Galeazzo Maria, managed to secure the succession, but Venice decided to exploit the favourable opportunity. Opposed to Venice was an alliance of Florence, Naples, and Milan that had been concluded at Rome, with the Pope's cooperation, in January 1467. The general of the Most Serene Republic, Colleoni, first moved against Florence, where the Medici were menaced by a great internal opposition. But they contrived to suppress a rising. The Pope intervened in the dispute and commanded peace in a manifest overestimation of his effective power. Gradually the Italian states adhered to the peace but only for a short time. A new quarrel erupted over the cities of the Malatesta, which the Curia was unwilling to let slip from its hold, but it encountered resistance from Milan and Florence. A general alliance, concluded at Rome in 1470 under pressure from the Turkish threat, brought a temporary calm. But the spirit of Lodi could not be reawakened, and, despite his claims, the Pope played a subordinate role.[35]

Shortly before his death Pius II had summoned the Bohemian King, George of Podiebrad, to Rome. With the accession of Paul II the affair came to a standstill and at first efforts were made to settle it amicably. The Emperor, powerfully supported in his difficulties by Podiebrad, interceded for him, as did a group of German princes. However, after the Bohemian had quarrelled with the Emperor and with King Matthias Corvinus of Hungary, the Pope pronounced his excommunication and deposition at the end of December 1466 and called for a crusade against the heretic.[36] Despite threats from within and without, the Bohemian King managed to maintain himself until his death in March 1471, when at Rome there was a willingness to reach an agreement through negotiations.[37]

When Negroponte (Euboea), the last bulwark of Venice in the Levant, was taken by Muhammad II in 1470, the Pope issued a new general sum-

---

[35] *Storia di Milano,* VII (1956), 246–49.

[36] K. A. Fink, "Der Kreuzablass gegen Georg Podiebrad in Süd- und Westdeutschland," *QFIAB,* 24 (1932 f.), 207–43.

[37] *Handbuch der Geschichte der böhmischen Länder,* I (1967), 549–54 (with bibliography).

mons to the crusade against the Turks and sent invitations to a congress at Rome. But nothing more than the previously mentioned league of Italian states came into being. [38]

The project of a general council became ever more prominent under Paul II in his constant disputes with France. In his election capitulation the holding of such a council within three years had been demanded. It was not only the understandable dislike of the Curia for a council, which it feared would seek reform of the head, that posed obstacles; with Peter Barbo there was added his own authoritarian and aristocratic concept of his office. When in 1468 the Emperor Frederick III paid a private visit to Rome, he suggested to Paul the organizing of a general assembly, with the participation of Pope and Emperor, at Constance, but he could get only the vain promise of a congress of envoys at Rome. [39] Quite unexpectedly the Pope died in July 1471 at the age of only fifty-three.

CHAPTER 57

The Popes of the High Renaissance

Sixtus IV (1471–84)

With the pontificate of the former minister general of the Franciscans, Francis della Rovere, one may correctly say that the High Renaissance had begun. For, contrary to all expectations, this son of Saint Francis did not emulate his master. This appears in the election itself, which occurred on 9 April 1471 after a conclave of three days. The election capitulation is extant and offers the usual picture of the last two decades. [1] These regulations, though sworn to by the one elected, were hardly observed by the Popes, and Sixtus IV was no exception. His election was especially promoted by the Duke of Milan, and rich presents were made to him and all the electors. [2] The Franciscan, a native of Liguria, was regarded as an outstanding theologian, who successfully devoted himself to timely controversies, and was a well known and much sought preacher. People were thus all the more amazed at the rapid change in his views, at the preeminence of politics which could not be reconciled with the papacy's religious tasks, at the

---

[38] Babinger, *op. cit.*, 299–308.
[39] H. Jedin, "Sánchez de Arévalo und die Konzilsfrage unter Paul II.," *HJ*, 73 (1954), 95–119; other literature in A. Strnad, "Francesco Todeschini-Piccolomini," *loc cit.*, 213, footnote 21.
[1] U. Manucci, "Le capitolazioni del conclave di Sisto IV, 1471," *RQ*, 29 (1915), 73–90.
[2] For the balloting see *Pastor*, IV, 505–07.

making of the Papal State into an Italian principality by recourse to all means, lawful and unlawful, and at the unseemly promoting of the Pope's relatives.

As early as two weeks after his election, the Pope, in flagrant disregard of the sworn election capitulation, raised two nephews, the Franciscans Peter Riario and Julian della Rovere, to the cardinalate; they had already been richly endowed with bishoprics and abbeys. In the election capitulation of 1471 there had been included a tightening of the regulations in regard to additions to the Sacred College. If the Pope were to make creations against the will of the cardinals, at the Pope's death such persons were to lose their dignity and their active and passive vote. If the creation of Julian della Rovere, later Pope Julius II, can be defended, the papal favour shown to Peter Riario fell upon one who was unworthy, who after a life of luxury and vice died in 1474. His position of influence was assumed by still another nephew, Jerome Riario, who became the Pope's evil genius. Married to Catherine Sforza, a natural daughter of Galeazzo Maria Sforza, Duke of Milan, and raised to the rank of Count, he obtained the territories of Imola and Forlì in Romagna, thus anticipating the later Borgia policy. He bears most of the guilt for a policy that was unbecoming to a Pope and that was also unfortunate.

The Pope's strained relations with Florence, which could only regard the consolidation of the neighbouring ecclesiastical political power with opposition and suspicion, came to a climax in the so-called Pazzi conspiracy.[3] Under pressure from his nephew, Jerome Riario, he supported the Florentine banking family of the Pazzi, who were hostile to the Medici, and Siena, which was menaced by Florence. In accord with the manner of the age, the heads of the Medici family were to be disposed of by a *coup de main* during a visit to Florence by the eighteen-year-old Cardinal Sansoni-Riario, a relative of the Pope, and their rule was to be overthrown by attacks on their territory from various quarters. The question whether the Pope had agreed to the intended assassination of Lawrence and Julian Medici can probably be answered in the negative. But he did not keep himself sufficiently aloof from these dangerous plans and he shares complicity in the infamous deed that was perpetrated in the cathedral of Florence during High Mass on 26 April 1478. Julian was killed, but the wounded Lawrence managed to escape. The rising was put down and the adherents of the Medici took a fearful vengeance; among the victims was the young Archbishop of Pisa, Francis Salviati, who was involved in the conspiracy. This violation of ecclesiastical jurisdiction and the imprisonment of the Cardinal induced the Pope to excom-

[3] Angelo Poliziano, *Della congiura dei Pazzi a cura di A. Perosa* (Padua 1958), standard edition with important appendixes; F. Morandini, "Il conflitto tra Lorenzo il Magnifico e Sisto IV dopo la congiura de' Pazzi. Dal Carteggio di Lorenzo con Girolamo Morelli, ambasciatore Fiorentino a Milano," *AstIt,* 107 (1949), 113–54.

municate the Medici and later to lay Florence under an interdict. Even
though the deploying of troops against Florence accomplished little, the
political situation worsened and forced Lawrence to conclude peace with
Naples, to the great irritation of the Pope, who was little influenced by the
serious remonstrances of Italian and foreign princes.

Two groups now stood in confrontation: Florence, Naples, Milan, and
Ferrara on the one side, and on the other the Pope, Venice, and the Angevins,
who now renewed their old claims to Naples with favourable prospects.
And Jerome Riario, who, like the Borgias later, intended to construct for
himself in Romagna a state of his own that should, so far as possible, survive
the death of his uncle, was once again the author of a new war in Italy.
Once he had added Forlì to Imola, he cast his glance on Ferrara, in which
Venice also was interested. The year 1482 saw almost all the Italian powers
engaged in the new war.[4] The victory of the papal and Venetian troops
under Robert Malatesta at Campo Morto in the Pontine Marshes in the
summer of 1482 brought no decision, for in this period political negotiations
were almost always more successful than military operations. A conference
at Cremona in 1483 was unable to end the disputes, and the Pope, once
again rapidly changing his allies, proceeded against Venice with spiritual
penalties. The Peace of Bagnolo in 1484 confirmed the *status quo* and brought
the Pope and his nephew, not the expected acquisition of territory in
Romagna, but instead dangerous risings in Rome and Latium and strife
between Colonna and Orsini. The eventful years 1482–84 also witnessed
the threat of an attempt to convoke a council.

The election capitulations made it clear that the decrees of the reform
Councils of Constance and Basel were not forgotten, even though here too
they gradually became a *topos*. The opinions on the conciliar idea that were
often defended in the course of the fifteenth century, the numerous appeals
to a council, and the efforts to convoke one also showed this. The papal
prohibitions made no difference, for they were rightly regarded as the
measures of one faction and a council could be prevented by them at any
time. The threat of a reform council was one of the means resorted to in the
political struggle with the papacy and the Papal State, but it seldom materialized.[5] However, it did go that far in the pontificate of Sixtus IV. Andrew
Zamometič, titular Bishop of Granea, near Saloniki, tried to revive the

---

[4] R. Cessi, "Per la storia della guerra di Ferrara, 1482–1483," *Notizie degli Archivi di
Stato*, 8 (1948), 63–72; G. Coniglio, "La participazione del Regno di Napoli alla guerra di
Ferrara 1482–1484," *Partenope* (Naples), 2 (1961), 53–74.

[5] *Jedin*, II, 73–79 (English translation, I, 92–100); *idem, Giovanni Gozzadini, ein Konzi-
liarist am Hofe Julius' II. Ausgewählte Aufsätze und Vorträge*, II (1966), 17–74; *idem*,
"Sánchez de Arévalo und die Konzilsfrage unter Paul II.," *HJ*, 73 (1954), 95–119; K. A.
Fink, "Die konziliare Idee im späten Mittelalter," *Vorträge und Forschungen*, 9 (1965),
119–34.

Council of Basel, which in his view had not yet been concluded. [6] His summons, proclaimed in the Basel Münster in March 1482, with its citation of the Pope, was anything but politically clever, and what induced him to make it has never been clarified. By origin a South Slav, he entered the Dominican order in his youth and studied at Padua, where he became a friend of Francis della Rovere. For some time he acted in a diplomatic capacity for the Emperor Frederick III but became unpopular because of his sharp criticism of the Curia and for a time was detained in the Castel Sant'Angelo. He apparently decided that the Pope's embarrassment in the Ferrara War was the proper moment for taking action on the council that had so often been called for, for deposing the Pope, and for finally undertaking and carrying through the reform of Curia and Church. The survival of the conciliar idea was not without the assent and encouragement of all the opponents of the Rovere Pope, who laid an interdict on Basel. The council did not actually materialize and the Emperor, after some wavering, finally came out against both the council and the conciliar city and had Zamometič imprisoned. The Bishop died at Basel two years later, probably by suicide. [7]

The first task of the new Pope mentioned in the election capitulation of 1471, the crusade against the Turks, was taken very seriously by Sixtus IV in the first years of his pontificate, and immediately after his accession he issued a solemn summons and dispatched five cardinal legates to all the greater states of the West. A fleet was equipped at great expense, but after modest successes on the coast of Asia Minor it returned to Italy. The succeeding undertakings were not in keeping with the great plans at the beginning, and the hope aroused by the marriage at Rome of the Great Prince of Russia, Ivan III, and the niece of the last Byzantine Emperor in regard to union with the Russian Church remained only a wish. That nothing really decisive occurred at a time so favourable for an attack on Muhammad II — the Sultan was seriously threatened in the eastern part of his realm by the Turcoman chief, Usun Hasan — was due to the lack of determination in the commanders of the Venetian fleet and especially to the failure of the Emperor and the other Western princes to participate and must not be blamed on the Pope. This procrastinating attitude of the West did not change during the remainder of his pontificate, and Italian politics and the effort to provide for his importunate relatives claimed his energies to an ever greater degree. The outcome was actually a landing of Turkish troops in Apulia, where Otranto was occupied by them for more than a year. The news of the Muslim

---

[6] J. Schlecht, *Andrea Zamometič und der Basler Konzilsversuch vom Jahre 1482* (Paderborn 1903); A. Stoecklin, *Der Basler Konzilsversuch des Andrea Zamometič vom Jahre 1482* (Basel 1938); *Jedin*, I, 101–06 (English version).

[7] Sixtus IV's interest in the reform councils, understandable in view of the circumstances of the time, is reflected in his notes on *Cod. Vat. lat.* 1335; see H. Finke, *Acta conc. Constant.*, IV (1928), p. XIX.

invasion of the Italian peninsula aroused fear and dread. However, even this extremely grave situation was unable to induce Western Christendom to a common energetic action against the infidel, especially since the great Sultan died in 1481 and the peril now seemed to have been exorcised for some time. [8]

From the religious viewpoint also the pontificate of Sixtus IV cannot be described as fortunate. The thirty-four cardinals — six of them were his nephews — whom he created contrary to the electoral capitulations were for the most part hardly worthy men and carried further the secularization of the papacy and of the Sacred College. Consequently, the Rovere Pope bears a heavy responsibility for the history of Christianity and of the Church. The reckless multiplication of curial posts and the increase of the Roman court also belong to the shady side of his reign. The Curia's fiscality mounted rapidly under Sixtus IV, as the need for money for the numerous costly undertakings and the paying of the mercenaries required for these, the expenditures on art and luxury, on the maintenance of the court, and on providing for the papal relatives increased just as rapidly. [9] The instituting of many new marketable posts and the frequent granting of indulgences brought in important revenue.[10] The financial administration, in particular the extraordinary, came more and more into the hands of the *Datarius,* who thereby became the most powerful figure in the Curia. His competence included the money for the crusade, the sale of offices, and indulgences, and the composition, or "deal," acted essentially as his method of procedure. In such a system it is obvious that much was possible. On the other hand, one must not fail to mention the care, reminiscent of Nicholas V, for humanists and men of letters and for scholarship, the refurnishing of the Vatican Library, and the establishing of the Vatican archives; the most important documents of *privilegia* were taken to Sant'Angelo. [11] With the name of Sixtus IV is forever connected the transformation of mediaeval Rome into a Renaissance city. This includes the new streets, as the need for these was made clear by the crowds of pilgrims in the Jubilee of 1475, the Ponte Sisto over the Tiber, the churches of Santa Maria del Popolo, burial place of the della Rovere, and Santa Maria della Pace, the new hospital of Santo Spirito, numerous palaces of cardinals and other high prelates, and especially the great new palace chapel in the Vatican, the Sistine Chapel, which received its first decorations from

[8] F. Babinger, *Mehmed der Eroberer,* 430–35; O. Halecki, "Sixte IV et la Chrétienté orientale," *SteT,* 232 (1964), 241–64, seeks to give greater stress than has hitherto been accorded to Sixtus IV's interest in the East.

[9] C. Bauer, "Studi per la storia delle finanze papali durante il pontificato di Sisto IV," *ASRomana,* 50 (1927), 319–400; P. Partner, "The 'Budget' of the Roman Church in the Renaissance Period," *Italian Renaissance Studies,* ed. E. F. Jacob (London 1960), 256–78.

[10] E. Göller, "Deutsche Kirchenablässe unter Papst Sixtus IV.," *RQ,* 31 (1923), 55–70.

[11] K. A. Fink, *Das Vatikanische Archiv* (Rome, 2nd ed. 1951), 2.

the Umbrian masters. The Pope's bronze monument by Pollaiuolo, now in the crypts under Saint Peter's, is one of the finest of papal graves.

The stressing of the personal goodness and piety of Sixtus IV cannot prevent our seeing in him the one who upset the Italian balance of power by his unfortunate political enterprises. And he bears the chief guilt for the further progress of the Roman Curia into unbridled nepotism and worldliness.

Innocent VIII (1484–92)

The death of Sixtus IV was followed in Rome by a storm against the "Genoese," who, so the Romans and the inhabitants of the Papal State thought, had occupied all the good positions under the Ligurian Pope; it was a repetition of what had happened earlier to the "Catalans" and the "Sienese" on the deaths of Calixtus III and Pius II. The chroniclers do not tire of reporting the insecurity, the unrest, the plundering, and the street fighting during the vacancy, but these lasted throughout the reign of the new Pope. The hitherto all powerful Jerome Riario was away from Rome, campaigning against the Colonna, but his undaunted wife, Catherine Sforza, seized the Castel Sant'Angelo and thereby maintained his rule for a while. After lengthy negotiations between the Sacred College and the mutually hostile groups it was possible to remove the many troops from Rome, and the conclave could begin in the Vatican. It lasted only from 26 to 29 August. Twenty-five cardinals took part, and they were again split into two factions: on the one side was the Vice-chancellor Borgia, the Orsini, Milan, and Naples; on the other side, Julian della Rovere with the Colonna and Venice. The election capitulation, transmitted by the master of ceremonies, Burckard of Strasbourg, differs in form from earlier ones by its strict distinction between the general arrangements in regard to a council, the Turkish War, and reform of Church and Curia and the special regulations for the cardinals, but in content it scarcely deviates from the previous rules.[12] After it had become clear that he had no prospects, Cardinal Julian della Rovere managed to carry the election of Cardinal John Baptist Cibò, Bishop of Molfetta, who belonged to a Genoese noble family and was sickly and totally dependent on him. His having signed the petitions of several cardinals in his cell on the night before his election can scarcely be regarded as other than transparent bribery and simony.[13] Formally elected on the following morning, he called

---

[12] *Burckardi Liber notarum*, ed. Celani, I, 30–43.

[13] *Ibid.*, 47: "facte sunt diverse practice et tandem XVII vel circa, rr. morum dd. cardinalium vota addicta in favorem r.mi d. cardinalis Melfitensis, qui in nocte sequenti, ante horam sextam noctis, incepit in camera sua signare supplicationes ad instantiam quorundam cardinalium; genuflexus super uno genu, supplicationes super quodam forzerio ante se positas signabat, cardinalibus aliquibus circumstantibus, qui signaturas huiusmodi expectabant."

himself Innocent VIII, thereby acknowledging the Roman line of claimants in the Western Schism. From the period preceding his entry into the clergy he had several bastards, who, in accord with the new style, were now suitably provided for by marriage into Italian princely houses.

In politics the Pope, who was a lover of peace, opposed the great league of Naples, Milan, Florence, Siena, Lucca, Spain, and the Orsini, while Venice remained neutral. His most bitter opponent was Ferrante of Naples, who created anxiety for the Pope by the threat of a council, by risings in the Papal State, and by stirring up the Hungarian King, Matthias Corvinus, after Innocent had allied with the rebel barons of the Neapolitan Kingdom in a manner that was both awkward and not welcome to the other powers. Appeals to France for help were unsuccessful and so in the summer of 1486 the Papal State had to accept a peace that was scarcely favourable. The marriage of Maddalena, daughter of Lawrence de' Medici, with the Pope's son, Franceschetto, brought about a temporary reconciliation with Florence. But the smouldering opposition to Naples led in 1489 to a new war and to the imposing of ecclesiastical censures on the King and his territory. Peace and an understanding with Naples were reached shortly before the Pope's death in 1492.[14]

The chronically ill Pope was subject to the influence, really to the domination, of the strong personality of Julian della Rovere. Only during the Cardinal's absence from Rome did the Pope make any decisions of his own, and for the most part these sought weakly to effect compromise. The constant lack of money could not be corrected even by the multiplying of marketable offices and similar practices. Thus the traditional six posts in the ancient College of Apostolic Secretaries, which had become renowned because of the humanist culture of their holders, were increased to thirty and disposed of in return for appropriate payments.

A remarkable figure arrived at the Curia in the person of the Turkish Prince Dschem, son of Muhammad II and brother of the reigning Sultan Bajazet II. He fled from snares laid by his brother, who rightly saw in him a rival to his authority, first to Rhodes and, at the price of a cardinal's hat for the grand master of the Hospitallers, was handed over to the Pope as an extremely valuable political pawn. The Sultan paid a large sum annually to keep him confined and abstained from direct undertakings against Italy. It is going too far to say that this arrangement meant an alliance with infidels. A conference at Rome in 1490, which was intended to unite the West for

[14] P. Fedele, "La pace del 1468 tra Ferdinando d'Aragona e Innocenzo VIII," *Archivio storico per le province Napoletane*, 30 (1905), 480–503; R. Palmarocchi, "La politica italiana di Lorenzo de' Medici. Firenze nella guerra contro Innocenzo VIII," *Biblioteca storica Toscana*, 8 (Florence 1933); E. Pontieri, "L'atteggiamento di Venezia nel conflitto tra papa Innocenzo VIII e Ferrante I d'Aragona, 1483–1492," *Archivio storico Napoletano*, 81 (1962), 197–324.

a crusade against the Turks, was without results. The reign of the Cibò Pope was almost constantly filled with disturbances in Rome, and it was necessary to fortify the Vatican and the palaces of the cardinals. On the whole it was an unfortunate and weak pontificate in an age which needed a strong, reform-minded personality.

Alexander VI (1492–1503)

Innocent VIII died on the night of 25–26 July 1492. Because of his poor health and his repeated sicknesses there had been much concern about the succession in both the Sacred College and the chanceries of Europe. Among the twenty-three cardinals who entered the conclave at the Vatican on 6 August there can be discerned two factions, one of them centring on Ascanius Sforza and the Vice-Chancellor Rodrigo Borgia, the other on Sixtus IV's nephew, Julian della Rovere, who had exercised the greatest influence on Innocent. In these factions was reflected the rivalry between Louis *il Moro* of Milan and King Ferrante of Naples. Pretty reliable reports tell of the availability of large sums for the conclave in various quarters. No election capitulation has thus far come to light; apparently the Sacred College was satisfied with the detailed capitulation of the previous conclave and made a few alterations. The votes in the three ballotings of 8 to 10 August have come down to us, even though the lists must be used with great care. In any event they show that neither faction could expect a quick achieving of the two-thirds majority. But then, in the late evening of 10 August, the election of the Vice-chancellor was assured for the following morning. Since the Dean of the Sacred College, Cardinal Borgia, was not at first regarded as a serious candidate — though from national rather than moral considerations, — an explanation of the sudden turn of events is desired. It is hardly possible to doubt that simoniacal intrigues produced the change. Even if in earlier cases, following the completing of an election, gifts that were at times of considerable value were distributed among the electors, it appears to have become customary in the second half of the fifteenth century to reach precise agreements beforehand in regard to money, benefices, and curial posts in return for the gaining of votes, and this is certainly simony. In this election simony was openly admitted by contemporaries and was mentioned as a possible point of attack on the new Pope in case of need. [15]

Not much exception was taken to his moral defects in the conclave and just as little in the chanceries of kings, princes, and cities when the outcome

---

[15] Soranzo, *Studi intorno a Papa Alessandro VI*, 1–33: "L'assunzione al pontificato del cardinale Rodrigo Borgia"; F. La Torre, *Del conclave di Alessandro VI, papa Borgia* (Florence and Rome 1933); Picotti, *Nuovi studi*, 181–207, lists of balloting, 243–47.

of the election was made known. The obedience and joy over this election, as expressed by numerous embassies, indicate, even while taking into consideration the formalities and flattery usual on this occasion, the gratification that, after the sickly Innocent VIII, an important politician and a capable statesman was elected. If difficulties should occur, one could always go back to the simoniacal election and the unspiritual manner of life.[16]

Alexander VI, as he styled himself, was born around 1430 at Játiva near Valencia; a nephew of Cardinal Borja (Borgia in Italian), he came to Italy and studied at Bologna. When his uncle had become Pope Calixtus III, he was admitted to the Sacred College, with the assent of all the cardinals present, in the very first year of the pontificate, and a year later he obtained the very lucrative post of Vice-Chancellor of the Roman Church. Because of the large number of his benefices, among them several bishoprics and rich abbeys, he was regarded as being the richest Cardinal of his time next to the French Cardinal d'Estouteville. Corresponding to this wealth was a mode of life that was decidedly not exemplary, the sort that had, it is true, become widespread at the Curia and especially among the cardinals and other high prelates since the pontificate of Sixtus IV. Since, as Cardinal and even as Pope, he had no concern for popular gossip, the curiosity of those responsible for the *chronique scandaleuse* then and later could amply occupy itself with the alleged or real number of his children. In the years 1462–71 were born to him Peter Louis, Jerónima, and Isabella, the names of whose mothers have not come down to us. Best known are those born of his liaison with Vannozza de Cattaneis, Caesar, John, Geoffrey, and Lucretia, who, after his election to the papacy, were at once provided for in the manner of princes and who claimed an excessive share of the Pope's interests.[17] John, born in 1476, became, after the early death of his brother Peter Louis, Duke of Gandía in Spain and then, despite his unfitness, was given honorary posts in Rome, made captain general of the papal troops in the struggle against the Orsini, and enfeoffed with the Duchy of Benevento, which was detached from the Papal State. His sensational assassination in 1497 has never been cleared up, though suspicion was directed against Cardinal Ascanius Sforza, the Orsini, and later even Caesar Borgia.

Most pernicious of all was Caesar's influence on the Pope. Born in 1475, he was richly endowed with benefices while still a youth by Sixtus IV and Innocent VIII. After his father's election as Pope he obtained at the age of eighteen several bishoprics, including the wealthy see of Valencia, and in

---

[16] G. Soranzo, "Documenti inediti o poco noti all'assunzione al pontificato di Alessandro VI," *Archivi*, serie II, 19 (1952), 157–78.

[17] On the order of births of Vannozza's children — Caesar, John, Lucretia, Geoffrey — see Bellonici, 27, 71, Schüller-Piroli, 179, 559. On Vannozza's tombstone, formerly in Santa Maria del Popolo, now in San Marco, see A. Ferrua, "Ritrovamento dell'epitafio di Vannozza Cattaneo," *ASRomana*, 71 (1948), 139–41.

1493 he was made a Cardinal. On the death of his brother John he resigned the cardinalate, without serious objections from the Sacred College; he had advanced only to the diaconate. He now became Duke of Valentinois and married a French princess. His sphere of action was especially Romagna, where, supported by copiously flowing streams of money from the Curia and given the title of Duke of Romagna by the Pope, he began to bring together the small petty lordships into a large territorial state and threatened Tuscany. Caesar's administration was esteemed by the inhabitants but distrusted by the nearby city states, since an alteration of the balance of power was feared. These enterprises helped to centralize the Papal State and could later be regarded as a model for the policy of Julius II. Just the same, this grand-style nepotism involved the danger that such territory would be severed from the ancient possessions of the Roman Church. The Pope's death caused Caesar's star to fade rapidly, and the unscrupulous and brutal man found a soldier's death in Navarre in 1507 after various changes of fate.[18]

The favourite daughter, Lucretia, was born in 1480 and was destined for a princely future through great projects of marriage. After earlier engagements to various Spanish nobles she first contracted marriage in 1493: the Count of Pesaro, a relative of the House of Sforza, was chosen for political reasons. A declaration of nullity because of the husband's alleged impotence brought about the dissolution of the marriage in 1497. This was soon followed by Lucretia's marriage to the Neapolitan, Alfonso, Duke of Bisceglie. With the changing of papal policy in the direction of France, he was murdered by Caesar's minions in the Vatican palace during the Holy Year 1500. The next year saw Lucretia's third marriage, this time to Alfonso d'Este of Ferrara. The Pope's daughter survived the ruin of the House of Borgia until her death in 1519.[19]

Vannozza's youngest child, Geoffrey, was born in 1482. In 1494 he married Sancia of Aragón, a bastard daughter of Alfonso II of Naples, and became Prince of Squillace. He died in 1517.

Great difficulties await any effort to pass judgment on Alexander's relationship with Julia Farnese, sister of Cardinal Alexander Farnese, the later Pope Paul III. As a Cardinal he had himself blessed her marriage to Orsino Orsini. Soranzo's attempt to prove that Rodrigo Borgia's connection with "la bella Giulia" while he was a Cardinal and when he was Pope was innocent is probably not successful, despite the ingenuity devoted to the interpretation of the Pope's celebrated letters.[20] And the two boys born during

---

[18] C. Fusero, *Cesare Borgia* (Milan 1958); Schüller-Piroli, 319–97.

[19] M. Bellonci, *Lucrezia Borgia*, German trans. *Lucrezia Borgia, nicht Teufel, nicht Engel, nur Weib* (Berlin, Vienna, and Leipzig 1941).

[20] G. Soranzo, "Orsino Orsini, Adriana di Mila sua madre, e Giulia Farnese, sua moglie, nei loro rapporti con papa Alessandro VI," *Archivi*, 26 (1959), 119–50; *idem, Studi intorno a papa Alessandro VI*, 92–129: "Il presunto scandalo di Giulia Farnese e papa Alessandro

Alexander's pontificate, John, the *Infans Romanus,* in 1498 and Rodrigo in 1503, very probably had the Pope for their father; but these continue to be open questions, since such matters, for obvious reasons, lacked clarity from the outset.[21]

Alexander's policies as ruler of the Papal State were generally shrewd. This was of great importance, since in the epoch of the Renaissance papacy, far more so than previously or later, the administration of the Papal State was regarded as a standard for evaluating a pontificate. The Italian peninsula was the site where the great European contests were decided. The political entities of Italy were, despite their widely divergent interests, deeply concerned for the preserving of the laboriously achieved balance of power and reacted very sensitively to outside interference. As interference must be understood the constant wrangling between Spain and France, which had gained a footing in Naples and Milan. After first inclining toward the Sforza of Milan, the Pope veered to Naples and maintained this position when Charles VIII of France in 1494–95 undertook his famous but ill-starred expedition through Italy *en route* to Naples. Although the French King put strong pressure on the Pope at Rome, Alexander did not yield to the demand for investiture with the Neapolitan Kingdom; he alone energetically represented an Italy free from foreigners. When the French army decided to withdraw because of the concluding in March 1495 of the Holy League between the Pope, Venice, Milan, the Emperor Maximilian I, and Spain, the Pope avoided a meeting with the foreign King and vanished into the strongholds of Orvieto and Perugia. In the second half of his pontificate he moved ever closer to France under Caesar's influence and agreed to the partition of Naples between France and Spain. The enduring quarrels of the petty lords in the Papal State, especially the rivalries of the Roman families of Colonna, Orsini, and Savelli, caused him great difficulties. Quite often the Pope had to seek shelter in Sant'Angelo, and he did not hesitate to proceed with severe ecclesiastical penalties against the disturbers of peace. He was not prudish in his choice of means and in this respect conformed to the style of other princely courts. This is the explanation of his dealings with the Turkish Sultan Bajazet II to keep the French out of South Italy.[22]

VI"; G. Gasca Queirazza, *Gli scritti autografi di Alessandro VI nell' "Archivum Arcis":* *Studi intorno alla Lingua* (Quaderni di filologia Romanza, 3 [Turin 1959]).

[21] G. Soranzo, "La più grave accusa data a papa Borgia," *Archivi,* 28 (1961), 179–88.

[22] G. Soranzo, *Il tempo di Alessandro VI papa,* 53–157: "Papa Alessandro VI e la discesa di Carlo VIII, re di Francia, in Italia"; H. Pfeffermann, *Die Zusammenarbeit der Renaissancepäpste mit den Türken* (Winterthur 1946), 93–121, where the case is overstated; *cf.* F. Babinger, "Mehmed II., der Eroberer, und Italien," *Aufsätze und Abhandlungen zur Geschichte Südosteuropas und der Levante,* 1 (1962), 172–200, especially 185; A. Strnad, "Francesco Todeschini-Piccolomini," *RömHM,* 8/9 (1964–66), 373, footnote 78, with copious bibliography; G. Soranzo, "Due singolari giudizi sul governo temporale dei Papi

With regard to the figure of the Prior of San Marco at Florence, Jerome Savonarola, persons are greatly divided, and on their interpretations depends to a great extent their judgment of the Borgia Pope. A learned and mystically gifted theologian and ardent advocate of a strict religious discipline, he was drawn into politics as a passionate preacher of reform and was especially involved in a leading capacity in the upheavals at Florence in the last decade of the fifteenth century. His prophetic preaching, originating in a consciousness of a special mission, seemed to be confirmed in the French King's expedition to Italy and the ensuing overthrow of the House of Medici. The religious and democratic system of government that he brought about at Florence and the conversion of large groups to an edifying life were, however, of only brief duration. His clash with the Pope had political rather than theological causes, namely his support of the refusal by the Florentine *signoria* to join the great Italian league against France. For the King of France was intended, in a total misunderstanding of reality, the task of reforming Church and Curia by the convoking of a general council and of replacing Alexander by a more worthy Pope. After long and patient waiting the Curia took action by excommunicating Savonarola and threatening Florence with interdict. The disregard of the ecclesiastical censures and the ordeal by fire, which was tensely awaited by the public but which did not materialize, produced a quick revulsion and imprisonment, torture, and execution in May 1498, after an obliging ecclesiastical court had condemned Savonarola as a heretic. The controversial Dominican was obviously a victim of the rapidly changing sympathy of the Florentine masses, of the hostility of some of his own confrères, and of the rivalry of other orders. If Pastor has judged him one-sidedly, especially on the question of his obedience or disobedience to the Curia, and has rendered too superficial a decision, more recent critics incline to regard him as a martyr and, in the query whether he was a heretic or a saint, to opt for the latter.[23]

della fine del secolo XV e dei primi anni del secolo XVI," *Studi Romagnoli* (Faenza), 11 (1960), 335–47.

[23] *Edizione nazionale delle opere di Girolamo Savonarola* (Rome 1955 ff.); M. Ferrara, *Savonarola, Prediche e scritti commentati e collegati da un racconto biografico*, 2 vols. (Florence 1952), II, 75–234, bibliografia ragionata; J. Schnitzer, *Savonarola. Ein Kulturbild aus der Zeit der Renaissance*, 2 vols. (Munich 1924); S. Merkle, "Der Streit um Savonarola," *Hochland*, 27, 2 (1929 f.), 462–85, also in S. Merkle, *Ausgewählte Reden und Aufsätze* (Würzburg 1965), 177–98; R. Ridolfi, *Studi Savonaroliani*, 2 vols. (Florence 1935); *idem, Vita di G. Savonarola*, 2 vols. (Florence 1952); *Studi Savonaroliani: Deputazione provinciale Ferrarese di storia patria, Atti e memorie*, Nuova serie, vol. 7 (1952), parte prima; M. Ferrara, *Discorso*, parte seconda: I. Farneti, *Luoghi e tempi di edizioni e di raccolte Savonaroliane; Accademia d'Oropa. Alessandro VI e Savonarola. Brevi e lettere* (Turin 1950), various contributions, 217–45: Saggio bibliografico; M. de la Bedoyère, *The Meddlesome Friar* (London 1958); G. Soranzo, *Il tempo di Alessandro VI Papa e di Fra G. Savonarola* (Milan 1960); G. Picotti, *Alessandro VI, Savonarola*, etc., 60–67; G. Gieraths, *Savonarola. Ketzer oder Heiliger* (Freiburg, Basel, and Vienna 1961, with bibliography);

Despite all the evil that can be said of Alexander VI, in the external ecclesiastical sphere he can seldom be taken to task. Well known is his predilection for magnificent liturgical displays, to which his imposing figure gave particular splendour. The Jubilee of 1500 was celebrated in Rome with many ecclesiastical rites in which the Pope usually took part. The ceremonies of the opening of the holy door at the beginning of the Jubilee Year go back to him. The assassination of his favourite son, John, and the collapsing of a ceiling in the Vatican palace during a severe storm, with great danger to the Pope, provided the occasion for taking up the long discussed questions of Church reform. Alexander appointed a reform commission of worthy and learned cardinals and competent theologians. It worked hard and drew up an admirable program for reform of head and members, but the reform bull that was prepared was never issued. Its draft holds an important place in the long series of reform testimonials. Patronage of the religious orders, especially of the Augustinians and the Minims, lay very close to the Pope's heart.

The drawing of the famous line of demarcation 100 leagues west of the Azores between Spanish and Portuguese possessions and newly discovered areas confirms the prestige enjoyed by the Holy See and even by Alexander. Agreements over the lands wrested from the Muslims and the recently discovered islands had been reached earlier by the two seafaring powers and were ratified by the Curia. The bulls issued in 1493, shortly after the discovery of America by Columbus, dealt with what was clearly an act of investiture in favour of Castile, and in 1494 this was followed by the important Treaty of Tordesillas. An expert knowledge of the questions at stake seems not to have been present at the Curia or anywhere else. [24]

E. Garin, *G. Savonarola: La cultura filosofica del Rinascimento italiano* (Florence 1961), 183–212; G. Schwaiger, "Savonarola und seine Zeit," *MThZ*, 12 (1961), 210–14; R. Elia, "Precisazioni sulla figura del Savonarola," *Sapienza*, 17 (Rome 1964), 545–50; C. Loubet, *Savonarole prophète assassiné?* (Paris 1967).

[24] P. de Leturia, *Relaciones entre la S. Sede e Hispanoamérica*, I (*An Gr* 101, Rome 1959), especially 153–204; *Las grandes bulas misionales de Alejandro VI, 1493* (with very detailed literature), 511–19: "La bula Alejandrina 'Inter coetera' del 4 de mayo de 1493 (with literature); E. Staedler, "Die 'donatio Alexandrina' und die 'divisio mundi' von 1493," *AkathKR*, 117 (1937), 363–402; *idem*, "Die Urkunde Alexanders VI. zur westindischen Investitur der Krone Spaniens von 1493," *AUF*, 15 (1938), 145–58; *idem*, "Die sog. westindische Schenkung Alexanders VI. von 1493 als kirchengeschichtliches Rechtsproblem," *ZKG*, 62 (1943 f.), 127–63; *idem*, "Die westindischen Lehnsedikte Alexanders VI. (1493)," *AkathKR*, 118 (1938), 337–78; *idem*, "Zum Datierungsproblem der vier vatikanischen Westindien-Urkunden vom 3. und 4. Mai 1493," *AUF*, 18 (1944), 196–209; C. de Witte, "Les bulles pontificales et l'expansion portugaise au XVe siècle," *RHE*, 48 (1953), 683–718, 49 (1954), 438–61, 51 (1956), 413–53, 809–36, 53 (1958), 5–46; A. García Gallo, *Las bulas de Alejandro VI y el ordenamiento jurídico de la expansión portuguesa y castellana en África e Indias* (Madrid 1958); A. de la Hera, "El tema de la bulas indianas de Alejandro VI," *Estudios Americanos*, 19 (1960), 257–68.

In regard to the Pope's death in August 1503, following a severe fever, there are varying reports and varying interpretations. A mix-up in a poisoned drink destined for the host at a garden party is said to have resulted in the Pope's death a few days later, while the equally ill Caesar escaped with his life. Many historians, however, defend the more probable view that the dangerous Roman fever was the cause of death.[25]

No other pontificate has evoked so much lively discussion and disagreement. Of fundamental importance is the question of the reliability of the data in the diary of the papal master of ceremonies, Burckard of Strasbourg. If he has been only too easily trusted in the past and his often exaggerated accounts have been taken literally, today he is evaluated with considerably more caution and with attention to his pathological traits. His statements on Alexander were certainly prompted by hatred and hence require a careful investigation to the extent this is possible from the sources.[26] If one disregards the many fictitious writings, composed to satisfy the need for the sensational and historically worthless, there is still left a sufficient quantity of literature that is to be taken seriously. During Alexander's own pontificate there were many critical voices, which, it is true, often had a political origin. In more recent times the dispute broke out especially because of Pastor's estimation of Savonarola in his *History of the Popes,* and a group of critics made their appearance. In addition, several Catalan and Spanish authors sought to refute the charges against their countryman, but without great success. Ferrara's book, appearing in many editions, took the easy way out by passing off as later fabrications the for the most part undoubtedly authentic documents in the Vatican archives. Thus, while his attempted rehabilitation may contain occasional correctives, it loses its credibility.[27]

The vindication of Alexander by Olmos y Canalda is of even less value. On the other hand, the dispute that went on for years between two Italian historians, Soranzo and Picotti, is of great importance. Soranzo's many studies deal with almost all the charges against the Pope, but, while they correct numerous details, they are unable to avoid an apologetic warmth. Picotti seems to come closer to historical truth, but one will always have to take both authors into consideration in order to arrive at a judgment.

The Renaissance papacy reached its climax in the remarkable personality

---

[25] J. Schnitzer, *Der Tod Alexanders VI., eine quellenkritische Untersuchung* (Munich 1929); *idem,* "Um den Tod Alexanders VI.," *HJ,* 50 (1930), 256–60; *Seppelt-Schwaiger,* IV (1957), 387.

[26] J. Lesellier, "Les méfaits du cérémonier Jean Burckard," *MAH,* 44 (1927), 11–34; Picotti, *Nuovi Studi,* 173–80: II. "La tradizione manoscritta e il valore storico dei 'Libri' di Giovanni Burckard"; F. Wasner, "Eine unbekannte Handschrift des Diarium Burckardi," *HJ,* 83 (1964), 300–31, indicates Burckard's tendentious reporting in regard to Alexander VI, especially in the interpolations, from a hitherto unknown codex in Naples.

[27] See the titles in the bibliography for this chapter.

of Alexander VI, for evil practices that had been hitherto customary were now present in abundance and were tolerated by the cardinals: a failure to observe celibacy even as Pope, dissolution of marriages from purely political motives, granting of high ecclesiastical office, including the cardinalate, in return for considerable sums, extremes of nepotism in the providing for children to the detriment of the Papal State, the administering of the apostolic palace by the Pope's daughter Lucretia, who was also regent of Spoleto for a year, — and yet Rodrigo Borgia refused to be outdone by anyone in the firmness of his faith.

Pius III (1503)

The unexpected death of Alexander VI produced much commotion in Rome and the Papal State. The opponents of the Borgia saw that their hour had struck, especially since Caesar lay seriously ill. But he still exercised a great influence and he intended to use it. The College of Cardinals contrived to induce him to leave Rome, and hence the conclave of 16–21 September could proceed calmly with its business in the Vatican. This time, however, the election capitulation of 1484 was adopted with the express injunction that a general council had to be convoked within two years, and then one was to meet every five years, especially for the reform of the Church. Apparently these details in regard to time in what was otherwise a general formula in every election capitulation came from the Sienese Cardinal Piccolomini, who also inserted the maximum of twenty-four cardinals, which was contained in the reform decrees and agreements of the past century. The candidates with the best prospects were Julian della Rovere and the French Cardinal George d'Amboise, Archbishop of Rouen. But since neither could gain the required number of votes, Pius II's nephew, Francis Todeschini-Piccolomini, who was seriously ill, was elected as a "caretaker" Pope. The pontificate of Pius III lasted only twenty-six days. Contemporaries and posterity regarded the briefness of his reign as a great misfortune, since the convoking of a general council and serious reform measures could have been expected from him. [28]

Julius II (1503–13)

Matters were to turn out quite differently and a man was to obtain the tiara who would be reckoned among the forceful and great Popes, at least from a worldly viewpoint: Julius II.

The few days of the pontificate of Pius III did not suffice to alter the general situation and so the same groups confronted each other in the new

[28] A. A. Strnad, "Francesco Todeschini-Piccolomini," *RömHM*, 8/9 (1964/66), 101–425.

conclave. But now Julian della Rovere, whom people on all sides wanted as Pope, succeeded in outwitting the crafty Caesar Borgia while assuring him of his good will. This got him the votes of the Spanish cardinals. They, like many others, were won by generous bribes, so that without doubt the election must be called simoniacal. One of the shortest conclaves in papal history ended on the very first day with the election of della Rovere, who styled himself Julius II. Although, as was customary after the completion of the election, he swore to abide by the arrangements of the Sacred College, he had no intention of keeping these and other promises, as Caesar Borgia especially was to learn. With a firm grip the new Pope took hold of the reins and inaugurated a pontificate which was filled with great policies and military enterprises such as no other could claim. He was now sixty years old and had been made a Cardinal by his uncle, Sixtus IV, as long ago as 1471 when he was a young Franciscan. He had had great experience in all secular affairs and ways of life and was brilliantly gifted. Under Innocent VIII he was regarded as the reigning Pope, but under Alexander VI he left Italy for France, only to return for a short time with the French King on his expedition to Naples.

Building on the political successes of the Borgia in the Papal State, his goal was the consolidation of his state — something which could be achieved only by keeping the great powers out of Italy. His policy was pursued in three stages: the assuring of papal authority in Rome and the Papal State, the winning back of lost territories, and the expelling of the "foreigners" from the Italian peninsula. And so he is regarded in Italian historiography as a proponent of Italian unification. In the very first year of his reign he undertook the celebrated expedition to wrest the two important cities of Perugia and Bologna from their local tyrants, the Baglioni and the Bentivogli. It was more difficult to persuade Venice to give back the areas occupied in Romagna on the collapse of the Borgia power.[29] When all negotiations and threats came to nothing, the Pope resorted to force and in 1509 allied with France, the Emperor Maximilian, and the Swiss, the old enemies of the Most Serene Republic, in the League of Cambrai. The frightful defeat of Agnadello in 1509, the blackest day in the history of Venice, induced the Republic to give up the cities it had seized and ostensibly to abandon its state Church policy. It also induced the Pope, in order not to weaken too severely one of Italy's *cinque principati*, to make a new alliance with Venice and Spain in the Holy League of 1511 against the French. But the winning of Parma, Piacenza, and Reggio-Emilia was too dearly purchased, for France replied to the papal offensive in the ecclesiastical sphere by renewing the Pragmatic Sanction of Bourges and getting Francophile cardinals to summon a council to Pisa in the summer of 1511, with

[29] F. Seneca, *Venezia e papa Giulio II* (Padua 1962).

the aim of deposing the Pope. To counter the threatening danger, especially since even the Emperor Maximilian showed himself favourable to the Council of Pisa, the Pope now summoned the Fifth Lateran Council to meet at Rome in 1512.[30]

This year did not at first grant the Holy League the desired success. Quite the contrary: under the leadership of the young and capable Gaston de Foix the French inflicted a severe defeat on the Spanish and papal army at Ravenna on Easter Sunday, and the papal legate, Cardinal John de' Medici, was captured. But luck changed sides after the death of the French general, and some months later the troops of France had to leave Italian soil. The Medici returned to power at Florence, Maximilian Sforza, son of Louis *il Moro,* at Milan, and the Emperor deserted the Council of Pisa and recognized the Lateran Council. The latter continued in several sessions until 1517, but with the collapse of the schismatic synod it had really accomplished its intended task.

To what extent politics dominated all else appears in the Pope's relations to the Emperor Maximilian. Julius sought in every way to keep him out of Italy and from his imperial coronation, even if he occasionally had to ally with him for the sake of his Italian policy. He was not displeased by the obstacles which Venice put in the way of a journey to Rome. He agreed when in 1508 Maximilian had himself designed as "Roman Emperor-elect" at Trent.[31] The Emperor was unwilling to renounce the rich provinces of Italy and the financial power of the German Church and hoped to achieve his goal in the ecclesiastical sphere. Hence a matter which has received very different evaluations becomes understandable: the Emperor's plan of acquiring the tiara. If until recently it has been necessary in this question to depend upon a tradition which left room for doubt, new finds have confirmed the seriousness of the plan and of the steps taken. When in the summer of 1511 the Pope became seriously ill and his end was expected, Maximilian, like everyone else, readied himself for the impending conclave, but in such a way that he himself appeared as a candidate. An old desire seemed about to be fulfilled. Since as early as the last decade of the fifteenth century persons had heard of Maximilian's intention of controlling at least the German Church, on the French model, either through a reform council or through a withdrawal of obedience and a schism.[32] The schismatic Council of Pisa

---

[30] *Jedin,* I, 106–12 (English version).

[31] H. Wiesflecker, "Maximilians I. Kaiserproklamation zu Trient (4. 2. 1508). Das Ereignis und seine Bedeutung," *Österreich und Europa. Festgabe für Hugo Hantsch* (Graz, Vienna, and Cologne 1965), 15–38; W. Stelzer, "Konstantin Arianiti als Diplomat zwischen König Maximilian I. und Papst Julius II. in den Jahren 1503–1508," *RQ,* 63 (1968), 29–48.

[32] H. Wiesflecker, "Neue Beiträge zur Frage des Kaiser-Papstplanes Maximilians I. im Jahre 1511," *MIÖG,* 71 (1963), 311–32; J. M. Doussinague, *Fernando el Católico y el cisma de Pisa* (Madrid 1946).

was a favourable opportunity for such an undertaking. But now, with the serious illness of the Pope, it was important to act quickly in order "to arrive at the papacy" or at least to acquire the disposal of the rights and finances of the German Church. In a detailed letter, whose authenticity has recently been proved, several possibilities emerge: that Maximilian should become the coadjutor of the reigning Pope or of an Antipope, that he should himself become Antipope or even, and this was hardly probable, the lawfully elected Pope after the death of Julius II. There were long discussions on the subject with France and Spain, with the intention on both sides of outwitting the other partner. The masterful diplomacy of the Spanish court, vis-à-vis the imperial intermediary, Bishop Matthew Lang of Gurk, succeeded in dragging out the business and, after the Pope's recovery, in detaching the Emperor from the alliance with France and from supporting the Council of Pisa. [33]

In an attempt to extol the Pope's ecclesiastical activity a group of individual items has been compiled: participation in solemn liturgical services, procedure against heretics, reform of monasteries and orders, and edicts against duels and the pillaging of wrecks. All this, however, pertains to the normal duties of the papal office and of the Curia. Hence it hardly modifies the well known remark of the Florentine historian, Guicciardini, that Julius II had nothing of the priest except the dress and the name. The four solemn sessions of the Fifth Lateran Council in his pontificate were devoted essentially to combatting the Council of Pisa and counteracting its encouragement by France. In this connection one must not forget that, as a Cardinal, Julius had suggested to the French King the convoking of a council to depose Alexander VI. The important prohibition of simony in future papal elections would have acquired a great significance if it had been heeded. [34]

Although he was personally neither a theologian nor a man of letters, the Pope acquired immortal fame as a Maecenas. The rebuilding of Saint Peter's and the ruthless tearing down of the venerable Constantinian basilica, the painting of the ceiling of the Sistine Chapel by Michelangelo, and the frescoes of Raffael in the stanze of the Vatican palace must especially be mentioned here. The plan for his tomb in Saint Peter's can be called gigantic but also daring; of it there survives the always impressive monument in his former titular church of San Pietro in Vincoli with the figure of Moses, in which is materialized the overwhelming personality of the Pope. The homage which Pastor pays to his hero can apply only to the politician. And even there reservations must be made. If the Papal State became temporarily through the policy and military abilities of its kingly ruler the first power in Italy and for a while played a leading role in European politics, this situation changed in the last weeks of the second Rovere Pope with the

[33] H. Wiesflecker, loc cit., 315, footnote 23.
[34] Pastor, VI, 440.

rapprochement of Venice to France and the growth, dangerous for the "freedom of Italy," of Spanish influence. To style Julius II, as Pastor does, the "saviour" of the papacy will not do. For the tasks of the papacy lie not in politics, however clever, successful, mighty, and violent, but in an intellectual and spiritual ministry that follows the example of Christ.

Leo X (1513–21)

Julius II left a conflicting legacy: on the one hand, the Papal State in a position which again deserved the name of state and a considerable treasure in the Castel Sant'Angelo; on the other, the enmity with France and an ecclesiastical opposition, called into being for political reasons but not without its dangers. In addition was the fact that really nothing had yet been done in the ecclesiastical sphere for the reform that was so urgently necessary and was being energetically demanded on all sides.

Twenty-five cardinals took part in the conclave, which began in the Vatican palace on 4 March 1513; the schismatics of Pisa, whom Julius had deposed, were not admitted. As had long been customary, an election capitulation was first decided and sworn to by all the cardinals present. The great concerns and tasks that had persisted for decades recurred here in their traditional form: efforts for peace among Christian nations and states so that the war against the Turks could at length be taken up, reform of the Church and of the Curia, and continuation of the Fifth Lateran Council. The special regulations concerning the College of Cardinals must be understood with reference to the authoritarian rule of the dead Pope: the necessary assent of two-thirds for proceedings against cardinals, for the naming of new members, and for important measures in the Papal State and in foreign policy. In addition, there was so large a number of particular promises as to money, offices, and benefices that the new Pope could not do justice to all desires. Two factions, the "old" and the "young," confronted each other. But agreement quickly occurred, and on 11 March the thirty-seven-year-old John de' Medici was elected. The fact that he was carried into the conclave ill and at once had to undergo an operation is said to have made it easier to gain the assent of the old cardinals; but, more than this acute illness, the zealous but probably not simoniacal activity of his secretary, Bibbiena, seems to have gained the decision for him. [35] His great political experience and his activity as ruler of Florence made him probably the most qualified candidate.

[35] G. L. Moncallero, *Il cardinale Bernardo Dovizi da Bibbiena, Umanista e Diplomatico 1470–1520* (Florence 1953), 333–43; *idem, Epistolario di Bernardo Dovizi da Bibbiena,* I, *1496–1513* (Florence 1955).

His home was Florence, his father was Lawrence *il Magnifico*. Admitted to the clerical state by receiving the tonsure at the age of seven, he soon obtained a series of lucrative benefices, including the abbey of Montecassino. When not yet fourteen he was secretly named a Cardinal by Innocent VIII and in his seventeenth year, as the Pope had arranged, he entered the Sacred College. The letter which his father sent him at Rome on this occasion is, in its lack of genuine religious sentiment and its refined worldliness, a striking mirror for a cardinal of this epoch. [36]

Because of a careful education the young Cardinal had the aristocratic culture and manners of a Renaissance prince. And such he remained when, following the death of the forceful Julius II, he was elected Pope. He was above all the prince in politics, the chief activity of a Pope in the age of the Renaissance. Not without skill in all the arts of diplomacy, he sought to keep the Papal State and his own Florence out of the struggle of the great European powers, France, Spain, and Austria, over Italy and to acquire for his family at the favourable moment a position of predominance in Italy, even outside Florence. The ceaseless changes in high politics forced him to adapt himself to and to take part in rapidly alternating alliances. The aim of the papal and Florentine policy was to prevent the uniting of Naples with Milan, which was disputed and often changed lords, and to maintain and assure the rule of the Medici in Florence. Hence throughout most of his pontificate the Pope also conducted the government of often refractory Florence, and the members of his family, such as Lawrence *il Pensieroso*, who acted there in administrative capacities were only his agents. [37] If his political practices — simultaneous negotiations and alliances with different and mutually hostile partners and equivocal treaties — were often condemned, still, despite deceit and double dealing, the concern for peace in his balance of power policy was prominent. He deviated from it only in a few cases. And his wavering and hesitation, his postponing of urgent decisions have often been represented merely as weakness and too little notice has been taken of his statesmanship and the successes it achieved.

At his accession the Papal State belonged to an anti-French coalition. Leo accepted this situation without sincerely agreeing to it and without openly supporting the alliance against France. From the outset he was concerned to preserve the independence of Milan with the aid of the Swiss and not to let it fall into the hands of a foreign power. To this corresponded his great exertions for an Italian league, but they were unsuccessful because of the opposition of Venice and of the great powers. French reverses in North Italy and the new anti-French alliances as well as the Pope's willingness to

[36] *Pastor*, V, 358–61.

[37] H. Reinhard, *Lorenzo von Medici, Herzog von Urbino 1492–1515* (Diss. phil., Heidelberg 1935).

oblige led to an understanding and especially to the abandonment of the Council of Pisa and the acceptance of the Fifth Lateran Council. New difficulties arose when in 1515 Francis I ascended the throne and at once prepared for an expedition to Italy. Only after long hesitation did the Pope join a large league against France, but, after the French King's victory at Marignano, he was forced to make important concessions in the Treaty of Viterbo. At a meeting of the Pope and the King at Bologna in December 1515 the Papal State had to surrender Parma and Piacenza, territories that had been destined for the Medici family, and the King seems even to have obtained the prospect of investiture with Naples. From the ecclesiastical viewpoint the discussions at Bologna were of special importance because of agreement on a concordat and the annulling of the Pragmatic Sanction of Bourges. The concordat made hitherto unprecedented concessions to the French crown. The King obtained the full right of nomination to almost all benefices that were conferred in consistory, that is, bishoprics and abbeys. The Pope could fill only a small number of lesser benefices. Expectatives and reservations were abolished for France, and only *causae maiores* could be carried to the Curia. In addition, the King personally received a number of privileges.[38] The Pope had great difficulty in having so far-reaching a concordat approved in consistory, and only the fear that the French Church would separate itself entirely from Rome facilitated the consent of the cardinals. Nevertheless, the French *parlements* were not satisfied with the concordat. In the course of the pontificate and especially in its last years relations with France grew worse. Apart from Venice it was chiefly the French King who obstructed Leo's serious efforts for a crusade against the Turks, even though he collected large sums in crusade tithes and managed to use them for his enterprises in Italy. The religious situation in Germany brought the Pope to an understanding with the new King of the Romans, with the result that the French troops in North Italy were compelled to withdraw.

After his earlier mishaps, especially in the war against Venice, the Emperor Maximilian had been able to take only a slight part in the struggle for predominance in Italy. When the question of the imperial succession became acute, the Curia acquired an important role because the candidates were Francis I of France and Charles I of Spain. Because of their great power and their position in Italy both presented a danger to the Papal State, especially Charles as ruler of Naples. Hence Rome desired a candidate from among the German princes and thought of the Elector Frederick of Saxony. When he declined, the three spiritual Electors were to be gained for the French King by tempting offers. Not until Charles's election was certain

[38] Mercati, *Raccolta di concordati*, 233–51.

did the Curia yield. The Pope's simultaneous treaties of alliance with Francis and Charles have gone down in history as masterstrokes of diplomacy.[39]

The importance attaching to high politics also explains the enigmatic hesitations in the proceedings against Martin Luther and the delaying of the process that had been instituted. Politics also determined the continuation and conclusion of the Fifth Lateran Council, convoked by Julius II as a political chess move against France and the rebel cardinals.[40] The sixth session took place on 27 April 1513, a few weeks after Leo's election. As already noted, Leo contrived an understanding with France and hence the submission of the schismatic cardinals and the acknowledgement of his own Council. The twelfth and final session was held on 16 March 1517. It cannot be denied that in the discussions of the reform commission, lasting for years, and in the great reform bull of the ninth session on 5 May 1514 considerable work was accomplished, but mostly in theory only. Of the few other decrees the definition of the individuality of the human soul and the condemnation of the doctrine of the double truth deserve mention.[41] If one looks at the meagre participation and the routine, it was a papal Council, but with no representation of the Universal Church in the manner now customary for centuries. Activities on the part of the few episcopal participants for solidarity in maintaining their rights were rejected as attacks on the divinely intended monarchical constitution of the Church. Interest in having the Council attended by representatives from Germany, France, and Spain was not very great. Quite the contrary: the Pope feared from such a Council too thoroughgoing a reform in head and members. Hence it is difficult to assign to this Fifth Lateran Council the rank of a general council.

A great sensation was produced by the proceedings against several cardinals on the charge of conspiracy. The Sienese Cardinal Alfonso Petrucci was alienated by the expulsion in 1516 of his brother from Siena, in which the Pope had played a role, and he was soon regarded as the head of a dangerous *fronde* of cardinals. He is said to have tried to have the Pope poisoned by a Florentine physician. As a result of confessions obtained by torture from Petrucci's servants, he and Cardinal Sauli were arrested as they entered the Vatican and imprisoned in the dungeons of Sant'Angelo,

[39] G. L. Moncallero, "La politica di Leone X e di Francesco I nella progettata crociata contro i Turchi e nella lotta per la successione imperiale," *Rinascimento*, 8 (1957), 61–109.
[40] *Mansi*, XXXII; *Hefele-Leclercq*, VIII, 297–558; *Pastor*, VIII, 384–410; J. Klotzner, *Kardinal Dominikus Jacobazzi und sein Konzilswerk* (Rome 1948); A. Deneffe, "Die Absicht des V. Laterankonzils," *Scholastik*, 8 (1933), 359–79.
[41] S. Offelli, "Il pensiero del concilio Lateranense V sulla dimostrabilità razionale dell'immortalità dell'anima umana," *Studia Patavina*, 1 (1954), 7–40, 2 (1955), 3–17; new summary by F. Favale, *I concili ecumenici nella storia della chiesa* (Turin 1962); Jedin, I, 102–10; O. de la Brosse, *Le Pape et le Concile. La comparaison de leurs pouvoirs à la Veille de la Réforme* (Paris 1965).

and later the Dean of the Sacred College and *Camerlengo* of the Roman Church, Cardinal Riario, was also incarcerated there. Long and stormy discussions in several consistories attended the rather murky process. Petrucci was executed; the other accused cardinals were deprived of their dignities, benefices, and revenues for a long time and punished with enormous fines. The financial aspect of the matter occasioned the widespread view that it was merely a pretext for getting money, together with the immediately subsequent great creation of cardinals, to which the intimidated Princes of the Church had to assent. Recent studies take a more serious view of the conspiracy and approve the Pope's proceedings, which have so often been condemned as inhuman. [42]

Church History has taken Leo X severely to task for his nepotism. Since he was actually ruling Florence also, his concern for the Medici family is understandable. He rejected many demands of his relatives, such as their claims to Piombino and Siena. That he wanted to obtain Parma, Piacenza, Modena, and Reggio, and perhaps Ferrara also, for his brother Julian can be regarded as means of guaranteeing the Papal State, but less can be said for his covetous glances at Naples. [43] The war over Urbino on behalf of his nephew Lawrence was a great political and financial misfortune. The property expropriated from the Medici at the time of their expulsion was repurchased with money belonging to the Church and the Papal State. The finances of the Papal State endured an enormous burden because of the gigantic expenses for politics, for the luxurious court, and for the grand-scale patronage of art and scholarship. According to a contemporary saying, he squandered the treasure amassed by his predecessor, the income of his own pontificate, and that of his successor's reign. Through highly questionable financial practices the administration of the Papal State and of ecclesiastical benefices was further demoralized, the number of vendible offices was irresponsibly increased, and even admittance to the College of Cardinals was made dependent on the payment of large sums. Objections to such methods cannot be invalidated by reference to the immortal achievements of Michelangelo and Raffael. Leo X was an almost unfathomable personality, a refined gourmet, a Maecenas, but without creative qualities. From genuine artist and inspired man of letters to buffoon — all were represented at his court. He took particular delight in festive cavalcades and pageantry. The theatrical performances in the papal palace did not, for the most part, correspond to a spiritual mode of life, and Leo's predilection for hunting

[42] F. Winspeare, "La congiura dei cardinali contro Leone X," *Biblioteca dell'Archivio storico italiano,* 5 (Florence 1957); A. Mercati, "Minuzie intorno ad una lettera di Pietro Bembo," *RSTI,* 9 (1955), 92–99; A. Schiavo, "Profilo e testamento di Raffaele Riario," *StRom,* 8 (1960), 414–29.

[43] E. Dupré-Theseider, *I papi Medicei,* 295 ff.

has often been censured. And yet the blame affects not so much his person as the system that he took over and further developed, a system which could not be justified from a religious viewpoint.

CHAPTER 58

The Inner Life of the Church

The Urban Parish

The Church life of the late Middle Ages, like that of the early Church, once again was centred around the urban parish. Cities had experienced a vigorous growth in the thirteenth and fourteenth centuries. If there were some 250 cities in Germany around 1200, about 800 more were founded during the thirteenth century alone, and by the close of the Middle Ages approximately 3,000 places possessed city rights. The European city owes its growth to commerce rather than to the trades. As soon as and so long as commerce linked the lesser economic systems to an extensive area — the Hansa is the prime example, — cities flourished, whereas they stagnated wherever the gilds with their efforts for self-sufficiency prevailed. All the more the small political units of the territorial principalities impeded the development of cities at the end of the Middle Ages.

> In the place of the proud and erect bearing of a *bourgeoisie*, master of its destiny and acting upon wide areas, appeared the small, congested, submissive bearing of the subject of later centuries... In and among territories the German cities from now on eked out an unassuming life, until the Thirty Years' War ruined for most of them a still considerable prosperity.[1]

Notwithstanding their importance, their inhabitants were not numerous. Of the 3,000 German cities, 2,800 had less than 1,000 inhabitants, and 150 between 1,000 and 2,000. Only the remaining 50, with more than 2,000 citizens, were of real significance for the economy. A mere fifteen of them exceeded a population of 10,000; the largest, Cologne, surpassed 30,000. Then came Lübeck with about 25,000. Next, probably only Nürnberg, Strasbourg, Danzig, and Ulm reached a figure of 20,000. In 1493 the population of Erfurt was reckoned as about 18,500, whereas that of Leipzig was estimated as only 4,000 in 1474.[2] Among the inhabitants of the cities women predominated. "In cities like Nürnberg, Basel, and Rostock in the fifteenth

---

[1] F. Röhrig, *Die europäische Stadt im Mittelalter* (Göttingen n. d.), 124.
[2] *Ibid.*, 75 f.

or sixteenth century, for each 1,000 men there were 1,207, 1,246, and even 1,295 women."[3] The causes of this were male military service, greater male licentiousness, and the greater susceptibility of males to contagious diseases. Also responsible is the fact that a relatively large number of males were out of the question as far as marriage was concerned because they were diocesan or religious priests — Lübeck's 300 to 400 were less than the average. With this surplus of females the convents and, in the case of the middle and lower classes, the houses of Beguines had a considerable social importance as places for the support of unmarried women. Between 1250 and 1350 some 100 Beguine houses are said to have been founded in Cologne, and they provided shelter and a meaningful life for at least 1,000 women. If, as places devoted to the fostering of a specific kind of religious life, they had a great significance for the life of devotion in the mediaeval city, on the other hand the deficiencies in religious spirit, the idleness and laxity of morals in the convents and Beguine houses could only have increased the alarmingly great spread of public lewdness at the close of the Middle Ages.

The large number of priests and religious in the cities, constituting as much as one-tenth of the total population, gave rise to serious social and economic problems. Clerics and religious claimed immunity from taxation for themselves and for the property of their church or monastery. Yet they not infrequently possessed as much as half of the real estate in a city. They claimed the advantages of urban life, for example its security and commerce, without contributing a corresponding share to bearing the city's burdens. Hence, after 1300 the cities' defensive measures to halt the expansion of the untaxable property of monasteries and churches were stepped up. Further acquisitions of real property in mortmain were either forbidden or it was established that citizens' properties should remain subject to taxation when they passed to ecclesiastical ownership. In the country too efforts were made to restrict the exemption of ecclesiastics from taxation or at least to guard against its consequences. Thus, for example, it was forbidden for the only son of a tax-paying peasant to become a cleric, and churchmen were excluded from acquiring peasant property, or it was expressly stipulated that such property should remain taxable. Hence in the fifteenth century clerical privileges declined increasingly in importance.[4]

Special grounds for conflict developed in the episcopal cities. In contrast to most secular princes, bishops resided in cities and sought to maintain their supremacy against the townsmen's aspirations for freedom. Probably no episcopal city was spared a struggle with its bishop. Cologne obtained its independence in 1288 as a result of ceaseless bitter quarrels with its

[3] *Ibid.*, 78 f.
[4] F. X. Künstle, *Die deutsche Pfarrei und ihr Recht zu Ausgang des Mittelalters* (Stuttgart 1905), 28.

archbishops, but only in 1475 was it formally recognized as a Free Imperial City by Frederick III. By the close of the thirteenth century most of the important cities of Germany and of the Low Countries had self-government. The administration of bishops or other city lords was supplanted by that of the council as organ of the urban upper class. Some spiritual lords contrived to maintain their influence, as, for example, at Trier and Bamberg, where, even in the fourteenth and fifteenth centuries, the council remained dependent on the episcopal justices of the peace, who participated in the sessions of the council.[5] As in the case of immunity from taxation, the conflict in the cities was concerned also with clerical freedom from lay courts. On the other hand, in the thirteenth century a growing number of complaints were heard at synods in regard to the violence and encroachments of which lay persons, authorities and private individuals, were guilty.[6]

The fight against the privileges of the clergy was conducted under the auspices of quite modern principles, such as public safety and general welfare. While a lay authority was established, there was no abdication of an interference in ecclesiastical matters. On the contrary, cities sought more and more to assume control of Church life.

The development of the parochial system in the cities was essentially complete in the thirteenth century. For a long time the cathedral had ceased to be the only parish church in the city. Collegiate churches and at times even abbeys had obtained parochial rights in the cities and their own parishes. But the self-reliance of the now independent *bourgeoisie* went beyond this to demand its own parish churches or at least its own priest from its own ranks (*plebanus*, people's priest). This priest and often also the pastors were frequently considered to be city officials, like the justice of the peace, schoolmaster, and councillors; they formed part of the *officiales civitatis*, as the Bern municipal law of 1218 expressed it. This led logically to the demand on the part of the citizens or of the party in political control in the cities to elect their pastor like other officials. The right of electing the pastor was granted especially to newly founded cities. But, much as this did occur, it was not universally established. Frequently the citizens contrived to acquire patronage over their city churches and hence the right to name or to present the pastor. The citizens took care of their churches and in accord with the cooperative principle wanted a share in the administration and supervision of church property. For this purpose they made use of the church custodian, whose function more and more became part of the urban administrative system and was subject to the council. Cities made the

---

[5] W. Neukamm, "Immunitäten und Civitas in Bamberg von der Gründung des Bistums 1007 bis zum Ausgang des Immunitätsstreites 1410," *78. Bericht und Jb. 1922/24 des Hist. Vereins für die Pflege der Geschichte des ehem. Fürstbistums Bamberg* (n. d. [1925]), 189 to 369 (especially pages 337–41).

[6] *Cf.* the Cologne Synod of 1266 (*Mansi*, XXIII, 1140).

building of their churches and the administration of the church property their own monopoly and responsibility.[7] The Würzburg Synod of 1287 complained "that in a number of places, on the pretext of improving the economic administration of the Church, lay persons are appointed by lay persons, without the consent of prelates and chapters, to receive the offerings and the income from other sources."[8]

But the city council not only supervised the church plant and controlled the offerings and other donations of the faithful through the custodian. It also exercised a decisive influence on the appointment of clerics to Mass benefices and the administration of the endowment funds. Like the monasteries, the canonries, vicarships, pastorships, and benefices to provide Masses and hospital chaplains were means of support for younger children. If the canonries were reserved to the city patriciate, then the rest of the citizens and the artisans sought to provide for their sons as pastors or Mass-priests. Hence there existed quite often a close bond of life and interests between *bourgeoisie* and clergy.[9]

The absorption of the ecclesiastical organization into the *bourgeoisie* included also the school and the care of the poor and the sick. These passed increasingly into the hands of the laity or of the secular officialdom. The hospital organization was probably the starting-point of this development. The office of the city hospital custodian appears to be older than that of the church custodian.[10] The close connection of hospital and religious corporation or monastery dissolved. Hospitals became autonomous, and hospital fraternities assumed care of them. The Council of Vienne (1311–12) called for the appointing, not of clerics, but of efficient and experienced laymen for the direction of hospices and hospitals. They were to be under the bishop and answerable to him.[11] The development often proceeded further, however, and led to the transformation of the church hospital into a municipal institution. The administration frequently passed exclusively to the city council, which appointed the supervisor and had the right to present and to remove the hospital chaplain.[12]

The establishing of city schools meant that the school system also passed from the clergy to control by the city. But even so, the post of schoolmaster,

[7] *Feine, RG,* I, 371; in almost all cities new parish churches appeared or old ones were rebuilt in the late Middle Ages: e.g., at Munich Sankt Peter (thirteenth century, rebuilt in 1368) and the Frauenkirche (1468–88); at Nürnberg Sankt Lorenz (1439–77) and Sankt Sebaldus (choir 1361–79); at Ulm the Münster (1377–1452); at Münster Sankt Lamberti (1350–1450).

[8] *Mansi,* XXIV, 863 f.

[9] K. Fröhlich, "Kirche und städt. Verfassungsleben im Mittelalter," *ZSavRGkan,* 22 (1933), 188–287 (especially pages 252 ff.).

[10] S. Reicke, *Das deutsche Spital und sein Recht im Mittelalter* (Stuttgart 1932), I, 200.

[11] E. Müller, *Das Konzil von Vienne* (Münster 1934), 575 f.

[12] *Hauck,* IV, 57 f.; *Feine, RG,* I, 371 f.

like that of town clerk, frequently continued to be filled by clerics. Cities founded universities by papal privilege: Cologne in 1389, Erfurt in 1392, Basel in 1460, and Breslau in 1507. At Trier the university was able to become a reality in 1473, once the Archbishop had ceded to the city the right of foundation granted to him by the Pope in 1454.

Even "the monasteries became more *bourgeois.*"[13] The cities increasingly secured control of monastic property and in many cases monasteries were regularly included in the sphere of city government. In the pastoral care of the city populations great credit belongs to the mendicant orders of Franciscans and Dominicans, whose houses were to be found in every city of any importance. Because they carried out their care of souls among the people without regard to the boundaries of dioceses or parishes, they came into conflict with bishops and diocesan clergy. When Martin IV in the bull "Ad Fructus Uberes" of 13 December 1281 even authorized mendicants delegated by their superiors as confessors or preachers to fulfill their office without the consent and even against the will of bishops and pastors, a violent quarrel ensued. In particular the French bishops and the University of Paris attacked the bull in the interests of an orderly and proper care of souls. As Cardinal Legate, the future Boniface VIII rejected the complaints, but as Pope he had to cancel the privileges to a great extent in the bull "Super Cathedram" of 18 February 1300. The mendicants should be permitted to preach freely in their churches and in the public squares outside the hours of parochial services, but, like the diocesan clergy, they needed the bishop's authorization for hearing confessions. The less the parish priests took into account the new needs and, because of pluralism and disregard of the duty of residence, did not even carry out their traditional obligations, the mendicant orders gained popular favour.

The Liturgy

The Church's worship, with the Mass as its centre and climax, underwent a further elaboration, not in the sense of a real enrichment but rather of a multiplication and continuation of the existing rite. New starts cannot be ascertained, but, all the more, a proliferation of external forms. The personal and the subjective elements came into prominence, the tangible and concrete and the particular that could be counted were stressed. The community nature of the celebration of the Eucharist became constantly less clear, and the "private" Mass more and more preempted the field. It gradually determined the very form of the solemn Mass.

From the thirteenth century, when the complete missal superseded the

---

[13] E. Schiller, *Bürgerschaft und Geistlichkeit in Goslar (1290–1365)* (Stuttgart 1912), 124.

sacramentary, the priest had also to read, for himself, the parts sung by the choir and soon even to read the Epistle and the Gospel while they were being sung by the sacred ministers. The liturgy was no longer understood as the service of the whole Church, whose membership was expressed in the distribution of functions among priest, choir, and community, but was a clerical or even a priestly liturgy. Only what the priest did was "valid," and hence he had to recite everything himself. The people were even debarred from the readings. No effort was made to translate them, and frequently they were drowned out by the playing of the organ. Even in parish churches, for example at Breisach, a rood-screen separated the sanctuary from the nave of the laity and kept the community from participating in the solemn liturgy. The Mass had ceased to be a proclamation of the word. The unintelligible language barred any approach by the people to an understanding. All the more importance was attached to the ritual — the external ceremonies and the sacramental signs — but without the word this threatened to become a splendid but empty covering. The liturgy became a performance — beautiful and intricate but really mute. From outside it efforts were made, by means of allegory, to give it an artificial voice. Sermons on the Mass, which could have unlocked the mystery, were inadequate as regards both number and content. [14] Thus the Eucharistic celebration, called by the missal the "source of all sanctity," was able to exercise a fruitful influence on popular piety only in a very limited sense.

Popular piety invented substitutes for the liturgy, and these succumbed all the more easily to the danger of superficiality to the extent that they were no longer connected with the centre of the mystery. What was unfamiliar and inaccessible had to be praised. Sermons and speculation on the fruits of the Mass and the value of attendance at Mass dominated the otherwise jejune theology of the Mass and the instruction in it. The fruits of the Mass were understood at the close of the Middle Ages in an increasingly massive and this-worldly manner. [15]

If there was nothing to listen to, even greater prominence was given to seeing. Popular devotion at Mass concentrated on gazing at the Host at the elevation following the consecration, and this became of the greatest importance from the thirteenth century. William of Auxerre (d. 1230) had already taught: "Many prayers are answered while looking at the Lord's body, and many graces are poured out." [16] Synods urged priests to elevate the Host so high that it could be seen by the people. But soon measures had to be taken against those who all too often complied with popular demand

[14] A. Franz, *Die Messe im deutschen Mittelalter* (Freiburg 1902), 676.
[15] *Ibid.*, 40.
[16] *Summa aurea* (Paris 1500), 260. Quoted in E. Demoutet, *Le désir de voir l'hostie* (Paris 1926), 18; *cf.* P. Browe, *Die Verehrung der Eucharistie im Mittelalter* (Munich 1933).

and increased the number of elevations to three or continued the elevation for an excessively long time.[17] The elevation acquired such importance that in some places "to go to Mass" meant to arrive for the consecration and to look at the Host. At the end of the fifteenth century the describing of the effects resulting from gazing at the Host became ever more extravagant and superstitious. This led to the nonsense of running from one altar to another, in churches that had several, to catch a glimpse of the elevation. The popular demand for looking was met from the fourteenth century by numerous Eucharistic processions, exposition, and benediction with the Sacrament. All of this caused the Eucharistic celebration as sacrifice and banquet to retire more and more into the background.

In the fifteenth century there were not lacking voices protesting the multiplication of processions and expositions. The Papal Legate Nicholas of Cusa emphasized that the Eucharist "was instituted as food and not for show,"[18] and in his reform decrees he forbade processions and expositions outside the octave of Corpus Christi.[19] His prohibition of venerating bleeding Hosts and of the pilgrimage to Wilsnack foundered on the resistance of local authorities, which obtained support at the Curia.

Abuses and superstition in regard to the Blessed Sacrament could spread all the more since the word, the *verbum sacramenti* in the strict sense and that of the liturgy in general, was not only not understood but was not even heard. The word is of course intended to remove from the sensible element its ambiguity and elevate it to the clarity and precision of the intellect.[20] Without the accomplishing of the word there is the risk of missing the meaning of the Sacrament or even of falsifying it. The word, not understood by the layman and often only pitifully by the priest, became paralyzed in formalism. Too easily what took place became congealed into a thing or ran the risk of magic. A thing can be reproduced at pleasure, something not possible to processes in life and personal actions.

As a matter of fact, in the later Middle Ages the Mass was stamped by individualization and multiplication. Every gild and confraternity, even a family which thought highly of itself, wanted to have its Mass and, so far as possible, at its own altar. This striving was encouraged by a theology which taught the finite value of the Mass and defended the view that an *a priori* determined number of Mass fruits was divided among the participating group; hence it was better to live in a smaller parish because then the share in the Mass offered by the pastor on Sundays for his flock was greater.[21]

---

[17] P. Browe, *op. cit.*, 49–69.

[18] A. Krautzius, *Metropolis* (Frankfurt a. M. 1576), XI, c. 39; P. Browe, *op. cit.*, 170.

[19] J. Koch, *Der deutsche Kardinal in deutschen Landen* (Trier 1964), 15.

[20] *Cf.* Thomas Aquinas, *Summa Theologica*, III, q. 60, a. 6.

[21] *Cf.* E. Iserloh, "Der Wert der Messe in der Diskussion der Theologen vom Mittelalter bis zum Ausgang des 16. Jahrhunderts," *ZKTh*, 83 (1961), 44–79 (especially page 61).

To satisfy all these demands the number of Masses and of altars had to be greatly multiplied. This also led to an unhealthy growth in the number of Masspriests — those who had nothing else to do but celebrate Mass and on occasion take part in the choral office. Parish churches, like cathedrals and collegiate churches, had a large number of altars, for which to some extent several priests were beneficed. For example, "the Constance cathedral at the close of the Middle Ages possessed fifty-four endowments for Mass-priests; the Ulm Münster, the largest parish church in the diocese, more than sixty; 122 Mass-priests occupied forty-seven altars at Breslau's Elisabeth-kirche; while at the Magdalenenkirche there were fifty-eight altars and 114 Mass-endowments." [22] A place like Breisach had at the parish church, besides the pastor and curates, sixteen chaplaincies for twelve altars. [23]

The duties of Mass-priests were not sufficient to keep them occupied, and the income was not enough to assure them adequate support. The only natural attempt to escape pauperization by means of pluralism led to further abuses. Mass-benefices were subject to the surveillance of the pastor and the bishop and often of the secular patron. Ever greater became the influence of the city officials on the conferring of Mass-benefices at the city churches and on the administration of the capital endowment.

The multiplication of Mass-endowments made necessary a rapid succession of the most varied services. If there was a question of chanted Masses, then, even with so many altars, it was difficult to celebrate them. Hence there arose abuses such as "curtailed Masses," that is, sung Mass became a low Mass from the Creed to enable another sung Mass to begin, or *Missae bifaciatae* or *trifaciatae* were held. In these several "liturgies of the Word" were combined with one sacrificial Mass. The "dry Mass", that is, Mass without the Canon and the narrative of the institution of the Eucharist, which had some meaning as the administering of communion in a sick-room, was debased in order that a priest might accept a stipend without having celebrated the consecration and communion. In Thuringia, around 1470, preachers of indulgences had to be reprimanded for finishing the Mass as a "dry Mass" when they were informed before the sacrificial part that the collection of indulgence alms did not come up to their expectations. [24]

Criticism of the practices in regard to Mass was not wanting. John Gerson (d. 1429) took preachers to task who hoodwinked the people into believing that on the day of attending Mass a person did not become older, could not lose his sight, and would not die a sudden death. Such a thing, he said, was a

---

[22] *Feine, RG,* I, 373.
[23] W. Müller, "Der Wandel des kirchlichen Lebens vom Mittelalter in die Neuzeit, erörtert am Beispiel Breisach," *FreibDiözArch,* 82/83 (1962–63), 227–47 (especially page 229).
[24] L. A. Veit, *Volksfrommes Brauchtum und Kirche im deutschen Mittelalter* (Freiburg 1936), 25.

temptation to Judaism and superstition.[25] This notion of the Mass, connected with the characteristic late mediaeval inclination to the individual and the subjective, led to the endeavour to put it as far as possible at the service of the individual's needs and desires. The result was a tremendous increase in the number of votive Masses.

There were votive Masses of the twenty-four patriarchs or elders; of the fourteen, fifteen, and more "holy helpers"; of the seven joys and sorrows of Mary; votive Masses against sicknesses, including one against pestilence, one of Holy Job against syphilis, one of Saint Christopher against sudden death, one each of Saint Roch and Saint Sebastian against pestilence, one of Saint Sigismund against fever; votive Masses for special requests: in honour of the Archangel Raphael or of the Three Magi for a safe journey, a Mass to keep away thieves and to recover stolen property, a Mass before a duel or ordeals, one against Hussites and Turks and against witches; the seven-day, thirteen-day, or thirty-day Masses of emergency, which had to be offered by one priest for seven, thirteen, or thirty days respectively, at the end of which interval guaranteed liberation from sickness and distress was expected, and in addition the three Masses of Saint Nicholas for needs.[26]

These last mentioned series of Masses, which increased to forty-five in number for all possible concerns, were all the more dubious in that they held out the prospect of a guaranteed outcome for the living and the dead. On the eve of the Reformation the gloomy statement is true, that

The holiest of the Church's possessions remained, it is true, the centre of genuine piety. But alas, the clouds and shadows surrounding this centre brought matters to such a pass that the Institution of Jesus, that well of life from which the Church had drawn for fifteen hundred years, became an object of scorn and ridicule and was repudiated as a horrible idolatry by entire peoples.[27]

Preaching

If, because of the Latin language, the liturgy itself was in no position to introduce the faithful to Christian doctrine, this assignment became the monopoly of preaching. There was much preaching in the late Middle Ages, perhaps more than in more recent ages. Preaching in German on Sundays and holy days, during or before Mass, was probably the rule in city and country.[28] In addition there often were also special afternoon preaching

---

[25] *Opera*, ed. by Du Pin, II (Antwerp 1706), 521–23.
[26] L. A. Veit, *op. cit.*, 26; A. Franz, *op. cit.*, 169–217.
[27] Jungmann, *The Mass of the Roman Rite*, I, 132.
[28] R. Cruel, *Geschichte der deutschen Predigt im Mittelalter* (Detmold 1879), 674.

services. Before or after the sermon the feasts of the coming week and the annual commemorations were announced, the names of the dead and of benefactors were read out, prayers of intercession for all classes in the Church, the Our Father, the Hail Mary, the Creed, and the ten commandments were recited. To the sermon were added, though in some places only on specified days, a general confession of sins and absolution.[29] There was preaching on week-days too, especially on the Wednesdays and Fridays of Advent and Lent. The duty of preaching on the part of clerics occupied in the care of souls goes without saying, but the frequent insistence on this duty by synods[30] proves that it was not seldom neglected, less in cities than in the country. "The poor peasants ask for bread but rare are the pastors who break it for them," complained Cornelius de Suckis around 1500.[31] If it was demanded time and again that the priest must recite the Our Father, the creed, and the commandments to the people in their vernacular on Sundays,[32] then we should probably not entertain any high expectations of pastoral preaching. It is difficult to form a picture. The material left by diocesan priests is naturally scanty. Complaints extend from the charge of scholastic sophistry and a mania for distinctions to indignation over the absurdities and banalities of the preachers.

The basic source of these shortcomings was the inadequate education of priests, especially of the poorly paid vicars, by whom the frequently absentee holders of pastoral benefices had their functions performed. The dearth of a priestly spirit and of a pastoral sense of responsibility in the bishops had an especially unhealthy effect in this regard. It was left to the individual, after attending the Latin school in his town, to acquire the necessary knowledge from a pastor or in a monastery. One could obtain ordination from a bishop, usually without any special examination. The cathedral *scholasticus*, and in the fifteenth century also a special cathedral preacher, had charge of the instructing of clerics and of the examining of candidates for ordination. Only a small percentage of clerics attended a university; a high estimate gives one-fifth. But most of these did not continue the study of the liberal arts more than one or two years, and so they obtained no special preparation for the clerical office.

Shockingly slight was the indispensable minimum of knowledge which thirteenth-century theologians required of the priest and with which persons were probably satisfied in practice. The Dominican Ulric of Strasbourg

---

[29] J. U. Surgant, *Manuale curatorum praedicandi praebens modum* (1506), Liber II, Consideratio 3–6; 16. *Cf.* E. Iserloh, *Die Eucharistie in der Darstellung des Johannes Eck* (Münster 1950), 255 f.; Jungmann, *op. cit.*, I, 480–94.

[30] F. W. Oediger, *Über die Bildung der Geistlichen im späten Mittelalter* (Leiden and Cologne 1953), 115, footnote 5.

[31] *Ibid.*, 116, footnote 1.

[32] *Der Katholik*, 71 (1891), II, 383 f.; F. W. Oediger, *op. cit.*, 51, footnote 5.

(d. 1277) expressed it in the following manner and this was adopted by the canonists:

> To the extent that the priest is obliged to the celebration of the worship of God, he must know enough grammar to be able to pronounce and accent the words correctly and to understand at least the literal sense of what he reads. As minister of the Sacraments he must know the essential form of a Sacrament and the correct manner of administering it. As teacher he must know at least the basic doctrine of faith proving itself effective in charity. As judge in matters of conscience he must be able to distinguish between what is sin and what is not and between sin and sin. [33]

It was certainly no mere chance that the mendicant orders, which were especially concerned for the extensive theological education of their members, assumed in the thirteenth and fourteenth centuries the task of preaching, rendered more urgent by the enhanced religious interests of the city populations and because of the sects. From the end of the fourteenth century they were joined by educated priests from the diocesan clergy. At that time in many places, especially in South Germany, a few preaching offices were created for them by private bequests or by action of a city council. They were supposed to satisfy the more rigorous claims of their listeners and hence as far as possible were to have earned a degree in theology. But this *sine qua non* stipulation again made it difficult, considering the educational status of priests, to fill the posts. These preachers were not to replace the customary preaching in the parochial liturgy. Frequently in the foundation charters a defining of rights and duties was envisaged or it was specified that this preacher had to withdraw if the pastor himself wanted to preach. When the canons would not accept John Eck, presented for the preaching office at Sankt Moritz on 29 January 1518, James Fugger wrote: "A parish is in greater need of preaching and hearing confessions than of the choral chanting of the entire chapter." [34] He thereby expressed vividly the esteem in which preaching was held by the upper *bourgeois* and the responsibility which they felt for it.

In addition to the principal categories of sermons for Sundays *(de tempore)* and for feasts of saints *(de sanctis)*, in the late Middle Ages there appeared sermons on the Passion, Lenten sermons, and catechetical sermons, that is, on the various points of Christian doctrine which were later compiled in the catechism under the headings: articles of faith, prayers, the ten commandments, and the seven Sacraments. There were also sermons on the seven capital sins, the cardinal virtues, and other moral questions. The sermon based on the scholastic method was fostered by scholars such as

---

[33] *Summa de bono*, 6, tr. 4, c. 24; quoted in F. W. Oediger, *op. cit.*, 55 f.
[34] G. von Pölnitz, *Jakob Fugger*, I (Tübingen 1949), 381.

Henry Heinbuche von Langenstein (d. 1397), Francis de Maironis (d. 1328), Robert Holcot (d. 1349), John Gerson (d. 1429), Nicholas of Dinkelsbühl (d. 1433), Nicholas of Cusa (d. 1464), and Gabriel Biel (d. 1495). More popular and more adapted to ordinary Christian life were the great itinerant preachers of penance, like Vincent Ferrer (d. 1419), Bernardine of Siena (d. 1456), John of Capestrano (d. 1456), Robert Caracciolo (d. 1495), Olivier Maillard (d. 1502), Gabriel Barletta (d. 1480), and Jerome Savonarola (d. 1498), probably the most powerful and ardent preacher of the Middle Ages. To precision of thought Savonarola joined mystical depth and warm emotion. Disregarding all scholarly and ornamental formality, he preached Holy Scripture and with unheard of prophetical frankness arraigned before its tribunal life in the world and in the Church. In the area of German speech the most important popular preacher at the end of the Middle Ages was Johannes Geiler von Kaysersberg (d. 1510). Before going to the Strasbourg Münster as preacher in 1478, he had taught at Freiburg (1465–70) as a master of philosophy and had received the doctorate in theology at Basel in 1476. He understood both life and man and had the special gift of expressing himself in a clear and down-to-earth and oftentimes coarse manner. With great frankness he condemned the immorality of the people and that of persons of high rank in Church and State, humorously but frequently with biting irony and devastating ridicule. In him the proclaiming of the faith very definitely took a second place after moral teaching — something characteristic of late mediaeval religious instruction generally.

An influence was exercised on preaching by various reference books for homiletics: preaching cycles, collections of topics and examples, lives of saints, and postils. Particularly important were those by such authors as James a Voragine (d. 1298), author of the *Legenda aurea* and *Sermones super Evangelia*, Jordan of Quedlinburg or of Saxony (d. *ca.* 1380), an Augustinian Hermit, John Nider (d. 1438), Dominican and author of *Formicarius* and *Sermones aurei*, John of Werden (d. 1437), Franciscan, author of *Dormi secure*, John of Herolt (d. 1468), a Dominican, and others. Furthermore, textbooks of homiletics were not lacking. Widely circulated were the *Tractatus de modo discendi et docendi ad populum sacra seu de modo praedicandi* (printed, among other places, at Landshut in 1514) of Jerome Dungersheym (1465–1540) and the *Manuale curatorum praedicandi praebens modum* (1503 and later) of John Ulric Surgant (1450–1503),[35] pastor and professor at Basel. From Surgant has come down one of the first baptismal registers, which he kept as pastor of Sankt Theodor in Basel from

---

[35] Reproduced in substance and in part *verbatim* in *Katholik*, 69 (1889), II, 166–86, 302–22, 432–44, 496–523. *Cf.* D. Roth, *Die mittelalterliche Predigttheorie und das Manuale Curatorum des Joh. U. Surgant* (Basel 1956).

1490 to 1497. While church records were kept in Italy and the Midi already in the fourteenth century, this was not the practice in Germany. At the end of the fifteenth century synods more and more frequently admonished or obliged pastors to keep lists of the baptized, the dead, those going to confession, and the excommunicated. But it was not until the Council of Trent that it became a duty to keep records of baptisms and marriages. [36]

Catechesis

The baptism of infants put an end to the catechumenate of adults, but in the Middle Ages no regular Church instruction of children took its place. Only sporadically and rather late do we find synodal decrees that oblige pastors to instruct the young in faith and morals, [37] for this was regarded as the duty of parents and godparents. They were supposed to teach the children the creed and the Our Father, and in the late Middle Ages care was taken to include the Hail Mary and the ten commandments. Works of edification, such as the *Himmelsstrasse (The Way to Heaven)* of the Vienna provost, Stephen of Landskron (d. 1477), and the *Christenspiegel (The Mirror for Christians)* of Dietrich Kolde (1435–1515), urged parents to carry out this duty. The *Seelenführer (Director of Souls)* charges the mother: "You must bless your child, teach him the faith, and bring him early to confession, instructing him in all he needs to know in order to confess properly." Hence even the preparation for confession and communion was the business of the parents. The Middle Ages knew no special instruction for these two Sacraments. [38] Add to this that the role of the school in direct religious instruction was slight. There was no separate subject of religious education, but in the other aspects of instruction much religious knowledge was probably imparted in a practical manner, for example, by teaching to read the Our Father and other prayers. But the school comprised only a part of the city youth, while country youngsters seldom had an opportunity to go to school. How meagre religious knowledge was can be gathered from the fact that Nicholas of Cusa, as Cardinal Legate in Germany in 1451–52, felt obliged to have wooden tablets giving the Our Father, the creed, and the ten commandments set up in the churches for the religious instruction of the people. [39]

[36] H. Börsting, *Geschichte der Matrikeln von der Frühkirche bis zur Gegenwart* (Freiburg 1959); M. Simon, "Zur Entstehung der Kirchenbücher," *ZBKG*, 28 (1959), 129–42; F. W. Oediger, *op. cit.*, 119 f.

[37] Béziers, 1246 *(Mansi, XXIII, 693)*; Albi, 1254 *(Mansi, XXIII, 837)*; *cf.* Decretals of Gregory IX, 1. 3, t. 1, c. 3.

[38] P. Browe, "Der Beichtunterricht im Mittelalter," *ThGl*, 26 (1934), 427–42.

[39] *Pastor*, II, 123. Reproduction of tablet and text in J. Koch and H. Teske, "Die Auslegung des Vaterunsers in vier Predigten," *Cusanus-Texte*, I, *Predigten*, 6 (Heidelberg 1940), 280–85.

Because of this lack of direct and systematic instruction, this "catechetical vacuum of the Middle Ages," [40] people were for the most part left to learn the Christian faith by life and experience in a Christian environment. The paintings on the walls, in the windows, and on the altars were the Bible of the illiterate. Mystery plays, Christmas, Holy Week, and Easter plays, and other dramatic presentations brought sacred history to men and held up to their gaze morally good conduct. An abundance of religious customs attended the day-to-day life of the individual and the community from cradle to grave. The educative power of Christian morality and a Christian *milieu* must certainly not be underestimated. But there is also no question that such a Christianity of mere custom, without adequate clarification by knowledge and understanding, was particularly susceptible to mass-suggestion and superstition and was hardly a match for serious crises.

The vast deficiency in personal instruction and formation of consciences lent an enhanced importance to the annual confession, the preparation for it, and the actual making of the confession. Helps were provided by the outlines for examining the conscience and, at the end of the Middle Ages, the confession brochures. [41] In Latin or in the vernacular, these were aids for the proper administration and the fruitful reception of the Sacrament of penance. About fifty printings of such little books are known for the period 1450 to 1520. This clearly indicates the new possibilities for religious instruction latent in the invention of printing. The same is true of other works of prayer and edification and above all of the brief summaries of Christian doctrine and morality which Luther later called the catechism. There had already earlier been such compilations of the chief catechetical points for the use of pastors and teachers, such as the *Opus tripartitum de praeceptis decalogi, de confessione et de arte moriendi* of John Gerson (d. 1429), [42] or the *Discipulus de eruditione Christifidelium* of the Dominican John of Herolt (d. 1468). The latter work was printed twelve times between 1490 and 1521. In his translation of Gerson's *Opus tripartitum*, Geiler of Kaysersberg admonished priests, parents, schoolmasters, and hospital directors to see to it that the doctrine of this brief book is inscribed on tablets and hung up in public places, such as churches, schools, and hospitals; but now the art of book printing made it possible to provide the pupil with works of this sort as his textbook. In such works of the fifteenth century the form of a catechism is not yet clearly developed. They are equally prayerbooks and books of edification, as is evident from such titles as *Der Seele Trost (Consolation of Soul), Die Himmelsstrasse (The Way to Heaven)*, and *Spiegel der Laien*

---

[40] R. Padberg, *Erasmus als Katechet* (Freiburg 1956), 27.
[41] F. Falk, *Drei Beichtbüchlein nach den Zehn Geboten* (Münster 1907); C. H. Zimmermann, *Die deutsche Beichte vom 9. Jahrhundert bis zur Reformation* (Veida 1934), with the literature; R. Rudolf, *Ars moriendi* (Cologne and Graz 1957); *LThK*, II (2nd ed. 1958), 126.
[42] *Opera,* ed. by Du Pin, I (Antwerp 1706), 425–50.

(Mirror for the Laity).[43] The best known of these popular books is *Der Christenspiegel (The Mirror for Christians)* by the Franciscan Dietrich Kolde (d. 1515), which appeared in many editions from 1470.[44]

Printing was of special importance for the spread of the Bible. Around 100 printings of the Vulgate had appeared by 1500. From the first printed German translation in 1461, or at the latest in 1466,[45] until Luther's edition of the New Testament in 1522 fourteen High German and four Low German complete Bibles appeared in print, in addition to a large number of German psalters, other printings of parts of Scripture, and editions of Gospels and Epistles (postils and *plenaria*). In France there appeared after 1200 the so-called "Bible History," following an abridgement of biblical historical material, the *Historia scholastica* of Peter Comestor (d. 1179). Greatly enlarged, this came out in print in 1477 and 1487. And the first printed Bible in Dutch, at Delft in 1477, was a Bible History of this sort. Two separate Italian translations appeared at Venice in 1471.

Religious Orders

The religious institutes of the late Middle Ages were in a state of decay, arising from many causes. Its progress in the individual orders was also quite varied and did not follow one pattern. When the mendicant orders experienced their tremendous growth early in the thirteenth century, the Benedictine family was in decline, and it was the mendicants that responded to the needs of the new situation. Hence they exerted a powerful attraction on the young, whereas the old orders were in no position to proclaim and to live their ideal in a manner adapted to gaining in any great numbers young men of deep religious convictions. In Germany at the beginning of the twelfth century there were about 260 Benedictine monasteries. Thereafter there were no new foundations, and from the twelfth to the fifteenth century a large number of houses disappeared because of secularization or of transformation into communities of canons. Too closely identified with feudalism, the order had as slight a connection with the new social and economic conditions as with the new educational system of *studia generalia* and universities. In a sense the Benedictines retired from religious, intellectual, and cultural life without their wealthy and imposing monasteries

---

[43] P. Bahlmann, *Deutschlands katholische Katechismen bis zum Ende des 16. Jahrhunderts* (Münster 1894), 12–23.

[44] *Der Christenspiegel des Deutschen Katechismus von Münster*, ed. by C. Drees (Werl 1954); in High German in C. Moufang, *Katholische Katechismen des 16. Jahrhunderts* (Mainz 1881), I–L; on the editions see A. Groeteken, "Der älteste gedruckte deutsche Katechismus und die Volksbücher Dietrich Koldes," *FStud*, 37 (1955), 53–74, 189–217, 388–410.

[45] J. Mentel, *Strassburg;* new ed. by W. Kurrelmeyer, 10 vols. (Tübingen 1904–15).

ceasing to offer material inducements. The nobility saw them as places for providing for younger sons. But these wanted to continue in the monastery to live the life of their own social class and frequently disregarded the vow of poverty as well as inclosure. It became more and more common for the monastic property and income to be divided between abbot and community, with the abbacy and the claustral offices being regarded as benefices and the monks being allowed to have property (*peculium*) for their personal use. Abbeys were conferred *in commendam* on cardinals, bishops, and even lay persons, who drew the income without being concerned for the internal life of the monasteries.

The Black Death of 1348 involved grave material distress in most religious communities and carried off a large number of the members. In general it produced a serious breakdown of religious and moral discipline. Monks who had fled from the plague and had lived in freedom in the world were no longer willing to submit to the rule as formerly. In an effort to replenish the thinned ranks people ceased to be very particular about accepting candidates. Before long the Western Schism gave rise to serious shocks in the orders as well as in the Church at large. The split showed itself in the orders and at times in individual monasteries. At Montserrat the monks recognized Rome, whereas the Abbot looked to Avignon. In other monasteries each faction elected its own abbot; at Korvey, for example, the two rival abbots engaged in violent struggle.[46] Some orders, like the Carthusians, Cistercians, and Carmelites, split into two branches, each with its general.

All this naturally caused grave damage to the spiritual life and discipline of the monasteries. Under these circumstances reform was not possible, because its opponents contrived to play off the one authority against the other. But reform efforts were made in the fourteenth and fifteenth centuries. Mention has already been made of the quarrels in the Franciscan family, which resulted in 1517 in the separation of the Conventuals and the Observants, and also of the reform congregation of the Windesheim Augustinians. In other orders, too, observant circles were formed to live the rule in its original austerity. Among the Augustinian Hermits the reformed houses united into a special reformed congregation directly subject to the general.

Benedict XII (1334–42) seriously sought a reform of the orders. He tried first of all to bring back his own Cistercian Order to its former spirit. In the constitution "Fulgens sicut Stella" (1335) he issued detailed regulations on claustral life, the monks' theological studies, and the management of monastic property. He made a deep inroad into the traditional structure of the Benedictine Order in the bull "Summi Magistri Dignatio" (1336), called

---

[46] J. Evelt, "Die Anfänge der Bursfelder Benediktiner-Congregation," *Zeitschrift für vaterländische Geschichte und Altertumskunde Westfalens* (3rd series), 5 (1865), 125–27.

for short the "Benedictina." In this he aimed to assure the economic basis of the monasteries by a definitely regulated administration and, aware of the value of a good education and of serious intellectual discipline for monastic observance, enacted regulations for the monks' studies. The centralization of the order which he decreed was thorough. The order was to be divided into thirty-six precisely defined provinces. Provincial chapters were to meet every three years. At these the visitors elected by the chapter were to make their report and the accounts of each monastery were to be examined. Although the Pope personally tried to implement his reform decrees in practice, he had no success. The reform not infrequently collapsed in the face of the resistance of the secular rulers, who forbade abbots to attend the provincial chapters for fear lest decrees would be issued which would run counter to the lord's interests.

Benedict XII had no greater luck with his endeavours for a reform of canons regular, and serious disputes arose with the Dominicans and Franciscans. The reason was not merely the absence of a desire for reform in the orders, but also the fact that the Pope's regulations were often lacking in a correct understanding of the peculiar nature of each order.

If the "Benedictina" had had hardly any effect, the idea of merging individual monasteries into provinces or congregations remained alive, and all reform efforts of the fifteenth century were characterized by it. From Santa Giustina at Padua Abbot Louis Barbo founded in 1419, under Martin V, a reform congregation which obtained its definitive form in 1432 under Eugene IV. All authority was vested in the annual general chapter of delegates and superiors of the monasteries. The individual abbey was a member of the congregation and was administered by it. The abbots were elected for life but they changed monasteries every year and later every six years. The monks were professed for the congregation rather than for a particular monastery and could be transferred to another monastery by the president of the congregation or the visitor. Thereby the abbatial dignity and the claustral offices were stripped completely of their character as benefices and the abuses of *commenda* and prebends were effectively obviated. In the course of time almost all the Italian monasteries, including Montecassino, Subiaco, La Cava, and Cervara, themselves reformed houses, joined the Congregation of Santa Giustina. And though it continued to be restricted to the peninsula, it still exercised a great influence on the organization of many other congregations.

In Germany the reform movement received a stimulus from the Council of Constance, in which, among the numerous regulars, many Benedictines took part. Under the very eyes of the Council Fathers, as it were, there took place at the Abbey of Petershausen near Constance in 1417 a chapter attended by the Benedictines present in Constance and the superiors of the Mainz-Bamberg province. The "Benedictina" was to be again observed and, above all, poverty and the common life were again enjoined. Furthermore, the chapter issued decrees against the nobility's monopoly of certain monasteries. But there was no central tribunal to see to the implementation of the decrees. Many abbeys resisted the reforms, and some sought to escape them by having their monks transformed into secular canons. Just the same, the idea of reform had awakened. Centres of renewal were the abbeys at Kastl in the Upper Palatinate, Melk on the Danube, Sankt Matthias in Trier, Tegernsee, the Vienna Schottenkloster, and Bursfeld on the Weser.

The customs of Kastl, which, in addition to the liturgy, especially stressed silence, poverty, and obedience, determined the monastic reform decrees of the Petershausen Chapter and of the Council of Basel. Twenty-five abbeys were revived by Kastl, directly or indirectly. But neither this reform nor that of Melk resulted in the establishing of a congregation. This work was initiated by German monks from Subiaco and spread from Melk to monasteries in Austria, Bavaria (Tegernsee), Swabia, and Hungary. The starting point of reform in North and West Germany was the monastery of Bursfeld near Göttingen, where John Dederoth became Abbot in 1433. During a stay in Italy he had come to know the Congregation of Santa Giustina and as Abbot of Clus had introduced the reform. In 1434 he went to Trier to visit Abbot John Rode of Sankt Matthias, who as a Carthusian monk had assumed the direction of this Benedictine monastery in 1421 and had drawn up new statutes for it after lengthy study. The Council of Basel had appointed him reformer and visitor of the monasteries of southwestern Germany. From him the new Abbot of Bursfeld, John Dederoth, obtained the reform statutes and four of his best monks. Thus Bursfeld was able to experience a new flowering and to become under the direction of Abbot John von Hagen from 1439 the nucleus of a strictly organized congregation with a chapter that met annually from 1446. In 1469 thirty-six monasteries, including Hirsau, belonged to it; in 1530, ninety-four. The abbots had to take an oath to be loyal to the union and to follow or introduce the Bursfeld observance in their monasteries. The Bursfeld reform received stimulation and encouragement from the Provost John Busch (d. 1479) and the Cardinal Legate Nicholas of Cusa (d. 1464).

Religious life in France sank to its nadir in the fifteenth century as a consequence of the Hundred Years' War and the far-reaching encroachments of the secular authorities, notably through the Pragmatic Sanction of Bourges in 1438. Within the Benedictine Order there were reform endeavours at Cluny, Tiron, and especially Chezal-Benoît in the diocese of Bourges. But the Concordat of 1516 hurt reform by giving the King the right to name the abbots.

In Spain the monastery of Valladolid, founded as recently as 1390, became the centre of a reform congregation which almost all the Spanish monasteries joined. To avoid the abuses of *commenda* the abbatial title was abolished and the duration of office of the claustral appointments was restricted to a few years.

In the Cistercian Order the symptoms of decay were not so alarming, and the twenty-four new foundations of the fifteenth century testify to a certain vitality. The Carthusian Order experienced a real flowering in the fourteenth and fifteenth centuries. Despite numerous afflictions and persecutions at the hands of Hussites and Turks, in 1510 there were 195 charterhouses in seventeen provinces. Of great significance for the spiritual life of the late Middle Ages beyond the limits of their order were Ludolf of Saxony (d. 1378), Henry of Kalkar (d. 1408), Henry of Coesfeld (d. 1410), and Dionysius the Carthusian (d. 1471).

The founding of new orders and of communities and confraternities resembling orders proves that the seeking of Christian perfection was still alive. In addition to the Brothers and Sisters of the Common Life, still other lay confraternities were formed to devote themselves to active charity for the neighbour in the care of the poor and the sick and the burial of the dead. The Alexians, also called Cellites, Lollards, or Rollbrüder (Burial Brothers), came together after the Black Death of 1348–49 in Flanders and on the Lower Rhine. Those of Aachen made vows in 1469. In 1472 Sixtus IV gave them the Augustinian rule.

Originally a lay confraternity founded by John Colombini at Siena in 1360, the Jesuates aimed to devote themselves to the salvation of their fellowmen by prayer, mortification, and the care of the sick. They lived at first according to the Benedictine rule but later adopted that of the Augustinians. They were called "Apostolic Clerics of Saint Jerome," after their patron.

As patron of hermits he also gave his name to the Hieronymites, who followed the Augustinian rule as expanded by ideas from Jerome. There were originally four congregations in Italy and Spain. In Castile they united under Peter Fernández Pecha. Confirmed as an order in 1373, they were subordinated in 1415 to a superior general in Spain.

The Minims are a mendicant order founded in Calabria in 1454 by Francis of Paula under the title of "Hermits of Saint Francis." Their rule is the Franciscan, but made more austere in regard to diet. Referred to as Paulans from their founder, they were called "Bons hommes" in France and "Fratres de Victoria" in Spain in connection with the victory over the Muslims. In 1520 they had around 450 monasteries.

The Birgittines, or Order of the Saviour, were founded by Saint Birgitta of Sweden (1303–73). She lived a happy married life with a noble to whom she bore eight children, among them Saint Catherine of Sweden. Following a pilgrimage to Santiago de Compostela (1341–42), her husband retired to a Cistercian monastery, where he died in 1344. Around this time began the "heavenly revelations," which she recorded in the Swedish language and which her confessors translated into Latin. She founded the first monastery at Vadstena in 1346 and in 1349 went to Rome to secure the establishment of her order. She spent the last twenty-four years of her life in the Eternal City. In burning words she lashed out at the abuses in the Church and implored the Popes in the name of Christ to return to Rome. The constitutions of her foundation were confirmed by Urban V in 1370; but the definitive approval did not come until 1378, after her death, when Urban VI added them as a supplement to the Augustinian rule. Like Vadstena, the houses were to be double monasteries, both being under the direction of an abbess. For sixty nuns there were to be thirteen monks, four deacons, and eight lay brothers. The order spread quickly throughout Europe and is said to have soon comprised seventy-nine monasteries, which were of great religious and cultural importance, especially for Scandinavia. Birgitta died at Rome in 1373, after a pilgrimage to the Holy Land. She was canonized by Boniface IX in 1391.

CHAPTER 59

Theology in the Age of Transition

Nicholas of Cusa

At the point where the Middle Ages gave way to modern times there was in Nicholas of Cusa a mind which, with headstrong and obstinate will power to create a whole, compelled the antagonistic forces of his day into a "Catholic concordance" and at the same time held out the creative beginnings of a possible bridge connecting with a new age.

Son of the sailor Henne Krebs (Chryfftz), Nicholas was born in 1401 at Kues (Cusa) on the Moselle. It cannot be proved that he attended the school of the Brothers of the Common Life in Deventer, nor is it likely that he did so. He matriculated at Heidelberg as a *clericus* as early as 1416 and became bachelor of arts in 1417. In the same year he took up the study of canon law at Padua, where he became acquainted with the doctrine of consent elaborated by Francis Zabarella (d. 1417). According to this, what affects all must be approved by all. At the same time he came in contact with Italian humanism, gained the friendship of Paul del Pozzo Toscanelli, and studied mathematics, physics, and astronomy. In 1423 he became *doctor decretorum*. Back home he obtained the parish of Altrich in 1425, without having received the priesthood.[1] From Easter 1425 he lectured on canon law and studied

---

[1] He was still a deacon in 1436 and received the priesthood before 1440. *Cf.* E. Meuthen, *Mitteilungen und Forschungsbeiträge der Cusanusgesellschaft*, 2 (Mainz 1962), 33 f.

theology at Cologne. His teacher, or rather his stimulating friend, was Heymeric de Campo, the chief protagonist of the Albertists, a strongly Platonic version of scholasticism, which gave him the intellectual treasures of pseudo-Dionysius and Raymond Lull and probably of Master Eckhart.

The discovery of twelve comedies of Plautus and of other Latin classics, his demonstration of the spuriousness of the Donation of Constance by a critical investigation of its sources, and his doubts as to the identification of the highly esteemed Dionysius with Dionysius the Areopagite made him a pioneer of German humanism.

His services to the Archbishop of Trier yielded a number of benefices, including in 1427 the deanery of the Stift Sankt Florin in Koblenz. He made this his residence. At the beginning of 1433 he went to the Council of Basel to uphold the claims of Ulric von Manderscheid to the archbishopric of Trier.[2] Here he finished his *De concordantia catholica*. Originally this seems to have been projected only as a "Libellus de ecclesiastica concordantia," which was to treat in two books of the Church, her nature, her reform, and the tasks of the council. The adding of a third book on reform of the Empire produced a significant work on the all-embracing Christian concord in Church and Empire.[3] In accord with the pattern of Neoplatonic anthropology — spirit, soul, body — Nicholas developed the exemplar of a Christian order, in which "the one Church of all believers in Christ" displays "a harmonious accord of the divine Spirit, the priestly soul, and the body of believers."[4]

In the *Concordantia catholica* and in the testimonial "De auctoritate praesidendi in concilio generali" (1434),[5] Nicholas of Cusa was a moderate conciliarist. "The Roman Pontiff, who is a member of the Church, even though the highest ranking in administration, is subject to the general council" (p. 24). The council represents the Universal Church more truly than does the Pope alone. The Pope represents the Church only in an indefinite manner ("confuse"). Hence the Church, "for the sake of her own welfare or in urgent need, [can] dispose of the papacy at her discretion" (p. 26). The Pope holds the first place at the council and must be regarded as its head and judge. Hence he or his legates must be allowed to participate in the council.

---

[2] See also E. Meuthen, *Das Trierer Schisma von 1430 auf dem Basler Konzil* (Münster 1964); *idem*, "Nikolaus von Kues und der Laie in der Kirche," *HJ*, 81 (1962), 101–22 (especially pp. 110 f.).

[3] *Cf.* G. Kallen, *Die handschriftliche Überlieferung der "Concordantia catholica" des Nikolaus von Kues* (Heidelberg 1963).

[4] "Deus enim spiritus est, qui per medium sacramentorum, quorum ministri sunt domini sacerdotes, tamquam per animas corpori id est fideli populo gratiose coniungitur, ut homo sit in deo" (III, 41).

[5] Ed. by G. Kallen, *Cusanus-Texte*, II, 1 (Heidelberg 1935); the quotations that follow are taken from here.

586

In fact, if he wishes to attend and is able to do so, no council can take place without him (p. 32).

The unity, or *consensus*, of pope and council is for Nicholas the sign of truth. And so his sudden *volte-face*, his change from the Council of Basel to Eugene IV, was not so radical as it seemed, for the Pope offered a Council which promised unity with the East, whereas at Basel controversy and uproar became increasingly open. To leave Basel meant to decide for Pope and Council. Because unity is the proof of truth, and the Council of Basel on the other hand was working for a schism, "the Holy Spirit could not be there."[6]

For Nicholas the unity of the Church was more and more guaranteed in her single head. "The Christian people, united to the one Shepherd of the one *Cathedra Petri* and to the one High Priest, constitutes the one Church, just as man is one because all his members are united to one head."[7] His previous view, that the unity of the Church is the result of the orderly cooperation of the various degrees of the one priesthood and of the consent of all believers (*concordantia catholica*), was replaced, in connection with the philosophical insights of the *Docta ignorantia* (1440) in the sign of the double concept "complicatio-explicatio," by the knowledge that plurality is the unfolding (*explicatio*) of unity, which precedes everything as *complicatio*. Folded up in unity in God is everything that in the world is unfolded in plurality and differentiation. Because all things are in him as their effective and formal cause, though not in their multiplicity but in unity, he is the "coincidentia oppositorum." He, however, does not comprise the contradictories in their opposition; rather he is above every opposition. "God is not the root of the contradiction but the unity before every root."[8] This one and first before all else is beyond our intellect.

Where all plurality is abolished in unity, all definability by means of otherness ceases, and the contradictories fall together, there, so to speak, the intellect loses all the ground under its feet. There begins that unknowing, which is at the same time the single possibility for the human mind to somehow behold anywhere the infinite, to "touch" the incomprehensible "incomprehensibly."[9]

Just as now the plural is explained only by the one, and the beneath can

---

[6] Discourse at Mainz in 1441, *RTA*, 15, 643: "... legittimum esse Florentinum concilium constaret ex effectu unionis Graecorum, quia 'arbor bona fructus bonos faceret,' ex fine vero Basiliense illegittimum, quia scisma fecisset, et ubi scissio, non poterat esse spiritus sanctus." Cf. *Cusanus-Texte*, IV, 1, ed. by J. Koch (Heidelberg 1944), 46.

[7] Letter of 1439 to a Carthusian monastery, in *Cusanus-Texte*, IV, 1, p. 38.

[8] "Nam non est radix contradictionis Deus, sed est ipsa simplicitas ante omnem radicem" (ed. Basel, 339; ed. A. Petzelt, 206).

[9] J. Stallmach, "Zusammenfall der Gegensätze," *Mitteilungen und Forschungsbeiträge der Cusanusgesellschaft*, 1 (Mainz 1961), 52–75 (especially p. 62).

be understood only by the above, so the unity of the Church is based also on the one supreme head. His authority is the *complicatio* of all powers requisite for the maintenance and guidance of the Church.[10]

Nicholas distinguishes the mystical body of Christ as the invisible Church, which is nothing other than the unfolded grace of Christ, from the visible Church, the *ecclesia coniecturalis*. The latter embraces good and bad, but it can be recognized as the Holy Church, and to some extent comprehended, by its marks. It possesses a visible head in the Pope. In him the Church is given *complicative,* and, vice versa, the Pope is in her in so far as she has developed on the basis of Peter's confession and preaching.[11]

"The Hercules of the Eugenians" — so he was called by Aeneas Silvius Piccolomini, later Pope Pius II, — Nicholas of Cusa in the succeeding years fought for the recognition of the papal authority and at imperial and princely diets came out for the reconciliation of Pope and Empire. His exertions had their successful conclusion at the Princely Diet of Aschaffenburg in 1447, where Nicholas V obtained general recognition and the Vienna Concordat of 1448 was arranged. The tireless interventions of the legate for the restoration of the unity of the Church as understood by the papacy were rewarded by his elevation to the cardinalate in 1448 and his promotion to the bishopric of Brixen in 1450. But in his see he had to wage a protracted and less successful struggle to assure or restore respectively the spiritual and temporal independence of the prince-bishopric *vis-à-vis* the efforts of Archduke Sigismund, Count of Tirol, to consolidate an independent state and a territorial Church.

However, the Cardinal was not to assume the government of his diocese until April 1452. Before doing so he traveled through the Empire as papal legate for a year and a quarter, from Vienna to Brussels, from Magdeburg to Trier, preaching the jubilee indulgence. To effect in clergy and people a religious and moral renewal, to visit monasteries, to make peace, to summon aid against the Turks, in brief to reform the German Church and activate its forces — such was his task. The Cardinal Legate began the work of reform in February 1451 at Salzburg,[12] where he held a provincial council and prepared for the reform of the monasteries. At Easter he held a diocesan synod at Bamberg, while in May he held at Würzburg a chapter at

---

[10] "Et hoc est iuxta regulam intellectualem doctae ignorantiae in pontifice esse ecclesiam complicative et ipsum esse pariter in ecclesia" — letter of 1442 to Rodrigo Sánchez de Arévalo, ed. by G. Kallen, *Cusanus-Texte*, II, 1 (Heidelberg 1935), 111; cf. J. Koch, *Nikolaus von Cues und seine Umwelt*, 22.

[11] "Sensibilem enim ecclesiam sensibile caput habere convenit. Et ob hoc caput huius ecclesiae sensibile est pontifex ... In quo est haec ipsa ecclesia complicative ... et ob hoc Petrus a confessione petrae, quae Christus est, nomen accipiens, complicatam in se ecclesiam explicavit verbo doctrinae primo omnium ..." (G. Kallen, *Cusanus-Texte*, II, 1, 108).

[12] For the itinerary of the legatine journey *cf.* Koch, *op. cit.*, 111–52.

which seventy Benedictine abbots obliged themselves to the reform of their monasteries within a year (24 May 1451). At Magdeburg monastic reform involved chiefly the Augustinians. John Busch, provost of Neuwerk and historian of the Windesheim Congregation, was an energetic and competent assistant in this. In the Benedictine monasteries of Erfurt, Hildesheim, and Minden, Nicholas enabled the Bursfeld Reform to achieve a break-through. At the provincial councils of Magdeburg (18–28 June 1451), Mainz (14 November–3 December), and Cologne (23 February–8 March 1452) he proclaimed the jubilee indulgence, emphasizing that the important thing was, not the indulgence, but a genuine and sincere conversion, which must begin with a worthy reception of the Sacrament of penance. The Legate strictly forbade the accepting or offering of money for absolution. The amount of the alms given to gain the indulgence was to be left to the conscience of the individual. The decrees published at the synods ordered prayers for Pope and Bishop at Mass, gave directions for the dignified celebration of the liturgy and the honouring of the Eucharist, forbade the founding of new confraternities, the venerating of bleeding Hosts, and the laying of an interdict in order to collect debts, attacked simoniacal intrigues in the conferring of benefices, clerical concubinage, and the disregard of the inclosure of nuns, and required in general a reform of religious orders by strict fidelity to the rule within one year. Jews were to make themselves known by special badges and thereafter they were no longer to engage in lending money to Christians. [13] In his numerous sermons the Cardinal insisted upon a deepened and intensified religious feeling. He denounced the excessive attention given to pilgrimages, especially to the bleeding Host of Wilsnack, and the superstitious veneration of images and saints. He dispensed from pilgrimage vows and ordered those thus dispensed to visit instead the Blessed Sacrament in their parish church; here divine power really lay concealed.

Nicholas had carefully prepared for his legatine journey in the hope of achieving or at least starting a far-reaching religious reform of the German people. A profound success was granted him only where a will to be reformed was present, as in Archbishop Frederick of Magdeburg, Provost John Busch, and the monks of the Bursfeld Congregation. The Cardinal's at times stubborn views, out of touch with the reality of the situation, were responsible for some failures. The questionable measures against the Jews, for example, were wrecked by economic necessities, as is clear from the Pope's annulling of the prohibition of money transactions at the urging of the Emperor and of the Archbishop of Salzburg. [14] Religious superiors frequently promised reform but thought no more of implementing it.

[13] Koch, *op. cit.*, 112.
[14] J. Uebinger, "Kardinal Nicolaus Cusanus in Deutschland 1451/52," *HJ*, 8 (1887), 639.

But the Legate did not only encounter hidden resistance. The opposition in Liège was especially serious. The Cardinal had been solemnly received there on 13 October 1451, but on the very next day the canons of Maastricht and an abbess complained of the severity of his reform and he soon saw himself involved in a heated controversy with the clergy. Serious accusations against his person were uttered.[15] The clergy of Utrecht appealed to Rome against his reform decrees. In a letter of admonition the Cardinal Legate severely rebuked the clergy and stressed how different they were from the faithful. Whereas the latter were hurrying back to Christ, the clergy, "who drew fat incomes from the blood of Christ and of the martyrs," persisted "in their war against Christ."[16] Among the religious orders the Legate met opposition especially from the mendicants. When he required those in Cologne and Trier to adopt reform they appealed to the Pope and insisted on their exemption. As already in regard to the decree on the Jews and the prohibition of the Wilsnack pilgrimage, here too the Pope decided against his Legate, who, he said, had exceeded his authority.

If the refractory refused to change their mind, Nicholas threatened with the secular arm. In general he had few reservations in regard to calling upon political power for the sake of reform, though he must have known from his own bishopric that to allow the secular authorities to intervene within the ecclesiastical sphere was to draw a two-edged sword. In the next years monastic reform in Brixen would be tedious and finally collapse, precisely because circles unwilling to be reformed, such as Verena von Stuben, Abbess of Sonnenburg, found support in the territorial nobility and especially in Archduke Sigismund against the Bishop. On the other hand, Nicholas had to restore his own territorial authority as a Prince-Bishop if he wished to carry out his reform. This in turn entangled him in a disastrous political power struggle.

In these very years of controversy over his bishopric (1453–60), a time of exasperating disputes over reforms and feudal rights, over spiritual and secular judicial supremacy, which were carried on by means of force on the one side and excommunication and interdict on the other, Nicholas of Cusa found time and leisure for speculative writings such as *De visione Dei* (1453), *De Beryllo* (1458), and *De principio* (1459). The fall of Constantinople in 1453 and the impotence of divided Christianity, made clear in the event, provided Nicholas with a sad opportunity to ponder more deeply *On Peace and Unity in the Faith* (1453). In a vision he has seventeen representatives of the various nations and religions discuss the differences and similarities of all religions before the throne of God. In them is sought, in different ways and under manifold names, the one God, who remains

---

[15] Koch, *op. cit.*, 46.
[16] *Cusanus-Texte*, IV, 1, p. 64.

concealed and ineffable in his true essence. The aim of this is the under-standing, made possible by the mercy of God, "that amidst the diversity of religious customs there is only one religion" (chapter 1).

It may, then, be enough to fortify peace in faith and in the command-ment of love, but to tolerate the various customs on both sides (chapter 17). For to strive for exact uniformity in everything would be rather to disturb peace ... Where a uniformity cannot actually be realized, the nations may retain their own forms in the exercises of piety and ceremonies, to the extent that faith and peace are preserved (chapter 20).

In all forms of divine adoration the one true God of Jesus Christ is meant and in Christianity the religious concerns of all are capable of realization. Nicholas later sought to prove this in regard to Islam. According to his *Cribatio Alchorani* (1461) the Koran contains the Christian message, but distorted and abridged; it needs only a "sifting."

With the pontificate of Pius II (1458–64) Nicholas of Cusa obtained the opportunity to escape from the increasingly hopeless guerilla warfare over his bishopric and to make his energies and reform will available to the entire Church. As early as the beginning of 1457 he had received from Aeneas Silvius Piccolomini, just made a Cardinal, the pressing invitation to come to Rome so that they might bear the burden of responsibility together. The future Pope wrote:

Unacceptable is the excuse, "I am not listened to, when I urge to what is right." Fortunes change, and he who was once scorned is now espe-cially honoured. Come then, I implore you, come. For it is precisely your strength that must not languish there, inclosed in snow and dark vales. I know that there are many who wish to see, hear, and follow you, among whom you will always find me as your obedient listener and pupil. [17]

On 30 September 1458, after the accession of Pius II, Nicholas arrived in Rome. Frustrated in his bishopric, he seemed to have come to his exile, but in reality he experienced at the side of Pius II a climax in his ecclesiastical and reform activity. He was a member of the reform commission of cardi-nals, bishops, and prelates, appointed by the Pope in the autumn of 1458 to determine and report on what needed changing and reforming at the Curia. Of the deliberations and testimonials there are extant only the *De reforma-tionibus romanae curiae* of Dominic de' Domenichi, Bishop of Torcello, [18] and Nicholas's *Reformatio generalis*, a sketch of a reform bull. [19] Pius II's

---

[17] Letter of 27 December 1456, in E. Meuthen, *Die letzten Jahre des Nikolaus von Kues*, 133; cf. ibid., 15.
[18] On the manuscripts and their content cf. H. Jedin, "Studien über Domenico de' Do-menichi (1416–78)," *AAMz*, 5 (Wiesbaden 1957), 117–300 (especially pp. 247 ff.).
[19] Edited by S. Ehses in *HJ*, 32 (1911), 281–97; cf. E. Iserloh, *Reform der Kirche bei Niko-laus von Kues* (Wiesbaden 1965).

reform program in the bull "Pastor aeternus" was based on the latter,[20] but because of the Pope's death it was never published.

As early as 11 December 1458, Pius II, before his departure for the Congress of Princes at Mantua, had confided the reform of the Roman clergy to Nicholas of Cusa by naming him *Legatus Urbis* and governor of the part of the Papal State south of the Apennines. The Cardinal had at once taken up the task at a synod but he was hardly successful.[21] Failure, however, was unable to break his reform will. In order to gain a free hand with regard to France and Germany, in 1461 he recommended a council at Mantua, which should deal with crusade and reform.[22] If as Legate in Germany he had impressed upon visitors always to begin the reform of a monastery with its superior, so, according to the *Reformatio generalis*, the reform of the Universal Church should begin with the "Church of Rome and the Curia."[23] Nicholas knew only too well to what extent since the beginning of the fifteenth century the opinion had gained ground that the Popes and the Curia were chiefly responsible for the decay of the Church and how little the self-reform of the Curia was trusted. How justified this mistrust was he had himself abundantly experienced already.[24] The visitors should not even hesitate to visit the Pope. Though he is the Vicar of Christ, he is also a sinful and mortal man.[25] The cardinals should be exemplary men and faithful advisers of the Pope, subject to no one. As a continuing council in miniature, at the Pope's disposal, the College should have a share in the government of the Church.

The general rules given to the visitors aimed to lead every member of the Church, from the baptized Christian through monk, priest, canon, and cardinal, to Pope, to the manner of life which his name signifies and which he assumed in solemn promise. Steps should especially be taken against any pluralism, which impedes the celebration of the liturgy and the care of souls, against embezzlement of the property of hospitals and parishes, against humbug on the part of indulgence dealers, against false relics and allegedly miraculous Hosts, invented for the sake of indecent profit.

> It should be sufficient for Christians to have Christ really in their churches in the Sacrament of the Eucharist. In it they have everything that they can desire for their salvation (p. 291).

Nicholas sought, not radical changes, but reform, a leading back to Christ, the archetype of all Christians. "We who wish to reform all Christians can

---

[20] R. Haubst, "Der Reformentwurf Pius' II.," *RQ*, 49 (1954), 188–242.

[21] E. Meuthen, *Die letzten Jahre des Nikolaus von Kues*, 32.

[22] *Ibid.*, 78, 84, 250–53.

[23] Edition of S. Ehses, 286.

[24] *Cf.* the statements quoted by E. Meuthen, *Die letzten Jahre des Nikolaus von Kues*, 81, 108; for example, "When I at last speak of reform in the consistory, they laugh at me."

[25] Edition of S. Ehses, 292.

provide them with no other model for their imitation than Christ, from whom they have obtained their name" (p. 285). God the Father, so we read at the very beginning of the introduction to the reform treatise, has revealed himself in the Word, his beloved Son, full of grace and truth, in order to enable all who accept him to share in his life.

The Father's only commandment is to believe in his Son and ambassador, who is his Word . . . This faith bestows all sanctity, wisdom, justice, and beatitude. For he who truly believes this keeps his commandments and does not sin . . . He knows that true life is found only in the promises of Christ and no one is justified whom he does not justify by the merit of his death. He can say with the Apostle that he knows only Christ, and him crucified, in whom he achieves the highest and perfect faith, the faith whereby the just man lives (p. 282).

If a person seizes hold of Christ

as the unique teacher of life, to him he gives in faith and work the figure which qualifies him for eternal life . . . However, Christ must impart and give it . . . For we are appointed out of grace to the inheritance. We can acquire it only by justice [based on] the merits of Christ . . . Hence he became justice for us . . . And so it is only from him that we have everything necessary for perfect bliss, whether it be grace or justice. And he is the sole mediator in whom is everything and without whom we cannot possibly be truly happy (pp. 284 f.).

Justification by faith can probably not be more clearly formulated, rejection of all justification by works cannot be more firmly stated. This is especially noteworthy in a summons to reform, in which one would expect to find stress placed rather on human activity. There is no question here of any isolated expression in Nicholas. For example, there occurs in *De pace fidei* (1453): "For man's justification consists in this — that he obtains the promise on the sole ground that he believes God and hopes for the fulfillment of God's word" (chapter 17).

If it is desired to represent the Cardinal as a reformer before the Reformation because of this teaching of his on justification by faith,[26] then it must be said simultaneously that at that time the Reformation was still a Catholic possibility.

Impressed with the stamp of a realistic scholasticism that was influenced by Platonism, Nicholas of Cusa freed himself in method from the Procrustean bed of the questions, objections, and responses of the philosophy of the schools and its cult of authorities. Related to humanism in this respect

---

[26] The Hesse reformer John Kymeus (d. 1552) included the section quoted from *De pace fidei* in his pamphlet *Des Babsts Hercules wider die Deutschen* (1538, ed. by O. Menzel in *Cusanusstudien*, VI, 6 [Heidelberg 1941]). Chapter 4 reads: "That in regard to our justification, Cardinal Cusanus has written contrary to the Pope's views and in conformity with our Gospel."

as well as in his renewed connection with antiquity and in his inclination to historical criticism, on the other hand he pressed too much for a speculative grasp of being in its unity and totality to be satisfied with the world of rhetorical literature of the humanists as he had encountered these in Italy. With Nicholas the philosophy of being became a philosophy of consciousness, of knowledge, even of the knowledge of not knowing. In this reflecting of the mind upon itself, in the question of one's own subjectivity and of the personal mind seizing hold of and touching upon everything, Nicholas probably most unambiguously showed himself to be a modern thinker. Furthermore, he took up the initial steps, later on so significant, toward mathematical and scientific thought in late scholasticism and in the Byzantine mathematicians and carried them forward creatively.

Above all, Nicholas of Cusa was a churchman, for whom the receptacle of all philosophy, all exertions of the mind, was theology; in the final analysis they had to serve to conduct man and history back to their divine origin. On the other hand he also again and again withdrew himself from the leisure of speculation in order to intervene in a responsible fashion in the exasperating real world of Church and Empire, though here compromises were at most to be expected. He stood in the "autumn of the Middle Ages," but also in the spring of the modern world. He proved that it would have been possible for the latter to come forth in continuity with the Middle Ages and in harmony with the Church and that, accordingly, the revolution was as yet not an unconditional historical necessity. It was all the more portentous that, after Pius II, began the series of Renaissance Popes in the bad sense and the papacy long refused to have anything to do with the reform that was so urgently demanded.

Johannes von Wesel

Compared with Nicholas of Cusa, the men who, like Johannes von Wesel, Johannes von Goch, and Wessel Gansfort, have been called "reformers before the Reformation," seem small in regard to religious depth, reform *élan*, and inner proximity to Luther, unless the essence of the reform movement is understood simply as criticism of the Church. As has already been said, the fifteenth century was characterized by a looking back to tradition. Aquinas and the *via antiqua* experienced a renaissance. People were weary of the extravagant sophistries of the *via moderna* and found it painful that what had been achieved should again and again be questioned. In particular the second half of this century was under the sign "of romantic restoration tendencies." [27] Furthermore, if one reckoned oneself in the Ockhamist school,

[27] G. Ritter, *Spätscholastik*, III, 4.

one strove to bring all radical theses into harmony with pedantic orthodoxy. Problems became superficial, contradictions were smoothed over. The *collectorium,* the anthology, and collections of maxims from available works became the desirable literary *genre;* the repeating of the "ancients" in paraphrase became the customary method. If the German universities already had displayed the most timid hesitation in regard to the radical tendencies of the Council of Basel, people were especially suspicious and aloof in regard to whatever seemed to be connected with the Hussite disturbances. What was to be read in fourteenth century treatises, such as those of Marsilius of Padua or William of Ockham, could no longer be repeated without opposition, just as it was, and even less could it be withdrawn from the sphere of academic disputation and set before the mob.

This explains the fate of a mind, hardly original and rather mediocre, condemned by the Inquisition and regarded by later generations as a "reformer before the Reformation":[28] Johannes Rucherath von Oberwesel. From 1441 he studied at Erfurt, where he became master of arts in 1445 and doctor of theology in 1456. Immediately afterwards he was rector of the University. From his Erfurt period came his commentaries on the *Physics* of Aristotle and on *The Sentences* of Peter Lombard, which offered a simple and shallow Ockhamism. "The infinite mass of learned ballast drives out the spirit at the same time."[29] For unknown reasons Johannes von Wesel went to Worms, where in 1460 he was a canon. In the spring of 1461 he took up at Basel a professorship in theology that had been offered him. But he soon (1463) returned to Worms as cathedral preacher. In addition to his preaching activity, he published a series of popular theological works, in which the practical pastor of souls answered questions of moral theology and canon law. They dealt with the artificial discharge of the semen for reasons of health, the obligations of a husband whose wife had made a vow of chastity before marriage, the Immaculate Conception of Mary; they opposed astrology, the instituting of the feast of Mary's presentation in the temple, and indulgences. The author directed an often bold and challenging criticism to Church life and institutions, but there is no trace of a deeper religious concern, not to mention the proclaiming of a new, reforming sense. Decisive for him were the Ockhamist viewpoints of the sovereignty of God and the freedom of man. This caused him to write against astrology and above all to place limits to the legislative authority of the Church. He clearly expounds the difference between the divine and the merely ecclesiastical law. God bestows grace in absolute freedom; but he can even grant it when man does not do "what is in him." Grace places man in a position to gain eternal life. God acts directly in the Sacraments if the priestly minister

[28] C. Ullmann, *Reformatoren vor der Reformation,* I (Gotha, 2nd ed. 1866), 202–346.
[29] Ritter, *op. cit.,* III, 9.

effects the sign. Johannes von Wesel rejects indulgences because the temporal punishments for sin, such as sickness, age, death, and the pains of purgatory, have to be endured and only God can dispose of the merits of the saints. The establishing of the temporal punishments of sin must be left to him alone. According to God's determination, the Church's power of the keys refers only to the guilt of sin. To conclude from the *de facto* instituting of indulgences by the Church a justification of the practice is unlawful, for the Church, like councils, can err. Only the Church of Christ, contained in the Universal Church but not empirically demonstrable, is holy and immaculate.[30] According to Matthew 28: 20, Christ himself is always with his Church and guiding her. He needs no vicar, and he alone, in the final analysis, has the power of the keys. The Pope is the executor of his commands. For the building up of the Church he has a certain authority in the framework of positive law. He can establish feasts and order fasts and other things, but he cannot impose them under pain of mortal sin. Ultimately authoritative is the truth recorded in Holy Scripture. This truth is authority; in comparison with it knowledge acquired by reason and revelation by means of miracles have only a secondary importance. What is necessary for salvation is contained in the Bible.[31]

According to Johannes von Wesel, a scriptural proof of transubstantiation cannot be given. Though, like Ockham, he inclined to consubstantiation, also like Ockham he held to the substantial change as being the teaching of the Church. And he adhered to the Ockhamist school also in the doctrine of original sin. With Anselm he saw its essence in the absence of the justice of the original state of man, with no further injuring of nature which would be transmitted by procreation. Because original sin is thus the mere lack of something not of itself belonging to man, Johannes von Wesel could designate it as a "nothing";[32] but this does not imply that he denied it, as G. Ritter and others have said of him.[33] Apart from the denial of the *Filioque*, for

---

[30] "Ecclesiam Christi sic intelligit: Ecclesia est collectio omnium fidelium caritate copulatorum, iuxta opinionem suam motus verbis sequentibus in evangelio, 'Et portae inferi non praevalebunt adversus eam' (Mt. 16:18). Et credit eandem esse Christi ecclesiam quam nemo sciat nisi deus" — in O. Clemen, "Über Leben und Schriften des Johannes von Wesel," *DZGw*, NF, 2 (1898), 143–73 (especially p. 170).

[31] "In quibus mysteria salutis plurima et fortassis omnia ad salutem necessaria continentur" — "Disputatio gegen die Ablässe," ed. by Walch, *Monimenta medii aevi*, I, 1, pp. 111–56 (especially p. 113).

[32] ". . . quidam ponunt aliquid reale parvulos contrahere a parentibus alii autem ponunt nihil reale esse peccatum originale, sed tantum esse privacionem iusticie originalis debite inesse. De numero eorum ego sum, qui dico: Peccatum originale nihil est" — Ritter, *op. cit.*, III, 88.

[33] O. Clemen, "Zu dem Ketzerprozess Johannes' von Wesel," *DZGw*, NF, 2 (1898), 168, speaks of a "denial of the doctrine of original sin"; so does G. Ritter, *Spätscholastik*, III, 18. He is followed by R. Samoray, *Johannes von Wesel* (typewritten diss., Münster 1954), who makes also the serious mistake of always translating "iustitia originalis" as "natural justice" (e. g., 60 f., 66, 68).

which he saw no scriptural basis, in his trial for heresy he could not really be charged with any formal heresies,[34] but only with brazenly formulated opinions which had already been expounded for decades. But is was fatal to him that, as Wessel Gansfort complained,[35] he brought everything into the pulpit before the people and brought suspicion upon himself through his relations with the Hussites.

In 1477 he was dismissed from his posts as cathedral preacher and canon at Worms, but found temporarily a situation as rector of the cathedral at Mainz; however, he was soon again accused of heresy and of relations with the Hussites. In February 1479 he had to defend himself before a tribunal of the Inquisition, consisting of professors from the Universities of Heidelberg, Cologne, and Mainz and of members of the Mainz cathedral chapter. The presidency was exercised by the Cologne Dominican and Inquisitor Gerard von Elten, together with the Dominican James Sprenger, the future coauthor of the *Malleus Maleficarum* (Cologne 1489). After almost fourteen days of discussion, when he had recanted nineteen propositions that had been branded as heretical and his books had been burned, he was condemned on 21 February 1479 to life-imprisonment among the Mainz Augustinians. There he soon died, probably in 1481, after reception of the Sacraments.

Johannes von Goch

In contrast to the frequently challenging criticism of Johannes von Wesel, Johannes Pupper von Goch remained in the sphere of a "theology of calm edification" in the spirit of the *devotio moderna*.[36] Born at Goch on the lower Rhine early in the fifteenth century and educated by the Brothers of the Common Life, as a priest he studied law at Cologne, perhaps in 1454. In 1459 he founded near Mechlin the Augustinian monastery of Thabor for canonesses, which he governed until his death on 28 March 1475. His works were circulated in manuscript and did not appear in print until after 1520. Opposing every institutional rigidity, he stressed the free operation of the Holy Spirit in the free activity of the man of a pious disposition. Tradition has authority only in so far as it is close to the Bible.

> Faith without doubt and authority without opposition belong only to the canonical Scripture. The writings of the ancient Fathers have authority to the extent that they conform to the canonical truth . . . The writings of modern teachers, especially of those from the mendicant orders, . . . serve rather empty show than truth *(Epistola apologetica)*.

[34] This is also the opinion of the glossator of the report of the trial; *cf.* Ritter, *op. cit.*, III, 25, 10; O. Clemen in *DZGw*, NF, 2 (1898), 167–69.

[35] Letter to Ludolf van Veen, *Opera* (Groningen 1614), 920 f.; Ritter, *op. cit.*, III, 28.

[36] G. Ritter, "Romantische und revolutionäre Elemente," *DVfLG*, 5 (1927), 363.

But the Church attests to Scripture; John agreed with Augustine's statement that he would not believe the Gospel if he did not believe the Church. However, incontestable authority belongs to the Church only in matters of faith and not in practical directions. Hence John could criticize monasticism and vows. The evangelical counsels must, in a sense, be observed by all Christians as means for the observing of the commandments. They call upon us to do good works out of pure love.

As a nominalist, Johannes von Goch separated philosophy and theology, but he rejected the thesis of the double truth. The one truth can be recognized only in the light of faith. His doctrine of acceptance leaned heavily on Augustinian thought. It rests with God's discretion whether to behold and accept man's works with forbearance or to regard them as they actually are, as a bloodstained clout (Is 64:6). Finally, Johannes von Goch was a mystic, concerned for union with God in love. Man must let himself be filled by the divine love and arrive, by means of love of God and neighbour, at likeness to God and union with him. The permeation of the human will by the divine love leads to the *fruitio dei,* which is not an act of knowledge but of will, namely, the ability for the highest love.

Wessel Gansfort

Like Johannes von Goch, the more important and bolder Wessel Gansfort (1419–89) came from the world of the *devotio moderna.* Born at Groningen, he studied there with the Brothers of the Common Life and then taught at Zwolle (1432–49). His profound uneasiness drove him into the world. He studied first at Cologne (1449) and then at Heidelberg (1456–57); in 1458 he was in Paris and around 1470 he went to Italy. He zealously applied himself to languages, learning Greek, Hebrew, Aramaic, and Arabic. But he found as little satisfaction in early humanism as he had in scholasticism. He had started out as a champion of Cologne Neo-Thomism; then, one after another, he took up all the schools of the existing universities and learned to scorn them all together.[37] Externally he included himself in the Ockhamist school, without sacrificing his independence to a professorial chair. He was critical of the authority of Pope and council, of the Church's power of binding and loosing, of indulgences and purgatory, of the efficacy of the Sacraments. Only Scripture is binding. The apostolic traditions interpret the content of the canonical Scriptures. We believe with the Church, not in the Church.[38]

It cannot be said that Wessel Gansfort in his teaching overstepped the

[37] *Ibid.,* 372.
[38] *Opera* (Groningen 1614), 888.

limits of what was then possible within the Church. He actually proved how much latitude there was in the fifteenth century or how extensive was the dogmatic uncertainty. After long years of travelling — he had to leave Paris in 1475, probably because of the royal prohibition of nominalism — he returned to his point of departure, the world of the *devotio moderna*. From 1477 to 1482 he lived on the Agnetenberg, enjoying the protection of Bishop David of Utrecht. In his last years he devoted himself at Groningen to study and meditation.

Though a layman, he composed for the pious canons of Agnetenberg a series of treatises as an introduction to prayer and meditation. These were, among others, *De Oratione*, with an explanation of the Our Father, *Scala Meditationis, Exempla scalae Meditationis, De magnitudine Dominicae Passionis,* and *De Sacramento Eucharistiae.* He was concerned about the encounter with Christ, especially with him crucified, in the faith given by God. "God has been pleased to impart justice to those who believe, to bestow on them a greater righteousness and integrity than the justice of the angels." [39] Also in the Eucharist Christ wants to be received in faith. Hence a purely spiritual communion in faith and love can produce more fruit than a sacramental reception which is lacking in disposition, in a real spiritual hunger and thirst. Through his introduction to meditation Wessel Gansfort became one of the teachers of the *devotio moderna*, especially influencing John Mombaer (d. 1501) and his *Rosetum*. Luther felt a spiritual relationship with him. In 1522 Luther published *Farrago rerum theologicarum,* a collection of essays, and remarked in the introduction that the malicious might be able to think that he had taken everything from Wessel Gansfort, "so much were both minds in accord" (*WA*, 10, II, 317). But we have to see in Wessel Gansfort a connecting link from the *devotio moderna* to criticism of the Church and to the spiritualistic Bible Christianity of Erasmus.

Gabriel Biel

Gabriel Biel (d. 1495) represents the direct connection between late mediaeval theology and piety and the modern age. He ranks as the "last of the scholastics" of the Middle Ages and exercised a strong influence on both Luther and Luther's Catholic opponents. At the same time as Luther was doing so at Erfurt, his future opponent John Eck was lecturing at Freiburg (1509–10) on *The Sentences* of Peter Lombard, following Biel.

Gabriel Biel was born at Speyer around 1410. As morning sacristan of Sankt Peter there, he matriculated at Heidelberg in 1432, becoming master of arts in 1438. In 1442–43 and again in 1452 he was on the theological

[39] *De magnitudine passionis,* chapter 45, *Opera,* 551.

faculty at Erfurt and in 1453 on that at Cologne. It cannot be determined where he obtained his licentiate in theology. In any case, he got to know not only Ockham at Erfurt but also Aquinas and Albert at Cologne. At the beginning of the sixties he became vicar and cathedral preacher at Mainz. In the struggle over the see between Dieter von Isenburg and Adolf von Nassau, he supported the latter and hence the Pope. He justified his position in *Defensorium oboedientiae apostolicae ad Pium Papam II* (1462). Around 1468 he joined the Brothers of the Common Life at Marienthal in the Rheingau and soon became provost of Sankt Markus, their house at Butzbach. From 1476 he collaborated with Count Eberhard the Bearded in the Württemberg Church reform initiated by the latter, and in 1479 he became provost of Eberhard's foundation, the monastery at Urach. On 22 November 1484 he assumed a professorship at the University of Tübingen, founded in 1477; he made possible there the break-through of the *via moderna*. Following his retirement in 1491, he directed the new house of the Brothers of the Common Life, Sankt Peter at Einsiedel in the Schönbuch near Tübingen, and there he died on 7 December 1495.

Gabriel Biel was not especially independent. He communicated to his epoch the nominalist theology in a form supplemented and toned down in accord with a pastoral outlook. His works are compilations, very popular because of their practical usefulness. His dependence on the topic of the moment is apparent, for example, in the fact that, in his commentary on *The Sentences*, in the doctrine of the Eucharist he in no way discusses the Mass as a sacrifice, but in the *Expositio* he allows it much space.

The commentary on *The Sentences* is a summary of and addition to Ockham's *Quaestiones in IV libros Sententiarum* and hence is also called the *Epitome* or *Collectorium*. According to F. Stegmüller it became "the classical work of theological nominalism." Biel finished the first book before 1 May 1486 and the third on 13 August 1488, while the fourth probably preoccupied him until his death.

But the crucial point of Biel's work is found in the religious and pastoral sphere, in his sermons and his explanation of the Canon of the Mass. His lengthy sermons prove a high opinion of the dignity and importance of the word of God. He who does not devote a proper attention to preaching is no less guilty than one who out of carelessness lets the body of Christ fall to the ground. Preaching is really more important than the Blessed Sacrament, for the former leads to faith and penitence and hence is necessary for salvation, whereas the latter only increases grace.[40] The *Canonis missae Expositio*, completed on 4 November 1488, is a lecture, closely dependent on the discourses which his friend, Master Egeling Becker of Braunschweig, had

---

[40] *Sermones dominicales* (Hagenau 1510), 59 D; *cf.* H. A. Obermann, *The Harvest of Medieval Theology* (Cambridge, Mass. 1963), 23.

delivered at Mainz at the close of the 1450's. Biel claims he omitted only a
little but "added or changed some." A comparison of both texts shows "that
more than three-fourths of the *Expositio* belongs to Master Egeling." [41] This
work, at the reading of which Luther had felt his heart bleed from emotion,[42] stands between scholastic theology — for those untrained in
"scholastic subtleties" Biel published an abridged version, the *Epitome* —
and pastoral theology.

In his theology Biel closely follows Ockham. But he does not propound
it so defiantly and takes care that its philosophical permeation does not
undermine faith. Throughout, he has rather the actual way of salvation in
mind. *De potentia dei absoluta* God can accept anyone for salvation without
caritas creata, but conversely he does not have to bestow eternal life on
anyone who possesses *caritas.* He is absolutely free and not bound by any form
or available gift. Thus Biel, like Ockham, seeks to exclude any Pelagianism. [43]
The divine will has no superior rule to which it must conform itself. A thing
is right and just because God wills it to be so. [44] He can do something which
in itself is unjust. If he were to do it, then it would be just for it to happen. [45]
One can rightly speak here of a "divine caprice." But actually God has
bound himself. Since Biel now discusses the actual way of salvation in more
detail and treats the question of preparation for grace by applying the
proposition: "God does not deny grace to one who does his best," he suc-
cumbs to the danger of Semipelagianism. For now the initiative lies with
man. *Facere quod est in se* is understood as natural activity with the exclusion
of actual grace. Man for his part is in the position of doing his first duty,
and God, because he has so bound himself, is obliged to give his grace to
everyone who does his best. [46] Thus, grace is "not the root but the fruit of

---

[41] A. Franz, *Messe im Mittelalter* (Freiburg 1902), 553. That this dependence is not clear
in the edition of H. A. Obermann and N. J. Courtenay is a serious defect.

[42] "Gabriel scribens librum super canonem missae, qui liber meo iudicio tum optimus fuerat;
when I read it, my heart bled. Bibliae autoritas nulla fuit erga Gabrielem" (*WA, Tr,* III,
no. 3722).

[43] "Et hoc dictum maxime recedit ab errore Pelagii . . ." (1 *Sent.,* d. 17, q. 1, a. 2, F); L.
Grane, *Contra Gabrielem* (Copenhagen 1962), 149–53.

[44] "Non enim habet aliam regulam, cui teneatur se conformare, sed ipsa divina voluntas
est regula omnium contingentium. Nec enim quia aliquid rectum est aut iustum, ideo deus
vult, sed quia deus vult, ideo iustum et rectum" (1 *Sent.,* d. 17, q. 1, a. 3, L).

[45] "Deus potest aliquid facere, quod non est iustum fieri a deo; si tamen faceret, iustum
esse fieri" (1 *Sent.,* d. 41, a. 1, E); *cf.* W. Dettloff, *Die Entwicklung der Akzeptations- und
Verdienstlehre von Duns Scotus bis Luther* (Münster 1963), 357 f.

[46] *Canonis missae Expositio,* Lect. 59 P: "Ex quo hoc elicitur, quod iste facit quod est in
se, qui illuminatus lumine rationis naturalis aut (!) fidei vel utroque cognoscit peccati tur-
pitudinem et proponens ab ipso resurgere desiderat divinum adiutorium quo possit a peccato
mundari et deo suo creatori adhaerere. Haec facienti deus gratiam suam tribuit necessario,
necessitate non coactionis sed immutabilitatis." *Cf.* Obermann, *op. cit.,* 132 ff. On Ockham
see E. Iserloh, *Gnade und Eucharistie* (Wiesbaden 1956), 126–33.

the preparatory good works," [47] God's reply to man's free act. Here Gabriel Biel finds himself opposing Gregory of Rimini, who credits man's free will with too little (II *Sent.*, d. 28, q. 1, A). Man does his best if he loves God above all. As Ockham had already taught, this love lies in the possibility of man's natural powers. All the more must man struggle for it or be anxious about possessing it. Accordingly, in such a strongly Pelagian system anxiety over salvation is not less but greater. "The dialectic between fear and love is [also] the general topic of Biel's preaching." [48] Thus Gabriel Biel became Luther's chief opponent in the latter's "Disputation against Scholastic Theology" of 4 September 1517, in which Luther sought to prove that modern theology was Pelagian. "All the antitheses which dealt directly with the theological theme of the disputation were either directly taken from Biel's *Collectorium* or at least are to be found there." [49]

In his explanation of the Canon of the Mass Biel emphasizes that the Mass is not a repetition of the sacrifice once directly offered by Christ on the cross, but a calling to mind and representation of it. [50] The related concepts, *memoria, recordatio,* and *repraesentatio,* are not explained with regard to content. There is no question in all this of an identity with the sacrifice of the cross but of a difference in the manner of offering. The Mass is a symbol of the sacrifice of the cross, a recalling of the historical past as a psychological representation. The "moment of truth" and the unity of the sacrifice are based on the sacrificial gift which is offered by the Church in the Mass. Since the Mass is "only" a symbol, in value it is far inferior to the sacrifice of the cross. [51] Biel understands the "once for all" of Hebrews (7, 27; 9, 11; 10, 10) to refer to the bloody sacrifice on the cross and not to the daily sacrifice under the appearances of bread and wine. [52] Hence it is

---

[47] Obermann, *op. cit.,* 141, 176; Grane, *op. cit.,* 214–22; II *Sent.,* q. 1, a. 2, concl. 1: "Item voluntas ex suis naturalibus potest se disponere ad gratiae dispositionem"; *Sermones dominicales,* 99 F: "peccator disponens se recipit gratiam."

[48] Obermann, *op. cit.,* 133. He reaches a conclusion which at most can be toned down but can hardly be refuted: "It is therefore evident that Biel's doctrine of justification is essentially Pelagian" (177).

[49] Grane, *op. cit.,* 46.

[50] "In cruce enim Christus se immediate obtulit, factus verum sacrificium... In officio autem missae idem sacrificium est et oblatio, non per iteratam mortem sed per mortis semel passae rememorativam repraesentationem" (Lect. 27 K). "Unde nostra oblatio non est reiteratio suae oblationis sed repraesentatio" (Lect. 53 U). "...illius sacrificii veri et immolationis sanctae factae in cruce repraesentativa est et memoriale... imago quaedam est passionis Christi repraesentativa, quae est vera eius immolatio, ideo et ipsa immolatio nominatur" (Lect. 85 F).

[51] "Quis autem dubitat esse maioris efficaciae mortem semel in sanguinis effusione... quam tantum mortis semel passae memoriam" (Lect. 27 K).

[52] "Quamvis autem semel oblatus est Christus in aperta carnis effigie, offertur nihilominus quottidie in altari velatus in panis vinique specie" (Lect. 85 F).

unexplained how the Church can have a sacrifice without the unity of the New Testament sacrifice being jeopardized — a question which, a few decades later, would come decisively between Luther and the Church.

CHAPTER 60

The Jews in Mediaeval Christendom

Despite national and political variety, Western Christendom was, until the beginning of modern times, united in the one faith in Christ in the one Church. Paganism and especially Islam were thought of as both a foreign threat and a religious danger. In day-to-day consciousness the world as a reality determined and formed by religion was identical with Christianity.

The Jews were an exception, constituting a special religious and national group and, as such, exposed to all prejudices and resentments. Unintelligible rites, not open to everyone, increased the mistrust and dread. In the abstract Judaism was far closer to Christianity than was paganism. According to the mosaics in the apses of Christian basilicas, the Christian congregation even in the early Middle Ages regarded itself as the Church of Jews (Jerusalem) and pagans (Bethlehem). In crucifixion scenes in manuscript illuminations and on the portals or in the narthex of Gothic cathedrals the synagogue proclaimed through the majesty of her aspect the dignity of the Chosen People, while the blindfold and the broken lance indicated that this people missed its destiny and in its obstinacy called down the blood of the Messiah upon itself and its children. The less this understanding was dominated, in the course of the Middle Ages, by the Pauline message that God had not retracted his promise to Israel but rather that finally this nation, whose "rejection had brought the reconciliation of the world," would be saved as a whole, and the less people took to heart with Gregory the Great the reflection that the death of Jesus was caused by all mankind, the accusation of deicide became the root of a religiously determined anti-Semitism.

Patristic theology established the notion of Jewish servitude (servitus Iudaeorum). According to Augustine,[1] who was here following Tertullian and Justin, the older (Esau) shall, according to Genesis 25:23, serve the younger (Jacob), and the Jewish people, having forfeited its inheritance, had become the slave of the younger Christian people.[2] This idea was adopted by mediaeval theologians, including Rupert of Deutz (d. 1129), Peter the

---

[1] Epistolae, III, 196, PL, 33, 897, CSEL, 57, 226 f.; Sermones de script., 5, PL, 38, 56; De civit., XVI, c. 35, CSEL, 40 II, 187, PL, 41, 513.
[2] G. Kisch, Forschungen, 64 f.

Venerable (d. 1156), Bernard of Clairvaux (d. 1153), and Thomas Aquinas (d. 1274). The Jews were scattered among the nations as witnesses to the prophecies and are reserved for the end. They are "bookkeepers of the Christians,"[3] as slaves they carry the Holy Scripture for them but without understanding it. Thus the pagans cannot assert that the Christians had invented the prophecies. These theologians envisaged only individual conversions; the people as a whole will not be converted and will persist in its blindness and slavery till the end of the world as witness of Christ's death, and hence no one is allowed to do violence to it.

At first this "servitude of the Jews" was valid only in the spiritual and not the legal sense. Decisions in Roman Law in regard to the Jews, made last of all under Justinian (527–65), were transmitted into the Middle Ages and were not expressly abolished. According to these, religious toleration was basically accorded them, but it was subjected to various restrictions. Conversion to Judaism was forbidden. The Jews were free and could possess property, but they were excluded from public office and military service and could not keep Christian slaves or domestics. At first in the Middle Ages they could freely engage in commerce and industry and did not have to reside in ghettos. Perhaps the common practice of their religion in a hostile environment induced the Jews on their own to live in special residential quarters. But it was only in the late Middle Ages that the Jewish quarter became a ghetto, walled in and sealed off by gates. In the early Middle Ages Christians and Jews lived together on relatively friendly terms; the anti-Semitic writings of Agobard of Lyons (d. 840) and of Claudius of Turin (d. *ca.* 827) were an exception and were motivated by local frictions. Bishops and kings issued letters of safe-conduct for the Jews, who in return paid fees. Thus privileges were granted to the Jews of Speyer by Bishop Rüdiger in 1084 and to those of Worms and Speyer by the Emperor Henry IV in 1090.

Shortly afterwards severe persecutions of Jews occurred in connection with the crusades. As early as 1063 when aid was being hurried to the Christians of Spain in their war against Islam, *en route* attacks were made on Jews. Pope Alexander II censured the blind passion which then raged against those whom the divine goodness perhaps destined for salvation.[4] And the same Pope cited greed as the motive for persecution of Jews. Frightful excesses took place when the crusaders from northern France moved up

---

[3] Augustinus, *Enarrationes in Ps.* 56, 9, *PL*, 36, 666; *CSEL*, 39, 699 f.; P. Browe, "Die Judengesetzgebung Justinians," *Miscellanea iuridica Iustiniani et Gregorii IX*, ed. by the Pontificia Universitas Gregoriana (Rome 1935), 109–46 (especially pp. 140 f.).

[4] "Epistola ad omnes episcopos Hispaniae": "Illi quippe stulta ignorantia, vel forte caeca cupiditate commoti, in eorum necem volebant saevire, quos fortasse divina pietas ad salutem praedestinavit" (*PL*, 146, 1386 f.).

the Rhine toward the southeast. In the Jews people saw "enemies of Christ" who had to be liquidated in one's own country before the Holy Land could be set free. The chronicler Ekkehard of Aura, who took part in the crusade in 1101, reported:

> In all cities through which they went they either completely exterminated or forced baptism on the remnants of the wicked Jews, those internal enemies of the Church. But very many of them returned to their former faith, as the dog to his vomit. [5]

These excesses became still worse in the next crusades. The Cistercian Radulf, who was inciting religious fanatics and the economically discontented to murder the "enemies of the Christian religion," encountered opposition at Mainz from Saint Bernard of Clairvaux. According to the latter, the Jews must be neither persecuted nor banished; for they are living witnesses of our redemption, who set the Lord's sufferings before our eyes.

Bishops and Emperors undertook the protection of Jews and in times of persecution placed their castles and strongholds at their disposal. They punished extravagances. The public peace promulgated at Mainz in 1103 subjected any attack on the life and property of Jews to the threat of punishment, including the death penalty. [6] On the occasion of the pogroms in connection with the Third Crusade, Frederick I issued an edict whereby the hand that injured a Jew was to be cut off and murder of a Jew was to be punished by death. [7] This Emperor considered the Jews as belonging to the imperial fisc.

In the thirteenth century the legal situation of the Jews deteriorated. Their "servitude," originally understood as spiritual, became legal, and, as "slaves of the imperial chamber," the Jews were placed under a particular law. [8] The privilege of the Emperor Frederick II for Vienna in 1237 states:

> Faithful to the obligations of a Catholic prince, we exclude the Jews from public office so that they may not exploit the power of office to oppress Christians. For the imperial authority from time immemorial has imposed perpetual servitude on the Jews as punishment for Jewish crime. [9]

As slaves of the chamber the Jews and their belongings were the possession of the Emperor, taxable by him and at the same time under his protection. In 1342 Louis the Bavarian demanded a tax of a florin, the *guldin pfenning*, from every Jew at least twelve years of age and imposed on them a regular

---

[5] *MGSS*, VI, 208, *PL*, 154, 959.

[6] Kisch, *op. cit.*, 57.

[7] I. Ellbogen *et al.*, *Germania Judaica*, I, 182.

[8] Kisch, *op. cit.*, 59 ff.

[9] J. Aronius, *Regesten zur Geschichte der Juden in Deutschland bis zum Jahre 1273* (Berlin 1902), no. 509; Kisch, *op. cit.*, 67.

poll-tax, "in return for which he intended to protect the Jews so much the better." [10] Protection of the Jews thus became a source of revenue, which, with the decay of the central power, was claimed by bishops and princes also or was regularly sold or pawned to them. In the fourteenth century the right to protect the Jews became more and more an object of traffic.

The Jews' route into bondage from the thirteenth century onward was accompanied by fearful pogroms, for which the charge of ritual murder and of desecration of the Blessed Sacrament supplied the pretext. According to this the Jews were said to have given vent to their hatred of Christians by outraging the Host and innocent members of Christ's body. The first case referred to by name of an alleged ritual murder was that of William of Norwich (d. 1147), a twelve-year-old tanner's apprentice. The Jews were supposed to have enticed him into a trap in order to repeat on him the cruci-fixion of Christ, including the crowning with thorns and the piercing of the side. Other well-known cases were the murder of a boy at Blois in 1171, of Richard of Paris in 1179, of five children at Fulda in 1235, of Hugh of Lincoln in 1255, of Werner of Oberwesel in 1287, of Rudolf of Bern in 1294, of Andrew of Rinn in 1462, and of Simon of Trent in 1475. In the case of Werner of Oberwesel the two themes, murder and desecration of the Host, coalesced in the process of the development of the legend. The Jews were supposed to have wanted to obtain possession of the Host received by the boy; when they failed in this, they vented their fury on the mystical rather than the real body of Christ and tortured the youngster to death. [11]

Besides religious fanaticism and naked greed, which afforded a pretext for the pillaging of Jewish property or for the cancelling of debts, supersti-tion led to this charge of murder. From Innocent IV (1243–54) the Popes had repeatedly opposed this, but their voices, like the voices of Emperors and bishops, went unheeded. They could not prevent persons "from maliciously charging the Jews with murder whenever a corpse was discovered" or from

> stirring fury against them by these and many other atrocity stories,
> depriving them of all their property without accusation, confession and
> conviction ... against God and justice, oppressing them with hunger,
> imprisonment, and many tortures and torments ... and condemning
> as many as possible to a shameful death. [12]

In the often renewed bull "Sicut Iudaeis" the Popes assured the Jews of

[10] M. Wiener, *Regesten zur Geschichte der Juden in Deutschland während des Mittelalters* (Hanover 1862), no. 137, p. 44; Kisch, *op. cit.*, 89.

[11] E. Iserloh, *Werner von Oberwesel*, 274 f.

[12] Pope Innocent IV on 5 July 1247 (*MGEp*, saec. XIII, II, 298); M. Stern, *Die päpstlichen Bullen über die Blutbeschuldigungen* (Munich 1900), 10–13; S. Grayzel, *The Church and the Jews*, 268–71.

freedom of religion, forbade compulsory baptism, and under threat of excommunication demanded unqualified respect for property and life.[13] Thus at the end of the Middle Ages the Jews in Italy were relatively very secure.

However, at most the Church tolerated the Jews; in other respects she restricted them as far as possible. There could be only one synagogue in one place and this had to be as unassuming as possible.[14] Ecclesiastical regulations which sought to prevent endangering Christians by means of Jewish teaching and the association of Jews and Christians, above all in mixed marriages, contributed much to the hatred of Jews. The Fourth Lateran Council (1215) decreed that "Jews and Saracens of both sexes in every Christian country and at all times should be distinguished in public from other persons by their dress, especially since Numbers 15:37–41 has already imposed this on them."[15] These prescriptions in regard to dress were not applied in Germany, however, before the fifteenth century. Cardinal Nicholas of Cusa had them prescribed during his legatine journey of 1451–52 by the provincial councils of Salzburg, Bamberg, Magdeburg, Mainz, and Cologne as canonical regulation and as the legal usage in Rome and at the same time had all money-lending by Jews to Christians forbidden.[16]

As a result of the remonstrances of the Emperor and the Archbishop of Salzburg this last prescription was annulled by the Pope, because it was too harmful to their private interests. For money-lending, to which the Jews were reduced after they had been excluded from the wholesale trade and in the late Middle Ages also from acquiring real estate, was thoroughly exploited for the public treasury by the Emperor and the princes, not excluding the bishops. These last often determined the excessive interest which branded the Jews as usurers. The Bishop of Minden, for example, in 1270 decided the maximum interest for the week as four pfennig in the mark — that is, 2.7 percent or 140 percent per year.

In the fifteenth century the Jews were almost completely annihilated in the Rhineland and many cities of South Germany. As early as the mid-fourteenth century frightful pogroms had occurred throughout Germany. The occasion was, among other things, the Black Death of 1348–49, which was attributed to the poisoning of wells by the Jews. In addition, flagellants on their journeys stirred up a blind religious hatred, which was whipped into a mass hysteria and in regard to which the exhortations of the Emperor

---

[13] *Decret. Greg. IX*, 1. 5, t. 6, c. 9, Friedberg, II, 774.

[14] P. Browe, *Die religiöse Duldung der Juden*, 34 ff.; *Decret. Greg. IX*, 1. 5, t. 6, c. 7, Friedberg, II, 773.

[15] *Decret. Greg. IX*, 1. 5, t. 6, c. 15, Friedberg, II, 776 f.

[16] J. Koch, "Nikolaus von Kues und seine Umwelt," *SAH* 1944/48, 2 (Heidelberg 1948), 112; J. Uebinger, "Kardinal Nicolaus Cusanus in Deutschland," *HJ*, 8 (1887), 638 f.

Charles IV (1346–78) and Pope Clement VI (1342–52) were of no avail. The real cause was envy and greed and the driving forces were often the gilds. In Basel the city council was forced to burn the Jews, and in Strasbourg the majority of the approximately 2,000 Jews were delivered to the flames in their cemetery. This example was followed at Speyer, Worms, Cologne, and many other places. At Mainz, which had the largest Jewish community in Germany, the Jews, after a fruitless defense, surrendered themselves to the fire. Although many cities again allowed them to take up residence and even exerted themselves to this end for the sake of financial gain, the Jewish communities never recovered after the Black Death. They were unable to cope with financial demands from three quarters: king, territorial prince, and city. Controversy between bishop and city council in regard to the protection of Jews led to new expulsions of Jews at the end of the fourteenth and the beginning of the fifteenth century: from Strasbourg (1386), the Palatinate (1390), Freiburg (1401 and 1424), Speyer (1405 and 1435), Trier (1418), Mainz (1420 and several times later), and Cologne (1423). The Emperor Frederick III (1440–93), who because of concern for taxes on Jews wanted to keep on the good side of his slaves of the chamber and therefore undertook their protection against princes and cities, was unable to prevent their extermination. Many of the Jews who were banished from western and southern Germany settled in lands east of the Elbe and in Italy.

Jews were expelled also from England, France, and especially Spain. After the fall of Granada in 1492 the *reyes católicos* enacted a law whereby everyone who did not attend proselytizing sermons and was unwilling to receive baptism within four months had to emigrate.[17] Some 50,000 may have avoided loss of home and property by means of baptism, but the majority left Spain. Feigned baptisms, however, were the source of new misgivings and of suspicions which went so far as to call for Inquisition procedures.

The Popes of the Renaissance, especially those of the Medici family, were kindly disposed to the Jews, and Leo X took Reuchlin under his protection. But a reaction began under Julius II when there was mention of a condemnation of the Talmud. It was completed by Paul IV, who in the bull of 14 July 1555 confined the Jews of Rome and of all other cities of the Papal State to ghettos, forbade them to possess real estate, and forced them to wear the yellow "Jewish hat."[18]

---

[17] P. Browe, *Die Judenbekämpfung*, 357.
[18] *Pastor*, XIV, 272; P. Rieger - H. Vogelstein, *Geschichte der Juden in Rom*, 2 vols. (Berlin 1895 f.).

Of special significance for the intellectual life were the Jews of Provence and Spain, where Christian and Muslim cultures were in contact and where especially Jewish and Arabic intellectual endeavours were in competition. Not only Arabic philosophers such as Averroes (d. 1198) but also Jews handed on to the West the writings and intellectual legacy of Aristotle. The philosopher and religious poet Avicebron or Solomon Ibn Gabirol (d. *ca.* 1070), who was born at Málaga around 1020, provided in a strongly pantheistic system a farrago of Jewish religious doctrines with Aristotelian and Catholic ideas. He influenced both high and late scholasticism through his chief work, *Fons Vitae,* [19] very well known in the Middle Ages. Against him Aquinas wrote *De substantiis separatis.*

The most significant representative of Jewish theology and philosophy in the Middle Ages was Moses Maimonides, who was born at Córdoba in 1135 and died at Cairo in 1204. He sought by means of commentaries on the Talmud and systematic presentations *(Recapitulation of the Law)* to explain Jewish doctrine and make the simple Jew acquainted with it. In his chief philosophical work, *Guide of the Wavering,* [20] he wanted to demonstrate the reasonableness of the faith of their fathers to those of his fellows who had been made unsure of it by Arabic philosophy. Philosophical knowledge, whose highest authority is Aristotle, is independent of revealed faith; it does not contradict it but rather helps to grasp it more deeply. Himself strongly affected by the Arabic Aristotelian philosophy, Maimonides acquired an influence on thinkers and mystics such as Albertus Magnus, Thomas Aquinas, Master Eckhart, and Nicholas of Cusa.

Chasdai ben Abraham Crescas (1340–1412) in his *Light of God* definitely rejected Moses Maimonides and his Aristotelianism. For Crescas God is especially the supreme love and not the supreme reason. The route to God leads, for man, not by way of knowledge but of love.

Opposed to the rationalism of a Maimonides was likewise the *Cabala*, or tradition, a mystic and theosophic secret doctrine of Judaism. It originated in Provence between 1150 and 1250, spread to Spain, and, following the expulsion of 1492, became a national religious movement. Its chief work, *Zohar* ("Brilliance"), was attributed to the doctor of the law, Simon bar Jochai, of the second century, but must be regarded as composed by Moses de León (d. 1305) from Castile. According to it, the hidden God ("En Soph,"

---

[19] Hebrew and German, ed. by S. Munk (Paris 1859; new edition 1927); Latin translation by John of Spain, ed. by C. Baeumker (Münster 1895); French translation by F. Brunner (Paris 1950). Bibliography in G. Vajda, *Jüdische Philosophie* (Bern 1950).

[20] S. Munk, *Le guide des égarés* (Arabic with French translation), 3 vols. (Paris 1856–66; 2nd ed. 1960, French only); German translation by A. Weiss (Leipzig 1923 f.).

the infinite, the first cause) reveals and unfolds himself in the ten "Sephirot" (spheres). Through them, as though through doors, the devout one, by proper fulfillment of the law, prayer, and contemplation, can gain access to the mystery of God and contribute to the restoration of the fallen world. In itself the world was created according to the model of the Sephirot and hence is a mirror of the divine wisdom revealing itself in them. Man and world are evil only to the extent that they have broken the connection with divine love and grace and depend upon themselves alone. The expanding of the *Cabala* from an esoteric teaching to a national movement after 1492 gave a new stimulus to messianism and contributed to intensification of internal life, but it also led to magic and to abuses of superstition. Beyond Judaism, the *Cabala* also influenced humanists such as Pico della Mirandola (d. 1494) and John Reuchlin (d. 1522).

Efforts to Convert the Jews

With all the persecuting of the Jews, efforts were made time and again to win them to Christian truth. One means of this was the religious discussion. Far too often, it is true, this became an argument or dispute in which the important thing was to vanquish the opponent rather than to understand and win him over. Occasionally, especially in the earlier Middle Ages, there were real discussions. Abbot Gilbert Crispin of Westminster (1084–1117) tells that he had engaged in one with a friendly London Jew and thereupon another Jew of the city had been converted and had entered a monastery.[21] In discussions of this sort Archbishop Bruno of Trier (1102–24) succeeded in convincing his Jewish physician Josuah and in inducing him to be baptized.[22] The most celebrated example of such a conversion was Hermann Judaeus. He had money transactions with the Archbishop of Cologne and thereby came into contact with Abbot Rupert of Deutz. This led to exhaustive religious discussions. After severe struggles he had himself baptized, became a Premonstratensian at Kappenberg, and finally was made first prior of Scheda, founded in 1143. In his account of his conversion he laments that Christians' hatred for Jews kept Jews from belief in Christ.[23]

---

[21] Disputatio iudaei cum christiano, *PL*, 159, 1006; P. Browe, *Die Judenmission*, 61; according to Z. Werblowsky, "Crispins Disputation," *JJS*, 11 (1960), 69–77, it was only a fictional discussion.

[22] *Gesta Treverorum*, c. 21; *MGSS*, VII, 195; *Die Taten der Trierer*, ed. by E. Zenz, I (Trier 1955), 68.

[23] *De conversione sua opusculum*, *PL*, 170, 805–36; an amended text in J. Greven, "Die Schrift des Herimannus quondam iudaeus, 'De conversione sua opusculum,'" *AHVNrh*, 115 (1929), 111–33; G. Misch, *Geschichte der Autobiographie*, III, part 2/1 (Frankfurt 1959), 505–22.

From the thirteenth century ecclesiastical authorities regarded religious discussions between Jews and Christians with an ever growing distrust. Jews were often ahead of Christians in a knowledge of the Old Testament, and they did not find it difficult at all to refute irresponsible charges by means of the Talmud. Hence the Trier Provincial Council of 1227 forbade uneducated priests ("sacerdotes illiterati") to engage in such conversations.[24] Alexander IV's prohibition of disputes by the laity with heretics, which in 1298 became a part of the common law,[25] covered also colloquies with Jews. Rules of this sort were not intended to prevent disputations in which persons who had studied theology and clerics familiar with Hebrew and with the Talmud took part and which held out the prospect of demonstrating the superiority of the Christian faith. Particularly in Spain such public disputations took place in the high and late Middle Ages. Famous were that at Barcelona in 1263 and that at Tortosa. This last was spread out over sixty-nine sessions, from 7 February 1413 to 13 November 1414, most of which were guided by Benedict XIII, Peter de Luna, himself. The discussion was rather an invitation to conversion than a real and candid dispute. Just the same, the most famed Aragonese rabbis and scholars upheld the Jewish side, while the Christian side was chiefly represented by the converts Andrew Bertram (Mosse) and Jerome de Sancta Fide (Josua Halorqui).[26] In his bull on the Jews Benedict XIII gives the number of Jews converted following the disputation as 3,000.

Polemical writings were often not real dialogues, even though they were often so called. The Jewish participants were for the most part invented in order to demonstrate the truth of the Christian faith by their objections. In the *Annulus sive Dialogus inter Christianum et Iudaeum*[27] Rupert of Deutz aims to prove from the prophecies of the Old Testament the truth of the Christian faith, in particular the mysteries of the Trinity and the Incarnation. For him the Jew was the older brother, to whom the Father was still offering the ring, the mark of faith. Saint Hildegarde of Bingen in her visions argued in a similar fashion, using the same religious and conciliatory language. But the farther we get from the early Middle Ages, the more inconsiderate, contemptuous, and ironical becomes the tone of the discussion. "This is especially true of the disputations introduced into the dramatic presentations of the later period, the Passion Plays, Corpus Christi Plays, and Shrove Tuesday Plays, which were presented for the amusement of the audience."[28]

---

[24] *Mansi*, XIII, 32.
[25] *Liber Sextus Decret.*, 1. 5, t. 2, c. 2.
[26] P. Browe, *Die Judenmission*, 79–85.
[27] *PL*, 170, 559–610.
[28] P. Browe, *Die Judenmission*, 113; *cf.* here (pp. 99–110) the list of polemical works composed from the seventh century to 1560.

Of greater importance among polemical writings were the chief work of the Dominican Raymond Martí (d. 1286), *Pugio fidei adversus Mauros et Iudaeos;* the religious discussion, *Liber de gentili et tribus sapientibus,* by the learned missionary Raymond Lull (d. 1315/16), which avoided all invective; the *Pharetra fidei Catholicae contra Iudaeos,* attributed to the Paris Dominican Theobald; and the strongly anti-Jewish *Fortalitium fidei* of the Spanish Franciscan convert Alfonso de Spina (d. 1491). The *Tractatus contra perfidos Iudaeos* and *Der stern Meschiah* by the Dominican Peter Schwarz (Petrus Nigri, d. 1481) were widely circulated.

Mediaeval theologians and canonists forbade Jews to attend Christian worship. For Thomas Aquinas it was not fitting that infidels and Jews should look at the sacred Host.[29] Jews were, however, allowed to hear sermons. In 1278 Pope Nicholas III asked the superiors of the Franciscans and Dominicans to select qualified preachers who would be able to bring the Jews to the truth of the Gospel. If necessary, they should enlist the aid of the secular authorities in this. Not much came of this decree. Only in Spain did persons go to great trouble from the thirteenth century to convert Muslims and Jews and to fit them into Christian society. Since they did not come voluntarily, the authorities resorted to force. These compulsory sermons, occurring several times a year in churches, public squares, or even in synagogues, had, understandably, only slight and, for the most part, merely external success, especially when the preachers, annoyed by their failure, began to revile the Jews.

Sermons of this sort are not heard of in Germany until the fifteenth century. On the occasion of his legatine activity against the Hussites, John of Capestrano (d. 1456) preached also to the Jews at Vienna and Nürnberg. They were required to attend. Otherwise we know only of the grand-scale but likewise fruitless proselytizing effort of the Dominican Peter Schwarz. At Regensburg in 1474 and at Frankfurt, Worms, Bamberg, and Nürnberg later, he delivered lectures in the Hebrew and German languages which the Jews had to attend. In fifteenth-century Italy proselytizing attempts of this sort were undertaken by great preachers, such as John of Capestrano and Bernardine of Siena (d. 1444). But in their exertions to alleviate the economic misery of the people they seem to have preached rather against the Jews and their usury than for their conversion. This contributed to stir up excesses, hardly known before in Italy, against the Jews, so that the Popes had to call the preachers to order. Under the influence of Spanish bishops, the Council of Basel decreed in 1434 that several times a year bishops should have the Christian faith preached to the Jews; all Jews should be compelled under penalties to hear these sermons. The Council also admonished the bishops and preachers to behave so that they might win the Jews not only by means

[29] *S. th.,* III, q. 80, a. 4.

of the truth but also by works of charity.[30] In Germany, however, except for the already mentioned efforts of Peter Schwarz, nothing came of this.

If the number of converts remained extremely slight, the explanation is not to be sought only in the curious missionary methods or lack of a genuine missionary spirit in accord with the Gospel among Christians nor in the loyalty and love of the Jews for the faith of their ancestors and their tradition. Not the least important reason is the fact that their conversion was opposed to the financial interests of the princes, not excluding the bishops, and these made it almost impossible by legal measures. The source of revenue which every Jew represented on the basis of the right of protection and especially of the cameral servitude dried up with his baptism. To balance matters converts were to renounce their property. Already in 1090 the Emperor Henry IV had demanded this of the Jews of Worms and Speyer who desired to became his brothers in the faith. In his privilege for the Jews of Vienna Frederick II decreed:

> If one, for his part, desires baptism, . . . he shall give up his inheritance, just as he has abandoned the law of his fathers.[31]

Naturally, this total loss of property kept many from being baptized. That from Alexander III in 1179 the Popes took measures against this practice and threatened excommunication for those who caused converts to lose their inheritances or confiscated their property[32] seems to have had little effect. It seems sheer mockery that Archbishop Kuno II of Trier (1362–88) granted an indulgence of twenty days to those who assisted a Jewish family, which, after receiving baptism, had deposited before the church door all that it had possessed in Judaism.[33] At Constance Cardinal d'Ailly protested that people did not leave the converted Jews even the necessities of life, with the result that they fell away and accused the Christians of uncharitableness.[34] The Council forbade under excommunication the seizing of the goods of the newly converted. Nevertheless, the confiscation of property after baptism remained a sort of prescriptive right, and in 1542 Paul III had to forbid it again.[35]

---

[30] *Mansi*, XXIX, 98.

[31] *MGConst*, I, 228; P. Browe, *Die Judenmission*, 180, 144.

[32] *Decret. Greg. IX*, 1. 5, t. 6, c. 5, Friedberg, II, 773; *Extravag. comm.*, 1. 5, t. 2, c. 2, Friedberg, II, 1290; for other examples see P. Browe, *Die Judenmission*, 188 f.

[33] A. Goerz, *Regesten der Erzbischöfe zu Trier* (Trier 1861), 120.

[34] J. Gerson, *Opera*, ed. Du Pin, II (Antwerp 1706), App. 915; P. Browe, *Die Judenmission*, 193.

[35] P. Browe, *Die Judenmission*, 183, 195.

CHAPTER 61

German Humanism

Much more so than south of the Alps, in Germany humanism was a matter of education, the concern of scholars and restricted circles. Hence it appears more independent in comparison with the general cultural movement of the Renaissance, of which it was actually the effect in the field of literary culture, language, and education. Indeed, German princes and German cities also made use of the writers, jurists, and medical men trained by the new lay education, but this did not result in a Renaissance state or a Renaissance society as in Italy, or a corresponding political theory similar to that of Machiavelli. In regard to German territory one cannot speak of a "Renaissance culture" but of German humanism.[1] The connection with antiquity was not so direct here; there was no unbroken continuity. Therefore the encounter with antiquity was also not so elementary but rather the object of the educational endeavour, and the temptation to paganism was less real than in Italy. In art Gothic was so deeply rooted and still so alive that the new style had a difficult time establishing itself.

Already at the Council of Constance (1414–18) and especially at Basel (1431–49) closer contacts were made with Italian humanism. Here, and through his later diplomatic and courtly career, Aeneas Silvius Piccolomini, the later Pope Pius II, became, in Joachimsen's words, the "Apostle of German humanism." The new education had its first centre, not at the universities, but in the chanceries of princely courts and cities, the living quarters of scholars, the monasteries, and a number of city schools. The universities were too institutionalized and too dominated by the traditional scholasticism. The liberal arts were above all preparatory stages for the other sciences, especially theology. Little wonder that homeless poets and *rhetores,* who as itinerant teachers gave only occasional lectures and courses, as for example Peter Luder (d. after 1474) and Samuel Karoch of Lichtenberg in Upper Franconia, became the most active opponents of scholasticism. It was not until the turn of the century that special chairs were established within the faculty of arts or even special courses in poetry were given, as at Vienna under the direction of Conrad Celtis (1459–1508). This "German arch-humanist," as David Frederick Strauss termed him, the vintner's son, Conrad Bickel of Wipfeld near Würzburg, was crowned at Nürnberg in

[1] The term "humanism" was coined in 1808 by the Bavarian educational reformer, F. J. Niethammer. In fourteenth-century Italy the expression *studia humanitatis* is found, borrowed from Cicero, for the study of rhetoric and politics. The teachers of these arts were called *oratores* and *poetae.* The term *umanista* is found only from the end of the fifteenth century.

1487 by the Emperor Frederick III with the laurel of the poet, the first German to be so honoured. In the course of his restless wandering he founded learned societies (*sodalitates litterariae*) in many places, such as Cracow, Prague, Bratislava, Buda, Heidelberg (1491), and Vienna (1497). At Vienna he also established, at the request of the Emperor Maximilian I, a college of poetry and mathematics in 1502, and as its president he had the right of conferring the poet's laurel. From his journeys he expected to obtain material for a "Germania illustrata," in which he apparently intended to describe Germany in four books according to the four points of the compass. But only the *Norimberger* (1495) was published, — a song of praise to the city of Nürnberg. In poetic form some of his planned work was issued in the *Quatuor libri Amorum secundum quatuor latera Germaniae* (1502), a mixture of love lyric and description of countries and peoples. With his edition of the *Germania* of Tacitus and the discovery of the *Tabula Peutingeriana*, of the works of Roswitha of Gandersheim, and of the Barbarossa epic *Ligurinus*, Celtis laid the foundation for the study of German history and antiquities. He is an early example of the manner in which the German humanists, in a sort of hate-love for Italy, which had handed on to them the treasures of ancient civilization, came to extol extravagantly the value of German nationality and of German history in order to give the lie to the charge of barbaric origin. His polemic against abuses in the Church, against indulgence fraud and "stinking cowls," was conditioned by the struggle against the foreign spiritual domination and material exploitation by the Roman Curia.

As willingly as he, like many other humanists, abandoned himself to pagan ideas and took delight in frivolity, a break with the Church never entered his mind. Above all, what the circle of the initiated was free to choose to do and think should remain forbidden to "the people." "For if the masses were to understand certain secrets as we philosophers do, it would then be difficult to keep their turbulence under control."[2]

The men who in Italy became enthusiastic over antiquity, its language, art, and way of life, and sought to pass on these treasures to their countrymen were first in the circles of the patrician class of the cities. These were the Augsburg merchant Sigismund Gossembrot (d. after 1488); the Augsburg city physician Hermann Schedel, who died at Nürnberg in 1485; Niklas von Wyle (d. 1478), town-clerk of Esslingen; the Ulm city physician Henry Steinhövel (d. 1482); Albert von Eyb (d. 1475), canon of Eichstatt and Augsburg; and the jurist and diplomat Gregory von Heimburg (d. 1472). Through the stimulation they provided and their work the Free Cities of South Germany became centres of humanism.

At Nürnberg Willibald Pirkheimer (1470–1530) was the celebrated leader

---

[2] Ingolstadt inaugural lecture of 31 August 1492, ed. by J. Rupprich (Leipzig 1932), 8.

of a humanist circle. Liberally educated, he was as much at home in law, history, and geography as in theology. He translated ancient and patristic Greek authors and wrote a geography of ancient Germany dominated by a nationalistic enthusiasm, and the *Description of the Swiss War,* in which he had led the Nürnberg contingent. In other respects too his interest in scholarship and art was not that of a dilettante. Versatile as he was, Pirkheimer devoted himself to the public service of his city as a diplomat and promoter of schools.

The most important humanist among the patrician middle class of Augsburg was Conrad Peutinger (1465–1542). In the controversy concerning interest and monopoly he took the side of early capitalism. His history of the Emperors and collecting and publishing of the sources of German history served the imperial patriotic endeavours of the circle surrounding the Emperor Maximilian I.

The strongly pedagogical character of German humanism is made clear in a group of scholars from the Netherlands and Westphalia, who were often closely connected with the *devotio moderna.* The Frisian Rudolf Agricola (1444–85) had studied philosophy at Erfurt, Cologne, and Louvain in the traditional way, then had concentrated on humanistic studies in Italy, and finally in 1484 went to Heidelberg. Here he delivered talks and lectures in connection with the University, learned Hebrew, and developed a program for the reform of university studies. He himself never sacrificed his freedom as a man of letters to a set teaching assignment, regarded marriage as an intolerable restraint, and even considered his obligation to his benefactor, Bishop Dalberg of Worms, as a grievous slavery.

Alexander Hegius (1433–98) learned Greek from Agricola. According to his pupil Erasmus, Hegius raised the school at Deventer from a barbaric educational establishment to a humanistic school. He was one of the early Christian humanists, who emphatically sought the association of scholarship and religion. He considered any "knowledge injurious which [was] gained at the cost of integrity."

Rudolf von Langen (1438–1520) effected the reform of the cathedral school of Münster along humanistic lines and summoned Hegius's pupil, John Murmellius (1480–1517), to be associate director. The Westphalian Hermann von dem Busche (1468–1534)[3] was a pupil of both Hegius and Agricola. In the course of his restless existence as an itinerant teacher he came into contact with the Erfurt humanistic circle and belonged to the group of humanists whose path led away from the Church.

Through the Westphalian Louis Dringenberg, director of the school at Schlettstadt from 1441 to 1477, the association with the humanism of the upper Rhine, having its centres at Schlettstadt, Strasbourg, Freiburg, and

[3] *Cf. LThK,* II (2nd ed. 1958), 800.

Basel, was established. The patriotic tendency in German humanism found a congenial environment especially in Alsace. In addition to the pleasure derived from collecting the antiquarian and historical evidence of the German past and criticism of the Roman Curia, here in the west the resistance to French claims afforded a special stimulus to enthusiasts for German greatness and the declaration of national interests. The poet and journalist Sebastian Brant (1457–1521), born in Strasbourg, who had served in his native city as legal adviser and clerk from 1500, was still strongly attached to scholasticism. In popular legal collections (*Layenspiegel* of 1509 and *Klagspiegel* of 1516), in religious poems *(Carmina in laudem beatae Mariae)*, and in moral treatises he developed a heavily didactic method. He became famed for his *Narrenschiff* (1494), in which, in popular language, he provided a mirror of the failings and vices of all contemporary classes and professions.

The diocesan priest James Wimpheling (1450–1528) became the herald of German national greatness in his *Germania* (1501); the German translation bore the title *Tutschland zu Ere der Statt Strassburg und des Rinstroms*. He sought to prove that the left bank of the Rhine had never formed part of Gaul, that the Vosges and not the Rhine formed Germany's boundary, and that all Roman Emperors since Charles the Great had been Germans. Moreover, he composed the first extensive history of the German people, placing great emphasis on the history of the Emperors and of culture: the *Epitome rerum Germanicarum* of 1505. Wimpheling devoted the second part of his *Germania* to his reflections on schools and education. He called for a "Fechtschul," which, after elementary school, should prepare for the university, thereby developing the program of the later Latin *Gymnasium*. It should envisage not only the future clergy but should also take care of young men who intended to devote themselves to a "middle-class, knightly, or town-councillor's career." Hence, the curriculum should include, among other things, history, public administration, military science, architecture, and agriculture.

It was hardly sympathy for the French or concern for the existence of monastic schools but rather a humanist's delight in polemics and satire that caused the Strasbourg Franciscan, Thomas Murner (1475–1537), in *Germania Nova* pitilessly to tear to shreds Wimpheling's pompously patriotic but uncritical arguments. The language of the popular preacher, satirist, and poet Murner was merciless and blunt, not so solemn and ponderous as Wimpheling's, but therefore all the more to the point. In his moral satires, influenced by Brant's *Narrenschiff* — *Narrenbeschwörung* (1512), *Schelmenzunft* (1512), *Mühle von Schwindelsheim* (1515), and *Gäuchmatt* (1519) — he skilfully developed it and used it as a weapon against abuses and vices of all classes. In his *Geistliche Badenfahrt* (1514), an edifying rhymed poem, and in the first translation of the *Aeneid* into German verse he demonstrated

617

his linguistic skill more seriously. Both Wimpheling and Murner were not sparing in criticism of conditions in the Church. Doubtless, in the heat of the attack, they may often have gone too far. That they remained in the Church is beyond doubt. In 1510, at the request of the Emperor, Wimpheling published the Pragmatic Sanction and the "Grievances of the German Nation" of 1455–57, more or less unchanged. It was in this connection that at first he welcomed the reformer in Luther. But it was equally consistent that, like Murner, he turned against him when Luther shattered the doctrinal structure of the ancient Church. The Alsatians Geiler von Kaysersberg (1445–1510), Sebastian Brant, Thomas Murner, James Wimpheling, and Beatus Rhenanus (1485–1547) are thus to be regarded as representatives of a moralizing humanism, which was concerned not only for the reform of the Church but equally for the maintaining of the old order.

Wimpheling's friends included the Freiburg jurist Ulric Zasius (1461 to 1536) and Abbot John Trithemius (1462–1516), a Benedictine of Sponheim and later of Würzburg. In his works, dealing with history and the history of literature, such as *Catalogus scriptorum ecclesiasticorum* (1494) and *De viris illustribus Germaniae* (1495), Trithemius collected abundant material which is still of value today. However, when his sources failed him, he often gave free rein to his imagination. In his enthusiasm for the greatness of Germany he went so far as to "discover" in "Hunibald" an historian of the origins of the Franks, who was supposed to have attested the existence of a Frankish kingdom, independent of Rome, 500 years before the birth of Christ.

The anticlercial spirit and radical criticism, aloof and sarcastic, gained the firmest foothold in the humanist circle at Erfurt. Here Peter Luder (*ca.* 1460) and Conrad Celtis (1486) had worked and Mutianus Rufus (Conrad Muth, 1470–1526) had studied. The last named, after a rather long stay in Italy and close contact with Florentine Platonism, returned in 1503 to Gotha as a canon and from there took care of the Erfurt circle, to which Eobanus Hessus (1488–1540), Euricius Cordus (1486–1535), Ulric von Hutten (1488 to 1523), Crotus Rubeanus (1468–1534), Justus Jonas (1493–1555), and George Spalatin (1484–1545) belonged. In order to live "beata tranquillitas," Mutianus declined every professorship and wrote no books, just as "Socrates and Christ." He expressed his convictions exclusively in letters, which, in his opinion, were open only to the small circle of the initiated and unsuited to be exposed to the mob. He made all the more fun of the follies and weaknesses of men, especially the narrow-mindedness of the devout and most of all the hypocrisy and narrowness of monks. For him Christianity was the same as monotheism, but this can have numerous forms.

There are only one God and one Goddess, but many forms and names, such as Jupiter, Sol, Apollo, Moses, Christ, Luna, Ceres, Proserpina, Tellus, Mary. But be on your guard against uttering this. For, like the mysteries of the Eleusinian goddesses, it must be cloaked in silence. In

618

matters of religion one must make use of fables and veils of images . . .
The one I call Jupiter I know as Christ and as true God . . . [4]

He read Paul through the spectacles of the Stoa and gave him a moral interpretation.

The occasion for open war against scholasticism and the hollow ecclesiasticism was provided by the Reuchlin dispute. Born at Pforzheim in 1455, John Reuchlin (d. 1522) had, while pursuing studies at Paris and Basel in 1474, learned Greek through association with Byzantine emigrants, and, after 1482, Hebrew also from Jews in Italy. Through his *Rudimenta linguae Hebraicae* (1506) he became the founder of Hebrew linguistics in Germany. He took great pains with the study of the *Cabala*, to which he devoted his treatises *De verbo mirifico* (1494) and *De arte cabbalistica* (1517). In 1482 he entered the service of Count Eberhard V of Württemberg as a jurist, accompanied him to Italy, and served him as adviser and agent. From 1499 he lived at Stuttgart as a private scholar and was acting as a judge of the Swabian League (1502–13) when his name became the war-cry of the younger humanists in the struggle against scholasticism.

The convert's zeal of the ex-Jew, John Pfefferkorn, baptized at Cologne in 1507, was not satisfied with working for the conversion of his former co-religionists by writings only. In 1500 he secured an imperial order for the confiscation of all Jewish works of a theological content. In an opinion sent to the Emperor in 1510 Reuchlin proposed that only those Jewish writings should be destroyed which contained clear defamation of Christianity. The Talmud and the *Cabala* could be used to support the Christian faith. Against this Pfefferkorn wrote the *Handspiegel*, to which Reuchlin replied with the *Augenspiegel*. Meanwhile, the theological faculty of Cologne had become involved in the question. In the Dominican Inquisitor James von Hoogstraeten (1460–1527) an important man sided with Pfefferkorn. He declared the *Augenspiegel* heretical and instituted a process against Reuchlin. The Pope referred it to the Bishop of Speyer. The humanist was acquitted at this tribunal and silence was imposed on his opponents (1514), but Hoogstraeten appealed to the Pope.

In the meantime attention was less centred on Jewish writings, for in Reuchlin the humanists saw themselves and the new style of thought and scholarship attacked. As proof of his integrity, Reuchlin in 1514 published under the title *Clarorum virorum epistolae* letters which the most illustrious minds of the day had written to him. The preface was written by his great-nephew and pupil, Philip Melanchthon. More attention was attracted the next year by another collection of letters, the *Epistolae obscurorum virorum* (1515–17), addressed to Master Ortwinus Gratius, spokesman of the Cologne

---

[4] Letter of 1505 to the Cistercian H. Urban, in *Der Briefwechsel des Mutianus Rufus,* ed. by C. Krause (Kassel 1885), 28.

scholastics. These "letters of obscure men" are fictitious and composed in barbarous "kitchen Latin." They were supposed to make Reuchlin's opponents look ridiculous and to present them as uneducated and hypocritical. Ultimately all monks appeared as stupid, vain, untruthful, and lewd, and theologians got their delight in empty and ridiculous subtleties. In coarse and obscene humour the Church and what is sacred were exposed to ridicule, along with the orders, relics, and indulgences. Here humanism stood in hostility to the Church, but this hostility was originally foreign to it. Thus, as Lortz says, the Reuchlin dispute became an "immediate prelude to the Reformation." The authors of the "letters of obscure men" belonged to the Erfurt circle: Crotus Rubeanus, who contributed letters 1 to 41, and Ulric von Hutten, responsible for the seven additional letters of the second edition (Cologne 1516) and the sixty-two letters of Part II (1517). The proceedings against Reuchlin were long drawn out and were finally affected by the case against Luther. Hence the *Augenspiegel* was condemned under Leo X in 1520. Nevertheless, Reuchlin, who was active in his last years as professor of Greek and Hebrew at Ingolstadt (1520–21) and Tübingen (1521–22), remained loyal to the ancient Church. He died at Stuttgart on 30 June 1522.

German humanism reached its zenith in Desiderius Erasmus. The second illegitimate son of the priest Rotger Gerard, he was born at Rotterdam on 28 October 1466[5] (or 1469). At about the age of fourteen he lost his parents. The taint of illegitimacy, which he never overcame, and the lack of family and home contribute much to make his restlessness, his suspicious withdrawal, his fear of committing himself, his sensitivity, and his need to be accepted understandable. The description of himself as a citizen of the world, "civis totius mundi," cannot completely conceal this homelessness. His last words in his otherwise unused mother tongue, "Lieve God," can be understood as a cry for security and a home on the lips of the man whom through years and decades seven European states considered it an honour to have lodged. Even in regard to the chronic anxiety about his "frail little body" more was involved than concern for an easily upset stomach, a nausea produced by the smell of fish, kidney stones, and insomnia. Erasmus did not get away from himself. For example, again and again he encountered the painful reminder of his birth when he had to obtain a dispensation in order to acquire a benefice.

His schooling at Deventer and 's-Hertogenbosch was marked by the spirit of the *devotio moderna*. He claims that he was forced by his guardian to enter the Augustinian monastery at Steyn near Gouda (1486–88). However,

---

[5] Thus E. W. Kohls, "Das Geburtsjahr des Erasmus," *ThZ*, 22 (1966), 96–121, against R. R. Post, "Geboortejaar en opleiding van Erasmus," *Mededelingen der Koninklijke Nederlandse Akademie van Wetenschapen*, N. R. 16, Afdeling Letterkunde (1953), 327–48, who, contrary to what Erasmus himself says, regards 1469 as the year of his birth.

his enthusiastic friendship with a former fellow student from Deventer and the opportunity for abundant reading of the ancient and patristic authors at first reconciled him to the monastery. Jerome became his ideal as a synthesis of Christianity and classical culture. Later (1496) he adopted the name of Jerome's friend, Desiderius. Soon after his ordination to the priesthood on 25 April 1492, Erasmus became secretary of Henry von Bergen, Bishop of Cambrai. The trip to Italy, which he had hoped for as the Bishop's companion, did not materialize, but the Bishop made it possible for him to study at Paris from the autumn of 1495. The barbarous severity at the Collège Montaigu pleased Erasmus as little as did scholasticism and its "barbarous" Latin. His humanist writings, which were printed later, *Antibarbari* (1520), *Adagia* (1500), *Colloquia* (1518), and others, took form in these years. Following a wandering life Erasmus went to England in 1499. This first stop there was of decisive importance, for in men such as John Colet (1466–1519), Dean of St. Paul's at London, Thomas More (1478–1535), and John Fisher (1469–1535), he met a Christian humanism and a theology based on the Bible and the Church Fathers. His enthusiasm found expression in the words: "For one who knows England a journey to Italy is superfluous." Erasmus achieved a conscious turn to theology. The importance of the biblical languages became clear. Thereafter he wanted to "apply himself with all his heart to Holy Scripture" and to "dedicate the rest of [his] life" to it. He refused a call to Louvain (1502), just as later he never renounced his independence.

The first result of his turning to theology was the *Enchiridion militis Christiani* (1503), the manual or small weapon of the Christian warrior, intended as an introduction to Christian life for the laity. For piety and even perfection are not monopolies of clergy and monks. Only the reprintings from 1515 gained for this work a wider circle. The edition of 1518, with a foreword addressed to Abbot Paul Volz, made it a huge success. In the foreword Erasmus summarizes the basic ideas of the *Enchiridion* and gives an insight into his own religious outlook. For the simple man, who is unable to pour over the thick and detailed volumes of the scholastics, but for whom also Christ died, one should "condense the entire philosophy of Christ in its fundamental traits from the purest sources of the Gospels and the Apostles, from the most trustworthy exegetes, and this should be simple but scholarly, brief but clear." [6] Clarity, simplicity, and purity through going back to the sources, Holy Scripture and the Fathers — such are the goals of Christian humanism as Erasmus advocated it.

The goal is thus one: Christ and his holy teaching . . . No type of vocation is excluded from this goal . . . One must not stain the heavenly

[6] *Desiderius Erasmus, Ausgewählte Werke,* ed. by H. Holborn (Munich 1933; reprinted 1964), 7.

philosophy of Christ with man's work...He who kindles love for Christ teaches the essence of Christian piety.

Christian perfection is not a matter of subtle reflection but of a loving act. "It manifests itself in warmth of feeling, not in a special state [monasticism], in the heart, not in holy garments or foods."[7] All ceremonies are only helps for those not of age; the perfect is the invisible, the religion of the heart. The spiritual man no longer needs the aid of the external. In Erasmus the effort for biblical simplicity and inwardness is connected with a Platonic spiritualism, which underestimates external form and the corporeal and hence cannot do justice to the Incarnation, the mystery of the Church, and the Sacraments. All the more reckless is his criticism of the numerous ceremonies, theology, and the morals of the clergy and monks.

This criticism was expressed in a particularly clever manner, but also especially frivolously and maliciously, in the "intimate conversations" which Erasmus had written at Paris in 1500 but which only appeared in Basel in 1518 under the title *Familiarium colloquiorum formulae*. This work was intended as a school textbook; as a collection of Latin idioms and of examples of cultured conversation it was to instruct the pupil in Latin eloquence and impart to him proper conduct of life. The Italian sojourn of 1506–09, during which he became doctor of theology at Turin, did not have for the great humanist the significance that we might suppose. It was only the finishing touch in his humanist education. At the beginning of his third visit in England (1509–14) Erasmus wrote *Encomium Moriae* (1511), the *Praise of Folly*, in the house of Thomas More, who was bound to him in a close friendship. In it folly has its say. This literary artifice made it possible to say serious things without committing oneself. If the author even wanted to express risky views, he could not be pinned down but always had an alibi. It was only folly speaking. This "cunningly indirect procedure," as Meissinger calls it, promoted a levity which could not but operate destructively in the religious field.

As early as 1504 Erasmus had discovered Lawrence Valla's *Adnotationes* to the New Testament, which he published in 1505. Thereafter he had eagerly studied Greek and preoccupied himself with the text of Scripture. These studies bore fruit when in 1514 he moved to Basel for two years and in John Froben found a qualified printer and publisher for his *Novum Instrumentum*. Appearing in 1516, this was the Greek text of the New Testament with notes and a Latin translation differing from the Vulgate. In the introduction, under "Paraclesis, Methodus, Apologia," Erasmus outlined a biblical theology, his "Philosophia Christi," which, as "renascentia," that is, as "the renewal *(instauratio)* of the originally good nature," should be

[7] *Ibid.*, 12.

simple, clear, devout, and practical. In the dedicatory letter to Leo X he wrote:

.... since I see that that doctrine of salvation is found much purer and more alive in the veins themselves, from which sources it is drawn, than from pools or drained-off streams, I have revised the entire Greek New Testament in fidelity to the original text, not frivolously or with slight exertion but by recourse to several Greek and Latin manuscripts, and those that are the oldest and the best, not those that are entirely more agreeable. [8]

In the "Paraclesis," the admonition to the pious reader, he wrote:
At best few can be scholars, but everyone can be a Christian, everyone can be devout, yes, I will boldly add, everyone can be a theologian. What is in conformity with nature easily becomes common property. But what is Christ's philosophy, which he himself calls a rebirth *(renascentia)*, but a renewal of the originally good nature? [9] ... That rich and genuine philosophy of Christ is obtained nowhere more happily than from the Gospels and the other Apostolic writings. [10]

In "Methodus," Erasmus demands:
The young theologian must learn to quote well from Sacred Scripture, not from manuals, musty tomes, or God knows what kind of *collectanea,* which have already been shaken together and hodge-podged hundreds of times, but according to the sources themselves. [11] ... Make your own heart a library of Christ; from it, as from a treasury, bring forth new or old, as the matter requires. That which flows live from the heart penetrates much more vitally into the heart of the hearer than what has been picked up from someone else's crib. [12]

With the edition of the New Testament and that of the works of Jerome (1517 ff.), "by far the first and most learned" of the Church Fathers, Erasmus moved into the front rank of theologians of his day. At the same time, having taken up residence in the Netherlands again in May 1516 and having become a princely councillor, he entered upon the political scene with his *Institutio principis christiani* (1516) for the future Charles V and with the *Querela pacis* (1517). Through his English connections in 1517 he obtained from Rome the privilege of living free in the world without his religious habit and of accepting benefices unimpeded by his illegitimate birth. [13] In accord with his demand that theologians should open up Scripture instead

[8] *Opus epistularum*, edited by P. S. Allen, II (Oxford 1910), 185.
[9] *Ausgewählte Werke,* 145.
[10] *Ibid.,* 146.
[11] *Ibid.,* 158.
[12] *Ibid.,* 160.
[13] Leo X's brief of dispensation (26 January 1517) in *Opus epistularum,* nos. 517 f.

of treating silly questions, he wrote paraphrases of Romans (1517), the other Epistles (1517–21), the Gospels (1522 ff.), and Acts. At the same time he worked on the writings of the Fathers. Their printed editions were to occupy the rest of his life: Cyprian (1521), Arnobius (1522), Hilary (1523), Irenaeus (1526), Ambrose (1527), Origen (1527), Augustine (1527–29), and Chrysostom (1530).

In the years 1516–18 Erasmus was at the height of his reputation. By means of scholarship and education and more particularly through his exertions in regard to the text of the Bible and of the Fathers — *"ad fontes!"* — he expected to bring about renewal, and not a few contemporaries looked to him as the man of the longed-for reform. Then, with the appearance of Luther, forces emerged which were strange and even repugnant to the prince of humanists in their elemental power and existential importance, especially since they did not remain within the sphere of the "good sciences" but appealed also to the man in the street and demanded of Erasmus, "vir duplex," [14] a clear taking of sides.

[14] Martin Luther, *WA, Tr,* 1, no. 131.

BIBLIOGRAPHY

GENERAL BIBLIOGRAPHY

A. The Western Church

I. SOURCES FOR THE HISTORY OF THE WESTERN CHURCH

1. ANCILLARY SCIENCES

For the ancillary sciences (Chronology, Palaeography, Libraries, Diplomatics, Archives, Heraldry, Geography and Cartography, Statistics) see Volume I of this *Handbook,* 435–46.

2. SOURCES

See Volume III, 475. Also: R. C. van Caenegem and F. L. Ganshof, *Kurze Quellenkunde des westeuropäischen Mittelalters* (Göttingen 1963). K. Jacob and H. Hohenleutner, *Quellenkunde der deutschen Geschichte im Mittelalter,* III: *Das Spätmittelalter.* Edited by F. Weden (Berlin, 2d ed. 1968).

3. THE MORE IMPORTANT GENERAL COLLECTIONS OF SOURCES

See Volume III, 476.

4. COUNCILS, DOCTRINAL AND CANONICAL DECISIONS, CANON LAW

See Volume III, 476 f. Also: J. F. von Schulte, *Geschichte der Quellen und Literatur des kanonischen Rechts von Gratian bis auf die Gegenwart,* 3 vols. (Stuttgart 1875–80); Fr. Maasen, *Geschichte der Quellen und Literatur des kanonischen Rechts im Abendland bis zum Ausgang des Mittelalters,* I (Graz 1870); G. Le Bras, *Prolégomènes* (Vol. I of *Histoire du droit et des institutions de l'Église en Occident* [Paris 1955]).

5. PAPACY

See Volume III, 477. Also: S. Baluze, *Vitae Paparum Avenionensium,* ed. G. Mollat, 4 vols. (Paris 1916–28); A. Potthast, *Regesta Pontificum Romanorum inde ab anno 1198 ad annum 1304,* 2 vols. (Berlin 1874 f., reprinted Graz 1957). A collection of documents hitherto unprinted, and hence not in Potthast, is in progress; it will cover the years 1198–1417 and will appear in *Index Romanorum Pontificum ab Innocentio III usque ad Martinum V electum. Registra* of papal letters are continuous only from Innocent III; the various editions in L. Santifaller, *Neuere Editionen mittelalterlicher Königs- und Papsturkunden* (Vienna 1958), 40–43; *ibid.,* 43–58, list the more important territorial collections from the papal *registra.*

6. SECULAR LAW AND CONCORDATS

See Volume III, 477. Also: A. Mercati, *Raccolta di Concordati su materie ecclesiastiche tra la S. Sede e le autorità civili (1098–1954),* 2 vols. (Rome, 2d ed. 1954).

7. Historical-Statistical Works With or Without Source Editions

See Volume III, 478. Also: C. Eubel, *Hierarchia catholica medii aevi,* 3 vols., new ed. by L. Schmitz-Kallenberg (Münster, 2d ed. 1913–23; reprinted Padua 1960).

8. Religious Orders

See Volume III, 478. Also: *Bullarium Franciscanum,* I–IV, edited by H. Sbaralea and B. de Rossi (Rome 1759–68); V–VII, by K. Eubel (Rome 1898–1904); VIII (new series, I), by U. Hüntemann (Quaracchi 1929); IX–X (new series II–III), by J. Pou y Marti (Quaracchi 1939–49); Suppl. I, by F. Annibali de Latera (Rome 1780); Suppl. II, by K. Eubel (Quaracchi 1908). *Acta Ordinis Fratrum Minorum vel ad Ordinem quoquomodo pertinentia,* I–V (Rome 1882–86), VI ff. (Quaracchi 1887 ff.); L. Wadding, *Annales Ordinis Minorum,* 8 vols. (Lyons 1625–54); continued by J. M. Fonseca *et al.,* 25 vols. (Rome, 2d ed. 1731–1886); continued by A. Chiappini *et. al.,* thus far 30 vols. (Quaracchi, 3d ed. 1931 ff.). *Bullarium Ordinis Fratrum Praedicatorum,* ed. T. Ripoll and A. Bremond, 8 vols. (Rome 1729–49); *Monumenta Ordinis Fratrum Praedicatorum Historica,* ed. B. M. Reichert, 14 vols. (Rome 1896–1904); continued, Paris 1931 ff. K. Eubel, *Die avignonesische Obedienz der Mendikanten-Orden sowie der Orden der Mercedarier und Trinitarier zur Zeit des Grossen Schismas. Beleuchtet durch die von Clemens VII. und Benedikt XIII. an dieselben gerichteten Schreiben. Quellen und Forschungen aus dem Gebiete der Geschichte* (Paderborn 1900), published by the Görres-Gesellschaft; K. Hallinger, *Corpus consuetudinum monasticarum,* cura Pont. Athenaei S. Anselmi de Urbe editum; of the approximately 25 vols. planned 3 have thus far appeared (Siegburg 1963–67).

9. Liturgy   See Volume III, 478.

10. Hagiography   See Volume III, 478 f.

11. Philosophy and Theology

See Volume III, 479. Also: *Bibliotheca Franciscana scholastica medii aevi,* cura PP. collegii S. Bonaventurae ad Claras Aquas, 23 vols. (Quaracchi and Florence 1903 ff.); *RepFont,* I, 73 f.

12. Crusades

A. S. Atiya, *The Crusade. Historiography and Bibliography* (Bloomington, Ind. 1962); H. E. Mayer, *Bibliographie zur Geschichte der Kreuzzüge* (Hanover, 2d ed. 1965); *Recueil des historiens des croisades,* ed. Académie des Inscriptions et Belles-Lettres: *Historiens occidentaux,* 5 vols. (Paris 1844–95); *Historiens orientaux,* 5 vols. (Paris 1872–1906); *Historiens grecs,* 2 vols. (Paris 1875–81); *Documents arméniens,* 2 vols. (Paris 1869–1906); *Lois. Les Assises de Jérusalem,* 2 vols. (Paris 1841–43).

13. History of the Missions

Bibliotheca Missionum, ed. R. Streit, IV: *Asiatische Missionsliteratur (1245–1599)* (Aachen 1928; reprinted Freiburg im Breisgau 1964); G. Golubovich, *Biblioteca Bio-Bibliografica della Terra Santa e dell'Oriente francescano,* 5 vols. (Quaracchi 1906–27); *Sinica Franciscana,* Vol. I, ed. A. van den Wyngaert (Quaracchi 1929).

II. ACCOUNTS OF WESTERN HISTORY

1. UNIVERSAL HISTORY

a) LARGER WORKS: See Volume III, 479. Also: *Peuples et Civilisations. Histoire générale*, ed. L. Halphen and P. Sagnac (Paris 1926 ff.), VII, 1: H. Pirenne *et al.*, *La désagrégation du monde médiéval* (1931 and at other dates); *Histoire générale*, ed. G. Glotz (and successors) (Paris 1925 ff.), IV, 1: E. Jordan, *L'Allemagne et l'Italie aux XIIe et XIIIe siècles* (1939); IV, 2: C. Petit-Dutaillis and P. Guinard, *L'essor des états d'occident* (2d ed. 1944); VI, 1–2: R. Fawtier and A. Coville, *L'Europe occidentale de 1270 à 1380* (1940 f.); D. J. Geanakoplos, *Byzantine East and Latin West* (New York 1967).

b) SHORTER SUMMARIES: R. Morghen, *Medioevo cristiano* (Bari 1951); J. Le Goff, *Das Hochmittelalter* (Frankfurt am Main 1965); E. Hassinger, *Das Werden des neuzeitlichen Europa (1300–1600)* (Braunschweig, 2d ed. 1966); W. K. Ferguson, *Europe in Transition, 1300–1520* (New York 1962); E. P. Cheyney, *The Dawn of a New Era, 1250–1453* (New York 1936); *Cambridge Medieval History*, Vols. VII and VIII (Cambridge 1932, 1936); G. Mattingly, *Renaissance Diplomacy* (Boston 1955); D. M. Vaughan, *Europe and the Turk: A Pattern of Alliances, 1350–1700* (Liverpool 1954); J. W. Thompson, *Economic and Social History of Europe* (New York 1931; reprint 1960); *The Cambridge Economic History of Europe*, Vol. II: *Trade and Industry in the Middle Ages* (Cambridge 1954); D. Hay, *Europe in the Fourteenth and Fifteenth Centuries* (London 1966); B. H. Slicher van Bath, *Agrarian History of Western Europe* (London 1963).

c) WORKS ON CULTURAL AND INTELLECTUAL HISTORY: K. Bosl, *Frühformen der Gesellschaft im mittelalterlichen Europa* (Munich and Vienna 1964); J. Huizinga, *The Waning of the Middle Ages* (London 1924); R. Stadelmann, *Vom Geist des ausgehenden Mittelalters* (Halle 1929); A. Ehrhard, *Das Mittelalter und seine kirchliche Entwicklung* (Munich 1908); G. Leff, *Heresy in the Later Middle Ages*, 2 vols. (Manchester 1967); *Klassiker des Protestantismus*, I: *Wegbereiter der Reformation*, ed. G. A. Benrath (Bremen 1967).

2. NATIONAL HISTORY   See Volume III, 480 f.

ENGLAND: *The Oxford History of England*, ed. G. N. Clark (Oxford 1934 ff.); IV: F. M. Powicke, *The Thirteenth Century 1216–1307* (2d ed. 1962); V: M. McKisack, *The Fourteenth Century (1307–1399)* (1959); VI: E. F. Jacob, *The Fifteenth Century (1399–1485)* (1961); A. R. Myers, *England in the Late Middle Ages, 1307–1536* (Baltimore 1952); B. Wilkinson, *The Constitutional History of Medieval England, 1216–1485* (New York 1948–1964); S. B. Chrimes, *English Constitutional History*, 2d ed. (Oxford 1953); V. H. H. Green, *The Later Plantagenets* (London 1955).

FRANCE: E. Lavisse, *Histoire de France depuis les origines jusqu'à la Révolution* (Paris 1900 ff.), III, 1: A. Luchaire, *Louis VII, Philippe-Auguste, Louis VIII 1137–1226* (1901); III, 2: C. de Langlois, *Saint Louis, Philippe le Bel, les derniers Capétiens directs 1226–1328* (1901); IV, 1: A. Coville, *Les premiers Valois et la Guerre de Cent Ans (1328–1422)* (1902); IV, 2: C. Petit-Dutaillis, *Charles VII, Louis XI, Charles VIII (1422–1492)* (1902).

ITALY: N. Valeri, *L'Italia nell'età dei principati dal 1343 al 1516* (Verona 1949); *Storia d'Italia*, ed. N. Valeri, I: *Il Medioevo;* II: *Dalla crisi della libertà agli arbori dell'illuminismo* (Turin 1959).

SPAIN AND PORTUGAL: H. V. Livermore, *A History of Portugal* (Cambridge, Mass. 1947); J. Vicens Vives, *Historia social y económica de España y América*, 2 (Barcelona 1957);

J. H. Mariejol, *The Spain of Ferdinand and Isabella*, ed. B. Kenn (New Brunswick, N. J. 1961); R. B. Merriman, *The Rise of the Spanish Empire in the Old World and the New* (New York 1918); Burgundy: R. Vaughan, *Philip the Bold* (Cambridge 1962); *idem, John the Fearless* (New York 1966). For other lands their national histories are cited, as occasion demands, in their respective chapters.

3. General Church History

P. Hughes, *A History of the Church*, Vol. III: *The Revolt against the Church* (London 1947); A. C. Flick, *The Decline of the Medieval Church* (London 1930); *Histoire de l'Église depuis les origines jusqu'à nos jours*, ed. A. Fliche and V. Martin (and their successors) (Paris 1934 ff.), IX: A. Fliche, R. Foreville, and J. Rousset, *Du premier concile du Latran à l'avènement d'Innocent III (1123–1198)*, in 2 parts (1946–53); X: A. Fliche, C. Thouzellier, and Y. Azais, *La chrétienté romaine (1198–1274)* (1950); XIV: É. Delaruelle, R. Labande, and P. Ourliac, *L'Église au temps du Grand Schisme et de la crise conciliaire (1378–1449)*, in 2 parts (1962–64); XV: R. Aubenas and R. Ricard, *L'Église et la Renaissance (1449–1517)* (1951); B. Moeller, *Spätmittelalter* (Göttingen 1966); M. A. Schmidt and K. Goldammer, *Scholastik/Christliche Kunst im Mittelalter* (1968); García Villada Zaccarias, *Historia eclesiástica de España*, 5 vols. (Madrid 1926–36); G. de Lagarde, *La naissance de l'esprit laïque du moyen âge*, 5 vols. (Louvain 1956–63); V. Martin, *Les origines du Gallicanisme*, 2 vols. (Paris 1939); G. Falco, *Geist des Mittelalters* (Frankfurt 1958).

4. Church History of Individual Lands

Belgium: E. de Moreau, *Histoire de l'Église en Belgique*, 5 vols. and suppl. (Brussels 1940 ff.), III: *L'Église féodale 1122–1318* (1945), Tome complémentaire I (Texte) (1948); IV (1949).

England: *History of the English Church*, ed. W. R. W. Stephens and W. Hunt, 8 vols. in 9 (London 1899–1910, frequently reprinted), III: W. W. Capes, *The English Church in the Fourteenth and Fifteenth Centuries* (1909); W. A. Pantin, *The English Church in the Fourteenth Century* (Cambridge 1955); *Ecclesiastical History of England*, ed. J. C. Dickinson (London 1961).

France: N. Valois, *La France et le Grand Schisme d'Occident*, 1–4 (Paris 1896–1902); A. Latreille, *Histoire du catholicisme en France*, 2 (Paris 1960).

Portugal: P. Miguel de Oliveira, *Historia eclesiastica de Portugal* (Lisbon, 2d ed. 1948).

5. Conciliar and Papal History

See Volume III, 482 f. Also: C. J. von Hefele and H. Leclercq, *Histoire des conciles*, V: 1073–1250; VI: 1250–1409; VII: 1409–1447; *Histoire des conciles œcuméniques*, ed. G. Dumeige (Paris 1961 ff.); G. Mollat, *The Popes at Avignon*, translated by Janet Love (London and New York 1963); F. X. Seppelt, *Geschichte des Papsttums*, IV: *Das Papsttum im Spätmittelalter und in der Zeit der Renaissance*, revised by G. Schwaiger (Munich, 2d ed. 1957).

Rome and the Papal State: *Storia di Roma*, published by the Istituto di Studi Romani (Bologna 1938 ff.), XI: E. Dupré-Theseider, *Roma dal comune di popolo alla signoria Pontificia 1252–1377* (1952); D. Waley, *The Papal State in the Thirteenth Century* (London 1961); P. Paschini, *Roma nel Rinascimento* (1940).

6. Ecclesiastical Legal and Constitutional History

See Volume III, 483. Also:

Legal History: G. Le Bras, C. Lefèbvre, and J. Rambaud, *L'âge classique 1140–1378. Sources et théorie du droit* (Paris 1965).

7. Secular Legal and Constitutional History

See Volume III, 483 f.

8. Monographs on Ecclesiastical and Secular Legal History

See Volume III, 484. Also:

b) History of Political Ideas: F. A. von der Heydte, *Die Geburtsstunde des modernen Staates. Ein Beitrag zur Geschichte der Völkerrechte, der allgemeinen Staatslehre und des politischen Denkens* (Regensburg 1952); F. Calasso, *I glossatori e la teoria della sovranità* (Milan, 2d ed. 1957); S. Mochi Onory, *Fonti canonistiche dell'idea moderna dello Stato* (Milan 1951).

9. History of Religious Orders

See Volume III, 484 f. Also: P. Cousin, *Précis d'histoire monastique* (Paris n. d. [1958]); L. Lekai and A. Schneider, *Geschichte und Wirken der weissen Mönche* (Cologne 1958); B. Grassl, *Der Prämonstratenser-Orden* (Tongerloo 1934); H. Holzapfel, *Handbuch der Geschichte des Franziskanerordens* (Freiburg 1909); R. M. Huber, *A Documented History of the Franciscan Order (1182–1517)* (Milwaukee 1954); A. Léon, *Histoire de l'Ordre des Frères Mineurs* (Paris 1954); T. Nyberg, *Birgittinische Klostergründungen des Mittelalters* (Leiden 1967); A. Walz, *Compendium historiae Ordinis Praedicatorum* (Rome, 2d ed. 1948); A. Mortier, *Histoire des maîtres généraux de l'ordre des frères prêcheurs* (Paris 1903 ff.).

For Individual Lands: D. Knowles, *The Religious Orders in England*, 3 vols. (Cambridge 1961); T. W. Parker, *The Knights Templar in England* (Tucson, Ariz. 1963); J. Hasenberg and A. Wienand, *Das Wirken der Orden und Klöster in Deutschland* (Cologne 1957).

10. Liturgy and Hagiography

See Volume III, 485. Also: F. Doyé, *Heilige und Selige der römisch-katholischen Kirche,* 2 vols. (Leipzig 1930–32); F. G. Holweck, *A Biographical Dictionary of the Saints* (St. Louis and London 1924); *Bibliotheca Sanctorum,* published by the Istituto Giovanni XXIII (Rome 1961 ff., thus far 9 vols.).

11. Literature and General Cultural History

Literature: See Volume III, 485. Also: W. Stammler and K. Langosch, *Deutsche Literatur des Mittelalters. Verfasserlexikon,* 5 vols. (Berlin and Leipzig 1933–55); A. W. Ward and A. R. Waller, *Cambridge History of English Literature,* Vols. I and II (Cambridge 1908); G. Paris, *La littérature française du Moyen Âge, XIe–XIVe siècle* (Paris 1913); F. Flora, *Storia della Letteratura Italiana,* vol. I: *Dal medio evo alla fine del Quattrocento* (Milan 1955).

SCHOOLS AND UNIVERSITIES: H. Denifle, *Die Entstehung der Universitäten des Mittelalters bis 1400* (Berlin 1885); G. Kaufmann, *Die Geschichte der deutschen Universitäten*, I: *Vorgeschichte* (Stuttgart 1888); S. d'Irsay, *Histoire des universités françaises et étrangères*, I: *Moyen Âge et Renaissance* (Paris 1933); H. Rashdall, *The Universities of Europe in the Middle Ages,* ed. F. M. Powicke and A. B. Emden, 3 vols. (Oxford 1936).

12. PHILOSOPHY, THEOLOGY, SPIRITUALITY

See Volume III, 485 f. Also:

PHILOSOPHY: H. H. Heimsoeth, *Die sechs grossen Themen der abendländischen Metaphysik und der Ausgang des Mittelalters* (Berlin, 3d ed. 1954).

THEOLOGY: K. Werner, *Die Scholastik des späteren Mittelalters*, 5 vols. (Vienna 1881–87); G. Ritter, *Studien zur Spätscholastik*, 3 vols. (Heidelberg 1921–27); H. Obermann, *The Harvest of Medieval Theology, Gabriel Biel and Late Medieval Nominalism* (Cambridge, Mass. 1963); *idem, Forerunners of the Reformation: The Shape of Late Medieval Thought* (New York 1966).

SPIRITUALITY: S. Axters, *Geschiedenis van de vroomheid in de Nederlanden,* 3 vols. (Antwerp 1950–56).

13. CRUSADES

R. Grousset, *Histoire des croisades et du royaume franc de Jérusalem,* 3 vols. (Paris 1934–36); S. Runciman, *A History of the Crusades,* 3 vols. (Cambridge 1951–54); A. Waas, *Geschichte der Kreuzzüge,* 2 vols. (Freiburg im Breisgau 1956); *A History of the Crusades,* ed. K. M. Setton; the following volumes have thus far appeared: I: *The First Hundred Years,* ed. M. W. Baldwin (Philadelphia 1955), II: *The Later Crusades,* ed. R. L. Wolff and W. Hazard (Philadelphia 1962); H. E. Mayer, *Geschichte der Kreuzzüge* (Stuttgart 1965).

14. HISTORY OF THE MISSIONS

J. Schmidlin, *Katholische Missionsgeschichte* (Steyl n. d. [1925]); A. Mulders, *Missionsgeschichte. Die Ausbreitung des katholischen Glaubens* (Regensburg 1960); T. Ohm, *Wichtige Daten der Missionsgeschichte* (Münster, 2d ed. 1961); K. S. Latourette, *A History of the Expansion of Christianity,* II: *The Thousand Years of Uncertainty (500–1500)* (New York and London 1938); *Histoire universelle des missions catholiques,* ed. S. Delacroix, I: *Les missions des origines au XIVe siècle* (Paris 1956).

B. The Eastern Church

See General Bibliography, Volume III, 487–95.

BIBLIOGRAPHY FOR INDIVIDUAL CHAPTERS

Part one:
The High Middle Ages

SECTION ONE

The Post-Gregorian Epoch: 1124-1153

SOURCES

Mansi, XXI: *Hefele-Leclercq*, V, 645–847; *MGLiblit*, III; *Duchesne LP*, II and III; *Watterich*, II, 157–322; *Jaffé*, nos. 7182–9942; *Bullarium Taur.*, II, 349–621. Papal documents in Germany, Italy, France, England, and Portugal: see Gen. Bibliog., I, 5; also M. P. Sheehy, *Pontificia Hibernica*, 2 vols. (Dublin 1962). Letters of the Popes in this period: Honorius II, *PL*, 166; Innocent II, *PL*, 197; Anacletus II, *PL*, 179; Celestine II, *PL*, 179; Lucius II, *PL*, 179; Eugene III, *PL*, 180; Anastasius IV, *PL*, 188. *Acta* and documents of emperors and kings: Lothar, *MGDD*, 8; *MGConst*, I; H. C. W. Davis, *Regesta regum anglo-normannorum*, II (Henry I), ed. C. Johnson and H. A. Cronne (Oxford 1956); A. Luchaire, *Louis VI, Annales de sa vie et de son règne* (Paris 1890); J. F. Böhmer, *Regesten des Kaiserreiches* (Frankfurt am Main 1831), 108–23; K. F. Stumpf-Brentano "*Die Reichskanzler,*" 2 vols. (Innsbruck 1868–72). Important are the collections of letters: *Reinhardsbrunner Briefsammlung*, ed. Peeck, *MGEp. sel.*, 5 (1952); *Epistolae Wibaldi*, ed. P. Jaffé, *Bibl. rer. germ.*, I, 76–616 (Gen. Bibliog., I, 3); *Codex Udalrici* (in the appendix letters from 1125–34), ed. P. Jaffé, *ibid.*, V, 17–469; also now F. J. Schmale, "Die Bemühungen Innocenz' II. um seine Anerkennung in Deutschland," *ZKG*, 65 (1953 f.), 240–65; letters of Bernard of Clairvaux in *PL*, 182 (a critical edition is still wanting); letters of Peter the Venerable in *PL*, 189; letters of Hildebert of Lavardin in *PL*, 171; *Briefwechsel der heiligen Hildegard von Bingen*, ed. A. Führkötter (Salzburg 1965).

NARRATIVE SOURCES

Germany: Annalista Saxo (to 1139), *MGSS*, 6, 553–777; *Chronica S. Petri Erfordensis*, ed. O. Holder-Egger, *MGSS*, 30/1, 335–457; *Chronica Regia Coloniensis*, ed. G. Waitz, *MGSS rer. Germ.* (1880); in the *Gesta Treverorum* the *Vita Adalberonis archiepiscopi Trevirensis*, *MGSS*, 8, 243–60; the Annals of Paderborn, ed. P. Scheffer-Boichorst (1870); *Gesta archiepiscoporum Magdeburgensium*, *MGSS*, 14, 361–484; Otto of Freising, *Chronica*, ed. A. Hofmeister, *MGSS rer. Germ.* (2d ed. 1912); *Gesta Friderici I Imperatoris*, ed. A. Schmidt and F. J. Schmale (Darmstadt 1965); also *Otto von Freising, Gedenkgabe zu seinem 800. Todesjahr*, ed. J. A. Fischer (Hist. Verein Freising 1958); *Lauterberg Chronicle (Chronicon Montis Sereni)*, *MGSS*, 23, 138–226; *Gesta pontificum Leodiensium*, *MGSS*, 25, 1–129; lives of Otto of Bamberg, *MGSS*, 12, 746–902; the *Kaiserchronik* (to 1147), *MG, Deutsche Chroniken*, 1 (1892), and now E. Nellmann, *Die Reichsidee in deutschen Dichtungen der Salier- und frühen Stauferzeit. Annolied-Kaiserchronik-Rolandslied-Eraclius*, Philologische Studien und Quellen, 16 (Berlin 1963).

Italy: Caffaro, Annals of Genoa, I (1099–1174), ed. L. T. Belgrano (1890), *Fonti per la storia d'Italia*, 11; Romuald of Salerno, *Chronicon* (to 1178), ed. C. A. Garufi, *SS Rer. Ital.*

(2d ed. 1935), *MGSS*, 19, 398–461; Alexander of Telese, *De rebus gestis Rogerii Siciliae regis* (to 1136), ed. G. Del Re, *Cronisti e scrittori sincroni napolitani*, 1 (Naples 1845); *ibid.*, also Falco of Benevento, *Chronicon;* Peter the Deacon, *Chronica monasterii Casinensis* (to 1139), *MGSS*, 7, 574–844, *PL*, 183, 479–978 (for the period under consideration there is question only of the continuation of the *Chronicle* of Leo Marsicanus by Peter the Deacon); Annals of Pisa, *MGSS*, 19, 236–66; Annals of Ceccano, *MGSS*, 19, 275–302. On Alexander of Telese see now M. Reichenmiller, "Bisher unbekannte Traumerzählungen Alexanders von Telese," *DA*, 19 (1963), 339–52.

England: William of Malmesbury, *Gesta pontificum Anglorum*, ed. N. E. S. A. Hamilton (London 1870), *Rolls Series*, 52; *idem, Gesta regum Anglorum and Historia novella*, ed. W. Stubbs, 2 vols. (London 1887–89), *Rolls Series*, 90; the *Historia Novella*, text, translation, and commentary by K. R. Potter, Nelson's Medieval Texts (London 1955); *Gesta Stephani* (to 1154), ed. R. Howlett, *Chronicles of the Reigns of Stephen, Henry II, and Richard I*, III, *Rolls Series*, 82 (London 1884), text, translation, and commentary by K. R. Potter, Nelson's Medieval Texts (London 1955); Robert of Torigny, *Chronicle*, ed. W. Stubbs (see *supra*), Vol. 4, there also as Vol. 1, William of Newburgh, *Historia rerum anglicarum* (to 1198); Ordericus Vitalis, *Historia ecclesiastica* (to 1141), ed. A. Le Prévost and L. Delisle, 5 vols. (Paris 1838–55), in the edition by A. Duchesne also in *PL*, 188; see H. Wolter, *Ordericus Vitalis* (Wiesbaden 1955); Henry of Huntingdon, *Historia Anglorum* (to 1154), ed. T. Arnold, *Rolls Series*, 74 (London 1879); John of Salisbury, *Historia Pontificalis* (to 1152), ed. R. L. Poole, with translation and commentary, ed. M. Chibnall, Nelson's Medieval Texts (London 1956).

France: Ordericus Vitalis (see *supra*); *Vita Ludovici Grossi von Suger von Saint-Denis*, ed. H. Waquet (Paris 1929); *Historia pontificum et comitum Engolismensium*, ed. J. Boussard (Paris 1957); *Chronicle of Morigny* (to 1147), ed. A. Duchesne, *PL*, 180, 131–76; M. Bouquet, *Recueil des historiens de la France*, Vols. 12–15 (Gen. Bibliog, I, 3); Herman of Tournai, *De restauratione monasterii S. Martini Tornacensis*, *MGSS*, 14, 274–327; *Chronicle of Saint-Bertin* (extracts in *MGSS*, 25, 747–866, ed. O. Holder-Egger).

Other lands: Helmold of Bosau, *Chronica Slavorum*, ed. B. Schmeidler (ed. tertia), *MGSS rer. Germ.*, 32 (Hanover 1937); *Chronica Adefonsi Imperatoris* (to 1147), H. Flórez, *España Sagrada*, 21, 320–409, *RepFont*, I, 254; William of Tyre, *Historia rerum in partibus transmarinis gestarum*, *RecHistCrois*, *HistOcc*, 1 (*PL* 201); Saxo Grammaticus, *Gesta Danorum*, ed. J. Olrik, H. Raeder, *et al.*, 2 vols. (Copenhagen 1931–57); John, prior Haugustaldensis ecclesiae, *Historia de regibus Anglorum et Danorum*, ed. T. Arnold, *Symeonis monachi opera*, 2, *Rolls Series*, 75 (London 1885), *MGSS*, 27, 14–16; *Historia Compostellana*, ed. H. Flórez, *España Sagrada*, 20 (*PL*, 170, 889–1236), translated into Spanish by Manuel Suárez, with notes and introduction by José Campelo (Santiago de Compostela 1950).

General Literature

Historia Mundi, VI; *The Cambridge Medieval History*, V; L. Halphen; H. Pirenne, G. Cohen, and H. Focillon (see Volume III, 479, Gen. Bibliog., II, 1, a). A. Cartellieri, *Der Vorrang des Papsttums zur Zeit der Kreuzzüge 1095–1150* (Munich and Berlin 1941); *Gebhardt-Grundmann*, I; O. Brandt, A. O. Meyer, and L. Just, *Handbuch der deutschen Geschichte*, I; P. Rassow, *Deutsche Geschichte im Überblick; Giesebrecht*, IV (2d ed. 1877) (Gen. Bibliog., II, 2); K. Hampe and F. Baethgen, *Deutsche Kaisergeschichte in der Zeit der Salier und Staufer* (Heidelberg, 11th ed. 1963); F. Heer, *Aufgang Europas*, 2 vols. (Vienna and Zurich 1949); *idem, Die Tragödie des Heiligen Reiches*, 2 vols. (Stuttgart

1952); W. von den Steinen, *Der Kosmos des Mittelalters. Von Karl dem Grossen zu Bernhard von Clairvaux* (Munich 1959); R. Folz, *L'idée d'empire en Occident du Ve au XIVe siècle* (Paris 1953); E. E. Stengel, *Abhandlungen und Untersuchungen zur Geschichte des Kaisergedankens im Mittelalter* (Cologne 1965); F. L. Ganshof, *Le moyen âge. Histoire des relations internationales*, I, ed. P. Renouvin (Paris, 2d ed. 1958); E. Jordan, *L'Allemagne et l'Italie aux XIIe et XIIIe siècles*, G. Glotz, *Histoire du moyen âge*, VI, 1 (Gen. Bibliog. II, 1, a) (Paris 1939). A. L. Poole, *From Domesday Book to Magna Carta 1087–1216* (Oxford, 2d ed. 1955, reprinted 1964); *idem, Medieval England*, 2 vols. (Oxford, 2d ed. 1960); D. M. Stenton, *English Society in the Early Middle Ages* (1066–1307) (Harmondsworth, 4th ed. 1965); G. Barraclough, *The Medieval Empire, Idea and Reality* (Historical Association, Series G, 17) (London 1960); H. W. C. Davis, *England under the Normans and Angevins* (London, 13th ed. 1961); A. Luchaire, *Les premiers Capétiens (987–1137)* (Paris 1901); *idem, Louis VII-Philippe Auguste-Louis VIII (1137–1226)* (Paris 1902); *Lavisse*, II, 2, III, 1; J. Le Goff, *La civilisation de l'Occident mediéval* (Paris 1964); *Storia politica d'Italia*, dir. da A. Solmi, IV (see Volume III, 480, Gen. Bibliog., II, 2); R. Soldevilla, *Historia de España* (see Volume III, 481, Gen. Bibliog., II, 2); P. Peres, *Historia de Portugal*, 2 vols. (Barcelos 1928 f.) (see Volume III, 481, Gen. Bibliog., II, 2). *Fliche-Martin*, IX, 1; R. García Villoslada, *Edad media 800–1303* (Madrid, 2d. ed. 1958); *Hauck*, IV (5th ed. 1925); R. W. Southern, *The Medieval Church* (Harmondsworth 1966); *The English Church and* the *Papacy*, ed. C. W. Lawrence (London 1965). For further literature on the Church History of individual lands see Gen. Bibliog., II, 4. J. Haller, *Das Papsttum, Idee und Wirklichkeit*, III, ed. H. Dannenbauer (Esslingen, 3d ed. 1962); *Seppelt*, III: *Die Vormachtstellung des Papsttums von der Mitte des 11. Jahrhunderts bis zu Cölestin V.* (Munich 1956); K. Bierbach, *Kurie und Nationalstaaten im früheren Mittelalter (1032–1245)* (Dresden 1938); R. Foreville, *Latran I, II, III et Latran IV, Histoire des conciles œcuméniques*, 6 (Paris 1965). Further literature in the individual chapters.

1. *Honorius II, The Schism of 1130, and The Second Lateran Council*

Sources

For Honorius II: *PL*, 166, 1217–1320 (letters); *Jaffé*, I, 2d ed., nos. 823–39, II, 755; *Duchesne LP*, II, 327 f., 379, III, 136 f., 170 f., *LPM*, 203–17 (Pandulf's *Vita* from the *Liber Pontificalis Dertusensis); Watterich*, II, 157–73; *Hefele-Leclercq*, V, 645–75. For Innocent II: *PL*, 179, 21–674 (letters); Jaffé, I, 2d ed., nos. 840–911; *Duchesne LP*, II, 379–85, 449, III, 138; *Watterich*, II, 174–275. For Anacletus II: *PL*, 179, 687–732; *Jaffé*, I, 2d ed., nos. 911–19; *Duchesne LP*, II, 319, 328, 379 f., 382 f.; Arnulf of Lisieux, *Tractatus de schismate Petri Leonis orto post Honorii papae decessum*, L. d'Achéry, *Spicilegium*, I, 2d ed., 152 ff., *PL*, 201, 173–194; *Historia Compostellana, España Sagrada*, XX, 513–17.

Literature

G. Tellenbach, "Der Sturz des Abtes Pontius von Cluny und seine geschichtliche Bedeutung," *QFIAB*, 42/43 (1963), 13–55; L. M. Smith, *Cluny in the Eleventh and Twelfth Centuries* (London 1930); J. Leclercq, *La vie de Pierre le Vénérable* (Paris 1946); A. Wilmart, "Deux pièces relatives à l'abdication de Pons abbé de Cluny en 1122," *RBén*, 44 (1932), 351–53; H. V. White, "Pontius of Cluny, the Curia Romana and the End of Gregorianism in Rome," *Church History*, 27 (1958), 195–219; U. Berlière, "Le cardinal Matthieu d'Albano," *RBén*, 18 (1901), 113–40, 280–303.

U. Balzani, *Italia, papato e impero nella prima metà del secolo XII (1124–1167)* (Messina 1930); *JbbDG:* W. Bernhardi, *Lothar von Supplinburg* (Leipzig 1879); *idem, Konrad III.* (Leipzig 1883); J. Bachmann, *Die päpstlichen Legaten in Deutschland und Skandinavien (1125–1159)* (Berlin 1913); W. Janssen, *Die päpstlichen Legaten vom Schisma Anaklets II. bis zum Tode Coelestins III.*, Kölner historische Abhandlungen, 6 (Cologne 1961).

The Schism of 1130: R. Zoepffel, "Die Doppelwahl des Jahres 1130" (appendix to his *Die Papstwahlen vom 11. bis zum 14. Jahrhundert* [Göttingen 1871]); E. Mühlbacher, *Die streitige Papstwahl des Jahres 1130* (Innsbruck 1876, reprinted *ibid.* 1966); H. W. Klewitz, "Das Ende des Reformpapsttums," *DA*, 3 (1939), 372–412 (now also H. W. Klewitz, *Reformpapsttum und Kardinalkolleg* [Darmstadt 1957], 209–59); P. F. Palumbo, "Lo scisma del MCXXX, i precedenti, la vicenda Romana e le ripercussioni europee della lotta tra Anacleto ed Innocenzo II col regesto degli'atti di Anacleto II," *Miscellanea della Reale Deputazione di Storia Patria* (Rome 1942); *idem,* "La cancelleria di Anacleto II," *Scritti di paleografia e diplomatica in onore di V. Federici* (Florence 1944), 79 ff. (now also: *Studi Salentini*, 17 [1964], 5–52); H. Bloch, "The Schism of Anacletus and the Glanfeuil Forgeries of Peter the Deacon," *Tr*, 8 (1952), 159–264; F. J. Schmale, "Die Bemühungen Innocenz' II. um seine Anerkennung in Deutschland," *ZKG*, 65 (1954), 240–65; *idem, Studien zum Schisma des Jahres 1130, Forschungen zur kirchlichen Rechtsgeschichte und zum Kirchenrecht*, 3 (Cologne and Graz 1961); *idem,* "Papsttum und Kurie zwischen Gregor VII. und Innocenz II.," *HZ*, 193 (1961), 265–85; P. F. Palumbo, "Nuovi studi (1942–1962) sullo scisma di Anacleto II," *BIStIAM*, 75 (1963), 71–103.

The Normans: F. Chalandon, *Histoire de la domination normande en Italie et en Sicile*, 2 vols. (Paris 1907, reprinted New York 1960); G. Pepe, *I normanni in Italia meridionale (1060–1194)*, ed. G. Musca (Bari 1964); D. Clementi, "Alexandri Telesini 'Ystoria serenissimi Rogerii primi regis Sicilie,' Lib. IV, 6–10 (Twelfth Century Political Propaganda)," *BIStIAM*, 77 (1965), 105–26; J. R. Ménager, "L'institution monarchique dans les états normands d'Italie," *CCivMéd*, 2 (1959), 303–31, 445–68 (important); J. Béraud Villars, *Les Normands en Méditerranée* (Paris 1951); E. Caspar, *Roger II (1101–1154) und die Gründung der normannisch-sicilischen Monarchie* (Innsbruck 1904, reprinted Darmstadt 1963); P. F. Kehr, "Belehnungen der Normannenfürsten durch die Päpste (1059–1192)," *SAB*, 1934, 1; W. Holtzmann, *Il regno di Ruggero II e gli inizi di un sistema di stati europei, Atti del Convegno internazionale di Studi Ruggeriani* (Palermo 1955); J. Déer, "Der Anspruch der Herrscher des 12. Jahrhunderts auf die apostolische Legation," *AHPont*, 2 (1964), 115–86; W. Holtzmann, "Papsttum, Normannen und die griechische Kirche," *Miscellanea Bibl. Herzianae* (Munich 1961), 68–76; P. Andrieu-Guitrancourt, *Histoire de l'empire normand et de sa civilisation* (Paris 1952); A. de Stefano, *La cultura in Sicilia nel periodo normanno* (Bologna, 2d ed. 1954); L. T. White, *Latin Monasticism in Norman Sicily* (Cambridge, Mass. 1938); L. R. Ménager, "Les fondations monastiques de Robert Guiscard, duc de Pouille et de Calabre," *QFIAB*, 39 (1959), 1–116; *idem,* "La 'byzantinisation' religieuse de l'Italie méridionale et la pratique monastique des Normands d'Italie," *RHE*, 53 (1958), 747–74, 54 (1959), 5–40; H. Niese, *Die Gesetzgebung der normannischen Dynastie im regnum Siciliae* (Halle 1910); E. Pontieri, *Tra i normanni nell'Italia meridionale* (Naples, 2d ed. 1964). *Roger II: Atti del Convegno internazionale di Studi Ruggeriani*, 2 vols. (Palermo 1955); H. Wieruszowski, "Roger II of Sicily, Rex Tyrannus, in Twelfth-Century Political Thought," *Speculum*, 38 (1963), 46–78; R. Elze, "Zum Königtum Rogers II. von Sizilien," *Festschrift P. E. Schramm*, I (Wiesbaden 1964), 102–16; W. Holtzmann, "Maximilla regina, soror Rogeri regis," *DA*, 19 (1963), 149–57.

Lateran II: Latran I, II, III, et Latran IV, Histoire des conciles œcuméniques, 6 (Paris 1965); R. L. Poole, "The English Bishops at the Lateran Council of 1138," *EHR*, 38 (1923), 61–63; C. Leonardi, "Per la tradizione dei concili di Ardara, Lateranensi I–II e Tolosa," *BIStIAM*, 75 (1963), 57–70.

2. *The Reform Orders of the Twelfth Century and Bernard of Clairvaux*

Cistercians

SOURCES

J. Laurent, *Cartulaires de l'abbaye de Molesme,* I (Paris 1907); *Vita Roberti,* ed. K. Spahr, *Das Leben des heiligen Robert von Molesme* (Fribourg 1944); J. Marlier, *Chartes et documents concernant l'abbaye de Cîteaux (1098–1182)* (Rome 1961); J. Turk, *Cistercii statuta antiquissima* (Rome 1949); J. Wacquet, *Recueil des chartes de l'abbaye de Clairvaux* (Troyes 1950); J. B. Van Damme, *Documenta pro Cisterciensis Ordinis historiae ac iuris studio* (Westmalle 1959); "Exordium Cistercii nach Ms. 1207 von Ste-Geneviève-Paris," ed. J. A. Lefèvre, *CollOCR,* 16 (1954), 96–104; "Exordium parvum," ed. C. Noschitzka, *AnOCist,* 6 (1950), 6–22; *Nomasticon Cisterciense seu antiquiores Ordinis Cisterciensis constitutiones,* ed. H. Séjalon (Solesmes, 2d ed. 1892); *Statuta capitulorum generalium Ordinis Cisterciensis 1116/1786,* 8 vols., ed. J. M. Canivez (Louvain 1933–41); C. de Visch, *Bibliotheca Scriptorum Ordinis Cist.* (Cologne, 2d ed. 1656); M. A. Dimier, *Recueil de plans d'églises cisterciennes,* 2 vols. (Paris 1949); M. Aubert, *L'architecture cistercienne en France* (Paris 1955); *Menologium Cisterciense* (Westmale 1952); C. H. Talbot, "A Cistercian Commentary on the Benedictine Rule," *Analecta monastica,* V, *Studia Anselmiana,* 43 (Rome 1958), 101–58.

LITERATURE

L. J. Lekai, *Les moines blancs* (Paris 1957); J. B. Mahn, *L'ordre cistercien et son gouvernement des origines au milieu du XIII° siècle* (Paris, 2d ed. 1951); G. Müller, *Vom Cistercienserorden* (Bregenz 1927); G. Schreiber, "Studien zur Exemptionsgeschichte der Zisterzienser," *ZSavRGkan,* 4 (1914), 74–116; old, but still indispensable is F. Winter, *Die Cistercienser des nordöstlichen Deutschland,* 3 vols. (Gotha 1868–71); M. Gloning, "Verzeichnis der deutschen Cistercienser-Abteien und -Priorate", *SM,* 36 (1915), 1–42; R. Ohle, *Die Bedeutung der Zisterzienser für die Besiedelung der Mark Brandenburg* (Prenzlau 1922, polemical); J. Eicheler, *Die Kongregationen des Zisterzienserordens* (diss., Fribourg 1931); J Rambaud-Buhot, "L'Abbaye normande de Savigny, chef d'Ordre et fille de Cîteaux," *MA* (1936), 1–19, 249–72; A. A. King, *Cîteaux and Her Elder Daughters* (London 1954); L. Bouyer, *La spiritualité de Cîteaux* (Paris 1955). On the origin of the *Carta Caritatis:* D. Knowles, "The Primitive Cistercian Documents," *Great Historical Enterprises. Problems in Monastic History* (London 1963), 197–224, with a report on the studies of J. Turk and J. A. Lefèvre (to 1956) and the research continued by J. B. Van Damme, "Formation de la Constitution Cistercienne. Esquisse historique," *StudMon,* 4 (1962), 111–37 (completed in July 1961); J. M. Canivez, "L'Abbaye de Cîteaux," *DHGE,* 12 (1953), 852–74; *idem,* "L'Ordre de Cîteaux," *DHGE,* 12 (1953), 874–997 (sources, literature, and maps); C. Bock, *Les codifications du droit cistercien* (Westmalle 1955); K. Spahr, "Die Zisterzienser," *LThK,* X (2d ed. 1965), 1382–87; annual bibliography in *CollOCR* (Westmalle), *AnOCist* (Rome), *Cist* (Mehrerau and Bregenz), *Cîteaux in de Nederlanden* (Westmalle), *Cistercium* (Palencia), *RBén* (Bulletin d'histoire bénédictine) (Maredsous); L. Janauschek, *Originum Cisterciensium,* I (Vienna 1877); P. Zakar, "Die Anfänge des Zisterzienserordens," *AnOCist,* 20 (1964), 103–38; J. B. Van Damme in *AnOCist,* 21 (1965), 128–37 (criticism and supplement); B. Schneider, "Cîteaux und die benediktinische Tradition," *AnOCist,* 16 (1960), 160–254, 17 (1961), 73–114; S. Roisin, "L'efflorescence cistercienne et le courant féminin de piété au XIII° siècle," *RHE,* 39 (1943), 342–78. On devotion to Mary: *Maria,* II, 581–624, and *LM,* 710–20. On liturgy: S. Marosszeki, "Les origines du chant cistercien," *AnOCist,* 8 (1952), 1–179; M. Cocheril, "Le 'Tonale Sancti Bernardi' et la définition du 'ton,'" *Cîteaux,*

13 (1962), 35–66. On the pursuit of study: A. Dimier, "Les premiers Cisterciens étaient-ils ennemis des études?" *Los Monjes y los Estudios* (Poblet 1963), 119–46. On economic history: H. Wiswe, "Grangien niedersächsischer Zisterzienserklöster," *Braunschweig, Jb.,* 34 (1953), 5–134 (bibliog.); R. A. Donkin, "The Cistercian Grange in England in the 12th and 13th Centuries, with Special Reference to Yorkshire," *StudMon,* 6 (1964), 95–144 (maps); F. Van Der Meer, *Atlas de l'ordre cistercien* (Haarlem 1965).

Canons Regular

SOURCES

E. Amort, *Vetus disciplina canonicorum regularium et saecularium* (Venice 1747); *Institutio canonicorum Aquisgranensis,* ed. A. Werminghoff, *MGLL,* s. III, *Concilia,* 3 *(Concilia aevi karolini,* pars I) (Hanover 1906), 307–421; Arno of Reichersberg, *Scutum canonicorum, PL,* 194, 1493–1528; A. Carrier de Belleuse, *Coutumier du XI*ᵉ *siècle de l'Ordre de Saint-Ruf en usage à la cathédrale de Maguelone, Études et documents sur l'Ordre de Saint-Ruf,* 8 (Sherbroke 1950); C. Dereine, "Saint-Ruf et ses coutumes au XI*ᵉ* et XII*ᵉ* siècle," *RBén,* 59 (1949), 161–82; *Die Chronik des Klosters Petershausen,* ed. and trans. O. Feger, *Casus Monasterii Petrishusensis, Schwäbische Chroniken der Stauferzeit,* 3 (Lindau and Constance 1956); A. Hänggi, *Der Rheinauer Liber Ordinarius, Spicilegium Friburgense. Texte der Geschichte des kirchlichen Lebens,* 1 (Fribourg 1957); C. Hoffmann, "L'abbaye de Marbach et le nécrologe de 1241," *Bulletin de la société pour la conservation des monuments historiques d'Alsace – Mitteilungen der Gesellschaft für Erhaltung der geschichtlichen Denkmäler im Elsass,* 2d series, 20 (Strasbourg 1902), 67–230 (list of confreres and obituary).

LITERATURE

F. Bonnard, *Histoire de l'abbaye royale et de l'ordre des chanoines réguliers de Saint-Victor de Paris,* 2 vols. (Paris 1907); J. Siegwart, *Die Chorherren- und Chorfrauengemeinschaften in der deutschen Schweiz vom 6. Jahrhundert bis 1160. Mit einem Überblick über die deutsche Kanonikerreform des 10. und 11. Jahrhunderts, Studia Friburgensia,* new series, 30 (Fribourg 1962), with ample bibliographical citations for the entire reform movement; important are the results of the studies of C. Dereine, summarized up to 1953 in his article "Chanoines," *DHGE,* 12 (1953), 353–405; A. Smith, "Chanoines réguliers," *DSAM,* 2 (1953), 463–77; J. C. Dickinson, *The Origins of the Austin Canons and their Introduction into England* (London 1950); C. Dereine, *Les chanoines réguliers au diocèse de Liège avant Saint Norbert* (Brussels 1952); F. A. Goehlinger, *Histoire de l'Abbaye de Marbach* (Colmar 1954); T. Humpert, *Chorherrenstift, Pfarrei und Kirche St. Stephan in Konstanz* (Constance 1957); J. Mois, *Das Stift Rottenbuch in der Kirchenreform des XI. bis XII. Jahrhunderts. Ein Beitrag zur Ordensgeschichte der Augustinerchorherren, Beiträge zur altbayerischen Kirchengeschichte,* 3d series, 19 (Munich 1953); C. Giroud, *L'ordre des chanoines réguliers de Saint-Augustin et ses diverses formes de régime interne* (Martigny 1961).

Premonstratensians

J. Le Paige, *Bibliotheca Ordinis Praem.* (Paris 1633); C. L. Hugo, *S. Ordinis Praemonstratensis annales,* 2 vols. (Nancy 1734–36); P. Winter, *Die Prämonstratenser des 12. Jahrhunderts und ihre Bedeutung für das nordöstliche Deutschland* (Berlin 1865); L. A. Goovaerts, *Dictionnaire bio-bibliographique des écrivains, artistes et savants de l'Ordre de Prémontré,* 4 vols. (Brussels 1900–09); G. Schreiber, *Kurie und Kloster,* 2 vols. (Stuttgart 1910, reprinted Amsterdam 1965); R. van Waefelghem, *Les premiers statuts de Prémontré* (Louvain and Brussels 1913); A. Zak, *Der Prämonstratenserorden in den alten deutschen Metropolen* (Vienna 1919); U. Berlière, *Les monastères doubles aux XIIe et XIIIe siècles, Mémoires de l'Académie Royale de Belgique*, 18 (Brussels 1923); F. Petit, *L'ordre de Prémontré* (Paris 1927); H. Heijman, *Untersuchungen über die Prämonstratensergewohnheiten* (Tongerloo 1928); B. Grassl, *Der Prämonstratenserorden* (Tongerloo 1934); G. Schreiber, "Prämonstratensische Frömmigkeit," *ZKTh*, 64 (1940), 181–201; *idem*, "Prämonstratenserkultur des 12. Jahrhunderts," *APraem*, 16 (1940), 41–108, 17 (1941), 5–33; *idem*, "Gregor VII., Cluny, Cîteaux, Prémontré zu Eigenkirche, Parochie und Seelsorge," *Gemeinschaften des Mittelalters* (Münster 1948), 283–370; P. Lefèvre, *Les statuts de Prémontré* (Louvain 1946); F. Petit, *La spiritualité de l'ordre de Prémontré aux XIIe et XIIIe siècles* (Paris 1947); C. Dereine, "Les origines de Prémontré," *RHE*, 42 (1947), 352–78; *idem*, "Le premier ordo de Prémontré," *RBén*, 58 (1948), 84–92; H. M. Colvin, *The White Canons in England* (Oxford 1951); *Monasticon Praemonstratense*, ed. N. Backmund, 3 vols. (Straubing 1949–56; rich bibliography); annual bibliography in *Analecta Praemonstratensia* (Tongerloo; from 1953: Averbode); R. van Waefelghem, *Répertoire des sources imprimées et manuscrites relatives à l'histoire et à la liturgie des monastères de l'ordre de Prémontré* (Brussels 1930); A. Huber, *Die Prämonstratenser* (Baden-Baden 1955); P. Lefèvre, *La liturgie de Prémontré* (Louvain 1957); N. Backmund, "Die Prämonstratenser," *LThK*, VIII (2d ed. 1963), 688–94; H. L. Martin, *Initia historico-iuridica Capituli Generalis Ordinis Praemonstratensis* (diss., Rome 1964).

Bernard of Clairvaux

BIBLIOGRAPHY

L. Janauschek, *Bibliographia Bernardina* (to 1890), *Xenia Bernardina*, 4 (Vienna 1891, reprinted Hildesheim 1959); M. Bernards, "Der Stand der Bernhardforschung" (to 1955), *Bernhard von Clairvaux. Mönch und Mystiker*. Internationaler Bernhardkongress Mainz 1953, *Veröffentlichungen des Instituts für europäische Geschichte*, 6 (Wiesbaden 1955), 3–43; J. de la Croix Bouton, *Bibliographie Bernardine (1891–1957), Commission d'histoire de l'ordre de Cîteaux*, 5 (Paris 1958); J. Leclercq, the chief representative of the studies stimulated by the 1953 jubilee of Bernard's death, gives a critical report on the results in "Les études bernardines en 1963," *Bulletin de la Société internationale pour l'étude de la philosophie médiévale*, 5 (1963), 121–38.

WORKS

Sancti Bernardi Opera, ed. J. Leclercq, C. H. Talbot, and H. M. Rochais: *Sermones super Cantica Canticorum*, I (Rome 1957), II (Rome 1958), Treatises, III (Rome 1963). All other works, especially the letters, are in *PL: Sermones, PL*, 183 and 184, Letters, *PL*, 182, Parables and Sentences, *PL*, 183 and 184. Other works, hitherto unprinted, have been edited by J. Leclercq, P. Séjourné, G. Hüffer, A. Wilmart, C. H. Talbot, *et al.; cf.* the list in D. Farkasfalvy, "L'inspiration de l'Écriture Sainte dans la théologie de Saint Bernard," *Studia Anselmiana*, 53 (Rome 1964), 18 f. For Bernard's correspondence: D. Van den Eynde, "La correspondance de Saint Bernard de 1115 à 1126," *Antonianum*, 41 (1966), 189–259 (with further bibliography). Bernard's attitude to Peter Abelard: "Capitula haeresum Petri Abaelardi," *PL*, 182, 1049–54, "De erroribus Abaelardi," *PL*, 182, 1053–72, "Sermo de conversione ad clericos," *PL*, 182, 833–56; *Briefe des heiligen Bernhard von Clairvaux*, trans. H. Michel (Mainz 1928); *Schriften des heiligen Bernhard von Clairvaux*, 6 vols., trans. A.

Wolters and H. Michel (Wittlich 1935–38); B. Scott James, *The Letters of St. Bernard of Clairvaux* (London 1953); H. M. Rochais, "Inédits bernardins dans le manuscrit Harvard 185," *Studia Anselmiana*, 50 (n. d.), 53–175; *idem*, "Enquête sur les sermons divers et les sentences de saint Bernard," *AnOCist*, 18 (1962). A glance at the several aspects of research is provided by the Congress reports and the jubilee writings of 1953 (J. de la Croix Bouton, *Bibliographie Bernardine*, 709–75), especially by the Mainz collection (Wiesbaden 1955), cited *supra*; the *Mélanges Saint Bernard* (Congress of Dijon) (Dijon 1954); *San Bernardo* (Congress of Milan) (Milan 1954); *Saint Bernard Théologien* (Second Congress of Dijon), *AnOCist*, 9 (Rome 1953), fascicles 3–4; the important collection *Bernard de Clairvaux, Commission d'histoire de l'Ordre de Cîteaux*, 3 (Paris 1953); the commemorative publication of the Dutch Cistercians, *Sint Bernardus van Clairvaux* (Achel and Rotterdam 1953); and the commemorative issue of the *Collectanea OCistReform, 1953* (Westmalle); the *Festschrift der österreichischen Cistercienserkongregation, Österreichische Beiträge zur Geschichte des Cistercienserordens* (Vienna 1953), *cf.* F. Grass, "Das Bernhardjubiläum 1953 im Spiegel des Schrifttums," *ZSavRGkan*, 41 (1955), 415–21; J. Leclercq, *Études sur Saint Bernard et le texte de ses écrits, AnOCist*, 9 (Rome 1953), fascicles 1–2; K. Spahr, "Festgabe und Festgaben zum Bernhardsjubiläum," *Cist*, 61 (1954), 43–52, 108–15, 62 (1955), 35–48, 84–94; J. Leclercq, *Recueil d'études sur saint Bernard et ses écrits* (Rome 1962); J. Leclercq, "Aspects littéraires de l'œuvre de saint Bernard," *CCivMéd*, 1 (1958), 435–50; D. Van den Eynde, "Les débuts littéraires de Saint Bernard," *AnOCist*, 19 (1963), 189–98; J. Leclercq, "Nouveaux aspects littéraires de l'œuvre de Saint Bernard," *CCivMéd*, 8 (1965), 299–326; *idem*, "L'art de la composition dans les traités de Saint Bernard," *RBén*, 76 (1966), 87–115.

BIOGRAPHY

BHL, 1207–38; the oldest piece is *Fragmenta Gaufridi de Vita et Miraculis S. Bernardi*, ed. R. Lechat, *AnBoll*, 50 (1932), 83–122; the first important source is the *Vita Prima*, by William of Saint-Thierry, Arnold of Bonnevale, and Godfrey of Auxerre, in *PL*, 185, 225–466; see A. H. Bredero, "Études sur la 'Vita prima' de S. Bernard," *AnOCist*, 17 (1961), 3–72, 215–60, 18 (1962), 3–59, as the basis for a critical edition of the oldest biographies; P. Sinz, *Das Leben des heiligen Bernhard von Clairvaux ("Vita Prima")*, ed. and trans. (Düsseldorf 1962); the classic biography by E. Vacandard, 2 vols. (Paris, 4th ed. 1910), is still important for chronology and routes of journeys, even though in some particulars it is outdated. For the older biographies, by A. Neander and S. M. Deutsch, G. Hofmeister, A. Luchaire, A. K. Luddy, and others, see M. Bernards *(supra)*, 24, footnote 29. There are many popular accounts, by R. Linhardt, H. Höver, G. Goyau, P. Miterre, A. Martin, J. Schuck, and fictional romances, such as those by J. Weingärtner, K. Vogt, J. Schenk, E. Schmidt-Pauli, and others. More important for the scholar are: É. Gilson, *La théologie mystique de Saint Bernard* (Paris 1932); W. W. Williams, *S. Bernard of Clairvaux, Publications of the University of Manchester*, Historical Series, 69 (Manchester, 2d ed. 1953); J. Calmette and H. David, *S. Bernard, Les grandes études historiques* (Paris 1953); A. Dimier, *Saint Bernard, "Pêcheur de Dieu"* (Paris 1953); A. Dimier, "C'est en 1174, et non en 1175, que Saint Bernard fut canonisé," *Cîteaux*, 12 (1961), 79–85; I. Vallery-Radot, *Bernard de Fontaines, abbé de Clairvaux, ou les noces de la grâce et de la nature. Les années de formation (1090–1130)* (Paris 1963); J. Leclercq, "Saint Bernard, le dernier des Pères," *La spiritualité du moyen âge* (Paris 1961), 238–49; *idem, Saint Bernard mystique* (Paris and Bruges 1948); E. Bertola, *S. Bernardo e la teologia speculativa* (Padua 1959); M. Dumontier, *Saint Bernard et la Bible* (Bruges and Paris 1953); P. Delhaye, *Le problème de la conscience morale chez Saint Bernard* (Namur 1957); A. van den Bosch, *La personne du Christ dans l'œuvre de Saint Bernard* (Rome 1957); R. Fritegotta, "De vocatione christiana

S. Bernardi doctrina," *Studia Antoniana,* 15 (Rome 1961); A. H. Bredero, "Studien zu den Kreuzzugsbriefen Bernhards von Clairvaux und seine Reise nach Deutschland im Jahre 1142," *MIÖG,* 66 (1958), 331–43; R. Kereszty, "Die Weisheit in der mystischen Erfahrung beim heiligen Bernhard von Clairvaux," *Cîteaux,* 16 (1963), 6–24, 105–34, 185–201; the work, cited *supra,* by D. Farkasfalvy (Rome 1964); P. Zerbi, "Bernardo di Chiaravalle," *Bibliotheca sanctorum,* 3 (Rome 1963), 1–37; B. Jacqueline, *Papauté et Épiscopat selon Saint Bernard de Clairvaux* (Paris 1963); K. Knotzinger, "Das Amt des Bischofs nach Bernhard von Clairvaux. Ein Traditionsbeitrag," *Scholastik,* 38 (1963), 519–35; L. Grill, "Bernhard von Clairvaux und die Ostkirche," *AnOCist,* 19 (1963), 165–88; R. Bultot, *S. Bernard, la Somme, le Roi et le double idéal antique de la magnanimité* (Westmalle 1964). *Bernard and Gilbert de la Porrée:* N. M. Häring, "Dialogus Ratii et Everardi," *MS,* 15 (1953), 243–89; *idem,* "Everard von Ypern als Autor des gen. Dialogs," *MS,* 17 (1955), 143–72; S. Gammersbach, *Gilbert von Poitiers und seine Prozesse im Urteil der Zeitgenossen* (Cologne and Graz 1959).

Bernard and Peter Abelard: A. M. Landgraf, "Probleme um den heiligen Bernhard von Clairvaux," *Cist,* 61 (1954), 1–16; A. Borst, "Abälard und Bernhard," *HZ,* 186 (1958), 497–526; R. Klibansky, "Peter Abailard and Bernard of Clairvaux. A Letter by Abailard," *MRS,* 5 (1961), 1–27; J. R. Sommerfeldt, "Abelard and Bernard of Clairvaux," *Papers of the Michigan Academy of Science, Arts and Letters,* 46 (1961), 493–501; P. Zerbi, "I rapporti di san Bernardo di Chiaravalle con i vescovi e le diocesi d'Italia," *Vescovi e diocesi in Italia nel medioevo* (Padua 1964), 219–314; K. H. Esser, "Der Kirchenbau des heiligen Bernhard von Clairvaux," *AMrhKG,* 5 (1953), 195–222.

3. *The Papacy and the Western Kings in the Age of Saint Bernard*

Sources

Mansi, XXI, 540–785; *Hefele-Leclercq,* V, 747–847; *Duchesne LP,* II and III. For Celestine II: *Watterich,* II, 276–78; *Duchesne LP,* II, 385, 449, III, 138; *Jaffé,* II, 2d ed., 1–7, 716, 758; *PL,* 179, 765–822. For Lucius II: *Watterich,* II, 278–81; *Duchesne LP,* II, 385 f., 449, III, 138; *Jaffé,* II, 2d ed., 7–9, 717, 758; *PL,* 179, 819–938. For Eugene III: *Watterich,* II, 281–321; *Duchesne LP,* II, 386 f., 449, III, 138 f., *Jaffé,* II, 2d ed., 20–89; supplements in H. Gleber (see *infra*), 191–208; John of Salisbury, *Historia pontificalis,* ed. R. L. Poole (1927), English translation by M. Chibnall (London 1956); Bernard of Clairvaux, *De consideratione,* ed. J. Leclercq and H. M. Rochais, *Sancti Bernardi Opera Omnia,* III (Rome 1963), 379–493; and the narrative sources listed in the bibliography for this section *(supra)*. For Anastasius IV: *Watterich,* II, 321 f.; *Duchesne LP,* II, 388, 449, III, 139; *Jaffé,* II, 2d ed., 89–102.

Literature

In addition to the works already listed for Chapter 1: J. Bachmann, *Die päpstlichen Legaten in Deutschland und Skandinavien (1125–59), HStud,* 115 (Berlin 1913); G. Säbekow, *Die päpstlichen Legationen nach Spanien und Portugal bis zum Ausgang des 12. Jahrhunderts* (diss., Berlin 1931); H. Tillmann, *Die päpstlichen Legaten in England bis zur Beendigung der Legation Gualas (1218)* (diss., Bonn 1926); L. Spätling, "Kardinal Guido und seine Legation in Böhmen-Mähren (1142–46)," *MIÖG,* 66 (1958), 306–30; R. Manselli, *Alberico, cardinale vescovo d'Ostia e la sua attività di legato pontificio, ADRomana,* 78 (1955); O. Kolsrud, *Kardinal-legaten Nicolaus av Albano i Norge 1152* (Oslo 1943–46); A. O. Johnsen, *Studier vedrørende kardinal Nicolaus Breakspears legasjon til Norden* (diss.,

Oslo 1945); A. Gwynn, "Papal Legates in Ireland during the Twelfth Century," *IER*, 63 (1941), 361–70.

H. Gleber, *Papst Eugen III. (1145–53) unter besonderer Berücksichtigung seiner politischen Tätigkeit* (Jena 1936); review of the preceding by E. Jordan in *RHE*, 33 (1937), 367–72, which supplies a more sober perspective; G. Del Guerra, N. Caturegli, and G. L. Bentivoglio, *Il beato Eugenio III* (Pisa 1954); the bibliography on Saint Bernard is given in that for Chapter 2; P. Rassow, *Honor Imperii* (Munich 1940); P. Brezzi, *Roma e l'impero medioevale* (Bologna 1947); P. Lamma, *Comneni e Staufer*, 2 vols. (Rome 1955–57); G. Edelsbrunner, *Arnold von Brescia. Untersuchungen über die weltliche Herrschaft der Kurie und die häretischen Bewegungen um die Mitte des 12. Jahrhunderts* (typed diss., Graz 1958). (More detailed bibliography on Arnold of Brescia *infra*, for Chapters 8 and 13.)

The Curia and England: A. L. Poole, *From Domesday Book to Magna Carta* (Oxford, 2d ed. 1964), 190–96; H. Böhmer, *Kirche und Staat in England und in der Normandie im 11. und 12. Jahrhundert* (to 1154) (Leipzig 1899; standard); Z. N. Brooke, *The English Church and the Papacy* (Cambridge 1931); D. Knowles, *The Monastic Order in England* (Cambridge, 2d ed. 1963); C. R. Cheney, *English Bishops' Chanceries (1100–1250)* (Manchester 1950); L. Voss, *Heinrich von Blois, Bischof von Winchester (1129–71)* (Berlin 1932).

The Curia and France: Lavisse, III/1, 1–11; E. R. Labande, "Pour une image véridique d'Aliénor d'Aquitaine," *Bulletin de la Société des Antiquaires de l'Ouest*, 4th series, II (1952), 175–234; M. Pacaut, *Louis VII et les élections épiscopales dans le royaume de France* (Paris 1958); C. Petit-Dutaillis, *La monarchie féodale en France et en Angleterre (X^e–XIIIe siècles)* (Paris 1933).

The Curia and Germany: Hauck, IV, 5th ed., 114–95; *Gebhardt-Grundmann*, I, 285–301; R. Holtzmann, "Der Kaiser als Marschall des Papstes," *SAB*, 1928; E. Eichmann, "Das Officium stratoris et strepae," *HZ*, 142 (1930), 16–40; R. Holtzmann, "Zum Strator- und Marschalldienst," *HZ*, 145 (1932), 301–50; G. Ladner, "I mosaici e gli affreschi ecclesiastico-politici nell'antico Palazzo Lateranense," *RAC*, 12 (1935), 265–92. On the situation in South Italy at the time of the Emperor Lothar's second Italian expedition: P. F. Kehr, *Italia pontificia*, 8 (1935), 40–43; *idem*, "Die Belehnungen der süditalienischen Normannenfürsten durch die Päpste," *SAB*, 1934; H. Zatschek, "Wibald von Stablo. Studien zur Geschichte der Reichskanzlei und Reichspolitik unter den älteren Staufern," *MIÖG*, suppl. vol. 10 (Vienna 1928), 237–92; W. Ohnsorge, "'Kaiser' Konrad III.," *MIÖG*, 46 (1932); F. Geldner, "Zur neueren Beurteilung König Konrads III.," *Monumentum Bamburgense. Festgabe für B. Kraft* (Munich 1955), 395–412; P. Acht, "Die Gesandtschaft König Konrads III. an Papst Eugen III. in Dijon," *HJ*, 74 (1955), 668–73.

The Curia and Spain: J. Vincke, *Staat und Kirche in Katalonien und Aragón* (Münster 1931); G. Säbekow (*supra*).

Eastward expansion: M. Bünding, *Das Imperium Christianum und die deutschen Ostkriege vom 10. bis zum 12. Jahrhundert*, HStud, 366 (Berlin 1940); H. Beumann, "Kreuzzugsgedanke und Ostpolitik im hohen Mittelalter," *HJ*, 72 (1953), 112–32; *Heidenmission und Kreuzzugsgedanke in der deutschen Ostpolitik des Mittelalters*, ed. H. Beumann (Darmstadt 1963).

4. *Elaboration of the Curia and Criticism of Church and Papacy*

SOURCES

M. Andrieu, *Le Pontifical Romain au moyen âge*, I: *Le Pontifical Romain du XIIe siècle*, SteT, 86 (Rome 1938); R. Elze, *Die Ordines für die Weihe und Krönung des Kaisers und der Kaiserin*, MGFont. iur., 9 (Hanover 1960); *Duchesne LP*, I–III; P. Fabre, L. Duchesne, and G. Mollat, *Le Liber Censuum de l'Église Romaine*, 3 vols.; Bernard of Clairvaux, *De* *consideratione libri quinque,* ed. J. Leclercq and H. M. Rochais, *Sancti Bernardi Opera Omnia,* III (Rome 1963), 379–493 (*PL,* 182, 727–808); *Sancti Bernardi Sermo de conversione ad clericos, PL,* 182, 833–56 (a more concise redaction of this sermon in J. Leclercq, "Deux sermons de S. Bernard selon une rédaction inédite," *Analecta monastica,* I [Rome 1948], 127–33); Gerhoh of Reichersberg: E. Sackur, *MGLiblit,* III, 131–525, supplies extracts from his works with a political content; *Gerhohi Praepositi Reichersbergensis Opera inedita, Tractatus et Libelli,* ed. D. and O. Van den Eynde and P. A. Rijmersdael (Rome 1955), 309–50 ("Opusculum ad Cardinales"; extract in Sackur, *MGLiblit,* III, 400–11); most of Gerhoh's works are accessible in *PL,* 193 and 194, while P. Classen (see *infra*), 407–44, lists new and supplementary editions; John of Salisbury, *Policraticus (Joannis Saresberiensis Episcopi Carnotensis Policratici sive de nugis curialium libri VIII),* ed. C. C. J. Webb, 2 vols. (Oxford 1909); *The Letters of John of Salisbury,* I (1153–61), ed. W. J. Millor, H. E. Butler, and C. N. L. Brooke, *Nelson's Medieval Texts* (London 1955); A. Frugoni, *Arnaldo da Brescia nelle fonti del secolo XII* (Rome 1954).

LITERATURE

For the elaboration of the Curia: B. Rusch, *Die Behörden und Hofbeamten der päpstlichen Kurie des 13. Jahrhunderts, Schriften der Albertusuniversität,* Arts Series, 3 (Königsberg and Berlin 1936); K. Jordan, "Die Entstehung der römischen Kurie, Ein Versuch," *ZSav RGkan,* 28 (1939), 97–152; *idem,* "Das Eindringen der Lehnsidee in das Rechtsleben der römischen Kurie," *AUF,* 12 (1932), 13–110; *idem,* "Zur päpstlichen Finanzgeschichte im 11. und 12. Jahrhundert," *QFIAB,* 25 (1933 f.), 61–104; J. Sydow, "Untersuchungen zur kurialen Verwaltungsgeschichte im Zeitalter des Reformpapsttums," *DA,* 11 (1954), 18–73; F. Salerno, "Problemi costituzionali nelle vicende storiche della Curia Romana," *Rev. it. Sc. Giur,* 10 (1959–62), 327–96; C. Bauer, "Die Epochen der Papstfinanz," *HZ,* 133 (1928), 457–504; R. Elze, "Die päpstliche Kapelle im 12. und 13. Jahrhundert," *ZSavRGkan,* 36 (1950), 145–204; E. Eichmann, *Die Kaiserkrönung im Abendland,* II (Würzburg 1942), 210–79 (Palatium Lateranense); for particular offices see the bibliography in *Feine RG,* 287–89.

For criticism of the Curia: P. Lehmann, *Die Parodie im Mittelalter* (Stuttgart, 2d ed. 1963), 25–68 (against the Roman Curia and the higher clergy); B. Jacqueline, *Papauté et Épiscopat selon Saint Bernard de Clairvaux* (Paris 1963); E. Meuthen, *Kirche und Heilsgeschichte bei Gerhoh von Reichersberg* (Leiden and Cologne 1959), 94–110 (Chapter 6, "Regnum und Sacerdotium: Die moralische Beurteilung der Reformträger"); P. Classen, *Gerhoh von Reichersberg. Eine Biographie* (Wiesbaden 1960), standard, 141–49 (Zion and Babel), 173–83 (against the innovations of this age), 215–33 (vestiges of Antichrist), and much else; C. C. J. Webb, *John of Salisbury* (London 1932); H. Liebeschütz, *Mediaeval Humanism in the Life and Writings of John of Salisbury* (London 1950); see also the introductions to the editions listed *supra; cf. Haller,* III, 104–15 (criticism and self-criticism).

5. *The Second Crusade and the Wars in Spain and the Slavic East*

SOURCES

The chief Latin source for the Second Crusade is Odo of Deuil, *La croisade de Louis VII Roi de France,* ed. H. Wacquet (Paris 1949); Suger of Saint-Denis, *Vie de Louis le Gros* (which includes also his history of Louis VII), ed. A. Moliner (Paris 1887); Suger's correspondence is found in his *Œuvres complètes,* ed. A. Lecoy de la Marche (Paris 1867); Otto of Freising, *Chronica sive Historia de duabus civitatibus,* ed. A. Hofmeister, *MGSS*

rer. Germ. (Hanover and Leipzig, 2d ed. 1912); *idem, Gesta Friderici I Imperatoris,* ed.
G. Waitz and B. von Simson (Hanover and Leipzig, 3d ed. 1912); Wibald of Stablo,
Epistolae, ed. P. Jaffé, *Bibl. rer. germ.,* I (Berlin 1864); Bernard of Clairvaux, *Epistolae,*
PL, 182, 67–716; William of Tyre, *Historia rerum in partibus transmarinis gestarum,* ed.
RecHistCrois, Hist. Occ., 1 (an edition is being prepared by R. B. C. Huygens and H. E.
Mayer), English trans. by E. A. Babcock and A. C. Krey, 2 vols. (New York 1943); Osbern,
De expugnatione Lyxbonensi, ed. with English trans. by C. W. David (New York 1933).
For William of Tyre: Cf. A. C. Krey, "William of Tyre. The Making of an Historian in
the Middle Ages," *Speculum,* 16 (1941), 149–66; *The Chronicle of Morea (Crusaders as*
Conquerors), ed. and trans. by H. E. Lurier (New York 1964); John of Salisbury, *Historia*
pontificalis, ed. M. Chibnall (London 1956; based on R. L. Poole's edition of 1927); Gerhoh
of Reichersberg, *Die investigatione Antichristi,* ed. E. Sackur, *MGLiblit,* III, 304–95
(extracts), complete edition by F. Scheibelberger, 2 vols. (Linz 1875); *The First and Second*
Crusades from an Anonymous Syriac Chronicle, ed. A. S. Tritton and H. A. R. Gibb, *JRAS,*
1933, 69–101, 273–305; *Chronicle* of Michael the Syrian, ed. J. B. Chabot, 4 vols. (Paris
1899–1924); John Konnamos, *Epitome historiarum,* ed. A. Meinecke (Bonn 1836; Migne,
Patrologia graeca, 133), extracts with Latin translation as *De secunda expeditione, RecHist*
Crois, Hist Grecs, 1; Nicetas Choniates, *Historia,* ed. I. Bekker (Bonn 1835; Migne, *Patro-*
logia graeca, 139), extracts with Latin translation as *De secunda tertiaque expeditionibus,*
RecHistCrois, HistGrecs, 1; the Arab, Syriac, and Armenian sources are listed and discussed
by V. G. Berry, "The Second Crusade," *A History of the Crusades,* ed. K. M. Setton, I
(Philadelphia 1955), 463, footnote.

Literature

H. E. Mayer, *Bibliographie der Kreuzzüge,* nos. 2015–61; B. Kugler, *Studien zur Ge-*
schichte des zweiten Kreuzzuges (Stuttgart 1866); *idem, Analekten zur Geschichte des*
zweiten Kreuzzuges (Tübingen 1878); *idem, Neue Analekten* (Tübingen 1883); G. Hüffner,
"Die Anfänge des zweiten Kreuzzugs," *HJ,* 8 (1887), 391–429; F. Chalandon, *Les Com-*
nènes: Jean II Comnène (1118–43) et Manuel I Comnène (1143–80) (Paris 1912); H. Co-
sack, "Konrads III. Entschluss zum Kreuzzug," *MIÖG,* 35 (1914), 278–96; P. Rassow, "Die
Kanzlei St. Bernhards von Clairvaux," *SM,* 34 (1913), 1–62, 201–42; E. Caspar, "Die
Kreuzzugsbullen Eugens III.," *NA,* 45 (1924), 285–300; J. L. La Monte, *Feudal Monarchy*
in the Latin Kingdom of Jerusalem (1100–1291) (Cambridge 1932); H. Gleber, *Eugen III.*
(Jena 1936); E. Pfeiffer, "Die Cistercienser und der zweite Kreuzzug," *Cist,* 47 (1935),
78–150; H. Conrad, "Gottesfrieden und Heersverfassung in der Zeit der Kreuzzüge,"
ZSavRGgerm, 61 (1941), 71–126; C. Cahen, *La Syrie du Nord à l'époque des croisades et*
la principauté d'Antioche (Paris 1940); E. Delaruelle, "L'idée de croisade chez Saint Bernard," *Mélanges de Saint Bernard* (Dijon 1953), 53–67; A. Seguin, "Bernard et la seconde
croisade," *Bernard de Clairvaux* (Paris 1953), 379–409; E. Willems, "Cîteaux et la seconde
croisade," *RHE,* 49 (1954), 116–51; P. Lamma, *Comneni e Staufer,* 2 vols. (Rome 1955–57);
V. G. Berry, "The Second Crusade," *A History of the Crusades,* ed. K. M. Setton, I (Philadelphia 1955), 463–512; S. Runciman, *A History of the Crusades,* 3 vols. (Cambridge
1951–54), II, 247–88; R. Grousset, *Histoire des croisades,* 3 vols. (Paris 1934–36), II, 225–70;
A. Waas, *Geschichte der Kreuzzüge,* 2 vols. (Freiburg im Breisgau 1956), I, 166–82; R. L.
Nicholson, *Jocelyn I, Prince of Edessa* (Urbana, Ill. 1954); H. E. Mayer, *Geschichte der*
Kreuzzüge (Stuttgart 1965), 96–108.
Crusades in Spain and the Slavic East: F. Kurth, "Der Anteil der niederdeutschen Kreuzfahrer an den Kämpfen der Portugiesen gegen die Mauren," *MIÖG,* Suppl. Volume 8 (1911),
133 ff.; H. A. R. Gibb, *English Crusaders in Portugal: Chapters in Anglo-Portuguese Re-*
lations, ed. E. Prestage (London 1935); G. Constable, "The Route of the Anglo-Flemish

Crusaders," *Speculum*, 28 (1953), 525 f.; M. Bünding, *Das Imperium christianum und die deutschen Ostkriege vom 10.–12. Jahrhundert, HStud,* 366 (Berlin 1940); H. Beumann (ed.), *Heidenmission und Kreuzzugsgedanke in der deutschen Ostpolitik des Mittelalters* (co-operative work) (Darmstadt 1963).

6. *Monastic Humanism*

Sources

The sources for this chapter are mostly the works of the writers and theologians mentioned in it. The old editions of them were collected by J. P. Migne, *PL*, but since his time un-remitting labour has produced new editions and made other manuscripts available. Worthy of special mention are, among others: *Studia Anselmiana* (Rome 1933 ff.); *Studies in Mediaeval and Renaissance Latin* (Washington 1933 ff.); *Studies of the Warburg Institute* (London 1936 ff.); *Textes philosophiques du moyen âge* (Paris 1955 ff.); *Beiträge zur Geschichte der Philosophie und Theologie des Mittelalters* (Münster i. W. 1891 ff.); *Medieval Classics-Medieval Texts* (London 1949 ff.); *Sources chrétiennes* (Paris 1942 ff.); *cf.* Volume III, 485, Gen. Bibliog., II, 11.

Literature

See Volume III, 485, Gen. Bibliog., II, 11. C. H. Haskins, *The Renaissance of the Twelfth Century* (Cambridge, Mass. 1927); R. W. Southern, "The Place of England in the Twelfth Century Renaissance," *History*, 45 (1960), 201–16; *Ueberweg*, II (Berlin, 11th ed. 1928); *Manitius*, III (Munich 1931); F. J. E. Raby, *A History of Christian Latin Poetry* (Oxford, 2d ed. 1953); *idem, A History of Secular Latin Poetry in the Middle Ages* (Oxford, 2d ed. 1957); J. de Ghellinck, *L'essor de la littérature latine au XIIe siècle,* 2 vols. (Brussels 1946); E. R. Curtius, *European Literature and the Latin Middle Ages* (New York 1953; reprint 1963); R. W. Southern, *The Making of the Middle Ages* (London 1953); P. Lehmann, *Erforschung des Mittelalters, Ausgewählte Abhandlungen und Aufsätze,* 5 vols. (Stuttgart 1959–62); G. Misch, *Geschichte der Autobiographie,* III: *Das Mittelalter,* 2: *Das Hochmittelalter,* 2 vols. (Frankfurt 1959–62); M. D. Chenu, *La théologie au douzième siècle* (Paris 1957); J. Leclercq. *L'amour des lettres et le désir de Dieu* (Paris 1957), English translation: *The Love of Learning and the Desire for God* (New York 1961); J. Leclercq, F. Vandenbroucke, and L. Bouyer, *Histoire de la spiritualité chrétienne,* II: *La spiritualité du moyen âge* (Paris 1961); M. N. Scivoletto, *Spiritualità medioevale e tradizione scolastica nel secolo XII in Francia* (Naples 1954); P. Vignaux, *La philosophie au moyen âge* (Paris 1958); *Artes liberales. Von der antiken Bildung zur Wissenschaft des Mittelalters,* ed. J. Koch (Leiden and Cologne 1959).
Peter the Venerable: works in *PL*, 189; G. Constable and J. Kritzeck, "Petrus Venerabilis (1156–1956): Studies and Texts commemorating the Eighth Centenary of his Death," *SA,* 40 (Rome 1956); J. Leclercq, *Pierre le Vénérable* (Saint-Wandrille 1946); D. Knowles, "Peter the Venerable," *BJRL*, 39 (1956), 132–45; J. Leclercq, "Cluny fut-il ennemi de la culture?" *RMab*, 47 (1957), 172–82; P. Lamma, *Momenti di storiografia cluniacense* (Rome 1961); G. Vinay, *Spiritualità cluniacense* (Todi 1960).
Ordericus Vitalis: Historia ecclesiastica, PL, 188, ed. A. Le Prévost and L. Delisle, 5 vols. (Paris 1838–55) (M. Chibnall is preparing a new edition); H. Wolter, *Ordericus Vitalis. Ein Beitrag zur kluniazensischen Geschichtsschreibung* (Wiesbaden 1955).
Guibert de Nogent: works in *PL*, 156; edition of the autobiography by G. Bourgin (Paris 1907); G. Misch (see *supra*), III/2/1, 108–62.

William of Malmesbury: works: ed. W. Stubbs in *Rolls Series,* 90 (London 1887–89); ed. N. E. S. A. Hamilton in *Rolls Series,* 52 (London 1870); ed. R. R. Darlington, *Vita Wulfstani* (London 1928); H. Farmer, "William of Malmesbury's Commentary of Lamentations," *StudMon,* 4 (1962), 283–311.

Hariulf of Saint-Riquier: works in *PL,* 174; Chronicle, ed. F. Lot (Paris 1894); H. Wolter, "La Chronique de l'abbaye de Saint-Riquier, témoin de l'humanisme bénédictin," *Saint-Riquier, Études concernant l'Abbaye depuis le huitième siècle jusqu'à la Révolution,* I (Saint-Riquier 1962), 68–86.

Rupert of Deutz: works in *PL,* 167–70; in regard to the spurious character of the *Chronicon* see H. Silvestre, *Le Chronicon s. Laurentii Leodiensis* (Louvain 1952); M. Magrassi, *Teologia e Storia nel pensiero di Ruperto da Deutz* (Rome 1959); M. Bernards, "Die Welt der Laien in der kölnischen Theologie des 12. Jahrhunderts. Beobachtungen zur Ekklesiologie Ruperts von Deutz," *Die Kirche und ihre Ämter und Stände. Festschrift Kardinal Frings* (Cologne 1960), 391–416 (bibliography). There is no modern study of Rupert's life and works; *cf.* P. Classen, *Gerhoch von Reichersberg,* 36–40; R. Haacke is preparing a new edition; see *idem,* "Die Überlieferung der Schriften Ruperts von Deutz," *DA,* 16 (1960), 397–436.

William of Saint-Thierry: works in *PL,* 180, 184, 185; M. M. Davy, *Théologie et Mystique de Guillaume de Saint-Thierry* (Paris 1954); the best bibliography in M. M. Davy, "Wilhelm von St-Thierry," *LThK,* X (2d ed. 1965), 1150–52.

Aelred of Rievaulx: works in *PL,* 195; *Sermones inediti,* ed. C. H. Talbot (Rome 1952); *Speculum charitatis,* ed. A. Hoste, *SourcesChr* (Paris 1958); his life was written by Walter Daniel, ed. F. M. Powicke (London 1950); A. Hallier, *Un éducateur monastique: Aelred de Rievaulx* (Paris 1959).

Hugh of Saint-Victor: works: index in R. Baron, *Études sur Hugues de Saint-Victor* (Paris 1963), 261–67; *PL,* 175–77; *Didascalicon,* ed. C. H. Buttimer (Washington 1939); *De contemplatione,* ed. R. Baron (Toulouse and Paris 1958); L. Ott , "Hugo von St-Victor," *LThK,* V (2d ed. 1960), 518 f. (bibliography); R. Baron is preparing further editions.

Gerhoh of Reichersberg: works: index in P. Classen, *Gerhoch von Reichersberg, eine Biographie. Mit einem Anhang über die Quellen, ihre handschriftliche Überlieferung und ihre Chronologie* (Wiesbaden 1960), 407–44; *PL,* 193–94; E. Meuthen, *Kirche und Heilsgeschichte bei Gerhoch von Reichersberg* (Cologne 1959). Classen's biography is standard.

Premonstratensians: F. Petit, *La spiritualité des Prémontrés aux XIIe et XIIIe siècles* (Paris 1947); H. M. Colvin, *The White Canons in England* (London 1951); P. Lefèvre, *La liturgie de Prémontré* (Louvain 1957).

Guigues du Châtel: works in *PL,* 153; *Meditationes,* ed. A. Wilmart (Paris 1936), German translation by P. A. Schlüter, *Guigo von Kastell, Tagebuch eines Mönchs* (Paderborn 1952); C. A. de Meyer and J. M. de Smet, "Notes sur quelques sources littéraires relatives à Guiges Ier," *RHE,* 48 (1953), 168–95; G. Hocquard, "La vie cartusienne d'après le prieur Guiges Ier," *RevSR,* 31 (1957), 364–82.

7. *The New Theology: Abelard, Peter Lombard, Gratian*

GENERAL LITERATURE

See Volume III, 485 f., Gen. Bibliog., II, 11 and 12, especially *Fliche-Martin,* XIII; Z. Alszeghy, "Frühscholastik," *LThK,* IV (2d ed. 1960), 433–38; M. Grabmann, *Geschichte der scholastischen Methode,* 2 vols. (Freiburg im Breisgau 1909–11, reprinted Graz 1956); *Ueberweg,* II (11th ed. 1928, reprinted 1951); *Wulf;* J. Hirschberger, *Geschichte der Philo-*

sophie, 2 vols. (Freiburg im Breisgau, 8th ed. 1965); F. Copleston, *A History of Philosophy*, II: *Mediaeval Philosophy* (Westminster, Md., 4th ed. 1957); *Grabmann MGL*; *Grabmann G*; O. Lottin, *Psychologie et morale aux XII* et XIII* siècles*, 6 vols. (Louvain 1942–60); M. D. Chenu, *La théologie au douzième siècle, Études de philosophie médiévale*, 45 (Paris 1957); A. M. Landgraf, *Einführung in die Geschichte der theologischen Literatur der Frühscholastik* (Regensburg 1948); Spanish translation with supplements: *Introducción a la historia de la literatura teológica de la escolástica incipiente* (Barcelona 1956); idem, *Dogmengeschichte der Frühscholastik*, I/1–IV/2 (Regensburg 1952–56); S. Otto, *Die Funktion des Bildbegriffs in der Theologie des 12. Jahrhunderts, BGPhMA*, 40, 1 (Münster i. W. 1963) (copious bibliography on Anselm of Laon, Abelard, Robert of Melun, and their schools, the Victorines, Gilbert de la Porrée, Peter Lombard, and their schools, and the monastic theologians [cf. preceding chapter]: Rupert of Deutz, William of Saint-Thierry, Hugh of Amiens, Aelred of Rievaulx).

Anselm of Laon: E. Michaud, *Guillaume de Champeaux et les écoles de Paris au XII* siècle* (Paris 1867); G. Lefèvre, *Anselmi Laudunensis et Radulphi fratris eius sententiae excerptae* (Évreux 1895); idem, *Les variations de Guillaume de Champeaux et la question des universaux* (Lille 1898); J. de Ghellinck, "The Sentences of Anselm de Laon and their Place in the Codification of Theology during the Twelfth Century," *IThQ*, 6 (1911), 427–41; F. Bliemetzrieder, *Anselms von Laon systematische Sentenzen, BGPhMA*, 18, 2–3 (Münster i. W. 1919); idem, "Autour de l'œuvre théologique d'Anselm de Laon," *RThAM*, 1 (1929), 435–83; idem, "Trente-trois pièces inédites de l'œuvre théologique d'Anselme de Laon," *RThAM*, 2 (1930), 54–79; idem, "Gratian und die Schule Anselms von Laon," *AkathKR*, 112 (1932), 37–63; H. Weisweiler, "L'école d'Anselme de Laon et de Guillaume de Champeaux," *RThAM*, 4 (1932), 237–69; F. Bliemetzrieder, "L'œuvre d'Anselme de Laon et la littérature théologique contemporaine, I: Honorius d'Autun," *RThAM*, 5 (1933), 275–291, II: "Hugues de Rouen," *RThAM*, 6 (1934), 261–83, 7 (1935), 28–51; H. Weisweiler, *Das Schrifttum der Schule Anselms von Laon und Wilhelms von Champeaux in deutschen Bibliotheken, BGPhMA*, 33, 1–2 (Münster i. W. 1936); A. M. Landgraf, "Werke aus dem Bereich der Summa Sententiarum und Anselms von Laon," *DTh*, 14 (1936), 209–20; O. Lottin, "Aux origines de l'école théologique d'Anselme de Laon," *RThAM*, 10 (1938), 101–22; E. Lesne, *Les écoles de la fin du VIII* siècle à la fin du XII* siècle* (Lille 1940); R. Silvain, "La tradition des Sentences d'Anselme de Laon," *AHD*, 22/23, (1947 f.), 1–52; H. Cloes, "La systématisation théologique pendant la première moitié du XII* siècle," *EThL*, 14 (1958), 277–328; H. Weisweiler, "Die Arbeitsweise der sogenannten Sententiae Anselmi," *Scholastik*, 34 (1959), 190–233; idem, "Paschasius Radbertus als Vermittler des Gedankenguts der karolingischen Renaissance in den Matthäuskommentaren des Kreises um Anselm von Laon," *Scholastik*, 35 (1960), 363–402. Bibliography and treatment of this school and its works in S. Otto in *BGPhMA*, 40, 1, 24–69 *(supra)*.

School of Saint-Victor: L. Ott, *Untersuchungen zur theologischen Briefliteratur der Frühscholastik, BGPhMA*, 34 (Münster i. W. 1937); J. Châtillon, "De Guillaume de Champeaux à Thomas Gallus. Chronique d'histoire littéraire et doctrinale de l'école de Saint-Victor," *RMA*, 8 (1952), 139–62; R. Baron, "L'influence de Hugues de Saint-Victor," *RThAM*, 22 (1955), 56–71; idem, *Science et sagesse chez Hugues de Saint-Victor* (Paris 1957); idem, *Études sur Hugues de Saint-Victor* (biographiques, critique chronologique, stylistique, doctrinale [Le Commentaire de la 'Hierarchie Celeste'], textes inédites) (Paris 1963); D. Van den Eynde, *Essai sur la succession et la date des écrits de Hugues de Saint-Victor* (Rome 1960); H. R. Schlette, *Die Nichtigkeit der Welt. Der philosophische Horizont des Hugo von St. Viktor* (Munich 1961); H. Weisweiler, "Die Arbeitsweise Hugos von St. Viktor," *Scholastik*, 24 (1949), 59–87, 232–67; idem, "Sakrament als Symbol und Teilhabe—Der Einfluss des Ps-Dionysius auf die allgemeine Sakramentenlehre Hugos von St. Viktor," *Scholastik*, 27 (1952), 321–43.

Richard of Saint-Victor: C. Ottaviano, *Riccardo di S. Vittore. La vita, le opere, il pensiero* (Rome 1933); G. Dumeige, *Richard de Saint-Victor et l'idée chrétienne de l'amour* (Paris 1952); C. Kirchberger, *Richard of St. Victor* (London 1957). Godfrey of Saint-Victor must be listed as witness for the Victorines' connection with the school of Chartres: P. Delhaye, *Godefroy de Saint-Victor, Microcosmus, Mémoires et travaux publiés par les professeurs des Facultés catholiques de Lille*, fasc. 56 (Lille 1951).

Peter Abelard: works: *Œuvres inédites d'Abélard*, ed. V. Cousin (Paris 1836); *Petri Abaelardi Opera*, ed. V. Cousin, 2 vols. (Paris 1849–59); *PL*, 178; *De unitate et trinitate divina*, ed. R. Stölzle (Freiburg 1891); *Theologia "Summi Boni,"* ed. H. Ostlender, *BGPhMA*, 35, 2–3 (Münster i. W. 1939); *Dialectica*, ed. L. M. de Rijk (Assen 1956); *Historia calamitatum*, ed. J. Monfrin (Paris 1959); *Abaelards philosophische Schriften*, ed. B. Geyer, *BGPhMA*, 21, 1–4 (Münster i. W. 1919–33); *Scito te ipsum*, Italian translation by M. Dal Pra (Vincenza 1941); *Œuvres choisis d'Abélard*, M. de Gandillac (Paris 1945); *Hymnarius*, ed. G. Dreves, *AH*, 48 (1905), 141–232; *Astrolabius, Gedicht Abälards an seinen Sohn*, ed. H. Brinkmann, *Münchener Museum für Philologie*, 5 (1928–33), 168–201; *Epistola consolatoria*, ed. J. T. Muckle *(Abelard's Letter of Consolation to a Friend)*, *MS*, 12 (1950), 163–213; *Heloissae epistola*, ed. J. T. Muckle, "The Personal Letters between Abelard and Heloise," *MS*, 15 (1953), 47–94; *Epistolario completo di Pietro Abelardo*, ed. C. Ottaviano (Rome 1934); *Petri Abaelardi Dialogus inter Philosophum, Judaeum et Christianum*, ed. F. H. Rheinwald (Berlin 1831); *Petri Abaelardi Sic et Non*, ed. E. L. T. Henke and G. S. Lindenkohl (Marburg 1851); P. Ruf and M. Grabmann, *Ein neu aufgefundenes Bruchstück der Apologie Abaelards*, *SAM* (1930), no. 5; *Abaelards Leidensgeschichte und Briefwechsel mit Heloisa*, German translation by E. Brost (Heidelberg, 2d ed. 1954); "Epistola Petri Abailardi contra Bernhardum Abbatem," ed. J. Leclercq, *Études sur saint Bernard et le texte de ses écrits*, *AnOCist*, IX, 1–2 (Rome 1953); 104 f.; T. P. McLaughlin, "Abelard's Rule for Religious Women," *MS*, 18 (1956), 241–92.

Literature: H. Reuter, *Die Geschichte der religiösen Aufklärung im Mittelalter* (Berlin 1875); S. M. Deutsch, *Peter Abälard. Ein kritischer Theologe des zwölften Jahrhunderts* (Leipzig 1883); E. Portalié in *DThC*, I (1903), 36–55; E. Vacandard in *DHGE*, I (1912) 71–91; *Fliche-Martin*, XIII, 93–105; R. L. Poole, *Illustrations of the History of Medieval Thought and Learning* (London, 2d ed. 1920), 116–45; É. Gilson, *Héloïse und Abaelard, zugleich ein Beitrag zum Problem von Mittelalter und Humanismus* (Freiburg, 3d ed. 1955). The best biography is that by J. G. Sikes, *Peter Abailard* (Cambridge, 2d ed. 1946). M. Grabmann, *Geschichte der scholastischen Methode*, II, 168–229; *Manitius*, III, 105–12; J. de Ghellinck, *L'essor* (see bibliog. for Chapter 6), I, 41–50; *idem, Le mouvement théologique du XIIᵉ siècle* (Bruges, 2d ed. 1948), 149–75; A. M. Landgraf, *Einführung (supra)*, 62–72.

Monographs: H. Denifle, "Die Sentenzen Abaelards und die Bearbeitungen seiner 'Theologia' vor der Mitte des 12. Jahrhunderts," *ALKGMA*, I (1885), 402–624; B. Geyer, "Die Stellung Abaelards in der Universalienfrage nach neuen handschriftlichen Texten," *Festgabe Bäumker*, *BGPhMA*, Suppl. I (1913), 101–27; W. Betzendörfer, "Glauben und Wissen bei Peter Abälard," *ZSTh*, 3 (1925), 334–52; J. Rivière, "Le dogme de la Rédemption chez Abélard," *RevSR*, 12 (1932), 355–88; J. Cottiaux, "La conception de la théologie chez Abélard," *RHE*, 28 (1932), 247–95, 533–51, 788–828; H. Weisweiler, "Eine neue Bearbeitung von Abaelards 'Introductio' und der Summa Sententiarum," *Scholastik*, 9 (1934), 346–71; B. Schmeidler, "Der Briefwechsel zwischen Abälard und Heloïse als eine literarische Fiktion Abälards," *ZKG*, 54 (1935), 323–38 (this view is no longer defended, following É. Gilson's attack on it); A. Borst, "Abälard und Bernhard," *HZ*, 186 (1958), 497–526; R. Oursel, *La dispute et la grâce. Essai sur la Rédemption d'Abélard, Publications de l'Université de Dijon*, 19 (Paris 1959); R. Klibansky, "Peter Abailard and Bernard de Clairvaux," *MRS*, 5 (1961), 1–27 (without reference to A. Borst); J. Jolivet, "Abélard et la philosophie,"

RHR, 164 (1963), 181–89; *idem,* "Sur quelques critiques de la théologie d'Abélard," *AHD,* 30 (1963), 7–51; M. Buytaert, "Thomas of Morigny and the 'Theologia Scholarium' of Abelard," *Antonianum,* 40 (1965), 71–95; R. Thomas, *Der philosophisch-theologische Erkenntnisweg Peter Abaelards im Dialogus inter Philosophum, Judaeum et Christianum, Untersuchungen zur allgemeinen Religionsgeschichte,* new series, 6 (Bonn 1966).

Abelard's School: A. M. Landgraf, *Écrits théologiques de l'école d'Abélard.* Textes inédits (Louvain 1934); *idem, Commentarius Cantabrigiensis in Epistolas Pauli e schola Abaelardi,* 2 vols. (Notre Dame 1937–48); H. Ostlender, "Die Sentenzenbücher der Schule Abaelards," *ThQ,* 117 (1936), 208–52; A. M. Landgraf, "Beiträge zur Erkenntnis der Schule Abälards," *ZKTh,* 54 (1930), 367–405; H. Ostlender, "Die 'Theologia scholarium' des Peter Abälard," *BGPhMA,* Suppl. III, 1 (Münster i. W. 1935), 263–81; A. M. Gietl, *Die Sentenzen Rolands, nachmals Papstes Alexander III.* (Freiburg im Breisgau 1891); L. Ostlender, *Sententiae Florianenses, FlorPatr,* 19 (Bonn 1929); *idem, Peter Abaelards Theologia und die Sentenzenbücher seiner Schule* (Breslau 1926).

Peter Lombard: works: *Petri Lombardi Libri IV Sententiarum,* ed. studio et cura PP. Collegii S. Bonaventurae, 2 vols. (Quaracchi 1916); *PL,* 192, 521–962; *Commentarius in Psalmos, PL,* 191, 55–1296; *Collectanea in Epistolas Pauli, PL,* 191, 1297–1696; *PL,* 192, 9–520; 29 *sermones* (scattered among the *sermones* of Hildebert of Lavardin) in PL, 171, 339–963; fragments of exegetical works in B. Smalley and G. Lacombe, "The Lombard's Commentary on Isaias and Other Fragments," *The New Scholasticism,* 5 (1931), 123–62; F. Stegmüller, *Repertorium commentariorum in Sententias Petri Lombardi,* 2 vols. (Würzburg 1947), and supplement by V. Doucet (Quaracchi 1954); F. Stegmüller, *Repertorium Biblicum Medii Aevi,* thus far 7 vols. (Madrid 1953–61).

Literature: J. de Ghellinck in *DThC,* 12 (1935), 1941–2019 (bibliography); *idem, L'essor* (see bibliog. for Chapter 6), I, 70–76; *idem, Le mouvement théologique du XIIe siècle* (Bruges, 2d ed. 1948), 213–77; *idem,* "La carrière de Pierre Lombard," *RHE,* 27 (1931), 792–830, 30 (1934), 95–100; I. Brady, "Peter Lombard, Canon of Notre-Dame," *RThAM,* 32 (1965), 277–95; A. M. Landgraf, *Einführung,* 93–109; F. Stegmüller, *Repertorium Biblicum* (see *supra*), IV, nos. 6624–69; *Miscellanea Lombardiana* (Novara 1957) (acts of the centenary congress with contributions by L. Ott, "Pietro Lombardo: Personalità e opera"; D. Van den Eynde, "Essai chronologique sur l'œuvre de Pierre Lombard"; F. Pelster, "Petrus Lombardus und die Verhandlungen über die Streitfrage des Gilbertus Porreta in Paris [1147] und Reims [1148]"; N. M. Häring, "Petrus Lombardus und die Sprachlogik in der Trinitätslehre der Porretanerschule"; G. Le Bras, "Pierre Lombard, prince du droit canon"; A. Gambaro, "Pier Lombardo e la civiltà del suo secolo"; *et al.*); from 1957 there also appears in Novara a periodical: *Pier Lombardo.* For Peter Lombard's method see J. Schupp, *Die Gnadenlehre des Petrus Lombardus* (Freiburg 1932), 289–98; E. M. Buytaert, "St. John Damascene, Peter Lombard and Gerhoh of Reichersberg," *FStudies,* 10 (1950), 323–43; L. Ott, "Walter von Mortagne und Petrus Lombardus in ihrem Verhältnis zueinander," *Mélanges J. de Ghellinck,* II (Gembloux 1951), 646–97; H. Weisweiler, "La 'Summa Sententiarum' source de Pierre Lombard," *RThAM,* 6 (1934), 143–83; L. Ott, "Die Trinitätslehre der 'Summa Sententiarum' als Quelle des Petrus Lombardus," *DTh,* 21 (1943), 159–86; P. Delhaye, *Pierre Lombard* (Montreal and Paris 1961). For Peter Lombard's piety see F. Vandenbroucke, *Histoire de la spiritualité du moyen âge* (Paris 1961), 280–83. For the more than 500 commentators see F. Stegmüller, *Repertorium* (see *supra*); A. M. Landgraf, *Dogmengeschichte der Frühscholastik* (Regensburg 1952–56), *passim; Fliche-Martin,* XIII, 157–60.

Gratian's Decretum: until the projected new edition appears the standard work is still that of E. Friedberg (Leipzig 1879, reprinted 1955); the centenary congress at Bologna in 1952 resulted in the *Studia Gratiana* (from 1953), thus far 7 vols., ed. G. Forchielli and A. M. Stickler; *Fliche-Martin,* XII, 1 (1959): G. Le Bras, *Institutions ecclésiastiques de la chré-*

tienté médiévale, 45–55; G. Fransen, "La date du Décret de Gratien," *RHE*, 51 (1956), 521–31; P. Pinedo, "Intorno al titulo del Decreto de Graziano," *Anuario de Historia del Derecho español*, 25 (1955), 845–68; preparations for a critical edition: *Tr*, 11 (1955), 12 (1956), etc., as annual report. J. F. McCarthy, "The Genius of Concord in Gratian's Decree," *EIC*, 19 (1963), 105–51, 259–95; C. Munier, "Droit canonique et Droit romain d'après Gratien et les Décrétistes," *Études d'histoire du droit canonique dédiées à Gabriel Le Bras* (Paris 1965), 943–54.

Biography of Gratian by S. Kuttner, *StG*, I (Bologna 1953), 15–29. For the content, structure, and importance of the *Decretum* see A. M. Stickler, *Historia Iuris Canonici Latini*, I: *Historia Fontium* (Turin 1950), 200–16; S. Kuttner, "Zur Frage der theologischen Vorlagen Gratians," *ZSavRGkan*, 23 (1934), 243–68; *Feine RG*, I, 276–82; G. Le Bras, *Histoire du Droit et des Institutions de l'Église en Occident, 7: L'âge classique (1140–1378)*, by G. Le Bras, C. Lefèbvre, and J. Rambaud (Paris 1965), 52–99.

SECTION TWO

The Threats to the Freedom of the Church: 1153-1198

8. *The Popes, the Emperor Frederick I, and the Third Lateran Council*

SOURCES

Mansi XXI, 786–1222, XXII, 1–686; *Hefele-Leclercq*, V, 849–1178; *Duchesne LP*, II, 351–446 (Boso, *Gesta pontificum Romanorum*), III, 139; *Watterich*, II, 321–748; *Jaffé*, II, nos. 9736–17679; *Bullarium Taur.*, II, 596–836, III, 7–112. Letters and documents of the Popes of this period: Anastasius IV and Hadrian IV, *PL*, 188; Alexander III, *PL*, 200; Lucius III, *PL*, 201; Urban III and Gregory VIII, *PL*, 202; Clement III, *PL*, 204; Celestine III, *PL*, 206. *Acta* and documents of kings and emperors: *MGConst*, I; J. F. Böhmer, *Regesten des Kaiserreiches* (Frankfurt am Main 1831); K. F. Stumpf-Brentano, *"Die Reichskanzler,"* 2 vols. (Innsbruck 1868–72, reprinted 1960); J. F. Böhmer and J. Ficker, *Acta imperii selecta* (Innsbruck 1870); E. Winkelmann, *Acta imperii inedita*, 2 vols. (Innsbruck 1880–85); K. Jordan, *Die Urkunden Heinrichs des Löwen* (Stuttgart 1949, reprinted 1960); *Urkundenbuch zur Geschichte der Babenberger in Österreich*, ed. H. Fichtenau and E. Zöllner, I: *Die Siegelurkunden der Babenberger bis 1215* (Vienna 1950); *Dahlmann-Waitz*, 76–90; L. Delisle and E. Berger, *Recueil des actes de Henri II*, 3 vols. (Paris 1909–27); L. Landon, *The Itinerary of King Richard I* (London 1935), Pipe Roll Society, new series, 13; H. F. Delaborde, E. Berger, C. Petit-Dutaillis, J. Monicat, and C. Bunel, *Recueil des actes de Philippe Auguste, roi de France*, 2 vols. (Paris 1916–43).

Chronicles, Annals, and Letters: Otto of Freising and Rahewin, *Gesta Frederici I Imperatoris*, ed. G. Waitz and B. von Simson, *MGSS rer. Germ.* (Hanover, 3d ed. 1912); *Otto Morena et continuatorum Historia Frederici I*, ed. F. Güterbock, *MGSS rer. Germ.*, new series, 7 (Berlin 1930); Helmold of Bosau, *Slawenchronik*, ed. B. Schmeidler, *MGSS rer. Germ.* (2d ed. 1937); *Chronica regia Coloniensis*, ed. G. Waitz, *MGSS rer. Germ.* (1880); Hugh of Poitiers, *Liber de libertate monasterii Vizeliacensis*, *MGSS*, 26, 143–50; John of Salisbury, *Letters* (see bibliog. for Chapter 4), I (1153–61); Gilbert Foliot, *The Letters and Charters*, ed. A. Morey and C. L. N. Brooke (Cambridge 1966), *cf*. A. Morey and C. N. L. Brooke, *Gilbert Foliot and his Letters* (Cambridge 1965); the "Ligurinus" (Frederick's acts to 1160), ed. C. G. Dumgé (1812), new edition in preparation, *PL*, 212, 327–476; E. Assmann, "Bleibt der Ligurinus anonym?" *DA*, 12 (1956), 453–72 (Gunther of Pairis in Upper

Alsace is now regarded as the author); Godfrey of Viterbo, *Gesta Frederici* (to 1181), ed. G. Waitz, *MGSS rer. Germ.*, 30 (Hanover 1870); *Lauterberg Chronicle (Chronicon Montis Sereni),* ed. E. Ehrenfeuchter, *MGSS,* 23, 138–226; for other chronicles and annals of the period see K. Jacob and H. Hohenleutner, *Quellenkunde der deutschen Geschichte im Mittelalter,* II (1961), 100–19; also important are the *Annals of Genoa* by Caffaro (to 1163), by Obertus (to 1173), by Ottobonus (to 1196), *MGSS,* 18, 11–356 (Leipzig 1863), and the edition of L. T. Belgrano *et al., FontiStIt,* 11–14, 5 vols. (Rome 1890–1929); Bernardo Marago, *Chronicle of Pisa* (to 1181), continued to 1192, *MGSS,* 19, 236–66, ed. M. Lupo Gentile (Muratori, 2d ed., VI/2) (Bologna 1930–36); Romuald of Salerno, *Chronicle* (to 1178), ed. C. A. Garufi (Muratori, 2d ed., VII/1) (Bologna 1935); Arnold of Lübeck, *Chronicle,* ed. J. M. Lappenberg, *MGSS rer. Germ.,* 14 (reprinted 1930, new edition in preparation).

Literature

Gen. Bibliog., II; *Historia Mundi,* VI; F. L. Ganshof, *Le moyen-âge,* I (Paris 1953); *Giesebrecht,* IV (2d ed. 1877), V (1880), VI, ed. B. von Simson (Leipzig 1895); A. L. Poole, *From Domesday Book to Magna Carta* (Oxford, 2d ed. 1964); *Lavisse,* III/1, ed. A. Luchaire (Paris 1902); N. Valeri, *Storia d'Italia,* I: *Il medioevo* (Turin 1959); R. Soldevilla, *Historia de España,* 2 vols. (Barcelona 1952 f.); P. Peres, *Historia de Portugal,* 2 vols. (Barcelos 1928 f.). *Fliche-Martin,* IX/2; for handbooks see Gen. Bibliog., II, 3; *Hauck,* IV (Leipzig, 5th ed. 1925), 196–685; for the more recent histories of the Church in various lands see Gen. Bibliog., II, 4; C. W. Lawrence, *The English Church and the Papacy* (London 1965, cooperative work); *Histoire du catholicisme en France,* by A. Latreille, E. Delaruelle, and J. R. Palanque, 2 vols. (Paris 1957–60); *Haller,* III (Darmstadt, 2d ed. 1962), 116–295; *Seppelt,* III, 213–318 (bibliography); B. Tierney, *The Crisis of Church and State (1050–1300), with selected documents* (Englewood, N. J. 1964); J. G. Rowe, "The Papacy and the Ecclesiastical Province of Tyre (1100–1187)," *BJRL,* 43 (1960), 160–89; M. Schwarz, "Heiligsprechungen im 12. Jahrhundert und die Beweggründe ihrer Urheber," *AKG,* 39 (1957), 43–62.

Hadrian IV: Epistolae et privilegia, PL, 188, 1349–1644; *Duchesne LP,* II, 388–97 (Boso); *Jaffé,* II (2d ed.), 102–45, 720 f., 760 f.; H. Schrörs, *Untersuchungen zu dem Streite Friedrichs I. mit Hadrian IV.* (Freiburg im Breisgau 1916); E. M. Almedinger, *Hadrian IV* (London 1925); A. O. Johnsen, *Studier vedrørende Kardinal Nicolaus Breakspears Legasjon til Norden* (Oslo 1945); O. Kolsrud, *Kardinal-legaten Nicolaus av Albano i Norge (1152),* Hist. Tidskrift Oslo, 33 (1945), 485–512; W. Ullmann, "Cardinal Roland and the Incident at Besançon," *Misc. Hist. Pont.,* 18 (Rome 1954); *idem,* "The Pontificate of Hadrian IV," *CambrHJ,* 11 (1955), 233–52; P. Lamma, *Comneni e Staufer,* I (Rome 1955); M. Maccarone, "La coronazione imperiale di 1155," *Studi Romani,* 6 (1958), 16–38; P. Lamma, "Adriano IV," *Dizionario biografico degli Italiani,* I (1960), 330–35; M. Maccarone, *Papato e Impero dalla elezione di Federico I alla morte di Adriano IV (1152–59)* (Rome 1959); M. P. Sheehy, "The Bull Laudabiliter: a Problem in Medieval Diplomacy and History," *Galway Archaeological and Historical Society Journal,* 29 (1961), 45–70; *idem, Pontificia Hibernica,* I (Dublin 1962), no. 4, pp. 15 f.; G. Inger, *Das kirchliche Visitationsinstitut im mittelalterlichen Schweden* (Lund 1961; bibliography).

Alexander III: Epistolae et privilegia, PL, 200; *Duchesne LP,* II, 397–446; *Jaffé,* II (2d ed.), 145–431; *Watterich,* II, 377–649; *Hefele-Leclercq,* V, 916–1114; *Die Summa Magistri Rolandi nachmals Papstes Alexander III.,* ed. F. Thaner (Innsbruck 1874, reprinted Aalen 1962); G. Möser-Mersky, "Das österreichische 'Chronicon rhythmicum,'" *MIÖG,* 73 (1965), 17–38; W. Holtzmann and E. W. Kemp, *Papal Decretals in the Diocese of Lincoln in the Twelfth Century* (Lincoln 1954) (363 out of 713 decretals of Alexander were directed to

England); M. Pacaut, *Alexandre III. Étude sur la conception du pouvoir pontifical dans sa pensée et dans son œuvre* (Paris 1956), in regard to which see F. Kempf in *RHE*, 52 (1957), 932–37; *idem*, "Louis VII et Alessandre III," *RHÉF*, 39 (1953), 5–45; there is no modern biography of Alexander III but mention must be made of the outdated work by H. Reuter, *Geschichte Alexanders III. und der Kirche seiner Zeit*, 3 vols. (Leipzig 1860); W. Ullmann in *Misc. Hist. Pont.*, 18 (1954), 107.

B. W. Scholtz, "The Canonisation of Edward the Confessor (1161)," *Speculum*, 36 (1961), 38–60; J. Schlafke, "Das Recht der Bischöfe in causis Sanctorum bis zum Jahre 1234," *Die Kirche und ihre Ämter, Festschrift Kardinal Frings* (Cologne 1960), 417–33; G. Miletti, "Il monumento di Alessandro III nella Basilica Lateranense," *Saggi d'istoria dell'architettura in onore [di] V. Fasolo* (Rome 1961), 269–72; N. M. Häring, "The Eulogium ad Alexandrum Papam tertium of John of Cornwall," *MS*, 13 (1951), 253–300.

J. M. Brixius, *Die Mitglieder des Kardinalkollegiums von 1130–1181* (Berlin 1912); J. Bachmann, *Die päpstlichen Legaten in Deutschland und Skandinavien 1125–1159* (Marburg 1913); H. Tillmann, *Die päpstlichen Legaten in England bis zur Beendigung der Legation Gualas* (Bonn 1926); W. Ohnsorge, *Die Legaten Alexanders III. im ersten Jahrzehnt seines Pontifikats (1159–1169)* (Berlin 1928); G. Dunken, *Die politische Wirksamkeit der päpstlichen Legaten in der Zeit des Kampfes zwischen Kaisertum und Papsttum in Oberitalien unter Friedrich I.* (Berlin 1931); I. Friedländer, *Die päpstlichen Legaten in Deutschland und Italien am Ende des 12. Jahrhunderts (1181–98)* (Berlin 1928); W. Ohnsorge, *Päpstliche und gegenpäpstliche Legaten in Deutschland und Skandinavien 1159 bis 1181* (Berlin 1929); M. Pacaut, "Les légats d'Alexandre III (1159–81)," *RHE*, 50 (1955), 821–38; K. Ruess, *Die rechtliche Stellung der päpstlichen Legaten bis Bonifaz VIII.* (Paderborn 1912); K. Walf, *Die Entwicklung des päpstlichen Gesandtschaftswesens in dem Zeitabschnitt zwischen Dekretalenrecht und Wiener Kongress (1159–1815)*, MthSt, Kan. Abt., 24 (Munich 1966); W. Janssen, *Die päpstlichen Legaten in Frankreich vom Schisma Anaklets II. bis zum Tode Cölestins III.*, *Kölner Historische Abhandlungen*, 6 (Cologne and Graz 1961).

The Schism of 1159: Sources: S. Tengnagel, *Vetera Monumenta contra Schismaticos* (Ingolstadt 1612); John of Salisbury, letter to *Magister* Ralph of Sarre (June–July 1160), *The Letters of John of Salisbury* (see bibliography for Chapter 4), I, 204–15; Anonymous, *Tractatus de Schismaticis*, ed. J. Dieterich and H. Böhmer, *MGLiblit*, III, 109–30; Gerhoh of Reichersberg, *De investigatione Antichristi* (1160–62), *PL*, 194, 1445–80, ed. H. Böhmer, *MGLiblit*, III, 309–95; Rahewin, *Dialogus de Pontificatu sanctae Romanae Ecclesiae inter Victorem IV et Alexandrum III*, ed. H. Böhmer, *MGLiblit*, III, 526–46; Abbot John of Santa Maria in Trastevere, *De vera pace contra schisma sedis apostolicae*, ed. A. Wilmart, *Lateranum*, new series (Rome 1938). Literature: in addition to the older works, such as M. Meyer, *Die Wahl Alexanders III. und Viktors IV., ein Beitrag zur Kirchenspaltung unter Kaiser Friedrich I.* (Göttingen 1871), and W. Ribbeck, "Der Traktat über die Papstwahl des Jahres 1159," *FDG*, 25 (1885), 354–64, see also I. Schnack, *Richard von Cluny, seine Chronik und sein Kloster in den Anfängen der Kirchenspaltung von 1159. Ein Beitrag zur Geschichte der Anschauungen vom Kardinalkolleg und Papsttum im 12. und 13. Jahrhundert* (Berlin 1921); P. Kehr, "Zur Geschichte Viktors IV.," *NA*, 46 (1926), 53–85; W. Holtzmann, "Quellen und Forschungen zur Geschichte Friedrich Barbarossas," *NA*, 48 (1930), 284–413; J. Engel, *Das Schisma Barbarossas im Bistum und Hochstift Freising (1159–1177)* (dissertation, Freiburg im Breisgau 1930); M. Preiss, *Die politische Tätigkeit der Cisterzienser im Schisma von 1159–1177* (Berlin 1934); R. Jordan, *Die Stellung des deutschen Episkopats im Kampf um die Universalmacht unter Friedrich I. bis zum Frieden von Venedig (1177)* (Würzburg 1939); L. J. Barmann, "The Papal Election of 1159," *AER* (1963), 37–43.

Lateran II: *COD*, 181–201; *Hefele-Leclercq*, V, 1086–1112; Roger of Howden, *Chronicle*, ed. W. Stubbs (London 1869), *Rolls Series*, 51/2, II, 173–89; *Gesta regis* (once attributed to

Benedict of Peterborough, now regarded as probably a redaction of the *Chronicle* of Roger of Howden), ed. W. Stubbs (London 1867), *Rolls Series*, 49/1, I, 222–38; letters of convocation: *Jaffé*, 13097–99, 13070; S. Löwenfeld, *Epistolae pontificum Romanorum ineditae* (Leipzig 1855), 154 f., no. 271; *PL*, 200, 1357 f.; signatures in *Mansi*, 22, 213–17, 239 f.; *cf.* G. Tangl, *Die Teilnehmer an den allgemeinen Konzilien des Mittelalters* (Weimar 1922), 196–201, 210–19; G. Morin, "Le discours d'ouverture du concile général de Latran (1179) et l'œuvre littéraire de maître Rufin, évêque d'Assise," *AttiPontAc*, Ser. III, Memoire, 2 (Rome 1928), 116–20. The canons can be best consulted in *COD*, 187–201; see the introductory comments on them and their sources in the decretal collections; S. Kuttner, *Repertorium der Kanonistik (1140–1234), SteT*, 71 (Rome 1937); the holding of the Council was based on an *Ordo Romanus*, ed. M. Andrieu, *Le Pontifical romain au moyen âge*, I, *SteT*, 86 (Rome 1938), 255–60; the best account is now that by R. Foreville, *Latran I, II, III, et Latran IV, Histoire des conciles œcuméniques*, 6 (Paris 1965), 116–62, 194–223 (Text).

The Emperor Frederick I: H. Haimpel in *NDB*, 5 (1961), 459–78; *Dahlmann-Waitz*, 6330–33, 6557–6619; P. Kehr, "Der Vertrag von Anagni im Jahre 1176," *NA*, 13 (1888), 75–118; H. Simonsfeld, *Jahrbücher des Deutschen Reiches unter Friedrich I.*, 1 *(1152–1158)* (Leipzig 1908); K. Hampe and F. Baethgen, *Deutsche Kaisergeschichte in der Zeit der Salier und Staufer* (Heidelberg 1949); K. Hampe, *Herrschergestalten des deutschen Mittelalters* (Leipzig, 6th ed. 1955); W. Kamlah, "Der Ludus de Antichristo," *HV*, 28 (1933), 53–87; E. Rundnagel, "Die Ehescheidung Friedrich Barbarossas," *Festschrift R. Holtzmann* (Berlin 1933), 145–59; H. H. Jacobs, "Friedrich Barbarossa und Heinrich der Löwe," *Die Grossen Deutschen*, I (1935), 94–123; W. Föhl, "Bischof Eberhard von Bamberg, ein Staatsmann Friedrichs I.," *MIÖG*, 50 (1936), 73–131; F. Böhm, *Das Bild Friedrich Barbarossas in den ausländischen Quellen seiner Zeit* (Berlin 1937); T. Mayer, K. Heilig, and C. Erdmann, *Kaisertum und Herzogsgewalt im Zeitalter Friedrichs I., Schriften des Reichsinstituts für ältere deutsche Geschichtskunde*, 9 (Stuttgart 1944, reprinted 1952); F. B. Koeppler, "Frederick Barbarossa and the School of Bologna," *EHR*, 54 (1939); E. F. Otto, *Friedrich Barbarossa* (Potsdam 1940); *idem*, "Friedrich Barbarossa in seinen Briefen," *DA*, 5 (1941 f.), 72–111; P. Rassow, *Honor imperii* (Munich 1940, reprinted Darmstadt 1961); *idem, Der Prinzgemahl, ein Pactum matrimoniale aus dem Jahre 1188* (Weimar 1950); P. Brezzi, *Caratteri, momenti e protagonisti dell'azione politica di Federico Barbarossa, RSIt*, 5 (Naples 1940); W. Ohnsorge, "Das Mitkaisertum in der abendländischen Geschichte des frühen Mittelalters," *ZSavRGgerm*, 67 (1950), reprint in *Abendland und Byzanz* (Homburg v. d. Höhe 1958), 261–87; K. Langosch, *Politische Dichtung um Kaiser Friedrich Barbarossa* (Berlin 1943); K. Bosl, *Die Reichsministerialität der Salier und Staufer*, 2 vols., Schriften der *MG*, 10, 1–2 (Stuttgart 1950 f.); F. Heer, *Die Tragödie des Heiligen Reichs* (Stuttgart 1952), commentary (*ibid.*, 1953); E. Maschke, *Der Kampf zwischen Kaisertum und Papsttum, Handbuch der deutschen Geschichte*, ed. Leo Just, I (1957), 4. Abschnitt; W. Heinemeyer, "Der Friede von Montebello (1175)," *DA*, 11 (1954), 101–39; P. Lamma, *Comneni e Staufer*, 2 vols. (Rome 1955–57); G. de Vergottini, *Lo Studio di Bologna, l'Impero, il Papato, Studi e Memorie Stor. Univ. di Bologna*, new series, 1 (1956); H. Büttner, "Erzbischof Heinrich von Mainz und die Staufer (1142–53)," *ZKG*, 69 (1958), 247–67; K. Jordan, *Friedrich Barbarossa, Kaiser des christlichen Abendlandes, Persönlichkeit und Geschichte*, 13 (Göttingen 1959); H. Appelt, "Der Vorbehalt kaiserlicher Rechte in den Diplomen Friedrich Barbarossas," *MIÖG*, 68 (1960), 81–97; P. Klopsch, *Zum Kaiserhymnus des Archipoeta, Euphorion*, 54 (1960); W. Heinemeyer, "Die Verhandlungen an der Saône im Jahre 1162," *DA*, 20 (1964), 155–89; J. Y. Mariotte, *Le comté de Bourgogne sous les Hohenstaufen (1156–1208), Annales littéraires de l'université de Besançon*, 56 (Paris 1963); H. J. Kirfel, *Weltherrschaftsidee und Bündnispolitik. Untersuchungen zur auswärtigen Politik der Staufer, Bonner Historische Forschungen*, 12 (Bonn 1959); J. Déer, "Die

Siegel Kaiser Friedrichs I. Barbarossa und Heinrichs VI. in der Kunst und Politik ihrer Zeit," *Festschrift H. R. Hahnloser*, ed. E. J. Beer, P. Hofer, and L. Mojon (Basel and Stuttgart 1961), 47–102; H. Appelt, "Friedrich Barbarossa und das römische Recht," *RömHM*, 5 (1961 f.), 18–34; P. Munz, "Frederick Barbarossa and the 'Holy Empire'," *JRelH*, 3 (1964 f.), 20–37; W. Ohnsorge, "Zu den aussenpolitischen Anfängen Friedrich Barbarossas," *Abendland und Byzanz* (Bad Homburg v. d. Höhe 1963), 411–33; *idem*, "Ein Beitrag zur Geschichte Manuels I. von Byzanz," *Abendland und Byzanz (ibid.* 1963), 387–410; F. Kempf, "Der 'favor apostolicus' bei der Wahl Friedrich Barbarossas und im deutschen Thronstreit (1189–1208)," *Festschrift Spörl, Speculum historiale. Geschichte im Spiegel von Geschichtsschreibung und Geschichtsdeutung*, ed. C. Bauer (Freiburg im Breisgau and Munich 1965), 469–78; J. Ficker, *Rainald von Dassel, Reichskanzler und Erzbischof von Köln* (Cologne 1855, reprinted Aalen 1966); R. M. Herkenrath, *Rainald von Dassel, Reichskanzler und Erzbischof von Köln* (typed dissertation, Graz 1962).

9. *Thomas Becket and Henry II of England*

Sources

Materials for the History of Thomas Becket, Archbishop of Canterbury, canonized by Pope Alexander III, A.D. 1173, ed. J. Craigie Robertson (Vols. 1–6) and J. C. Robertson and J. Brigstocke Sheppard (Vol. 7), *Rolls Series*, 67 (London 1875–85); they contain the biographies by William of Canterbury (Vol. 1), Benedict of Peterborough, John of Salisbury, Alan of Tewkesbury, Edward Grim (Vol. 2), William Fitzstephen and Herbert of Bosham (Vol. 3), anonymous authors and the *Quadrilogus* (Vol. 4), letters from and to Becket (Vols. 5–7); this work supersedes the two-volume edition by J. A. Giles (Oxford and London 1845), which was reprinted in extracts in *PL*, 190, 1–745. E. Magnússon edited the Icelandic vita, *Thómas saga erkibyskups. A life of Archbishop Thomas Becket in Icelandic, with English translation, notes and glossary*, 2 vols., *Rolls Series*, 65 (London 1875–83). A French vita in verse was edited by E. Walberg, *La vie de S. Thomas le Martyr par Guernes de Pont-Sainte-Maxence* (Lund 1922). Cf. E. Walberg, *La tradition hagiographique de Saint Thomas Becket avant la fin du XIIᵉ siècle* (Paris 1929). A vita, no longer extant, by Robert of Cricklade, was reconstructed by M. Orme, "A Reconstruction of Robert of Cricklade's *Vita et Miracula S. Thomae Cantuariensis*," *AnBoll*, 84 (1966), 379–98; *BHL*, 8170–8248; P. G. Foote, "On the Fragmentary Text Concerning Thomas Becket in Stock. per. fol. nr. 2," *Saga-Book*, 4 (1961), 407–50; an Anglo-Norman poem on Thomas Becket by the monk Benedict of St. Alban's, ed. B. Schlyter, *La vie de Thomas Becket par Benoît, Études romanes de Lund*, 4 (Lund 1941). Also important are the collections of the letters of contemporaries: Gilbert Foliot (*The Letters and Charters of Gilbert Foliot*, ed. A. Morey and C. N. L. Brooke [Cambridge 1966], *PL*, 190, 739–1068, ed. J. A. Giles [Oxford 1845]); Arnulf of Lisieux (*The Letters of Arnulf of Lisieux*, ed. F. Barlow, Camden Society, Third Series, 61 [London 1939], *PL*, 201, 17–152); John of Salisbury (*The Letters of John of Salisbury*, ed. W. J. Millor, H. E. Butler, and C. N. L. Brooke, 1, *Nelson's Medieval Texts* [London 1956]; this edition extends only to 1161; the rest are in the edition by J. A. Giles, 2 vols. [Oxford 1845–48], *PL*, 199, 1–378). *Annales monastici*, 5 vols., ed. H. R. Luard, *Rolls Series*, 36 (London 1864–69); *Historia et Cartularium monasterii sancti Petri Gloucestriae*, 3 vols., ed. W. H. Hart, *Rolls Series*, 33 (London 1863–67); the historical writings of Ralph of Diceto were edited by W. Stubbs, 2 vols., *Rolls Series*, 68 (London 1876); the works of Gervase of Canterbury were also edited by W. Stubbs, 2 vols., *Rolls Series*, 73 (London 1879 f.); Walter Map, *De nugis curialium*, ed. T. Wright, Camden Society, Old Series, 50 (London 1850), English translation by M. R. James, with commentary by J. E.

Lloyd, ed. E. Sidney Hartland, *Cymmrodorion Record Series*, 9 (1923); Roger of Howden, *Gesta Henrici Secundi* and *Gesta Ricardi*, ed. W. Stubbs, 2 vols., *Rolls Series*, 49 (London 1867); Stubbs attributed the preceding *Gesta* to Benedict of Peterborough, but D. M. Stenton in *EHR*, 68 (1953), 574–82, proved that their author was Roger of Howden; Giraldus Cambrensis, *Opera*, 8 vols., ed. J. S. Brewer and J. F. Dimock, *Rolls Series*, 21 (London 1861–91); William of Newburgh, *Historia rerum anglicarum: Chronicles of the Reigns of Stephen, Henry II, and Richard I*, ed. R. Howlett, *Rolls Series*, 82, I (London 1884). On the sources see the detailed presentation in R. Foreville, *L'Église et la Royauté en Angleterre sous Henri II Plantagenet (1154–1189)* (Paris 1943), XI–XXXV.

Literature

L. B. Radford, *Thomas of London* (Cambridge 1894), important for Becket's youth; T. F. Tout, "The Place of St. Thomas of Canterbury in History," *BJRL*, 6 (1921), 244–58; D. M. Stenton, "England: Henry II," *The Cambridge Medieval History*, V (Cambridge 1926), 554–91, 895–900; Z. N. Brooke, *The English Church and the Papacy* (Cambridge 1931); C. R. Cheney, *From Becket to Langton* (Manchester 1956); J. Boussard, *Le gouvernement d'Henri Plantagenet* (Paris 1956); J. Haller, "Die Tragödie des Thomas Becket," *Die Welt als Geschichte*, 4 (1938), 97–124; *Haller*, III, 200–24; the most detailed treatment is in the above mentioned work by R. Foreville, 77–428, with a comprehensive bibliography up to 1943, 565–84; R. Foreville in *Fliche-Martin*, IX/2, 83–126; A. L. Poole, *From Domesday Book to Magna Carta* (Oxford, 2d ed. 1964), says that Foreville's work displays exhaustive scholarship but is "marred by bias and lack of judgement" (500), whereas David Knowles, *The Episcopal Colleagues of Archbishop Thomas Becket* (Cambridge 1951), 4, regards it as indispensable, despite certain limitations. D. Knowles has written the best character study in "Archbishop Thomas Becket," *Proceedings of the British Academy*, 35 (1949), 177–205, now also in *The Historian and Character and Other Essays* (Cambridge 1963), 98–129; A. Duggan, *Thomas Becket* (London 1952), is a popular account; T. Borenius, *The Iconography of St. Thomas of Canterbury* (Oxford 1929); P. A. Brown, *The Development of the Legend of Thomas Becket* (Philadelphia 1930); R. Foreville, *Le Jubilé de Saint Thomas Becket du XIIIᵉ au XVᵉ siècle (1220–1470). Études et documents, Bibliothèque Générale de l'École des Hautes Études*, VIᵉ Section (Paris 1958); cf. L. Buisson in *ZSavRGkan*, 46 (1960), 536–39; *idem*, "Tradition et comput dans la chronologie de Thomas Becket," *Bulletin historique et philologique … du comité des travaux historiques et scientifiques 1955/56* (1957), 7–20; M. Barth, "Zum Kult des heiligen Thomas Becket im deutschen Sprachgebiet, in Skandinavien und Italien," *FreibDiözArch*, 80 (1960), 96–166; S. A. Morey, *Bartholomew of Exeter, Bishop and Canonist* (Cambridge 1937); A. Saltman, *Theobald, Archbishop of Canterbury* (London 1956); A. Morey and C. N. L. Brooke, *Gilbert Foliot and his Letters, Cambridge Studies in Medieval Life and Thought*, new series, 11 (Cambridge 1965); C. Duggan, "The Becket Dispute and the Criminous Clerks," *Bulletin of the Institute of Historical Research*, 35 (1962), 1–28; F. J. West, *The Justiciarship in England (1066–1232), Cambridge Studies in Medieval Life and Thought*, new series, 12 (Cambridge 1966); H. Tillmann, *Die päpstlichen Legaten in England bis zur Beendigung der Legation Gualas 1218* (Bonn 1926); R. A. L. Smith, *The Canterbury Cathedral Priory* (Cambridge 1943); C. R. Cheney, *English Bishops' Chanceries (1100–1250)* (Manchester 1950); M. Pacaut, "Les légats d'Alexandre III (1159–1181)," *RHE*, 50 (1955), 821–38.

10. The Heritage of Alexander III

SOURCES

Watterich, II, 650–748; *Liber censuum Romanae Ecclesiae* (drawn up in 1192 by Cencius Savelli, *Camerlengo* of the Curia and later Pope Honorius III), ed. P. Fabre and L. Duchesne, 3 vols. (Paris 1889–92); *Annals of Montecassino*, ed. G. H. Pertz, *MGSS*, 19 (Hanover 1866); Annals of Marbach, ed. H. Block, *MGSS rer. Germ.* (Hanover 1907); *Gesta Treverorum* (continuatio III), *MGSS*, 24, 384–90; Arnold of Lübeck, continuation of the *Chronica Slavorum*, ed. J. M. Lappenberg, *MGSS rer. Germ.* (2d ed. 1930); *Gesta Henrici* by Roger of Howden (see bibliog. for Chapter 9); Robert of Torigny, *Chronicon* (see bibliog. for Chapter 1); *Chronica regia Coloniensis* (see bibliog. for Chapter 8); Ralph of Diceto, *Chronicon* (see bibliog. of Chapter 9); *Annals of Pegau;* William of Newburgh (see the bibliog. for Chapter 9); *Chronicle of Laon* (see the bibliog. for Section Two); *Cronaca di Pisa di Raineri Sardo*, ed. *FontiStIt*, 99 (Rome 1963); *Constitutiones*, I; K. F. Stumpf-Brentano, *"Die Reichskanzler,"* 3 vols. (Innsbruck 1865–81, reprinted Aalen 1964); R. Ries, "Regesten der Kaiserin Konstanze," *QFIAB*, 18 (1926), 30–100.

LITERATURE

Fliche-Martin, IX, 2, 189–230; *Hefele-Leclercq*, V, 1114–78; *Hauck*, IV (5th ed. 1925), 307–24, 686–711; *Gebhardt-Grundmann*, I (8th ed. 1954), 322–40; F. L. Ganshof, *Le Moyen-Age* (Paris, 3d ed. 1964); *idem, Das Hochmittelalter: Propyläen Weltgeschichte*, ed. G. Mann and A. Nitschke, V (1963), 395–488, esp. 435–55; J. T. Appleby, *England without Richard (1189–1199)* (London 1965); M. Powicke, *The Loss of Normandy (1189–1204)* (Manchester, 2d ed. 1961); A. Marongiu, "A Model State in the Middle Ages: The Norman and Swabian Kingdom of Sicily," *Comparative Studies in Society and History*, 6 (1963 f.), 307–20; A. Cartellieri, *Philipp II. August, König von Frankreich*, 4 vols. (Leipzig 1899–1921); *idem*, "Das deutsch-französische Bündnis von 1187 und seine Wandlungen," *HV*, 27 (1932), 111–23; M. Jallut, *Philippe Auguste, fondateur de l'unité française* (Paris 1963); G. Falco, *La Santa Romana Repubblica, Profilo storico del Medio Evo* (Naples, 4th ed. 1963), English translation: *The Holy Roman Republic: A Historical Profile of the Middle Ages* (London 1964); L. Salvatorelli, *L'Italia comunale del secolo XI alla metà del secolo XIV* (Milan 1940); E. Jordan, *L'Allemagne et l'Italie au XIIᵉ siècle, Glotz*, III (Paris 1939); K. Bosl, "Das Hochmittelalter in der Deutschen und Europäischen Geschichte," *HZ*, 194 (1962), 529–67 (good structural analysis, especially of the twelfth century).

Seppelt, III (1956), 213–318; *Haller*, III (3d ed. 1962), 225–95; *Giesebrecht*, VI; W. Lehnel, "Der Konstanzer Friede von 1183 und die italienische Politik Friedrichs I.," *HZ*, 128 (1923), 189–261; K. Wenk, "Die römischen Päpste zwischen Alexander III. und Innocenz III. und der Designationsversuch Weihnachten 1197," *Papsttum und Kaisertum. Festschrift P. Kehr.* (Munich 1926), 415–74; F. Güterbock, "Kaiser, Papst und Lombardenbund nach dem Frieden von Venedig," *QFIAB*, 25 (1933 f.), 158–91; H. Müller, *Die Mitglieder des Kardinalskollegiums von 1181–1216* (typed dissertation, Göttingen 1941); H. Grundmann, "Die Papstprophetien des Mittelalters," *AKG*, 19 (1928), 77–138; M. Maccarone, "Il Papa 'Vicarius Christi,'" *Miscellanea P. Paschini*, I (Rome 1948), 437–500; I. Friedländer, *Die päpstlichen Legaten in Deutschland und Italien (1181–1198)* (Berlin 1928); G. Säbekow, *Die päpstlichen Legationen nach Spanien und Portugal bis zum Ausgang des 12. Jahrhunderts* (dissertation, Berlin 1931); W. Janssen, *Die päpstlichen Legaten in Frankreich (1130–1198)* (Cologne and Graz 1961); V. Pfaff, "Die Einnahmen der römischen Kurie am Ende des 12. Jahrhunderts," *Vierteljahresschrift für Sozialwissenschaft und Wirtschaftsgeschichte*, 40 (1953), 97–118; P. Zerbi, *Papato, Impero e "respublica Christiana" dal 1187 al 1198*

(Milan 1955); J. A. Yunck, "Economic Conservatism, Papal Finance and the Medieval Satires on Rome," *MS*, 23 (1961), 334–51; G. V. Scammel, *Hugh de Puiset, Bishop of Durham (1153–95)* (Cambridge 1956); P. L. Feser, "Bischof Berthold von Livland (1196–98)," *FreibGeschBl*, 27 (1963 f.), 101–28.

Lucius III: PL, 201, 1067–1380; *Jaffé*, II (2d ed.), 431–92, 725 f., 766–69; S. Kuttner, "Pope Lucius III and the Bigamous Archbishop of Palermo," *MS, Festschrift für A. Gwynn* (Dublin 1961), 409–53; J. Ramackers, "Eine Kassation von Papstbriefen unter Lucius III," *HJ*, 55 (1935), 547–51.

Urban III: PL, 202, 1331–1534; *Jaffé*, II (2d ed.), 492–528, 726, 769 f.; P. Scheffer-Boichorst, *Kaiser Friedrichs I. letzter Streit mit der Kurie* (Berlin 1866); H. Kauffmann, *Die italienische Politik Kaiser Friedrichs I. nach dem Frieden von Konstanz (1183–89)* (dissertation, Greifswald 1933); M. C. de Fischer-Reichenbach, *Urban III et Barberousse et les trois cardinaux Crivelli* (Bern 1940).

Gregory VIII: PL, 202, 1537–64; *Jaffé*, II (2d ed.), 528–35; C. D. Fonseca, "La professione canonicale del cardinale Alberto de Mora," *RSTI*, 16 (1962), 136 f.; P. Kehr, "Papst Gregor VIII. als Ordensgründer," *Miscellanea F. Ehrle*, II, *SteT*, 38 (Rome 1924), 248–76, supersedes the older works by G. Kleemann, *Papst Gregor VIII. (1187)* (Bonn 1912), and P. Nadig, *Gregor VIII.* (Basel 1890); W. Holtzmann, "Die Dekretalen Gregors VIII.," *MIÖG*, 58 (1950), 113–23.

Clement III: PL, 204, 1273–1506; *Jaffé*, II (2d ed.), 535–76, 727, 770; R. Foreville in *DHGE*, 12 (1953), 1096–1109; J. Geyer, *Papst Clemens III. (1187–91)* (dissertation, Bonn 1914).

Celestine III: PL, 206, 863–1280; *Jaffé*, II (2d ed.), 577–644, 727, 771 f.; R. Mols in *DHGE*, 12 (1953), 62–77 (bibliography); J. Leinenweber, *Studien zur Geschichte Cölestins III.* (dissertation, Jena 1905); O. Thielepape, *Das Verhältnis Papst Cölestins III. zu den Klöstern* (dissertation, Greifswald 1913); V. Laurent, "Rome et Byzance sous le pontificat de Célestin III," *ÉO*, 39 (1940), 26–58; V. Pfaff, "Die Kardinäle unter Papst Cölestin III. (1191–98)," *ZSavRGkan*, 41 (1955), 58–94; *idem*, "Pro posse nostro. Die Ausübung der Kirchengewalt durch Papst Cölestin III.," *ZSavRGkan*, 43 (1957), 89–131; *idem*, "Feststellungen zu den Urkunden und dem Itinerar Papst Cölestins III.," *HJ*, 78 (1959), 110–39; *idem*, "Die soziale Stellung des Judentums in den Auseinandersetzungen zwischen Kaiser und Kirche vom 3. zum 4. Laterankonzil," *Vierteljahresschrift für Sozialwissenschaft und Wirtschaftsgeschichte*, 52 (1965), 168–206; W. Holtzmann, "La 'Collectio Seguntina' et les décrétales de Clément III et de Célestin III," *RHE*, 50 (1955), 400–53; V. Pfaff, "Papst Cölestin III.," *ZSavRGkan*, 47 (1961), 109–28.

The Emperor Henry VI: JbbDG; T. Toeche, *Heinrich VI.* (Leipzig 1867), which, though old and useful only as incomplete collection of materials, was reprinted at Darmstadt in 1965; J. Haller, "Heinrich VI. und die römische Kirche," *MIÖG*, 35 (1914), 384–454, 545–669 (reprinted Darmstadt 1962); W. Wohlfahrt, *Kaiser Heinrich VI. und die oberitalienischen Städte* (Heidelberg 1939); E. Perels, *Der Erbreichsplan Heinrichs VI.* (Berlin 1927); V. Pfaff, *Kaiser Heinrichs VI. höchstes Angebot an die römische Kurie (1196), Heidelberger Abhandlungen*, 55 (Heidelberg 1927); E. Jordan, "Henri VI a-t-il offert à Clément III de lui faire hommage pour l'empire?" *Mélanges F. Lot* (Paris 1925), 285–306; M. C. E. Perrin, "Les négociations de 1196 entre l'empereur Henri VI et le pape Célestin III," *Mélanges L. Halphen* (Paris 1951), 565–72; W. Leonhardt, *Der Kreuzzugsplan Kaiser Heinrichs VI.* (dissertation, Giessen 1913); J. Heinrich, "Kaiser Heinrich VI. und die Besetzung der deutschen Bistümer," *RQ*, 51 (1956), 189–227. On Henry's coronation see P. Zerbi in *Miscellanea G. Belvederi* (Rome 1954), 517–28; D. Clementi, "Calendar of the Diplomas of the Hohenstaufen Emperor Henry VI Concerning the Kingdom of Sicily," *QFIAB*, 35 (1955), 86–225; E. Moreau, *Albert de Louvain, prince-évêque de Liège* (Brussels 1946); G. Bullinger, *König Richard Löwenherz und Kaiser Heinrich VI.* (typed dissertation, Tübingen 1947); W. Holtzmann, *Das Ende des Bischofs Heinrich von Chur. Ein Beitrag zur Geschichte von Reich und Kirche in den Zeiten Heinrichs VI.*, Zeitschrift für Schweizer Geschichte, 29 (1949); D. von der Nahmer, *Die Reichsverwaltung in Toscana unter Friedrich I. und Heinrich VI.* (Aalen 1966); H. Grundmann, "Kirchenfreiheit und Kaisermacht um 1190 in der Sicht Joachims von Fiore," *DA*, 19 (1962), 353–96; D. Clementi, *Some Unnoticed Aspects of the Emperor Henry VI's Conquest of the Norman Kingdom of Sicily*, BJRL, 36 (1954).

11. *The Third Crusade*

SOURCES

Anonymi Chronicon Terrae Sanctae (to 1187), ed. H. Prutz, *Quellenbeiträge zur Geschichte der Kreuzzüge* (Danzig 1876); Nicetas Choniates, *Historia* (to 1206), ed. I. Bekker, *CSHB* (Bonn 1835), also *RecHistCrois, HistGrecs*, I, 319–37, German translation of selections in F. Grabler, *Byzantinische Geschichtsschreiber*, 7/9 (Graz and Cologne 1938); for the Arabic sources see H. A. R. Gibb, "The Arabic Sources for the Life of Saladin," *Speculum*, 25 (1950), 58–72; *Quellen zur Geschichte des Kreuzzuges Kaiser Friedrichs I.* (*Historia de expeditione Friderici imperatoris, Historia peregrinorum, Epistola de morte Friderici imperatoris, Narratio itineris navalis ad Terram sanctam*), ed. A. Chroust, *MGSS rer. Germ.*, new series, 5 (Berlin 1928); *cf.* A. Chroust, *Tageno, Ansbert und die Historia peregrinorum* (Graz 1892); some information in Arnold of Lübeck, *Chronica Slavorum, MGSS*, 21, ed. I. M. Lappenberg, *MGSS rer. Germ.* (Hanover 1868), and in the *Chronicle* of Otto of Sankt Blasien, ed. A. Hofmeister, *MGSS rer. Germ.* (Hanover and Leipzig 1912); Ambroise, *L'estoire de la Guerre Sainte*, ed. G. Paris, English translation and commentary by M. J. Hubert, *The Crusade of Richard Lionhearted* (New York 1941); L. Landon, *The Itinerary of King Richard I*, Pipe Roll Society, 51 (London 1935); *Das Itinerarium peregrinorum. Eine zeitgenössische Chronik zum 3. Kreuzzug in ursprünglicher Gestalt*, ed. H. E. Mayer, Schriften der *MG*, 18 (Stuttgart 1962); on the preceding see the review by M. L. Bulst in *HZ*, 198 (1964), 380–87, the reply by H. E. Mayer in *DA*, 20 (1964), 210–21, and the refutation by M. L. Bulst in *DA*, 21 (1965), 593–606; Roger of Howden, *Gesta regis Henrici II* and *Chronica* (report of an eyewitness), ed. W. Stubbs, *Rolls Series*, 49, 51 (London 1867–71); Richard of Devizes, *De rebus gestis Ricardi primi*, ed. R. Howlett, *Rolls Series*, 82 (London 1884–89), *Chronicles of the Reigns of Stephen, Henry II and Richard I*, 3; Ralph of Diceto, *Opera historica*, 2 vols., ed. W. Stubbs, *Rolls Series*, 68 (London 1876); Rigord, *Gesta Philippi Augusti*, ed. H. F. Delaborde (Paris 1871), *Œuvres de Rigord et Guillaume le Breton*, 1; Baha-ad-Din's biography of Saladin in *RecHistCrois, HistOr*, III; H. A. R. Gibb, "The Achievement of Saladin," *BJRL*, 35 (1952 f.), 44–60; J. Hartmann, *Die Persönlichkeit des Sultans Saladin im Urteil der abendländischen Quellen*, HStud, 239 (Berlin 1933); M. Salloch, *Die lateinische Fortsetzung Wilhelms von Tyrus* (dissertation, Berlin 1934); Sicard of Cremona, *Chronicle*, MGSS, 31, 22–185; *cf.* E. Brocchieri, *Sicardo di Cremona e la sua opera letteraria* (Cremona 1958).

LITERATURE

H. E. Mayer, *Geschichte der Kreuzzüge* (Stuttgart 1965), bibliography, nos. 2066–2188. For the Crusade of Richard and Philip Augustus: K. Norgate, *Richard the Lion Heart* (London 1924); A. Cartellieri, *Philipp II. August*, 2 (Leipzig 1906); Y. M. J. Congar, "Henri de Marcy, abbé de Clairvaux, Cardinal-évêque d'Albano," *SA*, 43 (1958), 1–90; M. W. Baldwin, *Raymond III of Tripolis and the Fall of Jerusalem* (Princeton 1936);

F. Groh, *Der Zusammenbruch des Reiches Jerusalem (1187–89)* (Jena 1909); E. Jamison, *Admiral Eugenius of Sicily. His Life and Work* (London 1957); L. Usseglio, *I marchesi di Monferrato in Italia ed in Oriente durante i secoli XII e XIII*, 2 vols. (Turin 1926); H. Bettin, *Heinrich II. von Champagne, seine Kreuzfahrt und Wirksamkeit im Heiligen Lande (1190–97)* (Berlin 1910).

For the Crusades of Frederick I and Henry VI: K. Fischer, *Geschichte des Kreuzzugs Kaiser Friedrichs I.* (Leipzig 1870); S. O. Riezler, "Der Kreuzzug Kaiser Friedrichs I.," *FDG,* 10 (1870), 3–149; R. Röhricht, "Die Rüstungen des Abendlandes zum dritten grossen Kreuzzuge," *HZ,* 34 (1875), 1–73; *Giesebrecht,* VI; A. Fürst, *Der Kreuzzugsbrief Kaiser Friedrichs I. an Saladin,* Programm zum Jahresbericht des Königlichen Neuen Gymnasiums in Regensburg 1907/08 (Regensburg 1908); H. E. Mayer, "Der Brief Kaiser Friedrichs I. an Saladin vom Jahre 1188," *DA,* 14 (1958), 488–94; K. Zimmer, "Der Friede von Adrianopel (Februar 1190)," *ByZ,* 11 (1902), 302–20; *idem,* "Der deutsch-byzantinische Konflikt vom Juli 1189 bis Februar 1190," *ByZ,* 12 (1903), 42–77; P. Scheffer-Boichorst, "Barbarossas Grab," *Gesammelte Schriften von Paul Scheffer-Boichorst,* 2, *HStud,* 43, 2 (Berlin 1905), 154–64; E. Traub, *Der Kreuzzugsplan Kaiser Heinrichs VI. im Zusammenhang mit der Politik der Jahre 1195–97* (Jena 1910). The other literature will be found in the bibliography for Chapter 10.

A History of the Crusades, ed. K. M. Setton *et al.,* II (Philadelphia 1962): H. Wieruszowski, "The Norman Kingdom of Sicily and the Crusades," 3–44; S. Painter, "The Third Crusade: Richard the Lionhearted and Philip Augustus," 45–86; E. N. Johnson, "The Crusades of Frederick Barbarossa and Henry VI," 87–122; S. Runciman, *A History of the Crusades,* III (Cambridge 1954), 3–75; R. Grousset, *Histoire des Croisades,* III (Paris 1936), 1–121; A. Waas, *Geschichte der Kreuzzüge,* I (Freiburg im Breisgau 1956), 184–225; copious bibliography in H. E. Mayer, *Das Itinerarium peregrinorum,* XI–XXXIV; F. Kurth, "Der Anteil niederdeutscher Kreuzfahrer an den Kämpfen der Portugiesen gegen die Mauren," *MIÖG,* suppl. Vol. 8 (1911), 131–252; C. Cahen, *La Syrie du Nord à l'époque des croisades et la principauté franque d'Antioche,* Institut de Damas. Bibliothèque orientale, 1 (Paris 1940); *idem,* "Selğukides, Turcomans et Allemands au temps de la troisième croisade," *Wiener Zeitschrift für die Kunde des Morgenlandes,* 56 *(Festschrift H. W. Duda)* (1960), 21–31; A. Cartellieri, "Landgraf Ludwig III. von Thüringen und der dritte Kreuzzug," *Zeitschrift des Vereins für thür. Geschichte und Altertumskunde,* 42 (new series, 34) (1940), 42–64.

Crusade Piety: H. E. Mayer *(Geschichte der Kreuzzüge, supra),* bibliography, nos. 1735–97, 4091–4111, 5291–5311; F. Vandenbroucke, *La piété des laïcs au XIIe siècle;* J. Leclercq, F. Vandenbroucke, and L. Bouyer, *La spiritualité du moyen âge* (Paris 1961), 299–344; H. Wolter, *Elemente der Kreuzzugsfrömmigkeit in der Spiritualität des heiligen Ignatius;* F. Wulf, *Ignatius von Loyola. Seine geistliche Gestalt und sein Vermächtnis* (Würzburg 1956), 111–150; C. Erdmann, *Die Entstehung des Kreuzzugsgedankens,* Forschungen zur Kirchen- und Geistesgeschichte, 6 (Stuttgart 1935); P. Alphandéry, *La Chrétienté et l'idée de Croisade,* I: *Les premières croisades* (texte établi par A. Dupront) (Paris 1954); P. Rousset, "L'idée de croisade chez les chroniqueurs d'Occident," *Relazioni del X congresso internazionale di Scienze storiche,* 3. *Storia del Medio Evo* (Florence 1956), 547–63; Y. M. J. Congar, "Henri de Marcy, abbé de Clairvaux, Cardinal-évêque d'Albano et légat pontifical," *SA,* 43 (1958), 1–90 (esp. pages 77–90); A. Waas, *Geschichte der Kreuzzüge,* I, 1–53; F. W. Wentzlaff-Eggebert, "Kreuzzugsidee und mittelalterliches Weltbild," *DVfLG,* 30 (1956); *idem, Geschichtliche und dichterische Wirklichkeit in der deutschen Kreuzzugslyrik,* Festschrift J. Lortz, 2 (Mainz 1958); *idem, Die Kreuzzugslyrik des Mittelalters* (Berlin 1960).

12. *Scholasticism, Canon Law, and the Universities*

SOURCES

General Bibliography, I, 11; H. Denifle and A. Chatelain, *Chartularium Universitatis Parisiensis*, I (Paris 1889); the works of the theologians and canonists named in this chapter.

ACCOUNTS

General Bibliography, II, 11 and 12, in particular the works of F. Ueberweg and B. Geyer, M. de Wulf, É. Bréhier, É. Gilson and P. Böhner, P. F. Cayré, M. Grabmann, F. Stegmüller, H. Rost, B. Smalley, C. Spicq, H. de Lubac, *Exégèse médiévale*, now complete in 4 vols. (Paris 1960–64); in General Bibliography, II, 6, the works of H. E. Feine, G. Le Bras, B. Kurtscheid, A. Van Hove, *Commentarium Lovaniense in Codicem Iuris Canonici*, I/1, *Prolegomena* (Malines and Rome, 2d ed. 1945); A. M. Stickler, *Historia Iuris Canonici Latini*, I: *Historia Fontium* (Turin 1950); *Fliche-Martin*, XIII (Paris 1951), 147–78; the best introduction to the early science of canon law is G. Le Bras, C. Lefèbvre, and J. Rambaud, *L'âge classique (1140–1378), Sources et théorie du droit, Histoire du droit et des institutions de l'Église en Occident*, 7 (Paris 1965), 266–91; S. Kuttner, *Repertorium der Kanonistik (1140–1234), Prodromus Corporis Glossarum*, I, *SteT*, 71 (Rome 1937).

For the beginnings of the universities: General Bibliography, II, 11 (works of J. van den Driesch, W. Wühr, L. Maître, E. Lesne); also: G. Paré, A. Brunet, and P. Tremblay, *La renaissance du XIIe siècle. Les écoles et l'enseignement* (Ottawa 1933); S. d'Irsay, *Histoire des universités françaises et étrangères des origines à nos jours*, I: *Moyen-âge et Renaissance* (Paris 1933); H. Rashdall, *The Universities of Europe in the Middle Ages*, ed. F. M. Powicke and A. B. Emden, 3 vols. (Oxford 1936); H. Denifle, *Die Universitäten des Mittelalters bis 1400* (Berlin 1885), is still valuable; G. Post, "Alexander III. The licentia docendi and the Rise of the Universities," *Anniversary Essays in Medieval History by Students of C. H. Haskins* (Boston 1929), 255–77; P. Delhaye, "L'organisation scolaire au XIIe siècle," *Tr*, 5 (1947), 211–68; F. Battaglia, "L'unità del sapere nelle prime Università occidentali," *Rivista internazionale di filosofia del diritto* (1955), 190–201; H. Grundmann, *Vom Ursprung der Universitäten im Mittelalter* (Darmstadt, 2d ed. 1960, supplements); R. Meister, "Beiträge zur Gründungsgeschichte der mittelalterlichen Universitäten," *AnzAW*, Phil.-hist. Kl., 49 (1957), 27–50; S. Stelling-Michaud, "L'histoire des universités au moyen-âge et à la renaissance au cours des vingt-cinq dernières années," *Rapport I Comité International des Sciences historiques, XIe Congrès Internat. Stockholm* (1960), 97–143.

Bologna: C. Calcaterra, *Alma Mater Studiorum* (Bologna 1948); G. de Vergottini, *Lo studio di Bologna, l'Impero, il Papato, Studi e memorie per la storia dell'Università di Bologna*, new series, 1 (Bologna 1954).

Paris: L. Halphen, *Les origines de l'Université de Paris: A travers l'histoire du moyen-âge* (Paris 1950); S. Kuttner, "Les débuts de l'école canoniste française," *Studia et documenta historiae et iuris*, 4 (1938), 1–14; *Fliche-Martin*, IX/2, 371–81; E. Behler, "Die Entstehung der mittelalterlichen Universität von Paris," *Perennitas. Festschrift für Thomas Michels*, ed. H. Rahner and E. von Severus (Münster 1963), 294–321; A. L. Gabriel, "Les écoles de la Cathédrale de Notre-Dame et le commencement de l'Université de Paris," *RHÉF*, 50 (1964), 73–99.

13. *Heresy and the Beginnings of the Inquisition*

SOURCES

Ekbert of Schönau, *Sermones adversus Catharorum errores (ca.* 1163), *PL*, 195, 11–98; on the preceding, A. Borst, *Die Katharer* (Stuttgart 1953), 6 f.; Alain de Lille, *De fide catholica contra hereticos sui temporis praesertim Albigenses, PL*, 205, 306–430; Bonacorsi, *Manifestatio heresis Catarorum, PL*, 204, 775–94, ed. Ilarino da Milano, "La 'Manifestatio heresis Catarorum quam fecit Bonacursus,' secondo il cod. Ott. lat. 136 della Bibl. Vaticana," *Aevum*, 12 (1938), 281–333; *idem, L'eresia di Ugo Speroni nella confutazione del Maestro Vacario. Testo inedito del secolo XII con studio storico e dottrinale, SteT*, 115 (Rome 1945); E. Turdeanu, "Apocryphes bogomiles et apocryphes pseudo-bogomiles," *RHR*, 138 (1950), 22–52, 176–218; A. Dondaine, "Aux origines du Valdéisme. Une profession de foi de Valdès," *AFP*, 16 (1946), 191–235; *idem*, "Nouvelles sources de l'histoire doctrinale du néo-manichéisme au moyen-âge," *RSPhTh*, 28 (1939), 465–88; Peter the Venerable, *Epistola sive tractatus adversus petrobrusianos* (1139–42), *PL*, 189, 719–850; Hugh of Amiens, *Contra hereticos sui temporis sive de Ecclesia et eius ministris, PL*, 192, 1141–1352; Bernard of Fontcaude, *Adversus Waldenses Liber, PL*, 204, 793–840; *Epistola Evervini* (provost of Steinfeld) to Bernard of Clairvaux, *PL*, 182, 676–80; Bernard of Clairvaux, *Sermones 65 et 66 super Cantica Canticorum*, ed. J. Leclercq, C. H. Talbot, and H. M. Rochais, *S. Bernardi Opera*, II (Rome 1958), 172–88; *Epistola Leodiensis ecclesie ad papam Lucium II* (1144–45), *PL*, 179, 937 f.; Letters of the Cardinal Bishop Henry of Albano and of Cardinal Peter of San Crisogono (1178), *PL*, 199, 1120–24, 204, 235–40; *Epistola Henrici VI Romanorum imperatoris ad Coelestinum III papam de legatis et haereticis, MGConst*, I, no. 370, p. 519; Walter Map, *De nugis curialium*, ed. T. Wright, Camden Society, Old Series, 50 (London 1850), translation and commentary by M. R. James and J. E. Lloyd, ed. E. S. Hartland, *Cymmrodorion Record Series*, 9 (1923); Roger of Howden, *Chronica*, ed. W. Stubbs, *Rolls Series*, 51 (London 1871); see the bibliography for Chapter 8 for Otto of Freising, *Gesta Friderici*, and Hugh of Poitiers, *Liber de Libertate Monasterii Vizeliacensis; Akten des Albigenserkonzils von Saint-Félix de Caraman*, ed. A. Dondaine, *MiscMercati*, V (1946), 326 f.; analysis of the sources in J. Guiraud, *Histoire (infra)*, I, XI–XLIII, and A. Borst, *Die Katharer* (Stuttgart 1953), 3–12; C. du Plessis d'Argentré, *Collectio iudiciorum de novis erroribus qui ab initio XII seculi usque ad annum 1735 in Ecclesia proscripti sunt et notati*, 3 vols. (Paris 1724–36); I. von Döllinger, *Beiträge zur Sektengeschichte des Mittelalters*, II: *Dokumente vornehmlich zur Geschichte der Valdensier und Katharer* (Munich 1890); P. Frédéricq, *Corpus documentorum inquisitionis haereticae pravitatis Neerlandicae*, 5 vols. (Ghent 1889–1906).

LITERATURE

C. U. Hahn, *Geschichte der Ketzer im Mittelalter, besonders im 11., 12. und 13. Jahrhundert*, 3 vols. (Stuttgart 1845–50); H. Reuter, *Geschichte der religiösen Aufklärung im Mittelalter*, 2 vols. (Berlin 1875–77); F. Tocco, *L'eresia nel medio evo* (Florence 1884); H. C. Lea, *A History of the Inquisition in the Middle Ages*, 3 vols. (London 1888, reprinted New York 1955); on the preceding see J. Dalberg-Acton in *EHR*, 3 (1888), 773–88; P. Frédéricq, *Geschiedenis der Inquisitie in de Nederlanden (1025–1528)* (Ghent 1892); A. S. Turberville, *Medieval Heresy and the Inquisition* (London 1920, reprinted London 1964); G. Volpe, *Movimenti religiosi e sette ereticali nella società medioevale italiana sec. XI–XIV* (1922, 2d ed. 1926, reprinted Florence 1961); H. Grundmann, *Religiöse Bewegungen im Mittelalter* (Berlin 1935, reprinted with supplement Darmstadt 1961); J. Guiraud, *Histoire de l'Inquisition au moyen-âge*, 2 vols. (Paris 1935–38); A. Aegerter, *Les hérésies du moyen-âge* (Paris 1939); W. Nigg, *Das Buch der Ketzer* (Zürich 1949); G. Welter, *Histoire des sectes chrétiennes des origines à nos jours* (Paris 1950); R. Morghen, *Medioevo cristiano* (Bari 1951, 2d ed. 1958), 204–81; L. Sommariva, "Studi recenti sulle eresie medioevali," *RSIt*, 64 (1952), 237–68; E. Dupré-Theseider, *Introduzione alle eresie medioevali* (Bologna 1953); P. Ilarino da Milano, "Le eresie medioevali," *Grande Antologia Filosofica*, II/4 (Milan 1954), 1599–1689; R. R. Betts, E. Delaruelle, H. Grundmann, R. Morghen, and L. Salvatorelli, "Movimenti religiosi popolari ed eresie del Medioevo," *Relazioni del X Congresso Internazionale di Scienze storiche*, III (Florence 1955), 305–541; H. Grundmann, *Ketzergeschichte des Mittelalters* (Göttingen 1963), fasc. 2 G, 1, of *Die Kirche in ihrer Geschichte*, ed. K. D. Schmidt and E. Wolf; J. Russell, "Interpretations of the Origins of Medieval Heresy," *MS*, 25 (1963), 26–53; E. Van der Vekené, *Bibliographie der Inquisition. Ein Versuch* (Hildesheim 1963), and, in regard to it, B. A. Vermaseren, "Een bibl. over de inquisitie," *Tijdschr. v. Geschiedenis*, 77 (1964), 472–77; C. Pozo, "La noción de 'herejía' en el derecho canónico medieval," *Misc. Pérez Goyena* (Madrid 1960), 235–51; H. Flatten, *Der Häresieverdacht im Codex Iuris Canonici, Kan. Studien und Texte*, 21 (Amsterdam 1963); H. Grundmann, "Oportet et haereses esse. Das Problem der Ketzerei im Spiegel der mittelalterlichen Bibelexegese," *AKG*, 45 (1963), 129–64; *idem*, "Der Typus des Ketzers in mittelalterlicher Anschauung," *Kultur- und Universalgeschichte, Festschrift für W. Goetz* (Leipzig 1927), 91–107.

The Cathari: E. Broeckx, *Le Catharisme* (Hoogstraten 1916); S. Runciman, *The Medieval Manichee* (Cambridge 1947); A. Borst, *Die Katharer*, Schriften der *MG*, 12 (Stuttgart 1953); F. Niel, *Albigeois et Cathares* (Paris 1955); E. Delaruelle, "Le Catharisme en Languedoc vers 1200, une enquête," *Annales du Midi*, 72 (1960), 149–67; P. de Berne-Lagarde, *Bibliographie du catharisme languedocien*, Institut des Études cathares, Collection de textes et documents, 1 (Toulouse 1957); D. Walther, "A Survey of Recent Research on the Albigensian Cathari," *Church History*, 34 (1965), 146–77; C. Thouzellier, *Catharisme et valdéisme en Languedoc à la fin du XIIe et au début du XIIIe siècle. Politique pontificale. Controverses* (Paris 1966).

The Waldensians: A. Armand-Hugon and G. Gonnet, *Bibliografia valdese* (Torre Pellice 1953); G. Gonnet, *Enchiridion fontium Valdensium* (Torre Pellice 1953; Vol. I to 1218); *idem, Il Valdismo medioevale, Prolegomeni* (1942); A. Dondaine, "Aux origines du Valdéisme," *AFP*, 16 (1946), 191–235, 17 (1947), 85–194, 29 (1959), 228–76; G. Gonnet, "Waldensia," *RHPhR*, 33 (1953), 202–54; G. Koch, "Neue Quellen und Forschungen über die Anfänge der Waldenser," *FF*, 32 (1958), 141–49; W. Mohr, "Waldes und das frühe Waldensertum," *ZRGG*, 9 (1957), 357–63; H. Wolter, "Aufbruch und Tragik der apostolischen Laienbewegung im Mittelalter. Die Anfänge der Waldenserbewegung," *GuL*, 30 (1957), 357–69; S. Dupré-Theseider, "Gli eretici sul mondo comunale italiano," *Bollettino della Società di Studi Valdesi*, no. 114 (1963), 3–23.

The Humiliati: H. Tiraboschi, *Vetera Humiliatorum monumenta* (Milan 1766–68); A. de Stefano, "Le origini dell'Ordine degli Umiliati," *Riv. stor.-crit. delle scienze teol.*, 2 (1906), 851–71; *idem.* in *Arch. Roman.*, 11 (1927), 31–75; P. Guerrini, "Gli Umiliati a Brescia," *Miscellanea P. Paschini*, I (1948), 187–214; G. Mercati, "Due ricerche per la storia degli Umiliati," *RSTI*, 11 (1957), 167–94.

The beginnings of the Inquisition: H. Maisonneuve, *Études sur les origines de l'Inquisition, L'Église et l'État au Moyen-Age*, ed. G. Le Bras, 7 (Paris 1960); H. C. Lea, *The Inquisition of the Middle Ages: Its Organisation and Operation. With an historical introduction by W. Ullman* (London 1963); Y. Dossat, "Les débuts de l'Inquisition à Montpellier et en Provence," *Bull. Phil. et Hist. du Comité des Travaux historiques et scientifiques* (1961), 561–79; M. Bévenot, "The Inquisition and its Antecedents," *Heythrop Journal*, 7 (1966), 257–68, 381–93, 8 (1967), 52–69.

14. Lay Movements of the Twelfth Century, Christian Knighthood, Pastoral Care, Popular Piety, and Mystical Theology

LITERATURE

Lay Movements: G. Le Bras, *Fliche-Martin,* XII, 2 parts (Paris 1959–64); Y. M. J. Congar, *Jalons pour une théologie du laïcat* (Paris 1953), with many historical references; J. Fichet, *Histoire du laïcat dans l'Église: Le rôle des laïcs dans l'Église* (Carrefour 1951, Montreal 1952); L. Leitmaier, "Der Laie in der Kirche im Mittelalter und im 20. Jahrhundert," *ZSavRGkan,* 39 (1953), 28–45; H. Grundmann, *Religiöse Bewegungen im Mittelalter. Untersuchungen über die geschichtlichen Zusammenhänge zwischen der Ketzerei, den Bettelorden und den religiösen Frauenbewegungen im 12. und 13. Jahrhundert und über die geschichtlichen Grundlagen der deutschen Mystik,* 2d ed., expanded and supplemented, with a report on the research by the Tenth International Congress of Historians at Rome in 1955 (Darmstadt 1961); *idem,* "Literatus, illiteratus . . .," *AKG,* 40 (1958), 1–65; G. Volpe, *Movimenti religiosi e sette ereticali nella società medioevale italiana* (Florence 1961); A. Auer, *Weltoffener Christ. Grundsätzliches und Geschichtliches zur Laienfrömmigkeit* (Düsseldorf 1960).

Confraternities: G. Le Bras, "Les confréries chrétiennes," *RHD* (1940 f.), 310–363; *idem* in *Études de sociologie religieuse,* II (Paris 1956), 432–62; P. Dubarc, "Confréries du Saint-Esprit et communautés d'habitants au moyen-âge," *RHD* (1958), 349–67; *Fliche-Martin,* IX/2 (Paris 1953), 317–29; C. Petit-Dutaillis, *Les communes françaises, caractères et évolution des origines au XVIIIe siècle* (Paris 1947); E. C. Lodge, "The Communal Movement, especially in France," *The Cambridge Medieval History,* 5 (1926), 624–57, 903–08 (bibliography).

The ius patronatus: S. Schröcker, *Die Kirchenpflegschaft* (Paderborn 1934); F. Fournier, *Le droit de propriété exercé par les laïcs sur les biens de l'église dans le haut moyen-âge* (Lille 1943); F. J. Schmale, "Kanonie, Seelsorge und Eigenkirche," *HJ,* 78 (1959), 38–63; V. Chomel, "Droit de patronage et pratique religieuse dans l'archevêché de Narbonne," *BÉCh,* 115 (1957), 58–137.

Knighthood: C. Cohen, *Histoire de la chevalerie en France au moyen-âge* (Paris 1949); H. Naumann, *Deutsche Kultur im Zeitalter des Rittertums, Handbuch der Kulturgeschichte* (Potsdam 1938); *idem, Der staufische Ritter* (Leipzig 1936); G. Fliegner, *Geistliches und weltliches Rittertum im Rolandslied des Pfaffen Konrad* (dissertation, Breslau 1937); W. Berges, *Die Fürstenspiegel des hohen und späten Mittelalters,* Schriften der *MG,* 1 (Leipzig 1938); W. Kleineke, *Englische Fürstenspiegel vom Policraticus des Johannes von Salisbury bis zum Basilikon Doron Jakobs I.* (Halle 1937); G. Ehrismann, "Die Grundlagen des ritterlichen Tugendsystems," *ZdAdL,* 56 (1919), 137–216; E. R. Curtius, "Das ritterliche Tugendsystem," *DVfLG,* 21 (1943), 343–68; F. W. Wentzlaff-Eggebert, "Ritterliche Lebenslehre und antike Ethik," *DVfLG,* 23 (1949), 252–73; F. Maurer, "Das ritterliche Tugendsystem," *DVfLG,* 23 (1949), 274–85; *idem,* "Zum ritterlichen 'Tugendsystem'," *DVfLG,* 24 (1950), 526–29; E. Neumann, "Der Streit um das ritterliche Tugendsystem," *Festschrift K. Helm* (Tübingen 1951), 137–55; S. Pivano, "Lineamenti storici e giuridici della cavalleria medioevale," *Memorie della Reale Accademia delle Scienze di Torino,* series 2, 55, *Scienze morali* (Turin 1905), 255–336; K. E. Löfqvist, *Om Riddarväsen och Frälse i Nordisk Medeltid* (Lund 1935); Z. Wojciechowski, *Das Ritterrecht in Polen vor den Statuten Kasimirs des Grossen, Bibliothek geschichtlicher Werke aus den Literaturen Osteuropas,* 5 (Breslau 1930); C. Sánchez-Albornoz, *Entorno a los orígenes del feudalismo,* 2 vols. (Mendoza 1942); P. B. Wessels, *Der höfische Ritter, ein Wanderer zwischen zwei Welten* (Nijmegen and Utrecht 1952); U. T. Holmes, *Daily Living in the Twelfth Century. Based on Observations of Alexander Neckam in London and Paris* (Madison 1952); P. Alphandéry, *La chrétienté et l'idée de croisade,* II: *Recommencements nécessaires (XIIe–XIIIe siècles)* (Paris 1959); D. Zorgi, *Valori religiosi nella letteratura provenzale. La spiritualità trinitaria* (Milan 1954); E. R. Labande, "Le 'Credo' épique. A propos des prières dans les chansons de geste," *Recueil M. C. Brunel* (Paris 1955), 62–80; J. P. Ritter, *Ministérialité et chevalerie. Dignité humaine et liberté dans le droit médiéval* (typed dissertation, Lausanne 1955); R. Coulborn *et al., Feudalism in History* (Princeton 1956); S. Painter, *French Chivalry, Chivalric Ideas and Practices in Medieval France* (new printing, Ithaca, N. Y., 2d ed. 1957); O. Brunner, *Feudalismus, Sb. Mainz 1958,* 10 (Wiesbaden 1959); H. de Boor, *Die höfische Literatur* (Munich 1964), *passim;* H. J. Koppitz, *Wolframs Religiosität. Beobachtungen über das Verhältnis Wolframs von Eschenbach zur religiösen Tradition des Mittelalters, Abhandlungen zur Kunst-, Musik- und Literaturgeschichte,* 7 (Bonn 1959); A. Borst, "Das Rittertum im Hochmittelalter," *Saeculum,* 10 (1959), 213–31 (bibliography); D. M. Stenton, *English Society in the Early Middle Ages (1066–1307)* (Harmondsworth, 4th ed. 1965), 60–99; H. Kuhn, *Rittertum und Mystik* (Munich 1963); A. Waas, *Der Mensch im deutschen Mittelalter* (Graz and Cologne 1964); E. H. Massmann, *Schwertleite und Ritterschlag, dargestellt auf Grund der mittelhochdeutschen literarischen Quellen* (dissertation, Hamburg 1932); induction into knighthood: M. Andrieu, *Le Pontificat romain au moyen-âge,* III, *SteT,* 88 (Rome 1940), 447–50, 549 f.; F. M. Stenton, *The First Century of English Feudalism (1066–1166)* (Oxford, 2d ed. 1950); H. Spranaym, "Zu Hartmanns Kreuzzugslyrik," *DVfLG,* 26 (1952), 162–77.

Pastoral Care: Sacraments: D. Van den Eynde, *Les définitions des sacrements (1050–1240)* (Rome 1950); A. M. Landgraf, *Dogmengeschichte der Frühscholastik,* III (Regensburg 1954 f.); A. Franz, *Die Messe im deutschen Mittelalter* (Freiburg 1902); F. Gillmann, *Die Siebenzahl der Sakramente bei den Glossatoren des Gratianischen Dekrets* (Mainz 1909); J. de Ghellinck, "Über den Sakramentsbegriff des 12. Jahrhunderts," *Mélanges Mandonnet,* II (Paris 1930), 79–96; H. Weisweiler, *Die Wirksamkeit der Sakramente nach Hugo von Sankt Viktor* (Freiburg 1932).

P. Browe, "Die Kinderkommunion im Mittelalter," *Scholastik,* 5 (1930), 1–45; J. Baumgärtler, *Die Erstkommunion der Kinder bis zum Ausgang des Mittelalters* (Munich 1929); C. Clinton, *The Paschal Precept* (dissertation, Washington 1932); P. Browe, *Die Verehrung der Eucharistie im Mittelalter* (Munich 1933); *idem,* "Die Elevation in der Messe," *JLW,* 9 (1929), 20–66; *idem, Die häufige Kommunion im Mittelalter* (Münster 1938); *idem,* "Die Kommunionvorbereitung im Mittelalter," *RKTh,* 56 (1932), 375–415; *idem,* "Die eucharistischen Verwandlungswunder des Mittelalters," *RQ,* 38 (1929), 137–69; *idem, Die Pflichtkommunion im Mittelalter* (Münster 1940); *idem,* "Die Kommunion der Heiligen im Mittelalter," *StdZ,* 117 (1929), 425–37; *idem,* "Mittelalterliche Kommunionriten—Die Sterbekommunion," *JLW,* 15 (1941), 23–66; E. Maffei, *La réservation eucharistique jusqu'à la Renaissance* (Brussels 1942); E. Dumoutet, *Le désir de voir l'Hostie et les origines de la dévotion au S. Sacrement* (Paris 1926); *idem, Le Christ selon la chair et la vie liturgique au moyen-âge* (Paris 1932); A. L. Mayer, "Die 'heilbringende' Schau in Sitte und Kult," *Festschrift I. Herwegen* (Münster 1938), 234–61; M. Andrieu, *Le Pontificat romain au moyen-âge,* 4 vols. (Rome 1938–41), *SteT,* 86–88, 99.

P. Schmoll, *Die Busslehre der Frühscholastik* (Munich 1909); J. A. Spitzig, *Sacramental Penance in the Twelfth and Thirteenth Centuries* (Washington 1947); P. Anciaux, *La théologie du sacrement de Pénitence au XIIe siècle* (Louvain 1947); R. Blomme, *La doctrine du péché dans les écoles théologiques de la première moitié du XIIe siècle* (Louvain 1958); N. Paulus, *Die Geschichte des Ablasses im Mittelalter,* 3 vols. (Paderborn 1922 f.), basic work; B. Poschmann, *Der Ablass im Lichte der Bussgeschichte* (Bonn 1948); A. Teetaert, *La confession aux laïques dans l'Église latine du VIIIe au XIVe siècle* (Bruges 1926); F. Billmann in *AkathKR,* 107 (1927), 360–78, and H. Weisweiler in *Scholastik,* 3 (1928), 574–80.

H. Thurston, *Familiar Prayers. Their Origin and History* (London 1953), Chapter VI; L. Gougaud, *Dévotion et pratiques ascétiques du moyen-âge* (Maredsous 1925); A. Wilmart, *Auteurs spirituels et textes dévots du moyen-âge latin* (Paris 1932); J. Leclercq, "Dévotion privée, piété populaire et liturgie au moyen-âge," *Études de pastorale liturgique* (Paris 1944), 149–83; F. Vandenbroucke, "La piété des laïcs au XIIe siècle," *Histoire de la spiritualité chrétienne*, II (Paris 1961), 299–344.

Pastoral Care: Preaching: J. B. Schneyer, "Die Predigt im Mittelalter," *LThK*, VIII (2d ed. 1963), 708–10, 713; W. Wackernagel, *Altdeutsche Predigten und Gebete* (Basel 1876); L. Bourgain, *La chaire française au XIIe siècle* (Paris 1879); R. Cruel, *Geschichte der deutschen Predigt im Mittelalter* (Detmold 1879); A. Lecoy de la Marche, *La chaire française au moyen-âge* (Paris, 2d ed. 1886); A. Linsenmayer, *Geschichte der Predigt in Deutschland von Karl dem Grossen bis zum Ausgang des 14. Jahrhunderts* (Munich 1886); G. R. Owst, *Preaching in Medieval England* (Oxford and Cambridge, 2d ed. 1926); *idem, Literature and Pulpit in Medieval England* (Oxford, 2d ed. 1961); H. Caplan, *Mediaeval Artes Praedicandi. A Handlist* (Ithaca, N. Y. 1934), supplementary volume (1936); T. M. Charland, *Artes Praedicandi. Contributions à l'histoire de la rhétorique au moyen-âge* (Paris and Ottawa 1936); J. B. Schneyer, *Wegweiser zu lateinischen Predigtreihen des Mittelalters* (Munich 1965); J. Châtillon, "Sermons et prédicateurs victorins de la seconde moitié du XIIe siècle," *AHD*, 32 (1965), 7–60.

Devotion to Mary: Maria, Études sur la Sainte Vierge, ed. H. du Manoir, 7 vols. (Paris 1949–64); T. Meier, *Die Gestalt Mariens im geistlichen Schauspiel des deutschen Mittelalters* (Berlin 1959); R. W. Southern, "The English Origins of the 'Miracles of the Virgin,'" *MRS*, 4 (1958), 176–216; H. Graef, *Maria. Eine Geschichte der Lehre und Verehrung* (Freiburg 1964), Chapter 5; E. Baumann, *Histoire des pèlerinages de la Sainte Vierge* (Paris 1941); M. V. Gripkey, *The Blessed Virgin Mary as Mediatrix in the Latin and Old French Legend prior to the Fourteenth Century* (Washington 1938).

Mystical Theology: J. Leclercq, F. Vandenbroucke, and L. Bouyer, *La spiritualité du moyen-âge* (Paris 1961), 161–298; M. N. Scivoletto, *Spiritualità medioevale e tradizione scolastica nel secolo XII in Francia* (Naples 1954); M. D. Chenu, *La théologie au XIIe siècle* (Paris 1957); P. Wolff, *Die Viktoriner mystischen Schriften* (Vienna 1936); R. Roques, "Connaissance de Dieu et théologie symbolique d'après 'In Hierarchiam coelestem' de Hugues de Saint Victor: De la connaissance de Dieu," *Recherches de philosophie*, III–IV (Paris 1958), 187–266; R. Javelet, *Psychologie des auteurs spirituels du XIIe siècle* (Épinal 1959); D. Lasic, *Hugonis a S. Victore theologia perfectiva, eius fundamentum philosophicum ac theologicum* (Rome 1956); G. Dumeige, *Richard de Saint-Victor et l'idée chrétienne de l'amour* (Paris 1952); *Liber exceptionum,* ed. J. Châtillon (Paris 1958); J. Beumer, "Richard von St. Viktor, Theologe und Mystiker," *Scholastik*, 31 (1956), 213–38; Godfrey of Saint-Victor, *Microcosmus,* ed. P. Delhaye, 2 vols. (Lille 1951), with a theological interpretation. The best introduction to Rupert of Deutz is now M. Bernards, "Die Welt der Laien in der kölnischen Theologie des 12. Jahrhunderts. Beobachtungen zur Ekklesiologie Ruperts von Deutz," *Die Kirche und ihre Ämter und Stände, Festschrift Kardinal Frings* (Cologne 1960), 391–416; comprehensive treatment of Gerhoh of Reichersberg in P. Classen's biography (Wiesbaden 1960).

The Byzantine Church in the Epoch of the Crusades

15. *The Byzantine Church from 1054 to 1203*

LITERATURE

F. Chalandon, *Essai sur le règne d'Alexis I Comnène* (Paris 1900); *idem, Jean Comnène et Manuel Comnène* (Paris 1912); S. Runciman, *A History of the Crusades*, 3 vols. (Cambridge 1951–54); *idem, The Eastern Schism* (Oxford 1955); *A History of the Crusades*, ed. K. M. Setton, I–II (Philadelphia 1955–62); P. Lamma, *Comneni e Staufer*, I–II (Rome 1955–57); A. Frolow, *Recherches sur la déviation de la IVe croisade vers Constantinople* (Paris 1955); W. Norden, *Das Papsttum und Byzanz* (Berlin 1903; reprint 1965).

16. *The Byzantine Church from 1203 to 1282*

LITERATURE

A. Heisenberg, *Neue Quellen zur Geschichte des lateinischen Kaisertums und der Kirchenunion*, I–III, *SAM*, 1922, 5; 1923, 2; 1923, 3 (Munich 1922 f.); W. Miller, *The Latins in the Levant* (London 1908); J. Lognon, *L'empire latin de Constantinople et la principauté de Morée* (Paris 1949); S. Lampros, Αὐτοκρατόρων τοῦ Βυζαντρίου χρυσόβουλλα καὶ χρυσᾶ γράμματα ἀναφερόμενα εἰς τὴν ἔνωσιν τῶν ἐκκλησιῶν: Νέος Ἑλληνομήμων 11 (1904), 94–128, 241–54; A. L. Tautu, *Acta Urbani IV, Clementis IV, Gregorii X* (Vatican City 1953); A. Gardner, *The Lascarids of Nicaea* (London 1912); D. J. Geanakoplos, *Emperor Michael Palaeologus and the West* (Cambridge, Mass. 1959).

17. *The Inner Life of the Byzantine Church in the Age of the Crusades*

SECTION FOUR

The Papacy at the Height of Its Power: 1198 - 1216

SOURCES

Mansi, XXII–XXIV; *Hefele-Leclercq*, V, 2 (Paris 1913); *Potthast R; Liber Censuum Romanae Ecclesiae*, compiled by Cencius Savelli (Pope Honorius III), ed. P. Fabre, L. Duchesne, and G. Mollat, 3 vols. (Paris 1889–1952), and, in regard to it, V. Pfaff in *Vierteljahresschrift für Sozial- und Wirtschaftsgeschichte*, 44 (1957), 87–96, 105–20, 220–42, 325–51; J. F. Böhmer, *Regesta Imperii*, V (1198–1272), revised by J. Ficker and E. Winkelmann, 5 parts (Innsbruck 1881–1901), supplements by P. Zinsmaier, *ZGObrh*, 102 (1954), 183–273; *MGConst*, II (1198–1272); A. Huillard-Bréholles, *Historia diplomatica Frederici Secundi*, 12 vols. in 6 (Paris 1852–61, reprinted Turin 1963); *MG Epistolae s. XIII e regestis Pontificum Romanorum selectae* (Honorius III to Clement IV), ed. C. Rodenberg, 3 vols. (Hanover 1883–94); *Regesta Honorii Papae III*, ed. P. Pressuti, 2 vols. (Rome 1888–95);

the École française de Rome has edited the *registra* of the Popes following Honorius III (see the respective chapters). *Chronica Fratris Salimbene de Adam* (1168–1287), ed. O. Holder-Egger, *MGSS*, 32 (Hanover 1905–13), German translation by A. Doren, 2 vols. (Leipzig 1914), *cf.* O. Holder-Egger in *NA*, 37 (1912), 163–218, 38 (1913), 469–81; Salimbene's *Chronicle* is now also edited by G. Scalia, *Scrittori d'Italia*, 232/233, 2 vols. (Bari 1966); Burchard of Ursperg, *Chronicle* (1126–1225), ed. O. Holder-Egger and E. von Simson, *MGSS rer. Germ.* (Hanover, 2d ed. 1916); Roland of Padua, *Liber chronicorum in factis et circa facta Marchie Treviciane*, Muratori, 8, 169–360; Richard of San Germano, *Chronica regni Siciliae*, Muratori, 7, 967–1052; *Annales Placentini* (1012–1235), ed. O. Holder-Egger, *MGSS rer. Germ.* (Hanover 1901); Matthew Paris, *Chronica maiora*, ed. H. R. Luard, *Rolls Series*, 57, 7 vols. (London 1872–83); Walther von der Vogelweide, *Gedichte*, ed. K. Lachmann, 10th ed. by C. von Kraus (Berlin and Leipzig 1936); Martin of Troppau (Polonus), *Chronica summorum Pontificum Imperatorumque de VII aetatibus mundi* (to 1277, but often legendary), ed. L. Weiland, *MGSS*, 22, 377–475, and, in regard to it, H. Grundmann, *Geschichtsschreibung im Mittelalter* (Göttingen 1965); Vincent of Beauvais, *Speculum maius (historiale)* (to 1250) (Douai 1624); continuation of the *Chronica Regia Coloniensis* (to 1220), ed. G. Waitz, *MGSS rer. Germ.*, 18 (1880); Annals of Marbach (to 1238), ed. H. Bloch, *MGSS rer. Germ.*, 9 (1907); continuation of the *Casus S. Galli* (1203–33 by Conrad of Fabaria), ed. G. Meyer von Knonau, *St. Gallische Geschichtsquellen*, IV (1879); *Saxon World Chronicle*, in Low German (to 1248), *MG Deutsche Chroniken* II, 65–258 (Hanover 1877); T. Rymer, *Foedera, conventiones, litterae et cuiuscumque generis acta publica inter reges Angliae et alios quosvis*, 6 vols. (London 1816–30), ed. A. Clarke, J. Caley, and F. Holbrooke; L. Landon, *The Itinerary of King Richard I*, Pipe Roll Society, new series, 13 (London 1935); *Monasticon Anglicanum*, ed. J. Caley *et al.* (London 1849); Ralph of Diceto, *Imagines Historiarum*, ed. W. Stubbs, *Rolls Series*, 68 (London 1876); Gervase of Canterbury, *Opera historica*, ed. W. Stubbs, *Rolls Series*, 73, 2 vols. (London 1879 f.); Ralph of Coggeshall, *Chronicon Anglicanum*, ed. J. Stevenson, *Rolls Series*, 66 (London 1875); Walter of Coventry, *Memoriale*, ed. W. Stubbs, *Rolls Series*, 58 (London 1873); Roger of Wendover, *Flores Historiarum*, ed. H. O. Coxe, English Historical Society (London 1841 f.), adopted and polished by Matthew Paris in his historical works, *cf.* V. H. Galbraith, *Roger Wendover and Matthew Paris* (Glasgow 1944); *Histoire des ducs de Normandie et des rois d'Angleterre*, ed. F. Michel, *Société de l'histoire de France* (Paris 1840); Giraldus Cambrensis, *Opera*, ed. J. S. Brewer, 4 vols. (London 1861–65); *Histoire de Guillaume le Maréchal*, ed. P. Meyer, 2 vols. (Paris 1891–1901); *Epistolae Cantuarienses*, ed. W. Stubbs, *Rolls Series*, 38 (London 1865); *Gesta Philippi Augusti* by Rigord and William the Breton, ed. H. F. Delaborde (Paris 1882); *Philippide* of William the Breton, ed. H. F. Delaborde (Paris 1885); H. F. Delaborde, E. Berger, C. Petit-Dutaillis, J. Monicat, and C. Bunel, *Recueil des actes de Philippe Auguste, roi de France*, 2 vols. (Paris 1916–43); Robert of Auxerre, *Chronicle* (to 1211), ed. O. Holder-Egger, *MGSS*, 26, 226–87.

LITERATURE

Fliche-Martin, X (Paris 1950); *Kirchengeschichte*, ed. P. J. Kisch, II, 2: J. Hollnsteiner, *Die Kirche vom Anfang des 13. bis zur Mitte des 15. Jahrhunderts* (Freiburg 1940); *Seppelt*, III (Munich 1956); *Haller*, III–IV (Esslingen, 2d ed. 1962); E. Delaruelle *et al.*, *Histoire du catholicisme en France*, II (Paris 1960); *Lavisse*, III, 1–2 (Paris 1901); A. Cartellieri, *Philipp II. August*, IV (Leipzig 1921 f.); R. Davidsohn, *Geschichte von Florenz*, I–IV, 3 (Berlin 1896–1927); F. Gregorovius, *Geschichte der Stadt Rom im Mittelalter*, ed. W. Kampf, 3 vols. (Darmstadt 1953–57); K. Völker, *Kirchengeschichte Polens* (Berlin 1930); B. Hóman, *Geschichte des ungarischen Mittelalters*, 2 vols. (Berlin 1940–43); *idem*, *König*

Stephan 1. der Heilige. Die Gründung des ungarischen Königtums (Pécs 1935); G. Stadt-müller, "Die ungarische Grossmacht des Mittelalters," *HJ,* 70 (1951), 65–105; K. Hampe, *Das Hochmittelalter* (Graz, Vienna, and Cologne, 5th ed. 1963), with an epilogue by G. Tellenbach; *Hauck,* IV, 686–776 (Leipzig, 5th ed. 1925, reprinted Berlin 1954); A. L. Poole, *From Domesday Book to Magna Carta* (Oxford, 2d ed. 1964); M. Powicke, *The Thirteenth Century (1216–1307)* (Oxford, 2d ed. 1962); J. E. A. Joliffe, *Angevin Kingship* (London, 2d ed. 1963); C. Duggan, "From the Conquest to the Death of John," *The English Church and the Papacy,* ed. C. H. Lawrence (London 1965), 63–115; L. Salvatorelli, *L'Italia medioevale: L'Italia comunale dal secolo XI alla metà del secolo XIV* (Milan 1940); J. Ficker, *Forschungen zur Reichs- und Rechtsgeschichte Italiens,* 4 vols. (Innsbruck 1864–74); F. Soldevilla, *Historia de España,* 3 vols. (Barcelona 1952–54); D. Peres, *Historia de Portugal,* 8 vols. (Barcelos 1928–37); *idem, Como nasceu Portugal* (Barcelos 1938); D. Mansilla, *Iglesia castellano-leonesa y Curia Romana en los tiempos del Rey San Fernando* (Madrid 1945); O. H. Green, *Spain and the Western Tradition. The Castilian Mind from El Cid to Calderón* (Madison 1963; rich bibliography); C. Erdmann, *Das Papsttum in Portugal im 1. Jahrhundert der portugiesischen Geschichte, AAB* (1938), no. 5; M. de Oli-veira, *Historia eclesiástica de Portugal* (Lisbon, 3d ed. 1958); L. Musset, *Les peuples scan-dinaves au moyen-âge* (Paris 1951); H. Koch, *Danmarks Kirke i den begynende Højmid-delalder,* 2 vols. (Copenhagen 1936).

18. *Personality and Program of Innocent III*

SOURCES

Letters, Documents, Works: PL, 214–217; *Regestum super negotio Romani Imperii,* ed. W. M. Peitz (Rome 1927), W. Holtzmann (1947 f.), F. Kempf (Rome 1947); selections in German translation by G. Tangl (Leipzig 1923); Innocent's *registra* are now critically edited by the Österreichisches Kulturinstitut in Rome under O. Hageneder and A. Haid-acher, *Die Register Innozenz' III.,* I, Publikationen der Abteilung für Historische Studien des Österreichischen Kulturinstituts, published in connection with the Österreichische Aka-demie der Wissenschaften by L. Santifaller, II Abteilung, Quellen, first series (Graz and Cologne 1964); on the preceding see H. Tillmann in *RQ,* 61 (1966), 228–36, with important corrections of the historical commentary. Studies and preparatory work are reported by the *MIÖG* and the *RömHM.* On the investigation of the *registra* see, among other works, H. Tillmann in *QFIAB,* 23 (1931 f.), 53–79, R. von Heckel in *HJ,* 57 (1937), 258–89, F. Bock in *AZ,* 50/51 (1955), 329–64; F. Kempf, *Die Register Innocenz' III.* (Rome 1945); *idem* in *QFIAB,* 36 (1956), 86–137; E. Pásztor, *Annali della Scuola Speciale per Archivisti e Bibliotecari dell'Università di Roma,* 2 (1962), 287–304; A. Haidacher, *Sachkommentar zur Edition des ersten Jahrgangs der Register Papst Innocenz' III. Vorarbeiten aus dem Institut für österreichische Geschichtsforschung* (Vienna 1965). For further bibliography see P. Arató, "Bibliografia Historiae Pontificiae," *AHPont,* 1 (1963), 465–719, 4 (1966), 401–669 (thus far the best bibliography for the history of the papacy and of the Church); *Pontificia Hibernica. Medieval Papal Chancery Documents concerning Ireland (640–1261),* I (Dublin 1962), 91–182, ed. M. P. Sheehy; F. J. Dunning, "The Letters of Innocent III to Ireland," *Tr,* 18 (1962), 229–53; *Selected Letters of Pope Innocent III concerning England (1198–1216),* ed. C. R. Cheney and W. H. Semple (London 1953); C. R. Cheney, "The Letters of Pope Innocent III," *BJRL,* 35 (1952), 23–43; *Acta Innocentii Papae III (1198–1216),* ed. T. Haluscynsky, Pontificia Commissio ad redigendum codicem iuris orientalis, *Fontes,* series III, Vol. II (Vatican City 1944). *Gesta Innocentii III papae* (anonymous, to 1208), ed. L. G. O. F. de Bréquigny and F. J. G. La Porte du Theil (Paris 1791), *PL,* 214, XVII–CCXXVIII, and H. Elkan, *Die Gesta Innocentii III. im Verhältnis zu den Registern desselben Papstes* (dissertation, Heidelberg 1876); Y. Lefèvre, "Innocent III et son temps vu de Rome. Étude sur la biographie anonyme de ce pape," *MAH*, 61 (1949), 242–45, regards the *Gesta* as a collection of materials; V. Pfaff, "Die Gesta Innocenz' III. und das Testament Heinrichs VI.," *ZSavRGkan*, 50 (1964), 78–126. There is no adequate scholarly edition. Sermons: *PL*, 217, 313–688, and, in this connection, J. Scuppa, *I sermoni di Innocenzo III* (dissertation, Lateran, Rome 1962). *De sacro altaris mysterio*, *PL*, 217, 763–964, and, in regard to it, M. Maccarone, "Innocenzo III teologo dell'Eucharistia," *Divinitas*, 10 (1966), 362–412. *De contemptu mundi sive de miseria conditionis humanae,PL,*217,701–46. *Biographies and Monographs:* F. Hurter, *Geschichte Innocenz' III. und seiner Zeitgenossen*, 4 vols. (Hamburg, 3d ed. 1841–43); A. Luchaire, *Innocent III*, 6 vols. (Paris 1904–08); C. H. C. Pirie-Gordon, *Innocent the Great. An Essay on his Life and Times* (London 1907); J. Haller, *Innocenz III.*, "Meister der Politik," I (Stuttgart, 2d ed. 1923), 517–59; M. Florin, "Innocenz III. als Schriftsteller und als Papst," *ZKG*, 45 (1926), 344–58; L. E. Binns, *Innocent III* (London 1931); J. Clayton, *Pope Innocent III and his Times* (Milwaukee 1940); C. E. Smith, *Innocent III, Church Defender* (Baton Rouge 1951); S. Packard, *Europe and the Church under Innocent III* (New York 1927); S. Sibilia, *Innocenzo III* (Rome 1951); H. Tillmann, *Papst Innocenz III., Bonner Historische Forschungen*, 3 (Bonn 1954); F. Kempf, *Papsttum und Kaisertum bei Innocenz III., Misc. Hist. Pont.*, 19 (Rome 1954); E. F. Jacob, "Innocent III," *Cambridge Medieval History*, 6 (1926), 1–43, 857–62; M. Maccarone, "Innocenzo III prima del suo Pontificato," *ADRomana*, 66 (1943), 59–134; A. Fliche in *Fliche-Martin*, X, 11–216; G. Martini, *Il pontificato d'Innocenzo III* (Rome 1952); R. Schneider, *Innocenz der Dritte* (Munich 1963, poetical interpretation); J. M. Powell, *Innocent III. Vicar of Christ or Lord of the World?* (Boston 1963).

E. W. Meyer, *Staatstheorien Papst Innocenz' III.* (Bonn 1920); G. Martini, "Traslazione dell'Impero e donazione di Costantino nel pensiero e nella politica d'Innocenzo III," *ASRomana*, 56/57 (1933 f.), 219–362; E. von Strube, *Innocenz' III. politische Korrespondenz und die religiöse Weltherrschaftsidee der Kurie* (dissertation, Berlin 1936); M. Maccarone, *Chiesa e Stato nella dottrina del papa Innocenzo III* (Rome 1941); H. Tillmann, "Zur Frage des Verhältnisses von Kirche und Staat in Lehre und Praxis Papst Innocenz' III.," *DA*, 9 (1951), 136–81; A. M. Stickler, "Imperator vicarius papae," *MIÖG*, 62 (1954), 165–212; A. Hof, " 'Plenitudo potestatis' und 'Imitatio Imperii' zur Zeit Innocenz' III.," *ZKG*, 66 (1954 f.), 39–71; P. A. Van den Baar, *Die kirchliche Lehre der Translatio Imperii Romani* (Rome 1956); W. Goez, *Translatio Imperii* (Tübingen 1958); O. Hageneder, "Über das Sonne-Mond-Gleichnis bei Innocenz III.," *MIÖG*, 65 (1957), 340–68; *idem*, "Exkommunikation und Thronverlust bei Innozenz III.," *RömHM*, 2 (1959), 9–50; *idem*, "Das päpstliche Recht der Fürstenabsetzung (1150–1250)," *AHPont*, 1 (1963), 53–95; D. Waley, *The Papal State in the Thirteenth Century* (London 1961); H. Hoffmann, "Die beiden Schwerter im hohen Mittelalter," *DA*, 20 (1965), 78–114 (Innocent's contribution to the theory); B. Tierney, "The Continuity of Papal Political Theory in the Thirteenth Century. Some Methodological Considerations," *MS*, 27 (1965), 227–45; J. A. Watt, *The Theory of Papal Monarchy in the Thirteenth Century* (London 1965).

19. *The Spiritual Monarch as Arbiter Mundi*

Sources

Innocent's *gesta* and *registra* (see bibliography for Chapter 18).

LITERATURE

The Papal State: G. Ermini, *La libertà comunale nello Stato della Chiesa*, 2 vols. (Rome 1926 f.); H. Tillmann, "Das Schicksal der päpstlichen Rekuperationen nach dem Friedens-abkommen zwischen Philipp von Schwaben und der römischen Kirche," *HJ*, 45 (1931), 341–65; J. Seeger, *Die Reorganisation des Kirchenstaates unter Innocenz III. Grundlagen und Durchführung* (dissertation, Kiel 1937); G. Ermini, "Caratteri della sovranità tem-porale dei papi nel secolo XIII e XIV," *ZSavRGkan*, 27 (1938); many of Ermini's works have to do with the material treated in this chapter, *cf.* the list in D. Waley *(infra)*, 332 f.; B. Bartolini, "Per la storia del Senato Romano nei secoli XII e XIII," *BIStIAM*, 60 (1946); D. Waley, *The Papal State in the Thirteenth Century* (London 1961). Waley, 325–31, also lists the written sources for local history.

The Vassal States: F. Baethgen, *Die Regentschaft Papst Innocenz' III. im Königreich Sizi-lien, Heidelberger Abhandlungen zur mittleren und neueren Geschichte*, 44 (Heidelberg 1914); R. Ries, "Regesten der Kaiserin Constanze, Königin von Sizilien, Gemahlin Heinrichs VI.," *QFIAB*, 18 (1926), 30–100; T. C. van Cleve, *Markward of Annweiler and the Sici-lian Regency* (Princeton 1937); L. Böhm, *Johann von Brienne, König von Jerusalem, Kaiser von Konstantinopel* (Heidelberg 1938); N. Kamp, *Istituzioni comunali in Viterbo nel Medioevo*, I: *Consoli, Podestà, Balivi e Capitani nei secoli XII e XIII, Biblioteca di Studi Viterbesi*, 1 (Viterbo 1963); A. Sacchetti-Sassetti, "Rieti e gli Urslingen," *ADRomana*, 85/86 (1962 f.), 3–24; A. Marongiu, "A Model State in the Middle Ages: the Norman and Swabian Kingdom of Sicily," *Comparative Studies in Society and History*, 6 (1963 f.), 307–24.

Spain: D. Mansilla, "Innocencio III y los reinos hispanos," *Anthologica annua. Publica-ciones del instituto español de estudios eclesiásticos*, 2 (1954), 9 ff.; J. Vincke, "Estado e Iglesia en la historia de la Corona de Aragón (siglos XI–XIV)," *Ponencias VII. Congreso de Historia de la Corona de Aragón* (Barcelona 1962), 289–326; D. Mansilla, "El Cardenal hispano Pelayo Gaitán (1206–1213)," *Anthologica annua*, 1 (1953), 11–66; J. Vincke, "Der Eheprozess Peters II. von Aragón (1206–1213)," *Gesammelte Aufsätze zur Kulturgeschichte Spaniens*, 5 (Münster 1935), 108–89.

Portugal: A. Herculana, F. L. Gonzaga de Azevedo, and D. M. Gomes dos Santos, *Historia de Portugal* (to 1250), 6 vols. (Lisbon 1940–44), especially Vols. IV and V; H. V. Liver-more, *A New History of Portugal* (Cambridge 1966), 50–99; *Cronica dos sete primeiros reis de Portugal*, ed. C. Silva Tarouca, 3 vols. (Lisbon 1952 f.); *Cronica de cinco reis*, ed. A. Magalhãis Basto (Oporto 1945); C. Erdmann, *Papsturkunden in Portugal* (Göttingen 1927); *idem, O Papado e Portugal* (Lisbon 1935); D. Mansilla, "Disputas diocesanas entre Toledo, Braga y Compostela en los siglos XII al XV," *Anthologica annua*, 3 (1955).

Hungary: A. Theiner, *Vetera monumenta historica Hungariam sacram illustrantia*, 2 vols. (Rome 1859 f.); W. Fraknói, *Monumenta Vaticana historiam Hungariae illustrantia*, 6 vols. (Budapest 1884–91); *idem, The Ecclesiastical and Political Relations of Hungary with the Holy See*, 3 vols. (Budapest 1901–03, in Hungarian).

The Bulgarian Question: see the introduction to T. Haluscynsky, *Acta Innocentii papae III. (1198–1216)* (Rome 1944).

England: see the bibliography for this section. Also: K. Norgate, *John Lackland* (London 1902); E. Gütschow, *Innocenz III. und England* (Berlin 1905); K. Norgate, *Richard the Lion Heart* (London 1924); H. Tillmann, *Die päpstlichen Legaten in England bis zur Be-endigung der Legation Gualas 1218* (Bonn 1926); Z. N. Brooke, *The English Church and the Papacy* (Cambridge 1931); F. M. Powicke, *Stephan Langton* (Oxford 1935); M. D. Knowles, "The Canterbury Election of 1205/6," *EHR*, 53 (1938), 211–30; H. G. Richard-son, "The Morrow of the Great Charter," *BJRL*, 28 (1944), 422–43, 29 (1945), 184–200; F. M. Powicke, *King Henry III and the Lord Edward*, 2 vols. (Oxford 1947); C. R. Cheney, "King John and the Papal Interdict," *BJRL*, 31 (1948), 295–317; S. Painter, *The Reign of*

King John (London 1950, Baltimore 1949); *Acta Stephani Langton*, ed. K. Major, Canterbury and York Society, 118 (Oxford 1950); C. R. Cheney, "King John's Reaction to the Interdict on England," *Transactions of the Royal Historical Society*, 31 (1949), 129–50; *Magna Carta Libertatum*, ed. H. Wagner (Bern 1951); C. R. Cheney, "The Letters of Pope Innocent III," *BJRL*, 35 (1952), 23–43; *idem*, "The Eve of Magna Carta," *BJRL*, 38 (1956), 311–41; J. C. Holt, "The Making of the Magna Carta," *EHR*, 72 (1957), 401–22; *idem*, *The Northerners. A Study in the Reign of King John* (Oxford 1961); W. L. Warren, *King John* (London 1961); J. C. Holt, *King John* (London 1963).

The Empire: F. Kempf, *Papsttum und Kaisertum bei Innocenz III. Die geistigen und rechtlichen Grundlagen seiner Thronstreitpolitik* (Rome 1954), basic; *idem, Regestum Innocentii III papae super negotio Romani Imperii, Misc. Hist. Pont.*, 9 (Rome 1947); *idem*, "Die zwei Versprechen Ottos IV. an die römische Kirche," *Festschrift für E. E. Stengel* (Münster and Cologne 1952), 359–84; J. Haller, "Innocenz III. und Otto IV.," *Papsttum und Kaisertum, Festschrift P. Kehr* (Munich 1926), 475–507; H. Hirsch, "Das Recht auf die Königserhebung durch Papst und Kaiser im hohen Mittelalter," *Festschrift E. Heymann* (Weimar 1940), 209–49; H. Mitteis, *Die deutsche Königswahl. Ihre Rechtsgrundlagen bis zur Goldenen Bulle* (Munich and Vienna, 2d ed. 1944, reprinted Darmstadt 1965); A. Stickler, "Imperator Vicarius Papae. Die Lehren der französisch-deutschen Dekretistenschule des 12. und beginnenden 13. Jahrhunderts über die Beziehungen zwischen Papst und Kaiser," *MIÖG*, 62 (1954), 165–212; R. Folz, *L'idée d'empire en Occident* (Paris 1953); W. Winkelmann, *König Philipp von Schwaben (1197–1208), JbbDG* (Leipzig 1873, reprinted Darmstadt 1963); *idem, Kaiser Otto IV. von Braunschweig (1208–18)* (Leipzig 1878, reprinted Darmstadt 1963); F. Baethgen, "Die Exkommunikation Philipps von Schwaben" (first 1913), *Mediaevalia*, I (Stuttgart 1960), 85–92; *idem*, "Kaiser Friedrich II. (1194–1250)" (first 1956), *Mediaevalia*, I (Stuttgart 1960), 93–109; A. J. Walter, *Die deutsche Reichskanzlei während des Endkampfes zwischen Staufern und Welfen* (Innsbruck and Leipzig 1938), and, in this connection, the sources and literature for Chapter 25.

France: see the bibliography for this section. Also: O. Cartellieri, *Die Schlacht bei Bouvines (27. Juli 1214) im Rahmen der europäischen Politik* (Leipzig 1914); R. H. Tenbrock, *Eherecht und Ehepolitik bei Innocenz III.* (dissertation, Münster 1933); A. Hadengue, *Bouvines, victoire créatrice* (Paris 1935); C. Petit-Dutaillis, *The Feudal Monarchy in France and England from the Tenth to the Thirteenth Century* (reprinted London 1964); R. Davidsohn, *Philipp II. August von Frankreich und Ingeborg* (Stuttgart 1888), and E. Michael in *ZKTh*, 14 (1890), 562–69; M. Jallut, *Philippe-Auguste, fondateur de l'unité française* (Paris 1963). *Scandinavia, Poland, and the Balkan Peninsula:* G. Inger, *Das kirchliche Visitationsinstitut im mittelalterlichen Schweden* (Lund 1961); *Monumenta Poloniae Vaticana. Analecta Vaticana 1207–1366*, ed. L. Ptasnik, 2 vols. (Cracow 1903–04); K. Völker, *Kirchengeschichte Polens* (Berlin and Leipzig 1930), 37–41; N. Banescu, *Un problème d'histoire médiévale: création et caractère du second empire bulgare (1185)* (Bucharest 1943); R. L. Wolff, "The 'Second Bulgarian Empire.' Its Origin and History to 1204," *Speculum*, 24 (1949), 167–206; L. Tautu, "Le Conflit entre Johanitsa Asen et Émeric roi de Hongrie (1202–04). Contribution à l'étude du problème du second empire valaque-bulgare," *Mélanges Eugene Tisserant*, III, *SteT*, 233 (Rome 1964), 367–93.

20. *The Fourth Crusade and the Latin Empire*

SOURCES

Geoffrey of Villehardouin, *La conquête de Constantinople*, edited and translated by E. Faral, *Classiques de l'histoire de France au moyen-âge*, 2 vols. (Paris 1938 f.); Robert of Clari, *La conquête de Constantinople*, ed. P. Lauer, *Classiques de l'histoire de France au moyen-âge* (Paris 1924); Gunther of Paris, *Historia Constantinopolitana,* ed. P. Riant (Geneva 1875); P. Riant, *Exuviae sacrae Constantinopolitanae* (Geneva 1877), contains, among other things, the brief reports of the Anonymous of Halberstadt, *De peregrinacione in Graeciam,* of the Anonymous of Soissons, and of the Anonymous of Langres; C. Hopf, *Chroniques gréco-romanes inédites ou peu connues* (Berlin 1873), gives (93–98) a Latin translation of a section of the Russian *Chronicle of Novgorod* on the conquest of Constantinople, which is presumably the work of a Russian eyewitness. Accounts of the Fourth Crusade are also given in the chronicles already cited in the bibliography for this section: *Chronica Regia Coloniensis,* Alberic of Trois-Fontaines, Rigord's *Gesta Philippi Augusti,* Roger of Howden, etc. Important sources are also the *Gesta Innocentii III* and that pope's letters (bibliography for this section). The most important Greek source is the work of Nicetas Choniates, ed. J. Bekker, *Historia, CSHB* (Bonn 1835), selections from which are translated into German, with introduction and commentary, by F. Grabler, *Die Kreuzfahrer erobern Konstantinopel, Byzantinische Geschichtsschreiber,* 9 (Graz, Vienna, and Cologne 1958); *Crusaders as Conquerors. The Chronicle of Morea,* translated and edited by H. E. Lurier (New York 1964), and, in this connection, P. Topping in *Speculum,* 40 (1965), 735–42.

LITERATURE

H. E. Mayer, *Geschichte der Kreuzzüge,* bibliography, nos. 2119–59; A. Luchaire, *Innocent III: La Question d'Orient* (Paris 1907); C. Diehl, "The Fourth Crusade and the Latin Empire," *Cambridge Medieval History,* 4 (1923), 415–43; 850 f., new ed., IV, 1 (1966), 275–330; *Grousset,* III (1936), 169–77; *Runciman,* III (1954), 107–131; E. H. McNeal, "The Fourth Crusade," *A History of the Crusades,* ed. K. M. Setton, II (1962), 153–85; S. de Mundo Lo, *Cruzados en Byzancio. La cuarta cruzada a la luz de las fuentes latinas y orientales* (Buenos Aires 1958); J. Lognon, *Recherches sur la vie de Geoffroi de Villehardouin* (Paris 1939); H. Kretschmayr, *Geschichte von Venedig,* 2 vols. (Gotha 1905–20); A. Frolow, *Recherches sur la déviation de la IVe croisade vers Constantinople* (Paris 1955); R. Cressi, "Venezia e la quarta crociata," *Archivio Veneto,* 81 (1951), 1 ff.; W. M. Daly, "Christian Fraternity, the Crusaders and the Security of Constantinople," *MS,* 22 (1960), 43–91 (especially 78–91); B. Primov, "The Papacy, the Fourth Crusade and Bulgaria," *Byzantino Bulgarica,* 1 (1962), 183–211; D. E. Queller, "Innocent III and the Crusader-Venetian Treaty of 1201," *Med et Hum,* 15 (1963), 31–34.

The Latin Empire: Sources: the same as those for the Fourth Crusade. Also: Henry of Valenciennes, *Histoire de l'Empereur Henri de Constantinople,* ed. J. Lognon (Paris 1948); A. Heisenberg, *Neue Quellen zur Geschichte des lateinischen Kaisertums und der Kirchenunion, AAM* (1922 f.).

Literature: H. E. Mayer, *Geschichte der Kreuzzüge,* bibliography, nos. 2771–88; J. Lognon, *L'Empire latin de Constantinople et la principauté de Morée* (Paris 1949); E. Gerland, *Geschichte des lateinischen Kaiserreichs* (Homburg v. d. Höhe 1905), only Vol. I, extending to 1216, appeared (reprinted Darmstadt 1966); R. L. Wolff, "Romania. The Latin Empire of Constantinople," *Speculum,* 23 (1948), 1–34; *idem,* "Baldwin of Flanders and Hainaut, First Latin Emperor of Constantinople. His Life, Death and Resurrection (1172–1225)," *Speculum,* 27 (1952), 281–322; *idem,* "Mortgage and Redemption of an Emperor's Son. Castile and the Latin Empire of Constantinople," *Speculum,* 29 (1954), 45–84; *idem,* "The Latin Empire of Constantinople (1204–1261)," *A History of the Crusades,* ed. K. M. Setton, II (1962), 187–234; L. Santifaller, *Beiträge zur Geschichte des lateinischen Patriarchats von Konstantinopel* (Weimar 1938); R. L. Wolff, "Politics in the Latin Patriarchate of Constantinople (1204–1261)," *Dumbarton Oaks Papers,* 8 (1954), 225–303; *idem,* "The Organisation of the Latin Patriarchate of Constantinople," *Tr,* 6 (1948), 33–60; P. L'Huillier, "La nature des relations ecclésiastiques gréco-latines après la prise de Constantinople par les croisés," *XI. Intern. Byzantinisten-Kongress* (Munich 1958), 314–20; A. Gardner, *The Lascarids of Nicaea. The Story of an Empire in Exile* (Amsterdam 1964); J. Folda, "The Fourth Crusade, 1201–1203. Some Reconsiderations," *Byzslav,* 26 (1965), 277–90; W. Miller, *The Latins in the Levant: A History of Frankish Greece, 1204–1566* (London 1908; reprint 1964).

21. Reform and the Struggle against Heresy

Sources

The Albigensian Crusade: Peter of Les Vaux-de-Cernay, *Hystoria Albigensis,* ed. P. Guébin and E. Lyon, 3 vols. (Paris 1926–39), the best eyewitness report (the author was a nephew of Abbot Guy of Les Vaux-de-Cernay, who in 1212 became Bishop of Carcassonne); French translation of the preceding, *Histoire Albigeoise,* by P. Guébin and H. Maisonneuve (Paris 1951); William of Tudela, *Chanson de la croisade contre les Albigeois,* ed. P. Meyer, 2 vols. (Paris 1875–79) (a new edition by E. Martin-Chabot [Paris 1931–57] is available thus far in 2 vols., bringing text and a new French translation down to 1217; William of Tudela narrates to the summer of 1213, when an anonymous writer continues the story); William of Puylaurens, *Cronica* or *Historia Albigensium,* latest edition by Beyssier, "Guillaume de Puylaurens et sa chronique," *Troisième Mélange d'histoire du moyen-âge* (Paris 1904), 85–175; on the preceding see Y. Dosset, "Le Chroniqueur Guillaume de Puylaurens," *Annales du Midi,* 65 (1953), 343–53; the chronicle goes to 1272, and it is thought that William composed the parts on the crusade *ca.* 1250. Important are the letters of Innocent III and Honorius III. The conciliar *acta* are in *Mansi,* XXII and XXIII. Also to be consulted are A. Molinier, "Catalogue des actes de Raimond VI et de Raimond VII," *Histoire générale de Languedoc,* VIII, 1940–2008, and *idem,* "Catalogue des actes de Simon et d'Amauri de Montfort," *BÉCh,* 34 (1873), 153–203, 445–501.

Literature

Reform: Fliche-Martin, X, 139–93; H. Tillman, *Papst Innocenz III.* (Bonn 1954), 152–85; M. Maccarone, "Riforma e sviluppo della vita religiosa con Innocenzo III," *RSTI,* 16 (1962), 29–72; U. Berlière, "Les chapitres généraux de l'ordre de saint Benoît," *RBén,* 18 (1901), 364–71; *idem,* "Innocent III et la réorganisation des monastères bénédictins," *RBén,* 32 (1920), 22–42, 145–59; J. B. Mahn, *L'ordre cistercien et son gouvernement des origines au milieu du XIIIᵉ siècle (1098–1265)* (Paris 1945); P. Viard, *Histoire de la dîme ecclésiastique dans le royaume de France aux XIIᵉ et XIIIᵉ siècles (1150–1313)* (Paris 1912); D. W. Robertson, "Frequency of Preaching in Thirteenth-Century England," *Speculum,* 24 (1949), 377–88; H. Winterer, "Zur Priesterehe in Spanien bis zum Ausgang des Mittelalters," *ZSavRGkan,* 52 (1966), 370–83.

The Albigensian Crusade: basic is the *Histoire générale de Languedoc,* by C. Devic and J. Vaissette, vols. 6–8 in the edition by A. Molinier *et al.* (Toulouse 1879–1904); A. Luchaire, *Innocent III: La Croisade des Albigeois* (Paris, 3d ed. 1911); P. Belperron, *La Croisade contre les Albigeois et l'union du Languedoc à la France (1209–49)* (Paris 1942); A. P. Evans, "The Albigensian Crusade," *A History of the Crusades,* ed. K. M. Setton, II (Philadelphia 1962), 277–324, with bibliography for particular questions.

The Cathari and the Waldensians: see the bibliography for Chapter 13. Also: A. Dondaine, *Un traité néo-manichéen du XIIIᵉ siècle: Le Liber de duobus principiis, suivi d'un fragment de rituel cathare*, Institutum Historicum Fratrum Praedicatorum (Rome 1939); C. Thouzellier, "La profession trinitaire du vaudois Durand de Huesca," *RThAM*, 27 (1960), 267–89; *idem*, "Controverses vaudoises-cathares à la fin du XIIᵉ siècle," *AHD*, 35 (1960), 137–227; *idem*, *Un traité cathare inédit du début du XIIIᵉ siècle d'après le Liber contra Manicheos de Durand de Huesca, Bibliothèque de la Revue d'histoire ecclésiastique*, 37 (Louvain 1961); *idem, Une somme anti-cathare. Le Liber contra Manicheos de Durand de Huesca, Spicilegium Sacrum Lovaniense*, 32 (Louvain 1964), and, in regard to it, B. Töpfer in *ThL*, 92 (1967), 118–20; *Hauck*, IV (Leipzig, 5th ed. 1925), 891–910.

22. The Fourth Lateran Council

Sources

A critical edition of the conciliar texts is still lacking; those collected in *Mansi*, XXII, 953–1086, must be examined individually in regard to their trustworthiness. The last edition, by C. Leonardi in *COD* (Freiburg im Breisgau, 2d ed. 1962), 203–47, is not definitive. The decrees were transmitted especially by the *Compilatio IV* of Johannes Teutonicus (1216), which gives all of them except canon 42; from here they were all adopted into Gregory IX's *Liber Extra*, except canons 42 and 49. Their impact on the provincial and diocesan synods of the thirteenth century can be demonstrated by means of the relevant editions. For France see O. Pontal, *Statuts synodaux des diocèses de l'ancienne France du XIIIᵉ à la fin du XVIIIᵉ siècle* (Paris 1964); for Poland, J. Sawicki, *Concilia Poloniae*, 9 vols. (Warsaw, Lublin, Poznań, and Breslau 1943 ff.); for England, F. M. Powicke and C. R. Cheney, *Councils and Synods with other Documents relating to the English Church*, II, 1 (Oxford 1964), continuation of *Councils and Ecclesiastical Documents*, ed. A. West Haddan and W. Stubbs, 3 vols. (Oxford 1871–73).

For lists of participants: A. Luchaire, "Un document retrouvé," *Journal des Savants*, new series, 3 (1905), 557–67; S. Ketrzynski, "Wiadomosc o udziale Polski w IV soborze Lateranenskim," *Przeglad Historyczny*, 3 (1906), 139–42; J. Werner, "Die Teilnehmerliste des Laterankonzils vom Jahre 1215," *NA*, 31 (1906), 577–92; J. F. Rivera, "Personajes hispanos asistentes en 1215 al IV concilio de Letrán," *Hispania Sacra*, 4 (1951), 335–55.

Contemporary Reports: Richard of San Germano, *Chronica priora*, ed. A. Gaudenzi (Naples 1888), 90–94, ed. C. A. Garufi, *Rerum Italicarum Scriptores*, VII, 2 (2d ed. 1938), 61–73; the Anonymous of Giessen, "A New Eyewitness Account of the Fourth Lateran Council," ed. S. Kuttner and A. García y García, *Tr*, 20 (1964), 123–29, together with commentary, 115–78; English voices in: Matthew Paris, *Chronica maiora*, II, ed. H. R. Luard, *Rolls Series*, 57 (London 1874); Walter of Coventry, *Memoriale*, ed. W. Stubbs, *Rolls Series*, 58 (London 1865); *Gesta abbatum S. Albani*, ed. H. T. Riley, *Rolls Series*, 28 (London 1865).

The treatise of Joachim of Fiore on the Trinity is lost, but one should consult *Joachimi abbatis Liber contra Lombardum. Scuola di Gioacchino da Fiore*, ed. C. Ottaviano (Rome 1934); *Scritti minori*, ed. E. Buonaiutti, *FontiStIt*, 78 (Rome 1936); F. Russo, "Un documento sulla condanna di Gioacchino da Fiore nel 1215," *Archivio storico per la Calabria e la Lucania*, 20 (1951), 69–73.

The discussions dealing with the Albigensian problem: *Chanson de la croisade albigeoise*, ed. P. Meyer, II (Paris 1879) (Société de l'Histoire de France au moyen-âge); Peter of Les Vaux-de-Cernay, *Hystoria Albigensis*, ed. P. Guébin and E. Lyon. Société de l'Histoire de France, 3 vols. (Paris 1926–39), French translation, *Histoire Albigeoise*, by P. Guébin and H. Maisonneuve (Paris 1951).

Literature

Hefele-Leclercq, V, 1316–18; A. Luchaire, *Innocent III: Le concile de Latran et la réforme de l'Église* (Paris 1908); M. Gibbs and J. Lang, *Bishops and Reform, 1215–1272, with Special Reference to the Lateran Council of 1215* (Oxford 1934); H. Tillmann, *Innocenz III.* (Bonn 1954), 152–68; A. García y García, "El concilio IV de Letrán (1215) y sus comentarios," *Tr*, 14 (1958), 484–502; M. Maccarone, "Il IV Concilio Lateranense," *Divinitas*, 5 (1961), 270–98; R. Foreville, *Latran I, II, III et Latran IV, Histoire des Conciles Œcuméniques*, 6 (Paris 1965), the best presentation thus far.

Participants: G. Tangl, *Die Teilnehmer an den allgemeinen Konzilien des Mittelalters* (Weimar 1922); H. Krabbo, "Die deutschen Bischöfe auf dem 4. Laterankonzil von 1215," *QFIAB*, 10 (1907), 275–300; M. and C. Dickson, "Le Cardinal Robert de Courson. Sa vie," *AHD*, 9 (1934), 53–142.

Preparation: J. W. Baldwin, "The Intellectual Preparation for the Canon of 1215 against Ordeals," *Speculum*, 36 (1961), 613–36; B. Tierney, " 'Tria quippe distinguit iudicia.' A Note on Innocent III's Decretal 'Per Venerabilem'," *Speculum*, 37 (1962), 48–59.

The Decrees: E. Friedberg, *Die Canones-Sammlungen zwischen Gratian und Bernhard von Pavia* (Leipzig 1887); F. Gillmann, "Der Kommentar des Vincentius Hispanus zu den Kanones des vierten Laterankonzils (1215)," *AkathKR*, 109 (1929), 223–74; S. Kuttner, *Repertorium der Kanonistik*, I (Vatican City 1937), 369–71; *idem*, "Johannes Teutonicus, das vierte Laterankonzil und die Compilatio Quarta," *Miscellanea Giovanni Mercati*, V, *SteT*, 125 (Rome 1946), 608–34; F. Gillmann, "Hat Johannes Teutonicus zu den Konstitutionen des 4. Laterankonzils (1215) als solchen einen Apparat verfasst?" *AkathKR*, 117 (1937), 55–68; A. García y García, "Los comentarios de los canonistas a las constituciones del Concilio IV de Letrán (1215)," *Congrès de droit canonique médiéval de Louvain et Bruxelles (22–26 juillet 1956)* (Louvain 1959), 151–60; C. R. Cheney, "The Decretal Collections before Compilatio IV, Pragensis, Palatina I and Abrincensis II," *Tr*, 15 (1959), 464–83; H. J. Schroeder, *Disciplinary Decrees of the General Councils* (Saint Louis 1937), 236–96.

Effect of the Decrees: M. Maccarone, "Riforma e sviluppo della vita religiosa con Innocenzo III," *RSTI*, 16 (1962), 29–72; U. Berlière, "Les chapitres généraux de l'ordre de Saint Benoît," *RBén*, 18 (1901), 364–71; *idem*, "Innocent III et la réorganisation des monastères bénédictins," *RBén*, 32 (1920), 22–42, 145–59; J. B. Mahn, *L'ordre cistercien et son gouvernement des origines au milieu du XIIIᵉ siècle (1098–1265)* (Paris 1945); P. Viard, *Histoire de la dîme ecclésiastique dans le royaume de France aux XIIᵉ et XIIIᵉ siècles (1150–1313)* (Paris 1912); D. W. Robertson, "Frequency of Preaching in Thirteenth-Century England," *Speculum*, 24 (1949), 377–88; K. G. Hugelmann, "Der Sachsenspiegel und das vierte Lateranische Konzil," *ZSavRGkan*, 13 (1924), 427–87; J. Dauvillier, *Le mariage dans le droit classique de l'Église depuis le Décret de Gratien (1140) jusqu'à la mort de Clément V (1314)* (Paris 1933); M. Peuchmaurd, "Le prêtre ministre de la parole dans la théologie du XIIᵉ siècle," *RThAM*, 29 (1962), 52–76; A. McDevitt, "The Episcopate as an Order and Sacrament on the Eve of the High Scholastic Period," *FStudies*, 20 (1960), 96–148; P. A. Kirsch, "Der sacerdos proprius in der abendländischen Kirche vor dem Jahre 1215," *AkathKR*, 84 (1904), 527–37; A. Teetaert, *La confession aux laïques dans l'Église latine depuis le VIIIᵉ jusqu'au XIVᵉ siècle . . .* (Paris 1926); P. Browe, *Die Pflichtkommunion im Mittelalter* (Münster 1940); G. G. Meersseman, *Dossier de l'ordre de la pénitence au XIIIᵉ siècle* (Fribourg 1961); R. Foreville, "L'idée de Jubilé chez les théologiens et les canonistes (XIIᵉ–XIIIᵉ siècles) avant l'institution du Jubilé romain (1300)," *RHE*, 56 (1961), 401–23; P. Michaud-Quantin, *Sommes de casuistique et manuels de confession au moyen âge XIIᵉ–XVIᵉ siècles, Analecta Mediaevalia Namurcensia*, 13 (Louvain 1962); R. von Heckel, "Das Aufkommen der ständigen Prokuratoren an der päpstlichen Kurie im 13. Jahrhundert," *Miscellanea Francesco Ehrle*, II, *SteT*, 38 (Rome 1924), 290–321.

Effect of the Decrees on Provincial and Diocesan Synods: C. R. Cheney, *English Synodalia of the Thirteenth Century* (Oxford 1940); *idem,* "The Earliest English Diocesan Statutes," *EHR,* 50 (1935), 198–216; L. Guizard, "Recherches sur le texte des statuts synodaux d'Eudes de Sully, évêque de Paris," *Bulletin d'Information de l'Institut de Recherche et d'Histoire des Textes,* 5 (1956), 53–59; P. C. Boeren, "Les plus anciens statuts du diocèse de Cambrai (XIIIᵉ siècle)," *RDC,* 3 (1953); O. Pontal, "Les plus anciens statuts synodaux d'Angers et leur expansion dans les diocèses de l'Ouest de la France," *RHÉF,* 46 (1960), 54–67; O. Dobiache-Rojdestvensky, *La vie paroissiale en France d'après les actes épiscopaux* (Paris 1911); E. Diebold, *La pratique religieuse d'après les statuts synodaux (du IVᵉ concile du Latran au concile de Trente). Mémoire de l'École pratique des Hautes Études* (Paris, n. d.); *idem,* "L'application en France du canon 51 du IVᵉ concile du Latran d'après les anciens statuts synodaux," *L'année canonique,* 2 (1951), 187–95.

23. *The Mendicant Orders*

Francis of Assisi

Sources

Opuscula S. Francisci, ed. L. Lemmens (Florence and Quaracchi, 2d ed. 1941); H. Boehmer, *Analekten zur Geschichte des Franciscus von Assisi* (Tübingen and Leipzig, 1904, 2d ed. 1930); K. Esser and L. Hardick, *Die Schriften des heiligen Franz von Assisi* (Werl, 2d ed. 1956); K. Esser, *Das Testament des heiligen Franz von Assisi, Vorreformationsgeschichtliche Forschungen,* 15 (Münster 1949); *idem,* "Der Brief des heiligen Franziskus an den heiligen Antonius von Padua," *FStud,* 31 (1949), 135–51; Vittorio Branca, "Cantico di Frate Sole," *AFrH,* 41 (1949), 1–87; *Canticle of the Sun* in German translation by O. Karrer (Zürich 1942); G. Sabatelli, "Neue Literatur zum Sonnengesang," *AFrH,* 51 (1958), 3–24; Thomas of Celano, *Vita I* (1228) *et Vita II* (1247) *S. Francisci Assis.* and *Tractatus de miraculis S. Francisci, AFranc,* 10 (Quaracchi 1926–28); Bonaventure, *Legendae duae de vita S. Francisci* (1263), *Opera S. Bonaventurae,* 8 (Quaracchi 1898), published separately 1941; *Testimonia minora saeculi XIII de S. Francisco Assis.,* ed. L. Lemmens (Quaracchi 1926); *Legenda trium sociorum,* ed. G. Abate, *MF,* 39 (1939), 375–432; *Speculum perfectionis, auctore fratre Leone,* ed. P. Sabatier (Paris 1898); in 2 vols., *British Society of Franciscan Studies,* 13, 17 (Manchester 1928–31); also, ed. L. Lemmens (Quaracchi 1901); *Actus S. Francisci et sociorum eius,* ed. P. Sabatier (Paris 1902); *I Fioretti di San Francesco,* ed. P. Sabatier (Paris 1902); also ed. G. Pagnani (Rome 1959); A. G. Little, *Some Recently Discovered Franciscan Documents* (London 1926); *idem, Franciscan Papers, Lists and Documents* (Manchester 1943); criticism and account of the problems raised by the sources especially in A. Fortini, *Nova Vita di San Francesco,* 4 vols. (Assisi, 2d ed. 1959); J. R. H. Moorman, *The Sources for the Life of St. Francis* (Manchester 1940).

Literature

Biographies: P. Sabatier (Paris 1893, last ed., Paris 1931); C. Schnürer (Mainz, 2d ed. 1907); J. Jørgensen (Copenhagen 1907 and later); C. Cuthbert (London 1912); A. Fortini (Milan 1926); *idem, Nova Vita di S. Francesco,* 4 vols. (Assisi, 2d ed. 1959); J. R. H. Moorman (London 1950); O. Englebert (Paris, 2d ed. 1957); H. Felder, *Die Ideale des heiligen Franz von Assisi* (Paderborn, 4th ed. 1951); P. Sabatier, *Collection d'Études et de Documents sur l'histoire religieuse et littéraire du moyen-âge,* 8 vols. (Paris 1898 ff.); W. Goetz, *Die Quellen zur Geschichte des heiligen Franziskus* (Gotha 1904); J. Campbell, *Les écrits de s. François devant la critique* (Werl 1954).

The Stigmata: *cf.* F. van den Borne in *FStud,* 6 (1917), 67–71, with bibliography; A. Groeteken, *Franz von Assisi in der Poesie der Völker* (Mönchen-Gladbach 1912); E. Scott

Davison, *Forerunners of St. Francis* (Boston 1927); A. Styra, *Franz von Assisi in der neueren deutschen Literatur* (Breslau 1928); F. van den Borne, "Een rondgang langs de moderne F.-biografieën," *Franciscana* (St. Truiden 1949, 1950); K. Esser, "Franziskus von Assisi und die Katharer seiner Zeit," *AFrH*, 51 (1958), 225–64; O. Bonmann, "Franziskus von Assisi," *LThK*, IV (2d ed. 1960), 231–34.

Iconography: H. Thode, *Franz von Assisi* (Vienna, 4th ed. 1934); V. Facchinetti, *L'Iconografia Francescana* (Milan 1924); B. Kleinschmidt, *St. Franziskus in Kunst und Legende* (Mönchen-Gladbach, 5th ed. 1926); B. Bughetti in *AFrH*, 19 (1926), 636–732; M. Villain, *St. François et les peintres d'Assise* (Paris 1941); L. Cellucci, *Le leggende franciscane del secolo XIII nel loro aspetto artistico* (Modena, 2d ed. 1957).

Spirituality: H. Felder, *Die Ideale des heiligen Franziskus von Assisi* (Paderborn, 4th ed. 1951); J. Leclercq and F. Vandenbroucke, *La spiritualité du moyen-âge* (Paris 1961), 299–344; E. Longpré, "Saint François d'Assise," *DSAM*, 5 (1964), 1268–1303, with comprehensive bibliography. Up-to-date bibliographies in *AFrH, FStud, MF, AnBoll, RHE*; complete from 1931 in *CollFr;* also in individual editions.

The Friars Minor

Sources

BullFr; Bullarii Franciscani Epitome, ed. C. Eufel (Quaracchi 1908); L. Wadding, *Annales Minorum*, 8 vols. (to 1540) (Lyons and Rome, 1625–54), 2d ed., 25 vols. (to 1622) (Rome, Naples and Quaracchi, 1731–1886), reprinted as Editio III auctior et emendata, 31 vols. (Quaracchi 1931–56); *Annales Minorum continuati*, by A. Chiappini *et al.*, Vols. 26–31 (1623–70) (Quaracchi and Rome 1933–56); *Documenta antiqua Franciscana*, ed. L. Lemmens, 3 vols. (Quaracchi 1901 f.); L. Wadding, *Scriptores Ordinis Minorum* (Rome, 3d ed. 1906), Supplementum, 2 vols., ed. J. H. Sbaralea (Rome 1805 f.); Wadding-Sbaralea, *Scriptores Ordinis Minorum*, nova editio (to 1780), by A. Nardecchia and A. Chiappini, 4 vols. (Rome 1906–36); *Chronologia historico-legalis seraphici ordinis*, 4 vols. (Naples, Venice, and Rome 1650–1795); *Analecta Franciscana* (chronicles, etc.), 10 vols. (Quaracchi 1885–1951); *Chronica Fratris Jordani de Jano, Collection d'études et de documents*, 6, ed. H. Boehmer (Paris 1908); *Chronica Fratris Salimbene de Adam* (to 1272), ed. O. Holder-Egger, *MGSS*, 32 (1905–13), and O. Holder-Egger in *NA*, 37 (1912), 163–218, 38 (1913), 469–81; ed. F. Bernini, 2 vols. (Bari 1942), and, in this connection, *AFrH*, 48 (1955), 436–41; F. Ehrle, "Die ältesten Redaktionen der Generalkonstitutionen des Franziskanerordens," *ALKGMA*, 6 (1892), 1–138; D. Mandic, *De legislatione antiqua Ordinis Fratrum Minorum*, I (1210–21) (Mostar 1924).

Literature

Heimbucher, 3d ed., I, 656–828, II, 661–63; K. Müller, *Die Anfänge des Minoritenordens und der Bussbruderschaften* (Breslau 1885); H. Felder, *Geschichte der wissenschaftlichen Studien im Franziskanerorden bis um die Mitte des 13. Jahrhunderts* (Freiburg 1904); H. Holzapfel, *Handbuch der Geschichte des Franziskanerordens* (Freiburg im Breisgau 1909); A. Léon, *Histoire de l'ordre des Frères Mineurs* (Paris 1954); Gratien de Paris, *Histoire de la fondation et de l'évolution de l'Ordre des Frères Mineurs au XIIIᵉ siècle* (Paris 1928); P. M. Sevesi, *L'ordine dei frati minori*, 3 vols. (Milan 1942–60); A. Gemelli, *Il Francescanesimo* (Milan, 7th ed. 1956); A. Zawart, *A History of Franciscan Preaching and Preachers (1209–1927)* (New York 1928); A. Masseron, *Les Franciscains* (Paris 1931); F. Vernet, *Les ordres mendiants* (Paris 1933); E. Benz, *Ecclesia spiritualis, Kirchenidee und Geschichtstheologie der franziskanischen Reformation* (Stuttgart 1934); F. de Sessevalle, *Histoire* générale de l'Ordre de S. François, Part I: Le Moyen-Age, 2 vols. (Paris 1935–37); R. M. Huber, A Documented History of the Franciscan Order (1182–1517) (Milwaukee 1944); A. Matanic, Compendio di storia dell'Ordine dei frati minori, I (Rome 1956); D. Knowles, The Religious Orders in England, I (Cambridge 1948); L. Cassut, Die älteste franziskanische Lebensform (Graz, Vienna, and Cologne 1955); S. Clasen, "Franziskaner," LThK, IV (2d ed. 1960), 273–79; B. Mathis, Die Privilegien des Franziskanerordens (Paderborn 1927); B. von Wolfenhagen, "Das franziskanische Privilegienrecht," CollFr, 4 (1934), 337–62; R. B. Brooke, Early Franciscan Government (Elias to Bonaventure) (Cambridge 1959); P. Gemelli, "Giacomo da Vitry e le origini del movimento francescano," Aevum, 39 (1965), 474–95; K. Esser, Anfänge und ursprüngliche Zielsetzungen des Ordens der Minderbrüder, Studia et documenta franciscana, 4 (Leiden 1966); R. de Nantes, "La première prédication franciscaine," Éfranc, 30 (1913), 357–77; A. Murith, "Pour l'histoire de la prédication franciscaine," MF, 39 (1939), 433–48; L. Zarncke, Der Anteil des Kardinal Ugolino an der Ausbildung der drei Orden des heiligen Franz (Leipzig 1930).

Periodicals: Éfranc; AFrH; FStud; MF; CollFr; Antonianum; Analecta ordinis minorum capuccinorum (1937 ff.); Wissenschaft und Weisheit (Düsseldorf 1934 f.); etc.

Spread of the Order: Provinciale ordinis fratrum minorum vetustissimum, ed. C. Eubel (Quaracchi 1892); Die Chroniken der Minderbrüder Jordan von Giano und Thomas von Eccleston, ed. L. Hardick (Werl 1957) (Germany and England); Bavaria Franciscana antiqua, ed. J. Glatz (Ulm 1954 ff.); Alemania Franciscana antique, ed. J. Glatz (Ulm 1956 ff.); C. Eubel, Geschichte der oberdeutschen Minoritenprovinz (Würzburg 1886); Thomas de Eccleston, Liber de adventu Fratrum Minorum in Angliam, ed. A. G. Little and J. R. H. Moorman (Manchester, 2d ed. 1951); V. Green, The Franciscans in Medieval English Life (1224–1348) (Paterson, N. J. 1939); J. R. H. Moorman, The Grey Friars in Cambridge (1225–1538) (Cambridge 1952); M. Schoengen, Monasticon Batavum, I (Amsterdam 1941); M. Roncaglia, Biblioteca bio-bibliografica della Terra Santa e dell'Ordine Francescano, I, Storia della provincia della Terra Santa, 1: I Francescani in Oriente durante la crociata (Cairo 1954); E. Lempp, Frère Élie de Cortone, Étude biographique, Collection d'études et de documents, 3 (Paris 1901); S. Attal, Frate Elia, Compagno di San Francesco (Rome 1936); C. L. Sagui, Frate Elia e la lotta fra la Chiesa e l'Impero nel tredicesimo secolo (Assisi 1928); J. Toussaert, Saint Antoine de Padoue, German translation by S. Summerer and G. Kurz, Antonius von Padua. Versuch einer kritischen Biographie (Cologne 1967).

Dominic Guzmán

SOURCES

B. Altaner, Der heilige Dominikus. Untersuchungen und Texte (Breslau 1922); M. H. Vicaire, S. Dominique de Caleruega d'après les documents du XIIIe siècle (Paris 1955); Bullarium Ordinis Fratrum Praedicatorum, I, ed. A. Bremond (Rome 1729); Cartulaire ou histoire diplomatique de S. Dominique, ed. Balme, Lelaidier, and Colomb, 3 vols. (Paris 1893–1901); M. H. Laurent, Historia Diplomatica S. Dominici, MOP, XV (Paris 1933); Libellus, Legenden und Kanonisationsverfahren, MOP, XVI (Rome 1935); Gérard de Frachet, Vitae Fratrum Ordinis Praedicatorum, MOP, I (Louvain 1896); Anecdotes historiques et apologues tirés du recueil inédit d'Étienne de Bourbon, dominicain du XIIIe siècle, ed. A. Lecoy de la Marche (Paris 1877); Thomas de Cantinpré, Bonum universale de apibus (Douai 1605); Sister Cécile, Miracula beati Dominici, ed. A. Walz, Miscellanea Pio Paschini (Rome 1949), 306–26; Étienne de Salagnac, De quatuor in quibus Deus praedicatorum ordinem insignivit, ed. T. Kaeppeli, MOP, XXII (Rome 1949); Dietrich of Apolda, Life of Saint Dominic, ActaSS, Augusti I, 558–628.

Literature

Biographies: H. D. Lacordaire, *Vie de S. Dominique* (Paris 1841); H. Petitot, *Vie de S. Dominique* (Saint-Maximin 1926); H. C. Scheeben, *Der heilige Dominikus* (Freiburg 1927); P. Mandonnet, M. H. Vicaire, and R. Ladner, *S. Dominique, l'idée, l'homme et l'œuvre*, 2 vols. (Paris 1938); L. A. Getinom, *Santo Domingo de Guzmán . . .* (Madrid 1939); M. H. Vicaire, *Histoire de S. Dominique*, 2 vols. (Paris 1957); W. J. Koudelka, "St. Dominicus," *Biblioteca Sanctorum*, 4 (1964), 692–727; *Saint Dominique en Languedoc, Cahiers de Fanjeaux*, 1 (Toulouse 1966); P. M. Amato, G. G. Palmieri, F. Frassetto, *et al.*, *Le reliquie di S. Domenico. Storia e leggende, ricerche scientifiche, recostruzione fisica* (Bologna 1946). Iconography: M. C. Nieuwbarn, *Verherrlichung des heiligen Dominikus in der Kunst* (Mönchen-Gladbach 1906); F. Ferretti, *S. Domenico. Biografia e Iconografia* (Florence 1921); L. G. Alonso-Getino, *Santo Domingo en el arte* (Madrid 1922); G. Bazin, *S. Dominique* (Paris 1937); G. Kaftal, *St. Dominic in Early Tuscan Painting* (Oxford 1948); M. H. Vicaire and L. von Matt, *S. Dominique* (Paris 1957); A. Walz, "Zur dominikanischen Ikonographie," *AFP*, 35 (1965), 255–63.

The Order of Preachers

Sources

T. Ripoll and A. Bremond, *Bullarium Ordinis Fratrum Praedicatorum*, 8 vols. (Rome 1729–40); *Epitome Bullarii OP*, ed. V. Ligiez and P. Mothon (Rome 1898); *Monumenta Ordinis Fratrum Praedicatorum historica*, 14 vols. (Louvain and Rome 1896–1904), Vols. 15 ff. (Rome 1933); *Analecta Ordinis Fratrum Praedicatorum* (Rome 1893 ff.); *AFP*; J. Quétif and J. Échard, *Scriptores OP*, 2 vols. (Paris 1719–21), editio altera emendata, aucta . . ., ed. R. Coulon and A. Papillon (Paris 1909–34).

Literature

Heimbucher, I (3d ed.), 469–536; D. A. Mortier, *Histoire des maîtres généraux de l'ordre des Frères Prêcheurs*, 8 vols. (Paris 1903–20); A. M. Walz, *Compendium historiae OP* (Rome, 2d ed. 1948); H. Denifle, "Die Constitutionen des Prediger-Ordens vom Jahre 1228," *ALKGMA*, I (1885), 165–227; *idem*, "Die Constitutionen des Predigerordens in der Redaction Raimunds von Peñafort," *ALKGMA*, V (1889), 530–64, and now R. Creytens, "Les Constitutions des Frères Prêcheurs dans la rédaction de S. Raymond de Peñafort," *AFP*, 18 (1948), 5–68; H. C. Scheeben, *Die Konstitutionen des Predigerordens unter Jordan von Sachsen* (Cologne 1939); G. R. Galbraith, *The Constitution of the Dominican Order (1216–1360)* (Manchester 1926); J. Meyer, *Liber de illustribus viris OP*, ed. P. Loe, *Quellen und Forschungen* (see *infra*), 12 (Leipzig 1918); B. Altaner, *Die Dominikanermissionen des 13. Jahrhunderts* (Habelschwerdt 1924); R. C. T. Zeller, *La vie dominicaine* (Paris 1927); O. Decker, *Die Stellung des Predigerordens zu den Dominikanerinnen (1207–67)* (Vechta 1935); R. F. Bennet, *The Early Dominicans* (London 1937); J. Guiraud, *Cartulaire de Notre Dame de Prouille*, 2 vols. (Paris 1907); H. C. Scheeben, *Die Anfänge des zweiten Ordens des heiligen Dominikus*, 2 (1932), 284–315; P. Mandonnet, *Les règles et le gouvernement de l'Ordre de Paenitentia au XIIIᵉ siècle* (Paris 1902); G. Meersseman, "Études sur les anciens confréries dominicaines, I: Les confréries de Saint-Dominique," *AFP*, 20 (1950), 1–113, "II: Les confréries de Saint-Pierre Martyr," *AFP*, 21 (1951), 51–196, "III: Les congrégations de la Vierge," *AFP*, 22 (1952), 5–176, "IV: Les milices de Jésus-Christ," *AFP*, 23 (1953), 275–308; R. L. Oechslin, "Les origines du Tiers-Ordre et les Milices de Jésus-Christ," *Vie dominicaine*, 18 (1959), 57–65, 83–87; *Quellen und Forschungen zur Ge-*

schichte des Dominikanerordens in Deutschland, ed. P. von Loe, B. M. Reichert, H. Wilms, *et al.* (Leipzig and Cologne 1907 ff.); H. D. Simonin, R. L. Oechslin, *et al.,* "La spiritualité des Frères Prêcheurs," *DSAM,* 5 (1964), 1422–1524.

Individual Lands: B. Jarrett, *The English Dominicans* (London, 2d ed. 1937); W. A. Hinnebusch, *The Early Friars Preachers* (Rome 1951); D. Knowles, *The Religious Orders in England,* I (Cambridge 1948); J. Gallén, *La province de Dacie de l'Ordre des Frères Prêcheurs* (Helsinki 1946); N. Pfeiffer, *Die ungarische Dominikanerprovinz (1221–42)* (Zürich 1913); M. D. Chapotin, *Histoire des Dominicains de la province de France. Le siècle des fondations* (Rouen 1898); M. Aron, *Un animateur de la jeunesse au XIIIe siècle. Vie, voyages du bienheureux Jourdain de Saxe* (Paris 1930); A. Zucchi, *Roma domenicana. Note storiche,* I (Florence 1938).

The Carmelites

Sources

E. Monsignani, *Bullarium Carmelitanum,* 4 vols. (Rome 1715–68); B. Zimmermann, *Monumenta historiae Carmelitana,* I (Lérins 1907); *Acta capitulorum generalium Ordinis Fratrum B. V. Mariae de Monte Carmelo,* I (1318–1593), ed. G. Wessels (Rome 1914); Cosmas de Viliers, *Bibliotheca Carmelitana,* 2 vols. (Orléans 1752), new edition by G. Wessels (Rome 1927); B. M. Xiberta, *De scriptoribus scholasticis saeculi XIV ex ordine Carmelitarum* (Louvain 1931).

Literature

Heimbucher, II (3d ed.), 54–95; André de Sainte-Marie, *L'Ordre de Notre-Dame du Mont Carmel* (Bruges 1910), translated into English and enlarged, *The Order of Our Lady of Mount Carmel* (Bruges 1913); Benoît Marie de la Sainte Croix (i. e., B. Zimmermann), *Les saints déserts des Carmes déchaussés* (Paris 1927); L. Van den Bossche, *Les Carmes* (Paris 1930); Melchior de Sainte-Marie, "Carmel," *DHGE,* 11 (1949), 1070–1104, with bibliography ("L'histoire de cet ordre est encore à faire," 1070); P. McCaffrey, *The White Friars* (Dublin 1926); Silverius a S. Teresia, *Historia del Carmen Descalzo,* 14 vols. (Burgos 1935–43); G. Mesters, *Geschichte des Karmeliterordens* (Mainz 1958).

Germany: H. Koch, *Die Karmeliterklöster der niederdeutschen Provinz (13. bis 16. Jahrhundert)* (Freiburg 1889); C. Martini, *Der deutsche Karmel,* 2 vols. (Bamberg 1922); G. Mesters, *Die rheinische Karmeliterprovinz während der Gegenreformation* (Speyer 1958).

England: L. Sheppard, *The English Carmelites* (London 1943); D. Knowles, *The Religious Orders in England,* I (Cambridge 1948).

France: Antoine M. de la Présentation, *Le Carmel en France,* 7 vols. (Toulouse 1936–39).

Spirituality: Jérôme de la Mère de Dieu, *La tradition mystique du Carmel* (Paris 1929); Gabriel a S. Magdalena, *Les plus vieux textes du Carmel* (Paris 1945); T. Brandsma, *Das Erbe des Propheten* (Cologne 1958); idem, *Karmel. Gesetz und Geheimnis* (Cologne 1960); idem, "La spiritualité de l'ordre des Carmes," *DSAM,* 2 (1953), 156–71.

Periodicals: *Analecta Ordinis Carmelitani* (Rome 1909 ff.); *Études carmélitaines* (Paris 1911 ff.); *Rivista storica Carmelit,* 3 vols. (Florence 1929–32); *Carmelus* (Rome 1954 ff.); *Ephemerides Carmeliticae* (Rome 1947 ff.); *Carmel* (Tilburg 1948 ff.).

BIBLIOGRAPHY

The Hermits of Saint Augustine

SOURCES

L. Empoli, *Bullarium Ordinis Eremitarum S. Augustini* (Rome 1628); *Jordani de Saxonia Liber Vitasfratrum,* ed. R. Arbesmann and W. Hümpfner (New York 1943); Henry of Friemar, *De origine et progressu ordinis ...,* ed. R. Arbesmann, *Augustiniana,* 6 (1956), 37–145; P. M. Vélez, *Leyendo nuestra Crónicas,* 2 vols. (Escorial 1932), gives critical notes on all the chronicles.

Bibliography: A. Perini, *Bibliographia Augustiniana,* 4 vols. (Florence 1929–35); A. de Meijer and R. Kuiters, "Licet Ecclesiae Catholicae. Text, Commentary," *Augustiniana,* 6 (1956), 9–36; A. Zumkeller, *Manuskripte von Werken der Autoren des Augustiner-Eremiten-Ordens in mitteleuropäischen Bibliotheken, Augustiniana,* 11–16 (1961–66), especially I. Anhang, "Manuskripte zur Geschichte des Augustinerordens," *ibid.,* 15 (1965), 73–130.

LITERATURE

Heimbucher, I (3d ed.), 537–70; T. Kolde, *Die deutsche Augustiner-Kongregation* (Gotha 1879); A. Sans, *Historia de los agostinos españoles* (Madrid 1948); W. Hümpfner, "Äussere Geschichte der Augustinereremiten in Deutschland," *Festschrift St. Augustinus* (Würzburg 1930), 147–96; U. Mariani, *Gli Agostiniani e la grande unione del 1256* (Rome 1957); V. Maturana, *Historia general de los Eremitanos de San Agostín,* 6 vols. (Santiago de Chile 1912–31); A. C. de Romanis, *L'Ordine Agostiniano* (Florence 1935); E. van Moé, "Recherches sur les Ermites de Saint Augustin entre 1250 et 1350," *RQH,* 60 (1932), 257–316; F. Roth, "Die Augustiner-Generale des 13. Jahrhunderts," *Cor Unum,* 8–9 (Würzburg 1950); *idem,* "Cardinal Richard Annibaldi, First Protector of the Augustinian Order (1243–76)," *Augustiniana,* 2–4 (1952–54); J. Hemmerk, "Die Augustiner-Eremiten in Bayern," *Augustiniana,* 6 (1956), 385–490; S. Rennhofer, "Augustinerklöster in Österreich," *Augustiniana,* 6 (1956), 491–536; A. Zumkeller, "Zur Frühgeschichte der Augustiner in Deutschland," *Augustiniana,* 9 (1959), 93–104; *700 Jahre Augustiner-Eremiten in Würzburg (1263–1963)* (Würzburg 1963); E. Braem and N. Teeuwen, *Augustiniana Belgica Illustrata* (Louvain 1956); F. Roth, "A History of the English Austin Friars," *Augustiniana,* 8 (1958), 16 (1966); D. Knowles, *The Religious Orders in England,* I (Cambridge 1948).

Spirituality: D. Gutiérrez, "Ermites de Saint-Augustin," *DSAM,* 4 (1960), 983–1042.

Other Mendicant Orders

Williamites: F. Roth, "Die Wilhelmiten," *Cor Unum,* 8 (1950), 78–81; K. Elm, *Beiträge zur Geschichte des Wilhelmitenordens* (Cologne and Graz 1962); P. Janssens, "De Wilhelmieten en de Magna Unio Augustiniana," *Augustiniana,* 12 (1962), 451–72; K. Elm, "Die Bulle 'Ea quae iudicio' Clemens' IV. (30. 8. 1266). Vorgeschichte, Überlieferung, Text und Bedeutung," *Augustiniana,* 14 (1964), 500–22, 15 (1965), 54–67, 493–520, 16 (1966).

Servites: Heimbucher, I (3d ed.), 576–88; A. Morini and P. Soulier, *Monumenta Ordinis Servorum S. Mariae,* 20 vols. (Brussels and Florence 1897–1930); A. P. M. Piermejus, *Memorabilium S. Ordinis Servorum B. M. V. Breviarium,* 3 vols. (Rome 1927–31); A. M. Rossi, *Man. di Storia dell'Ord. dei Servi di Maria* (Rome 1956); *Studi storici sull'Ord. dei Servi di Maria* (Rome 1933 ff.); P. Soulier, *Vie de S. Philippe Benizi* (Paris 1886); A. M. Wimmer, *Der heilige Philipp Benizi* (Freiburg 1932); M. Courayville, *Giuliana Falconieri* (Florence 1938).

Mercedarians: Heimbucher, I (3d ed.), 571–76; M. Even, *L'ordre de la Merci* (Rome, 2d ed. 1918); G. Vázquez Núñez, *Manual de Historia de la Orden de N. Señora de la Merced* (Toledo 1931); F. Gazulla, *La Orden de Nuestra Señora de la Merced* (Barcelona 1934);

681

M. Aime-Anizan, *Le quatrième vœu, Notre-Dame de la Merci et les captifs* (Paris 1958); P. N. Pérez, *San Pedro Nolasco* (Barcelona 1915); J. Rius Serra, *S. Raymundo de Peñafort. Diplomatario* (Barcelona 1954).

24. *The Western Mediaeval Hospital*

SOURCES

Chronicles and cartularies of cities, monasteries, hospitals, religious orders, and confraternities, tax books, transcripts, episcopal *registra*, etc.

LITERATURE

L. Le Grand, *Statuts d'hôtels-Dieu et de léproseries* (Paris 1901); A. Hauck "Wohltätigkeitsanstalten," *RE*, XXI (3d ed. 1908), 435–52; W. Schönfeld, "Die Xenodochien in Italien und Frankreich im frühen Mittelalter," *ZSavRGkan*, 12 (1922), 1–54, basic; W. Liese, *Geschichte der Caritas*, 2 vols. (Freiburg 1922), with bibliography; D. L. Mackay, *Les hôpitaux et la charité à Paris au XIII° siècle* (Paris 1923); G. Schnürer, *Kirche und Kultur im Mittelalter*, II (Paderborn 1926), 456–78; F. Meffert, *Caritas und Krankenwesen bis zum Ausgang des Mittelalters* (Freiburg 1927); S. Reicke, *Das deutsche Spital und sein Recht im Mittelalter, Kirchenrechtliche Abhandlungen*, 111–114, 2 vols. (Stuttgart 1932), with bibliography; supplementary to the preceding is J. Sydow, "Kanonistische Fragen zur Geschichte des Spitals in Südwestdeutschland," *HJ*, 83 (1964), 54–68; S. Reicke, "Stiftungsbegriff und Stiftungsrecht im Mittelalter," *ZSavRGgerm*, 53 (1933), 247–76; W. J. Marx, *The Development of Charity in Medieval Louvain* (New York 1936); J. Imbert, *Les hôpitaux en droit canonique, L'Église et l'État au moyen âge*, 8 (Paris 1947); G. Schreiber, "Byzantinisches und abendländisches Hospital," *Gemeinschaften des Mittelalters* (Münster 1948), 3–80; P. de Angelis, *L'arci-confraternità ospitaliera di S. Spirito in Saxia* (Terni 1951); E. Nasalli-Rocca, *Il diritto ospedaliero nei suoi lineamenti storici* (Milan 1956); *Atti del primo congresso italiano di storia ospedaliera (1956)* (Reggio d'Emilia 1957); B. Tierney, *Medieval Poor Law* (Berkeley, Los Angeles 1959); *Fliche-Martin*, XII, 2 (Paris 1964), 472–75; *Atti del primo Congresso Europeo di Storia Ospitaliera (1960)* (Reggio d'Emilia 1962); J. H. Mundy, "Charity and Social Work in Toulouse (1100–1250)," *Tr*, 22 (1966), 203–87; D. Jetter, *Geschichte des Hospitals, I: Westdeutschland von den Anfängen bis 1850* (Wiesbaden 1966); R. M. Clay, *The Mediaeval Hospitals of England* (New York, 2d ed. 1966).

Particular Hospitals (only a few of the more recent works will be listed out of an extensive special literature): F. F. Schäfer, *Das Hospital zum Heiligen Geist auf dem Domhofe zu Köln* (Cologne 1910), with a list of the German Hospitals of the Holy Spirit, supplemented by G. Schreiber in *HV*, 15 (1912), 136 f.; O. Ulm, *Das Heilig-Geist-Hospital zu Überlingen am Bodensee im Mittelalter* (Heidelberg 1913); J. Kuhn, *Aus der Geschichte des Heiliggeistspitals zu Freiburg im Breisgau* (Hildesheim 1914); H. Kluge, *Das Heilig-Geist-Hospital zu Schondorf* (Marbach 1936); A. Englisch, *Über Leproserien in Württemberg* (typed dissertation, Frankfurt am Main 1951); B. Zeller, *Das Heilig-Geist-Spital zu Lindau im Bodensee, Schwäbische Geschichtsquellen und Forschungen*, 4 (Lindau 1952); E. Wyde-Leemann, *Rechtsgeschichte des alten Spitals in Zürich* (Zürich 1952); W. D. von Kunatowski, *St. Leonhard vor Braunschweig, Braunschweiger Werkstücke*, 23 (Braunschweig 1958); P. Gradauer, *Spital am Pyhrn in Oberösterreich* (Linz 1957), and, in this connection, H. E. Feine in *ZSavRGkan*, 45 (1959), 622 f.; V. M. I. Ottazzi, "Le principali fundazioni ospitaliere d'Italia nei loro statuti dal secolo XI fino al secolo XIV," *Atti del primo congresso italiano di storia ospedaliera (1956)* (Reggio d'Emilia 1957), 508–22; G. Strodel, *Das Heiliggeistspital von Ravensburg* (typed dissertation, Tübingen 1958); R. van der Made, *Le grand hôpital de Huy* (Louvain 1960); P. de Angelis, *L'ospedale di Santo Spirito in Saxia*, I: *Delle origini al 1300* (Rome 1960); W. Haug, *Das St.-Katharinen-Hospital Esslingen a. N.* (typed dissertation, Tübingen 1961); A. Stollenwerk, *Zur Geschichte des Heilig-Geist-Hospitals in Boppard* (Boppard 1961); R. Kleiminger, *Das Heilig-Geist-Hospital in Wismar* (Weimar 1962); K. Wellschmied, *Die Hospitäler der Stadt Göttingen, Studien zur Geschichte der Stadt Göttingen*, 4 (Göttingen 1963); W. Berweck, *Das Heilig-Geist-Hospital zu Villingen im Schwarzwald* (Villingen 1963); H. Muschel, *Das Spital der Reichen Siechen zu St. Katharina in Ulm, Forschungen zur Geschichte der Stadt Ulm*, 5 (Ulm 1965).

The Hospitallers: Heimbucher, I (3d ed.), 615–17; J. von Pflugk-Harttung, *Die Anfänge des Johanniterordens in Deutschland* (Berlin 1899); J. Delaville Le Roulx, *Cartulaire générale de l'ordre des Hospitaliers de St. Jean de Jérusalem*, 4 vols. (Paris 1894–1906); idem, *Les Hospitaliers en Terre Sainte et à Chypre (1100–1310)* (Paris 1904); idem, *Les Hospitaliers à Rhodos* (Paris 1913); M. Ambrazicjute, *Studien über die Johanniterregel* (Fribourg 1929); E. J. King, *The Rule, Statutes and Customs of the Hospitallers (1099–1310)* (London 1934); C. H. C. Flugi van Aspermont, *De Johanniterorde in het Heilige Land (1100–1292)* (Assen 1957); S. Reicke, *Das deutsche Spital* (see *supra*), I, 93–111.

The Teutonic Knights: Heimbucher, I (3d ed.), 617–20. Only a select few of the virtually countless number of source publications and presentations can be listed here: R. ten Haaf, *Kurze Bibliographie zur Geschichte des Deutschen Ordens (1198–1561)* (Kitzingen 1949); J. Rink, *Die christliche Liebestätigkeit im Ordensland Preussen bis 1525* (Breslau 1911); M. Tumler, *Der Deutsche Orden im Werden, Wachsen und Wirken bis 1400* (Vienna 1955), bibliography, 631–72; P. G. Thielen, *Die Verwaltung des Ordensstaates Preussen, vornehmlich im 15. Jahrhundert* (Cologne and Graz 1965), with bibliography; see also the bibliography for Chapter 29.

Order of Lazarus: Heimbucher, I (3d ed.), 612 f.; E. Sauer, *Der Lazariter-Orden und das Statutenbuch von Seedorf* (Freiburg 1930); P. Bertrand, *Histoire des Chevaliers-Hospitaliers de St-Lazare* (Paris 1932); S. Reicke, *Das deutsche Spital* (see *supra*), I, 132–48.

Order of Saint Anthony: Heimbucher, I (3d ed.), 611–15; V. Advielle, *Histoire de l'ordre hospitalier de Saint-Antoine de Viennois* (Paris 1883); H. Dijon, *L'église abbatiale de Saint-Antoine en Dauphiné* (Grenoble and Paris 1902); L. Maillet-Guy, *Les origines de Saint-Antoine* (Valence 1908); other monographs by Maillet-Guy on the parishes, priories, grand masters, and commendatory prelates of the order in the Midi appear in the *Bulletin de la Société archéologique de la Drôme* and in *RMab* (1926–28); idem, *Les commanderies de l'ordre de Saint Antoine de Viennois* (Ligugé 1928); A. C. Wand, "La chiesa di S. Antonio Abbate sull'Esquilino," *RivAC*, 10 (1933), 71–104; H. Chaumartin, *Le Mal des Ardents et le Feu St. Antoine* (Vienne 1946); J. Rauch, "Der Antoniterorden in Deutschland," *AMrhKG*, 9 (1957), 33–50; A. Mischlewski, "Der Antoniterorden in Deutschland," *AMrhKG*, 10 (1958), 39–66; J. Rauch and H. Becker, "Geschichte des Antoniterhauses Rossdorf-Höchst," *AMrhKG*, 11 (1959), 76–159, with bibliography; S. Reicke, *Das deutsche Spital* (see *supra*), I, 156–66.

Order of the Holy Spirit: Heimbucher, I (3d ed.), 417–19; S. Reicke, *Das deutsche Spital* (see *supra*), I, 166–81; K. Hofmann, "Hospitaliter," *LThK*, V (2d ed. 1960), 492–94; P. Brune, *Histoire de l'ordre hospitalier du Saint-Esprit* (Paris 1892).

Bearers of the Cross: Heimbucher, I (3d ed.), 419–22; F. Jacksche, *Geschichte des ritterlichen Ordens der Kreuzherren mit dem roten Stern* (Prague 1904); S. Reicke, *Das deutsche Spital* (see *supra*), I, 182–89.

Brothers of the Holy Sepulchre at Jerusalem: F. Pasini, *Il sacro militare ordine Gerosolimitano del santo Sepolcro* (Pisa 1888); S. Reicke, *Das deutsche Spital* (see *supra*), I, 189–95.

Hospital Confraternities: S. Reicke, *Das deutsche Spital* (see *supra*), I, 48–71; G. Le Bras "Les confréries chrétiennes. Problèmes et propositions," *Études de sociologie religieuse*, 2 (Paris 1956), 423–62; G. Schreiber, "Religiöse Verbände in mittelalterlicher Wertung," *HJ*, 62–69 (1949), 284–358; also the abundant bibliography for the various lands.

SECTION FIVE

The Contest for the Leadership of the West: 1216-1274

25. *The Papacy's Victory over Frederick II*

SOURCES

Mansi, XXII–XXIV; *Hefele-Leclercq,* V, 1409–1759, VI, 1–228; P. Pressutti, *Regesta Honorii Papae III,* 2 vols. (Rome 1888–95); L. Auvray *et al., Les Registres de Grégoire IX,* 4 vols. (Paris 1896–1955); E. Berger, *Les Registres d'Innocent IV,* 4 vols. (Paris 1884–1921); C. de la Roncière, J. de Loye, and P. de Céneval, *Les Registres d'Alexandre IV,* 3 vols. (Paris 1902–59); J. Guiraud, *Les Registres d'Urbain IV,* 4 vols. (Paris 1901–58); E. Jordan, *Les Registres de Clément IV* (Paris 1893–1945); J. Guiraud, *Les Registres de Grégoire X* (Paris 1892–1960); C. Rodenberg, *Epistolae Saeculi XIII e regestis Pontificum Romanorum, MG,* 3 vols. (Berlin 1883–94); *Corpus Iuris Canonici,* ed. E. Friedberg (Freiburg 1881), in Volume II Gregory IX's *Liber Extra; Innocentii IV Commentaria super Libros quinque Decretalium,* Apparatus (Frankfurt am Main 1570); Hostiensis (Henry of Susa), *Summa aurea* (Basel 1573); *idem, Lectura seu commentaria* (Venice 1581); J. F. Böhmer, *Regesta Imperii,* V, 1–2, ed. F. Ficker (Innsbruck 1881 f.); *idem, Regesta Imperii,* V, 3–5, ed. J. Ficker and E. Winkelmann (Innsbruck 1892–1901); *MGConst,* II, ed. L. Weiland (Hanover 1896); E. Winkelmann, *Acta Imperii inedita a saeculis XIII et XIV,* 2 vols. (Innsbruck 1880–85); J. L. A. Huillard-Bréholles, *Historia diplomatica Friderici II,* 6 vols. (Paris 1852–61, reprinted Turin 1963); *idem, Vie et correspondance de Pierre de la Vigne, ministre de l'empereur Frédéric II. Avec une étude sur le mouvement réformiste au XIII⁰ siècle* (Paris 1864, reprinted Aalen 1966); T. Rymer, *Foedera, conventiones, litterae et cuiuscumque generis acta publica inter reges Angliae et alios quosvis,* ed. A. Clarke, J. Caley, and F. Holbrooke, 6 vols. (London 1816–30).
Eike of Repgow, *Die sächsische Weltchronik* (to 1248), ed. L. Weiland, *MG deutsche Chroniken,* II, 65–258 (Hanover 1877); Alberic of Troisfontaines, *Chronicon* (to 1241), ed. P. Scheffer-Boichorst, *MGSS,* 26, 226–950; Vincent of Beauvais, *Speculum historiale* (to 1250) (Douai 1624), in *Speculum maius,* and, in this connection, A. L. Gabriel, *The Educational Ideas of Vincent of Beauvais* (Notre Dame, 2d ed. 1962); Martin of Troppau, *Chronicon pontificum et imperatorum* (to 1277), ed. L. Weiland, *MGSS,* 22, 377–475; Martinus Minorita, *Flores temporum* (to 1292), *MGSS,* 24, 230–50; Albert of Stade, *Annals* (to 1256), *MGSS,* 16, 283–378; *Gesta Treverorum* (to 1259), especially for the time of Archbishop Arnold II, *MGSS,* 24, 376–414, translated into German by E. Zenz, *Die Taten der Trierer,* Teil 3 (1152–1259) (Trier 1959); under Frederick II the Italian sources are especially important: Rolandin of Padua, *Chronicle* (to 1262), *MGSS,* 19, 38–147, and *Muratori,* new edition, VIII, 1; Albert Milioli (Reggio) (to 1285), *MGSS,* 31; Salimbene de Adam, *Chronica* (to 1287), *MGSS,* 32; Thomas of Pavia, *Gesta imperatorum et pontificum* (to 1278), *MGSS,* 22, 490–528; Richard of San Germano, *Chronica Regni Siciliae* (to 1243), *MGSS,* 19, and *Muratori,* new edition, VII, 2 (1938); Roger of Wendover, *Flores historiarum* (to 1235), ed. H. G. Howlett, *Rolls Series,* 84, 3 vols. (London 1886–89); Matthew Paris,

BIBLIOGRAPHY

Chronica maiora (to 1259), ed. H. Luard, *Rolls Series*, 57, 7 vols. (London 1872–84), with extracts in *MGSS*, 27, 107–473; see also R. Vaughan, *Matthew Paris, Cambridge Studies in Medieval Life and Thought*, new series (Cambridge 1958), and H. V. Galbraith, *Roger Wendover and Matthew Paris* (Glasgow 1944).

LITERATURE

Historia Mundi, VI; *Propyläen-Weltgeschichte*, V; *The Cambridge Medieval History*, VI; *Peuples et Civilisations*, VI (see Vol. III, Gen. Bibliog., II, 1, a); *Glotz*, VIII; see the General Bibliography, II, 1, a–c, and the works listed for Section I on national history; *Fliche-Martin*, X; *Hauck*, IV and V, 1; R. García Villoslada, *Edad media (800–1303)* (Madrid, 2d ed. 1958); *The English Church and the Papacy*, ed. C. H. Lawrence (London 1965); *Seppelt*, III; *Haller*, IV, ed. H. Dannenbauer (Esslingen 1962); H. Wolter and H. Holstein, *Lyon I et Lyon II, Histoire des Conciles Œcuméniques*, 7 (Paris 1966). Further bibliography in the individual chapters.
Honorius III: Potthast R, I, 468–679; Böhmer-Ficker, *Regesten*, V, 3 (Innsbruck 1892), 1120–70; *Honorii III Opera*, ed. C. A. Horoy, *Medii aevi bibliotheca patristica*, 5 vols. (Paris 1879–83); letters in *MGEp saec. XIII*, I, 1–260; *Regesta*, ed. P. Pressutti, 2 vols. (Rome 1888–95); A. L. Tautu, *Acta Honorii III et Gregorii IX* (Rome 1950); D. Mansilla, *La documentación pontificia de Honorio III (1216–1227)* (Rome 1965), *Monumenta Hispaniae Vat. Registros*, 2; J. Clausen, *Papst Honorius III. (1216–1227)* (Bonn 1895); W. Knebel, *Kaiser Friedrich II. und Honorius III.* (Münster 1905); N. Mengozzi, *Onorio III e le sue relazioni col regno d'Inghilterra* (Siena 1911); A. Keutner, *Papsttum und Krieg unter dem Pontifikat Honorius' III.* (dissertation, Münster 1935); S. Kuttner, "Papst Honorius III. und das Studium des Zivilrechts," *Festschrift für Martin Wolff* (Tübingen 1952), 79–101; R. Manselli, "Onorio III e Federico II (Revisione d'un giudizio?)," *StRom*, 11 (1963), 142–59.
Gregory IX: Potthast R, I, 680–942; Böhmer-Ficker, *Regesten*, V, 3 (Innsbruck 1892), 1170–1258; *Vita e curia* and *Vita* by Bernard Guidonis, ed. *Muratori*, III, 575–87; G. Levi, *Registro del Card. Ugolino d'Ostia* (Rome 1890); L. Auvray *et al., Les Registres de Grégoire IX*, 4 vols. (Paris 1896–1955); H. Golubovich, "Disputatio seu Relatio Apocrisiariorum Gregorii IX de gestis (1234)," *AFrH*, 12 (1919), 418–70; J. Felten, *Papst Gregor IX.* (Freiburg 1886); E. Brem, *Gregor IX. bis zum Beginn seines Pontifikates* (Heidelberg 1911); W. Fuchs, *Die Besetzung der deutschen Bistümer unter Gregor IX. und bis zum Regierungsantritt Papst Innocenz' IV. (1243)* (dissertation, Berlin 1911); W. Reich, *Die Besetzung der sizilischen Bistümer unter Friedrich II.* (Heidelberg 1923); G. A. Donner, *Kardinal Wilhelm von Sabina, Bischof von Modena (1222–34). Päpstlicher Legat in den nordischen Ländern († 1251)* (Helsingfors 1929); L. Zarncke, *Der Anteil des Kardinal Ugolino an der Ausbildung der drei Orden des heiligen Franziskus* (Leipzig 1930); B. Zöllig, *Die Beziehungen des Kardinal Hugolin zum heiligen Franziskus und seinem I. Orden* (Münster 1934); G. Marchetti-Longhi, "Ricerche sulla famiglia di Gregorio IX," *ADRomana*, 67 (1944), 275–307; C. Thouzellier, "La légation du cardinal Hugolin en Lombardie (1221)," *RHE*, 45 (1950), 508–42; H. M. Schaller, "Die Antwort Gregors IX. auf Petrus de Vinea, I, 1, 'Collegerunt pontifices,'" *DA*, 11 (1954), 140–65; S. Sibilia, *Gregorio IX (1227–1241)* (Milan 1961).
Innocent IV: Potthast R, II, 943–1285, 2110–24; Böhmer-Ficker, *Regesten*, V, 3 (Innsbruck 1892), 1260–1407; E. Berger, *Les Registres d'Innocent IV*, 4 vols. (Paris 1884–1921); Nicholas of Calvi, *Vita Innocentii IV Papae*, ed. F. Pagnotti, *ASRomana*, 21 (1898); P. Vogel, *Nikolaus von Calvi und seine Lebensbeschreibung des Papstes Innocenz IV. mit besonderer Berücksichtigung der Friedensverhandlungen zwischen Papst Innocenz IV. und Kaiser Friedrich II. in den Jahren 1243/44* (dissertation, Münster 1939); G. Abate, "Lettere secrete d'Innocenzo IV," *MF*, 55 (1955), 317–73; P. Sambin, *Problemi politici attraverso*

685

lettere inedite di Innocenzo IV (Venice 1955); *Acta Innocentii PP. IV (1243–1254) e regestis vaticanis*, ed. T. T. Haluscynskyj and M. M. Wojnar, Pontificia commissio ad redigendum Codicem Iuris Canonici Orientalis, *Fontes*, series III, IV, 1 (Vatican City 1962); F. Bock, "Studien zu den Registern Innozenz' IV.," *AZ*, 52 (1956), 11–48. There is no critical biography of Innocent IV; H. Schulz in *RE*, IX (Leipzig, 3d ed. 1901), 122–30, assembled the pertinent sources from the contemporary chronicles; F. Bernini, "Innocenzo IV e il suo parentado," *Nuova Rivista storica*, 24 (1940), 178–97; G. von Puttkamer, *Papst Innocenz IV. Versuch einer Gesamtcharakteristik aus seiner Wirkung* (Münster 1930); J. A. Cantini and C. Lefèbvre in *DDC*, VII (Paris 1958–62), 1029–62; K. Hampe, "Ein ungedruckter Bericht über das Konklave von 1241 im römischen Septizonium," *SAH* (1913), 1; K. Wenck, "Das erste Konklave der Papstgeschichte (August bis Oktober 1941)," *QFIAB*, 18 (1926), 101–70; W. de Vries, "Innozenz IV. und der christliche Osten," *OstKSt*, 12 (1963), 113–31; P. L. Pisanu, *L'attività politica d'Innocenzo IV e i Francescani, Annuario dell'Istituto superiore di scienze e lettere Santa Chiara* (Naples 1957); J. A. Cantini, "De autonomia iudicis saecularis et de romani pontificis plenitudine potestatis in temporalibus secundum Innocentium IV," *Salesianum*, 23 (1961), 407–80; H. Weber, *Kampf zwischen Innocenz IV. und Kaiser Friedrich II. bis zur Flucht des Papstes nach Lyon* (Berlin 1900); A. Folz, *Kaiser Friedrich II. und Papst Innocenz IV. Ihr Kampf in den Jahren 1244 und 1245* (Strasbourg 1905); C. Rodenberg, "Die Friedensverhandlungen zwischen Friedrich II. und Innocenz IV. 1243–1244," *Festgabe für Gerold Meyer von Knonau* (Zürich 1913), 165–204; P. Aldinger, *Die Neubesetzung der deutschen Bistümer unter Papst Innocenz IV. (1243–54)* (Leipzig 1900); H. Kroppmann, *Ehedispensübung und Stauferkampf unter Innocenz IV.* (Berlin 1937); R. Morghen, *Il tramonto della potenza sueva in Italia* (Rome 1936); F. Bernini, "Come si preparò la rovina di Federico II," *RSIt*, 60 (1948), 204–49; C. Rodenberg, *Innocenz IV. und das Königreich Sizilien (1245–1254)* (Halle 1892); K. Hampe, "Papst Innocenz IV. und die sizilische Verschwörung von 1246," *SAH* (1923); W. Gross, *Die Revolutionen in der Stadt Rom (1219–1254)* (Berlin 1934); E. Berger, *Saint Louis et Innocent IV* (Paris 1893); W. Meyer, *Ludwig IX. von Frankreich und Innocenz IV. (1244–1247)* (dissertation, Berlin 1915); G. Martini, *La politica finanziaria dei papi in Francia alla metà del secolo 13* (Rome 1950); L. Dehio, *Innocenz IV. und England* (Leipzig 1914).

The Emperor Frederick II: acta in Huillard-Bréholles *(supra)* and *MGConst*, II, 54–389; Böhmer-Ficker, *Regesten*, I, 1–2 (Innsbruck 1881 f.), 153–692; E. Sthamer, "Die sizilischen Register Friedrichs II.," *SAB* (1925); *Dahlmann-Waitz*, 6713–96; the standard scholarly biography is that by E. Kantorowicz, *Kaiser Friedrich der Zweite* (Berlin 1927, 4th ed. 1936), supplementary volume (Berlin 1931, reprinted 1963), English translation: *Frederick II* (New York 1957); E. Winkelmann, *Kaiser Friedrich II., JbbDG*, 2 vols. (to 1233) (Leipzig 1889–97); K. Hampe, *Kaiser Friedrich II. in der Auffassung der Nachwelt* (Stuttgart 1925); W. E. Heupel, *Der sizilische Grosshof unter Kaiser Friedrich II.* (Leipzig 1940); A. de Stefano, *L'idea imperiale di Federico II* (Florence, 2d ed. 1952); F. Cognasso, *Il pensiero e l'opera politica di Federico II* (Turin 1951); A. de Stefano, *La cultura alla corte di Federico II* (Palermo, 2d ed. 1951); G. Vergottini, *Studi sulla legislazione imperiale di Federico II in Italia* (Milan 1952); R. M. Kloos, "Kaiser Friedrich II.: Literaturbericht 1950–1955," *Tr*, 12 (1956), 426–56; *Atti del convegno internazionale di studi federiciani 1950* (Palermo 1952); recent biographies by E. Mogliano, *Federico II. di Svevia* (Milan and Verona 1948); M. Brion, *Frédéric II de Hohenstaufen* (Paris 1948); E. Pontieri, *Federico d'Hohenstaufen e i suoi tempi* (Naples n. d. [1959]); H. M. Schaller, *Kaiser Friedrich II., Persönlichkeit und Geschichte*, 34 (Göttingen 1964); *idem*, "Friedrich II.," *NDB*, 5 (1961), 478–84; *Stupor Mundi. Zur Geschichte Friedrichs II. von Hohenstaufen*, ed. G. Wolf, *Wege der Forschung*, 101 (Darmstadt 1966).

Political Propaganda: F. Graefe, *Die Publizistik in der letzten Epoche Kaiser Friedrichs II.* (Heidelberg 1909); W. von den Steinen, *Das Kaisertum Friedrichs II. nach den Anschau-*

ungen seiner Staatsbriefe (Berlin and Leipzig 1922); O. Vehse, *Die amtliche Propaganda in der Staatskunst Kaiser Friedrichs II.* (Munich 1929); H. Wieruszowski, *Vom Imperium zum nationalen Königtum. Vergleichende Studien über die publizistischen Kämpfe Kaiser Friedrichs II. und König Philipps des Schönen mit der Kurie* (Munich and Berlin 1933, reprinted Aalen 1965); P. E. Schramm, *Kaiser Friedrichs II. Herrschaftszeichen* (Göttingen 1955); H. M. Schaller, "Die Kanzlei Friedrichs II.," *ADipl*, 3 (1957), 207–86, 4 (1958), 264–327; F. Fehling, *Kaiser Friedrich II. und die römischen Kardinäle (1227–1239)* (Berlin 1901); B. Sütterlin, *Die Politik Kaiser Friedrichs II. und die römischen Kardinäle in den Jahren 1239–1250* (Heidelberg 1929); E. and O. Schönbauer, "Die Imperiumspolitik Kaiser Friedrichs II. in rechtsgeschichtlicher Bedeutung," *Festschrift K. G. Hugelmann*, II (Aalen 1959), 523–59.

The Fifth Crusade: H. E. Mayer, *Geschichte der Kreuzzüge*, Bibliog., 2171–80. Sources: James of Vitry, *Letters*, ed. R. B. C. Huygens (Leiden 1960); James of Vitry, *Historia Hierosolimitana*, ed. J. Bongars, *Gesta Dei per Francos*, I, 1047–1124 (Hanover 1611); Oliver Scholasticus, *Historia Damiatina*, ed. H. Hoogeweg, *Die Schriften des Kölner Domscholasters, späteren Bischofs von Paderborn und Kardinal-Bischofs von S. Sabina, Bibliothek des litterarischen Vereins in Stuttgart*, 202 (Tübingen 1894), 159–282; R. Röhricht, *Quinti belli sacri scriptores minores* (Geneva 1879); *idem*, *Testimonia minora de quinto bello sacro* (Geneva 1882); *Chronique d'Ernoul et de Bernard le trésorier*, ed. L. de Mas Latrie (Paris 1871). Literature: T. C. van Cleve, "The Fifth Crusade," *A History of the Crusades*, ed. K. M. Setton, II (Philadelphia 1962), 377–428; H. E. Mayer, *Geschichte der Kreuzzüge* (Stuttgart 1965), 188–203; *Grousset*, III, 196–245; *Waas*, I, 258–73; *Runciman*, III, 132–70; H. L. Gottschalk, *Al-Malik al-Kamil von Ägypten und seine Zeit* (Wiesbaden 1958); R. Röhricht, *Studien zur Geschichte des fünften Kreuzzugs* (Innsbruck 1891); J. P. Donovan, *Pelagius and the Fifth Crusade* (Philadelphia 1950); D. Mansilla, "El Cardenal hispano Pelayo Gaitán (1206–1230)," *Anthologica Annua*, 1 (1953), 11–66; L. Böhm, *Johann von Brienne, König von Jerusalem, Kaiser von Konstantinopel* (Heidelberg 1938); G. Golubovich, "San Francesco e i Francescani in Damiata, 5. Nov. 1219–2. Febr. 1220," *StudFr*, 23 (1926), 307–30; L. Lemmens, "De Sancto Francisco Christum praedicante coram Sultano Aegypti," *AFrH*, 19 (1926), 559–78; M. Roncaglia, "San Francesco d'Assisi in Oriente," *StudFr*, 50 (1953), 97–106.

The Crusade of Frederick II: H. E. Mayer, *Geschichte der Kreuzzüge*, Bibliog., 2181–95. Sources: there is no special account of this crusade; the reports must be gathered from the general sources for the period (*supra*, for this section and chapter). Literature: T. C. van Cleve, "The Crusade of Frederick II," *A History of the Crusades*, ed. K. M. Setton, II (Philadelphia 1962), 429–62; H. E. Mayer, *Geschichte der Kreuzzüge*, 204–14; *Grousset*, III, 271–326; *Waas*, I, 274–89; *Runciman*, III, 177–93; see also the literature on Frederick II (*supra*); an important monograph is R. Röhricht, *Die Kreuzfahrt Kaiser Friedrichs des Zweiten* (Berlin 1872), expanded in *Beitr. zur Geschichte der Kreuzzüge*, I (Berlin 1874), 1–112; Philip of Novara, *The Wars of Frederick II against the Ibelins in Syria and Cyprus*, ed. J. L. La Monte (New York 1936); H. Heimpel, "Hermann von Salza," *Der Mensch in seiner Gegenwart* (Göttingen 1954), 87–108; for the older literature see T. C. van Cleve, "The Crusade of Frederick II" (*supra*), 429 f.

Lyons I: Decrees: *COD*, 249–77, with critical introduction to the sources; for the course of the Council see the "Brevis Nota" of the Curia, *MGConst*, II, 513–16, and M. Tangl, "Die sogenannte Brevis Nota über das Lyoner Concil von 1245," *MIÖG*, 12 (1891), 246–53; Matthew Paris, *Chronica maiora*, ed. H. R. Luard, IV, 430–37, 445, 456–78, also the edition of F. Liebermann, *MGSS*, 28, 250, 256–68; a few texts on the Council are also in H. Cole, *Documents illustrative of English History in the Thirteenth-Fourteenth Centuries* (London 1884), 351–56; T. von Karajan, "Zur Geschichte des Concils von Lyon 1245," *SAW* (1851), 67–118; A. Folz, *Kaiser Friedrich II. und der Papst Innocenz IV. Ihr Kampf in den Jahren*

1244 und 1245 (Strasbourg 1905); S. Kuttner, "Die Konstitutionen des ersten allgemeinen Konzils von Lyon," *Studia et documenta historiae et iuris,* 6 (1940), 70–131; idem, *L'édition romaine des conciles généraux et les actes du premier concile de Lyon, Misc. Hist. Pont.,* III, 5 (Rome 1940); P. J. Kessler, "Untersuchungen über die Novellengesetzgebung Papst Innocenz' IV., ein Beitrag zur Geschichte des kanonischen Rechts," *RSavRGkan,* 31 (1942), 142–320, 32 (1943), 300–83, 33 (1944), 56–128; H. Wolter and H. Holstein, *Lyon I et Lyon II, Histoire des Conciles Œcuméniques,* 7 (Paris 1966).

26. *The Veering of the Papacy to France and the Angevin Domination in Italy*

SOURCES AND LITERATURE

Alexander IV: Potthast R, 1286–1473, 2124–29; Böhmer-Ficker-Winkelmann, *Regesten,* V/3, 1407–41; *registra* (see the bibliography for this section); *Registro degli atti e delle lettere di Gregorio de Monte Longo (1233–69)* (Rome 1965); *Acta Alexandri PP. IV,* ed. T. T. Haluscynskyj and M. M. Wojnar (Rome 1966); F. Tenckhoff, *Papst Alexander IV.* (Paderborn 1907); S. Sibilia, *Alessandro IV (1254–61)* (Anagni 1961); J. Haller, "Die Herkunft Papst Alexanders IV.," *QFIAB,* 32 (1942), 254–59; S. Andreotta, "La famiglia di Alessandro IV e l'Abbazia di Subiaco," *Atti e Memorie della Società Tiburtina di Storia e d'Arte,* 35 (1962), 63–126, 36 (1963), 5–87.

Urban IV: Potthast R, 1474–1542; RI, V/3, 1441–65; *MGEp s. XIII,* III, 474–626; *registra* (see the bibliography for this section). W. Sievert, "Das Vorleben des Papstes Urban IV.," *RQ,* 10 (1896), 451–505, 12 (1898), 127–61; K. Hampe, *Urban IV. und Manfred (1261–64)* (Heidelberg 1905); *AAM,* 27 (Munich 1912); R. Davidsohn, "Beiträge zur Geschichte Manfreds," *QFIAB,* 17 (1914–24), 78–107; H. Grauert, "Magister Heinrich der Poet in Würzburg und die römische Kurie," *VII Centenario della Bolla "Transiturus" (1264–1964). Studi eucaristici* (Orvieto 1966); F. Callaey, "Documentazione eucaristica liegese, dal vescovo di Liegi Roberto di Torote al Papa Urbano IV (1240–64)," *Miscellanea Pio Paschini,* I (Rome 1948), 215–37; F. Schneider, "Manfreds Versöhnungspolitik," *QFIAB,* 15 (1913), 17–52.

Clement IV: Potthast R, 1542–1650; RI, V/3, 1465–1512; *MGEp s. XIII,* III, 627–726; *registra* (see the bibliography for this section). P. Brayda, *La responsabilità di Clemente IV e di Carlo I d'Anjou nella morte di Corradino di Svevia* (Naples 1900); U. Bünger, *Ludwig IX. von Frankreich und die Kurie (1265–68)* (Berlin 1898); J. Heidemann, *Papst Clemens IV., Vorleben und Legationsregister* (Münster 1903); E. Horn, "Le rôle politique de Clément IV," *Comtes rendues de l'Académie des sciences morales et politiques 1925,* 273–300; G. Mollat, "Clément IV," *DHGE,* 12 (1953), 1109–15; K. Elm, "Die Bulle 'Ea quae iudicio' Clemens' IV. (30. 8. 1266). Vorgeschichte, Überlieferung und Bedeutung," *Augustiniana,* 14 (1964), 500–22, 15 (1965), 54–67, 492–520, 16 (1966), 95–145.

The Last Hohenstaufen: Conrad IV: H. Hartmann, "Die Urkunden Konrads IV.," *AUF,* 18 (1944), 108–32; G. Zeller, *Konrad IV. in Italien 1252–54* (Strasbourg 1907); W. Puhlmann, *Konrad IV. im Lichte der augustinisch-eschatologischen Geschichtsauffassung* (Greifswald 1914); K. G. Hugelmann, *Die Wahl Konrads IV. zu Wien 1237* (Weimar 1914); E. Michael, "Innocenz IV. und Konrad IV.," *ZKTh,* 18 (1894), 457–72. Manfred: A. Bertmann, *König Manfred von Sizilien (1264–66)* (Heidelberg 1909); O. Cartellieri, *König Manfred* (Palermo 1910); K. Hampe, "Zum Manifest Manfreds an die Römer vom 24. Mai 1265," *NA,* 36 (1911); C. Brückner, *Die Auffassung des Staufers Manfred und seiner Gegner im Licht der augustinisch-eschatologischen Geschichtsauffassung* (Greifswald 1914); P. F. Palumbo, "Per una biografia di Manfredi," *Studi Salentini,* 15 (1963), 193–205; H. M. Schaller, "König Manfred und die Assassinen," *DA,* 21 (1965), 173–93. Conradin: K.

Hampe, *Geschichte Konradins von Hohenstaufen* (Innsbruck 1894), with an appendix by H. Kämpf (3d ed. 1942); K. Pfister, *Konradin. Der Untergang der Hohenstaufen* (Munich 1941); A. Nitschke, "Der Prozess gegen Konradin," *ZSavRGkan*, 42 (1956), 25–54; on the preceding *cf.* H. M. Schaller in *QFIAB*, 37 (1957), 311–27, and A. Nitschke in *QFIAB*, 38 (1958), 268–77; L. Oelenheim, *Konradin von Hohenstaufen, König von Jerusalem und seine Vermählung auf der Coburg 1266* (Coburg 1930); R. Kohlrausch, *Herrschaft und Untergang der Hohenstaufen in Italien* (Jena 1926); J. Maubach, *Die Kardinäle und ihre Politik um die Mitte des 13. Jahrhunderts* (Bonn 1902); H. L. Gottschalk, "Der Untergang der Hohenstaufen," *WZKM*, 53 (1957), 267–82, shows the keen sympathy of the Islamic world for the fate of the last Hohenstaufen; P. F. Palumbo, "L'età sveva: i protagonisti," *Studi Salentini*, 13 (1962), 3–37.

Charles of Anjou: G. del Giudice, *Codice diplomatico del regno di Carlo I e II*, 3 vols. (Naples 1863–1902); R. Sternfeld, *Karl von Anjou als Graf der Provence (1245–65)* (Berlin 1888); E. Jordan, *Les origines de la domination angevine en Italie* (Paris 1909); F. Kern, *Die Anfänge der französischen Ausdehnungspolitik bis zum Jahre 1308* (Tübingen 1910), with bibliography; E. Sthamer, "Die verlorenen Register Karls I. von Anjou," *AAB* (Berlin 1923); R. Trifone, *La legislazione angioina* (Naples 1921); R. Filangieri, *I registri della cancelleria angioina*, 13 vols. (Naples 1950–59); G. M. Monti, *Da Carlo I a Roberto di Angiò, Ricerche e documenti* (Naples 1932); A Cutolo, *Gli Angioini* (Florence 1934); R. Morghen, *Il tramonto della potenza sueva in Italia (1250–66)* (Rome 1936); C. W. Previté-Orton, "Italy (1250–90)," *Cambridge Medieval History*, VI (Cambridge 1929, reprinted 1957), 166–204, bibliography, 869–74; E. G. Léonard, *Les Angevins de Naples* (Paris 1954); C. Rodenberg, *Innocenz IV. und das Königreich Sizilien* (Halle 1892); F. Baethgen, "Der Anspruch des Papsttums auf das Reichsvikariat," *ZSavKGkan*, 10 (1920), 168–268, now also in *Mediaevalia, Gesammelte Aufsätze von F. Baethgen*, I (Stuttgart 1960), 110–85; A. Wachtel, "Die sizilische Thronkandidatur des Prinzen Edmund von England," *DA*, 4 (1941), 98–178; N. Denholm-Young, *Richard of Cornwall* (Oxford 1947); H. Marc-Bonnet, "Le Saint-Siège et Charles d'Anjou sous Innocent IV et Alexandre IV (1245–61)," *RH*, 200 (1948), 38–65; *idem*, "Richard de Cornouailles et la Couronne de Sicile," *Mélanges L. Halphen* (Paris 1951), 483–89; A. Hauss, *Kardinal Oktavian Ubaldini, ein Staatsmann des 13. Jahrhunderts* (Heidelberg 1913); F. Reh, *Kardinal Peter Capocci, ein Staatsmann und Feldherr des 13. Jahrhunderts* (Berlin 1933); N. Schöpp, *Papst Hadrian V. (Kardinal Ottobuono Fieschi)* (Heidelberg 1916).

The Interregnum: Dahlmann-Waitz, 7033–35, 8351, 7025–31, 7040. W. Neumann, *Die deutschen Königswahlen und die päpstlichen Machtansprüche während des Interregnums (1257–73)* (Berlin 1921); M. Lintzel, "Die Entstehung des Kurfürstenkollegs," *AAL*, 99/2 (Berlin 1952); I. Llampayas, *Alfonso X-El hombre, el rey y el sabio* (Madrid 1947); N. Denholm-Young, *Richard of Cornwall* (Oxford 1947); W. von Schoen, *Alfons X. von Kastilien* (Munich 1957); A. de Bouard, *Le régime politique et les institutions de Rome au moyen âge (1253–1347)* (Paris 1920); P. Schmitthenner, *Die Ansprüche des Adels und des Volkes der Stadt Rom auf Vergebung der Kaiserkrone während des Interregnums (1250–73)* (Berlin 1923); E. Dupré-Theseider, *Roma dal Comune di popolo alla signoria pontificia* (Bologna 1952).

27. *Pope Gregory X and The Second Council of Lyons*

Gregory X: Potthast R, 1651–1703; *RI*, VI/1; J. Guiraud and L. Cadier, *Les Registres de Grégoire X (1272–76)* (Paris 1892–1960); P. Glorieux, "Autour des registres de Grégoire X," *RSTI*, 5 (1951), 305–25; F. Bock, "Autour des registres de Grégoire X," *RSTI*, 7 (1953), 307–36; A. L. Tautu, *Acta Urbani IV, Clementis IV, Gregorii X (1261–76)*, Pontificia commissio ad redigendum Codicem Iuris Canonici Orientalis, *Fontes*, series III, V/1 (Vatican

City 1953); F. Walter, *Die Politik der Kurie unter Gregor X.* (Berlin 1894); H. Otto, *Die Beziehungen Rudolfs von Habsburg zu Papst Gregor X.* (Innsbruck 1895); R. Diaccini, "Gregorio X e i domenicani," *Memorie domenicane,* 43 (1926), 22–29; J. Müller, *Studien zur Geschichte Gregors X.* (Freiburg im Breisgau 1929); idem, "Die Legationen unter Gregor X.," *RQ,* 37 (1929), 57–135; E. Nasalli-Rocca, *Problemi religiosi e politici del Duecento nell'opera di due grandi italiani* (Piacenza 1938); W. Hotzelt, "Gregor X., der letzte Kreuzzugspapst," *Das Heilige Land in Vergangenheit und Gegenwart,* III (Cologne 1941), 92–110; V. Laurent, "La croisade et la question d'Orient sous le pontificat de Grégoire X," *Revue historique du Sud-Est européen* (Bucharest 1945), 105–37; L. Gatto, *Il pontificato di Gregorio X* (Rome 1959); R. Pasini, *Un sommo conciliatore (Gregorio X)* (Milan 1962); B. Roberg, "Die Abdankung Alfons' X. von Kastilien als deutscher König," *HJ,* 84 (1964), 334–51.

Lyons II: J. B. Martin, *Conciles et bullaires du diocèse de Lyon* (Lyons 1905); *Mansi,* XXIV, 61–68; A. Franchi, *Il Concilio II di Lione (1274) secondo la Ordinatio Concilii Lugdunensis* (text and notes) (Rome 1965); Humbert of Romans, *Opus tripartitum,* ed. P. Crabbe, *Concilia omnia,* II (Cologne 1551), 967–1003; the shorter redaction is in *Mansi,* XXIV, 109–32; K. Michel, *Das Opus tripartitum des Humbertus de Romanis O. P. Ein Beitrag zur Geschichte der Kreuzzugsidee und der kirchlichen Unionsbestrebungen* (Graz, 2d ed. 1926); "Das Memorandum des Bischofs von Olmütz, Bruno von Holstein-Schaumburg," ed. *MGLL,* IV/3, 589–94; Gilbert of Tournai, *Collectio de scandalis,* most recently edited by A. Stroick, *AFrH,* 24 (1931), 35–62; on the preceding see J. Auer, *Studien zu den Reformschriften für das II. Lyoner Konzil* (Freiburg 1910); A. Stroick, "Verfasser und Quellen der 'Collectio de scandalis Ecclesiae,'" *AFrH,* 23 (1930), 3–41, 273–99, 433–66; further documents on the Council in B. Roberg, "Die Union zwischen der griechischen und der lateinischen Kirche auf dem II. Konzil von Lyon (1274)," *Bonner historische Studien,* 24 (Bonn 1964). Decrees of the Council in *COD,* 279–307; *Disciplinary Decrees of the General Councils,* ed. H. J. Schroeder (Saint Louis and London 1937), 324–64, 595–606; S. Kuttner, "Conciliar Law in the Making. The Lyonese Constitutions (1274) of Gregory X," *Miscellanea Pio Paschini,* II (Rome 1949), 39–81; H. Finke, *Konzilienstudien zur Geschichte des 13. Jahrhunderts. Ergänzungen und Berichtigungen zu Hefele-Knöpfler, "Conciliengeschichte"* V und VI (Münster 1891); *Hefele-Leclercq,* VI, 153–218; *Fliche-Martin,* X, 487–503; H. Wolter and H. Holstein, *Lyon I et Lyon II, Histoire des Conciles Œcuméniques,* 7 (Paris 1966), with copious bibliography.

The Union with the Greeks: see the bibliography for Chapter 16, *supra;* D. J. Geanakoplos, *Emperor Michael Palaeologus and the West (1258–1282). A Study in Byzantine-Latin Relations* (Cambridge, Mass. 1959).

28. *Heresy and the Inquisition in the Thirteenth Century*

Heresy: see the bibliographies for Chapters 13 and 21, in particular C. du Plessis d'Argentré, *Collectio iudiciorum,* I. von Döllinger, *Beiträge zur Sektengeschichte,* and P. Frédéricq, *Corpus documentorum.* The best survey so far is the concise work by H. Grundmann, *Ketzergeschichte des Mittelalters, Die Kirche in ihrer Geschichte,* ed. K. D. Schmidt and E. Wolf, II, G, 1 (Göttingen 1963), with its rich bibliography; L. Zanoni, "Valdesi a Milano nel secolo XIII," *Archivio storico lombardo,* IV/17 (1912), 5–22; H. Haupt, *Waldensertum und Inquisition im südöstlichen Deutschland* (Freiburg 1890); A. E. Schönbach, "Das Wirken Bertholds von Regensburg gegen die Ketzer," *SAW,* 147 (1904), 99–107; W. Preger, "Der Traktat des David von Augsburg gegen die Waldenser," *SAM,* 14/2 (1879), 181–235; G. Biscaro, "Inquisitori ed eretici lombardi (1292–1318)," *Misc. di Storia Ital.,* series 3, 19 (1922), 445–557; idem, "Eretici ed inquisitori nella Marca Trevisana (1280–1308)," *Archivio Veneto,* series 5, 11 (1932), 148–80; R. Manselli, "Per la storia dell'eresia catara nella Firenze del tempo di Dante," *BISI*, 62 (1950), 123–38; E. Dupré-Theseider, "L'eresia a Bologna nei tempi di Dante," *Studi storici in onore di G. Volpe*, 2 (1958), 383–444; E. Renan, *Averroès et l'averroïsme* (Paris 1852, 4th ed. 1882); P. Mandonnet, *Siger de Brabant et l'averroïsme latin au XIIIᵉ siècle* (Louvain 1908–11); F. van Steenberghen, *Siger de Brabant d'après ses œuvres inédits* (Louvain 1931–42); *idem*, "Averroismus," *LThK*, I (2d ed. 1957), 1144–46; A. C. Shannon, *The Popes and Heresy in the Thirteenth Century* (Villanova 1949).

The Inquisition: Sources: C. Douais, *Les sources de l'histoire de l'Inquisition dans le midi de la France* (Paris 1882); Bernard Guy, *Practica officii inquisitionis haeretice pravitatis*, ed. C. Douais (Paris 1886), ed. G. Mollat (Paris 1926); *Manuel de l'inquisiteur*, ed. G. Mollat and G. Drioux, 2 vols. (Paris 1937); A. Dondaine, "Le manuel de l'inquisiteur," *AFP*, 17 (1947), 85–194; P. Frédéricq, *Corpus documentorum* (see bibliog. for Chapter 13); A. Dondaine, *Un traité néo-manichéen du XIIIᵉ siècle. Le Liber de duobus principiis* (Rome 1939); J. N. Garvin and J. A. Corbett, *The Summa contra haereticos, ascribed to Praepositinus of Cremona* (Notre Dame 1958); G. Lacombe, *La vie et les oeuvres de Prévostin* (Paris 1927); James de Capellis, *De erroribus catharorum*, ed. De Bazzocchi, *L'eresia catara* (Bologna 1920), in the appendix; *De heresi catharorum in Lombardia*, ed. A. Dondaine, *AFP*, 19 (1949), 280–312; on the *Tractatus de hereticis* by Anselm of Alessandria see A. Dondaine, *AFP*, 20 (1950), 234–324 (text 308–24); Peter Martyr of Verona, *Summa contra Paterenos*, ed. T. Kaeppeli, *AFP*, 17 (1947), 295–335; on the preceding see A. Dondaine, "S. Pierre Martyr," *AFP*, 23 (1953), 66–162; Moneta of Cremona, *Summa adversus Catharos et Valdenses*, ed. T. A. Ricchini (Rome 1743); Rainer Sacconi, *Summa de Catharis et Pauperibus de Lugduno*, ed. A. Dondaine, *Un traité néo-manichéen (supra)*, 64–78.

Literature: *Hinschius*, V, 449–92, VI, 328–96 (reprinted Graz 1959); J. Ficker, "Die gesetzliche Einführung der Todesstrafe für Ketzerei," *MIÖG*, 1 (1880), 177–226; H. C. Lea, *History of the Inquisition in the Middle Ages*, 3 vols. (New York 1888, reprinted 1955); P. Frédéricq, *Geschiedenis de Inquisitie in de Nederlanden*, 2 vols. (Ghent 1892–98); C. Douais, *L'Inquisition, ses origines, sa procédure* (Paris 1906); R. Gandrille, *L'Organisation de l'Inquisition en France de 1233 à 1500* (Paris 1908); H. Maillet, *L'Église et la répression sanglante de l'hérésie* (Liège 1909); C. Vacandard, *L'Inquisition* (Paris 1912); H. Köhler, *Die Ketzerpolitik der deutschen Könige und Kaiser (1152–54)* (Bonn 1913); R. Schmidt, *Königsrecht, Kirchenrecht und Stadtrecht beim Aufbau des Inquisitionsprozesses* (Munich 1915); E. Tuberville, *Mediaeval Heresy and the Inquisition* (London 1920); C. H. Haskins, "Robert le Bougre and the Beginnings of the Inquisition in Northern France," *AHR*, 7 (1902), 437–57, supplemented in *Studies in Mediaeval Culture* (Oxford 1929), 193–244; L. Förg, *Die Ketzerverfolgungen in Deutschland unter Gregor IX.* (Berlin 1932); J. Guiraud, *Histoire de l'Inquisition au moyen âge*, 2 vols. (Paris 1935–38), important; G. della Veneria, *L'inquisizione medioevale e il processo inquisitorio* (Milan 1939); B. Llorca, *La Inquisición en España* (Madrid, 2d ed. 1946, 3d ed. 1954); Y. Dossat, *Les crises de l'Inquisition toulousaine* (Bordeaux 1959); H. Maisonneuve, *Études sur les origines de l'Inquisition* (Paris 1942, 2d ed. 1960); *Fliche-Martin*, X, 291–340; J. Lecler, "Inquisition," *Catholicisme*, 5 (1963), 1682–93; H. Grundmann, "Ketzerverhöre des Spätmittelalters als quellenkritisches Problem," *DA*, 21 (1965), 519–75; M. Bévenot, "The Inquisition and its Antecedents," *The Heythrop Journal*, 7 (1966), 257–68, 381–93, 8 (1967), 52–69, 152–68.

29. The Missionary Work of the Church in the Twelfth and Thirteenth Centuries

See Vol. III, bibliographies for Chapters 30 and 31. J. Schmidlin, *Katholische Missionsgeschichte* (Kaldenkirchen 1925), English translation (expanded) by M. Braun, *Catholic Mission History* (Techny, Ill. 1933); K. S. Latourette, *A History of the Expansion of*

Christianity, II: *The Thousand Years of Uncertainty (500–1500)* (London 1938), 150–222; *Hauck,* IV (5th ed. 1925), 576–685; *Dahlmann-Waitz,* 6872–6963; P. David in *The Cambridge History of Poland,* ed. W. F. Riddaway, J. H. Halecki, and P. Diboski (Cambridge 1950), Chapter 4; S. Delacroix, *Histoire universelle des missions catholiques,* I: *Les missions des origines au XVIᵉ siècle* (Paris 1956).

EASTERN EUROPE

R. Kötzschke, *Quellen zur Geschichte der ostdeutschen Kolonisation im 12./14. Jahrhundert* (Leipzig, 2d ed. 1931); K. Hampe, *Der Zug nach Osten, die kolonisatorische Grosstadt des deutschen Volkes im Mittelalter* (Leipzig, 5th ed. 1939); A. Hofmeister, *Der Kampf um die Ostsee vom 9.–12. Jahrhundert* (Greifswald 1931); M. Seidlmayer in *RQ* (1935), 187–204; F. Baethgen, "Die Kurie und der Osten im Mittelalter," *Mediaevalia,* I (Stuttgart 1960), 51–70; B. Stasiewski, "Ostmission," *LThK,* VII (2d ed. 1962), 1289–92, with bibliography; H. Beumann, "Kreuzzugsgedanke und Ostpolitik im hohen Mittelalter," *HJ,* 72 (1953), 112–32, now in *Heidenmission und Kreuzzugsgedanke in der deutschen Ostpolitik des Mittelalters,* ed. H. Beumann (Darmstadt 1963), 121–45; M. Bünding-Naujoks, "Das Imperium Christianum und die deutschen Ostkriege vom 10. bis zum 12. Jahrhundert," *ibid.,* 65–120; H. D. Kahl, "Zum Geist der deutschen Slawenmission des Hochmittelalters," *ibid.,* 156–76; *idem,* "Zum Ergebnis des Wendenkreuzzuges von 1147. Zugleich ein Beitrag zur Geschichte des sächsischen Frühchristentums," *ibid.,* 275–316; W. Berges, "Reform und Ostmission im 12. Jahrhundert," *ibid.,* 317–36.
Pomerania: Pommersches Urkundenbuch, 8 vols. (Stettin and Cologne 1868–1961); H. Heyden, *Verzeichnis von Büchern zur Kirchengeschichte Pommerns* (Blomberg 1952); *Vita* of Otto of Bamberg by Wolfger of Prüfening, ed. A Hofmeister (Greifswald 1924), German translation by A. Hofmeister (Leipzig 1928); M. Wehrmann, *Die Lehr- und Predigttätigkeit des Bischofs Otto von Bamberg in Pommern, Baltische Studien,* 26 (Stettin 1924); W. Kümmel, *Die Missionsmethode des Bischofs Otto von Bamberg und seiner Vorläufer in Pommern* (Gütersloh 1926); P. Grosskopf, *Otto von Bamberg, der Pommernapostel* (Berlin, 2 ed. 1932); P. David, *La Pologne et l'évangélisation de la Poméranie au XIᵉ et XIIᵉ siècle* (Paris 1928); H. Heyden, *Kirchengeschichte Pommerns,* I (Cologne, 2d ed. 1957).
The Wends: Helmold of Bosau, *Chronica Slavorum* (to 1171), ed. B. Schmeidler (Leipzig, 3d ed. 1937); H. von Schubert, *Kirchengeschichte Schleswig-Holsteins,* I (Kiel 1907); F. Hestermann, *St. Vizelin* (Dülmen 1926); W. Lammers, *Geschichte Schleswig-Holsteins,* ed. O. Klose, IV (Neumünster 1961 ff.), 3d issue; W. Brüske, *Untersuchungen zur Geschichte des Liutizenbundes* (Münster and Cologne 1955); G. Labuda, *Fragments for the History of the Western Slavs* (in Polish), 2 vols. (Poznań 1960–64); H. D. Kahl, "Heidnisches Wendentum und christliche Stammesfürsten," *AKG,* 44 (1962), 72–119, with bibliography.
Livonia: Sources: Scriptores rerum Livonicarum, I (Riga and Leipzig 1853); *Liv-, est- und kurländische Urkundenregesten bis zum Jahre 1300,* by F. G. von Bunge, with supplements by L. Arbusow, new edition by F. Benninghoven (Hamburg 1959); *Urkundenbuch der alten sächsischen Franziskanerprovinzen,* ed. members of the Saxon and Silesian Province, I: *Die Observantenkustodie Livland und Preussen,* revised by L. Lemmens (Düsseldorf n. d. [1913]); *Heinrichs livländische Chronik,* reedited by L. Arbusow and A. Bauer, *MGSS rer. Germ.* (Hanover 1955); Henry of Latvia, *Livländische Chronik,* new German translation by A. Bauer (Darmstadt 1959); Hermann of Arthberge, *Chronicon Livoniae,* ed. E. Strehlke (Leipzig 1863); "Hartmann von Heldrungen, Hochmeister des deutschen Ordens, Bericht über die Vereinigung des Schwertordens mit dem deutschen Orden und über die Erwerbung Livlands durch den letzteren," ed. E. Strehlke, *Mitteilungen aus dem Gebiete der Geschichte Liv-, Est- und Kurlands,* 11 (1868), 76–90; *Die ältere livländische Reimchronik,* ed. L.

Meyer (Paderborn 1876); Bartholomäus Hoeneke, *Die jüngere livländische Reimchronik*, ed. K. Höhlbaum (Leipzig 1872); *Livonica, vornähmlich aus dem 13. Jahrhundert im Vatikanischen Archiv*, ed. H. Hildebrand (Riga 1887).

Literature: P. von Goetze, *Albert Suerbeer, Erzbischof von Preussen, Livland und Estland* (St. Petersburg 1854); L. Arbusow, *Grundriss der Geschichte Liv-, Est- und Kurlands* (Riga, 4th ed. 1918); H. Laakmann, "Zur Geschichte Heinrichs von Lettland und seiner Zeit," *Beiträge zur Kunde Estlands*, 18 (1933), 57–102; P. Johansen, *Die Estlandliste des Liber Census Daniae* (Copenhagen and Reval 1933); L. Arbusow, "Zur Würdigung des Kultur Altlivlands im Mittelalter," *HZ*, 151 (1935), 18–47; A. M. Ammann, *Kirchenpolitische Wandlungen im Ostbaltikum bis zum Tode Alexander Newskis* (Rome 1936); M. von Taube, "Internationale und kirchenpolitische Wandlungen im Ostbaltikum und Russland zur Zeit der deutschen Eroberung," *Jbb. für Geschichte Osteuropas*, 3 (1938), 11 ff.; L. Arbusow, *Livland—Mark des Reiches (1207–1561)* (Riga 1944); P. Johansen, *Nordische Mission, Revals Gründung und die Schwedensiedlung in Estland* (Stockholm 1951); M. Hellmann, *Das Lettenland im Mittelalter* (Münster and Cologne 1954); P. Johansen, "Lippstadt, Freckenhorst und Fellin in Livland. Werk und Wirkung Bernhards II. zur Lippe im Ostseeraum," *Veröff. des Prov.-Inst. für westf. Landes- und Volkskunde*, 7: *Westfalen, Hanse, Ostseeraum* (Münster 1955), 97–160; A. Bauer, "Der Livlandkreuzzug," *Baltische Kirchengeschichte*, ed. R. Wittram (Göttingen 1956), 26–34; B. Abers, "Zur päpstlichen Missionspolitik in Lettland und Estland zur Zeit Innocenz' III.," *Commentationes Balticae*, 4/5 (1956 f.) (Bonn 1958), 1–18; H. Biezais, "Der friedliche Zeitabschnitt der katholischen Mission in Lettland bis zum Jahre 1196," *Kyrkohistorisk Arsskrift* (Uppsala 1956), 13–29; T. Grentrup, "Der Zisterzienser Dietrich in der altlivländischen Mission," *ZMR*, 40 (1956), 265–81; G. Gnegel-Waitschies, *Bischof Albert von Riga. Ein Bremer Domherr als Kirchenfürst im Osten* (Hamburg 1958); M. Hellmann, *Die Verfassungsgrundlagen Livlands und Preussens im Mittelalter. Ein Beitrag zur vergleichenden Verfassungsgeschichte* (Munich 1958); E. Weise, "Über die Herkunft Erzbischof Friedrichs I. von Bremen-Hamburg und Bischof Bertolds von Livland," *Stader Jb. 1959*, 95–101; A. von Transche-Roseneck, *Die ritterlichen Livlandfahrer des 13. Jahrhunderts, eine genealogische Untersuchung*, ed. W. Lenz (Würzburg 1960); F. Benninghoven, *Der Orden der Schwertbrüder, Fratres milicie Christi de Livonia* (Cologne and Graz 1965), with bibliography.

Prussia: J. Voigt, *Geschichte Preussens* (to 1525), 9 vols. (Königsberg 1827–39), standard; W. Roth, *Die Dominikaner und Franziskaner im Ordensland Preussen bis 1466* (Königsberg 1919); P. Ostwald, *Das Werk des Deutschen Ritterordens in Preussen* (Berlin 1926); F. Blanke, "Die Missionsmethode des Bischofs Christian von Preussen," *Altpreussische Forschungen*, 4 (1927), 3–25, now in H. Beumann, *Heidenmission (supra)*, 337–63; F. Blanke, "Die Entscheidungsjahre der Preussenmission (1206–1274)," *ZKG*, 47 (1928), 18–40, or H. Beumann, *Heidenmission (supra)*, 389–416; E. Maschke, *Der Deutsche Orden und die Preussen. Unterwerfung und Bekehrung* (Berlin 1928); idem, "Polen und die Berufung des Deutschen Ordens nach Preussen," *Ostländische Forschungen*, 4 (Berlin 1934); idem, *Der Deutsche Orden* (Jena 1939); G. A. Donner, *Kardinal Wilhelm von S. Sabina, Bischof von Modena* (Helsingfors 1929); W. Loos, *Die Beziehungen zwischen dem Deutschen Ordensstaat und Pommern* (Königsberg 1937); E. E. Stengel, *Hochmeister und Reich* (Weimar 1938); G. Kunze, *Glaube und Politik. Zur Idee des Deutschen Ordens* (Jena 1938); K. Forstreuter, *Preussen und Russland im Mittelalter (13.–17. Jahrhundert)* (Berlin 1938); idem, "Die Gründung des Erzbistums Preussen," *Jb. der Albertus-Universität in Königsberg*, 10 (1960), 9–31; *Festschrift Kurt Forstreuter: Preussenland und Deutscher Orden* (Würzburg 1958).

Hermann of Salza: A. Lorck, *Hermann von Salza, sein Itinerar* (Kiel 1908); E. Caspar, *Hermann von Salza und die Gründung des Deutschordensstaates* (Tübingen 1924); W. Cohn, *Hermann von Salza* (Breslau 1930); E. Maschke, "Die Herkunft Hermanns von

Salza," *Zeitschrift des Vereins für thüring. Geschichte und Altertumskunde*, new series, 34 (1940), 372–89; H. Heimpel, *Der Mensch in seiner Gegenwart* (Göttingen 1954), 87–108. *The Teutonic Order: Scriptores rerum Prussicarum, Die Geschichtsschreiber der preussischen Vorzeit*, ed. T. Hirsch, M. Toeppen, and E. Strehlke, 5 vols. (Leipzig 1861–74); *Preussisches Urkundenbuch*, ed. F. Philippi, C. P. Woelky, *et al.*, I–III/2 (Königsberg and Marburg 1882–1958); E. Joachim and W. Hubatsch, *Regesta Ordinis S. Mariae Theutonicorum*, 4 vols. (Göttingen 1948–50); R. ten Haaf, *Kurze Bibliographie des Deutschen Ordens* (Göttingen 1949); M. Hellmann, "Neue Arbeiten zur Geschichte des Deutschen Ordens," *HJ*, 75 (1956), 201–13; W. Kuhn, "Ritterorden als Grenzhüter des Abendlandes gegen das östliche Heidentum," *Ostdeutsche Wissenschaft*, 6 (1959), 7–70; M. Hellmann, "Über die Grundlagen und die Entstehung des Ordensstaates in Preussen," *Nachr. der Giessener Hochschulgesellschaft*, 31 (1962), 108–26; B. Poschmann, "Bistümer und Deutscher Orden in Preussen," *Zeitschrift für Geschichte und Altertumskunde Ermlands*, 30 (1962), 227–356; H. H. Hofmann, *Der Staat des Deutschmeisters. Studien zu einer Geschichte des Deutschen Ordens im Heiligen Römischen Reich deutscher Nation* (Munich 1964); E. Weise, "Der Heidenkampf des Deutschen Ordens," *Zeitschrift für Ostforschung*, 12 (1963), 420–73, 622–73, 13 (1964), 401–20; I. Matison, "Die Lehnsexemtion des Deutschen Ordens und dessen staatsrechtliche Stellung in Preussen," *DA*, 21 (1965), 194–248; O. Engels, "Zur Historiographie des Deutschen Ordens im Mittelalter," *AKG*, 48 (1966), 336–63.

ASIA

R. Streit, *Bibliotheca Missionum*, IV (Aachen 1928), 1245–1599; R. Hennig, *Terrae incognitae*, II–III (Leiden, 2d ed. 1950–53); *Sinica Franciscana*, I: *Itinera et Relationes Fratrum Minorum saec. XIII et XIV*, ed. A. van den Wyngaert (Quaracchi 1929); J. Becquet and L. Hambis, *Jean de Plan Carpin, Histoire des Mongols*, traduit et annoté (Paris 1965); H. Matrod, *Miscellanea nel 7. centenario della sua* [John of Piano di Carpine] *morte* (Assisi 1952); William of Ruysbroeck, *Reisebericht*, translated into German by F. Risch (Leipzig 1934); F. Soldi, *Undecima hora. La missione di Bartolomeo da Cremona al Gran Khan di Karakorum nel 1254* (Cremona 1954); H. Dörrie, *Drei Texte zur Geschichte der Ungarn und Mongolen. Die Missionsreisen des Fr. Julianus O. P. ins Uralgebiet (1234/35) und nach Russland (1237) und der Bericht des Erzbischofs Peter über die Tartaren*, *Nachrichten der Akademie der Wissenschaften Göttingen 1956*, 6 (Göttingen 1956); D. Sinor, "Les relations entre les Mongols et l'Europe jusqu'à la mort d'Arghum," *Cahiers d'histoire mondiale*, 3 (1956), 39–62; G. Vernadsky, *The Mongols and Russia* (New Haven 1953); C. Cahen, "The Mongols and the Near East," *A History of the Crusades*, ed. K. M. Setton, II, 715–34, with bibliography.

The Papacy and the Mongols: P. Pelliot, "Les Mongols et la papauté," *ROC*, 23 (1922 f.), 3–30, 24 (1924), 225–335, 28 (1931 f.), 3–84; G. Soranzo, *Il papato, l'Europa e i Tartari* (Milan 1930); G. Rocheau, "Innocent IV devant le péril tartare. Ses lettres à Daniel de Galicie et à Alexandre Nevsky," *Istina*, 6 (1959), 167–86; H. Serruys, "Early Mongols and the Catholic Church," *NZM*, 19 (1963), 161–69.

China: B. Altaner, *Die Dominikanermission des 13. Jahrhunderts* (Habelschwerdt 1924); J. de Ghellinck, *Les Franciscains en Chine au XIII*ᵉ *et XIV*ᵉ *siècle* (Louvain 1927); J. Stewart, *Nestorian Missionary Enterprise* (Edinburgh 1928); L. Lemmens, *Geschichte der Franziskanermissionen* (Münster 1929); A. C. Moule, *Christians in China before 1550* (London 1930); L. E. Browne, *The Eclipse of Christianity in Asia from Muhammed till the Fourteenth Century* (Cambridge 1933); O. van den Vat, *Die Anfänge der Franziskanermission . . . während des 13. Jahrhunderts* (Werl 1934); M. d'Elia, "Katholische Kirche in China 635/1294/1948," *StMis* (1950 f.), 3–67; P. S. Hsiang, *The Catholic Missions in China 1294–1368* (Washington 1949); F. Soldi, *Undecima hora (supra)*; C. Cary-Elwes,

China and the Cross (London 1957); C. W. Troll, "Die Chinamission im Mittelalter," *FStud*, 48 (1966), 109–50, 49 (1967), 22–78, with bibliography.

30. *Canon Law and the Constitution of the Church in the Thirteenth Century*

Sources

The five great compilations: ed. E. Friedberg, *Quinque compilationes antiquae* (Leipzig 1882); the Decretals of Gregory IX, *Liber Extra:* last edition by E. Friedberg (Leipzig 1881, often reprinted); on this edition *cf.* A. M. Stickler, *Historia Iuris Canonici Latini*, I: *Historia Fontium* (Turin 1950), 249 f.; Innocent IV's collection of *novellae:* latest edition by P. J. Kessler, "Untersuchungen über die Novellen-Gesetzgebung Papst Innocenz' IV. Ein Beitrag zur Geschichte des kanonischen Rechts," *ZSavRGkan*, 31 (1942), 142–320, 32 (1943), 300–83, 33 (1944), 56–128; the Decretals of Gregory X (almost exclusively the constitutions of Lyons II): ed. J. H. Böhmer, *Corpus Iuris Canonici*, II, Anhang 4; Nicholas III's collection of *novellae:* partly edited by F. von Schulte, *SAW*, 55 (1867), 718–22; Boniface VIII's *Liber Sextus:* last edition by E. Friedberg (Leipzig 1881) (see *supra*).

Literature

Feine RG, I, 283–92; G. Le Bras, C. Lefèbvre, J. Rambaud, *Histoire du Droit et des Institutions de l'Église en Occident*, VII: *L'âge classique (1140–1378)* (Paris 1965), 133–351; H. Singer, *Neue Beiträge über die Dekretalen-Sammlungen vor und nach Bernhard von Pavia*, *SAW*, 171 (Vienna 1914), and, in connection with this work, the discussion by F. Heyer in *ZSavKGkan*, 3 (1913), 615–42, 4 (1914), 583–608; on the collections between Gratian and Gregory IX *cf.* S. Kuttner, *Repertorium der Kanonistik*, *SteT*, 71 (Rome 1937), 272–385; on the five great compilations *cf.*, *inter alia*, G. Fransen, "Les diverses formes de la Compilatio Ia," *Scrinium lovaniense*, Mélanges historiques E. van Cauwenbergh (Louvain 1961), 235–53; C. R. Cheney, "Three Decretal Collections before Compilatio IVa," *Tr*, 15 (1959), 464–83; S. Kuttner, "Johannes Teutonicus, das vierte Laterankonzil und die Compilatio IVa," *MiscMercati*, V, *SteT*, 125 (Rome 1946), 608–34; on the *Liber Extra: Feine RG*, I, 287; *Le Bras D*, 233–43; on the *novellae* of Innocent IV: P. J. Kessler, *Untersuchungen* (see *supra*); on the *Liber Sextus: Feine RG*, I, 288 f.; *Le Bras D*, 247–51. S. Gagner, *Studien zur Ideengeschichte der Gesetzgebung* (Uppsala 1960), is an important work on the legislative achievements of the thirteenth-century Popes.

The Decretalists: Bernard of Pavia, *Summa decretalium*, ed. E. A. T. Laspeyres (Regensburg 1860); Sinibaldo Fieschi (Innocent IV), *Apparatus in V libros Decretalium* (Frankfurt am Main 1570; editio princeps, Strasbourg 1477); Henry of Susa (Hostiensis), *Summa super titulis Decretalium* (Rome 1473); A. Rivera Damas, *Pensamiento político de Hostiensis* (Zürich 1964). Only the most famous have been listed; a distinction is made between the older decretalists (up to the *Liber Extra*) and the later. On the *apparatus* and glosses *cf. Le Bras D*, 292–301; on Innocent IV as a canonist *cf.* J. A. Cantini and C. Lefèbvre in *DDC*, 7 (1958–62), 1029–62; on Henry of Susa *cf. Le Bras D*, 312–14; G. Le Bras, "Théologie et droit canonique dans l'oeuvre de Henri de Suse," *Études Didier* (Paris 1961), 195–204.

Constitution of the Church: the following are the most important works: *Hinschius*; J. B. Sägmüller, *Lehrbuch des katholischen Kirchenrechts*, I (Freiburg, 4th ed. 1934); W. M. Plöchl, *Geschichte des Kirchenrechts*, II: *Das Kirchenrecht der abendländischen Christenheit 1055–1517* (Vienna, 2d ed. 1961); *Fliche-Martin*, 12/1; *Feine RG*. All the works just mentioned include a comprehensive bibliography for individual chapters and problems.

The Papacy: W. Ullmann, *The Growth of Papal Government in the Middle Ages* (London, 2d ed. 1962); *idem, Principles of Government and Politics in the Middle Ages* (London 1961); *Hinschius,* I, 163–308; *Feine RG,* 299–321; *Le Bras D,* 305–333; M. Wilks, *The Problem of Sovereignty in the Later Middle Ages* (Cambridge 1963), especially 354–407; criticism of Ullmann by F. Kempf, "Die päpstliche Gewalt in der mittelalterlichen Welt," *Saggi storici intorno al papato* (Rome 1959), 117–69; on the dispute whether the thirteenth-century Popes were "hierocrats" or "dualists" *cf.* now the important remarks by B. Tierney, "The Continuity of Papal Political Theory in the Thirteenth Century," *MS,* 27 (1965), 227–45; M. Pacaut, "L'autorité pontificale selon Innocent IV," *MA,* 66 (1960), 85–119; M. Maccarone, *Vicarius Christi. Storia del titolo papale* (Rome 1952); D. P. Waley, *The Papal State in the Thirteenth Century* (London 1961); J. H. Hackett, "State of the Church. A concept of the medieval canonists," *The Jurist* (1963), 259–90.

Councils: A. Hauck, "Die Rezeption und Umbildung der allgemeinen Synode im Mittelalter," *HV,* 10 (1907), 465–82; H. Fuhrmann, "Das ökumenische Konzil und seine historischen Grundlagen," *Geschichte in Wissenschaft und Unterricht,* 12 (1961), 672–95; F. Dvornik, *Histoire des conciles* (Paris 1962); G. Tangl, *Die Teilnehmer an den allgemeinen Konzilien des Mittelalters* (Weimar 1922); B. Tierney, *Foundations of the Conciliar Theory* (Cambridge 1955); J. Leclercq, *Jean de Paris et l'ecclésiologie du XIII*ᵉ *siècle* (Paris 1942).

Bishops: Hinschius, II, 1–48, also I, 538–632; *Feine RG,* 366–69; *Le Bras D,* 365–76. There is a copious literature on the history of dioceses in Germany, France, England, and Spain, which usually also treats questions of organization. Important biographies of English bishops have recently appeared: D. L. Douie, *Archbishop Pecham* (Oxford 1952); D. A. Callus, *Robert Grosseteste, Scholar and Bishop* (Oxford 1955); C. M. Fraser, *A History of Antony Bek, Bishop of Durham* (Oxford 1957); C. H. Lawrence, *St. Edmund of Abingdon, Archbishop of Canterbury* (Oxford 1960). Special problems are treated in: K. Rahner and J. Ratzinger, *Episkopat und Primat* (Freiburg im Breisgau 1961); G. Barraclough, "The Making of a Bishop in the Middle Ages," *CHR,* 19 (1933), 275–319; P. Hofmeister, "Die kanonischen und nichtkanonischen Wahlen," *ZKTh,* 77 (1955), 432–71; A. Desprairies, *L'élection des évêques par les chapitres au XIII*ᵉ *siècle* (Paris 1922); A. Diegel, *Der päpstliche Einfluss auf die Bischofswahlen in Deutschland während des 13. Jahrhunderts* (Berlin 1932); R. L. Benson, *The Bishop-Elect: A Study in Medieval Ecclesiastical Office* (Princeton 1968); R. Brentano, *Two Churches: England and Italy in the Thirteenth Century* (Princeton 1968); J. J. Smith, *The Attitude of John Pecham toward Monastic Houses under His Jurisdiction* (Washington 1949).

Archdeacons: J. B. Sägmüller, *Lehrbuch* (see *supra*), 1 467–69, with the older literature; *Hinschius,* II, 183–204; *Feine RG,* 369–75; *Le Bras D,* 391–94. The series of monographs on the archdeaconry begins with N. Hilling for Münster (1902) and Halberstadt (1902), after which come those by H. Bastgen for Trier (1906), E. Baumgartner for the Rhenish dioceses (1907), G. Gescher for Cologne (1920), J. Machens for Hildesheim (1921), A. Schröder for Augsburg (1925), B. Panzram for Silesia (1937), M. Hannappel for Erfurt (1941), H. Mulders for Utrecht (1943), and A. Szentirmai for Hungary (*ZSavRGkan,* 43 [1957], 132–201); J. Frieg, *Kampf der Bischöfe gegen die Archidiakonate im Bistum Würzburg* (Stuttgart 1914); A. Franzen, *Die Kölner Archdiakonate in vor- und nachtridentinischer Zeit* (Münster 1953), with bibliography.

Parishes: Hinschius, II, 261–328; *Feine RG,* 391–427; *Le Bras D,* 404–23. The older bibliography is in *Feine RG,* 411–14 and 424–27 (urban parish). A. Schultze, "Stadtgemeinde und Kirche im Mittelalter," *Festschrift Rudolf Sohm* (Munich and Leipzig 1914), 105–42, and, in connection with this essay, K. Frölich in *HV,* 20 (1920), 37–46; R. A. R. Hartridge, *A History of Vicarages in the Middle Ages* (Cambridge 1930); K. Frölich, "Die Rechtsformen der mittelalterlichen Altarpfründen," *ZSavRGkan,* 20 (1931), 457–544, with bibliography; *idem,* "Kirche und städtisches Verfassungsleben im Mittelalter,"

ZSavRGkan, 22 (1933), 188–287; L. Pfleger, *Untersuchungen zur Geschichte des Pfarr-Instituts im Elsass* (Strasbourg 1936); G. Mollat, "Le droit de patronage en Normandie du XIe au XVe siècle," *RHE*, 33 (1937), 464–84, 725–88, 34 (1938), 21–69; B. Panzram, *Geschichtliche Grundlage der ältesten schlesischen Pfarreiorganisation* (Breslau 1940); L. Manni, *La parrocchia studiata nei documenti lucchesi dei secoli VIII–XIII* (Rome 1948); H. T. Hoederath, "Forensis Ecclesia," *ZSavRGkan*, 36 (1950), 390–99; H. Lentze, "Die Rechtsform der Altarpfründen im mittelalterlichen Wien," *ZSavRGkan*, 37 (1951), 221–302; E. O. Kuujo, *Die rechtliche und wirtschaftliche Stellung der Pfarrkirchen in Alt-Livland* (Helsinki 1953); J. Nylander, *The Origins of the Office of Churchwarden* (York 1954); G. H. Cook, *The English Medieval Parish Church* (London 1954); H. B. Noser, *Pfarrei und Kirchgemeinde. Studie zu ihrem rechtlichen Begriff und grundsätzlichen Verhältnis* (Fribourg 1957); H. E. Feine, "Kirche und Gemeindebildung," *Recht und Kirche, ausgewählte Abhandlungen*, ed. F. Merzbacher (Aalen 1966), 101–18.

Cathedral Chapters: Hinschius, II, 49–160; *Feine RG*, 379–91; *Le Bras D*, 376–90; A. Schulte, *Der Adel und die deutsche Kirche* (Darmstadt, 3d ed. 1958); G. von Below, *Die Entstehung des ausschliesslichen Wahlrechts der Domkapitel* (Leipzig 1883); P. Schneider, *Die Entwicklung der bischöflichen Domkapitel* (Mainz 1892); E. Mayer, "Der Ursprung der Domkapitel," *ZSavRGkan*, 7 (1917), 1–33. Monographs on the history of cathedral chapters in Germany, France, England, Ireland, Italy, Switzerland, Belgium, and Poland are listed in *Fliche-Martin*, 12, 377, footnote 3; L. Santifaller, *Das Brixener Domkapitel in seiner persönlichen Zusammensetzung im Mittelalter*, 2 vols. (Innsbruck 1924 f.); A. Hamilton-Thompson, *The Cathedral Churches of England* (Oxford 1925); P. Hofmeister, *Bischof und Domkapitel nach altem und nach neuem Recht* (Neresheim 1931); J. Oswald, *Das alte Passauer Domkapitel* (Munich 1933); M. Gibbs and J. Lang, *Bishops and Reform (1215–1272)* (London 1934); R. Samulski, *Untersuchungen über die persönliche Zusammensetzung des Breslauer Domkapitels im Mittelalter (to 1341)* (Weimar 1940); E. Fournier, *Nouvelles recherches sur les curies, chapitres et universités de l'Église de France* (Arras 1942); L. Santifaller, *Urkunden und Forschungen zur Geschichte des Trienter Domkapitels im Mittelalter*, I (Vienna 1948); C. N. L. Brooke, "The Composition of the Chapter of St. Paul's (1086–1163)," *CambrHJ*, 10 (1951), 111–32; J. Szymanski, "Les recherches sur l'histoire des chapitres polonais effectuées de 1945 à 1960," *RHE*, 57 (1962), 484–92.

SECTION SIX

The Crisis of the Papacy and of the Church: 1274 - 1303

Sources

Mansi, XXIV and XXV; *Hefele-Leclercq*, VI/1, 229–467; *Bullarium Taur.*, IV, 35–174; *Potthast R*, 1704–2024; *Duchesne LP*, II, 457–71; *MGConst*, III and IV, ed. J. Schwalm (Hanover and Leipzig 1904–11); E. Winkelmann, *Acta Imperii inedita saec. XIII et XIV (1198–1400)*, 2 vols. (Innsbruck 1880–85, reprinted Aalen 1964). Papal *registra*: Gregory X and John XXI, ed. J. Guiraud and E. Cadier (Paris 1892–1960); Nicholas III, ed. J. Guy and S. Vitte (Paris 1938); Martin IV, ed. M. Olier-Martin (Paris 1901–35); Honorius IV, ed. M. Prou (Paris 1888); Nicholas IV, 2 vols., ed. E. Langlois (Paris 1905); Boniface VIII, 4 vols., ed. G. Digard, M. Faucon, A. Thomas, and R. Fawtier (Paris 1907–39). *Regesta Imperii*, VI/1 (Rudolf of Habsburg), ed. O. Redlich (Innsbruck 1898); *Regesta Imperii*, VI/2 (Adolf of Nassau), ed. V. Samanek (Innsbruck 1948); there is not yet available a new revision for Albert I, but A. Hessel, *Jahrbücher des Deutschen Reiches unter König Albrecht von Habsburg* (Munich 1931, with all the literature), should be consulted; Y.

Lanhers, *Le dossier d'Albert d'Autriche aux Archives et à la Bibliothèque Nationale de Paris, Festschrift . . . des Haus-, Hof- und Staatsarchivs*, I, *Mitteilungen des Österreichischen Staatsarchivs*, supplementary Volume 2 (Vienna 1949); F. Kern, *Acta Imperii, Angliae et Franciae* (Berlin 1911); H. Finke, *Acta Aragonensia*, 3 vols. (Berlin 1908–22), supplemented by *Gesammelte Aufsätze zur Kulturgeschichte Spaniens*, 4 (1933), 355–536; J. Vincke, *Documenta selecta mutuas civitatis Arago-Cathalaunicae et Ecclesiae relationes illustrantia* (Barcelona 1936). Most of the historical writing of this period—frequently the work of mendicant friars—is confined to particular territories, but the compendia of Martin of Troppau and Martinus Minorita (see the bibliog. for Section V) are more comprehensive.

The continuations of the Italian annals are valuable: of Piacenza to 1284, *MGSS*, 17, 457–81 (Ghibelline); of Genoa to 1294, *MGSS*, 18, 11–356; of Parma to 1335, *MGSS*, 18, 664–790; of Albert Milioli (Reggio) to 1285, *MGSS*, 31, 336–668; Tolomeo of Lucca, *Historia ecclesiastica nova* (to 1294), ed. *Muratori*, XI, 753–1216; Saba Malaspina, *Rerum Sicularum libri VI* (1250–76) and Continuatio (to 1285), ed. *Muratori*, VIII, 785–874; Bartholomew of Neocastro, *Historia Sicula*, ed. G. Paladino (Bologna 1921 f.).

Germany: the Great Annals of Marbach (to 1305), *MGSS*, 17, 142–80; Ottakar's *Österreichische Reimchronik*, ed. J. Seemüller, *MG Deutsche Chroniken*, 5 (Hanover 1890–93); the Chronicle of Colmar (to 1304), *MGSS*, 17, 183–270; the Annals of Altaich, with their continuations, ed. F. von Oefele, *MGSS rer. Germ.* (Hanover 1891); the Chronicles of Erfurt (to 1355), ed. O. Holder-Egger, *MGSS rer. Germ.* (Hanover 1899); the Chronicle of Reinhardsbrunner (to 1338), ed. O. Holder-Egger, *MGSS*, 30, 490–656; see K. Jacob and F. Werden, *Quellenkunde der deutschen Geschichte im Mittelalter*, III (Berlin 1952), 22–42.

England: Chronicles of Bury St. Edmunds (to 1301), latest edition by V. H. Galbraith, *EHR*, 53 (1943), 51–78 (important); Bartholomew Cotton of Norwich, *Historia Anglicana* (to 1298), ed. H. R. Luard, *Rolls Series*, 16 (London 1859); monastic annals are numerous and in this field also the mendicants undertook the writing toward the close of the century, as, for example, the Lanerost Chronicle (1201–1346), ed. J. Stevenson, Bannatyne Club (1839), translated by W. Maxwell, introduction by J. Wilson (London 1913); the Chronicle of Walter of Guisborough (formerly: Walter of Hemmingford) (to 1312), ed. H. Rothwell, Camden Society, Third Series, 89 (London 1957); for other English sources *cf.* F. M. Powicke, *The Thirteenth Century* (Oxford, 2d ed. 1962), 730–43.

France: especially important is the Chronicle of William of Nangis (1113–1300), ed. H. Géraud, 2 vols. (New York and London 1964).

Spain: James I, *Crónica*, ed. J. M. Casacuberta *et al.*, 9 vols. (Barcelona 1926–62); B. Desclot, *Libre del rey en Pere de Aragó e dels seus antecessors passats*, ed. M. Coll i Alentorn (Barcelona 1949); R. Muntaner, *Crónica*, ed. E. Bagué (Barcelona 1927), and, in connection with it, F. Soldevilla, *Les gestes de Pere el Gran* (Barcelona 1926).

LITERATURE

See the works already listed for Section Five. Also: H. Heimpel, *Deutschland im späteren Mittelalter, Handbuch der Deutschen Geschichte*, ed. L. Just, I, V. Abschnitt (Constance 1957); E. de Moreau, *Histoire de l'Église en Belgique*, III (Brussels 1945); E. G. Léonard, *Les Angevins de Naples* (Paris 1954); F. M. Powicke, *The Thirteenth Century (1216–1307)* (Oxford, 2d ed. 1962); *idem*, *King Henry III and the Lord Edward*, 2 vols. (Oxford 1947); *The Cambridge Medieval History*, VII (London 1932, reprinted 1957); *Lavisse*, III/2; H. Hantsch, *Die Geschichte Österreichs*, I (Vienna, 4th ed. 1959).

31. *The Papacy Subject to Angevin Influence*

LITERATURE

Seppelt, III, 534–80; *Haller*, V, 42–89.

Innocent V: H. M. Laurent, *Le bienheureux Innocent V et son temps, SteT,* 129 (Rome 1947); E. A. van Moe, "L'envoi des nonces à Constantinople par les papes Innocent V et Jean XXI (1276)," *MAH,* 47 (1930), 39–62; H. M. Laurent, "Georges le Métochite, ambassadeur de Michel VIII Paléologue auprès d'Innocent V," *MiscMercati,* 3 (Rome 1956), 136–56; L. F. Barmann, "Peter of Tarentaise, a Biographical Study," *Revue de l'Université d'Ottawa,* 31 (1961), 96–125; *Beatus Innocentius Papa V (Petrus de Tarantasia). Studia et documenta* (Rome 1943).

Adrian V: R. Graham, "Letters of Cardinal Ottoboni," *EHR,* 15 (1900), 87–120; N. Schöpp, *Papst Hadrian V. (Kardinal Ottobuono Fieschi)* (Heidelberg 1916).

John XXI: R. Stapper, *Papst Johannes XXI. Eine Monographie* (Münster i. W. 1898); *Obras filosóficas,* 3 vols., ed. M. A. Alonso (Madrid 1941–52, Barcelona, 2d ed. 1961); *Summulae logicales,* ed. J. P. Mullally (Notre Dame 1945); V. Ludovisi, "Vocabor Joannes. Il papa Giovanni [XXI] nel periodo ducentesco della sede Viterbese," *Viterbo città dei papi* (Viterbo 1961), 9–16; *Peter of Spain, Tractatus syncategorematum and Selected Anonymous Treatises,* translated by J. P. Mullally, with introduction by J. P. Mullally and R. Houde (Milwaukee 1964).

Nicholas III: A. Demski, *Papst Nikolaus III.* (Munich 1903); R. Sternfeld, *Der Kardinal Johann Gaetan Orsini (Papst Nikolaus III. 1244–77)* (Berlin 1905); E. Dupré-Theseider, *Roma dal Comune di popolo alla Signoria pontificia* (Bologna 1952); G. Barraclough, "The Chancery Ordinance of Nicholas III," *QFIAB,* 25 (1933 f.), 192–250; F. Baethgen, "Ein Pamphlet Karls I. von Anjou zur Wahl Papst Nikolaus' III.," *SAM* (1906–07); R. J. Loenertz, "Mémoire d'Ogier protonotaire, pour Marco et Marchetto nonces de Michel VIII Paléologue auprès du pape Nicholas III 1278," *OrChrP,* 31 (1965), 374–408.

Martin IV: N. Backes, *Kardinal Simon de Brion* (Breslau 1910); R. Sternfeld, "Das Konklave von 1280 und die Wahl Martins IV.," *MIÖG,* 31 (1910), 1–53; J. R. Strayer, "The Crusade against Aragon," *Speculum,* 28 (1953), 102–13; A. Fabrega Grau, "Actitud de Pedro III el Grande de Aragón ante la propia deposición fulminada por Martín IV," *Sacerdozio e regno da Gregorio VII a Bonifacio VIII, Misc. Hist. Pont.,* 18 (Rome 1954), 161–80; R. Kay, "Martin IV and the Fugitive Bishop of Bayeux," *Speculum,* 40 (1965), 460–83.

Honorius IV: B. Pawlicki, *Papst Honorius IV.* (Münster 1896); G. von Gaisberg-Schöckingen, *Das Konzil und der Reichstag von Würzburg 1287* (Marburg 1928).

Nicholas IV: O. Schiff, *Studien zur Geschichte Papst Nikolaus' IV.* (Berlin 1897); G. I. Bratianu, "Autour du projet de croisade de Nicolas IV: la guerre ou le commerce avec l'Infidèle," *Revue historique du Sud-Est européen,* 22 (Bucharest 1945), 250–55.

The Angevins and Sicily: see the bibliography for Chapter 26. Also: V. Nicolini, *Codice diplomatico sui rapporti veneto-napoletani durante il regno di Carlo I d'Angiò* (Rome 1965); O. Cartellieri, *Peter von Aragón und die sizilianische Vesper* (Heidelberg 1904); E. Sthamer, "Aus der Vorgeschichte der sizilischen Vesper," *QFIAB,* 19 (1927), 262–372; H. Wieruszowski, "Der Anteil Johannes von Procida an der Verschwörung gegen Karl von Anjou," *Gesammelte Aufsätze zur Kulturgeschichte Spaniens,* I/5 (Münster 1935), 230–39; *eadem,* "Le corte di Pietro d'Aragona e i precedenti dell'impresa siciliana," *AstIt,* 96 (1938), I, 141–62, II, 200–17; G. La Mantia, "Studi sulla rivoluzione siciliana del 1282," *Archivio storico per la Sicilia,* 6 (1939), 97–140; M. Amari, *La guerra del Vespro Siciliano* (Mazara 1947); S. Runciman, *The Sicilian Vespers* (Cambridge 1958); A. Nitschke, "Karl von Anjou und Peter von Aragón. Ihre Stellung zur sizilianischen Bevölkerung," *Fest-*

schrift P. E. Schramm, I (1964), 322–33; *idem*, "Der sizilische Adel unter Karl von Anjou und Peter von Aragón," *QFIAB*, 45 (1965), 241–73.

Spain: J. Vincke, *Staat und Kirche in Katalonien und Aragón während des Mittelalters* (Münster 1931); H. J. Chaytor, *A History of Aragon and Catalonia* (London 1933); J. B. Strayer, "The Crusade against Aragon," *Speculum*, 28 (1953), 102–13; J. M. Pou y Martí, "Conflictos entre el Pontificado y los reyes de Aragón en el siglo XIII," *Sacerdozio e regno da Gregorio VII a Bonifacio VIII, Misc. Hist. Pont.*, 18 (Rome 1954), 139–60; H. Wieruszowski, "Politische Verschwörungen und Bündnisse König Peters von Aragón gegen Karl von Anjou am Vorabend der Sizilianischen Vesper," *QFIAB*, 37 (1957), 136–91; F. Soldevilla, "L'ambaixada de Pere el Gran a l'emperador Rudolf de Habsburg," *Homenaje a Aime Vicens Vives*, I (Barcelona 1965), 651–59.

Germany: O. Redlich, *Rudolf von Habsburg. Das deutsche Reich nach dem Untergange des Kaisertums* (Innsbruck 1903, reprinted Aalen 1965); the older literature in *Dahlmann-Waitz*, 7581–97; F. Baethgen, "Ein Versuch Rudolfs von Habsburg, die Reichsrechte in der Toskana wahrzunehmen," *HV*, 22 (1924 f.), 70–75. For the plan to make the Empire hereditary: W. Neumann, "Reichsreformpläne im 13. Jahrhundert," *Festschrift für Hermann Reincke-Bloch* (Breslau 1927), 37–47; H. Hempel, "Alexander von Roes und das deutsche Selbstbewusstsein des 13. Jahrhunderts," *AKG*, 26 (1935), 19–60; *Die Schriften des Alexander von Roes*, ed. and trans. H. Grundmann and H. Heimpel (Weimar 1949); H. Grundmann, "Über die Schriften des Alexander von Roes," *DA*, 8 (1950), 154–237; *idem*, "Sacerdotium—Regnum—Studium," *AKG*, 34 (1951), 5–21; H. Heimpel, "Über den Pavo des Alexander von Roes," *DA*, 13 (1957), 171–227; H. Otto, *Die Beziehungen Rudolfs von Habsburg zu Gregor X.* (Innsbruck 1895); A. Demski, *Rudolf von Habsburg und die römische Kaiserkrone unter Nikolaus III.* (Breslau 1906); H. Roeder, *Rudolf von Habsburg als römischer König* (Bonn 1926); H. Rössler, *Ein König für Deutschland* (Munich 1960); K. and M. Uhlirz, *Handbuch der Geschichte Österreich-Ungarns*, I (Graz, Vienna, and Cologne, 2d ed. 1963), 263–66, 274–78, with bibliography; V. Samanek, *Studien zur Geschichte König Adolfs I, SAW*, 20 (Vienna 1929); G. Barraclough, "Edward I and Adolf of Nassau," *CambrHJ*, 6 (1940), 225–62; F. J. Schmale, "Eine thüringische Briefsammlung aus der Zeit Adolfs von Nassau," *DA*, 9 (1952), 464–93; W. H. Struck, "Eine neue Quelle zur Geschichte König Adolfs von Nassau," *Nassauische Annalen*, 63 (1952), 72–105; F. Baethgen, "Zur Wahl Adolfs von Nassau," *DA*, 12 (1956), 536–43; the older literature in *Dahlmann-Waitz*, 7598–7602; O. Herding, *Das Römisch-Deutsche Reich in deutschen und italienischen Beurteilungen von Rudolf von Habsburg zu Heinrich VII.* (Erlangen 1937).

32. *Christian Fanaticism in the Thirteenth Century*

LITERATURE

H. Grundmann, *Religiöse Bewegungen im Mittelalter. Untersuchungen über die geschichtlichen Zusammenhänge zwischen der Ketzerei, den Bettelorden und den religiösen Frauenbewegungen im 12. und 13. Jahrhundert und über die geschichtlichen Grundlagen der deutschen Mystik* (Darmstadt, 2d ed. 1961), in the appendix: "neue Beiträge zur Geschichte der religiösen Bewegungen im Mittelalter," also in *AKG*, 37 (1955), 129–82; E. Dupré-Theseider, *Introduzione alle eresie medioevali* (Bologna 1952); H. Grundmann, *Ketzergeschichte des Mittelalters* (Göttingen 1963); G. Leff, *Heresy in the Later Middle Ages*, 2 vols. (Manchester 1967).

Joachim of Fiore: Works: *Concordia novi ac veteris testamenti* (Venice 1519); *Expositio in Apocalypsim* (Venice 1527); *Psalterium decem chordarum* (Venice 1527); *Tractatus super quatuor evangelia*, ed. E. Buonaiuti (Rome 1930); *De articulis fidei*, ed. E. Buonaiuti (Rome 1936); *Liber figurarum*, ed. L. Tondelli (Turin, 2d ed. 1953); *De vita et regula S.*

Benedicti, ed. C. Baraut, *AST,* 24 (1951), 33–122; *De septem sigillis,* ed. M. Reeves and B. Hirsch-Reich, *RThAM,* 21 (1954), 211–47; *Adversus Iudeos,* ed. A. Frugoni, *Fonti-StIt,* 95 (Rome 1957). Literature: F. Russo, *Bibliografia gioachimita* (Florence 1954), and, in connection with it, *RThAM,* 24 (1957), 27–44; M. W. Bloomfield, "Joachim of Fiore, a Critical Survey," *Tr,* 13 (1957), 249–311, with bibliography; H. Denifle, "Das Evangelium aeternum und die Commission zu Anagni," *ALKGMA,* 1 (1885), 49–142; H. Grundmann, *Studien über Joachim von Fiore* (Leipzig 1927); biographies by. H. Bett (London 1931) and E. Buonaiuti (Rome 1931); E. Benz in *ZKG,* 50 (1931), 24–111, 51 (1932), 415–55; *idem, Ecclesia spiritualis* (Stuttgart 1934); J. C. Huck, *Joachim von Floris und die joachitische Literatur* (Freiburg 1938); H. Grundmann, *Neue Forschungen über Joachim von Fiore* (Marburg 1950); M. W. Bloomfield and M. Reeves, "The Penetration of Joachim into Northern Europe," *Speculum,* 29 (1954), 773–93; F. Russo, *Gioacchino da Fiore e le fondazioni florensi* (Naples 1959); H. Grundmann, "Zur Biographie Joachims von Fiore und Rainers von Ponza," *DA,* 16 (1960), 437–546 *(Vita beati Ioachimi abbatis,* 528–44); R. Manselli, "L'attesa dell'età nuova e il gioachimismo," *L'attesa dell'età nuova nella spiritualità della fine del medioevo* (Todi 1962), 145–70.

The Spirituals: E. Benz, *Ecclesia spiritualis. Kirchenidee und Geschichtstheologie der franziskanischen Reformation* (Stuttgart 1934); L. Oliger, "Beiträge zur Geschichte der Spiritualen, Fratizellen und Clarener in Mittelitalien," *ZKG,* 45 (1926), 215–42; J. M. Pou y Martí, *Visionarios, beguinos y fraticelos catalanes (siglos XIII a XV)* (Vich 1930); D. Douie, *The Nature and the Effect of the Heresy of the Fraticelli* (Manchester 1932); L. von Auw, *Angelo Clareno et les Spirituels Franciscains* (Lausanne 1952); M. D. Lambert, *Franciscan Poverty. The Doctrine of the Absolute Poverty of Christ and the Apostles in the Franciscan Order (1210–1323)* (London 1961).

Arnald of Villanova: Obras catalanes, ed. M. Batllori and J. Carreras, 2 vols. (Barcelona 1947); M. Menéndez y Pelayo, *Historia de los heterodoxos españoles,* 2 vols. (Madrid 1880–82), ed. Madrid, *BAC,* 1956, I, 539–76; R. Verrier, *Études sur Arnauld de Villeneuve,* 2 vols. (Leiden 1947–49); J. A. Paniagua, *Estudios y notas sobre Arnau de Vilanova* (Madrid 1963); P. Diepgen, *Arnald von Villanova als Politiker und Laientheologe* (Berlin 1909); R. Manselli, "La religiosità d'Arnaldo da Villanova," *BIStIAM,* 63 (1951), 1–100; *idem,* "Arnaldo da Villanova e i papi del suo tempo tra religione e politica," *Studi Romani,* 7 (1959), 146–61.

Beguines and Beghards: basic is E. W. MacDonnell, *The Beguines and Beghards in Medieval Culture with Special Emphasis on the Belgian Scene* (New Brunswick 1954); J. Greven, *Die Anfänge der Beginen* (Münster 1912); H. Grundmann, "Zur Geschichte der Beginen im 13. Jahrhundert," *AKG,* 21 (1931), 296–320; A. Mens, *Oorsprong en betekenis van de nederlandse Begijnen- en Begardenbeweging* (Brussels and Antwerp 1947); R. Manselli, *Spirituali e Beghini in Provenza* (Rome 1959); E. G. Neumann, *Rheinisches Beginen- und Begardenwesen* (Meisenheim 1960); J. Koch, *Frauenfrage und Ketzertum* (Berlin 1962), Marxist interpretation; in addition, there are many studies on the history of local Beguine houses.

33. *The Flowering of Scholasticism and of the Western Universities*

LITERATURE

See the General Bibliography I, 11, and II, 11 and 12, and the bibliographies for Chapters 7 and 12, especially *Fliche-Martin,* 13, *Ueberweg-Geyer, Wulf,* J. Hirschberger, *Grabmann G, Grabmann MGL,* É. Gilson, *Stegmüller RS,* O. Lottin, H. de Lubac, F. Copleston, P. Glorieux, L. Bréhier, F. Cayré; for the universities, especially the works of S. d'Irsay, Rashdall-Powicke-Emden, H. Denifle, H. Grundmann, S. Stelling-Michaud. Also: H.

Mayer, "Über den klerikalen Charakter der mittelalterlichen Universität," *FreibDiözArch*, 36 (1935), 152–83; N. Schachner, *The Medieval Universities* (New York 1938); M. Bechthum, *Beweggründe und Bedeutung des Vagantentums in der lateinischen Kirche des Mittelalters* (Jena 1941); P. Kibre, *The Nations in the Medieval Universities* (Cambridge 1950); F. Pegues, "Ecclesiastical Provisions for the Support of Students in the Thirteenth Century," *Church History*, 26 (1957), 307–17; H. Wieruszowski, *The Medieval University* (New York 1966); G. Ajo and C. M. Sáinz de Zuñiga, *Historia de las Universidades Hispánicas*, I: *Medievo* (Ávila 1957), II: *Carlu Cario* (Ávila 1960).

Paris: H. Denifle, E. Chatelain, *et al.*, *Chartularium Universitatis Parisiensis*, 4 vols. (Paris 1889–97), *Auctarium*, 5 vols. (Paris 1894–1952); P. Perdrizet, *Le Calendrier de la Nation d'Allemagne de l'ancienne Université de Paris* (Strasbourg 1937); M. Fournier, *Les statuts et privilèges des universités françaises*, 4 vols. (Paris 1890–94); P. Féret, *La faculté de théologie de Paris et ses docteurs les plus célèbres au moyen âge*, 3 vols. (Paris 1894–96); M. Davy, *Les sermons universitaires parisiens de 1230/31* (Paris 1931); P. Glorieux, *Les origines du Collège de Sorbonne* (Notre Dame 1959); A. L. Gabriel, *Student Life in Ave Maria College* (Paris) (Notre Dame 1955).

Bologna: Chartularium Studii Bononiensis, 12 vols., ed. L. Nardi and E. Orioli (Imola and Bologna 1909–41); F. Ehrle, *I più antichi statuti della facoltà teologica dell'università di Bologna (1364)* (Bologna 1932); A. Sorbelli, *Storia della università di Bologna*, I (Bologna 1940); C. Calcaterra, *Alma mater studiorum* (Bologna 1948); G. Le Bras, "Bologne, monarchie médiévale des droits savants," *Memorie per la storia dell'Università di Bologna* (1956), 1–18; G. Masi, "L'università di Bologna al suo primo albeggiare," *Rivista di storia del diritto italiano*, 31 (1958), 269–331.

Oxford: C. E. Mallet, *History of the University of Oxford*, 3 vols. (London 1924–26); A. B. Emden, *A Biographical Register of the University of Oxford to A.D. 1500*, 3 vols. (Oxford 1957–59).

The Aristotelian Corpus: G. Théry, *Tolède, ville de la renaissance médiévale, point de jonction entre la philosophie musulmane et la pensée chrétienne* (Oran 1944); Dominic Gundisalvi, *De divisione philosophiae*, ed. L. Bauer, *BGPhMA* (1903); H. Bédoret in *RNPh*, 4 (1938), 374–400. On the schools of translators at Naples see *Fliche-Martin*, 13, 180. É. Gilson in *AHD*, 4 (1929), 5–107, treats the Greek and Arabic sources of scholasticism; for Latin Averroism see M. Grabmann in *SAM* (1931 f.), and *Notes et textes sur l'Averroïsme latin* (Paris 1934); *Aristoteles latinus* (Rome, Cambridge, and Paris 1939 ff.); M. Grabmann, *Forschungen über die lateinischen Aristoteles-Übersetzungen des 13. Jahrhunderts*, *SAM* (1916); Grabmann *MGL*, III, 36–231; M. Grabmann, *I divieti ecclesiastici di Aristotele sotto Innocenzo III e Gregorio IX* (Rome 1941); idem, *Methoden und Hilfsmittel des Aristoteles-Studiums im Mittelalter* (Munich 1939); idem, *Guglielmo da Moerbeke e le sue traduzioni d'Aristotele* (Rome 1946). F. Ehrle, *Xenia Thomistica*, III (Rome 1925), discusses Aristotle and Augustine in thirteenth-century scholasticism; S. D. Wingate, *The Medieval Latin Versions of the Aristotelian Scientific Corpus* (London 1931); E. Franceschini, *Aristotele nel medio evo* (Padua 1935); D. A. Callus, *Introduction of Aristotelian Learning to Oxford* (London 1944); F. van Steenberghen, *Aristotle in the West* (London 1955).

Franciscans: H. Felder, *Geschichte der wissenschaftlichen Studien im Franziskanerorden bis um die Mitte des 13. Jahrhunderts* (Freiburg 1904); on the Franciscan school in general see B. Vogt in *FStud*, 9 (1922), 137–53; on this school at Oxford, A. G. Little in *AFrH*, 19 (1926), 803–74, and D. E. Sharp, *Franciscan Philosophy at Oxford in the Thirteenth Century* (Oxford 1930); on the Franciscan masters at Paris, V. Doucet in *AFrH*, 26 (1933), 257–81, 27 (1934), 531–64, 585–89; G. Bonafede, *Il pensiero francescano nel secolo 13* (Palermo 1952); on the beginnings of the Franciscan school and Thomism, H. a Krizovljan in *CollFr*, 31 (1961), 133–75.

Dominicans: see P. Mandonnet in *DTC,* 6 (1924), 863–924; R. M. Martin in *RSPhTh,* 9 (1920), 556–80, treats of the Dominican theologians at Paris and Oxford from 1229 to 1279; F. Ehrle in *Miscellanea Dominicana* (Rome 1923), 85–138, discusses the Dominican *studium* at Paris; E. Filthaut, *Roland von Cremona († 1259) und die Anfänge der Scholastik im Predigerorden* (Vechta 1936).

Alexander of Hales: Works: *Summa theologica,* 5 vols. (Quaracchi 1924–48); *Glossa in 4 libros sententiarum Petri Lombardi,* 4 vols. (Quaracchi 1951–57); *Quaestiones disputatae,* 3 vols. (Quaracchi 1960); J. A. Endres in *PhJ* (1888), 24 f., 203–25, 257–96, discusses the life and the psychological doctrine of Alexander of Hales. Literature: up to 1948 in V. Doucet, *Prolegomena ad Summam,* IV (Quaracchi 1948), supplemented to 1951 in the introduction to the *Glossa;* A. Hufnagel, "Über das Wesen der Person bei Alexander von Hales," *FZThPh,* 4 (1957), 148–74.

Bonaventure: Works: *Opera omnia,* 11 vols. (Quaracchi 1882–1902); *Opera theologica selecta,* 5 vols. (Quaracchi 1934–64); *De reductione artium ad theologiam,* ed. E. T. Healy (New York 1940); German translation of his mystical and ascetical works by S. J. Hamburger, I (Munich 1923); German translation of the *Breviloquium* by F. Imle (Werl 1931); German translation of the *Itinerarium mentis in Deum* by J. Kaup and P. Böhner (Werl 1932); *Obras de san Buenaventura,* 6 vols., ed. L. Amoros et al., *BAC* (Madrid 1946); *De triplici via,* edited and translated by K. Ruh (Munich 1957); *Soliloquium,* Latin and German, by J. Hosse (Cologne 1958); *Itinerarium mentis in Deum,* Latin and German (Munich 1961); *Collationes in Hexaemeron,* Latin and German (Munich 1964). Literature: biographies by L. Lemmens (Munich 1909), V. Breton (Paris 1943), E. Bettoni (Brescia 1945), and R. Lazzarini (Milan 1946). O Righi, *Il pensiero e l'opera di S. Bonaventura* (Florence 1932); É. Gilson, *La philosophie de saint Bonaventure, Études de philosophie médiévale,* IV (Paris, 2d ed. 1943); É. Gilson, *The Philosophy of St. Bonaventure* (London 1935); Eng. A. Borak, *Philosophia S. Bonaventurae* (Rome 1956); F. Imle and J. Kaup, *Die Theologie des heiligen Bonaventura* (Werl 1931); J. Kaup, *Das geistliche Leben nach der Lehre des heiligen Bonaventura* (Werl 1939); J. F. Bonnefoy, *Une somme bonaventurienne de théologie mystique* (Paris 1949); J. Ratzinger, *Die Geschichstheologie des heiligen Bonaventura* (Munich and Zürich 1959); J. G. Bougerol, *Introduction à l'étude de Saint Bonaventure* (Paris 1961).

Duns Scotus: Works: *Opera omnia,* ed. L. Wadding (Lyons 1639, Paris 1891–95); critical edition, thus far 9 vols. (Rome 1950–66); on the critical edition *cf.* C. Balič, *Ratio editionis criticae operum omnium J. Duns Scoti,* 3 vols. (Rome 1939–51); *A Treatise on God as First Principle,* ed. A. B. Wolter (Chicago 1966). Literature: E. Longpré, *La philosophie du B. Duns Scot* (Paris 1924); P. Minges, *J. Duns Scoti doctrina philosophica et theologica* (Quaracchi 1930); É. Gilson, *Jean Duns Scot. Introduction à ses positions fondamentales* (Paris 1952); H. Mühlen, *Sein und Person nach Johannes Duns Scotus* (Werl 1954); W. Pannenberg, *Die Prädestinationslehre des Johannes Dun Scotus* (Göttingen 1954); bibliography by O. Schäfer (Rome 1955); J. F. Bonnefoy, *Le vénérable Jean Duns Scot* (Rome 1960); C. Bérubé, "L'année scotiste et le septième centenaire de la naissance de Jean Duns Scot" (report of research), *CollFr,* 37 (1967), 145–85.

Siger of Brabant: Works: *De aeternitate mundi,* ed. R. Barsotti (Münster 1933); *Questions sur la Physique d'Aristote,* ed. P. Delhaye (Louvain 1941); *Questions sur la metaphysique,* ed. C. A. Graiff (Louvain 1948). Literature: report of research by A. A. Mauer in *Speculum,* 31 (1956), 49–56; P. Mandonnet, *Siger de Brabant et l'Averroïsme latin au XIIIe siècle,* 2 vols. (Louvain 1908–11); F. van Steenberghen, *Siger de Brabant d'après ses œuvres inédites,* 2 vols. (Louvain 1931–42), basic. On the question whether Siger maintained the double truth see J. P. Müller in *Studia Anselmiana* (1941), 35–50; M. Grabmann, "Siger und Dante," *Deutsches Dante-Jahrbuch 1939,* 109–30; G. Sajó, *Un traité récemment découvert de Boèce de Dacie "De aeternitate mundi"* (Budapest 1954). H. a

Krizovljan in *CollFr,* 27 (1957), 121–65, treats the relationship of the Franciscans to Siger.

Albertus Magnus: Works: the critical *editio Coloniensis,* 40 vols., by B. Geyer *et al.,* published by the Albertus-Magnus-Institut (Cologne) from 1951; *Ueberweg-Geyer* (12th ed. 1951), 402, 739–43 (bibliography); regular reports in *RThAM* and *BThAM* from 1929; M. H. Laurent and Y. Congar, "Essai bibliographique albertienne," *RThom,* 36 (1931), 260–92; F. J. Catania, "A Bibliography of St. Albert the Great (1931–1958)," *The Modern Schoolman,* 37 (1959), 11–28. Literature: H. Wilms, *Albert der Grosse* (Munich 1930); G. Meersseman, *Introductio in opera omnia B. Alberti Magni* (Bruges 1931); H. C. Scheeben, *Albert der Grosse* (Vechta and Leipzig 1931); idem, *Albertus Magnus* (Cologne, 2d ed. 1955); B. Geyer, "Albertus Magnus," *Die Grossen Deutschen,* I (Berlin 1956), 201–16. *Festschriften: RThom,* 36 (1931), 225–468; *DTh,* 10 (1932), 1–304; *Angelicum,* 9 (1932), 2d and 3d Hefte; *Serta Albertina* (Rome 1944); *Studia Albertina, Festschrift B. Geyer* (Münster 1952); M. Gorce, *L'essor de la pensée au moyen âge, Albert le Grand et Thomas d'Aquin* (Paris 1933); H. C. Scheeben and A. Walz, *Iconographia Albertina* (Freiburg 1932); A. Wendehorst, "Albertus Magnus und die Kirchenreform," *MIÖG,* 64 (1956), 241–61; G. Meersseman, *Geschichte des Albertismus,* 2 vols. (Rome 1933–35); D. Salman, "Über Albert den Grossen und den Averroismus," *RSPhTh,* 24 (1935), 38–64; on the same topic, M. Feigl in *PhJ,* 63 (1955), 131–50; A. Schneider, *Die Psychologie Alberts des Grossen,* 2 vols. (Münster 1903–06); H. Doms, *Die Gnadenlehre des seligen Albertus Magnus* (Breslau 1929); W. Arendt, *Die Staats- und Gesellschaftslehre Albertus des Grossen* (Jena 1929); J. Goergen, *Des heiligen Albertus Magnus Lehre von der göttlichen Vorsehung und von dem Fatum* (Vechta 1932); K. Schmieder, *Alberts des Grossen Lehre vom natürlichen Gottwissen* (Freiburg 1932); F. Haberl, *Die Incarnationslehre des heiligen Albertus Magnus* (Freiburg 1939); J. M. Vosté, *S. Albertus Magnus Sacrae Paginae Magister,* 2 vols. (Rome 1932 f.); U. Daehnert, *Die Erkenntnislehre des Albertus Magnus* (Leipzig 1934), with bibliography; B. Korosak, *Mariologia S. Alberti Magni eiusque coaequalium* (Rome 1954); A. Hufnagel, *Die Wahrheit als philosophisch-theologisches Problem bei Albert dem Deutschen* (Bonn 1940); R. Erni, *Die Herz-Jesu-Lehre Alberts des Grossen* (Lucerne 1941); A. Piolanti, *Il corpo mistico e le sue relazioni con l'Eucaristia in S. Alberto Magno* (Rome 1939); J. Rinna, *Die Kirche als Corpus Christi mysticum beim heiligen Albertus* (Rome 1940); L. Brandl, *Die Sexualethik des heiligen Albertus Magnus* (Regensburg 1955); H. Balss, *Albertus Magnus als Zoologe* (Munich 1928); idem, *Albertus Magnus als Biologe* (Stuttgart 1947); R. Liertz, *Die Naturkunde von der menschlichen Seele nach Albert dem Grossen* (Cologne 1933).

Thomas Aquinas: P. Mandonnet, *Bibliographie thomiste* (Le Saulchoir, 2d ed. 1960). Works: *Opera omnia,* 18 vols. (Rome 1570–71, *Editio Piana*) 25 vols. (Parma 1852–1873); 34 vols., ed. L. Vivès (Paris 1871–90); *Editio Leonina,* thus far 26 vols. (Rome 1882–1967); *Opuscula omnia,* ed. P. Mandonnet, 5 vols. (Paris 1927), ed. J. Perrier (Paris 1949 ff.); *Scriptum super libros Sententiarum Petri Lombardi,* ed. P. Mandonnet, 3 vols., Vol. IV, ed. M. F. Moos (Paris 1929–47); *Quaestiones disputatae et quodlibetales,* ed. R. Spiazzi *et al.* (Turin 1949); *Expositio super librum Boethii de Trinitate,* ed. B. Decker (Leiden, 2d ed. 1959); *The Summa Theologica,* 22 vols. (London 1912–26); *The Summa contra Gentiles,* 5 vols. (London 1928–29); *The Catechetical Instructions of St. Thomas* (London 1939); *The Most Devout Exposition of the Lord's Prayer* (London 1927); *Basic Writings of St. Thomas,* 2 vols. (New York 1945); *On the Governance of Rulers* (Toronto 1935). V. J. Bourke, *Thomistic Bibliography: 1920–1940* (St. Louis, Mo., 1945); R. Erni, *Die theologische Summa des Thomas von Aquin in ihrem Grundaufbau,* 4 vols. (Lucerne 1947–50); R. J. Deferrari and M. I. Barry, *Lexicon of St. Thomas Aquinas* (Washington 1948–54). *Fontes vitae S. Thomae Aquinatis,* ed. D. Prümmer and H. M. Laurent, 6 vols. (Saint-Maximin [Var] 1911–37); "Processus canonizationis S. Thomae

Aquinatis," *RThom*, 39–41 (1934–36). Biographies by A. D. Sertillanges, 2 vols. (Paris 1910), M. Grabmann (Munich 1949), É. Gilson (Paris 1925), A. D. Sertillanges (Paris 1931), A. Cresson (Paris 1942), A. Walz (Basel 1953), M. D'Arcy (London 1954), F. Copleston (London 1955), K. Foster (London 1959), P. Novarina (Louvain and Paris 1962). Chronology and authenticity of his works: P. Mandonnet, *Des écrits authentiques de S. Thomas d'Aquin* (Fribourg, 2d ed. 1910); M. Grabmann, *Die Werke des heiligen Thomas von Aquin* (Munich, 2d ed. 1949); J. Destrez, *Études critiques sur les œuvres de S. Thomas d'Aquin d'après la tradition manuscrite*, I (Paris 1933), and, in regard to this work, A. Pelzer in *BullThomiste*, 11 (1934), 225–40; A. Dondaine, *Secrétaires de S. Thomas*, 2 vols. (Rome 1956). Introductions: M. Grabmann, *Einführung in die Summa Theologica des heiligen Thomas von Aquin* (Munich, 2d ed. 1928); R. Sineu, *Initiation à la théologie de S. Thomas d'Aquin* (Tournai 1953); M. D. Chenu, *Introduction à l'étude de S. Thomas d'Aquin* (Paris, 2d ed. 1954); J. Pieper, *Hinführung zu Thomas von Aquin* (Munich 1958); A. Michelitsch, *Kommentatoren zur Summa Theologica des heiligen Thomas von Aquin* (Graz and Vienna 1924). Thomism: É. Gilson, *Le Thomisme* (Paris, 5th ed. 1945), Eng. *The Philosophy of St. Thomas* (Cambridge 1937); J. Maritain, *Le docteur angélique* (Paris 1930), Eng. *St. Thomas Aquinas* (London 1946); G. M. Manser, *Das Wesen des Thomismus* (Fribourg, 3d ed. 1949); P. Wyser, *Der Thomismus* (Bern 1951); J. Ude, *Die Autorität des heiligen Thomas von Aquin als Kirchenlehrer und seine Summa theologica* (Salzburg 1932). *Festschriften: Mélanges thomistes* (Le Saulchoir 1923); *Xenia thomistica*, ed. S. Szabó, 3 vols. (Rome 1925). Philosophy: A. D. Sertillanges, *La philosophie de S. Thomas* (1907, Paris, 3d ed. 1955); H. D. Gardeil, *Initiation à la philosophie de S. Thomas*, 4 vols. (Paris 1952 f.); G. Siewerth, *Der Thomismus als Identitätssystem* (1938, Frankfurt am Main, 2d ed. 1961); L. Legrand, *L'univers et l'homme dans la philosophie de S. Thomas*, 2 vols. (Brussels and Paris 1946); L. B. Geiger, *Le problème de l'amour chez S. Thomas* (Montreal and Paris 1952); B. Lakebrink, *Hegels dialektische Ontologie und die thomistische Analektik* (Cologne 1955); R. J. Henle, *St. Thomas and Platonism* (The Hague 1956); A. Hayen, *La communication de l'être d'après S. Thomas*, 2 vols. (Paris and Louvain 1957–59); C. Fabro, *Participation et causalité selon S. Thomas* (Louvain and Paris 1961); F. J. Kovach, *Die Ästhetik des heiligen Thomas* (Berlin 1961); A. Antweiler, *Die Anfangslosigkeit der Welt nach Thomas und Kant*, 2 vols. (Trier 1961); B. Montagnes, *La doctrine de l'analogie de l'être d'après S. Thomas* (Louvain and Paris 1963); W. Kluxen, *Philosophische Ethik bei Thomas von Aquin* (Mainz 1964). Theology: H. Meyer, *Thomas von Aquin, Sein System und seine geistesgeschichtliche Stellung* (Paderborn, 2d ed. 1901); M. D. Chenu, *S. Thomas et la théologie* (Paris 1959); I. Backes, *Die Christologie des heiligen Thomas und die griechischen Kirchenväter* (Paderborn 1931); H. Bouillard, *Conversion et grâce chez S. Thomas* (Paris 1944); H. Lais, *Die Gnadenlehre des heiligen Thomas in der Summa contra Gentiles* (Munich 1951); P. Vanier, *Théologie trinitaire chez S. Thomas. Évolution du concept d'action notionelle* (Paris 1953); A. Horvath, *Studien zum Gottesbegriff* (Freiburg 1954); Q. van Roo, *Grace and Original Justice according to St. Thomas* (Rome 1955); A. Mallet, *Personne et amour dans la théologie trinitaire de S. Thomas* (Paris 1956); R. Guindon, *Béatitude et théologie morale chez S. Thomas* (Ottawa 1956); R. Völkl, *Die Selbstliebe in der Heiligen Schrift und bei Thomas* (Munich 1956); O. Schweizer, *Person und hypostatische Union bei Thomas* (Fribourg 1957); S. Pfürtner, *Triebleben und sittliche Vollendung nach Thomas* (Fribourg 1958); H. Christmann, *Thomas als Theologe der Liebe* (Heidelberg 1958); T. Bonhoeffer, *Die Gotteslehre des Thomas als Sprachproblem* (Tübingen 1961); M. Seckler, *Instinkt und Glaubenswille nach Thomas* (Mainz 1961); B. Duroux, *La psychologie de la foi chez S. Thomas* (Toulouse 1963); M. Seckler, *Das Heil in der Geschichte, Geschichtstheologisches Denken bei Thomas* (Munich 1964); G. Ebeling, "Der hermeneutische Ort der Gotteslehre bei Petrus Lombardus und Thomas von Aquin" *ZThK*, 61 (1964), 283–326; H. Vorster,

Das Freiheitsverständnis bei Thomas und Martin Luther (Göttingen 1965); U. Kühn, *Via caritatis. Theologie des Gesetzes bei Thomas* (Göttingen 1965); H. O. Pesch, *Theologie der Rechtfertigung bei Martin Luther und Thomas von Aquin* (Mainz 1966).

Robert Grosseteste: Works: *Epistolae,* ed. H. R. Luard (London 1861); philosophical works, ed. L. Baur (Münster 1912); S. H. Thomson, *The Writings of Robert Grosseteste* (Cambridge 1940); U. Gamba, *Il commento di Roberto Grosseteste al "de mystica theologia" del Ps. Dionigi Areopagita* (Milan 1942). Literature: B. C. Boulter, *Robert Grosseteste* (London 1936); D. A. Callus, F. M. Powicke, *et al., Robert Grosseteste, Scholar and Bishop. Essays in Commemoration of the Seventh Centenary of his Death* (Oxford 1955); A. C. Crombie, *Robert Grosseteste and the Origins of the Experimental Science* (Oxford 1953); S. Gieben, "Robert Grosseteste on Preaching (with the edition of the 'sermo ex rerum initiatarum' on redemption)," *CollFr,* 37 (1967), 100–41.

Roger Bacon: Works: *Opus maius sive de utilitate scientiarum,* ed. J. H. Bridges, 2 vols. (Oxford 1897); *Opera quaedam hactenus inedita (Opus tertium, Opus minus, Compendium philosophiae),* ed. J. S. Brewer (London 1859); *Opera hactenus inedita,* ed. R. Steele, A. G. Little, E. Withington, F. M. Delorme, 16 fasc. (Oxford 1905–40); R. B. Burke, *The Opus Maius of Roger Bacon,* 2 vols., Eng. (Philadelphia 1928); *Compendium studii theologiae,* ed. H. Rashdall (Aberdeen 1911); *Summa Grammatica,* ed. R. Steele (London 1940); *Moralis Philosophiae,* ed. E. Massa (Rome 1953). Literature: *Roger Bacon Essays,* ed. A. G. Little *et al.* (Oxford 1914); T. Crowley, *Roger Bacon. The Problem of the Soul* (Dublin 1950); F. Alessio, *Mito e scienza in R. Bacone* (Milan 1957); E. Heck, *Roger Bacon, ein mittelalterlicher Versuch einer historischen und systematischen Religionswissenschaft* (Bonn 1957). R. Carton, *La synthèse doctrinale de Roger Bacon* (Paris 1929).

34. *The Cardinals and the Curia in the Thirteenth Century*

Literature

The Cardinals: A. Ciaconius, *Vitae et res gestae Pontificum Romanorum et S. R. E. Cardinalium ab A. Oldonio recognitae,* I (Rome 1677); *Hinschius,* I, 309–72 (cardinals), 373–497 (curia); J. P. Kirsch, *Die Finanzverwaltung des Kardinalskollegiums im 13. und 14. Jahrhundert* (Münster 1895); J. B. Sägmüller, *Die Thätigkeit und Stellung der Cardinäle bis Papst Bonifaz VIII.* (Freiburg im Breisgau 1896); P. M. Baumgarten, *Untersuchungen und Urkunden über die Camera Collegii Cardinalium für die Zeit von 1225 bis 1437* (Leipzig 1898); J. B. Sägmüller, "Die oligarchischen Tendenzen des Kardinalskollegs bis Bonifaz VIII.," *ThQ,* 83 (1901), 45–93; J. Maubach, *Die Kardinäle und ihre Politik um die Mitte des XIII. Jahrhunderts* (Bonn 1902); J. Lulvès, *Die Machtbestrebungen des Kardinalats bis zur Aufstellung der ersten päpstlichen Wahlkapitulationen* (Rome 1910); idem, "Die Machtbestrebungen des Kardinalskollegiums gegenüber dem Papsttum," *MIÖG,* 35 (1914), 455–83; E. Schelenz, *Studien zur Geschichte des Kardinalats im 13. und 14. Jahrhundert* (Marburg 1913); B. Katterbach and W. M. Peitz, "Die Unterschriften der Päpste und Kardinäle in den 'Bullae maiores' vom 11. bis 14. Jahrhundert," *Misc. F. Ehrle,* IV (Rome 1924), 177–274; H. Hofmann, *Kardinalat und kuriale Politik in der ersten Hälfte des 14. Jahrhunderts* (dissertation, Leipzig 1935); E. Kartusch, *Das Kardinalskollegium (1181–1227)* (dissertation, Vienna 1948); enlightening in retrospect is G. Mollat, "Le Sacré Collège de Clément V à Eugène IV," *RHE,* 46 (1951), 22–112, 566–94; K. Ganzer, *Die Entwicklung des auswärtigen Kardinalats im hohen Mittelalter. Ein Beitrag zur Geschichte des Kardinalskollegiums vom 11. bis 13. Jahrhundert* (Tübingen 1963); C. G. Fürst, "Die 'geborenen' Kardinäle," *ZKTh,* 88 (1966), 51–74; P. Hofmeister, "Die Titelkirchen der Kardinäle," *MThZ,* 17 (1966), 13–23.

The Curia: Liber diurnus, ed. H. Foerster (Bern 1958); M. Tangl, *Die päpstlichen Kanzleiordnungen von 1200–1500* (Innsbruck 1894); J. Teige, "Beiträge zum päpstlichen Kanzleiwesen des 13. und 14. Jahrhunderts," *MIÖG*, 17 (1896), 408–39; P. M. Baumgarten, *Aus Kanzlei und Kammer* (Freiburg im Breisgau 1907); W. V. Hofmann, *Forschungen zur Geschichte der Kurialbehörden* (Rome 1914); R. L. Poole, *Lectures on the History of the Papal Chancery down to the Time of Innocent III* (London 1916); R. Göller, "Die Kubikulare im Dienste der päpstlichen Hofverwaltung vom 12. bis 15. Jahrhundert," *Festschrift P. Kehr* (Munich 1926), 622–44; C. Bauer, "Epochen der Papstfinanz," *HZ*, 133 (1928), 457–504; F. Baethgen, "Quellen und Untersuchungen zur Geschichte der päpstlichen Hof- und Finanzverwaltung unter Bonifaz VIII.," *QFIAB*, 20 (1928 f.), 114–95, also in *Mediaevalia*, I, 228–95; G. Barraclough, "The Chancery Ordinance of Nicholas III," *QFIAB*, 25 (1933 f.), 192–250; H. Göring, *Die Beamten der Kurie unter Bonifaz VIII.* (dissertation, Königsberg 1934); W. E. Lunt, *Papal Revenues in the Middle Ages*, 2 vols. (New York 1934); L. Nina, *Le finanze pontificie nel medioevo*, 3 vols. (Milan 1929–32); B. Rusch, *Die Behörden und Hofbeamten der päpstlichen Kurie des 13. Jahrhunderts* (Königsberg and Berlin 1936); G. Felici, *La Reverenda Camera Apostolica* (Rome 1940); R. Elze, "Die päpstliche Kapelle im 12. und 13. Jahrhundert," *ZSavRGkan*, 36 (1950), 145–204; R. Brentano, *York Metropolitan Jurisdiction and Papal Judges Delegate (1279–96)* (Berkeley 1959); P. Herde, *Beiträge zum päpstlichen Kanzlei- und Urkundenwesen im 13. Jahrhundert* (Kallmünz 1961); J. Sayers, "Canterbury Proctors at the Court of 'Audientia litterarum contradictarum,'" *Tr*, 22 (1966), 311–45; C. R. Cheney, *The Study of the Medieval Papal Chancery* (Glasgow 1966); W. Ullmann, "On the Heuristic Value of Medieval Chancery Products with Special Reference to Papal Documents," *Annali della Fondazione italiana per la storia amministrativa*, 1 (Milan 1964), 117–34; P. Herde, "Marinus von Eboli 'Super revocatoriis' und 'De confirmationibus,'" *QFIAB*, 42/43 (1964), 119–264.

35. *Celestine V and Boniface VIII*

LITERATURE

Celestine V: ActaSS, Maii IV (1685), 419–61; P. M. Baumgarten, *Il regesto di Celestino V* (Chieti 1896); F. X. Seppelt, *Studien zum Pontifikat Cölestins V.* (Berlin 1910); *idem*, *Monumenta Coelestiniana* (Paderborn 1921); J. Hollnsteiner, "Die 'Autobiographie' Cölestins V.," *RQ*, 31 (1923), 29–40; F. Baethgen, *Beiträge zur Geschichte Coelestins V.* (Halle 1934); P. Laurelli, *Dante e Celestino V* (Isernia 1939); F. Baethgen, *Der Engelpapst* (Leipzig 1943); R. Mols, "Célestin V," *DHGE*, 12 (1953), 79–101, with bibliography; A. Frugoni, *Celestiniana, Studi storici*, 6–7 (Rome 1954); G. Celidonio, *S. Pietro del Morrone (Celestino V)* (Pescara, 2d ed. 1954); G. Marchetti-Longhi, "Considerazione sull'accettazione e la rinunzia di Celestino V al pontificato," *Benedictina*, 11 (1957), 219–33; *idem*, "Castel Fumone e la prigione di Papa Celestino V," *Strenna Ciociaria* (Rome 1965), 81–90; I. Hösl, *Kardinal Jacobus Gaetani Stefaneschi* (Berlin 1908). Cardinal Stefaneschi composed an *opus metricum* on Celestine V, ed. F. X. Seppelt, *Monumenta Coelestiniana*, 3–146, see also R. Morghen in *BIStIAM*, 46 (1931), 1–39. Celestine's abdication: A. Graf, "Il rifiuto di Celestino V," *Miti, leggende e superstizioni del Medio Evo*, II (Bologna 1965), 223–35 (reprint of the Turin edition of 1893); J. Leclercq, "La renonciation de Célestin V et l'opinion théologique en France du vivant de Boniface VIII," *RHÉF*, 15 (1939), 183–92; S. García Palou, "El Beato Ramon Llul y la cuestión de la renunciabilidad de la Sede romana," *AST*, 17 (1944), 67–96; W. Ullmann, "Medieval Views concerning Papal Abdication," *IER*, 71 (1949), 125–33; F. Schneider, "Der grosse Verzicht Cölestins V.," *Deutsches Dante-Jahrbuch*, 33 (1954), 212–14.

BIBLIOGRAPHY

Boniface VIII: H. Finke, *Aus den Tagen Bonifaz' VIII. Funde und Forschungen* (Münster 1902, reprinted Rome 1964); R. Scholz, *Die Publizistik zur Zeit Philipps des Schönen und Bonifaz' VIII., ein Beitrag zur Geschichte der politischen Anschauungen des Mittelalters* (Stuttgart 1903, reprinted Amsterdam 1962); M. Brosch, "Bonifaz VIII. und die Republik Florenz," *ZKG,* 25 (1904), 233–47; K. Wenck, "War Bonifaz VIII. ein Ketzer?" *HZ,* 94 (1904), 1–66; R. Holtzmann, "Papst Bonifaz VIII. ein Ketzer?" *MIÖG,* 26 (1905), 488–98; R. Scholz, "Zur Beurteilung Bonifaz' VIII. und seines sittlichen Charakters," *HV,* 9 (1906), 470–515; H. Finke, *Acta Aragonensia,* 3 vols. (Berlin 1908–22); P. Fedele, "Per la storia dell'attentato di Anagni," *BISI,* 41 (1921), 195–232; J. Rivière, *Le problème de l'Église et de l'État au temps de Philippe le Bel* (Louvain and Paris 1926); G. Caetani, *Domus Caetana,* I (Sancasciano and Pesa 1927); F. Baethgen, "Quellen und Untersuchungen zur Geschichte der päpstlichen Hof- und Finanzverwaltung unter Bonifaz VIII.," *QFIAB,* 20 (1928 f.), 114–95, now also in *Mediaevalia,* I, 228–95; T. S. R. Boase, *Boniface VIII* (London 1933), hitherto the latest scholarly biography; H. K. Mann, *The Lives of the Popes in the Middle Ages,* 18 (London 1932); G. de Lagarde, *La naissance de l'esprit laïque au déclin du moyen âge,* I: *Bilan du XIIIe siècle* (Louvain and Paris, 3d ed. 1956); F. M. Powicke, "Pope Boniface VIII," *History,* 18 (1934), 307–29; G. Digard, *Philippe le Bel et le Saint-Siège de 1285 à 1304,* 2 vols. (Paris 1936); R. Fawtier, *Introduction* [to the completed volumes of papal chancery registers] (Paris 1939); *idem* in *Glotz,* VI/1; M. Seidlmayer, "Papst Bonifaz VIII. und der Kirchenstaat," *HJ,* 60 (1940), 78–87; F. Bock, *Reichsidee und Nationalstaaten vom Untergang des alten Reiches bis zur Kündigung des deutsch-englischen Bündnisses* (Munich 1943), 82–116; A. de Stefano, *Correnti politiche,* I: *La polemica bonifaciana* (Palermo 1948); R. Fawtier, "L'attentat d'Anagni," *MAH* (1948), 153–79; S. Sibilia, *Bonifacio VIII* (Rome 1949), survey with no new research; M. Melville, "Guillaume de Nogaret et Philippe le Bel," *RHÉF,* 36 (1950), 56–66; G. Le Bras, "Boniface VIII, symphoniste et modérateur," *Mélanges Louis Halphen* (Paris 1951), 383–94; *Seppelt,* IV (2d ed. 1957), 9–55; S. Gagner, *Studien zur Ideengeschichte der Gesetzgebung* (Uppsala 1960), 121–79; R. Foreville, "L'idée de jubilé chez les théologiens et les canonistes avant l'institution du jubilé romain (1300)," *RHE,* 56 (1961), 401–23; *Haller,* V (2d ed. 1962), 91–216; P. Dupuy, *Histoire du différend d'entre le Pape Boniface VIII et Philippe le Bel Roy de France* (Paris 1655, reprinted Tucson 1963), basic as a collection of sources; H. Wieruszowski, *Vom Imperium zum nationalen Königtum. Vergleichende Studien über die publizistischen Kämpfe Kaiser Friedrichs II. und König Philipps des Schönen mit der Kurie* (Munich 1933, reprinted Aalen 1964); H. Schmidinger, "Ein vergessener Bericht über das Attentat von Anagni," *Mélanges Tisserant, SteT,* 235, V (1964), 373–88.

Boniface VIII and France: the works listed *supra* by Dupuy, Wieruszowski, Schmidinger, Rivière, Digard, Fedele, Fawtier, and Melville. Also: F. Kern, *Die Anfänge der französischen Ausdehnungspolitik bis zum Jahre 1308* (Tübingen 1910); W. Kienast, "Der Kreuzkrieg Philipps des Schönen von Frankreich gegen Aragón," *HV,* 28 (1934), 673–98; M. Curley, *The Conflict between Pope Boniface VIII and King Philip IV the Fair* (dissertation, Washington 1927); Y. Renouard, "Les papes et le conflit franco-aragonais en Aquitaine de 1259 à 1337," *MAH,* 51 (1934), 258–92; R. Holtzmann, *Wilhelm von Nogaret* (Freiburg im Breisgau 1898); Y. Dossat, "Guillaume de Nogaret, petit-fils d'hérétique," *Annales du Midi,* 53 (1941), 391–402; M. Delle Piane, "Vecchio e nuovo nelle idee politiche di Pietro Dubois," *Studi Senesi,* 65 (1953), 299–349, 454–91; J. M. Vidal, "Bernard Saisset, évêque de Pamiers (1232–1311)," *RSR,* 5 (1925), 416–38, 565–90, 6 (1926), 50–77, 177–98, 371–93; A. Baumhauer, *Philipp der Schöne und Bonifaz VIII. in ihrer Stellung zur französischen Kirche* (Freiburg im Breisgau 1920); *idem,* "Die Gründung des französischen Bistums Pamiers in Zusammenhang mit dem Streit zwischen Philipp dem Schönen und Papst Bonifaz VIII.," *ZKG,* 45 (1926), 358–69; B. A. Poquet de Haut Jussé, "Le second différend entre Boniface VIII et Philippe le Bel," *Mélanges A. Dufourcq* (Paris 1932),

708

73–108; F. Bock, "Musciatto dei Francesi," *DA*, 6 (1943), 521–44; *idem*, "Bonifacio VIII nella storiografia francese," *RSTI*, 6 (1952), 248–59.

Boniface VIII and Sicily: H. E. Rohde, *Der Kampf um Sizilien in den Jahren 1291–1302* (Berlin 1913); E. Haberkorn, *Der Kampf um Sizilien in den Jahren 1302–37* (Berlin 1923); A. de Stefano, *Federico II d'Aragona, re di Sicilia (1296–1337)* (Palermo 1937); J. Vincke, "Krone, Kardinalat und Kirchenpfründe in Aragón zu Beginn des 14. Jahrhunderts," *RQ*, 51 (1956), 34–53.

Boniface VIII and the Colonna: H. Denifle, "Die Denkschriften der Colonna gegen Bonifaz VIII.," *ALKGMA*, 5 (1889), 403–520; L. Mohler, *Die Kardinäle Jakob und Peter Colonna. Ein Beitrag zur Geschichte des Zeitalters Bonifaz' VIII.* (Paderborn 1914); R. Neumann, *Die Colonna und ihre Politik von der Zeit Nikolaus' IV. bis zum Abzuge Ludwigs des Bayern aus Rom* (Berlin 1914); A. Maier, "Due documenti nuovi relativi alla lotta dei cardinali Colonna contro Bonifacio VIII," *RSTI*, 3 (1949), 344–64.

Boniface VIII and the Poets: H. Grundmann, "Bonifaz VIII. und Dante," *Dante und die Mächtigen seiner Zeit* (Munich 1960), 1–27; F. Schneider, "Dantes Hass und Verachtung gegen Papst Bonifaz VIII.," *HZ*, 193 (1962), 574–80; F. Brambilla Ageno, "Sull'invettiva di Iacopone da Todi contro Bonifacio VIII," *Lettere Italiane*, 16 (1964), 373–414; F. Grisi, "Iacopone da Todi contro Bonifacio VIII," *Nuova Antologia*, 100 (1965), 362–77; S. Nessi, "Iacopone da Todi al vaglio della critica moderna," *MiscFranc*, 64 (1964), 404–32.

V. Fenicchia, "Il sepolcro del vescovo Pietro Caetani, qui nutrivit dominum Bonifacium pp. VIII," *RSTI*, 2 (1948), 338–61; R. Weiss, "Cinque lettere inedite del Card. Benedetto Caetani," *RSTI*, 3 (1949), 157–64; P. H. Schmidt, *Bullarium Anni Sancti* (Rome 1949); A. Frugoni, "Il giubileo di Bonifacio VIII," *BIStIAM*, 62 (1950) 1–121; *idem, De centesimo anno seu jubileo liber (Il libro del card. Stefaneschi)* (Brescia 1950); C. Stange, "Der Jubelablass Bonifaz' VIII. in Dantes Commedia," *ZKG*, 63 (1950 f.), 145–65. C. Paulus, *Welt- und Ordensklerus beim Ausgang des 13. Jahrhunderts im Kampf um die Pfarr-Rechte* (Essen 1900); B. Mathis, *Die Privilegien des Franziskanerordens bis zum Konzil von Vienne (1311)* (Paderborn 1928); K. L. Hitzfeld, "Krise in den Bettelorden im Pontifikat Bonifaz' VIII.?" *HJ*, 48 (1928), 1–30; K. Schleyer, *Anfänge des Gallikanismus im 13. Jahrhundert. Der Widerstand des französischen Klerus gegen die Privilegierung der Bettelorden* (Berlin 1937); G. Ladner, "Die Statue Bonifaz' VIII. in der Lateranbasilika und die Entstehung der dreifach gekrönten Tiara," *RQ*, 42 (1934), 35–69, and, in this connection, P. E. Schramm in *HZ*, 152 (1935), 307–12.

Iconography: C. Sommer, *Die Anklage der Idololatrie gegen Papst Bonifaz VIII. und seine Porträtstatuen* (Freiburg im Breisgau 1920); C. Ricci, "I ritratti di Bonifacio VIII," *L'Italia artistica industriale*, I (Rome 1893), fasc. 4; S. Sibilia, "L'Iconografia di Bonifacio VIII," *Boll. della Sezione di Anagni della Soc. Rom. di Storia Patria*, 1 (1951), 10–13; C. Mitchell, "The Lateran Fresco of Boniface VIII," *Journal of the Warburg and Courtauld Institutes*, 14 (1951), 1–6.

36. *The End of the Crusading Epoch*

See the bibliographies for the individual crusades in the preceding chapters. Also: G. Mazzoni, *La crociata alla fine del secolo XIII ed al principio del secolo XIV* (Urbino 1938); A. S. Atiya, *The Crusades in the Later Middle Ages* (London 1938); *Heidenmission und Kreuzzugsgedanke in der deutschen Ostpolitik des Mittelalters*, ed. H. Beumann (Darmstadt 1963); A. S. Atiya, *Crusade, Commerce and Culture* (Bloomington 1962); H. E. Mayer, *Bibliographie zur Geschichte der Kreuzzüge* (Hanover, 2d ed. 1965); *idem, Geschichte der Kreuzzüge* (Stuttgart 1965); *idem, Idee und Wirklichkeit der Kreuzzüge* (texts) (Germering 1966).

709

Part Two:
The Late Middle Ages

SECTION ONE

The Popes at Avignon

Sources

Baluze-Mollat; G. Mollat, Étude critique sur les Vitae Paparum Avenionensium d'Étienne Baluze (Paris 1917); *idem,* "Baluze," *DHGE,* 6 (1932), 439–52; *MGHConst,* IV–VI; H. Finke, *Acta Aragonensia. Quellen zur deutschen, italienischen, französischen, spanischen, Kirchen- und Kulturgeschichte aus der diplomatischen Korrespondenz Jaymes II. 1291–1327,* I and II (Berlin and Leipzig 1908), III (Berlin and Leipzig 1922). Appendices and supplements to the *Acta Aragonensia* (I–III): *Gesammelte Aufsätze zur Kulturgeschichte Spaniens,* IV (1933), 355–536. For the correspondence of the German Kings and princes with the rulers of Aragón in the fourteenth and fifteenth centuries: *Gesammelte Aufsätze,* V (1935), 458–505. Appendices and supplements to the *Acta Aragonensia,* I–III. On the cultural importance of the royal Aragonese archives: *Gesammelte Aufsätze,* VII (1938), 326–46. E. E. Stengel, *Nova Alamanniae. Urkunden, Briefe und andere Quellen besonders zur deutschen Geschichte des 14. Jahrhunderts vornehmlich aus den Sammlungen des Trierers Notars und Offizials, Domdekans von Mainz Rudolf Losse aus Eisenach in der ständischen Landesbibliothek zu Kassel und im Staatsarchiv zu Darmstadt,* I (Berlin 1921), II, 1 (Berlin 1930); T. Mommsen, *Italienische Analekten zur Reichsgeschichte des 14. Jahrhunderts, 1310–1378, Schriften der Monumenta Germaniae historica,* 11 (1952); K. A. Fink, *Das Vatikanische Archiv. Einführung in die Bestände und ihre Erforschung* (Rome, 2d ed. 1951).

Literature

Glotz, VI, 1 and 2; M. McKisack, *The Fourteenth Century 1307–1399, The Oxford History of England,* V (Oxford 1959); E. F. Jacob, *The Fifteenth Century 1399–1485, The Oxford History of England,* VI (Oxford 1962); E. Perroy, *The Hundred Years War with an Introduction to the English edition* by D. C. Douglas (London 1951); E. R. Labande, *L'Italie de la Renaissance. Duecento-Trecento-Quattrocento. Évolution d'une société* (Paris 1954); N. Valeri, *L'Italia nell'età dei principati dal 1343 al 1516* (Verona 1949); L. Simeoni, *Storia politica d'Italia,* VII: *Le signorie,* I (Milan 1950); *Storia d'Italia,* I: *Il Medioevo,* ed. G. Arnaldi, C. Violante, P. Lamma, E. Christiani, and N. Valerie (Turin 1959); M. Seidlmayer, *Geschichte Italiens. Vom Zusammenbruch des römischen Reiches bis zum ersten Weltkrieg* (Stuttgart 1962); D. Hay, *Geschichte Italiens in der Renaissance* (Stuttgart 1962); G. Peyronnet, "Les relations politiques entre la France et l'Italie, principalement au XIVe et dans la première moitié du XVe siècle," *MA,* 55 (1949), 301–42, 56 (1950), 85–113; A. Latreille, E. Delaruelle, and J. R. Palanque, *Histoire du catholicisme en France,* II (Paris 1960); E. E. Stengel, *Avignon und Rhens. Forschungen zur Geschichte des Kampfes um das Recht am Reich in der ersten Hälfte des 14. Jahrhunderts* (Weimar 1930); F. Bock,

Reichsidee und Nationalstaaten. Vom Untergang des alten Reiches bis zur Kündigung des deutsch-englischen Bündnisses im Jahre 1341 (Munich 1943); F. Trautz, *Die Könige von England und das Reich 1272–1377* (Heidelberg 1961); E. Léonard, *Les Angevins de Naples* (Paris 1954); A. de Stefano, *Federico II d'Aragona re di Sicilia 1296–1337* (Palermo 1937); R. Davidsohn, *Geschichte von Florenz*, III (Berlin 1912); G. A. Brucker, *Florentine Politics and Society 1343–1378* (Princeton 1962); *Storia di Milano*, V, VI (Milan 1955); F. Cognasso, *I Visconti* (Milan 1965); *Storia di Brescia*, I (Brescia 1963); G. Mollat, *The Popes at Avignon* (London and New York 1963; reprinted New York 1965); E. Dupré-Theseider, *I papi di Avignone e la questione Romana* (Florence 1939); idem, *Roma dal comune di popolo alla signoria pontificia 1252–1377* (Bologna 1952); idem, *Problemi del papato avignonese* (Bologna 1961); Y. Renouard, *La papauté à Avignon* (Paris 1954); B. Guillemain, *La cour pontificale d'Avignon 1309–1376* (Paris 1962); *Runciman*, III (Cambridge 1954); J. Goñi Gaztambide, *Historia de la bula de la cruzada en España* (Vitoria 1958); P. Piur, *Petrarcas "Buch ohne Namen" und die päpstliche Kurie. Ein Beitrag zur Geistesgeschichte der Frührenaissance* (Halle 1925); V. Martin, *Les origines du Gallicanisme*, 2 vols. (Paris 1939); G. Mollat, "Les origines du gallicanisme parlementaire aux XIV⁰ et XV⁰ siècles," *RHE*, 43 (1948), 90–147; J. Rivière, *Le problème de l'Église et de l'État au temps de Philippe le Bel* (Louvain and Paris 1926); M. Pacaut, *La théocratie, l'église et le pouvoir au moyen âge* (Paris 1957); F. Merzbacher, "Wandlungen des Kirchenbegriffs im Spätmittelalter. Grundzüge der Ekklesiologie des ausgehenden 13., des 14. und 15. Jahrhunderts," *ZSavRGkan*, 39 (1953), 274–361; H. Helbling, *Saeculum Humanum. Ansätze zu einem Versuch über spätmittelalterliches Geschichtsdenken* (Naples 1958); M. J. Wilks, *The Problem of Sovereignty in the Later Middle Ages* (Cambridge 1963); J. Haller, *Papsttum und Kirchenreform*, I (Berlin 1903); L. Buisson, *Potestas und Caritas. Die päpstliche Gewalt im Spätmittelalter* (Cologne and Graz 1958).

37. The Situation after the Death of Boniface VIII: Benedict XI and Clement V

SOURCES

C. Grandjean, *Le registre de Benoît XI* (Paris 1905); *Regestum Clementis papae V ex Vaticanis archetypis ... nunc primum editum,* cura et studio monachorum OSB, I–IX (Rome 1885–92), appendices, I (1892); *Tables des registres de Clément V publiés par les Bénédictins, Bibliothèque des Écoles françaises d'Athènes et de Rome*, 3d series (Paris 1948), includes a chronological list of bulls, a list of *incipit*, and the itinerary of Clement V; *Tables des registres de Clément V publiées par les Bénédictins*, établies par Y. Lanhers, C. Vogel sous la direction de R. Fawtier et G. Mollat (Paris 1957); T. Lecisotti, "Note in margine all'edizione dei regesti di Clemente V," *SteT*, 235 (1964), 15–45; "Benedetto XI papa," *Dizionario biografico degli Italiani*, 8 (1966), 370–78.

LITERATURE

"Benoît XI," *DHGE*, 8 (1935), 106–16; "Clément V," *DHGE*, 8 (1935), 1115–29; H. Finke, *Aus den Tagen Bonifaz' VIII.* (Münster 1902); K. Wenck, *Philipp der Schöne von Frankreich, seine Persönlichkeit und das Urteil seiner Zeitgenossen* (Marburg 1905); G. Lizerand, *Clément V et Philippe le Bel* (Paris 1910); M. Delle Piane, "Vecchio e nuovo nelle idee politiche di Pietro Dubois," *Studi Senesi*, 65 (1953), 299–349, 454–91; E. Müller, *Das Konzil von Vienne 1311–1312, Seine Quellen und seine Geschichte* (Münster 1934); J. Lecler, *Vienne, Histoire des Conciles Œcuméniques*, 8 (Paris 1964); G. Mollat, *The Popes at Avignon* (1965), 3–8.

The Templars: H. Finke, *Papsttum und Untergang des Templerordens,* 2 vols. (Münster 1907), the standard work; R. Gilles, *Les templiers sont-ils coupables? Leur histoire, leur règle, leur procès* (Paris 1957); G. Charpentier, *L'ordre des Templiers* (Paris, 2d ed. 1961); H. Neu, *Bibliographie des Templer-Ordens 1927–65* (Bonn 1965).

38. *From John XXII to Clement VI*

SOURCES

S. Reizler, *Vatikanische Akten zur deutschen Geschichte in der Zeit Kaiser Ludwigs des Bayern* (Innsbruck 1891); C. Erdmann, "Vatikanische Analekten zur Geschichte Ludwigs des Bayern," *AZ,* 41 (1932), 1–47; H. Schröder, "Die Protokollbücher der päpstlichen Kammerkleriker 1329–1347," *AKG,* 27 (1937), 121–286.

LITERATURE

E. Déprez, *Les préliminaires de la guerre de Cent Ans* (Paris 1902); E. E. Stengel, *Avignon und Rhens* (see the bibliography for this section); *idem,* "Baldewin von Luxemburg, ein grenzdeutscher Staatsmann des 14. Jahrhunderts," *Abhandlungen und Untersuchungen zur mittelalterlichen Geschichte* (Cologne and Graz 1960), 180–215; O. Bornhak, *Staatskirchliche Anschauungen und Handlungen am Hofe Kaiser Ludwigs des Bayern* (Weimar 1933); K. Bosl, "Die 'geistliche Hofakademie' Kaiser Ludwigs des Bayern im alten Franziskanerkloster zu München," *Der Mönch im Wappen. Aus Geschichte und Gegenwart des katholischen München* (Munich 1960), 97–129; C. K. Brampton, "Okham, Bonagratia and the Emperor Lewis IV," *Medium Aevum,* 31 (1962), 81–87; H. S. Offler, "Über die Prokuratorien Ludwigs des Bayern für die römische Kirche," *DA,* 8 (1951), 461–87; Conrad of Megenberg, *Klagelied der Kirche in Deutschland (Planctus ecclesiae in Germaniam),* ed. H. Kusch, *Leipziger Übersetzungen und Abhandlungen zum Mittelalter,* series A, I (Berlin 1956); *Kaiser, Volk und Avignon. Ausgewählte Quellen zur antikurialen Bewegung in Deutschland in der ersten Hälfte des 14. Jahrhunderts,* edited and translated by O. Berthold, *Leipziger Übersetzungen,* series A, III (Berlin 1960); F. Bock, "Roma al tempo di Roberto d'Angiò," *ASRomana,* 65 (1942), 163–208; *idem,* "Bemerkungen zur Beurteilung Kaiser Ludwigs IV. in der neueren Literatur," *ZBLG,* 23 (1960), 115–27.
John XXII: G. Mollat, *Lettres communes analysées d'après les registres dits d'Avignon et du Vatican,* 16 vols. (Paris 1904–46); A. Coulon and S. Clemencet, *Lettres secrètes et curiales du pape Jean XXII relatives à la France,* 8 fasc. (Paris 1900–65); G. Mollat, *The Popes at Avignon* (1965), 9–25; N. Valois, "Jacques Duèse, pape sous le nom de Jean XXII," *Histoire littéraire de la France,* 34 (1915), 391–630; B. Guillemain, *La cour pontificale d'Avignon,* gives detailed bibliography; H. Otto, "Zur italienischen Politik Johanns XXII.," *QFIAB,* 14 (1911), 140–265; G. Tabacco, *La casa di Francia nell'azione politica di papa Giovanni XXII,* Istituto storico italiano per il medio evo. *Studi storici,* fasc. 1–4 (Rome 1953); G. Dürrholder, *Die Kreuzzugspolitik unter Papst Johann XXII.* (dissertation, Strasbourg 1913); F. Bock, "Studien zum politischen Inquisitionsprozess Johanns XXII.," *QFIAB,* 26 (1935 f.), 21–142; *idem,* "Processi di Giovanni XXII contro i ghibellini italiani," *ASRomana,* 63 (1940), 129–43; *idem,* "Die Appellationsschriften König Ludwigs IV. in den Jahren 1323/24," *DA,* 4 (1940), 179–205; *idem,* "Politik und kanonischer Prozess zur Zeit Johanns XXII.," *ZBLG,* 22 (1959), 1–12.
Benedict XII: J. M. Vidal, *Lettres communes,* 3 vols. (Paris 1903–11); C. Daumet, *Lettres closes, patentes et curiales se rapportant à la France,* 2 vols. (Paris 1899–1920); J. M. Vidal and G. Mollat, *Lettres closes et patentes intéressant les pays autres que la France,* 8 fasc.

(Paris 1913–52); *DHGE*, 8 (1935), 116–35, with detailed bibliography; G. Mollat, *The Popes at Avignon* (1965), 26–36; K. Jacob, *Studien über Papst Benedikt XII.* (Berlin 1910); B. Guillemain, *La politique bénéficiale du pape Benoît XII (1334–1342)*, *BÉH*, 299 (Paris 1952); C. Schmitt, *Un pape réformateur et un défenseur de l'unité de l'église. Benoît XII et l'ordre des frères mineurs* (Florence and Quaracchi 1959), with detailed bibliography; B. Guillemain, *La cour pontificale d'Avignon*, gives detailed bibliography; F. Wetter, "Die Lehre Benedikts XII. vom intensiven Wachstum der Gottesschau," *AnGr*, 92 (Rome 1958); H. Otto, "Benedikt XII. als Reformer des Kirchenstaates," *RQ*, 36 (1928), 59–110; F. Bock, "Die Prokuratorien Kaiser Ludwigs IV. an Papst Benedikt XII.," *QFIAB*, 25 (1933 f.), 251–91; "Benedetto papa XII," *Dizionario biografico degli Italiani*, 8 (1966), 378–84.

Clement VI: E. Déprez, J. Glénisson, and G. Mollat, *Lettres closes, patentes et curiales se rapportant à la France*, 3 vols. (Paris 1901–61); E. Déprez and G. Mollat, *Lettres closes, patentes et curiales intéressant les pays autres que la France*, 3 fasc. (Paris 1960 f.); T. Gasparini Leporace, *Le suppliche di Clemente VI* (Rome 1948); *DHGE*, 12 (1953), 1129–62; G. Mollat, *The Popes at Avignon* (1965), 37–43; B. Guillemain, *La cour pontificale d'Avignon*, gives detailed bibliography; A. Pélissier, *Clément VI le magnifique, premier pape limousin* (Brive 1951); G. Mollat, "Le St-Siège et la France sous le pontificat de Clément VI (1342–1352)," *RHE*, 55 (1960), 5–24; *idem*, "Clément VI et la péninsule ibérique," *Journal des Savants* (1960), 122–29.

39. *From Innocent VI to Gregory XI*

SOURCES

Innocent VI: P. Gasnault and M. H. Laurent, *Lettres secrètes et curiales* (Paris 1959 ff.). *Urban V:* M. H. Laurent, P. Gasnault, and M. Hayez, *Lettres communes* (Paris 1954 ff.); P. Lecacheux and G. Mollat, *Lettres secrètes et curiales se rapportant à la France* (Paris 1902–55). *Gregory XI:* L. Mirot, H. Jassemin, J. Vielliard, G. Mollat, and E. R. Labande, *Lettres secrètes et curiales relatives à la France* (Paris 1935–57); G. Mollat, *Lettres secrètes et curiales intéressant les pays autres que la France* (Paris 1962–65); A. Segre, "I dispacci di Cristoforo da Piacenza, procuratore Mantovano alla corte pontificia 1371–83," *AstIt*, V series, 43 (1909), 27–95, 44 (1909), 253–326; G. Mollat, "Relations politiques de Grégoire XI avec les Siennois et les Florentins," *MAH*, 68 (1956), 335–76. The publications of the series of *registra* in the Vatican Archives for the individual lands and copious bibliography are given in B. Guillemain, *La cour pontificale d'Avignon*, 11–13.

LITERATURE

G. Mollat, *The Popes at Avignon* (1965), 44–63; *Storia di Milano*, VI (Milan 1955); J. P. Kirsch, *Die Rückkehr der Päpste Urban V. und Gregor XI. von Avignon nach Rom* (Paderborn 1898); L. Mirot, *La politique pontificale et le retour du Saint-Siège à Rome en 1376* (Paris 1899); A. Pélissier, *Innocent VI le réformateur, deuxième pape Limousin* (Tulle 1961); G. Mollat, "Grégoire XI et sa légende," *RHE*, 49 (1954), 873–77; A. Pélissier, *Grégoire XI ramène la papauté à Rome, troisième pape Limousin* (Tulle 1962); G. Pirchan, *Italien und Kaiser Karl IV. in der Zeit seiner zweiten Romfahrt*, 2 vols. (Prague 1930).

40. *The Curia at Avignon*

SOURCES

Vatikanische Quellen zur Geschichte der päpstlichen Hof- und Finanzverwaltung 1316–1378, published by the Görres-Gesellschaft (Paderborn): I: E. Göller, *Die Einnahmen der apostolischen Kammer unter Johann XXII.* (1910), II: K. H. Schäfer, *Die Ausgaben der apostolischen Kammer unter Johann XXII., nebst den Jahresbilanzen von 1316–1375* (1914), III: K. H. Schäfer, *Die Ausgaben der apostolischen Kammer unter Benedikt XII., Klemens VI. und Innocenz VI., 1335–1362* (1914), IV: E. Göller, *Die Einnahmen der apostolischen Kammer unter Benedikt XII.* (1920), V: L. Mohler, *Die Einnahmen der apostolischen Kammer unter Klemens VI.* (1931), VI: K. H. Schäfer, *Die Ausgaben der apostolischen Kammer unter den Päpsten Urban V. und Gregor XI., 1362–1378, nebst Nachträgen und einem Glossar für alle drei Ausgabenbände* (1937), VII: H. Hoberg, *Die Einnahmen der apostolischen Kammer unter Innocenz VI.* (1955). Publications of the *registra* of the Popes are listed under the respective pontificates.

LITERATURE

B. Guillemain, *La cour pontificale d'Avignon, 1309–1376. Étude d'une société* (Paris 1962), gives a broad presentation, with charts, statistics, and a copious bibliography. F. Lot and R. Fawtier, *Histoire des institutions françaises au moyen âge.* III: *Institutions ecclésiastiques* (Paris 1962); C. Lux, *Constitutionum apostolicarum de generali beneficiorum reservatione ab anno 1265 usque ad annum 1378 emissarum, tam intra quam extra corpus iuris exstantium, collectio et interpretatio* (Breslau 1904); G. Mollat, *La collation des bénéfices ecclésiastiques à l'époque des papes d'Avignon, 1305–1378* (Paris 1921); G. Barraclough, *Papal Provisions* (Oxford 1935); G. Mollat, "La diplomatie pontificale au XIVᵉ siècle," *Mélanges Louis Halphen* (Paris 1951); Y. Renouard, *Les relations des papes d'Avignon et des compagnies commerciales et bancaires de 1316 à 1378* (Paris 1941); C. Bauer, "Die Epochen der Papstfinanz," *HZ,* 138 (1928), 457–503; P. D. Partner, "Camera papae: Problems of the Papal Finance in the Later Middle Ages," *JEH,* 4 (1953), 55–68; R. de Roover, *The Rise and Decline of the Medici Bank* (Harvard 1963); G. Mollat, *The Popes at Avignon* (1965), 279–342; A. Esch, "Bankiers der Kirche im Grossen Schisma," *QFIAB,* 46 (1966), 277–398 (important also for the period preceding the Schism and supplying bibliography); T. Majic, "Die apostolische Pönitentiarie im 14. Jahrhundert," *RQ,* 50 (1955), 129–77.

41. *Nominalism. The Universities Between Via Antiqua and Via Moderna*

LITERATURE

K. Werner, *Die Scholastik des späteren Mittelalters,* II–IV (Vienna 1881–87); *Ueberweg,* II; *Wulf,* III; *Gilson-Böhner; Fliche-Martin,* 13, 417–73; F. Copleston, *A History of Philosophy* (Westminster, Md., 2d ed. 1959); *Grabmann G;* G. Ritter, *Studien zur Spätscholastik,* I–III (Heidelberg 1921–27); *idem, Die Heidelberger Universität* (Heidelberg 1936); F. Ehrle, *Der Sentenzenkommentar Peters von Candia* (Münster 1925); P. Vignaux, *Justification et prédestination au XIVᵉ siècle* (Paris 1934); *idem, Nominalisme au XIVᵉ siècle* (Montreal 1948); *Stegmüller RS;* A. Maier, *Studien zur Naturphilosophie der Spätscholastik,* 5 vols. (Rome 1949–58); G. de Lagarde, *La naissance de l'esprit laïque,* 5 vols. (Paris,

3d ed. 1956–63); W. Dettloff, *Die Entwicklung der Akzeptations- und Verdienstlehre von Duns Scotus bis Luther* (Münster 1963); H. Oberman, *The Harvest of Medieval Theology. Gabriel Biel and Late Medieval Nominalism* (Cambridge, Mass. 1963).

William of Ockham: Works: P. Böhner, "Die unpolemischen Schriften Ockhams," *FStud,* 32 (1950), 156–63; *De sacramento altaris,* ed. T. Bruce Birch (Burlington 1930); *Quaestio prima principalis Prologi in I Sent.,* ed. P. Böhner (Paterson 1939); *Centiloquium,* ed. P. Böhner, *FStudies,* 1 (1941), 2 (1942); *Summa logicae,* I–III/I, ed. P. Böhner (St. Bonaventure, N. Y., 2d ed. 1957–62); *Philosophical Writings,* selections edited and translated by P. Böhner (Edinburgh and London 1957); *Quodlibeta septem* and *Tractatus de sacramento altaris* (Strasbourg 1491, facsimile Louvain 1962); *Opera plurima* (Lyons 1494–96, reprinted London 1962). Literature: W. Heynck, "Ockham-Literatur 1919–1949," *FStud,* 32 (1950), 164–83; R. Guelluy, *Philosophie et théologie chez Guillaume d'Ockham* (Paris 1947); L. Baudry, *Guillaume d'Ockham, sa vie, ses œuvres, ses idées sociales et politiques,* I: *L'homme et les œuvres* (Paris 1950); idem, *Lexique philosophique de Guillaume d'Ockham* (Paris 1958); T. Barth, "Wilhelm von Ockham und die Philosophie der Ordnungen," *PhJ,* 60 (1950), 323–34; idem, "Nuove interpretazioni della filosofia di Ockham," *StudFr,* 52 (1955), 187–204; C. Vasoli, *Guillaume d'Ockham* (Florence 1953); W. Kölmel, "Von Ockham zu Gabriel Biel," *FStud,* 37 (1955), 218–59; E. Iserloh, *Gnade und Eucharistie in der philosophischen Theologie des Wilhelm von Ockham* (Wiesbaden 1956); H. Shapiro, *Motion, Time and Place according to William Ockham* (St. Bonaventure, N. Y. 1957); P. Böhner, *Collected Articles on Ockham,* ed. E. Buytaert (St. Bonaventure, N. Y. 1958); F. Hoffmann, *Die erste Kritik des Ockhamismus durch den Oxforder Kanzler Johann Lutterell* (Breslau 1941); idem, *Die Schriften des Oxforder Kanzlers Johann Lutterell* (Leipzig 1959).

Nicholas of Autrecourt: J. Lappe, *Nikolaus von Autrecourt* (Münster 1908); J. R. O'Donnel, "Nicholas of Autrecourt," *MS,* 1 (1939), 179–280, 4 (1942), 97–125; J. R. Weinberg, *Nicholas of Autrecourt* (Princeton 1948); E. Maccagnolo, "Metafisica e gnoseologia in Niccolò d'Autrecourt," *RFN,* 45 (1952), 36–53.

John of Mirecourt: F. Stegmüller, "Die 2 Apologien des Johanns de Mirecourt," *RThAM,* 5 (1933), 46–78, 192–204; A. Franzinelli in *RSF,* 13 (1958), 319–40, 415–19.

Robert Holkot: A. Meissner, *Gotteserkenntnis und Gotteslehre nach dem englischen Dominikanertheologen Robert Holkot* (Limburg 1953); P. Molteni, *Robert Holkot. Dottrina della grazia et della giustificazione* (typed dissertation, Bonn 1962).

Gregory of Rimini: Super I et II Sent. (reprinted St. Bonaventure, N. Y. 1955); M. Schüler, *Prädestination, Sünde und Freiheit bei Gregor von Rimini* (Stuttgart 1934); *ECatt,* VI, 1156 f.; D. Trapp in *Augustiniana,* 6 (1956), 182 ff., 8 (1958), 425 ff.

Marsilius of Inghen: G. Ritter, *Studien zur Spätscholastik,* I: *Marsilius von Inghen und die okkamistische Schule in Deutschland* (Heidelberg 1921); A. Lang, *Die Wege der Glaubensbegründung bei den Scholastikern des 14. Jahrhunderts* (Münster 1930); W. Möhler, *Die Trinitätslehre des Marsilius von Inghen* (Limburg 1949).

Henry Heinbuche of Langenstein: A. Lang, "Die Katharinenpredigt Heinrichs von Langenstein," *DTh,* 26 (1948), 123–59, 233–58, 361–94; A. Emmen, "Heinrich von Langenstein und die Diskussion über die Empfängnis Mariens," *Schmaus ThGG,* 625–50.

Henry Totting of Oyta: A. Lang, *Heinrich Totting von Oyta* (Münster 1937); F. Rosenthal, "Heinrich von Oyta and Biblical Criticism in the Fourteenth Century," *Speculum,* 25 (1950), 178–83.

Nicholas of Dinkelsbühl: A. Madre, *Nikolaus' von Dinkelsbühl Leben und Schriften* (Münster 1965).

Peter d'Ailly: B. Meller, *Studien zur Erkenntnislehre des Peters von Ailly* (Freiburg 1954); M. Liebermann, "Gerson et d'Ailly," *Romania,* 78 (Paris 1957), 433–62, 79 (1958), 339–75, 80 (1959), 289–336, 81 (1960), 44–98.

John Gerson: Œuvres complètes, Introduction, texte et notes, ed. P. Glorieux, thus far 6 vols. (Paris, Tournai, Rome, and New York 1960–66); J. B. Schwab, *J. Gerson* (Würzburg 1858); W. Dress, *Die Theologie Johanns Gerson* (Gütersloh 1931); A. Combes, *Jean Gerson: commentateur dionysien* (Paris 1940); idem, *Essai sur la critique de Ruysbroeck par Gerson,* 3 vols. (Paris 1945–59); L. Mourin, *Jean Gerson prédicateur français* (Bruges 1952); G. H. M. Posthumus Meyjes, *J. Gerson zijn kerkpolitiek en ecclesiologie* ('s-Gravenhage 1963); further literature in the bibliography for Chapter 44.

John Wenck: E. Vansteenberghe, *Le "De ignota litteratura"* (Münster 1910); R. Haubst, *Studien zu Nikolaus von Kues und Johannes Wenck* (Münster 1955), and, in connection with the preceding, *RQ,* 53 (1958), 81–88.

Henry of Gorkum: A. G. Weiler, *Heinrich von Gorkum († 1431). Seine Stellung in der Philosophie und Theologie des Spätmittelalters* (Hilversum and Einsiedeln 1962).

Dionysius the Carthusian: Opera omnia, 1–44 (Montreuil and Tournai 1896–1935); *DHGE,* XIV, 256–60, with bibliography; A. Mougel, *Dionysius der Kartäuser* (Mülheim an der Ruhr 1898); E. Ewig, *Die Anschauungen des Kartäusers Dionysius von Roermond über den christlichen Ordo in Staat und Kirche* (Bonn 1936); H. Pohlen, *Die Erkenntnislehre Dionysius' des Kartäusers* (Leipzig 1941); M. Beer, *Dionysius des Kartäusers Lehre vom Desiderium naturale* (Munich 1963).

42. Concept of the Church and Idea of the State in the Polemics of the Fourteenth Century, The Laicized State in Marsilius of Padua

Sources and Literature

M. Goldast, *Monarchia S. Romani Imperii,* 3 vols. (Hanover and Frankfurt 1611–14, reprinted Graz 1960); S. Riezler, *Die literarischen Widersacher der Päpste zur Zeit Ludwigs des Bayern* (Leipzig 1874); R. Scholz, *Die Publizistik zur Zeit Philipps des Schönen und Bonifaz' VIII.* (Stuttgart 1903); idem, *Unbekannte kirchenpolitische Streitschriften aus der Zeit Ludwigs des Bayern,* 2 vols. (Rome 1911–14); J. Rivière, *Le problème de l'Église et de l'État au temps de Philippe le Bel* (Louvain 1926); U. Mariani, *Scrittori politici Agostiniani del secolo XIV* (Florence 1930); O. Bornhak, *Staatskirchliche Anschauungen und Handlungen am Hofe Ludwigs des Bayern* (Weimar 1933); V. Martin, *Les origines du gallicanisme,* 2 vols. (Paris 1939); G. de Lagarde, *La naissance de l'esprit laïque au déclin du moyen âge.* 5 vols. (Louvain and Paris, 3d ed. 1956–63); F. Merzbacher, "Wandlungen des Kirchenbegriffs im Spätmittelalter," *ZSavRGkan,* 39 (1953), 274–361.

Aegidius Romanus (Giles of Rome): De ecclesiastica sive summi pontificis potestate, ed. R. Scholz (Weimar 1929, reprinted Aalen 1961); discussion of the preceding in R. Scholz, *Die Publizistik,* 46–129, J. Rivière, *Le problème,* 191–228, and G. de Lagarde, *La naissance,* I, 230–41; G. Santonastoco, *Il pensiero politico di Egidio Romano* (Florence 1939); E. Moody, "Ockham and Aegidius Romanus," *RStudies,* 9 (1949), 417–42; R. Kuiters, *De ecclesiastica sive de summi pontificis potestate secundum Aegidium Romanum* (Rome 1948), with bibliography.

James of Viterbo: De regimine christiano, ed. H. X. Arquillière (Paris 1926); discussion of the preceding in R. Scholz, *Die Publizistik,* 131–52, and J. Rivière, *Le problème,* 228–52.

Augustinus Triumphus: D. A. Perini, *Bibliographia Augustiniana,* IV (Florence 1935), 20–28; R. Scholz, *Die Publizistik,* 172–89; idem, *Unbekannte Streitschriften,* I, 191–96, II, 481–90; R. van Gerven, *De wereldlijke macht van den paus volgens Augustinus Triumphus in het licht van het politiek Augustinisme* (Louvain 1946); F. Merzbacher, "Wandlungen," *loc. cit.;* M. J. Wilks, "Papa est nomen iurisdictionis: Augustinus Triumphus and the Papal Vicariate of Christ," *JThS,* 8 (1957), 71–91; W. Kölmel, "Einheit und Zweiheit der Gewalt im Corpus Mysticum. Zur Souveränitätslehre des Augustinus Triumphus," *HJ*, 82 (1963), 103–47.

Marsilius of Padua: Works: *Defensor pacis,* ed. C. W. Previté-Orton (Cambridge 1928); R. Scholz, *MG Fontes iuris,* 2 vols. (Hanover 1932 f.); A. Gewirth (New York 1956), with English translation; H. Kusch, 2 vols. (Darmstadt 1958), with German translation and bibliography; *Defensor minor,* ed. C. K. Brampton (Birmingham 1922); *Tractatus de translatione Romani imperii,* M. Goldast, *Monarchia,* II, 147–53; *Tractatus de iurisdictione imperatoris in causis matrimonialibus, ibid.,* 1383–91. Literature: F. Battaglia, "Marsilio da Padova e il Defensor pacis," *Rivista internazionale di filosofia del diritto,* 4 (Rome 1924), 398 ff.; *idem, Marsilio e la filosofia politica del medio evo* (Florence 1928); J. Haller, "Zur Lebensgeschichte des Marsilius von Padua," *ZKG,* 48 (1929), 166–99; M. Grabmann, "Studien über den Einfluß der aristotelischen Philosophie auf die mittelalterlichen Theorien über das Verhältnis von Kirche und Staat," *SAM,* 2 (1934), 41–60; R. Scholz, "Marsilius und die Genesis des modernen Staatsbewusstseins," *HZ,* 156 (1937), 88–103; A. Checchini and N. Bobbio (ed.), *Marsilio da Padova, Studi raccolti nel VI centenario della morte* (Padua 1942); A. Dordett, *Der geistliche Charakter der kirchlichen Gerichtsbarkeit* (Vienna 1954); A. Gewirth, *Marsilius and Medieval Political Philosophy* (New York 1951); J. Heckel, "Marsilius und Martin Luther," *ZSavRGkan,* 75 (1958), 268–336; H. Segall, *Der "Defensor pacis" des Marsilius* (Wiesbaden 1959); P. Mikat in *LThK,* VII (2d ed. 1962), 108–10; G. de Lagarde, "Marsile de Padoue et Guillaume d'Ockham," *Études d'histoire du droit canonique dédiées à Gabriel Le Bras,* I (Paris 1965), 593–605.

William of Ockham: Works: *Opera plurima* (Lyons 1494–96, reprinted London 1962); M. Goldast, *Monarchia,* I, II; R. Scholz, *Unbekannte Streitschriften,* II; *Guilielmi de Ockham opera politica,* ed. J. G. Sikes *et al.,* 3 vols. (Manchester 1940–56); *Opus XC dierum,* M. Goldast, *Monarchia,* II, 993–1236, and Sikes, I and II; *Dialogus,* Goldast, *Monarchia,* II, 398–957 (continuation in R. Scholz, *Unbekannte Streitschriften,* II, 392–95); *Monumenta politica,* ser. I, no. I, ed. L. Firpo (reprinted Turin 1959); *Octo quaestiones,* M. Goldast, *Monarchia,* II, 314–91, and Sikes, I, 12–221; *Breviloquium de principatu tyrannico,* ed. R. Scholz (Leipzig 1944, reprinted Stuttgart 1952) and V. L. Baudry (Paris 1937); *De imperatorum et pontificum potestate,* R. Scholz, *Unbekannte Streitschriften,* II, 453–80 (continuation in W. Mulder, *AFrH,* 16 [1923], 469–92, 17 [1924], 72–97), ed. C. K. Brampton (New York 1927). Literature: H. Köhler, *Der Kirchenbegriff bei Wilhelm von Ockham* (dissertation, Würzburg 1937); A. Hamman, "La doctrine de l'église et de l'état d'après le Breviloquium d'Occam," *FStud,* 32 (1950), 135–41; W. Kölmel, "Das Naturrecht bei Wilhelm von Ockham," *FStud,* 35 (1953), 35–85; *idem, Wilhelm Ockham und seine kirchenpolitischen Schriften* (Essen 1962), with bibliography; E. F. Jacob, "Ockham as a Political Thinker," *Essays in the Conciliar Epoch* (Manchester 1953), 85–105; B. Tierney, "Ockham, The Conciliar Theory and the Canonists," *Journal of the History of Ideas,* 16 (1954), 40–70; *idem, Foundations of the Conciliar Theory* (Cambridge 1955); F. Hofmann, *Der Anteil der Minoriten am Kampf Ludwigs des Bayern gegen Johannes XXII., unter besonderer Berücksichtigung des Wilhelms von Ockham* (dissertation, Münster 1959); E. K. Brampton, "Ockham, Bonagratia and the Emperor Lewis IV," *Medium aevum,* 31 (1962).

43. *The Spiritual Movement and the Poverty Dispute*

LITERATURE

BullFr, I–V; *ALKGMA,* II–IV; *Holzapfel;* K. Balthasar, *Geschichte des Armutsstreites im Franziskanerorden* (Münster 1911); L. Oliger, *Documenta inedita ad historiam Fraticellorum specantia* (Quaracchi 1913); *idem,* "Beiträge zur Geschichte der Spiritualen, Fratizellen und Clarener im Mittelalter," *ZKG,* 45 (1926), 215–42; *idem,* "Bonagratia de Bergamo et eius Tractatus ... de paupertate," *AFrH*, 22 (1929), 292–335, 487–511; cf. *AFrH*, 23 (1930), 57–69, 106–71, 32 (1939), 274–411; L. Oliger, *De secta spiritus libertatis in Umbria* (Rome 1943); M. Bierbaum, *Bettelorden und Weltgeistlichkeit an der Universität Paris* (Münster 1920); P. Gratien, *Histoire de la fondation et de l'évolution de l'ordre des Frères Mineurs au XIIIe siècle* (Paris 1930); E. Müller, *Das Konzil von Vienne* (Münster 1934); E. Benz, *Ecclesia spiritualis* (Stuttgart 1934); F. Sessevalle, *Histoire générale de l'ordre de s. François* I, 1–2 (Paris 1935–37); R. M. Huber, *A Documented History of the Franciscan Order (1182–1517)* (Milwaukee 1944); A. Léon, *Histoire de l'ordre des Frères Mineurs* (Paris 1954); E. Wagner, *Historia constitutionum generalium OFM* (Würzburg and Rome 1954); H. S. Offler, "Meinungsverschiedenheiten am Hofe Ludwigs des Bayern," *DA*, 11 (1954), 191–206; K. Bosl, "Die 'Geistliche Hofakademie' Kaiser Ludwigs des Bayern im alten Franziskanerkloster zu München," *Der Mönch im Wappen* (Munich 1960), 97–129; M. D. Lamtert, *Franciscan Poverty* (London 1961); Thaddeus of New Durham, *The Doctrine of the Franciscan Spirituals* (Rome 1963); *LThK*, I (2d ed. 1957), 886 f., and IX (2d ed. 1964), 974 f.

44. *The German Mystics*

TEXTS

F. Pfeiffer, *Deutsche Mystiker des 14. Jahrhunderts*, 2 vols. (Göttingen, 2d ed. 1906–07, reprinted Aalen 1962); A. Spamer, *Texte aus der deutschen Mystik des 14. und 15. Jahrhunderts* (Jena 1912); F. Schulze-Maizier, *Mystische Dichtung aus 7 Jahrhunderten* (Leipzig 1925); O. Karrer, *Die grosse Glut. Textgeschichte der Mystik im Mittelalter* (Munich 1926); W. Oehl, *Deutsche Mystikerbriefe des Mittelalters* (Munich 1931); W. Stammler, *Gottsuchende Seelen* (Munich 1948); J. Quint, *Textbuch zur Mystik des deutschen Mittelalters* (Tübingen and Halle, 2d ed. 1957); M. Kunisch (ed.), *Eckhart, Tauler, Seuse. Ein Textbuch aus der altdeutschen Mystik* (Hamburg 1958).

LITERATURE

Stammler-Langosch; C. Greith, *Die deutsche Mystik im Predigerorden* (Freiburg 1861); *Preger;* H. Denifle, "Über die Anfänge der Predigtweise der deutschen Mystiker," *ALKGMA*, 2 (1886), 641–52; J. Bernhart, *Die philosophische Mystik des Mittelalters* (Munich 1922); J. Quint, "Mystik," *RDL*, IV (1933), 65–88; W. Muschg, *Die Mystik in der Schweiz 1200–1500* (Fravenfeld and Leipzig 1935); *Pourrat;* F. W. Wentzlaff-Eggebert, *Deutsche Mystik zwischen Mittelalter und Neuzeit* (Tübingen 1947); H. Dénifle and O. Spiess, *Die deutschen Mystiker des 14. Jahrhunderts* (Fribourg 1951); E. von Ivánka, "Wanderung und Wandlung eines stoischen Terminus," *ZKTh*, 72 (1950), 149–55; H. Grundmann, *Religiöse Bewegungen im Mittelalter* (Darmstadt, 2d ed. 1961); *idem,* "Die geschichtlichen Grundlagen der deutschen Mystik," *DVfLG*, 12 (1934), 400–29; K. Ruh, "Altdeutsche Mystik," *Wirkendes Wort*, 7 (1957), 135–46, 211–31 (report of research); K. Ruh (ed.), *Altdeutsche und altniederländische Mystik* (Darmstadt 1964).
Mechtilde of Magdeburg: Texts: G. Morel, *Das fliessende Licht der Gottheit* (Middle High German) (1863 Darmstadt, 2d ed. 1963), partial printing in accordance with a recently discovered manuscript, ed. W. Schleussner (Mainz 1929); *Revelationes Gertrudianae ac Mechtildianae*, II (Poitiers 1877), 435–707; M. Schmidt (trans.), *Das fliessende Licht der Gottheit* (Einsiedeln 1956). Literature: *Stammler-Langosch*, III, 323–26; H. Stierling, *Studien zu Mechtild von Magdeburg* (dissertation, Göttingen 1907); G. Lüers, *Die Sprache der deutschen Mystik des Mittelalters im Werke der Mechthild von Magdeburg* (Munich 1926); M. S. C. Molenaar, *Die Frau vom anderen Ufer* (Heidelberg 1946); H. Neu-

mann, "Beiträge zur Textgeschichte des 'Fliessenden Lichts' und zur Lebensgeschichte Mechthilds von Magdeburg," *NAG* (1954), no. 3, 28–80.

Mechtilde of Hackeborn: Texts: *Revelationes Gertrudianae ac Mechtildianae*, II (Poitiers 1877), 1–442; J. Müller, *Leben und Offenbarung der heiligen Mechthild*, 2 vols. (Regensburg 1880 f.); H. U. von Balthasar, *Mechthild von Hackeborn. Das Buch vom strömenden Lob* (Einsiedeln 1956), with bibliography. Literature: *Stammler-Langosch,* III, 321 ff.; C. Vagaggini, *Cor Iesu,* II (Rome 1959), 31–48.

Gertrude: Texts: *Revelationes Gertrudianae,* I (Poitiers 1875); *Exercitia spiritualia,* Latin and Italian, ed. R. Medici (Praglia 1924); P. Doyère (ed. and trans.), *Le mémorial spirituel de Ste Gertrude* (Books I and II of the *Legatus divinae pietatis*) (Paris 1954); Gertrudis Sancta, *Œuvres spirituelles,* Latin and French, ed. J. Honlier and A. Schmitt (Paris 1967). Literature: G. Ledos, *Ste Gertrude* (Paris 1901, 6th ed. 1916); A. Vollmer, *Die heilige Gertrud die Grosse* (Kevelaer 1937); *Baudot-Chaussin,* IX, 520–36, with bibliography; C. Vagaggini, *Cor Iesu,* II (Rome 1959), 29–48.

Dietrich of Freiberg: E. Krebs, "Meister Dietrich," *BGPhMA,* 5 (1906), 5 f.; *idem* in *RNPh,* 18 (1911), 516–36; J. Würschmidt (ed.), *De iride, BGPhMA,* 12 (1914), 5; F. Stegmüller, "Meister Dietrich von Freiberg über die Zeit und das Sein," *AHD,* 13 (1942), 153–221; A. Maurer in *MS,* 18 (1956), 173–203; A. Wallace, *The Scientific Methodology of Theoderic of Freiberg* (Fribourg 1959); W. Eckert in *LThK,* III (2d ed. 1959), 384.

Master Eckhart: Texts: German works ed. J. Quint, I (Stuttgart 1958), V (Stuttgart 1963), Latin works ed. J. Koch, E. Benz, K. Weiss, *et al.,* IV (Stuttgart 1956); F. Pfeiffer, *Deutsche Mystiker,* II (Leipzig 1857, reprinted Aalen 1962); J. Quint (ed. and trans.), *Meister Eckhart. Deutsche Predigten und Traktate* (Munich 1955); E. K. Pohl (trans.), *Meister Eckhart. Von der Geburt der Seele. Predigten und Traktate* (Gütersloh 1959). Acts of his trial: A. Daniels (ed.), "Eine lateinische Rechtfertigungsschrift," *BGPhMA,* 23 (1923), 5; G. Théry, "Édition critique des pièces relatives au procès d'Eckhart," *AHD,* 1 (1926), 129–268; O. Karrer and H. Piesch, *Meister Eckharts Rechtfertigungsschrift* (Erfurt 1927); M. H. Laurent, "Autour du procès de Maître Eckhart," *DTh(P)* (1936), 331–48. Literature: *Stammler-Langosch,* I, 485–502, V, 163–71, with bibliography; H. Denifle, "Meister Eckharts lateinische Schriften und die Grundanschauungen seiner Lehre," *ALKGMA,* II (1886), 417–562, 672–87 (reprinted 1956); O. Karrer, *Meister Eckhart. Das System seiner religiösen Lehre und Lebensweisheit* (Munich 1923); *idem, Das Göttliche in der Seele bei Meister Eckhart* (Würzburg 1928); E. Seeberg, *Meister Eckhart* (Tübingen 1934); A. Dempf, *Meister Eckhart* (Leipzig 1934, Freiburg 1960); W. Bange, *Meister Eckharts Lehre vom göttlichen und geschöpflichen Sein* (Limburg 1937); O. Bolza, *Meister Eckhart als Mystiker* (Munich 1938); H. Ebeling, *Meister Eckharts Mystik* (Stuttgart 1941); H. Piesch, *Meister Eckharts Ethik* (Lucerne 1935, 2d ed. 1948); H. Hof, *Scintilla animae* (Lund 1952); K. Weiss, *Meister Eckharts Stellung innerhalb der theologischen Entwicklung des Spätmittelalters* (Berlin 1953); M. Bindschedler, "Meister Eckharts Lehre von der Gerechtigkeit," *Studia philosophica,* 13 (Basel 1953), 58–71; B. Schmoldt, *Die deutsche Begriffssprache Meister Eckharts* (Heidelberg 1954); J. Kopper, *Die Metaphysik Meister Eckharts* (Saarbrücken 1955); J. Ancelet-Hustache, *Maître Eckhart et la mystique rhénane* (Paris 1956); J. M. Clark, *Meister Eckhart* (London 1957); U. M. Nix and R. Öchslin (ed.), *Meister Eckhart der Prediger* (Freiburg 1960); V. Lossky, *Théologie negative et connaissance de Dieu chez Maître Eckhart* (Paris 1960); *NDB,* IV, 295–301; *DSAM,* IV, 93–116.

John Tauler: Texts: the only authentic works are the sermons and one each of the letters to E. Schappach and M. Ebner. Printings: Leipzig 1498, Basel 1521, Cologne 1543 (ed. P. Vanisius *et al.*); F. Vetter, *Die Predigten Taulers* (Berlin 1910); A. L. Corin, *Sermons de J. Tauler,* 2 vols. (Paris 1924–29); J. Quint, *Textbuch zur Mystik des deutschen Mittelalters* (Tübingen, 2d ed. 1957). Literature: *Stammler-Langosch,* IV, 375–86, V, 1078; G. Siedel, *Die Mystik Taulers* (Leipzig 1911); A. Vogt-Terhost, *Der bildliche Ausdruck in den Pre-*

digten Taulers (Breslau 1920); J. Zahn, "Taulers Mystik in ihrer Stellung zur Kirche," *Festschrift J. G. von Sachsen* (Freiburg 1920), 120–46; E. Hugueny, "La doctrine mystique de Tauler," *RSPhTh*, 15 (1921), 194–291; D. Helander, *Johannes Tauler als Prediger* (Lund 1923); T. Absil, "Die Gaben des Heiligen Geistes in der Mystik Taulers," *ZAM*, 2 (1927), 254–64; A. Korn, *Tauler als Redner* (Münster 1928); K. Grunewald, *Studien zu Johannes Taulers Frömmigkeit* (Leipzig 1930); C. Kirmsse, *Die Terminologie des Mystikers Johannes Tauler* (dissertation, Leipzig) (Engelsdorf 1930); E. Holzmair, *Eckhart und Tauler* (Vienna 1931); F. W. Wentzlaff-Eggebert, *Studien zur Lebenslehre Taulers* (Berlin 1940); P. Wyser, "Der 'Seelengrund' in Taulers Predigten," *Lebendiges Mittelalter* (Fribourg 1958), 204–311; M. de Gandillac, "De Jean Tauler à Henri Seuse," *Études Germaniques*, 5 (Lyons 1950), 241–56; *idem, Valeur du temps dans la pédagogie spirituelle de Jean Tauler* (Paris 1956); E. Filthaut (ed.), *Johannes Tauler, Gedenkschrift zum 600. Todestag* (Essen 1961), with bibliography; I. Weilner, *Johannes Taulers Bekehrungsweg* (Regensburg 1961).

Henry Suso: Texts: *Büchlein der ewigen Weisheit, Büchlein der Wahrheit, Grosses und Kleines Briefbuch*, K. Bihlmeyer (ed.), *Heinrich Seuse, Deutsche Schriften* (Stuttgart 1907, reprinted Freiburg 1961); in New High German, M. Diepenbrock (Regensburg 1829, 4th ed. 1884), H. S. Denifle (Munich 1876–80), N. Heller (Heidelberg 1926), W. Lehmann, 2 vols. (Jena, 2d ed. 1922). Literature: *Stammler-Langosch*, IV, 164–80, V, 1047; H. Lichtenberg, "Le mysticisme allemand," *Revue des Cours et Conférences*, 18 (Paris 1909), 600–12, 19 (Paris 1910), 683–95; A. Niklas, *Die Terminologie des Mystikers Heinrich Seuse* (dissertation, Königsberg 1914); C. Heyer, *Stilgeschichtliche Studien über Heinrich Seuses Büchlein der ewigen Weisheit* (dissertation, Kiel 1915); R. Senn, *Die Echtheit der Vita Heinrich Seuses* (dissertation, Bonn 1930); R. Schwarz, *Das Christusbild des deutschen Mystikers Heinrich Seuse* (Greifswald 1934); M. A. Fischer, *Die Heilige Schrift in den Werken des deutschen Mystikers Heinrich Seuse* (Speyer 1936); D. Planzer, *Das Horologium Sapientiae des seligen Heinrich Seuse* (Rome 1937); C. Gröber, *Der Mystiker Heinrich Seuse* (Freiburg 1941); J. Bühlmann, *Christuslehre und Christusmystik des Heinrich Seuse* (Lucerne 1942); J. A. Bizet, *Henri Suso et le déclin de la scholastique* (Paris 1946), with bibliography; *idem, Suso et le Minnesang ou la morale de l'amour courtois* (Paris 1947); D. Planzer, "Henry Suso on the Spiritual Life," *Cross and Crown*, 2 (St. Louis 1960), 58–79; J. Schwietering, "Zur Autorschaft von Seuses Vita," *Mystik und höfische Dichtung im Hochmittelalter* (Darmstadt 1960), 107–22; J. Ancelet-Hustache, "Le problème de l'autenticité de la vie de Suso," *La mystique rhénane* (Paris 1963), 193–205; E. Filthaut, *Heinrich Seuse. Studien zum 600. Geburtstag (1366–1966)* (Cologne 1966).

The Friends of God: R. Egenter, *Die Lehre von der Gottesfreundschaft in der Scholastik und Mystik des 12. und 13. Jahrhunderts* (Augsburg 1928); *idem,* "Die Idee der Gottesfreunde im 14. Jahrhundert," *BGPhMA*, Suppl. III (Münster 1935), 1021–36; P. Strauch (ed.), *M. Ebner und Heinrich von Nördlingen* (Freiburg and Tübingen 1882); H. Wilms (ed.), *Der seligen Margarete Ebner Offenbarungen und Briefe* (Vechta 1928); J. Prestel (ed.), *Die Offenbarungen der Margarete Ebner und Adelheid Langmann* (Weimar 1939); A. Walz, "Gottesfreunde um Margarete Ebner," *HJ*, 72 (1953), 253–65.

John van Ruysbroeck: Works: ed. J. B. David, 6 vols. (Ghent 1858–68), according to the standard edition of Groenendael ed. by the Ruusbroec-Gesellschaft at Antwerp, 4 vols. (Cologne, 2d ed. 1950), Latin ed. L. Surius (Cologne 1552), French translation ed. by the Benedictines of St-Paul des Wisques, 6 vols. (Brussels 1912–38); German translation, *Zierde der geistlichen Hochzeit* by F. A. Lambert (Leipzig 1901), W. Verkade (Mainz 1922), F. Hübner (Leipzig 1924); J. Kuckhoff, *J. van Ruysbroeck. Einführung in sein Leben. Auswahl aus seinen Werken* (Munich 1938). Literature: *Jan van Ruusbroec, Leven, werken,* ed. by the Ruusbroec-Genootschaft (Malines 1931), with bibliography; A. Auger, *Étude sur les mystiques des Pays-Bas au moyen-âge* (Brussels 1892); A. Wautier d'Aygalliers, *Ruysbroeck l'Admirable* (Paris 1923); L. Reypens, *Ruusbroec* (Brussels 1926); *idem,*

"Ruusbroec-studien," *OGE*, 12 (1938), 158–86, 392–411; M. d'Asbeck, *La mystique de Ruysbroeck l'Admirable* (Paris 1930); G. Dolezich, *Die Mystik Johannes van Ruysbroecks des Wunderbaren* (Habelschwerdt 1926); M. J. Smits van Waesberghe, *Katholieke Nederlandse Mystiek* (Amsterdam 1947); A. Ampe, *Kernproblemen uit de leer van Ruusbroec*, 3 vols. (Tielt 1950–57); P. Henry, "La mystique trinitaire du bienheureux J. Ruysbroeck," *RSR*, 40 (1952), 335–68, 51 (1953), 51–75; A. Combes, *Essai sur la critique de Ruysbroeck par Gerson*, 3 vols. (Paris 1945–59); S. Axters, *Geschiedenis van de vroomheid in de Nederlanden*, II: *De eeuw van Ruusbroec* (Antwerp 1953); F. Hermans, *Ruysbroeck l'Admirable et son école* (Paris 1958); B. Fraling, *Der Mensch vor dem Geheimnis Gottes* (Würzburg 1967); L. Moereels, *Ruusbroec en het rel. Leven* (Tielt and The Hague 1962).

Sisters' Lives: F. Vetter (ed.), *Das Leben der Schwestern zu Töss* (Berlin 1906); C. Schröder (ed.), *Der Nonne von Engelthal Büchlein von der Gnadenüberlast* (Tübingen 1871), German translation by W. Oehl (Paderborn 1924); M. Weinhandl (ed.), *Deutsches Nonnenleben. Das Leben der Schwestern zu Töss und der Nonne von Engelthal Büchlein von der Gnaden Überlast* (Munich 1921); W. Blank, *Die Nonnenviten des 14. Jahrhunderts* (Freiburg 1962).

John Gerson: Texts: *Opera omnia*, ed. L. E. Du Pin, 5 vols. (Antwerp 1706); *Œuvres complètes*, ed. P. Glorieux (Paris 1960 ff.); *Initiation à la vie mystique*, ed. P. Pascal (Paris 1945); *De mystica theologia*, ed. A. Combes (Lugano 1958). Literature: J. L. Connolly, *John Gerson, Reformer and Mystic* (Louvain 1928); J. Stelzenberger, *Die Mystik des Johannes Gerson* (Breslau 1928); W. Dress, *Die Theologie Johannes Gersons* (Gütersloh 1931); C. J. Corcoran, *John Gerson, Champion of Parish Priests* (Washington, D. C., 1944); P. Glorieux, "La vie et les œuvres de Gerson," *AHD*, 18 (1950 f.), 149–92; A. Combes, *La théologie mystique de Gerson*, 2 vols. (Rome 1963 f.); further literature in the bibliography for Chapter 41.

Rulman Merswin: Texts: F. Lauchert (ed.), *Des Gottesfreundes im Oberland Buch von den zwei Mannen* (Bonn 1896); P. H. Strauch (ed.), "Schriften aus der Gottesfreund-Literatur," *Altdeutsche Textbibliothek*, nos. 22, 23 (Halle 1927), no. 27 (Halle 1929). Literature: H. Denifle in *ZdAdL*, 24 (1880), 200–19, 280–324, 463 ff., 25 (1881), 101 ff.; *RE*, XVII, 203–27; K. Rieder, *Der Gottesfreund vom Oberland* (Innsbruck 1905); A. Chiquot, *Histoire ou légende* (Strasbourg and Paris 1922); W. Oehl, *Deutsche Mystikerbriefe* (Munich 1931), 397–424; E. Dehnhardt, *Die Metaphorik der Mystiker Meister Eckhart und Tauler in den Schriften des Rulman Merswin* (dissertation, Marburg 1940); *Stammler-Langosch*, III, 355–68, V, 682, with bibliography.

Theologia Deutsch: Editions: *Theologia Deutsch*, ed. H. Mandel (Leipzig 1908); F. Pfeiffer (Gütersloh, 5th ed. 1923); *Der Franckforter*, ed. Willo Uhl (Bonn 1912) from manuscript of 1497; G. Siedel (Gotha 1929), Luther's imprint of 1518. German translations: J. Bernhart (Munich 1946), and others; G. Baring, *Bibliographie der Ausgaben der Theologia Deutsch* (Baden-Baden 1963). Literature: F. G. Lisco, *Die Heilslehre der Theologia Deutsch* (Stuttgart 1857); J. Paquiers, *Un mystique allemand du XIVe siècle* (Paris 1922); K. Müller, "Zum Text der Deutschen Theologie," *ZKG*, 49 (1930), 306–35; E. Schröder, "Die Überlieferung des 'Franckforters,'" *NGG*, new series, II, 2 (1937), 49–65; *RE*, XIX, 626–31, XXIV, 561–63; R. Haubst in *Scholastik*, 33 (1958), 375–98.

45. Missionary Work of the Mendicants outside Europe

Sources

In addition to the papal *registra* and the *bullaria* of the orders, G. Golubovich, *Biblioteca Bio-Bibliografica della Terra Santa e dell'Ordine Francescano* (Quaracchi 1906–27) and the related *Documenti* (Quaracchi since 1921); A. van den Wyngaert, *Sinica Franciscana*, I (Quaracchi 1929).

BIBLIOGRAPHY

Bibliotheca Missionum, ed. R. Streit and J. Dindinger, IV: *Asiatische Missionsliteratur 1245–1599* (Aachen 1928), XV: *Afrikanische Missionsliteratur 1053–1599* (Freiburg 1951); J. Beckmann, "Neuerscheinungen zur chinesischen Missionsgeschichte 1945–1955," *Monumenta Serica*, 15 (Tokyo 1956), 378–462.

LITERATURE

In addition to the handbooks on mission history by J. Schmidlin, *Catholic Mission History*, K. S. Latourette, *A History of the Expansion of Christianity*, II, S. Delacroix, *Histoire universelle des missions catholiques*, I, A. Mulders, *Missionsgeschichte*, and others, see also: L. Lemmens, *Die Heidenmissionen des Spätmittelalters* (Münster 1919); B. Altaner, *Die Dominikanermissionen des 13. Jahrhunderts* (Habelschwerdt 1924); K. S. Latourette, *A History of Christian Missions in China* (New York 1929); G. Soranzo, *Il Papato, l'Europa cristiana e i Tartari* (Milan 1930); O. van der Vat, *Die Anfänge der Franziskanermissionen im nahen Orient und in den mohammedanischen Ländern während des 13. Jahrhunderts* (Werl 1934); N. Simonut, *Il metodo d'evangelizzazione dei Francescani tra Musulmani e Mongoli nei secoli XIII–XIV* (Milan 1947); M. Roncaglia, *I Francescani in Oriente durante le Crociate* (Cairo 1954).

SECTION TWO

The Western Schism and the Councils

46. The Western Schism to the Council of Pisa

SOURCES

Mansi, XXVI–XXVII; *RepGerm*, I: *Clemens VII. von Avignon (1378–1394)*, ed. E. Göller (Berlin 1916), II: *Urban VI., Bonifaz IX., Innocenz VII. und Gregor XII. (1378–1415)*, ed. G. Tellenbach (Berlin 1933–62), III: *Alexander V., Johann XXIIII., Konstanzer Konzil (1409–17)*, ed. U. Kühne (Berlin 1935); *Analecta Vaticano-Belgica*, VIII (Brussels and Rome 1924), XII (1930), XIII (1932); *Monumenta Vaticana res gestas Bohemiae illustrantia*, V (1903–05); *Deutsche Reichstagsakten*, older series, I–VI (reprinted 1956); Dietrich of Niem, *De schismate libri tres*, ed. G. Erler (Leipzig 1890); F. Ehrle, "Neue Materialien zur Geschichte Peters von Luna (Benedikt XIII.)," *ALKGMA*, 6 (1892), 7 (1900); *Baluze-Mollat*, I–IV; F. Ehrle, *Martin de Alpartils chronica actitatorum temporibus domini Benedicti XIII.* (Paderborn 1906); J. Vincke, *Briefe zum Pisaner Konzil* (Bonn 1940); idem, "Acta concilii Pisani," *RQ*, 46 (1941), 81–331; idem, *Schriftstücke zum Pisaner Konzil* (Bonn 1942).

LITERATURE

Fliche-Martin, 14, 1–2 (Paris 1962–64), with copious bibliography; L. Gayet, *Le grand schisme d'occident. Les origines*, 2 vols. (Florence and Berlin 1889); L. Salembier, *Le grand schisme d'occident* (Paris, 5th ed. 1922); N. Valois, *La France et le grand schisme d'occident*, 4 vols. (Paris 1896–1902); M. Seidlmayer, *Die Anfänge des grossen abendländischen Schismas* (Münster 1940); W. Ullmann, *The Origins of the Great Schism* (London 1948); E. F. Jacob, *Essays in the Conciliar Epoch* (Manchester, 3d ed. 1963); O. Přerovský,

"L'elezione di Urbano VI e l'insorgere dello scisma d'occidente," *Miscellanea della società Romana di storia patria*, XX (Rome 1960); H. Angermeier, "Das Reich und der Konziliarismus," *HZ*, 192 (1961), 529–83; P. Brezzi, "Lo scisma d'occidente come problema italiano," *ADRomana*, 67 (1944), 391–450; A. Cutolo, *Re Ladislao d'Angiò-Durazzo*, 2 vols. (Milan 1936); M. de Boüard, *La France et l'Italie au temps du grand schisme d'occident* (Paris 1936); E. Perroy, *L'Angleterre et le grand schisme d'occident. Étude sur la politique religieuse de l'Angleterre sous Richard II, 1378–1399* (Paris 1933); W. Ullmann, "The University of Cambridge and the Great Schism," *JThS*, new series, 9 (1958), 53–77; A. M. Rodríguez, "Benedicto XIII y el reino de Aragón," *Hispania*, 19 (1959), 163–91; L. Suárez Fernández, *Castilla, el cisma y la crisis conciliar 1378–1440* (Madrid 1960); A. Boscolo, *La politica italiana di Martino il vecchio re d'Aragona* (Padua 1962); S. Puig y Puig, *Pedro de Luna último papa de Aviñón* (Barcelona 1920); G. Pillement, *Pedro de Luna, le dernier pape d'Avignon* (Paris 1955); A. Glasfurd, *The Antipope (Peter de Luna, 1342–1423). A Study in Obstinacy* (London 1965); G. J. Jordan, *The Inner History of the Great Schism of the West. A Problem in Church Unity* (London 1930); K. A. Fink, "Zur Beurteilung des grossen abendländischen Schismas," *ZKG*, 73 (1962), 335–43; R. G. Trexler, "Rome on the Eve of the Great Schism," *Speculum*, 42 (1967), 489–509; J. Favier, *Les finances pontificales à l'époque du grand schisme d'occident* (Paris 1966).

The Council of Pisa: Hefele-Leclercq, VI; F. Stuhr, *Organisation und Geschäftsordnung des Pisaner und Konstanzer Konzils* (Schwerin 1891); L. Schmitz, "Zur Geschichte des Konzils von Pisa," *RQ*, 9 (1895), 351–75; L. Dax, *Die Universitäten und die Konzilien von Pisa und Konstanz* (dissertation, Freiburg 1910); A. Brüggen, *Die Predigten des Pisaner Konzils* (typed dissertation, Freiburg 1963).

The Conciliar Idea: F. Bliemetzrieder, *Das Generalkonzil im grossen abendländischen Schisma* (Paderborn 1904); R. Scholz, "Eine Geschichte und Kritik der Kirchenverfassung vom Jahre 1406," *Papsttum und Kaisertum, Festschrift P. Kehr* (Berlin 1926), 595–621; J. Klotzner, *Kardinal Dominikus Jacobazzi und sein Konzilswerk, AnGr*, 45 (1948); F. Merzbacher, "Wandlungen des Kirchenbegriffs im Spätmittelalter. Grundzüge der Ekklesiologie des ausgehenden 13., des 14. und 15. Jahrhunderts," *ZSavRGkan*, 39 (1953), 274–361; B. Tierney, *Foundations of the Conciliar Theory* (Cambridge 1955); L. Buisson, *Potestas und Caritas* (Cologne and Graz 1958); J. M. Moynihan, *Papal Immunity and Liability in the Writings of the Medieval Canonists, AnGr*, 120 (1961); A. Marongiu, "Il principio della democrazia e del consenso (quod omnes tangit, ab omnibus approbari debet) nel XIV secolo," *StG*, 8 (1962), 553–75; M. J. Wilks, *The Problem of Sovereignty in the Later Middle Ages* (Cambridge 1963); H. Jedin, *Bischöfliches Konzil oder Kirchenparlament* (Basel 1963); K. W. Nörr, *Kirche und Konzil bei Nicolaus de Tudeschis, Panormitanus* (Cologne and Graz 1964); U. Horst, "Papst, Bischöfe und Konzil nach Antonin von Florenz," *RThAM*, 32 (1965), 76–116; K. A. Fink, "Die konziliare Idee im späten Mittelalter," *Vorträge und Forschungen*, 9 (1965), 119–34; F. Merzbacher, "Die ekklesiologische Konzeption des Kardinals Francesco Zabarella," *Innsbrucker Beiträge zur Kulturwissenschaft*, 12 (1966), 279–87; J. Lecler, "La crise conciliaire du XVᵉ siècle," *RSR*, 55 (1967), 76–87.

47. *The Devotio Moderna*

Literature

J. M. Dols, *Bibliographie der Moderne Devotie* (Nijmegen 1941); W. Nijhoff and M. E. Kronenberg, *Nederlandsche Bibliogr. von 1500–1540*, 3 vols. ('s-Gravenhage 1923–54); W. Jappe Alberts, "Zur Historiographie der Devotio moderna und ihre Erforschung," *Westfälische Forschungen*, 11 (1958), 51–67; G. Dumbar, *Analecta seu vetera aliquot scripta,* I (Deventer 1719); J. Acquoy, *Het klooster te Windesheim en zijn invloed,* 3 vols. (Utrecht 1875–80); K. Grube (ed.), *Des Augustinerpropstes Johannes Busch Chronicon Windeshemense und Liber de reformatione monasteriorum* (Halle 1886); P. Mestwerdt, *Die Anfänge des Erasmus. Humanismus und Devotio moderna* (Leipzig 1917); A. Hyma, *The Christian Renaissance, A history of the Devotio Moderna* (Grand Rapids, Mich. 1924), partially revised in *The Brethren of the Common Life (ibid.* 1950) and *Renaissance to Reformation (ibid.* 1951); on the preceding *cf.* J. De Jong, "Het karakter en de invloed van de 'moderne devotie,'" *Historisch Tijdschrift,* 4 (1925), 26–58; R. Stadelmann, *Vom Geist des ausgehenden Mittelalters* (Halle 1929); P. Debognie in *DSAM,* III, 727–47; R. Post, *De moderne Devotie* (Amsterdam, 2d ed. 1950); *idem, Kerkgeschiedenis van Nederland in de middeleeuwen,* 2 vols. (Utrecht and Antwerp 1957); S. Axters, *Geschiedenis van de vroomheid in de Nederlanden,* III: *De moderne Devotie 1380–1550* (Antwerp 1956). *Gerard Groote:* Sources: *Gerardi magni epistolae,* ed. W. Mulder (Antwerp 1933); *Tractatus de quatuor generibus meditationum,* ed. A. Hyma, *AGAU,* 49 (1924), 296–326; M. H. Mulders, *Geert Groote en het huvelijk* (ed. of *De Matrimonio*) (Nijmegen 1941); *Incipiunt aliqua verba notabilia Domini Florencii et Magistri Gherardi Magni,* ed. F. van Vree and J. Vregt, *AGAU,* 10 (1882), 427–72; Petrus Horn, *Vita Magistri Gerardi Magni,* ed. W. J. Kühler, *NAKG,* 6 (1909), 332–70; Rudolf Dier van Muiden, *Scriptum de magistro Gherardo Grote, Domino Florencio et multis aliis devotis fratribus,* ed. G. Dumbar, *Analecta,* I (Deventer 1719), 1–87; Thomas a Kempis, *Vita Gerardi Magni, Opera omnia,* ed. J. Pohl, VII (Freiburg 1927), 31–115; Gerrit Grote, *Die Nachfolge Christi,* ed. and trans. by F. Kern (Olten 1947). Literature: L. Smit, "Geert Groote over de Kerk," *StC,* 10 (1934), 257–68, 367–77; K. de Beer, *Studie over de spiritualiteit van Geert Groote* (Brussels and Nijmegen 1938); J. Tiecke, *De Werken van Geert Groote* (Utrecht and Nijmegen 1941); J. van Ginneken, *Geert Groote's Levensbeeld naar de oudste gegevens bewerkt* (Amsterdam 1942); T. P. van Zyl, *Gerard Groote, Ascetic and Reformer* (Washington 1963). *The Brothers of the Common Life:* J. Gerretsen, *Florentius Radewijns* (Nijmegen 1891); M. v. Woerkum, "Florentius Radewijns. Schets van zijn leven, geschriften persoonlijkheid en ideeën," *OGE,* 24 (1950), 337–64; C. van der Wansem, *Het ontstaan ende geschiedenis der Broederschap van het Gemene Leven tot 1400* (Louvain 1958).

The Windesheim Congregation: V. Becker, "Eene onbekende kronijk van het klooster te Windesheim," *Bijdragen en Mededeeligen van Historisch Genootschap,* 10 (1887), 376–445; W. J. Kühler, *Joh. Brinckerinck en zijn klooster te Diepenveen* (Rotterdam 1908); L. Schmitz-Kallenberg, "Die Windesheimer Kongregation," *HJ,* 36 (1915), 306–16, 598–608; E. de Schaepdrijver, "De congregatie van Windesheim gedurende de 16. eeuw," *Bijdragen tot de Geschiedenis,* 14 (1924), 15 (1924), 16 (1925); P. Hofmeister, "Die Verfassung der Windesheimer Augustinerkongregation," *ZSavRGkan,* 30 (1941), 165–270; K. Löffler, *Quellen zur Geschichte des Augustiner-Chorherrenstiftes Frenswegen* (Soest 1930); J. A. Bemolt van Longhum Slaterus, *Het klooster Frenswegen* (Arnheim 1938); W. J. Alberts and A. L. Hulshoff, *Het Frensweger Handschrift* (Leiden 1958); S. van der Woude, *Joh. Busch Windesheimer kloosterreformator en kroniekschrijver* (Edam 1947); *idem, Acta Capituli Windeshemensis* ('s-Gravenhage 1953); W. Lourdaux and E. Persoons, "De Statuten van de Windesheimse mannenkloosters," *Archief voor de geschiedenis van de Kath. Kerk in Nederland,* 6 (Utrecht 1964), 180–224; *LThK,* X (2d ed. 1965), 1177 f.

The Brothers of the Common Life in Germany: Sources: "Urkunden der Brüder vom gemeinsamen Leben zu St. Michael in Rostock," *Jahrbuch des Vereins für Mecklenburgische Geschichte und Altertumskunde,* 4 (Schwerin 1839), 211–81; H. A. Erhard, *Gedächtnisbuch des Fraterhauses in Münster,*" *Zeitschrift für vaterländische Geschichte und Altertumskunde,* 6 (1843), 89–126; F. J. Mone, "Jahresgeschichten der Stiftskirche zu Wolf," *ZGObrh,* 18 (1865), 74–83; J. Petry, "Die Hausordnung der Fraterherren ... zu Emmerich," *Programm des Progymnasiums zu Steele* (1899); *idem,* "Die Satzungen des St. Gre-

724

goriushauses zu Emmerich," *AHVNrh*, 93 (1912), 103–22; H. Doebner, *Annalen und Akten der Brüder vom gemeinsamen Leben im Lüchtenhof zu Hildesheim, Quellen und Darstellungen zur Geschichte Niedersachsens*, IV (Hanover 1903); H. A. Grimm, *Die Annalen des Klosters Wolf, 1478–1503, Trierer Chronik*, 12 (1916), 10–17; K. Löffler, "Das Gedächtnisbuch des Kölner Fraterhauses Weidenbach," *AHVNrh*, 103 (1919), 1–47; *idem*, *Quellen zur Geschichte des Augustinerchorherrenstiftes Frenswegen* (Soest 1930); F. W. Oediger (ed.), *Schriften des Arnold Heymerik* (Bonn 1939). Literature: L. Schulze, "Heinrich von Ahaus, der Stifter der Brüder vom gemeinsamen Leben in Deutschland," *Zeitschrift für kirchliche Wissenschaft und kirchliches Leben*, 3 (Leipzig 1882), 38–48; O. Gerland, "Beiträge zur Geschichte der Brüder vom gemeinsamen Leben in Hessen," *Hessenland*, 18 (1904), 218–21, 232–35, 249–51, 265 ff.; G. Boerner, *Die Annalen und Akten der Brüder vom gemeinsamen Leben im Lüchtenhofe zu Hildesheim* (Berlin and Fürstenwalde 1905); K. Löffler, "Heinrich von Ahaus und die Brüder vom gemeinsamen Leben," *HJ*, 30 (1909), 762–98, and, in connection with it, *cf. Zeitschrift für vaterländische Geschichte und Altertumskunde Westfalens*, 74 (1916), 229–40; *idem*, "Das Fraterhaus Weidenbach in Köln," *AHVNrh*, 102 (1918), 99–128, and *cf. AHVNrh*, 104 (1920), 174–77; O. Meyer, "Die Brüder vom gemeinsamen Leben in Württemberg," *Blätter für württembergische Kirchengeschichte*, 17 (1913), 97–138, 18 (1914), 142–60; J. H. Richter, *Geschichte des Augustinerklosters Frenswegen in der Grafschaft Bentheim* (Hildesheim 1913); E. Barnikol, *Studien zur Geschichte der Brüder vom gemeinsamen Leben* (Tübingen 1917); H. Gleumes, "Das Wirken der Fraterherren in Emmerich," *AHVNrh*, 124 (1934), 143–46; H. Draht, *St. Martini Wesel* (Gladbeck 1936); W. Brüggeboes, *Die Fraterherren (Brüder vom gemeinsamen Leben) im Lüchtenhofe zu Hildesheim* (dissertation, Münster 1939); H. Nottarp, "Die Brüder vom gemeinsamen Leben," *ZSavRGkan*, 32 (1943), 384–418; H. Stiesberg, *Die Wirksamkeit der Fraterherren in Emmerich* (typed, 1950); B. Windeck, *Die Anfänge der Brüder vom gemeinsamen Leben* (typed dissertation, Bonn 1951); W. M. Landeen, "The Beginnings of the Devotio Moderna in Germany," *Research Studies of the State College of Washington*, 19 (1951), 162–202, 221–53, 21 (1953), 275–309, 22 (1954), 53–75; *idem*, "Gabriel Biel and the Devotio Moderna in Germany," *ibid.*, 27 (1959), 135–213, 28 (1960), 21–45, 61–95; F. J. Heyen, "Die Brüder vom gemeinsamen Leben in St. German," *Neues Trierisches Jahrbuch*, 1 (1962), 16–27.

Literature and Spirituality: J. F. Vregt, "Eenige ascetische tractaten, afkomstig van de Deventersche Broederschap van het Gemene Leven," *AGAU*, 10 (1882), 321–498; G. G. Wilbrink, *Das geistliche Lied der Devotio moderna* (Nijmegen 1930); J. J. Mak, "Christus bij de Moderne Devoten," *OGE*, 9 (1935), 106–66; M. Goossens, *De Meditatie in de eerste tijd van de Moderne Devotie* (Haarlem and Antwerp 1954); F. van d. Borne, "Geert Groote en de Moderne Devotie in de geschiedenis van het middeleeuwse ordewezen," *StC*, 16 (1940), 397–414, 17 (1941), 120–33, 197–209, 18 (1942), 19–40, 203–24; H. Watrigant, "La méditation méthodique et l'École des Frères de la vie commune," *RAM*, 3 (1922), 134–55.

Sources of Spirituality; M. Viller, "Le speculum monachorum et la Devotio moderna," *RAM*, 3 (1922), 45–56; C. Smits, "David van Augsburg en de invloed van zijn Profectus op de Moderne Devotie," *Coll. franciscana neerlandica* (1927), 171–203; H. Gleumes, "G. Groot und die Windesheimer als Verehrer des heiligen Bernhard von Clairvaux," *ZAM*, 10 (1935), 90–112; E. Mikkers, "Sint Bernardus en de Moderne Devotie," *Cîteaux en de Nederlanden*, 10 (Westmalle 1953), 149–86; M. A. Lücker, *Meister Eckhard und die Devotio Moderna* (Leiden 1950), and, in this regard, L. Reypens in *OGE*, 25 (1951), 215; D. de Man, "Heinrich Suso en de Moderne Devotie," *NAKG*, 19 (1926), 279–83; P. Debongnie, "Henri Suso et l'Imitation de Jésus-Christ," *RAM*, 21 (1940), 242–68.

Florens Radewijns: "Het libellus 'Omnes, inquit, artes' een rapiarium van Florentius Radewijns," *OGE*, 25 (1951), 113–58, 225–68; *Het libellus "Multum valet,"* ed. J. F. Vregt, *AGAU*, 10 (1882), 383–427.

Gerard Zerbolt van Zutphen: De spiritualibus ascensionibus, ed. J. Mathieu (Bruges 1941); J. van Rooij, *Gerard Zerbolt van Zutphen. Leven en Geschriften* (Nijmegen and Utrecht 1936); A. Hyma, "Is Gerard Zerbolt of Zutphen the Author of the 'Super modo vivendi'?" *NAKG*, 16 (1921), 107–28; *idem* (ed.), *Super modo vivendi devotorum hominum simul commorantium, AGAU*, 52 (1926), 1–100.

Dirc van Herxen: De libris teutonicalibus, ed. A. Hyma, *NAKG*, 17 (1924), 42–70; P. H. J. Knierim, *Dirc van Herxen (1381–1457) rector van het Zwolse fraterhuis* (Amsterdam 1926).

Hendrik Mande: G. Visser, *Hendrik Mande, Bijdrage tot de kennis de Noord-Nederlandse mystiek* ('s-Gravenhage 1899); A. Combes, "Essai sur la critique de Ruysbroeck par Gerson," *Études de théologie et d'histoire de la spiritualité*, 3 vols. (Paris 1945–59).

Gerlach Peters: Soliloquium, ed. J. Strange (Cologne, Bonn, and Brussels 1849); W. Moll, "Gerlach Peters en zijne schriften," *Kerkhistorisch Archief*, 2 (1859), 174–99; E. Assemaine, "Gerlach Peters," *VS*, 5 (1921), 117–23; *idem* (trans. and introduction), *Gerlach Peters, Le soliloque enflammé* (Juvisy 1936); J. J. Mak, *De Dietse vertaling van Gerlach Peters' Soliloquium* (Rotterdam 1936); M. van Rijn, *Wessel Gansfort* (The Hague 1917); *idem, Studien over Wessel Gansfort en zijn tijd* (Utrecht 1933).

John Mombaer: Exercitia utilissima pro horis solvendis et pro devota communione sacramentali cum considerationibus variis de vita et passione domini et sacramento eucharistiae (Zwolle 1491); *Rosetum exercitiorum spiritualium et sacrarum meditationum* (Basel 1504); H. Watrigant, "La méditation méthodique et Jean Mauburnus," *RAM*, 4 (1923), 13–29; P. Debongnie, *Jean Mombaer de Bruxelles, ses écrits et ses réformes* (Louvain and Toulouse 1927); J. Donndorf, *Das Rosetum des Johannes Mauburnus* (dissertation, Halle 1929).

John Veghe: Lectulus noster floridus. Unser Blumenbettchen, ed. H. Rademacher (Hiltrup 1938); *Wyngarden der sele*, ed. H. Rademacher (Hiltrup 1940); F. Jostes, *Johannes Veghe. Ein deutscher Prediger des 15. Jahrhunderts* (Halle 1883); *idem*, "Drei unbekannte deutsche Schriften von Johannes Veghe," *HJ*, 6 (1885), 345–412; H. Triloff, *Die Traktate und Predigten Veghes* (Halle 1904); A. Bömer, "Johannes Veghe," *Westfälische Lebensbilder*, I (Münster 1930), 166–82; H. Rademacher, *Mystik und Humanismus der Devotio moderna in den Predigten und Traktaten des Johannes Veghe* (Hiltrup 1935); H. Kunisch, "Johannes Veghe und die oberdeutsche Mystik des 14. Jahrhunderts," *Zeitschrift für deutsches Altertum*, 75 (1938), 141–71.

Imitatio Christi: Thomas a Kempis, *Omnia opera*, ed. J. Pohl, I–VII (Freiburg 1902–22); French translation by L. Baudry (Paris 1950) gives the literature and a survey of the history of the question of authorship; L. M. J. Delaissé, *Le manuscrit autographe de Thomas a Kempis et "L'Imitation de Jésus-Christ,"* 2 vols. (Brussels 1956); P. E. Puyol, *Descriptions des manuscrits et des principales éditions du livre De Imitatione Christi* (Paris 1898); *idem, L'auteur du livre De Imitatione Christi*, 2 vols. (Paris 1899 f.); R. Storr, *Concordantia ad IV libros a Thoma Kempensi* (London, 2d ed. 1911).

Question of authorship: C. Wolfsgruber, *Giovanni Gersen, sein Leben und sein Werk de Imitatione Christi* (Augsburg 1880); R. Pitigliani, *L'Abbate Giovanni Gersenio autore dell'Imitazione di Cristo* (Turin 1937); *idem, Le fonti dell'Imitazione di Cristo, SC*, 65 (1937); T. Lupo, "Validità della tesi gerseniana sull'autore della 'Imitazione di Cristo'," *Salesianum*, 12 (Turin 1960), 56–106; P. Bonardi and T. Lupo, *L'Imitazione di Cristo e il suo autore*, 2 vols. (Turin 1964); H. Denifle in *ZKTh*, 6 (1882), 692–718, 7 (1883), 692–743. J. B. Monnoyeur, *Gerson, l'auteur de l'Imitation de Jésus-Christ* (Paris 1936). J. Huijben and P. Debongnie, *L'auteur ou les auteurs de l'Imitation* (Louvain 1957); C. C. de Bruin, *De middelnederlandse vertaling van de Imitatio Christi in hs. Leiden ... 339* (Leiden 1954), synopsis in German in *Altdeutsche und Altniederländische Mystik*, ed. K. Ruh (Darmstadt 1964), 462–96. P. Hagen, *Zwei Urschriften der Imitatio Christi in mittelniederdeutschen Übersetzungen* (Berlin 1930); *idem, De Imitatione Christi libri qui dicitur tractatus secun-*

dus et tertius recognovit et ad auctorem anonymum atque Thomam Kempensem reduxit (The Hague 1935); *idem, Untersuchungen über Buch II und III der Imitatio Christi, Verhandlelingen d. k. Ak. v. Wet. Afd. Letterk.*, 34 (Amsterdam 1935); J. van Ginneken, *Trois textes pré-kempistes du premier livre de l'Imitation, ibid.*, 44 (Amsterdam 1940); *idem, Trois textes pré-kempistes du second livre de l'Imitation, ibid.*, 46 (Amsterdam 1941); *idem, De Navolging van Christus* (Amsterdam, 2d ed. 1947); L. Kern, "Zur Verfasserfrage der Imitatio Christi," *OGE*, 28 (1954), 27–44, 151–71; A. Hyma, "The Original Version of de Imitatione Christi by Gerard Zerbolt of Zutphen," *AGAU*, 69 (1950), 1–41; J. Huby, "Les origines de l'Imitation de Jésus-Christ de G. Groote à T. a Kempis," *RSR*, 31 (1943), 102–39, 32 (1944), 211–44; J. Tesser, "De eerste en de laatste faze van het auteursproblem der Navolging in Italië," *OGE*, 23 (1949); M. Lücker in *GuL*, 22 (1949), 228–32; B. Spaapen in *GuL*, 31 (1958), 303–08; *idem* in *OGE*, 23 (1949); L. Fernández, "El autor de 'La Imitación de Christo,'" *Manresa*, 32 (1960), 33–44.

Content: P. E. Puyol, *La doctrine du livre De Imitatione Christi* (Paris, 2d ed. 1898); G. Clamens, *La dévotion à l'humanité du Christ dans la spiritualité de Thomas a Kempis* (Lyons 1931); P. Debongnie, "Les thèmes de l'Imitation de Jésus-Christ," *RHE*, 36 (1940), 289–344; E. Iserloh, "Die Kirchenfrömmigkeit in der Imitatio Christi," *Sentire Ecclesiam* (Freiburg 1961), 251–67; *idem*, "Die Nachfolge Christi," *Bücher der Entscheidung*, ed. W. Sandfuchs (Würzburg 1964), 55–66.

Influence: H. Watrigant, *La méditation fondamentale avant saint Ignace* (Enghin 1907); P. Groult, *Les Mystiques des Pays-Bas et la littérature espagnole du seizième siècle* (Louvain 1927); H. Gleumes, "Niederländische und spanische Mystik im 16. Jahrhundert," *ZAM*, 11 (1936), 323–28; J. Hashagen, "Die Devotio moderna in ihrer Einwirkung auf Humanismus, Reformation und Gegenreformation," *ZKG*, 55 (1936), 523–31; A. Suquia Goicoechea, "El Epistolario de Gerardo de Groote y el Libro de Ejercicios de San Ignacio de Loyola," *Manresa*, 21 (1949), 305–24; *idem, La santa Misa en la espiritualidad de San Ignacio de Loyola* (Madrid 1950).

48. *The Nationalist Heresies: Wyclif and Hus*

Wyclif

SOURCES

John Wyclif, The Latin Works, 35 vols. (London 1883–1922, reprinted Frankfurt 1964); Thomas Netter of Walden, *Fasciculi zizaniorum magistri Ioannis Wyclif cum tritico*, ed. W. Waddington Shirley (London 1858); F. Palacký, *Documenta Magistri Ioannis Hus vitam, doctrinam, causam in Constantiensi concilio actam et controversias de religione in Bohemia annis 1403–1418 motas illustrantia* (Prague 1869, reprinted Osnabrück 1966).

LITERATURE

Fliche-Martin, 14, 2, 943–88; *LThK*, X (2d ed. 1965), 1278–81; *Hefele-Leclercq*, VII; H. Grundmann, "Ketzergeschichte des Mittelalters," *Die Kirche in ihrer Geschichte*, 2, series G, 1 (Göttingen 1963), G 60–G 62; M. McKisack, *The Fourteenth Century 1307–1399*, 510–24, 554; A. Molnár, "Recent Literature on Wyclif's Theology," *Communio viatorum*, 7 (1964), 186–92; B. A. Vermaseren, "Niewe studies over Wyclif en Hus," *Tijdschrift voor Geschiedenis*, 76 (1963), 190–212; H. B. Workmann, *John Wyclif*, 2 vols. (Oxford 1926); J. H. Dahmus, *The Prosecution of John Wyclyf* (New Haven 1952); J. A. Robson, *Wyclif and the Oxford Schools* (Cambridge 1961); L. J. Daly, *The Political Theory of John Wyclif* (Chicago 1962); P. de Vooght, "Wiclif et la 'Scriptura sola,'" *EThL*, 39 (1963),

50–86; G. A. Benrath, *Wyclifs Bibelkommentar* (Berlin 1966); *idem*, "Wyclif und Hus," *ZThK*, 62, 196–216; A. Zumkeller, "Die Augustinereremiten in der Auseinandersetzung mit Wyclif und Hus, ihre Beteiligung an den Konzilien von Konstanz und Basel," *AAug*, 28 (1965), 5–56; G. Wendelborn, *Das Verhältnis von Schrift und Vernunft im Werk John Wiclifs* (typed dissertation, Rostock 1964); F. de Boor, *Die neue Definition der Simonie bei John Wyclif* (typed dissertation, Halle 1964); M. Wilks, "Predestination, Property and Power. Wyclif's Theory of Dominion and Grace," *Studies in Church History*, 2 (1965), 220–36; J. Dahmus, *William Courtenay, Archbishop of Canterbury 1381–1396* (London 1966); G. A. Benrath, "Stand und Aufgaben der Wyclif-Forschung," *ThLZ*, 92 (1967), 261–64.

Hus

SOURCES

Ioannis Hus atque Hieronymi Pragensis confessorum Christi historia et monumenta, 2 vols. (Nürnberg 1588); *Magistri Ioannis Hus Opera omnia*, ed. W. Flajšhans and M. Kominková, 3 vols. (Prague 1903–07, reprinted Osnabrück 1966); *Magistri Ioannis Hus Opera omnia*, 8: *Sermones de tempore qui collecta dicuntur*, ed. A. Schmidtová (Prague 1959), 22: *Polemica*, ed. F. Graus (Prague 1966); *Magistri Ioannis Hus Tractatus de ecclesia*, ed. S. Harrison Thomson (Cambridge, Mass. 1956); F. Palacký, *Documenta Magistri Ioannis Hus vitam, doctrinam, causam . . . illustrantia (supra)*. Writings and sermons in Czech are listed under the literature *(infra)*, as are also the most important works on Hus in Czech by F. M. Bartoš, V. Novotný, V. Kybal, J. Sedlák, *et. al.*

LITERATURE

Fliche-Martin, 14, 2, 989–1029, with bibliography; *LThK*, V (2d ed. 1960), 543–45, with bibliography; H. Grundmann, "Ketzergeschichte" *(supra)*, G 62–G 65; *Hefele-Leclercq*, VII, 110–66; *Hauck*, V, 870–950; P. De Vooght, *L'hérésie de Jean Hus* (Louvain 1960); *idem, Hussiana* (Louvain 1960); *idem*, "Jean Hus au Symposium Hussianum Pragense," *Istina*, 11 (1965 f.), 41–60; D. Girgensohn, *Peter von Pulkau und die Wiedereinführung des Laienkelches* (Göttingen 1964); H. Köpstein, "Über die Teilnahme von Deutschen an der hussitischen revolutionären Bewegung—speziell in Böhmen," *Zeitschrift für Geschichtswissenschaft*, 11 (1963), 116–45; J. Kejř, "Zur Entstehungsgeschichte des Hussitentums," *Die Welt zur Zeit des Konstanzer Konzils* (Constance 1965), 47–61; A. Zumkeller, "Die Augustinereremiten in der Auseinandersetzung mit Wyclif und Hus" *(supra)*, *AAug*, 28 (1965), 5–56; F. Seibt, "Hus und die Hussiten in der tschechischen wissenschaftlichen Literatur seit 1945," *Zeitschrift für Ostforschung*, 8 (1958), 566–90; *idem, Hussitica. Zur Struktur einer Revolution* (Cologne and Graz 1965), with detailed bibliography; A. Molnár, "Gli studi su Jean Hus nel 550⁰ anniversario della morte," *Nuova Rivista storica*, 49 (1965), 696–99; Jiři Kejř, *Husitský Právnik M. Jan z Jesenice* (Prague 1965), with German summary; M. Spinka, *John Hus' Concept of the Church* (Princeton 1966); F. M. Bartoš, *Husitská revoluce. Doba Žižkova 1415–1426*, 2 vols. (Prague 1965 f.), with bibliography; I. Hlavacek, "Bohemicale Literatur in den mittelalterlichen Bibliotheken des Auslandes (nach den mittelalterlichen Bibliotheksverzeichnissen)," *Historica*, 13 (1966), 113–55; M. Kudelásek, "Bibliographie des travaux sélectionnés des historiens tchécoslovaques parus au cours des années 1963–64," *Historica*, 13 (1966), 233–71; J. Macek, "Jean Hus et son époque," *Historica*, 13 (1966), 51–80; *idem*, "Giovanni Hus e la riforma Boema," *BIStIAM*, 78 (1967), 45–73; *Handbuch der Geschichte der böhmischen Länder*, ed. K. Bosl, I (Stuttgart 1957), 494–531; R. Kalivoda, *Husitská Ideologie* (Prague 1961); *idem*, "Seibt's 'Hussitica' und die Hussitische Revolution," *Historica*, 14 (1967), 225–46; F. Šmahel, "Le mouvement des étudiants à Prague dans les années 1408–1412," *Historica*, 14 (1967), 33–75, with bibliography; H. Kaminsky, *A History of the Hussite Revolution* (Berkeley, Los Angeles 1967); E. Werner, "Der Kirchenbegriff bei Jan Hus, Jakoubek von Mies, Jan Zelivsky und den linken Taboriten," *SAB*, Klasse für Philosophie, Geschichte, Staats-, Rechts- und Wirtschaftswissenschaften (1967), no. 10.

49. *The Council of Constance. Martin V*

Sources

Acta scitu dignissima docteque concinnata Constantiensis concilii celebratissimi (Hagenau 1500); H. von der Hardt, *Magnum œcumenicum Constantiense concilium,* 6 vols. (Frankfurt and Leipzig 1696–1700), index volume (1742); J. Lenfant, *Histoire du concile de Constance,* new ed., 2 vols. (Paris 1727); H. Bourgeois du Chastenet, *Nouvelle histoire du concile de Constance* (Paris 1718); *Mansi,* XXVII–XXVIII; H. Finke, *Acta concilii Constanciensis,* 4 vols. (Münster 1896–1928); Ulrich Richental, *Das Konzil zu Konstanz. Faksimileausgabe und Kommentarband* (Constance 1964); H. Heimpel, "Aus der Kanzlei Kaiser Sigismunds," *AUF,* 12 (1932), 111–80; *idem,* "Regensburger Berichte vom Konstanzer Konzil," *Festschrift G. Hugelmann,* I (Aalen 1959), 213–72; H. Koeppen, *Die Berichte der Generalprokuratoren des Deutschen Ordens an die Kurie, 2: Peter von Wormditt (1403–19); Veröffentlichungen der Niedersächsischen Archivverwaltung,* Heft 13 (Göttingen 1960); C. M. D. Crowder, "Constance Acta in English Libraries," Franzen-Müller, *Das Konzil von Konstanz (infra),* 477–517; *idem,* "Correspondence between England and the Council of Constance 1414–1418," *Studies in Church History,* I (London 1964), 184–206; H. Finke, *Forschungen und Quellen zur Geschichte des Konstanzer Konzils* (Paderborn 1889); K. A. Fink, "Zu den Quellen für die Geschichte des Konstanzer Konzils," Franzen-Müller, *Das Konzil von Konstanz (infra),* 471–76; L. R. Loomis, *The Council of Constance* (New York 1961), contains selections from Richental's Chronicle, Fillastre's Diary and Cerretano's Journal.

Literature

Hefele-Leclercq, VII: *Fliche-Martin,* 14, 1; E. F. Jacob, "Reflections upon the Study of the General Councils in the Fifteenth Century," *Studies in Church History,* I (1964), 80–97; A. Franzen and W. Müller, *Das Konzil von Konstanz. Beiträge zu seiner Geschichte und Theologie* (Freiburg 1964), with detailed bibliography; E. Hänggi, "Zur Geschichte des Konzils von Konstanz," *ZSKG,* 60 (1966), 187–94; "Die Welt zur Zeit des Konstanzer Konzils," *Vorträge und Forschungen,* 9 (Constance 1964); K. A. Fink, "Die weltgeschichtliche Bedeutung des Konstanzer Konzils," *ZSavRGkan,* 51 (1965), 1–23; P. Glorieux, *Le concile de Constance au jour le jour* (Tournai 1964); J. Gill, *Constance et Bâle-Florence* (Paris 1965); A. Franzen, "Das Konstanzer Konzil: Probleme, Aufgaben und Stand der Konzilsforschung," *Concilium,* I (1965), 555–74 (English translation: "The Council of Constance: Present State of the Problem," *Concilium,* 7, *Historical Problems of Church Renewal* [Glen Rock, N. J. 1965], 29–68); F. Stuhr, *Die Organisation und Geschäftsordnung des Pisaner und Konstanzer Konzils* (dissertation in philosophy, Breslau 1891); H. Finke, *Bilder vom Konstanzer Konzil* (Heidelberg 1903); P. Arendt, *Die Predigten des Konstanzer Konzils. Ein Beitrag zur Predigt- und Kirchengeschichte des ausgehenden Mittelalters* (Freiburg 1933); J. B. Schneyer, "Konstanzer Konzilspredigten. Eine Ergänzung zu H. Finkes Sermones- und Handschriftenlisten," *ZGObRh,* 113 (1965), 361–88; O. Engels, "Der Reichsgedanke auf dem Konstanzer Konzil," *HJ,* 86 (1966), 80–106; Graziano di S. Teresa, "Contributi alla Libellistica dello scisma occidentale (1378–1417)," *ECarm,* 15 (1964), 387–424.

Prehistory of Constance: E. Göller, *König Sigismunds Kirchenpolitik vom Tode Bonifaz' IX. bis zur Berufung des Konstanzer Konzils 1404–1413* (Freiburg 1902); F. Schoenstedt, "König Sigismund und die Westmächte," *Die Welt als Geschichte*, 14 (1954), 149–64; A. Franzen, "Die Vorgeschichte des Konstanzer Konzils. Vom Ausbruch des Schismas bis zum Pisanum," Franzen-Müller, *Das Konzil von Konstanz*, 3–35; J. Lenzenweger, "Von Pisa nach Konstanz," *ibid.*, 36–54.

Participants: J. Riegel, *Die Teilnehmerlisten des Konstanzer Konzils* (dissertation in philosophy, Freiburg 1916); P. Lehmann, "Konstanz und Basel als Büchermärkte während der grossen Kirchenversammlungen," *Erforschung des Mittelalters*, 1 (1941), 253–80; J. Goñi Gaztambide, "Los españoles en el concilio de Constanza. Notas biográficas," *HS*, 15 (1962), 253–386, 18 (1965), 103–58, 265–332; *idem*, "Los obispos de Pamplona del siglo XV y los Navarros en los Concilios de Constanza y Basilea," *Estudios de Edad Media de la Corona de Aragón*, 7 (1962), 358–547; B. Fromme, *Die spanische Nation und das Konstanzer Konzil* (Münster 1896); L. Suárez Fernández, *Castilla, el cisma y la crisis conciliar 1378–1440* (Madrid 1960); K. Dieterle, "Die Stellung Neapels und der grossen italienischen Kommunen zum Konstanzer Konzil," *RQ*, 29 (1915), 3–21, 45–72; J. Hollerbach, "Die gregorianische Partei. Sigismund und das Konstanzer Konzil," *RQ*, 23 (1909), 129–65, 24 (1910), 3–39, 121–40; H. Keusen, "Die Stellung der Universität Köln im grossen Schisma und zu den Reformkonzilien des 15. Jahrhunderts," *AHVNrh*, 115 (1929), 225–54; D. Girgensohn, "Die Universität Wien und das Konstanzer Konzil," Franzen-Müller, *Das Konzil von Konstanz*, 252–81; T. Straub, *Herzog Ludwig der Bärtige von Bayern-Ingolstadt und seine Beziehungen zu Frankreich in der Zeit von 1391–1415*, Münchener historische Studien, Abt. Bayer. Gesch., VII (1965); J. Keppler, *Die Politik des Kardinals-Kollegiums in Konstanz vom Januar bis März 1415* (dissertation in philosophy, Münster 1899); K. Zähringer, *Das Kardinalkollegium auf dem Konstanzer Konzil bis zur Absetzung Papst Johannes' XXIII.*, Münsterische Beiträge zur Geschichtsforschung, 59 (1935); K. Gatzemeier, *Stellung und Politik der Kardinäle auf dem Konstanzer Konzil nach der Absetzung Johanns XXIII.* (dissertation in philosophy, Münster 1937); J. Rest, *Kardinal Fillastre bis zur Absetzung Johanns XXIII. auf dem Konstanzer Konzil* (dissertation in philosophy, Freiburg 1908); W. Hasenohr, *Patriarch Johannes Maurosii von Antiochien* (dissertation in philosophy, Freiburg 1909). For Cardinal d'Ailly see the bibliography for Chapter 41; also: A. Gómez Moriana, "El pensamiento eclesiológico de Pierre d'Ailly," *Anales de la cátedra Francisco Suárez* (Granada), 3 (1963), 1–43; F. Oakley, *The Political Thought of Pierre d'Ailly. The voluntarist tradition* (New Haven and London 1964); P. Glorieux, "Pierre d'Ailly, Jean XXIII et Thierry de Nieheim," *RThAM*, 31 (1964), 100–21. For Gerson see the bibliography for Chapter 41; also: G. H. M. Posthumus Meyjes, *Jean Gerson, zijn Kerkpolitiek en ecclesiologie* ('s-Gravenhage 1963); J. B. Morall, *Gerson and the Great Schism* (Manchester 1960); P. Glorieux, *Jean Gerson. Œuvres complètes*, I: *Introduction générale* (1960), thus far 6 vols.

Causa unionis: A. Lenné, *Der erste literarische Kampf auf dem Konstanzer Konzil im November und Dezember 1414* (dissertation in philosophy, Freiburg 1913); J. Katterbach, *Der zweite literarische Kampf auf dem Konstanzer Konzil im Januar und Februar 1415* (dissertation in philosophy, Freiburg 1919); H. G. Peter, *Die Informationen Papst Johanns XXIII. und dessen Flucht von Konstanz bis Schaffhausen* (Freiburg 1926); J. A. Rubio, *La política de Benedicto XIII desde la substracción de Aragón a su obediencia hasta su destitución en el concilio de Constanza* (Zamora 1926); K. A. Fink, "Die Wahl Martins V.," Franzen-Müller, *Das Konzil von Konstanz*, 138–51; J. Goñi Gaztambide, "Recompensas de Martín V a sus electores españoles," *Hispania sacra*, 11 (1958), 259–97; H. Zimmermann, "Die Absetzung der Päpste auf dem Konstanzer Konzil," Franzen-Müller, *Das Konzil von Konstanz*, 113–37.

Causa fidei: D. Girgensohn, *Peter von Pulkau und die Wiedereinführung des Laienkelches, Veröffentlichungen des Max-Planck-Instituts für Geschichte,* 12 (Göttingen 1964), with detailed bibliography; J. Kejř, "Zur Entstehungsgeschichte des Hussitentums," *Die Welt zur Zeit des Konstanzer Konzils* (Constance 1965), 47–61; F. Seibt, *Hussitica. Zur Struktur einer Revolution* (Cologne and Graz 1965); P. De Vooght, *L'hérésie de Jean Hus* (Louvain 1960); *idem, Hussiana* (Louvain 1960); *idem,* "Jean Huss et ses juges," Franzen-Müller, *Das Konzil von Konstanz,* 152–73; *Hus in Konstanz, Der Bericht des Peter von Mladoniowitz,* translation into German, with introduction and comment by J. Bujnoch, *Slavische Geschichtsschreiber,* 3 (Graz, Vienna and Cologne 1963); F. Machilek, "Hus in Konstanz. Zu einer deutschen Übersetzung der relatio de magistro Iohanne Hus des Peter von Mladoñovic," *ZRGG,* 18 (1966), 163–70; bibliography on Hus and Hussitism in H. Grundmann, "Ketzergeschichte des Mittelalters," *Die Kirche in ihrer Geschichte,* 2, series G, 1 (Göttingen 1963), 62–65; A. Coville, *Jean Petit. La question du tyrannicide au commencement du XVe siècle* (Paris 1932); F. Schoenstedt, *Der Tyrannenmord im Spätmittelalter. Studien zum Begriff des Tyrannen und zum Problem des Tyrannenmordes im Spätmittelalter, insbesondere in Frankreich, Neue deutsche Forschungen,* 198 (Berlin 1938); H. Koeppen, *Die Berichte der Generalprokuratoren des Deutschen Ordens an der Kurie,* 2: *Peter von Wormditt* (Göttingen 1960); S. Belch, "Magistri Pauli Wladimiri decr. doct. scriptum denunciatorium errorum Satyrae Ioannis Falkenberg OP concilio Constantiensi datum," *Sacrum Poloniae millennium,* 2 (1955), 165–92; *idem,* "Tractatus 'opinio Hostiensis,'" *ibid.,* 3 (1956), 385–431; *idem, Paulus Wladimiri and his Doctrine concerning International Law and Politics,* 2 vols. (London, The Hague, and Paris 1965); R. Bäumer, "Das Verbot der Konzilsappellation Martins V. in Konstanz," Franzen-Müller, *Das Konzil von Konstanz,* 187–213; E. Weise, "Der Heidenkampf des Deutschen Ordens," *Zeitschrift für Ostforschung,* 12 (1963), 420–73, 622–72, 13 (1964), 401–20; K. A. Fink, "Zum Streit zwischen dem Deutschen Orden und Polen auf den Konzilien zu Konstanz und Basel," *Reformata reformanda, Festgabe H. Jedin,* I (Münster 1965), 74–86; A. D. De Sousa Costa, "Canonistarum doctrina de Iudaeis et Saracenis tempore concilii Constantiensis," *Antonianum,* 40 (1965), 3–70; F. Machilek, *Ludolf von Sagan und seine Stellung in der Auseinandersetzung um Konziliarismus und Hussitismus* (dissertation in philosophy, Munich 1967).

Causa reformationis: B. Hübler, *Die Constanzer Reformation und die Concordate von 1418* (Leipzig 1867); J. Haller, *Papsttum und Kirchenreform* (Berlin 1903); H. Heimpel, *Dietrich von Niem* (Münster 1932); *idem, Dietrich von Niem, Dialog über Union und Reform der Kirche 1410* (Leipzig and Berlin 1933); *idem, Studien zur Kirchen- und Reichsreform des 15. Jahrhunderts, SAH* (1929 f.); F. Merzbacher, "Wandlungen des Kirchenbegriffs im Spätmittelalter," *ZSavRGkan,* 39 (1953), 274–361; L. Buisson, *Potestas und Caritas* (Cologne and Graz 1958); H. Jedin, *Bischöfliches Konzil oder Kirchenparlament. Ein Beitrag zur Ekklesiologie der Konzilien von Konstanz und Basel* (Basel 1963); K. A. Fink, "Die konziliare Idee im späten Mittelalter," *Vorträge und Forschungen,* 9 (1965), 119–34; P. De Vooght, *Les pouvoirs du concile et l'autorité du pape au concile de Constance* (Paris 1965).

Martin V: Mansi, XXVIII; K. A. Fink, *RepGerm,* IV, 1–3 (Berlin 1943–58); *idem,* "Die ältesten Breven und Brevenregister," *QFIAB,* 25 (1933 f.), 292–307; *idem,* "Die politische Korrespondenz Martins V. nach den Brevenregistern," *QFIAB,* 26 (1935 f.), 172–244; *idem, Martin V. und Aragón* (Berlin 1938); *idem,* "Martin V. und Bologna," *QFIAB,* 23 (1931 f.), 182–217; *idem,* "Papsttum und Kirchenreform nach dem Grossen Schisma," *ThQ,* 126 (1946), 110–22; B. Partner, *The Papal State under Martin V* (London 1958); J. Haller, "England und Rom unter Martin V.," *QFIAB,* 8 (1905), 249–304; N. Valois, *Le Pape et le Concile,* I (Paris 1909); R. Valentini, "Lo Stato di Braccio," *ASRomana,* 52 (1931), 223–379.

50. *Eugene IV and The Council of Basel-Ferrara-Florence*

SOURCES

Deutsche Reichstagsakten, 9–17 (reprinted Göttingen 1957–63); *RepGerm*, *Pontifikat Eugens IV.*, I (Berlin 1897); *Mansi*, XXIX–XXXII; *Monumenta conciliorum generalium saeculi decimi quinti*, I–IV (Vienna 1857–1935); *Concilium Basiliense, Studien und Quellen zur Geschichte des Concils von Basel*, I–VIII (Basel 1896–1936). In regard to the transmission of the sources for the Council of Basel: *Deutsche Reichstagsakten*, 10, pp. xlv–cix; *Concilium Florentinum. Documenta et scriptores*, I–VIII (Rome 1940–64), not yet completed.

LITERATURE

Hefele-Leclercq, VII; J. Gill, *Constance et Bâle-Florence* (Paris 1965); *Fliche-Martin*, 14, 1–2; N. Valois, *Le Pape et le Concile*, 2 vols. (Paris 1909); J. Gill, *Eugenius IV Pope of Christian Union* (Westminster, Md. 1961); idem, *The Council of Florence* (Cambridge 1959), with copious bibliography; idem, *Personalities of the Council of Florence* (Oxford 1964); A. N. E. D. Schofield, "The Second English Delegation to the Council of Basel," *JEH*, 17 (1966), 29–64; W. Küchler, "Alfons V. von Aragón und das Basler Konzil," *Gesammelte Aufsätze zur Kulturgeschichte Spaniens*, 23 (1967), 131–46; J. Décarreaux, "L'arrivée des Grecs en Italie pour le concile de l'union des églises d'après les mémoires de Siropoulos 1437–1438," *Revue des études italiennes*, 8 (1961); idem, "Les Grecs à Florence pour le concile de l'union des églises d'après les mémoires de Siropoulos," *ibid.*, 9 (1962–63), 33–99, 10 (1964), 219–39; D. Caccamo, "Eugenio IV e la crociata di Varna," *ADRomana*, 79 (1956), 35–87; R. Bäumer, "Eugen IV. und der Plan eines 'Dritten Konzils' zur Beilegung des Basler Schismas," *Reformata reformanda, Festgabe für H. Jedin*, I (1965), 87–128; J. Dephoff, *Zum Urkunden- und Kanzleiwesen des Konzils von Basel* (Hildesheim 1930); U. Frommherz, *Johannes von Segovia als Geschichtsschreiber des Konzils von Basel* (Basel and Stuttgart 1960); M. Lehmann, *Die Teilnehmer des Basler Konzils* (dissertation, Vienna 1945); H. Angermeier, "Das Reich und der Konziliarismus," *HZ*, 192 (1961), 529–83; H. Stutt, "Die nordwestdeutschen Diözesen und das Basler Konzil in den Jahren 1431 bis 1441," *Niedersächsisches Jahrbuch*, 5 (1928), 1–97; C. Hanna, *Die südwestdeutschen Diözesen und das Baseler Konzil in den Jahren 1431 bis 1441* (dissertation in philosophy, Erlangen 1929); R. Wittram, *Die französische Politik auf dem Basler Konzil während der Zeit seiner Blüte* (dissertation in philosophy, Tübingen 1927); N. Valois, *Histoire de la Pragmatique Sanction de Bourges sous Charles VII* (Paris 1906), and, in this connection, J. Haller in *HZ*, 103 (1909), 1–51; A. N. E. D. Schofield, "England, the Pope and the Council of Basel," *Church History*, 33 (1964), 248–78; J. H. Burns, *Scottish Churchmen and the Council of Basle* (Glasgow 1962); L. Suárez Fernández, *Castilla, el cisma y la crisis conciliar 1378–1440* (Madrid 1960); V. Beltrán de Heredia, "La embajada de Castilla en el concilio de Basilea y su discusión con los ingleses acerca de la precedencia," *HS*, 10 (1957), 1–27; J. Toussaint, *Philippe le Bon et le concile de Bâle* (Brussels 1942); idem, *Les relations diplomatiques de Philippe le Bon avec le concile de Bâle* (Louvain 1942); J. Goñi Gaztambide, "Los obispos de Pamplona del siglo XV y los Navarros en los concilios de Constanza y Basilea," *Estudios de edad media de la corona de Aragón*, 7 (1962), 358–547; A. Zumkeller, "Die Augustinereremiten in der Auseinandersetzung mit Wyclif und Hus, ihre Beteiligung an den Konzilien von Konstanz und Basel," *AAug*, 28 (1965), 5–56; R. Zwölfer, "Die Reform der Kirchenverfassung auf dem Konzil zu Basel," *Basler Zeitschrift für Geschichte und Altertumskunde*, 28 (1929), 141–247, 29 (1930), 1–58; P. Clausen, *Heinrich Toke, ein Beitrag zur Geschichte der Reichs- und Kirchenreform in der Zeit des Baseler Konzils* (dissertation in philosophy, Jena 1939); H. Dannenbauer, "Ein deutscher Reformantrag vom Konzil zu Ferrara 1438," *HJ*, 62 (1942), 279–85, extant only as an off-print; P. Becker, "Fragen um den Verfasser einer benediktinischen Reformschrift ans Basler Konzil. Studie über die Wirksamkeit des Abtes Johannes Rode von St. Matthias in Trier," *SM*, 74 (1963), 293–301; H. Hürten, "Die Mainzer Akzeptation von 1439," *AMrhKG*, 11 (1959), 42–75; J. B. Toews, "Pope Eugenius IV and the Concordat of Vienna 1448," *Church History*, 34 (1965), 178–94; H. Koller, *Reformation Kaiser Sigismunds* (Stuttgart 1964); L. Hödl, "Kirchengewalt und Kirchenverfassung nach dem liber de ecclesiastica potestate des Laurentius von Arezzo. Eine Studie zur Ekklesiologie des Basler Konzils," *Theologie in Geschichte und Gegenwart* (Munich 1957), 255–78; F. Boularand, "La primauté du pape au concile de Florence," *BLE*, 61 (1960), 161–203; H. Hürten, " Zur Ekklesiologie der Konzilien von Konstanz und Basel," *ThRv*, 59 (1963), 362–72; K. Binder, *Wesen und Eigenschaften der Kirche bei Kardinal J. de Torquemada* (Innsbruck 1955); H. Jedin, *Bischöfliches Konzil oder Kirchenparlament* (Basel and Stuttgart 1963); B. Duda, *Johannes Stojković OP: doctrina de cognoscibilitate ecclesiae, Studia Antoniana*, 9 (1958); N. López, "El cardenal Torquemada y la unidad de la iglesia," *Burgense*, 1 (1960), 45–71; V. Proaño, "Doctrina de Juan de Torquemada sobre el concilio," *ibid.*, 1 (1960), 73–96; C. Lefèbvre, "L'enseignement de Nicolas de Tudeschis et l'autorité pontificale," *EIC*, 14 (1958), 312–39; K. N. Nörr, *Kirche und Konzil bei Nikolaus de Tudeschis, Panormitanus* (Cologne and Graz 1964); E. F. Jacob, "Reflections upon the Study of the General Councils in the Fifteenth Century," *Studies in Church History*, I (1964), 80–97; B. Schultze, "Das letzte ökumenische Einigungskonzil theologisch gesehen," *OrChrP*, 25 (1959), 288–309; H. G. Beck, "Byzanz und der Westen im Zeitalter des Konziliarismus," *Die Welt zur Zeit des Konstanzer Konzils* (Constance and Stuttgart 1965), 134–48; A. Leidl, *Die Einheit der Kirchen auf den spätmittelalterlichen Konzilien von Konstanz bis Florenz* (Paderborn 1966); G. Hödl, "Zur Reichspolitik des Basler Konzils: Bischof Johannes Schele von Lübeck," *MIÖG*, 75 (1967), 46–65.

SECTION THREE

The Byzantine Church: The Age of Palamism

51. *From the Second Council of Lyons to the Council of Ferrara-Florence*

LITERATURE

W. Norden, *Das Papsttum und Byzanz. Die Trennung beider Mächte und das Problem ihrer Wiedervereinigung bis zum Untergange des byzantinischen Reiches* (Berlin 1903); M. Viller, "La question de l'union des églises entre Grecs et Latins depuis le concile de Lyon jusqu'à celui de Florence," *RHE*, 17 (1921), 260–305, 515–33, 18 (1922), 20–60; M. Jugie, *Le schisme byzantin. Aperçu historique et doctrinal* (Paris 1941); *Runciman*, III; Aziz S. Atiya, *The Crusade in the Later Middle Ages* (London 1938).

52. *Hesychasm and Palamism*

SOURCES

The chief sources are the synodal decrees *(tomoi)*, which will be cited in the chapter footnotes. For the numerous polemical writings and reports see the references in *Beck*, 712 ff. New material since 1959; Gregory Palamas, *Défense des saints hésychastes*, ed. J. Meyendorff, 2 vols. (Louvain 1959), in Greek and French; other new editions of texts are listed in H. G. Beck, "Humanismus und Palamismus," *XIIe Congrès Intern. des Études byzantines, Ohrid 1961,* Rapports, III (Belgrade 1961), 63–82.

LITERATURE

M. Jugie, *Theologia dogmatica christianorum orientalium,* II (Paris 1933), 48–183; *idem,* "Palamite, Controverse," *DThC,* XI/2, 1777–1818; I. Hausherr, "L'hésychasme," *OrChrP,* 22 (1956), 5–40, 247–85; S. Guichardan, *Le problème de la simplicité divine en Orient et en Occident aux XIVe et XVe siècles* (Lyons 1933); G. Mercati, *Notizie di Procoro e Demetrio Cidone . . . ed altri appunti . . .* (Vatican City 1931); E. von Ivánka, "Hesychasmus und Palamismus," *JÖByzG,* 2 (1952), 23–34. On Palamas in particular: V. Krivošein, *Die asketische und theologische Lehre des heiligen Gregorios Palamas* (Würzburg 1939); J. Meyendorff, *Introduction à l'étude de Grégoire Palamas* (Paris 1959), the best monograph. On Barlaam see especially the introduction to G. Schirò, *Barlaam Calabro: Epistole greche* (Palermo 1954); M. Jugie in *DHGE,* VI, 817–34. On Akindynos: M. T. Disdier in *DSAM,* I, 263–68. On Gregoras: R. Guilland, *Essai sur Nicéphore Grégoras* (Paris 1926).

53. *Intellectual Life in the Late Mediaeval Byzantine Church*

LITERATURE

F. Dölger, "Politische und geistige Strömungen im sterbenden Byzanz," *JÖByzG,* 3 (1954), 3–18; H. Hunger, "Von Wissenschaft und Kunst der frühen Palaeologenzeit," *ibid.,* 8 (1959), 123–55; I. Ševčenko, "The Decline of Byzantium seen through the Eyes of its Intellectuals," *DOP,* 15 (1961), 169–86; *idem,* "Intellectual Repercussions of the Council of Florence," *CHR,* 24 (1955), 291–323; E. Bouvy, "Saint Thomas. Ses traducteurs byzantins," *Revue Augustinienne,* 9 (1910), 401–08; M. Rackl, "Die griechische Übersetzung der Summa theologiae des heiligen Thomas von Aquin," *ByZ,* 24 (1923 f.), 48–60; *idem,* "Die griechischen Augustinusübersetzungen," *Miscellanea F. Ehrle,* I (Rome 1924), 1–38; G. Mercati, *Notizie di Procoro e Demetrio Cidone, Manuele Caleca e Teodoro Meliteniota ed altri appunti per la storia della teologia e della letteratura bizantina del secolo XIV* (Vatican City 1931).

54. *Patriarchate-Emperor and Church-Missions-Monasticism*

SECTION FOUR

From the Middle Ages to the Reformation

55. *Renaissance and Humanism*

SOURCES

V. Ilardi, "Fifteenth-century Diplomatic Documents in Western European Archives and Libraries 1450–1494," *Studies in the Renaissance,* 9 (1962), 64–112; *Calendar of Entries in the Papal Registers relating to Great Britain and Ireland,* X–XIV, *1447–1492* (1915–60); *RepGerm,* VI: *Nikolaus V.* (in preparation); Vespasiano da Bisticci, *Vite di Uomini illustri del secolo XV,* ed. P. D'Ancona and E. Aeschlimann (Milan 1951); L. Pastor, *Ungedruckte Akten zur Geschichte der Päpste,* I: *1376–1464* (Freiburg 1904).

BIBLIOGRAPHY

Literature

Fliche-Martin, 15 (1951); *Pastor*, I–IV, English translation: *The History of the Popes from the Close of the Middle Ages*, II–VIII (St. Louis 1891–1908), and, in this connection, A. Strnad, "Francesco Todeschini-Piccolomini. Politik und Mäzenatentum im Quattrocento," *RömHM*, 8/9 (1964–66), 101–425, with supplements and corrections for *Pastor* and very copious bibliography; *Seppelt-Schwaiger*, IV (1957); *Storia d'Italia*, ed. N. Valeri, II (Turin 1959); N. Valeri, *L'Italia nell'Età dei Principati* (Verona 1949); P. Paschini, *Roma nel Rinascimento* (Bologna 1940), 477–88 (bibliography); H. Marc-Bonnet, *Les papes de la Renaissance 1447–1527* (Paris 1953); D. Hay, *The Italian Renaissance on its Historical Background* (Cambridge 1961); F. Bérence, *Les papes de la Renaissance* (Paris 1966); F. Cognasso, *L'Italia nel Rinascimento. Società e Costume*, II (Turin 1965), 275–372; J. H. Plumb, *The Italian Renaissance. A Concise Survey of its History and Culture* (New York 1965); F. Babinger, *Mehmed der Eroberer und seine Zeit* (Munich 1953); S. Schüller-Piroli, *Borgia. Die Zerstörung einer Legende, die Geschichte einer Dynastie* (Olten and Freiburg 1963); *Handbuch der Geschichte der böhmischen Länder*, ed. K. Bosl, I (Stuttgart 1967); G. Urban, "Die Kirchenbaukunst des Quattrocento in Rom," *Römisches Jahrbuch für Kunstgeschichte*, 9/10 (1961 f.), 73–287; D. Redig de Campos, *I palazzi Vaticani* (Bologna 1967); R. U. Montini, *Le Tombe dei Papi* (Rome 1957); G. Ladner, "Die mittelalterliche Reform-Idee und ihr Verhältnis zur Idee der Renaissance," *MIÖG*, 60 (1952), 31–59; B. L. Ullmann, *Studies in the Italian Renaissance* (Rome 1955); P. O. Kristeller, "Studies on Renaissance Humanism during the Last Twenty Years," *Studies in the Renaissance*, 9 (1962), 7–30; *Bibliographie internationale de l'Humanisme et de la Renaissance*, I: *Travaux parus en 1965* (Geneva 1966); *The Renaissance. A Reconsideration of the Theories and Interpretation of the Age*, ed. T. Helton (Madison 1964); E. Raimondi, *Rinascimento inquieto* (Palermo 1965); F. Chabod, *Scritti sul Rinascimento* (Turin 1967); *Begriff und Problem der Renaissance. Wege der Forschung*, ed. A. Buck (Darmstadt 1968); H. Baron, "Die politische Entwicklung der italienischen Renaissance," *HZ*, 174 (1952), 31–56; *idem*, *Humanistic and Political Literature in Florence and Venice at the Beginning of the Quattrocento* (Cambridge, Mass. 1955); *idem*, *The Crisis of the Early Italian Renaissance. Civic Humanism and Republican Liberty in an Age of Classicism and Tyranny*, 2 vols. (Princeton 1955); in regard to the preceding see M. Seidlmayer, *Wege und Wandlungen des Humanismus* (Göttingen 1965), 47–74, and Ferguson and Baron in *Journal of the History of Ideas*, 19 (1958), 14–34; P. Herde, "Politik und Rhetorik in Florenz am Vorabend der Renaissance," *AKG*, 47 (1965), 141–220; G. Toffanin, *La religione degli Umanisti* (Bologna 1950); *idem*, *Storia dell'Umanesimo*, 3 vols. (Bologna 1950); E. Garin, *La cultura filosofica del Rinascimento Italiano* (Florence 1961); *idem*, *Medioevo e Rinascimento* (Bari, 2d ed. 1961); *idem*, *Storia della Filosofia Italiana*, 3 vols. (Turin 1966); *idem*, *Die Kultur der Renaissance, Propyläen-Weltgeschichte*, VI (1964); R. Weiss, *Humanism in England during the Fifteenth Century* (Oxford, 2d ed. 1957); *Renaissance und Humanismus in Mittel- und Osteuropa*, I, directed by J. Irmscher (Berlin 1962); M. Gritz, *Die Stellungnahme der katholischen Kirchenhistoriker Deutschlands im 19. Jahrhundert zu Renaissance und Humanismus* (typed dissertation in theology, Tübingen 1955).
R. Weiss, *The Spread of Italian Humanism* (London/New York 1964); R. A. Goldthwaite, *Private Wealth in Renaissance Florence* (Princeton, 1968); L. Martines, *Lawyers and Statecraft in Renaissance Florence* (Princeton 1968); J. E. Seigel, *Rhetoric and Philosophy in Renaissance Humanism: The Union of Eloquence and Wisdom, Petrarch to Valla* (Princeton 1968); W. K. Ferguson, *The Renaissance in Historical Thought* (Boston 1948); T. Helton (ed.), *The Renaissance: A Reconsideration of the Theories and Interpretations of the Age* (Madison 1961); W. K. Ferguson, et al., *The Renaissance: Six Essays* (New York 1953); D. Herlihy, *Medieval and Renaissance Pistoia: the Social History of an Italian Town, 1200–1430* (New Haven/London 1967): Charles G. Nauert, Jr., *Agrippa and the Crisis of Renais-*

sance Thought (Urbana, 1965); P. G. Bietenholz, *History and Biography in the Work of Erasmus of Rotterdam* (Geneva 1966); M. E. Cosenza, *Biographical and Bibliographical Dictionary of the Italian Printers and of Foreign Printers in Italy from the Introduction of the Art of Printing into Italy to 1800* (Boston 1968); and *idem, Biographical and Bibliographical Dictionary of the Italian Humanists and of the World of Classical Scholarship in Italy, 1300–1800*, 5 vols. (Boston 1968); B. Berenson, *The Italian Painters of the Renaissance* (London 1967); H. Baron, *From Petrarch to Leonardo Bruni* (Chicago 1968); L. Martines, *Lawyers and Statecraft in Renaissance Florence* (Princeton 1968); H. Baker, *The Race of Time: Three Lectures on Renaissance Historiography* (Toronto 1967); C. H. Clough, *Machiavelli Researches* (Naples 1967); R. Ergang, *The Renaissance* (Princeton 1967).

Christian Humanism: A. Della Torre, *Storia dell' Accademia Platonica di Firenze* (Florence 1902, reprinted Turin 1960); M. Becker, *Florence in Transition* (Baltimore, Maryland, 1967); P. O. Kristeller, *Studies in the Renaissance Thought and Letters* (Rome 1956); A. Soria, *Los Humanistas de la Corte de Alfonso el Magnánimo* (Granada 1956); E. Garin, *Studi sul Platonismo medioevale* (Florence 1958); F. Secret, *Les Kabbalistes chrétiens de la Renaissance* (Paris 1964); P. O. Kristeller, *Eight Philosophers of the Italian Renaissance* (London 1965); E. Wind, *Pagan Mysteries in the Renaissance* (Bungay, Suffolk 1967). On Valla: *Laurentii Vallae Opera* (Basel 1540, 1543), ed. E. Garin (Turin 1962 ff.); G. Radetti, *L. Valla, Scritti filosofici e religiosi* (Florence 1953); F. Gaeta, *Lorenzo Valla* (Naples 1955); *Convegno di Studi per il V centenario della morte di L. Valla, Archivio storico per le province Parmensi*, IV, 9th series (1957). On Marsilius Ficinus: *Marsilii Ficini Florentini Opera*, 2 vols. (Basel 1561, 1576, reprinted Turin 1959); P. O. Kristeller, *Supplementum Ficinianum*, 2 vols. (Florence 1937); W. Dress, *Die Mystik des Marsilius Ficinus* (Berlin and Leipzig 1929); P. O. Kristeller, *Il Pensiero filosofico di Marsilio Ficino* (Florence 1953); M. Schiavone, *Problemi filosofici in Marsilio Ficino* (Milan 1957). On Pico della Mirandola: *Opera* (Basel 1572), ed. E. Garin, 3 vols. (Florence 1942–52); E. Monnerjahn, *Giovanni Pico della Mirandola. Ein Beitrag zur philosophischen Theologie des italienischen Humanismus* (Wiesbaden 1960); P. Rocca, *Studi in onore di Giovanni Pico della Mirandola nel V centenario della nascita, Atti e memorie della Dep. prov. Ferrarese di storia patria*, new series, 26 (Ferrara 1963); E. Garin, *Giovanni Pico della Mirandola* (Parma 1963); G. Di Napoli, *Giovanni Pico della Mirandola e la Problematica dottrinale del suo tempo* (Rome 1965); *L'Opera e il Pensiero di Giovanni Pico della Mirandola nella storia dell'umanesimo.* I: *Relazioni,* II: *Communicazioni* (Florence 1966). *Important Periodicals and Series: MRS; Renaissance News;* since 1967 *Renaissance Quarterly,* Renaissance Society of America Publications (New York 1948 ff.); *Rinascimento.* Rivista dell'Istituto Nazionale di Studi sul Rinascimento (Rome 1950 ff., 2d series, 1961 ff.); *Studies in the Renaissance.* Publications of the Renaissance Society of America (New York 1954 ff.).

56. *The Popes of the Early Renaissance*

LITERATURE

A. A. Strnad, "Francesco Todeschini-Piccolomini," *RömHM,* 8/9 (1964–66), 101–425, the most important supplement to *Pastor,* II–IV, with very detailed bibliography; *Storia d'Italia,* ed. N. Valeri, II (Turin 1959); *Storia di Milano,* VI–VIII (Milan 1955 f.); F. Babinger, *Mehmed der Eroberer und seine Zeit* (Munich 1953); H. Pfeffermann, *Die Zusammenarbeit der Renaissancepäpste mit den Türken* (Winterthur 1946); *Handbuch der Geschichte der böhmischen Länder,* ed. K. Bosl, I (Stuttgart 1967); F. G. Heymann, *George of Bohemia. King of Heretics* (Princeton 1965); O. Odložilík, *The Hussite King. Bohemia in European Affairs 1440–1471* (New Brunswick 1965); V. Ilardi "The Italian League, Francesco Sforza, and Charles VII (1454–1461)," *Studies in the Renaissance*. Publications of the Renaissance Society of America, VI (New York 1959), 129–66; E. Dupré-Theseider, *La politica italiana di Alfonso d'Aragona. Lezioni tenuti nell'Università di Bologna durante l'anno accademico 1955–1956* (Bologna 1956); G. F. Ryder, "La politica italiana di Alfonso d'Aragona 1442–1458," *Archivio storico per le province Napoletane*, new series, 38 (1959), 43–106; J. Hofer, *Johannes Kapistran. Ein Leben im Kampf um die Reform der Kirche*, new ed. O. Bonmann, 2 vols. (Rome 1966); C. Santoro, *Gli Sforza* (Milan 1968).

Nicholas V: Sources: Vespasiano da Bisticci, *Vite di Uomini illustri del secolo XV* (Milan 1951), 21–47; I. Manetti, *Vita Nicolai V summi pontificis ex manuscripto Florentino, Muratori*, III, 2 (Milan 1734), 908–60; *RepGerm*, VI (in preparation). Literature: *Pastor*, II, with bibliography; *Seppelt-Schwaiger*, IV, 306–26, with bibliography; F. K. Pleyer, *Die Politik Nikolaus' V.* (dissertation in philosophy, Tübingen 1927); G. Soranzo, *La Lega Italica 1454–1455* (Milan 1924); *idem*, "Studi e Discussioni su la Lega Italica del 1454–1455," *Studi storici in onore di G. Volpe* (Florence 1958), 969–95; V. Ferrando, *Vita del Papa Niccolò V-Tommaso Parentucelli* (Sarzana 1929).

Calixtus III: Sources: J. Rius Serra, *Regesto Ibérico de Calixto III*, I (Barcelona 1947); *RepGerm*, VII (in preparation). Literature: *Pastor*, II, with bibliography; *Seppelt-Schwaiger*, IV, 326–31, with bibliography; J. Rius Serra, *Catalanes y Aragoneses en la Corte de Calixto III* (Barcelona 1927); P. Brezzi, "La Politica di Callisto III. Equilibrio italiano e difesa dell'Europa alla metà del secolo XV," *StRom*, 7 (1959), 31–41; S. Schüller-Piroli, *Borgia* (see bibliog. for Chapter 55), 100–39.

Pius II: Sources: *Opera quae extant omnia* (Basel 1551, 1571, reprinted Frankfurt 1967); *Briefwechsel des Aeneas Silvius Piccolomini*, ed. R. Wolkan, *Fontes rerum Austriacarum*, 61, 62, 67, 68 (Vienna 1909–20); *Pii II Pont. Max. olim Aeneae Sylvii Piccolomini Senensis orationes politicae et ecclesiasticae*, ed. G. D. Mansi (Lucca 1755–59); *Aeneae Silvii Piccolomini Senensis opera inedita*, 3 vols., ed. G. Cugnoni, *Atti della Real Accademia Nazionale dei Lincei*, 3d series (1882 f.); *Commentarii rerum memorabilium*, considerably modified, ed. F. Bandini-Piccolomini (Rome 1584), Book 13 by C. Voigt, *Enea Silvio Piccolomini als Papst Pius II. (infra)*, 359–77, complete English translation, *The Commentaries of Pius II*, 5 vols. (Northampton 1937–57), by F. A. Gragg, abbreviated edition (New York 1962); on the preceding *cf.* G. C. Zimolo, *Le vite di Pio II (infra)*, 73 f.; H. Kramer, "Untersuchungen über die Commentarii Pius' II.," *MIÖG*, 48 (1934), 58–92; R. Avesani, "Per la biblioteca di Agostino Patrizi Piccolomini, vescovi di Pienza," *SteT*, 236 (1964), 1–87 (a critical edition is being prepared by F. Gaeta and G. Bernetti according to Cod. Vat. Regin. lat. 1995); L. Pastor, *Ungedruckte Akten zur Geschichte der Päpste* (Rome 1904), 88–331; *Le Vite di Pio II di Giovanni Antonio Campano e Bartolomeo Platina* a cura di G. C. Zimolo, *Muratori*, III, part II (Bologna 1964), with an important introduction. Literature: *Pastor*, III, with bibliography; *Seppelt-Schwaiger*, IV, 331–48, with bibliography; G. Voigt, *Enea Silvio Piccolomini als Papst Pius II. und sein Zeitalter*, 3 vols. (Berlin 1856–63, reprinted Berlin 1967); J. Paparelli, *Enea Silvio Piccolomini* (Bari 1950); G. Bürck, *Selbstdarstellung und Personenbildnis bei Enea Silvio Piccolomini (Pius II.)* (Basel and Stuttgart 1956); E. Dupré-Theseider, *Enea Silvio Piccolomini umanista* (Bologna 1957); E. Garin, "Ritratto di Enea Silvio Piccolomini," *La cultura filosofica del Rinascimento italiano* (Florence 1961), 38–59; B. Widmer, *Enea Silvio Piccolomini, Papst Pius II. Ausgewählte Texte* (Basel 1960), with a biographical introduction, 13–139; *idem, Enea Silvio Piccolomini in der sittlichen und politischen Entscheidung* (Basel 1963); R. J. Mitchell, *The Laurels and the Tiara, Pope Pius II* (London 1962); L. M. Veit, *Pensiero e vita religiosa di Enea Silvio Piccolomini prima della sua consacrazione episcopale, AnGr*, 139 (Rome 1964); G. Toffanin, "Cicerone fra i padri della chiesa e gli umanisti (per il centenario di Pio II)," *AHPont*, 2 (1964), 187–210; G. B. Picotti, *La dieta di Mantova e la politica de' Veneziani. Miscellanea di storia Veneta*, 3d series, 4 (1912); E. Meuthen, *Die letzten Jahre des Nikolaus von Kues*

(Cologne and Opladen 1958); A. Matanič, "L'idea per la crociata anti-turca del papa Pio II," *StudFr*, 61 (1964), 382–94; F. Wasner, "Piccolominibriefe. Ein Beitrag zum italienischen Humanismus," *HJ*, 79 (1960), 199–219; A. Lhotsky, *Aeneas Silvius und Österreich* (Basel and Stuttgart 1965); "Il Convegno Senese per il V centenario della morte di Pio II," *RSTI*, 20 (1966), 204–06; *Atti del Convegno storico Piccolominiano Ancona 9 maggio 1965. Estratto da Atti e Memorie*, series VIII, vol. 4, fasc. 2 (Ancona 1967); L. F. Smith, "Lodrisio Crivelli of Milan and Aeneas Sylvius, 1457–1464," *Studies in the Renaissance*, 9 (1962), 31–63; H. Diener, "Enea Silvio Piccolominis Weg von Basel nach Rom. Aus päpstlichen Registern der Jahre 1442–1447," *Adel und Kirche. Festschrift Tellenbach* (Freiburg 1968).

Paul II: Sources: *Le Vite di Paolo II di Gaspare da Verona e Michele Canensi* a cura di G. Zippel, *Muratori*, III, part XVI (1904); B. Platina, *Liber de Vita Christi ac omnium Pontificum*, ed. G. Gaida, *Muratori*, III, 1, 363–98. Literature: *Pastor*, IV, with bibliography; *Seppelt-Schwaiger*, IV, 348–53, with bibliography; R. Weiss, *Un Umanista Veneziano Papa Paolo II* (Venice 1958); G. Soranzo, "Giovanni Battista Zeno, Nipote di Paolo II, cardinale di S. Maria in Portico (1469–1501)," *RSTI*, 16 (1962), 249–74; *Storia di Milano*, VII (Milan 1966); other special literature in A. A. Strnad, "Francesco Todeschini-Piccolomini," *RömHM*, 8/9 (1964–66), 101–425.

57. *The Popes of the High Renaissance*

SOURCES

Stefano Infessura, *Diario della Città di Roma*, ed. O. Tommassini (Rome 1890); Sigismondo dei Conti da Foligno, *Le storie de' suoi tempi (1475–1510)*, 2 vols. (Rome 1883); Jacopo da Volterra, *Diarium Romanum (1479–1484)*, ed. E. Carusi, *Muratori*, XXIII, 3 (1904); Jacopo Ammanati-Piccolomini, *Diario Concistoriale (1472–1479)*, ed. E. Carusi, *Muratori*, XXIII, 3 (1904–11); Sebastiano de Branco Tedalini, *Diario (1492–1524)*, ed. P. Piccolomini, *Muratori*, XXIII (1906–11); Antonio de Vascho, *Il diario della Città di Roma (1480–1492)*, ed. G. Chiesa, *Muratori*, XXIII, 3 (1910 f.); *Iohannis Burckhardi Liber notarum ab anno 1483 usque ad annum 1506*, ed. E. Celani, *Muratori*, XXIII, 1, 2 (1911–42), incomplete; Paris de Grassis, *Il diario di Leone X*, ed. P. Delicati and M. Armellini (Rome 1884); Marino Sanudo, *I diarii*, 58 vols. (Venice 1879–1903); *Les "libri Annatarum" pour les pontificats d'Eugène IV à Alexandre VI*. IV: *Pontificats d'Innocent VIII et d'Alexandre VI 1484–1503*. Textes publiés par E. Brouette, *Analecta Vaticano Belgica*, XXIV (Brussels 1963).

LITERATURE

E. Rodocanacchi, *Histoire de Rome. Une cour princière au Vatican pendant la Renaissance. Sixte IV, Innocent VIII, Alexandre VI Borgia* (Paris 1925); idem, *Le pontificat de Jules II, 1503–1513* (Paris 1928); idem, *Le pontificat de Léon X, 1513–1521* (Paris 1931); *Storia d'Italia*, ed. N. Valeri, II (Turin 1959); *Storia di Milano*, VII–VIII (Milan 1956 f.); F. Babinger, *Mehmed der Eroberer und seine Zeit* (Munich 1953); P. Partner, "The 'Budget' of the Roman Church in the Renaissance Period," *Italian Renaissance Studies* by E. F. Jacob (London 1960), 256–78; E. Gagliardi, *Der Anteil der Schweizer an den italienischen Kriegen 1494–1516* (Zürich 1918); A. Büchi, *Kardinal Matthäus Schiner als Staatsmann und Kirchenfürst*, 2 vols. (Fribourg 1923–37); H. Pfeffermann, *Die Zusammenarbeit der Renaissancepäpste mit den Türken* (Winterthur 1946); J. Fernández Alonso, *Legaciones y nunciaturas en España de 1466 a 1521*, I: *1466–1484* (Rome 1963); E. Breisach, *Caterina Sforza. A Renaissance Virago* (Chicago and London 1967).

Sixtus IV and Innocent VIII: B. Platina, *Liber de Vita Christi ac omnium Pontificum,* ed. G. Gaida, *Muratori,* III, 1 (Bologna 1913–32), gives detailed treatment of Sixtus IV to 1475); E. Carusi, *Dispacci e lettere di Giacomo Gheradi nunzio pontificio 1487–90, SteT,* 21 (Rome 1909); *I diarii di Cicco Simonetta,* ed. A. R. Natale, I: *1473–1478* (Milan 1962); *Pastor,* IV; further literature in the footnotes for this chapter.

Alexander VI: Dizionario biografico degli Italiani, II (1960), 196–205, with copious bibliography; G. Pepe, *La politica dei Borgia* (Naples 1946); E. Olmos y Canalda, *Reivindicación de Alejandro VI* (Valencia, 7th ed. 1954); O. Ferrara, *El papa Borgia* (Madrid, 4th ed. 1956), English translation by F. J. Sheed, *The Borgia Pope, Alexander VI* (New York 1940); G. Schwaiger, "Savonarola und seine Zeit," *MThZ,* 12 (1961), 210–14, with bibliography; S. Schüller-Piroli, *Borgia. Die Zerstörung einer Legende, die Geschichte einer Dynastie* (Olten and Freiburg 1963); M. Batllori, *Alejandro VI y la casa real de Aragón 1492–1498, Real academia de la historia* (Madrid 1958); H. Kühner, "Der Charakter Alexanders VI.," *ThZ,* 14 (1958), 214–21; G. Soranzo, *Studi intorno a Papa Alessandro VI Borgia* (Milan 1950); *idem,* "Risposta al Prof. Giovanni Picotti," *RSTI,* 6 (1952), 96–107; *idem,* "Documenti inediti o poco noti relativi all'assunzione al pontificato di Alessandro VI." *Archivi,* 19 (1952), 157–78; *idem,* "Orsino Orsini, Adriana di Mila sua madre, e Giulia Farnese, sua moglie, nei loro rapporti con papa Alessandro VI," *Archivi,* 26 (1959), 119–50; *idem, Il tempo di Alessandro VI Papa e di Fra Girolamo Savonarola* (Milan 1960); *idem,* "La più grave accusa data al papa Borgia," *Archivi,* 28 (1961), 179–88; G. B. Picotti, "Nuovi studi e documenti intorno a Papa Alessandro VI," *RSTI,* 5 (1951), 169–262; *idem,* "Replica al Prof. Giovanni Soranzo," *RSTI,* 6 (1952), 107–10; *idem,* "Ancora sul Borgia," *RSTI,* 8 (1954), 313–55; *idem,* "Alessandro VI, il Savonarola ed il cardinale Giuliano della Rovere in una pubblicazione recente," *ASRomana,* 83 (1960, published 1963), 51–72; *Pastor,* V–VI.

Pius III: A. A. Strnad, "Francesco Todeschini-Piccolomini. Politik und Mäzenatentum im Quattrocento," *RömHM,* 8/9 (1964–66), 101–425; this detailed study treats the entire second half of the fifteenth century and must be used to supplement *Pastor,* II–IV; it includes a copious bibliography; *Pastor,* VI.

Julius II: De Terrateig, *Politica en Italia del Rey Católico 1507–1516. Correspondencia inédita con el embajador Vich,* 2 vols. (Madrid 1963); M. Brosch, *Papst Julius II. und die Gründung des Kirchenstaates* (Gotha 1878); E. Rodocanacchi, *Le pontificat de Jules II, 1503–1513* (Paris 1928); G. B. Picotti, *La giovinezza di Leone X* (Milan 1928); *idem, La politica italiana sotto il pontificato di Giulio II* (Pisa 1949); A. Luzio, "I Preliminari della Lega di Cambrai concordati a Milan ed a Mantova," *Archivio storico Lombardo,* 38 (1911), 245–310; *idem, Isabella d'Este di fronte a Giulio II negli ultimi tre anni del suo pontificato* (Milan 1912); C. Fusero, *Giulio II* (Milan 1965); G. de Beauville, *Jules II, Sauveur de la Papauté* (Paris 1965); L. Bindi Senesi, *Giulio II. Un Papa con l'archibugio* (Milan 1967); D. S. Chambers, *Cardinal Bainbridge in the Court of Rome 1509 to 1514* (London 1965); R. Cessi, *Dispacci degli ambasciatori veneziani alla corte di Roma presso Giulio II* (Venice 1932) *Storia di Milano,* VIII (Milan 1957); F. Seneca, *Venezia e Papa Giulio II* (Padua 1962); *Pastor,* VI.

Leo X: J. Hergenröther, *Regesta Leonis X,* fasc. 1–8, 1514–1515 (Freiburg 1884–91); P. Bembo, *Libri XVI epistolarum Leonis P. M. nomine scriptarum* (Basel 1539 and later); Paris de Grassis, *Diario di Leone X,* ed. D. Delicati and M. Armellini (Rome 1884); M. Sanudo, *I diarii,* XVI–LVIII (Venice 1886–1903); S. Camerani, *Bibliografia Medicea, Biblioteca di Bibliografia Italiana,* XLV (Florence 1964); F. Nitti, *Leone X e la sua politica* (Florence 1892); G. B. Picotti, *La giovinezza di Leone X* (Milan 1928); E. Rodocanacchi, *Le pontificat de Léon X* (Paris 1951); D. Gnoli, *La Roma di Leone X* (Milan 1938); P. Prodi, "Relazioni diplomatiche fra il Ducato di Milano e Roma sotto il Duca Massimiliano Sforza 1512–1515," *Aevum,* 30 (1956), 437–94; *Storia di Milano,* VIII (Milan 1957); E. Dupré-

Theseider, "I Papi Medicei e la loro politica domestica," *Studi Fiorentini* (Florence 1963), 271–324; *Pastor, VII–VIII.*

58. *The Inner Life of the Church*

LITERATURE

The Urban Parish: Feine RG; F. X. Künstle, *Die deutsche Pfarrei und ihr Recht zu Ausgang des Mittelalters* (Stuttgart 1905); A. Schultze, *Stadtgemeinde und Kirche im Mittelalter, Festgabe R. Sohm* (Munich and Leipzig 1914); A. Störmann, *Die städtischen Gravamina gegen den Klerus am Ausgange des Mittelalters und in der Reformationszeit* (Münster 1916); L. von Muralt, *Stadtgemeinde und Reformation, Recht und Staat in Geschichte und Gegenwart,* 11 (Tübingen 1918); E. Rütimeyer, *Stadtherr und Stadtbürgerschaft in den rheinischen Bischofsstädten* (Stuttgart 1928); S. Reicke, *Das deutsche Spital und sein Recht im Mittelalter* (Stuttgart 1932); K. Fröhlich, "Kirche und städtisches Verfassungsleben im Mittelalter," *ZSavRGkan,* 22 (1933), 188–287; S. Schröcker, *Die Kirchenpflegschaft. Die Verwaltung des Niederkirchenwesens durch Laien seit dem ausgehenden Mittelalter* (Paderborn 1934); F. Röhrig, *Die europäische Stadt im Mittelalter* (Göttingen n. d.); E. Hegel, "Städtische Pfarrseelsorge im deutschen Spätmittelalter, *TThZ,* 57 (1948), 207–20. A. H. Thompson, *The English Clergy and Their Organization in the Later Middle Ages* (Oxford 1947); K. Edwards, *The English Secular Cathedrals in the Middle Ages* (Manchester 1949); W. A. Pantin, *The English Church in the Fourteenth Century* (London 1955); K. L. Wood-Legh, *Studies in Church Life Under Edward III* (Cambridge, 1934); E. L. Cutts, *Parish Priests and Their People in the Middle Ages* (London 1898); B. L. Manning, *The People's Faith in the Time of Wycliffe* (Cambridge 1919); R. A. Smith, *Canterbury Cathedral Priory* (Cambridge 1943); M. Aston, *Thomas Arundel: A Study of Church Life in the Reign of Richard II* (Oxford 1967); H. B. Workman, *John Wyclif: A Study of the English Medieval Church* (Hamden, Conn., 1966); R. Brentano, *Two Churches: England and Italy in the Thirteenth Century* (Princeton 1968); L. Gabel, *Benefit of Clergy in England in the Later Middle Ages* (New York 1967); L. B. Betcherman, "The Making of Bishops in the Lancastrian Period," *Speculum,* XLI (April, 1966), 397–419; W. O. Ault, "Manor Court and Parish Church in Fifteenth-Century England: A Study of Village By-Laws," *Speculum,* XLII (January, 1967), 53–67; W. M. Brady, *The Episcopal Succession in England, Scotland and Ireland AD 1400 to 1875* (Rome 1876–77); N. Harpsfield, *Historia Anglicana Ecclesiastica* (Douay 1622).

Parish Books: F. Falk, *Die pfarramtlichen Aufzeichnungen des Fl. Diel zu St. Christoph in Mainz (1491–1518)* (Freiburg 1904); J. Greving, *Joh. Ecks Pfarrbuch für U. L. Frau in Ingolstadt* (Münster 1908); J. B. Götz, *Das Pfarrbuch des Stephan May in Hilpoltstein vom Jahre 1511* (Münster 1926).

Pastoral Privileges of the Mendicant Friars: C. Paulus, *Welt- und Ordensklerus beim Ausgang des 13. Jahrhunderts im Kampf um die Pfarrechte* (Essen 1900); B. Mathis, *Die Privilegien des Franziskanerordens bis zum Konzil von Vienne (1311)* (Paderborn 1928); K. L. Hitzfeld, "Krise in den Bettelorden im Pontifikat Bonifaz' VIII.," *HJ,* 48 (1928), 1–30; K. Schleyer, *Anfänge des Gallikanismus im 13. Jahrhundert* (Berlin 1937); Sisino de Romallo, *Il ministero della confessione nei primordi dell'ordine francescano in relazione ai diritti parrocchiali* (Milan 1949); L. Hödl, "Zum Streit um die Busprivilegien der Mendikantenorden in Wien im 14. und beginnenden 15. Jahrhundert," *ZKTh,* 79 (1957), 170–89.

The Liturgy: A. Franz, *Die Messe im deutschen Mittelalter* (Freiburg 1902); *idem, Die kirchlichen Benediktionen im Mittelalter,* 2 vols. (Freiburg 1909); L. A. Veit, *Volksfrommes Brauchtum und Kirche im deutschen Mittelalter* (Freiburg 1936); P. Browe, *Die Verehrung der Eucharistie im Mittelalter* (Munich 1933); *idem, Die häufige Kommunion im Mittelalter* (Münster 1938); *idem, Die Pflichtkommunion im Mittelalter* (Münster 1940); *Jungmann*

MS, I; *idem*, "Der Stand des liturgischen Lebens am Vorabend der Reformation," *Liturgisches Erbe und pastorale Gegenwart* (Innsbruck 1960), 87–107; A. L. Mayer, "Die Liturgie und der Geist der Gotik," *JL*, 6 (1926), 68–97; A. Kolping, "Eucharistie als bona gratia. Die Messauffassung Alberts des Grossen," *Studia Albertina* (Münster 1952), 249–78.

Preaching: M. Kerker, "Die Predigt in der letzten Zeit des Mittelalters," *ThQ*, 43 (1861), 373–410, 44 (1862), 267–301; R. Cruel, *Geschichte der deutschen Predigt im Mittelalter* (Detmold 1879); A. Linsenmayer, *Geschichte der Predigt in Deutschland von Karl dem Grossen bis zum Ausgang des 14. Jahrhunderts* (Munich 1886); N. Paulus, "Zur Geschichte der Predigt des ausgehenden Mittelalters," *Katholik*, 10 (1894), 279–87; F. Landmann, *Das Predigtwesen in Westfalen in der letzten Zeit des Mittelalters* (Münster 1900); J. Rauscher, "Die Prädikaturen in Württemberg vor der Reformation," *Württembergische Jahrbücher für Statistik und Landeskunde*, 2 (1908), 152 ff.; *idem*, "Die ältesten Prädikaturen Württembergs," *Blätter für württembergische Kirchengeschichte*, new series, 25 (1921), 107–11; R. Herrmann, "Die Prediger im ausgehenden Mittelalter," *Beiträge zur Thüringischen Kirchengeschichte*, 1 (1929), 20–68; F. W. Oediger, *Über die Bildung der Geistlichen im Spätmittelalter* (Leiden and Cologne 1953); T. Freudenberger, *Der Würzburger Domprediger Dr. Joh. Rayss* (Münster 1954); C. R. Owst, *Preaching in Medieval England* (Cambridge 1926); *idem, Literature and Pulpit in Medieval England* (Cambridge 1933); T. M. Charland, *Artes Praedicandi* (Paris 1936); M. A. Devlin, "Bishop Brunton and his Sermons," *Speculum*, XIV (1939), 324–344; D. Robertson, "The Frequency of Preaching in 13th Century England," *Speculum*, XXIV (1949), 376–388.

Catechesis. J. Geffken, *Der Bilderkatechismus des 15. Jahrhunderts und die katechetischen Hauptstücke bis auf Luther* (Leipzig 1855); P. Göbl, *Geschichte der Katechese im Abendland* (Cologne 1880); F. Probst, *Geschichte der katholischen Katechese* (Breslau 1886); F. Falk, "Der Unterricht des Volkes in den katechetischen Hauptstücken am Ende des Mittelalters," *HPBl*, 108 (1891), 553–60, 682–94; P. Bahlmann, *Deutschlands katholische Katechismen bis zum Ende des 16. Jahrhunderts* (Münster 1894); W. Burger, "Römische Beiträge zur Geschichte der Katechese im Mittelalter," *RQ*, 21 (1907), II, 159–97; L. Pfleger, "Beiträge zur Geschichte der Predigt und des religiösen Volksunterrichtes im Elsass während des Mittelalters," *HJ*, 38 (1917), 661–717; K. Schrems, *Die religiöse Volks- und Jugendunterweisung in der Diöcese Regensburg vom Anfang des 15. Jahrhunderts bis gegen Ende des 18. Jahrhunderts. Ein Beitrag zur Geschichte der Katechese* (Munich 1929); P. Browe, "Der Beichtunterricht im Mittelalter," *ThGl*, 26 (1934), 427–42; *Jungmann K*; E. Schoelen and W. Haerten, *Pädagogisches Gedankengut des christlichen Mittelalters* (Freiburg 1956); R. Padberg, *Erasmus als Katechet* (Freiburg 1956).

Scripture: translations of the Bible: *LThK*, II (2d ed. 1958), 401–11, with bibliography; W. Walther, *Die deutschen Bibelübersetzungen des Mittelalters*, 3 parts (Braunschweig 1889–92); F. Falk, *Die Bibel am Ausgang des Mittelalters* (Cologne 1905); H. Vollmer, *Materialien zur Bibelgeschichte und religiösen Volkskunde des Mittelalters*, 4 vols. (Berlin 1912–29); *idem, Neuere Beiträge zur Geschichte der Bibel im Mittelalter* (Berlin 1938); *idem, Die Bibel im deutschen Kulturleben* (Salzburg and Leipzig 1938); *Bibel und deutsche Kultur*, I–XI (Potsdam 1931–41); W. Hadorn, *Die deutsche Bibel in der Schweiz* (Leipzig 1925); H. Rost, *Die Bibel im Mittelalter* (Augsburg 1939); A. Schramer, *Die ersten deutschen Bibelübersetzungen und Bibeldrucke* (Einsiedeln 1952); W. Ziesemer, *Studien zur mittelalterlichen Bibelübersetzung* (Halle 1928); F. Maurer, *Studien zur mitteldeutschen Bibelübersetzung vor Luther* (Heidelberg 1929); H. Volz, *Bibel und Bibeldruck im 15. und 16. Jahrhundert* (Mainz 1960); S. Berger, *La Bible française au moyen âge* (Paris 1884); D. Lortsch, *Histoire de la Bible en France* (Paris 1915); H. H. Glunz, *History of the Vulgate in England* (Cambridge 1933); B. Smalley, *The Study of the Bible in the Middle Ages* (New York, 1952); A. Gasquet, *The Old English Bible and other Essays* (London 1897); M. Deanesly, *The Lollard Bible* (Cambridge 1920).

Religious Orders: Heimbucher; S. Hilpisch, *Geschichte des benediktinischen Mönchtums,* III (Freiburg 1929), 253–365, with bibliography; P. Schmitz, *Histoire de l'ordre de Saint Benoît,* 7 vols. (Maredsous 1948–56), Vols. III–VII; J. Zeller, "Das Provinzkapitel im Stift Petershausen im Jahre 1417," *SM,* 41 (1921), 1–73; V. Redlich, *Joh. Rode von St. Matthias bei Trier. Ein deutscher Reformabt des 15. Jahrhunderts* (Münster 1923). Kastl: B. Wöhrmüller, "Beiträge zur Geschichte der Kastler Reform," *SM,* 42 (1924), 10–40; J. Hemmerle, *Die Benediktinerklöster in Bayern* (Munich 1951), 60 ff. (bibliography); J. Sudbrack, *Die geistliche Theologie des Joh. von Kastl,* 2 vols. (Münster 1967), with bibliography. Melk: F. X. Thoma, "Petrus von Rosenheim und die Melker Benediktinerreformbewegung," *SM,* 45 (1927), 94–222. Bursfeld: P. Volk, *Die Generalkapitel der Bursfelder Benediktinerkongregation* (Münster 1928); *idem, 500 Jahre Bursfelder Kongregation* (Münster 1950); H. Herbst, "Die Anfänge der Bursfelder Reform," *Zeitschrift für niedersächsische Kirchengeschichte,* 36 (1931), 13–30; *idem, Das Benediktinerkloster Klus und die Bursfelder Reform* (Leipzig 1932); A. G. Little, *Studies in English Franciscan History* (Manchester 1917); A. Gwynn, *The English Austen Friars in the Time of Wycliffe* (Oxford 1940); A. F. C. Bourdillon, *The Order of Minoresses in England* (Manchester 1926); T. Burke (ed.), *Hibernia dominicana, sive historia provinciae Hiberniae ordinis praedicatorum* (Cologne 1762, 1772); C. Cotton, *The Grey Friars of Canterbury* (Manchester 1924); C. L. Kingsford, *The Grey Friars of London* (Manchester 1924); A. R. Martin, *Franciscan Architecture in England* (Manchester 1937).

France: P. Imbart de la Tour, *Les origines de la Réforme,* II (Melun, 2d ed. 1946). Valladolid: M. del Alamo in *Enciclopedia España,* 66 (Barcelona 1929), 930–87, with bibliography; P. Hofmeister, "Die Verfassung der Benediktinerkongregation von Valladolid," H. Finke, *Gesammelte Aufsätze zur Kulturgeschichte Spaniens,* 5 (1935), 311–36. St. Birgitta: *Revelationes celestes domine Birgitte de Swedia* (Lübeck 1492, Rome 1628); *Revelationes S. Birgittae,* ed. E. and M. Wessén, *Corpus codicum Suecicorum medii aevi,* 10 (Copenhagen 1949), 13 (1952); *Acta et processus canonisationis Beatae Birgittae,* ed. I. Collijn (Uppsala 1924–31); E. Fogelklon, *Die heilige Birgitta* (German trans., Munich 1929); K. Adalsten, *Licht aus dem Norden* (Freiburg 1951). Order of the Saviour (Birgittines): *DHGE,* X, 728–31, with bibliography; B. Berthelson, *Studier i birgittinordens byggnadsskick* (Stockholm 1946); T. Ahldén, *Nonnenspiegel und Mönchsvorschriften der Danziger Birgittinerkonvente* (Göteborg 1952); T. Nyberg, *Birgittinische Klostergründungen des Mittelalters* (Lund 1965).

59. *Theology in the Age of Transition*

Nicholas of Cusa: Works: *Opera omnia,* ed. Faber Stapulensis (Favre d'Étaples) (Paris 1514, reprinted Frankfurt 1962); ed. H. Petri (Basel 1565); ed. Heidelberger Akademie der Wissenschaften (Leipzig and Hamburg 1932 ff.); *Cusanus-Texte,* I (sermons), II (treatises), IV (correspondence), V (documents from Brixen), *SAH* (1929 ff.); texts of his philosophical works, I, ed. A. Petzelt (Stuttgart 1949). German translation sponsored by the Heidelberger Akademie der Wissenschaften, 15 vols. (Leipzig and Hamburg 1936–64), 3 vols. (Heidelberg 1949–60); philosophical and theological works in Latin and German, ed. L. Gabriel, 3 vols. (Vienna 1964–67). Bibliography: *Mitteilungen und Forschungsbeiträge der Cusanusgesellschaft,* 1 (Mainz 1961), 95–126, 3 (1963), 223–37; J. Koch, *Untersuchungen über Datierung, Form, Sprache und Quellen. Kritisches Verzeichnis sämtlicher Predigten* (Heidelberg 1942); *Cusanus-Konkordanz,* ed. E. Zellinger (Munich 1960). Literature: F. A. Scharpff, *Der Kardinal und Bischof Nicolaus von Cusa,* I (Mainz 1843); J. M. Düx, *Der deutsche Cardinal Nicolaus von Cusa,* 2 vols. (Regensburg 1847); E. Vansteenberghe, *Le cardinal Nicolas de Cues* (Paris 1920, reprinted Frankfurt 1963); P. Mennicken, *Nikolaus von Kues* (Trier, 2d ed. 1950); J. Koch, *Nikolaus von Cues und seine Umwelt* (Heidelberg 1948); E. Meuthen, *Die letzten Jahre des Nikolaus von Kues* (Cologne and Opladen 1958); *idem, Nikolaus von Kues* (Münster 1964); *idem, Das Trierer Schisma von 1430 auf dem Basler Konzil* (Münster 1964); S. Ehses, "Der Reformentwurf des Kardinals Nicolaus Cusanus," *HJ*, 32 (1911), 281–97; J. Lenz, *Die docta ignorantia des Nikolaus Cusanus* (Würzburg 1923); J. Hommes, *Die philosophische Gotteslehre des Nikolaus Kusanus* (Munich 1926); A. Posch, *Die "Concordantia catholica" des Nikolaus von Cusa* (Paderborn 1930); M. de Gandillac, *La philosophie de Nicolas de Cues* (Paris 1942); R. Haubst, *Das Bild des Einen und Dreieinen Gottes in der Welt nach Nikolaus von Kues* (Trier 1952); *idem, Nikolaus von Kues und Johannes Wenck* (Münster 1955); *idem, Die Christologie des Nikolaus von Kues* (Freiburg 1956); M. Seidlmayer, "'Una religio in rituum varietate' zur Religionsauffassung des Nikolaus von Kues," *AKG*, 36 (1954), 145–207; G. Pöppel, *Die docta ignorantia des Nicolaus Cusanus als Bildungsprinzip* (Freiburg 1956); K. H. Volkmann-Schluck, *Nicolaus Cusanus* (Frankfurt 1957); G. Heinz-Mohr, *Unitas Christiana* (Trier 1958); E. Colomer, *Nikolaus von Kues und Raimund Llull* (Berlin 1961); E. Iserloh, *Reform der Kirche bei Nikolaus von Kues* (Wiesbaden 1965); H. Bett, *Nicholas of Cusa* (London 1932); P. E. Sigmund, *Nicholas of Cusa and Medieval Political Thought* (Cambridge, Mass., 1963); J. P. Dolan, *Unity and Reform: Selected Writings of Nicholas of Cusa* (Notre Dame 1962); M. Watanabe, *The Political Ideas of Nicholas of Cusa, with Special Reference to his De Concordantia Catholica* (Geneva 1963). Also, see the following articles: R. Bauer, "Sacrum imperium et imperium germanicum chez Nicholas de Cues," *Archives d'histoire*, 12, 28–54 (1949); F. E. Cranz, "St. Augustine and Nicholas of Cusa in the Tradition of Western Christian Thought," *Speculum*, 28, 297–315 (April, 1953); B. Decker, "Die Toleranzidee bei Nikolaus von Kues und in der Neuzeit," in *Nicolo Cusano, Relazioni presentate al Convegno Interuniversitario di Bressanone* (Florence 1962), pp. 5–24; L. Duhem, "Thierry de Chartres et Nicolas de Cues," *Revue des sciences philosophiques et theologiques*, 3, 525–531 (1909); E. F. Jacob, "Nicholas of Cusa," in *Social and Political Ideas of Some Great Thinkers of the Renaissance and Reformation*, ed. F. J. C. Hearnshaw (London 1925), pp. 31–60; R. Klibansky, "Copernic et Nicolas de Cues," in *Leonard de Vinci et l'expérience scientifique au seizième siècle*, pub. by Centre National de la Recherche Scientifique (Paris 1953); B. L. Ullmann, "Manuscripts of Nicholas of Cues," *Speculum*, 13, 194–197 (1938).

John von Wesel: Sources: *Disputatio adversus indulgentias* (1475), ed. C. W. F. Walch, *Monimenta medii aevi*, I/1 (Göttingen 1757), 111–56; Relatio A of the process: Orthuinus Gratius, *Fasciculus rerum expetendarum et fugiendarum* (Cologne 1535), and D. d'Argentré, *Collectio iudiciorum de novis erroribus*, I/2 (Paris 1724), 291 ff. Literature: O. Clemen, "Über Leben und Schriften des Johannes von Wesel," *DZGw*, new series, 2 (Freiburg 1898), 143–73 (with Relatio B of the process); *idem*, "Zu dem Ketzerprozess Johannes' von Wesel," *HV*, 3 (1900), 521–23 (with the 19 recanted propositions; *idem* in RE, 21, 127–31; N. Paulus, "Johannes von Wesel über Bussakrament und Ablass," *ZKTh*, 24 (1900), 644–56; *idem* in *ZKTh*, 27 (1903), 601; *idem, Geschichte des Ablasses*, III (Paderborn 1923), 524–27; *idem*, "Wimpheling als Verfasser eines Berichtes über den Prozess gegen Johannes von Wesel," *ZGObrh*, 81, new series 42 (1929), 296–300, 451 ff.; G. Ritter, *Studien zur Spätscholastik*, III (Heidelberg 1927); R. Samoray, *Johannes von Wesel* (typed dissertation, Münster 1954); J. F. G. Goeters, "J. Ruchrat von Wesel," *Monatshefte für ev. Kirchengeschichte des Rheinlands*, 16 (1967), 184–91, with bibliography.

John von Goch: Works: *De libertate christiana* (1473; Antwerp 1521); *Epistola apologetica* (1474, Antwerp 1520); *Dialogus de 4 erroribus circa evangelicam legem* (Antwerp 1523); *In divinae gratiae et christianae fidei commendationem ... fragmenta* (Antwerp 1523). Editions: C. W. F. Walch, *Monimenta medii aevi*, I/4 (Göttingen 1760), 73–239 *(Dialogus)*, II/1 (Göttingen 1761), 3–24 *(Epistola apologetica)*; F. Pijper in *BNR*, VI (The Hague

1909), *De libertate christiana, Fragmenta, Epistola apologetica;* Luther's Foreword to the *Fragmenta* in *WA,* 10, II, 327–30. Literature: C. Ullmann, *Reformatoren vor der Reformation,* I (Gotha, 2d ed. 1866), 17–148; C. Clemen, *Johannes Pupper von Goch* (Leipzig 1896); *idem* in *RE,* 6, 740–43, 23, 565; G. Ritter, *Studien zur Spätscholastik,* I–III (Heidelberg 1921–27); *idem,* "Romantische und revolutionäre Elemente in der deutschen Theologie am Vorabend der Reformation," *DVfLG,* 5 (1927), 342–80; R. R. Post, "Joh. Pupper von Goch," *Nederlands Archief voor Kerkgeschiedenis,* 47 (1965 f.), 71–97; L. Abramowski, "Die Lehre vom Gesetz und Evangelium bei Joh. Pupper von Goch im Rahmen seines nominalistischen Augustinismus," *ZThK,* 64 (1967), 83–98.

Wessel Gansfort: Works: *Opera* (Groningen 1614). Literature: *RE,* 21, 131–47; E. W. Miller, *Wessel Gansfort, Life and Writings,* 2 vols. (New York and London 1917); M. van Rhijn, *Wessel Gansfort* (The Hague 1917); *idem, Studien over Wessel Gansfort* (Utrecht 1933); H. J. J. Wachters, *Wessel Gansfort* (Nijmegen 1940); R. R. Post, *Kerkgeschiedenis van Nederland in de Middeleeuwen,* I (Utrecht 1957), 397 ff.

Gabriel Biel: Works: *Sermones,* 4 vols. (Tübingen 1499 f., Hagenau 1510 and later); *Passionis dominicae sermo historialis* (Tübingen 1489 and later); *Canonis missae expositio* (Reutlingen 1488, Tübingen 1499 and later), ed. H. A. Oberman and W. J. Courtenay, 4 vols. (Wiesbaden 1963–67); *Epitoma expositionis canonis missae* (Tübingen 1499 and later; Antwerp 1565); from the preceding: *Sacri canonis missae expositio brevis et interlinearis* (after 1499); *Epithoma et collectorium circa IV libros Sententiarum* (Tübingen 1501 and later; reprinted Frankfurt 1965); extract (IV Sent., d. 15, g. 9): *De potestate et utilitate monetarum* (Oppenheim 1516), English translation by R. B. Burke (Philadelphia 1930); *Regula puerorum* (Urach 1483, Leipzig *ca.* 1497); *De communi vita clericorum* (MS, The Hague 75–958), ed. W. M. Landren, *Research Studies, Washington State University,* 28 (1960), 79–95. Literature: G. Plitt, *Gabriel Biel als Prediger* (Erlangen 1879); H. Hermelink, *Geschichte der theologischen Fakultät in Tübingen vor der Reformation 1477–1534* (Tübingen 1906), 204–07; O. Meyer, "Die Brüder des gemeinsamen Lebens in Württemberg 1477–1517," *Blätter für württembergische Kirchengeschichte,* 17 (1913), 109–38; C. Feckes, *Die Rechtfertigungslehre des Gabriel Biel* (Münster 1925); *idem,* "Der erste Dogmatiker der Universität Tübingen in seiner wissenschaftlichen Bedeutung," *ThQ,* 118 (1927), 50–76; J. Haller, *Die Anfänge der Universität Tübingen 1477–1537* (Stuttgart 1927–29), I, 153–72, II, 54–64; *DHGE,* VIII (1935), 1429–35; P. Anatriello, *La Dottrina di Gabriele Biel sull'Eucaristia* (Milan 1937); A. M. Jodice, "L'efficacia del Sacramento della Penitenza negli Scolastici e in Gabriele Biel," *SC,* 66 (1938), 141–60, 430–42; *idem* in *DTh(P),* 41 (1938), 113–29, 44 (1941), 273–92; E. Bonke, "Doctrina nominalistica de fundamento ordinis moralis apud Gulielmum de Ockham et Gabrielem Biel," *CollFr,* 14 (1944), 57–83; W. M. Landren, "Gabriel Biel and the Brethren of the Common Life," *Church History,* 20 (1951), 23–36; *idem,* "Gabriel Biel and the Devotio Moderna in Germany," *Research Studies, Washington State University,* 27 (1959), 135–76, 214–29, 28 (1960), 21–45, 61–78; L. Grane, "Gabriel Biels Lehre von der Allmacht Gottes," *ZThK,* 53 (1956), 53–75; *idem, Contra Gabrielem* (Copenhagen 1962); H. A. Obermann, *The Harvest of Medieval Theology. Gabriel Biel and Late Medieval Nominalism* (Cambridge, Mass. 1963), with bibliography; R. Damerau, *Die Abendmahlslehre des Nominalismus insbesondere die des Gabriel Biel* (Giessen 1963).

60. *The Jews in Mediaeval Christendom*

LITERATURE

J. Aronius, *Regesten zur Geschichte der Juden in Deutschland bis zum Jahre 1273* (Berlin 1902); I. Elbogen, A. Freimann, and H. Tykocinski, *Germania Iudaica. Von den ältesten Zeiten bis 1238* (Breslau 1934, reprinted Tübingen 1963); H. Graetz, *Geschichte der Juden von den ältesten Zeiten bis auf die Gegenwart*, 11 vols. in 13 (Leipzig, 4th ed. n. d. [1894–1908]); S. Dubnow, *Weltgeschichte des jüdischen Volkes*, 10 vols. (Berlin 1928–30); I. Elbogen, *Geschichte der Juden in Deutschland* (Berlin 1935); H. Fischer, *Die verfassungsrechtliche Stellung der Juden in den deutschen Städten des 13. Jahrhunderts* (Breslau 1931); E. L. Dietrich, "Das Judentum im Zeitalter der Kreuzzüge," *Saeculum*, 3 (1952), 94–131; G. Kisch, *Forschungen zur Rechts- und Sozialgeschichte der Juden in Deutschland während des Mittelalters* (Zürich 1955); idem, *Die Universitäten und die Juden* (Tübingen 1961); E. L. Ehrlich, *Geschichte der Juden in Deutschland* (Düsseldorf, 2d ed. 1958); E. Meyer, *Juden und Judenfeinde in der christlichen Welt* (Cologne 1962); P. Wilpert (ed.), *Judentum im Mittelalter. Beiträge zum Christlich-Jüdischen Gespräch* (Berlin 1966).

The Church and the Jews: M. Stern, *Urkundliche Beiträge über die Stellung der Päpste zu den Juden*, 2 vols. (Kiel 1893–95); idem, *Die päpstlichen Bullen über Blutbeschuldigung* (Munich 1900); L. Erler, "Die Juden des Mittelalters: Die Päpste und die Juden," *AkathKR*, 48 (1882), 369–416, 50 (1883), 3–64, 53 (1885), 3–70; H. Loewe, *Die Juden in der katholischen Legende* (Berlin 1912); P. Browe, "Die Hostienschändung der Juden im Mittelalter," *RQ*, 34 (1926), 167–97; idem, "Die religiöse Duldung der Juden im Mittelalter," *AkathKR*, 118 (1938), 3–76; idem, "Die Judenbekämpfung im Mittelalter," *ZKTh*, 62 (1938), 197–231, 349–84; idem, *Die Judenmission im Mittelalter und die Päpste* (Rome 1942); S. Grayzel, *The Church and the Jews in the Thirteenth Century* (Philadelphia 1933); H. Pflaum, *Die religiöse Disputation in der europäischen Dichtung des Mittelalters*, I: *Der allegorische Streit zwischen Synagoge und Kirche* (Geneva and Florence 1935); G. La Piana, "The Church and the Jews," *Historia Iudaica*, 11 (1949), 117–44; E. Peterson, "Perfidia Iudaica," *ELit*, 50 (1936), 296–311; on the preceding see J. Oesterreicher in *Cahiers Sioniens*, I (1947), 85–101, H. Schmeck in *VigChr*, 5 (1951), 129–47, B. Blumenkranz in *ALMA*, 22 (1952), 157–70; E. Iserloh, "Werner von Oberwesel," *TThZ*, 72 (1963), 270–85; W. P. Eckert, "Das Verhältnis von Christen und Juden im Mittelalter und Humanismus," *Monumenta Iudaica. Handbuch*, ed. K. Schilling (Cologne 1963), 131–98; K. Schilling and E. L. Ehrlich, *Judenhass—Schuld der Christen* (Essen 1964); W. Seiferth, *Synagoge und Kirche im Mittelalter* (Munich 1964); K. H. Rengstorf and S. von Kortzfleisch (ed.), *Kirche und Synagoge. Handbuch zur Geschichte von Christen und Juden*, I (Stuttgart 1968).

Jewish Philosophy and Theology: Bibliography: G. Vajda, *Jüdische Philosophie* (Bern 1950). Texts: *Jüdischer Glaube*, ed. K. Wilhelm (Bremen 1961); A. Franck, *Die Kabbala oder die Religionsphilosophie der Hebräer* (Leipzig 1844); D. Neumark, *Geschichte der jüdischen Philosophie des Mittelalters*, 2 vols. (Berlin 1907–20); J. Guttmann, *Philosophie des Judentums* (Munich 1933); L. G. Lévy, *Maimonide* (Paris 1911, 2d ed. 1932); *Moses ben Maimon*, ed. W. Bacher *et al.*, 2 vols. (Leipzig 1908–14); G. Vajda, *Introduction à la pensée juive du moyen-âge* (Paris 1947); H. Köhler, *Wirkung des Judentums auf das abendländische Geistesleben* (Berlin 1952); A. Altmann, *Jewish Philosophy* (New York 1953); K. Schubert, *Die Religion des nachbiblischen Judentums* (Vienna 1955); idem, "Kabbala," *LThK*, V (2d ed. 1960), 1233–36; G. Scholem, *Die jüdische Mystik in ihren Hauptströmungen* (Frankfurt 1957); idem, *Ursprung und Anfänge der Kabbala* (Berlin 1962); C. Roth, *History of the Jews in England*, 3d ed. (Oxford 1964); S. Stern, *Josel of Rosheim, Commander of Jewry in the Holy Roman Empire of the German Nation* (Philadelphia 1965); A. Altmann (ed.), *Jewish Medieval and Renaissance Studies* (Cambridge, Mass. 1967); E. A. Ashtor, *A History of the Jews in Muslim Spain*, 2 vols. (Jerusalem 1967); Z. W. Falk,

Jewish Matrimonial Law in the Middle Ages (Oxford/New York 1966); B. Blumenkranz, *Le Juif Mediéval au Miroir de l'Art Chrétien* (Paris 1966); J. P. Dolan, "A Note on Emperor Frederick II and Jewish Tolerance," in *Jewish Social Studies,* XXII, No. 3, 165–175; J. Starr, "The Mass Conversion of the Jews in Southern Italy (1290–1293)," in *Speculum,* XXI (1946), 203–211; J. W. Baron, *A Social and Religious History of the Jews* (New York 1959); *idem, Essays on Maimonides* (New York 1941); I. Husik, *A History of Medieval Jewish Philosophy* (Philadelphia 1941).

61. *German Humanism*

LITERATURE

Schottenloher, 37909–70, 63158–210; R. Stupperich, "Vom Humanismus zur Reformation. Literaturbericht," *AKG,* 36 (1954), 338–401; P. Joachimsen, *Geschichtsauffassung und Geschichtsschreibung in Deutschland unter dem Einfluss des Humanismus* (Leipzig and Berlin 1910); *idem,* "Der Humanismus und die Entwicklung des deutschen Geistes," *DVfLG,* 8 (1930), 419–80; *idem,* "Loci communes. Untersuchungen zur Geistesgeschichte des Humanismus und der Reformation," *LuJ,* 8 (1926), 27–97; H. Hermelink, *Die religiösen Reformbestrebungen des deutschen Humanismus* (Tübingen 1907); P. Mestwerdt, *Die Anfänge des Erasmus. Humanismus und Devotio Moderna* (Leipzig 1917); G. Ritter, "Die geschichtliche Bedeutung des deutschen Humanismus," *HZ,* 127 (1923), 393–453; M. P. Gilmore, *The World of Humanism (1453–1517)* (New York 1925); H. Baron, "Die religiösen Reformbestrebungen des deutschen Humanismus," *HZ,* 132 (1925), 413–46; H. von Schubert, "Reformation und Humanismus," *LuJ,* 8 (1926), 1–26; P. Kalkhoff, "Die Stellung der deutschen Humanisten zur Reformation," *ZKG,* 46 (1928), 161–231; H. Rupprich, *Humanismus und Renaissance in den deutschen Städten und an den Universitäten* (Leipzig 1935); *idem, Die Frühzeit des Humanismus und die Renaissance in Deutschland* (Leipzig 1938); R. Newald, "Deutsche Literatur im Zeitalter des Humanismus (Literatur-Übersicht 1939/53)," *DVfLG,* 27 (1953), 309–26; A. Schreiber, *Petrarca und Erasmus. Der Humanismus in Italien und im Norden* (Heidelberg 1947); J. Sellmair, *Humanitas christiana. Geschichte des christlichen Humanismus* (Munich, 2d ed. 1948); H. von Srbik, *Geist und Geschichte vom deutschen Humanismus bis zur Gegenwart,* I (Munich and Salzburg 1950); P. Renucci, *L'aventure de l'humanisme européen* (Paris 1953); A. Renaudet, *Préreforme et Humanisme à Paris (1494–1517)* (Paris 1953); P. Lehmann, "Grundzüge des Humanismus deutscher Lande," *Aevum,* 31 (1957), 253–68; H. Lutz, *Conrad Peutinger* (Augsburg 1958); B. Moeller, "Die deutschen Humanisten und die Anfänge der Reformation," *ZKG,* 70 (1959), 46–61; L. W. Spitz, *The Religious Renaissance of the German Humanists* (Cambridge, Mass. 1963).

Conrad Celtis: Works: *Fünf Bücher Epigramme von Konrad Celtis,* ed. K. Hartfelder (Berlin 1881); *Briefwechsel,* ed. H. Rupprich (Munich 1934); *Quatuor libri Amorum, Germania generalis,* ed. F. Pindter (Leipzig 1934); *Libri Odarum, Liber Epodon, Carmen saeculare,* ed. F. Pindter (Leipzig 1937); *Oratio in Gymnasio in Ingolstadio recitata,* ed. J. (H.) Rupprich (Leipzig 1932). Literature: F. von Bezold, *Konrad Celtis der deutsche Erzhumanist* ([1883] Darmstadt 1959); E. Novotny, *Die Weltanschauung des Konrad Celtis* (typed dissertation, Vienna 1938); L. Sponagel, *Konrad Celtis und das deutsche Nationalbewusstsein* (dissertation, Heidelberg 1939); D. Narr, "Conrad Celtis," *Württembergisches Jahrbuch für Volkskunde* (Stuttgart 1955), 66–78; H. Drewinc, *Vier Gestalten aus der Zeit des Humanismus* (St. Gallen 1946), 60–124; L. W. Spitz, *Conrad Celtis, The German Arch-Humanist* (Cambridge, Mass. 1957); M. Seidlmayer, "Konrad Celtis," *Wege und Wandlungen des Humanismus* (Göttingen 1965), 174–96.

BIBLIOGRAPHY

The Alsace Circle: O. Herding, "Probleme des frühen Humanismus in Deutschland," *AKG,* 38 (1956), 344–89; R. Newald, *Elsässische Charakterköpfe aus dem Zeitalter des Humanismus* (Colmar 1944); W. Gilbert, "Sebastian Brant, Conservative Humanist," *ARG,* 46 (1955), 145–67; J. Knepper, *J. Wimpheling* (Freiburg 1902), with list of writings; E. von Borries, *Wimpheling und Murner im Kampf um die ältere Geschichte des Elsasses* (Heidelberg 1926).

The Erfurt Circle: Der Briefwechsel des Mutianus Rufus, ed. C. Krause (Kassel 1885); *Der Briefwechsel des Conradus Mutianus,* ed. K. Gilbert (Halle 1890); L. Geiger, *Humanismus und Renaissance* (Berlin 1882), 132–35; G. Bauch, *Die Universität Erfurt im Zeitalter des Frühhumanismus* (Breslau 1904); P. Kalkhoff, *Humanismus und Reformation in Erfurt* (Halle 1926); M. Burgdorf, *Der Einfluss des Erfurter Humanismus auf Luthers Entwicklung bis 1510* (Leipzig 1928); P. Halbauer, *Mutianus Rufus und seine geistesgeschichtliche Stellung* (Leipzig and Berlin 1929); L. W. Spitz, "The Conflict of Ideals in Mutianus Rufus," *Journal of the Warburg Institute,* 16 (London 1953), 121–43; E. W. Krapp, *Der Erfurter Mutiankreis und seine Auswirkungen* (dissertation, Cologne 1954).

Epistolae obscurorum virorum: Editions: E. Böcking, 2 vols. (Leipzig 1864–70); F. G. Stokes (London 1909, 2d ed. 1925); A. Bömer, 2 vols. (Heidelberg 1924). Literature: *Schottenloher,* 36720–35; W. Brecht, *Die Verfasser der Epistolae obscurorum virorum* (Strasbourg 1904); P. Merker, *Die Verfasser des Eccius dedolatus und anderer Reformationsdialoge* (Halle 1923); A. Bömer, "Verfasser und Drucke der Epistolae obscurorum virorum," *ZblB,* 41 (1924), 1–12; L. Blum, "La part de l'Alsace à l'origine des 'Epistolae obscurorum virorum'," *Arch. de l'Église d'Alsace,* 19 (Rixheim 1949 f.), 99–128.

John Reuchlin: Works: *Codex Reuchlinianus,* 3, with introduction by A. Sperber (Copenhagen 1956); *Augenspiegel,* ed. J. Benzing (Munich 1961); *Johannes Reuchlins Briefwechsel,* ed. L. Geiger (Stuttgart 1875, reprinted Hildesheim 1962). Literature: *Schottenloher,* 17841–89a, 48848–57a, 57727–38; L. Geiger, *Johannes Reuchlin* (Leipzig 1871); J. Wille, "Johannes Reuchlin," *ZGObrh,* 76 (1922), 249–75; T. Schmid, *Reuchlins Anschauung von Wesen und Sinn der Sprache* (dissertation, Vienna 1938); W. Maurer, "Reuchlin und das Judentum," *ThLZ,* 77 (1952), 539–44; *Johannes Reuchlin,* ed. M. Krebs (Pforzheim 1955); J. Benzing, *Bibliographie der Schriften Johannes Reuchlins im 15. und 16. Jahrhundert* (Bad Bocklet 1955); L. W. Spitz, "Reuchlin's Philosophy," *ARG,* 47 (1956), 1–20; W. Maurer, "Melanchthon und Reuchlin," *Philipp Melanchthon,* ed. W. Elliger (Göttingen 1961), 116–20.

Desiderius Erasmus: Works: ed. Beatus Rhenanus, 9 vols. (Basel 1540), J. Clericus, 10 vols. (Leiden 1703–06, reprinted Hildesheim 1961); selected works ed. H. Holborn (Munich 1933, reprinted 1964); *Opuscula,* ed. W. K. Ferguson (The Hague 1933); *Ausgewählte Schriften. Ausgabe in 8 Bänden,* Latin and German, ed. W. Welzig, I (Darmstadt 1967); *Opus Epistularum,* ed. P. S. Allen, 12 vols. (Oxford 1906–58); *De libero arbitrio,* ed. J. von Walter (Leipzig, 2d ed. 1935); *Encomium Moriae,* ed. H. A. Schmid (Basel 1931). Translations: *Erasmus and His Times: A Shortened Version of the Adages of Erasmus,* trans. M. M. Phillips (Cambridge 1967); L. K. Born (ed.), *Education of a Christian Prince* (New York 1965); *Julius Exclusus,* trans. P. Pascal (Bloomington, Ind. 1968); *Enchiridion of Erasmus,* trans. R. Himelick (Bloomington, Ind. 1963); *Epistles of Erasmus,* trans. F. M. Nichols, 3 vols. (New York 1918); *On Copia of Words and Ideas,* trans. D. B. King and H. D. Rix (Milwaukee 1963); *The Colloquies of Erasmus,* trans. C. R. Thompson (Chicago 1965); *Discourse on Free Will,* trans. E. F. Winter (New York 1961); J. P. Dolan (ed. and trans.), *The Essential Erasmus* (New York 1963).

Literature: *Schottenloher,* 5492–845, 46065–187, 54278–477; P. Mestwerdt, *Die Anfänge des Erasmus* (Leipzig 1917); A. Renaudet, *Études érasmiennes (1521–29)* (Paris 1939); idem, *Érasme et l'Italie* (Geneva 1954); R. Newald, *Erasmus* (Freiburg 1947); K. A. Meissinger, *Erasmus* (Berlin, 2d ed. 1948); W. E. Campbell, *Erasmus, Tyndale and More* (London 1949); J. Lortz, "Erasmus—kirchengeschichtlich," *Aus Theologie und Philosophie, Festschrift für F. Tillmann* (Düsseldorf 1950), 271–326; J. Huizinga, *Erasmus;* A. Flitner, *Erasmus im Urteil seiner Nachwelt* (Tübingen 1952); A. Auer, *Die vollkommene Frömmigkeit des Christen nach dem Enchiridion* (Düsseldorf 1954); K. Schätti, *Erasmus und die römische Kurie* (Basel 1954); L. Bouyer, *Autour d'Érasme* (Paris 1955); E. Schneider, *Das Bild der Frau im Werk des Erasmus* (Basel 1955); J. Étienne, *Spiritualisme érasmien et théologiens louvanistes* (Louvain and Gembloux 1956); R. Padberg, *Erasmus als Katechet* (Freiburg 1956); C. Augustijn, "Die religiöse Gedankenwelt des Erasmus," *Rheinische Vierteljahresblätter,* 28 (1963), 218–30; G. Gebhardt, *Die Stellung des Erasmus von Rotterdam zur römischen Kirche* (Hamburg 1966); E. W. Kohls, *Die Theologie des Erasmus,* 2 vols. (Basel 1966), with bibliography. M. M. Philipps, *Erasmus and the Northern Renaissance* (New York/London 1949); P. S. Smith, *Erasmus, A Study of His Life, Ideals and Place in History* (New York 1962); *idem, A Key to the Colloquies of Erasmus* (Cambridge/London 1927); P. S. Allen, *Lectures and Wayfaring Sketches* (Oxford / New York 1934); L. Bouyer, *Erasmus and His Times* (Westminster, Md./London 1959); M. P. Gilmore, *The World of Humanism* (New York / London 1952); E. H. Harbison, *The Christian Scholar in the Age of the Reformation* (New York 1956); J. Huizinga, *Erasmus and the Age of Reformation* (New York 1957).

LIST OF POPES

Rival claimants are preceded by an asterisk.

Calixtus II	1119–1124	Honorius IV	1285–1287
Honorius II	1124–1130	Nicholas IV	1288–1292
*Celestine II	1124	Celestine V	1294
Innocent II	1130–1143	Boniface VIII	1294–1303
*Anacletus II	1130–1138	Benedict XI	1303–1304
*Victor IV	1138	Clement V	1305–1314
Celestine II	1143–1144	John XXII	1316–1334
Lucius II	1144–1145	*Nicholas V	1328–1330
Eugene III	1145–1153	Benedict XII	1334–1342
Anastasius IV	1153–1154	Clement VI	1342–1352
Hadrian IV	1154–1159	Innocent VI	1352–1362
Alexander III	1159–1181	Urban V	1362–1370
*Victor IV	1159–1164	Gregory XI	1370–1378
*Paschal III	1164–1168	Urban VI	1378–1389
*Calixtus III	1168–1178	*Clement VII	1378–1394
*Innocent III	1179–1180	Boniface IX	1389–1404
Lucius III	1181–1185	*Benedict XIII	1394–1423
Urban III	1185–1187	Innocent VII	1404–1406
Gregory VIII	1187	Gregory XII	1406–1415
Clement III	1187–1191	*Alexander V	1409–1410
Celestine III	1191–1198	*John XXIII	1410–1415
Innocent III	1198–1216	Martin V	1417–1431
Honorius III	1216–1227	Eugene IV	1431–1447
Gregory IX	1227–1241	*Felix V	1439–1449
Celestine IV	1241	Nicholas V	1447–1455
Innocent IV	1243–1254	Calixtus III	1455–1458
Alexander IV	1254–1261	Pius II	1458–1464
Urban IV	1261–1264	Paul II	1464–1471
Clement IV	1265–1268	Sixtus IV	1471–1484
Gregory X	1271–1276	Innocent VIII	1484–1492
Innocent V	1276	Alexander VI	1492–1503
Adrian V	1276	Pius III	1503
John XXI	1276–1277	Julius II	1503–1513
Nicholas III	1277–1280	Leo X	1513–1521
Martin IV	1281–1285		

GENERAL INDEX

Figures in italics denote pages where the subject receives more intensive treatment.